Handbook of
AMERICAN
WOMEN'S
HISTORY

Second Edition

To
Ida Marie Habben Weber,
Sis (Louise) Weber Howard,
Christina Assunta Ricci Kavenik, and
Elizabeth Kavenik Ward,
women ahead of their time,
who taught us how to be strong, smart, courageous, and resourceful.

Handbook of
AMERICAN
WOMEN'S
HISTORY

Second Edition

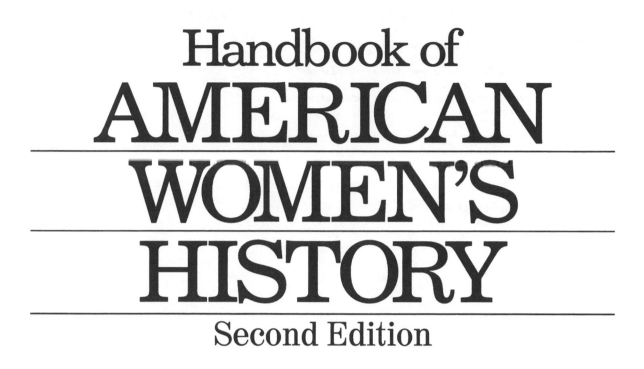

Angela M. Howard & Frances M. Kavenik

EDITORS

Sage Publications, Inc.
International Educational and Professional Publisher
Thousand Oaks ■ London ■ New Delhi

For information:

Sage Publications, Inc.
2455 Teller Road
Thousand Oaks, California 91320
E-mail: order@sagepub.com

Sage Publications Ltd.
6 Bonhill Street
London EC2A 4PU
United Kingdom

Sage Publications India Pvt. Ltd.
M-32 Market
Greater Kailash I
New Delhi 110 048 India

Printed in the United States of America

Library of Congress Cataloging-in-Publication Data

Main entry under title:

Handbook of American women's history / edited by Angela M. Howard and Frances M. Kavenik.— 2nd ed.
    p. cm.
    Includes bibliographical references and index.
    ISBN 0-7619-1635-0 (cloth: alk. paper)
    1. Women—United States—History—Handbooks, manuals, etc. I. Howard, Angela. II. Kavenik, Frances M., 1944–
    HQ1410 .H36 2000
    305.4'0973—dc21

                                                                99-050812

05 06 7 6 5 4 3

Acquiring Editors:	Catherine Rossbach and Peter Labella
Editorial Assistant:	Caroline Reynolds Sherman
Production Editor:	Diana E. Axelsen
Editorial Assistant:	Nevair Kabakian
Copy Editor:	Linda Gray
Permissions Editor:	Jennifer Maxon Morgan
Typesetter/Interior Designer:	Christina M. Hill
Cover Designer:	Ravi Balasuriya

Contents

List of Illustrations

Foreword

What an honor to introduce this *Handbook* of U.S. women's history, representing the *summa* of scholarly usefulness and fulfilling centuries-long ambitions in the field. In the past two decades, we have seen several biographical dictionaries, many anthologies of women's creative writing, and bibliographies in both women's studies and women's history. These kinds of works have antecedents from at least the eighteenth century on, and biographical compendia of women's lives date from much earlier. An encyclopedic undertaking has an equally honorable pedigree: One thinks of the French stenographer Marie-Louise Bouglé, who in the 1920s and 1930s envisioned a multivolumed encyclopedia with 250,000 entries on women's history. Wearing a single skirt for eight years and devising other money-saving ploys, she scrimped to collect and house primary materials for it. Others have similarly aspired to an encyclopedic knowledge of women's past, hoping to build comprehensive archives of raw data and sometimes even achieving their dream.

This work by Angela Howard and Frances Kavenik is a unique accomplishment for many reasons. First and foremost, it has aimed at covering the important issues, events, and personages in U.S. women's history, while avoiding the avid encyclopedist's unachievable dream of capturing every minute fact—a dream that ultimately stymied someone like Marie-Louise Bouglé. Second, using the talents of a wide range of historians, this handbook provides a mature representation of the work since the 1960s in the field of U.S. women's history. This second edition integrates the findings and scholarship of the 1990s, making the work even more up-to-date. Finally, the editors have chosen trends and events for their utility to those inside and outside academe, to the specialist and non-specialist, to the historian, and to the curious citizen.

The product of cooperation and consensus, the *Handbook of American Women's History* is interdisciplinary, bringing under its lens the novelist, physician, and movie star. The *Handbook* builds bridges across scholarly fields and thus demonstrates the interconnectedness of knowledge that has characterized scholarship on women over the past two centuries. High politics and popular culture, everyday life issues and industrialization cohabit these pages. Such is an accurate representation of the real accomplishment of women's history, for the broadening of what we consider important to history has resulted from the cogent writings by the contributors to this work. In their selection of topics, the editors have done hard thinking to purge the least essential and explore the most relevant themes.

The *Handbook* grows out of a commitment to feminist research and networking that so influenced the rebirth of scholarship on women more than three decades ago. Professors Howard and Kavenik were both activists and scholars in Wisconsin, and they tapped some of the scholar-activists they had heard about or worked with in many parts of the country. The scholarly networks that women's history and the feminist movement engendered long ago also shape this handbook. As users come to learn from and appreciate the vast knowledge represented in this work, that web of women's history will grow even thicker, even stronger.

—Bonnie G. Smith
Rutgers University

Introduction to the Second Edition

A decade has passed since the first edition of the *Handbook of American Women's History* was published. Since 1990, the field of women's history has assumed a respected place within the curriculum of public schools as well as within the discrete fields offered by university and college history departments across the nation. The first generation of self-taught women's historians has witnessed the emergence of succeeding generations of historians formally prepared to teach and research all aspects of women's history. Germinal works among the secondary sources published in the 1960s and 1970s launched further inquiry, informed through research into the gender-specific experience of women that was informed by the increased body of recovered, reclaimed, and restored primary source materials. The editors of the *Handbook* take pride in the contribution of the first edition to the expansion in the reference sources for women's history since 1990.

There are three obvious alterations in this revised edition of our *Handbook*. First, the recognition of the enormous contribution of Frances M. Kavenik, associate editor of the first edition, required her acknowledgment as an editor of the second edition. Second, Sage Publications, Inc. is the publisher of the Second Edition. Third, the *Handbook of American Women's History, Second Edition* features the addition of 69 illustrations and 142 new entries; the editors are proud to announce that 93 new contributors are among those who have authored or revised and adapted the 922 entries in the expanded text of our second edition.

In keeping with the design of the first edition as a reference to assist students, teachers, and librarians who are new to the field of American women's history, the *Handbook of American Women's History, Second Edition* offers introductory and fundamental information necessary for a general understanding of the field through a readily accessible collection of summary definitions for crucial concepts, events, organizations, and various historical persons. The entries include references to relevant and basic bibliography on each topic. Since 1990, a multitude of specialized references works supplement the *Handbook* in providing a variety and breadth of information regarding accessible sources and research in American women's history; therefore, although the second edition of the *Handbook* does not include an entry for every person, place, event, organization, or concept within this discrete field of historical inquiry, its entries focus on those events, organizations, concepts, and individuals that constitute a core of pertinent information regarding the basic materials and sources, as did the entries of the first edition. Many of the monographs and other sources that served as reference material for entries in the first edition have been replaced by more current scholarship; however, to assist contemporary readers in understanding the historiography of American women's history, the editors offer at the end of this introduction to the second edition a general listing of established sources in the field that includes reference works, monographs, and collections of primary sources.

Arranged alphabetically, the entries include both a concise definition that establishes the historical significance of the subject and a basic bibliography to indicate available primary and secondary sources to which the reader may refer for additional, more detailed information. The internal cross-references at the end of each entry refer the reader to related entries in the *Handbook*, second edition. Following the comprehensive index, the "About the Contributors" section provides vital information concerning the authors of the entries.

The second edition was not intended to include everything that is significant to the field of American women's history. Some of its entries reflect the specialized interests of the contributors; other entries supply fundamental information for those new to the field. The editors chose to emphasize historical information rather than attempt to provide a repository of current events in women's history at the close of the twentieth century. The *Handbook* was intended to supplement, not duplicate, existing and newly developed reference and bibliographic sources; for a referral to such sources, readers are encouraged to consult the entry "Archives and Sources."

Our efforts on the second edition have made us keenly aware that there remain significant and intriguing areas yet to be researched by women's history scholars. There is still much to be done in this vast and vital field. Despite the dedicated five-year effort of the editors (who have grown older in this endeavor), the expertise of our patient contributors (who have been so accommodating during the long interval between their submissions and the actual event of the second edition's publication), and the careful supervision of the manuscript by the seemingly indefatigable publishing staff (who often humbled us with their energy, precision, and perseverance), the editors anticipate that the second edition will receive constructive criticism. We accept full responsibility for all limitations and omissions in our revision of the *Handbook*.

The field of women's history for the past three decades has documented and affirmed the validity of historical inquiry regarding women's presence, participation, and contributions. Patterns and trends that were detected and assessed early on have been tested, contested, and reexamined by successive generations of historians who specialized in American women's history. To assist the reader in identifying works that have become standard in the field, we offer the following list of monographs and anthologies, reference works, and a select few collections of primary sources. Many of these publications, listed with their original publication dates, were often cited in first edition entries that now offer more specific references.

General Surveys and Anthologies

These works provide the reader with historical narratives, overviews, syntheses, and analyses of aspects of American women's history, with special concern for information regarding women of color and minority women.

Acosta-Belen, Edna, ed. *The Puerto Rican Woman,* 2d ed. New York: Praeger, 1986.

Asian Women United of California, eds. *Making Waves: An Anthology of Writings by and about Asian American Women.* Boston: Beacon, 1989.

Banner, Lois. *Women in Modern America: A Brief History.* San Diego: Harcourt, Brace, Jovanovich, 1984.

Berkin, Carol, and Mary Beth Norton, eds. *Women of America: A History.* Boston: Houghton Mifflin, 1979.

Chafe, William. *The American Woman: Her Changing Social, Economic, and Political Roles, 1920–1970.* New York: Oxford University Press, 1972.

Cott, Nancy. *The Grounding of Modern Feminism.* New Haven, CT: Yale University Press, 1988.

Daniel, Robert. *American Women in the Twentieth Century: The Festival of Life.* San Diego: Harcourt, Brace, Jovanovich, 1987.

Degler, Carl. *At Odds: Women and the Family in America from the Revolution to the Present.* New York: Oxford University Press, 1980.

de la Torre, Adela, and Beatriz Paquera. *Building with Our Hands: New Directions in Chicana Studies.* Berkeley: University of California Press, 1993.

Douglas, Ann. *The Feminization of American Culture.* New York: Knopf, 1977.

Evans, Sara. *Born for Liberty: A History of American Women.* New York: Free Press, 1989.

———. *Personal Politics: The Roots of Women's Liberation in the Civil Rights Movement and the New Left.* New York: Knopf, 1979.

Flexner, Eleanor. *Century of Struggle: The Woman's Rights Movement in the United States.* Cambridge, MA: Belknap Press/Harvard University Press, 1959, 1975.

Giddings, Paula. *When and Where I Enter: The Impact of Black Women on Race and Sex in America.* New York: William Morrow, 1984.

Gordon, Linda. *Woman's Body, Woman's Right: Birth Control in America.* Rev. ed. New York: Penguin, 1990.

Green, Rayna. *Women in American Indian Society.* New York: Chelsea House, 1992.

Hine, Darlene Clark, Wilma King, and Linda Reed. *"We Specialize in the Wholly Impossible": A Reader in Black Women's History.* Brooklyn: Carlson, 1995.

Kerber, Linda, and Jane DeHart Mathews, eds. *Women's America: Refocusing the Past,* 4th ed. New York: Oxford University Press, 1995.

Lerner, Gerda. *The Majority Finds Its Past: Placing Women in History.* Oxford, UK: Oxford University Press, 1979.

———. *The Woman in American History.* Reading, MA: Addison-Wesley, 1971.

O'Neill, William. *Everyone Was Brave: A History of Feminism in America.* Chicago: Quadrangle, 1969.

Riley, Glenda. *Inventing the American Woman: A Perspective on Women's History.* Arlington Heights, IL: Harlan Davidson, 1986, 1987.

Ruiz, Vicki L., and Ellen Carol DuBois, eds. *Unequal Sisters: A Multicultural Reader in U.S. Women's History,* 2d ed. New York: Routledge, 1994.

Scott, Anne Firor. *Making the Invisible Woman Visible.* Urbana: University of Illinois Press, 1984.

———. *Natural Allies: Women's Association in American History.* Chicago: University of Illinois Press, 1992.

Woloch, Nancy. *Women and the American Experience: A Concise History.* New York: McGraw-Hill, 1996.

Reference Works

These collections of biographic and bibliographic information inform the reader about specific women, issues, and events in American women's history.

Bataille, Gretchen M., ed. *Native American Women: A Biographical Dictionary.* New York: Garland, 1993.

Bataille, Gretchen M., and Kathleen M. Sands. *American Indian Women: A Guide to Research.* New York: Garland, 1991.

Cott, Nancy, ed. *The Young Oxford History of Women in the United States,* 11 vols. New York: Oxford University Press, 1995-96. [For younger readers.]

Edward, James, Janet Wilson James, Paul Boyer, Barbara Sicherman, and Carol Green, eds. *Notable American Women: A Biographical Dictionary,* 4 vols., 2d ed. Cambridge, MA: Harvard University Press, 1980.

Hine, Darlene Clark, ed. *Black Women in America: An Historical Encyclopedia,* 2 vols. Brooklyn: Carlson, 1993.

Journal of Women's History: Guide to Periodical Literature, compiled by Gayle Fischer. Bloomington: Indiana University Press, 1992.

Lerner, Gerda. *Bibliography in the History of American Women,* 2d ed. Bronxville, NY: Sarah Lawrence College, 1975.

Sweeney, Patricia. *Biographies of American Women: An Annotated Bibliography.* Santa Barbara, CA: ABC-CLIO, 1990.

Collections of Documents

These edited collections provide the reader immediate access to primary source material related to the experience of the diverse population of women in the United States from 1607 to the present. The final text by Norton and Alexander also provides representative historiography for the field.

Lerner, Gerda, ed. *The Female Experience: An American Documentary.* New York: Oxford University Press, 1992.

Moynihan, Ruth Barnes, Cynthia Russett, and Laurie Crumpacker, eds. *Second to None: A Documentary History of American Women,* 2 vols. Lincoln: University of Nebraska Press, 1993.

Norton, Mary Beth, and Ruth Alexander, eds. *Major Problems in American Women's History: Documents and Essays,* 2d ed. Lexington, MA: D. C. Heath, 1996.

—Angela Howard
University of Houston–Clear Lake, Texas

Acknowledgments for the
Second Edition

Revising the *Handbook of American Women's History* for a second edition seemed like such an obvious and, ostensibly, uncomplicated two-year task in 1995. The project started where we finished—with the 1990 edition and our Women's Studies editor Marie Ellen Larcada at Garland Publishing—but ended in a joint effort with the Books Division and Senior Production Editor Diana Axelsen at Sage Publications. As editors of this revised reference work, Frances Kavenik and I presided over what started as a sort of late 1990s women's studies revival among the original *Handbook* contributors; our reunion of women's studies veterans from the 1980s was transformed into a recruitment drive among the '90s generation of newcomers to the now well-established interdisciplinary field. The careers of the contributors to the second edition reflect the last decade's developments in women's studies.

Not all of the contributors to the first edition were where we left them in 1990, to be sure. Among those who agreed to revise their first edition entries, many are now recognized authorities in their fields of specialization. Their participation in the first edition testified to the collective commitment to supporting women's history and women's studies that secured recognition and legitimacy of the interdisciplinary field within the academy. However, to revise the entries of those original contributors who declined our invitation to "reenlist," we sought out "new" contributors, many of whom supplied additional entries as well as undertaking the responsibility of revising, rewriting, or updating first-edition entries and references. Carol Cyganowski once again offered her good offices for referrals from her vast network of colleagues in literature and women's studies. Joyce Keivit and Jonathan Zophy also shared their networks of scholars as possible contributors. If we gave an award for most helpful contributor, Robert Waite would be accepting a small but tasteful golden statue right this minute. We thank each of our contributors, especially for their patience as the revision process was extended by our change of publisher for the revised *Handbook* in 1997.

We are grateful for the good offices of my friend Gary Kuris for his counsel regarding possible publishers, and we thank Theresa Leuck, a contributor to both editions of the *Handbook,* for recommending Sage Publications. The capable and enthusiastic staff at Sage suggested further improvements for the *Handbook:* Catherine Rossbach, Peter Labella, Caroline Sherman, and Linda Gray contributed much to preparation of the final text. Diana Axelsen's dedication and professionalism kept our eyes on the prize and brought our much transformed manuscript to press. We conducted a concerted good faith effort to contact even the first-edition contributors who opted out of participating in the revisions. Although there were moments when we suspected that several of those contributors had been absorbed into some sort of witness protection program, the tenacity of the Sage staff and the assistance of friends such as Kelly Jamison and Verva Densmore and of professionals like Phyllis Holman Weisbard, the women's studies librarian for the University of

Wisconsin System, facilitated our location of most of the "missing" original contributors. If "I Get By with a Little Help from My Friends" remained the appropriate theme song for the *Handbook,* we added a corollary to all contributors: "You can run, but you cannot hide!"

Fran and I worked on the revisions, as we had on the original edition, in probable violation of the interstate commerce regulations, she at the University of Wisconsin–Parkside and I at the University of Houston–Clear Lake in Texas. She would like to thank the following folks at the University of Wisconsin–Parkside: Judith Pryor and the staff of the Library/Learning Center, who helped find people, places, and things; Tim Fossum, chair of the Computer Science Department, who kept "stretching" Frances's PC to accommodate software upgrades and more data; Kate Pietri, Pat Eaton, and other networking and microcomputer specialists, who helped her keep in reasonable proximity to new research tools and techniques; and Kathy Caskey, English Department Program Assistant, who helped in multitudinous ways to keep this project moving steadily and smoothly forward. I am indebted to the following colleagues, administrators, staff, and students at the University of Houston–Clear Lake: the administrative team of the School of Human Sciences and Humanities; my faculty suite secretary, Gloria Eby, and Rosalind Franklin; the reference staff of the Alfred R. Newmann Library, especially Gerald Churchill, Patricia Pate, Gay E. Carter, Susan Steele, and the staff in the Inter-library Loan office. My graduate student Pamela F. Wille, as assistant to the editors, launched our 1994–1995 effort to contact the original contributors and maintained crucial records on the second-edition contributors and entries; we were especially indebted to Pam for those records after we changed publishers in 1997. Her successors, Sasha Renaé Adams Tarrant, Rae Fuller Wilson, Susanne Grooms, and Richard Wilson, provided crucial expertise in researching as well as technological support as we rushed to complete the final draft of the manuscript by the fall of 1996.

Fran and I established, early on, a working division of editorial labors: She handled all things textual, and I worked with the people involved in our effort, the contributors and publishing staff particularly. The very existence of this second edition and all that is "right" about its format and content resulted from her dedication and expertise; I am honored to have been able to work beside her on this project. My duties sometimes resembled the challenge of "herding cats"—I had the privilege of working with talented scholars and colleagues nationwide who joined our project. My editorial responsibilities included handling questions, criticisms, and complaints from all involved, which is appropriate because I am the probable source of the errors of fact and judgment that may have escaped the sharp eyes of Fran and Laura Stempel, our proofreader, as well as the professional vetting of the manuscript by the Sage production staff. Fran and I offer the *Handbook of American Women's History, Second Edition* as an addition to the women's studies reference works that assist students, teachers, and librarians in their research efforts.

—Angela Howard
University of Houston–Clear Lake, Texas

Introduction to the
First Edition

The *Handbook of American Women's History* was conceived and designed as a reference to assist students, teachers, and librarians who are new to the field of American women's history. It offers introductory and fundamental information necessary for a general understanding of the field through a readily accessible collection of summary definitions with focused bibliography for crucial concepts, events, organizations, and various historical persons. The *Handbook* was not intended to contain references to all of the past or current research in American women's history nor to include an entry for every person, place, event, organization, or concept within this discrete field of historical inquiry. It does, however, attempt to provide entries for those events, organizations, concepts, and individuals that constitute a core of pertinent information regarding the basic materials and sources.

Arranged alphabetically, the entries include both a concise definition that establishes the historical significance of the subject and a basic bibliography to indicate available primary and secondary sources to which the reader may refer for additional, more detailed information. The internal cross references at the end of each entry refer the reader to related entries in the *Handbook*. There is also a comprehensive Index. Notes on the Contributors provides vital information concerning the authors of the entries.

In the past decade, women's history has become established as a recognized field of historical inquiry. Contemporary women's historians have built upon the seminal work of previous generations of scholars and, thus, have produced an expansive body of scholarship that informs the discipline of history regarding women's presence, participation, and contributions. Scholarly debates over discerned trends within women's history have produced contending "schools" of interpretation. Women's history has developed terms and references that have become central to the scholarly vocabulary of historians in the field but are not yet well known in the mainstream of American history. Women's historians now allude to certain individuals, groups, events, and to certain primary and secondary sources without including accompanying descriptions or definitions. This development is especially apparent in the concentrated area of American women's history. As a reference work, the *Handbook* utilizes an alphabetical approach to its entries to render accessible introductory information required by nonspecialists as well as to assist those who have considerable exposure to the discipline.

The *Handbook* is encyclopedic in the sense that it includes much that is well known and much that is not. While great effort was made to include entries that cover the fundamental concepts and sources of American women's history, this *Handbook* does not purport to include everything that is significant to the field. Some of its entries reflect the interests and expertise of its editor and its contributors, and therefore it includes entries on many little-known persons, topics, and events. However, the *Handbook* does not contain all of the entries that every historian of women's history might desire. Only those contemporary persons, events, and issues that the editor deemed crucial to provide critical background for the post-1960 phase of the modern women's movement have been included, since the emphasis of the *Handbook* is history, not current events. The *Handbook* was intended to supplement, not duplicate, existing reference and bibliographic sources; for referral to such sources, readers are encouraged to consult the entry "Archives and Sources."

Readers of the *Handbook* are encouraged to take note of areas that have not yet been well researched. Despite the increased scholarly activity in the field of women's history, clearly there are crucial areas yet to be investigated. Thus,

the editor is hopeful that the *Handbook* will not only provide some basic answers to questions but will inspire and direct additional research in this vast and vital field.

The *Handbook* has had the benefit of a superb associate editor, outstanding assistants to the editor who were effective beyond the editor's capability to reward properly their efforts and time given, and fine individual contributors. However, it has limitations and deficiencies, which are the sole responsibility of its editor who has every confidence that both will be duly noted and reported to her for correction by those who use this book.

Acknowledgments for the
First Edition

This *Handbook* is the result of networking among women's history and women's studies colleagues. I owe special gratitude to the Women's Studies Minor Program of the University of Wisconsin–Parkside, chaired by Teresa Peck, Professor of Education. In a meeting of the women's studies faculty and staff that focused on available resources in women's studies, I boldly asserted the need for such a reference as this *Handbook* in the presence of our guest presenter, the women's studies librarian for the University of Wisconsin System, Susan E. Searing. Susan passed the suggestion along to Marie Ellen Larcada, reference editor of Garland Publishing, Inc., who sent me a request for a proposal for such a reference handbook. My friend and colleague in women's studies, tennis, and life, Frances M. Kavenik, Assistant Professor of English, taught me enough "remedial" WordPerfect word-processing skills to allow me to produce the requested prospectus, which Marie Ellen found acceptable. My commitment to the need for such a guide, coupled with the support of outstanding women like these, impelled me to accept the challenge of compiling and editing the *Handbook*.

Once I had committed to this insane undertaking for one, I was further encouraged by the unstinting support of the Social Science Division of the University of Wisconsin–Parkside. For everything from paper clips to staff support, I thank Division Chair Larry Duetsch, professor of economics, and his predecessor, Leon Applebaum, professor of economics, and the division's program assistant, Arlene D. Monson. The generosity and collegial support of the division for its part-time member merits grateful, even extravagant, acknowledgment. Within the Social Science Division office staff, Josephine McCool and Bonnie F. Andrews ably and good-humoredly facilitated the logistical nightmare of recruiting and securing contributors, constantly bailed me out of my circular arguments with my WordPerfect program, and worked closely with my student assistants to get the project off the ground and keep it running smoothly. My student assistants at UW–Parkside were Rose Kolbasnik Callahan, Carol Waterloo, and Marge Reimann. Rose served the longest and, I think, the most difficult tour of duty, for she capably assumed time-consuming clerical tasks with a commitment that was inspiring. Many of my UW–Parkside students in women's history volunteered to contribute entries.

The women's studies liaison librarian, Judith M. Pryor, trained Rose Callahan, Carol Waterloo, and (her greatest challenge) me in the mysteries of the computerized reference and bibliographic search capability of the Wylie Library Learning Center of the University of Wisconsin–Parkside. Robert T. Maleske, academic services consultant for the Computing Support Center, offered his considerable services to assist me in applying the possibilities of the WordPerfect program to the needs of the *Handbook*.

Halfway through the project, Frances M. Kavenik accepted the post of associate editor and thus brought vigor and rigor to the processing of the *Handbook* manuscript. Its form and style benefited greatly from her dedication and professionalism. I just hope Frances recovers her health. She also referred me to Carol Klimick Cyganowski, Assistant Professor of English at DePaul University, who served as assistant to the editor for entry assignments. It is entirely probable that Carol has not a friend, colleague, associate, or acquaintance remaining who was not drafted into our contributor ranks. For her enthusiasm and perseverance, no less than for her excellent contacts, I thank Carol especially.

As we entered the last few months allocated to completing the *Handbook,* I accepted the position of Assistant Professor of Historical Studies at the University of Houston at Clear Lake. Despite this change, the *Handbook* still received crucial support from UW–Parkside: to assist Frances's work on the *Handbook,* the able staff of the Humanities Division took up the daunting task of processing all the original copy of the *Handbook* entries onto floppy diskettes. For this support, Frances and I are inestimably indebted to Humanities Chair Eugene L. Norwood, professor of German, and the division staff: program assistants Marge Rowley, Trudy M. Rivest, Pam LeClaire, and Mildred A. Nutini (who said she thought of all this work for the *Handbook* as job security), and to Marcella Ricciardi, program assistant for the ACCESS Program.

I found commensurate institutional and collegial support upon my arrival at the University of Houston at Clear Lake. Within the School for Human Sciences/Humanities, Dean Wayne Charles Miller, Associate Dean for Faculty Affairs Rita R. Culross, and Associate Dean for Administration Robert Wegmann provided essential assistance. I received a generous grant from the UH–Clear Lake Faculty Research and Support Fund to cover the telephone and mailing costs attendant to completing the *Handbook.* The staff of the Alfred R. Neumann Library at UH–Clear Lake were predictably patient in their assistance with verifying entry references; I am especially indebted to Patricia J. Garrett, Associate Dean for Public Services, and reference librarians Gay E. Carter, Rebecca Christman, and Patricia M. Pate.

Within my faculty suite, our secretary, Tamia L. Leger, picked up the burden of the typing for the editor that had been carried by the staff of the UW–Parkside Social Science Division, and my new colleagues generously shared the limited faculty suite supplies. Gloria D. Rodrigues, microcomputer specialist for the Computing Services, graciously and patiently instructed and reinstructed me in the wonders of the WordPerfect program. In addition to UH–Clear Lake students who volunteered to assist in the completion of the *Handbook* by writing entries, several undertook the unglamorous work of verifying bibliographic details: Barbara Bradford Novy, Ginger Rae Allee, Cynthia A. Bragg, and Barbara Jean Hayes deserve more than honorable mention for their library research contributions. Another of their number, Jean McGrath Hayes, proofread the first draft of the *Handbook* manuscript. La Donna Williams, as student assistant to the editor, and Merri J. Scheibe, graduate student assistant, worked with dedication as we completed the *Handbook* manuscript at UHCL.

The contributors provided the most essential element of the *Handbook,* the entries. I thank them for their expertise, their professional commitment to a project that offered neither fame nor fortune, and their patience with the editor once their entries were submitted. Especially to those contributors who submitted many entries, and those who accepted "emergency" assignments with very short deadlines, I give my heartfelt gratitude.

My final acknowledgment of gratitude goes to my friend, colleague, and spouse, Jonathan W. Zophy. His reference work *The Holy Roman Empire: A Dictionary Handbook* inspired me to propose such a tool for American women's history. From the inception of this project, he cheerfully and consistently provided consultation, expertise, and advice. As of the fall 1987, he formally accepted the responsibility of serving as an assistant to the editor.

I credit the unbounded support of Jonathan and Frances for having brought me and the *Handbook* this far. If this undertaking were to have had a patron saint, it could have been Blanche Du Bois: I often received the kindest of responses and timely assistance from colleagues whom I had not known before. If this project had a theme song, it must have been "I Get By with a Little Help from My Friends." All those listed above share in whatever praise accrues to the *Handbook.* The editor accepts sole responsibility for its limitations.

Abbott, Berenice (1889–1991)

Berenice Abbott was a photographer who documented people, places, and scientific phenomena during a lengthy, critically acclaimed career. She is almost as well-known for her role in the preservation and promotion of the images of nineteenth-century French photographer Eugene Atget, whose life's work she brought to the attention of the art world.

Born in Ohio, she studied journalism briefly at Columbia University before embarking on a trip to Europe in 1921. She learned photography in Paris in 1925 as the darkroom assistant of avant-garde artist Man Ray. Her own portraits were first exhibited in Paris in 1926. These early images, characterized by their directness and the use of natural light, remain highly regarded to this day.

In 1929, she returned to New York. At a time when the city was undergoing enormous change, she captured the old as it gave way to the new in images imbued with a sense of the tempo and character of the city. In 1935, the Federal Art Project of the Works Progress Administration (WPA) underwrote this venture, which Abbott called *Changing New York*. Ninety-seven photographs appear in a book of the same title published in 1939, the first of many books focusing on her work produced during her long career.

Abbott first became aware of the work of Eugene Atget through Man Ray, who admired its "surreal" documentation of Paris. Not only did Abbott seek out the old man and take the only extant portrait of the artist just before his death in 1927, she bought the bulk of his negatives from his estate. His entire archive was purchased from her by the Museum of Modern Art in 1968.

She first turned her attention to the interpretation of science in the 1940s. In 1958, she was hired by the Physical Science Study Committee to illustrate a new textbook, *Physics,* which was published in 1960.

Abbott taught photography at the New School for Social Research in New York from 1934 to 1958. She wrote articles and book introductions about Atget, Nadar, and Lisette Model. In later years, she exhibited images from all periods of her career in many galleries and institutions, among them the Museum of Modern Art in 1970, the Smithsonian in 1982, and the International Center for Photography in 1989. As an artist and a historian she occupies a major position in the history of twentieth-century photography. *(See also: Photography)*

—**Allison Bertrand**

Further Reading

Abbott, Berenice. *The World of Atget.* New York: Horizon, 1964.

Berenice Abbott: Photographs. New York: Horizon, 1970. Reprint, Washington, DC: Smithsonian Institution Press, 1990.

Jones, Kurt. "Berenice Abbott, 1898–1991," *Afterimage* 19 (February 1992): 2.

McCausland, Elizabeth, and Berenice Abbott. *Changing New York.* New York: E. P. Dutton, 1939. Revised and reprinted as *New York in the Thirties, as Photographed by Berenice Abbott.* New York: Dover, 1973.

Van Haaften, Julia. *Berenice Abbott,* Aperture Masters of Photography, no. 9. New York: Aperture Foundation, 1988.

Abbott, Edith (1876–1957)

Recognized for her contributions to social work education, Edith Abbott lived most of her life in Chicago, teaching, writing, and championing the poor. Born in Nebraska, she earned a doctorate in economics from the University of Chicago (1905), studied at the London School of Economics, and worked for the Women's Trade Union League, the American Economic Association, the Carnegie Institution, Wellesley College, and St. Hilda's Settlement (London) before moving with her sister Grace to Hull House (1908), where she participated in the settlement house movement with Jane Addams, Julia Lathrop, and Florence Kelley. The movement encouraged educated young people to "settle" and work among the urban poor and serve as catalysts for social reform. Abbott joined the Chicago School of Civics and Philanthropy, teaching social research, her hallmark, and by 1919 was helping to organize the first national association of schools of social work. In 1920, she negotiated a merger that resulted in the establishment of the Graduate School of Social Service Administration of the University of Chicago. She advocated "professional education," placing social work under university auspices despite criticism from supporters of the concept of apprenticeship in programs controlled by the charity organizations. By 1924, the University of Chicago had named Abbott a dean, a position she held until her retirement in 1942.

While the casework method became prevalent in eastern schools, Abbott's curriculum emphasized the structures of government, legislation, economics, social research, and the history of social welfare. Her graduates were sought for their expertise in social administration, especially during the post-Depression recovery period. Abbott and her colleague Sophonisba Breckinridge established the *Social Service Review,* which Abbott edited for many years. Her influence on the development of social work education and public policy remains in the more than one hundred books and papers she published. *(See also: Abbott, Grace; Hull House; Social Work; University of Chicago)*

—Beverly G. Toomey

Further Reading

Costin, Lela. *Two Sisters for Social Justice: A Biography of Grace and Edith Abbott.* Urbana: University of Illinois Press, 1983.

Abbott, Grace (1878–1939)

Best known for her advocacy of women and children, this outstanding social reformer and public administrator influenced the social welfare policies of five presidential administrations. Trained as a teacher in her native Nebraska, Grace Abbott went to Chicago to study political science at the University of Chicago but was truly educated at Hull House in the social activism of Jane Addams and Julia Lathrop. In 1908, she began serving the immigrant community, and from this experience she developed a lifelong commitment to the causes of women and children as well as to world peace, representing Hull House at the International Congress of Women, an antiwar meeting in 1916.

Guided by Lathrop, who became the first director of the U.S. Children's Bureau, Abbott was instrumental in the development of child labor laws, and in 1917, she took her first Washington appointment to administer them. When they were declared unconstitutional, Abbott returned to the Immigrant Protective League in Chicago until President Harding appointed her to head the Children's Bureau in 1921. Under her leadership, the bureau led the fight for maternal and child health care, child welfare, and child labor laws. Abbott also continued to work for international peace by organizing numerous international conferences on child welfare issues. She left the bureau in 1934 to join the faculty at the University of Chicago but remained active as a member of the President's Advisory Council on Economic Security and is credited with having significantly influenced the final passage of the Social Security Act.

Grace Abbott's death from cancer in 1939 left her sister Edith, close compatriot in ideology and activism, in despair. Her legacy lies in the influence she brought to bear on behalf of the needy in America. *(See also: Abbott, Edith; Hull House; Immigrant Protective League; Protective Legislation; Social Security Act of 1935; United States Children's Bureau)*

—Beverly G. Toomey

Further Reading

Abbott, Edith. "Grace Abbott: A Sister's Memories," *Social Service Review* 4 (September 1939): 351-407.
Abbott, Grace. *The Child and the State,* 2 vols. Chicago: University of Chicago Press, 1945.
———. *From Relief to Social Security.* Chicago: University of Chicago Press, 1941.
Costin, Lela. *Two Sisters for Social Justice: A Biography of Grace and Edith Abbott.* Urbana: University of Illinois Press, 1983.
Parker, Jacqueline K. "Women at the Helm: Succession Politics at the Children's Bureau," *Social Work* 39 (September 1994): 551-59.

Abolition and the Antislavery Movement

Thousands of American women in the early nineteenth century braved public disapproval to participate in the antislavery movement. Often veterans of moral reform activities, these women were inspired by a blend of religious principles and republican ideology to call for an immediate end to slavery. Fighting for a place in moral reform activities outside a narrow, domestically defined sphere, the female abolitionists helped set in motion the organized women's rights campaign.

A few women attended the founding convention of the American Anti-Slavery Society (AASS) in 1833, but that organization at first barred female members. Abolitionist women instead formed their own local organizations, which held national conventions in 1837 and 1838. By sponsoring events such as bazaars and picnics, these women's groups soon became invaluable fund-raisers for the abolitionist movement. In the late 1830s, female abolitionists entered the political arena by sending large numbers of antislavery petitions to Congress.

The question of the proper role of women in the abolitionist movement surfaced in 1837, when Angelina and Sarah Grimké, expatriate sisters from South Carolina, broke social convention by lecturing to mixed audiences of males and females. When several Massachusetts clergymen condemned the Grimkés, a radical male abolitionist faction led by William Lloyd Garrison championed the right of women to participate in every part of the movement. Many other male abolitionists opposed a public role for female abolitionists—some because of antifeminist principles, and others because they feared a backlash from linking antislavery to an even more unpopular cause. The "woman's issue" became enmeshed with other quarrels among abolitionists regarding tactics in the religious and political spheres. After gaining the right to vote in the AASS's annual meeting in 1839, women provided the Garrisonians with the strength to win control of the society the following year, when their opponents quit to protest the election of a female officer.

Women played key roles in the AASS after 1840. Maria Weston Chapman of Boston served as one of the society's principal propagandists and oversaw the operation of its main office. Lydia Maria Child edited the AASS's official newspaper for almost two years. Abby Kelley, Lucy Stone, Sojourner Truth, Elizabeth Cady Stanton, and dozens of other women braved insults and threats of physical harm to serve as traveling lecturers and organizers. These public figures became important role models for women seeking to overcome other barriers to their sex.

In contrast to the Garrisonians, political and religious abolitionists allowed women little role in their organized activities. The one prominent antislavery woman outside the Garrisonian ranks was Harriet Beecher Stowe, whose novel *Uncle Tom's Cabin* proved the most effective piece of propaganda of the entire abolitionist movement.

The abolitionist ideology of inalienable rights for all gave early feminists powerful arguments with which to challenge the strictures placed on their sex by institutions such as church and state. Elizabeth Cady Stanton, Susan B. Anthony, Lucy Stone, and hundreds of other female abolitionists also learned valuable organizational and agitational skills that they later brought to the women's rights campaign. Having fought for equal participation in the antislavery movement, these women would continue to struggle to be equal in society. *(See also: American Antislavery Societies; Garrisonians; Grimké, Angelina Emily; Grimké, Sarah Moore; Public Speakers: Nineteenth Century; Stowe, Harriet Beecher; Women's Rights Movements: Nineteenth and Twentieth Centuries)*

—**John R. McKivigan**

Further Reading

DuBois, Ellen. "Women Rights and Abolition: The Nature of the Connection." In *Antislavery Reconsidered: New Perspectives on the Abolitionists,* edited by Lewis Perry and Michael Fellman, 238-51. Baton Rouge: Louisiana University Press, 1979.

Friedman, Lawrence J. *Gregarious Saints: Self and Community in American Abolitionism, 1830–1879.* New York: Cambridge University Press, 1982.

Hersh, Blanche Glassman. *The Slavery of Sex: Feminist-Abolitionists in America.* Urbana: University of Illinois Press, 1978.

Hewitt, Nancy A. *Women's Activism and Social Change: Rochester, New York, 1822–1872.* Ithaca, NY: Cornell University Press, 1984.

Yellin, Jean Fagin. *Women and Sisters: The Antislavery Feminists in American Culture.* New Haven, CT: Yale University Press, 1989.

ᴥ Abortion

In medical terms, abortion is the termination of a pregnancy, whether spontaneous or induced. Reports of the practice of abortion for purposes of selective birth control and maternal health date back to ancient times, and the controversy surrounding this practice also appears to have arisen then. One finds a proscription of the practice in the Hippocratic oath taken by Greek physicians.

In the United States, until the latter half of the nineteenth century, physicians regularly performed abortions at the request of pregnant women prior to "quickening." Quicken-

Figure 1. Abortion Rights
Protest surrounded the U.S. Supreme Court hearing of *Webster v. Reproductive Health Services.* The Court's ruling alllowed states to impose restrictions on a woman's right to an abortion during the first trimester of pregnancy. Used by permission of UPI/Corbis-Bettmann.

ing, the point at which the mother first feels the fetus move, normally occurs between the twelfth and fourteenth weeks. Throughout the eighteenth and early nineteenth centuries, women acknowledged that voluntary abortion was illegal, but generally, they did not perceive the practice as a sin. The movement to establish abortion as both criminal and sinful was led by male physicians as part of a crusade from the 1860s to the 1880s to outlaw all forms of contraception. In 1821, Connecticut became the first state to pass legislation restricting abortion, and by 1860, twenty states and territories in the United States had such laws.

By 1965, all fifty states had passed legislation prohibiting abortion during all stages of pregnancy. These laws allowed only therapeutic abortions, generally restricted to life-threatening situations. Women of means were forced to travel at great expense to procure abortions in other countries. Less fortunate women resorted to dangerous, often fatal, illegal abortions or, worse still, attempts at self-induced abortion. It is important to note that legal prohibition did not have the effect of reducing the incidence of abortion.

In the 1960s, under pressure from the feminist movement, a number of states liberalized their laws to allow abortions for reasons other than the endangerment of a woman's life or physical well-being. The new grounds included rape, incest, and, in several states, fetal deformity. Most feminists saw these changes as welcome but far from ideal. In many states, for example, abortion required the consent of the spouse or parent. Without the availability of abortion on demand, the decision of whether to continue a pregnancy remained under the control of the legal and medical communities, not the woman herself.

In the early 1970s, legal challenges were increasingly mounted against any prohibition of a woman's ability to obtain an abortion. The resulting Supreme Court decision in *Roe v. Wade* (1973) struck down all state laws prohibiting abortion on any grounds during the first trimester of pregnancy (the first twelve weeks after conception). Furthermore, *Roe v. Wade* allowed state regulation of abortion after the first trimester but before viability (the point at which the fetus can survive outside the womb) only to protect the pregnant woman's health and safety. *Roe v. Wade* did not, however, strike down the requirement that a woman obtain spousal or parental consent. Subsequent court action has removed this requirement except in cases of immature, unemancipated minors.

Since *Roe v. Wade*, antiabortion forces have tried in various ways to restrict women's ability to obtain abortions. In 1981, a Human Life Amendment, which declared that human life begins at conception, was introduced in Congress. This proposal, which would have had the effect of giving unicellular conceptuses equal legal status with any U.S. citizen, failed to make it out of committee. The city of Akron, Ohio, passed legislation that required (a) that physicians inform women seeking abortions of various details of fetal development and of the physical and emotional risks of abortion; (b) that abortions be performed only at hospitals, not clinics (where most early abortions are performed); and (c) that a physician not perform an abortion until at least twenty-four hours after an informed consent form has been signed. This law was subsequently found unconstitutional by the Supreme Court in *City of Akron v. Akron Center for Reproductive Health* (1983). Perhaps the most significant antiabortion legislation since *Roe v. Wade*, however, has been the Hyde Amendment, which restricts federal Medicaid funding for abortion to cases in which the mother's life is endangered by continuing the pregnancy or when the pregnancy is the result of rape or incest. The Supreme Court upheld the constitutionality of this legislation in a 1980 decision, *Harris v. McRae*. Although the Court reaffirmed the central holding of *Roe v. Wade* in 1986, a newly constituted Court agreed to hear *Webster v. Reproductive Health Services* in 1989. The Supreme Court decision on the *Webster* case opened the door for states to assume the authority to limit a woman's right to a legal abortion.

In 1992, *Planned Parenthood of Southeastern Pennsylvania v. Casey* set a new precedent for consideration of state regulations on a woman's right to choose. Until *Casey*, the Court had interpreted the right articulated in *Roe v. Wade* as a "fundamental" right that could not be restricted by requirements such as parental notification, waiting periods, and requirements that the woman be provided state-mandated information about abortion and fetal development. With *Casey*, the Court adopted a new standard to the effect that states can regulate abortion, provided that the regulation does not place an "undue burden" on the woman seeking an abortion. With *Casey*, the burden of proof in abortion rulings has shifted from requiring that the state prove that its regulation does not impinge on a woman's right to an abortion to requiring that the plaintiff prove that the regulation does not place an undue burden on the woman seeking an abortion. This new test has allowed many states to place conditions such as waiting periods, parental notification, and requiring that women seeking abortions be given state-mandated information.

By the mid-1990s, concern regarding the impact of technology on abortion practices replaced focus on state or federal control of abortion laws that characterized the debates over abortion in the 1980s. Availability of mifepristone (known also as RU-486, the "French pill" or the "morning-after" pill) became an issue within the abortion debate in the 1990s, as did "partial-birth" abortion. *(See also: Birth Control; Right-Wing Political Movements;* Roe v. Wade)

—**David Levin**

Further Reading

Bogavoglia, Angela. "Later-Term Abortion: Separating Fact from Fiction," *Ms.* 7 (May/ June 1997): 54-63.

Callahan, Daniel. *Abortion: Law, Choice, and Morality.* New York: Macmillan, 1970.

City of Akron v. Akron Center for Reproductive Health, 462 U.S. 416, 76 L. Ed. 2d 687 (1983).

Davis, Nanette J. *From Crime to Choice: The Transformation of Abortion in America.* Westport, CT: Greenwood, 1985.

Faux, Marion. Roe v. Wade: *The Untold Story of the Landmark Decision That Made Abortion Legal.* New York: Mentor, 1989.

Gordon, Linda. *Woman's Body, Woman's Right: A Social History of Birth Control in America.* New York: Penguin, 1974, 1976.

Harper, John Paull. "Be Fruitful and Multiply: Origins of Legal Restrictions on Planned Parenthood in Nineteenth Century America." In *Women of America: A History,* edited by Carol Ruth Berkin and Mary Beth Norton, 245-69. Boston: Houghton Mifflin, 1979.

Harris v. McRae, 48 U.S. 917 (1980).

Mohr, James. *Abortion in America: The Origins and Evolution of National Policy.* New York: Oxford University Press, 1978.

Planned Parenthood of Southeastern Pennsylvania v. Casey, 112 S. Ct. 2791 (1992).

Roe v. Wade, 410 U.S. 113, 35 L. Ed. 2d, 147. 93 S. Ct. 705 (1973).

Webster v. Reproductive Health Services, 851 F. 2d 1074 (8th. Cir. 1988), probable jurisdiction noted, 109 S. Ct. 780 (1989).

◄ Abzug, Bella Savitsky (1920–1998)

Bella Abzug was a civil rights and labor lawyer, lobbyist, sociopolitical activist, and congressional representative.

Born into a Russian-Jewish immigrant family, she received her A.B. from Hunter College and graduated from Columbia Law School in 1947. As a law student, Abzug edited the *Columbia Law Review.*

After graduation, Abzug offered free legal services in cases involving civil rights and civil liberties issues and defended individuals accused of subversion by Joe McCarthy. During the 1950s, Abzug helped author legislation included in the Civil Rights Act of 1954 and the Voting Rights Act of 1965. Her activism increased during the 1960s. She served as a political action director for the Women's Strike for Peace, and she led nuclear disarmament and antiwar lobbies and demonstrations in Washington.

After her election to Congress in 1971, Abzug immediately filed a resolution calling for the end of the war in Vietnam. As a congresswoman, she was appointed to the prestigious Public Works and Government Operations Committees. While in Congress, Abzug was instrumental in founding the National Women's Political Caucus, co-authored the Freedom of Information Act, proposed the bill that federally financed the National Women's Conference of 1977, and worked on behalf of the Equal Rights Amendment.

Abzug was defeated by Daniel Patrick Moynihan in her bid for a U.S. Senate seat in 1976. She also competed unsuccessfully in the 1977 New York mayoral primary. She subsequently served as cochair of the President's National Advisory Committee on Women in the Carter administration until her dismissal in 1979. As a member of the Democratic National Committee and secretary to the General U.N. Conference on Environment and Development, she continued to work on behalf of women's rights.

In 1990, Abzug and her associate Mim Kelber created the Women's Environment & Development Organization (WEDO), an organization that worked to give power to women within the U.N. system. This worldwide network has its secretariat in New York City, near U.N. headquarters, but also holds international meetings that have focused on the environment at a conference in Brazil, on human rights (Vienna), population (Cairo), and women (Beijing). The group analyzes all U.N. documents to determine their impact on women and monitors government action in response to U.N. directives. Although Abzug died on March 31, 1998, her influence as a champion of women's rights, as an advocate of economic, environmental, and racial justice, and as a peace activist continues. *(See also: Democratic Party; Gender Gap; Politics)*

—**Donald R. Martin**

Further Reading

Abzug, Bella S. *Bella! Ms. Abzug Goes to Washington.* New York: Saturday Review Press, 1972.

———. "If Women Had a Foreign Policy," *Ms.* 13 (March 1985): 42-50.

Abzug, Bella S., and Mim Kelber. *Gender Gap.* New York: Houghton Mifflin, 1984.

———. "Three Scenarios for the '84 Election," *Ms.* 12 (March 1984): 39-42.

Faber, Doris. *Bella Abzug.* New York: Lothrop, 1976.

Malanowski, Jamie. "Running with the Also Rans," *Harper's* 267 (November 1983): 69-73.

Mathews, Tom, and Lucy Howard. "Bye, Bye, Bella," *Newsweek* 93 (January 22, 1979): 27-28.

Matson, Rosemary. "Nairobi—Where the End Is the Beginning," *The Humanist* 45 (November/ December 1985): 12-16.

Steinem, Gloria. "Remembering Bella," *Ms.* 9 (July/August 1998): 79-80.

⟍ Acquaintance/Date Rape

Acquaintance or date rape is sexual assault by someone known to the victim who is not related by blood or marriage. Date rape is, by definition, sexual assault that occurs while on a date or between persons who expect to have (or already have) an intimate relationship.

Primary targets of acquaintance rape or date rape are girls and women in their last year of high school or freshman year of college. Acquaintance rapes tend to occur primarily on weekends, are usually committed in the rapist's own environment, and occur indoors. The date rapist rarely uses lethal weapons; he relies instead on verbal threats and physical force to intimidate and overpower. Such sexual assault tends to be longer in duration, sometimes stretching over hours, and is likely to occur on first or blind dates and when both the victim and the perpetrator have been drinking.

Some studies estimate that up to 89 percent of rapes that occur in this country are committed by someone known to the victim. Fifty-seven percent of these occurred on dates. Yet despite these high incidence rates, fewer than 1 percent of these sexual assaults are reported. If the victim/survivor does report, she is more likely to drop out of the legal system before prosecution of the crime. If a trial occurs, jurors are hesitant to convict if the rapist and victim knew each other.

Myths about rape contribute substantially to both the high incidence of acquaintance rape and the lack of reporting. Date rape is not provoked by the victim. This mistaken belief holds that women "ask to be raped" through their actions or dress. Men may overestimate their date's interest in sex and may later feel "led on," which some males regard as justification for rape. Situations rated as most indicative that the woman wanted sex were when she asked the man out, went to his apartment, or let him pay the dating expenses. Beliefs that women "tease" men sexually and that women cry "rape" after initially agreeing to have sex are also unfounded; the FBI indicates that false reports of rape occur in the same percentage as that of any other crime, 5 percent.

In our society, both males and females have been taught many half-truths about each other. Males are taught to "score" with women sexually; they believe women say no but really mean yes and just need a little persuasion. Women are taught that they are responsible if things get out of hand sexually. All too frequently, the result of this social conditioning is rape.

However, rape on a date is not a communication problem; it is coercive sex. New coercive techniques include the use of Rohypnol, GHB, and Ketamine, the so-called date rape drugs. Inducing sedation and amnesia, rapists give these drugs to potential victims to ensure cooperation and make prosecution difficult. Due to the drug-induced amnesia, it is impossible to estimate the frequency of use of these substances. Their use is increasing, however.

Victim/survivors experience equal, if not greater, trauma than that experienced by victims of stranger rape. However, due to societal attitudes of disbelief, they are less likely to seek psychological help or support. They are more likely to blame themselves and feel betrayed by their own judgment. They may also have to face the rapist again, especially in school settings.

Because female high school students and college freshmen are at risk, many campuses are developing policies, as well as educational programs at freshman orientations. Peer education has been effective in reducing date rape and in helping men rethink their attitudes about sexual activity on dates. *(See also: Dating; Marital Rape; Rape/Sexual Assault)*

—**Susan C. Turell**

Further Reading

Brownmiller, Susan. *Against Our Will*. New York: Bantam, 1988.

Calhoun, S., D. Wesson, G. Galloway, and D. Smith. "Abuse of Fluritrazepam (Rohypnol) and Other Benzodiazepines in Austin and South Texas," *Journal of Psychoactive Drugs* 28 (1996): 183-89.

Koss, M. P., T. E. Dinero, C. Siebel, and S. Cox. "Stranger, Acquaintance, and Date Rape: Is There a Difference in the Victim's Experience?" *Psychology of Women Quarterly* 12 (1988): 1-24.

Koss, M. P., C. A. Gidycz, and N. Wisniewski. "The Scope of Rape: Incidence and Prevalence of Sexual Aggression and Victimization in a National Sample of Higher Education Students," *Journal of Consulting and Clinical Psychology* 55 (1987): 162-70.

✦ Adams, Abigail (1744–1818)

Abigail Adams was a prodigious letter writer and an astute observer of the revolutionary American political system. As the wife of John Adams, prominent lawyer, legislator, and second president of the United States, she exerted an influence over his political decisions and also had a strong voice in the domestic decisions that affected them both. A champion of the American Revolution, Adams believed in America's right to free itself from Britain's rule. Although she supported America's right to rebel, she also held deeply conservative political views regarding the right of others to revolt, especially those who questioned the nature of the newly formed government in America.

Adams held similarly contrasting views about the role of women in society. She believed, for example, that women were the intellectual equals of men and therefore had a right to an equal education. In her philosophy, education symbolized the role of women in the social sphere, and Adams often lamented her own lack of education. Yet she also felt that the proper place for women was in the home, taking care of the children and ensuring a proper environment for the family. Adams thought she herself was unable to manage responsibilities outside the domestic sphere, yet during the extended periods when her husband was in Philadelphia or abroad, she ran the family farm, managed all of the finances, made most of the financial decisions, and raised her children alone.

In her many letters to friends, family, and especially her husband, Adams discussed the role of women in eighteenth-century life. She criticized the legal and social status of women, particularly the lack of available public education. During her husband's absences, she relayed vital political information to him. Abigail Adams enjoyed the excitement of politics and exercised considerable influence over President Adams, who relied heavily on her judgment. *(See also: Revolutionary War)*

—**Lynn E. Lipor**

Further Reading

Adams, Abigail. *Familiar Letters of John Adams and His Wife Abigail Adams during the Revolution, with a Memoir of Mrs. Adams*. Edited by Charles Francis Adams. Boston: Houghton Mifflin, 1875. Reprint, Freeport, NY: Books for Library Press, 1970.

Levin, Phyllis Lee. *Abigail Adams: A Biography*. New York: Ballantine, 1987.

Withey, Lynn. *Dearest Friend: A Life of Abigail Adams*. New York: Free Press, 1981.

✦ Addams, Jane (1860–1935)

Pioneer in the settlement house movement, social worker, and peace advocate, Jane Addams was among America's most influential reformers in the late nineteenth and early twentieth centuries. As the founder of Chicago's Hull House settlement—which served the neighborhood poor and served as a center for social reform activities—she rejected women's traditional role in the home for a career in the public sector. Through her speaking and writing, she encouraged other women, particularly those with an advanced education, to abandon the domestic sphere for the world of social activism. By the time the settlement was a few years old, it had become a virtual clearinghouse of reform and home to an amazing array of talented women and men. Together, they worked to improve the lives of their immigrant neighbors while finding an outlet for their own education, skills, and ambitions.

Addams was born and raised in rural Cedarville, Illinois. Her mother died when she was two years old, and Addams grew up with an unusually strong attachment to her father, a prominent local businessman and politician. In 1877, she enrolled at nearby Rockford Female Seminary. Her father died the summer after her graduation, and Addams plunged into a decade-long period of depression and indecision. She attempted medical school, underwent spinal surgery, and twice journeyed abroad. While in London, she visited

Toynbee Hall settlement and determined to launch a similar project when she returned to America.

In September 1889, Addams fulfilled that promise when she and Rockford classmate Ellen Gates Starr moved into the decaying Hull mansion in the heart of Chicago's teeming Nineteenth Ward. By 1893, the settlement housed the regular meetings of over forty different groups that attracted approximately two thousand participants weekly. Moreover, it was a center of scholarly inquiry, as Addams and other practitioners of the new social work methodology attempted to define and describe their environment.

Addams wrote numerous books and articles outlining her experiences at Hull House. In addition, she was a leader in other contemporary reform efforts, including the woman suffrage and peace movements. Her pacifist opposition to World War I eroded her popularity during the war years, but by the 1930s, she had regained prominence. Addams shared the 1931 Nobel Peace Prize, evidence of the recognition she earned by dedicating almost fifty years to social activism and service. *(See also: Hull House; Pacifism and the Peace Movement; Settlement House Movement; Social Work; Starr, Ellen Gates)*

—**Rebecca L. Sherrick**

Further Reading

Addams, Jane. *The Second Twenty Years at Hull-House.* New York: Macmillan, 1930.
———. *Twenty Years at Hull-House.* New York: Macmillan, 1910.
Davis, Allen F. *American Heroine.* New York: Oxford University Press, 1973.
Jane Addams Papers. Swarthmore College Peace Collection. Swarthmore, PA.

Adkins v. Children's Hospital (1923)

Adkins v. Children's Hospital was a decision by the conservative majority of the Supreme Court in 1923 that a District of Columbia minimum wage law for women was unconstitutional. The Court ruled that such a federal law deprived a woman of the liberty to bargain in making contracts.

The *Adkins* decision struck a blow at Progressive Era reform groups because it removed the principal grounds on which they sought legislative assistance. In addition, it further divided the already polarized National Woman's Party (NWP). Labor activist and NWP leader Florence Kelley, along with her followers, worked to create and support minimum wage laws for women. This position was based on the traditional view of women as dependent on males. Alice Paul, also a leader in the NWP, resented the implications of such legislation for women. She and her followers preferred to regard women as equals, a view that led to Paul's development of the first proposed Equal Rights Amendment.

The Court's ruling struck down minimum wage laws for women in the District of Columbia, Arizona, Kansas, and Wisconsin. Elsewhere, the law fell into disuse. As Kelley noted, the Court had, in reality, affirmed "the inalienable right of women to starve." *(See also: Kelley, Florence; Progressive Legislation; Protective Legislation)*

—**Karen Raines-Pate**
—**Jonathan W. Zophy**

Further Reading

Adkins v. Children's Hospital, 261 U.S. 525 (1923).
Baer, Judith A. *The Chains of Protection: The Judicial Response to Women's Labor Legislation.* Westport, CT: Greenwood, 1978.
Zimmerman, Joan G. "The Jurisprudence of Equality: The Women's Minimum Wage, the First Equal Rights Amendment, and *Adkins v. Children's Hospital,* 1905–1923," *Journal of American History* (June 1991): 188-225.

Advertising

Advertising is commercial messages, the majority of which are directed at women as consumers of products and that use women in their content to attract men as consumers. National advertising became a significant feature of industrial capitalism at the end of the nineteenth century as a means to create markets for newly mass-produced products. As separate public and private spheres were imagined in order to create distinct roles for women and men in the new economic order, women came to be seen as the primary household consumer to whom advertising was directed.

Advertising content over the past one hundred years has reflected changing expectations for women. For example, after World War II, advertising content echoed the national drive to establish homemaking and motherhood as women's highest aspiration. In the 1960s, advertising directed to men began the now well-established tradition of using white women as beauty objects, capitalizing on the "sexual revolution" touted by the mass media.

Feminist activists and scholars have seen advertising as a critical part of the symbol system that defines women in limited and negative ways. A beauty and fashion standard is set by white women models that is impossible for white women and women of color to attain. A historic black mammy figure in advertising, characterized by Aunt Jemima, shadows many of the black women models used in contemporary ads. Native women are relegated to "Indian Princess" characters. During the last decades of the twentieth century, advertising that used images of women as victims of sexual and other violence became increasingly widespread. The trend, as well as gender and ethnic stereotyping, has been effectively described and illustrated in Jane Kilbourne's documentary *Still Killing Us Softly,* which began as a slide show in the Boston area.

Advertising representations rely on a "visual grammar" that codes power relations between women and men in both overt and covert ways. Visual advertising messages are linked to other genres of texts, including magazines, fashion photography, and pornography, making intervention in the production of such images difficult but critical. *(See also:*

Consumerism; Mass Communication Media; Popular Culture; Pornography)

—Lana F. Rakow

Further Reading
Bartels, Diana. *Putting on Appearances: Gender and Advertising.* Philadelphia: Temple University Press, 1988.
Goffman, Irving. *Gender Advertisements.* New York: Harper & Row, 1979.
Kern-Foxworth, Marilyn. *Aunt Jemima, Uncle Ben, and Rastus: Blacks in Advertising, Yesterday, Today, and Tomorrow.* Westport, CT: Greenwood, 1994.
Kilbourne, Jean. *Still Killing Us Softly.* Film. Cambridge, MA: Cambridge Documentary Films. [Available from Cambridge Documentary Films, Inc., P.O. Box 390385, Cambridge, MA 02139-0004; phone: 617-484-3993; fax: 617-484-0754]
Warlaumont, Hazel G. "Visual Grammars of Gender: The Gaze and Psychoanalytic Theory in Advertisements," *Journal of Communication Inquiry* 17 (Winter 1993): 25-40.
Wolf, Naomi. *The Beauty Myth: How Images of Beauty Are Used Against Women.* New York: William Morrow, 1991.

✎ Advice to a Daughter (1688)

Advice to a Daughter is an early example of the prescriptive literature for girls that influenced early American women writers of that genre in the nineteenth century. Originally a letter written by the Marquis of Halifax to his daughter, it was one of the first etiquette documents directing a woman of the upper class about what to think and how to act in different situations. The letter begins with an explanation by the Marquis of his reasons for writing it: so his daughter will know what to expect and how to behave in life, and will exemplify "the Picture of a fine Woman." Nine chapters of advice follow, beginning with the most important, Religion, and continuing with Husbands, House and Family and Children, Behavior and Conversation, Friendships, Censure, Vanity, Pride, and, finally, Diversions.

The Marquis's belief in his daughter's intelligence is revealed in his advice. The longest chapter, on husbands, explains how she should deal with men of different temperaments without appearing superior. In the chapter on the management of the house, the father discusses how to balance different areas of expense, such as decoration, menu, clothing, and entertainment. The idea of correct behavior in the company of different people, such as men, friends, servants, and children, is also explained.

While *Advice to a Daughter* considers the proper attitudes necessary for a woman to live comfortably and be well respected by her family and peers, it also acknowledges the difficulties of a woman's life and the intelligence needed to balance her responsibilities, behave correctly, and be happy. Victorian women writers relied heavily on such seventeenth- and eighteenth-century prescriptive literature in the development of their works that promoted the cult of true womanhood. *(See also: Cult of True Womanhood; Prescriptive Literature)*

—Theresa A. McGeary

Further Reading
Marquis of Halifax. *Advice to a Daughter.* London: Matt, Gillyflower, 1688.

✎ Affirmative Action

Affirmative action refers to a series of federal regulations, based on executive orders and federal statutes, that prohibit employment discrimination by employers who hold contracts with the federal government and require such employers to make "good faith" efforts to remedy past discrimination by recruiting, hiring, and promoting minority group members. Currently, affirmative action regulations apply to businesses and institutions that employ about a third of the U.S. labor force.

Originally promulgated under Executive Order 11246 in 1964, affirmative action forbade discrimination only on the basis of race, color, religion, or national origin; sex was added in 1968 through Executive Order 11375. As an executive order, issued by the president, affirmative action is not a law, but the courts have ruled that it has the "force and effect of law." It is enforced, however, differently than a law.

The Office of Federal Contract Compliance (OFCC) has been charged with enforcing affirmative action regulations, and it, in turn, has delegated the responsibility to fifteen government departments or compliance agencies. Each compliance agency is supposed to conduct periodic reviews of government contractors, and every contractor scheduled to receive $1 million or more in federal funds must pass a compliance review before the money is actually awarded. Each contractor must establish a program of goals for recruitment with a fixed timetable for achievement in the hiring of women and minorities. In addition, individuals and groups may file a discrimination complaint with the OFCC or a compliance agency against a federal contractor. After an investigation in which the employer has been found in violation of affirmative action regulations, the OFCC or compliance agency may (a) withhold funds until compliance is achieved, (b) cancel the federal contract, (c) bar the employer from receiving future federal contracts, or (d) refer the case to the Justice Department or the Equal Employment Opportunity Commission for suit in the federal courts.

Despite these provisions, affirmative action has been largely ineffective in preventing and remedying discrimination. One important reason is that the departments and agencies responsible for enforcement are not adequately staffed to carry out effective reviews and investigations. As a result, relatively few employers have actually been sanctioned for violations. In addition, since 1980, the federal government has undertaken to weaken the regulations and to limit their protective applicability. At the same time, the Justice Department has gone to court to oppose the use of numerical goals in affirmative action plans and to argue against programs that provide preferential treatment for women and minorities. Such actions signal the dismantling of affirmative action, but the congressional override of President Reagan's veto of the Civil Rights Restoration Act in 1988 reestablished the intent of Congress and, therefore, the constitutionality of requiring institution-wide compliance with antidiscrimination laws whenever federal funds are accepted by that institution.

Although the Clinton administration publicly defended affirmative action, it simultaneously implemented the most drastic reduction in affirmative action programs since the 1960s. In addition, during the 1990s, voters in California and Washington supported propositions to repeal affirmative action programs in their states, and a federal appeals court in Texas ruled that the affirmative action program at the University of Texas, Austin, law school was unconstitutional because it allowed for reverse discrimination. Thus, the future of affirmative action appears uncertain. *(See also: Equal Employment Opportunity Commission)*

—**Claire M. Renzetti**

Further Reading

Guinier, L., and S. Strum. "The Future of Affirmative Action: Reclaiming the Innovative Idea," *California Law Review* (1996): 953-1037.

Hanmer, Trudy J. *Affirmative Action: Opportunity for All?* Hillside, NJ: Enslow, 1993.

Pottinger, J. Stanley. "Race, Sex, and Jobs: The Drive Toward Equality," *Change Magazine* 4 (October 1972): 24, 26-29.

Lindgren, J. R., and N. Traub. *The Law of Sexual Discrimination.* Minneapolis, MN: West, 1993.

African American Benevolent Societies

As far back as the late eighteenth century, black Americans, many of them African-born ex-slaves, joined together in mutual benefit societies. The Free African Societies of Philadelphia and of Newport, Rhode Island, were founded in 1787. Along with the church, these fraternal groups formed the basis for the early institutional organization of the black community in America.

The benevolent societies had both economic and social purposes. Informally, they offered a meeting place where African Americans could gather for friendship, recreation, and a sense of racial solidarity. On a more formal level, they provided economic assistance to members and to the local black community. Dues and other money raised paid for sickness and death benefits to widows and children and for schools and other community needs.

Perhaps because economic relief for widows and children was an important issue in their lives, black women participated as much as and more than men in the African benevolent societies. The Philadelphia Benevolent Society, established in 1793, was the first African American mutual aid organization of its kind. Male societies such as the African Benevolent Society of Newport (1808) stated that they were

open "to any person of colour whether male or female," but only men could vote or hold office. As a result, women organized an autonomous group, the African Female Benevolent Society of Newport (1809). The earliest recorded female group was the Female Benevolent Society of St. Thomas, founded in 1793. By 1830, there were more female societies (twenty-seven) in existence than male (sixteen), according to a study done in Philadelphia in that year.

These autonomous female associations successfully raised money for the "mutual relief" of their communities. The Philadelphia study, for instance, showed that the female societies distributed over $3,500 in benefits, compared with just over $2,000 raised by their male counterparts. The largest amount raised that year, over $400, came from the African Female Band Benevolent Society of Bethel, New York. In the case of at least one female organization, however, the African Dorcas Association of New York City (1827), men, predominantly black ministers, supervised meetings and kept financial records, while women mainly sewed the clothes supplied to children attending the African free schools.

The African female benevolent societies can be seen as part of the religious reform movements found in New York State and New England in the early nineteenth century. These charitable and missionary groups were formed primarily by white middle-class women whose goals and priorities revolved around moral guidance and religious conversion. While both types of groups were charitable, there were major differences. Chief among these was the greater emphasis of the African female benevolent societies on real economic assistance to themselves and their communities. Some of the black women's groups were explicitly working class in nature, such as the Daughters of Africa, whose approximately two hundred members joined together to help themselves economically. Other groups directed their aid to the larger black community, such as the African Dorcas Association or the Female Benevolent Society of Newport, whose main goal was to raise money for a black school.

By the 1830s, these organizations were beginning to take on a more middle-class focus. Instead of "benevolent" or "relief" societies, they began to be known as "mutual improvement" or literary societies. Yet the emphases on economic aid, racial solidarity, and community assistance found in the early African benevolent societies continued to be important throughout the nineteenth century. The early benevolent societies laid the groundwork for late-nineteenth-century black-run banks and insurance companies, as well as many political and community assistance organizations. *(See also: Black Women; Black Women's Clubs)*

—**Mary Battenfeld**

Further Reading

Bracey, John, August Meier, and Elliot Rudwick, eds. *Black Nationalism in America.* New York: Bobbs-Merrill, 1970.

Sterling, Dorothy. *Turning the World Upside Down.* New York: Feminist Press, 1987.

African American Domestic Workers

African American domestic workers are women employed in private homes to perform tasks commonly done by the housewife-mother. African American female slaves, like their male counterparts, were always forced to labor in both the master's field and family home without compensation. After emancipation, the majority of African American women lived in the South, where only sporadic wage-earning opportunities were available to African American men. Working within the southern racial and occupational restrictions to avoid starvation and homelessness, over 80 percent of the employed African American women worked as either laundry or domestic service workers. By 1920, European immigrant and native-born white women servants were replaced by African American servants in households all over the North and West. Thus, the entire nation adopted the long-standing racial, gender, and caste system of the South, and African American women's work was synonymous with household work.

It is difficult to investigate African American household workers for the period prior to 1920 because the government excluded servants from its official definition of working women; however, housework would continue to rank first among these women's occupations through the 1940 census. During the Great Depression of the 1930s, when many white women returned to household employment, African American women faced a deterioration in both working conditions and salaries. During the 1940s, as a result of World War II's expanding employment opportunities, a small percentage of African American household workers found higher-paying jobs in other areas. By the 1950s, however, household workers still received some of the nation's lowest salaries and benefits.

As recently as 1984, the federal government's efforts at "domestic service" reform were halfhearted and haphazard because federal labor researchers never saw housework as contributing to the national economy. During the twentieth century, employment reform laws of the states, originally designed to protect factory workers, have not easily been applied to domestic employees. Even today, it is estimated that less than 9 percent of the household workers receive federal or state employment benefits, because employers and legislators believe the regulation of household service is a threat to domestic privacy and family autonomy. Without question, the low racial and gender status of African American household workers has prolonged government insensitivity to their requests for employment justice. *(See also: Black Women; Domestic Service; Housework; Slavery)*

—**Elizabeth Clark-Lewis**

Further Reading

Basler, Barbara. "Underpaid, Overworked and from the Philippines," *New York Times International* (August 28, 1990): 3.

Clark-Lewis, Elizabeth. *Living In, Living Out: African-American Domestics in Washington, D.C., 1910–1940.* Washington, DC: Smithsonian Press, 1994.

"Domestic Workers Organizing Project," *Metropolitan Women's Organizing Newsletter* (December 1993): 3ff.

Giddings, Paula. *When and Where I Enter.* New York: Random House, 1984.

Jones, Jacqueline. *Labor of Love, Labor of Sorrow.* New York: Basic Books, 1985.

African Free Schools

African Free Schools were the first free secular schools in New York for African American youth. Opened on November 1, 1787, by the New York Manumission Society, the first African Free School was part of a broadly based effort by religious and philanthropic societies to provide free education to Negro freedmen. The first governing Board of Trustees of the school was composed of members of the Manumission Society. In 1834, however, the school's administration was placed under the New York Public School Society. By 1853, authority was entirely relinquished to the New York City Board of Education. In its first three decades, the student body grew from forty to two hundred scholars. By 1847, over five thousand Negro children were enrolled in the New York public school system.

From its inception, all fundamental subjects of instruction were offered, including astronomy and navigation for boys; needlework was added for girls in 1791 when a female teacher joined the faculty. In 1830, separate libraries for male and female students held 450 and 200 volumes, respectively. Moral instruction was emphasized; morning sessions began with Scripture reading. A school fair was held every three months to display the students' best achievements.

In 1809, the school adopted the Lancasterian or Monitorial system of instruction whereby more advanced pupils helped to instruct and discipline those less qualified. A "Class of Merit" composed of the best behaved and most advanced boys met monthly and inspired others with their superior character and achievement.

Parents and guardians were encouraged to participate in the training of students. Toward this end, school agents, one of whom was the Reverend Samuel Cornish, were sent to homes to encourage regular attendance and to advance the educational goals of the institution. Each household was also presented with the printed regulations of the school.

The academic achievement and moral character of students at the African Free Schools was widely recognized and earned the praise of General Lafayette when he visited in 1824. *(See also: Crandall, Prudence; Education)*

—**Marilyn Demarest Button**

Further Reading

Andrews, Charles C. *The History of the African Free Schools.* 1830. Reprint, New York: Greenwood, 1969.

Bond, Horace Mann. *The Education of the Negro in the American Social Order.* New York: Octagon, 1966.

ᴧ Afro-American

The names that persons of African descent in America have used to identify themselves have changed over the years in response to political and social influences. From the colonial and revolutionary era through the early national period, *African* was generally preferred but was frowned on after the founding of the American Colonization Society (1816), an organization whose purpose was to return free persons to Africa and rid the United States of what Henry Clay and others regarded as a social anomaly and political danger. Next the term *colored* was used, but it became unpopular after emancipation because, generally written in lowercase, it was thought to lack specificity and dignity. By the early twentieth century, *Negro* was considered more proper because it was consistent with the so-called scientific racialism of the times. The term served as a rallying point for international racial solidarity, and a major battle was fought to have it capitalized in written usage. *Negro* fell out of favor in the 1960s, however, when "blackness" became glorified as a positive cultural characteristic, in contrast to its negative connotations in the past. Critics argued, moreover, that the term *Negro* was a racist invention and cultural trap because it suggested neither a geographical or national homeland nor an ethnic identity and thus seemed to rest primarily on the legacy of slavery. The terms *Afro-American* and *African-American* have been used during both the nineteenth and twentieth centuries before the 1980s, and many believe that they most accurately reflect the ethnic heritage and national identity of persons of African descent in the United States and that their usage may also help to eliminate our society's preoccupation with skin color. In the 1990s, *African American* and *black* became the terms most commonly employed to designate a person of African descent. *(See also: Black Women)*

—**Gwendolyn Keita Robinson**

ᴧ Age of Consent

Age of consent defines the age at which a girl can be assumed to be acting consensually in "carnal relations with the other sex." Laws setting the age of consent have had mixed aims, which include protecting girls from rape or seduction, regulating prostitution, and policing women's sexual activity.

In common law, the age of consent was ten, which was reflected in the law of many states. Beginning in the 1880s, efforts to raise the age at which a woman could agree to sexual intercourse formed part of a broad series of social purity reforms spearheaded by women. Reformers—a coalition of feminists, Woman's Christian Temperance Union members, and other middle-class white women—often characterized young women as innocents lured into sexual activity by unscrupulous men and in need of protection. These campaigns, which focused on working-class white women, met with some success; by the turn of the century, the age of consent ranged from ten to twenty-one, and by the 1920s, most states set it at sixteen or above. Sexual relations with a girl under the legal age of consent exposed her male partner to criminal penalties, regardless of her consent. Many legislators opposed age-of-consent legislation, fearing that it would allow women to blackmail men. The laws were also sometimes used by families wishing to discipline recalcitrant daughters.

Age-of-consent laws reflected a number of changes in American life by structuring life stages and participating in the construction of female adolescence as a distinct phase. They also reflected the shift from familial to state regulation of youth behavior. Most important, they have defined female maturity in sexual terms and have been used to regulate women's sexual behavior. *(See also: Prostitution; Social Purity Movement; Woman's Christian Temperance Union)*

—**Miriam Reumann**
—**William G. Shade**

Further Reading

Degler, Carl N. *At Odds: Women and the Family in America from the Revolution to the Present.* New York: Oxford University Press, 1980.

D'Emilio, John, and Estelle B. Freedman. *Intimate Matters: A History of Sexuality in America,* 2d ed. Chicago: University of Chicago Press, 1997.

Nathanson, Constance. *Dangerous Passage: The Social Control of Sexuality in Women's Adolescence.* Philadelphia: Temple University Press, 1992.

Odem, Mary E. *Delinquent Daughters: Protecting and Policing Adolescent Female Sexuality in the United States, 1885–1920.* Chapel Hill: University of North Carolina Press, 1995.

Pivar, David J. *Purity Crusade: Sexual Morality and Social Control, 1869–1900.* Westport, CT: Greenwood, 1973.

ᴧ Agriculture: Preindustrial and Nineteenth-Century United States

The role of women in agriculture reflects both the implicit partnership and the inequality of men and women in the agricultural world. The nature of women's participation was altered by the transitions of agriculture on the single-family farm, from colonial- and frontier-era subsistence farming to semisubsistence farming as settlement progressed, to the raising of commercial crops adapted to the particular region in the nineteenth century. Into the twentieth century, there remained strong holdovers of the family economy that required all members of a family to cooperate in producing the means of family survival and, when cash was involved, the family wage. For women, this meant participating in the agricultural cycles of planting, cultivating, and harvesting, as well as maintaining the household. Because subsistence was often the key, some women engaged in poultry production and garden work, both to supply family needs and to provide a meager supplemental cash income. Women also contributed the labor for the home manufacturing that coexisted with factory labor through the nineteenth century.

In the primarily agricultural South, planters' wives faced a variation of this reality. Originally, the relative scarcity of white women in the South allowed them more autonomy than women elsewhere enjoyed. Competition for women as wives declined by the early eighteenth century, but although the demographic inequality disappeared, some of its effect continued in the occasional exercise of women's rights under a more traditional system of social inequality. The planter's wife assumed a dual role, serving as mistress of the household and as overseer of the plantation, with authority over the slaves and hired staff who were responsible for crop production. The household was her primary responsibility, but in the absence of the planter-husband, the entire plantation was subject to her direction.

Southern black women faced a more complex agricultural reality. If they were slaves, they were subject to the work and discipline requirements of slavery. While alterations in work assignments because of sex (half tasks, shorter hours, and the like) were possible, female slaves usually assumed workloads identical to those of male slaves. Within their own frequently disrupted families, they played a domestic role as well, responsible for most of the child care and the laundry, cooking, and rudimentary cleaning tasks that were possible in slave quarters. Finally, the female slave's situation was often complicated by a sexual liaison with the master.

Frontier women, although seldom credited with occupations within census data, performed myriad tasks associated with child rearing and household maintenance and at the same time worked as partners with their husbands in crop production. They were full economic partners in the agricultural world, yet like other women in agriculture, they lacked social and legal equality.

By the mid-twentieth century, the impact of demographic change, technology, and the reform of property rights legislation had improved but not substantially altered the secondary status of women as agricultural workers. *(See also: Black Women; Migration and Frontier Women; Patrons of Husbandry)*

—**Thomas F. Armstrong**

Further Reading

Carr, Lois Green, and Lorena S. Walsh. "The Planter's Wife: The Experience of White Women in Seventeenth Century Maryland," *William and Mary Quarterly* 34 (1977): 542-71.

Janiewski, Dolores E. *Sisterhood Denied: Race, Gender, and Class in a New South Community.* Philadelphia: Temple University Press, 1985.

Jansen, Joan M. *Loosening the Bonds: Mid-Atlantic Farm Women, 1750-1850.* New Haven, CT: Yale University Press, 1986.

Jones, Jacqueline. *Labor of Love/ Labor of Sorrow.* New York: Basic Books, 1985.

———. " 'Tore Up and A-Movin': Perspectives on the Work of Black and Poor White Women in the Rural South, 1865–1920." In *Women and Farming: Changing Roles, Changing*

Structures, edited by Wava G. Haney and Jane B. Knowles, 15-34. Boulder, CO: Westview, 1988.

Riley, Glenda. "Not Gainfully Employed: Women on the Iowa Frontier," *Pacific Historical Review* 49 (May 1980): 237-64.

❧ Ahern, Mary Eileen (1868–1938)

The indefatigable editor of *Public Libraries* from 1896 to 1931, Mary Ahern began her library career as Indiana assistant state librarian in 1889, then became state librarian in 1893. She organized and ran the Indiana Library Association from 1889 to 1896, first as secretary, then as president. After attending library school at Armour Institute in Chicago in 1895, she became editor of a new periodical created to meet the needs of small public libraries recently established throughout the Midwest. *Public Libraries* was intended to rival the older and more genteel New York-based *Library Journal* and emphasized practical information for staff members of small public libraries who could not acquire an apprenticeship or formal library education.

As editor, Ahern was a vocal and articulate critic of professional matters. She regularly battled male leaders of this feminized profession, although usually in private correspondence rather than in the pages of *Public Libraries,* which may have served as a check on their chauvinistic excesses. Ahern was instrumental in wresting the American Library Association headquarters away from New England control and relocating it in Chicago in 1909. She also engaged in a relatively unsuccessful attempt to bring the education and library communities together through her activities as secretary of the library department of the National Education Association. *(See also: Librarianship)*

—**Wayne A. Wiegand**

Further Reading

Dale, Doris Cruger. "Ahern, Mary Eileen (1860–1938)." In *Dictionary of American Library Biography,* edited by Bohdan S. Wynar, 5-7. Littleton, CO: Libraries Unlimited, 1978.

Wiegand, Wayne A. *Politics of an Emerging Profession: The American Library Association, 1876–1917.* Westport, CT: Greenwood, 1986.

❧ AIDS

AIDS, or acquired immune deficiency syndrome, is a fatal, sexually transmitted disease, which first appeared in the United States in approximately 1977. AIDS is caused by a virus transmitted through the exchange of bodily fluids. The main routes of infection have been from transfusions with infected blood, the sharing of hypodermic needles, sexual intercourse (homosexual and heterosexual), and from an infected mother during birth. People infected with the AIDS virus (HIV) are often asymptomatic for many years, after which the virus attacks and destroys the helper T-cells, a vital part of the body's immune system. At this point, a variety of opportunistic illnesses appear.

Political considerations quickly attended the public policy debate over the proper response to what was perceived as an AIDS crisis. Groups that had argued over the political and social consequences of the sexual revolution of the 1960s offered predictably conflicting interpretations of the significance of AIDS as they proposed political and medical policy to meet the crisis.

The U.S. government has been extremely slow in recognizing the risk to women and even slower in recognizing and dealing with this threat appropriately as a community public health issue. AIDS was so strongly presented as a plague on gay men and drug addicts that the federal Centers for Disease Control (CDC) did not establish "heterosexual contact" as an official risk category until 1984 and made the criteria for inclusion in this category so rigid that few cases could unequivocally qualify. However, by 1986, the number of cases among women acquired through sexual contact began to grow faster than those acquired through shared needles, and currently, heterosexual contact is the primary mode of transmission for women.

The proportion of AIDS cases reported for adolescent and adult women continues to grow, and by 1997, women accounted for 22 percent of the cases of AIDS. By 1996, AIDS was the leading cause of death among African American women in the twenty-five- to forty-four-year age group and the fourth leading cause of death among all U.S. women in that age group. Women of color have been most strongly affected by HIV/AIDS. More than three-fourths of the AIDS cases among women were accounted for by African American and Hispanic women, although this group accounts for only one-fourth of the female U.S. population. Between July 1998 and June 1999, 17,142 new cases of AIDS in women were reported.

Women are now the fastest growing group of AIDS patients. Among adolescent girls, the trend has been even more alarming: In 1998, girls constituted 39 percent of all AIDS cases among thirteen- to nineteen-year-olds.

Despite advances in treatment that slow down the progression from HIV infection to AIDS, data on HIV infection in the United States suggests that HIV and AIDS will remain a major public health concern for women. *(See also: Sexual Revolution; Venereal Disease/Sexually Transmitted Diseases)*

—**Hilary Jo Karp**

Further Reading

Cohen, Felissa, and Jerry D. Durham, eds. *Women, Children, and HIV-AIDS.* New York: Springer, 1993.
Corea, Gena. *The Invisible Epidemic: The Story of Women and AIDS.* New York: HarperCollins, 1992.
"Critical Need to Pay Attention to HIV Prevention for Women: Minority and Young Women Bear Greatest Burden." Archived at http://www.cdcnpin.org/geneva98/issues/fwomen.htm [Center for Disease Control and Prevention National AIDS Clearinghouse]
Kloser, Patricia, and Jane M. Craig. *The Women's HIV Sourcebook: A Guide to Better Health and Well-Being.* Dallas, TX: Taylor, 1994.
Koop, C. E. *Surgeon General's Report on Acquired Immune Deficiency Syndrome.* Washington, DC: U.S. Public Health Service, 1986.
Norwood, Chris. *Advice for Life: A Woman's Guide to AIDS Risks and Prevention.* New York: Pantheon, 1987.
Rieder, Ines, and Patricia Ruppelt. *AIDS: The Women.* San Francisco: Cleis, 1988.
Sauire, Corinne, ed. *Women and AIDS: Psychological Perspectives.* Newbury Park, CA: Sage, 1993.
http://www.cdcnpin.org [CDC National AIDS Clearinghouse Website]
http://www.sfaf.org [San Francisco AIDS Foundation]

~ Albright, Madeleine Korbel (b. 1937)

The first female U.S. secretary of state, Madeleine Albright was born in Czechoslovakia. Her family was forced to leave Czechoslovakia twice, first in 1938 to escape the Nazis and then again in the wake of a communist coup in 1948. The Korbels settled permanently in Colorado where her father, Josef Korbel, a former Czech diplomat, taught at the University of Denver. Soon after her confirmation as Secretary of State, Albright discovered that her family was Jewish. Albright attributes her belief in the wise usage of American power and military might to her refugee childhood. Albright is also an outspoken advocate of hard work, tireless preparation, and prudent networking, all hallmarks of her path to success in the male-dominated world of foreign policy making.

Albright graduated from Wellesley College in 1959 with a B.A. in political science. She married Joseph Albright shortly after graduation. In an age when few single women attempted graduate studies, Albright combined raising three daughters with coursework at Columbia University's Russian Institute. Albright went on to earn a master's (1968) and a doctorate (1976) in public law and government from Columbia University. After earning her Ph.D., Albright juggled family and career, serving as chief legislative assistant to Senator Edmund Muskie from 1976 to 1978 and later as the congressional relations liaison to her former adviser at Columbia, Zbigniew Brzezinski, national security adviser to President Jimmy Carter.

After her daughters had grown and she was divorced in 1982, Albright immersed herself full-time in her career at Georgetown University's School of Foreign Service, where she taught international relations and established mentoring programs for women interested in international relations careers. Albright also served as the unpaid foreign policy adviser to Democratic presidential candidates Walter Mondale (1984) and Michael Dukakis (1988), increasing her visibility within the Democratic Party. In 1989, Albright became president of the high-profile Center for National Policy, a nonprofit organization devoted to the study and discussion of domestic and international issues. In 1993, President Bill Clinton tapped Albright as the U.S. ambassador to the United Nations where she soon became known for her personal and insistent lobbying (Albright is fluent in French and

Czech with reading and conversational skills in Russian and Polish), easy charm, and blunt speaking style, transforming the usually insignificant office into a policy-making arm.

Her emphasis on "pragmatic idealism" in handling both foreign policy making and foreign leaders impressed President Clinton, who nominated Albright for secretary of state in December 1996. Albright was confirmed unanimously by the Senate and sworn in on January 23, 1997. She is the subject of several full-length autographies, including *Madeleine Albright: A Twentieth-Century Odyssey* (Michael Dobbs, 1999) and *Madam Secretary: The Biography of Madeleine Albright* (Thomas Blood, 1999). *(See also: Democratic Party; Politics)*

—**Victoria C. Allison**

Further Reading

Albright, Madeleine. Interview by Ed Bradley on *60 Minutes*. CBS-TV. February 9, 1997.

Chesnoff, Richard. "Clinton's Gung-ho Voice at the U.N.," *U.S. News and World Report* 118 (February 13, 1995): 60-62.

Cooper, Matthew, and Melinda Liu. "Bright Light," *Newsweek* 129 (February 10, 1997): 22-29.

Gibbs, Nancy. "The Many Lives of Madeleine," *Time* 149 (February 17, 1997): 52-61.

Whitelaw, Kevin, and Thomas Omestad. "For Albright, an All Right Year," *U.S. News and World Report* 121 (January 19, 1998): 46-49.

ᦉ Alcott, Abby (May) (1800–1877)

Abby May Alcott, matriarch of the New England transcendentalist family, was a radical thinker, an early feminist, and a prototype of the modern social worker while employed as a missionary to the poor of Boston.

Born into the prominent Quincy and Sewall families, Abigail Alcott grew up amid the reformist fervor of early nineteenth-century America. Her family and friends supported women's rights, the humane treatment of Native Americans, and abolition. She married Amos Bronson Alcott, the transcendental philosopher and educator, in 1830 and raised four daughters. Bronson Alcott was a genius but improvident and impractical; thus, much of their married life was marred by severe financial problems that necessitated her employment.

Alcott had an unusual ability to empathize with others and to identify with oppressed women, especially slave mothers whose conjugal and maternal rights were unprotected by law. This commitment to the oppressed led her to a career of "servicing the poor." In 1850, she opened an "intelligence service" (employment agency) in Boston. Each month, she reported her results in finding jobs for people as well as her views of American society. These reports, reprinted by the press, show the problems of the social welfare movement of the mid-nineteenth century.

Alcott advocated fair and equal wages for immigrant women. She believed that the whole system of servitude in New England was almost as false and dehumanizing as slavery in the South. Alcott walked miles a day, conferring, visiting, preaching, and teaching in the slums of Boston. In the evenings, she studied and attended lectures on social conditions. Eventually, she established a successful central "relief room" that operated as charity headquarters for Boston.

Along with such practical projects, Alcott also analyzed the fundamental causes of poverty and its effect on urban America. She considered unfair wages the major problem and advocated government programs to relocate immigrants to the western areas of the United States. Alcott eventually turned her attention to the emerging women's rights movement and worked with her good friend Lucretia Mott, the abolitionist and Quaker leader. Alcott organized a petition to the Massachusetts State Constitutional Convention for women to have the right to vote on amendments to the state constitution.

Alcott began as a liberal and became increasingly radical as she aged. Her diaries reflect a commitment to the "new poor." Moreover, as the model for "Marmee," the central character in her daughter Louisa's *Little Women,* she served as an example for late-nineteenth-century motherhood. Alcott's life reflected her credo: "Every woman with a feeling heart is answerable to her God if she does not plead the cause of the oppressed." *(See also: Alcott, Louisa May)*

—**Linda Noer**

Further Reading

Abigail May Alcott Diary. Houghton Library. Harvard University, Cambridge, MA.

Bedell, Madelon. *Alcotts: Biography of a Family.* New York: Potter, 1980.

ᦉ Alcott, Louisa May (1832–1888)

Louisa May Alcott was born into an era of social upheaval that radically transformed Western culture on both sides of the Atlantic. In 1832, the year of Alcott's birth, the British Parliament passed its first Reform Bill. In Massachusetts, the recently organized Anti-Slavery Society agitated for emancipation, an activity that contributed significantly to the eventual outbreak of the Civil War. Reform was thus inescapably a part of Alcott's physical and spiritual environment.

Bronson and Abby (Abigail) Alcott, her parents, enthusiastically supported both the antislavery and the woman's rights movements of the day. At one point, Alcott's mother ran a shelter for lost girls and abused wives. In 1836, Margaret Fuller became a teacher at Bronson Alcott's experimental Temple School in Boston. Fuller, who later wrote the landmark feminist work *Woman in the Nineteenth Century* (1845), was to become Alcott's lifelong heroine. Through Fuller and her own long-suffering, activist mother, Alcott became particularly sensitive to the apparently insurmountable contradiction in Western culture between femininity—especially in its domestic form—and individuality. That contradiction and the attempt to resolve it supplied the force behind most of Alcott's work.

Besides the celebrated and perennially popular *Little Women* series, Alcott wrote several novels, dozens of "blood-and-thunder" thrillers, numerous short stories, and a diary of her own experiences as a Civil War nurse. Taken as a whole, these works provide a multifaceted reflection of women's life in nineteenth-century America. Unlike her contemporary Emily Dickinson, who depicted the restrictive life of women in poems elaborated out of imagined experiences, Alcott always actively engaged life. At the age of eighteen, she determined to support herself and her family. From then on, Alcott held every type of legitimate job then available to a female: governess, maid, seamstress, teacher, and nurse.

Her experiences with other writers were equally diverse. Dickens, George Eliot, Dante, Shakespeare, and Carlyle all left their marks on her work. Perhaps the most indelible literary brand was left by *The Pilgrim's Progress,* a favorite of her father's and a work that Alcott incorporated into *Little Women.* In many ways, the Pilgrim in the Alcott canon is "woman" seeking salvation in the discovery of her own individuality. Also, despite obvious differences in style, *Little Women* has much in common with the British children's classic *Alice's Adventures in Wonderland.* Like Alice, Jo March breaks through conventional prescriptions for ladylike behavior. Both works lack the preachiness then considered necessary in a children's work, and both challenge the model of the simplemindedly domestic, self-effacing young girl. In fact, the two works aroused similarly critical responses for their revolutionary approaches to budding femininity.

Little Women was an instant best-seller and has become an American classic. Although Alcott first published Part I in 1868 and Part II in 1869, since the 1880s, the two parts of *Little Women* have usually been combined into one volume. Alcott's fictional tale of the generic New England March family drew heavily on her personal experience as one of four daughters. *Little Women* begins vaguely during a civil war that remains nameless throughout Part I, whose plot spans only one crucial year in the March girls' adolescence. Covering a longer period of the girls' development, Part II charts each daughter's odyssey into adulthood. Its original illustrations by Alcott's sister May were replaced by the work of professional artists in subsequent and lavishly illustrated editions, for *Little Women* quickly became a perennially popular children's book. However, *Little Women* is more than merely a children's classic: It is a quintessentially American Victorian domestic morality tale focusing on the passage of the four March daughters from girlhood into True Womanhood.

Underlying its deceptively simple story, *Little Women* presents universal and feminist themes about women's autonomy that transcend the lives of these nineteenth-century fictional characters. The girls and their mother, "Marmee,"

represent archetypal aspects of nineteenth-century womanhood based on the cult of true womanhood; their attendant spiritual struggle in an age of rising consumerism represents the conflict of an idealistic middle class with the rising materialism of urban and industrial Victorian America. Moreover, Alcott has woven the national work ethic into the fabric of *Little Women.* Thus, this unimpeachably respectable story about Victorian girls who are becoming women contains the subversive message that economic self-sufficiency and independence were as important for women's social and personal integrity as for men's.

The inherent contradictions within the cult of true womanhood between women's self-esteem and their obligatory obedience and self-sacrifice is most apparent in Jo's struggle for autonomy, since Jo avoids a direct challenge to her father's patriarchal authority and the circumscribing influence of her strongest role model, Marmee. Marmee represents the fulfillment of True Womanhood as she bravely and resourcefully bears the economic consequences of her husband's patriotic voluntary service in the military as well as her additional home front duties. Despite their differing female temperaments, which must be overcome to achieve Marmee's ideal, the daughters represent the development of True Womanhood. The oldest, Meg, represents the ordinary and conventional girl who struggles against her vanity and susceptibility to the materialism of her peers both before and after her marriage to John Brooke, while the second-born, Jo, is a tomboy and incipient author for whom the transition into womanhood means repeatedly coming to terms with the limitations of the gender system in general and of woman's sphere in particular. The next younger sister, Beth, suffers from a domestic femininity too pure to survive beyond the family sphere in the real world; and the youngest daughter, Amy, represents the adaptive and ambitious girlhood of the family "princess."

In the allegorical Part I, all four March girls confront the challenge of maintaining their middle-class lifestyle and values in the reduced circumstances of their now all-female household. Their contact with the all-male inhabitants of the "palace Beautiful" of their wealthy neighbors, the Laurences, draws them beyond their domestic circle and provides contrast between the genteel but enriched poverty of the March women and the wealth of their next-door neighbor Mr. Laurence and his grandson, "Laurie," whose wealth does not ensure the men's happiness or contentment. The girls learn one moral lesson after another under the guidance of Marmee so that within this one year each daughter has confronted and acknowledged her major character flaw. When Marmee is called away to nurse the wounded Mr. March at the war front, the girls face Beth's critical illness, which is resolved by Marmee's return. Part I ends with the family circle completed as the convalescent Mr. March also returns, but Meg's engagement to Laurie's tutor, John Brooke, marks the end of girlhood for all the daughters.

Beginning three years later with Meg's wedding, Part II abandons the allegorical approach and charts the four girls' entry into womanhood. Meg's struggle with domesticity and caring for her twins, Daisy and Demi, parallels Jo's conflict with romance and career. In flight from the former and pursuit of the latter (like Alcott herself), Jo goes to New York as a governess and writes trashy thrillers for the "penny dreadfuls," cheap commercial adventure periodicals, until her new friend, Professor Bhaer, persuades her to eschew writing vulgar but quickly profitable sensational short stories in order to apply her talent to more worthy work. The death of Beth marks a turning point for Jo and Amy. The second part lacks the satisfying ending of the first but leaves Marmee content that her surviving daughters have become True Women and are well married.

Offering a surprisingly sophisticated critique of the expectations of womanhood in the nineteenth and twentieth centuries, *Little Women* defies and challenges classification as a simple children's book. A female Peter Pan, the central character, Jo, resists the constraints of both girlhood and imminent womanhood, but in the end, she does not escape her womanly destiny of marriage and domesticity.

The popularity of the trilogy of *Little Women, Little Men* (1871), and *Jo's Boys* (1886), and the wealth of Alcott's other works classified as children's literature, eclipsed the feminist implications of *Little Women* and some of her other novels. *Moods* (1865) explored the myth and realities of love and marriage for nineteenth-century American women; *Old Fashioned Girl* (1870), *Eight Cousins* (1875), and its sequel *Rose in Bloom* (1876) offered incisive social commentary on the lifestyle of Victorian women and insights into the social history of the era. Drawn from her own employment experiences, *Work* (1873) presents a devastatingly accurate picture of the conditions of the classic women's employments during the mid-Victorian period.

In *Work: A Story of Experience,* Christie Devon, a nineteenth-century, 21-year-old working girl holds jobs as parlor maid, paid companion, governess, actress, and seamstress. By the end of the story, Christie has been married and widowed, given birth to a daughter, become wealthy, and emerged as a spokesperson for women's rights. Unlike Alcott, Christie is an orphan with no family to support, but like Alcott, Christie suffers from exhaustion and depression and even attempts suicide. Characters in *Work* are based on people Alcott knew: Thomas Power is based on Thomas Parker, a minister who helped Alcott, and David Sterling is based on Henry David Thoreau, whose transcendental ideals permeate the story. Alcott extols the benefits of sexual equality, racial equality, and education for all. Women's rights and unity among women appear as strong messages. The closing scene best illustrates Alcott's philosophies: Christie, the matriarch, sits with her young daughter and their friends of differing ages, social classes, and upbringings, all holding hands and rejoicing in their experience and womanhood.

Louisa May Alcott died in 1888, never having married, on the same day as her father; the two were eulogized at a double funeral ceremony. It seems appropriate that they received a joint tribute, for Bronson Alcott inspired both his daughter's love of literature and her lifelong conflict about the restrictions imposed on the wife in a marriage. *(See also: Alcott, Abby; Cult of True Womanhood; Fuller, Margaret; Transcendentalism; Women Writers)*

—Mary Lowe-Evans
—Angela M. Howard

Further Reading

Alcott, Louisa May. *Jo's Boys.* 1886. Reprint, Boston: Little, Brown, 1930.

———. *Little Women.* Boston: Roberts Brothers, 1868, 1869.

———. *Little Women.* Introduction by Madelon Bedell. New York: Modern Library, 1983.

———. *Moods.* Boston: Loring, 1865.

———. *Work: A Story of Experience.* 1873. Reprint, Introduction by Sarah Elbert. New York: Schocken, 1977.

Bedell, Madelon. *The Alcotts: Biography of a Family.* New York: Potter, 1980.

Boos, Clair, ed. *Works of Louisa May Alcott.* New York: Avenel, 1982.

Cheney, Ednah Dow. *Louisa May Alcott, Her Life, Letters and Journals.* Boston: Roberts Brothers, 1889.

Elbert, Sarah. *A Hunger for Home.* Philadelphia: Temple University Press, 1984.

———. *So Sweet to Remember: Feminism and Fiction of Louisa May Alcott.* Philadelphia: Temple University Press, 1983.

Payne, Alma J. *Louisa May Alcott: A Reference Guide.* Boston: G. K. Hall, 1980.

Stern, Madeleine. *Behind a Mask: The Unknown Thrillers of Louisa May Alcott.* New York: William Morrow, 1975.

———. *Critical Essays on Louisa May Alcott.* Boston: G. K. Hall, 1984.

———. *Louisa May Alcott.* Norman: University of Oklahoma Press, 1971.

American Antislavery Societies

Modeled after organizations in England and spurred by the publication of William Lloyd Garrison's abolitionist paper, the *Liberator* (1831), American antislavery societies were begun in the United States in the 1830s. Garrison's New England Anti-Slavery Society, founded early in 1832, was the first such group.

From the beginning, women, particularly free black women, played a large role in the antislavery societies. Just after Garrison's New England Society was formed, a group of black women in Salem, Massachusetts, began the Female Anti-Slavery Society, the first in America (February 1832). Shortly thereafter, Maria Weston Chapman, a member of Boston's Brahmin elite, organized the Boston Female Anti-Slavery Society as an auxiliary to Garrison's all-male group. Black women worked alongside white women in the Boston group, as well as in the integrated Female Anti-Slavery Societies of Lynn, Massachusetts, Philadelphia, Pennsylvania, and Rochester, New York. In New York City, however, black women were turned away by the existing antislavery societies and formed their own group.

The presence of women in the antislavery societies inevitably raised questions about the position of women in nineteenth-century American society. When the American Anti-Slavery Society held its first convention in Philadelphia in 1833, women were not allowed to join the society or sign the founding statement of purpose. After the meeting, twenty women, including Lucretia Mott, met and formed the Philadelphia Female Anti-Slavery Society. By 1837, when the first National Female Anti-Slavery convention was held in New York, eighty-one delegates from twelve states attended.

Some of the activities of the female antislavery societies were consistent with the nineteenth-century ideology of separate spheres for men and women. These activities included raising money through annual fairs, circulating petitions, and bringing in male speakers for the antislavery cause. But increasingly, women themselves began speaking publicly for the cause of abolition: notably, Angelina and Sarah Grimké, and Maria Stewart, a free black woman. Women speakers were attacked both by those opposed to abolition and by antifeminists within the antislavery movement for daring to step outside their "proper sphere."

In 1840 the "woman question" came to a head when the American Anti-Slavery Society split into two separate organizations, ostensibly over the appointment of Abby Kelley to a leadership position within the group. The issue also dominated that year's World Anti-Slavery Convention in London, at which women delegates were required to sit in a screened-off balcony. Present at that meeting were women like Elizabeth Cady Stanton and Lucretia Mott, who would later become leaders of the woman suffrage movement.

The participation of women in the American antislavery societies thus helped pave the way for the suffrage movement by raising the issue of women's access to a broader sphere of activity. Nineteenth-century women gained significant leadership skills and organizational training from their experiences in the antislavery societies and, importantly, developed a consciousness of their own oppression as women. *(See also: Abolition and the Antislavery Movement; Foster, Abby Kelley; Public Speakers: Nineteenth Century; Slavery; Woman Question)*

—Mary Battenfeld

Further Reading

Hersh, Blanche Glassman. *The Slavery of Sex: Feminist-Abolitionists in America.* Urbana: University of Illinois Press, 1978.

Lerner, Gerda. "The Political Activities of Antislavery Women." In *The Majority Finds Its Past,* edited by Gerda Lerner, 112-28. New York: Oxford University Press, 1979.

Yellin, Jean Fagan. *Women and Sisters: The Antislavery Feminists in American Culture.* New Haven, CT: Yale University Press, 1989.

🕭 American Association of University Women (AAUW)

The American Association of University Women (AAUW) was the first organization of university women in the United States. It was founded in 1882 as the Association of Collegiate Alumnae and became the American Association of University Women in 1921 after merging with the Southern Association of College Women and the Western Association of Collegiate Alumnae. In 1881, Marion Talbot, Emily Fairbanks Talbot, Alice Hayes, and Ellen Richards organized a meeting for a group of seventeen young women representing eight colleges and universities. These women notified alumnae of their respective institutions, and sixty-five women from Boston University, the universities of Michigan and Wisconsin, Cornell, Oberlin, Smith, Vassar, and Wellesley gathered in Boston on January 14, 1882, for the first organizational meeting of the Association of Collegiate Alumnae.

The AAUW can be credited with leading the movement to improve conditions and facilities for women in many colleges and universities. Early administrators used AAUW institutional admission as leverage to obtain funding for women's dormitories, improve the salaries of women instructors, and encourage the hiring of women in positions beyond the instructor level, as well as to promote a cordial attitude for women students. Today, the association promotes the advancement of women's education and women in society and contributes to the betterment of the community. It funds projects of branch and state divisions and individual members through research and project grants and fellowship programs. The AAUW maintains a comprehensive library and archival collection on women and supports one of the largest lobbying teams on women's issues.

In 1991, the AAUW published "Shortchanging Girls, Shortchanging America," a nationwide survey of attitudes concerning educational experiences, math and science interest, and career aspirations of girls and boys from ages nine to fifteen years. This study was followed by "The AAUW Report: How Schools Shortchange Girls," a synthesis of research of girls in school that revealed significant patterns of gender bias and inequity. This report prompted the AAUW Educational Foundation to commission a survey on sexual harassment in America's schools titled "Hostile Hallways: The AAUW Survey on Sexual Harassment in America's Schools." This was the first nationally representative survey of adolescent sexual harassment in schools and confirmed that sexual harassment is a major problem.

In addition to many brochures, research studies, study guides, and booklets, the association publishes *Action Alert* while Congress is in session, *Graduate Woman,* and *Leader in Action,* as well as *AAUW Outlook.* There are branches in every state and a membership of over 200,000. *(See also: Association of Collegiate Alumnae; Education; Higher Educa-*

tion; Sex Equity/Comparable Worth; Sexual Harassment; Talbot, Marion)

—Sandra M. Fox

Further Reading
"Achieving Gender Equity in the Classroom and on the Campus: The Next Steps." Symposium Proceedings. Washington, DC: AAUW, 1995.

"Gender and Race on the Campus and in the School: Beyond Affirmative Action." Symposium Proceedings. Washington, DC: AAUW, 1997.

"Girls in the Middle: Working to Succeed in School." Washington, DC: AAUW, 1996.

"Growing Smart: What's Working for Girls in School." Washington, DC: AAUW, 1995.

"Hostile Hallways: The AAUW Survey on Sexual Harassment in America's Schools." Commissioned by the AAUW Educational Foundation and conducted by Louis Harris and Associates. Washington, DC: AAUW, 1993.

"How Schools Shortchange Girls: The AAUW Report." Commissioned by the AAUW Educational Foundation and researched by the Wellesley College Center for Research on Women. Washington, DC: AAUW, 1992.

Levin, S. *Degrees of Equality: The American Association of University Women and the Challenge of Twentieth-Century Feminism.* Philadelphia: Temple University Press, 1995.

Orenstein, Peggy. *School Girls: Young Women, Self-Esteem, and the Confidence Gap.* New York: Doubleday, 1994.

"Separated by Sex: A Critical Look at Single-Sex Education for Girls." Washington, DC: AAUW Educational Foundation, 1998.

"Shortchanging Girls, Shortchanging America: A Call to Action." Rev. ed. AAUW Initiative for Educational Equity. Washington, DC: AAUW, 1994.

http://www.aauw.org/ [American Association of University Women Website]

❧ American Birth Control League (ABCL)

The American Birth Control League (ABCL) was founded by Margaret Sanger (1879–1966) at the first American Birth Control Conference in New York City in 1921. The ABCL had broader ambitions than its rival, the Voluntary Parenthood League, working simultaneously for legislation, education, clinical services, and popularizing the message of birth control. Led by Sanger and a small group of upper- and middle-class women, the ABCL successfully encouraged state affiliates and made strides toward winning support for birth control from the medical community.

Under Sanger's presidency, from 1921 to 1928 the ABCL quickly became the largest birth control organization in the country. It served as an organizational base for Sanger's national lecture tours, which, in turn, sparked the organization of state leagues that affiliated with the ABCL. The ABCL also published the *Birth Control Review,* a monthly journal that provided news about the state of birth control in the United States and abroad. Because Sanger was the most well-known exponent of birth control in the United States, the

ABCL handled the hundreds of thousands of requests for birth control information she received between 1921 and 1928. Because the federal Comstock laws prohibited sending birth control information through the mail, the ABCL developed a referral service by which they could refer women to local leagues or sympathetic doctors who would provide the sought-after information.

In 1923, Sanger founded the first legal American birth control clinic, the Clinical Research Bureau (CRB) of the ABCL. Other clinics around the country looked to the ABCL for advice on how to establish their own contraceptive services, and the ABCL published a wide range of materials to help such leagues.

For Sanger, birth control was a health issue, and securing the support of the medical profession was paramount to securing general acceptance of birth control. To further medical acceptance of birth control, the ABCL hired Dr. James Cooper to speak to medical groups around the country from 1925 to 1929. Sanger and the ABCL also lobbied for state and federal legislation exempting doctors from the restrictions on providing contraceptive information. Although "doctor's only" bills garnered more support than the free speech arguments of the rival Voluntary Parenthood League, the ABCL was unable to convince any representatives to sponsor their bill.

As the ABCL grew larger, tensions arose between Margaret Sanger and the Board of Directors. Sanger resigned from the ABCL in 1928, dissatisfied with her inability to direct the league as she saw fit. Sanger took with her several loyal officers, the Clinical Research Bureau, and much of the media attention and contributions. Under the direction of the new president, Eleanor Dwight Jones, and her successors, the ABCL continued to manage state leagues, foster clinics, and seek endorsements from national and state organizations throughout the 1930s.

By the end of the decade, it became clear to both Sanger and the ABCL that dividing the birth control movement into two rival factions did not serve the movement. In 1939, the ABCL and Sanger's Birth Control Clinical Research Bureau (the new name of the CRB) merged to form the Birth Control Federation of America (BCFA). Although Sanger was made honorary chairman of the BCFA, she had little real power in the new organization. In 1942, against her wishes, the BCFA was renamed the Planned Parenthood Federation of America. *(See also: Birth Control; Birth Control Clinical Research Bureau; Planned Parenthood Federation of America, Inc.; Sanger, Margaret Louise)*

—Cathy Moran Hajo

Further Reading
The Margaret Sanger Papers, Smith College Collections and Collected Documents Series. Bethesda, MD: University Publications of America, 1995-1996. Microform.

Chesler, Ellen. *Woman of Valor: Margaret Sanger and the Birth Control Movement in America.* New York: Simon & Schuster, 1992.

Gordon, Linda. *Woman's Body, Woman's Right: A Social History of the Birth Control Movement.* New York: Grossman, 1976.

McCann, Carole R. *Birth Control Politics in the United States, 1916–1945.* Ithaca, NY: Cornell University Press, 1994.

Sanger, Margaret. *Margaret Sanger, an Autobiography.* New York: Norton, 1938.

———. *My Fight for Birth Control.* 1931. Reprint, Elmsford, NY: Maxwell Reprint Co., 1969.

ᵥ American Federation of Labor (AFL)

The Federation of Organized Trade and Labor Unions of the United States and Canada was organized in 1881. At its sixth annual session in 1886, the American Federation of Labor (AFL) was formed, absorbing the original organization. Under the direction of Samuel Gompers, the AFL became the most significant labor organization in the United States, emphasizing labor's immediate concerns: wages, hours, and working conditions. In addition, the AFL stood ready to employ the strike when necessary to achieve its ends. As the name implies, the AFL was a federation of trade unions that rejected the idea of individual membership in one all-inclusive union. Instead, the AFL stressed the organization of skilled workers into separate craft unions, each belonging to the larger federation.

While the name Federation of Organized Trade and Labor Unions implies the inclusion of all laborers, not just males, no women were present at the founding convention in 1881. In 1882, the organization urged the women's labor organizations to join the federation "upon an equal footing . . . with men." The following year, Mrs. Charlotte Smith, president of the Women's National Industrial League, was admitted to the AFL convention and was granted a seat at the 1884 convention. At that convention, a proposal was drafted titled "An Address to Worker Girls and Women," which urged women to organize and to support the federation in the premise that "equal amounts of work should bring the same prices whether performed by man or woman." Other than recognizing the problems of women workers, however, the AFL did little by way of concrete action to improve the status or organization of American female laborers. Although the federation's first woman delegate, Mary Burke, introduced a resolution in 1890 to have women appointed to organize women in the trades under AFL jurisdiction, federation action was slow and limited: Mary Kenney was given a fixed, unrenewed five-month appointment in 1892.

Since the AFL concentrated on and consisted primarily of skilled workers, it tended to offer little to workers on the lower rungs of the industrial ladder, where, to a great extent, women and blacks were located. Typical of the problem facing women interested in participating in the AFL was the stance of the Baker, Carpenter, and Molder Union affiliates of the AFL: Each barred women members until well into the twentieth century. Even when women were admitted to a constituent union, the tendency was to establish separate sex-segregated locals for women workers, which proved to be extremely ineffective and therefore languished for members. With the approval of the AFL leadership, the National Women's Trade Union League (NWTUL) was organized at the 1903 AFL convention, but this merely reinforced the inadequate representation of women workers in American labor organizations. Until the Great Depression, the NWTUL supported protective legislation that perpetuated wage discrimination and sex segregation of the labor force.

The National Recovery Act (1933) and the National Labor Relations Act (1935) benefited the industrial workforce, 20 percent of whom were women. The New Deal labor policies facilitated the revitalization of the International Ladies Garment Workers Union, but the reluctance of the AFL male membership to accept women in union leadership remained and resurfaced after World War II. Women continued to enter the industrial labor force during the 1950s and 1960s, however, which enabled AFL women to assert their presence and demand union attention to their issues. The Coalition of Labor Union Women, organized in 1974, influenced the AFL to reconsider its traditional opposition to the Equal Rights Amendment, which dated from the 1950s and reflected its support of protective legislation for women workers. The AFL merger with the Congress of Industrial Organizations (CIO) did not increase the union's attention to the needs of women workers. By the mid-1970s, the AFL-CIO had only two women in national leadership posts, an associate director of its civil rights department to service women's activities and the director of the union library.

Linda Chavez-Thompson, executive vice president since October 25, 1995, is the first person of color ever elected to an executive office of the AFL-CIO and the highest-ranking woman in the labor movement. Affiliated with the AFL-CIO are the American Federation of State, County, and Municipal Employees (AFSCME) and the United Farm Workers (UFW), chartered on August 22, 1972. Current membership of the AFL-CIO is 5.6 million women. *(See also: American Federation of State, County, and Municipal Employees; Congress of Industrial Organizations; Huerta, Dolores; International Ladies Garment Workers Union; National Women's Trade Union League; Protective Legislation; Unions; United Farm Workers)*

—Maureen Anna Harp

Further Reading

Kaufman, Stuart. *Samuel Gompers and the Origins of the American Federation of Labor.* Westport, CT: Greenwood, 1973.

Kennedy, Susan E. *If All We Did Was to Weep at Home.* Bloomington: Indiana University Press, 1979.

Kessler-Harris, Alice. *Out to Work: A History of Wage-Earning Women in the United States.* New York: Oxford University Press, 1982.

Morris, James. *Conflict within the AFL.* Ithaca, NY: Cornell University Press, 1958.

Richards, Yevette. " 'My Passionate Feeling about Africa': Maida Springer-Kemp and the American Labor Movement." Ph.D diss., Yale University, 1994.

Taft, Philip. *The AF of L from the Death of Gompers to the Merger.* New York: Harper, 1959.

————. *The AF of L in the Time of Gompers*, 2 vols. New York: Harper, 1957.

http://www.aflcio.org/home.htm [AFL-CIO Website]

⁊ American Federation of State, County, and Municipal Employees (AFSCME)

In 1932, a group of fifty state employees that included professionals, supervisors, and department heads but few rank-and-filers met in the assembly chambers of the Wisconsin State Capitol to organize a union for state employees from the top down. Among the organizers themselves there was controversy over whether to form an independent professional organization or an affiliate of organized labor. Proponents of unionization argued that labor conventions and meetings would publicize state employees' contributions to good government as well as their struggle for reasonable wages, hours, and conditions of employment. Within six months, the new union, named the Wisconsin State Employees Association, had won affiliation with the American Federation of Labor.

The unemployed in Wisconsin at the depths of the Great Depression in 1933 numbered 200,000, which equaled a quarter of the workers in the state. Another 100,000 workers had only part-time jobs. Conservative Democrats swept into office by the Roosevelt landslide had campaigned to repeal the civil service law, to provide jobs for the party faithful. When the Wisconsin legislature convened in 1933, hordes of unemployed people camped in the corridors of the capitol building in anticipation of appointments to those civil service positions. With the help of the AFL and other citizen groups interested in good government, the new union successfully campaigned to defeat the civil service repeal.

The executive secretary of the union, Arnold Zander, and organizer Roy Kubista drafted a call for a convention in Chicago in December 1935 to form an international union of public employees, over the objections of AFL president William Green. Twenty-six delegates attended the first constitutional convention of AFSCME to elect officers, adopt resolutions, and sign an application for an AFL charter that designated Madison, Wisconsin, as AFSCME headquarters.

The new international union doubled its membership between 1937 and 1938. After its first decade, AFSCME had 73,000 members; by the 1955 AFL-CIO merger, its membership topped 100,00, and in 1957 AFSCME transferred its headquarters to Washington, D.C. By the 1980s, the AFSCME constituency in the tertiary sector of the economy made it the fastest-growing union in the United States with more than a million members in local chapters throughout the states, Puerto Rico, and Panama.

Because AFSCME targeted unionization of clerical occupations in local and state government, it recruited many women members and became a pioneer in the struggle to achieve pay equity for working women. Women constitute over half of the 800,000 members and hold 40 percent of AFSCME leadership positions. AFSCME has confronted the sex discrimination in jobs traditionally held by women who have been underpaid for work that requires skill, effort, and responsibility equal to or exceeding that of male-dominated occupations. AFSCME worked to secure state legislatures' funding of job evaluation studies as well as passage of legislation that committed states to follow the principles of pay equity in their pay scales and employment policies. Through legal action and collective bargaining, AFSCME has won substantial pay increases for its women members in Washington, California, Illinois, and Wisconsin.

AFSCME represents public employees and health care workers throughout the United States, Panama, and Puerto Rico. They include employees of state, county, and municipal governments; school districts; public and private hospitals; universities; and nonprofit agencies who work in a cross section of jobs, ranging from blue collar to clerical, professional, and paraprofessional. White-collar employees account for one-third of the membership, while health and hospital workers constitute the largest sector with more than 325,000 members. About 325,000 AFSCME members are clerical and secretarial employees, making AFSCME the largest union of office workers. One hundred thousand members are corrections officers, making AFSCME the largest union in that profession. Total membership in AFSCME in 1998 was more than 1.3 million. Although the highest-ranking officers were male, seven of the thirty-one international vice presidents are women. *(See also: American Federation of Labor; Sex Equity; Unions)*

—**Mary Lou France**

Further Reading
American Federation of State, County, and Municipal Employees. *AFSCME: Decade for Decisions.* Washington, DC: AFSCME, 1980.

Billings, Richard N. *Power to the Public Worker.* Washington, DC: R. B. Luce, 1974.

Kubista, Roy. *Wisconsin State Employees Union.* Madison, WI: AFSCME, 1982.

http://www.afscme.org [American Federation of State, County, and Municipal Employees Website]

⁊ American Home Economics Association (AHEA)

Founded in 1909, the American Home Economics Association (AHEA) was one of several organizations that grew out of the home economics or domestic science movement in the late 1800s. During this time, women's seminaries and, later, women's colleges began offering training in home economics, public schools began to offer domestic science, and cooking schools were developed to train teachers of cooking. The AHEA was the culmination of a series of ten conferences, known as the Lake Placid Conferences, that began in 1899. Ellen Richards was instrumental in setting up the conferences; a chemist, she felt that scientific principles should be applied to household work and that homemaking was the most natural and desirable occupation for women. Richards had been working on a new science that she called *oekology*, the science of right living. Mevil Dewey, president of the New York Efficiency Society, encouraged Richards to organize the new discipline and suggested it be called home economics.

Through the nineteenth century, as home economics was becoming part of American education at all levels, it lacked a body of literature that clarified its philosophy and place in the overall educational system. The Lake Placid Conferences were held to deal with these concerns. During the ten years of its existence, the group attempted to work with other groups such as the National Education Association (NEA), resulting in the formation of sections within the NEA on home economics and manual training. The Lake Placid group had less success with the Association of Collegiate Alumnae (later the American Association of University Women), at whose meeting in June 1905 a resolution was passed that home economics had no place in a college course for women. This was a blow for Richards and Marion Talbot, another leader of the Lake Placid Conferences, because they had been cofounders of the Association of Collegiate Alumnae. The suffrage movement embraced the home economics movement, however. At the 1897 meeting of the National American Woman Suffrage Association, the keynote address was on the topic of domestic science, which was in keeping with the feeling of many women that they deserved the vote because they were homemakers.

By the time the tenth conference was planned, the leaders decided that an organization was needed to carry on their work. The first official meeting of the American Home Economics Association was held in Washington, and Richards was elected president. There were 143 delegates and 700 charter members at this convention. The organization had 30,000 members in 1985 and is still active today.

The establishment of the AHEA testified to the success of the domestic science movement and to the influence of the Victorian cult of domesticity on women's education. Courses in home economics at the secondary and postsecondary levels of public education were intended to maintain and enhance the status of homemaking as a respected profession; however, this specialized curriculum served to reinforce the domestic identity of women, regardless of their endeavors in traditional academic fields or their aspirations to careers outside the home. *(See also: Association of Collegiate Alumnae; Home Economics; National Education Association; Talbot, Marion)*

—**Judith Pryor**

Further Reading

Baldwin, Keturah E. *The AHEA Saga: A Brief History of the Origin and Development of the American Home Economics Association and a Glimpse at the Grass Roots from Which It Grew.* Washington, DC: American Home Economics Association, 1949.

Ehrenreich, Barbara, and Deirdre English. *For Her Own Good: 150 Years of the Experts' Advice to Women.* Garden City, NY: Anchor, 1978.
Hunt, Caroline Louisa. *The Life of Ellen H. Richards, 1842–1911.* 1912. Reprint, Washington, DC: American Home Economics Association, 1958.
Weigley, Emma Seifrit. "It Might Have Been Euthenics: The Lake Placid Conferences and the Home Economics Movement," *American Quarterly* 26 (March 1974): 79-97.

American Jewess

The first national Jewish women's magazine in the United States, *American Jewess* was published in Chicago by Rosa Sonneschein from 1895 to 1899. It encouraged women from German Jewish immigrant stock to continue Jewish life in America. Sonneschein was the upper-middle-class wife of a prominent Reform rabbi whom she later divorced. Her 29,000 readers were also largely upper-middle-class Reform Jews.

The magazine promoted domestic feminism and Zionism, and its features included stories for children and columns on scientific housekeeping, medicine, and the social sciences. It also provided reviews of both Jewish and secular literature, music, art, and drama, as well as short stories by popular female authors. Every issue also contained an editorial by Sonneschein, reports of international and national feminist and Jewish activities, and articles by prominent feminists.

Sonneschein hoped that the magazine would become the official publication of the National Council of Jewish Women (NCJW), but the organization turned down the offer of eight pages per issue in favor of printing its own newsletter. Still, Sonneschein believed that the aims of the NCJW and the *American Jewess* were identical, so she devoted a major portion of the magazine to reporting NCJW activities, even ignoring the presidential election of 1896 to cover the council's first convention. Despite its steady readership, the magazine folded in 1899 when Sonneschein's health failed and no one stepped in to fill her shoes. *(See also: Domestic Feminism; Jewish Women; Sonneschein, Rosa Fassel)*

—**Faith Rogow**

Further Reading

See *Rosa Sonneschein* in the Small Collections File, American Jewish Archives, Cincinnati, Ohio.

American Missionary Association (AMA)

Founded in 1846 as a domestic mission for the Congregational Church, the American Missionary Association (AMA) combined radical abolitionism with Protestant evangelicalism. The AMA sent its missionaries to follow northern armies in the latter years of the Civil War to convert slaves to the abolitionist and to the evangelical

Protestant causes. From early efforts at Hampton, Virginia, and Port Royal, South Carolina, the AMA became the most active sponsor of northern teachers in the immediate postwar period. In Georgia, for example, the AMA funded and sponsored 80 percent of the northern teacher-missionaries after the war (1865–1873).

The narrow focus of this organization had been influenced by the antebellum movement among churchwomen to fund the education, training, and placement of young women missionaries who were to take the gospel to the sequestered women of Asia, Africa, and the Middle East. While the women missionaries were encouraged to wed male missionaries, those who refused were nonetheless supported as independent single missionaries. By the 1850s, medical training was added to the program for women missionaries. The placements offered to medically trained graduates of women's nursing and medical institutions provided an outlet for a new professional class of educated women.

The specific thrust of the AMA was to develop schools and churches. Several hundred primary schools were established in the South, many housed on former plantations in crude buildings built by freedmen. The society was always short of funds, and many of the schools survived on a combination of northern donations and frugality. The society acknowledged the economic realities of the freedmen's lives by operating the schools when seasonal agricultural work was least demanding. Although many of these primary schools closed their doors after a few years, some survived to bear testimony to AMA efforts—for example, the Dorchester Academy in Liberty County, Georgia, which remained open until the 1930s. A more concentrated educational effort of the AMA led to the founding of several black colleges, including Nashville's Fisk and the Atlanta University complex. These colleges, in turn, trained black ministers to continue the work of the AMA throughout the South.

The AMA came to mirror mid-nineteenth-century society and challenge it through the roles women played in the organization. Although the bureaucracy of the AMA was fundamentally male, more than 90 percent of the volunteers for southern service were female and disproportionately single, young, and New England-born. The AMA service experience of these women paralleled that of the next generation in the settlement house movement. Expected to demonstrate the modesty and decorum of the cult of true womanhood, AMA women missionaries in fact had to join freedmen and freedwomen in the fields, challenge local authorities who often wished to close their schools, and organize the efforts to support their establishments. They demonstrated perseverance and professionalism despite inequities within the AMA that reflected those of the larger society. As the focus of the AMA shifted to the black colleges by the mid-1870s, the role of women diminished. By the 1890s, AMA activity in the South had all but disappeared. *(See also: Abolition and the Antislavery Movement; Education)*

—**Thomas F. Armstrong**

Further Reading

Hill, Patricia. *The World Their Household: American Women's Foreign Mission Movement and Cultural Transformation.* Ann Arbor: University of Michigan Press, 1985.

Jones, Jacqueline. *Soldiers of Light and Love: Northern Teachers and Georgia Blacks, 1865–1873.* Chapel Hill: University of North Carolina Press, 1980.

Rose, Willie Lee. *Rehearsal for Reconstruction: The Port Royal Experiment.* Indianapolis, IN: Bobbs-Merrill, 1964.

Saunders, Frank, and George Rogers. "Eliza Ann Ward: Teacher and Missionary to the Freedman." In *Swampwater and Wiregrass: Historical Sketches of Coastal Georgia,* edited by R. Frank Saunders and George Rogers, 139-50. Macon, GA: Mercer University Press, 1984.

✍ American Negro Academy (ANA)

The American Negro Academy (ANA) was the first major learned society in science and the humanities for African Americans. The academy was formally inaugurated on March 5, 1897 in Washington, D.C., by eighteen prominent members of the African American community. Alexander Crummell, a Cambridge-trained Episcopalian clergyman, served as its first president for eighteen months and was succeeded in this position by W. E. B. Du Bois, Archibald Grimké, John Cromwell, and Arthur Schomburg.

The purpose of the academy was to encourage intellectual activity among American Negroes and to affirm racial equality. Specifically, the constitution proposed "an organization of Colored authors, scholars, and artists" whose goals included the publication of literary and scholarly works by Negro authors, the promotion of culture among youths of genius, the establishment of archives to house historical data and publications by Negro authors, and the creation of an annual volume of original works by American Negroes. Its creation reflected a broadly based proliferation of ethnic historical societies and learned and professional associations among the educated American middle class of all races.

Annual meetings included the presentation of scholarly papers on a range of subjects related to race; some were published in an attempt to publicize the academy's intellectual activity. Media coverage of the academy's activities was consistently limited.

Membership of the ANA during the thirty-one years of its existence included outstanding African American intellectuals such as Francis J. Grimké, Paul Laurence Dunbar, Alain Locke, Carter Woodson, William Pickens, and James Weldon Johnson. Edward Blyden and Henry Ossawa Tanner were among the foreign members whose inclusion was designed to promote links among blacks worldwide. The constitution did not provide for female membership, although women were invited to give papers at annual meetings. Maritcha Lyons was the only woman to have her paper read at the academy's meeting in 1898.

The academy grew slowly, and full membership never reached the constitutional limit of fifty. Throughout its history, the academy suffered from small membership growth, high attrition rate of old and new members, limited financial resources, and lack of public interest in the group's activities. It is generally agreed that the academy failed to meet its goals as defined in the constitution, but its existence until its last meeting in December 1928 testifies to the intellectual vigor of the African American community. *(See also: Lyons, Maritcha Remond)*

—**Marilyn Demarest Button**

Further Reading

Bennett, Lerone, Jr. *Before the Mayflower: A History of Black America.* Chicago: Johnson, 1987, 292-93.
Moss, Alfred A., Jr. *The American Negro Academy.* Baton Rouge: Louisiana State University Press, 1981.

~ American Red Cross

An outgrowth of the International Red Cross, the American Red Cross was established in the United States largely through the exertions of Clara Barton. She was made aware of the work of the parent organization, established in Geneva in 1864, by Dr. Louis Appia, whom she met while staying with friends in Geneva in 1869. She was distressed to learn that her own country had declined membership because the government thought it might constitute an "entangling alliance," against which President Washington had warned in his Farewell Address of 1797. Before Barton could return home, she was witness to the Franco-Prussian War and, while working as a relief organizer under the flag of the Red Cross, provided assistance to civilian women devastated by the war.

Once back in the United States, Barton began a campaign to win American participation in the Red Cross movement, only to meet objections from successive secretaries of state that membership ran counter to historic national policy. Undaunted, she wrote widely in support of American membership, used her numerous high-level contacts inside and outside the government, and set up a Washington, D.C., chapter to keep up pressure on the administration in office. Finally, in March 1884, the U.S. Senate affirmed the Geneva Treaty, and in 1900, Congress gave the American Red Cross a federal charter.

The American branch almost at once undertook to make assistance available to victims of natural as well as man-made disasters. Clara Barton viewed the Red Cross as a standby organization to give aid in the wake of fire, flood, hurricane, or tidal wave. It did an exceptional job of aiding the Cuban wounded in the Spanish-American War.

As the American Red Cross grew, it became increasingly difficult for its president, Clara Barton, to keep a firm hand on its operation. She was not an organization woman, and in 1904, she was succeeded by William Howard Taft, then secretary of war, in a change literally forced on Barton. As it turned out, Taft was but a figurehead. Mabel Boardman was the driving force in reorganizing the American branch, put-

ting its finances in order and enlarging active membership throughout the country. In the long view, it was both the inspirational efforts of Clara Barton and the organizational skill of Mabel Boardman that helped make the Red Cross a permanent and respected institution in American life. *(See also: Barton, Clara; Civil War)*

—**David H. Burton**

Further Reading

Barton, Clara. *The Red Cross: A History.* Washington, DC: American Red Cross, 1898.
Bicknell, Ernest P. *Pioneering with the Red Cross.* New York: Macmillan, 1935.
Dulles, Rhea Foster. *The American Red Cross: A History.* Westport, CT: Greenwood, 1971.

~ American Revolutionary Era

Women participated in the events that culminated in the American Revolution, contributing crucial cooperation with prewar colonial resistance, especially economic sanctions and, after 1774, providing labor on the home front and support on the battlefield. During the turbulent 1760s and early 1770s, women's anti-tea leagues and ladies' associations provided crucial support for the boycotts and nonimportation efforts of the aggrieved colonists. Patriot women increased their production and use of homespun goods and eschewed British-made or imported luxury items. Women's political activities through the Daughters of Liberty paralleled those of men; women attended and sponsored bonfire rallies, burnt tax collectors' effigies, and produced their own anti-British propaganda. As individuals, women influenced their spouses, brothers, and suitors to support the Revolutionary cause or lose their womanly favors, services, and esteem; as professional printers and propagandists, women printers produced crucial Revolutionary broadsides, newspapers, and documents such as the Declaration of Independence. Mercy Otis Warren wrote patriotic plays and poems that satirized the British and lauded the Revolutionary cause. Sarah Bradless Fulton instigated the Boston Tea Party.

After the Declaration of Independence, women on farms and in towns assumed the responsibilities and positions of their men who volunteered and served in the Continental Army as well as participating in the more traditional women's wartime activities of sewing clothes for the soldiers, rolling bandages, and preparing foodstuffs for the front. The local production of shot for the soldiers' rifles and often the manufacture and assembly of arms were undertaken by women who converted their peacetime facilities to war production. Women took direct action in policing uncooperative merchants, British sympathizers, and collaborators. Through fund-raising fairs, patriotic groups such as the Ladies Association of Philadelphia raised large sums to purchase food, clothing, and medical supplies for the Continental Army. Many women courageously opted for a scorched-earth policy, destroying their farms rather than allowing their crops to fall into British hands.

At the battle lines, women were present as camp followers who served as cooks, nurses, washerwomen, and under takers for the fallen. Most of the camp followers were wives and family members of the soldiers, but the term has come to connote only the prostitutes, who were a minority of these women who lived in the Army camps. Whether disguised as men or merely harmless females, women served heroically as spies, saboteurs, and couriers.

While the Revolution did not bring full legal and political equality to women in North America, it did bring subtle but significant changes to women's lives in the latter eighteenth century. Women's patriotic wartime activities initiated them into business and politics beyond the domestic realm and gave them a sense of the importance of their contributions. With the absence of men at the home front, the status of women advanced due to both their proven capabilities and their sense of their potential. Women benefited from the post-Revolutionary changes in the family and the rise of the image of the republican mother: The family structure became smaller and less authoritarian, and the role of the republican mother fused the revolutionary patriotism of women with their traditional duties. Republican motherhood laid the foundations for the domestic feminism that would progress during the nineteenth century from the cult of true womanhood to the cult of domesticity that has endured into the late twentieth century. *(See also: Ladies Association of Philadelphia; Pitcher, Molly; Republican Motherhood; Warren, Mercy)*

—Angela M. Howard

Further Reading

Kerber, Linda K. *Women of the Republic: Intellect and Ideology in Revolutionary America.* Chapel Hill: University of North Carolina Press, 1980.

Norton, Mary Beth. *Liberty's Daughters: The Revolutionary Experiences of American Women.* Boston: Little, Brown, 1980.

⟳ American Woman Suffrage Association (AWSA)

The American Woman Suffrage Association (AWSA) was founded at a convention held in Cleveland, November 24-25, 1869. It was promoted by Lucy Stone and other prominent members of the New England Woman Suffrage Association who disapproved of the program and tactics of the National Woman Suffrage Association (NWSA) started by Elizabeth Cady Stanton, Susan B. Anthony, and their supporters earlier that year. In contrast to NWSA, which was at first loosely structured, largely New York based, and strongly influenced by Stanton's radical feminist ideas, AWSA took a more moderate stance. AWSA claimed, through its formal delegate system, to represent more accurately the state suffrage associations that were springing up across the nation. In fact, AWSA tended to reflect the views of a core of influential New England members, many of them former abolitionists. Thus, the new organization looked to the Republican Party as the most likely source of progress on the suffrage issue, supported the Fifteenth Amendment (guaranteeing black male suffrage without reference to women) as the fulfillment of the abolition crusade, and chose to support a separate federal amendment for woman suffrage.

Although individual members favored various reform and philanthropic causes, AWSA officially confined its work to suffrage and avoided taking positions on related but more controversial feminist issues. Men were conspicuous in the AWSA leadership; its first two presidents were Henry Ward Beecher and T. W. Higginson. Beginning in 1874, Julia Ward Howe was president for many years, but Lucy Stone and her husband, Henry B. Blackwell, continued as guiding spirits. Through lecture tours, an ambitious publication program, and the convening of annual conventions in midwestern cities, AWSA attempted to build a national membership. Outside New England, it had considerable success in New Jersey, Ohio, Illinois, Indiana, Maryland, and several other states. But these efforts were soon outstripped by Susan B. Anthony's organizing zeal, and almost from the start, NWSA led in both membership and fund-raising.

AWSA lobbied steadily for a federal suffrage amendment but concentrated its energies at the state level, supporting several campaigns for school and municipal suffrage. It gained a wide audience through *Woman's Journal,* a Boston weekly. Founded in 1870 and edited from 1872 by Lucy Stone, *Woman's Journal* became the most influential and longest lived of nineteenth-century feminist newspapers.

In response to pressure from younger members, a joint committee met in 1887 to begin negotiating terms under which the two rival wings of the suffrage movement could be reconciled. After long deliberation, agreement was reached, and in 1890, AWSA and NWSA were merged as the National American Woman Suffrage Association. *(See also: Abolition and the Antislavery Movement; Anthony, Susan B.; Blackwell, Alice Stone; Equal Rights Association; National American Woman Suffrage Association; National Woman Suffrage Association; Stanton, Elizabeth Cady; Stone, Lucy; Suffrage, Woman's Journal)*

—Gail Malmgreen

Further Reading

Blackwell, Alice Stone. *Lucy Stone, Pioneer of Woman's Rights.* Boston: Little, Brown, 1930.

Buechler, Steven M. *The Transformation of the Woman Suffrage Movement: The Case of Illinois, 1850–1920.* New Brunswick, NJ: Rutgers University Press, 1986.

Kerr, Andrea Moore. *Lucy Stone: Speaking Out for Equality.* New Brunswick, NJ: Rutgers University Press, 1992.

Stanton, Elizabeth Cady, et al., eds. *History of Woman Suffrage.* Vols. 2, 4. Rochester, NY: Privately printed, 1881, 1902.

Wagner, Sally Roesch. *A Time of Protest: Suffragists Challenge the Republic, 1870–1887.* Sacramento, CA: Spectrum, 1987.

ᴈ American Women's Education Association

The American Women's Education Association was founded in 1852 by noted educator and author Catharine Beecher. The purpose of the organization was to help women secure a liberal education and appropriate employment, which according to the association, was training the mind, taking care of the body, and preserving the family state. In pursuit of these goals, the association provided funding for women's colleges, particularly Milwaukee Female College (later called Milwaukee Normal Institute), which had been started by Beecher. The association supported three other colleges, too, but only Milwaukee Normal Institute survived for more than a few years.

Beecher believed that women, especially unmarried women, must be prepared to earn an independent livelihood. But she had the view, conservative even for her time, that women's proper role lay in the traditional domestic areas of housework or working with children. She therefore wanted to head a department of domestic economy at Milwaukee Normal Institute.

For several years, the association had provided money for salaries, but its aim had always been to fund the establishment of departments. This it was unable to do, so Beecher went east to raise money for the college, hoping to raise enough to build a home for herself on the Milwaukee campus that would also serve as the domestic economy department. The trustees of the college declined her request for help because they thought it inappropriate to fund a place of residence for Beecher on the campus. Greatly disappointed, Beecher resigned from the association and ended her relationship with the college. In her letter of resignation, she stated that should the association decide to fund a health and domestic department at Milwaukee or anywhere else, she would rejoin. Beecher later rescinded her resignation, but soon thereafter, the association lost effectiveness.

The college did later erect a building to be used as a department of domestic education (not funded by the association) and asked Beecher to lead the department, but she declined. By 1862, the association had voted to disband, feeling there was little left that it could accomplish. Beecher ignored this decision and continued its activities alone until her death in 1878. (See also: Beecher, Catharine; Education; Normal Schools)

—Judith Pryor

Further Reading

Harveson, Mae Elizabeth. *Catharine Esther Beecher.* New York: Arno, 1969.

Milwaukee-Downer College Records, 1852–1964, Milwaukee Manuscript College. http://www.uwm.edu/Dept/Library/arch/findaids/mssl.htm

Sklar, Kathryn Kish. *Catharine Beecher: A Study in American Domesticity.* New Haven, CT: Yale University Press, 1973.

ᴈ American Women's Hospitals Service (AWHS)

Established at the second annual meeting of the Medical Women's National Association (American Medical Women's Association [AMWA]), June 5-6, 1917, the American Women's Hospitals Service (AWHS) was the primary organization through which women doctors used their professional skills during World War I. Because women physicians were refused entry into the armed forces, AWHS—operating as an AMWA committee—provided an all-female force of doctors, nurses, and ambulance drivers; it organized hospitals in the French war zone, setting up dispensaries to serve the civilian population in the outlying areas. Barely under way when the armistice was signed, AWHS refocused its efforts on reconstruction in Europe and in Serbia (the former Yugoslavia) beginning in 1918. Reaching its peak in overseas service in 1923, when approximately twelve thousand refugees from Turkey were treated on the offshore Greek island of Macronissi, the organization turned its attention to the Appalachian area of the United States in 1931. Medical service was continued in other parts of the world, however, extending throughout the Near East, Far East, and later into South America, although largely without American women doctors.

Dr. Rosalie Slaughter Morton chaired the AWHS committee the first year, followed by Dr. Mary M. Crawford the second year, then by Dr. Esther Pohl Lovejoy, who retained the position for forty-eight years. AWHS functioned officially under AMWA, but Lovejoy ran the organization independently. In 1959, AWHS separated from AWMA until 1980, when it rejoined the parent organization in its original status as a committee.

The history of AWHS does not bear out the contention that women's rights advance in wartime. Despite the organization's impressive record overseas during and after World War I, World War II began with the same refusal to accept women physicians into the armed forces. Restrictions barring women doctors from service were lifted in 1943 but were reinstituted at the war's end. Not until the 1950s did women doctors win rank and commissions in the armed forces permanently. (See also: Military Service; Physicians; World War I)

—Jayne Crumpler DeFiore

Further Reading

Archives and Special Collections on Women in Medicine. Philadelphia: Medical College of Pennsylvania. [Alumnae Files; American Medical Women's Association Papers; American Women's Hospitals Service Papers]

Lovejoy, Esther Pohl. *Certain Samaritans,* 2d ed. New York: Macmillan, 1933.

———. *The House of the Good Neighbor,* 2d ed. New York: Macmillan, 1920.

———. *Women Doctors of the World.* New York: Macmillan, 1957.

———. *Women Physicians and Surgeons National and International Organizations.* Livingston, NY: Livingston, 1939.

Americans with Disabilities Act (ADA)

The Americans with Disabilities Act (ADA) guarantees persons with physical or mental disabilities access to and participation in employment, public accommodations, public services, transportation, and telecommunications. President George Bush signed the law on July 26, 1990.

Under the ADA, employers may not discriminate against qualified individuals with disabilities in preemployment screening, hiring, benefits, promotions, or termination. Employers need to provide "reasonable accommodation" to individuals with disabilities to enable them to fulfill their duties. In addition, public transportation must be accessible by persons with disabilities. Public accommodations must not discriminate against the disabled and must provide auxiliary aids and services to disabled users. Telephone companies must offer relay services for the deaf.

Opponents of the ADA say it is an intrusive federal mandate, producing unfair compliance costs. However, "reasonable accommodations" under the law are required only when "readily achievable" and they can be provided "without much difficulty or expense." Implementation of the ADA has not resulted in large numbers of lawsuits as some had predicted.

The ADA is the most far-reaching civil rights legislation since the 1964 Civil Rights Act. The law grants persons with mental or physical disabilities broad civil rights protections already available to racial groups and women. The disabilities rights movement has paralleled the women's rights movement in its emphasis on equality versus difference and on personal characteristics and abilities versus social bias. In the workplace, advocates for disabled and female workers stress equal opportunity in employment and wages, training on nondiscrimination practices, employer flexibility, and examination of employee evaluation and reward structures. *(See also: Civil Rights)*

—**Anne Hudson Bolin**

Further Reading

The Americans with Disabilities Act: Ensuring Equal Access to the American Dream. Washington, DC: National Council on Disability, 1995.

The Americans with Disabilities Act: A Practical and Legal Guide to Impact, Enforcement, and Compliance. Washington, DC: Bureau of National Affairs, 1990.

Americans with Disabilities Handbook. Washington, DC: Equal Employment Opportunity Commission and the U.S. Department of Justice, 1991.

Disability Discrimination: Employment Discrimination Prohibited by the Americans with Disabilities Act of 1990. Washington, DC: U.S. Equal Opportunity Commission Technical Assistance Program, 1995.

Ames, Jessie Daniel (1883–1972)

Suffragist and civil rights activist, Jessie Daniel Ames led a campaign against lynching in a Ku Klux Klan-dominated era. As founder and director of the Association of Southern Women for the Prevention of Lynching (ASWPL; 1930-1942), Ames exposed the link between sexual and racial repression that lay at the root of mob violence in the South. She argued that "false chivalry," built on the myth of the black rapist and the pure white "southern lady" in need of protection, demeaned white women even as it terrorized blacks. Ames also criticized the double standard that simultaneously condoned white men's lynching of black men and their sexual exploitation of black women.

Ames grew up in Texas, graduating from Southwestern University at Georgetown in 1902. At the age of thirty-one, she found herself widowed with three young children to support. The self-confidence and economic independence Ames gained during this period nurtured a growing feminism, and in 1916, she began her public career as a suffragist. Throughout the 1920s, Ames mobilized newly enfranchised women behind the social welfare goals of southern progressivism. But she soon became dissatisfied with the contradiction between social feminism and the exclusion of black women and racial concerns and turned to the South's chief interracial reform organization, the Commission on Interracial Cooperation (CIC). In 1929, she moved to Georgia as director of the CIC Women's Committee, where she sought to bridge the color line separating black and white middle-class women, calling for female solidarity in the fight against racist stereotypes.

Ames's major contribution came in the 1930s, with the founding of the ASWPL. The association worked through established women's networks to fight mob violence with speeches, writings, investigations, and even intervention. The women combined a nineteenth-century reputation for moral superiority with a twentieth-century potential for political power in their efforts to convince local leaders to denounce lynching. Blending their traditional roles as moral guardians with their resistance to the suppression of women for their own "protection," Ames and her followers made progress in their feminist revolt against chivalry, while still holding to some of the trappings of the traditional "southern lady." *(See also: Association of Southern Women for the Prevention of Lynching; Commission on Interracial Cooperation; Southern Lady; Southern Women's History; Wells-Barnett, Ida B.)*

—**Misti Turbeville**

Further Reading

ASWPL Papers. Trevor Arnett Library. Atlanta University, Atlanta, GA.

Hall, Jacquelyn Dowd. *Revolt against Chivalry: Jessie Daniel Ames and the Women's Campaign against Lynching.* New York: Columbia University Press, 1979.

Figure 2. Marian Anderson
Contralto Marian Anderson performed everything from Schubert to gospel for a crowd of 75,000 as she sang from the steps of the Lincoln Memorial in 1939. Used by permission of UPI/Corbis-Bettmann.

New York Philharmonic. By the 1930s, she was well received on tours throughout Europe and the United States.

She gained notoriety in 1939 when the Daughters of the American Revolution (DAR), a patriotic white women's organization, barred her from performing a concert in Constitution Hall in Washington, D.C. Amid a wave of public outcry, a prominent group of civil rights organizers and government officials arranged for her to sing at the Lincoln Memorial. Some 75,000 people attended the Easter Sunday concert in support of Anderson and in opposition to racial discrimination. Eleanor Roosevelt's decision to resign from the DAR in protest of its treatment of Anderson added to the national visibility and political meaning of the event. Anderson went on to have an illustrious career, which included performances at the White House and on *The Ed Sullivan Show,* and she was the first African American to sing at the Metropolitan Opera. *(See also: Black Women; Civil Rights; Daughters of the American Revolution; Music; Roosevelt, Eleanor)*

—**Susan Lynn Smith**

Further Reading

Anderson, Marian. *My Lord, What a Morning: An Autobiography.* New York: Viking, 1956.

Patterson, Charles. *Marian Anderson.* New York: Watts, 1988.

Sandage, Scott A. "A Marble House Divided: The Lincoln Memorial, the Civil Rights Movement, and the Politics of Memory, 1939–1963," *Journal of American History* 80 (June 1993): 135-67.

Story, Rosalyn M. "Marian Anderson, a DAR-ing Lady," *American Visions* 7 (1993): 44-46.

Tobias, Toby. *Marian Anderson.* New York: Crowell, 1972.

Jessie Daniel Ames Papers. Southern Historical Collection. University of North Carolina, Chapel Hill.

Miller, Kathleen Atkinson. "The Ladies and the Lynchers: A Look at the Association of Southern Women for the Prevention of Lynching," *Southern Studies* 17 (Fall 1978): 221-40.

Scott, Anne Firor. *The Southern Lady: From Pedestal to Politics, 1830–1930.* Chicago: University of Chicago Press, 1970.

❧ Anderson, Marian (1902–1993)

A successful African American singer, Marian Anderson performed a famous concert at the Lincoln Memorial in 1939 that came to symbolize the promise of black protest. Born in Philadelphia, this contralto began to sing publicly at the age of six in a local Union Baptist Church. Recognizing her talent, church members raised $600 to pay for her singing lessons under the renowned teacher Giuseppe Boghetti. After graduating from high school, she won several major music competitions, including contests sponsored by the Philadelphia Philharmonic Society and the

❧ Androgyny

Androgyny is the condition of being both male and female, of having both male and female characteristics.

Aristophanes, greatest of the Greek comic playwrights, tells the story of the androgynes in Plato's *Symposium.* When the world was new, Aristophanes explains, Zeus peopled it with complete beings. Each had two faces, four legs, and four arms and was at once male and female. Very soon, however, these prototypical humans became so powerful that they threatened the gods, and so Zeus sliced them in two. Desperate for their original wholeness, the severed halves clung together, refusing to eat or drink, and soon many of them were dying. Zeus saved the race and created human beings as we now know them, by making it possible for the halved androgynes to unite sexually and so experience some semblance of their archetypal selves. Romantic lovers, then, are people who have found their other halves.

Within feminism, androgyny has been seen as both a goal and a delusive solution. Virginia Woolf, in *A Room of One's Own,* praises great writers—Shakespeare, Keats, and

Coleridge, for instance—for their androgyny: their capacity to write without insistent sexual identification. "[I]t is fatal for anyone who writes to think of their sex," Woolf says, and she looks forward to a time when women and men will be able to accept each other without the sexual resentment she sees pervading early twentieth-century literature. Adrienne Rich, on the other hand, in *The Dream of a Common Language,* writes

> There are words I cannot choose again:
> humanism androgyny
> Such words have no shame in them, no diffidence
>   before the raging stoic grandmothers . . .
>   *("Natural Resources" 66)*

Rich rejects the inadequate goal of androgyny in favor of women's strength, gentleness, and persistence in reconstituting a culture imperiled by competition and male violence. *(See also: European Influences; Rich, Adrienne)*

—**Gretchen Mieszkowski**

Further Reading

Heilbrun, Carolyn G. *Toward a Recognition of Androgyny.* New York: Norton, 1982.

Piel Cook, Ellen. *Psychological Androgyny.* New York: Pergamon, 1985.

Rich, Adrienne. "Natural Resources." In *The Dream of a Common Language: Poems 1974–1977,* p. 66. New York: Norton, 1978.

Weil, Kari. *Androgyny and the Denial of Difference.* Charlottesville: University Press of Virginia, 1992.

Women's Studies 2 (1974). [Androgyny issue]

❧ Angelou, Maya (b. 1928)

Through her autobiographies, poetry, articles, interviews, performances, and presence, Maya Angelou has profoundly influenced black American women since the 1960s. Her gentle outspokenness and rich prose inspired novice writers and her reading public of all races and both genders to overcome heartache and hardship through her series of five autobiographical volumes: *I Know Why the Caged Bird Sings* (1970), *Gather Together in My Name* (1974), *Singin' and Swingin' and Gettin' Merry Like Christmas* (1977), *The Heart of a Woman* (1981), and *All God's Children Need Traveling Shoes* (1986).

The first volume is the most famous, describing Angelou's childhood during the Depression with her brother, Bailey, and their courageous grandmother, who owned and operated the general store in the poor black community of rural Stamps, Arkansas. When she was eight years old, Angelou's brief reunion with her mother in East St. Louis resulted in her being raped. When she returned to Stamps, her state of guilt induced a self-imposed silence broken only when her grandmother's friend Mrs. Bertha Flowers insisted that Maya read aloud the great literature of the world. With ex-

traordinary candor and compassion, Angelou presents a textured picture of the kinship and church-centered community of these southern blacks. As a teenager during World War II, she lived with her mother in California, becoming the first black woman fare collector with the San Francisco Streetcar Company. The initial autobiography ends with sixteen-year-old Angelou giving birth to her son, Guy, "the best thing that ever happened to me." Her later books record her development and maturity as an artist and writer during the 1960s and 1970s in New York and Europe. The latest volume relates her travels to Africa, where "she became a hunter for that elusive place and much longed for place the heart could call home."

Singer, dancer, playwright, and political activist, Angelou has accomplished much in diverse areas. During the 1960s, she performed in the Obie-award-winning play *The Blacks,* by Jean Genet. Shortly afterward, she served as the northern coordinator for the Reverend Dr. Martin Luther King's Southern Christian Leadership Conference. As a student of the classics, Angelou recalled the experience of being asked by her teacher Mrs. Flowers to memorize and recite poetry: "I have often tried to search behind the sophistication of years for the enchantment I so easily found in those gifts."

The enchantment of those gifts has created such diverse opportunities as reading her poem, "On the Pulse of Morning," at the inauguration of President William J. Clinton in 1993 and speaking at the Million Man March in October 1995. The enchantment of those gifts has spanned acting roles in the movies *Roots* (1975), *Poetic Justice* (1993), and *How to Make an American Quilt* (1995). She is a living treasure, a wonder. She is also a Reynolds Professor at Wake Forest University in Winston-Salem, North Carolina and a Living Legacy Award recipient. She has called her connection to "everything and everybody delicious and wonderful." Her writing gifts, presence, and voice make our lives "delicious and wonderful." *(See also: Black Women; Women Writers)*

—**R. Janie Isackson**

Further Reading

Angelou, Maya. *All God's Children Need Traveling Shoes.* New York: Random House, 1986.

———. *And Still I Rise.* New York: Random House, 1978.

———. *The Complete Collected Poems of Maya Angelou.* New York: Random House, 1994.

———. *Gather Together in My Name.* New York: Random House, 1974.

———. *The Heart of a Woman.* New York: Random House, 1981.

———. *I Know Why the Caged Bird Sings.* New York: Random House, 1970.

———. *I Shall Not Be Moved.* New York: Random House, 1990.

———. *Just Give Me a Cool Drink of Water 'fore I Die: The Poetry of Maya Angelou.* New York: Random House, 1971.

———. *Life Doesn't Frighten Me.* New York: Random House, 1993.

———. "No Longer Out of Africa," *Ms.* 14 (August 1986): 36-38.

———. *Now Sheba Sings the Song.* New York: Dutton/Dial, 1987.

———. *Oh, Pray My Wings Are Gonna Fit Me Well.* New York: Random House, 1975.

———. *Phenomenal Woman: Four Poems Celebrating Women.* New York: Random House, 1994.

———. *Shaker, Why Don't You Sing?* New York: Random House, 1983.

———. *Singin' and Swingin' and Gettin' Merry Like Christmas.* New York: Bantam, 1977.

Christian, Barbara T. "Maya Angelou's African Sojourn Links Two Worlds," *Chicago Tribune* 6 (March 23, 1987): 37-38.

Gross, Robert A. "Growing Up Black," *Newsweek* 75 (March 2, 1970): 89-90.

& Antebellum Era (1812–1860)

This era extended from the end of the War of 1812 to the beginning of the Civil War and was characterized by industrial and economic growth and westward expansion, which had substantial impact on American women. The mainstream ideal of the antebellum True Woman defined her as a wife and mother whose place was in the home. As the moral guardian of society, she possessed the four cardinal virtues: purity, piety, submissiveness, and domesticity. However, this ideal was not the reality for most women in the antebellum era, whose lives were largely determined by class, race, and geographic location.

Between 1830 and 1860, women became involved in efforts to reshape American society. Writer and editor Sarah Josepha Hale (1788–1879) sought to improve women's effectiveness as moral reformers by expanding their sphere of influence through increased educational opportunity, simplification of women's clothing, and promotion of women authors, teachers, medical practitioners, and missionaries. Catharine Beecher (1800–1878) opened Hartford Female Seminary in the 1820s, and Mary Mason Lyon (1797–1849) founded the first women's college, Mount Holyoke.

Other women eluded the limitations of women's sphere through active involvement in reform movements such as the temperance and abolition movements, which led women like Angelina (1805–1879) and Sarah Grimké (1792–1873), Lucretia Mott (1783–1880), and Elizabeth Cady Stanton (1815–1902) to question the cult of domesticity. Such women began to develop an intricate philosophy based on the political liberal doctrines of the American Revolution, ideas of eighteenth-century British reformers, and nineteenth-century transcendentalism. In 1848, in Seneca Falls, New York, women activists organized the first formal women's rights convention to discuss the status of women. Some abolitionist groups and other reform movements began to add selected women's rights issues to their agendas: married women's property rights, divorce and custody laws, and woman suffrage. These reforms appealed primarily to upper- and middle-class white women; therefore, the participants in these movements were neither numerous nor representative of the female population as a whole.

Upper- and middle-class northern white women sometimes were able to fit into the model of the ideal woman.

More women, however, had to enter the American workforce in the early nineteenth century because farm families often needed cash income. Some young women, especially in New England, moved to new mill towns such as Lowell, Massachusetts, to work in the mills for low wages. Frequently, they sent their meager earnings home to support their families or finance their brothers' education. Many women also worked as domestics, farmhands, piece workers in the garment trades, teachers, and prostitutes.

In the South, upper- and middle-class women were restricted by the cult of white womanhood that characterized them as weak, fragile, and in need of protection and guidance. Despite this stereotype, upper- and middle-class southern white women frequently participated in the running of plantations and were important economic and moral forces in their families and communities. Poor southern women did farm labor and many of the same jobs as their northern counterparts and slave women.

Black women in the South were generally slaves, sold and treated like livestock. They labored as domestics, farmhands, servants, nurses, and dairymaids; rarely were they permitted to pursue crafts and trades as black slave men could. Although black women were regarded as chattel rather than human beings, they were the glue that held slave families together. Free black women in both the North and the South were the lowest paid and most exploited of all free women in the workforce.

Immigrant women, like black women, had tremendous problems finding employment. Mostly unskilled and non-English speaking, they generally found work in the needle trades, as domestics, or as prostitutes at less than subsistence wages. On the West Coast, Chinese groups known as *tongs* regularly imported young Chinese women as prostitutes, and they led miserable lives. A small number of them became wives or self-supporting business owners whose opportunities were limited by anti-Chinese sentiment as well as by racism and sexism in the western territories.

Native American women also began to lose status during the early nineteenth century. Among some indigenous groups such as the Cherokee, land was traditionally owned by the women, who kept custody of their children after a divorce. As the tribes adopted European-style constitutions and legal codes, the matrilineal system changed to a patrilineal system of inheritance. The depleted game supply resulting from the fur trade caused Native American men to take over the agricultural tasks that formerly belonged to women. In addition, white men refused to negotiate with indigenous women as tribal representatives; consequently, opportunities decreased for women to become political leaders, shamans, or warriors in their communities. Similarly, Chicanas in the Southwest experienced loss of status and property rights as a result of Texas's independence from Mexico, the annexation of the Lone Star Republic by the United States, and the Mexican War.

Despite some improvements in women's access to education, increase in women's self-esteem, and society's respect for motherhood, the antebellum era failed to produce a single standard for all women. Some women began to question the restrictions on their lives and to expand their activities into the community. Women reformers educated the public on issues affecting women's status. These efforts challenged the proscribed role for women prior to the Civil War and laid the groundwork for the American feminist movement of the late nineteenth and early twentieth centuries. *(See also: Asian American Women; Beecher, Catharine; Black Women; Chicana; Cult of True Womanhood; Grimké, Angelina Emily; Grimké, Sarah Moore; Hale, Sarah Josepha; Immigration; Lowell Mill Girls; Mott, Lucretia Coffin; Mount Holyoke Seminary; Native American Women; Stanton, Elizabeth Cady; Women's Rights Movements: Nineteenth and Twentieth Centuries)*

—**Joyce Ann Kievit**

Further Reading

Brownlee, W. Elliot. "Household Values, Women's Work, and Economic Growth, 1800–1923," *Journal of Economic History* 39 (March 1979): 199-209.

Clinton, Catherine. *The Other Civil War: American Women in the Nineteenth Century.* New York: Hill & Wang, 1984.

Cotera, Martha. *Diosa y Hembra: The History and Heritage of Chicanas in the United States.* Austin, TX: University Information Systems, 1976.

Fox-Genovese, Elizabeth. *Within the Plantation Household: Black and White Women of the Old South.* Chapel Hill: University of North Carolina Press, 1988.

Niethammer, Carolyn J. *Daughters of the Earth: The Lives and Legends of American Indian Women.* New York: Colliers, 1977.

Yung, Judy. *Unbound Feet: A Social History of Chinese Women in San Francisco.* Berkeley: University of California Press, 1995.

◈ Antenuptial Agreements

Antenuptial agreements, or marriage settlements, were made in early America in an effort to circumvent coverture, the merging of a woman's legal existence with that of her husband at marriage. A contract was signed before marriage, specifying the rights that a wife could continue to hold. Usually, it gave a married woman some control over the property she brought to a marriage. Parents used this device to protect a daughter in the event that she was widowed. It was more often used by a widow to protect her own wealth after remarriage.

A study of eighteenth-century Pennsylvania marriage settlements shows that, at first, antenuptial agreements were allowable only when placed in trust (supervised by a third party). Increasingly, the Pennsylvania courts recognized simple agreements between engaged couples; settlements made after marriage still required the administration of trustees. An examination of South Carolina marriage settlements indicates that they were employed by 1 to 2 percent of all married couples, were largely confined to the upper classes, and involved property in personalty (which was not protected by common law) and slaves rather than land.

SUSAN B. ANTHONY.

Figure 3. Susan B. Anthony
An engraving of Susan B. Anthony, who helped build the National American Women Suffrage Association. Used by permission of Corbis-Bettmann.

Equity courts enforced marriage settlements, particularly in the late eighteenth and early nineteenth centuries when such settlements became more numerous. *(See also: Coverture; Equity Courts; Marriage; Married Women's Property Acts)*

—**Barbara E. Lacey**

Further Reading

Salmon, Marylynn. *Women and the Law of Property in Early America.* Chapel Hill: University of North Carolina Press, 1986.

◈ Anthony, Susan B. (1820–1906)

Suffragist Susan B. Anthony was the preeminent organizer and strategist of the nineteenth-century agitation for woman's enfranchisement. From 1851, when she met suffragist Elizabeth Cady Stanton, until the end of her life Anthony worked full-time to build a political movement among women and direct it toward gaining equal rights. Recognizing Anthony's significance early on, the federal government singled her out for prosecution when she voted in Rochester, New York, in 1872, while it ignored scores of women voting elsewhere. Persistence and intensity made her the symbol of political equality; a popular symbol, she inspired suffragists to coalesce for several decades until a mature political organization could grow.

Born in South Adams, Massachusetts, but associated primarily with her family's later home in Rochester, New York, Anthony received a Quaker education and taught school for a decade before finding her vocation in reform. In the 1850s, she threw herself into mobilizing public opinion behind abolition and temperance as well as women's rights. After the Civil War, she singled out woman suffrage as her primary goal. Her personal and political lives were virtually inseparable. Political engagements dictated her yearly schedules, and for months at a time, she stayed at hotels or the homes of co-workers, calling no place her home until 1890.

Anthony, along with Stanton, set goals for the National Woman Suffrage Association (NWSA) during postwar Reconstruction. Mindful of how quickly Republicans forgot the cause of women when the war ended, they insisted on an independent movement that would be free to help the party that helped the cause. This stance contributed to the formation of the rival, and soundly Republican, American Woman Suffrage Association in 1869.

The women of NWSA were Republican enough, however, to take the constitutional amendments of Reconstruction as their model of how woman suffrage should be won. A federal amendment offered women the surest protection and most significant recognition of equal rights. To attain a federal amendment, NWSA made Congress its target and met annually in Washington, D.C., where its members became proficient and familiar lobbyists.

In the 1880s, Anthony built bridges between suffragists and the mushrooming woman's movement. She courted the Woman's Christian Temperance Union, directed the establishment of the International and National Councils of Women, and saw to it that by 1890 the two major suffrage organizations were united as the National American Woman Suffrage Association. Results were mixed. On the one hand, her constituency multiplied; on the other, it became far more difficult to lead. Lacking the ideal of universal rights that had inspired the pioneers, the later suffrage movement combined various and often rival claims about how women should use the vote.

Eighty years old before she retired from the National American Woman Suffrage Association (NAWSA) presidency, Anthony kept her sights set on "the right protective of all other rights." She acted defensively to stop efforts to make the suffrage movement an instrument of policy. She appeared tolerant when the demand was to exclude Mormons and intolerant when the demand was to condemn racial discrimination. Nonetheless, she kept alive the dream and the demand for equal rights against half a century of male opposition and female indecisiveness. *(See also: Abolition and the Antislavery Movement; American Woman Suffrage Association; National American Woman Suffrage Association; National Woman Suffrage Association; Stanton, Elizabeth Cady; Suffrage)*

—**Ann D. Gordon**

Further Reading

Anthony, Susan B., and Ida Husted Harper, eds. *History of Woman Suffrage.* Vol. 4. Rochester, 1902. Reprint, New York: Arno, 1969.

Barry, Kathleen. *Susan B. Anthony.* New York: New York University Press, 1988.

Gordon, Ann D., ed. *The Papers of Elizabeth Cady Stanton and Susan B. Anthony.* Vol. 1, *In the School of Anti-Slavery, 1840–1866.* New Brunswick, NJ: Rutgers University Press, 1997.

Gordon, Ann D., and Patricia G. Holland, eds. *The Papers of Elizabeth Cady Stanton and Susan B. Anthony.* Wilmington, DE: Scholarly Resources, 1991, 1992. Microfilm.

Harper, Ida Husted. *The Life and Work of Susan B. Anthony,* 3 vols. Indianapolis, IN: Bowen-Merrill, 1898–1908. Reprint, Salem, NH: Ayer, 1983.

Stanton, Elizabeth Cady, Susan B. Anthony, and Matilda Joslyn Gage, eds. *History of Woman Suffrage,* 3 vols. New York: Fowler & Wells, 1881–1886. Reprint, New York: Arno, 1969.

~ Antifeminism

Twentieth-century women's historians use the term *antifeminism* to designate opposition to either the assumption or the advocacy of women's equality. An aspect of political fundamentalism of the 1920s, antifeminism gained recognition in women's participation in the Ku Klux Klan and reflected the Klan's nativist concerns as well as a reaction to potential freedom for woman inherent in cultural perceptions of flappers. After World War II, antifeminism in the late 1940s and 1950s focused on definitions of female psychology as quintessentially passive, a definition popularized by postwar American disciples of Freudian theory. Antifeminism of the 1970s, however, criticized feminism and the movement for women's equality as lethal to the divinely ordained domestic role of woman within the patriarchal family unit. Thus, historically, antifeminism arose to defend gender systems from potential public acceptance of a feminist definition of womanhood that promotes woman's autonomy at the expense of her thralldom to the family.

Categorically defining feminist criticism of the cult of domesticity as neurotic, proponents of Freudian-based antifeminism argued that they alone understood women's sexuality and therefore possessed authority to define women's proper social (and economic) roles. Responding to acceleration of social and economic changes that presented even married women with new opportunities in education and employment during World War II, antifeminists offered little more than a "psychobabble" version of the biological determination argument that relegated women to a primarily reproductive function and used Freudian theory to justify sexual inequality as both natural and physically unavoidable. Antifeminists such as Helene Deutsch, Marynia Farnham, and Marie Robinson dismissed previous woman's rights advocates and challenges to "traditional" women's roles as psychologically deviant but offered no scientific evidence to support their contention that women remained little more than castrated males and pathetic masochistic narcissists. Antifeminists of the 1940s and 1950s remained primarily architects of a new cult of motherhood later called the "feminine mystique."

In response to a 1960s resurgence of the women's movement, antifeminism in the 1970s focused its defense of the cult of domesticity on women's inescapable responsibility to fulfill a maternal role to ensure survival of the patriarchal family. A strain of political fundamentalism permeated the hostile view that women's liberation threatened traditional sex roles. Social and economic changes in 1970s American society brought more middle-class women into the labor force, regardless of their marital status or political persuasion, and forced antifeminists such as Phyllis Schlafly and Mirabelle Morgan to accommodate their definition of women's role. Nevertheless, antifeminists clung to their emphasis on the necessity and propriety of women's maternal destiny and subordination within the family. Evoking the twin specters of divorce and the displaced homemaker to politicize a group strongly identified with traditional apolitical domesticity, the antifeminists used "pro-family" and antiabortion rhetoric to recruit conservative middle-class housewives to their cause, co-opting effective strategies of their feminist opponents to pursue their goal of preserving woman's traditional role.

By the 1980s, antifeminism represented the concerns of a vocal minority that championed a Protestant fundamentalist interpretation of woman's proper role. After efforts to ratify the Equal Rights Amendment failed, national antifeminist leadership reflected a shift in focus from political conservatism to religious fundamentalism.

Thus, the intensity of antifeminism through the twentieth century increased in proportion to national economic and political trends that altered the nature and function of women's role in the nuclear family and to increased opportunities for women. *(See also: Antisuffragism; Flapper; Freudianism; Modern Woman: The Lost Sex; Right-Wing Political Movements; Schlafly, Phyllis MacAlpin)*

—Angela M. Howard
—Sasha Ranaé Adams Tarrant

Further Reading

Conover, Pamela J., and Virginia Gray. *Feminism and the New Right: Conflict over the American Family.* New York: Praeger, 1983.

Kinnard, Cynthia D. *Antifeminism in American Thought: An Annotated Bibliography.* Boston: G. K. Hall, 1986.

Marshall, Susan E. "Who Speaks for American Women? The Future of Antifeminism." *Annals of the American Academy of Political and Social Science* 515 (1991): 50-62.

McElroy, Wendy. *Freedom, Feminism, and the State.* Washington, DC: CATO Institute, 1982.

Mitchell, Juliet. *Psychoanalysis and Feminism.* New York: Vintage, 1975.

~ Antisuffragism

A predominantly female movement to oppose the enfranchisement of women, antisuffragism began with local organized protests in 1868 in Massachusetts, eventually spreading to more than twenty states. In 1911, the National Association Opposed to Woman Suffrage (NAOWS) was formed in New York with Mrs. Josephine Dodge as president. Opposition to woman suffrage was also promoted by separate male organizations, such as the Man-Suffrage Associations in various states and the national American Constitutional League, as well as by conservative ethnic and religious groups and by business and liquor interests.

As a group, antisuffrage leaders were Protestant middle-class, middle-aged women who were less well educated and more religiously conservative than suffragists. In legislative testimony, petitions, and publications such as *Remonstrance* (1890–1920), *Anti-Suffragist* (1908–1911), and *Woman's Protest* (1912–1918), they rejected suffragists' claims to sex equality. Although they participated in many of the same social welfare activities as suffragists, antisuffragists used biological and theological arguments that women could best effect reform through their influence within the patriarchal nuclear family, which they claimed to be the basis of social order.

In 1917, NAOWS headquarters moved to Washington, D.C., and new leadership emerged that accorded more influence in the organization to men. *Woman's Protest* was replaced by *Woman Patriot,* and reasoned arguments about the place of women in society gave way to vituperative accusations linking women's feminist and pacifist activities to radicalism, socialism, and treason. After ratification of the Nineteenth Amendment, antisuffragists, calling themselves the Woman Patriots, continued to oppose federal welfare legislation through the 1920s. *(See also: Antifeminism; Suffrage)*

—Joyce Follet
—Andrea Moore Kerr

Further Reading

Benjamin, Anne Myra Goodman. *A History of the Anti-Suffrage Movement in the United States from 1895 to 1920.* Lewiston, NY: Edwin Mellen, 1991.

Camhi, Jane Jerome. *Women against Women: American Anti-Suffragism.* Brooklyn, NY: Carlson, 1994.

Jablonsky, Thomas J. *The Home, Heaven, and Mother Party: Female Anti-Suffragists in the United States, 1868–1920.* Brooklyn, NY: Carlson, 1994.

~ Arbus, Diane Nemerov (1923–1971)

Photographer Diane Arbus is internationally renowned for her images that integrate portraiture of people who are abnormal, grotesque, or eccentric with images of more mainstream American society.

Arbus was born in New York City to David and Gertrude Nemerov. Her father owned the fashionable Russek's Fifth Avenue, and Arbus rebelled against the security and sense of unreality of this upper-middle-class background. She was educated at the progressive Fieldston School, and although she never went to college, she was widely read and studied art in museums. At eighteen, she married Allan Arbus, and the couple had two daughters. The Arbuses became prominent as a fashion photography team. Diane, however, left full-time fashion work to develop the artistic vision that made her famous.

Between 1955 and 1957, she studied with Lisette Model, an Austrian-born social documentary photographer. Arbus told Model that she wished to photograph "evil," in the sense of the forbidden. She then began to photograph "people who had passed their test in life"—midgets, giants, transvestites, and nudists—as well as the banality of middle-class life. During the 1960s, she also photographed celebrities. Norman Mailer, Susan Sontag, and Mae West were among the many artists, writers, and film stars she recorded. Many of these images appeared in major publications such as *Vogue, Harper's Bazaar,* and *Esquire.*

To supplement her income, Arbus taught photography from 1965 to 1971 at the Parsons School of Design, Cooper Union, Hampshire College, and Rhode Island School of Design. She received Guggenheim fellowships in 1963 and 1966, and her work was part of the important *New Documents* exhibit at the Museum of Modern Art, New York, in 1967. Despite her increasing reputation, Arbus committed suicide in 1971. A retrospective of Diane Arbus photographs opened at the Museum of Modern Art in 1972 and traveled throughout the United States. That same year, she also became the first American photographer whose works were exhibited at the Venice Biennale, attesting to her status as a major twentieth-century artist. *(See also: Photography)*

—C. Jane Gover
Adapted for the second edition by Diana Emery Hulick.

Further Reading

Arbus, Doon, and Marvin Israel, eds. Essay by Thomas Southhall. *Diane Arbus Magazine Work.* Millerton, NY: Aperture, 1984.
Bosworth, Patricia. *Diane Arbus.* New York: Avon, 1984.
Tucker, Anne, ed. *The Woman's Eye.* New York: Knopf, 1973.

~ Architecture

Until the end of the nineteenth century, any man or woman engaged in building could call himself or herself an architect. Architecture did not establish itself in the United States as a formal profession until the founding of the first academic programs at the Massachusetts Institute of Technology (1868), Cornell University (1871), and the University of Illinois (1897), and the enactment of the first licensing law in Illinois in 1897. Historically, entry into the profession was accomplished either by gaining practical experience as an apprentice in the atelier of a master architect or by obtaining a formal architectural education. Both routes presented formidable obstacles for women.

The personal prejudices of individual males made it difficult for women to obtain professional training through apprenticeship, and discriminatory policies in the academy made it equally difficult for women to obtain architectural degrees. These egregious policies indirectly led to the establishment of two unique architectural schools open only to women. The Cambridge School was founded in 1915 by Henry Atherton Frost, an instructor at the Harvard School of Architecture who agreed to tutor a young woman in his own office when Harvard refused to instruct the woman directly. During its twenty-seven-year history, the Cambridge School (staffed by Harvard's best faculty) enrolled nearly five hundred women, the majority graduating to become able and active practitioners. The Women's School of Planning and Architecture (WSPA) was founded in 1974 as a national summer program—the only school of its kind to be completely conceived of, founded, financed, and run by women for women. During its years of operation, 1975 to 1981, more than three hundred women participated in WSPA's annual two-week residential sessions, held on different college campuses around the United States. Many went on to found construction companies and development corporations, design and build housing for low-income and single-parent women, and develop new feminist scholarship on women and the built environment.

The percentage of women in architecture in the United States has gone up and down but has remained consistently small. Between 1950 and 1970, the proportion of women architects declined from 3.8 percent to 3.6 percent; by 1988, it had risen to 14.6 percent, and by the early 1990s, 18 percent of all architects were women. Women as a percentage of total employment in architecture in 1995 were 19.8 percent. The enrollment of women students in collegiate schools of architecture is generally increasing, making up 30 percent of the bachelor's programs and 40 percent of the master's programs in 1993–1994. However, enrollment patterns are very uneven among schools; in some, women may number as high as 50 percent; in others, there are too few to count. Among the total number of architecture faculty teaching in 1990, women represented only 15.7 percent, and of this total, only 2.8 percent were tenured. As of June 1995, about 10.5 percent of American Institute of Architecture members were women (5,622 of a total membership of almost 53,706).

The obstacles women historically faced that hindered their careers as architectural practitioners have ensured that relatively few achieved more than a modest reputation. However, there are some notable exceptions. Julia Morgan (1872–1957) designed an estimated eight hundred buildings during some fifty years of private practice in the San Francisco Bay Area. (Her best-known work is William Randolph Hearst's palatial residence, La Casa Grande, near San Simeon, California.) She graduated from the University of California at Berkeley in engineering in 1894 and the Ecole des Beaux Arts in Paris in architecture in 1901 and was the first woman to receive degrees in these subjects from either school.

Marion Mahony Griffin (1871–1961) worked in the Chicago office of the preeminent American architect, Frank Lloyd Wright, for some fourteen years as the gifted delineator of some of "Wright's" most acclaimed work. In 1911, she married Walter Burley Griffin, a colleague in Wright's office, and in 1912, they moved to Australia (where her work is best remembered) where they won the competition for the Australian capital of Canberra.

Eleanor Raymond enrolled in the Cambridge School in 1917, beginning a productive career that produced innovative domestic architecture and spanned over fifty years. In 1919, she opened an office in partnership with Henry Atherton Frost, and in 1928, she began her own office in Boston where she broke away from her traditional Beaux Arts training, developing her own modern architectural vocabulary using experimental building materials such as plywood and masonite and new technologies such as solar energy.

Chloethiel Woodard Smith (born in Peoria, Illinois, in 1910) has been a principal in several architectural firms since 1946 and was elected to the College of Fellows of the American Institute of Architects in 1960. Smith has been responsible for numerous urban design studies and multifamily housing complexes, including La Clede Town in St. Louis, designed in the 1960s as a racially and economically integrated community.

Denise Scott Brown, born in Zambia in 1931, is a principal in Venturi Scott Brown and Associates, Inc. in Philadelphia. She is a well-known theorist, educator, and writer as well as practitioner, whose work over the last thirty years has earned her numerous professional honors. She is widely published, including the seminal book *Learning from Las Vegas* (with Robert Venturi and Steven Izenour, 1972).

Other American women architects who are well-known and highly respected include Elizabeth Plater-Zyberk, Adel Naude Santos, and Jane Thompson. In the coming decades, the number of nationally and internationally known American architects who are women will no doubt increase, as will the impressive collection of books written by women in architectural education and practice on a wide range of subjects, along with the numbers of biographies, monographs, and anthologies documenting their lives and work. *(See also: Higher Education)*

—**Leslie Kanes Weisman**

Further Reading

Berkeley, Ellen Perry, ed. *Architecture: A Place for Women.* Washington, DC: Smithsonian Institution, 1989.

Boutelle, Sara Holmes. *Julia Morgan, Architect.* New York: Abbeville, 1988.

Cole, Doris. *From Tipi to Skyscraper.* Boston: I Press, 1973.

Lorenz, Clare. *Women in Architecture.* New York: Rizzoli, 1990.

Torre, Susana. *Women in American Architecture: A Historic and Contemporary Perspective.* New York: Whitney Library of Design, 1977.

Weisman, Leslie Kanes. *Discrimination by Design: A Feminist Critique of the Man-Made Environment.* Urbana: University of Illinois Press, 1992.

⧫ Archives and Sources

In the 1930s, women's historian Mary Ritter Beard envisioned a World Center for Women's Archives. Although she failed to realize her dream, she influenced the founding of the rich archives at Radcliffe College and Smith College. Today, the Arthur and Elizabeth Schlesinger Library at Radcliffe houses some fifty thousand published volumes and hundreds of periodicals, plus microforms, pamphlets, and clipping files. Its impressive collection of primary documents includes personal papers of notable women, archives of organizations, diaries, letters, oral histories, and photographs. The library's collecting policy emphasizes suffrage, feminism, and women's rights; social welfare and reform; women in the professions and the labor movement; women's organizations; and the history of the family. A special Culinary Collection houses both historic cookbooks and recipes in manuscript. Library staff have made a concerted effort to gather materials reflecting the lives and experiences of "ordinary" women, the contemporary women's movement, and the academic practice of women's history.

The Sophia Smith Collection consists of over 100,000 manuscripts, diaries, letters, photographs, memorabilia, and books. Its scope is international, with emphasis on the history of the birth control movement and women in the professions. These holdings are complemented by Smith College's institutional archives, which illuminate the history of women's higher education and college athletics.

Other academic collections specialize in a locale, period, or subject. The Woman's Collection at Texas Woman's University, for example, emphasizes the lives and accomplishments of Texan women; the Cairns Collection of American Women Writers at the University of Wisconsin—Madison documents the writing and publishing activities of women authors, primarily in the nineteenth century; the Medical College of Pennsylvania concentrates on the history of women physicians in its Archives and Special Collections on Women in Medicine. Among the more recently established archives are the National Women and Media Collection at the University of Missouri School of Journalism, the International Archive of Women in Architecture at Virginia Polytechnic Institute, and the Archives of Women in Science and Engineering at Iowa State University Library.

Many libraries not devoted solely to women's materials hold valuable resources for feminist scholars. The Library of Congress retains the personal papers of prominent suffragists and reformers, along with records of the National American Woman Suffrage Association, the National Women's Party, and the League of Women Voters, and its Prints and Photographs Division is a fine source of visual documentation in American women's history. The Special Collections Library of Duke University boasts strong holdings in southern women's culture and pro-women activism, from the time of slavery to the present. Many historical societies and state libraries likewise house manuscripts, organizational and governmental archives, memorabilia, and locally printed materials on women. Some associations and agencies maintain their own archives. For example, the

Dexter McCormick Library of the Planned Parenthood Federation documents the history of birth control in the United States.

Even with this wealth of resources, the experiences of American women of color remain inadequately documented. The Bethune Museum-Archives in Washington, D.C., has gathered the nation's largest collection of manuscripts on the contributions of individual African American women and women's associations. The Schlesinger Library sponsored the Black Woman Oral History Project, recording and transcribing the life stories of numerous influential women. The Black Women in the Middle West Project assembled primary materials from Illinois and Indiana. There is much work still to be done before historians have ready access to sources about women of all racial and ethnic backgrounds.

Lesbians, another underrepresented group, have recovered their heritage largely through independent grassroots archives. The Lesbian Herstory Archives in New York City and the June L. Mazer Collection in West Hollywood preserve both personal and organizational materials, including rare photographs, diaries, and letters. Cornell University's Human Sexuality Collection emphasizes gay and lesbian history and the politics of pornography; its establishment in 1989 signaled a growing scholarly interest in lesbian sources.

How does the American historian identify relevant archival collections? *Women's History Sources* (1979), edited by Andrea Hinding, is a landmark volume describing more than eighteen thousand collections. A new edition is sorely needed. Another vital finding aid is *Women's Periodicals and Newspapers from the 18th Century to 1981* (1982), offering full bibliographic and location data for nearly fifteen hundred periodicals. The Schlesinger Library has issued a *Directory of Repositories Collecting Records of Women's Organizations* (1994). The seventh edition of the general guide, *Subject Collections* (1993), lists hundreds of specialized collections on women in North American libraries, many of them including archival materials.

Commercial microfilming is the usual solution to the problem of preserving and disseminating unique primary materials. Sources available in microformat include women's magazines; records of women's organizations, such as the National Association of Colored Women's Clubs and the Women's Trade Union League; and personal papers of luminaries such as Jane Addams, Emma Goldman, Eleanor Roosevelt, Margaret Sanger, and the combined papers of Elizabeth Cady Stanton and Susan B. Anthony. The Schlesinger Library's collection has been mined for several microform sets, including an edition of its vertical file of clippings, pamphlets, and other ephemeral items and extensive thematic collections on "Woman's Suffrage," "Women in National Politics," and "Sexuality, Sex Education, and Reproductive Rights." The *History of Women* microfilm collection preserves thousands of books, pamphlets, periodicals, manuscripts, and photographs relating to American and European women through 1920, drawn from the holdings of nine U.S. libraries. For the history of women's liberation, the *Herstory* microfilms are essential sources. They reproduce women's newsletters, journals, and newspapers from 1956 to 1974; supplemental sets cover law and health/mental health. Other key microform sources include *Pamphlets in American History: Women* and *American Women's Diaries.*

Automation promises to enhance scholarly access to primary documents. New imaging technologies enable the preservation and transmission of facsimile documents and visual archives, and records for archival materials are being integrated into electronic finding aids, including library catalogs and bibliographic databases. As more information by and about women is created and disseminated solely in electronic formats such as e-mail messages and computerized news groups, archivists are developing new methods to capture and preserve source materials for future historians. *(See also: Internet Resources)*

—Susan E. Searing

Further Reading

Ash, Lee. *Subject Collections*. New Providence, NJ: R. R. Bowker, 1993.

Directory of Repositories Collecting Records of Women's Organizations. Schlesinger Library, Radcliffe College, Cambridge, MA, 1994.

Hady, Maureen E. *Women's Periodicals and Newspapers from the 18th Century to 1981*. Edited by James P. Dankey; compiled by Maureen E. Hady, Christopher Noonan, and Neil E. Strache; in association with the State Historical Society of Wisconsin. Boston: G. K. Hall, 1982.

Hildebrand, Suzanne, ed. *Women's Collections: Libraries, Archives, and Consciousness*. New York: Haworth, 1986.

Women's History Sources: A Guide to Archives and Manuscript Collections in the United States. New York: Bowker, 1979.

ᴧ Arendt, Hannah (1906–1975)

Hannah Arendt was an editor, educator, social worker, political theorist, and philosopher. She was born in Hannover, Germany, and matriculated at Marburg and Freiburg. Arendt completed her Ph.D. at Heidelberg, where she studied under Karl Jaspers. When Hitler and the Nazis took power in 1933, she fled to Paris and did social work for Youth Aliyah, a relief organization placing Jewish orphans. With the fall of France to the Nazis in 1940, Arendt was again forced to flee, this time to the United States.

In the United States, Arendt found work as a research director for the Conference on Jewish Relations. She then became head editor for Schocken Books. Between 1949 and 1952, she served as the executive secretary of the Jewish Cultural Reconstruction, a group that collected and relocated Jewish writings dispersed by the Nazis. Then she entered the academy in America and was the first woman appointed a full professor at Princeton University. Arendt also taught at Brooklyn College, the University of Chicago, the University of California at Berkeley, and finally at the New School for Social Research in New York. Arendt became famous for her controversial writings, in which she argued that revolution and war constitute the central forces of our time. She also advocated greater participation in democracy and citizenship by all. A naturalized citizen since 1950, Arendt was one of the most influential postwar academics. *(See also: Jewish Women; World War II)*

—Jonathan W. Zophy

Further Reading

Arendt, Hannah. *The Human Condition.* Chicago: University of Chicago Press, 1958.

———. *On Revolution.* New York: Harcourt Brace, 1958.

———. *On Violence.* New York: Faber, 1962.

———. *The Origins of Totalitarianism*, 3 vols. New York: Harcourt Brace, 1951.

Benhabib, Seyla. *The Reluctant Modernism of Hannah Arendt.* Thousand Oaks, CA: Sage, 1996.

Brightman, Carol, ed. *Between Friends: The Correspondence of Hannah Arendt and Mary McCarthy, 1949–1975.* New York: Harcourt Brace, 1995.

Canovan, Margaret. *Hannah Arendt: A Reinterpretation of Her Political Thought.* New York: Cambridge University Press, 1992.

d'Entreves, Maurizio Passerin. *The Political Philosophy of Hannah Arendt.* New York: Routledge, 1993.

Isaac, Jeffrey. *Arendt, Camus, and Modern Rebellion.* New Haven, CT: Yale University Press, 1992.

Young-Bruehl, Elisabeth. *For Love of the World.* New Haven, CT: Yale University Press, 1982.

~ Army Nurse Corps (ANC)

The Army Nurse Corps (ANC) was created in recognition of the need for military nurses during the Spanish-American War. Some military personnel maintained that untrained corpsmen actually helped to spread disease, so military leaders and the surgeon general started lobbying for the creation of a nurse corps. Dr. Anita Newcomb McGee, a practicing physician, was instrumental in coordinating nursing efforts during the Spanish-American War and in selecting the ANC's first superintendent, Mrs. Dita Kenney, a forty-four-year-old widowed nurse. The Army created the first nurse corps in 1901; the Navy followed suit in 1908. Poor pay, high educational requirements, and inadequate leadership stifled enlistment efforts for the first decade of the corps' existence. By World War I, the ANC had been reorganized, nurses' pay was increased, and the Red Cross was designated as the ANC's reserve in case of war.

Nurses had to lobby for years to gain a rank commensurate with their skills and to improve their status. From the beginning, it was assumed that nurses would not be associated with enlisted personnel. But their initial status was similar to that of a cadet. Finally, in 1920 they were granted "relative rank," or approximate rank, which meant that women officers were designated as having the same rank as men officers in the Army and Navy but not the same pay or benefits normally associated with that rank. Not until 1944 did nurses gain the same rank and status as the men (see WAAC,

WAC, WAVES for a different model). Disability benefits were granted ANC members for the first time in 1926.

During World War I, at peak strength, 8,538 nurses served with the American Expeditionary Forces in Europe. At peak strength during World War II, 47,000 nurses served in the ANC. While exact figures are unknown, nurses also served in large numbers during the Korean War and Vietnam War.

In 1955, male nurses were allowed to join the ANC. Until then, the men had to serve as corpsmen, without hope of becoming officers. While only about 6 percent of America's 2 million registered nurses are male, about 25 percent of today's ANC is male. In part, this is a tribute to the excellent benefits and high status that the ANC has been able to achieve compared with civilian nursing.

Nursing came of age during World War II when the American Nursing Association replaced the American Red Cross as the premier advocate for nurses. Veteran nurses had a rude shock when they returned to America after World War II; they were offered low-paying, low-status positions, whereas in the Army and Navy, because of the shortage of doctors, they had been doing highly responsible work. According to the 1990 census, women make up 1.2 million veterans, or about 4 percent of the veteran population.

While nursing and other traditionally female occupations provided women with the opportunity to enter the military, women now make up a significant portion of the active duty (11 percent) and reserve forces (14 percent). *(See also: Military Service; Nursing)*

—D'Ann Campbell

Further Reading

Aynes, Edith A. *From Nightingale to Eagle: An Army Nurse's History.* Englewood Cliffs, NJ: Prentice Hall, 1973.

Bellafaire, Judith. *The Army Nurse Corps in World War II.* Washington, DC: U.S. Army Center of Military History, 1993.

Buchanan, Margaret S. *Reminiscing: An Account of the 300th Army General Hospital in World War II.* Nashville, TN: Williams Printing, 1988.

Campbell, D'Ann. *Women at War with America: Private Lives in a Patriotic Era.* Cambridge, MA: Harvard University Press, 1984.

Cooper, Page. *Navy Nurse.* New York: Whittlesey House, 1946.

Flikke, Julia, Col. A.U.S. (ret.). *Nurse in Action.* Philadelphia: J. B. Lippincott, 1943.

Hine, Darlene Clark. *Black Women in White: Racial Conflict and Cooperation in the Nursing Profession, 1890–1950.* Bloomington: Indiana University Press, 1989.

Jopling, Lucy Wilson. *War in White.* San Antonio, TX: Watercress Press, 1990.

Kalisch, Philip A., and Beatrice Kalisch. *The Advance of American Nursing.* Boston: Little, Brown, 1978.

Maxwell, Pauline. "History of the Army Nurse Corps." Unpublished multivolume history housed at the Center for Military History, Washington DC. [The ANC has commissioned a history that will draw heavily on Maxwell's materials.]

Melosh, Barbara. *"The Physician's Hand": Work Culture and Conflict in American Nursing.* Philadelphia: Temple University Press, 1982.

Norman, Elizabeth M. *Women at War: The Story of Fifty Military Nurses Who Served in Vietnam.* Philadelphia: Pennsylvania University Press, 1990.

Premonte, Robert V., and Cindy Gurney, eds. *Highlights in the History of the Army Nurse Corps.* Washington, DC: U.S. Army Center of Military History, 1987.

Redmond, Juanita. *I Served on Bataan.* Philadelphia: J. B. Lippincott, 1943.

Reverby, Susan. *Ordered to Care: The Dilemma of American Nursing, 1850–1945.* Cambridge, MA: Harvard University Press, 1987.

Shields, Elizabeth A. "A History of the United States Army Nurse Corps (Female): 1901–1937." Ph.D. diss., Columbia University Teachers College, 1980.

Staupers, Mabel Keaton. *No Time for Prejudice: A Story of the Integration of Negroes in Nursing in the United States.* New York: Macmillan, 1961.

Stinson, Julia Catherine. *Finding Themselves: The Letters of an American Army Chief Nurse in a British Hospital in France.* New York: Macmillan, 1918.

The United States Cadet Nurse Corps and Other Federal Nurse Training Programs. Washington, DC: Government Printing Office, 1950.

Wandrey, June. *Bedpan Commando: The Story of a Combat Nurse During World War II,* 2d ed. Elmore, OH: Elmore, 1991.

◆ Art

Women have contributed to every major art movement between America's shores. From the work of the first Native American women who incorporated geometric abstract designs into their weaving, pottery, painted leather, beadwork, and quillwork to the latest developments in contemporary art, American women have displayed their talents.

Although life for colonial women left little leisure time for art, they channeled their creativity into practical and strikingly beautiful works of stitchery, woven rugs, and quilts. One such woman, Henrietta Deering Johnston, was America's first pastel artist, completing over forty pastel portraits of the leading citizens of Charleston, South Carolina. Considered America's first sculptor, Patience Lovell Wright (1725–1786) modeled life-sized portraits in wax. Unfortunately, documentation of other women artists from colonial times through the eighteenth century remains scant.

The first artistic field into which a significant number of women entered was miniature painting, a style popular in the late eighteenth and early nineteenth centuries. Miniature painting attracted women artists who lacked access to studio space and materials. Their limited training in life drawing and modeling at this time also led them to concentrate on the face or bust-length poses. One of the earliest miniaturists, Ann Hall of Pomfret, Connecticut, exhibited in New York City as early as 1817. Hall also had the distinction of being the first woman to become a full member of the National Academy of Design. Other miniaturists included Sarah Goodridge, Anna Claypoole Peale, Mary Ann Hardy, and Lucia Fuller.

By the beginning of the nineteenth century, evidence suggests, the number of women artists substantially increased.

At this time, nearly all of them were related to male artists—fathers, brothers, and uncles—who recognized their talents and shared studio space with them. The best example of an artistically supportive family is the Peale family, in which the daughters of artist James Peale and nieces of artist Charles Willson Peale assisted and learned from their relatives. Without access to studios or built-in family instruction, other American women artists were left on their own to perfect their artistic talents.

Although the Pennsylvania Academy of the Fine Arts allowed women to exhibit in annual shows from its conception in 1805, the first documentation of women students in an American art school occurs only in 1844. At this time, women's drawing from a live nude model was unthinkable, but the Pennsylvania Academy did permit the women students to draw from nude antique plaster casts for one hour on Monday, Wednesday, and Friday in a segregated class. In 1856, "Ladies' Day" was abolished, and women drew from the plaster casts of the Apollo Belvedere and Laocoön with the men, but not before the instructor placed a "close-fitting but inconspicuous fig-leaf" on the offending works.

By 1868, the Pennsylvania Academy established the first Ladies' Life Class with a live nude female model, depicted by Alice Barber Stephens ten years later in her work *Female Life Class.* The academy regularly used nude male models in 1877 but was severely criticized by the public for allowing young ladies to view them. Thomas Eakins, who instituted an experimental life drawing class in the 1870s, was dismissed from the academy in 1886 when he removed the loincloth from a male model in an anatomy lecture before a mixed audience.

The conservative National Academy of Design in New York permitted women students to attend its Antique School (drawing from casts) in 1831, but regular enrollment of female students did not occur until 1846. A women's life drawing class opened in 1871, but women could not attend anatomy lectures until 1914. From 1825 to 1953, the National Academy of Design offered membership and associate membership to only seventy-five women of a total of 1,300 members. A more liberal institution in New York, the Art Students' League, which opened in 1875, not only included women art students but placed women on its governing board.

Without mastery of anatomy and human proportions, women artists focused primarily on still life and portraiture, which in the hierarchy of the art world were considered far less important than history painting. History painting depicted Biblical, mythological, and historical themes, which often involved an abundance of human figures. Once admitted to art institutions and life drawing classes, women had the opportunity to master the human figure for history painting.

As America expanded westward, new schools such as the Cincinnati Art Academy, the St. Louis Art Academy, and the Art Institute of Chicago became available to women. Contributing to the range of artistic opportunities was the in-

Figure 4. Maya Lin

Maya Lin was a college senior at Yale when she was chosen as the winner of the Vietnam memorial competition for her design of names engraved on black granite. After the protests of veterans' groups, a representational statue of three soldiers was also placed at the entrance to the memorial. Used by permission of UPI/Corbis-Bettmann.

volvement of the women's clubs with the arts. Associations and groups of women artists formed all across the country. The membership of the National Association of Women Painters and Sculptors in America grew large enough to administer its own academy, sponsor exhibits, and fund scholarships. In 1876, a community of women pioneered the Women's Pavilion at the Philadelphia Centennial Exposition. Displayed along with other accomplishments by women, the art dominated the all-female exhibition space. In 1893, at the Women's Building at the Chicago World's Columbian Exposition, major sculpture and painting commissions enabled women such as Mary Cassatt and Mary MacMonnies, who painted a monumental mural in the great hall, to produce works of great scale.

In sculpture in the mid-nineteenth century, a maverick group of American women left the United States for Rome to work in the neoclassical style. They chose Rome because it offered an excellent source of marble, readily available trained artisans, and inexpensive living conditions. Harriet

Hosmer, for example, arrived in Rome in 1852 and studied with the leading English sculptor John Gibson. Other women artists joined her. Emma Stebbins and Vinnie Ream Hoxie used the skills they mastered in Rome to garner major commissions in the United States. Stebbins's work *Angel of the Water* remains in New York's Central Park. These women, along with Edmonia Lewis, Margaret Foley, Louisa Landers, Elizabet Ney, Anne Whitney, and fellow male sculptors helped to create the first major school of American Neoclassical sculpture.

During the last quarter of the century, another wave of American women participated in the major art movement called impressionism. In Europe, particularly France, artists moved their canvases outdoors and developed the *en plein air* technique to capture the effects of natural light. Devoted to light and color, impressionism is characterized by loose brushstrokes, thick application of paint, and interest in everyday subject matter as opposed to the historical subjects of realism. Among the American women artists who traveled to France to explore the avant-garde technique were Mary Cassatt, Cecilia Beaux, Lilla Cabot Perry, and Elizabeth Nourse.

By the close of the century, women's position within the artistic community had clearly changed. Educational opportunities had expanded, and increasingly, women entered art institutions, traveled abroad, and received awards and commissions for their work. In 1895, Cecilia Beaux became the first woman professor of art at the Pennsylvania Academy of the Fine Arts.

Despite the difficulty women faced in obtaining appropriate training for their art and exhibition opportunities for their work, one medium was available to them from its first development—photography. Perhaps because this medium was somewhat problematic in terms of its place within the fine arts and the training required was quite different from that of painting or sculpture, women were routinely included in photographic exhibitions and took their place beside their male colleagues in the development of the art. Frances Benjamin Johnston, Gertrude Käsebier, Berenice Abbott, and Diane Arbus, among a host of other women, recorded their view of society through portraiture. Although their styles are vastly different and the ways in which they portray their subjects vary considerably, all captured aspects of their personal experience and their culture at large in ways that still have an impact on their viewers.

The character and composition of America dramatically altered in the twentieth century, and art reflected those changes. Neither past realism nor avant-garde impressionism could adequately express the pace and clamor of industrial society. Skyscrapers, fast trains, bright city lights, photography, factories and their poor working conditions, waves of homeless immigrants, and the theories of Einstein, Freud, and Marx all affected America and its art scene as well. Like changing seasonal fashions, art movements matched the fast pace. The first of the shocking new art waves was the Ash Can School of 1908. Ash Can artists portrayed street life and the slums of New York realistically, departing from the color and light of the impressionists in their severe examination of the dirty urbanization of America.

A prominent Ash Can sculptor, Mary Abastenia St. Leger Eberle (1878–1942), moved to New York from Ohio to study at the Art Students' League, sharing a studio with another sculptor, Anna Hyatt Huntington. Eberle furthered her studies in Europe and returned to take trips into Manhattan's Lower East Side, which inspired her compassionate and lively works. Eberle's sculptures, small-scale bronzes, evoke motion—a child roller-skating or an immigrant woman sweeping. Other women painters and illustrators in the Ash Can School included May Wilson Preston, Florence Shinn, Marjorie Organ, and Marianna Sloan.

The 1913 Armory Show in New York City brought radical American and European styles such as cubism and fauvism to the American public. More than forty American women participated in the Armory Show, including Marguerite Thompson Zorach and Katherine Sophie Dreier.

The development of new exhibition spaces, as well as experience with the modernists, helped foster a more egalitarian environment for women artists. The authority of the traditional art institutions was challenged by galleries such as Alfred Stieglitz's "291." The first nonphotographic art exhibited, in January 1907, was that of artist Pamela Coleman Smith. "291" also showed the work of photographers Gertrude Käsebier and Alice Boughton. Painters such as Marion H. Beckett, Katherine N. Rhodes, and Georgia O'Keeffe gained valuable exposure from such galleries, and other women found encouragement in the liberal environment of the New York School of Art (later the Art Students' League), studying with Henri and William Merritt Chase.

The woman suffrage movement during the early 1900s, together with the rise of labor unions and women's clubs, contributed to women's self-awareness and feelings of independence. Katherine Sophie Dreier, a modernist-cubist painter, opened the Société Anonyme with Marcel Duchamp in 1920. It was the first gallery devoted entirely to modern art. Dreier's collection now forms the core of Yale University's modern art holdings.

Promoter, patron, and sculptor, Gertrude Vanderbilt Whitney founded the Whitney Studio Club in New York. Here, artists met, shared creative talents, and displayed their works. In 1931, she opened the Whitney Museum of American Art, devoted to America's avant-garde. As a sculptor, Whitney produced many works herself and won the *Titanic Memorial* commission in 1931 in Washington, D.C.

As American art expanded, women continued as forerunners in major movements. New materials and techniques opened new avenues for artistic expression. Canvases expanded, and color, line, and form dominated compositions. Surrealists Kay Sage and Dorothea Tanning contributed to America's interest in this mysterious movement. Lee Krasner and Joan Mitchell both practiced abstract expressionism, while Alma Thomas experimented with blocks of color, allowing a bit of the canvas to show through. America's renewed interest in the figure is partly due to the work of artists Elaine de Kooning, Marcia Marcus, and Grace Hartigan.

In 1952, Helen Frankenthaler took an unprimed canvas and poured paint on it. Without the gesso, the paint soaked into the surface, staining the canvas. This piece, *Mountains and Sea*, began a whole new art movement called color-field or stain painting. Landscapes continued to be a theme for Frankenthaler as she allowed the pigments to flow and to create their own shapes and forms. Frankenthaler's technique inspired others, chiefly Morris Louis and Kenneth Noland.

In sculpture, Louise Nevelson used scraps of wood to create unique environmental works. Lee Bontecou, Anna Hyatt Huntington, Marisol, and Anne Truitt all employed a variety of materials in their sculptures.

Coincident with the formation of the women's movement in the 1970s, artists began to turn to ideas of feminine and feminist subject matter, media, and process as new ways for women to work. Taking traditional areas of "women's work," such as quilting and textile and fabric design, and incorporating these media into collaborative pieces—another example of women's work—artists such as Miriam Schapiro and Judy Chicago created installations that brought together women's history and women's art and created a new method for contemporary artists to work. These ideas have influenced a generation of artists, freeing their imaginations and their media.

American women continue to make history with their artistic endeavors. The opening of the National Museum of Women in the Arts in 1987, with over eighty thousand members, both celebrates women artists and encourages scholarship on the subject. Only through increased research, exhibitions, and continued integration into art history will the full impact of women artists on art in America be realized in the 21st century. *(See also: Abbott, Berenice; Arbus, Diane Nemerov; Beaux, Cecilia; Cassatt, Mary Stevenson; Dreier, Katherine Sophie; Hosmer, Harriet Goodhue; Hoxie, Vinnie; Johnston, Henrietta Deering; Käsebier, Gertrude Stanton; Krasner, Lee; Lewis, Edmonia; National Museum of Women in the Arts; Neel, Alice; O'Keeffe, Georgia; Peale Family, Women Artists of the; Perry, Lilla Cabot; Photography; Spencer, Lilly Martin; Thomas, Alma; World's Columbian Exposition; Zorach, Marguerite Thompson)*

—**Cynthia Lynn Gould**

—**Marian J. Hollinger**

Further Reading

Broude, Norma, and Mary D. Garrard. *The Power of Feminist Art.* New York: Harry N. Abrams, 1994.

Chadwick, Whitney. *Women, Art, and Society,* 2d ed. New York: Thames & Hudson, 1996.

———. *Women Artists and the Surrealist Movement.* Boston: Little, Brown, 1985.

Frueh, Joanna, Cassandra L. Langer, and Arlene Raven, eds. *New Feminist Criticism: Art, Identity, Action.* New York: Icon/HarperCollins, 1994.

Gerdts, William H. *Women Artists of America, 1707–1964.* Newark, NJ: Newark Museum, 1965.

Greer, Germaine. *The Fortunes of Women Painters and Their Work.* London: Farrar, Straus, & Giroux, 1979.

Harris, Ann Sutherland, and Linda Nochlin. *Women Artists: 1550–1950.* New York: Knopf, 1976.

Hulick, Diana Emery, with Joseph Marshall. *National Museum of Women in the Arts.* Washington, DC: National Museum of the Women in the Arts, 1987.

———. *Photography, 1900 to the Present.* Upper Saddle River, NJ: Prentice Hall, 1998.

Munro, Eleanor. *Originals: American Women Artists.* New York: Touchstone, 1979.

Nochlin, Linda. *Women, Art, and Power, and Other Essays.* New York: Harper & Row, 1988.

Parker, Rozsica, and Griselda Streifer. *Old Mistresses: Women, Art, and Ideology.* New York: Pantheon, 1981.

Raven, Arlene, Cassandra L. Langer, and Joanna Frueh, eds. *Feminist Art Criticism.* Ann Arbor: University of Michigan Research Press, 1988.

Rubenstein, Charlotte Streifer. *American Women Artists from Early Indian Times to the Present.* Boston: G. K. Hall, 1982.

Tufts, Eleanor. *American Women Artists, 1830–1930.* Washington, DC: National Museum of Women in the Arts, 1987.

⮑ Arzner, Dorothy (1900–1979)

Along with Lois Weber and Ida Lupino, Dorothy Arzner was one of the few women to direct more than a single major film between 1925 and 1960. Many of her films addressed women's issues of the period when she was most active (1927–1942) and have been at the heart of the reexamination of the Hollywood feature film by feminist critics for two decades.

After a childhood on the fringes of the developing California film colony, Arzner left the study of medicine at the University of California shortly after World War I to enter the film industry. She worked her way up through the already rigidly defined segregated crafts system. There, although patterns of promotion were circumscribed, there were nonetheless more opportunities for women than were to be found later, after the innovation of sound. Arzner began as a script typist and moved on to become a manuscript reader, script girl, cutter, and finally editor-in-chief and scenario writer. Her work on prestige films such as *Blood and Sand* (1922) and James Cruze's *The Covered Wagon* (1923) gained her a directing opportunity at Paramount Studios.

When her first film as director, *Fashions for Women* (1927), was a success, Arzner was typed as a "women's film" specialist—which suited her. "The greater part of the motion picture audience is feminine," she said in a 1936 interview. "Box office appeal is thought of largely in terms of the women lined up at the ticket window. If there are no women directors, there ought to be." In important "flapper" films with Esther Ralston and Clara Bow such as *The Wild Party* (1929), Arzner became a key figure in dramatizing "the new attention to sexuality [that] colored a whole range of related behavior" (Fass 279).

Arzner's career from 1930 to 1943 was spent freelancing at different studios; in all, she directed sixteen features. Her work with Joan Crawford, Rosalind Russell, Katharine Hepburn, and other actresses during this period includes direct examinations of the many paradoxes 1920s feminism had brought to light. Films such as *Merrily We Go to Hell* (1932) and *Craig's Wife* (1936) display Arzner's ability to rechannel the currents of the melodramatic "woman's film" away from sexist ideological obstacles into the realm of ambivalence and, occasionally, even outright feminist postures. *Working Girls* (1931) and *Dance, Girl, Dance* (1940) were among several Arzner films that dealt sensitively with the lives of working women. And *Nana* (1934) showed a deft yet sympathetic touch with conflict among female characters in classical literature. For all its variety, her *oeuvre* was remarkably unified: "Communities of women function, in Arzner's career as well as in her films, as perhaps the most consistent and important feature" (Mayne, *Directed* 131).

Cast by the popular media as an "exotic" in the Hollywood community, Arzner seems to have viewed her career

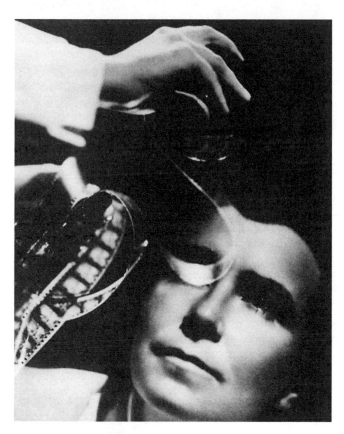

Figure 5. Dorothy Arzner
This 1937 photo of filmmaker Dorothy Arzner was originally accompanied by a caption that marveled at the success of a woman in what was termed "a man's job." Used by permission of UPI/Corbis-Bettmann.

with almost clinical detachment. Her greatest work, *Dance, Girl, Dance*, reflects this objectivity; it is a near-Brechtian analysis of the nature of celebrity and the power and manipulative potential of gender representation—all set in a Brooklyn vaudeville house. Perhaps the film was a personal allegory, for, as Judith Mayne's exhaustive research has shown, Arzner's own lesbian life subtly informed her films and made her wary of publicity.

Illness brought her career to a premature end. Cryptically saying she had "had enough" of the film industry, Arzner finished her career by directing Women's Army Auxilary Corps (WAAC) training shorts during World War II. In the years to follow, she directed television commercials and set up filmmaking programs at UCLA and the Pasadena Playhouse.

Dance, Girl, Dance was a crucial text in the renaissance of interest in mainstream women's filmmaking that developed in the early 1970s. Tributes to her work (by the Directors Guild in 1975 and many film festivals over the years) continue, and Arzner lived long enough to see her films accorded the status of American feminist cultural landmarks. *(See also: Hepburn, Katharine; Lupino, Ida; Weber, Lois; Woman's Film)*

—**Kevin Jack Hagopian**

Further Reading

"Distaff Side Director," *New York Times Magazine* (September 27, 1936): 4.

Fass, Paula. *The Damned and the Beautiful: American Youth in the 1920's*. Oxford, UK: Oxford University Press, 1977.

"Hommage à Dorothy Arzner." In *Films de Femmes: Festival International de Créteil 8, 1986*, pp. 39-45. Créteil, France: International Women's Film Festival, 1986.

Johnston, Claire, ed. *The Work of Dorothy Arzner: Towards a Feminist Cinema*. London: British Film Institute, 1975.

Mayne, Judith. *Directed by Dorothy Arzner*. Bloomington: University of Indiana Press, 1994.

———. *The Woman at the Keyhole: Feminism and Women's Cinema*. Bloomington: University of Indiana Press, 1990.

∼ Ashbridge, Elizabeth Sampson
(1713–1755)

Quaker preacher and American autobiographer, Elizabeth Ashbridge wrote a personal narrative of her early years and her conversion to the Quaker faith, *Some Account of the Fore-Part of the Life of Elizabeth Ashbridge*, that serves as the main source of information about her life. Numerous editions of this narrative were printed throughout the nineteenth and early twentieth centuries, with some minor variations in the title, and it is important for the challenges it poses to traditional understandings of early British North America, shaped largely from primary documents written by male members of the dominant Puritan culture. Ashbridge's narrative documents a life lived outside the dominant culture and provides the perspective of someone marginalized by her religious beliefs as well as by her gender.

Born in England the only child of Thomas and Mary Sampson, Ashbridge eloped at the age of fourteen against her parents' wishes and was thereby estranged from her father. Widowed only a few months after her marriage, she was unable to return to her childhood home and went instead to live with relatives in Ireland. In 1732, she emigrated to New York as an indentured servant and began a period of servitude to a master who treated her cruelly. Owing to her skill at needlework, she earned enough money to pay off the last year of her indentureship, and a few months after gaining her freedom, she married a man named Sullivan, who was attracted to her because of her ability to dance.

Throughout her marriage to Sullivan, Ashbridge, dissatisfied with her Anglican heritage, explored a variety of religions. Her search ended during a visit to relatives in Pennsylvania, where she encountered Quaker teachings. Her conversion to the Quaker faith and the accompanying changes in her lifestyle occasioned abusive behavior by her husband, and her life became a series of daily trials during which her faith grew.

In 1746, after Sullivan's death in Cuba where he refused to engage in combat even though he had enlisted in the British Army, Ashbridge married her third husband. Aaron Ashbridge, a Quaker, shared her religious convictions and supported her work as an itinerant preacher. Her preaching took her to Ireland in 1753, where she remained until her death. *(See also: Society of Friends)*

—**Cristine M. Levenduski**

Further Reading

Ashbridge, Elizabeth. "Some Account of the Fore-Part of the Life of Elizabeth Ashbridge." Edited with an introduction by Daniel B. Shea. In *Journeys in New Worlds: Early American Women's Narratives*, edited by William L. Andrews, 117-80. Madison: University of Wisconsin Press, 1990.

Shea, Daniel B. *Spiritual Autobiography in Early America*. Princeton, NJ: Princeton University Press, 1968.

❧ Asian American Women

Asian American women include women whose ancestral background links them to China, Japan, Korea, the Philippines, India, Pakistan, Bangladesh, Thailand, Vietnam, Laos, Cambodia, Indonesia, and a dozen other Asian countries. Although ethnically diverse, Asian American women share a common history as women of color in the United States that makes them a distinct racial/ethnic and political entity among Americans.

The Chinese were the first Asians to emigrate to the United States. Driven overseas by war and poverty in China during the time of the California gold rush, early Chinese sojourners, who intended to strike it rich and return home, did not bring their families with them. Cultural restrictions at home, lack of traveling funds, and anti-Chinese violence in the West further discouraged the early immigration of women. Only the merchant class, which made up less than 1 percent of the immigrant population, could afford to bring their wives and children to America. In 1860, there were only 1,784 Chinese women among 33,149 Chinese men.

This sexual imbalance, combined with antimiscegenation attitudes and laws that discouraged Asian men from marrying white women, created a demand for prostitution. Most white prostitutes were independent professionals or worked in brothels for wages, but Chinese prostitutes, who formed an estimated 85 percent of the Chinese female population in San Francisco in 1860 and 71 percent in 1870, were uniquely indentured servants who had been kidnapped, lured, or purchased from poor parents in China and resold in America for high profits. Treated as chattel and subjected to physical and mental abuse, the average prostitute did not outlive her contract term of four to five years. Some were redeemed by wealthy clients; others sought refuge at Protestant mission homes and were later married to Chinese Christians. By 1920, organized prostitution had declined due to antiprostitution laws; the Chinese Exclusion Act of 1882, which barred the further entry of Chinese laborers and their families; and successful rescue raids by Protestant missionaries.

Although a few women other than prostitutes did emigrate alone, most of the remaining Chinese women were wives who lived in urban Chinatowns or in remote rural areas where their husbands could find work. Following Chinese decorum, Chinatown wives seldom left their homes, where, in addition to housework and caring for their children, they often worked for low wages—sewing, washing, rolling cigars, and making slippers and brooms. In rural areas, Chinese wives also tended livestock and vegetable gardens, hauled in the catch and dried seafood for export, or took in boarders to help with the family income. Regardless of their residence or their husbands' social status, throughout the nineteenth century Chinese immigrant wives led hard-working lives and remained subordinate to their husbands and confined to the domestic sphere.

The second Asian group to emigrate to the United States in large numbers was the Japanese, followed by the Koreans and Filipinos. Few Japanese women emigrated before 1900, when the ratio of Japanese men to women was twenty-four to one. Among the early Japanese immigrant women there were prostitutes who worked in Hawaii, California, the Pacific Northwest, and the Rocky Mountain states, but the combined efforts of Japanese government officials and community leaders who were anxious to promote a positive image of Japan in America, as well as the institution of "picture brides," soon put an end to Japanese prostitution.

The Gentleman's Agreement of 1907–1908 between Japan and the United States barred the further entry of Japanese, and later Korean, laborers. However, Japanese and Korean men in Hawaii and on the mainland were allowed to send for picture brides until 1921. The Immigration Act of 1924 denied further entry to virtually all Asians. Matched through photographs according to the *omaiai-kekkon* or arranged marriage custom, more than 21,000 Japanese and Korean women arrived in America this way, often misled by visions of wealth and photographs of younger versions of their new husbands. Their willingness to assume the double burden of housewife and laborer allowed for the establishment of families and enabled their husbands to leave plantation and migrant farmwork and move into family-operated farms growing rice, vegetables, and grapes or into family enterprises such as laundries, bathhouses, restaurants, grocery stores, and boardinghouses. Life for these picture brides was marked by toil—working alongside their husbands in the fields or in their small businesses, or as domestic servants, seamstresses, or cannery workers—while assuming the responsibilities of homemaker and mother, often under primitive living conditions.

Filipino wives also migrated to Hawaii, California, and Washington between 1907 and 1934, when the Tydings-McDuffie Act reduced Filipino immigration to fifty persons a year. Having lived under Spanish and American colonialism, they were different from other Asian women in being educated, Catholics, and Westernized. But subjected to the same discrimination as other Asian immigrants, they also led burdensome lives, working in the fields, doing domestic chores, or managing restaurants, pool halls, and stores, as well as taking care of their own homes. By 1930, there were

2,500 Filipino women among a total population of 45,200 Filipinos in America; some of them were teachers, nurses, and pharmacists—occupations denied their men, who were still relegated to culinary and custodial jobs regardless of their educational background.

Despite their hard-working lives, the Chinese, Japanese, Korean, and Filipino immigrant women did not forget their obligations to their children, home country, or new communities in America. They ensured that cultural traditions and language were maintained among the second generation, and contributions were made to overseas independence movements—the Chinese revolution of 1911, the War of Resistance against Japan in the 1930s, and Korean independence from Japanese domination. At the same time, they worked to improve their communities by participating in church activities and women's clubs organized to promote education and charitable work. Women were also visibly active in labor protests such as the 1920 strike by plantation workers in Hawaii and the 1938 strike by garment workers in San Francisco.

World War II heralded profound changes in the lives of Asian American women. After Japan bombed Pearl Harbor, 120,000 Japanese Americans were deprived of their civil rights and lifelong investments and possessions, uprooted from their homes on the West Coast, and incarcerated in concentration camps in desolate desert areas. Family life was rudely disrupted by the makeshift conditions of camp life. Fathers lost their means of livelihood and status as head of the household, while sons were forced to choose between enlistment or imprisonment at Tule Lake, a camp set up for dissidents. Although women also suffered, camp life provided mothers with time for educational and leisure activities and accelerated the Americanization of daughters through peer group influence within the camps and educational and employment opportunities outside the camps.

Although Japan was seen as the enemy during World War II, China and the Philippines were considered allies, which helped to improve conditions for Chinese and Filipino women working in the war factories and filling jobs in the private sector once closed to them. After the war, legislation was passed allowing a few thousand Asian Americans to send for war brides, wives, and families previously barred from immigrating. Women and children could now come from China, Japan, Korea, the Philippines, and India as nonquota immigrants. Often, the differences in age and educational background between war brides and their husbands made these marriages difficult. Like the picture brides before them, war brides and reunited wives and families infused the Asian American communities with a new vitality.

Thousands of Japanese, Filipino, and Korean women also came as wives of non-Asian U.S. servicemen after World War II and the Korean conflict. Although many of these marriages proved to be happy and stable, others were troubled by serious problems: language and cultural adjustment difficulties, wife abuse, and alienation caused by racial isolation on scattered military bases or ostracism from ethnic communities.

Each successive wave of immigrant women from Asia was followed by the birth of a second generation and the establishment of family life in America. Like other children of immigrant parents, American-born Asian daughters experienced cultural conflicts and identity crises in attempting to follow Asian traditions and at the same time adjust to American society. In addition, their sex and race often proved to be liabilities, both within and outside their ethnic communities. Despite their ability to speak English, their high educational attainment, and their Western outlook, Chinese and Japanese American women of the 1920s and 1930s had difficulty finding gainful employment in their chosen fields as well as acceptance in the larger American society.

Assimilation became easier for Asian Americans after World War II, as educational and employment opportunities opened up and laws limiting their civil rights and social interactions were repealed. Increased numbers of Asian American women began leaving domestic and clerical work and entering technical, sales, and professional fields, but their earning power was often not commensurate with their level of education. At the same time, stereotypes of Asian American women as passive, exotic China dolls impeded their advancement up the managerial ladder. Subtle discrimination barred Asian American women from living in the most desirable neighborhoods and joining the most prestigious social groups. Yet if outmarriage rates are any indication of assimilation, one-fourth of all Asian American women were marrying outside their race according to the 1970 U.S. census.

The Immigration and Naturalization Act of 1965, which established an annual quota of twenty thousand immigrants from each country under a preference system favoring family reunification, skilled and professional labor, and refugee resettlement, resulted in increased immigration and a more diversified population of Chinese, Koreans, Filipinos, and South Asians (Indians, Pakistanis, and Bangladeshis) in America. Refugees from China and Southeast Asia (Vietnam, Laos, and Cambodia) were admitted under special refugee acts. Over half of these newcomers have been women, some separated from their husbands for as long as ten to thirty years due to immigration restrictions. Many others have been highly educated, urban women from China, Korea, the Philippines, and South Asia—doctors, nurses, teachers, and scientists—who have come for economic opportunities but often found themselves locked out of professional jobs because of language barriers and discriminatory licensing examinations.

Women from Southeast Asia face unique problems due to the aftereffects of war in their homeland. Like other immigrant women, they confront the difficulties of language and cultural adjustment and economic survival in America. As refugees from Southeast Asia, they also carry deep psychological scars from the traumatic experiences of war, dispossession, family separation, harsh treatment under the new government, rape and pillage at sea, and the ordeal of resettlement. While those with education and entrepreneurial skills have found paraprofessional or high-technology jobs or have established small family businesses, women from preindustrial, rural societies in Laos and Cambodia have been concentrated in truck farming or fruit growing or have required intensive education and employment training to survive in urban America.

According to the 1990 U.S. census, there are approximately 3.5 million Asian American women, composing 51 percent of the total Asian American population. Forty-eight percent of Asian American women are married. Their nativity and socioeconomic backgrounds vary among the ethnic groups. The Japanese are 68 percent native-born, while the majority of all other Asian groups are foreign-born. As a group, 74 percent of all Asian American women have a high school education, and 41 percent have college degrees, but the majority of Cambodian and Lao women have less than a fifth-grade education. Sixty percent of Asian American women are in the labor force (higher than all women in the United States), earning a median annual income of $21,691 (slightly higher than the median income for the U.S. female population but lower than for any group of males). Of these, 39 percent are in technical, clerical, and sales positions; 27 percent are in managerial and professional jobs; and 31 percent hold service, low-skilled, and semiskilled jobs. Regardless of comparable educational background, because of racism and sexism in the labor market, Asian American women earn less than their male counterparts. About 14 percent of Asian Americans live in poverty, a rate slightly higher than the 13 percent for the entire nation. Thus, economic survival and parity remain a major concern of Asian American women in the 1990s.

In addition to economic concerns, Asian American women today are committed, like their predecessors, to maintaining their families, communities, and cultures. As wage earners, wives, and mothers, they have been able to keep a tenuous balance between these roles, a balance easily upset if husbands choose to be patriarchal or if social changes gained through the civil rights and women's liberation movements are reversed. Because women are also concerned about the lack of affordable health care, child care, and housing, as well as increased sexual harassment and violence in the workplace and larger society, they have been active in educational, religious, ethnic, women's, and political organizations, often assuming leadership to bring about improvements in the overall quality of life. *(See also: Japanese Relocation Camps: World War II; Kingston, Maxine Hong; Triple Jeopardy)*

—**Judy Yung**

Further Reading

Asian Women United, ed. *Making Waves: Writings by and about Asian American Women.* Boston: Beacon, 1989.

Espiritu, Yen Le. *Asian American Women and Men: Labor, Laws, and Love.* Thousand Oaks, CA: Sage, 1996.

Glenn, Evelyn Nakano. *Issei, Nisei, War Bride: Three Generations of Japanese American Women in Domestic Service.* Philadelphia: Temple University Press, 1986.

Hirata, Lucie Cheng. "Chinese Immigrant Women in Nineteenth-Century California." In *Women of America,* edited by C. R.

Berkin and M. B. Norton, 223-44. Boston: Houghton Mifflin, 1979.

Kim, Elaine, and Lilia Villanueva, eds. *Making More Waves: New Writing by Asian American Women.* Boston: Beacon, 1997.

Nakano, Mei. *Japanese American Women: Three Generations, 1890–1990.* Berkeley, CA: Mina, 1990.

Root, Maria P., ed. *Filipino Americans: Transformation and Identity.* Thousand Oaks, CA: Sage, 1997.

The Women of South Asian Descent Collective. *Our Feet Walk the Sky: Women of the South Asian Diaspora.* San Francisco: Aunt Lute, 1993.

Yang, Eun Sik. "Korean Women of America: From Subordination to Partnership, 1903–1930," *Amerasia Journal* 11 (Fall/Winter 1984): 1-28.

Yung, Judy. *Chinese Women of America: A Pictorial History.* Seattle: University of Washington Press, 1986.

———. *Unbound Feet: A Social History of Chinese Women in San Francisco.* Berkeley and Los Angeles: University of California Press, 1995.

⌘ Association for Women in Mathematics (AWM)

The Association for Women in Mathematics (AWM) was founded in 1971 to promote the status of women in mathematics. A speakers' bureau provides opportunities for students to learn more about careers in the mathematical sciences. The Alice T. Schafer Mathematics Prize and the Louise Hay Award in Mathematics Education are awarded annually to outstanding women researchers. The association publishes pamphlets on careers in mathematics and a bimonthly newsletter containing employment opportunities and articles by and about women in mathematics. The AWM currently has more that 4,100 members (women and men), representing a broad spectrum of the mathematical community, both in the United States and internationally. *(See also: Mathematics)*

—**Jonell Duda Comerford**

Further Reading

Daniels, Peggy Kneffel, and Carol A. Schwartz, eds. *Encyclopedia of Associations,* 28th ed., p. 825. Detroit, MI: Gale Research, 1994.

http://www.awm-math.org [Association for Women in Mathematics Website]

⌘ Association of Collegiate Alumnae (ACA)

In 1882 Marion Talbot, Alice Freeman (Palmer), Alice Hayes, Ellen Swallow Richards, and thirteen other women met in Boston to establish the Association of Collegiate Alumnae (ACA), uniting college graduates for "practical educational work." Members of the first generation of college-educated women, they had struggled for an education only to find that society had no place for them and no interest in using their abilities. Through the new organization, they hoped to promote and raise standards for women's higher education. To distinguish themselves from normal school and academy graduates, they limited membership to alumnae of specified, carefully selected four-year colleges and universities. In addition, they expected the ACA to help end the social isolation often faced by women college graduates when they returned home. Women in other regions responded enthusiastically and set up ACA branches across the country. Founded in 1901, the Southern Association of College Women (SACW) served a similar community. In 1921, the ACA and the SACW merged, forming the American Association of University Women (AAUW). Although the ACA, the SACW, and later the AAUW were committed to equal access to education, they avoided identification as explicitly feminist organizations. Until the 1970s, AAUW leaders rejected controversial and potentially divisive issues, such as woman suffrage and the Equal Rights Amendment.

During its first fifty years, the ACA studied a variety of issues related to women's education. In the 1880s, it sponsored and published research refuting Dr. Edward Clarke's dictum that females ruined their health when they attended college. ACA members promoted the scientific study of child development and euthenics, believing that as mothers and teachers, college women were uniquely qualified to pave the way for more enlightened methods of child rearing and thus for a more efficient society. They addressed the status of women within the academy by lobbying for women to serve as college trustees, fought discrimination on coeducational campuses, and argued for inclusion in the curriculum of home economics courses designed to make homemaking more professional and scientific. In addition, the ACA provided fellowships for undergraduate, graduate, and postdoctoral study and encouraged women's careers, particularly in the social sciences. Activities of regional branches and local groups of the ACA varied a good deal. Particularly during the Progressive Era, some ACA members formed industrial committees and engaged in reform work; others, more concerned with self-improvement, practiced French conversation.

World War I temporarily disrupted the customary work of the ACA, as members directed their energies toward educating the public on the need for U.S. intervention. The internationalism of the war years carried over into the 1920s, when the AAUW joined similar organizations from eight other countries to promote women's education around the world and to create an international community of college women through the International Federation of College Women. (See also: American Association of University Women; Higher Education)

—Catherine E. Kelly

Further Reading
ACA Publications (1888–1911).
The Graduate Woman (1978).
Journal of the American Association of University Women (1912–1978).
Papers of the American Association of University Women. Washington, DC: AAUW Archives. [Also available on microfilm; records of regional ACA/ AAUW groups are often available in local archives]
Talbot, Marion, and Lois Kimball Mathews Rosenberry. The History of the American Association of University Women, 1881–1931. Boston: Houghton Mifflin, 1931.

~ Association of Southern Women for the Prevention of Lynching (ASWPL) (1930–1942)

The Association of Southern Women for the Prevention of Lynching (ASWPL) was founded and directed by feminist reformer Jessie Daniel Ames. Recognizing a link between racial and sexual repression, Ames challenged the justification commonly given for lynching: that it was necessary for the defense of white southern womanhood. Through the ASWPL, she hoped to use the moral and social leverage of enfranchised white women to prevent mob violence in the rural South.

The ASWPL was sponsored and financed primarily by the Commission on Interracial Cooperation (CIC), the South's major interracial reform organization. For years, black women had pressed the issue within the CIC Women's Committee. "When Southern white women get ready to stop lynching, it will be stopped, and not before," they said. In the ASWPL, southern white women accepted this challenge, working through missionary societies to denounce the claim that lynchers acted in the defense of womanhood. With pledges and press statements, informal talks and public speeches, investigations and local intervention, ASWPL members hammered home their argument that black men did not provoke lynching by raping white women and that the "false chivalry" of lynching demeaned white women even as it terrorized blacks.

Just as the temperance movement had earlier channeled women into the political arena, the ASWPL linked mob violence to the special concerns of women and brought them to the forefront of the antilynching campaign. Ames made ingenious use of southern institutions and the modes of influence available to middle-class women, drawing eclectically on nineteenth-century feminist ideals of sisterhood, moral superiority, and a separate public sphere for women. At the same time, she presented an implicitly feminist antiracism and led ASWPL members toward an understanding of lynching's deepest roots. (See also: Ames, Jessie Daniel; Commission on Interracial Cooperation)

—Misti Turbeville

Further Reading
ASWPL Papers. Trevor Arnett Library. Clark Atlanta University, Atlanta, GA.
ASWPL Papers, 1930–1942. Sanford, NC: Microfilming Corporation of America.
Jessie Daniel Ames Papers. Southern Historical Collection. University of North Carolina, Chapel Hill.

Hall, Jacquelyn Dowd. *Revolt against Chivalry: Jessie Daniel Ames and the Women's Campaign Against Lynching.* New York: Columbia University Press, 1979.

Miller, Kathleen Atkinson. "The Ladies and the Lynchers: A Look at the Association of Southern Women for the Prevention of Lynching," *Southern Studies* 17 (Fall 1978): 221-40.

✒ Atherton, Gertrude Franklin Horn
(1857–1948)

Gertrude Atherton was the author of forty novels, an autobiography, and numerous short stories and prose essays. Although she was descended from northern businessmen (including Benjamin Franklin) and southern landowners and was the widow of a wealthy Californian, Atherton, due to family estrangement and financial disaster, earned her living entirely from writing. Her works were best-sellers on both sides of the Atlantic by the turn of the century.

She criticized the "thin, anemic" realist presentation of the dull lives of the bourgeoisie epitomized by W. D. Howells and countered with her own romantic realism, influenced in part by Taine and Saint-Beuve, in which the conflict of character with the forces of heredity and environment create a highly dramatic course of cause and effect. She was especially interested in characters who transcended limitations, forged new personalities, and sought new life adventures. Most of her novels focus on women. A few, such as *Julia France and Her Times,* dealt directly with the women's rights movement. In fact, she believed that the real birth of democracy lay in the awakening of women to the pursuit of their own happiness. Ever the energetic individualist, she had little patience with the domestic woman or with pacifist or collectivist reformers.

Atherton was known for her attention to historical detail both as an observer of her own time and as a student of the past. She wrote three very successful historical novels about antiquity, inaugurated the form of the biographical novel, and fictionalized well-researched contemporary issues, personalities, and scenes. Although she was often associated with California as a regional writer or viewed mainly as an interesting personality, Atherton may more appropriately be seen as a gifted literary observer of American culture. *(See also: Women Writers)*

—Anne O. Dzamba (Sessa)

Further Reading

Atherton, Gertrude. *Adventures of a Novelist.* New York: Liveright, 1932.

Leider, Emily Wortis. *California's Daughter: Gertrude Atherton and Her Times.* Stanford, CA: Stanford University Press, 1991.

McClure, Charlotte S. *Gertrude Atherton.* Boston: G. K. Hall, 1979.

✒ Athletics/Sports

Although, traditionally, women have been encouraged less than men to develop athletic ability, they have always been active in sports. In the nineteenth century, some upper- and middle-class women engaged in physical exercises and recreational sports, although lower-class women were generally unable to find time for any sport activity. Toward the end of the century, some women were able to participate in a limited number of intercollegiate games and occasional private tournaments. In the 1870s, socialite Mary Ewing Outerbridge helped popularize lawn tennis in the United States, and by 1887, interest in women's tennis had grown so much that the first national competition for women in the sport was held at the Philadelphia Cricket Club.

Fears that women would lose "femininity" by ruining their complexions and would injure themselves in strenuous physical activity, as well as Victorian notions about propriety, all worked to retard women's sports development well into the twentieth century. Despite these and other obstacles, such as limited access to athletic facilities and coaching and lack of societal support for women athletes, interest in women's athletics continued to grow, as evidenced by a White House conference on the subject in 1923.

The growth of interest in women's sports is also reflected in the participation by women in the modern Olympic Games. When the first modern games were held in Athens, Greece, no female athletes were allowed to compete. Four years later in the next round of the Olympics, eleven women took part, and that number has steadily increased. The 1984 Olympics in Los Angeles saw 1,620 women competing in seventy-three events. A number of American women have achieved international renown as Olympic athletes, including "Babe" Didrikson Zaharias in the 1932 games; sprinter Wilma Rudolph in the 1960 games; and gymnast Mary Lou Retton, sprinters Evelyn Ashford and Valerie Briscoe-Hooks, marathon runner Joan Benoite, volleyball star Flo Hyman, and basketball star Cheryl Miller in the 1984 games. Women stars of the 1988 Seoul Olympics included sprinter Florence Griffith Joyner, swimmer Janet Evans, and decathelete Jackie Joyner Kersee, who also starred in the 1992 summer games in Los Angeles. The winter games have produced celebrity athletes such as figure skaters Kristy Yamaguchi, Nancy Kerrigan, and Peggy Fleming, and Bonnie Blair in speed skating.

Olympian Babe Zaharias was one of the first women to gain international recognition as an athlete. Not only did she win gold medals in the javelin throw and the hurdles as well as a silver medal in the high jump in the 1932 Los Angeles Olympics, but she also had a glittering career in basketball and softball. One of the finest all-round athletes in the history of sport, Zaharias also gave tennis demonstrations and in her later years achieved fame as a golfer.

Golf and tennis have become the first women's sports to achieve lasting financial success as professional sports. The Ladies Professional Golf Association was formed in 1949 and has become a commercial success, annually awarding millions of dollars in prize money and making celebrities of performers such as Patty Berg, Joanne Carner, Nancy Lopez, and others.

Professional women's tennis has also become established as a viable spectator sport and achieved commercial success. Athletes such as Billie Jean King, Chris Evert, and Martina Navratilova have made great fortunes, and their names have become household words. King in particular has been an active feminist and has publicly linked the women's movement to women's sports. In 1957, Althea Gibson became the first black player to win a championship at Wimbledon, England, the most prestigious tennis tournament in the world. The talented Gibson had been restricted to blacks-only competitions for many years before her triumph at Wimbledon.

Other women's sports have not enjoyed the same commercial success as tennis and golf. For example, a professional women's basketball league proved short-lived in the late 1970s. A professional women's baseball league lasted from 1943 to 1954. It drew enthusiastic crowds to games in eight small midwestern cities, whose minor league teams had been depleted by World War II. Nevertheless, women's participation in athletics continues to grow dramatically. Between 1970 and 1984, the number of women in varsity high school sports rose by 600 percent; at the college level, by 900 percent.

The increase in women's participation in sports can be explained by a number of factors. Among them are the success of the women's movement in providing role models, concern for good health and physical fitness, the success of women in Olympic and professional competitions as well as subsequent publicity and recognition, and the implementation of Title IX of the Education Amendments of 1972. Title IX prohibited exclusion from participation in educational activities on the basis of sex at institutions receiving federal financial. The fear of losing federal revenues caused many colleges and universities to expand opportunities for women's athletics. During the Reagan years, the implementation of Title IX lacked the vigor of previous years, but it still served to ensure women access to scholarships, facilities, and coaching in most colleges and universities.

Ironically, while opportunities for women athletes have increased, the number of female college coaches has decreased in recent years. One reason for this was the demise of the Association for Intercollegiate Athletics for Women (AIAW) in 1983, as women's college sports came under the authority of the male-dominated National Collegiate Athletic Association. Also, as separate women's and men's athletic departments have merged, women have tended to lose athletic directorships and coaching positions.

In the 1990s, however, women athletes gained new prominence with the emergence of professional women's basketball. After appearances in the 1996 Olympics, many women who had been played abroad returned to the United States to play in the American Basketball League (ABL) and the Women's National Basketball Association (WNBA). Another milestone was the U.S. women's soccer team 1999 vic-

Figure 6. Aviation
The "First Lady of Aviation," Olive Ann Beech began as a secretary in the Travel Air Company, then founded Beech Aircraft with her husband Walter. She became president of the company in 1950 and pioneered post-WWII business air travel. Used by permission of UPI/Corbis-Bettmann.

tory over China in the Women's World Cup. The game was played at the Rose Bowl before a sellout crowd of more than 90,000, the largest ever for a women's soccer game, and it was the most-watched soccer game in U.S. television history. Although women's participation in sports at every level is still far from that of men's, women's sport continues to be an important part of North American culture and society. *(See also: Gibson, Althea; King, Billie Jean; Zaharias, "Babe" Didrikson)*

—Jonathan W. Zophy

Further Reading

Baker, W. J. *Sports in the Western World.* Totowa, NJ: Rowman & Littlefield, 1982.

Boutilier, Mary, and Lucinda San Giovanni, eds. *The Sporting Women.* Champaign, IL: Human Kinetics, 1983.

Cahn, Susan. *Coming on Strong: Gender and Sexuality in Twentieth-Century Women's Sport.* New York: Free Press, 1995.

Coakley, Jay. *Sport in Society,* 3d ed. St. Louis, MO: Times Mirror/ Mosby, 1986.

Guttmann, Allen. *Women's Sports: A History.* New York: College University Press, 1992.

Ingham, Gail. *Women in Baseball: The Forgotten History.* Westport, CT: Praeger, 1994.

Macy, Sue. *A Whole New Ball Game.* New York: Henry Holt, 1993.

Noverr, D. A., and Lawrence Ziewacz. *The Games They Played: Sports in American History.* Chicago: Nelson Hall, 1983.

⟶ Aviation

Almost from the beginning of manned flight, women have participated in aviation. In 1784, only months after the first free manned balloon flight was made, Madame Elisabeth

Thible became the first woman to ascend into the air, as a passenger in a Montgolfier balloon over Lyons, France. There is evidence that the first U.S. citizen to make a solo flight in this country was an exhibition balloonist who flew under the name of Madame Johnson in New York in 1825.

In the early 1900s, interest shifted from balloons to airplanes. In 1910, Blanche Stuart Scott became the first American woman to solo in an airplane. The following year, Harriet Quimby became the first American woman to receive a pilot's license. By World War I, eleven women in the United States had earned their pilots' licenses, and many others were flying without them.

During the 1920s, the era of barnstorming and stunt flying, women performed daredevil aerial feats along with men. One, Mabel Cody, ran her own "flying circus." In 1929, women competed in their first national aviation event—the Women's Air Derby. Although the prize money was good, the real incentive was for women to prove that they were competent professional pilots. The race was won by Louise Thaden, who in 1936 also became the first woman to win the prestigious cross-country Bendix Trophy Race.

The 1920s and 1930s were also the years of famous long-distance flights. Until 1928, no woman had flown across the Atlantic Ocean. That year, Amelia Earhart flew from Newfoundland to Ireland. Although she was only a passenger on that flight, it launched her career, and in 1932, she became the first woman to fly solo across the Atlantic. Three years later she became the first pilot, male or female, to fly solo from Hawaii to the U.S. mainland.

In 1943, the United States took the important step of initiating a program for women pilots. The Women's Airforce Service Pilots (WASPs) was established under the leadership of Jacqueline Cochran. The WASPs did almost all the domestic flying for the United States during World War II, including ferrying all types of aircraft, from fighters to heavy bombers, from factories to the coast for shipment overseas.

Today, there are many women flying for the airlines and for the military, serving as corporate pilots, and running their own aviation-related businesses and flight training centers. Women such as Olive Ann Beech, who headed Beech Aircraft for many years, are also prominent in the aviation industry at management levels. *(See also: Earhart, Amelia; Quimby, Harriet; Women's Airforce Service Pilots)*

—Claudia M. Oakes

Further Reading

Brooks-Pazmany, Kathleen. *United States Women in Aviation 1919–1929.* Washington, DC: Smithsonian Institution, 1983.

Douglas, Deborah G. *United States Women in Aviation, 1940–1985.* Washington, DC: Smithsonian Institution, 1990.

Dwiggins, Don. *They Flew the Bendix Race.* New York: J. B. Lippincott, 1965.

Oakes, Claudia M. *United States Women in Aviation 1930–1939.* Washington, DC: Smithsonian Institution, 1985.

———. *United States Women in Aviation through World War I.* Washington, DC: Smithsonian Institution, 1978.

Babcock, Caroline Lexow
(1882–1980)

Suffragist, pacifist, and feminist, Caroline Lexow Babcock was born in New York City, the eldest daughter of New York State Senator Clarence Lexow (1894–1898) and women's rights advocate Katharine Morrow Ferris. Although she lived most of her life in Nyack, New York, Babcock attended Barnard College from 1900 to 1904 and there met suffrage leader Harriet Stanton Blatch. In 1904, Babcock helped organize and became president of the Collegiate Equal Suffrage League of New York State. In 1908, she served as executive secretary of the National College Equal Suffrage League and, in 1910, as executive secretary and then field secretary for Blatch's Women's Political Union.

She married Philip Westerly Babcock in 1915, and they had three children by 1919. Although a member of the Woman's Peace Party during World War I, Babcock did not actively work for peace until 1919, when she became an executive board member of the Women's Peace Society and an organizer of the Women's Peace Union, an interwar pacifist organization that tried to outlaw war through a constitutional amendment. Because of the Great Depression, in 1935 Babcock took a paying position with the Women's International League for Peace and Freedom. This was followed by a nine-month term with the Campaign for World Government and then a longer position as executive secretary for the National Woman's Party (NWP) from 1938 to 1946. After leaving the NWP because of internal conflicts, Babcock retired at the age of sixty-four to her farm in Blairstown, New Jersey. *(See also: National Woman's Party; Women's International League for Peace and Freedom; Women's Peace Union)*

—**Harriet Hyman Alonso**

Further Reading

Babcock, Caroline Lexow, and Olive E. Hurlburt Papers. The Arthur and Elizabeth Schlesinger Library on the History of Women in America. Radcliffe College, Cambridge, MA.

Women's Peace Union Papers. Swarthmore College Peace Collection, Swarthmore, PA, and New York Public Library.

Alonso, Harriet Hyman. *The Women's Peace Union and the Outlawry of War, 1921–1942*. Syracuse, NY: Syracuse University Press, 1997.

Savell, Isabelle K. *Ladies' Lib: How Rockland Women Got the Vote*. New City, NY: Historical Society of Rockland County, 1979.

Baby Boom

"Baby boom" refers to the explosion of births in America—approximately 76,441,000—between 1946 and 1964. Although both Europe and America experienced a rapid rise in birthrates immediately following World War II as servicemen and their wives made up for lost time, the European boomlet faded quickly, while America's boom continued, peaking in 1957 with a record 4.3 million births.

America's baby boom was accompanied and made possible by a great marriage boom, as average age at marriage dropped from 24.3 to 22.6 for men and from 21.5 to 20.4 for women by 1951 and the marriage rate soared. The economic prosperity of the postwar era enabled men, especially those in the upper middle class, to provide for large families of four or more children, while an ideology that stressed "traditional" sex roles deemed childbearing and motherhood woman's highest callings. Finally, having many children made sense in the atmosphere of confidence and the strong, if sometimes confused, faith in the future that characterized postwar America.

America's baby boom generation is often defined, in popular culture and in the media, through its association with youth culture and protest movements of the 1960s, although given the eighteen-year span of the "boom" as well as the variables of class, race, and region, the experience of baby boomers varies greatly. Youthful rebellion against their parents' generation was central to the baby boomer public identity, but in the 1990s, a younger cohort emerged in the mass media as "Generation X" or "Thirteeners," railing against the aging "boomers."

The baby boom generation or "cohort" is often inelegantly referred to as the "pig in the python" because of the disconcerting bulge it makes in the population curve as baby boomers pass through the stages of life. Through sheer weight of numbers, this group has had and will continue to have a profound impact on American social and economic policy and on the shape of American culture. The women within the baby boom and their mothers played a significant role in the resurgence of the women's rights movement in the 1960s. Baby boomers began turning fifty in 1996, and in the coming decades, their cohort of seniors will put particular strains on Social Security and other programs to assist the elderly. *(See also: Demography)*

—**Beth L. Bailey**

Further Reading

Breines, Wini. *Young, White, and Miserable: Growing Up Female in the Fifties.* Boston: Beacon, 1992.

Douglas, Susan J. *Where the Girls Are: Growing Up Female with the Mass Media.* New York: Random House, 1994.

Jones, Landon Y. *Great Expectations: America and the Baby Boom Generation.* New York: Coward, McCann & Geoghegan, 1980.

Lyons, Paul. *Class of '66: Living in Suburban Middle America.* Philadelphia: Temple University Press, 1994.

May, Elaine Tyler. *Homeward Bound: American Families in the Cold War Era.* New York: Basic Books, 1988.

☙ Baez, Joan C. (b. 1941)

Musician and social activist Joan Baez is an advocate of nonviolence in the modern American movement for peace and justice. Having received national attention at the Newport Folk Festival in 1959, Baez began a musical career that she has combined with a life of political action through her music, writing, and speaking.

Baez's singing career began in the folk music renaissance of the 1960s. Her early albums were composed primarily of traditional songs, but as her career developed, her albums became more political—for example, *Carry It On, Where Are You Now, My Son?* and *Come from the Shadows.* Her later albums have become increasingly dependent on contemporary music that combines traditional roots with country, rock, and pop, much of it written by Baez. Her departure from pure folk music and her reluctance to research the folk music she performs have been criticized by purists, but both critics and audiences applaud her performance of both traditional and contemporary music.

While incorporating protest into her music, Baez does not limit her social activism to performance. During the 1960s and 1970s, Baez was an active participant in both the civil rights and anti-Vietnam War movements. In protest against the Vietnam war, Baez refused to pay war taxes, blocked induction centers, toured North Vietnam, and spoke in favor of draft resistance. During much of this period, Baez was married to imprisoned draft opponent David Harris. The marriage ended after the war. In the mid-1970s, Baez subordinated her musical career to her social activism, protesting in Belfast and meeting with dissidents in the former Soviet Union. Her condemnation of the government of the Socialist Republic of Vietnam was harshly criticized by her political allies on the Left. Despite this criticism, Baez continues to speak out against oppression wherever it exists, serving as founder of Humanitas International Human Rights Committee and as a member of the National Advisory Board of Amnesty International.

Into the 1990s, Baez continued her musical career. In 1992, Baez released a Grammy-nominated album *Play Me Backwards,* her first album for a major label since 1979. Still a socially conscious artist, Baez appears at numerous benefit concerts for organizations such as Amnesty International, We Are the World, and Bread and Roses. *(See also: Pacifism and the Peace Movement; Popular Vocalists; Vietnam War)*

—**Preston Lane**

Further Reading

Baez, Joan C. *And a Voice to Sing With.* New York: Summit, 1987.

———. *And Then I Wrote . . .* New York: Big 3 Music, 1979.

———. *Daybreak.* New York: Dial, 1968.

Playboy Interview: Joan Baez. Chicago: Playboy Press, 1971.

☙ Bagley, Sarah G. (?–1847?)

Sarah Bagley, the first notable woman trade unionist in the United States, was born in Meredith, New Hampshire, and received a typical New England common school education. She obtained employment as a weaver in the Hamilton Manufacturing Company, a cotton mill in Lowell, Massachusetts, in 1836. Working under the adverse conditions of a badly ventilated building, poor lighting, and a twelve-hour day stimulated her to join and become a leader in the labor battles for women mill workers during the 1840s.

In 1840, Bagley was contributing innocuous articles to the *Lowell Offering,* the apolitical magazine written by the mill girls, but as wages declined and working conditions deteriorated between 1844 and 1847, she voiced the workers' discontent in her speeches and writings. As the founder and first president of the Lowell Female Labor Reform Association in 1845, she argued for the ten-hour day in the New England Workingman's Association periodical *Voice of Industry.* She became editor after its purchase by the Lowell Female Labor Reform Association (LFLRA). With the aid of the LFLRA, she obtained two thousand signatures on petitions to the Massachusetts state legislature for a ten-hour day. Bagley and other female operatives testified in February 1845 at a public hearing, but without result; the legislature declined to interfere in the business of the mills.

Shortly thereafter, Bagley left her mill position and devoted herself to full-time labor activities through her organization of branches of the LFLRA in other mill towns, her speaking engagements for the New England Workingman's Association, her work as their corresponding secretary, and also her founding of the Lowell Industrial Reform Lyceum, a platform for speakers such as William Lloyd Garrison, George Ripley, and Horace Greeley.

When an article by Sarah Bagley was published in 1845 in the first of the *Factory Tracts* issued by the LFLRA, she seemed a militant radical, stating, "We will show those drivelling cotton lords . . . that our rights cannot be trampled upon with impunity." Bagley's courageous and innovative acts stood out as a beacon and unifying force for the early female factory operatives. Her health declined, and in February 1846, another mill girl replaced her as president of the LFLRA. But Sarah Bagley was not through: She blazed another trail as the first woman telegrapher in this country by accepting the position of superintendent of the Lowell Telegraph Office. *(See also: Lowell Female Industrial Reform and Mutual Aid Society; Lowell Mill Girls;* Voice of Industry)

—Virginia Beattie Mattes

Further Reading

Josephson, Hannah. *The Golden Threads, New England's Mill Girls and Magnates.* New York: Russell & Russell, 1967.

Stern, Madeline B. *We the Women: Career Firsts of Nineteenth Century America.* New York: Schulte, 1963.

❧ Baker, Josephine (1906–1975)

Singer, dancer, and comedienne, Josephine Baker was born in St. Louis and rose from an impoverished background to international acclaim as an entertainer. By the age of thirteen, Baker had begun to appear at the Booker T. Washington Club in St. Louis and soon afterward joined the Dixie Steppers and traveled on the Theatre Owner's Booking Association (TOBA) circuit through the South. TOBA was the booking agency for black entertainers in southern black theaters and a few northern theaters that sustained those entertainers in a segregated market. In 1921, she joined the Broadway company of the Eubie Blake and Noble Sissle musical *Shuffle Along* after originally being turned down for the road company production for being "too black." She became the hit of the show as a comedy chorus girl. In 1925, she starred in another Blake and Sissle musical, *Chocolate Dandies.*

Baker journeyed to Paris to be part of a black vaudeville show called "La Revue Négre" in October 1925. Her "Dance of the Savages" was soon the toast of Paris, and Baker became the quintessential "garçonne," the French version of the flapper. She later opened at the Folies-Bergére, where she appeared onstage wearing only a girdle of rhinestone-studded bananas, a costume that became her trademark.

In 1926, Baker opened up her own club in Paris called Chez Joséphine, which became a commercial and financial success. She returned to the United States to appear in the Ziegfeld Follies in 1936. The show was a critical and box office flop, and Baker returned to France. During World War II, Baker became a member of the Free French Forces, acting as a spy and entertaining troops in North Africa, where she was in exile. After the war, she received the Legion of Honor, the Rosette of the Resistance, and the Medallion of the City of Paris.

Radicalized by her wartime experiences, Baker returned to the United States in 1951. She lectured on racial equality and performed before mixed audiences. She received the National Association for the Advancement of Colored People's (NAACP's) Most Outstanding Woman of the Year

Figure 7. Josephine Baker

Shown here putting on makeup before a 1928 show in Vienna, performer Josephine Baker found greater freedom and acceptance in Europe than she could in the racially divided United States. Used by permission of UPI/Corbis-Bettmann.

Award for 1951. Between 1954 and 1965, Baker and her husband, Jo Bouillon, adopted twelve children of various races and nationalities. She came out of retirement for a triumphant seventeen-city tour of the United States in 1973. She returned to Paris and debuted a new stage show on April 8, 1975. Five days later she died of a cerebral hemorrhage. *(See also: Black Women; Dance; Popular Vocalists)*

—Rose Kolbasnik Callahan

Further Reading

Baker, Jean-Claude. *Josephine: The Hungry Heart.* New York: Random House, 1993.

Baker, Josephine, and Jo Bouillon. *Josephine.* Translated by Mariana Fitzpatrick. New York: Harper & Row, 1977.

Rose, Phyllis. *Jazz Cleopatra: Josephine Baker in her Time.* New York: Doubleday, 1989.

❧ Balch, Emily Greene (1867–1961)

Peace advocate, social reformer, and economist, Emily Greene Balch was born near Boston and educated at Bryn Mawr, where she earned her A.B. in 1889. She then went on to additional study at the Harvard Annex (later Radcliffe College), the University of Chicago, and the University of Berlin. Balch began her teaching career at Wellesley College in 1896 and remained there until dismissed in 1918 for her outspoken pacificism. From 1919 to 1922 she served as the international secretary-treasurer of the Women's International League for Peace and Freedom and continued to work for that organization for the rest of her life in a variety of capacities.

A prolific writer, Balch also promoted the cause of peace and social justice through numerous books and articles. She opposed and fought human oppression in a variety of forms. For this reason, she reluctantly sanctioned U.S. involvement in World War II, while continuing her peace efforts. After the war, she actively supported the creation of the United Nations. In 1946, she was awarded the Nobel Peace Prize. *(See also: Addams, Jane; Hamilton, Alice; Pacifism and the Peace Movement)*

—**Jonathan W. Zophy**
—**Karen Raines-Pate**

Further Reading

Balch, Emily Greene. *Occupied Haiti.* New York: Garland, 1972.
———. *Our Slavic Fellow Citizens.* New York: Arno, 1969.
Doenecke, Justus. "Balch, Emily Greene." In *Biographical Dictionary of Modern Peace Leaders,* edited by Harold Josephson. Westport, CT: Greenwood, 1985.
Faver, Catherine A. " 'Creative Apostle of Reconciliation': The Spirituality and Social Philosophy of Emily Greene Balch," *Women's Studies* 18 (1991): 335-51.
Randall, Mercedes. *Improper Bostonian: Emily Greene Balch.* New York: Twayne, 1964.
Solomon, Barbara. *Ancestors and Immigrants: A Changing New England.* Cambridge, MA: Harvard University Press, 1956.

⚫ Baldwin, Maria Louise (1856–1922)

Maria Louise Baldwin, educator, civic worker, first black female principal in Massachusetts, and clubwoman, was the first of three children born to Baltimore native Mary Blake and Haitian emigrant Peter Baldwin on September 13, 1856. An excellent student, Baldwin received her education in Cambridge, Massachusetts, attending Sargent Primary School and later Allston Grammar School. After graduating from Cambridge High School in 1874 and from the Cambridge Teachers' Training School in 1875, she taught for two years in Chestertown, Maryland, before returning in 1881 to Cambridge. At the Agassiz School, she taught all seven grades to the children of Harvard professors. Baldwin gained respect for her ability to motivate children to take on the responsibility of learning.

Her skills as an educator led to her becoming the first of her race and gender to assume various roles, first as principal in 1889 and later as master of Agassiz School in 1916, making her one of two women and the only black to hold such an important position in the state of Massachusetts. As the first

black female principal in Massachusetts, Baldwin served as a positive role model to young blacks and opened opportunities for black women in education throughout New England. She supervised a teaching staff of twelve white teachers and served five hundred students. In 1897, she delivered the annual George Washington Birthday Memorial Address, "The Life and Services of the Late Harriet Beecher Stowe," at the Brooklyn Institute, becoming the first woman to receive that honor. This honor led to public lectures throughout the United States, drawing crowds who listened to her dignified and beautiful voice as she presented topics on history, literature, woman suffrage, and racial justice.

Baldwin carried her role as educator into the Boston-Cambridge community. She tutored black students attending Harvard University. She held classes at the Robert Gould Shaw settlement house to improve basic skills among the community's poor. Her Prospect Street home was the site for many meetings to address social concerns through the clubs, literary societies, and racial advancement organizations to which she belonged: the Twentieth Century Club of Boston, the Boston Ethical Society, the League of Women for Community Service, the Cantabriga Club, the Teacher's Association, the Urban League of Greater Boston, and the local branch of the National Association for the Advancement of Colored People (NAACP).

On the night of January 9, 1922, Baldwin collapsed and died from progressive heart disease during an address to the Council of the Robert Gould Shaw House. Following services at Arlington Street Church, a center of early abolitionism, Baldwin was cremated. Forest Hills Cemetery in Boston contains her ashes. Her memory was honored. The memorial issue of *The Agassiz* contained tributes to her, and the class of 1922 provided a memorial tablet that was unveiled one year after her death. The auditorium at Agassiz School was renamed Baldwin Hall, a scholarship was established, and a memorial library was dedicated in her honor. In 1952, a newly constructed women's dormitory at Howard University was named Maria Baldwin Hall. *(See also: Black Women; Education; National Association for the Advancement of Colored People)*

—**Dorothy C. Salem**

Further Reading

Brawley, Benjamin. *Negro Builders and Heroes.* Chapel Hill: University of North Carolina Press, 1937.
Brown, Hallie Q. *Homespun Heroines and Other Women of Distinction.* Xenia, OH: Aldine, 1926. Reprint, Freeport, NY: Books for Libraries, 1971, pp. 182-93.
Daniels, John. *In Freedom's Birthplace: A Study of Boston Negroes.* Boston: Houghton-Mifflin, 1914.
Du Bois, W. E. B. "Maria Baldwin," *The Crisis* 22 (January 1922): 248-49.
Gibson, John W. *Progress of a Race . . .* Naperville, IL: J. L. Nichols, 1920.
Porter, Dorothy. "Maria Louise Baldwin, 1856–1922," *Journal of Negro Education* 21 (Winter 1952): 94-96.

～ Barnard, Kate (1875–1930)

Kate Barnard was the first woman in the nation to be elected to a major state office, serving as Commissioner of Charities and Corrections for Oklahoma from 1907 to 1914. A professional politician and a social justice progressive, she fought for the rights of children, workers, convicts, the insane, and the handicapped.

In many respects, Barnard's prepolitical life typified the lives of women in Oklahoma in the late nineteenth century. She helped her father homestead a claim, spent several years as a rural schoolteacher, then became a stenographer in Oklahoma City. However, she began to depart from the traditional role for single women when she became a labor organizer in Oklahoma City. In 1905, her career took a decided turn when she led a crusade to clothe every poor child in Oklahoma City before Thanksgiving. As a result of this successful drive, Barnard became head of the United Provident Association, a local charity organization. The discovery that giving away food and used clothing did not cure poverty convinced her to become a stalwart supporter of unions. Attracting statewide attention as a champion of laborers and children, she persuaded the Oklahoma Constitutional Convention (1906–1907) to adopt planks providing for compulsory education and protection for laboring children. In Oklahoma's first election in 1907, and again in 1910, Barnard won election as Commissioner of Charities and Corrections. She received more votes than any other candidate, a remarkable accomplishment considering that Oklahoma had not granted women suffrage at the time.

During her tenure in office, Barnard pushed through the state legislature measures implementing the constitutional provisions compelling the education of children and limiting their work outside the home. Owing to her persistent pressure, legislators also created a juvenile court system and reformed the criminal justice system. Her sensational investigations of asylum, jails, and penitentiaries resulted in improvements in the institutional care of the insane and the incarcerated As a labor advocate, Barnard was instrumental in persuading the legislature to establish a free state employment bureau and to pass laws concerning employer liability, mining safety, and factory inspection.

Barnard not only figured prominently in Oklahoma reform politics but also rose to national prominence through her work with the National Child Labor Committee, the National Conference of Charities and Corrections, the International Prison Commission, and the Lake Mohonk Conference on Indian rights.

Evidence of widespread fraud committed against Indian orphans prompted Barnard to undertake a crusade on their behalf in 1910. Barnard publicized the legal chicanery used to loot the orphans' estates. Subsequent attacks by the Oklahoma legislature, her own ill health, and waning enthusiasm for public office contributed to her retirement from politics in 1914. Sixteen years later, she died alone and obscure in an Oklahoma City hotel. *(See also: Politics; Prison Reform)*

—Suzanne Jones Crawford
—Lynn R. Musslewhite

Further Reading

Charities and Corrections Collection. State Archives of Oklahoma, Oklahoma City.

Bryant, Keith L., Jr. "The Juvenile Court Movement: Oklahoma as a Case Study," *Social Science Quarterly* 49 (September 1968): 368-76.

———. "Kate Barnard, Organized Labor and Social Justice in Oklahoma during the Progressive Era," *Journal of Southern History* 35 (1969): 145-64.

Crawford, Suzanne Jones, and Lynn Musslewhite. "Kate Barnard, Progressivism, and the West." In *An Oklahoma I Had Never Seen Before*, edited by Davis Joyce, 62-79. Norman: University of Oklahoma Press, 1994.

———. "Oklahoma Democrats and Progressive Reform: Kate Barnard vs. Bill Murray," *The Historian* 53 (Spring 1991): 473-88.

Houghen, H. R. "Kate Barnard and the Kansas Penitentiary Scandal," *Journal of the West* 17 (January 1978): 9-18.

Musslewhite, Lynn R., and Suzanne Jones Crawford. "Kate Barnard and Feminine Politics of the Progressive Era," *Mid-America* 75 (January 1993): 45-66.

～ Barnard College

In the late nineteenth century, increasing pressure was brought to bear on men's universities to admit women as students. By 1879, Columbia College in New York City had allowed females to attend selected classes, but when in 1882 appeals were made to the college by certain prominent New Yorkers urging the admittance of women as degree candidates, the proposal was overwhelmingly rejected by the Board of Trustees. Consequently, in 1883 "the Collegiate Course" was established, based on the Harvard precedent, whereby women could earn certificates of completion from Columbia College provided they passed the requisite examinations. Preparatory instruction for these examinations, however, was not provided.

In 1889, Barnard College was established, providing instruction and absorbing the work of the Collegiate Course. Barnard College was completely independent of Columbia College in nonacademic matters, but it did use Columbia College instructors and professors, library facilities, course standards, and examinations. As Columbia College professors became less available, Barnard College began to hire its own instructors. Early enrollments were low, with only nine graduates in the first class and only thirty-five graduates five years later.

Although the Barnard College curriculum was on a par with that of Columbia College, a chronic problem at Barnard (as well as at other female colleges) was the paucity of academically prepared women able to meet the rigors of legitimate university study. This was primarily because of the often inferior secondary preparation of the young women, particularly in the sciences, classics, and mathematics, which carried over into the university setting, where women were often discouraged from excelling in these typically "male" domains. Nonetheless, in 1900, Barnard College was incorporated into the Columbia University system, where it remains an integral part of the university to this day. *(See also: Higher Education; "Seven Sisters")*

—**Maureen Anna Harp**

Further Reading

"A History of Barnard College." Published in honor of the Seventy-fifth Anniversary of the College, 1964. New York: Columbia University Press, 1964.

Meyer, Annie Nathan. *Barnard Beginnings.* New York: Houghton Mifflin, 1935.

Miller, Alice Duer, and Susan Meyers. *Barnard College: The First Fifty Years.* New York: Columbia University Press, 1939.

White, Marian Churchill. *A History of Barnard College.* New York: Columbia University Press, 1954.

☙ Barry, Mother Gerald (1881–1961)

Mother Gerald Barry was prioress general of the Dominican Sisters of Adrian, Michigan (Congregation of the Most Holy Rosary), from 1933 to 1961. Born Bridget Catherine Barry in West Clare, Ireland, one of eighteen children of prosperous farmers, Michael and Catherine (Dixon) Barry, she was educated at Inagh National School in County Clare and emigrated to Chicago in 1896, where she studied business at Powers Business College. After teaching for four years, she worked as a secretary to her brother at a law firm at Nogales, Arizona. In 1912, she entered the Sisters of St. Dominic, Adrian, Michigan, and received the religious name "Mary Gerald." From 1914 to 1933, she served in various teaching and administrative positions in the community until she was elected prioress general of the congregation.

She served as leader of her community for over twenty-eight years and guided it through one of its most dynamic periods of growth and expansion. Not only did the numbers of Adrian Dominicans increase (930 to 2,480), but Mother Gerald pressed for expansion of the elementary, secondary, and higher education ministries of the order. Under her direction, the Adrian Dominicans accepted the staffing of seventy new parochial schools, established four high schools for girls, founded two colleges (Barry College, Florida, and Aquinas Teachers College, Nassau, Bahamas), and expanded the order's Siena Heights College in Adrian. Moreover, a number of missions in the Caribbean and Peru were accepted as well.

Mother Gerald was a firm advocate of higher education for nuns. To effect this, she not only established a house of studies in Washington, D.C., for her sisters studying at the Catholic University of America but also sent them to prestigious secular universities. She also recognized the great potential for uniting and coordinating the efforts of American religious women. In 1952, the Sacred Congregation for Religious called on her to act as executive chairperson of the National Committee for Sisters, a subgroup of the National Congress of Religious that met at the University of Notre Dame that year. Four years later, Rome appointed her to chair a meeting of Mothers General in the United States. Out of this grew the Conference of Major Superiors of Women Religious, now known as the Leadership Conference of Women Religious. She received honorary degrees from the University of Santo Domingo, Dominican Republic (Ph.D., 1949); University of Notre Dame (J.D., 1952); and Loyola University of Chicago (J.D., 1960). She died at the motherhouse of the Adrian Dominicans in 1961. *(See also: Christianity; Education; Religion)*

—**Steven M. Avella**

Further Reading

Barry, M. Gerald. *The Charity of Christ Presses Us: Letters to Her Community.* Edited by M. Philip Ryan. Milwaukee, WI: Bruce, 1962.

McKeough, M. Paul. "Mother Mary Gerald, O.P.," *Dominican Educational Bulletin* 3 (Winter 1962): 17-23.

☙ Barton, Clara (1821–1912)

Clara Barton, founder of the American branch of the International Red Cross, came to that enterprise in an indirect and far from predictable way. Born Clarissa Harlowe Barton, she was the fifth and last child of a family well established in the town of Oxford, Massachusetts. Somewhat spoiled by her older brothers and sister, she grew up a willful child and became a self-willed adult. Working under others was never easy for her, often impossible, and this personality trait contributed to both her successes and failures.

As a schoolteacher, Barton established the first free school in New Jersey in 1852; as an employee of the Patent Office in Washington in 1854, she made $1,400 a year. She then became a semirecluse—fits of physical lassitude and emotional deflation were common throughout her lifetime—until the Civil War provided the opportunity for her to fulfill what she saw as her great purpose in life—service to others. Her genius in wartime was not nursing as such but the gathering and distribution of supplies to supplement the work of the Union Army and, where needed, the efforts of the U.S. Sanitary Commission. For these efforts, she was celebrated as "the American Nightingale" and the "Angel of the Battlefield" for the rest of her life.

While visiting Europe in 1869, Barton first became aware of the relatively new organization, the International Red Cross, begun in 1864. She was taken with the Red Cross ideal: to succor all military and civilian casualties of war. Ready to return home to preach the idea in America, which had not joined the International Red Cross, Barton became involved in the Franco-Prussian War. Under the flag of the Red Cross, she worked to relieve the misery of the populations of Strasbourg, Metz, and Paris.

After a long, uphill fight on her part, the U.S. government finally joined the International Red Cross by signing the 1864 Geneva Convention in March 1882. Meanwhile, Barton saw the Red Cross as a standby organization, ready to offer aid in the wake of all manner of natural and man-made disasters. The organization was widely accepted in the United States and received a federal charter in 1900. But Clara Barton's egocentric leadership style fitted poorly into the formal structure of organizational charity, and she was forced to resign the presidency in 1904. *(See also: American Red Cross; Civil War; Nursing; United States Sanitary Commission)*

—**David H. Burton**

Further Reading

Barton, Clara. *The Story of My Childhood.* New York: Baker & Taylor, 1907.

Burton, David H. *Clara Barton: In the Service of Humanity.* Westport, CT: Greenwood, 1995.

Ross, Ishbel. *Angel of the Battlefield.* New York: Harper, 1956.

Williams, Blanche C. *Clara Barton, Daughter of Destiny.* Philadelphia: J. B. Lippincott, 1941.

☙ Baxter, Annie (1864–1944)

The first female county clerk in the United States and first elected female official in Missouri, Annie Baxter assumed her duties as Jasper County clerk in January 1891 at Carthage, Missouri. Nominated by the Democratic County Convention after years of service as deputy county clerk, her subsequent election was challenged by one of her opponents, Julius Fischer. When the Green County Circuit Court upheld her election in January 1892, Baxter had already served one year.

Born Anna White in Pittsburgh, Pennsylvania, she moved to Carthage in 1877, graduated from high school in 1882, then joined the staff of the county clerk. In 1888, she married Charles W. Baxter. Baxter lost her bid for reelection with the Republican landslide in 1894. After a short period in St. Louis, she moved to Jefferson City, Missouri, to work for the secretary of state. In 1913, Baxter became land registrar and held that position until 1921. In 1922, she became financial secretary to the Missouri Constitutional Commission and was the commission's only female staff member.

Baxter continued to be active in Missouri Democratic circles. However, her landmark 1890 election was not included in *Missouri Democracy,* her party's 1935 history. Included among Jasper County's "distinguished Democrats and partyworkers" were thirteen other women, including Emily Newell Blair, vice chairman of the National Democratic Committee in 1924.

Annie Baxter died on June 28, 1944. She is memorialized with a street named in her honor in Joplin, Missouri, and with a stone embedded at the east steps of the Jasper County Courthouse (1895), authorized and started during her term as county clerk. Baxter's election and public service were a milestone in the region and served as a source of inspiration to many Carthage women. Among these were Sara Frank, first woman to run for Jasper County school superintendent, 1894; Ella Harrison, president of the Missouri State Suffrage Association, 1896; the Reverend Lucy B. Lindsey, first ordained woman of the Christian denomination in Missouri, 1895; and Emma Knell, one of the first female morticians in Missouri in the late 1890s and first Republican woman elected to the Missouri House of Representatives, 1925. *(See also: Democratic Party; Politics)*

—**Michele A. Hansford**

Further Reading

Annie Baxter Research Files of the Powers Museum. Carthage, MO. Including Michelle Cheney. "Annie White Baxter: A Silent Movement for the Rights of the Individual Woman." Unpublished manuscript, 1987.

Dains, Mary K., ed. *Show Me Missouri Women.* Kirksville, MO: Thomas Jefferson University Press, 1989.

Logan, Mrs. John A. *The Part Taken by Women in American History.* Wilmington, DE: Perry-Nalle, 1912.

Willard, Frances, and Mary A. Livermore. *American Women.* New York: Mast, Crowell & Kirkpatrick, 1893.

☙ Beach, Amy Marcy Cheney (Mrs. H. H. A.) (1867–1944)

Amy Beach was a composer and pianist. She began as a pianist prodigy and had her first public appearance in 1883 at the age of sixteen. In 1885, she married Henry Harris Aubrey Beach, a distinguished surgeon, who encouraged her musicianship. Between 1885 and 1910, she concentrated on composition and then resumed her concert tours both in Europe and the United States. She settled in New York and often spent summers at the MacDowell Colony, a retreat for creative artists.

Her *"Gaelic"* Symphony, completed in 1896, was the first symphony by an American woman to be performed anywhere and the first by an American composer to quote folk songs as themes. She composed other large works, including an opera, *Cabildo,* op. 149; Piano Concerto, op. 45; Mass in E Flat Major, op. 5; and Sonata in A Minor for violin and piano, op. 34. In addition, she wrote many small works, including over 150 songs by which she became known to the general public. Beach was considered a leading representative of the late-nineteenth-century romantic style, with its emphasis on broad lines of melody and complex harmonies. Having little formal instruction in music theory, she taught herself orchestration and composition. Her works and performances received critical acclaim in her lifetime. *(See also: Music)*

—**Anne O. Dzamba (Sessa)**

Further Reading

Block, Adrienne Fried. *Amy Beach, Passionate Victorian: The Life and Work of an American Composer, 1867–1944.* New York: Oxford University Press, 1998.

———. "Dvorak, Beach, and American Music." In *A Celebration of American Music: Words and Music in Honor of H. Wiley Hitchcock,* edited by Richard Crawford, R. Allen Lott, and Carol J. Oja, 256-80. Ann Arbor: University of Michigan Press, 1990.

Pendle, Karin, ed. *Women and Music: A History.* Bloomington: Indiana University Press, 1991.

↝ Beard, Mary (Ritter) (1876–1958)

Historian, writer, and activist, Mary Beard was the founder of women's history and the inventor of women's studies, as well as an advocate for woman suffrage and better conditions for women workers. Born outside Indianapolis, Indiana, to a middle-class family, Beard graduated from DePauw University. She also attended Columbia University Graduate School but abandoned graduate work as too theoretical to effect social reform.

In the early 1900s, Beard actively fought for woman suffrage but opposed the Equal Rights Amendment because of her belief in protective legislation for women workers. With her husband Charles A. Beard, she coauthored several history texts that examined social and cultural issues in addition to traditional governmental issues and emphasized the utility of historical studies as a means of creating a better future. After passage of the Nineteenth Amendment, Beard focused on women's history as a discrete field of scholarship. In her major works, *On Understanding Women* (1931) and *Woman as Force in History* (1946), Beard exposed the lack of women in written histories and described women as central to the making of history and civilization.

Believing that women were hindered by traditional male-defined education, Beard invented the concept of women's studies. She proposed new women's universities and women's courses that would educate women about their important role in the world's development and would equip women to lead the world in their unique way. Beard had intended to develop just such a college around the short-lived World Center for Women's Archives, which she organized and directed. Instead, she promoted and supported women's studies at Radcliffe, Smith, Barnard, and Vassar colleges and Syracuse University.

Beard dedicated her life to studying and educating women with the goal of improving society by improving the personal and group status of women. She was a pioneer for women's rights and women's studies in the twentieth century. *(See also: Higher Education; Suffrage; Women's Studies)*

—**Piper Madland**

—**David H. Burton**

Figure 8. Mary Beard
Scholar and suffragist Mary Beard seated at her writing desk. Used by permissions of UPI/Corbis-Bettmann.

Further Reading

Beard, Mary R. *The Force of Women in Japanese History.* Washington, DC: Public Affairs Press, 1953.

———. *On Understanding Women.* New York: Longmans, Green & Co., 1931. Reprint, New York: Greenwood, 1968.

———. *Woman's Work in Municipalities.* New York: National Municipal League Series, 1915. Reprint, New York: Arno, 1972.

———. *Woman as Force in History: A Study in Traditions and Realities.* New York: Macmillan, 1946. Reprint, New York: Collier, 1962.

Cott, Nancy F., ed. *A Woman Making History: Mary R. Beard through Her Letters.* New Haven, CT: Yale University Press, 1991.

Lane, Ann J., ed. *Mary Ritter Beard: A Sourcebook.* New York: Schocken, 1977. Reprint, Boston: Northeastern University Press, 1988.

Turoff, Barbara K. *Mary Beard as Force in History.* Dayton, OH: Wright State University Press, 1979.

↝ Beauty Industry

From the earliest years, homemade cosmetics and shared advice on makeup were a part of women's culture in the United States despite other cultural perspectives that treated "powder and paint" as immoral. In the late nineteenth and early twentieth centuries, the beauty industry became an important arena for business. African American entrepreneurs Annie M. Turnbo Malone and Madam C. J. Walker built extremely successful businesses by concentrating on mass-based direct sales distribution. In contrast, upper-class white women were the clients targeted by Helena Rubinstein (1870–1965) and Elizabeth Arden (1878–1966). Though not a woman-owned company, Avon Cosmetics provided one of the first ways for women to earn an income of their own. The company's direct-selling method was pioneered by Mrs. P. F. E. Albee of Winchester, New Hampshire, the first "Avon Lady."

In the 1920s, corporations headed by men entered the beauty industry. Today, the beauty business is a male-dominated, multibillion-dollar enterprise. Nevertheless, the cosmetics industry continues to be highly profitable for women, as demonstrated by Mary Kay's more than $1 billion wholesale business in 1997, amounting to more than $2 billion at the retail level. Her operations have expanded to twenty-six countries, including the Ukraine and the Czech Republic. Anita Roddick, founder and CEO of The Body Shop, built a $500 million company operating in forty-four countries from a single storefront in 1976. Roddick has also been recognized for her no-advertising policy and for expanding the market for products of indigenous people. The Body Shop has also worked with numerous organizations on a variety of initiatives, including a ban on animal testing, protection of the ozone layer and of rain forests, and a variety of other environmental and social causes. Although not woman-owned, Avon has more women in management than any other Fortune 500 company, and since 1886, more than 25 million women in the United States have sold Avon products.

The relationship between the cosmetics industry and images of femininity continues to draw the attention of feminist scholars and activists. (See also: Malone, Annie Turnbo; Walker, Madame C. J.)

—Diana E. Axelsen

Further Reading

Columbia University Record 19 (June 10, 1994). [on Anita Roddick and The Body Shop]

Conger, Jay A., and Rabindra N. Kanungo. Charismatic Leadership in Organizations. Thousand Oaks, CA: Sage, 1998.

Gunn, Fenja. The Artificial Face: A History of Cosmetics. New York: Hippocrene, 1983.

Lauder, Estée. Estée: A Success Story. New York: Random House, 1985.

Peiss, Kathy. Hope in a Jar: The Making of America's Beauty Culture. New York: Henry Holt, 1998.

Rubinstein, Helena. My Life for Beauty. New York: Simon & Schuster, 1964.

✥ Beauty Pageants

Beauty contests were not American in origin. From feudal times, Austria, France, and Great Britain celebrated folk festivals, various holidays, and observances for which a beautiful female was crowned queen. May Day celebrations were the first competitions in the United States for a beauty queen; however, the Puritans of the Massachusetts Bay colonies replaced the May Day observance and all other English holidays with Thanksgiving. Nevertheless, May Day celebrations survived and expanded to include many other events.

By the middle of the nineteenth century, these festivals were popular in the West. They reached their height in the Pasadena Tournament of Roses, 1889, and in the Rose Festival of Portland, Oregon, 1909. Festivals also became popular in cities in the heartland of America. Surprisingly, the Victorians rarely protested the selection of queens for various festivals, despite their dislike of women displayed in public. As early as 1699, Mardi Gras, the common ancestor for all American festivals, legitimized queens and kings, using a selection process based on fate, luck, and a democratic process. The selection of queens demonstrated the social mobility of American society. For all festivals, queens were considered crucial, because women were the guardians of morality and a symbol of community values. The selection of festival queens was not always based on physical beauty. Early queens were selected for their civic leadership, community popularity, or in honor of a male relative. Nevertheless, May Day and other festival queens reinforced the importance of physical beauty as a matter of competition and elitism.

P. T. Barnum introduced photographic beauty contests, which became popular in the late 1800s and early 1900s. City newspapers spread this idea. Contests occurred in many cities and were popular because the women did not have to display themselves before the public or the judges. About the same time, the carnival that had won acceptance among the middle class began to promote local civic and business ventures. The main feature of this event was the selection of a queen based on physical beauty. The emergence of modeling as a respectable career for women in the twentieth century helped to popularize beauty contests. The fusion of the features of the lower-class carnivals with the upper-class festivals, however, would not occur in a natural and national setting until the first Miss America Pageant in 1921.

The Miss America Pageant had its beginning as an effort to keep tourists in Atlantic City past the Labor Day weekend. The organizers of the contest, attempting to offend no one, carefully emphasized the wholesome, natural qualities of the contestants and their athletic abilities. Herb Test, a reporter for the Atlantic City Press, was the creator of the title "Miss America." Margaret Gorman, a sixteen-year-old from Washington, D.C., won the first Miss America title and a Golden Mermaid Statue worth $5,000 on September 6, 1921.

The pageant grew in both size and budget, and by the late 1920s, people expressed concern for the exploitation of the morals of the contestants. Many contended that it remained closer to a carnival event than the high-class production they envisioned. As a result, the pageant was discontinued in 1927, not to return until 1933. The pageant continues to claim that the Great Depression was the reason for the discontinuance, although the stock market crash didn't occur until 1929.

The first year that the contest was officially titled the Miss America Pageant was 1941. The 1940s also brought the awarding of scholarships to contestants, as the pageant became the largest private endower of scholarships to women. Long-lasting changes to the pageant came about in the 1950s as it adapted to the needs of television. Bert Parks, a popular game show host, made his appearance and remained with the pageant until 1980. The song that almost everyone recognized, "There She Is" by Bernie Wayne, was sung for the first time at the pageant. Despite the resurgence of the women's movement in the 1960s, the pageant continued as usual.

Although the fiftieth anniversary of the pageant was celebrated in 1971, the decade of the 1970s saw less publicity than at any other time. This was only an interlude before the negative fallout of the 1980s. Bert Parks was replaced by other television celebrities, including Gary Collins, television personality and the husband of Mary Ann Mobley, Miss America 1959. Vanessa Williams, the first woman of color to earn the crown, became the first Miss America to be dethroned when *Penthouse* magazine printed nude pictures of her in its July 1984 issue, only two months before the 1985 pageant.

Each succeeding decade has brought new innovations and changes. Talent was introduced into the competition in 1938. In recent years, the winners have been requested to have an "official platform," in recognition of the changing roles of women. Another barrier was broken with the selection of Heather Whitestone in 1994 as the first Miss America with a disability. For the seventy-fifth anniversary, Leonard Horn, the chief executive of the Miss America Organization, conducted a telephone poll whereby viewers could call a "900" number to vote on the continuance of the swimsuit portion of the competition. On September 16, 1995, 79 percent of more than 898,000 callers paid 50 cents to retain the tradition.

Miss America, while not the only beauty pageant, is the only pageant that provides $3 million in scholarships for participants. The other two major pageants, Miss Universe and Miss USA, are strictly beauty contests. Pacific Knitting Mills created the Miss Universe Pageant as a protest when the Miss America Pageant refused to provide photographs of the contestants wearing Catalina swimsuits made by Pacific. A vehicle for advertising, the contest was first held in Long Beach, California, in 1951. The next year, it was moved to Miami, Florida, to accommodate its sole sponsor, Procter & Gamble. In 1981, Paramount Pictures took over the Miss Universe Pageant. The contestants for these pageants are differentiated on the state level—for instance, Miss Texas-USA. In 1984, Miss America was paid $25,000, while Miss Universe was paid $175,000; Miss Universe also receives as much as $2,500 for personal appearances, twice as much as Miss America receives. These pageants are held close to-

gether: Miss USA in April, Miss Universe in July, and Miss America in September. Prizes continue to reflect the assumption that women desire jewels and furs. In 1988, Bob Barker, the cohost of the Miss USA and Miss Universe Pageant for twenty-one years, resigned his six-figure salary because furs were given as prizes. An advocate for animals, Barker felt his credibility would be damaged if he continued to host the show.

The Miss Universe organization includes the Miss Teen-USA pageant. Other teenage pageants—such as America's Junior Miss, Miss Teenage America, and Miss United Teenager—include talent competitions, recognize high school academic standing and activities, and give scholarships. Special pageants include the Mrs. America Pageant in Palisades Park, New Jersey, and the local pageants for the very young, such as Our Little Miss. Competitions for men include Mr. America, Mr. Universe, and Mr. Olympia. These, however, are bodybuilding contests, and little emphasis is placed on the interview or formal evening wear.

Other countries have beauty contests and pageants, such as the Miss World Pageant in London, England. The U.S. contestant in this pageant is called Miss World-USA. Despite protests about pageants and some pageants protesting the others, the number of contests continues to grow. The current roster includes Ms. Long Distance, Miss Chinatown, Nubian Pageants, and the Asian Rose Ball Beauty. *(See also: Sexism; Women's Rights Movements: Nineteenth and Twentieth Centuries)*

—Judith Lucas

Further Reading
Banner, Lois W. *American Beauty*. New York: Knopf, 1983.

Bowen, Ezra, ed. *This Fabulous Century*. Vol. 3. New York: Time Life Books, 1969, 1974.

Funnel, Charles E. *By the Beautiful Sea: The Rise and High Times of That Resort, Atlantic City*. New York: Knopf, 1975.

Kindel, Stephen, ed. "Beauty You Can Take to the Bank," *Forbes* 133 (June 18, 1984): 136-39.

Martin, Nancie S. *Miss America through the Looking Glass*. New York: Messner, 1985.

Prewitt, Cheryl, and Katheryn Slattery. *A Bright and Shining Place*. New York: Viking, 1971.

∿ Beaux, Cecilia (1855–1942)

Cecilia Beaux was a painter of the early-twentieth-century elite. Raised in Philadelphia in a genteel tradition where appreciation for the arts was emphasized, she received early encouragement and support from relatives who recognized her talents.

After Beaux's first major composition, *Les Derniers Jours d'Enfance* ("The Last Days of Childhood"), was accepted by the Paris Salon in 1887, her career was launched and she became a well-established Philadelphia portraitist. In 1888, Beaux traveled for the first time to Europe. She entered classes in Paris at the Académie Julian, where she received criticism from painters William Bouguereau and Tony Robert-Fleury. She also studied the paintings of the Old Masters that she saw in the museums, particularly those by Titian, Rembrandt, and Rubens. Although aware of the impressionist movement, Beaux resisted any overpowering influences, determined to select from the diverse trends around her only those qualities that seemed appropriate to her emerging style.

In the 1890s, a surge of commissions caused Beaux to move to New York. She started a series of "white" paintings, followed by a series of impressive double portraits. Her portrait *Mother and Daughter* (1898) won four gold medals. Earlier, in 1887, she had received wide acclaim for her first painting in white tones, *A Little Girl* (Fanny Travis Cochran).

By 1900, Beaux was established as a leading portrait painter in New York. Her commissions came from prominent figures in the arts, finance, and government, among them Mrs. Theodore Roosevelt and Mrs. Andrew Carnegie. Her more academic portraits, such as those of Georges Clemenceau, Sir David Beatty, and Cardinal Mercier, were commissioned by the U.S. government. For the first Portrait Gallery (now the National Portrait Gallery), the artist successfully produced dignified portrayals of each sitter's office and position. Between 1897 and 1933, Beaux had fourteen one-woman shows, and her work was exhibited at the Pennsylvania Academy of Fine Arts, several New York galleries, and the Paris Salon. She received numerous prizes and awards.

Beaux's best work reveals simple forms and innovative figure placement, as well as an original compositional style. She was acclaimed for her psychological insight, rich brushwork, and subtle color. Her principal concerns, she claimed, were "imaginative insight and design." Beaux painted continuously until 1924, when she started her autobiography, *Background with Figures* (1930).

One of Beaux's greatest distinctions is that she was the first woman to be engaged as a full-time member of the Pennsylvania Academy of the Fine Arts faculty, thereby influencing the careers of countless women. In addition, the superior skills of Cecilia Beaux kept portraiture alive at a time when photography was rapidly replacing it in popularity. *(See also: Art)*

—**Florence Davis**

Further Reading

Beaux, Cecilia. *Background with Figures.* New York: Houghton Mifflin, 1930.

Cecilia Beaux and the Art of Portraiture. Washington, DC: Smithsonian Institution Press, 1995.

Cecilia Beaux: Portrait of an Artist. Exhibition catalog. Philadelphia: Pennsylvania Academy of the Fine Arts, 1974.

Harris, Ann Sutherland, and Linda Nochlin. *Women Artists, 1550–1950.* New York: Knopf, 1981.

Rubinstein, Charlotte Streifer. *American Women Artists: From Early Indian Times to the Present.* Boston: G. K. Hall, 1982.

Tappert, Tara L. "Cecilia Beaux: A Career as a Portraitist," *Women's Studies* 14 (1988): 389-411.

Tufts, Eleanor. *American Women Artists 1830–1930.* Washington, DC: National Museum of Women in the Arts, 1987.

❧ Beecher, Catharine (1800–1878)

Catharine Beecher was an educator and writer and a member of the famous New England Beecher family, sister to Henry Ward Beecher and Harriet Beecher Stowe. With other domestic feminists, Beecher saw the home as place and justification for women's separate and distinctive role in American society. While Beecher acknowledged that women were left aside in political and economic life, she promoted this disengagement as the means to an alternative role in advancing moral, cultural, psychological, and practical well-being. To prepare women properly for their roles as teachers of children, Beecher advocated women's education and involved herself in teaching and developing educational programs.

Looking for a means to support herself and her ideals, Beecher established the Western Female Institute in 1833 and then a succession of educational programs during the next decades: for example, in 1840, the Central Committee for Promoting National Education, to train teachers for the western settlements, and in 1851, the American Women's Educational Association. Beecher's involvement in these and other educational enterprises was always somewhat limited by her own finite interest in the daily chores of teaching and school administration.

During the 1840s, she attempted to publish as much as she could in magazines, but unlike many of her contemporaries, she was not able to make a living from writing for periodicals. *A Treatise on Domestic Economy* (1841) established Catharine Beecher's financial independence and national recognition. The first comprehensive American volume of household construction, management, and advice, Beecher's *Treatise* was based on the principles of domesticity as a social and moral value and of scientific understanding and laborsaving technology as mainstays of the self-sufficient American home. As Beecher made a virtue of nonparticipation in public life, she provided direction for a domesticity that included applying many professional competencies in the private home. From exceptional diagrams for construction of homes and explanations of technology, the *Treatise* moved to fulsome advice on family management, child care, prevention and identification of disease, and cookery. More scientific than its predecessors, Beecher's *Treatise* assumed that its readers could understand both the processes of modern domesticity and the reasons for them—and so, for example, provided advice not only on growing and preparing food but also on the human digestive and circulatory systems. Enormously popular on first publication, the *Treatise* continued to sell well for Beecher's lifetime. Expanded in 1869, including additions by Harriet Beecher Stowe, it reappeared as *The American Woman's Home;* revised in 1873, it was retitled *The New Housekeeper's Manual.*

Ironically, as Beecher advanced her own public career and promoted the creation of women's colleges, the domestic manual gained greater audiences than her other published works. Her 1851 *The True Remedy for the Wrongs of Women,* on women's colleges as "centers" of "influence," advanced homemaking and teaching as women's true professions. With the educational association and national fund-raising, Beecher attempted to embody and endow educational reform at her Milwaukee Female College. As before, royalties from publications—on health, domesticity, religion—were more profitable, and Beecher continued to alternate practical publishing with schemes for educational organizations. *(See also: Coeducation; Domestic Feminism; Education; Stowe, Harriet Beecher; Teaching)*

—**Carol Klimick Cyganowski**

Further Reading

Beecher, Catharine. *Treatise on Domestic Economy.* Boston: Marsh, Capen, Lyon & Webb, 1841.

Beecher, Catharine, and Harriet Beecher Stowe. *The American Woman's Home: Or, Principles of Domestic Science; Being a Guide to the Formation and Maintenance of Economical, Healthful, Beautiful, and Christian Homes.* 1869. Reprint, New York: Arno, 1971. Reprint, Ayer Co., American Education Series, 1972. Reprint, American Life Foundation, Library of Victorian Culture, 1975.

Sklar, Kathryn Kish. *Catharine Beecher: A Study in American Domesticity.* New Haven, CT: Yale University Press, 1973.

∞ Beijing Conference

The United Nations Fourth World Conference on Women, known as the Beijing Conference, was held September 4 through 15, 1995, in Beijing, China. This event brought together nearly 50,000 men and women from 189 governments, 32 U.N. organizations, 16 intergovernmental organizations, national liberation movements, 50 nongovernmental organizations (NGOs), and the private sector to review their efforts and renew their commitment to the theme of the conference: "Action for equality, development and peace."

The conference focused on persistent problems common to women from all parts of the globe and emphasized the crucial links between the advancement of women and the progress for society as a whole.

Although gathering and disseminating information on the situation of women was the primary activity at the conference and preparatory meetings, other objectives were to review and appraise the advancement of women since the previous World Conference on Women held in Nairobi, Kenya, in 1985; to mobilize women and men at both the policy-making and grassroots levels to achieve those objectives; to adopt a new platform for action; and to determine the priority actions to be taken between 1996 and 2001.

Participants assessed how women's lives had changed over the past decade and decided what steps needed to be taken to keep issues of concern to women high on the international agenda. They reviewed how women had fared in the areas of health, education, employment, family life, politics, and human rights.

These discussions resulted in the creation of the 150-page "Platform for Action," which noted that many of the goals adopted at Nairobi had not been achieved. The "Beijing Declaration and Plan for Action" established a precedent for the basic rights of women around the world. These two documents captured the gains made by women over the past twenty years and made numerous recommendations for action by governments, international institutions, NGOs, and the private sector, in respect to the twelve "critical areas of concern": women and poverty, the education and training of women, women and health, violence against women, women and armed conflict, women and the economy, women in power and decision making, institutional mechanisms for the advancement of women, the human rights of women, women and the media, women and the environment, and the future of the girl child.

For further information, contact the U.N. Department of Public Information, Room S-1040, New York, NY 10017, phone (212-963-1742), fax (212-963-3463); and the U.N. Division for the Advancement of Women, Room DC2-1220, New York, NY 10017, phone (212-963-5086), fax (212-963-3463). *(See also: Women's Rights Movements: Nineteenth and Twentieth Centuries)*

—**Diane DeVusser Fiero**

Further Reading

Auth, Janice, ed. *To Beijing and Back: Pittsburgh and the United Nations Fourth World Conference on Women.* Pittsburgh: University of Pittsburgh Press, 1998.

Blea, Irene I. *U.S. Chicanas and Latinas within a Global Context: Women of Color at the Fourth World Women's Conference.* Westport, CT: Praeger, 1997.

Chittister, Joan. *Beyond Beijing: The Next Step for Women, A Personal Journey.* Kansas City, MO: Sheed & Ward, 1996.

Heyzer, Noeleen, et al., eds. *A Commitment to the World's Women: Perspectives on Development for Beijing and Beyond.* New York: Women, Ink., 1996.

U.N. Department of Public Information. *Beijing Declaration & the Platform for Action: Fourth World Conference on Women, Beijing, China, 4-15 September 1995.* New York: U.N. Publishing, 1996.

U.N. Fund for Population Activities. *Proceedings of the Fourth World Conference on Women, Beijing, China, 1995.* New York: U.N. Publishing, 1996.

Websites of Note

http://www.undp.org/fwcw/daw1.htm [U.N. Fourth World conference on Women]

http://www.un.org/geninfo/bp/women.html [Fourth World Conference on Women (1995)]

http://www.igc.org/beijing/beijing.html [Bejing '95: Women, Power & Change]

http://www.iisd.ca/linkages/4wcw/ [Linkages: Fourth World Conference on Women]

∾ Benedict, Ruth Fulton
(1887–1948)

Ruth Fulton Benedict was one of the first women in the United States to become a professional anthropologist. At the time of her appointment as assistant professor in the Department of Anthropology of Columbia University in 1930, she was the first and only woman on the anthropology faculty. In 1936, her status was elevated to that of associate professor, and in 1948, just three months before her untimely death of coronary thrombosis at the age of sixtyone, she was made a full professor.

She studied as an undergraduate with Elsie Clews Parsons, who later helped to fund her research, and then as a graduate student with Franz Boas, one of the founders of anthropology in the United States. Benedict went on, with Margaret Mead and Edward Sapir, to help found "culture and personality" studies, which attempted to link personalities of individuals to the cultural form of their societies. Benedict believed that certain characteristic patterns of personalities could be found within each culture and that these overall patterns could be described in psychological terms. Her two most famous books, *Patterns of Culture* (1934) and *The Chrysanthemum and the Sword* (1946), helped to establish the legitimacy of anthropology in the minds of the American public. *Patterns of Culture* was written about three different cultures—the Zuñi, the Dobu, and the Kwakiutl—which she believed represented different cultural psychological "types," Apollonian and Dionysian. *The Chrysanthemum and the Sword* was written during World War II about the Japanese to help Americans understand the psychological makeup of an enemy culture.

One of her goals was to discover the mechanisms behind these patterns so that humans could ultimately determine the way their societies are patterned. She wanted human beings to be able to organize and shape their own cultures "with intelligence." She believed that complex behavior was learned, that biology did not determine cultural forms, and that all human "races" were equal. In 1940, she wrote *Race, Science and Politics,* in which she argued that differences between groups of people could be explained effectively only in terms of the different cultures from which they come rather than innate biological differences. The intent of the book was political; her aim was to show the fallacies on which Nazism and all other racist philosophies rest.

Because of a childhood illness, Benedict lost most of her hearing at a young age. Combined with her own shyness, her deafness made fieldwork an unpleasant chore for her. Nevertheless, she went out to the American Southwest and worked among the Serrano (summer 1922), the Zuñi (1924, 1925, and 1927), the Pima (1927), the Apache (summer 1930), and the Blackfoot (summer 1938). *(See also: Higher Education; Mead, Margaret)*

—**Steven Mandeville-Gamble**

Further Reading
Benedict, Ruth. *The Chrysanthemum and the Sword.* Boston: Houghton Mifflin, 1946.
———. *Patterns of Culture.* Boston: Houghton Mifflin, 1934.
———. *Race, Science and Politics.* New York: Viking, 1940.
Caffrey, Margaret. *Ruth Benedict.* Austin: University of Texas Press, 1989.
Mead, Margaret. *Ruth Benedict.* New York: Columbia University Press, 1974.
Wenner-Gren Foundation for Anthropological Research. *Ruth Fulton Benedict: A Memorial.* New York: Viking Fund, 1949.

∾ Benevolence

Benevolence refers to the charity and missionary activities of antebellum women, adapting the noblesse oblige of the European nobility to the rising middle class in the United States. From the colonial and revolutionary periods, benevolence was integrated into the prescribed activities for middle-class women, first as part of the late eighteenth-century concept of republican motherhood that defined women's role in the new nation and then during the nineteenth century as an aspect of woman's sphere and of its attendant concept of woman's influence. In addition to their educational, religious, and missionary efforts at home and abroad, middle-class women dispensed their aid and comfort to the deserving poor and needy of early industrial America through their voluntary associations.

Charity activities fell within the historic, preindustrial sexual division of labor, and therefore within the limits of the private, domestic woman's sphere, although these sanctioned benevolence efforts required women to enter the public sphere and to undertake organizational and fundraising enterprises that demanded both political and financial acumen. Through an astute application of piety, one of the traits of true womanhood, true women parlayed women's imperative to benevolence to support women's venture into the public and political arenas without challenging the legitimacy of the gender limitations imposed by woman's sphere. Thus, conservative spokeswomen and women's magazines could be and were enlisted to employ their unimpeachable respectability and their considerable influence to promote women's charity activities that established self-help agencies, educational institutions, and even small businesses to provide job training and employment for women and girls. Benevolence work provided a classic model of the dynamic of domestic feminism that expanded woman's sphere into the public arena without challenging its assumption that women belonged in the private sphere.

Benevolence efforts paved the way for women's entry into many Victorian reform movements. The earliest benevolent groups were sponsored by ministers, but it was the women in their congregations who provided the working membership. Eventually, women established separate voluntary associations such as the Boston Female Society for Missionary Purposes, founded in 1800, which financially supported educating ministers and sending male missionaries to serve the Native American tribes of the West in addition to providing material and spiritual assistance to the poor of Boston. By the 1820s, more secular women's benevolent groups were established that went beyond the traditional "Lady Bountiful" distribution of food and clothes to the deserving poor. For example, Boston women organized the Seaman's Aid Society to provide assistance for the widows and orphans of American sailors through establishing a sewing workshop to employ these women and their daughters. After the Civil War, such efforts focused women's energies on various causes and issues associated with social welfare and community improvement.

During the nineteenth century, women sponsored craft fairs and used the sale of their donated handcrafted items to raise the funds necessary to support their charity services and agencies. Ironically, the actual handling of the money required the presence and participation of male trustees because antebellum women lacked the legal identity required to manage their own or public funds. By the end of the nineteenth century, legal incorporation of women's benevolent institutions required that male boards of trustees replace the female volunteers who had established and capably managed thriving institutions.

The experience and success of women's benevolence activities before the Civil War made possible and respectable women's participation in latter-nineteenth-century civic politics. Ultimately, the development of social work as a woman's profession and many of the accomplishments of the Progressive Era can be traced to the humble amateur efforts of women's benevolence that began in the early nineteenth century. The rise and increase of governmentally supported social welfare programs before and after World War II depended on the participation of civic and religious women's groups to provide the volunteer workforce for such services to the community. By the 1980s, the increased participation of married women in the paid labor force drained the reservoir of volunteer middle-class matrons who historically had been crucial to the survival of community service organizations such as Meals on Wheels, the Girl Scouts, and the Boy Scouts. *(See also: Black Women's Clubs; Cult of True Womanhood; Republican Motherhood; Seamen's Aid Society; Voluntarism)*

—**Angela M. Howard**

Further Reading

Ginzberg, Lori D. *Women and the Work of Benevolence: Morality, Politics, and Class in the Nineteenth Century United States.* New Haven, CT: Yale University Press, 1990.

Scott, Anne Firor. "Women's Voluntary Associations in the Forming of American Society." In *Making the Invisible Woman Visible,* edited by Anne Fior Scott, 274-94. Urbana: University of Illinois Press, 1984.

Zophy, Angela Howard. "A True Woman's Duty 'To Do Good': Sarah Josepha Hale and Benevolence in Antebellum America."

In *The Moment of Decision: Biographical Essays on American Character and Regional Identity,* edited by Randall M. Miller and John R. McKivigan, 155-69. Westport, CT: Greenwood, 1994.

⌇ Berdache

Many Native American cultures accepted people who took on the gender roles associated with the biologically opposite sex. The controversial French/North African term *berdache* refers to these individuals. Such women or, more commonly, men were often accorded positions of high prestige as people possessing great spiritual power.

Commonly, women who became berdaches discovered their male identity in their dreams through the intercession of supernatural powers. Alternately, girl children who played with male-identified toys were allowed to take up male gender identities. From that time forward, they would live their lives as men, go on hunting parties, fight in battles, and take wives. Interestingly enough, their wives are rarely portrayed in ethnographic accounts as being different from other women. The cultures that accepted female homosexuality include Chiricahua, Creek, Crow, Hopi, Mandan, Maricopa, Menomini, Natchez, Navaho, Ojibwa, Omaha, Oto, Papago, Ponca, Quinault, Seminole, Tabatulabal, Yuma, Yurok, and Zuñi. *(See also: Lesbianism; Native American Women)*

—**Steven Mandeville-Gamble**

Further Reading

Denig, Edwin Thompson. *Five Indian Tribes of the Upper Missouri: Sioux, Arickaras, Assiniboines, Crees, Crows.* Edited by John C. Ewers. Norman: University of Oklahoma Press, 1961.

Ford, Clennan S., and Frank A. Beach. "Homosexual Behavior." In *Patterns of Sexual Behavior,* pp. 136-40. New York: Harper & Row, 1951.

Greenberg, David F. "Why Was the Berdache Ridiculed?" In *The Many Faces of Homosexuality,* edited by Evelyn Blackwood, 179-89. New York: Herrington, 1986.

Katz, Jonathan. *Gay American History.* Rev. ed. New York: Meridian, 1992.

Williams, Walter L. *The Spirit and the Flesh: Sexual Diversity in American Indian Culture.* Boston: Beacon, 1986.

⌇ Bernhard, Ruth (b. 1905)

Ruth Bernhard is a photographer whose *oeuvre* includes subjects as diverse as photomontages of found objects; detailed examinations of shells, leaves, or other natural commodities; and carefully lit studies of female nudes. The last twenty years have brought Bernhard growing recognition as a notable artist and increasing prominence as an important teacher.

Born in Berlin, she studied at the Berlin Academy of Art for two years before joining her father, designer and typographer Lucien Bernhard, in New York in 1927. She learned photography during a brief interlude as an assistant to an assistant of magazine photographer Ralph Steiner. Her early work attracted the attention of friends of her father who hired her to photograph industrial or architectural designs. She photographed her first nude, impulsively, while working on a commercial assignment in 1934.

She credits a chance meeting with Edward Weston in California in 1935 with inspiring her to work as an artist. She moved to the West Coast and opened a studio in Hollywood. During this period, she produced the surrealist photomontages that are among the most famous of her images. She moved back to the East Coast in 1939 and embarked on another personal project: photographing the shell collection of conchologist Dr. Jeanne S. Schwengel. *Natural History Magazine* purchased this series for a special issue in 1943.

She moved to San Francisco in 1953 and began to teach informally. As her career as an educator developed into workshops in university as well as studio settings, she gradually stopped working as a commercial photographer. In 1976, she completed two limited-edition portfolios of original prints, *The Eternal Body* and *The Gift of the Commonplace,* which showcased work dating from the 1930s to 1970. She received the Dorothea Lange award from the Oakland Museum in 1971. Her work appeared in several gallery and group exhibitions in the 1970s, among them a retrospective at the Friends of Photography Gallery in Carmel in 1979. In 1986, she had her first exhibition at the San Francisco Museum of Modern Art. In her ninth decade, she remains the subject of ever-growing critical acclaim and attention. *(See also: Photography)*

—**Allison Bertrand**

Further Reading

Alinder, James. *Collecting Light: The Photographs of Ruth Bernhard.* Untitled, no. 20. Carmel, CA: Friends of Photography, 1979.

"American Aces: Ruth Bernhard," *U.S. Camera* 1 (June 1939): 52-55.

Bernhard, Ruth. *The Eternal Body: A Collection of Fifty Nudes.* Text by Margaretta K. Mitchell. Carmel, CA: Photography West Graphics, 1986.

Lufkin, Liz. "Ruth Bernhard," *American Photographer* 20 (April 1988): 60-66.

Mitchell, Margaretta K. "Ruth Bernhard." In *Recollections: Ten Women of Photography,* edited by Margaretta K. Mitchell, 30-32. New York: Viking, 1979.

❧ Bethune, Mary McLeod (1875–1955)

Educator, clubwoman, and civil rights leader Mary McLeod Bethune grew up in an extended family on a farm near Mayesville, South Carolina. Born on July 10, 1875, the fifteenth of seventeen children, to former slaves Samuel and Patsy (McIntosh) McLeod, she became one of the most widely known African American women of the twentieth century. Her parents sacrificed so that Mary Jane McLeod could attend the Trinity Presbyterian Mission School for Negroes, where Emma Wilson, the African American mission school founder, gave her encouragement to pursue further education and found a white benefactor to finance her education at Scotia Seminary in Concord, North Carolina.

Her graduation in 1894 led to further education as an African missionary by attending Moody Bible Institute in Chicago, Illinois. Too young to secure a position following her graduation in 1895, she returned to the South to teach at Lucy Laney's Haines Institute in Augusta, Georgia, and later at Kendall Institute in Sumter, South Carolina, where she met and later married dry goods employee Albertus Bethune. In 1898, their only son, Albert McLeod Bethune, was born. The couple moved to Savannah, Georgia, where Albertus had been offered a teaching position, but soon, Mary took her infant son to her new teaching position at a missionary school in Palatka, Florida, where she established a Presbyterian school in 1900, followed by an independent school in 1902.

On a visit to Daytona Beach, she witnessed problems faced by black railroad workers. Bethune decided to follow the examples of her mentors, Wilson and Laney, and in October 1904, she founded the Daytona Normal and Industrial Institute for Negro Girls. To operate the school, Bethune initiated fund-raising techniques that included concerts, festivals, and lectures to purchase land, erect buildings, and pay for the educational services that expanded to 250 students and included boys two years later. She separated from her husband to continue her mission.

During the next twenty years, she built this school as a community asset. Day and night classes gave students the rudiments of literacy and the work ethic. Her students carried education to turpentine camps in the region through mission schools and received the help of the two black churches in the area. Bethune spoke to churches, lodges, clubs, and white philanthropists to solicit funds for the school. Her dedication gained the patronage of wealthy visitors to Daytona Beach: Thomas H. White of White Sewing Machine Company, John D. Rockefeller of Standard Oil, and James M. Gamble of Proctor & Gamble Enterprises. Wealthy white women of the Ladies' Advisory Board assisted Bethune's efforts. Students raised money as a traveling singing troupe that provided entertainment at jails and hotels. When white hospitals denied service to black patients and training for black residents and nurses, Bethune organized McLeod Hospital in 1911 to serve the community and to provide training for black physicians and nurses. By 1914, the school offered a full high school course, as well as training for cooks, nurses, teachers, and homemakers. Combining academic, manual, and moral education, the school had over three hundred students and a staff of twenty-five by 1922. A few years later, the school merged with a men's college to become Bethune-Cookman College, whose motto was "Enter to Learn/Depart to Serve." By 1943, the college awarded its first bachelor of science degree in elementary education and was accredited with an "A" rating.

Education and service had a broader meaning for Bethune. Within the black women's club movement, Bethune served as president of the Florida Federation of Colored Women's Clubs, as a Red Cross Lecturer of the Potomac Division, and a founder of the Circle of Negro War Relief of New York City during World War I, during which time her long-estranged husband died in 1918. She gave impetus for Florida clubwomen to open a home for wayward and delinquent girls in Ocala in 1920 and helped organize the Southeastern Association of Colored Women. She served as vice president of the Commission on Interracial Cooperation and helped to found both the National Association of Wage Earners and International Council of Women of the Darker Races of the World. As president for two terms in the National Association of Colored Women (NACW; 1924–1928), Bethune established the national headquarters for the NACW and advised the Coolidge and Hoover administrations on African American educational issues through the National Child Welfare Commission.

Bethune's role as political adviser raised her awareness about the need for black women to have a national coalition to effect political change. Thus, in 1935, she founded the National Council of Negro Women, an umbrella organization uniting various black women's groups to pressure the political system. She served as its president until 1949, while serving as a life member and president (1936–1951) of the Association for the Study of Negro Life and History, as president of the National Association of Teachers in Colored Schools, as vice president of the National Urban League, and on several committees in the National Association for the Advancement of Colored People (NAACP), an interracial organization that awarded her the Spingarn Medal in 1935, making her the second African American woman to receive this honor.

These political, club, and interracial activities brought her into regular contact with Eleanor Roosevelt, another humanitarian who shared Bethune's concern for youth and for the oppressed minorities. Bethune became the director of minority affairs in the New Deal's National Youth Administration (1936–1943). In August 1936, she brought black leaders serving in the Roosevelt administration to her home, leading to the formation of the Federal Council on Negro Affairs, often called the Black Cabinet.

All this activity took its toll on her health. Her chronic asthma forced her to restrict her travels and to relinquish the presidency of Bethune-Cookman College in 1942, yet she accepted the role as a second alternate for the NAACP to the San Francisco Conference charged with the writing of the charter of the United Nations. While she was en route to California, President Roosevelt died. Eleanor Roosevelt presented his cane to Bethune in remembrance of her service and their friendship. In addition to this personal honor,

Bethune won the Frances Drexel Award for Distinguished Service in 1937, the Thomas Jefferson Award in 1942, the Medal of Honor and Merit from Haiti in 1949, and the Star of Africa from Liberia in 1952.

On her seventy-fifth birthday in 1950, she settled into her home on the Bethune-Cookman campus, retiring from public life yet continuing the activity of handling the development of a black resort, Bethune-Volusia Beach; establishing the Bethune Foundation; receiving twelve honorary degrees; and serving as her country's representative at the inauguration of Liberian President William Tubman in January 1952. Bethune died of a heart attack on May 18, 1955. She was honored after death when her statue was dedicated on July 10, 1974, in Washington, D.C.'s Lincoln Park, the first public monument dedicated to an African American or woman in the nation's capital. (See also: Black Women; Democratic Party; Higher Education for Southern Women; National Association for the Advancement of Colored People; National Association of Colored Women; National Council of Negro Women; New Deal)

—Dorothy C. Salem

Further Reading

The National Black Women's History Archives is located in the Bethune home in Washington, D.C., a historical site. Her other "home" in Daytona Beach, Florida, at Bethune-Cookman College, holds the Mary Bethune Papers, Bethune Foundation.

Bennett, Lerone, Jr. "No Crystal Stair: The Black Woman in History," Ebony 32 (August 1977): 164-65, 167.

Brewer, William. "Personal: Mary McLeod Bethune," Journal of Negro History 40 (1955): 393-94.

Holt, Rackham. Mary McLeod Bethune. Garden City, NY: Doubleday, 1964.

Lefall, Dolores C., and Janet L. Sims. "Mary McLeod Bethune— The Educator," Journal of Negro Education 45 (Summer 1976): 342-59.

Mays, Benjamin. "The Most Extraordinary Black Woman I Have Ever Known," Ebony 32 (August 1977): 139-40.

Peare, Catherine Owen. Mary McLeod Bethune. New York: Vanguard, 1951.

Ross, B. Joyce. "Mary McLeod Bethune and the National Youth Administration: A Case Study of Power Relationships in the Black Cabinet of Franklin D. Roosevelt," Journal of Negro History 60 (January 1975): 1-28.

Smith, Elaine M. "Mary McLeod Bethune and the National Youth Administration." In Clio Was a Woman: Studies in the History of American Women, edited by Mabel E. Deutrich and Virginia C. Purdy, 1093-1121. Washington, DC: Howard University Press, 1980.

Sterne, Emma Gelders. Mary McLeod Bethune. New York: Knopf, 1957.

⤳ Bevier, Isabel (1860–1942)

Chemist, educator, and administrator, Isabel Bevier was a celebrated pioneer in the field of home economics. Trained in several leading scientific institutions, Bevier sought to develop an applied science that would address the interest of women. As head of the Department of Home Economics and vice president of the Home Economics Extension Department at the University of Illinois, Bevier became nationally known for her plans for developing and implementing a scientific curriculum dealing with household activities.

Born on an Ohio farm near Plymouth, to Calib Bevier and Cornella (Brinkerhoff) Bevier, Isabel was the youngest of nine children. Other than that she attended Wooster Preparatory and taught at a country school, little information exists about Bevier's early years and education. By her own account, Bevier decided to enter the field of science following the tragic death of her fiancé Elmer Strain in 1888. She became the first woman to apply to Chase School of Applied Science in Cleveland, where she studied with Albert A. Smith while teaching at the Pennsylvania College of Women. Smith encouraged Bevier to pursue a career in food chemistry, a new field that he felt would offer women secure positions in science. Taking his advice, Bevier contacted Professor Wilbur O. Atwater and Ellen Richards, both leaders in the field, and began working with them at the Massachusetts Institute of Technology. In 1898, Bevier took a position as professor at Lake Erie College for Women, where she taught and administrated the chemistry department and organized the college's domestic arrangements. Familiar with her work, President Andrew Sloan Draper of the University of Illinois asked Bevier to develop a department of household science at his university. Bevier, who felt more comfortable in a coeducational setting, jumped at the chance to head a department at a major land grant institution and joined the staff in 1900.

Bevier's work at the University of Illinois became one of the first serious efforts to establish home economics at the university level. Under her direction, students were taught to approach food as chemists would, and Bevier made courses in chemistry and natural science requirements for admission to the department. The success of her department won the continued support of President Draper and received high marks of excellence from the Carnegie Foundation. Given her reputation, various institutions and organizations frequently asked Bevier to lecture and lend her advice. As vice president of the American Home Economics Association (1908–1910) and later president (1911–1913), Bevier's ideals for the field became recognized nationally. At the University of Illinois, she directed the extension service that brought applied science to the noncollege farm population. Bevier continued to head the department until she retired from her post in 1921.

Bevier's work to expand the field of home economics did not end with her "retirement." She helped organize the home economics departments at the University of California at Los Angeles (1921–1923) and the University of Arizona (1925). She was the first woman named Professor Emerita at the University of Illinois and received honorary Ph.D.s from Iowa State in 1920 and Wooster University in 1936. Her articles appeared in *Women's World* and *Science*. Her major

work, *Home Economics in Education* (1924), documents the history of the movement and outlines her philosophy for developing an applied science that addresses the interests of women. At her death from a heart attack in 1942, Bevier left an endowment for a lecture series at the Department of Home Economics at the University of Illinois. These lectures, Bevier stipulated, would provide knowledge concerning science, economics, and aesthetics that women can apply to their daily tasks in homes, families, and the communities. These stipulations neatly summed up Bevier's mission throughout her distinguished career. *(See also: American Home Economics Association; Higher Education; Home Economics; Science)*

—**Barbara Shircliffe**

Further Reading

Bane, Juliet Lita. *The Story of Isabel Bevier.* Peoria, IL: Chas. A. Bennett, 1955.
Bevier, Isabel. *Home Economics in Education.* Philadelphia: J. B. Lippincott, 1928.
Matthews, G. *"Just a Housewife": The Rise and Fall of Domesticity in America.* New York: Oxford University Press, 1987.
Shapiro, L. *Perfection Salad: Women and Cooking at the Turn of the Century.* New York: Oxford University Press, 1987.

✑ Birth Control

The term *birth control* was first popularized by Margaret Sanger during a campaign for the legalization of contraception that began about 1914. But birth control in its generic sense—referring to any method of controlling reproduction, including abstinence and abortion—is as old as civilization. Traditional birth control arose from both women's desire for control over reproduction and community interests in controlling population size.

The first political campaign for birth control was not directly connected with women's rights agitation. Rather, it developed in early-nineteenth-century England out of the neo-Malthusians' attempt to reduce birthrates among the poor to improve their standard of living and thereby reduce their social radicalism. Utopian socialists in the United States also preached and practiced childbirth by choice. In the 1870s, U.S. feminists began to agitate quietly for birth control, using the slogan "Voluntary Motherhood." They sought not only control over reproduction but also over sexual activity, rejecting an ancient marital tradition that required women's sexual submission to their husbands. For these feminists, the recommended birth control method was abstinence except when conception was desired.

Contraception, a specific form of birth control, refers to methods that allow sexual intercourse without conception. Mechanical contraceptive techniques are of ancient origin and operate on the simple principle of blocking the cervical opening. Homemade pessaries were often combined with homemade spermicides and, if prepared and used carefully, could be effective. In the late nineteenth century, however, commercially produced thin rubber allowed the manufacture of modern vaginal diaphragms. In the first decades of the twentieth century, U.S. feminists active in the then-strong socialist movement became aware of the availability of these devices in European clinics; they began a civil disobedience campaign to resist the antiobscenity laws that made it illegal even to discuss contraception, and several served jail time for their convictions. Led by radical feminist activists such as Emma Goldman and, especially, Margaret Sanger and backed by a national grassroots agitation, they defied the law by distributing birth control leaflets and opening clinics that fitted women with diaphragms. They were gradually victorious. In the 1920s, most states legalized contraception by physicians' prescription.

The feminists' victories in making contraception legal and respectable created both gains and losses for women. Contraceptives were more available, but promoters of birth control increasingly separated themselves from women's-rights goals. While men could buy condoms over the counter in drugstores, access to effective women's contraceptives, such as diaphragms, IUDs, or hormones, was controlled by physicians rather than by women. Contraception helped women limit family size and permitted women more sexual freedom, and by mid-century, it had an enormous impact, strengthening the trend toward smaller families and women's employment. But it did not produce the radical increase in women's freedom and political power and participation that the early birth control campaigners had hoped for.

With the second wave of feminism in the late 1960s and 1970s, feminists reclaimed birth control in a renewed campaign for women's reproductive self-control, mainly focusing on the right to legal abortion but also taking in issues of better and safer contraception and noncoercive sterilization. States began repealing antiabortion laws in the 1960s, and by the time of the *Roe v. Wade* decision in 1973, eighteen states had already done so. Women's demand encouraged the development of a hormonal contraceptive pill, which entered the market in 1960 and was immediately successful. Soon afterward, a woman's health movement began protesting the pill's inadequate testing and exposed the health dangers of what was then a very high dosage of hormones; its pressure hastened the development of lower-dose pills. The women's movement also forced change in the double standard that governed sterilization up through the 1970s, a policy that made it difficult for young, middle-class, white women to get access to voluntary sterilization while imposing coercive, sometimes even undisclosed sterilizations on poor women of color. The last campaign was extremely effective, and today there is much less coercive sterilization and much easier access to sterilization as a freely chosen form of birth control.

A well-funded antiabortion movement started by the Catholic hierarchy in the 1970s picked up support from conservative Protestants in the 1980s and has succeeded not only in limiting women's access to abortion but also in hindering contraceptive developments. Both the "morning after" pill, a high hormonal dose that prevents uterine implantation, and RU-486, which causes shedding of the uterine lining, have been successfully opposed by the antiabortion forces. *(See also: Abortion; Sanger, Margaret Louise; Socialist Feminism; "Voluntary Motherhood")*

—**Linda Gordon**

Further Reading

Brodie, Janet Farrell. *Contraception and Abortion in Nineteenth-Century America*. Ithaca, NY: Cornell University Press, 1994.

Gordon, Linda. *Woman's Body, Woman's Right: A Social History of Birth Control in America*. New York: Viking/Penguin, 1976. Rev. ed., 1990.

McCann, Carole R. *Birth Control Politics in the United States, 1916–45*. Ithaca, NY: Cornell University Press, 1994.

Petchesky, Rosalind. *Abortion and Woman's Choice*. New York: Longman, 1984.

Reagan, Leslie. *When Abortion Was a Crime: Women, Medicine, and the Law in the United States, 1867–1973*. Berkeley: University of California Press, 1997.

Tone, Andrea, ed. *Controlling Reproduction: An American History*. Wilmington, DE: Scholarly Resources, 1996.

๛ Birth Control Clinical Research Bureau (BCCRB)

The Birth Control Clinical Research Bureau (BCCRB) was founded in New York City by Margaret Sanger (1879–1966) in 1923. The organization's history is somewhat tangled, but its services remained essentially the same despite myriad affiliations. The BCCRB was originally a department of the American Birth Control League (1923–1928), but when Sanger resigned from the league in 1928, she severed the clinic, retaining full control over it. Eleven years later, in 1939, the BCCRB rejoined the American Birth Control League to form the Birth Control Federation of America (BCFA). In 1940, the BCCRB changed its name to the Margaret Sanger Research Bureau (MSRB) to honor its founder, and in 1942, the BCFA became the Planned Parenthood Federation of America. In 1973, the MSRB became Planned Parenthood of New York City.

The BCCRB was the first American doctor-run birth control clinic and served as a model for the establishment of other clinics around the country. It provided not only contraceptive services but also gynecological exams, marriage counseling, and fertility services. Because the medical profession for the most part did not consider birth control safe or effective in the 1920s, a main goal of the clinic was to compile accurate patient statistics. Dr. Hannah Mayer Stone, medical director of the clinic from 1925 to 1942, proved through the analysis of nearly 100,000 patient records that the diaphragm/spermicidal jelly combination was both safe and effective. These tests also demonstrated that birth control could be successfully employed by the average woman.

Contraceptive research and training were other important services provided by the BCCRB in helping to establish birth control in America. Even if they were inclined to support birth control, the omission of contraceptive study from many medical schools made it difficult for doctors to advise their patients on the subject. The BCCRB offered training to doctors and medical students and conducted research on newly emerging contraceptive technologies, including the anovulant pill.

The BCCRB was the organization that best embodied Margaret Sanger's vision of birth control service and the one whose day-to-day operations she watched most closely. Sanger hoped that by providing the BCCRB as a model, other states, cities, and finally the federal government would be convinced of the merits of such clinics and that they would incorporate birth control into public health programs. Sanger's dream was not fully realized in her lifetime, but the BCCRB did provide the example for a chain of privately run birth control clinics across the country. *(See also: American Birth Control League; Birth Control; Sanger, Margaret Louise)*

—**Cathy Moran Hajo**

Further Reading

Chesler, Ellen. *Woman of Valor: Margaret Sanger and the Birth Control Movement in America.* New York: Simon & Schuster, 1992.

The Margaret Sanger Papers. Smith College Collections and Documents from Other Archives. Bethesda, MD, University Publications of America, 1995. Microform.

Reed, James. *The Birth Control Movement and American Society: From Private Vice to Public Virtue.* Princeton, NJ: Princeton University Press, 1978.

Stix, Regine K., and Frank W. Notestein. *Controlled Fertility.* Baltimore, MD: Johns Hopkins University Press, 1940.

❧ Birth Control Review (1917–1940)

The *Birth Control Review* was founded by Margaret Sanger as a vehicle for propagandizing her fight for the legalization of birth control in the United States. Until March 1929, Sanger's name remained on the masthead, although the actual managing editors were constantly changed, especially during the *Review*'s first five years.

Early issues reveal a radical tone. Sanger herself in a 1917 editorial called on mothers to take direct action to prevent the drafting of their sons. The very first issue included an article describing Sanger's own experience with the nation's first birth control clinic, which operated briefly in the Brownsville section of Brooklyn before it was shut down by the police in the fall of 1916. Left-wing influence can also be seen in articles by Eugene V. Debs and an organizer for the steelworkers union, as well as in the *Review*'s art, which was both avant-garde and feminist up to the middle 1920s. Feminist writers saw birth control as a fulfillment of woman's nature, rejecting celibacy as a method of contraception suited

only for monks and nuns. Even so, writers carefully avoided any direct reference to birth control as a means to female sexual fulfillment.

Sanger and her followers wanted the widest dissemination of their views, so the *Birth Control Review* was hawked on the streets of New York and other cities by volunteers. As late as 1926, one of the most zealous of these volunteers, Kitty Marion, was arrested for selling the *Birth Control Review* on the streets of Manhattan. Although the case was quickly dismissed, Sanger used it as an example of the continuing problem of censorship of even the public advocacy of birth control.

In 1924, the *Birth Control Review* became the official journal of Sanger's American Birth Control League. With a more conservative strategy appealing to wealthy, upper-class women and physicians, the *Review* lost its radical tone. Most articles were written by academics, physicians, and liberal Protestant and Jewish clergy, signifying the moral and social approval of birth control among the professional establishment. There were also frequent articles emphasizing the world population problem and birth control as an element in the eugenics movement. In fact, Sanger proposed that the *Birth Control Review* might become a joint publication of the Birth Control League and the Eugenics Society in 1928, but the readers of the journal were hostile to any such merger.

Much of the financial support for the *Review* came from advertisements and direct contributions from Sanger's second husband, J. Noah H. Slee. His company, Three In One Oil, was usually the only major advertiser in the journal. Consequently, when Sanger lost control of both the American Birth Control League and the *Birth Control Review* after her long stay in Europe during 1927 to 1928, Slee withdrew his advertisements and subsidies, and the *Review* declined accordingly. In the 1930s, it contained little or no art, and there were fewer articles by prominent advocates of birth control. Instead, the *Review* became mainly a newsletter for the American Birth Control League and its successor, the Birth Control Federation, although Pearl Buck wrote a brief article as late as November 1939. The last issue appeared in January 1940 as part of a program for the Birth Control Federation's annual meeting. *(See also: American Birth Control League; Birth Control; Sanger, Margaret Louise)*

—**Neil W. Hogan**

Further Reading

Birth Control Review. New York: Da Capo, 1970.

Chesler, Ellen. *Woman of Valor: Margaret Sanger and the Birth Control Movement in America.* New York: Doubleday, 1992.

Gordon, Linda. *Woman's Body, Woman's Right: A Social History of Birth Control in America.* Rev. ed. New York: Penguin Viking, 1990.

Hines, Norman E. *Medical History of Contraception.* New York: Schocken, 1970.

Kennedy, David M. *Birth Control in America: The Career of Margaret Sanger.* New Haven, CT: Yale University Press, 1970.

McCann, Carole R. *Birth Control Politics in the United States, 1916–1945*. Ithaca, NY: Cornell University Press, 1994.

⮞ Bishop, Elizabeth (1911–1979)

Elizabeth Bishop was a major twentieth-century poet whose life and work explored the tensions between her native New England's traditional past and her own restless career overseas and on both American continents. Bishop's paternal grandfather had directed construction of the Boston Public Library and Museum of Fine Arts. After her father died suddenly during her infancy and her mother suffered a nervous collapse, Bishop was reared by her maternal grandparents on their farm in Nova Scotia. (Her short stories "In the Village" and "Gwendolyn" record her life there.) At six, she returned to her father's family in Worcester, where her education was interrupted by illness. Yet she read widely, and her life's pattern was set. As she later said of her early years, "I was always a sort of a guest, and I think I've always felt like that."

Bishop began writing poetry at Vassar College, where her schoolmates included Eleanor Clark, Muriel Rukeyser, and Mary McCarthy. With the latter two, she edited and published a literary magazine, *Con Spirito*, which competed with the more traditional *Vassar Review*. In New York in 1934, Bishop met the poet Marianne Moore (1887–1972), who became her lifelong friend and, for a few years, her mentor and model. "From Brooklyn, over the Brooklyn Bridge," Bishop wrote in a poem to her, "on this fine morning, please come flying."

In the 1930s and 1940s, Bishop traveled and lived in Europe, North Africa, Florida, and Mexico; in 1945, her first collection of poems appeared as *North and South,* whose title embodied the geographic and temperamental poles of her life and work. In the next decade, she received a Guggenheim Fellowship (1947), served the Library of Congress as a consultant in poetry (1949–1950), and won the 1956 Pulitzer Prize for Poetry for an expanded collection, *North and South—A Cold Spring* (1955).

Supported by a small trust fund, Bishop shared a house in the Brazilian mountains near Petropolis and an apartment in Rio de Janeiro with architect Lota Costellat de Macedo Soares from 1951 to 1966. During these years, Bishop translated *The Diary of Helen Morley* (1957), originally written in the 1890s by a young girl in Diamantina, and with Emanuel Brasil she edited and translated *An Anthology of Twentieth-Century Brazilian Poetry* (1972). In a new book of poetry, *Questions of Travel* (1965), many pieces represented Brazil and its people.

In 1967, on a visit to New York, Bishop's companion committed suicide, after which the poet lived and worked mostly in the United States, from 1969 to 1977 as poet in residence at Harvard University. Her *Complete Poems* won the National Book Award in 1969, and a later collection, *Geography III,* won the 1977 *Books Abroad*/Neustadt International Prize for Literature—the first time this prize was awarded to a woman writer. Elizabeth Bishop died of a stroke in 1979, but the subtle voice of her poetry continues to balance the plain sense of her native north with the ravishing wonder of her journey south. "Think of the long trip home . . . ," she writes in "Questions of Travel":

> What childishness is it that . . .
> we are determined to rush
> to see the . . .
> tiniest green hummingbird in the world? . . .
> Oh, must we dream our dreams
> and have them, too?

(See also: Women Writers)

—**Craig White**

Further Reading

Austin, David Craig. "Elizabeth Bishop." In *Modern American Women Writers,* edited by Elaine Showalter, Lea Baechler, and A. Walton Litz, 9-22. New York: Scribner, 1991.

Costello, Bonnie. *Elizabeth Bishop: Questions of Mastery.* Cambridge, MA: Harvard University Press, 1991.

Goldensohn, Lorrie. *Elizabeth Bishop: The Biography of a Poet.* New York: Columbia University Press, 1992.

MacMahon, Candace W. *Elizabeth Bishop: A Bibliography, 1927–1979.* Charlottesville: University Press of Virginia, 1980.

Merrin, Jeredith. *An Enabling Humility: Marianne Moore, Elizabeth Bishop, and the Uses of Tradition.* New Brunswick, NJ: Rutgers University Press, 1990.

Millier, Brett C. *Elizabeth Bishop: Life and the Memory of It.* Berkeley: University of California Press, 1993.

Travisano, Thomas J. *Elizabeth Bishop: Her Artistic Development.* Charlottesville: University Press of Virginia, 1988.

⮞ Blaché, Alice Guy (1875–1968)

Alice Guy Blaché was a producer, director, inventor, writer, the first woman commercial filmmaker, and along with the Lumière brothers in France and the Edison group in the United States, one of the originators of film narrative itself.

A well-educated, middle-class Parisian, Alice Guy was working as industrialist Leon Gaumont's secretary in 1895 when she became interested in the brand new cinematographic apparatus that Louis Lumière was then perfecting. She shot her first film, a fantasy called *La Fée aux Choux,* at Gaumont's home early in 1896—surely one of the first narrative films ever made. Thereafter, she made dozens of films for Gaumont and helped in developing the cameras, processing equipment, and projectors used in early filmmaking, all with a careful eye toward technical standardization and exhibition of films in front of larger audiences.

Between 1896 and 1901, she was responsible for *all* of Gaumont's filmmaking projects, and as such, she was a founder of what would become France's largest media empire. Guy hired directors such as Louis Feuillade, Ferdinand Zecca, and others, many of whom would achieve international renown on their own. It seemed, according to one writer, that by surrounding herself with such remarkable subordinates, "with one mighty stroke, she had created the entire early French film industry."

She directed hundreds of short films during this time, and produced two of the earliest feature films: *Passion* (1902), one of the longest films of its period, and *Life of Christ* (1906). In 1906, she began some of the earliest experiments with synchronized sound, producing some one hundred films in the Chronophone system.

In 1907, she married Herbert Blaché and settled in the United States, where her husband was to act as Gaumont's U.S. distributor. Bored with domestic life, she returned to directing at a small studio in Flushing, New York. Released under the banner of the Solax Company, her films gained a reputation for quality with critics. Guy Blaché worked in thrillers, romances, and New Jersey-shot Westerns. At Solax, both filmmaking and processing were under her total control, and as Solax began to produce unusual longer films, the studio's output became eagerly sought after by distributors. By 1915, a trade publication could say that "to her, credit is due for many of the best-known features produced in the early days of feature productions." World War I brought great changes to the American film industry, and independent operations such as Guy Blaché's were soon swallowed up by large combines. She directed her last film, *Tarnished Reputations,* in 1920. In 1922, her marriage ended, leaving her disconsolate. Her own career ended precipitously, but Blaché argued tirelessly for programs in film education, believing this would open channels in the industry that were previously closed to women.

Although she was recognized as a Knight of the Legion of Honor in a ceremony at the Cinémathéque Française in 1953, she died in undeserved obscurity in the United States at the age of ninety-five. *(See also: Woman's Film)*

—**Kevin Jack Hagopian**

Further Reading

Blaché, Alice Guy. *The Memoirs of Alice Guy Blaché.* Edited by Anthony Slide, translated by Roberta and Simone Blaché. Metuchen, NJ: Scarecrow, 1986.

Heck-Rabi, Louise. "Alice Guy Blaché: Photoplay Pioneer." In *Women Filmmakers: A Critical Reception,* pp. 1-25. Metuchen, NJ: Scarecrow, 1984.

Lacassin, Francis. "Out of Oblivion: Alice Guy Blaché," *Sight and Sound* 40 (Summer 1971): 150-55.

Peary, Gerald. "Alice Guy Blaché: Czarina of the Silver Screen." In *Women and the Cinema,* edited by Karyn Kay and Gerald Pear, 139-45. New York: E. P. Dutton, 1977.

Slide, Anthony. *Early Women Directors.* New York: A. S. Barnes, 1977.

❧ Black Women

The African women who were captured, enslaved, and transported by ship to North America from the seventeenth through the nineteenth centuries were usually taken from the Bantu linguistic groups of West Africa that lived in the areas watered by the Gambia and Niger rivers. West African women were generally agriculturalists, an occupation that provided them with skills that would be exploited by their captors. Although slavery and warfare were common on the African continent, nothing like the Atlantic slave trade, with its alarming death toll, or North American chattel slavery were a part of the African woman's experience.

African women were first brought to Jamestown, Virginia, in 1619 to work as indentured servants, but within a generation, some had become slaves in various parts of the American colonies. Brought to the plantations of the South, to small farms and households of the North, black slave women served essentially an economic role. The majority of black women were slaves, but an increasing number achieved free status. A few emerged from slavery to receive recognition for literary creativity, as did colonial New England poets Lucy Terry and Phillis Wheatley. The presence of legal rights for slaves brought a few to the courts. The slave Jenny Slew filed suit in Massachusetts in 1765 for her freedom and won.

Following the American Revolution, northern states abolished slavery through court cases or through legislation calling for gradual emancipation. Although the upper South, Maryland, Delaware, and Virginia had been emancipating slaves in increasing numbers, this trend halted with the invention of the cotton gin, the acquisition of new lands in the West, and the legitimacy given slavery in the Constitution, which guaranteed the rights of slaveholders and guaranteed no tampering with importation until 1808.

The divisions between North and South increased during the nineteenth century. Free black women lived in both regions of the country, residing increasingly in the cities with black institutions such as churches, fraternal associations, schools, and businesses and with greater employment opportunities as domestics, laundresses, seamstresses, or teachers. Married black women worked predominantly in domestic service. Often, they took in boarders or did laundry to supplement the household income. Those with wealth or the privilege of education provided opportunities for the community. Sarah Mapps Douglass returned from her teaching position in New York to establish a high school for black girls in Philadelphia.

Black women formed gender-separate organizations for self-improvement and community uplift as ladies or female antislavery societies, literary societies, church circles, and study circles. Although more difficult to form in the South, black women used church and social clubs for self- and community improvement. With greater freedom in the North, many joined with men to eradicate the evils of society, especially slavery. They raised money for the antislavery movement through fairs and social events. Their homes provided shelter to fugitive slaves. Sojourner Truth, Mary Ann Shadd Cary, the Forten sisters, Frances Ellen Watkins Harper, and many others traveled throughout the North giving lectures against slavery. Cary founded a newspaper, *The Provincial*

Freeman, to aid fugitive slaves in their escape to Canada. From the parallels they saw in slavery, these leaders also fought for women's rights to property, children, divorce, and suffrage.

During the Civil War, they raised money for the Union, recruited black soldiers, nursed the injured in segregated medical facilities, and served as spies. As the fighting ceased, black women worked in their own communities and reached out to the freedmen. Boston women raised money to fund a school in Georgia. Teachers from the North came to establish schools and teach literacy skills in the South. Charlotte Forten left the comfort of Philadelphia to teach in the Port Royal (South Carolina) experiment to prove the freedmen worthy of freedom. Educated black women in the South established schools such as Emma Wilson's mission school in Mayesville, South Carolina; Lucy Laney's Haines Normal and Industrial School in August, Georgia; Mary McLeod Bethune's Daytona (Florida) Normal and Industrial Institute; and Olivia Davidson Washington's Tuskegee (Alabama) Institute.

Political rights also interested black women. Black men won the right to vote with the Fourteenth Amendment, an event that split the predominantly white woman's suffrage movement. Black women pursued the goal of woman suffrage through the American Woman Suffrage Association (AWSA) and the more militant National Woman Suffrage Association (NWSA). The vote was not the only tool for social change. They also worked for moral reform through emerging women's Christian organizations such as the Young Women's Christian Association (YWCA) and the Woman's Christian Temperance Union (WCTU). As women, they saw their calling to use their moral superiority to improve society.

Near the end of the nineteenth century, that moral superiority was not color blind. Increasingly, as local and regional groups merged to form national organizations during the Progressive Era, black women were segregated into racially separate units such as WCTU No. 2 or Phillis Wheatley Ys. Black women did not wait for inclusion to forge their own gender-specific organizations, such as the National Association of Colored Women (1896), the Alpha Suffrage Club (1913), Alpha Kappa Alpha (1908) and Delta Sigma Theta (1913) sororities, and the National Council of Negro Women (1935), or to anchor racial advancement organizations such as the National Association for the Advancement of Colored People (NAACP), Universal Negro Improvement Association, and National Urban League to the communities.

As conditions worsened in the South and opportunities opened in the North as a result of World War I, migrants streamed into cities. Black women organized to meet their needs for temporary shelter, employment, child care, training, and socialization through Cleveland's Phillis Wheatley Association, Brooklyn's Lincoln Settlement, Chicago's Negro Fellowship League, and Atlanta's Neighborhood Union. They added support for the war effort to their many respon-sibilities—hoping their patriotism would result in improved conditions in postwar America. Instead, racial violence increased, as witness to the Red Summer of 1919. By the 1920s, however, the influence of both the New Negro and New Woman was evident in black women. The black female presence was apparent through the cultural rebirth of the Harlem Renaissance, participation of black women in the federal government during the New Deal and World War II years, and the gradual erosion of legal discrimination.

The consistent role of black women in the community placed them in the front lines of the civil rights movement: for example, Rosa Parks and the Woman's Political Council in the Montgomery Bus Boycott; Septima Clark's Highlander Folk School; Diane Nash's role in the student sit-in movement and continuation of the Freedom Rides by representatives from Student Nonviolent Coordinating Committee; Fannie Lou Hamer's testimony at the 1964 Democratic Convention for recognition of the Mississippi Democratic Party delegation; Shirley Chisholm's 1972 bid for the Democratic presidential nomination; the 1977 appointment of the first black female cabinet member, Patricia Harris; and the 1992 election of Carol Moseley-Braun, the first black female in the U.S. Senate.

At the outset of the twenty-first century, close to 25 percent of black women work in skilled or professional occupations, distinguishing themselves in the arts, education, science, politics, religion, and business. The 1990s brought forth many firsts for black women: Mae Jemison became an astronaut; in 1993, Toni Morrison received the Nobel Prize for Literature; the first black woman to serve as U.S. Surgeon General, Joycelyn Elders, candidly confronted the practical issues of teenage sexuality despite the conservative backlash that demanded her resignation in 1995. These achievements cannot hide the problems still faced by many black women, who as single parents are raising children in poverty. Black women continue to address the problems of their less fortunate sisters through health networks such as Billye Avery's National Black Women's Health Project, Marian Edelman's Children's Defense Fund, and Katherine Dunham's Center for Performing Arts in East St. Louis, Illinois. Their tradition of service to community still prevails. *(See also: African American Domestic Workers; Afro-American; Slavery; Triple Jeopardy)*

—**Dorothy C. Salem**

—**Debra L. Newman Ham**

Further Reading

Dannett, Sylvia, ed. *Profiles of Negro Womanhood.* Chicago: Education Heritage, 1964.

Davis, Marianna. *Contributions of Black Women in America.* Columbia, SC: Kenday, 1982.

Harley, Sharon, and Rosalyn Terborg-Penn. *Afro-American Women: Struggles and Images.* New York: Kennikat, 1978.

Hine, Darlene Clark, ed. *Black Women in America: An Historical Encyclopedia.* Brooklyn: Carlson, 1993.

———. *Black Women in United States History.* 16 vols. Brooklyn: Carlson, 1990.

Jones, Jacqueline. *Labor of Love, Labor of Sorrow.* New York: Vintage, 1985.

Kranz, Rachel. *Biographical Dictionary of Black Americans.* New York: Facts on File, 1992.

Lerner, Gerda, ed. *Black Women in White America: A Documentary History.* New York: Random House, 1972.

Salem, Dorothy C. *African American Women: A Biographical Dictionary.* New York: Garland, 1993.

Smith, Jessie Carney. *Notable Black American Women.* 2 vols. Detroit, MI: Gale, 1992, 1996.

Sterling, Dorothy. *We Are Your Sisters: Black Women in the Nineteenth Century.* New York: Norton, 1984.

White, Deborah Gray. *Ar'n't I a Woman? Female Slaves in the Plantation South.* New York: Norton, 1985.

Lerner, Gerda. *The Majority Finds Its Past.* New York: Oxford University Press, 1979.

Neverdon-Morton, Cynthia. *Afro-American Women of the South and the Advancement of the Race, 1895–1925.* Knoxville: University of Tennessee Press, 1989.

Salem, Dorothy C. *To Better Our World: Black Women in Organized Reform, 1890–1920.* New York: Carlson, 1990.

Smith, Susan L. *Sick and Tired of Being Sick and Tired: Black Women's Health Activism in America, 1890–1950.* Philadelphia: University of Pennsylvania Press, 1995.

White, Deborah Gray. "The Cost of Club Work, the Price of Black Feminism." In *Visible Women: New Essays on American Activism,* edited by Nancy A. Hewitt and Suzanne Lebsock, 247-69. Urbana: University of Illinois Press, 1993.

⭐ Black Women's Clubs

Black women's clubs were organized in the late nineteenth century after the rise of a small, but vocal, black middle class. The national organization for the black women's club movement, the National Association of Colored Women, was formed in 1896. Club work was midway between the work of personal charity and professional institutions, and it influenced the direction of social welfare work during the Progressive Era. For African Americans, club work provided services denied because of segregation and discrimination. For black women, the club movement was a way of elevating the status of black womanhood.

Black club women believed that community improvement would uplift their race and that efforts on behalf of working women and girls would uplift their sex. Club women established day nurseries and kindergartens in response to the needs of working mothers. They opened working girls' homes to assist young, black migrants from rural areas with housing, employment information, job training, and moral instruction. Club women also helped to establish institutions such as hospitals and nurses' training schools. Their club activities laid the groundwork for the work of organizations such as the National Urban League and for the profession of social work. Self-respect, public respect, and self-sufficiency were the goals that club women set for themselves and for the women and girls they aided. *(See also: Black Women; National Association of Colored Women)*

—Susan Lynn Smith

Further Reading

Davis, Elizabeth Lindsay. *Lifting as They Climb.* Washington, DC: National Association of Colored Women, 1933.

Giddings, Paula. *When and Where I Enter: The Impact of Black Women on Race and Sex in America.* New York: William Morrow, 1984.

Harley, Sharon, and Rosalyn Terborg-Penn, eds. *The Afro-American Woman: Struggles and Images.* Port Washington, NY: National University Publications, Kennikat, 1978.

Hine, Darlene Clark. *When the Truth Is Told: A History of Black Women's Culture and Community in Indiana, 1875–1950.* Indianapolis, IN: National Council of Negro Women, 1981.

⭐ Blackwell, Alice Stone (1857–1950)

Daughter of nineteenth-century feminists Lucy Stone and Henry Brown Blackwell, Alice Stone Blackwell was involved throughout her life with the cause of feminism. For years, she edited the *Woman's Journal,* founded in 1870 by her mother. A brilliant theorist, writer, scholar, translator, and reformer, Blackwell was also responsible for editing and distributing the "Woman's Column," an early publicity release distributed nationwide for inclusion in the editorial columns and on the opinion pages of the nation's newspapers. She was instrumental in effecting the reunion in 1890 of the two wings of the woman suffrage movement, and later, it was she who prepared the notes used in 1916 by Woodrow Wilson in his historic speech declaring his support for woman suffrage.

In the decades leading to passage of the woman suffrage amendment, millions of flyers and leaflets were prepared and distributed nationwide, most of them signed by Alice Stone Blackwell. Her prose was forthright; her writing style a model of concise persuasion. In addition to the tracts, Alice translated Russian, Armenian, and Spanish poetry, and her biography of her mother, published in 1930, is still useful to scholars. Although she made many public speeches, extreme shyness kept Blackwell from attracting the widespread public and press attention her mother had enjoyed. As a consequence, the value of her contribution to theoretical and political feminism is underrated.

Blackwell was also directly involved in a number of other twentieth-century reform movements. She was a partisan of the Russian Revolution, a friend and publicist for the Russian noblewoman-turned-socialist Marie Breshkovsky, an outspoken opponent of the 1915 slaughter of the Armenians, and a leader in the fight to vindicate Sacco and Vanzetti. Nevertheless, her major efforts throughout her lifetime were on behalf of women. Old, impoverished, and nearly blind, Blackwell maintained her interest in woman's rights up until her death in 1950. *(See also: American Woman Suffrage Association; National American Woman Suffrage Association; Stone, Lucy; Suffrage; Woman's Journal)*

—Andrea Moore Kerr

Further Reading

Catt, Carrie Chapman. *The Ballot and the Bullet*. Philadelphia: A. J. Ferris, 1897.

Hays, Elinor Rice. *Those Extraordinary Blackwells*. New York: Harcourt, Brace & World, 1967.

Merrill, Marlene Deahl, ed. *Growing Up in Boston's Gilded Age: The Journal of Alice Stone Blackwell, 1872–1874*. New Haven, CT: Yale University Press, 1991.

Shaw, Anna Howard. *The Yellow Ribbon Speaker*. New York: C. T. Dillingham, 1891.

๛ Blackwell, Antoinette (Brown) (1825–1921)

Antoinette Blackwell, pioneer woman's rights reformer, theologian, and social scientist, is generally credited with having been the first ordained woman minister in the United States. Blackwell worked as a teacher until she could afford to attend Oberlin College, where she studied theology from 1846 to 1850.

At Oberlin, Blackwell befriended Lucy Stone, the fiery woman's rights activist and Garrisonian abolitionist. In 1850, Stone persuaded Blackwell to speak at the first National Woman's Rights Convention in Worcester, Massachusetts, and her speech repudiating the biblical argument that women should not speak in public established her as a premier feminist theorist. In 1853, she was invited to become pastor of the Congregational Church in South Butler, New York. There, on September 15, 1853, she was ordained a Congregational minister—an American first.

In January 1856, she married Samuel Chase Blackwell—brother of Dr. Elizabeth Blackwell, the first American female physician, and brother-in-law of Lucy Stone—who helped care for their five children, cooked meals, and aided his wife's career. In 1869, Blackwell published *Studies in General Science*, an attempt to integrate the growing body of scientific knowledge with her belief in woman's equality, a theme she later elaborated in *The Sexes Throughout Nature* (1875).

An active advocate of woman suffrage, Blackwell spoke frequently at woman's rights conventions. In 1881, she was elected to membership in the American Association for the Advancement of Science, one of the few women in that august body. She remained active into her old age in woman's rights and general social reform causes. *The Philosophy of Individuality*, published in 1893, was followed by *The Making of the Universe* (1914). At the age of ninety, Blackwell produced her last book, *The Social Side of Mind and Action*. Among pioneer woman suffragists, she alone lived to see the long-awaited suffrage legislation passed. On November 2, 1920, accompanied by her daughter, Blackwell rode to the local schoolhouse near Elizabeth, New Jersey, and cast her ballot. *(See also: Christianity; Religion; Stone, Lucy; Suffrage)*

—Andrea Moore Kerr

Further Reading

Cazden, Elizabeth. *Antoinette Brown Blackwell: A Biography*. Old Westbury, NY: Feminist Press, 1983.

Lasser, Carol, and Marlene Deahl Merrill, eds. *Friends and Sisters: Letters between Lucy Stone and Antoinette Brown Blackwell, 1846–93*. Urbana: University of Illinois Press, 1987.

๛ Blackwell, Elizabeth (1821–1910)

Elizabeth Blackwell was the first American female physician and, in 1859, became the first woman to be placed on the British Medical Register. Blackwell was born in Bristol, England, and in 1831, her family emigrated to the United States after losing its fortune in the sugar business. Blackwell's father, Samuel, encouraged her education and was an active abolitionist. William Lloyd Garrison was a frequent visitor in the family home, and Blackwell joined the Anti-Slavery Society at an early age.

After her father's death, Blackwell became a teacher in Henderson, Kentucky, in 1844, but disgusted by the abusive treatment slaves received in the area, she soon quit her post. She began to think of the possibility of becoming a doctor after a terminally ill female companion complained to her about the indignity of being examined and treated by men.

In 1847, at the age of twenty-six, Blackwell was finally accepted at Geneva College in upstate New York after being rejected by twenty-nine other American medical colleges. At first subjected to some harassment by male students and a failed attempt by a professor to keep her out of lectures dealing with the reproductive organs, Blackwell managed to prove herself a capable student. She passed her exams and graduated from Geneva on January 23, 1849. Blackwell served her residency at La Maternité Hospital in Paris and at St. Bartholemew's in London. After the initial publicity, much of it negative, surrounding Blackwell's degree, women's medical colleges were founded in Philadelphia and Boston. Blackwell returned to the United States to help with the effort. In 1851, with the aid of Horace Greeley, who agreed to run an ad for her in his newspaper, the *New York Tribune*, Blackwell set up a private practice in New York City. She was deluged with obscene letters and was subjected to epithets like "abortionist" and "harlot" on the streets. At first business was poor, but it improved greatly when Blackwell moved her office into the Eleventh Ward, a city slum.

Blackwell spent the later part of her life lecturing and writing on the subjects of hygiene and preventive medicine. In these areas, she proved to be ahead of her time. Late in her life, Blackwell lectured against prostitution and social disease and urged other physicians to be active in the campaign against vice, which she thought victimized women and children. Blackwell's pioneering effort to become a physician eased the way for other women to enter the profession in the late nineteenth century. *(See also: Abolition and the Antislavery Movement; Physicians)*

—Rose Kolbasnik Callahan

Further Reading
Blackwell, Elizabeth. *Pioneer Work in Opening the Medical Profession to Women: Autobiographical Sketches.* New York: Schocken, 1977.
Wilson, Dorothy Clarke. *Lone Woman.* Boston: Little, Brown, 1970.

Further Reading
"Missouri Women in History," *Missouri Historical Review* 63 (October 1968): inside back cover.
Thompson, Cheri. "Emily Newell Blair." In *Show Me Missouri Women: Selected Biographies,* Vol. I, edited by Mary K. Dains, 223-24. Kirksville, MO: Thomas Jefferson University Press, 1989.

∾ Blair, Emily Newell (1877–1952)

Writer, suffragist, and political figure, Emily Newell Blair led a campaign for the Missouri Equal Suffrage Association in 1914 and served as first editor of *Missouri Woman,* a suffrage magazine endorsed by the Missouri Parent-Teachers Association and the Federation of Women's Clubs. Blair saw the results of her labor in 1919, when the Missouri legislature ratified the Nineteenth Amendment, granting woman suffrage. She helped organize the League of Women Voters, believing that women could gain political power by holding office and taking part in political organizations.

A native of Joplin, Missouri, Blair graduated from Carthage High School in 1894 and attended Goucher College in Baltimore, Maryland, and the University of Missouri. In 1900, she married Harry W. Blair, a Carthage lawyer, and wrote about her life in "Letters of a Contented Wife," published in *Cosmopolitan* in 1910. She also wrote articles for *Lippincott's, Harper's, Outlook,* and *Woman's Home Companion.*

During World War I Blair worked in Washington, D.C., for the U.S. Council of National Defense, and in 1920, she wrote the official history of the council's work. That same year, she was elected to the National Democratic Committee and became the first woman to serve as the committee vice chairman (1922–1928). In this position, she organized women voters, formed Democratic women's clubs, and directed their party activities, traveling and speaking throughout the country. She helped organize the Woman's National Democratic Club, serving as secretary from 1922 to 1926 and president in 1928.

Blair continued her writing interests, serving as associate editor of *Good Housekeeping* from 1925 to 1933 and publishing *Creation of a Home* (1930) and *A Woman of Courage* (1931). Appointed to the consumer division of the National Industrial Recovery Act in the 1930s, she served as chairman in 1935. During World War II, she became public relations director for the women's interest section of the War Department.

In 1924, Blair was one of twenty-six Missouri women to have her name inscribed on a bronze tablet in Washington, D.C., honoring Missouri pioneers in the woman suffrage movement. Later, she became disillusioned with women's political accomplishments. Instead of working with men in existing parties, she began to urge women to band together, run for office, and support women candidates regardless of party affiliation. *(See also: Democratic Party; League of Women Voters; Magazines; Suffrage)*

—**Mary K. Dains**

∾ Blatch, Harriet Stanton (1856–1940)

Harriet Stanton Blatch, political organizer and woman's rights activist, was the sixth of seven children born to Henry and suffragist Elizabeth Cady Stanton. After graduating from Vassar College in 1878, she traveled in Europe. Returning, she assisted her mother with the preparation of Volume 2 of the *History of Woman Suffrage,* for which she wrote the chapter on the American Woman Suffrage Association. In 1882, she married Englishman William Henry Blatch and returned with him to Basingstoke, England, where she spent the next twenty years.

In England, she worked for woman suffrage, becoming one of its most effective speakers. A Fabian, she won the friendship and admiration of Beatrice and Sidney Webb and George Bernard Shaw. In 1892, while in England, she completed the degree requirements for an M.A. from Vassar, writing about English working-class women. Returning to America in 1902, Blatch became active in the National American Woman Suffrage Association and in the Woman's Trade Union League. In 1907, she was instrumental in organizing a coalition of industrial, business, and professional women that became the Equality League of Self-Supporting Women, later known as the Women's Political Union, which later still merged with the National Woman's Party.

In 1913 and 1914, Blatch edited a suffrage newspaper, *Women's Political World.* A tireless political organizer, she recalled a stormy evening in which she spoke at two separate trade union meetings as well as at a woman's industrial school, where an audience of more than a thousand women had gathered to hear her speak. In 1917, Blatch helped organize the group of one thousand women who picketed the White House to demand woman suffrage. During World War I, Blatch headed the Speakers Bureau of the Food Administration, serving simultaneously as director of the Woman's Land Army. In 1918, hoping to draw attention to women's contribution to the war effort, Blatch wrote *Mobilizing Woman Power,* with a foreword by Theodore Roosevelt.

Following passage of the suffrage amendment, Blatch worked for international peace, traveling and speaking throughout Europe, and in 1920 published *A Woman's Point of View: Some Roads to Peace.* She continued her political work through the 1920s and 1930s, channeling her efforts through the Progressive and Socialist parties.

Shortly after the publication in 1940 of her memoirs, *Challenging Years,* Harriet Blatch died of a stroke in Greenwich, Connecticut. Blatch's memoirs concluded: "The world is calling for women of vision and courage." Harriet

Stanton Blatch may justifiably have numbered herself among such women. *(See also:* History of Woman Suffrage; *Pacifism and the Peace Movement; Stanton, Elizabeth Cady; Suffrage)*

—Andrea Moore Kerr

Further Reading

Blatch, Harriet Stanton. *Challenging Years.* New York: G. R Putnam, 1940.

———. *Mobilizing Woman Power.* New York: Woman's Press, 1918.

———. *A Woman's Point of View.* New York: Woman's Press, 1920.

Blatch, Harriet Stanton, and Theodore Stanton, eds. *Elizabeth Cady Stanton as Revealed in Her Letters.* New York: Harper & Bros., 1922.

Bloomer, Amelia Jenks (1818–1894)

Amelia Bloomer, advocate for dress reform and women's rights, was born in Homer, New York, on May 27, 1818. She married Quaker reformer and editor Dexter C. Bloomer in 1840 and moved to Seneca Falls, New York. She was active in the temperance movement and was a frequent contributor to the temperance newspaper *Water Bucket,* writing under the pseudonym "Gloriana."

Temperance was an issue raised at the Women's Rights Convention held at Seneca Falls in 1848. As a result, Lucretia Mott and Elizabeth Cady Stanton organized the Ladies' Temperance Society, and Bloomer was appointed an officer. On January 1, 1849, the feminist and temperance newspaper *Lily* was launched, with Bloomer as editor and publisher. The editorial policy of the newspaper focused on temperance, dress reform, suffrage, women's rights, and repeal of unjust marriage and inheritance laws. The masthead included the words "Devoted to the Emancipation of Woman from Intemperance, Injustice, Prejudice, and Bigotry." Bloomer merged her advocacy for temperance and women's rights during her lecture tour of Rochester and New York City, as well as the state capitals of the Midwest in 1852 and 1853.

In the mid-nineteenth century, feminine attire consisted of restrictive corsets, layers of heavy petticoats, and a dress made up of at least twenty yards of fabric. Many early feminists urged dress reform, and the costume designed by Elizabeth Smith Miller was adapted and worn by Elizabeth Stanton, Lucretia Mott, Susan B. Anthony, Sarah and Angelina Grimké, and Amelia Bloomer. Bloomer publicized the costume in *Lily.* The costume consisted of a relatively short skirt reaching five inches below the knee and Turkish pants gathered at the ankles. Corsets and petticoats were discarded. The outfit was ridiculed in the press and denounced from the pulpit. Many goals of the women's movement had been advanced by the publicity lavished on the "Bloomer costume"; however, many feminists felt that the notoriety

Figure 9. Amelia Bloomer
An 1851 woodcut depicting what Amelia Bloomer referred to as a "rational dress." Used by permission of UPI/Corbis-Bettmann.

of the costume drew attention away from the more important issues of the movement. Stanton was the first to abandon the outfit, and the other women followed suit.

Bloomer's move to the Midwest in 1853 did not interrupt her activism for temperance and women's rights. She continued to edit *Lily,* now a nationally circulated magazine with six thousand subscribers, from her home in Ohio and then in Iowa. However, by 1856, the difficulties of its national distribution from the Midwest compelled her to sell it. With the outbreak of the Civil War, Bloomer organized the Soldiers Aid Society of Council Bluffs, Iowa, in 1861; by 1865, she was involved in coordinating the statewide contributions of Iowa women to the U.S. Sanitary Commission. Her postwar activities focused on the issues of woman suffrage and the revision of married women's property rights in Iowa.

Amelia Bloomer died in Council Bluffs on December 30, 1894. She was a prime force for woman suffrage in Iowa, an active feminist, lecturer, author, and editor, but generally, her name continued to be associated with the costume that bore her name. *(See also: Corset; Dress Reform: Nineteenth Century; Suffrage; Temperance Movement)*

—Therese M. Graziano

Further Reading

Bloomer, Dexter C. *Life and Times of Amelia Bloomer.* Boston: Arena, 1895.

Gattey, Charles Neilson. *The Bloomer Girls.* New York: Coward-McCann, 1968.

Gurko, Miriam. *The Ladies of Seneca Falls: The Birth of the Women's Rights Movement.* New York: Macmillan, 1974.

Russell, Frances F. "A Brief Summary of the American Dress Reform Movement of the Past with Views of Representative Women," *The Arena* 6 (August 6, 1892): 325-39.

✎ Blow, Susan Elizabeth (1843–1916)

Susan Blow, pioneer in the American kindergarten movement, advocated the plan of Friedrich Froebel, a German educator, for qualitative child nurture through the systematic training of women for their "divinely ordained mission" as nurturers. With the support of William Harris, superintendent of schools in St. Louis, socialite Blow organized and administered the first public school kindergarten in the United States there in 1873. Having successfully demonstrated the viability of Froebel's system of child nurture, in 1874 Blow established a training school geared to nurture the nurturers.

Working from an elevated sense of woman's status implicit in Froebel's assumption of the importance of the maternal sphere, Blow claimed the right to an appropriate education for those who nurtured others. Within the woman's world of Blow's kindergarten enterprise, apprenticing students were steeped in Froebelian principles and methods to learn the nature, means, and implications of their particular function. She augmented kindergarten training with an advanced course of study that stressed self-making through self-culture in literature, philosophy, religion, art, history, and education.

For a decade, Blow held a position of leadership in the movement. Her work in St. Louis was the subject of growing public attention. Then in 1884, ill health necessitated her withdrawal from kindergartening. By the time Blow recovered from her illness ten years later, the focus of the kindergarten movement had shifted from demonstrating the inherent validity of Froebel's ideas about the value and values of the domestic sphere to an emphasis on the utility of a modified kindergarten as an advocacy agency for the children of the immigrant poor.

Through lectures and writing, Blow attempted to reassert Froebelian ideology as the reason for the kindergarten, to urge that women hold fast to his ideal of nurture and to argue that any change in the Froebelian system be held in abeyance until his mission for women was understood and accepted. Despite the fact that Susan Blow was accorded much respect by her colleagues, the course of the kindergarten movement had undergone too fundamental a change for even a woman of her reputation to reverse. As kindergartens were increasingly assimilated within the schools, Blow's vision of the Froebelian ideal of nurture as the instrument of choice for empowering the woman's sphere within the culture was eclipsed by a new concentration on the kindergarten as a preparation for first grade. (*See also: Education; International Kindergarten Union; Teaching*)

—Catherine Cosgrove

Further Reading

Blow, Susan. "The History of the Kindergarten in the United States," *Outlook* 55 (April 1897): 932-38.
———. "The Ideal of Nurture," *Kindergarten Magazine* 14 (June 1902): 586-98.
———. "Kindergarten Ideal," *Outlook* 56 (August 1897): 890-94.
———. *Letters to a Mother on the Philosophy of Froebel.* New York: D. Appleton, 1896.

✎ "Bly, Nellie" (1865–1922)

Journalist "Nellie Bly" wrote social commentary urging reform of the conditions poor women faced in their workplaces and in charitable institutions. She made the working woman's plight visible to the general public and demonstrated that an American girl could take care of herself anywhere without an escort. Although not the first woman to be a serious reporter, she became one of the best known.

Her real name was Elizabeth Cochrane Seaman, but using her pen name Nellie Bly, she began writing as a teenager for the *Pittsburgh Dispatch,* where she faced stiff competition from other women journalists. In 1886, she traveled to Mexico. Her articles from this trip were widely reprinted, and from them, she wrote her first book, *Six Months in Mexico.* In 1887, she left Pittsburgh for New York to become a stunt writer for the *New York World.* For her first articles, she pretended insanity to get inside Blackwell's Island, a women's insane asylum, and expose the conditions there. These articles were revised and published as her second book, *Ten Days in a Madhouse.* The articles caused an investigation, resulting in increased funding and improved conditions for the insane. Nellie Bly continued to use undercover investigation to expose women's conditions in various factories, shops, and prisons. Her articles, sensationalized but factual, were tempered with just enough lighthearted humor to keep her popular.

She is best remembered for her attempt in 1889 to match the feat of Phineas Fogg, the fictional hero of Jules Verne's *Around the World in 80 Days.* Traveling alone, she cabled home articles of social commentary and amusing travelogue that made her famous and wrote her third book, *Nellie Bly's Book: Around the World in 72 Days,* from them. This trip by steamship, railroad, rickshaw, and sampan was important because it showed Americans that travel abroad was safe and fun even for a woman and that the age of lightning-fast travel had arrived. It was also one of the first times a celebrity was used to advertise everything from soaps to dolls.

On her return, Nellie Bly continued to write, exposing poor social conditions around the country until she married millionaire Robert Seaman in 1895. When he died in 1904, Nellie Bly took over his business but was unsuccessful. In 1919, she went back to writing for the *New York Journal.* She died relatively unknown and alone in 1922. (*See also: Journalism*)

—Terri Evert Karsten

Further Reading

Baker, Nina Brown. *Nellie Bly*. New York: Henry Holt, 1956.

Beasley, Maurine, and Sheila Gibbons. "Nellie Bly: Stunt Reporting." In *Women in Media: A Documentary Source Book*, pp. 47-53. Washington, DC: Women's Institute for Freedom of the Press, 1977.

Kroeger, Brooke. *Nellie Bly: Daredevil, Reporter, Feminist*. New York: Times Books, 1994.

New York World. October 1887–April 1895.

Noble, Iris. *Nellie Bly: First Woman Reporter*. New York: Messner, 1957.

Pittsburgh Dispatch. October 1885–March 1887.

Rittenhouse, Mignon. *The Amazing Nellie Bly*. New York: E. P. Dutton, 1956.

❧ Boarding/Housekeeping System

The boarding/housekeeping system was a common form of work for women, especially immigrant women, during the nineteenth and early twentieth centuries. Taking in boarders was an acceptable job for women and often an attractive choice in areas where positions in light industry and opportunities for homework were scarce.

Women provided lodging, food, and personal services such as cleaning and laundering for the boarder, usually an unmarried, foreign-born male who paid $3 to $4 per month at the turn of the century. Both parties benefited from this arrangement. The boarder could save money to send home to his family, and because he generally chose to live with fellow immigrants who were also in his age group, his adjustment to a new land and culture was eased. He could continue to eat familiar foods and speak his own language, although often the family with whom he boarded attempted to impose certain communally accepted norms of behavior on him. On the other hand, the woman was adding to the family income. The boarder's rent money was used for family living expenses, for a down payment on a house, for the education of children, or for paying off the mortgage. Such income often meant the difference between deprivation and starvation.

Boarding houses provided lodging on a larger scale than merely letting a room or a bed within a family's household to a nonfamily member; as small-scale enterprises, such establishments supplied housing to single men and women as well as to married couples who were "boarding out." Respectable widows or married women with houses could offer room and board to accommodate people in need of housing, both as a means of livelihood and as a way of maintaining their homes and middle-class lifestyle.

Recent immigrant families, families for whom the husband was the sole wage earner, and families whose heads had laboring positions were more likely to have a higher proportion of boarders than other families. Thus, the number of boarders who lived with a family varied with its income, the life cycles of the family members, and its other circumstances. All ethnic groups, including native-born whites, and all economic classes were likely to take in boarders at one time or another. For example, women of middle- and upper-class families often boarded their husbands' clerks or apprentices during the nineteenth century. By the end of the century, however, keeping boarders had become a common economic strategy mostly among working-class women, especially those in tenements.

The percentage of families housing boarders varied from 20 percent to 50 percent from the mid-nineteenth through the early twentieth centuries. Most scholars agree that boarding was not common after 1930. The U.S. Bureau of Labor reported in that year that only 11 percent of American families took in boarders. By the 1970s, that figure had fallen to less than 5 percent. A review of more recent census information kept by the Department of Commerce (Bureau of the Census) reveals that statistical information specifically for boarders has not been kept, suggesting either that such numbers are now negligible or that the concept and/or definition of "boarder" has changed and has been incorporated into another statistical analysis, such as nonfamily households. *The Statistical Abstract* produced by the Bureau of the Census defines the term *household* as comprising both related family members and unrelated persons, including *lodgers,* the closest term to *boarders,* thus making these persons statistically difficult to isolate, particularly in tables referring to nonfamily households. *(See also: Housework; Immigration)*

—Mary Jane Capozzoli Ingui

Further Reading

Bodnar, John, Roger Simon, and Michael P. Weber. *Lives of Their Own: Blacks, Italians, and Poles in Pittsburgh, 1900–1960*. Urbana: University of Illinois Press, 1982.

Boydston, Jeanne. *Home and Work: Housework, Wages, and the Ideology of Labor in the Early Republic*. New York: Oxford University Press, 1990.

Inskeep, Carolee. *The Children's Aid Society of New York: An Index to the Federal, State, and Local Census Records of Its Lodging Houses (1855–1925)*. Baltimore: Clearfield, 1996.

Modell, John, and Tamara K. Hareven. "Urbanization and the Malleable Household: An Examination of Boarding and Lodging in American Families," *Journal of Marriage and the Family* 35 (August 1973): 467-79.

Shelton, Beth Anne. *Women, Men and Time: Gender Differences in Paid Work, Housework and Leisure*. Westport, CT: Greenwood, 1992.

Strasser, Susan. *Never Done: A History of American Housework*. New York: Pantheon, 1982.

❧ Bonnin, Gertrude Simmons
(1876–1938)

Gertrude Simmons Bonnin (also known as Zitkala Sa or Redbird) was a Dakota Sioux author and political activist. After spending her first eight years on the Yankton Reservation in South Dakota, she attended White's Manual Institute in Wabash, Indiana, and later Earlham College in Richmond, Indiana, where she gained honors as an orator and poet. Both a musician and teacher, Simmons taught at Carlisle Indian School from 1898 to 1899. In 1902, she

Figure 10. Gertrude Simmons Bonnin
Among the prominent women who attended the meeting of the National Women's Party in Washington in 1921 was Gertrude Simmons Bonnin, née Princess Zitkala Sa of the Sioux. Used by permission of UPI/Corbis-Bettmann.

married Raymond T. Bonnin. She was an early contributor to the *Atlantic Monthly, Harper's Monthly,* and *American Indian Magazine,* as well as author of two collections: *Old Indian Legends* and *American Indian Stories.* Bonnin was a member of the Women's National Foundation, the League of American Pen-Women, and the Washington Salon and was active in the Society of American Indians organized at Ohio State University in 1911.

In 1916, Bonnin was elected secretary of the society and moved to Washington, D.C. She was acting editor of the society's publication *The American Indian Magazine* from 1918 to 1919. She lectured and campaigned for American Indian citizenship (finally granted in 1924) and worked for the employment of Indians in the Bureau of Indian Affairs as well as for settlement of land claims.

Until her death in 1938, Bonnin served as the president of the National Congress of American Indians, which she founded in 1926. She was instrumental in interesting the General Federation of Women's Clubs in issues concerning American Indians, persuading them to join with the Indian Rights Association to sponsor investigations of the government's relationship with tribes. Bonnin moved easily between the worlds of her tribe and the Eastern establishment;

both groups, however, found it difficult to reconcile her formal education with her tribal loyalty. *(See also: Native American Women; Native American Women's Literature)*

—**Gretchen M. Bataille**

Further Reading

Bonnin, Gertrude S. *American Indian Stories.* Washington, DC: Hayworth, 1921. Reprint, Lincoln: University of Nebraska Press, 1985.

————. *Old Indian Legends.* Boston: Ginn, 1901. Reprint, Lincoln: University of Nebraska Press, 1985.

Fisher, Dexter. "The Transformation of Tradition: A Study of Zitkala Sa and Mourning Dove, Two Transitional American Indian Writers." In *Critical Essays on Native American Literature,* edited by Andrew Wiget, 202-11. Boston: G. K. Hall, 1985.

————. "Zitkala Sa: The Evolution of a Writer," *American Indian Quarterly* 5 (August 1979): 229-38.

Johnson, David L., and Raymond Wilson. "Gertrude Simmons Bonnin, 1876–1938: 'Americanize the First Americans,'" *American Indian Quarterly* 12 (Winter 1988): 27-40.

Stout, Mary. "Zitkala Sa: The Literature of Politics." In *Coyote Was Here: Essays on Contemporary Native American Literary and Political Mobilization,* edited by Bo Scholer, 70-78. Aarhus, Denmark: University of Aarhus, 1984.

Susag, Dorothea M. "Zitkala Sa (Gertrude Simmons Bonnin): A Power(full) Literary Voice," *SAIL* Series 2. 5, 4 (Winter 1993): 2-24.

Willard, William. "Zitkala Sa: A Woman Who Would Be Heard," *Wicazo Sa Review* 1 (Spring 1985): 11-16.

Bookbinding

After the mid-1890s, bookbinding became an artistic handicraft dominated by women. Hundreds of women, mostly young and middle class, took up the craft during the early twentieth century either as professionals or as serious amateurs. Although a rather new pursuit for females, bookbinding conformed to the traditional sexual division of labor in that it was neither heavy nor dirty work but demanded patience, dexterity, and neatness. It could also be easily associated with the widely recognized literary interests of women.

The chief inspiration for this growth in bookbinding was Thomas James Cobden-Sanderson, a leading figure in the British arts and crafts movement and founder of the Doves Bindery in London. Although his own international reputation was based primarily on the sound construction of his books and their brilliantly designed and tooled covers, Cobden-Sanderson insisted in his teaching that the bookbinder not only be a skilled craftsman but also a liberally educated person able to express the spirit of the book's contents.

A small number of American women traveled to the Doves Bindery to study with Cobden-Sanderson. After their return, some established their own workshops and sometimes even a school where they passed on to others the methods of the British master. Evelyn Hunter Nordhoff, for example, founded the Elephant Bindery and a school in New York City. Among the more prominent students at

Nordhoff's school were Elizabeth Chapin, who set up a bindery in Brooklyn, and the Nova Scotia native Minnie Sophia Prat. Florence Foote worked at Nordhoff's and also gave lectures at the Pratt Institute.

Nordhoff's bindery, along with the establishment of the Guild of Book Workers in 1906, made New York the most important center of American artistic bookbinding. The most famous American woman to learn the craft, however, was Ellen Gates Starr, cofounder of the Hull House settlement in Chicago. She studied with Cobden-Sanderson in 1897–1898 and produced bindings that were highly praised and well publicized. In Philadelphia, both Elizabeth G. Marot and Mary Upton were former pupils at the Doves Bindery. Mary E. Bulkley was a prominent bookbinder in St. Louis, and Ida Meacham Strobridge founded the Artemisia Bindery in Los Angeles. The flowering of the bookbinding craft was truly national in scope. *(See also: Starr, Ellen Gates)*

—**Bruce R. Kahler**

Further Reading

Abbott, Leonard D. "Book Handicraft," *The Chautauquan* 30 (1899): 142-48.

Bowdoin, W. G. "Artistic Bookbinding in America," *Outlook* 71 (1902): 254-61.

Burleigh, G. "Some American Bindings, And the Guild of Book Workers," *Arts and Decoration* 5 (1915): 274-76.

White, Esther Griffin. "Some American Art Bookbinders," *Brush and Pencil* 13 (1904): 373-78.

⌒ Bosone, Reva Beck (1895–1978)

Congresswoman and judge Reva Beck Bosone was born in American Fork, Utah. At the age of thirty-one, after eight years as a high school teacher, Bosone followed her mother's advice to "go where the laws are made" if she wanted to benefit mankind, and like her brothers, she chose the law as her profession. In 1927, she enrolled in the College of Law at the University of Utah, where she met and married an Italian Catholic law student, Joseph P. Bosone. After law school and the birth of their daughter, Zilpha Teresa, the Bosones opened a law office in his hometown of Helper, a small coal-mining town in central Utah populated predominately by Italian and Greek coal miners. As a lawyer, she represented miners, gave legal advice to prostitutes, and gained notoriety for her defense of two young men charged with attempted rape.

During the early 1930s, she served two terms in the Utah state legislature, where she sponsored minimum wage and maximum-hour laws for women and children that resulted in the establishment of the Women's Division of the Utah State Industrial Commission. This legislation placed Utah in the forefront of social welfare legislation and won the state the praise of President Franklin D. Roosevelt and his secretary of labor, Frances Perkins.

In 1936, Bosone was elected to a city judgeship, becoming Utah's first woman judge. In her effort to decrease traffic fatalities, she increased fees for traffic violations and established a traffic school in Salt Lake City. Arguing that many defendants were sick people rather than criminals, she often ordered psychiatric and medical examinations for sex offenders and alcoholics. During World War II, she worked to counter the slander campaign against the Women's Army Corps, and when the United Nations was created in 1945, she participated in the development of the charter's equality clause for women.

Bosone was elected to the U.S. House of Representatives from Utah in 1948. She put forth bills to control the nation's natural resources, to provide a federal health insurance plan, to initiate programs to help juveniles, to promote international peace, to study alcoholism, to institute price controls, and to remove Indians from federal wardship by dissolving the Bureau of Indian Affairs. In 1950, she successfully campaigned for a second congressional term against the Republican candidate Ivy Baker Priest, who would later be appointed treasurer of the United States. During the 1952 campaign, she lost to William A. Dawson, who accused Bosone of being "soft on Communism," behaving in an "unladylike manner" in Congress, and violating the Corrupt Practices Act. (The last was a reference to Bosone's admission that she had accepted a $400 and a $250 donation for her reelection from two of her employees.) President John F. Kennedy appointed her to serve as the nation's first woman judicial officer and chairman of the Contract Board of Appeals for the U.S. Post Office Department. After seven years in this capacity, she retired in 1968. *(See also: Democratic Party; Legal Profession; Politics; Women's Army Corps)*

—**Beverly Beeton**

Further Reading

Bosone, Reva Beck. Special Collections Division, Marriott Library. University of Utah, Salt Lake City.

Congressional Record, Eighty-first and Eighty-second Congress. Washington, DC.

Walton, Juanita Irva Heath. "Reva Beck Bosone: Legislator, Judge, Congresswoman." Master's thesis. University of Utah, 1974.

⌒ Boston Marriages

A term from the late nineteenth century, *Boston marriage* refers to an intense relationship between two unrelated women, a relationship that usually endured throughout the life cycles of the pair whether they lived apart or in cohabitation. Some of these relationships included sexual intimacy, but others did not. The term was often applied to a cohabitational intimate relationship between women who for economic or affectional purposes combined their resources to create a home. Boston marriages also reflected the influences of the rigid sex segregation of male and female spheres that encouraged intense relationships between women. An almost separate culture for women in late-

Victorian society limited their casual interaction with the opposite sex while it facilitated intense female bonding in women's domestic circles, institutions of education, professions, and civic and political activities. For professional women at the turn of the century, living with another single woman would not entail the loss of their job as marriage would, since married women were not employable in teaching and other fields. Although their individual earnings were insufficient to support a separate household, independent single women required a more autonomous situation than one in which they would live as dependents with their families. Boston marriages provided them a reasonable alternative to remaining at home as well as a long-term relationship with a peer. *(See also: Friendships)*

—Angela M. Howard

Further Reading

Faderman, Lillian. *Surpassing the Love of Men: Love between Women from the Renaissance to the Present.* New York: Morrow, 1981.

James, Henry. *The Bostonians.* London: Macmillan, 1886. Reprint, Introduction by Irving Howe. New York: Modern Library, 1956.

～ Bourke-White, Margaret (1906–1971)

Margaret Bourke-White, one of the world's foremost photojournalists, was one of the first and perhaps the most notable woman to work in that field. As a member of the original staff of *Life* magazine, she helped to bring a new kind of visual communication, the photographic essay, into being. She used the camera not just to record an event but to say something about it, to place the subject in a social context to make a statement about the world and our place in it.

Bourke-White's rise to prominence in a male-dominated profession came from her singular devotion to her craft and her ideas, without any consideration to what was "woman's work" and what was not. She not only worked in a man's world but chose subjects—war and industry, to name two—that were "masculine." Bourke-White's work also took her to dangerous locations where few men, and almost certainly no women, dared to venture.

Bourke-White first gained recognition for her photographs of steel mills that captured the beauty and drama of industry, a subject she considered to be the vital force of her age. This work attracted the attention of Henry Luce, who wanted her to be a photographer for his new publication about business, *Fortune.* She traveled to Germany to photograph the steel industry and to Russia to document the birth of industrialism. In 1936, she began her work at *Life* magazine with the magazine's first cover photo and a photo essay. Throughout the 1930s, 1940s, and 1950s, Bourke-White traveled widely and photographed the events and leaders that shaped world history. In 1942, she became the first woman to be fitted with a war correspondent's uniform, as an official photographer for the U.S. Air Force. She photo-

Figure 11. Margaret Bourke-White
Portrait of internationally famous industrial photograher Margaret Bourke-White holding a camera. Used by permission of UPI/Corbis-Bettmann.

graphed the American forces in North Africa, Patton's entrance into Germany, the human devastation of the concentration camps at Buchenwald, and the effects of the guerrilla-style civil war in Korea. She captured Churchill, Gandhi, Haile Selassie, and other famous figures with her lens.

Bourke-White was also a writer, and she collaborated with her husband, Erskine Caldwell, on a number of books, including *You Have Seen Their Faces,* a social documentary about poverty in the rural South. As a world-renowned photojournalist and artist who often worked in spheres that had included only men, Bourke-White made a place for her own abilities and, certainly, for the women who follow her. *(See also: Journalism; Photography)*

—Carol Ann Sadtler

Further Reading

Bourke-White, Margaret. *Portrait of Myself.* New York: Simon & Schuster, 1963.

Goldberg, Vicki. *Margaret Bourke-White: A Biography.* New York: Harper & Row, 1986.

Silverman, Jonathan. *For the World to See: The Life of Margaret Bourke-White.* New York: Viking, 1983.

✎ Bowl and Dice Game

The Bowl and Dice Game is an American Indian women's game. Called the Bowl and Dice Game by scholars, it is referred to as Indian or Squaw Dice by native women who play this game of chance and skill with the same fervor seen in more athletic contests. Dates for the game's beginnings are not known, but it is as popular today as it was hundreds of years ago when white men first observed the game in villages.

Historically, the game is considered a woman's game although men are allowed to play. It was played at the end of female adoption ceremonies or as part of a woman's dance. In the early days, it was played in the winter instead of double ball, a kind of women's lacrosse.

Different versions of the game developed in different tribes. Potawatomie women play the game in two teams with a wooden bowl and eight bone dice. Oma Patrick, a Sac and Fox from Oklahoma, explains that in her tribe the game is played by five to nine women and not as a team. She recalls that in the old days it was played to see which one of them had to do the camp cooking. Mrs. Frank Smith, a full blood Sac and Fox from Oklahoma, called it Indian Dice or *Ko the ka no ke* in her native language. She said to use seven bone dice, hand carved into round shapes the size of a nickel and about one-eighth inch thick, with one side dyed black and the other side left natural; two game pieces carved in the shape of animals or animal heads (the turtle and the horse are favorites), also dyed black on one side and left natural on the other: and an Indian-made wooden bowl fifteen inches in diameter and two inches high.

To start the game, all the dice and heads are turned face down—black being the face—inside the bowl and the game begins. Each player has twelve buckeyes to be used as counters. The first player takes the bowl in both hands and bounces it one time on the matting in front of her. The number of dice turned face up determines her score. When she fails to score, the bowl is passed to the next player who in turn bounces the bowl. It goes around until a person wins the game. As each point is made, a buckeye is set out in front of the player and the first to get twelve points wins the game. *(See also: Native American Women)*

—**Jan Vassar**

Further Reading
Culin, Stewart. *Games of North American Indians.* New York: Dover, 1975.

Foreman, Grant, ed. *Indian-Pioneer History.* Works Progress Administration Project S-149. Vol. 9, pp. 480-82. Oklahoma City: Oklahoma Historical Society 1937.

Mueller, Kerstin. "The Changing Role of Algonkian Women: A Study on the Contemporary Sac and Fox of Oklahoma." Master thesis, University of Tulsa, 1991.

Time-Life, Inc. *Cycles of Life.* The American Indians Series, vol. 10. Alexandria, VA: Time-Life Books, 1994.

✎ Boyd, Louise A. (1877–1972)

An expert photographer, Louise Boyd led seven expeditions to Greenland between 1926 and 1941 and in 1955 was the first woman to fly over and around the North Pole. Her first expedition, from Norway to Franz Josef Land, was organized primarily to hunt and photograph landscape and wildlife. She canceled the second, scheduled for 1928, to help search for the missing Norwegian explorer Roald Amundsen. On subsequent trips, she combined her interest in photography with gathering geographic and scientific data. Although the press persisted in describing Boyd as a debutante and an "eccentric American millionairess," her work was taken seriously by those nations engaging in Arctic research and exploration.

Boyd's expeditions to Greenland in the 1930s resulted in the publication by the American Geographical Society of two major works, *The Fiord Region of East Greenland* (1935) and *The Coast Region of Northeast Greenland,* withheld from publication until 1948 because of the strategic importance of the information. The Swedish government awarded Boyd the Order of Saint Olaf for her courageous Arctic voyages, the only foreign woman to receive that honor, and in 1938, she received the Cullum Medal from the American Geographical Society, one of the only two women awarded a medal by that organization. Boyd continued her association with the American Geographical Society, attending the International Geophysical Congress at Warsaw in 1934, conducting investigations of magnetic radio phenomena in Greenland in 1941, and in 1960 serving as the society's first woman councillor. When queried about problems maintaining her "femininity" in such arduous conditions, Louise Boyd would answer that her primary concern was not the smoothness of her hands but avoiding frostbite. *(See also: Photography)*

—**Nancy Fogelson**

Further Reading
Wright, John Kirtland. *Geography in the Making.* New York: American Geographical Society, 1952.

✎ Bradstreet, Anne (Dudley) (1612–1672)

Anne Bradstreet is best known as the author of *The Tenth Muse Lately Sprung Up in America* (1650), the first book of poetry written in America. She received a classical education under the supervision of her English father, Thomas Dudley, steward to the Earl of Lincolnshire, and in 1628, she married Simon Bradstreet, a Cambridge graduate and assistant to her father. In 1630, she emigrated to America, where both her father and husband became governors of the Massachusetts Bay Colony.

Anne Bradstreet's colonial experience was shaped by her duties as wife of an important government official and as mother of eight children. Her first book, *The Tenth Muse,* was published in London by her brother-in-law, Reverend John Woodbridge, without her knowledge or approval, and was revised for posthumous publication as *Several Poems* (1678). The subjects of Bradstreet's early poems are largely secular, and they reflect a desire for literary recognition, a modest self-appraisal, and a sense of indebtedness to poets such as Sir Philip Sidney and Guillaume Du Bartas. Her later lyric poetry deals more directly with the experiences of motherhood and conjugal love. Bradstreet also experimented with short prose pieces, which she wrote especially for the instruction of her children (*Meditations Divine and Morale,* 1664). Underlying all of Bradstreet's work is a strong belief in God, although not to the exclusion of honest religious doubt.

Bradstreet's considerable volume of writing, produced despite the hardships of colonial life, attests to her extraordinary vitality and intellectual vigor. *(See also: Women Writers)*

—**Marilyn Demarest Button**

Further Reading

Bradstreet, Anne. *The Complete Works of Anne Bradstreet.* Edited by Joseph R. McElrath, Jr., and Allan P. Robb. Boston: Twayne, 1981.
———. *Several Poems.* Boston: John Foster, 1678.
———. *The Tenth Muse Lately Sprung Up in America.* London: Stephen Bowtell, 1650.
Martin, Wendy. *An American Triptych: Anne Bradstreet, Emily Dickinson, Adrienne Rich.* Chapel Hill: University of North Carolina Press, 1984.
Rosenmeier, Rosamond. *Anne Bradstreet Revisited.* Boston: Twayne, 1991.
Stanford, Ann. *Anne Bradstreet: The Worldly Puritan.* New York: Burt Franklin, 1975.
White, Elizabeth Wade. *Anne Bradstreet: The Tenth Muse.* New York: Oxford University Press, 1967.

Bratenahl, Florence (Brown) (1884–1940)

Florence Bratenahl served as landscape designer for the Washington National Cathedral from 1927 to 1936. Wife of the first Dean of the Cathedral, she was largely self-taught. Nevertheless, she sustained and built on the work of her predecessor Frederick Law Olmsted, Jr. by designing several major components of the cathedral close. Still visible today are Bratenahl's Pilgrim Steps, Norman Court, St. Catherine's Pool, and cloister garth of the College of Preachers.

During her years at the cathedral, Bratenahl was almost single-handedly responsible for raising funds and acquiring mature plantings and garden sculpture for the Bishop's Garden. To assist these efforts and to provide for a national support structure, in 1916, she founded All Hallows Guild, an

organization of volunteers to ensure the ongoing care and beautification of the fifty-seven acres making up the close. The guild exists to this day and remains actively involved in ensuring the integrity of the landscape that Bratenahl and others envisioned.

Bratenahl was also an enthusiastic writer, almost exclusively concerning her favorite cause—the Bishop's Garden. Her various publications in the 1920s and 1930s recount the trials and successes of developing a garden that would be in keeping with a fourteenth-century Gothic cathedral and yet be a "Garden for the Ages."

Bratenahl's contribution to the close is today commemorated by a plaque placed in the Bishop's Garden by All Hallows Guild. In 1962, the Herb Society of America planted a rare medlar tree nearby as further acknowledgment of her work. *(See also: Christianity; Religion; Voluntarism)*

—**Anne deHayden Neal**

Further Reading

The Bishop's Garden—A Revelation of God's Beauty. Washington, DC: All Hallows Guild, 1985.
Bratenahl, Florence Brown. *A Cathedral Hillside and Its Gardens.* Washington, DC: All Hallows Guild, 1931.
———. *The Pilgrim Steps and Other Cathedral Landscape Adventures.* Washington, DC: All Hallows Guild, 1930.
A Garden for the Ages. Washington, DC: All Hallows Guild, 1928.
Gardens of Washington National Cathedral—A Self-Guided Tour. Washington, DC: All Hallows Guild, 1985.
Klaus, Susan L. *Frederick Law Olmsted, Jr.—Cathedral Landscape Architect, 1907–1928.* Washington, DC: All Hallows Guild, 1991.

Bresette, Linna Eleanor (19??–1960)

Linna Bresette was a Catholic social activist and field secretary of the Social Action Department of the National Catholic Welfare Conference and of the Catholic Conference on Industrial Problems, 1921 to 1931. Born in Rossville, Kansas, she attended Kansas State Normal School and worked for a time as a teacher in the Topeka public schools. She lobbied Kansas state legislature for minimum wage and maximum-hour laws for women and in 1913 was appointed the first female factory inspector for the state. In 1915, she was chosen the secretary of the Kansas Industrial Welfare Commission. Later, she became chairperson of the women's division of the state industrial court and industrial mediation board. From this position, she helped write the minimum wage laws for women and the child labor laws for the state of Kansas. She also served as an inspector of mines, and her inspections became synonymous with improved working conditions.

After World War I, the reforming impulse in Kansas politics fell away, and Bresette was asked to resign. She was then employed by the Social Action Department of the National Catholic Welfare Conference, where her social vision and organizational skills were put to work in behalf of American Catholicism's progressive social agenda. She organized conferences on blacks and Mexicans in industry and the first Catholic summer schools for women and was the driving force behind traveling schools of social thought known as the Catholic Conference on Industrial Problems. Guided by the teachings of the social encyclicals, Bresette became one of the most influential Catholic social activists of her generation. She received honorary degrees from Conception College, Missouri, and Rosary College, Illinois. She retired from her position in 1951 and died in 1960. (See also: Christianity; Minimum Wage Laws; Religion)

—Steven M. Avella

Further Reading
Bresette, Linna Elizabeth. "Campaigning for Economic Justice," Catholic Action 19 (May 1937): 19.

———. "Negro in Industry Conference: New York City, September 1932," Interracial Review 5 (October 1932): 190-94.

———. "1941 Women's Industrial Institute," Catholic Action 23 (August 1941): 15.

～ Brewer, Lucy (c. 1800/1812)

Lucy Brewer (also known as Louisa Baker and Lucy West) dressed as a man and allegedly served aboard the U.S.S. Constitution during the War of 1812.

Little is known of Brewer that was not included in her memoirs, written under an alias. She was seduced by a family friend in rural Massachusetts at the turn of the nineteenth century. Pregnant and ashamed, she left her home for Boston, in search of work as a chambermaid. However, she was duped by a clever madame, told her baby had died at birth, and forced into prostitution. After three years, she disguised herself in the sailor uniform of a frequent customer and escaped the madame. Brewer then claimed to have cunningly circumvented the physical required to join the U.S. Navy and to have served on the illustrious U.S.S. Constitution for three years during the War of 1812 as a marine (one who shot muskets at passing ships in sea battles). She later returned to the family farm but found life as a woman confining and journeyed to New York for one last adventure. While in a carriage dressed as a man, she challenged a male passenger to a duel because he harassed a woman in the carriage, but the challenge was declined. Brewer eventually married and lived a conventional life.

The validity of her story is debatable. But regardless of its authenticity, Brewer's account was popular in 1815 and, most significantly, revealed the drawbacks of being a woman in a man's world during the nineteenth century. (See also: Military Service; Prostitution; Sampson, Deborah)

—Monica L. Everett

Further Reading
Brewer, Lucy. The Female Marine: Or Adventures of Miss Lucy Brewer. Edited by Alexander Medlicott, Jr. 1817. Reprint, New York: Da Capo, 1966.

Coles, Harry L. The War of 1812. Chicago: University of Chicago Press, 1965.

～ Brooks, Gwendolyn (b. 1917)

Poet, writer, and editor, Poet Laureate of the State of Illinois (1968–), Gwendolyn Brooks was the first African American to win the Pulitzer Prize (1950, for her poetry collection Annie Allen) and to be poetry consultant for the Library of Congress. Beyond her historical multiple firsts as a black poet, Brooks is outstanding for her formal adeptness and versatility, her invention of the sonnet ballad and of verse journalism, and her celebration of themes and characters in the everyday life of the black community. Writing of Chicago's south side, Brooks brought an accomplished poetic voice and a new sympathy and subject matter to American poetry.

Although born in Kansas, Brooks moved to Chicago in the same year, was educated in the city's public schools, and considers herself a Chicagoan. Brooks married Henry Blakely in 1939 and has a son and daughter.

Her first poetry collection, A Street in Bronzeville (1945), celebrated city voices, transforming traditional sonnet and ballad forms in lines such as, "Abortion will not let you forget. / You remember the children you got that you did not get." For Annie Allen, Brooks invented the sonnet ballad form, using its complex rhyme schemes to bring to life the children of the poor. A semiautobiographical novel, Maud Martha (1953), and another collection, The Bean Eaters (1960), increased Brooks's audience and established her as a major presence. Selected Poems (1963), drawn from her previously published work, is generally classed as one of the best twentieth-century poetry collections.

In 1967, at the age of fifty, Brooks radically reordered her life and work, as she discovered the black consciousness and black arts movement. Brooks ascribes the transforming experience to the 1967 Fisk University Black Writers' Conference, where she came to read and was caught by the spirit and engagement of black pride and a new generation of young black poets. Brooks gained a whole new perspective on poetry, changing her purpose and voice to address "all black people."

More forceful and more oral than her earlier work, the next collections—In the Mecca (1968), Riot (1969), Family Pictures (1970), and Beckonings (1975)—show a spare prosody directed to wide audiences. After In the Mecca, which was nominated for the National Book Award for Poetry, Brooks switched from her longtime publisher, Harper & Row, to the new black publishing firm, Broadside Press. Harper & Row reprinted Brooks's first five books in one volume: The World of Gwendolyn Brooks (1971).

Work in the community with young writers led to edited anthologies: A Broadside Treasury, 1965-70 and Jump Bad: A New Chicago Anthology (1971). For a time, Brooks conducted poetry workshops for members of the Blackstone Rangers, a Chicago street gang. Continually advocating empowerment through writing and developing young people as writers, Brooks now directs the Poet Laureate Awards for Illinois high school students.

In 1972, Brooks published an autobiography, *Report from Part One,* a compendium of earlier essays, transcripts of interviews, and a collage of personal notes and criticism. Brooks continues to publish regularly and be an active, public poet. Other volume publications include *To Disembark* (1981), *Primer for Blacks* (1981), *Mayor Harold Washington and Chicago, the "I Will" City* (1983), and *Very Young Poets* (1983), the last being advice to young poets with examples of Brooks's own writing. Recent publications include a compilation titled *Blacks* (1987), *The Gwendolyn Brooks Library* (1991), and an introduction to *Groundwork: New and Selected Poems of Don L. Lee/Haki R. Madhubuti from 1966–1996* (1997). *(See also: Black Women; Women Writers)*

—Carol Klimick Cyganowski

Further Reading

Brooks, Gwendolyn. *Report from Part One.* Prefaces by Don L. Lee and George Kent. Detroit, MI: Broadside, 1972.

————. *Selected Poems.* New York: Harper & Row, 1963.

Kent, George E. *A Life of Gwendolyn Brooks.* Lexington: University Press of Kentucky, 1990.

Madhubuti, Haki R., ed. *Say That the River Turns: The Impact of Gwendolyn Brooks.* Chicago: Third World Press, 1987.

Moore, Maxine Funderburk. *Gwendolyn Brooks: A Reference Guide.* New York: Garland, 1987.

Mootry, Maria K., and Gary Smith, eds. *A Life Distilled: Gwendolyn Brooks, Her Poetry and Fiction.* Urbana: University of Illinois Press, 1987.

Satz, Martha. "Honest Reporting: An Interview with Gwendolyn Brooks," *Southwest Review* 74 (Winter 1989): 25-35.

Shaw, Harry B. *Gwendolyn Brooks.* Boston: Twayne, 1980.

Wright, Stephen Caldwell, ed. *On Gwendolyn Brooks: Reliant Contemplation.* Ann Arbor, University of Michigan Press, 1996.

Brooks, Romaine (Goddard) (1874–1970)

Romaine Brooks, an American artist who painted the Parisian elite between the two world wars, created such penetrating and provocative portraits that she became known as the "thief of souls." Her sitters included vanguard personalities such as dancer Ida Rubenstein, poet Jean Cocteau, and longtime friend Natalie Barney, whose weekly literary salon was second in popularity only to that of Gertrude Stein. This dynamic, eccentric group made perfect subjects for Brooks's rather unorthodox portraits.

Brooks's own eccentric sense of independence dated back to her troubled childhood, during which she grew up alone with an irrational mother and a mentally ill brother. In her unpublished memoirs, "No Pleasant Memories," she described her childhood as an irrational circus of demons, apparitions, and fear. Out of this childhood came her highly acclaimed drawings, in which these unconscious fears take linear form. Perhaps most symbolic is her own artistic signature: a chained wing.

The melancholy of her life and drawings is also the core of her painting. On the advice of Charles Freer, a prominent art dealer whom she met while working in the artistic community of Capri, Brooks studied the work of James McNeill Whistler. His mastery of subtle gray tones fascinated her, and she learned to perfect her own shades of gray, incorporating them so well into her paintings that the critics pronounced her work bitterly beautiful, revealing as much about her own passionately despairing life as about the lives of her sitters.

The public agreed with this assessment; between 1910 and 1935, the work of Romaine Brooks was exhibited in Paris, London, and New York, and she was awarded the Cross of the French Legion of Honor in 1920. Although her ability to capture the soul of a personality was in great demand, Brooks was free, due to a family inheritance, to choose to paint only those individuals who intrigued her. In fact, she herself kept most of her paintings, preferring to remain out of the public eye.

The 1935 exhibition of her drawings in Chicago was her last; she then turned her attention away from art and spent the years after the war alone, composing her memoirs. Finally, in 1971, just a few months after her death, the National Collection of Fine Arts in Washington, D.C. (now the National Museum of American Art) organized her first exhibition since 1935. Reviews of this exhibition led modern critics to proclaim her (along with Mary Cassatt and Cecilia Beaux) one of the most important women artists in the history of America. *(See also: Art; Beaux, Cecilia; Cassatt, Mary Stevenson)*

—Karen P. Mattox

Further Reading

Barney, Natalie. *Romaine Brooks: Portraits, Tableaux, Dessins.* New York: Parno, 1952.

Breeskin, Adelyn D. *Romaine Brooks.* Washington, DC: Smithsonian Institution, 1986.

————. *Romaine Brooks: Thief of Souls.* Washington, DC: Smithsonian Institution, 1971.

Brooks, Romaine. "No Pleasant Memories." Unpublished manuscript. Washington, DC: National Museum of American Art, n.d.

Chadwick, Whitney. *Women, Art, and Society.* New York: Thames & Hudson, 1990.

Secrest, Meryl. *Between Me and Life: A Biography of Romaine Brooks.* Garden City, NY: Doubleday, 1974.

Brown, Alice M. (1857–1948)

Alice Brown was one of the most prolific writers in the local-color school of realistic fiction between the Civil War and the 1920s. Born on a small Hampton Falls, New Hampshire, farm in 1857, Brown was educated at the female academy in nearby Exeter. After a short career as a teacher, Brown migrated to Boston, where she began her writing career on the staff of the Unitarian-Universalist church publications office. She began to write and publish short stories in the early 1880s, and in 1884, her first novel,

Stratford by the Sea, appeared. Her first short-story collection to catch the notice of the critics and earn her recognition as one of the leading local colorists was *Meadow-Grass,* published in 1895.

Brown also began to take an increasingly active role in the life of literary Boston beginning in the 1890s; she became a member of the Boston Athenaeum and bought a town house on Beacon Hill. Brown and the poetess Louise Imogen Guiney—a lifelong friend—took many trips to explore literary England on foot, founding the Women's Rest Tour Association, which later became a part of the Women's Educational and Industrial Union in Boston. Elected president of the Boston Author's Club, Brown turned to writing poetry, novels, and one-act plays in the early years of the twentieth century. One of her plays, *Children of the Earth,* won a prize for the best new play of 1914, and several other plays were performed around the East and Midwest in small playhouses of the day. Although her novels reflected much that made her New England stories strong—the local-color realism of the post-Civil War era—none of her novels received major critical acclaim. She wrote prolifically and published more than one book a year until she was dropped by Houghton Mifflin and Macmillan during the early years of the Great Depression. She is remembered as a local colorist and as a woman writer who made a handsome living (she had a mountain farm in Hill, New Hampshire, and a home in Newburyport, Massachusetts, besides her residence on Beacon Hill). Brown also collaborated on a jointly written novel, *The Whole Family,* with a group of authors that included Henry James and Henry Van Dyke.

Brown died at the age of ninety-two in Boston. A proponent of peace, she had been greatly embittered after her struggles with the Creel Committee on Public Information in 1917, which defended U.S. entry into the "War to Prevent All Wars," and further disheartened by the advent of World War II. *(See also: Women Writers)*

—**Ellen D. Langill**

Further Reading

Alice Brown Letters. Holy Cross, Worcester, MA; Yale University, New Haven; The Library of Congress, Washington, DC; Huntington Library, San Marino, CA.

Langill, Ellen D. "Alice Brown: A Critical Study." Ph.D diss., University of Wisconsin, 1975.

Overton, Grant M. *The Women Who Make Our Novels.* New York: Dodd, Mead, 1918.

⤶ Brown, Margaret Tobin (1867–1932)

Political and social activist Margaret Brown (also known as Molly or Maggie) achieved fame when she survived the sinking of the *Titanic* in 1912. She was not known as "Molly" until her death. She was born July 18, 1867, in Hannibal, Missouri, where she attended grammar school until the age of thirteen. In 1886, she migrated to Leadville, Colorado, where she sewed carpets and draperies at the

Daniels, Fisher and Smith Dry Goods Store. Shortly thereafter, she married James J. (J. J.) Brown, a talented mining engineer, and had two children.

By 1893, the Browns had become extremely wealthy from a rich gold strike near Leadville and had moved to Denver. Brown then focused on entering "society," studying languages, literature, and dramatics to ease her acceptance into elite circles. She was successful despite being an Irish Catholic.

In 1909, Brown legally separated from her husband and began to spend much of her time in Europe. When her grandson became ill in 1912, she booked passage from England to the United States on the *Titanic* to care for him. Although a luxury passenger liner, the ship was hailed as "unsinkable." On April 14, 1912, while traveling at top speed during the night, the *Titanic* struck an iceberg and began sinking. Of the 2,201 passengers, the lifeboats accommodated only 1,178. Women and children, including Brown, were put in the lifeboats and sent to sea. In a matter of hours, the *Titanic* and those still aboard sank. Within two hours of the accident, Brown's boat was rescued.

Once on the rescue ship, Brown immediately began organizing rescue efforts; she made lists of survivors to be radioed to their families, raised $10,000 from wealthy survivors to aid destitute victims, and helped comfort immigrant families with her knowledge of foreign languages. After the incident, Brown was dubbed "unsinkable" by the press.

Following the tragedy, Brown petitioned Congress to change the tradition of saving women and children first, while leaving the men to die. Instead, steamers advertised "boats for all" to appease the public.

Brown continued her public service work and ran unsuccessfully for the U.S. Senate in 1914 before ratification of the Nineteenth Amendment. During World War I, she was awarded the French Legion of Honor for entertaining troops with dramatic roles made famous by Sarah Bernhardt. In 1923, as a member of the National Woman's Party, she met President Calvin Coolidge to encourage his support for the Equal Rights Amendment; however, he sided with the protective legislation advocates and the ERA failed.

In 1927, Brown began Denver's first historic homes preservation project. She then moved to New York City where she continued to turn heads with her flamboyant style until her death on October 26, 1932. Her fame was revived with the successful Broadway musical *The Unsinkable Molly Brown,* which was made into a feature film in 1964. *(See also: Equal Rights Amendment; National Woman's Party)*

—**Monica L. Everett**

Further Reading

Boles, Janet K. *The Politics of the Equal Rights Amendment: Conflict and the Decision Process.* New York: Longman, 1979.

Cott, Nancy F. "Equal Rights and Economic Roles: The Conflict over the Equal Rights Amendment in the 1920s." In *Women's America: Refocusing the Past,* edited by Linda K. Kerber and Jane Sherron de Hart, 356-68. New York: Oxford University Press, 1982, 1991.

Lord, Walter. *The Night Lives On.* New York: William Morrow, 1986.

Whitacre, Christine. *Molly Brown: Denver's Unsinkable Lady.* Denver: Historic Denver, Inc., 1984, 1993.

❧ Brown, Olympia (1835–1926)

Feminist, orator, minister, and lifetime activist for woman suffrage, Olympia Brown was born in rural Michigan. She entered Antioch College because its president, Horace Mann, admitted and encouraged education for women (although he discouraged their entering the professions). After graduation in 1860, Brown entered the St. Lawrence University theological school in Canton, New York. In 1863, she became a Universalist minister, the first woman to be ordained by full denominational authority. (Antoinette Brown Blackwell's Congregationalist ordination preceded hers but was performed by a local congregation without ecclesiastical jurisdiction.)

During those years when women fought for the right to speak in public, Brown was one of the very few who trained professionally as a public speaker. Determined to improve her somewhat high and shrill voice, she worked both in Boston and later in Racine, Wisconsin, at schools of gymnastics and voice culture, doing light gymnastics, studying elocution, breathing, and voice projection, and working with Indian clubs to strengthen her shoulder and arm muscles and improve her gestures.

Brown met woman's rights activists Susan B. Anthony, Lucy Stone, and Elizabeth Cady Stanton in 1866. Recognizing her intensity, her practical, political nature, and her speaking talents, they invited her to campaign in Kansas in 1867 for the first referendum on woman suffrage. The Kansas campaign was poorly planned, and Brown faced difficult conditions, including sabotage from within the ranks of the Republican Party. Yet she made almost three hundred speeches within four months.

Returning to parish work, Brown married John H. Willis in 1873 (although she continued to be known throughout her professional life as the Reverend Olympia Brown), had two children, and moved to Racine, Wisconsin, in 1878 to accept the pastorate of a Universalist church. There, she was elected president of the state Woman Suffrage Association, a position she maintained for twenty-eight years, and she worked ceaselessly on legislative reform and suffrage issues, eventually resigning from the church in 1887 to concentrate on politics. Surviving many factional splits within the movement, Brown continued to be an indefatigable activist for woman's suffrage. She was one of the few original suffrage workers to live to see the passage of the Nineteenth Amendment—for which she had worked for more than fifty-five years. *(See also: Blackwell, Antoinette Brown; Christianity; Public Speakers: Nineteenth Century; Religion; Suffrage; Unitarian-Universalism)*

—**Nan Nowik**

Further Reading

Brown, Olympia. *Acquaintances, Old and New, Among Reformers.* Privately printed, 1911.

Cote, Charlotte. *Olympia Brown: The Battle for Equality.* Racine, WI: Mother Courage Press, 1989.

Greene, Dana, ed. *Suffrage and Religious Principle: Speeches and Writings of Olympia Brown.* Metuchen, NJ: Scarecrow, 1983.

Neu, Charles E. "Olympia Brown and the Woman Suffrage Movement," *Wisconsin Magazine of History* 43 (Summer 1960): 277-87.

❧ Brown, Rita Mae (b. 1944)

Writer and political activist Rita Mae Brown was born in Hanover, Pennsylvania, then adopted and transplanted to Florida during childhood. In adolescence, Brown chose a lesbian lifestyle. A scholarship recipient at the University of Florida, she was ejected for civil rights activities in 1965. She traveled penniless to New York City, initially living on the street and eventually attending New York University, where she majored in English and classics and helped to form the first Student Homophile League in 1967. She did graduate work in comparative literature, studied cinematography, was a fellow of the Institute for Policy Studies, Washington, D.C., and holds a Ph.D. in political science.

Meanwhile, Brown joined the New York chapter of the National Organization for Women (1968) and marshaled the first postsuffrage White House picket in 1969, but mainstream feminists in NOW rejected her for her outspoken lesbianism and aggressive tactics. Brown moved similarly into and out of the feminist consciousness-raising Redstockings in 1969, then worked in Radicalesbians, the collective that shifted New Left newspaper *Rat* to a radical lesbian feminist forum and produced the landmark essay "The Woman-Identified Woman" (1970). Brown participated in the "Lavender Menace" lesbian takeover of the Second Congress to Unite Women (May 1970). As a lesbian separatist—one favoring the creation of an exclusively female culture—she helped form the Furies collective, which published a Washington, D.C., newspaper espousing separatist ideology from January 1972 to June 1973. Ousted again, the volatile Brown focused on her writing.

She had published two volumes of poetry—*The Hand That Cradles the Rock* (1971) and *Songs to a Handsome Woman* (1973), both reprinted as *Poems* (1987). When Brown's fabled first novel, *Rubyfruit Jungle,* came out in 1973, this founding mother of the 1960s women's movements became a preeminent feminist novelist. *Rubyfruit Jungle* has remained perennially popular, cementing Brown's literary reputation. No previous popular book detailed a lesbian life in realistic and positive terms: This semiautobiographical novel's main character, Molly Bolt, chose, accepted, and preferred life as a lesbian, with no guilty or pornographic overtones. Instituting the "coming-out novel" genre, *Rubyfruit* liberated fictional lesbianism, providing an affirmative text for newly raised consciousnesses, displacing

Radclyffe Hall's *Well of Loneliness* (1928) as "the" lesbian novel.

Molly constitutes a classic lesbian "type," a tomboy facing a variety of presumed handicaps: her poor white southern background, her sex, her adoption, her father's death, her college expulsion for lesbian activities, her struggle alone in New York City. But Molly overcomes all obstacles by relying on her intelligence, fortitude, and acid wit as she surveys modern lesbian culture. Molly also travels a remarkable sexual odyssey, from easygoing cousin LeRoy to Professor Polina's daughter Alice, with a football hero and a cheerleader thrown in for good measure. Molly is achingly All-American. *Rubyfruit* does suffer from an episodic plot and shallow minor characterizations; Brown favors verbal richness over visual detail, a storytelling effect.

A lesbian Huck Finn, Molly displays Brown's talent for comedy, especially in dialogue, which made *Rubyfruit* the first and foremost example of the lesbian comic novel. Brown revised the "postfeminist" lesbian image: the tough but funny, smart and seductive, tomboyish yet womanly dyke. Like Brown, Molly is assertive, always out of the closet, "liberated," a powerful role model dispelling negative stereotypes. Molly's ultimate rapprochement with her aging mother both resolves their lengthy hostility and illustrates a major concern of contemporary feminism. *Rubyfruit* remains significant and compelling in its readability, psychological honesty, and historicity.

After *Rubyfruit,* Brown published *In Her Day* (1976) and a collection of her political essays, *A Plain Brown Rapper* (1977), before Bantam republished *Rubyfruit* and Harper & Row published *Six of One,* perhaps her finest lesbian-content novel, in 1978. Set in the South, *Six* exhibits a tender hilarity as it bounces through 110 years of U.S. history recounting the exploits of several remarkable female "characters." *Bingo* (1988) extends the saga of Runnymede, Maryland, begun in *Six of One*. Brown's corpus includes many other novels, a writer's guide, and various screenplays.

Rita Mae Brown played an important part in the lesbian/feminist political actions of the 1960s and early 1970s—a strong figure with extremely radical views on the liberation of poor people, lesbians, and women, a controversial figure who once advocated revolt over revisionism. However, since 1973, Brown's commitment to social change has been expressed literarily rather than polemically, and her political stature has diminished in inverse proportion to her increasingly privileged posture. *(See also: Lesbian Separatism; Lesbianism; Radicalesbians)*

—**Penelope J. Engelbrecht**

Further Reading

Alexander, Dolores. "Rita Mae Brown: 'The Issue for the Future Is Power,' " *Ms.* 3 (September 1974): 110-13.

Brown, Katie. "*Rubyfruit Jungle:* The Greatest Movie Never Made," *Deneuve* 2 (May/June 1992): 6-9.

Brown, Rita Mae. *Rubyfruit Jungle.* New York: Daughters, 1973.

———. *Six of One.* New York: Harper & Row, 1978.

Faderman, Lillian. *Surpassing the Love of Men: Romantic Friendship and Love between Women from the Renaissance to the Present.* New York: Quill/William Morrow, 1981.

Radicalesbians. "The Woman-Identified Woman," 1970. Reprinted in *Radical Feminism,* edited by Anne Koedt, Ellen Levine, and Anita Rapone, 240-45. New York: Quandrangle, 1973.

"Redstockings Manifesto." In *Masculine/Feminine: Readings in Sexual Mythology and the Liberation of Women,* edited by Betty and Theodore Roszak, 272-74. New York: Harper Colophon, 1969.

Zimmerman, Bonnie. *The Safe Sea of Women: Lesbian Fiction, 1969–1989.* Boston: Beacon, 1990.

⚬ Brown, Ruth Winifred (1891–1975)

Ruth Winifred Brown, activist on behalf of civil rights for African Americans and the freedom to read, was born in Hiawatha, Kansas. A graduate of the Alva, Oklahoma, Normal School and the University of Oklahoma, she became librarian of the Bartlesville, Oklahoma, Public Library in 1919, a position she held for thirty years, until reaction to her activism brought about her firing.

In 1946, Brown helped organize an integrated group that became the first group in a Jim Crow state to affiliate with the Congress of Racial Equality (CORE). Committed to the principle of nonviolent direct action, in 1948 or 1949 Brown began to take some of her black friends to the Episcopal Church with her and launched a story hour for black children at the library. In February 1950, Brown and two black women friends asked to be served at a Bartlesville drug store lunch counter. Refused, they left without incident.

Shortly thereafter, however, a group composed of members of the American Legion and various conservative women's groups, supported by some of the executives of the community's largest employers, Phillips Petroleum and Cities' Service, charged Brown with having subversive materials, especially *The Nation* and *The New Republic,* in the Public Library. Aided by her Library Board, Brown defended her selections. The City Commission, however, dismissed the Library Board, named a new board, and fired Brown. A battle ensued, both in court and out, which lasted well into 1952.

The Oklahoma Library Association created a Committee on Intellectual Freedom to investigate the case. The American Library Association assisted Brown with information and condemned her firing. The case gained national attention. A letter to *The Saturday Review* written by one of Brown's supporters drew the attention of screenwriter Daniel Taradash, who seized on the case as inspiration for a script designed to attack McCarthyism. The film, *Storm Center* starring Bette Davis, was released in 1956.

Brown herself spent the ensuing years as librarian at the Piney Woods, Mississippi, Country Life School, and then at the Sterling, Colorado, Public Library. Following her 1962 retirement, she remained a member of CORE. Among those who knew her story, Ruth Brown has become a symbol of courage in the fight for freedom of access to information for all. *(See also: Civil Rights; Librarianship)*

—**Louise S. Robbins**

Further Reading

"Censorship in Bartlesville: A Report of the Oklahoma Library Association's Committee on Intellectual Freedom," *American Library Association Bulletin* 45 (March 1951): 87-90.

The Papers of the Congress of Racial Equality, 1941–1967. Executive Secretary's File, 1941–1962, Record Group 22. State Historical Society of Wisconsin, Madison. Microfilm.

Robbins, Louise S. *Censorship and the American Library: The American Library Association's Response to Threats to Intellectual Freedom, 1939-1969.* Westport, CT: Greenwood, 1996.

———. *The Dismissal of Miss Ruth Brown: Civil Rights, Censorship, and the American Public Library.* Norman, OK: University of Oklahoma Press, forthcoming.

Ruth W. Brown Archive, Kansas Collection. Pittsburg State University Library, Pittsburg, Kansas.

∾ Brown v. Board of Education of Topeka (1954)

In *Brown v. Board of Education of Topeka* (1954), the Supreme Court established the fundamental legal principle that "racial discrimination in public education is unconstitutional." The Court held that the "separate but equal" formula in public education is inherently unequal because it creates and perpetuates feelings of inferiority in members of minority groups. This decision rejected the legal assumption present in the United States from 1896 to 1954 that in areas of racial segregation "separate" can be equal.

The Fourteenth Amendment (1868) declares that "No state . . . shall deny any person within its jurisdiction the equal protection of the laws." *Brown* and some companion cases (e.g., *Bolling v. Sharpe,* 1954) extended this protection to the area of racial discrimination in public education. While the Court established this fundamental principle in the 1954 *Brown* decision, it postponed a decision on the application of this principle, inviting all interested parties to present their positions in the Court's next term. In *Brown v. Board of Education II* (1955), the original cases were remanded to the courts from which they originated to fashion decrees of enforcement on equitable principles and with regard to the "varied local school problems." *(See also: Civil Rights; Fourteenth Amendment to U.S. Constitution)*

—**Sue E. Strickler**

Further Reading

Bolling v. Sharpe, 347 U.S. 497; 74 S. Ct. 693; 98 L. Ed. 884 (1954).

Boozer, Michael, Alan B. Krueger, and Shari Wolkon. *Race and School Quality since* Brown vs. Board of Education. Cambridge, MA: National Bureau of Economic Research, 1992.

Brown v. Board of Education of Topeka, 347 U.S. 483; 74 S. Ct. 686; 98 L. Ed. 873 (1954).

Brown v. Board of Education of Topeka, 349 U.S. 294; 75 S. Ct. 753; 99 L. Ed. 1083 (1955).

Goldstein, Joseph. *The Intelligible Constitution: The Supreme Court's Obligation to Maintain the Constitution as Something We the People Can Understand.* New York: Oxford University Press, 1992.

Goldstein, Leslie Friedman. *The Constitutional Rights of Women.* New York: Longman, 1987.

Greenberg, Jack. *Crusaders in the Courts: How a Dedicated Band of Lawyers Fought for the Civil Rights Revolution.* New York: Basic Books, 1994.

Rossum, Ralph A., and G. Alan Tarr. *American Constitutional Law,* 2d ed. New York: St. Martin's, 1987.

Whitman, Mark, ed. *Removing a Badge of Slavery: The Record of* Brown vs. The Board of Education. Princeton, NJ: Markus Wiener, 1993.

Wilson, Paul E. *A Time to Lose: Representing Kansas in* Brown vs. The Board of Education. Lawrence: University Press of Kansas, 1995.

∾ Bryant, Louise (1887–1936)

Journalist, author, and suffragette, Louise Bryant was best known as the wife and widow of John Reed, the American communist and author of *Ten Days That Shook the World.* Although Bryant was married three times, it was her life with Reed that brought her to Greenwich Village and a circle of friends that included poetess Edna St. Vincent Millay, birth control pioneer Margaret Sanger, anarchist Emma Goldman, and playwright Eugene O'Neill, who became her lover. With Reed's help, she became an effective advocate of labor unions, equality of the sexes, communism, and pacifism. Bryant's articles and poems were published in, among others, *The Masses, Poetry, Dial,* and *Current Opinion.* She wrote several plays that were produced by the Provincetown Players, of which she, Reed, and O'Neill were founding members.

During World War I, Bryant traveled to Europe as a correspondent for the Bell News Syndicate. After her return to the United States in the late summer of 1917, Reed proposed a joint trip to witness and report the great events happening in Russia. They were in Petrograd (now Leningrad) during the Bolshevik Revolution, witnessed the storming of the Winter Palace, listened to Trotsky at the Petrograd Soviet, and interviewed revolutionary leaders. Bryant also interviewed heroines of the revolution such as Marie Spiridonova, leader of the Peasant Soviet; Alexandra Kollontai, welfare minister; and Katherine Breshko-Breshkovskaia, known as the "Babushka" (grandmother) of the Russian Revolution, who had survived half a century of Siberian exile. Bryant's best writing was done during these hectic months filled with the hardship and danger that both she and Reed seemed to relish. Her dispatches were compiled and published in 1918 as *Six Red Months in Russia.* On a lecture tour of major American cities in 1919, Bryant spoke glowingly of Soviet Russia and pleaded against American intervention in Russia's civil war.

Suffering the abuse of the Red Scare of 1919 in America, Bryant had joined Reed in 1920 during his second stay in Russia despite the revocation of her passport, and therefore she was with him when he died of typhus that year. In the years after Reed's death, Bryant reported for the Hearst press from Turkey and Russia. She wrote her second book, *Mirrors of Moscow* (published in 1923), during this period. Between 1923 and 1930 she was married to William C. Bullitt and gave birth to her only child, Anne. Following a divorce and the loss of Anne's custody, Bryant, now addicted to alcohol and drugs, spent her last years in Paris in poverty. She died of a cerebral hemorrhage at the age of forty-nine, on January 6, 1936, in Sèvres, France. *(See also: Journalism; Women Writers)*

—**Tamerin Mitchell Hayward**

Further Reading

Bryant, Louise. *Six Red Months in Russia.* New York: George H. Doran, 1918.
Gelb, Barbara. *So Short a Time: A Biography of John Reed and Louise Bryant.* New York: Norton, 1973.
Schneir, M. "Meet the Real Louise Bryant," *Ms.* 10 (April 1982): 43, 45-6, 92-3.

ᴈ Bryn Mawr College

Located on Philadelphia's suburban Main Line, Bryn Mawr College was originally founded by Dr. Joseph Taylor, a New Jersey physician, as a college for Quaker women, a counterpart to the then male-only Haverford College. Bryn Mawr's purpose changed radically even before it opened its doors in 1885. Although its first president was James E. Rhoades (1885–1894), a retired physician who provided stable financial administration, the real driving force behind Bryn Mawr's distinctive character was M. Carey Thomas, who served first as dean and then as the college's second president (1894–1922).

As one of the very first American women to earn a Ph.D., Thomas was determined to make Bryn Mawr a premier institution of women's learning comparable to the best of the elite eastern men's colleges. From the beginning, Bryn Mawr offered M.A. and Ph.D. degrees in addition to undergraduate education for women. It remains the only mainly women's college to have full-fledged doctoral programs.

Thomas wanted Bryn Mawr to be an institution devoted to scholarship like the Universities of Leipzig and Zurich where she had studied. She insisted on high admission standards, in contrast to some other women's colleges; there was no provision for students at Bryn Mawr who lacked its demanding academic prerequisites. Thomas tried to hire the best available scholars, male or female, as faculty. They also were paid high salaries, at least in the early years, and given time for scholarly work. Among the early faculty were Woodrow Wilson and Charles McLean Andrews, both in history, and later, Helen Taft Manning in English. Most of the campus buildings were, according to Thomas's plan, patterned after those of the traditional male colleges at Oxford, making Bryn Mawr a pioneer in the much copied collegiate Gothic style found in institutions across the United States.

Also, under Thomas's leadership, Bryn Mawr became the first college in the country to permit its students to organize a system of self-government that gave them the power to draw up their own code of discipline and punish infractions.

Bryn Mawr's tradition of concern for the disadvantaged was enhanced by the establishment of a Graduate Department of Social Economy and Social Research in 1912. The department became a full-fledged graduate school in 1970. In one of her last significant decisions, Thomas approved a summer school for working-class women. From 1921 to 1938, the summer school provided a creative cross-fertilization between college women and female industrial workers.

Thomas's autocratic rule provoked a revolt by the faculty in 1916. Her successor, President Marion Park (1922–1942), introduced a more open governance structure and new core curriculum. During Park's administration, a student honor code was developed. Although Bryn Mawr became nondenominational as early as 1893, much of the original Quaker philosophy has persisted into the late twentieth century, particularly in the honor code with its noncompetitive emphasis and in the college's tradition of independence. During the era of the Cold War in the 1950s and 1960s, Bryn Mawr was one of the few colleges that refused to require loyalty oaths from students requesting federal educational loans or grants. Alumnae raised money to provide alternatives for the students. A decade later during the Vietnam War protests, Bryn Mawr was the only college in Pennsylvania and one of a very few nationwide that refused to sign an agreement with the government to report student protesters as a condition for federal scholarships.

President Harris Wofford (1970–1978) improved ties with nearby Haverford College, enabling students to take advantage of the strengths of both institutions. Under its sixth president, Mary Patterson McPherson (1978–1997), Bryn Mawr substantially improved many of its academic facilities and enlarged its endowment while continuing the college's primary tradition of excellence in women's higher education. On December 6, 1997, Nancy J. Vickers was inaugurated, becoming Bryn Mawr's seventh president in its 112 years.

Bryn Mawr has a long list of distinguished alumnae, among whom are Emily Green Balch, 1889, economist, social reformer and winner of the Nobel Peace Prize; Hanna Holborn Gray, 1950, Renaissance historian and president of the University of Chicago; Katharine Hepburn, 1928, Academy Award winning actress; and Alice M. Rivlin, 1952, economist and director of the Office of Budget and Management in the Clinton administration. It is also the only women's college among the ten institutions in the nation with the highest percentage of winners in the National Science Foundation Graduate Fellowships. *(See also: Bryn Mawr Summer School for Women Workers; Higher Education; "Seven Sisters"; Thomas, M. Carey)*

—**Neil W. Hogan**

Further Reading
Bryn Mawr College Archives. Bryn Mawr, Pennsylvania.
Dobkin, Marjorie Housepian. *The Making of a Feminist*. Kent,
    OH: Kent State University Press, 1979.
Horowitz, Helen Lefkowitz. *Alma Mater*. New York: Knopf,
    1985.
———. *The Power and Passion of M. Carey Thomas*. New York:
    Knopf, 1994.
Meigs, Cornelia. *What Makes a College?* New York: Macmillan,
    1956.
West, Lucy Fisher, ed. *The Papers of M. Carey Thomas in the Bryn
    Mawr College Archives*. Woodbridge, CT: Research Publica-
    tions International, 1982. Index and microfilm.

ᔋ Bryn Mawr Summer School for Women Workers

The Bryn Mawr Summer School for Women Workers,
1921 to 1938, with Brookwood Labor College, launched
the American workers' education movement. It combined
the agendas of the suffragist, feminist, labor, progressive-
political, and progressive-educational movements into an
innovative residential program serving both organized and
unorganized blue-collar women workers from a cross section of geographic regions, occupations, and racial and ethnic groups.

The Bryn Mawr Summer School for Women Workers
quickly became the flagship humanistic program for women
workers of the loosely organized workers or labor education
movement. That movement, dedicated to broadening workers' consciousness and empowering them, experienced its
heyday in labor's years of struggle in the 1920s and 1930s.

The Bryn Mawr Summer School for Women Workers
drew its primary inspiration from organizations of the femi-
nist-progressive era: the National Women's Trade Union
League, the National Consumers' League, and the Young
Women's Christian Association. All were mixed-class undertakings engaged in promoting evolutionary change. While
the Bryn Mawr Summer School for Women Workers was a
product of its time, it required the catalytic force of educator
and Bryn Mawr president M. Carey Thomas to authorize its
creation within her elite domain. Thomas provided the vision and imprimatur and appointed the then-college dean,
Hilda Worthington Smith, as director.

The Bryn Mawr Summer School for Women Workers
forever changed not only the lives of many of its students but
also of its faculty, who were politicized by the experience.
Rita Heller's unique follow-up study of 3 percent of the students and twenty-eight teachers, conducted forty to sixty
years after school attendance, documented the experience's long-term effects. An overwhelming proportion of
the workers said the school had had a considerable impact
on their lives, self-image, and skill development. Many
moved into union leadership, with Carmen Lucia and
Elizabeth Nord becoming vice presidents of national unions.
Many faculty members turned to federal government and
other public service, the most renowned being Alice Hanson

Cook, Broadus Mitchell, Esther Peterson, Caroline Ware,
and Colston Warne.

The Bryn Mawr Summer School for Women Workers
meets contemporary definitions of feminist pedagogy because of its commitment to shared authority between administration and students and its engagement of students'
intellectual and emotional lives (Ard, 21-24). The school
linked Jane Addams's progressivism to Eleanor Roosevelt's
liberalism, connected educated elite women with blue-collar
workers, and thus fused an ebbing suffragism to militant
unionism and a dynamic New Deal. The Bryn Mawr Summer School for Women Workers constituted a powerful
force for change in the inter-World War decades. *(See also:
National Women's Trade Union League; New Deal; Peterson,
Esther; Thomas, M. Carey; Unions; Workers' Education for
Women)*

—Rita Rubinstein Heller

Further Reading
Several archival collections on the Bryn Mawr Summer School
are extant in the following locations: American Labor Education
Service Papers, School of Industrial and Labor Relations, Cornell
University, Ithaca, NY; American Labor Education Service Papers,
Wisconsin State Historical Society, Madison, WI; Bryn Mawr
Summer School Papers, Bryn Mawr College Archives, Bryn Mawr,
PA; Bryn Mawr Summer School Papers, Institute of Management
and Labor Relations Library, Rutgers University, New Brunswick,
NJ; Eleanor Coit Papers, Sophia Smith Collections, Smith Col-
lege, Northampton, MA; Hilda Worthington Smith Papers,
Schlesinger Library, Radcliffe College, Cambridge, MA.

Ard, Anne K. "Powerful Learning: A Study of the Bryn Mawr
    Summer School for Women Workers in Industry, 1921–1938."
    Paper presented at the annual meeting of the Association for
    the Study of Higher Education, September 1992.
Heller, Rita R. "Blue Collars and Blue Stockings: The Bryn Mawr
    Summer School for Women Workers." In *Sisterhood and Soli-
    darity: Workers Education for Women, 1918–1984,* edited by
    Joyce Kornbluh and Mary Frederickson, 107-45. Philadel-
    phia: Temple University Press, 1984.
———. "The Bryn Mawr Workers' Summer School, 1921–1938:
    A Surprising Alliance," *History of Higher Education Annual,*
    1981, pp. 110-13.
———. "The Women of Summer: The Bryn Mawr Summer
    School for Women Workers, 1921–1938." Ph.D. diss. Rutgers
    University, 1986.
———, co-producer. *The Women of Summer: The Bryn Mawr
    Summer School for Women Workers, 1921–1938.* A National
    Endowment for the Humanities Film, 1985.
Schneider, Florence Hemley. *Patterns of Workers' Education: The
    Story of the Bryn Mawr Summer School.* Washington, DC:
    American Council on Public Affairs, 1941.
Smith, Hilda Worthington. *Opening Vistas in Workers' Education:
    An Autobiography of Hilda Worthington Smith.* Washington,
    DC: Hilda Worthington Smith, 1978.

ᔋ Business

Women have been actively involved in the business life of
the United States since its inception. A female print shop

owner, Mary Katherine Goddard (1738–1816), was the official printer of the Declaration of Independence. During the New Nation period, enterprising women such as Abigail Adams (1744–1818) and Eliza Pinckney (1722–1793) managed their family businesses and property so well that their husbands, John and Charles, were able to devote themselves almost full-time to public service. America's first great fortune, that of John Jacob Astor in the fur trade, was helped greatly by the business skills of Astor's wife, Sarah Todd Astor (1762–1832). However, most of these women in business were unique cases to some extent because business was still predominantly a man's world in the early years of the United States.

The Industrial Revolution transformed the American economic landscape and increased nonagricultural and domestic-service employment opportunities for women. Iron magnate Rebecca Pennock Lukens (1794–1854) of Pennsylvania was one of those rare female entrepreneurs involved in the rise of early industrialism at the managerial level. Ellen Curtis Demorest (1824–1898) and Margaret Getchell La Forge (1824–1898) were on the cutting edge of the nineteenth-century fashion industry and were among the first to use the growing women's market.

In a few cases, women capitalists began to make large fortunes in business during the nineteenth and early twentieth centuries, although most of the great American fortunes were still controlled by men and most women were still expected to remain in their domestic sphere. Breakthrough women included Margaret Haughery (1813–1882), who made a fortune in the bakery business in New Orleans, and Susan King (1818–1880), who prospered with her Woman's Tea Company. Hetty Green (1834–1916) made $100 million speculating in the money market and became known as the "witch of Wall Street." Black entrepreneur and inventor Madame C. J. Walker (1867–1919) became wealthy in the cosmetics industry. On the American frontier, Henrietta Chamberlain King (1832–1925) successfully managed the huge King Ranch in Texas for many years.

Despite the few women who made large fortunes, most women in business did not, and few women obtained management positions even by the late nineteenth century. Women still held only 5 percent of the white-collar office jobs—as clerks, copyists, bookkeepers, stenographers, and typists. The business office from top to bottom was still predominantly a masculine environment. Mary Seymour Foot (1846–1893) was one of those who was determined to change all that. She set up a successful business school to train women in the new office skills, while also launching *Business Woman's Journal* in 1889. Foot's work was further extended by Katherine Gibbs (1865–1934), who developed a chain of business schools for women. The "Pink-Collar Ghetto" was on its way.

As business became more sophisticated and complex in the twentieth century, businesspeople began to turn to the new social science disciplines for guidance and ideas. Mary Parker Follett (1868–1933) was an influential pioneer in the new field of management theory. Her 1924 book *Creative Experience* was widely respected in business circles for its advice about decision making and the handling of labor problems. In the modern world, financial writer Sylvia Porter (1913–1991) was only one of a number of widely respected female business and financial advisers.

Women also became increasingly influential in the fashion world, especially after World War I. Ida Rosenthal (1889–1973) founded Maidenform, Inc., the first manufacturer of brassieres. Rosenthal also played a key role in developing the mass production, ready-to-wear industry. Nell Quinlan Donnelly (1889–1991) was also instrumental in transforming the garment industry.

While the contributions of Rosie the Riveter and her sisters to industrial production during the Second World War have not gone unrecognized, businesswomen also contributed to the war effort. Olive Ann Beech (1903–1993) converted a small commercial airplane operation into a major defense contractor that supplied 90 percent of the planes on which American bombardiers and navigators were trained. During the war, Tillie Lewis (1901–1977) introduced the Italian tomato industry to California. After the war, she developed the first artificially sweetened canned fruit and became the first woman director of the billion-dollar Ogden Corporation.

In recent decades, there has been a dramatic expansion of the role of women in business. Women are finding their way into the management structure of most large corporations at all levels. However, getting to the highest levels ("the glass ceiling") of many U.S. corporations is still problematic for many female executives. High-profile women such as advertising executive Mary Wells Lawrence (b. 1928), communications mogul Oprah Winfrey (b. 1954), and *Washington Post* publisher Katharine Meyer Graham (b. 1917) are no longer the rare exceptions that they would have been in the business world of previous eras. The beauty industry—with moguls such as Elizabeth Arden (1878–1966), Mary Kay Ash (b. 1915), and Helena Rubinstein (1870–1965)—is now only one of many industries in which women are in real positions of power, such as the movie industry with Barbra Streisand (b. 1942) and Jodie Foster (b. 1965), among others. In 1976, Martha Stewart (b. 1941) started a catering business that ten years later had become a $1 million enterprise through her writings for the *New York Times* and *House Beautiful* and her own magazine and television show, *Martha Stewart Living*. By the end of the twentieth century, women had become an increasingly active force in businesses ranging from professional sports franchises to computing firms. *(See also: Adams, Abigail; Beauty Industry; Industrial Revolution; Kreps, Juanita Morris; Pinckney, Eliza Lucas; Walker, Madame C. J.)*

—Jonathan W. Zophy

Further Reading

Bird, Caroline. *Enterprising Women.* New York: Norton, 1976.

Coffee, Robert, and Richard Scace. *Women in Charge: The Experience of Female Entrepreneurs.* Boston: Unwin, 1985.

Davidson, Marilyn, and Cary Cooper. *Shattering the Glass Ceiling: The Woman Manager.* Bristol, PA: Taylor & Francis, 1992.

Kanter, Rosabeth. *Men and Women of the Corporation.* New York: Basic Books, 1977.

Karsten, Margaret Foegen. *Management and Gender: Issues and Attitudes.* Westport, CT: Praeger, 1993.

Landrum, Gene. *Profiles of Female Genius: Thirteen Creative Women Who Changed the World.* Amherst, NY: Prometheus, 1993.

Leavitt, Judith. *Women in Management: An Annotated Bibliography and Sourcelist.* Phoenix, AZ: Oryx, 1987.

Matthaei, Julie A. *An Economic History of Women in America.* New York: Schocken, 1982.

Cabrini, Frances Xavier (1850–1917)

Frances Xavier Cabrini was the first citizen of the United States to be declared a saint by the Roman Catholic church. Frail but strong willed, this "Italian Immigrant of the Century" founded a worldwide religious community of missionary women.

Cabrini was born on July 15, 1850, at Sant'Angelo, near Lodi, in Lombardy, Italy. Her parents, Agostino and Stella, supported their thirteen children by farming. She attended private school in nearby Arluno, earned a teacher's certificate, and then taught for two years at the public school in Vidardo. In 1874, she went to Codogno to work at the House of Providence Orphanage and joined the Sisters of Providence, taking vows in 1877. When the House of Providence was dissolved in 1880, Cabrini, with seven young nuns, started her own community, called the Missionary Sisters of the Sacred Heart. As the number of sisters increased, new foundations were opened in Italy.

Although originally interested in missionary work in China, she was persuaded by Bishop Giovanni Battista Scalabrini of Piacenza and Pope Leo XIII to go to the United States and work among the Italian immigrants there. With a small group of nuns, Cabrini left for the United States in 1889. In New York City, she opened an orphanage, a school, and a hospital, with the sisters depending on gifts and begging to support their work. In the next fifteen years, she established similar institutions in New Orleans, Chicago, Scranton, Denver, Seattle, Los Angeles, and elsewhere. Cabrini also established predominantly educational foundations in Europe and Latin America. By 1905, Cabrini's community had spread into eight countries, the number of houses had grown to fifty, and the number of sisters totaled almost one thousand.

The community received papal approval in 1907. Two years later, Cabrini became a naturalized American citizen. She died of malaria in Chicago on December 22, 1917, and in 1946 she was canonized by the Roman Catholic church. *(See also: Christianity; Immigration; Religion)*

—**Edward C. Stibili**

Further Reading

Borden, Lucille P. *Francesca Cabrini: Without Staff or Scrip.* New York: Macmillan, 1945.

Dall'Ongaro, Giuseppe. *Francesca Cabrini, La Suora che Conquistò l'America.* Milan: Rusconi, 1983.

DeMaria, Saverio. *Mother Frances Xavier Cabrini.* Translated and edited by Rose Basile Green. Chicago: Missionary Sisters of the Sacred Heart of Jesus, 1984.

Maynard, Theodore. *Too Small a World: The Life of Francesca Cabrini.* Milwaukee: Bruce, 1945.

Sullivan, Mary L. *Mother Cabrini: Italian Immigrant of the Century.* New York: Center for Migration Studies, 1992.

Calderone, Mary Steichen (1904–1998)

Considered "the first lady of sex education," Mary Calderone was a leader in the movement to make sex education part of the public school curriculum. Calderone's decision to combine marriage, motherhood, and career was unconventional for a middle-class woman in the 1950s and 1960s. As a medical doctor and public health worker who advocated improvements in contraceptive technologies and sex education, Calderone became a controversial figure in American public life.

Born in New York City to Clara E. Smith and Edward J. Steichen, Calderone spent her first ten years at her parents' home in France. In 1911, with the approach of World War I, she returned to the United States and went to school in Connecticut and New York City. As a student at Vassar, she enrolled in the premedical program. Although she completed the program, her interest in acting led her to study acting for three years, during which time she married W. Lon Warting, also an actor, raised two daughters, and collaborated with her father on two children's photography books. Following her divorce and the death of her elder daughter, she returned to medicine, earning her M.D. from the University of Rochester in 1939 and an M.A. in Public Health in 1942. While continuing her education, she married Dr. Frank A. Calderone, a leading figure in public health.

In 1953, Calderone gave up her part-time job as a public school physician and took the position as medical director of Planned Parenthood, a leading birth control organization. Under her direction, Planned Parenthood introduced new methods in birth control, including the IUD, Emko Foam, and "the pill." Calderone edited and wrote several books on birth control, including *Abortion in the United States* (1958) and *Manual of Family Planning and Contraceptive Practice* (1970). Her interests expanded beyond techniques in birth control to many areas of human sexuality. Recognizing the importance of education for healthy sexual relations, Calderone launched her public career as a lecturer and writer on the need for sex education in the public schools. In 1964, Calderone left Planned Parenthood to become executive director of the Sex Information and Educational Council of the United States (SIECUS), which she helped found. Despite strong criticism from Christian groups and right-wing organizations, SIECUS, under Calderone's leadership, became the major clearinghouse for sex education in the early 1980s.

While working for SIECUS, Calderone published *The Family Book about Sex* (1981) and *Talking with Your Child about Sex* (1982). She traveled thousands of miles, lecturing to schools, parent groups, and organizations about the importance of educating children about the realities of sexual relationships. In her late seventies, Calderone continued her career as an adjunct professor of human sexuality at New York University. In 1988, Calderone retired and settled in a Quaker retirement community in Pennsylvania. She was the recipient of the Margaret Sanger Award from Planned Parenthood Foundation of America, the Lifetime Achievement Award from the Schlesinger Library of Radcliffe/Harvard College, and the Award for Human Service from the Mental Health Association of New York. She was inducted into the National Women's Hall of Fame in 1998. *(See also: Birth Control; Education; Planned Parenthood Federation of America)*

—**Barbara Shircliffe**

Further Reading

Calderone, Mary S., and Eric W. Johnson. *The Family Book about Sexuality.* New York: Harper, 1981.

Calderone, Mary S., and James W. Ramey. *Talking with Your Child about Sex.* New York: Random House, 1982.

Gilbert, Lynn, and Gaylen Moore. "Mary Steichen Calderone." Edited transcript of oral history interview in *Particular Passions: Talks with Women Who Have Shaped Our Times,* pp. 255-63. New York: Carkson N. Potter, 1981.

Naylor, Natalie A. "Mary Steichen Calderone." In *Women Educators in the United States, 1820–1993: A Bio-Bibliographical Source Book,* edited by M. S. Seller, 86-94. Westport, CT: Greenwood, 1994.

⮑ Campbell, Olive Dame (1882–1954)

Olive Dame Campbell was a folklorist, community developer, and founder of the John C. Campbell folk school in Brasstown, North Carolina. Together with her husband, John C. Campbell, she traveled the length and breadth of the southern Appalachian region for the Russell Sage Foundation's Department of the Southern Mountains between 1911 and 1919. After her husband's death in 1919, Campbell anonymously edited his notes and completed the manuscript for *The Southern Highlander and His Homeland,* considered the foundation document of Appalachian studies.

From her earliest travels throughout the Appalachian region, Campbell collected the folk ballads that she heard sung in different communities. In 1916, she persuaded Cecil J. Sharp, a famous English folklorist who was visiting America, to travel in the Appalachian region with her. In those nine weeks, they were able to expand her already substantial collection to 450 tunes, 325 of which were published the following year, in Sharp's words, "exactly as we took them down from the lips of the singers, without editing or adornment 'whatsoever.' " David E. Whisnant offers a balanced assessment of the Campbell-Sharp collaboration and its implications for cultural politics in the Appalachian region.

Olive Campbell was also a moving force (with assistance from Allen Eaton of the Russell Sage Foundation's Department of Art and Social Work and others) in the formation of the Appalachian Craft Guild, headquartered in Ashville, North Carolina, and (like her husband) was a formidable advocate of Danish folk schools for community development in rural America. The John C. Campbell Folk School in Brasstown, North Carolina, opened in January 1926, with financial assistance from the General Education Board. She also compiled a directory of mountain schools in the Appalachian Region from Russell Sage Foundation records, published in 1921. *(See also: Folklore; Music)*

—**Roger A. Lohmann**

Further Reading

Campbell, John C. *The Southern Highlander and His Homeland.* Lexington: University of Kentucky Press, 1921.

Campbell, Olive Dame. *Southern Highland Schools Maintained by Denominational and Independent Agencies.* Compiled by Olive D. Campbell. New York: Russell Sage Foundation, 1921.

Campbell, Olive Dame, and Cecil J. Sharp. *English Folk Songs from the Southern Appalachians.* New York: G. P. Putnam's, 1917.

Whisnant, David E. "All That Is Native and Fine: The Cultural Work of Olive Dame Campbell." In *All That Is Native and Fine,* edited by David E. Whisnant, 103-80. The Fred Morrison Series in Southern Studies. Chapel Hill: University of North Carolina Press, 1983.

⮑ Carson, Rachel (1885–1964)

Environmental writer and scientist Rachel Carson was born in Springdale, Pennsylvania. She earned her B.A. in science at the Pennsylvania College for Women in Pittsburgh and her M.A. in biology from Johns Hopkins University. Carson was affiliated with the zoology staff at the University of Maryland and did postgraduate work at the Marine Biological Laboratory in Woods Hole, Massachusetts.

In 1936, she joined the U.S. Fish and Wildlife Service as an aquatic biologist. She remained with the service until 1952, writing and editing many of their publications. Her own essays and books, beginning with *Under the Sea Wind* (1941) with its beautifully vivid descriptions of sea life,

Figure 12. Rachel Carson
Combining scientific knowledge with literary talent, Rachel Carson raised environmental awareness with her writings on the natural world. Used by permission of Underwood & Underwood/Corbis-Bettmann.

made her internationally famous. *The Sea Around Us* (1951) and *The Silent Spring* (1962) became best-sellers. *The Silent Spring* touched off an international controversy over the effects of pesticides on the environment. Her writings and concern for nature helped stimulate the larger movement to help save the environment from the depredations of modern industrialism. *(See also: Science; Women Writers)*

—**Jonathan W. Zophy**

Further Reading

Brooks, Paul. *The House of Life: Rachel Carson at Work*. Boston: Houghton Mifflin, 1972.

Carson, Rachel. *The Sea Around Us*. Boston: Houghton Mifflin, 1951.

———. *The Silent Spring*. Boston: Houghton Mifflin, 1962.

———. *Under the Sea Wind*. Boston: Houghton Mifflin, 1941.

Wadsworth, Ginger. *Rachel Carson: Voice for Earth*. New York: Lerner, 1991.

∽ Cary, Mary Ann Shadd (1823–1893)

Orator, educator, first black female editor of a weekly newspaper in North America, and lawyer, Mary Ann Shadd Cary was born October 9, 1823, in Wilmington, Delaware, the first of thirteen children of Abraham and Harriet Shadd, a well-to-do black family who provided models of racial commitment to the growing girl. Abraham, a shoemaker by trade, had invested in property to sustain his family while he worked for racial justice and advancement through the National Convention for the Improvement of Free People of Color. An advocate of self-help, Abraham Shadd opened his home to fugitive slaves and moved his entire family to Pennsylvania when education opportunities closed to his children.

Mary Ann Shadd embodied her father's values. Exposure to diverse beliefs was evident in her childhood and education. She was raised as a Roman Catholic, educated in a Quaker school in West Chester, Pennsylvania, and later espoused African Methodism when she felt that assimilation was impossible. Following her graduation from school at the age of sixteen, she returned to Wilmington, Delaware, to open a school for black children. She taught in Delaware, New York, and later in Pennsylvania, believing that education was the most important means for racial uplift.

In 1850, the passage of the Fugitive Slave Act changed the direction of Shadd's career. She accompanied her brother Isaac to Canada to help fugitive slaves to freedom in Canada. In 1852, her pamphlet informed fugitive slaves about the conditions in Canada, while she and her brother taught school in Windsor, Ontario. Her career in journalism started in 1853. After meeting antislavery journalist Samuel Ringgold Ward, Shadd cooperatively launched one of the best fugitive slave weeklies, the staunchly integrationist *Provincial Freeman*. Following her marriage to Thomas G. Cary in 1856, she shared the editorship with her brother and H. Ford Douglass. They found it increasingly difficult to find consistent financial backing, and the paper ceased publication in 1858.

Shadd returned to teaching following the death of her husband in 1860. She supported herself and her children as a teacher at an interracial school in Chatham. During the Civil War, she returned to the United States as a recruiter of "colored" volunteers for the Union Army in Indiana. Following the war, she went to Washington, D.C., where she served as public school principal, wrote for Frederick Douglass's *New National Era*, and entered Howard University to study for a law degree, becoming the first woman to do so.

In addition to her journalistic work for racial betterment, Shadd was active in women's rights organizations. She organized suffrage rallies, testified before the House Judiciary Committee, and spoke to audiences in churches and at the Bethel Literary and Historical Society for the "radical" National Woman Suffrage Association. She helped establish the Washington Colored Woman's League, but her death in 1893 of rheumatism and cancer prevented her from witnessing the national club movement for black women's rights. Her life served as a model for black women as a group to follow. *(See also: Black Women; Black Women's Clubs; Civil War; Colored Woman's League; Journalism; National Woman Suffrage Association)*

—**Dorothy C. Salem**

Further Reading

Bearden, James, and Linda Jean Butler. *Shadd: The Life and Times of Mary Shadd Cary.* Toronto: N. C. Press, 1977.

Brown, Hallie Q., ed. *Homespun Heroines.* Xenia, OH: Aldine, 1926.

Hancock, Harold B. "Mary Ann Shadd: Negro Editor, Educator, and Lawyer," *Delaware History* 15 (April 1973): 187-94.

Mary Ann Shadd Cary Papers. Howard University, Washington, D.C.

Murray, Alexander. "*The Provincial Freeman:* A New Source for the History of the Negro in Canada and the United States," *Journal of Negro History* 44 (April 1959): 123-35.

Silverman, Jason H. "Mary Ann Shadd and the Search for Equality." In *Black Leaders of the Nineteenth Century,* edited by Leon Litwack and August Meier, 87-100. Urbana: University of Illinois Press, 1988.

ᔨ Cassatt, Mary Stevenson (1844–1926)

A major American artist and the only American to win acceptance as a respected colleague of the French impressionists, Mary Cassatt was born in Allegheny City (now Pittsburgh), Pennsylvania. The daughter of the president of the Pennsylvania Railroad, she moved to Europe and lived in Germany and France with her family for nearly five years. While in Paris, she developed a fascination with that city that would last a lifetime. She worked there most of her adult life, although she always considered herself an American.

Over strong objections from her family, Cassatt began her art education at the Pennsylvania Academy of the Fine Arts at the age of seventeen. When she first announced her intention to become an artist, her father exclaimed, "I'd rather have you dead!" After four years of study in the United States, Cassatt prevailed on her family to permit her to go abroad, with a "proper chaperone," to study the Old Masters. She traveled to Spain and Italy first, then settled in Paris. In 1868, her first painting was accepted at the Paris Salon, and she continued sending works there until 1877, when Edgar Degas saw her work and invited her to join the impressionist group. Along with Japanese prints and photography, Degas profoundly influenced her later work.

Cassatt approached her subject matter—generally young women and children, many of them relatives who came to visit—with unsentimental, vigorous craftsmanship. Her keen interest in line and form, carefully modeled to exhibit her deep concern for fine drafting, resulted in a more realistic rendering than that of most of the impressionists. Working in both oils and pastels, Cassatt enjoyed highly successful one-woman shows. During the 1880s, she reached artistic maturity in both fine and graphic arts. Her other greatest contribution to the art world was her encouragement of American tourists abroad to purchase contemporary art and have it exhibited in the United States, as in the Havermeyer collection at the Metropolitan Museum of Art.

In 1904, Cassatt was made a Chevalier of the French Legion of Honor. By 1918, she had become blind from cataracts. At the time of her death in 1926, Mary Cassatt, because of her achievements, had raised the position of women artists to a higher level than anyone had previously considered possible. *(See also: Art)*

—**Janet G. Baldinger**

Further Reading

Boyle, Richard J. *American Impressionists.* Boston: New York Graphic Society, 1971.

Breeskin, Adelyn D. *Mary Cassatt, Catalogue Raisonné of the Oils, Pastels, Watercolors and Drawings.* Washington, DC: Smithsonian Institution, 1970.

Donegan, Frank. "American Impressionists," *Americana* 17 (January/February 1990): 66-69.

Johnson, Deborah J. "Mary Cassatt: The Color Prints," *Burlington Magazine* 132 (January 1990): 72-73.

Love, Richard. *Cassatt: The Independent.* Chicago: Milton H. Kreines, 1980.

Mathews, Nancy Mowll, and Barbara S. Shapiro. *Mary Cassatt: The Color Prints.* New York: Harry N. Abrams, 1989.

National Gallery of Art. *Mary Cassatt: A Private World.* New York: Universe, 1991.

ᔨ Cather, Willa (1873–1947)

Willa Cather, author, was born Wilella Cather in Back Creek, Virginia, the oldest of seven children. The family moved to Red Cloud, Nebraska, when Cather was nine; there, she encountered immigrants from various countries who later found their way into her fiction. Cather attended the University of Nebraska in Lincoln, where she studied Greek and Latin and wrote for several college papers. She also began to write for several Lincoln newspapers, and, by the time she graduated, she had written over three hundred columns.

In 1895, Cather moved to Pittsburgh to edit *Home Monthly* for a year and to work on the *Pittsburgh Daily Leader.* In 1903, she wrote *April Twilights,* a book of verse, and in 1905 *The Troll Garden,* a collection of short stories. Cather moved to New York City the following year to become managing editor of *McClure's Magazine.* Her first novel, *Alexander's Bridge* (1912), was serialized in *McClure's,* after which Cather left the magazine to devote herself to writing. In 1913, she began a relationship with Edith Lewis that lasted until Cather's death.

With Cather's next novel, *O Pioneers* (1913), she introduced one of the subjects to which she would return again and again in her fiction—the old American frontier experience and the heroism of those who lived there contrasted with twentieth-century America and the changes occurring in the new machine age. *The Song of the Lark* (1915) introduced the second of Cather's favorite subjects—the artist's struggle to adjust to society. *My Antonia* (1918) celebrates the courage of an immigrant pioneer woman. *Youth and the Bright Medusa* (1922) is a short-story collection centered around the lives of artists.

Although her nostalgia for the past brought her criticism from liberals who accused her of ignoring the present in her fiction, Cather was still considered one of the best regional writers in the country during the 1920s. Her later books are *A Lost Lady* (1923), *The Professor's House* (1925), *My Mortal Enemy* (1926), *Death Comes for the Archbishop* (1927), *Shadows on the Rock* (1931), *Obscure Destinies* (1932), *Lucy Gayheart* (1935), and *Sapphira and the Slave Girl* (1940). *One of Ours* (1922) won the Pulitzer Prize in 1923, making Cather only the second woman writer to have done so. *Not under Forty* (1936) is a collection of essays that includes pieces on various writers who influenced Cather, most notably Henry James, and presents her theory of fiction. Recent Cather scholarship tends to focus on how (or if) Cather's lesbianism affects gender construction, landscape, and point of view in her work. *(See also: Women Writers)*

—**Victoria L. Shannon**

Further Reading

Cather, Willa. *The Kingdom of Art: Willa Cather's First Principals and Critical Statements, 1893–1896.* Edited by Bernice Slote. Lincoln: University of Nebraska Press, 1966.
———. *On Writing.* New York: Knopf, 1949.
Lee, Hermoine. *Willa Cather: Double Lives.* New York: Pantheon, 1989.
Murphy, John J. *Critical Essays on Willa Cather.* Boston: G. K. Hall, 1984.
O'Brien, Sharon. *Willa Cather.* New York: Chelsea House, 1995.
———. *Willa Cather: The Emerging Voice.* New York: Oxford University Press, 1987.
Woodress, James Leslie. *Willa Cather: A Literary Life.* Lincoln: University of Nebraska Press, 1987.

๛ Catt, Carrie Chapman (Lane) (1859–1947)

Carrie Chapman Catt challenged social thinking in the late nineteenth and early twentieth centuries as a teacher, school administrator, suffragist, and peace advocate. After graduating from Iowa State College in 1880, she studied law but chose to become principal of the Mason City (Iowa) High School in 1881 and two years later became one of the first women superintendents of schools. Between 1887 and 1890, she established suffrage clubs in the state and eventually organized the Iowa Woman Suffrage Association. Recognizing her abilities, the National American Woman Suffrage Association (NAWSA) elected her in 1900 to succeed Susan B. Anthony as president, a post she held until 1904.

The next phase of Catt's career focused on international and New York suffrage. She founded the International Woman Suffrage Alliance and remained active in it until World War I intervened. While working on the international scene, she organized the New York woman suffrage movement and masterminded its unsuccessful campaign in 1915. These activities reveal her talents for leadership, organization, imaginativeness, and determination. With war hinder-

ing her participation in world suffrage, she thus became a viable candidate again for the national leadership of NAWSA.

Elected in 1915 to succeed Anna H. Shaw as president, Catt immediately set the national organization on course to win enfranchisement. Her insight suggested a shift from educational propaganda to political action, while her strategy included the development of a master plan for action. This represented a "turning of the corner" in the drive for the Nineteenth Amendment. She did not openly support either Woodrow Wilson or Republican Charles Evans Hughes in 1916. This foresight probably helped her to be able to call on Wilson for his support during the final drive for woman suffrage. Catt believed that women needed to support the war effort to gain the political favor needed to pass the woman suffrage amendment.

With successful ratification of woman suffrage in August 1920, Catt only slightly altered her course. She assisted in creating the League of Women Voters to continue the struggle to ensure full suffrage, remove legal discrimination, and democratize political structures. Also, during the 1920s, she urged women to support the League of Nations. Her later years were devoted to peace and disarmament through the National Committee on the Cause and Cure of War and the Woman's Peace Party. *(See also: League of Women Voters; National American Woman Suffrage Association; Suffrage; Woman's Peace Party)*

—**Ted C. Harris**

Further Reading

Catt, Carrie C., and Nettie R. Shuler. *Women Suffrage and Politics: The Inner Story of the Suffrage Movement.* New York: Scribner, 1923.
Fowler, Robert B. *Carrie Catt: Feminist Politician.* Boston: Northeastern University Press, 1986.
Peck, Mary Gray. *Carrie Chapman Catt, A Biography.* New York: Wilson, 1944.
Ziegler, Susan. "Finding a Cure for War: Women's Politics and the Peace Movement in the 1920s," *Journal of Social History* 24 (Fall 1990): 69-86.

๛ Center for Women and Religion

The Center for Women and Religion was founded in 1970 at the Graduate Theological Union in Berkeley, California, as a nondenominational and interfaith center "to end sexism, provide support and promote justice for women in religious institutions." More specifically, the center addresses "racism, classism, and economic justice issues for women, while retaining [its] interfaith commitment."

The center offers a wide variety of programs each year, ranging from networking services for women in religious academic and clerical professions to providing referrals for feminist psychotherapists and spiritual directors. The center offers one course per semester that can be taken for credit through the Graduate Theological Union, as well as funding distinguished guest lectures annually and sponsoring luncheon colloquia and seminars and retreats for center members and for the general public.

The center publishes a bimonthly newsletter as well as the more substantial *Journal of Women and Religion,* published annually, which offers articles on feminist ethics, theology and spirituality, and book reviews in addition to information about job openings and available grants and other resources.

More information is available from the Center for Women and Religion, 2400 Ridge Road, Berkeley, California 94709; phone (510) 649-2490; fax (510) 649-1730. *(See also: Christianity; Religion; Theologians)*

—**B. Jill Carroll**

Further Reading

"Center for Women and Religion Calendar (January-February 1996)." Pamphlet. Berkeley, CA: Center for Women and Religion.

Ray, Inna Jane, ed. "Membership Newsletter." Berkeley, CA: Center for Women and Religion, 1996.

～ *Charlotte Temple, A Tale of Truth*

Charlotte Temple, A Tale of Truth (1791), by Susanna Haswell Rowson, was intended, as the author mentions on the third page of the text, to be a guide "for the perusal of the young and thoughtless of the fair sex." While providing the story of the title character, Rowson hoped the book would enlighten those young women who had no friends to help them cope with life's evils. As a prototype of nineteenth-century prescriptive fiction for women, the book became more than a mere guidebook; by the early 1800s, this classic among the didactic literature that used the seduction theme had sold more copies than any other book in the history of either Britain or the United States.

The implicit moral enforced by the "seduced and abandoned" plot of *Charlotte Temple* entertained while instructing its readers that the unavoidable fate of a woman's fall from grace and respectability was the ruin of her character and her social status. Ultimately, the main character dies of heartache (her only option), and Rowson reveals Charlotte's death as a traumatic but inevitable incident; this popular cautionary tale for young women was far-reaching in its influence on the development of the genre of the domestic novel in the nineteenth century.

Rowson, one of the first professional women writers in the United States, was born in England and migrated permanently in 1793 to the United States where she became a stage actor and playwright. After leaving the theater, she opened a boarding school for girls in Boston and continued writing. *Charlotte Temple,* however, remained her most noted and popular text with over 160 editions published in its first three years of release. *(See also: Domestic Literature in the United States; Prescriptive Literature; Women Writers)*

—**James A. Howley**

Further Reading

Greenfield, Susan. "*Charlotte Temple* and *Charlotte's Daughter:* The Reproduction of Woman's Word," *Women's Studies* 18 (1990): 269-86.

Harris, L., and S. Fitzgerald, eds. *Nineteenth Century Literary Criticism.* Vol. 5. Detroit, MI: Gale, 1984.

Rowson, Susanna Haswell. *Charlotte Temple, A Tale of Truth.* London: William Lane, 1791; Philadelphia: Mathew Carey, 1794.

Well, Dorothy. *In Defense of Women: Susanna Rowson (1762–1824).* University Park: Pennsylvania State University Press, 1976.

～ Chesnut, Mary Boykin (Miller)
(1823–1886)

Mary Chesnut, Confederate diarist, was born into a socially and politically prominent South Carolina family and married James Chesnut, Jr., also of an important South Carolina family. Her upbringing included education in Charleston, wide reading in literature, life on plantations in South Carolina and Mississippi, and intense interest in Southern politics. Her husband's political career in federal and state government enlarged her social universe, including a brief stay in Washington, D.C. (1859–1860), during which she became friends with Southern families such as the Jefferson Davises. Secession brought the Chesnuts back to the South and gave Mary Chesnut an excellent vantage point to observe the social and political world of the Confederacy.

Accompanying her husband to Montgomery, Alabama, to Richmond, Virginia, to Columbia, South Carolina, and to their plantation home, Mulberry, near Camden, South Carolina, Chesnut lived intimately with the problems of nation building, war, and human relations within the Confederacy. Fiercely loyal to the Southern cause, she became intimate with the Davises and, while in Richmond, maintained a salon of sorts that wielded considerable influence.

During the war, Chesnut wrote a secret diary that formed the basis of her later writings. Her wartime diaries recorded penetrating sketches of numerous Confederate personalities, reactions to Southern fortunes in war, and Chesnut's hatred of slavery and the oppression of women that slavery encouraged. Her account is one of the most important primary sources on Confederate leaders and Southern society during the Civil War.

After the war, the Chesnuts lost most of their lands and political influence, but Mary Chesnut, who lived most of the postwar years in straitened circumstances in Camden, continued to write. She drafted three novels (never published), several stories, and a biography of her husband, and sought the proper genre to express her wartime experiences. She transcribed the diaries, adding material from memory to create narrative flow and fill in gaps in the original record, and revised and polished them over several years. By the 1880s, she had produced a massive manuscript. In adopting the diary form as the genre to give her experiences full literary expression, she blended autobiography, memoir, letters, history, and fiction to create what is now generally regarded as the best single literary contribution from the Civil War.

She never published her book. Two editions of it appeared that established Chesnut's reputation. In 1905, her friend Isabella Martin helped bring out an edition titled *A Diary from Dixie,* comprising less than half the original manuscript and cleansed of "offensive" material. Critics regarded the book as a classic example of Southern "Lost Cause" literature. In 1949, novelist Ben Ames Williams edited an even shorter version in which he altered Chesnut's original meaning in several ways. In 1981, historian C. Vann Woodward published the complete, unexpurgated 1880s manuscript under the title *Mary Chesnut's Civil War.* Chesnut's surviving Civil War diaries for 1861 and 1865 were published in 1984 as *The Private Mary Chesnut.*

Chesnut's book reveals an uncommon intellect. Her condemnations of slavery and women's plight in a slave society, even as she enjoyed the amenities of the "peculiar institution" and the indulgences of her class, have been cited repeatedly by historians as evidence of Southern guilt over slavery and an emerging feminine consciousness among privileged Southern white women. Chesnut's brilliant journal, with its full cast of characters embracing all strata of Southern society, captures the spirit of Southern resistance so well that it has become the metaphor for the historic crisis of her age. *(See also: Civil War; Slavery; Southern Lady)*

—**Randall M. Miller**

Further Reading

Chesnut, Mary Boykin. *Mary Chesnut's Civil War.* Edited by C. Vann Woodward. New Haven, CT: Yale University Press, 1981.

————. *The Private Mary Chesnut: The Unpublished Civil War Diaries.* Edited by C. Vann Woodward and Elisabeth Muhlenfeld. New York: Oxford University Press, 1984.

DeCredico, Mary A. *Mary Boykin Chesnut: A Confederate Woman's Life.* Madison, WI: Madison House, 1995.

Muhlenfeld, Elisabeth. *Mary Boykin Chesnut: A Biography.* Baton Rouge: Louisiana State University Press, 1981.

Rable, George C. *Civil Wars: Women and the Crisis of Southern Nationalism.* Urbana: University of Illinois Press, 1989.

Chicago, Judy (b. 1939)

Feminist artist Judy Chicago was born Judy Cohen in Chicago, Illinois. She received a B.A. in 1962 and an M.A. in 1964 from UCLA and became a successful West Coast minimal sculptor in the late 1960s, exhibiting in the Jewish Museum's *1966 Primary Structures* exhibition and in the Los Angeles County exhibition *Sculpture of the Sixties.* In 1972, Chicago finished her first collaborative project, titled *Womanhouse,* a literal house that became a metaphor for female captivity. During that same year, Chicago founded the first feminist art program, the Feminist Studio Workshop at the Women's Building in L.A. She also taught at California State University at Fresno and the California

Institute of Arts. Although she is primarily a sculptor and painter, her media have included ceramics, needlework, plastics, environments, and china painting.

Chicago worked on her famous project *The Dinner Party* for three years before she sought the help of others: artists, researchers, and administrative assistants, approximately 400 people altogether. *The Dinner Party* is one of the rich legacies of the feminist movement of Western women through the media of women's traditional crafts: china painting, embroidery, and weaving.

The centerpiece of *The Dinner Party* is a banquet table set with painted ceramic plates on richly embroidered place mats. Each plate evokes the accomplishments of an outstanding woman, from the Primordial Goddess and Ishtar to Sojourner Truth, Susan B. Anthony, Virginia Woolf, and Georgia O'Keeffe. The place mats are made with materials and techniques of embroidery appropriate for each subject, and their imagery develops the themes of the plates. An egg, crescent, breastplate, and double axe, for instance, appear on the Amazon's place mat, while Mary Wollstonecraft's is decorated with pictures of her life embroidered in stump work, a style of raised needlework popular in England in the seventeenth century.

The triangle, a sign of the goddess, appears repeatedly throughout *The Dinner Party.* The huge triangular banquet table stands on a "Heritage Floor" formed from triangular opalescent porcelain tiles. Each tile is inscribed with a woman's name, 999 in all. As light plays on the tiles, the names appear and disappear, symbolizing both Western woman's tenuous hold on her place in history and the rootedness of the thirty-nine honored guests in the lives and accomplishments of other women.

The Dinner Party made women's history at the same time that it honored the achievements of women of the past. Although Judy Chicago oversaw the production of every element of the work, an army of volunteers wove the tapestries, embroidered the place mats, amassed the 999 names, and painted the floor tiles—and most of those volunteers were women. Producing *The Dinner Party* yielded a new feminist approach to art in which mutually supportive women worked together to replace the isolated individual creator of traditional art.

Although record-breaking crowds of more than 100,000 people stood in line two to three hours to see *The Dinner Party* when it first opened at the San Francisco Museum of Modern Art in 1979, few museums were willing to show it. Its second opening was at the University of Houston–Clear Lake, after the Houston museums had refused it. Feminists charged that the major museums' neglect of *The Dinner Party* arose from a combination of hostility to feminist themes and disinterest in women's arts of needlework, weaving, and china painting. At present, *The Dinner Party* is in storage. Despite years of attempts, no permanent home has been found for it.

In 1980, Chicago began a needlepoint project titled *The Birth Project.* This project, which expresses the experience of childbirth that is central to so many women's lives, celebrates the mythical and the painful through creation and goddess images, images of women giving birth, and images of the birth trinity, the birth tear, and many other births.

Chicago changed her focus in her next project. In 1985, she and her husband Donald Woodman, both strong in their Jewish faith and sense of history, began to research the Holocaust. They visited Nazi concentration camps and Jewish grave sites. The result, titled *The Holocaust Project,* is a collaborative work of photography and painting on photolinen. Chicago returns to her focus on women in her most recent project, again a collaborative effort. The work features thirteen needlepoint artists in a multimedia project called *Resolutions for the Millennium—Stitch in Time* premiering at the American Craft Museum in 2000.

Her books include *The Dinner Party: A Symbol of Our Heritage* (1979), *Through the Flower: My Struggle as a Woman Artist* (1975), *Embroidering Our Heritage: Dinner Party Needlework* (1980), *The Birth Project* (1985), *The Holocaust Project* (1993), and *Beyond the Flower* (1996). She also made two films, *Womanhouse* and *Right Out of History: The Making of* The Dinner Party. *(See also: Anthony, Susan B.; Art; O'Keeffe, Georgia; Truth, Sojourner)*

—**Ginger Costello**

—**Gretchen Mieszkowski**

Further Reading

Chicago, Judy. *The Birth Project.* Garden City, NY: Doubleday, 1985.

———. *The Dinner Party: A Symbol of Our Heritage.* Garden City, NY: Anchor, 1979.

———. *Embroidering Our Heritage: The Dinner Party Needlework.* Garden City, NY: Doubleday, 1980.

———. *Holocaust Project: From Darkness into Light.* Donald Woodman, photographer. New York: Viking, 1993.

———. *Through the Flower: My Struggle as a Woman Artist.* Introduction by Anaïs Nin. Garden City, NY: Doubleday, 1975, 1977.

Lippard, Lucy. "Judy Chicago's Dinner Party," *Art in America* 68 (1980): 115-26.

Witzling, Mara R. "Through the Flower: Judy Chicago's Conflict between a Woman-Centered Vision and the Male Artist Hero." In *Writing the Woman Artist: Essays on Poetics, Politics, and Portraiture,* edited by Suzanne W. Jones, 196-213. Philadelphia: University of Pennsylvania Press, 1991.

౳ *Chicana*

The preferred term to refer to women of Mexican ancestry in the United States, *Chicana,* is the feminine form of *Chicano.* As with most terms of self-identity, the use of the term Chicana is a matter of individual preference and self-determination. Regional and generation differences exist with regard to its use as a self-referent. Thus, there is no one Chicana. There are different women who call themselves Chicana and who identify themselves with the Aztec culture and a mestizo heritage. In addition, Chicana also connotes the dignity and pride of Mexican Americans working to achieve political, economic, and social equality. Other umbrella terms such as *Latina* and *Hispanic* are deemed euphemistic and too imprecise to distinguish Chicanas from other Spanish-speaking peoples; they fail to acknowledge indigenous roots in favor of distant European roots.

Chicanas have significant diversity in their ethnic identity, primary language, education, occupations, and economic status. Common characteristics of Chicanas as resident members of a colonized minority within the United States include being of Mexican descent and yet of a unique culture with both Mexican and American influences. The unique blend of Mexican and American cultures as typified by Chicano culture is dynamic and as such is in a constant state of flux. As Chicanas gain more economic power, their traditional roles within the household, as well as their partners' or spouses' roles, are changing. Therefore, the stereotypical Chicano cultural concepts of *hembraismo* and *machismo* as defined by the mainstream of Anglo culture greatly oversimplify the gender patterns within the Chicano family. Hembraismo actually designates the time-honored matriarchal role of competent and enduring woman in the home rather than woman as only docile, weak, and submissive. Likewise, machismo encompasses the traditional patriarchal male role of protector and provider, not merely the male traits of power, assertion, and domination. Together, the terms form a familial whole around which individuals are strongly united. In today's families, the characteristics highlighted by each term are not as specifically gender linked as stereotypically portrayed.

Chicanas inherited the disenfranchisement and displacement of those Mexican people who were summarily absorbed by the United States after the Treaty of Guadalupe-Hidalgo in 1848, which ended the U.S.-Mexican War. As the victims of internal colonialism, Chicanas are Third World persons, discriminated against in terms of gender, class, and race. *(See also: Chicana/Latina Education; Mexican War; Triple Jeopardy)*

—**Patricia L. Prado-Olmos**

—**Angela M. Howard**

Further Reading

Anzaldua, Gloria. *Borderlands/La Frontera: The New Mestiza.* San Francisco: Spinsters/Aunt Lute, 1987.

DuBois, Ellen C., and Vicki L. Ruiz, eds. *Unequal Sisters: A Multicultural Reader in U.S. Women's History.* New York: Routledge, 1990.

Keefe, Susan E., and Amado M. Padilla. *Chicano Ethnicity.* Albuquerque: University of New Mexico Press, 1987.

Melville, Margarita, ed. *Twice a Minority.* London: C. V. Mosby, 1980.

Mirande, Alfredo, and Evangelina Enriquez. *La Chicana: The Mexican-American Woman.* Chicago: University of Chicago Press, 1979.

Zavella, Patricia. *Women's Work and Chicano Families: Cannery Workers of the Santa Clara Valley.* Ithaca, NY: Cornell University Press, 1989.

~ Chicana/Latina Education

Chicana/Latina education generally refers to the status of the identified group within the U.S. educational system. *Latina* generally refers to females of Mexican, Puerto Rican, Cuban, Central or South American, or other Spanish culture or origin. Dropout status is a widely used indicator of education status. A dropout is defined as a person who is not currently enrolled in school and does not have a high school diploma or an equivalent certificate. Graduation and dropout status tend to be used as convenient, if imprecise, measures of academic success and academic failure. These measures reveal little about how much or how little knowledge a student has acquired as well as the real learning opportunities and experiences students have.

Data from 1996 National Center for Education statistics indicate that among the population of sixteen- to twenty-four-year-olds the dropout rate for Latinos was 29.4 percent, compared with 13 percent for non-Latino blacks and 7.3 percent for non-Latino whites. Data from the 1990 census indicate that differences exist in the dropout rates for various Latino subgroups. Central Americans had the highest rate of 36 percent, followed by Chicanos with a rate of 34 percent. South Americans had the lowest dropout rate of 12 percent. The dropout rate for Latino males was 59 percent, for Latina females 41 percent. The overall dropout rate for Latinos has been relatively constant for the last 10 years in contrast to the declining dropout rate for white and black non-Latinos.

The data available indicate that Latinos most at risk of dropping out are those who fall into one or more of the following categories: (a) not born in the United States, (b) with limited English-speaking ability, (c) from poor families, and (d) either married or mothers. Latinas who had been married had a dropout rate about five times higher than those who had never been married. The dropout rate among married mothers was higher than the rates for married but childless females and unmarried mothers.

Numerous programmatic efforts for improving educational outcomes for Latinas and Chicanas have been undertaken. Among the most widely known efforts is bilingual education. Bilingual education is designed to provide instruction in the student's native language until such a time as he or she has acquired the necessary English language skills to participate in English-only classrooms. Research indicates that participation in bilingual education programs leads to positive academic outcomes. This body of research has explored the cognitive benefits of bilingualism, the continued academic success of bilingual students, and ways in which to provide the best instruction in a bilingual environment. However, in 1998, California voters passed the antibilingual education measure, Proposition 227. Proposition 227 requires non-English-speaking students to be placed in "English immersion" classrooms for one year and then moved into English-only instruction. No guidelines or models for "English immersion" exist, and school districts were in upheaval as the 1998–1999 school year began. The consequences of Proposition 227 will be far-reaching and are not predicted to be positive. *(See also:* Chicana; *Education)*

—Patricia L. Prado-Olmos

Further Reading

Arias, M. Beatriz, and Ursula Casanova, eds. *Bilingual Education: Politics, Practice, Research.* Chicago: University of Chicago Press, 1993.

Espinoza, James D., Terry Hanford, and Pamela Tumler. *Hispanics' Schooling. Risk Factors for Dropping Out and Barriers to Resuming Education.* Washington, DC: General Accounting Office, 1994.

Padilla, Amado M., Halford H. Fairchild, and Concepcion M. Valadez, eds. *Bilingual Education: Issues and Strategies.* Newbury Park, CA: Sage, 1990.

Trueba, Henry T., ed. *Success or Failure? Learning and the Language Minority Student.* Cambridge, MA: Newbury House, 1987.

U.S. Department of Education. National Center for Education Statistics. *Dropout Rates in the United States, 1996.* NCES 98-250. Marilyn McMillen, project officer. Washington, DC: Government Printing Office, 1997.

Valencia, Richard R., ed. *Chicano School Failure and Success: Research and Policy Agendas for the 1990s.* London: Falmer, 1991.

~ Child, Lydia Maria Francis
(1802–1880)

Lydia Maria Child, author and abolitionist, was born in Medford, Massachusetts, the youngest child of a prosperous baker, David Francis. After her mother died, she lived with a sister in Norridgewock, Maine; when her brother Convers settled near Boston, she joined his family. Among his friends were Emerson, Whittier, and other informed men whose conversation interested the young Maria Francis; both her antislavery attitudes and her desire to write grew in this congenial atmosphere.

Her first book, *Hobomok* (1824), was a romance based on the Abenaki Indian lore she had learned as a young girl in Norridgewock. Although she signed the book "An American," her name was soon known, and fame and attention followed. She wrote *The Rebels* (1825), a novel based on Revolutionary War history, and edited *Juvenile Miscellany,* the first American magazine for children. Other novels and collections of verse and prose followed. In October 1828, against the wishes of her family, she married the idealistic and improvident David Lee Child, a lawyer who shared her strong abolitionist sentiments. The establishment of their small household on her income led to *The Frugal Housewife* (1830), a very popular compendium of advice for the economical management of a home.

At their house in Roxbury, the Childs enjoyed entertaining their friends, chief among whom were abolitionists Theodore Parker, William Ellery Channing, and John Greenleaf Whittier. Child's antislavery commitment strengthened, and in 1833, she wrote *An Appeal in Favor of That Class of Americans Called Africans.* This reasoned appeal for just treatment and an end to slavery was too far ahead of its time to win popular approval. However, the book had a strong influence on Channing, other abolitionist leaders such as Thomas Wentworth Higginson, and most important, Wendell Phillips. Shortly thereafter, she wrote *The History of the Condition of Women* (1835) and *Philothea, A Story of Ancient Greece* (1836).

In 1839, David Francis bought a farm in Northampton, Massachusetts, where he hoped his daughter could live in comfort while his worthless son-in-law grew sugar beets. Mr. Francis lived with them there and, caught between her father and her husband, Maria felt trapped and exiled. She cherished the occasional drives with the Reverend John Sullivan Dwight to Boston, where she could visit friends, go to libraries or transcendentalist meetings, and attend the "conversations" run by her close friend Margaret Fuller.

When David Child refused the editorship of the New York *Anti-Slavery Standard* in 1841, Maria took the job instead, moving to New York and lodging with a Quaker family whose house was a station on the Underground Railroad. From New York, she wrote newsletters for the *Boston Courier,* which were eventually published as *Letters from New York* (1843, second series 1845). These widely read newsletters reestablished Child as a major literary figure. In 1843, she resigned, and David came to New York to replace her. They remained in New York until 1849; during that period, Maria wrote innumerable stories and articles for newspapers, magazines, and annuals, as well as her newsletters and many works for children.

They returned to live with her father in Wayland, Massachusetts. Francis died in 1856, leaving the farm to his daughter but carefully arranging matters so that control of money and property was kept from his son-in-law. A major work, *The Progress of Religious Ideas* (1855), a study of comparative religion, displayed her wide knowledge and intellect; it was admired by theologians and scholars, although it had no popular audience. She kept a steady income, however, with books for children and with anthologies.

Child's abolitionism and the fugitive slave controversy inspired her to write pamphlets and articles. *The Correspondence between Lydia Maria Child, Governor Wise, and Mrs. Mason* (1860), published by the Anti-Slavery Society, recorded her attempt to help John Brown in prison and with its aftereffects. It contained letters from Governor Wise of Virginia and an attack from Mrs. Mason, whose husband had written the Fugitive Slave Act; Mason accused Child of being un-Christian and not knowing her Bible; Child's response was informed, thorough, and scorching. She edited and wrote the introduction for *Incidents in the Life of a Slave Girl* by Harriet Brent Jacobs ("Linda Brent"), and in 1865, concerned for the newly freed slaves, she wrote *The Freedmen's Book,* a combination of inspiration and advice.

After David Child died in 1874, she wrote very little. In the last years of her life, she visited friends and relatives and lived with a companion. She died in October 1880. *(See also: Abolition and the Antislavery Movement; Domestic Feminism; Domestic Literature in the United States; Fuller, Margaret; Housework; Women Writers)*

—Theresa A. McGeary
Adapted for the second edition by Patricia R. Henschen.

Further Reading

Baer, Helene G. *The Heart Is Like Heaven.* Philadelphia: University of Pennsylvania Press, 1964.

Child, Lydia Maria. *The Freedmen's Book.* Boston: J. Allen, 1835.

———. *The Frugal Housewife: Dedicated to Those Who Are Not Ashamed of Economy.* London: T. T. & J. Tegg, 1832.

———. *The History of the Condition of Women in Various Ages and Nations.* Boston: Ticknor & Fields, 1865.

———. *The Mother's Book.* Boston: Carter & Hendee, 1831.

———. *Selected Letters, 1817–1880.* Edited by Milton Meltzer and Patricia G. Holland. Amherst: University of Massachusetts Press, 1982.

Karcher, Carolyn L. *The First Woman in the Republic: A Cultural Biography of Lydia Maria Child.* Durham, NC: Duke University Press, 1995.

Mills, Bruce. *Cultural Reformations: Lydia Maria Child and the Literature of Reform.* Athens: University of Georgia Press, 1994.

Osborne, William S. *Lydia Maria Child.* Boston: Twayne, 1980.

Yellin, Jean Fagan. *Women and Sisters: The Anti-Slavery Feminists in American Culture.* New Haven, CT: Yale University Press, 1989.

⮹ Childbirth

Childbirth, or parturition, is the act of giving birth. Early American women spent the majority of their married life either pregnant or nursing an infant. Childbirth was the culmination of nine months of preparation and pregnancy, as well as the precipitating event of usually thirteen months of breast-feeding an infant. Such childbirth matters occupied about sixteen years of a seventeenth-century woman's married life, during which she gave birth about ten times. By the last half of the nineteenth century, a woman gave birth closer to four times; a century later, typically, a woman will give birth twice or less.

In early America, childbirth was a women's rite. A woman recognized her own signs of the impending birth; she knew when to call "her women," when to send her husband for the midwife, and what to expect in the hours ahead. In a room or area set apart from the activity of the household, the women gathered. Soothing teas eased the expectant mother through the dilation stage of her labor. When she felt ready to deliver, she might do so on a birthing stool the midwife had brought, or she might choose another comfortable position. The midwife was in charge, but comments and suggestions from all were heard. The midwife was well equipped to handle difficulties such as excessive pain, slow progress, and a poorly positioned fetus, but most labors were normal, and the women were used to waiting.

When physicians moved into the birthing chamber in the second half of the eighteenth century, they were less willing to wait. They brought instruments—forceps in particular—to hurry along the delivery, and used bloodletting and other measures, such as tobacco enemas and later ergot (an oxytocic drug derived from a rye grain fungus), to speed up labor or opium to slow it down. By the mid-nineteenth century, doctors were using ether and chloroform to dull or erase childbirth pain.

With doctors' increasing role, childbirth was becoming a singular event to be managed medically rather than one part of the sequence from pregnancy through the nursing period that fit into the rhythms and rituals of everyday life. Women were still present at birth through the nineteenth century, but they were rarely in charge and were less often the only ones present. Attention at childbirth increasingly focused on medical aspects of the labor and delivery, on managing the woman's experience.

The twentieth century saw birth moved out of the home and into the hospital, where management could be controlled even more effectively. A variety of drugs and other interventions were introduced during the century as childbirth became thoroughly medicalized. But since the 1960s, a movement to reinstate "natural childbirth" has endeavored to return childbirth to its nonmedical state. The home birth and midwifery movements, as well as the establishment of birthing centers in hospitals, are working to return birth to the realm of women's experience in the family, to have it perceived as an essentially normal process that sometimes requires medical backup but that is not pathological and does not necessarily call for a medical response. *(See also: "Granny" Midwifery; Immigrant Midwifery; Midwifery)*

—**Janet Carlisle Bogdan**

Further Reading

Arms, Suzanne. *Immaculate Deception II.* Berkeley: Celestial Arts, 1994.

Bogdan, Janet Carlisle. "Care or Cure? Childbirth Practices in Nineteenth Century America," *Feminist Studies* 4 (1978): 92-99.

———. "Childbirth in America, 1650–1990." In *Women, Health, and Medicine in America: A Historical Handbook,* edited by Rima D. Apple, 101-20. New York: Garland, 1990.

Eakins, Pamela S., ed. *The American Way of Birth.* Philadelphia: Temple University Press, 1986.

Leavitt, Judith Waltzer. *Brought to Bed.* New York: Oxford University Press, 1986.

Rothman, Barbara K. *In Labor: Women and Power in the Birthplace.* 1982. Reprint, New York: Norton, 1991.

Child Rearing

The primary occupation of most women at some point in their lives, child rearing is both a source of emotional satisfaction and a stressful job that can tie women to the home. Colonial women typically spent most of their lives raising children, but household and farm chores left little time for child rearing per se. Mothers breast-fed infants but shared responsibility for child care with older children, neighbors,

and fathers. Children as young as six years old might be apprenticed outside the family.

The nineteenth and twentieth centuries saw the flowering of an ideology that placed children at the center of family life, glorified the mother-child relation, and stressed women's responsibility for the physical and psychological well-being of their offspring. Between 1800 and 1900, the number of living children born to married white women dropped from 7.04 to 3.56. This reduction in family size, along with the leisure afforded to middle-class women by the removal of industrial production from the home and a decline in infant mortality, changed the focus of middle-class child rearing from physical health to psychological development. Most middle-class women embraced the "professionalization" of motherhood by 1900, but many working-class women, immigrants, and women of color continued to follow traditional child-rearing practices.

At the turn of the twentieth century, experts taught mothers to raise children to succeed in an industrial world by adhering to strict schedules, beginning toilet training early, and bottle-feeding by the clock. In the 1920s, psychologists warned that excessive mother love obstructed children's personality development. By the 1950s, warnings against mothers' tendency to spoil children coexisted with a renewed idealization of the mother-child bond. Benjamin Spock's influential *Baby and Child Care* (1946) maintained that the mother's loving attention was essential to her child's emotional health and security and that women should structure household routines and careers around their children. By the 1980s, child care experts such as best-selling author Penelope Leach had discarded the idea that babies could be spoiled. They advised mothers to breast-feed on demand, to maintain close physical contact by carrying their baby as much as possible, and to follow the child's lead in toilet training.

Despite the existence of these experts, many women had neither the time nor financial resources to follow child-rearing advice. Although few mothers—with the exception of blacks—worked outside the home until World War II, housework and poverty took time away from child care. As the twentieth century drew to a close, most mothers of young children were in the labor force and shared the work of child care with relatives, babysitters, and day care providers. Despite the efforts of some feminists to establish affordable day care or to provide government allowances for women to care for children at home, most child rearing is still done without pay by mothers in private households. *(See also: Housework; Scientific Motherhood)*

—**Molly Ladd-Taylor**

Further Reading

Grant, Julia. *Raising Baby by the Book: The Education of American Mothers.* New Haven, CT: Yale University Press, 1998.

Hardyment, Christina. *Dream Babies.* New York: Harper & Row, 1983.

Hoffert, Sylvia D. *Private Matters: American Attitudes toward Childbearing and Infant Nurture in the Urban North, 1800–1860.* Urbana: University of Illinois Press, 1989.

Ladd-Taylor, Molly. *Mother-Work: Women, Child Welfare and the State, 1890–1930.* Urbana: University of Illinois Press, 1994.
———. *Raising a Baby the Government Way: Mothers' Letters to the Children's Bureau, 1915–1932.* New Brunswick, NJ: Rutgers University Press, 1986.

·~· Children's Library Movement (1876–1910)

The increasing presence of women on the staff of American public libraries from the mid-1870s brought with it the development of public library services to children. This development drew on several movements and attitudes common to the period. For example, the tendency of professional women to innovate new areas distinct from established male specialties is evident in the growth of children's services. The growing interest in the child during this period, as exemplified by the influential work of Evelyn Key, *The Century of the Child* (1909), which popularized modern child development principles, and the ongoing tradition that women had a special gift for working with children both contributed to the service. Finally, the middle-class women who promoted this service among poor immigrant children in the large industrial cities of the Northeast and Midwest remembered their own cultured upbringing and sought to re-create it for their charges. The growth of services to children in the public libraries brought those institutions into closer collaboration with schools, settlement houses, and hospitals caring for children, where many like-minded women were also building careers. Not surprisingly, considering the identification with women, the growth of services to children in public libraries is one of the most poorly researched areas in library history.

Minerva Saunders, librarian of the Pawtucket (Rhode Island) Public Library, is generally credited with being the first, beginning in 1877, to end age restrictions on access to the collection, provide suitable books for children, and provide suitable furniture in one corner of the reading room to be used by the children. The two major missing ingredients of modern children's services were soon added in 1894, when the Denver Public Library set aside a separate room, formerly a ladies' reading room, for children, and in 1898, when Anne Carroll Moore began giving courses in work with children at the Pratt Institute in Brooklyn. The first comprehensive children's department was opened in the Carnegie Library of Pittsburgh by Frances Jenkins Olcott in 1898. In 1910, this library issued a classic document authored by Olcott, titled *Rational Library Work with Children and the Preparation for It,* which summarizes the role of the children's library and librarians. The library, it said, should "take the place of a child's private library," giving the child a chance to browse among books of all kinds in a "beautifully proportioned and decorated room," assisted by a "genial and sympathetic woman" with a genuine interest in the child's personality. *(See also: Librarianship)*

—**Suzanne Hildenbrand**

Figure 13. Shirley Chisholm
Congresswoman Shirley Chisholm speaks at one of the the first pro-choice rallies in New York City. Used by permission of Bettye Lane.

Further Reading

Jagusch, Sybille A. "First among Equals: Caroline M. Hewins and Anne C. Moore. Foundations of Library Work with Children." Ph.D. diss., University of Maryland–College Park, 1990.
McNamara, Shelley G. "Early Public Library Work with Children," *Top of the News* 43 (Fall 1986): 59-71.
Smith, Karen Patricia, ed. "Imagination and Scholarship: The Contributions of Women to American Youth Services and Literature," *Library Trends* 44 (Spring 1996): 679-895.
Thomas, Fannette Henrietta. "The Genesis of Children's Services in the American Public Library: 1875–1906." Ph.D. diss., University of Wisconsin–Madison, 1982.

·~· Chisholm, Shirley (St. Hill) (b. 1924)

In 1968, Shirley Chisholm became the first black woman elected to the U.S. House of Representatives. From 1968 to 1982, she served in Congress as a Democrat representing the Twelfth district of Brooklyn, New York. For a while, she was Purrington Professor of Political Science at Mount Holyoke College in South Hadley, Massachusetts. She is the author of *Unbought and Unbossed* (1970) and *The Good Fight* (1973).

Chisholm was born in New York but went to live with her grandparents on their farm in Barbados at the age of four, living there and attending British schools until the age of ten, when she returned to her parents' home. She attended schools in Brooklyn and graduated from Brooklyn College in 1946, later receiving an M.A. in elementary education from Columbia University. After leaving school, she worked as a teacher and as assistant director of a nursery school in Harlem, director of a small private school, and director of the Hamilton-Madison Day Care Center in Manhattan.

Simultaneously, Chisholm became more involved in the politics of the Bedford-Stuyvesant area of New York. Capitalizing on her political tutelage in Democratic political clubs, she secured a vacant seat in the state assembly in 1964 and was reelected in 1965 and 1966. Race was less a factor in the Twelfth congressional district in Brooklyn than were sex or other topical issues. There were thirteen thousand more women than men in the district, and more than three times as many black women as black men were registered to vote. Chisholm mobilized this potential constituency and defeated James Farmer.

In 1972, Chisholm made history again by announcing her candidacy for the Democratic presidential nomination. Responding to the rising consciousness of women of all races and their increased interest and participation in politics, she and her running mate, Cissy Farenthal of Texas, introduced the major women's rights issues into the presidential primaries debate. The congresswoman emerged from the unsuccessful campaign a national spokesperson for women and the black community. Her dynamic speeches and adamant support of women's rights established her presence and prominence in the history of the modern women's movement.

During the Reagan administration, Chisholm decried cuts in federal grants for education agencies. On February 10, 1982, Chisholm announced that she would not run for reelection, favoring a return to private life over the difficult battles to effect change in an increasingly conservative political atmosphere. (See also: Black Women; Democratic Party; Politics)

—Susan Kinnell

Further Reading

Brownmiller, Susan. *Shirley Chisholm: A Biography*. Garden City, NY: Doubleday, 1971.
Chisholm, Shirley. *The Good Fight*. New York: Harper & Row, 1973.
Duffy, Susan. *Shirley Chisholm: A Bibliography of Writings by and about Her*. Metuchen, NJ: Scarecrow, 1988.
Haskins, James. *Fighting Shirley Chisholm*. New York: Dial, 1975.
http://www.triadntr.net/rdavis/chisholm.htm [A brief biography]
http://pathfinder.com/photo/essay/african/cap02.htm [A recent portrait]
http://www/ttemple.org/TrinityRd/AllSites/BlackHistoryMonth/People/shirleychisholm.htm [A biographical sketch]

~ Chopin, Kate (1850–1904)

Although Kate O'Flaherty Chopin lived forty of her fifty-four years in St. Louis, Missouri, the city of her birth, she is best known for the stories and novels whose Louisiana settings placed her among the southern "regionalist" and "lo-

cal color" writers of the late nineteenth century. In many ways, however, Chopin exceeded the bounds not only of region but also of nineteenth-century gender expectations. Fluent in French, she translated for American journals the stories of Guy de Maupassant, whose melancholy themes profoundly influenced her. But in applying similar themes to the situations of women in her own milieu, she created a body of work that explores virtually every convention restricting the lives of middle-class women at the turn of the century. Of French-Irish extraction, vivacious, well educated, tough-minded, and socially prominent, Chopin bore six children during her twelve-year marriage. She brought to her fiction a range of life experiences that authenticate the myriad characters in her stories. Her brother's service in the Civil War and her years in a convent school are among the facts of her life that find their way into her works.

Chopin began writing for publication six years after her husband's death from malaria in 1882. In the interim, she had successfully run the family store in Cloutierville, Louisiana, and paid off the debts Oscar Chopin (a cotton broker) had accumulated in the years before his death. Prior to their residence in Cloutierville, the Chopins had enjoyed a life of relative luxury, living successively in three different homes in the stylish "American" (as opposed to the Creole) sections of New Orleans. During these turbulent years of the Reconstruction era, the Chopins traveled abroad, kept servants, and spent summers on Grand Isle (a resort near New Orleans in the Gulf of Mexico where her most celebrated novel *The Awakening* is set). Unlike most women of her class, however, Chopin took solitary walks in the city, closely observing the multifaceted culture around her, sometimes smoking her favorite brand of little cigars.

Having put her financial life in order after Oscar's death, Chopin returned to her hometown of St. Louis, where between 1889 and her death in 1904 she produced an astonishing number of short stories, numerous critical reviews, social commentaries, and three novels. Most of her short stories—some of which were published in prestigious magazines, including *Vogue, The Youth's Companion, Atlantic Monthly, Harper,* and *Century*—are collected in three volumes: *Bayou Folk* (1894), *A Night in Acadie* (1897), and *A Vocation and a Voice* (published posthumously). From her first surviving story "Emancipation: A Life Fable" to *The Awakening,* Chopin is concerned with the ways in which the urge for independence within individuals is both manifest and stymied by cultural attitudes and conventions. This central theme is examined in the context of controversial issues such as miscegenation, suicide, social Darwinism, alcoholism, venereal disease, homosexual desire, and marital infidelity. Modern readers find Chopin's works remarkably insightful and courageous with regard to these rather sensitive subjects and thus view with irony that in her day Chopin was renowned almost exclusively for the atmosphere of "local color" she so aptly conveyed.

With the publication of *The Awakening* in 1899, however, critical attention focused on Chopin's previously unnoticed emphasis on female sexual desire and its relationship to a woman's drive for independence. Edna Pontellier, the heroine, was roundly criticized for her marital infidelity and apparent lack of maternal instincts. Most repellent of all to the critical public of 1899, however, was Edna's failure to repent and her purposeful, unsentimentalized suicide at the end of the novel.

Edna is initially awakened to sexuality by a young Creole but also experiences other awakenings as she moves toward life as an independent woman. A friend's torturous childbirth makes clear that, even if Edna struggles against society's demands, she cannot escape the fetters of motherhood. That episode, in conjunction with her lover's desertion, makes Edna believe the only way to avoid surrender is suicide, and she drowns herself.

The very strength of the critics' hostility—the book was called "moral poison" and was banned in St. Louis, Chopin's home—attested to the power of *The Awakening* when it appeared. Although Chopin accepted the novel's castigation with ironic equanimity, her failing health and untimely death, apparently from a brain hemorrhage, precluded her completing another full-length work. In the late 1950s, after fifty years of neglect, *The Awakening* and Kate Chopin began to receive the critical acclaim they deserved. Currently, the novel is among the top twenty of most frequently required literary texts on college syllabi in America. In terms of the questions it raises about women's various responsibilities, sexuality, differences one from another, and self-determination, it has seldom been equaled. The style, which combines naturalistic detail with mythic undertones, equals and surpasses many of the canonized male writers even of the modern period. *(See also: Women Writers)*

—**Mary Lowe-Evans**
—**Mabel Benson DuPriest**

Further Reading

Ewell, Barbara C. *Kate Chopin*. New York: Ungar, 1986.
Toth, Emily. *Kate Chopin*. New York: Morrow, 1990.
Walker, Nancy. "Introduction: Biographical and Historical Contexts." In *Case Studies in Contemporary Criticism: Kate Chopin*, The Awakening, edited by Nancy Walker, 3-18. Boston: Bedford Books of St. Martin's Press, 1993.

❧ Christianity (American)

Women have been involved in the Christian movement since its beginnings, although throughout most of Christian history, in the church and in society, they have not occupied positions of prominence, their involvement being largely limited to the private sphere. Christian immigrants to the United States brought with them many religious traditions, most of which excluded women from positions of leadership. However, there have been some exceptions. In the Colonial period, Anne Hutchinson (1591–1643) became the leader of the opposition party in the antiauthority crisis in seventeenth-century Massachusetts. She believed that individuals of both genders could communicate with the Spirit of Christ and interpret Scriptures and sermons on their own. Other colonial women such as Mary Dyer and Ann Easton also resisted the subordinate role that most religious communities assigned to women. Only a minority sect, the Society of Friends, or Quakers, granted Colonial women full participation in ministry.

One of the dominant paradigms throughout American Christianity has been revivalism, which emphasized personal regeneration, moral responsibility, the imminence of the Second Coming, and the need for individuals to bear "visible fruit." One result was often a blurring of the distinctions between the public and the private sphere, which in turn afforded women many new venues for participation in church and community. Between 1815 and 1840, a period often known as the Second Great Awakening, women prayed publicly, organized revival meetings, and published religious newspapers, such as the *Advocate of Moral Reform*. Women were especially active in a whole constellation of parachurch activities, including abolition, Moral Reform, dress and dietary reform, missionary movements, and the Sunday school movement. During this same time period, some women also exerted significant spiritual leadership within local congregations and even in several small, radically populist denominations, such as the Freewill Baptists and the Christian Connexion. A number of women preached and exhorted in their own congregations and as itinerate preachers throughout New England and the Eastern Seaboard. African American Jarena Lee (1783–?) and New Englander Harriet Livermore (1788–1868) were perhaps the preeminent female itinerants of the period: Livermore even preached on several occasions before the U.S. Congress.

The first known pastoral ordination of a woman took place in 1853 when Antoinette Brown Blackwell (1825–1921) was ordained into the Congregational ministry. But the window of leadership opportunity that had been open to women during this period shut soon after, owing to a variety of factors. Most significant was the new "higher criticism" of the Bible coming from Germany, the 1854 publication of Darwin's *Origin of the Species,* and the newly developing science of geology: These developments led many to question the authority and veracity of Scripture. Finding themselves on the defensive as the nineteenth century drew to a close, significant numbers of Protestants began to insist that Scripture should be interpreted "literally," and they constructed elaborate theories of biblical inspiration and infallibility to buttress the authority of Scripture. One unfortunate consequence of this development was the tendency to view the degree of women's leadership in church and society as a sort of litmus test of scriptural orthodoxy. It is not surprising, given the existence of passages such as 1 Timothy, that churches that allowed women a greater degree of involvement were often viewed as heterodox.

While women have usually made up the majority of active church members in the United States, well into the twentieth century they were denied admission to the professional ministry in most Protestant denominations. The Presbyterians began to ordain women in 1956, and several large Lutheran synods did so in 1970. The largest Protestant denomination in the United States, the Southern Baptists, does not ordain women, and the ordained leadership of the Roman Catholic and Orthodox churches remains exclusively male. Because the Episcopal Church, USA, does ordain women, individual bishops who refuse to ordain them request another bishop to perform the ordination so that there can be women priests in that diocese. Fundamentalist denominations do not ordain women, nor do many Evangelical denominations, although women are playing increasingly large roles in Evangelical church life. Although socially conservative, many charismatic groups are more open to women's leadership because they posit the Holy Spirit, rather than Scripture, as their primary source of authority.

Given the central importance of the Bible for most Protestant denominations, it is not surprising to see that some of the liveliest feminist religious scholarship in the nineteenth and twentieth centuries has focused on Scripture, especially those texts that have been regarded as most problematic for women. Innovative methodologies, careful readings of the text, and reconstruction of the cotext have enabled scholars such as Elizabeth Schussler Fiorenza, Phyllis Tribble, and others to bring fresh insights and new interpretations to bear on many biblical texts. Their work has occasioned a major reappraisal of traditional interpretations of several scriptural texts, including the accounts of the Creation and Fall in Genesis, the admonishments for women to remain silent in 1 Timothy, and Paul's personal greetings to his many co-workers in Romans 16. Newer interpretations of these texts have called into question long-standing assumptions that biblical women did not serve as religious leaders and spiritual authorities in their local religious communities.

In the last fifteen years, many Christians have begun to question the gender exclusivity of the language of Christian worship. That inclusive language is now such an important issue among so many Protestant churches is due almost entirely to the work of feminist Christian scholars who have argued persuasively that language does not just reflect reality but also creates it. Thus, they have worked to rid Christian worship and the lectionary system of exclusivistic and patriarchal language. Although this effort has met with resistance, many churches have become much more sensitized to the unjustifiably masculine nature of much liturgy, hymnody, and terminology for God.

The second half of the twentieth century has brought many changes to American Christianity, not the least of which has been the profound effect of feminist Christian scholarship on Christian theology, and the entry of women into positions of leadership in many denominations. This has irrevocably changed the landscape of American Christianity. Yet no woman has thus far occupied the highest office in any mainline denomination, and several denominations, including Roman Catholics and Southern Baptists, have become increasingly unwilling even to discuss the possibility of women's ordination. Women compose the majority of church members in most American denominations but are still underrepresented in leadership positions. *(See also: American Missionary Association; Blackwell, Antoinette Brown; Cabrini, Frances Xavier; Center for Women and Religion; Coughlin, Mother Mary Samuel; Episcopal Women; Fiorenza, Elizabeth Schussler; Lentfoehr, Sister Mary Therese; Lutheran Women; McPherson, Aimee Semple; Methodist Women in the Nineteenth Century; Presbyterian Women's Groups; Religion; Shakers; Society of Friends; Southern Baptist Woman's Missionary Society; Southern Christian Leadership Conference; Theologians; Women's Missionary Societies)*

—Sandra E. Roberts
—Jonathan W. Zophy
—Cynthia Jurisson

Further Reading

Carmody, Denise Lardner. *The Good Alliance: Feminism, Religion, and Education.* Lanham, MD: University Press of America, 1991.

Clark, Elizabeth A. *Women and Religion: The Original Sourcebook of Women in Christian Thought.* San Francisco: Harper, 1996.

Fiorenza, Elizabeth Schussler. *In Memory of Her: A Feminist Reconstruction of Christian Origins.* New York: Crossroad, 1983.

Fischer, Clare B., Betsy Brenneman, and Anne M. Bennett, eds. *Women in a Strange Land: Search for a New Image.* Philadelphia: Fortress, 1975.

Jewett, Paul K. *The Ordination of Women: An Essay on the Office of Christian Ministry.* Grand Rapids, MI: Eerdmans, 1980.

Mollenkott, Virginia. *The Divine Feminine: The Biblical Imagery of God as Female.* New York: Crossroad, 1983.

Ogden, Amy, ed. *In Her Words: Women's Writings in the History of Christian Thought.* Nashville, TN: Abingdon, 1994.

Ramshaw-Schmidt, Gail. *Christ in Sacred Speech: The Meaning of Liturgical Language.* Philadelphia: Fortress, 1986.

Ruether, Rosemary. *Sexism and God-Talk: Toward a Feminist Theology.* Boston: Beacon, 1983.

Scanzoni, Letha, and Nancy Hardesty. *All We're Meant to Be: A Biblical Approach to Women's Liberation.* Waco, TX: Word, 1975.

Wahlberg, Rachel Conrad. *Jesus and the Freed Woman.* New York: Paulist, 1978.

～ Cigar Makers/Tobacco Workers

Women's role in the tobacco, cigar, and cigarette industries has ranged from highly prized positions as hand rollers of fine cigars to lowly jobs in the stemming rooms. Skilled Bohemian and Cuban women cigar makers arrived in the United States beginning in the late nineteenth century, and manufacturers soon took advantage of their abilities. At the same time, unskilled immigrant and native-born black women stripped leaves from stems, earning low wages and suffering from the heat and humidity necessary to maintain quality tobacco.

Male cigar makers forged the powerful Cigar Makers International Union in the 1880s, but they generally excluded women from their ranks. The radical, Havana-based union, *La Resistencia,* which was active in Florida, was one of the few in which skilled and unskilled women and men were organized together. In most areas of the country, women's massive entry into the cigar industry rested on the union-busting tactics of the larger cigar manufacturers as well as on expanded production of cheaper cigars and automation. By 1919, these conditions prevailed, and women formed 58 percent of the total cigar factory labor force; by 1940, they made up 81.3 percent. Lower production figures and lower-priced cigars combined in the 1930s to reduce both workforce and wages, reductions halted only temporarily by World War II.

The cigarette industry was established in Virginia and North Carolina in the 1880s but expanded most rapidly in the early 1900s with the amalgamation of the tobacco trusts, which led to more centralized control of the market, and with the full automation of production. Although men served as machine operators and foremen, women early formed a significant portion of the cigarette labor force. Both black and white women from rural areas, equally unskilled, were drawn into the industry out of economic necessity. Yet white women soon dominated the more skilled positions, while black women were relegated to the stemmeries. Attempts to organize the cigarette industry, which peaked in the 1930s, were inhibited by the racial and sexual division of labor. In cities such as Durham, North Carolina, unionization reinforced racial tensions by protecting white but not black women's jobs. In the same period, more progressive organizers from the Congress of Industrial Organizations aided in organizing black stemmery workers in Richmond, Virginia, and Winston-Salem, North Carolina.

The tobacco, cigar, and cigarette industries were critical sources of employment for immigrant women in northern cities and in Florida and for black and white women in the Carolinas and Virginia. Although the sexual division of labor circumscribed women's opportunities in these industries, variations in skill, in levels of automation, and in the extent of unionization, in addition to racial tensions, placed women in competition with each other. Women's prominence in tobacco manufacturing occurred simultaneously with recognition of the product's damaging health effects. The latter has led to campaigns to limit consumption of cigarettes and force the industry to contribute to health care costs for long-time smokers. Thus, as women came to dominate the labor force, wages and working conditions deteriorated along with the public appeal of tobacco products. *(See also: Congress of Industrial Organizations; Industrial Revolution; Unions)*

—Nancy A. Hewitt

Further Reading

Cooper, Patricia. *Once a Cigar Maker: Men, Women and Work Culture in American Cigar Factories, 1900–1919.* Urbana: University of Illinois Press, 1987.

Hewitt, Nancy A. " 'The Voice of Virile Labor': Labor Militancy, Community Solidarity, and Gender Identity among Tampa's Latin Workers." In *Work Engendered: Toward a New History of American Labor,* edited by Ava Baron, 142-67. Ithaca, NY: Cornell University Press, 1991.

Janiewski, Dolores. *Sisterhood Denied: Race, Gender, and Class in a New South Community.* Philadelphia: Temple University Press, 1985.

⟡ Civil Liberties Movement During World War I

The United States declared war on Germany on April 6, 1917. One week later, New York City members of the Woman's Peace Party (WPP/NYC) initiated the establishment of the New York Bureau of Legal First Aid (later renamed and hereafter referred to as the New York Bureau of Legal Advice, or BLA), the first organization of the World War I era to offer free legal aid and counsel to draft-age men and conscientious objectors to military service. The executive secretary and directing force of the BLA was Frances Witherspoon, who, like many of her female comrades of the young peace movement generation, was a feminist, a pacifist, and a socialist. She enlisted the assistance of both women and men in civil liberties work, but capable women such as birth control advocate and lawyer Jessie Ashley and socialist labor organizer Ella Reeve Bloor provided the backbone of her organization.

At the same time that the WPP was helping to launch the BLA, several members of the American Union Against Militarism (AUAM)—notably Crystal Eastman, a feminist socialist labor lawyer and the head of the WPP/NYC, and Roger Baldwin, a social worker and the associate director of the AUAM—were establishing a legal aid committee within the AUAM that by fall 1917 had become autonomous, the National Civil Liberties Bureau (NCLB). Despite the involvement of a few women like Eastman on the initial directing committee, the NCLB, unlike Witherspoon's group, quickly became a predominantly male organization.

In 1917 and 1918, the BLA (for New York City) and the NCLB (for the rest of the country) provided legal assistance not only to draft-age men and conscientious objectors but also to labor leaders and rank-and-file members of "radical" labor groups such as the Industrial Workers of the World (IWW) and to political radicals (and liberals) arrested for alleged violations of wartime sedition laws. Both groups helped influence the federal government to eliminate one of the cruelest punishments of military prison: Manacling of prisoners to cell bars for nine hours per day for up to fourteen days was halted in late 1918. The BLA and NCLB, in concert with other associations, also lobbied, in this case unsuccessfully, for immediate amnesty for conscientious objectors and political prisoners after an armistice was declared on November 11, 1918. The BLA enjoyed a special triumph when in 1919 it was able to quash deportation proceedings for a number of IWW members with alien status.

The BLA and the NCLB shared leadership of the World War I civil liberties movement. But other organizations arose as well, sometimes as affiliates of the NCLB but often as autonomous groups that were nonetheless linked to the larger organizations by personal ties and common goals. Women were important in such associations—for example, Emma Goldman of the No-Conscription League, Eleanor Fitzgerald of the League for the Amnesty of Political Prisoners, and Lola Maverick Lloyd and Lenetta Cooper of the American Liberty Defense Union.

None of the wartime civil liberties groups in which women were so prominent existed beyond 1919, although the male-led and male-dominated NCLB survived, becoming the American Civil Liberties Union after the war. The reasons for the fading of women's involvement in civil liberties work are complex, but contributing factors include "burnout" of leaders such as Witherspoon, who needed time to recover from the demands of wartime activism; the reactionary antifeminist political climate of the 1920s, which demoralized many women activists; and factionalism in the feminist movement after 1920. Then, too, although women and men had worked shoulder to shoulder during the war and immediately thereafter in civil liberties work, a number of men, especially the "big guns," according to Witherspoon, were "antifeminist." This attitude influenced postwar developments, and women found themselves, to a degree, edged out of the civil liberties field, particularly at the leadership level. *(See also: Goldman, Emma; Industrial Workers of the World; Pacifism and the Peace Movement; Witherspoon, Frances M.; Woman's Peace Party)*

—Frances H. Early

Further Reading

Early, Frances H. "Feminism, Peace, and Civil Liberties: Women's Role in the Origins of the World War I Civil Liberties Movement," *Women's Studies* 18 (1990): 95-115.

———. *A World without War: How U.S. Feminists and Pacifists Resisted World War I.* Syracuse, NY: Syracuse University Press.

Records of the New York Bureau of Legal Advice. Tamiment Institute of Labor History at New York University.

Records of the New York Bureau of Legal Advice, the American Union Against Militarism, and the Woman's Peace Party. Swarthmore College Peace Collection, Swarthmore, PA.

ꙮ Civil Rights

Civil rights are governmental guarantees of equality. As we have interpreted the U.S. Constitution, we hold our rights as individuals, yet many of the basic rights and responsibilities of citizenship have been denied to individuals because of their membership in an oppressed group. The most historically obvious groups were women and slaves, but many other groups have been excluded because of prejudice, including all nonwhite peoples, gays and lesbians, the poor and working classes, and persons with disabilities. Historically, gaining civil rights has required struggle by those excluded.

The term *civil rights movement* usually refers to the struggle of African Americans since emancipation, particularly af-

ter World War II, to attain the basic rights of citizens guaranteed by the post-Civil War amendments; the term *women's rights movement* usually refers to the first wave of struggle by women in the nineteenth century, and contemporary liberal feminists are the primary inheritors of this struggle in the second wave. The movements are not always easily distinguishable, because many women are viewed, and view themselves, as participants in both race-based and gender-based movements. The civil rights movement can itself be defined more broadly, as the wave of mass protest by African Americans that emerged after World War II inspired other racially and otherwise excluded groups to organize large-scale protests aimed at attaining civil rights.

Civil rights struggles have pursued three interrelated goals. One set of goals was aimed at access to the responsibilities of full citizenship. While that included the right to vote, it also included the right to make contracts, own property, and sue and be sued (all necessities for economic autonomy) as well as the right to serve on juries, hold political and governmental office, and work in positions that require licensing by a governmental body. Because the rationales for excluding white women from these basics of citizenship differed from those that excluded women of color, attaining civil rights often came piecemeal and in ways that exacerbated racial, ethnic, and class tensions, both within women's movements and across progressive ones. Successful strategies sought legislation, executive enforcement, and court decisions. However, without the Equal Rights Amendment that would have placed gender at the same protected level as race in the Constitution, even these rights remain elusive for some women. Without the ability to exercise the responsibilities of citizen empowerment, struggling for further advances is difficult.

A second set of civil rights goals has aimed at striking down social and economic barriers, particularly those encoded into law. This struggle initially focused on achieving equal opportunity. The civil rights struggle to dismantle Jim Crow segregation in the South, including access to public schools, represents this form of struggle well. It highlighted the necessity for voting, jury service, and officeholding on the part of the excluded: Had they not claimed the right to make, enforce, and adjudicate policy, the dominant society could easily have reimposed de jure segregation. Equality-based legislation included the Equal Pay Act of 1963 that required equal pay for equal work and the Civil Rights Act of 1964 that forbade discrimination on the basis of race or sex in hiring, firing, and promotion and created the Equal Employment Opportunity Commission (EEOC) to review complaints. In 1972, education amendments to the Civil Rights Act prohibited schools that receive federal aid from discriminating on the basis of race or sex, while the Equal Employment Opportunity Act put teeth into the EEOC by empowering it to file lawsuits on behalf of complainants. The Equal Credit Opportunity Act of 1974 prohibited discrimination on the basis of sex or marital status in credit transactions.

As necessary as these achievements were, they did not necessarily gain women equality of outcomes or equity, and that became a further goal of civil rights struggles. The problem of economic autonomy for women provides a clear example. While the Equal Pay Act mandated equal pay for equal work, Congress chose not to enact the broader standard of equal pay for comparable work advocated by feminist organizations. Even so, businesses tried to avoid the pay increases the law required by titling the jobs held by men and women differently, a practice successfully challenged in the federal courts in 1970. The court decisions interpreted the law as prohibiting different pay for similar rather than identical work but still left women and racial minorities subject to race-, class-, and sex-segmented labor markets. As of 1998, women make 73 percent as much as men ("About the National Committee on Pay Equity"). *(See also: Affirmative Action; Civil Rights Act of 1964; Equal Employment Opportunity Commission; Equal Pay Act of 1963; Equal Rights Amendment; Politics; Sex Discrimination; Suffrage; United States Supreme Court; Voting Rights; Women's Rights Movements: Nineteenth and Twentieth Centuries)*

—**Deb Hoskins**

Further Reading

"About the National Committee on Pay Equity (NCPE)." Available at http://www.feminist.com/fairpay.htm

Button, James W., Barbara A. Rienzo, and Kenneth D. Wald. *Private Lives, Public Conflicts: Battles over Gay Rights in American Communities.* Washington, DC: C. Q. Press, 1997.

Evans, Sara M. *Personal Politics: The Origins of Women's Liberation in the Civil Rights Movement.* New York: Vintage, 1979.

Goldstein, Leslie Friedman. *Contemporary Cases in Women's Rights.* Madison: University of Wisconsin Press, 1994.

Hartmann, Susan M. *From Margin to Mainstream: American Women and Politics since 1960.* New York: Knopf, 1989.

Leavit, Nancy. *The Gender Line: Men, Women, and the Law.* New York: New York University Press, 1998.

Marcus, Erin. *Making History: The Struggle for Gay and Lesbian Equal Rights, 1945–1990: An Oral History.* New York: HarperCollins, 1992.

McClain, Charles, ed. *Asian Indians, Filipinos, Other Asian Communities, and the Law.* New York: Garland, 1994.

Miller, Diane Helene. *Freedom to Differ: The Shaping of the Gay and Lesbian Struggle for Civil Rights.* New York: New York University Press, 1998.

Otten, Laura A. *Women's Rights and the Law.* Westport, CT: Praeger, 1993.

Richards, David A. J. *Women, Gays, and the Constitution: The Grounds for Feminism and Gay Rights in Culture and Law.* Chicago: University of Chicago Press, 1998.

Roberts, Dorothy E. *Killing the Black Body: Race, Reproduction, and the Meaning of Liberty.* New York: Pantheon, 1997.

Robnett, Belinda. *How Long? How Long? African American Women in the Struggle for Civil Rights.* New York: Oxford University Press, 1997.

Robson, Ruthann. *Gay Men, Lesbians, and the Law.* New York: Chelsea House, 1997.

Schulman, Sarah. *My American History: Lesbian and Gay Life during the Reagan/Bush Years.* New York: Routledge, 1994.

Stetson, Dorothy McBride. *Women's Rights in the U.S.A.: Policy Debates and Gender Roles,* 2d ed. New York: Garland, 1997.

Williams, Patricia J. *The Alchemy of Race and Rights: Diary of a Law Professor.* Cambridge, MA: Harvard University Press, 1991.

Wunder, John R. *Retained by the People: A History of American Indians and the Bill of Rights.* New York: Oxford University Press, 1994.

Yarbrough, Tinsley E. *The Reagan Administration and Human Rights.* New York: Praeger, 1985.

⮑ Civil Rights Act of 1964

The Civil Rights Act of 1964 was a comprehensive law empowering the federal government to move against discrimination on a variety of fronts. Promoted by the civil rights movement and its supporters, the bill initially focused on racial discrimination. But Title VII of the act, which prohibited discrimination by employers and labor unions and created an Equal Employment Opportunity Commission (EEOC) to enforce the measure, included a ban on sex discrimination as well.

The amendment to insert "sex" into Title VII was introduced by a Virginia representative who supported legal equality for women but opposed civil rights legislation. Although liberals and civil rights supporters sought defeat of the amendment that they felt would jeopardize passage of the entire section, the amendment passed and was subsequently accepted by the Senate. While there was no mass women's movement demanding an attack on sex discrimination, a handful of congresswomen fought for the amendment, and a small group of women lobbyists exerted pressure from the outside.

Once enacted, the ban on sex discrimination spurred women's activism and helped launch a new surge of feminism. Frustration with the EEOC's failure to take sex discrimination seriously was an important catalyst for the founding of the National Organization for Women (NOW), the first national feminist organization. In addition, Title VII caused federal courts to strike down protective labor laws that applied only to women, thereby eliminating a major source of opposition to an equal rights amendment.

Since its passage, Title VII has been strengthened through amendment or interpretation. In 1972, Congress brought educational institutions and state and local governments under the law and empowered the EEOC to take cases to court on its own initiative. Congress amended the law again with the Pregnancy Discrimination Act of 1978, which banned discrimination against pregnant women in areas such as sick leave, medical benefits, and seniority. In 1986, the Supreme Court ruled that sexual harassment constituted sex discrimination under Title VII. And the Civil Rights Act of 1991 allowed women to win cash damages (up to $300,000) for intentional discrimination.

Tens of thousands of women have filed sex discrimination charges under Title VII. Feminist organizations and labor unions have also filed suits, and the EEOC has filed class action suits against a number of large corporations. Although overall occupational segregation by sex persisted and a large pay gap between men and women continued, Title VII diminished discrimination against women workers. Through out-of-court settlements or consent decrees, women won back pay and affirmative action remedies amounting to millions of dollars. *(See also: Affirmative Action; Civil Rights; Equal Employment Opportunity Commission; National Organization for Women; Sex Discrimination)*

—Susan M. Hartmann

Further Reading

Brauer, Carl M. "Women Activists, Southern Conservatives, and the Prohibition of Sex Discrimination in Title VII of the 1964 Civil Rights Act," *Journal of Southern History* 49 (1983): 37-57.

Harrison, Cynthia. *On Account of Sex: The Politics of Women's Issues, 1945–1968.* Berkeley: University of California Press, 1988.

Robinson, Donald A. "Two Movements in Pursuit of Equal Employment Opportunity," *Signs: Journal of Women in Culture and Society* 4 (Spring 1979): 413-33.

Wallace, Phyllis A. "Impact of Equal Employment Opportunity Laws." In *Women and the American Economy,* edited by Juanita M. Kreps, 123-45. Englewood Cliffs, NJ: Prentice Hall, 1976.

ᴥ Civil War (1861–1865)

The U.S. Civil War represented a watershed in national and regional history, but events of that era did not produce a total transformation of either American, northern, or southern society. Despite the tendency toward expansive estimates, gauging the war's impact on women's lives is best done in small increments. When this cataclysm had spent itself, the northern military victory had eliminated slavery, but it had hardly given rise to egalitarianism. Racism, sexism, and classism remained largely intact. Mary Todd Lincoln and Varina Howell Davis, the first ladies of the divided nation and both native southerners, drew criticism from contemporaries. Mrs. Lincoln came under suspicion for her southern sympathies; Mrs. Davis, for her northern connections.

As hostilities commenced, females as well as males in both the North and the South mobilized. Women continued to perform traditional roles as wives, mothers, daughters, and sisters, but in numerous instances, they moved beyond a circumscribed private sphere into what heretofore had largely been a public masculine world. When the slaughter had spent itself, leaving in its wake thousands of deaths, debilitating wounds, and recurring illnesses, the healing process most assuredly required enormous contributions and compromises by women. A sprinkling of northern females who had stepped from abolitionism into women's rights faced male colleagues who reminded them that this was "the black man's hour." In fact, southern white females may have experienced the most profound alteration in status because defeat in battle served to weaken the region's patriarchy and

to encourage female participation in public life. Ironically, black women who had reason to be the most hopeful probably knew the greatest disappointment.

The Civil War placed men center stage as generals, politicians, and diplomats and provided the cast of thousands for the armies. Females took supporting or lesser parts. For more southern women than ever before, the war and its aftermath meant "going out to work." Danger hung over those who filled cartridges for the Confederate Ordnance Department, and accidents at Brown's Island in the James River of Virginia and at a Jackson, Mississippi, factory killed or disfigured several young women, many of them just teenagers. Meanwhile, Yankee and Confederate women assumed responsibility for running farms and plantations and operating businesses. They rallied to collect and distribute supplies, establish hospitals, serve as nurses, and provide relief for widows, orphans, and disabled veterans. Northern heroines included Dorothea Lynde Dix, superintendent of nurses for the Union Army, along with nurses and U.S. Sanitary Commission agents such as Clara Barton and Mary Ann Ball "Mother" Bickerdyke. Confederate President Jefferson Davis commissioned Sally Louisa Tompkins a captain so that her hospital could be designated as an Army hospital in Richmond. From 1862 to 1865, Mrs. Phoebe Yates Pember served as chief matron of Chimborazo Hospital, which was also located in the Confederate capital. Mary Custis Lee, the wife of General Robert E. Lee, counted herself among the thousands of southern refugees. A few women disguised themselves as men and fought in the ranks of both the Union and Confederate armies, and still others, Rose O'Neal Greenhow, Belle Boyd, and Pauline Cushman, became spies, the first two for the South, the latter for the North. Female prostitutes serviced "Johnny Rebs" and "Billy Yanks."

The general acceptance of female subordination continued after the war and knew no geographical boundaries. Neither northerners nor southerners of the late nineteenth century seemed prepared to come to terms with the radical and fundamental changes that would have been required to afford the black race and the female gender a fair and equitable status in American society. Nonetheless, the war brought subtle although significant social, economic, and political alterations that heightened the expectations of some females. *(See also: Barton, Clara; Dix, Dorothea Lynde; United States Sanitary Commission)*

—Margaret Ripley Wolfe

Further Reading

Culpepper, Marilyn Mayer. *Trials and Triumphs: The Women of the American Civil War.* East Lansing: Michigan State University Press, 1991.

Faust, Drew Gilpin. *Mothers of Invention: Women of the Slaveholding South in the Civil War,* Fred W. Morrison Series in Southern Studies. Chapel Hill: University of North Carolina Press, 1996.

Jones, Jacqueline. *Labor of Love, Labor of Sorrow: Black Women, Work, and the Family from Slavery to the Present.* New York: Basic Books, 1985.

Massey, Mary Elizabeth. *Bonnet Brigades.* New York: Knopf, 1966.

Rable, George C. *Civil Wars: Women and the Crisis of Southern Nationalism.* Urbana: University of Illinois Press, 1989.

Scott, Anne Firor. *The Southern Lady: From Pedestal to Politics, 1830–1930.* Chicago: University of Chicago Press, 1970.

Wiley, Bell Irwin. *Confederate Women.* Westport, CT: Greenwood, 1975.

Wolfe, Margaret Ripley. *Daughters of Canaan: A Saga of Southern Women.* Lexington: University Press of Kentucky, 1995.

Clarke, Mary Elizabeth (Betty)
(b. 1924)

Mary Elizabeth Clarke began her military career as a private in the Women's Army Corps in August 1945 and completed it thirty-six years later in October 1981 as a major general. She was selected to fill positions in the Army never before held by a woman officer. One was as commander of the U.S. Army Military Police School and Training Center at Fort McClellan, Alabama (1978–1980). In this assignment, she was the first female commissioned officer to command an Army installation of great magnitude and extent. She was promoted to major general in November 1978, becoming the WAC's first two-star major general. Her next unique position was that of director of human relations in the Office of the Deputy Chief of Staff for Personnel of the Army (1980–1981)—a major executive position on the Army general staff.

Clarke was born December 3, 1924, in Rochester, New York. At age 20, she entered the Women's Army Corps and served as an enlisted woman and noncommissioned officer for over three years. After graduation from Officer Candidate School (1949), she commanded WAC units from company to battalion level, recruited enlisted women, and served in several staff officer positions. In September 1972 (then a colonel), she assumed command of the U.S. Women's Army Corps Center and School at Fort McClellan, Alabama. Her tenure included one of the most difficult periods in WAC history—a major expansion of the corps. In 1975, she was promoted to brigadier general and assigned as director of the Women's Army Corps at the Pentagon (1975–1978) where she supervised entry of the first women into the U.S. Military Academy at West Point in July 1976. She also supervised the introduction of mandatory weapons training for women officers and enlisted women beginning in 1976, the experiment of training men and women together in basic training, the participation of women in a major maneuver exercise in Germany, and the graduation of women from the Army Reserve Officer Training Program in 1976.

General Clarke received the Distinguished Service Medal when she retired in October 1981, the highest award a military person can receive for meritorious performance of duty. She resides in Jacksonville, Alabama, where she is active in retired Army personnel activities and in local community matters. *(See also: Military Service; United States Military Academy; Women's Army Corps)*

—**Colonel (Ret.) Bettie J. Morden**

Further Reading

Morden, Bettie J. *The Women's Army Corps, 1945–1978.* Washington, DC: Government Printing Office, 1990.

Cochran, Jacqueline (1910–1980)

Jacqueline Cochran was the first woman to fly faster than the speed of sound. At the time of her death in 1980, she held more speed, altitude, and distance records than any other pilot in aviation history.

Cochran began flying to help promote her fledgling cosmetics business, receiving her pilot's license in 1932. She began almost immediately entering major air races open to both male and female pilots. She strove for absolute records rather than women's records, because she believed that women's records would be broken by men. In 1938, she won the prestigious Bendix Trophy Race from Burbank to Cleveland against all male competition. Her record setting and air racing continued until World War II, when she went to England with a group of twenty-five other American women pilots to serve with the British Air Transport Auxiliary. In 1943, Cochran returned to the United States to head the Women's Airforce Service Pilots (WASPs), who did the majority of domestic flying during the war.

After the war, she returned to setting records, and on May 18, 1953, she became the first woman to fly faster than the speed of sound. Well into her sixties, she was setting speed records in aircraft capable of twice the speed of sound, flying over twelve hundred miles per hour. During her forty-year flying career, Cochran received many awards, including the French Legion of Honor, the U.S. Air Force Distinguished Flying Cross, and the Harmon Trophy for outstanding female pilot of the year, the latter awarded to her fourteen times. *(See also: Aviation; Women's Airforce Service Pilots)*

—**Claudia M. Oakes**

Further Reading

Cochran, Jacqueline. *The Stars at Noon.* Boston: Little, Brown, 1954.

Cochran, Jacqueline, and Maryann Bucknum Brinley. *Jackie Cochran: An Autobiography.* New York: Bantam, 1987.

Coeducation

The practice of educating women and men together has been an important theme in American history. While the earliest schools in English-speaking North America appear to have been for males alone, there is evidence that, by the mid-eighteenth century, many schools in New England enrolled both girls and boys. This was probably associated with the growing incidence of female church membership in this period and the need for women to be literate in order to read and understand the Bible and other religious writings. As common schools were established in Massachusetts and other states in the years following the American Revolution, coeducation appears to have become quite ordinary. It was considerably cheaper, after all, to educate girls and boys together than to conduct separate schools for each, especially in rural areas where school budgets (and the numbers of children) were meager. By the mid-nineteenth century, most schoolchildren in the United States probably attended coeducational schools.

Coeducation became a matter of controversy when women began to attend high schools and colleges in larger numbers after 1870. Some male scientists and educators argued that extended study threatened the health of young women, who were believed to be quite frail. A vigorous debate among educators on this issue continued into the opening decades of the twentieth century. Women continued to enroll in high schools and colleges, however, despite dire warnings from critics of coeducation. By 1900, more than three-quarters of all women enrolled in such institutions attended coeducational schools. After World War I, there appears to have been little debate about whether or not boys and girls should attend school together, although the development of home economics and other gender-specific courses in high schools and colleges may have diminished the extent to which they actually sat in the same classrooms. By the third decade of the twentieth century, in any case, coeducation had become a firmly established feature of American education. *(See also: Education; Higher Education; Morrill Land Grant Act; Sex in Education; or, A Fair Chance for the Girls)*

—**John L. Rury**

Further Reading

Hansot, Elisabeth, and David Tyack. *Learning Together: A History of Coeducation in American Schools.* New Haven, CT: Yale University Press, 1990.

Solomon, Barbara. *In the Company of Educated Women: A History of Women in Higher Education in America.* New Haven, CT: Yale University Press, 1986.

~ Colcord, Joanna Carver (1883–1960)

Author and social welfare administrator Joanna Colcord was born at sea aboard her father's sailing ship and spent her childhood on ships. Reflections of these years appear in her works *Sea Language Comes Ashore* (1945) and *Songs of American Sailormen* (1938).

Colcord received a B.S. from the University of Maine in 1906 and an M.S. there in 1909. In 1911, she received a certificate from the New York School of Philanthropy. She was assistant district secretary of the New York Charity Organization Society from 1914 to 1925. Under a leave of absence from that organization, she served with the Home Service Bureau of the American Red Cross, Virgin Islands, during 1920 and 1921. From 1925 to 1929, she was general secretary of the Family Welfare Association of Minneapolis and lecturer at the University of Minnesota.

Recognized as an outstanding practitioner of social research and community organization, Colcord succeeded Mary Richmond as director of the Charity Organization Department of the Russell Sage Foundation from 1929 to 1944.

Among her numerous publications are *Community Planning in Unemployment Emergencies* (1930), *Community Programs for Subsistence Gardens* (1933), *Richmond, Mary Ellen, 1861–1928—The Long View* (1930), *Cash Relief* (1936), *Your Community* (1939), and "Desertion and Non-Support in Family Case Work," in the *Annals of the Academy of Political and Social Science (May 1918)*. Her work *Emergency Work Relief* (1932) describes community models of administration in work relief programs. *Broken Homes* (1919, preface by Mary Richmond) was written in response to treatment needs in "social maladjustments."

Colcord was a member of Phi Kappa Phi, the American Association of University Women, and the Congregationalist church. In 1950, she married Frank Bruno, an authority on social welfare and the director of what was to become the George Warren Brown School of Social Work at Washington University, St. Louis. *(See also: Social Feminism; Social Work; Women Writers)*

—**Karen V. Harper-Dorton**

Further Reading

Colcord, Joanna Carver. *Broken Homes: A Study of Family Desertion and Its Social Treatment.* New York: Russell Sage Foundation, 1919.

Glenn, John M., Lilian Brandt, and F. Emerson Andrews. *Russell Sage Foundation.* Vols. 1-2. New York: Russell Sage Foundation, 1947.

Young, Whitney M., Jr., and Frankie V. Adams. *Some Pioneers in Social Work.* Atlanta, GA: University of Atlanta Press, 1957.

~ Coleman, Bessie (1896–1926)

Bessie Coleman was the first licensed black pilot in the world. In the early years of aviation, women, especially black women, had difficulty finding flying schools that would admit them for training. Determined to learn to fly, however, Coleman went to France and in June 1921 earned her pilot's license. After her return to the United States, she began a career as a barnstormer, or stunt pilot. Her goal was to earn enough money to open a flying school so that other blacks would not have to face the obstacles she did. However, on April 30, 1926, she was killed while practicing for an air meet in Orlando, Florida. Three years later, a group of black aviation enthusiasts in Los Angeles organized the Bessie Coleman Aero Clubs to promote aviation among blacks. Later, the Bessie Coleman School was established, and many young blacks learned to fly there. *(See also: Aviation; Black Women)*

—**Claudia M. Oakes**

Further Reading

Brooks-Pazmany, Kathleen. *United States Women in Aviation 1919–1929*. Washington, DC: Smithsonian Institution, 1983.

Hardesty, Von, and Dominick Pisano. *Black Wings: The American Black in Aviation*. Washington, DC: National Air and Space Museum, 1984.

Rich, Doris. *Queen Bess, Daredevil Aviator*. Washington, DC: Smithsonian Institution, 1993.

College Settlement

College Settlement (New York), which opened on the Lower East Side on September 1, 1889, was the second settlement house in the United States and the first to be established by women. The settlement was the first project of the College Settlements Association, which grew out of a Smith College reunion in 1887 and expanded to include graduates from other eastern women's colleges, such as Wellesley, Vassar, and Bryn Mawr. In 1892, the group began sponsoring Denison House in Boston and College Settlement in Philadelphia and added College Settlement in Baltimore in 1910. Of these, College Settlement in New York was most influential in popularizing among women the concept of college graduates' taking up residence in a settlement house in the slums and, as neighbors of the poor, providing a variety of educational and recreational services while also advocating social reform.

Although never generously funded, College Settlement attracted a number of influential women and provided a base for their social service activities. Lillian Wald lived at College Settlement while looking for a location for Henry Street Settlement, and Mary Kingsbury briefly headed College Settlement prior to marrying Vladimir Simkhovitch and founding Greenwich House. Florence Kelley used her College Settlement contacts to battle child labor. Frances Kellor, another resident, agitated to improve employment bureaus. The women of College Settlement also participated in a variety of civic improvement campaigns. College Settlement head residents included first Jean Fine, then Fannie W. McLean, Jane Robbins, Mary Kingsbury (Simkhovitch), and finally Elizabeth Williams.

By 1929, a number of College Settlement's services, such as its public library, playground, music lessons, and bathhouse, had been supplanted by other agencies, including additional settlement houses on the Lower East Side. Consequently, College Settlement decided to leave the neighborhood, cut its ties to the settlement house movement, and drop all activities other than creative arts for working-class women. In 1929, it reorganized as the Art Workshop. Although established and run entirely by women, College Settlement served neighbors of both sexes. *(See also: Henry Street Settlement; Kelley, Florence; Settlement House Movement; "Seven Sisters"; Social Feminism; Social Work; Wald, Lillian)*

—**Judith Ann Trolander**

Further Reading

Davis, Allen F. *Spearheads for Reform: The Social Settlements and the Progressive Movement, 1890–1914*. New York: Oxford University Press, 1967.

McFarland, Marjorie. "A Quarter Century of the College Settlements," *Survey* 33 (November 14, 1919): 170.

———. "Settlement for Sale," *Survey* 63 (March 15, 1930): 707, 733.

Scudder, Vida. *On Journey*. New York: E. P. Dutton, 1937.

Colonial Era Women

In the seventeenth century, European immigrants to North America found living conditions vastly different from those in Europe. Colonists, male and female, faced a lifetime of toil in an era that had no laborsaving devices or other amenities. Colonial women, in particular, endured arduous living conditions. In addition to tending the household—keeping the home, rearing the children, and providing moral instruction—women, from necessity, labored on the family's farm or in the family's trade. For many colonial women, frontier conditions imposed preindustrial gender roles.

Native American women played an eclectic role. Seen by many Europeans as the only true workers within the native community, Indian women, in fact, had a less strenuous life than their European counterparts, although native women farmed, fished, made crafts, produced household goods, and hunted. In addition, native women could have a public role, holding positions of power, such as shaman or priest, within their tribes, and trade or barter crops and goods among themselves and with Europeans. Occasionally, women served as warleaders. Many native groups were matrilineal and matrilocal in design, a notion foreign to European colonists.

In New England, women were expected to manage the home and care for the children. However, a shortage of manpower meant that women frequently worked in the family fields or assisted in the family business, while others filled voids in the trades or in professions. By no means freewheeling entrepreneurs, most women accepted the extended role they felt God had assigned them. Despite women's earning potential, this patriarchal society shortchanged them politically and legally: Women could not vote and had limited property rights.

In contrast, the egalitarian Society of Friends, or Quakers, found largely in the Middle Colonies, extended somewhat more equality toward their women. Women participated in the Quaker church—breaking with the doctrine of St. Paul that demanded silence in church for women. Quaker women also ran family farms, engaged in trade, and sold homemade goods. In addition, Quaker women participated in (Quaker) government through "women's meetings."

Most of the young European women arriving in the South came as indentured servants, outnumbered by their male counterparts six to one. Despite the sexual imbalance, most did not marry until their servitude was up, thus beginning their families later than their New England counterparts. Being an indentured servant meant years of exhausting labor, in an unhealthy subtropical climate; consequently, Southern women suffered a higher mortality rate than did other colonial era women.

The story of colonial black women took still another turn. The first black women in colonial America came as indentured servants but quickly became enslaved "for life." Black women served as a source of cheap labor and as the means for producing future workers. While white female servants rarely worked in the fields, black women routinely did. In addition to the heavy workload, black women in colonial America endured broken families, had a short life span, and suffered sexual exploitation—doubly oppressed as both slave and woman. *(See also: Black Women; Domestic Service; Native American Women; Slavery; Society of Friends)*

—**Mary Patterson**

Further Reading

Berkin, Carol Ruth. "Within the Conjurer's Circle: Women in Colonial America." In *The Underside of American History*, 3d ed., edited by Thomas R. Frazier, 79-105. New York: Harcourt, Brace & Jovanovich, 1978.

Dexter, Elisabeth Anthony. *Colonial Women of Affairs: Women in Business and the Professions in America Before 1776.* Boston: Houghton Mifflin, 1931.

Green, Rayna. "The Pocahontas Perplex: The Image of Indian Women in American Culture," *Massachusetts Review* 16 (1975): 698-714.

Morgan, Edmund S. *American Slavery, American Freedom: The Ordeal of Colonial Virginia.* New York: Norton, 1975.

Nash, Gary B. *Red, White & Black: The Peoples of Early North America*, 3d ed. Englewood Cliffs, NJ: Prentice Hall, 1992.

Norton, Mary Beth. "The Evolution of White Women's Experience in Early America," *William and Mary Quarterly* 39 (January 1982): 114-34.

〜 Colony Club

The Colony Club was formed at the beginning of the twentieth century as New York's first social club for women, and its first members were from some of the most exclusive families in New York. Having such a club for women was considered a daring innovation at the time. Florence Harriman, one of the founders and the first president of the club, felt that women would find the union in social life that men had discovered in business and working life.

The club set up a group to investigate working conditions in factories and stores. In 1909, Alva Belmont, a member of the club, enlisted the financial aid of the club in support of striking waist-makers. These workers, mostly single women under the age of twenty-five, had been striking for several months for better pay and working conditions. Belmont convinced the Colony Club to produce a fund-raiser for the strikers. Several waist-makers presented their stories to the

members, and $1,000 was contributed to the striking women. *(See also: National Women's Trade Union League; Shirtwaist Makers Strike of 1909; Social Feminism)*

—**Judith Pryor**

Further Reading

Flexner, Eleanor, and Ellen F. Fitzpatrick. *A Century of Struggle: The Women's Rights Movement in the United States.* Enlarged ed. Cambridge, MA: Belknap, 1996.

O'Neill, William L. *Everyone Was Brave: A History of Feminism in America.* New York: Quadrangle, 1971.

Woloch, Nancy. *Women and the American Experience.* New York: Knopf, 1984.

〜 Colored Woman's League

Black activist Hallie Q. Brown traveled from Wilberforce, Ohio, to Washington, D.C., several times in the early 1890s to meet with local black women and organize a group devoted to publicizing the accomplishments of African Americans. When planning began for the World's Columbian Exposition at Chicago in 1893, a Women's Board of Managers was established. Believing that blacks' contributions had been neither recognized nor compensated, Brown went to the chairperson and asked to be put on the board to represent the interests of black women. Told that members were selected as representatives of groups and not as individuals, Brown returned to Washington and held a rally at a Presbyterian church that resulted in the formation of the Colored Woman's League. However, Helen A. Cook was elected president and served as the group's representative to the World's Columbian Exposition.

Brown's desire to organize black women reflected a growing sentiment in favor of self-help. Local groups were springing up everywhere, and several sought to establish a national federation of these groups. Finally, in 1896, members of the Colored Woman's League joined with the women of the National Federation of Afro-American Women to form the National Association of Colored Women (NACW), which became a permanent and effective vehicle for self-help.

With the motto "Lifting as We Climb," the association was a confederation of local and state groups; it held biannual conventions and published *National Notes* and a literary organ, *Woman's Era*. The organization provided black women with a forum to express their concerns and a means of sharing ideas for the improvement of local conditions. Some of the group's activities included the organization of a "big sisters" movement to provide young girls with positive role models, the compilation of information to aid women going into business for themselves, and a campaign to improve traveling conditions on the railroads for blacks.

Reflecting the self-help mood of blacks at the turn of the century, the NACW tapped the resource of increasing numbers of well-educated black women to improve the conditions of the masses. It provided the impetus for the establishment of numerous local groups and in 1910 gained membership in the National Council of Women. Most of its leaders were busy professional women who found time to "lift others as they climbed." *(See also: Black Women; National Association of Colored Women; National Federation of Afro-American Women; World's Columbian Exposition)*

—Linda O. McMurry

Further Reading

Davis, Elizabeth Linsay. *Lifting as They Climb.* Washington, DC: National Association of Colored Women, 1933.

✍ Commission on Interracial Cooperation (1919–1944)

The Commission on Interracial Cooperation (CIC) was founded on April 9, 1919 in Atlanta, Georgia, by a group of white, Protestant churchmen who wanted to alleviate the racial tensions that surrounded the return of African American soldiers from World War I. The group sought to bring together black and white leaders at the state and local level who could "substitute reason for force" in the solution of racial conflict. The CIC did not attempt to dismantle racial segregation but instead sought accommodation through education and improvement of social conditions. During the 1920s, the organization grew rapidly and established chapters in thirteen southern states.

Starting in 1920, the CIC also provided a significant organization base for the interracial work of middle-class southern women. In October, the commission held its first women's conference in Memphis, Tennessee, which brought together ninety-one white and four black women from Protestant church reform networks, the burgeoning southern settlement movement, the Young Women's Christian Association, and the woman suffrage movement. The delegates, although initially tense and distrustful, quickly found a common bond in their religious faith and status as middle-class women. The white women were especially moved by the speeches of Charlotte Hawkins Brown and Margaret Murray Washington. By the end of the conference, the group had formed the Women's Division of the CIC and had determined to continue to work for racial harmony.

Despite the optimistic tone of the Memphis Conference, the group soon experienced conflicts over goals and strategies. White members were surprised by black women's demands that the new group take a stand on the issues of lynching, black suffrage, and the treatment of domestic workers. In 1929, the director of the Women's Division, Jessie Daniel Ames, formed the Association of Southern Women for the Prevention of Lynching (ASWPL), which became a sub-organization of the CIC. Although the ASWPL was all white, black women continued the interracial work as members of the CIC's women's division.

The women's committee had a regional leadership, but state and county chapters exercised a great amount of autonomy and interpreted interracial reform with varying degrees of activism. Thus, individual women shaped the character of the local groups. Some chapters met only in times of crisis, while other chapters worked for economic and social change and established educational campaigns.

Despite persistent distrust and conflicts over the group's goals, the CIC's women's division offered the strongest organizational base for women's interracial activism between the world wars. It created a bridge between black and white women's reform networks and opened up new channels of communication across the racial divide. *(See also: Ames, Jessie Daniel; Association of Southern Women for the Prevention of Lynching; Southern Women's History; Washington, Margaret Murray)*

—Caroline Cortina

Further Reading

Commission on Interracial Cooperation Papers. Trevor Arnett Library. Atlanta University, Atlanta, GA.

Giddings, Paula. *When and Where I Enter: The Impact of Black Women on Race and Sex in America.* New York: Bantam, 1984.

Hall, Jacquelyn Dowd. *Revolt against Chivalry: Jessie Daniel Ames and the Women's Campaign against Lynching.* New York: Columbia University Press, 1993.

Jessie Daniel Ames Papers. Southern Historical Collection. University of North Carolina, Chapel Hill.

Rouse, Jacqueline Anne. *Lugenia Burns Hope: Black Southern Reformer.* Athens: University of Georgia Press, 1989.

Scott, Ann Firor. *The Southern Lady: From Pedestal to Politics, 1830–1930.* Chicago: University of Chicago Press, 1970.

✍ Common Law

Common Law is the English system of judge-made law based on decrees and precedents that formed the basis for the American legal system in every state except Louisiana. Although not as oppressive to single women as Continental civil law, the common law placed severe restrictions on the legal status of married women. Under the doctrine of coverture, married women were legally merged with their husbands. As *feme covert,* meaning literally covered by her husband, a married woman could not own personal property nor keep any of her own wages or earnings. She could not make a contract nor draft a will, nor could she sue or be sued without being joined by her husband.

Real estate that a wife brought into the marriage could be used, mortgaged, or rented by her husband, but it could not be sold without her consent. Early American courts tried to make provisions for private hearings to determine if a wife's decision to sell had been made under duress, but these procedures were not always adequate for the protection of the few rights married women had under common law. Under the concept of dower rights, a wife was entitled to one-third of her husband's estate if there were children and one-half if there were none. This rule applied if the husband died without making a will or if he attempted to give less than her dower rights in his will. This portion might well be insufficient, especially if the wife had minor children to support from a previous marriage. Finally, if a tort, or legal wrong, was committed by the wife in the husband's presence, under common law only the husband was liable.

William Blackstone's widely read *Commentaries on the Laws of England,* first published in 1765, defended these restrictions as examples of the beneficial paternalism of English law for women. The popularity of Blackstone's interpretation of coverture later earned for his work the opprobrium of the early feminists.

Unlike their married sisters, single women under common law, known as *feme sol,* could sue and be sued, sign contracts, and consequently, carry on their own businesses. Realizing that certain categories of married women had to carry on their own businesses in the absence of their husbands, colonial legislatures passed laws also granting the status of *feme sol* to women married to seamen or women whose husbands had deserted them. The legal basis for these laws and similar court decisions was the existence of customary trading regulations in many English towns that permitted married women to engage in business independent of their husbands. These regulations benefited creditors as much as the women and their families and also reduced the need for public poor relief.

So limited were the rights of married women under the common law that another sort of legal remedy was needed, as for example to protect wealthy families from the spendthrift ways of sons-in-law. In England, this was provided by the system of equity jurisprudence, which was handled outside the common law in chancery proceedings. This system allowed married women and their families to protect their property through the legal concept of a separate equitable estate. A married woman could protect her property through the appointment of a trustee, whose role was to look after her interests. Under this arrangement, a wife could protect her property from a previous marriage or her family's property, and a husband could protect his wife's property in case his own estate was threatened by creditors.

While equity procedures were widely used in early American law, many states never had chancery courts, and judges often limited the rights of married women under the principles of equity. As a result of the efforts of feminists and legal reformers beginning around 1840, most states gave wives control of their personal and real estate property or adopted a community property system. The end of coverture brought significant benefits to married women, but it did not eliminate all of the partriarchal elements of the common law, some of which remained until the second half of the twentieth century. *(See also: Coverture; Divorce; Dower; Equity Courts; Feme Covert; Feme Sol; Married Women's Property Acts)*

—**Neil W. Hogan**

Further Reading

Blackstone, William. *Commentaries on the Laws of England.* Vol. 1, 1765. Reprint, Chicago: University of Chicago Press, 1979.

Hoff, Joan. *Law, Gender and Injustice, a Legal History of U.S. Women.* New York: New York University Press, 1991.

Holdsworth, Sir William. *A History of English Law,* 5th ed. Vol. 3. London: Methuen, Sweet & Maxwell, 1942.

Kerber, Linda K. *Women of the Republic.* Chapel Hill: University of North Carolina Press, 1980.

Rabken, Peggy. *The Legal Foundations of Female Emancipation.* Westport, CT: Greenwood, 1980.

Salmon, Marylynn. *Women and the Law of Property in Early America.* Chapel Hill: University of North Carolina Press, 1986.

Shammas, Carole. "Re-Assessing the Married Women's Property Acts," *Journal of Women's History* 6 (Spring 1994): 9-30.

Wortman, Marlene Stein. *Women in American Law.* Vol. 1. New York: Holmes & Meir, 1985.

❧ Communist Party

The first Marxist organization in the United States was founded by German immigrant Joseph Weydemeyer, who had participated in the Revolution of 1848 in Germany as an artillery officer and colleague of Karl Marx and Frederick Engels. According to Angela Davis, a noted scholar on women in the Communist Party, no women's names were associated with the Proletarian League when it was established by Weydemeyer in 1852. Other Marxist organizations, including the Communist Club and Workingmen's National Association, were also dominated by men.

However, the beginning of the twentieth century introduced a period of change to the socialist movement. As the broad plea for women's equality grew, women's interest in the Marxist Left also increased. The Socialist Party soon became an active advocate for women's equality. With the assistance of dedicated Socialist women such as Pauline Newman and Rose Schneiderman, a working-class suffrage movement was further advanced. The year 1908 introduced a national women's commission that had been established by the Socialist Party. Mass demonstrations in support of women's equality incited women nationwide to participate in the equal suffrage movement.

Many of the former Socialist Party women soon became leaders and activists of the Communist Party after its founding in 1919. According to Davis, Communist women with ties to the left wing of the Socialist party included Ella Reeve Bloor, Anita Whitney, Margaret Prevey, Kate Sadler Greenhalgh, Rose Pastor Stokes, and Jeanette Pearl.

Previously, in 1905, the Industrial Workers of the World (IWW) was founded. Although the IWW was an industrial union and not a political party, its main goal was socialism as a means to curb a growing class struggle. Women such as Mary Jones and Lucy Parsons were also active in this organization. In fact, the IWW encouraged women to become not only members of the group but also active leaders. In addition, only the IWW endorsed a policy of struggle against racism. The Socialist Party chose not to focus on the plight of black people. Davis notes the battle of black Socialist Helen Holman in her fight against the social dilemma of her race and gender: "As a black woman, Helen Holman was a rarity within the ranks of the Socialist party. The Socialists' posture of negligence vis-à-vis black women was one of the unfortunate legacies the Communist Party would have to overcome." However, the following decade brought a positive change in the black racial stance held by the Communist Party.

Other active participants in the Communist movement in the United States included Lucy Parsons, Elizabeth Gurley Flynn, and Claudia Jones. The endeavors of these women to achieve equality for both women and minorities greatly contributed to the growth of the Communist Party despite widespread antagonism against it. (See also: Davis, Angela Y.; Flynn, Elizabeth Gurley; Industrial Workers of the World; Jones, "Mother"; Schneiderman, Rose; Socialism)

—Amy Yeary Mangan

Further Reading

Dancis, Bruce. "Socialism and Women in the United States, 1900–1912," Socialist Revolution 6 (1976): 76-88.

Davis, Angela. "Communist Women." In Women, Race and Class, pp. 149-71. New York: Random House, 1981.

Foster, William. History of the Communist Party of the United States. New York: International Publishers, 1952.

⭐ Complex Marriage

Complex marriage was a form of group marriage practiced between 1846 and 1879 in communities founded by John Humphrey Noyes in Putney, Vermont; Oneida, New York; and Wallingford, Connecticut. At Oneida after 1848, approximately two hundred adults, equally balanced between the sexes, considered themselves married not as couples but to the entire group. Women and men frequently exchanged sexual partners; all exclusive interpersonal attachments, defined as "special love," were broken up because they were viewed as posing a threat to group stability. Central to the Oneida Community's functioning was loyalty to Noyes and his perfectionist religious principles: "male continence," a means of birth control by coitus reservatus; "mutual criticism," a system of group criticism; and "ascending and descending fellowship," the group's informal hierarchy. After 1868, a "stirpiculture" or eugenics experiment was also instituted among some members.

At Oneida, sex roles were perhaps more radically revised than in any similar American group for which extensive documentation exists. Both sexes worked alongside each other in many jobs; women served in some positions of authority over men, and there were no areas in which women were prohibited from working. Communal child rearing, involving both women and men, freed women to become a full part of community life. Women cut their hair short and wore an unusual outfit composed of a mid-length skirt over pants, similar to the attire popularized by Amelia Bloomer.

Noyes, however, was no feminist. Although he favored doing away with any distinctions between the sexes that were not intrinsic, he considered men to be ultimately superior to women, and he criticized the antebellum women's movement for helping to polarize relations between the sexes, thereby risking social chaos. His solution was to use complex marriage and other community practices to meet what he considered to be the true needs of both men and women. When internal and external pressures eventually convinced Noyes that his sexual system was no longer working, he recommended its abandonment in 1879. In 1881, the group also gave up its communistic form of economic organization, reorganized as a joint-stock corporation, and went on to become one of the most successful small businesses in the United States, best known for its silverware. Although the Oneida Community neither sought nor achieved full equality between the sexes, its experiment with complex marriage continues to raise many issues of importance for feminists today. (See also: Marriage; Oneida Community; Utopian Communities)

—Lawrence Foster

Further Reading

Carden, Maren Lockwood. Oneida: Utopian Community to Modern Corporation. Baltimore: Johns Hopkins University Press, 1969. Reprint, Syracuse, NY: Syracuse University Press, 1998.

Foster, Lawrence. "Free Love and Feminism: John Humphrey Noyes and the Oneida Community," Journal of the Early Republic 1 (Summer 1981): 165-83.

———. Religion and Sexuality: The Shakers, the Mormons, and the Oneida Community, pp. 72-122, 226-47. Urbana: University of Illinois Press, 1984.

Kern, Louis J. An Ordered Love: Sex Roles and Sexuality in Victorian Utopias—The Shakers, the Mormons, and the Oneida Community, pp. 207-79. Chapel Hill: University of North Carolina Press, 1981.

Klaw, Spencer. Without Sin: The Life and Death of the Oneida Community. New York: Allen Lane, Penguin, 1993.

Parker, Robert Allerton. A Yankee Saint: John Humphrey Noyes and the Oneida Community. New York: Putnam, 1935.

Robertson, Constance Noyes. Oneida Community: The Breakup, 1876–1881. Syracuse, NY: Syracuse University Press, 1972.

Wayland-Smith, Ellen. "The Status and Self-Perception of Women in the Oneida Community," Communal Societies 8 (1988): 18-53.

⭐ Comstock Law

A new era of repression of birth control material began with the passage of the Comstock Law. In 1873, the moral crusader Anthony Comstock (1844–1915) induced Congress to pass a bill strengthening the law (passed a year earlier) that forbade using the mails to circulate obscene materials. The 1873 law specified that birth control information was considered obscene. This definition ended the widespread appearance of advertisements in American newspapers for birth control devices, which had demonstrated the frank interest of Americans in obtaining means of controlling fertility. The anti-birth-control faction headed by Comstock, however, lumped together all such devices as inducements to debauchery. State laws that followed were modeled on the congressional statute banning birth control materials in the mails.

Subsequently appointed a special postal agent, Comstock set himself to enforce the law. He resorted to entrapment, writing under an assumed name to request articles advertised and then pouncing on the evidence that they were being sold for birth control. His actions also put a damper on the public discussion of birth control. Among the individuals accused of obscenity was the highly respected writer Edward Bliss Foote, as well as his son and his daughter-in-law, who were both doctors.

Birth control advocate Margaret Sanger ran afoul of the law in 1912. In a satirical response, the newspaper *Call* printed the title of Sanger's series of articles, "What Every Girl Should Know," and underneath it on an otherwise blank page, the legend: "Nothing, by order of the Post Office." Despite considered criticism of the law and opposition by the U.S. Army, which wanted to circulate information to protect against venereal disease, the Comstock Law was not rewritten to remove prohibitions against birth control material until 1971. *(See also: Birth Control; Obscenity; Pornography; Sanger, Margaret Louise)*

—Daryl M. Hafter

Further Reading
Gordon, Linda. *Woman's Body, Woman's Right: A Social History of Birth Control in America.* New York: Grossman, 1976.
Reed, James. *From Private Vice to Public Virtue: The Birth Control Movement and American Society since 1830.* New York: Basic Books, 1978.
Sanger, Margaret. *My Fight for Birth Control.* 1931. Reprint, Elmsford, NY: Maxwell, 1969.

Congress of Industrial Organizations (CIO)

Throughout the 1930s, the concept of industrial unionism had gained enough ground to prove a challenge to the traditional craft union approach to labor organization on which the American Federation of Labor (AFL), founded in 1886, was based. Industrial unionism advocated the inclusion in one union of all workers in a particular industry, regardless of skill or job, thereby increasing the potential power of the industry's workers in securing their demands and safeguarding their interests. Because this ran contrary to the approach of the AFL, that organization vigorously opposed this development in unionization. Nonetheless, on November 9, 1935, eight union affiliates of the AFL, led by John L. Lewis, head of the United Mine Workers, met and formed the Committee for Industrial Unionism. At its first convention (November 14-18, 1938) in Pittsburgh, the committee adopted a constitution and officially became the Congress of Industrial Organizations (CIO). As such, it was regarded as an autonomous body and a direct rival to the AFL.

The CIO was supported primarily by workers in mass production industries, especially the automobile, steel, electrical appliance, and textile industries, the latter encompassing a high percentage of women workers. Women constituted approximately 40 percent of the textile industry's workforce, and in this industry, the CIO made significant gains, winning over mill workers from the AFL's United Textile Workers, which refused to represent unskilled women textile workers. During the decade of the 1930s, hundreds of thousands of textile workers joined the CIO's Textile Workers Union of America. The TWUA, however, failed to win over the southern textile industry, where by 1939 less than 10 percent of textile workers, most of whom were women, remained unorganized.

It was precisely because American working women were located primarily in mass production industries that the CIO became extremely valuable to them. This does not mean the CIO was an avid supporter of feminist demands. Simply put, the CIO needed to win the support of women workers to attain a majority membership within a given industry. As in previous unions, very few women rose to any position of leadership in the CIO, and therefore, women had little control over CIO policy at any level of operation. On December 5, 1955, the AFL and the CIO formally merged to become the AFL-CIO, with little change in the status of women within the organization. *(See also: American Federation of Labor; Textiles: North and South; Unions)*

—Maureen Anna Harp

Further Reading
The AFL-CIO American Federationist, 1955—.
Foner, Philip S. *Women and the American Labor Movement: From World War I to the Present.* New York: Free Press, 1980.
Galenson, Walter. *The CIO Challenge to the AFL: A History of the American Labor Movement, 1935–1941.* Cambridge, MA: Harvard University Press, 1960.
Mason, Lucy Randolph. *To Win These Rights: A Personal History of the CIO in the South.* New York: Harper, 1952.
Preis, Art. *Labor's Giant Step: Twenty Years of the CIO.* New York: Pioneer, 1964. Reprint, New York: Pathfinder, 1972.
Salmond, John A. *Miss Lucy of the CIO: The Life and Times of Lucy Randolph Mason, 1882–1959.* Athens: University of Georgia Press, 1988.

Consciousness-Raising

Consciousness-raising or *C-R* is a term used to describe an intellectual process of self-realization and radicalization adapted by the women's liberation movement of the late 1960s as a tool of political organization. Practiced in small groups, C-R promoted women's awareness of the societal origins of "personal" problems that had influenced or limited their lives and encouraged collective action to seek positive changes for all women.

Many members of the women's liberation movement participated in the civil rights and New Left movements of the early and mid-1960s. These young women brought to their movement the egalitarian democratic ideologies and strategies that stressed a leaderless, participatory democratic approach to group action. As co-workers within the Student Non-Violent Coordinating Committee (SNCC) and Students for a Democratic Society (SDS), these women first recognized and confronted the sexist discrimination inherent in women's being treated as secondary and ancillary support workers regardless of the work they actually performed within those movements.

Derived from the earliest SNCC "rap groups" (which fostered uncensored candor and criticism among members), the SDS "Guatemala Guerrilla" group approach to organizing (which stressed an introspective, personalized sharing of individual experience), and the ruthless confrontational tactic of the "speaking truth" practiced by the Chinese revolutionaries, the feminist C-R group provided its members with a controlled and confidential environment for openly discussing and analyzing their past in a feminist perspective. This structured format fostered a sense of commonality that would impel not only personal but collective political action. Thus, "The Personal Is Political" became the slogan summarizing the C-R process that facilitated the women's liberation movement's development of theory and strategies for recruiting and organizing its members. In their structureless, supportive C-R groups, women became feminists as they explored the practical meaning in their lives of absolute equality of the sexes.

As the radical and leftist orientation of women's liberation gave way to a more mainstream emphasis in the 1970s, the National Organization for Women (NOW) used the C-R group to recruit and strengthen its members' stands on the more difficult feminist issues of abortion and lesbian rights. The C-R process fostered in group members a willingness to question authority as well as a sense of autonomy and a disposition to explore all their choices. NOW's formalization of the C-R process supplied the means to initiate its new members into the issues, theories, and strategies on the basis of the personal as political.

The process of C-R empowered not only individuals to change their lives but also provided the means to comfort and politicize self-help groups. The members of these self-help groups were organized around a shared problem, experience, or situation; within such groups, the members could confront the personal consequences of their common cause and shape an agenda of action to address that issue. Through self-help groups, C-R as a feminist process was mainstreamed and used around a single issue, such as sexual assault, single parents' special circumstances, or legal action against drunk drivers. *(See also: National Organization for Women; New Left; Women's Liberation Movement)*

—**Angela M. Howard**

Further Reading

Evans, Sara. *Personal Politics: The Roots of Women's Liberation in the Civil Rights Movement and the New Left.* New York: Random House, 1979.

NOW Guidelines for Feminist Consciousness-Raising. Rev. ed. Washington, DC: National Organization for Women, 1983.

❧ Consumerism

Consumerism is a basic principle of capitalism: Economic growth and vitality depend on individuals' purchasing (consuming) a never-ending quantity of goods and services. The society that develops within a consumerist economic system is democratic: Patterns of consumption are not regulated, and the only constraint on an individual's purchases is personal disposable wealth. Social status is, therefore, generally equal to economic status, and not determined by birth, intelligence, or nonmaterial factors.

Consumerism changed the lives of American women in the nineteenth and twentieth centuries. As the capitalist economy matured under the Industrial Revolution in the late nineteenth century, women were freed from producing goods needed by their families, such as food, thread, yarn, fabric, clothing, and household furnishings, and were able to buy them already manufactured. Between 1880 and 1930, a variety of new goods appeared that transformed women's work in the home: electricity and electric appliances, such as refrigerators, irons, vacuum cleaners, washing machines; indoor plumbing with running cold and hot water; the telephone, automobile, and radio; and movies.

With much of the drudgery of housework removed, women redefined their roles. Most middle-class women became purchasing agents for their families. While their husbands supported the family with their income, the women managed the family budget. They assessed their family's needs, then purchased the goods required. In some cases, discretionary income might be spent on material goods that could immediately enhance a family's social standing; in others, social mobility might be deferred for the next generation as parents saved money for their children's education. In either case, the woman's financial competence and personal taste affected the whole family's social standing.

After World War I, the service sector of the economy expanded dramatically, and many women, married and unmarried, moved into the newly created jobs. This movement into the labor force enhanced women's role as consumers; they had more money to spend and, because they were away from the home for extended periods, were obligated to purchase many of the goods they had earlier made at home.

Consumerism in the industrial age transformed American culture. The relentless search for novelty, fashion, and new technology accelerated changes in society. Companies developed products that anticipated or created what women and their families might want or need, then devised elaborate advertising campaigns to promote such products. Although women have played a critical role in maintaining the consumerist economy of the United States throughout the twentieth century, not until the 1970s did advertisers perceive and woo women as rational and practical adult consumers rather than as the easily manipulated "Mrs. Middle Majority" of the 1950s and 1960s. *(See also: Advertising; Housework; Industrial Revolution)*

—**Jane Crisler**

Further Reading

Matthaei, Julie A. *An Economic History of Women in America: Women's Work, the Sexual Division of Labor, and the Development of Capitalism.* New York: Schocken, 1982.

❧ Consumption

Consumption is a term used to describe tuberculosis between the eighteenth and mid-twentieth centuries. It generally referred to the pulmonary tuberculosis that tended to affect young adults and described the wasting of the flesh caused by accelerated metabolism and the deterioration of the lungs themselves. Although tuberculosis had been known in the Western world since ancient times, it acquired a particular cultural significance during the romantic age (late eighteenth to mid-nineteenth centuries), when major literary figures, such as Rousseau, Musset, Keats, Shelley, the Brontë sisters, Thoreau, and Edgar Allen Poe suffered from the disease and wrote about it in vivid terms.

The symptoms of "consumption"—thinness, pale skin, languor, and occasional physical and psychological excitation (especially when feverish)—were considered aesthetically attractive by the Romantics, signs of a refined, vulnerable sensibility. These characteristics, combined with the fact that tuberculosis has always been a disease that affects young people—children and young adults between twenty and thirty years old—provided the material for many tragic novels, plays, and poems, especially in nineteenth-century women's literature. Although drugs were developed between 1944 and 1952 that could cure and prevent tuberculosis, the aesthetic created by the disease—that thin, pale young adults are attractive—persists, although it is applied primarily to young women.

The social consequences of tuberculosis were dramatic at the beginning of the twentieth century; in 1900, it was the leading cause of death. As industrial growth attracted people into crowded urban centers, children and their young parents suffered in conditions that were far from romantic. Their desperate plight was a major impetus for the health and welfare reforms of the twentieth century. As reformers studied the course of tuberculosis, they realized that the entire family—father, mother, and children—had to be treated simultaneously. The resulting programs enhanced the civil rights of women and children and fostered many other social programs that promoted their welfare. *(See also: "The Vapors")*

—**Jane Crisler**

Further Reading

Dowling, Harry F. *Fighting Infection: Conquests of the Twentieth Century.* Cambridge, MA: Harvard University Press, 1977.

Sontag, Susan. *Illness as Metaphor.* New York: Vintage, 1977.

Figure 14. Cookbooks
Alice Waters with a copy of her cookbook, which contained recipes for many of the dishes served at the Chez Panisse restaurant. She said "not a single person" could resist her bouillabaisse. Used by permission of UPI/Corbis-Bettmann.

❧ Cookbooks

Until the 1960s, the vast majority of cookbooks in America were written by women. The publishing of cookbooks was one of the few areas of literary endeavor in which women were taken seriously. Consequently, women expressed their lives and times, not just recipes, in their cookbooks.

The earliest American cookbooks were reprints of European books, even when published under American imprints. Then in 1796, Amelia Simmons wrote *American Cookery,* in which she left out those dishes whose ingredients could not be obtained in America and established national dishes including Indian pudding, flapjacks, and johnnycake. This book was so successful that Lucy Emerson plagiarized it in its entirety in *New England Cookery* in 1808.

In the late 1820s, cooking practices, including measurements and cooking methods, began to be codified by Lydia Maria Child, Eliza Leslie, Sarah Hale, Esther Howland, and

Mary Randolph. Catharine Esther Beecher extended the idea of a code to household arts in *A Treatise on Domestic Economy for the Use of Young Ladies at Home and at School* published in 1841. This included instructions for setting a table; suggestions for serving special luncheons, teas, and large dinners; guidance for behavior at the table; and even recommendations on how to dress. This information was included because, with the onset of the industrial age, cooking and housekeeping were learned less from mother to daughter and more from books.

An interesting side note about Catharine Beecher is that she became a militant feminist and argued in her cookbooks that women's supremacy is clearly shown in the kitchen. To her, kitchen work was not demeaning but, in reality, gave women much control over other areas of the family and society.

The advent of ladies' cooking classes in the 1870s led to cooking's becoming an even more exact science. The most influential of these were offered at the Boston Cooking School, whose most famous principal, Fannie Merritt Farmer, known as the "mother of level measurement," in 1896 wrote the *Boston Cooking School Cook Book,* establishing the most exact possible standards for cooking. This book, *The Betty Crocker Cookbook,* and *The Good Housekeeping Cookbook,* both revised and reprinted on numerous occasions in the twentieth century, have become the standard cookbooks found in most American kitchens.

Two developments in American society in the past two decades have led to a sharp increase in the number of cookbooks published annually. The first is that the intense interest in the feminist movement has also opened up new opportunities for men. With the realization that women were much more than domestic servants, it became fashionable for men to do their share of the cooking. This led to an increased number of cookbooks written by and for men. The second is a general increase in the public's interest in physical health and nutritious foods. Dozens of cookbooks have been written as companions to specific fad diets and exercise programs. Thousands of church, school, and neighborhood groups have compiled their own suggestions for healthful eating, and each state or general area of the country seems to have its list of favorites. Cooking has become very specialized according to preference for certain ingredients and cooking methods, and there are sure to be several books available for each possible variable.

A revised edition of one of the mainstays of American cookery, *The Joy of Cooking,* was published in 1997. Signaling a return of interest in American recipes, there was considerable consternation over the cookbook's deletion of some traditional recipes and the inclusion of a multiethnic sampling. *(See also: Beecher, Catharine; Child, Lydia Maria Francis; Housework)*

—**Mari Lynn Dew**

Further Reading

The American Heritage Cookbook and Illustrated History of American Eating and Drinking. New York: American Heritage, 1964.

Dusablon, Mary Anna. *America's Collectible Cookbook: The History, the Politics, the Recipes.* Athens: Ohio University Press, 1994.

Harrison, Molly. *The Kitchen in History.* New York: Scribner, 1972.

Lincoln, Waldo. *American Cookery Books 1742–1860.* Worcester, MA: American Antiquarian Society, 1954.

Root, Waverly, and Richard de Rochemont. *Eating in America: A History.* New York: Morrow, 1976.

Schremp, Geraldine, and Gerry Schremp. *Celebration of American Food: Four Centuries in the Melting Pot.* Golden, CO: Fulcrum, 1996.

Shapiro, Laura. *Perfection Salad: Women and Cooking at the Turn of the Century.* New York: Farrar, Straus, & Giroux, 1986.

Simmons, Amelia. *American Cookery.* 1796. Reprint, Grand Rapids, MI: Eerdmans, 1965.

Tannahill, Reay. *Food in History.* New York: Stein & Day, 1973.

⌒ Corset

As a device for molding the thorax, particularly the waist (primarily female), for aesthetic, sexual, and status-expressive purposes (rather than orthopedic or protective purposes, not here considered), the corset may be said to have originated in Minoan Crete, but it disappears thereafter until the fourteenth century. A rigid and compressive garment, usually called "stays" until the nineteenth century, the corset became customary in the sixteenth century and was periodically subject to medical and clerical opposition, often in disapproval of décolletage. (The brassiere as a separate breast-supporting device did not arrive until the twentieth century.)

The hostility to a device deemed both unhealthy and provocative climaxed in the eighteenth century when the corset was blamed for just about every disease under the sun, gynecological and otherwise. In the nineteenth century, the abuse metastasized, on a popular level, in countless magazine articles, reaching vitriolic form by the 1870s and after. By this time, the opponents of the corset as such—especially its extreme form, known as tight lacing—began for the first time to reveal fully their misogynistic, antifeminist bias. While the relation of fashion and fashion reform campaigns to late-nineteenth-century feminism remains problematical, it is clear that the criticism of tight lacing (a minority habit, not a fashion) was used to castigate women generically as irrational, slavish, and deliberately and literally homicidal—of their God-given procreativity, which the corset seemed to jeopardize. Evidence of the use of the corset as an abortifacient added fuel to the fires of conservative male moral outrage. Tight lacing became a symbol of the New Woman's resistance to an age-old maternal stereotype and, insofar as it exposed and sexualized the body, a harbinger of a sexual revolution. Yet at the same time, the corset preserved an illusion

Figure 15. Corsets
Dr. Scott's electric corset was advertised in the 1880s as eliminating the need for painfully tight lacing and having beneficial effects for a woman's health. Used by permission of Corbis-Bettmann.

of bodily captivity deeply satisfying to male supremacist fantasies. The paradox is profound and subversive of the simplistic and traditional view, still upheld by feminists today, of the corset as a prime symbol and instrument of female slavery.

In fact, conspicuous tight lacing, always adduced by fashion and social history as a "fashion" of the dominant social classes, proves to have been the practice of a relatively few lower-class younger women (girls), who strove for what was deemed an upper-class appearance and were willing to risk social opprobrium to attract attention in a narcissistic and exhibitionistic way. Their sexual motivation, cruelly lambasted by the male moralists, was vaunted by the women themselves in pro-corset, "fetishist" correspondence in popular magazines, starting with the progressive but mainstream *English Woman's Domestic Magazine* in the 1860s.

After 1900, when fashion moved to looser and unencumbered styles (including shorter skirts), the waist-compressive

corset became functionally superfluous and incompatible with the rhetoric of female liberation. By the end of World War I, it was virtually dead, surviving in vestigial forms that were further attenuated as a result of World War II. The "soft" revival in the 1950s, manipulated by male-dominated corporate and consumerist interests, presents other problems. *(See also: Dress Reform: Nineteenth Century)*

—David Kunzle

Further Reading

Kunzle, David. *Fashion and Fetishism: A Social History of the Corset and Other Forms of Body Sculpture.* Totowa, NJ: Rowman & Littlefield, 1982.

Steele, Valerie. *Fashion and Eroticism: Ideals of Feminine Beauty from the Victorian Era to the Jazz Age.* London: Oxford University Press, 1985.

⚞ Coughlin, Mother Mary Samuel (1868–1959)

Mother Mary Samuel Coughlin was prioress general of the Dominican Sisters of Sinsinawa, Wisconsin (Congregation of the Most Holy Rosary), from 1909 to 1949 and a strong supporter of higher education for women. She was born Ellen Coughlin in Fairbault, Minnesota, the third child of Irish immigrant parents Daniel and Ellen (O'Mahoney) Coughlin, and graduated from Bethlehem Academy, Fairbault. She entered the teaching community of Dominican Sisters in 1886, at St. Clara's Convent, Sinsinawa, receiving the name "Mary Samuel." She served in mission grade schools of the congregation until 1901, when she was appointed bursar general. In 1904, she was appointed prioress of the motherhouse community at St. Clara's Convent. After the death of Mother Emily Power in 1909, Sister Mary Samuel assumed leadership of the Sinsinawa Dominicans and guided the community through an era of significant growth and development. Over fourteen hundred sisters entered the Dominicans under her administration, and sixty-three new foundations were made in various regions of the country.

Mother Samuel's greatest achievements lay in the field of higher education for women. She was responsible for the relocation of St. Clara's College, Sinsinawa, to River Forest, Illinois, where it was renamed Rosary College in 1922. She enhanced Rosary's program by founding two centers for European study: Villa de Fougères in Fribourg, Switzerland (1924), which she had acquired in 1917, and the Pius XII Institute (1948), a Florentine estate donated to the Holy See by Myron Taylor. Mother Samuel also established Edgewood College (1927) at Madison, Wisconsin, to prepare religious and lay women for teaching careers. In 1932, Loyola University of Chicago awarded her an honorary degree.

Mother Samuel welcomed black women to the Dominican community and was an early advocate of liturgical participation by the Catholic faithful. She was a shrewd and

astute manager, and the affairs of the congregation prospered under her guidance and assumed a more American
character. Mother Mary Samuel's spiritual life was the main-
spring of her activity. She cherished the communal prayer
life of her Dominican community. At the community's cen-
tenary in 1949, she relinquished her duties as prioress general. She lived ten more years at St. Clara's Convent until her
death on October 17, 1959, at the age of ninety-one. *(See
also: Christianity; Higher Education; Religion)*

—**Steven M. Avella**

Further Reading

McCarty, Sister Mary Eva. *The Sinsinawa Dominicans: Outlines
of Twentieth-Century Development, 1901–1949.* Dubuque,
IA: Hoermann, 1952.
O'Rourke, Sister Alice. *Let Us Set Out: Sinsinawa Dominicans
1949–1985.* Dubuque, IA: Union-Hoermann, 1986.

❧ Countryman, Gratia Alta (1866–1953)

An early leader in public library development, Gratia Alta
Countryman set professional standards for innovation and
energy as director of the Minneapolis Public Library from
1904 to 1936. Born in Hastings, Minnesota, she accepted a
job at the Minneapolis Public Library in 1889. She became
assistant librarian in 1892, then librarian in 1904, but only
after a successful letter-writing campaign from friends and
peers who had to convince trustees it was acceptable to hire
a woman as director. Still, Countryman was paid one-third
less than her predecessor; the board also eliminated the position she had just vacated.

Countryman was a tough manager with a vision for library service. During her tenure, she tried to de-emphasize
fiction, extend library services, and enhance the library's
role in Americanizing recent immigrants. Like most librarians of her time, she accepted the "uplift" theory, which
called for developing a collection endorsed by cultural, literary, and intellectual canons; she differed from her peers,
however, in the energy she applied to her work and her intense pursuit of nonlibrary users. During her tenure, the
Minneapolis Public Library system expanded by scores of
branches and library stations. Countryman was also very active in community affairs. She was first president of the Minneapolis Women's Welfare League, first president of the
Business Women's Club, and founding organizer of the
Woman's Club of Minneapolis. *(See also: Librarianship)*

—**Wayne A. Wiegand**

Further Reading

Benidt, Bruce Weir. *The Library Book: Centennial History of the
Minneapolis Public Library.* Minneapolis, MN: Minneapolis
Public Library and Information Center, 1984.
Dyste, Mena C. "Gratia Alta Countryman, Librarian." Master's
thesis, University of Minnesota, 1965.

Pejsa, Jane, *Gratia Countryman: Her Life, Her Loves, and Her
Library.* Minneapolis: Nodin, 1995.

❧ Coverture

Under English common law, which prevailed in the American colonies, married women were limited in their freedom
by the concept of coverture. While a single woman (*feme
sol*) had property rights but no political rights, a married
woman (*feme covert*) had her legal existence merged with
that of her husband. Her property, inheritance, and any
wages she earned legally became her husband's. She could
not sign contracts nor sue in court, and the children of the
marriage were under the custody of the father. Divorce was
rarely possible in cases of unhappy marriage, because it was
believed that human law should not dissolve marriage performed in accordance with God's law. The concept of coverture continued in the early years of the Republic, bolstered by the publication and dissemination in America of
William Blackstone's concise, readable *Commentaries on
the Laws of England* (1765). Typically, coverture was a permanent condition for women since most married early and
stayed married until they or their spouses died. Divorce
statutes varied by colony but were all based on the submersion of the wife's separate legal identity.

A married woman did have some protection under coverture. She had a right to a dower, or a life interest in one-third
of the family property at the husband's death. However, this
right eroded in the years after the Revolution. She also had
the right, in a private examination with a judge, to give or
withhold consent to any sale of the family real estate. But
since she would have to face her husband afterward, a
woman might have felt pressured to agree to the proposed
sale. Some married women gained rights during the Revolution when their husbands were away; they petitioned their
legislatures for designation as *feme sol* traders, enabling
them to engage in business and be self-supporting. In New
York and Virginia, some married women acted as agents for
their husbands and managed businesses without bothering
to have themselves declared *feme sol* traders.

The major recourse from coverture for married women
in the colonial period was in courts of equity that recognized
antenuptial agreements. By the mid-nineteenth century, the
passage of married women's property acts replaced equity
jurisdiction in safeguarding women's control of property.
*(See also: Common Law; Divorce; Dower; Equity Courts;
Feme Covert; Feme Sol; Married Women's Property Acts)*

—**Barbara E. Lacey**

Further Reading

Kerber, Linda K. *Women of the Republic: Intellect and Ideology in
Revolutionary America.* Chapel Hill: University of North
Carolina Press, 1980.

Norton, Mary Beth. *Liberty's Daughters: The Revolutionary Experience of American Women, 1750–1800.* Boston: Little, Brown, 1980.

❧ Coyle, Grace Longwell (1892–1962)

Grace Coyle was an educator and author who made a significant impact on the twentieth-century social group work movement as it evolved its purposes, methods, roles, and identity. Born in North Adams, Massachusetts, Coyle earned her A.B. from Wellesley College in 1914 and a year later completed a certificate from the New York School of Philanthropy (subsequently the Graduate School of Social Work of Columbia University). She became involved in social reform through settlement house work and other group work organizations, including the Industrial Women's Department of the YWCA, where she focused on adult education and recreation. She completed graduate study at Columbia with an M.A. in economics (1928) and a doctorate in sociology (1931).

As a result of her experiences with women in industry and children in groups, she began to appreciate the regularities that characterize the functioning of small groups. In 1930, she authored *Social Process in Organized Groups,* an insightful analysis of the universal processes that occur in small groups. This conceptual formulation was an important landmark that gave direction to subsequent research and knowledge about group behavior.

Coyle joined the faculty of the School of Applied Social Sciences at Western Reserve University of Cleveland (1934–1962). She was a prolific author and researcher on small groups, and her work shows the influence of John Dewey and the progressive education movement, with its emphasis on democratic ideals and learning by doing. She advocated for the small group as an effective vehicle for the attainment of educational and recreational goals, for promoting civic and social responsibility, and for its potential to enhance the social functioning of individual members. These themes were articulated in her writings in the late 1940s in *Group Experience and Democratic Values* (1947) and *Group Work with American Youth* (1948).

During the 1930s and 1940s, interest in small-group behavior grew rapidly, attracting professionals from diverse fields, including education, recreation, mental hygiene, and social work. They formed the American Association for the Study of Group Work in 1936, which provided for professional exchange, but they continued to feel ambivalence about group work's lack of alignment with an established field. In 1946, Coyle articulated the persuasive rationale for association with the field of social work. She was credited with stimulating the transition that resulted in group work's becoming identified as one of the basic social work methods.

Coyle's numerous leadership roles included those as president of the National Conference of Social Work (1940), the American Association of Social Workers (1942–1944), and the Council on Social Work Education (1958–1960). *(See also: Social Work)*

—Marie Schirtzinger Taris

Further Reading

Alissi, Albert S., ed. *Perspectives on Social Group Work Practice.* New York: Free Press, 1980.

Coyle, Grace L. *Group Experience and Democratic Values.* New York: Woman's Press, 1947.

———. *Group Work and American Youth: A Guide to the Practice of Leadership.* New York: Harper, 1948.

———. "On Becoming Professional." In *Toward Professional Standards.* Vol. 1. New York: Association Press, 1947.

———. *Social Process in Organized Groups.* New York: Smith, 1930.

Konopke, Gisela. *Social Group Work,* 3d ed. Englewood Cliffs, NJ: Prentice Hall, 1983.

Reid, Kenneth E. *From Character Building to Social Treatment.* Westport, CT: Greenwood, 1981.

Trecker, Harleigh B., ed. *Group Work Foundations and Frontiers.* New York: Whiteside & Morrow, 1955.

❧ Crandall, Prudence (1804–1889)

Teacher and abolitionist, Prudence Crandall was originally a Quaker from Rhode Island. In 1831, she founded a school for girls in Canterbury, Connecticut. Three years later, Crandall's school had gained a statewide reputation for excellence. Inspired by a copy of William Lloyd Garrison's the *Liberator,* Crandall admitted the first black girl to the school in 1833.

Immediately, white parents began withdrawing their children from the school. Crandall, ignoring community hostility, boldly announced that henceforth she would teach blacks exclusively. The residents of Canterbury reacted quickly. A town meeting was held, which Crandall could not attend because she was female. Crandall was accused of promoting racial amalgamation, and resolutions were passed to get rid of the school. Shopkeepers refused to supply the school, and vandalism to the property occurred. Students were pelted with manure, dead cats, and chicken heads when they attempted to exercise in the yard. Despite these brutal and inhumane acts, Crandall refused to close the school.

On May 24, 1833, the Connecticut state legislature passed the infamous "Black Law," making it illegal to set up a school for blacks not from Connecticut (many of Crandall's pupils were from out of state) or to set up a boarding school for blacks in a town where they were not residents, without prior written consent of the majority of the town's civil authority and selectmen. On June 27, Crandall was arrested for violating the "Black Law." Although she was convicted in 1834, the Court of Errors later reversed the decision. Crandall returned to Canterbury and reopened her school.

This time, harassment from local residents became more violent. Arson was attempted, and finally on September 9, 1834, men armed with iron bars and clubs rendered the school uninhabitable. The school was closed and put up for sale on September 11, 1834.

Crandall lived to see many of her former black pupils become teachers themselves. In 1886, Crandall was granted an annuity of $400 from the state legislature of Connecticut at the urging of Mark Twain. *(See also: Abolition and the Antislavery Movement; Black Women; Education)*

—**Rose Kolbasnik Callahan**

Further Reading

Foner, Phillip S., and Josephine F. Pacheco. *Three Who Dared: Prudence Crandall, Margaret Douglass, Myrtilla Miner—Champions of Antebellum Black Education.* Westport, CT: Greenwood, 1984.

Fuller, Edmund. *Prudence Crandall: An Incident of Racism in Nineteenth-Century Connecticut.* Middletown, CT: Wesleyan University Press, 1971.

Criminals

Although reliable criminal data exist only since the 1930s, broad historical patterns of female offenses are discernible. Since colonial New England, with its excessive concern with the individual's private behavior, status offenses such as truancy and promiscuity have predominated among women. Most of the colonial women punished by the criminal justice system were public order offenders. This concern with proper and accepted behavior remained strong through the eighteenth and nineteenth centuries, although property crimes, mostly theft, became more common. Crimes of violence remained rare.

In the 1870s, criminologists began predicting that the growing involvement of women outside the home would lead to an increase in crime among them. Common perceptions of female offenders shifted in the late 1800s from the idea of a sinister individual, a "Dark Lady," to that of a child-like individual, a fallen woman. The emphasis on status offenses intensified with the social purity reformers of the 1890s, who focused on venereal disease, white slavery, and prostitution. These reformers launched an influential national campaign to eradicate what they identified as serious female offenses. Society needed to be protected from those women who, as one reformer put it, "scatter disease through every community."

Similar concerns emerged in the 1930s and again during the Second World War, with the widespread campaigns against venereal disease. Since the 1960s, the number of women involved in crime, especially serious crime, has increased as their position in society has changed. Recently, scholars have studied women's offenses more intensely, often focusing on the role of women in contemporary society, and how these forces have affected their involvement in crime. During the 1960s, 1970s, and 1980s, for example,

the number of serious property offenses committed by women more than doubled, and criminologists maintain that with more women working outside the home and with greater opportunities to commit crimes, the rate will continue to increase. Over the same period, the proportion of females arrested for violent crimes hardly changed, and women continued to be prosecuted most often for property and status offenses.

FBI data from the 1990s show an increase in violent crimes and drug offenses by women. From 1992 to 1996, arrests of adult women for violent crimes (murder, forcible rape, robbery, aggravated assault) increased by nearly 23 percent, and over the same time period, arrests of adult women for drug offenses increased by just over 40 percent. Also during the same time period, arrests for women under the age of eighteen increased by 25.1 percent and 163.7 percent, respectively, for violent crimes and drug abuse violations. Even taking into consideration the percentage increases, women accounted for only 15 percent of 1996 arrests for violent crimes and 16.7 percent of drug offense arrests in the United States. Data from 1996 show larceny-theft to be the number-one cause of arrests of women. *(See also: Parker, Bonnie; Prison Reform; Prostitution; Venereal Disease/Sexually Transmitted Diseases; Women's Prisons)*

—**Robert G. Waite**

Further Reading

Freedman, Estelle. *Their Sisters' Keepers: Women's Prison Reform in America, 1830–1930.* Ann Arbor: University of Michigan Press, 1981.

Hull, N. E. H. *Female Felons: Women and Serious Crime in Colonial Massachusetts.* Champaign: University of Illinois Press, 1987.

Leonard, Eileen B. "Sexual Murder," *Gender & Society* 3 (1989): 572-77.

Mann, Coramae Richey. "Minority and Female: A Criminal Justice Double Bind," *Social Justice* 16 (1989): 95-114.

Pollak, Otto. *The Criminality of Women.* Philadelphia: University of Pennsylvania Press, 1950.

Pollack-Byrne, Joycelyn M. *Women, Prison and Crime.* Pacific Grove, CA: Brooks/Cole, 1990.

Rosen, Ruth. *The Lost Sisterhood: Prostitution in America, 1900–1918.* Baltimore: Johns Hopkins University Press, 1982.

Simon, Rita James. *The Contemporary Woman and Crime.* Rockville, MD: National Institute of Mental Health, 1975.

Crowell, Frances Elisabeth (1875–1950)

Frances Elisabeth Crowell was a leader in the international public health movement. Crowell was at the forefront of nursing from the beginning of her career: She was a member of the first class to graduate from St. Joseph's Hospital School of Nursing in Chicago, in 1895. The following year, she made a drastic change in her working environment, moving from a large city hospital to the Pensacola Infirmary, a small facility that served seamen on the Florida coast and treated a wide range of medical problems, including venereal disease, epidemics of yellow fever and other tropical diseases, and industrial accidents. In 1900, the infirmary moved to larger quarters, changed its name to St. Anthony's Hospital, and became a chartered corporation.

Crowell's role in the expanded enterprise was prominent and unusual for an unmarried woman: She was a major stockholder. In 1898, she had purchased a half-interest in the infirmary, an investment that appreciated as the medical establishment grew. Her concern for the financial security of unmarried working women, especially nurses, was a lifelong preoccupation and the topic of a number of her publications in nursing journals.

As a stockholder and nursing superintendent of St. Anthony's Hospital in Pensacola, Crowell grappled with the problems of providing nursing services to the indigent. In 1905, she moved to New York City to study social work for a year at the New York School of Philanthropy (subsequently the Graduate School of Social Work of Columbia University). After graduation, she went to work as a special investigator for the Association of Neighborhood Workers in the city and four years later became executive secretary of the Association of Tuberculosis Clinics in New York City, a post she held until 1917.

The education of health personnel was a continuing concern for Crowell. In Pensacola, she established her own nurses' training program to provide qualified nurses for St. Anthony's. While an administrator with the Association of Tuberculosis Clinics, she wrote a series of educational materials on tuberculosis and its control.

Her career as a leader of the international public health movement began when the Rockefeller Foundation appointed her to the commission it sent to France in 1917 to combat tuberculosis. She demonstrated her considerable skill as a diplomat and administrator in setting up schools to train French nursing personnel. She single-handedly established the public health nurse as the cornerstone of the antituberculosis programs in France. In recognition of her contribution, the French awarded her the Legion of Honor.

In 1922, when her work in France was completed, Crowell embarked on a new assignment for the Rockefeller Foundation: assessing nurse training programs in Europe and advising political and health leaders on quality education. Her assignment took her all over Europe, from Turkey to Spain, with frequent trips to England and the United States. She was an effective emissary who communicated equally well with physicians, nursing professionals, political leaders, and the board of the Rockefeller Foundation. She retired in 1941 to live in Italy, where she was an adviser to the Red Cross in the early days of World War II, but she spent most of the war years as a refugee confined to a convent. She died in 1950 of a stroke. *(See also: Consumption; Nursing)*

—**Jane Crisler**

Further Reading
Rockefeller Foundation Archives: RG 12.1, F. Elisabeth Crowell Diaries, 1926–1931. Rockefeller Foundation, New York.
Vickers, Elizabeth D. "F. Elisabeth Crowell: Pensacola's Pioneer Nurse," *Journal of the Florida Medical Association* 70 (1978): 642-46.

☙ Cult of True Womanhood

In her seminal article published in 1966, historian Barbara Welter analyzed the prescribed role of antebellum American women as the role was depicted in women's magazines, gift annuals, and religious literature of the nineteenth century. Enshrining the sexual division of labor that relegated women to the home, this prescriptive literature presented purity, piety, domesticity, and submission as the essential dogmas of the cult of true womanhood. As the hostage in the home and the moral guardian of an increasingly materialistic and secular national culture, the middle-class True Woman was to preserve the values of the family and the Republic, while the middle-class True Man forged an economic empire for himself and his family within the public sphere. As the "lady of leisure," displaced from the economic production of the rural woman, the matron of the rising urban middle-class family required a means of maintaining and enhancing her social esteem and status, one that would acknowledge the value of woman's unpaid labor in the home. The ideology of femininity presented within the cult of true womanhood ennobled woman's reproductive function while obscuring the sexual connotation inherent in motherhood.

The cult of true womanhood spawned a constellation of concepts to explain and enhance this essentially restricted role for woman in the nineteenth century. Marriage was deemed the only acceptable career for woman. Denied any political or economic participation in her own right, woman was to use her woman's influence (moral suasion exerted on men) to preserve the religious and social values of early America. Woman was to limit herself to the domestic concerns of family and home, woman's sphere. As the mother of the race, woman was to teach America's daughters to be dutiful helpmeets to her patriotic and achieving sons. Woman was to perform the household and child care chores of the home, woman's work. Woman was to be satisfied with her domestic role, woman's sphere.

As a form of social control of women in antebellum America, the cult of true womanhood was intended to emphasize the restrictions on respectable women's lives and choices. But even before the domestic feminists emerged after 1860, women discreetly continued to transform woman's sphere into a fortress, from which the True Woman could sally forth to do her duty even when that duty took her into the public sphere. In antebellum America, economic and social circumstances allowed—and sometimes required—the True Woman to seek paid employment to support herself and her family. The mother of the race became the teacher of the race, as women acquired education adequate to train them to achieve dominance of not only the profession of teaching but of nursing and the female-centered medical practices. As did the succeeding domestic feminists, true women ruthlessly appropriated industrial and technological occupations that could be defined as extensions of woman's work once found in the preindustrial home. The piety of the True Woman impelled her participation in the moral reform movements of the nineteenth century. The values of domesticity and True Woman's purity drove her to confront social and political graft, vice, and corruption in the public sphere because these contagions threatened the sanctity of the domestic sphere.

Thus the antebellum cult of true womanhood prepared the way for the domestic feminist throughout the nineteenth century to advance women's opportunities in education and employment as prerequisites to women's performance of their womanly duties rather than as challenges to the gender system. The development of the cult of true womanhood reflected the social and economic changes during the antebellum period; the refinement of its concepts after the Civil War provided a means of simultaneously accommodating Victorian America's emotional ties to the past and its contemporary economic and social needs. The seemingly stagnant cult of true womanhood actually provided a dynamic access tool for the domestic feminists such as Catharine Beecher, Sarah Josepha Hale, and Harriet Beecher Stowe to use as they sought to ensure due social regard for woman's sphere. The cultural definition of woman's role that developed among women of color and immigrant or ethnic women was also influenced by the cult of true womanhood. *(See also: Beecher, Catharine; Domestic Feminism; Education; Hale, Sarah Josepha; Stowe, Harriet Beecher; Women's Work: Nineteenth Century)*

—Angela M. Howard

Further Reading

Cott, Nancy. *The Bonds of Womanhood: "Woman's Sphere" in New England, 1780–1835.* New Haven, CT: Yale University Press, 1977.
Douglas, Ann. *The Feminization of American Culture.* New York: Knopf, 1977.
Perkins, Linda M. "The Impact of the 'Cult of True Womanhood' on the Education of Black Women," *Journal of Social Issues* 39 (1983): 17-28.
Sklar, Katharyn Kish. *Catharine Beecher: A Study in American Domesticity.* New Haven, CT: Yale University Press, 1973.
Welter, Barbara. "The Cult of True Womanhood: 1820–1860," *American Quarterly* 18 (Summer 1966): 151-74.
Zophy, Angela Howard. "Sarah Josepha Hale, Matron of Victorian Womanhood." In *For the General Welfare: Essays in*

Honor of Robert H. Bremner, edited by Frank Annunziata, Patrick D. Reagan, and Ray T. Wortman, 61-89. New York: Peter Lang, 1989.

Curtis, Emma Ghent (1860–1918)

Novelist, poet, editor, and suffragist, Emma Ghent Curtis was born in Frankfort, Indiana, to Ira and Mary (Palmer) Ghent. She graduated from Frankfort High School, moved to Canon City, Colorado, and married James Curtis, a rancher, in 1882. The couple had two children, Benjamin and Mary.

Curtis wrote several sentimental didactic novels including *The Administratrix* (1889) and *Fate of a Fool* (1890), and her poetry and short stories were printed in various Populist and suffrage newspapers. She was active in both Populist Party and woman suffrage campaigns in 1893 in southern Colorado, where the constituency was composed primarily of coal miners, many of whom did not speak English. In addition, she edited the *Royal Gorge,* a Populist newspaper.

In 1891, Curtis attended a convention of farm, labor, and reform organizations in Cincinnati to assist in the planning of the first Populist Party convention. To this end, Curtis worked on both the national organizing committee and the committee on resolutions. The following year, Curtis was a delegate to the National Conference of Industrial Associations of America, where the newly formed Populist Party organized the presidential nominating convention to be held several months later. In opposition to Woman's Christian Temperance Union president Frances Willard, who was also a delegate, Curtis supported separate planks for suffrage and temperance and offered a substitute to Willard's prohibition resolution. Curtis's action was approved by convention delegates. In 1894, following the election of Populist Davis Waite as governor of Colorado, Curtis was rewarded for her campaign efforts and appointed a commissioner on the Board of Control of the Colorado State Industrial School for Boys. *(See also: Politics; Populist Party; Suffrage in the American West; Women Writers)*

—MaryJo Wagner

Further Reading

Blocker, Jack S. "The Politics of Reform: Populism, Prohibition, and Woman Suffrage, 1891–1892," *Historian* 34 (1972): 628.
Brown, Joseph G. *The History of Equal Suffrage in Colorado, 1868–1898.* Denver: News Job Printing, 1898.
Curtis, Emma G. *The Administratrix.* New York: John B. Alden, 1889.
Diggs, Annie. "The Women in the Alliance Movement," *Arena* 6 (July 1892): 161-79.

Dall, Caroline Wells (Healey) (1822–1912)

Caroline Dall, feminist author, researched and wrote about women's economic, legal, and educational plight. The daughter of a wealthy businessman, she grew up in Boston, where she became a follower of Margaret Fuller, later publishing a book recounting her conversations with the famous transcendentalist. She was forced to find a job teaching school after her father experienced financial reverses. Her marriage to Charles Dall, a Unitarian clergyman, produced several children but eventually disintegrated. He left the United States to become a missionary in India, and Dall's experiences as a single parent sensitized her to the plight of women workers.

Dall lectured widely and wrote extensively, publishing *Women's Right to Labor* (1860), *Woman's Rights under the Law* (1862), and perhaps her best-known book, *The College, the Market, and the Court: or, Woman's Relation to Education, Politics, and Law* (1867). In these and other works, she argued that the relegation of women to only a few types of jobs led to competition and low pay. The end result was that many turned to prostitution. Critical of middle-class women whose lives were dominated by fashion and frivolity, Dall insisted that education and jobs could provide more women with financial and intellectual independence. Because of her tendency toward dogmatism and her emphasis on economics rather than suffrage, Dall was not closely allied with other late-nineteenth-century feminists. *(See also: Fuller, Margaret)*

—**Wendy Hamand Venet**

Further Reading
Caroline Wells Healey Dall Papers, 1811–1954. Bryn Mawr College Special Collections, Mariam Coffin Canaday Library.

Riegel, Robert E. *American Feminists.* Lawrence: University of Kansas Press, 1963.

Stanton, Elizabeth C., Susan B. Anthony, and Matilda J. Gage. *History of Woman Suffrage.* 6 vols. Rochester, NY: Charles Mann, 1886.

Welter, Barbara. "The Merchant's Daughter: A Tale from Life," *New England Quarterly* 42 (March 1969): 3-22.

Daly, Mary (b. 1928)

Renowned radical feminist and theologian Mary Daly was born October 16, 1928, in Schenectady, New York. She received her B.A. at the College of St. Rose in nearby Albany in 1950. Shortly after acquiring her M.A. at the Catholic University of America in 1952, she became a visiting lecturer in English at St. Mary's College in Notre Dame, Indiana, and started work on a Ph.D. In 1954, she completed her degree, then taught philosophy and theology, first at Cardinal Cushing College in Brookline, Massachusetts (1954–1959), then at the University of Fribourg in Switzerland (1959–1966). After returning to the United States, Daly began teaching at Boston College, a Catholic school, in 1966. Her first controversial book, *The Church and the Second Sex* (1968), exposed church policies that deny women full participation in the affairs of society; it almost cost her her tenure. Much of the same anger and hope of her first book appeared in its sequel, *Beyond God the Father* (1974), but the focus changed and the perception was deeper and wider.

Gyn/Ecology (1978), the first book in Daly's trilogy, focuses on a radical feminist voyage undertaken by a woman struggling to become herself. The book emphasizes women's need to rid themselves of patriarchy at its roots in everything from language, consciousness, myths, and institutions to ways of seeing, being, and doing. The second book in the trilogy, *Pure Lust* (1984), continues the journey and summons women to break through patriarchal barriers and live the feminist philosophy that reunites women with themselves and nature. Written in the powerful language that marks Daly's finest works, *Pure Lust,* in exploring the demands of the voyage, creates a shock of awakening for those strong enough to understand and accept new perceptions. Before Daly completed the third volume of the trilogy, *Outercourse* (1992), she published *Websters' First New Intergalactic Wickedary of the English Language* (1987) with Jane Caputi. The latter two books were republished in 1998.

Her most recent work, which further develops her elemental feminist philosophy, is *Realizing the Archaic Future: A Radical Elemental Feminist Manifesto* (1999). "This work," Daly says, "is in some respects a successor to my philosophical autobiography, *Outercourse,* and in other ways it is a logical/ontological successor to my earlier works. . . ."

All of Daly's books stress radical feminism as central to all causes and emphasize the importance of seeing connections between the women's movement and all other movements. Through her challenges to religion and patriarchy, as well as her exposure of the historic persecution of women, Daly has established her place among contemporary radical feminist theorists. *(See also: Feminism; Radical Feminism; Theologians)*

—**Ginger Costello**

Further Reading

Daly, Lois K., ed. *Feminist Theological Ethics: A Reader.* Louisville, KY: Westminster John Knox, 1994.

Daly, Mary. *Beyond God the Father.* Boston: Beacon, 1974.

———. *The Church and the Second Sex.* Rev. ed. Boston: Beacon, 1975.

———. *Gyn/Ecology: The Metaethics of Radical Feminism.* Boston: Beacon, 1978.

———. *Outercourse: The Be-Dazzling Voyage.* San Francisco: Harper & Row, 1992.

———. *Pure Lust: Elemental Feminist Philosophy.* 1984. Reprinted, San Francisco: Harper San Francisco, 1992.

———. *Websters' First New Intergalactic Wickedary of the English Language.* Conjured in Cahoots with Jane Caputi. 1987. Reprinted, Boston: Beacon, 1998.

Hampson, Daphne. *Theology and Feminism.* Cambridge, MA: Basil Blackwell, 1998.

Ratcliffe, Krista. *Anglo American Feminist Challenges to the Rhetorical Tradition: Virginia Woolf, Mary Daly, and Adrienne Rich.* Carbondale: Southern Illinois University Press, 1995.

http://womenbooks.com/mary_daly/index.html [Mary Daly page at women-writers.com]

⮥ Dance

During the nineteenth and twentieth centuries, American women dancers have served as models of innovation both as choreographers and performers. In the days of the Romantic ballet during the 1830s and 1840s, when America had yet to establish its own dance theater tradition, three ballerinas—Augusta Maywood (1825–1876), Mary Ann Lee (1823–1899), and Julia Turnbull (1822–1887)—emerged as stars. Maywood, noted for her technical virtuosity, danced at the Paris Opera in 1839 and achieved the title of *prima ballerina assoluta* at La Scala in Milan. Lee, a fine lyric dancer who came from a theatrical family, studied ballet in Philadelphia and Paris. After her return to America in 1846, Lee produced the first *Giselle,* which premiered in Boston, dancing the lead role with George Washington Smith as Albrecht. A third ballerina, Julia Turnbull, took Lee's place, dancing in *Giselle* and other Romantic ballets with Smith. During the second half of the nineteenth century, professional dance lost prestige. There were few opportunities for women to dance except in popular entertainments such as *The Black Crook* (1866), which promoted spectacular effects and simple choreographic patterns. Such extravaganzas led in the twentieth century to the development of musical theater productions such as the Ziegfeld Follies and others on Broadway in which tap dancing and ballroom formed the dance vocabulary. Out of these beginnings, American musical comedy flourished in subsequent decades.

New directions for dance came at the end of the nineteenth century with the appearance of Loie Fuller (1862–1928), Isadora Duncan (1877–1927), and Ruth St. Denis (1879–1968). Fuller was a pioneer not so much in dance technique as in lighting and costume. She took full advantage of the new electric lighting and manipulated yards of silk to catch the light in theatrical numbers such as *The Serpentine Dance, Fire Dance, The Butterfly,* and *Dance of Joy.* She was particularly successful in Europe; in Paris, she was the toast of the artistic elite. Isadora Duncan made a decided break with any earlier dance technique found either in vaudeville or classical ballet. Because America was not ready for her advanced style of modern dance, she established her reputation in Europe. She represents a major modernist force in her return to primitive simplicity. In her movement, she sought inspiration in walking, running, bending, skipping, and jumping and evolved a dance aesthetic that was at once expressive and hard to imitate. In her travels, she founded numerous schools and adopted various girls to carry on her style. She believed in the "New Woman," "the dancer of the future . . . more glorious than any woman that has yet been; more beautiful than the Egyptian, than the Greek, the early Italian, than all women of past centuries—the highest intelligence in the freest body." Similarly, Ruth St. Denis had a vision of a new, spiritual dance style. In time, she developed a series of evocative solos based on exotic Oriental dances. Among them were *Incense, Radha, The Cobras, Egypta,* and *Ishtar of the Seven Gates.* In 1914, she met and eventually married Ted Shawn, and together they founded the Denishawn school in Los Angeles, where they inculcated into their students an eclectic mixture of dance styles. Denishawn dancers made a name at home and on tour, and St. Denis and Shawn trained the next generation of dancers for the burgeoning movie industry along with serious innovators such as Martha Graham and Doris Humphrey.

The genuine new dance came into being in the late 1920s and 1930s. Martha Graham (1894–1991) broke from Denishawn in 1925 and over the years evolved a unique formal language independent of pseudo-Oriental or classical ballet. Hers is the first truly modern dance based on the principle of contract and release of the torso and pelvis. Graham floor exercises produce dancers with strength, flexibility, and virtuosity. Graham conceived the body's motion in both abstract form and potential expressiveness. Her nearly two hundred works explore all phases of human emotion from comedic to tragic. She choreographed for herself first, then for her group of female dancers, eventually admitting a series of fine male dancers into her small company beginning with Erick Hawkins in the mid-1930s. Among her masterpieces are *Lamentation* (1930), *Primitive Mysteries* (1931),

El Penitente and *Letter to the World* (1940), *Appalachian Spring* (1944), *Dark Meadow* and *Cave of the Heart* (1946), *Errand into the Maze* and *Night Journey* (1947), *Seraphic Dialogue* (1955), *Clytemnestra* (1958), *Episodes* (1959), *Acrobats of God* (1960), *Rite of Spring* (1984), and *Maple Leaf Rag* (1990). Graham's productions were often spare in costume, lighting, and set design, but she promoted the talents of artists such as Isamu Noguchi and Jean Rosenthal and collaborated with composers Louis Horst, Aaron Copland, Norman Dello Joio, William Schuman, Samuel Barber, and Paul Hindemith, among others.

Doris Humphrey (1895–1958) followed a parallel path to Martha Graham's, always in competition with her fellow Denishawn student. The Humphrey-Weidman technique, based on the principles of fall and recovery, came into being through the collaboration of Humphrey and Charles Weidman, who maintained a school and performing company in New York City for twenty years. In her choreography, Humphrey concentrated on the group more than on the individual. Among her masterpieces are the early *Soaring* (1920), produced with Ruth St. Denis, *Air for the G String* (1928), *Water Study* (1928), *The Shakers* (1931), *New Dance* trilogy (1935–1936), and *With My Red Fires* (1936). Due to crippling arthritis, Humphrey had to retire from the stage early, but she continued to teach in New York until the end of her life.

Three other women who developed in the difficult early days of American dance were Hanya Holm, Anna Sokolow, and Agnes de Mille. Holm (1893–1992) came to America from Germany where she had been a disciple of Mary Wigman. She arrived in New York to open a branch of the Wigman school in 1931 that continued until 1967. There she trained dancers such as Valerie Bettis, Glen Tetley, and Alwin Nikolais. A musician as well as dancer, Holm used percussion instruments in her classes to reinforce essential expressive movement. She also participated with Graham, Humphrey, Weidman, and José Limón in the summer dance institute at Bennington College during the 1930s. She founded her Center of the Dance in Colorado Springs in 1941. Of her choreographic pieces, the large-scale work *Trend,* first presented at Bennington in 1937, explores the themes of social decadence and collapse. Holm's solo performances tended toward the lyric, but *Trend* was the natural result of the synthesis between German expressionism and an American theme. Holm is best known for her choreography for the musical stage, including *Kiss Me, Kate* (1948), *My Fair Lady* (1956), and *Camelot* (1960).

Anna Sokolow (b. 1910) began at the Neighborhood Playhouse in New York with Martha Graham and Louis Horst whom she assisted for nine years. She joined Graham in 1929 and stayed until 1939, when she accepted the invitation to teach and choreograph in Mexico, remaining there for six months out of every year for ten years. She also worked in Israel, forming the Lyric Theatre Company in Tel Aviv in 1962. From 1959 on, Sokolow has been associated with the Julliard School as guest teacher. Of all the modern choreographers, Sokolow's vision of constant innovation remains the most insistent. She asserted that "the modern dance should be non-conformist. We should not try to create a tradition." A prolific choreographer for both ballet and modern dance companies, she embraces a social critique in her pieces. Among her works are *Lament for the Death of a Bullfighter* (1941), *Rooms* (1955), *Opus '60* (1960), *Dreams* (1961), *Seven Deadly Sins* (1967), and *Homage to Scriabin* (1977).

Although influenced in her early work by Martha Graham, with whom she maintained a lifelong friendship, Agnes de Mille (1905–1993) took a different track from the other early dancer/choreographers. Ballet rather than modern dance became the basis of her art. Informed by her exposure to Graham, she developed a unique vocabulary of movement and gesture, thus modifying classical technique. In the 1930s, she made a solo concert tour in Europe and then settled in London, studying with Marie Rambert and working alongside Antony Tudor and Frederick Ashton. Returning to America at the outbreak of World War II, de Mille created for Ballet Theatre *Three Virgins and a Devil* (1941), *Rodeo* (1942), *Fall River Legend* (1948), and *The Harvest According* (1952). In addition, she made a name on Broadway with *Oklahoma!* (1943), *Carousel* (1945), *Paint Your Wagon* (1951), and *110 in the Shade* (1963). In de Mille's synthesis of ballet and modern styles, one finds the expression of an identifiable American spirit. A superb writer, de Mille produced numerous books, including two autobiographies, *Dance to the Piper* (1952) and *And Promenade Home* (1956), as well as a biography of Martha Graham (1991).

Another pioneer of American ballet was Ruth Page (1899–1991) whose base was Chicago. After World War I, she joined Anna Pavlova's company and then danced with Adolph Bolm's company in Chicago and later with Ballets Russes under Diaghilev. Touring extensively with various companies during the 1920s and 1930s, she also appeared with Irving Berlin's Music Box Revue (1922–1923). During the next thirty years, Page was dancer, choreographer, or director for the Chicago Opera Ballet and acted as choreographer for the Ravinia Opera during its summer seasons. As choreographer of American themes, she is best known for *Frankie and Johnny* (1938), *Billy Sunday* (1948), and *The Bells* (1946), based on a work by Edgar Allan Poe, but her output also includes ballet adaptations of opera scenarios. Ruth Page's dynamism made Chicago into a ballet town, and her various companies provided work for generations of talented dancers.

One of those dancers was the African American Katherine Dunham (b. 1912), who danced in Page's *La Guiablesse* in 1933 and during that decade completed her Ph.D. at the University of Chicago in anthropology. As a dancer/choreographer, Dunham combined ballet with ethnic dance, especially central European, Caribbean, and African. In 1938, she became the director of the Negro Unit of the Chicago branch of the Federal Theatre Project, where she produced *L'Ag'Ya* (1938), based on folk material from Martinique.

Dunham performed extensively in solo concerts and with a small company of black dancers. She made her debut in New York in 1940 with *Tropics and Le Jazz Hot—From Haiti to Harlem,* which established her reputation. In the same year, she performed in the Broadway musical *Cabin in the Sky.* In following years, she appeared in numerous Hollywood films and black stage revues. From 1945 to 1955, Dunham trained dancers at her school in New York. Dunham has devoted her time in recent years to working with disadvantaged youth in East St. Louis, sponsored by Southern Illinois University's Performing Arts Training Center. Throughout her long career, Dunham's unique movement vocabulary has become part of American dance's mainstream.

Of the more recent dancer/choreographers, Twyla Tharp (b. 1941) stands out as an innovator, bringing together early training in ballet, tap, and jazz dance forms. She worked briefly with the Paul Taylor Dance Company (1963–1965) and then pursued freelance work with her own group or with various ballet companies. Her "cross-over" pieces not only demand mastery of multiple dance techniques but also meld high art dance with pop culture as exhibited in works such as *Deuce Coupe* and *As Time Goes By* for City Center Joffrey Ballet (1973), *Push Comes to Shove* (1976), and *Sinatra Suite* (1984) for American Ballet Theatre, and *The Catherine Wheel* (1981) to a commissioned score by David Byrne for her own company.

From the 1970s onward, many women have explored a range of postmodern strategies in dance from minimalism and improvisation to narrative and symbolist pieces. Among them are Lucinda Childs (b. 1940), Meredith Monk (b. 1942), Simone Forti (b. 1935), Deborah Hay (b. 1941), Yvonne Rainer (b. 1934), Laura Dean (b. 1945), Karole Armitage (b. 1955), Molissa Fenley (b. 1954), and Trisha Brown (b. 1936). The impetus for this phase of vanguard dance comes from Merce Cunningham and John Cage or from Ann Halprin's workshops or from the Judson Dance Theatre in Greenwich Village and its offshoots. Many pieces incorporate other media and art forms, such as visual arts, experimental music, and film. The process of making dances becomes as important as the product. American dance is being rejuvenated by these artists as they forge new formal and expressive languages; no one direction or one choreographer dominates. Every theoretical and practical approach is possible.

In addition to these dancer/choreographers, America has produced generation after generation of fine performers. Among the dancers working for George Balanchine in his various companies leading to the establishment of the New York City Ballet are Tanaquil Le Clercq (b. 1929), Maria Tallchief (b. 1925), Diana Adams (1926–1993), Melissa Hayden (b. 1923), Allegra Kent (b. 1937?), Suki Schorer (b. 1939), Patricia Wilde (b. 1928), Patricia McBride (b. 1942), Suzanne Farrell (b. 1945), Gelsey Kirkland (b. 1952), Kay Mazzo (b. 1946), Patricia Neary (b. 1942), Heather Watts (b. 1953), Kyra Nichols (b. 1958), Darci Kistler (b. 1964), and Merrill Ashley (b. 1950). American

Ballet Theatre (founded by Lucia Chase in 1940) has featured as principals Nora Kaye (1920–1987), Sallie Wilson (b. 1932), Toni Lander (1931–1985), Lupe Serrano (b. 1930), Cynthia Gregory (b. 1946), Martine van Hamel (b. 1945), Cynthia Harvey (b. 1957), Marianna Tcherkassky (b. 1955), Susan Jaffe (b. 1962), and Amanda McKerrow (b. 1963). Among modern dancers, women who have excelled are Yuriko (b. 1920), Sophie Maslow (b. 1911), Helen McGehee (b. 1921), Matt Turney (b. 1930?), Ethel Winter (b. 1924), Mary Hinkson (b. 1930), and Therese Capucilli (b. 1956) with the Martha Graham Dance Company; Pauline Koner (b. 1912) and Betty Jones (b. 1926) with the José Limón Company; Bettie de Jong (b. 1933) with the Paul Taylor Dance Company; Judith Jamison (b. 1943) with the Alvin Ailey American Dance Theatre (now its company director), and Carolyn Brown (b. 1927) with the Merce Cunningham Dance Company. These performers stand for the thousands of other American women who have dedicated their lives to forming and transforming the vital art of American dance during the twentieth century. *(See also: Duncan, Isadora; Graham, Martha; Music; Tallchief, Maria)*

—JoLynn Edwards

Further Reading

Anderson, Jack. *Ballet and Modern Dance: A Concise History,* 2d ed. Princeton, NJ: Princeton Book Company, 1992.

Au, Susan. *Ballet and Modern Dance.* London: Thames & Hudson, 1988.

Banes, Sally. *Writing Dancing in the Age of Postmodernism.* Middletown, CT: Wesleyan University Press, 1994.

de Mille, Agnes. *And Promenade Home.* Boston: Little, Brown, 1956.

———. *Dance to the Piper.* Boston: Little, Brown, 1952.

———. *Martha: The Life and Work of Martha Graham.* New York: Random House, 1991.

Duncan, Isadora. *My Life.* New York: Liveright, 1955.

Farrell, Suzanne, and Toni Bentley. *Holding on to the Air: An Autobiography.* New York: Summit, 1990.

Graham, Martha. *Blood Memory: An Autobiography.* New York: Doubleday, 1991.

Shelton, Suzanne. *Ruth St. Denis: A Biography of the Divine Dancer.* Austin: University of Texas Press, 1990.

Siegel, Marcia B. *The Shapes of Change.* Berkeley: University of California Press, 1985.

Sorell, Walter. *Hanya Holm: The Biography of an Artist.* Middletown, CT: Wesleyan University Press, 1969.

Tharp, Twyla. *Push Comes to Shove.* New York: Bantam, 1992.

Warren, Larry. *Anna Sokolow: The Rebellious Spirit.* Princeton, NJ: Princeton Book Company, 1991.

❧ Dating

Dating emerged in the early twentieth century as a new and peculiarly American form of courtship. It gradually replaced the nineteenth-century practice of "calling"—a system involving varying degrees of formality but that basically entailed a man's paying a call on a woman in her family's home. A date, in contrast, was an occasion on which a man invited a woman to "go out" with him to a public place and paid for her entertainment.

Although the rise of the dating system is traditionally traced to the automobile and the increased mobility it offered middle-class youth, the origins of dating actually lie with the urban lower classes. The term *date* first appears in lower-class slang in the 1880s. Pushed out of crowded apartments that lacked parlors for receiving callers, subject to decreasing parental authority, and enticed by the excitements of the city, young people took their courtships into the streets and to public places of amusement. Upper- and middle-class youth were also attracted by the freedoms offered by dating, and the term and the practice had achieved solid middle-class respectability by the 1920s.

By shifting the acts of courtship away from the watchful eyes of family and local community, dating lessened parental control over courtship. But dating also shifted the balance of power between men and women in courtship. According to the rules governing the calling system, the woman asked the man to call, and he was a guest in her home. In the dating system, the woman became the man's guest in the public sphere; he paid for her entertainment, and thus, she lost the power of initiative. Women did not ask men out on dates.

Between 1920 and the mid-1960s, dating was governed by a detailed set of rules that prescribed the appropriate behavior for each sex. The dating system yielded a mammoth body of advice literature and magazines primarily aimed at women and devoted to spelling out the arcane and changing rules of courtship. The dating system has gone through three major phases. From 1920 through World War II, men and women tried to demonstrate popularity by dating many different people. During the postwar era, "going steady" was the ideal. And from the mid-1960s on, the dating system has become more flexible, gradually incorporating the sexual revolution and making some accommodation to women's equality. *(See also: Gender Role Socialization; Sexual Revolution)*

—Beth L. Bailey

Further Reading

Bailey, Beth L. *From Front Porch to Back Seat: Courtship in 20th-Century America.* Baltimore: Johns Hopkins University Press, 1988.
Peiss, Kathy. *Cheap Amusements: Working Women and Leisure in Turn-of-the-Century New York.* Philadelphia: Temple University Press, 1986.
Seidman, Steven. *Romantic Longings: Love in America, 1830–1980.* New York: Routledge, 1991.
White, Kevin. *The First Sexual Revolution: The Emergence of Male Heterosexuality in Modern America.* New York: New York University Press, 1993.

∾ Daughters of Bilitis (DOB)

The Daughters of Bilitis (DOB) was a social and civil rights group for lesbians founded in 1955 by eight women in San Francisco. The name, taken from Pierre Louys's erotic poem "Songs of Bilitis," was intended to hold meaning for lesbians while protecting the anonymity of members by sounding like a traditional women's club.

By 1960, DOB had a membership of 110 women, a bimonthly newsletter called *The Ladder,* and four other chapters. The focus of the group was lesbian rights and culture. Education was seen as the most important avenue for achieving civil rights and higher status for lesbians. Like the primarily male Mattachine Society, with which it worked closely, DOB attempted to dispel myths and prejudice about homosexuality. To do this, DOB provided speakers for television and radio shows, colleges, and high schools. The organization also assisted in research projects and maintained a library for research and recreational reading.

In the late 1960s, the growing women's movement brought a more explicitly lesbian-feminist orientation to DOB. This new radicalism also caused conflicts in DOB, and in 1970, the national organization was dissolved, although *The Ladder* continued publication independently through 1972.

DOB's commitment to obtaining basic civil rights for lesbians made it an important and early forerunner of both the feminist and gay rights movements. *(See also: Lesbian Rights; Lesbianism)*

—Mary Battenfeld
Adapted for the second edition by Maureen R. Liston.

Further Reading

Damon, Gene [pseud. Barbara Grier]. "The Least of These: The Minority Whose Screams Haven't Yet Been Heard." In *Sisterhood Is Powerful,* edited by Robin Morgan, 333-43. New York: Vintage, 1970.
Daughters of Bilitis. *The Ladder.* 9 vols. 1956–1972. Reprinted, New York: Arno, 1975.
D'Emilio, John. *Sexual Politics, Sexual Communities: The Making of a Homosexual Minority in the U.S., 1940–1970.* Chicago: University of Chicago Press, 1983.
Faderman, Lillian. *Odd Girls and Twilight Lovers: A History of Lesbian Life in Twentieth-Century America.* New York: Columbia University Press, 1991.

∾ Daughters of Temperance

The Daughters of Temperance was founded in the 1840s as an auxiliary to the Sons of Temperance, a fraternal temperance organization begun in New York in 1842. The middle-class members of the Daughters helped the men by making meals for temperance meetings and collecting signatures on antiliquor petitions. In 1852, Susan B. Anthony, Mary C. Vaughn, and others attended a convention of the Sons as representatives of the Daughters group. The women's credentials were accepted, but they were not allowed to speak because the men felt that the women were there to listen and learn. A group of women left and organized their own group. Vaughn was elected president and spoke out strongly against the conventional image of women's role of meekness and submissiveness. She encouraged women to put that image aside to play a more active role in the reform movement. The Daughters of Temperance, with thirty thousand members, became the largest female organization of its kind and of its day; it sought passage of local and state ordinances to outlaw the sale of liquor. Anthony was appointed to prepare for a Women's State Temperance Convention in New York. This convention was held in April 1852 and led to the formation of the Woman's State Temperance Society. *(See also: Anthony, Susan B.; Temperance Movement)*

—Phyllis Holman Weisbard

Further Reading

Levine, Harry Gene. "Temperance and Women in Nineteenth-Century United States." In *Research Advances in Alcohol and Drug Problems*. Vol. 5, *Alcohol and Drug Problems in Women*, edited by Oriana Josseau Kalant, 25-67. New York: Plenum, 1980.

Stanton, Elizabeth Cady, Susan B. Anthony, and Matilda Joslyn Gage, eds. *History of Woman Suffrage*. Vol. 1. 1881. Reprinted, New York: Arno, 1969.

Tyrnell, Ian R. "Women and Temperance in Antebellum America, 1830–1860," *Civil War History* 28 (June 1982): 128-52.

⮜⮞ Daughters of the American Revolution (DAR)

The Daughters of the American Revolution (DAR) was founded in 1890. The founders, who included Eugenia Washington, Helen H. Walworth, Mary Desha, and Mary S. Lockwood, were encouraged to begin the society by the existing Sons of the American Revolution. The Sons excluded women from belonging to their organization, although they considered some women to be auxiliary members. After the annual convention of the Sons in 1890, when they flatly denied full membership to women descendants of revolutionary ancestors, these women, spurred on by a letter from Lockwood to the editor of the *Washington Post* concerning the convention's decision, founded their own group.

Although not one of the women active in founding the Daughters, Caroline Scott Harrison, wife of President Benjamin Harrison, was elected its first president-general. According to the constitution adopted at the first meeting, the purposes of the society are to perpetuate the memory and spirit of the men and women who achieved American independence, to promote education that would develop in the population the capacity for becoming good citizens, and to foster true patriotism and love of country. To be eligible for membership in the DAR, a woman must be eighteen years or older and be descended from a man or woman who served in the cause of independence during the Revolutionary War or who was a recognized patriot or gave material aid to the cause. In addition, the applicant must be personally acceptable to the society. The DAR has a special group for young women and also sponsors a National Society of the Children of the American Revolution, which is coeducational.

Both the membership and the activities of the society reflected the patriotism, nativism, and domestic feminism of the middle and upper classes in the late Victorian era in reaction to the influx of immigrants in the 1880s who were less well educated and tended to stay within their ethnic groups more than earlier groups. The DAR expressed concern for the cultural assimilation and political indoctrination of these new immigrants and prepared educational materials and inaugurated programs to help immigrant women. At the same time, the society made clear its support for restrictive immigration laws in the 1920s, in particular the law passed in 1924, which the members of the society saw as needed to protect the character of the country as they thought it should be.

Generally, the DAR did not get involved in the suffrage movement or on behalf of social issues. President-General Hazel Scott attempted to foster a social conscience in the society, but after her tenure, from 1909 to 1913, the society was more conservative in its involvement with social issues. It did not, however, completely abandon interest in national problems. For example, in 1919, the DAR joined with almost every other women's organization in supporting the League of Nations. Between the wars, the society hosted ceremonial social events for national governmental officials and their wives in Washington, D.C.

A controversial chapter in the society's history stemmed from the DAR's refusal to allow black opera star Marian Anderson to perform in its Constitution Hall in 1939. The society has made fewer headlines since the 1940s. The only exception to the lower profile that the society seems to have assumed after World War II came in 1967 when Joan Baez was denied permission to give a concert in Constitution Hall because she had refused to pay a part of her federal income taxes as a protest against the Vietnam War. Baez later gave an outdoor concert near the Washington Monument, despite the DARs' protest of this use of federal property to Interior Secretary Stewart L. Udall. The Daughters of the American Revolution continue to be identified with conservative patriotism and a primary concern for preserving genealogies and local history focused on the American Revolution. Current membership numbers nearly 180,000. *(See also: Anderson, Marian; Baez, Joan C.; Domestic Feminism; General Federation of Women's Clubs)*

—Phyllis Holman Weisbard

Further Reading

Anderson, Peggy. *The Daughters: An Unconventional Look at America's Fan Club—the D.A.R.* New York: St. Martin's, 1974.

Gibbs, Margaret. *The DAR.* New York: Henry Holt, 1969.

Hunter, Ann Arnold. *A Century of Service: The Story of the DAR.* Washington, DC: National Society Daughters of the American Revolution, 1991.

Somerville, Mollie. "A DAR Legacy: The Beginning," *Daughters of the American Revolution Magazine* 116 (1982): 568-73.

Strayer, Martha. *The D.A.R.: An Informal History.* Washington, DC: Public Affairs Press, 1958.

~ Davey v. Turner (1764)

Davey v. Turner was a colonial Pennsylvania Supreme Court decision that affirmed the joint deed system of conveyance, the legal procedure for the sale or transfer of property, in regard to married women's property rights in colonial America. The joint deed system required that the feme covert, or married woman, formally consent to the sale or transfer of property to protect the property that the woman brought into the marriage as well as to prove her relinquishment of her dower rights to the sold or transferred property. The formal consent was established by an oral examination of the wife by a justice of the peace. *(See also: Coverture; Dower; Feme Covert; Marriage; Married Women's Property Acts)*

—Angela M. Howard

Further Reading

Salmon, Marylynn. "Equality or Submersion? Feme Covert Status in Early Pennsylvania." In *Women of America: A History,* edited by Carol Ruth Berkin and Mary Beth Norton, 92-113. Boston: Houghton Mifflin, 1979.

~ Davis, Angela Yvonne (b. 1944)

Black scholar and social activist Angela Davis was born in Birmingham, Alabama, and grew up in a segregated, middle- class neighborhood, the daughter of two schoolteachers. Her father, B. Frank Davis, left teaching to operate a service station; her mother, Sallye Davis, taught primary school in Birmingham while working on an M.A. from New York University during the summers. Davis left home during high school to attend the progressive Elisabeth Irwin School in New York City and later went on to graduate with honors from Brandeis University.

As a major in French literature, Davis spent her junior year at the Sorbonne in Paris. During her senior year at Brandeis, she was tutored in philosophy by the legendary Marxist philosopher Herbert Marcuse, who regarded her as his best student in over thirty years of teaching. She went on to study philosophy at Goethe University in Frankfurt, West Germany but felt compelled to return to the United States to participate in the civil rights movement in this country. In September 1963, racist terrorists had blown up the Sixteenth Street Baptist Church in Birmingham, killing four young girls well known to the Davis family.

Following her return to the United States, Davis pursued graduate work in philosophy with Herbert Marcuse and others at the University of California at San Diego and also continued her career as a social activist. She was involved both with the Student Non-Violent Coordinating Committee (SNCC) and the Black Panthers. On June 22, 1968, Davis joined the Communist Party.

In the fall of 1969, Davis joined the philosophy faculty at the University of California at Los Angeles. An FBI informer wrote a letter to the UCLA student newspaper charging that an unnamed Communist had been hired to teach in the philosophy department contrary to the new state law that prohibited California universities from employing known Communists. (That law had been strongly supported by California's conservative governor, Ronald Reagan.) Although Davis had not been aware of the law at the time of her initial hiring, she was fired by the university system's board of regents under obvious political pressure on September 19, 1969. Quickly reinstated by the courts, she continued to teach with distinction until dismissed for making inflammatory speeches in defense of the Soledad brothers, three black convicts accused of killing a white prison guard the previous January. Davis had long been a defender of the three and had become especially close to one of them, George Jackson, mostly through correspondence.

On August 7, 1970, George Jackson's teenage brother Jonathan walked armed into a courtroom in San Rafael, California, where a case was being heard involving other black prisoners. He apparently wanted to make a political statement about the need to free his brother and other "black political prisoners." Instead, he ended up taking the presiding judge, the district attorney prosecuting the case, and several jurors hostage, leading them to a van parked in a lot outside the courthouse. A guard from San Quentin prison fired on the van, which set off a barrage of shots. Jonathan Jackson ended up dead, as did Judge James Haley and two of the black prisoners. District Attorney Garry Thomas and a woman juror were wounded. The carbine used by seventeen-year-old Jonathan Jackson had allegedly been purchased by Angela Davis, who was in the Bay Area doing research on her doctoral dissertation.

Fearing that as a known Communist who had been active in the black prisoners' rights movement she would not receive a fair trial, Davis fled from California and went underground. She soon found herself on the FBI's "ten most wanted" fugitive list and achieved additional media recognition as a black, Communist revolutionary who was brilliant, beautiful, and dangerous. Nearly two months later, on October 13, 1970, she was arrested in New York. Davis was held in jail for almost two months and had to endure the ordeal of a trial that lasted for nearly twenty months and attracted international attention. When it was finally over in June 1972, she was declared innocent of all charges.

Appealing to the coalition of minorities and sympathetic whites who had come together in her defense, Davis became a cause célèbre. In 1974, she published her autobiography in the hope that it might make "more people understand why so many of us have no alternative but to offer our lives—our bodies, our knowledge, our will—to the cause of our oppressed people" (p. x). Angela Davis has also resumed her academic career, teaching courses in black philosophy and aesthetics and women's studies at San Francisco State University. In 1998, Davis publicly affirmed that she is a lesbian. In that same year, she published her most recent book, *Blues Legacies and Black Feminism,* which takes her analysis of race and class into new areas of culture. Davis now holds the

University of California Presidential Chair at the University of California, Santa Cruz. *(See also: Civil Rights; Communist Party; New Left)*

—Jonathan W. Zophy

Further Reading

Bare, Barbara. "Davis, Angela." In *African American Women*, edited by Dorothy Salem, 142-45. New York: Garland, 1993.

Davis, Angela Yvonne. *Angela Davis: An Autobiography*. New York: Random House, 1974.

Blues Legacies and Black Feminism: Gertrude "Ma" Rainey, Bessie Smith, and Billie Holiday. New York: Random House, 1998.

———. *Women, Race and Class*. New York: Random House, 1981.

James, Joy, and Angela Y. Davis, eds. *The Angela Y. Davis Reader*. Malden, MA: Blackwell, 1998.

Major, Reginald. *Justice in the Round: The Trial of Angela Davis*. New York: Third Press, 1973.

Nadelson, Regina. *Who Is Angela Davis? The Biography of a Revolutionary*. New York: Wyden, 1972.

Noble, Jeanne. *Beautiful, Also, Are the Souls of My Black Sisters: A History of the Black Women in America*. Englewood Cliffs, NJ: Prentice Hall, 1978.

Parker, J. A. *Angela Davis: The Making of a Revolutionary*. New York: Arlington House, 1973.

⮟ Davis, Bette (1908–1989)

Bette Davis was an American film actor whose work and life epitomized the possibilities and pitfalls of the studio system. Neither conventionally beautiful nor acquiescent, she continually sought new challenges and unconventional roles over the course of her one-hundred-picture, sixty-year career. Among the awards she received were Best Actress Academy Awards for *Dangerous* (1935) and *Jezebel* (1938) and the New York Film Critics' Best Actress award for *All About Eve* (1950). In 1977, she became the fifth person, and the first woman, to receive the American Film Institute's Life Achievement Award.

Born Ruth Elizabeth Davis in Lowell, Massachusetts, she lived a peripatetic existence with her mother and sister after her parents' separation when she was ten. At age twenty, she joined a summer stock company, and within two years had advanced, first to Broadway, then to Hollywood, becoming part of the vast army of stage-trained actors who were to revolutionize the new "talkies." After a brief stint at Universal, Davis moved to Warner Bros., the working [wo]man's studio, where initially she found herself in a number of tight-budget, fast-talking films such as *Cabin in the Cotton* (1932) and *20,000 Years in Sing Sing* (1933). Her first demand of Warner's—to be released to play Mildred in *Of Human Bondage* (1934) at RKO—was reluctantly granted and gained her an Academy Award nomination. Back at Warner's, she squared off with Jack Warner himself over the roles the studio wanted to put her in, finally accepting an offer to make two films in England. Warner's successfully sued for breach of contract, and in November 1936, Davis returned to Hollywood, bloody but unbowed.

What followed was her most productive artistic period. Over the next decade, with the aid of directors like William Wyler and King Vidor, Davis turned out performances of astonishing variety and depth in films such as *Marked Woman* (1937), *Jezebel* (1938), *Dark Victory* (1939), *The Letter* (1940), *The Little Foxes* (1941), *Now, Voyager* (1942), *The Corn Is Green* (1945), and *A Stolen Life* (1946). During that same decade or so, she had numerous affairs, several abortions, was twice divorced, once widowed, became a mother, and was terminated by Warner's after eighteen years of honorable servitude.

Nonetheless, the 1950s began auspiciously, with what some believe to be her greatest film, *All About Eve* (1950), a new marriage to her costar in that film, Gary Merrill, and the adoption of two more children. But a succession of poor vehicles, health problems, and Merrill's alcoholism sent the marriage, and their professional reputations, into a decline; they were divorced in 1960. In 1957, Davis became one of the first Hollywood stars to appear on television, and she continued to do starring roles, bit parts, and talk shows over the next three decades, while still working in film and on stage. In 1987, at the age of seventy-nine, she appeared in her one hundredth film, *The Whales of August,* along with Lillian Gish, Vincent Price, and Ann Sothern.

Davis's life and career in many ways are a microcosm of the Hollywood studio system at its best and worst. Taken under contract by Warner Bros. at the age of twenty-two, she achieved stardom and developed her talent in collaborations with many of Hollywood's best writers and directors, staying at the top of her profession for nearly twenty years. Yet that success taxed her mental and physical health. Growing up in an era with firm notions about women's role, she was deeply ambivalent about her own identity. In her autobiography, *The Lonely Life,* she speaks obliquely of her failed marriages: "A woman has to fly high and fight to reach the top. She tires and needs a resting place. She should travel light—unburdened—but I've always done things the hard way" (13). Later, she speaks frankly of the hard lessons she learned: "It has been my experience that one cannot, in any shape or form, depend on human relationships for lasting reward. It is only work that truly satisfies" (251). In most of her personal relationships, Davis was the stronger partner, and that dominance often made her uncomfortable and built resentment in others, including her daughter. But that same strength went into her best roles, creating unforgettable portraits of extraordinary women. *(See also: Movie Stars; Woman's Film)*

—Frances M. Kavenik

Further Reading

Davis, Bette. *The Lonely Life: An Autobiography*. New York: G. P. Putnam, 1962.

Davis, Bette, with Michael Herskowitz. *This 'n That*. New York: G. P. Putnam, 1987.

Leaming, Barbara. *Bette Davis: A Biography*. New York: Simon & Schuster, 1992.

Ringgold, Gene. *The Films of Bette Davis*. Secaucus, NJ: Citadel, 1966.

Stine, Whitney. *"I'd Love to Kiss You . . .": Conversations with Bette Davis*. New York: Pocket Books, 1990.

Stine, Whitney, with Bette Davis. *Mother Goddam: The Story of the Career of Bette Davis*. New York: Hawthorn, 1974.

⁀ Davis, Katherine (1860–1935)

A prominent innovator in early twentieth-century prison reform, Katherine Davis engaged in many activities undertaken by women progressive reformers. While public opinion deemed some of these avenues acceptable for women—teaching in public schools and settlement work—others were more controversial, such as earning a doctorate in political science and becoming a prison administrator, the first woman appointed to the New York State cabinet, and, later, a sexologist.

Born in Buffalo, New York, in 1860, Davis was the eldest daughter of Oscar Bill and Frances Bement Davis. The family moved to Dunkirk, New York, and later to Rochester, where her father secured a managerial position in a credit-rating firm and Davis attended Rochester Free Academy. In 1890, after attending night school and working to help support her family, Davis entered the junior class at Vassar College at age thirty. Following her graduation, Davis continued her studies at Columbia University and taught at Brooklyn Heights Seminary for Girls. In 1893, Davis became head resident of the College Settlement in Philadelphia, where she organized reading and English classes and clubs for African Americans and Russian Jewish immigrants. Davis, however, left settlement work to attend graduate school at the University of Chicago from 1897 to 1900, becoming one of the first women to receive a Ph.D. in the United States.

Although Davis's studies focused on political economy, in 1901 she accepted a position to direct a new women's reformatory at Bedford Hills, New York. At the reformatory, she implemented educational programs, incorporated work routines into the daily activities of the inmates, and succeeded in developing several industries based on inmate labor. Retention among many inmates, however, led Davis to become an outspoken advocate for the need to classify "criminal types" before institutionalization. In 1912, Davis helped to establish the Laboratory of Social Hygiene (1912–1917), largely composed of female social scientists trained in psychology and eugenics who studied the inmate population. Not long after the laboratory opened, John Mitchell, the recently elected reform mayor of New York, offered Davis a position in his cabinet as commissioner of correction. Despite public controversy about her sex, Davis managed the position effectively until Mitchell lost the 1917 election.

After the Laboratory of Social Hygiene closed due to administrative problems, Davis continued her work as administrative secretary of the Bureau of Social Hygiene (1918–1928), an organization founded to investigate causes of and solutions for prostitution. At the bureau, Davis turned her research to female sexuality, resulting in one of the first major studies on the sexual desires and experiences of "normal" women. Published under the title *Factors in Sex Life of Twenty-Two Hundred Women* (1929), Davis's findings showed the benefits of sex education and challenged the stereotypes of female sexual passivity. In 1930, Davis retired, moving with her three younger sisters to California, where they resided together until Davis died of arteriosclerosis in 1935. Davis is remembered as one of the most innovative prison reformers at the turn of the century. *(See also: College Settlement; Criminals; Female Sexuality; Higher Education; Prison Reform; Settlement House Movement; University of Chicago)*

—Barbara Shircliffe

Further Reading

Davis, Katherine Bement. *Factors in Sex Life of Twenty-Two Hundred Women*. New York: Harper & Brothers, 1929.

———. "The Reformatory Method." In *Proceedings of the 37th National Conference of Charities and Correction*. St. Louis, 1910.

Fitzpatrick, Ellen. *Endless Crusade: Women Social Scientists and the Progress Reform*. New York: Oxford University Press, 1990.

Freedman, Estelle B. *Their Sisters' Keepers: Women's Prison Reform in America, 1830–1930*. Ann Arbor: University of Michigan Press, 1981, 1984.

⁀ Davis, Paulina Kellogg Wright (1813–1876)

Paulina Kellogg Davis, author and editor of the woman's suffrage paper, *Una*, from 1853 to 1855, played a prominent role in organizing the woman's rights movement in New England. She presided over the National Woman's Rights Convention in Worcester in 1850, helped found the New England Woman Suffrage Association in 1868, and was president of the Rhode Island Suffrage Association until 1869.

Davis's writings represented nineteenth-century feminist perspectives. She supported equality within marriage, health reform, and professions for women. She spoke out against contemporary mainstream magazines for "ladies" such as *Godey's Lady's Book*, and consequently established the *Una*, attempting to provide "stronger nourishment" for the fight for equality between the sexes.

Raised in New York by her aunt, a strict orthodox Presbyterian, Davis chose to marry Francis Wright, a New York merchant, instead of serving as a missionary. During their marriage, the Wrights became involved in temperance, abolition, and woman's rights issues. Davis supported herself after her first husband died by lecturing to women in anatomy and physiology, subjects in which she was self-taught. She was the first woman to use a mannequin in her classes, shocking some of her students but attracting others. Her second marriage to Thomas Davis, a Rhode Island legislator, allowed her to finance ventures such as the *Una* while speaking out on women's issues. Her writing career culminated with articles in *Revolution,* the periodical Elizabeth Cady Stanton and Susan B. Anthony founded when the national suffrage association split, and a pamphlet, *A History of the National Woman's Rights Movement,* in 1871. *(See also: Revolution; Suffrage; Una)*

—Karen C. Knowles

Further Reading

Riegel, R. E. *American Feminists.* Lawrence: University of Kansas Press, 1968.

Stanton, Elizabeth C., Susan B. Anthony, and Matilda J. Gage, eds. *History of Woman Suffrage,* 6 vols. New York: National American Woman Suffrage Association, 1888–1922.

Stearns, Bertha M. "New England Magazines for Ladies, 1830–1860," *New England Quarterly* 3 (October 1930): 653-54.

Stein, Karen F. "Paulina Kellogg Wright Davis." In *American Women Writers: A Critical Reference Guide from Colonial Times to the Present,* Vol. 1, edited by Lina Mainiero, 475-76. New York: Frederick Ungar, 1979.

The Una. Vols. 1-3. Boston: Sayles, Miller & Simons, 1853–1855.

❧ Day, Dorothy (1897–1980)

Author, activist, and cofounder of the Catholic Worker Movement, Dorothy Day was born in Brooklyn, New York, on November 8, 1897. Although her family did not practice any formal religion, Day converted to Catholicism at the age of twenty-seven and became one of the strongest lay leaders within the American Catholic Church.

Prior to her conversion, Day worked as a journalist for radical newspapers and journals such as the *Call, Masses,* and the *Liberator.* After her conversion, she sought to find a way to merge her religious beliefs with her political convictions. Her meeting with French philosopher Peter Maurin and their subsequent founding of the Catholic Worker Movement provided Day with an outlet for her energies. She became the editor of the movement's newspaper, the *Catholic Worker,* first published on May Day 1933, and continued in that position until the time of her death. As an author, Dorothy Day wrote articles continuously for the *Catholic Worker* from 1933 to 1980, as well as publishing works such as *From Union Square to Rome* and *Loaves and Fishes.*

Day was a devout and outspoken pacifist. She found herself in disagreement with the U.S. government regarding its involvement in World War II and with the Catholic Church and its stance on conscientious objection and the notion of a "just war." The civil rights movement, the anti-Vietnam movement, and the farmworkers campaign found Day as an active participant.

Dorothy Day referred to herself as a Christian anarchist and preached personal responsibility for political action. She distrusted government, and although she was jailed for marching with women suffragists in 1917, she never exercised her right to vote. Day lived and worked with the poor at the Catholic Worker Houses of Hospitality, espousing a belief in voluntary poverty and the importance of community, a practice that she said made people aware of their in-

terdependence. In 1972, she was recognized for her work among the poor when Notre Dame University presented her with the Laetare Medal. Dorothy Day died at Maryhouse, a Catholic Worker house for homeless women on New York's lower east side, in November of 1980. *(See also: Christianity; Journalism; Religion; Socialism)*

—Pamela F. Wille

Further Reading

Day, Dorothy. *The Long Loneliness: The Autobiography of Dorothy Day.* New York: Harper, 1952.

Ellesberg, Robert, ed. *By Little and By Little: The Selected Writings of Dorothy Day.* New York: Knopf, 1983.

Forest, Jim. *Love Is the Measure: A Biography of Dorothy Day.* New York: Paulist, 1986.

Miller, William. *Dorothy Day: A Biography.* San Francisco: Harper & Row, 1982.

———. *A Harsh and Dreadful Love: Dorothy Day and the Catholic Worker Movement.* Garden City, NY: Doubleday, 1974.

❧ Day Care

Day care, or day nurseries, became an important factor in mothers' lives with the onset of the Industrial Revolution. Before the mid-nineteenth century, women worked at home, had relatives living in the home providing child care, or were engaged in home-based cottage industry. The goal of the first day nursery that opened in New York City in 1852 was to support the impoverished woman who had to support her family. The need for day nurseries expanded during the Civil War. Federal funds were provided to meet the needs of children of war widows and women working in hospitals or industry. During this period, there were no guidelines for nurseries. The situations that surrounded the children varied from sturdy buildings to shabby rooms. Fear was a factor for the mother. If she complained, the child was dropped from the enrollment.

With the peak immigration in the early 1900s, the need for day care shifted from the single mother to working families. The programs began to change at this time from custodial care to child-centered programs with a nursery school as a model. The 1930s and 1940s brought about a greater need for quality child care. The federal government in 1942 established the Lanham Child Care Centers in forty-one states and closed them in 1946. In the 1960s, as more women joined the workforce, they became more selective about the center to which they would entrust their children.

Day care workers, as far back as 1892, began to look critically at their industry. In 1892, there were ninety recognized nurseries; by 1921, there were six hundred. In 1924, the Association of Day Nurseries published its annual report, which stated these concerns: Nurseries were poorly adapted due to inadequate quarters and personnel; nurseries that had the longest hours had the largest enrollment; 57 percent of the nurseries that belonged to the association had minimum standards. In 1960, Elinor Guggenheimer initiated a major campaign to bring day care needs to the attention of local community groups and organizations. The first federal funds since World War II were approved by Congress and signed into law by President John F. Kennedy in 1962. At that time, $4 million was allocated to be used throughout the country for day care. As a result of this funding, many states established day care guidelines. During the 1980s, the need for outstanding day care continued to be critical and became an issue during the 1988 presidential campaign.

Quality day care has become the concern of many in the 1990s. Four different national studies determined that between 12 percent and 21 percent of young children in child care are in situations rated as unsafe or harmful. For infants and toddlers the conditions are even worse, ranging from 35 percent to 40 percent in unsafe settings. With over 55 percent of mothers of preschool children in the workforce, the need for programs has become more acute. Day care is both a political and economic issue for many people. Federally supported day care programs have become a subject of controversy in the United States in the last ten years; several bills supporting comprehensive child care programs have been passed by Congress only to be vetoed by incumbent presidents. However, there have been significant, but not sufficient, increases in the number of programs addressing day care issues at the state and federal levels.

In 1997, the first White House Conferences on child care and early child development were held. In 1998, President Clinton announced a historic initiative to improve child care that proposed approximately $20 billion over the next five years and included programs to help working families pay for child care, build an adequate number of afterschool programs, improve the safety and quality of child care, and encourage early learning. The need to expand the program to full-day/full-year care because of parents moving into the workforce is great. The program now serves the needs of children from birth to age five and their families. The 105th Congress completed action on the fiscal year 1999 funding, which included appropriations for Head Start. The omnibus funding measure includes $4.66 billion for the fiscal year, which began October 1st and includes $337.5 million for Early Head Start.

Federal funding for child care has increased by nearly 70 percent since 1993 under the Clinton administration. The welfare reform law of 1996 increased child care funding by $4 billion over six years. The Healthy Child America Initiative ensures safe and healthy environments for all children in child care. This initiative arose from the concerns raised about monitoring child care centers. Quality and affordable day care for all children continues to be a foremost concern for women in the 21st century. *(See also: Child Rearing; Industrial Revolution; Lanham Act)*

—**Bonnie Lou Rayner**
—**Sandra M. Fox**

Further Reading

"Child Care That Strengthens American Families." *The White House at Work.* January 7, 1998. Archived at http://www.whitehouse.gov/WH/Work/010798.html

Goldsmith, Cornelia. *Better Day Care for the Young Child.* Washington, DC: National Association for the Education of the Young Child, 1972.

Hymes, Jr., James. *Living History Interviews—Book 2.* Carmel, CA: Hacienda, 1978.

Kagan, Sharon L. "Readying Schools for Young Children: Polemics and Priorities," *Phi Delta Kappan* 76 (November 1994): 226-33.

Maynard, Fredelle. *Child Care Crisis.* Markham, Ontario: Viking, 1985.

New, Caroline, and Miriam David. *For the Children's Sake.* Middlesex, England: Penguin, 1985.

Schultz, Tom, and M. Elena Lopez. "Early Childhood Reform: Local Innovations in a Flawed Policy System," *Phi Delta Kappan* 77 (September 1995): 60-63.

Watkins, Kathleen Pullan, and Lucius Durant, Jr. *Day Care: A Source Book.* New York: Garland, 1988.

Wetzstein, Cheryl. "Clinton's Child Care Boost Not a Big Priority on Hill," *Washington Times* (April 19, 1998).

ᵥ Declaration of Rights of Women (1876)

When America prepared to celebrate its centennial, the National Woman Suffrage Association declared that "the women of the United States, denied for one hundred years the only means of self-government, the ballot," are "political slaves" and "have greater cause for discontent, rebellion and revolution, than the men of 1776." "As Abigail Adams predicted," they continued, "we are determined to foment a rebellion, and will not hold ourselves bound by laws in which we have no voice or representation."

Renting headquarters in Philadelphia, where they held nightly meetings, the radical suffragists decided to "demand justice for the women of this land" by presenting a Declaration of Rights of Women at the official ceremonies on July 4. Matilda Joslyn Gage and Elizabeth Cady Stanton composed the document and then were denied permission to present it on the grounds that "if granted, it would be the event of the day—the topic of discussion to the exclusion of all others." The women decided to go ahead with their plan, risking the possibility of arrest to "place on record for the daughters of 1876, the fact that their mothers of 1876 had thus asserted their equality of rights, and thus impeached the government of today for its injustice towards women."

On July 4, 1876, five women—Matilda Joslyn Gage, Susan B. Anthony, Sara Andrews Spencer, Phoebe Couzins, and Lillie Devereux Blake—took their seats in the press section facing a crowd of 150,000 in Independence Square. They had only a few seconds to make their presentation after the reading of the Declaration of Independence, knowing there was a good chance they would be stopped before they reached the speakers' platform by the guards surrounding it. Anthony went first, followed by Gage, who held concealed the three-foot scroll containing the declaration. They moved rapidly, and as they approached the stand, the foreign guests, military officers, and guards—taken by surprise—all made way. Gage passed the document to Anthony, who placed it in the hand of a startled President *Pro Tempore* of the U.S. Senate Thomas W. Ferry, saying, "We present this Declaration of Rights of the women citizens of the United States." With his silent acceptance, the declaration became an official part of the day's proceedings.

The declaration ended with the words: "We ask justice, we ask equality, we ask that all the civil and political rights that belong to citizens of the United States, be guaranteed to us and our daughters forever." *(See also: Declaration of Sentiments and Resolutions; National American Woman Suffrage Association; Suffrage)*

—**Sally Roesch Wagner**

Further Reading
Stanton, Elizabeth C., Susan B. Anthony, and Matilda J. Gage, eds. *History of Woman Suffrage.* Vols. 1-3. New York: Fowler & Wells, 1881–1886.
Wagner, Sally Roesch. *A Time of Protest: Suffragists Challenge the Republic, 1870–1887.* Aberdeen, SD: Sky Carrier Press, 1998.

⟋ Declaration of Sentiments and Resolutions

The Declaration of Sentiments and Resolutions was written at the 1848 Seneca Falls Convention, held July 19-20 in Seneca Falls, New York, by the convention's leaders, Elizabeth Cady Stanton and Lucretia Mott, and the convention's female and male delegates, who numbered between one hundred and three hundred. The declaration became the first major document to define the issues and goals of the nineteenth-century woman's rights movement. Purposely modeled after the Declaration of Independence to invoke the political heritage of the American Revolution, this document broadly and candidly stated women's demands for legal, economic, social, and political equality and listed the convention's resolutions concerning women's rights.

The Declaration began: "We hold these truths to be self-evident; that all men and women are created equal; that they are endowed by their Creator with certain inalienable rights: that among these are life, liberty, and the pursuit of happiness . . ." It continued by condemning the unjust practices of men against women: "The history of mankind is a history of repeated injuries and usurpations on the part of man toward woman, having in direct object the establishment of an absolute tyranny over her. To prove this, let facts be submitted to a candid world."

After naming the abuses of women, the declaration offered eighteen resolutions that showed how society limited women's behavior, education, and opportunities and thus demonstrated women's need for equality in education, employment, and religious participation as well as for reformed property statutes for married women. Of all the resolutions, only one, pertaining to woman suffrage, received negative response. Eventually, although by a narrow margin, the woman suffrage resolution passed as well.

At the conclusion of the convention, sixty-eight women and thirty-two men signed the declaration, making it the first formal statement regarding women's rights. *(See also: Seneca Falls Convention; Suffrage; Women's Rights Movements: Nineteenth and Twentieth Centuries)*

—**Katherine Teschner**

Further Reading
Stanton, Elizabeth C., Susan B. Anthony, and Matilda J. Gage, eds. *History of Woman Suffrage,* 6 vols. New York: National American Woman Suffrage Association, 1888–1922.

⟋ Deconstruction

Deconstruction is a concept developed in the mid-twentieth century that has been increasingly employed among some women's studies scholars for the insights it provides into the workings of gender. Feminist scholars influenced by deconstruction look at the ways in which texts activate hierarchy and binary oppositions when it comes to terms having to do with gender. Many of these scholars are additionally influenced by contemporary psychoanalytic theory and thus regard language as inextricably bound up with intrapsychic systems of gender power and patriarchy. Deconstruction thus allows feminist scholars to scrutinize texts for evidence of gender power at work in language and the resistances offered to it.

Deconstruction is a poststructuralist twentieth-century conceptual position (equivalent to Heidegger's "destruction" or "dismantling") associated especially with Jacques Derrida and various American disciples in literary and historical theory. In general, it has a dual pedigree: (a) the sort of philosophical "destruction" implied by Nietzsche and Freud and (b) Saussurean linguistics, which stresses the relational rather than the referential character of language.

The theory and practice of deconstruction cannot be analyzed in the conventional terms of rational, "intentionalist" discourse. Rather, deconstruction offers fundamental critiques of conventional philosophical, linguistic, literary, and political assumptions. Philosophically, it rejects traditional metaphysics and all absolutist ideas in the theory of meaning, including ideas of historical continuity and "humanism." Linguistically, it denies the sovereignty of the self or "authorial will" in writing; assumes that speech is the operation of language, not of the individual; and in more radically textualist terms, assumes that there is no conceptual ground outside of the text. Politically, deconstruction insists on the correlation between language and power and by indirection seeks to dismantle, or to unmask, the "dominant" (institutional, social, sexual) discourse of conventional views of history and culture in the interests of egalitarian ideals and for the benefit of supposedly "marginal" groups.

The adoption of deconstruction by contemporary scholars and feminists has caused great debate precisely because it tends to examine structures of power in language and knowledge. Instead of investigating women's oppression in the workplace, for example, deconstructionists favor undermining texts and using wordplay. Nor in terms of deconstructive theory do texts ordinarily cited as oppressive to women always directly reveal such oppression. The growth of such scholarship has attracted the charge that it maintains a kind of irrelevant, hypersophisticated elitism, whereas scholarship should examine bread-and-butter issues. Issues raised by deconstruction and French feminist theory had an airing at a conference at Barnard College in 1979, and major journals such as *Signs* and *Feminist Studies* are clearly enmeshed in the deconstruction debate. The writings of Joan Scott and Gayatri Spivak were pivotal in promoting an understanding of deconstruction's usefulness to feminist scholars in the United States in the 1980s and 1990s. *(See also: Feminist Literary Criticism; Language and Linguistics; Women's History; Women's Studies)*

—Bonnie G. Smith

Further Reading

Culler, Jonathan. *On Deconstruction*. Ithaca, NY: Cornell University Press, 1984.

Derrida, Jacques. *A Derrida Reader: Between the Blinds*. Edited and notes by Peggy Kamuf. New York: Columbia University Press, 1991.

Eisenstein, Hester, and Alice Jardine, eds. *The Future of Difference*. New Brunswick, NJ: Rutgers University Press, 1985.

Jardine, Alice. *Gynesis: Configurations of Women and Modernity*. Ithaca, NY: Cornell University Press, 1985.

Niranjana, Tejaswini. *Siting Translation: History, Post-Structuralism and the Colonial Context*. Berkeley: University of California Press, 1992.

Scott, Joan Wallach. *Gender and the Politics of History*. New York: Columbia University Press, 1988.

Deer, Ada (b. 1935)

Social worker, educator, and activist, Ada Deer is best known for her leadership role in the struggle to regain federal recognition for the Menominee tribe after the Menominee Termination Act (implemented by 1961) ended federal aid and control on the tribal reservation. Born on the Menominee Indian Reservation in northern Wisconsin, Deer was the first Menominee to graduate from the University of Wisconsin–Madison, earning a B.A. degree in social work. Later, she was the first Native American to earn an M.A. in social work from Columbia University. She also briefly studied law and was a Fellow at the Harvard Institute of Politics, J.F.K. School of Government, in 1977. In 1970, Deer and others created a new Menominee political organization, Determination of the Rights and Unity for Menominee Shareholders (DRUMS). From 1972 to 1973, Deer served as vice president and chief lobbyist for the DRUMS-originated National Committee to Save the Menominee People and Forest, and their long-term goal—to repeal the Menominee Termination Act—was granted with the Menominee Restoration Act of 1973. After the Restoration Act, Deer was chair of the Menominee Restoration Committee, a position she held from 1974 to 1976.

Deer's political advocacy and crusade for social change have garnered her many awards, including the Politzer Award (1975), the White Buffalo Council Achievement Award (1974), the Wonder Woman Award (1982), the Indian Achievement Award (1984), and the Distinguished Service Award from the American Indian Resources Institute (1991). Deer's national visibility in cross-cultural endeavors has resulted in appointments such as serving on the boards of Girl Scouts of the USA, Americans for Indian Opportunity, the National Association of Social Workers, the National Women's Education Fund, and the Native American Rights Fund, on which she served as chair from 1989 to 1990. Active in local and state politics, Deer was a candidate for Wisconsin secretary of state and the U.S. House of Representatives. Since 1977, Deer has held the position of senior lecturer at the University of Wisconsin, Madison, in the School of Social Work and the Native American Studies Program. Ada Deer continues to inspire others with her devotion to social justice, particularly those issues dealing with women and Native Americans.

In 1993, Deer became the first American Indian woman to serve as Assistant Secretary for Indian Affairs in the U.S. Department of the Interior, a post she held until 1997. During her term, federal recognition was extended to 12 tribes, and tribal self-governance was expanded to 180 tribes through 54 annual funding agreements. She also was instrumental in the resolution of a century-old boundary dispute with the Crow Tribe. This settlement restored tribal lands and provided compensation for lost coal and reserves. Deer also participated in the development of U.S. policies in the international human rights arena and worked in support of a strong position on rights of indigenous persons in the United States. *(See also: Native American Women; Politics)*

—Laurie Lisa

Further Reading

Anderson, Owanah, ed. *Ohoyo One Thousand: A Resource Guide of American Indian/Alaska Native Women, 1982*. Wichita Falls, TX: Ohoyo Resource Center, 1982.

Bletzinger, Andrea, and Anne Short, eds. *Wisconsin Women: A Gifted Heritage*. Milwaukee: American Association of University Women, Wisconsin State Division, 1982.

Deer, Ada, with R. E. Simon, Jr. *Speaking Out*. Chicago: Children's Press Open Door Books, 1970.

Graf, Karen. "Ada Deer: Creating Opportunities for Minority Students," *On Wisconsin* 9 (April 1987): 8.

Peroff, Nicholas C. *Menominee Drums: Tribal Termination and Restoration, 1954–1974*. Norman: University of Oklahoma Press, 1982.

Democratic Party

The Democratic Party has been around in one form or another in the United States since the origins of the Republic in the eighteenth century. Because women were not eligible to vote until 1920, the Democrats, like the Republicans, were not overly concerned with women's issues. Throughout the early histories of both major political parties in the United States, women have had to exert their influence indirectly and through male politicians. The results have frequently been disappointing.

In the late 1860s, Elizabeth Cady Stanton and Susan B. Anthony looked to the Democratic Party for help in the struggle for woman suffrage, but the Democrats proved to be as unreliable as the Republicans, and the struggle for suffrage dragged on with little support from either major party. In 1913, Alice Paul and others organized a massive protest against the inauguration of Democratic president Woodrow Wilson, who had consistently failed to support a woman suffrage amendment to the Constitution. In 1914, the Congressional Union, a suffrage organization, actively campaigned against Democratic candidates for office. The union claimed that it had helped to defeat twenty-three of forty-three western Democratic congressional candidates in the 1914 elections. The union was later reorganized as the National Woman's Party in June 1916.

Partly in response to this kind of pressure, the Democratic platform of 1916 favored "the extension of suffrage to women, state by state, on the same terms as men." However, the Democrats continued to be divided on the issue, especially in the South, where traditional, conservative "Dixiecrats" were adamant in their opposition to votes for women. Nonetheless, conservative opposition to an increased political role for women was sufficiently overcome so that in 1920 the party's National Committee was reconstituted to include one female member from each state.

After women had secured the vote, they slowly but surely become more prominent actors in the politics of the 1920s and 1930s. Women such as Mary Norton began to get elected to Congress in 1924, although the number of women in the U.S. Congress has never much been greater than three dozen at any one time. Women were appointed as senators to finish the terms of their husbands, as was Hattie Caraway in 1931. Much the same thing occurred at the state level, where "Ma" Ferguson in Texas and Nellie Ross in Wyoming succeeded their deceased husbands as governors. Not until Democratic candidate Ella Grasso's election as governor of Connecticut in 1974 was a woman elected to a gubernatorial post.

The influence of women behind the scenes of Democratic Party life grew apace in the same period. New York social worker Belle Moskowitz became one of the top advisers to Democratic presidential candidate Al Smith in 1928. With the election of Franklin Delano Roosevelt to the White House in 1932, the role of women reached a new zenith. Acting partly under the influence of his talented wife, Eleanor, Roosevelt appointed Frances Perkins as secretary of labor, a post she maintained until 1945. Perkins, a graduate of Mount Holyoke, was the first woman to hold a cabinet position in the history of the United States, and she was one of a host of women who became a major part of Roosevelt's New Deal administration.

It is difficult to overestimate the importance of Eleanor Roosevelt in reshaping the attitudes of the Democratic Party and the nation toward political women and women's issues. A highly visible First Lady, Roosevelt published a daily newspaper column—"My Day"—and held weekly press conferences. A former teacher and social worker, she cared deeply about a host of reform issues and was influential in getting her husband's administration to hire women in record numbers. Women in Washington knew they had a friend in the White House in Eleanor Roosevelt.

In addition to Frances Perkins, the Roosevelt era women's network included Molly Dewson, who headed the Women's Division of the Democratic Party from 1932 to 1937 and was a member of the Social Security Board from 1937 to 1938. A close friend of the Roosevelts, Dewson spent a lot of time lobbying the president to hire more women and to respond to women's issues. Ellen Sullivan Woodward and Mary McLeod Bethune were among the many other women who were active in this period. Woodward helped set up relief programs for women under the auspices of the Federal Emergency Relief Administration and later became head of Women's and Professional Projects for the Works Progress Administration. She also served a six-year term on the Social Security Board. Bethune headed the Office of Minority Affairs from 1936 to 1944.

Ironically, Franklin Roosevelt did not use women, even his wife, as his top advisers, and neither he nor his wife supported the Equal Rights Amendment, which had first been proposed by the National Woman's Party in 1923. Indeed, the Equal Rights Amendment was not endorsed by the Democratic Party until 1944, although the party has remained faithful to it since that time.

Democratic women in Washington further enhanced their women's network by the creation of the Women's National Democratic Club, founded in 1924. Influential women within the Democratic Party, such as Emily Newell Blair, Marion Glass Banister, and Daisy Harriman, were important backers of this club, which became a significant meeting place for Democratic women.

The gains women had made in the Democratic Party during World War II were not lost in the aftermath of the war. The administration of Harry Truman continued to employ women in high places and low, and in 1948 Truman signed the Women's Armed Forces Integration Act, which gave women the chance for military careers.

In 1960, about 6 million women worked on the successful presidential campaign of John F. Kennedy, and he responded to his own failure to name a female cabinet member by accepting Esther Peterson's proposal for a Presidential Commission on the Status of Women. Peterson was the head of the Women's Bureau, and as assistant secretary of labor she held the highest position as a woman in the Kennedy administration. Eleanor Roosevelt headed the commission until her death in 1962, when she was succeeded by Peterson. Although a majority of the commission failed to support the ERA movement, it did produce the most comprehensive document about women ever produced by the federal government.

Women continued to be important, if underrepresented, voices into the administration of Lyndon Johnson. Johnson's wife, "Lady Bird," was an extremely active and effective First Lady. The Johnson years also featured the election of Shirley Chisholm to Congress in 1969—its first black female member. In 1972, Chisholm ran for the Democratic presidential nomination for president, while civil rights leader Fannie Lou Hamer fought for increased black representation.

During the presidency of Jimmy Carter (1978–1982), women reached a new peak of influence in the life of the Democratic Party and its administration. Influenced by a strong mother, Lillian, and a talented wife, Rosalynn, Carter had two women in his cabinet, and 12 percent of his presidential appointees in 1978 were women. The Carters were not afraid to let the world know that their marriage was a partnership and that talented people like Patricia Harris could rise to cabinet-level positions regardless of sex or race. By this time, Democratic women were rising to key positions in the party and the nation. For example, Jane Byrne was elected as Chicago's first woman mayor in 1979. In 1978, Diane Feinstein became mayor of San Francisco, Kathy Whitmire was elected mayor of Houston in 1981, and a number of women were elected to a host of local and state offices around the country. In 1984, the Democratic Party named Congresswoman Geraldine Ferraro as its vice presidential nominee.

The 1992 congressional elections brought the largest group of women members to the House and Senate in its history. The 1992 elections also brought William Clinton into the White House, and his administration has more women in politically influential positions than any other. For example, Madeleine Albright became the first woman secretary of state in 1997. His lawyer-wife, Hillary Rodham Clinton, has been highly influential and visible. She headed up the presidential Task Force on Health Care Reform and has been the most active First Lady since Eleanor Roosevelt. In 2000, she became the first presidential wife to run for public office when she entered the race for the U.S. Senate in New York. The Clintons are both avowed feminists.

President Clinton was reelected in 1996, and the Democratic minority in the U.S. Congress contained five women Democratic senators and thirty-seven women in the U.S. House of Representatives who had been elected on the Democratic ticket in their districts. Although Carole Mosely-Brown of Illinois lost her senate seat, the 1998 elections resulted in a U.S. Congress with fifty-seven women. Six of the nine women senators are Democrats. Among the victors in 1998 was Loretta Sanchez, who was reelected to the House of Representatives in the 46th District of California. In 1999, Sanchez became the first Latina to serve as cochair of the Democratic National Committee.

While women are still underrepresented in public life around the country, they have become a force to be reckoned with by both major political parties. How large the political "gender gap" continues to be remains open to question. Few dispute that it exists and that women will continue to play an increasingly powerful role in the future of the political life of the United States. *(See also: Abzug, Bella Savitsky; Bethune, Mary McLeod; Chisholm, Shirley; Douglas, Helen Mary; Ferraro, Geraldine; Gender Gap; New Deal; Perkins, Frances; Roosevelt, Eleanor; Suffrage)*

—Jonathan W. Zophy

Further Reading

Baker, Tod, Robert Steed, and Laurence Moreland. "Gender and Race among Democratic Party Activists in Two Southern States," *Social Science Quarterly* 65 (1984): 1088-91.

Belcher, Dixie. "A Democratic School for Democratic Women," *Chronicles of Oklahoma* 61 (1983–1984): 414-21.

Gruberg, Martin. *Women in American Politics: An Assessment and a Sourcebook.* Oshkosh, WI: Academia, 1968.

Jones, Jacqueline, ed. *Women in Politics.* New York: John Wiley, 1974.

Lash, Joseph. *Eleanor and Franklin.* New York: Norton, 1971.

———. *Eleanor: The Years Alone.* New York: Norton, 1972.

Martin, George. *Madam Secretary: Frances Perkins.* Boston: Houghton Mifflin, 1976.

～ Demography

Demography focuses on birth, death, marriage, migration, and life cycle patterns for women in American history within the study of the size, growth, density, distribution, and vital statistics of the national population. Among the significant changes in women's lives since the seventeenth century are a doubling of their life expectancy as well as a rise of female-headed households, reduced childbearing, a relatively stable age of marriage between twenty-one and twenty-three for nine of ten women, and a proportional divorce rate increase that parallels improvements in increased life expectancy. Among minority women, these trends are altered by a different, higher mortality. There were gender-specific results from the three great migrations in American history—to the New World in the seventeenth century, westward in the eighteenth and nineteenth centuries, and the rural/urban migration that began in the nineteenth century. Typically, women lacked authority in the family decision to migrate to the New World and then to the western frontier. They were a numerical minority in numbers in those migrations, and the rural-urban-suburban migration resulted in reduced family sizes that brought changes to women's social and economic lives. The specific pattern of women's migration was characterized in their moving shorter distances than men and by their urban rather than rural destination to seek employment opportunities in the cities. *(See also: Fertility; Immigration; Migration and Frontier Women)*

—Angela M. Howard

Further Reading

Degler, Carl N. *At Odds: Women and the Family in America from the American Revolution to the Present.* New York: Oxford University Press, 1980.

Federici, Nora, Karen O. Mason, and Sølvi Songer, eds. *Women's Position and Demographic Change.* New York: Oxford University Press, 1993.

Heitlinger, Alena. *Women's Equality, Demography, and Public Policies: A Comparative Perspective.* New York: St. Martin's, 1993.

Wells, Robert V. "Women's Lives Transformed: Demographic and Family Patterns in America, 1600–1970." In *Women of America: A History,* edited by Carol Ruth Berkin and Mary B. Norton, 16-33. Boston: Houghton Mifflin, 1979.

ᔰ Dennett, Mary Coffin (Ware)
(1872–1947)

Mary Dennett was a pioneer in the movements for woman suffrage, peace, birth control, and sex education. Married and divorced from architect William Hartley Dennett and the mother of three children, Dennett was trained as an artist and interior designer. Politically active and an ardent supporter of the growing peace movement during World War I, she was also deeply committed to the cause of woman suffrage, serving as secretary of the National American Woman Suffrage Association from 1912. Her support of women's rights soon led Dennett to a growing involvement in efforts to legalize birth control.

Opposed to the radical, confrontational tactics of Margaret Sanger, who challenged the laws prohibiting the dissemination of birth control, Dennett focused her efforts on lobbying for legislative reform. In 1915, she founded the first American birth control organization, the National Birth Control League (NBCL), to lobby for a bill that would allow the transmission of contraceptive information. Uncomfortable with the radical overtones associated with Sanger and birth control, Dennett reorganized the NBCL into the Voluntary Parenthood League in 1918 and emerged as Margaret Sanger's rival for leadership of the growing movement.

When Sanger and her American Birth Control League adopted the more conservative strategy of supporting laws that would allow physicians to disseminate birth control, Dennett was vehemently opposed. Promoting "doctors-only" laws, in her view, undermined the right of all citizens to have equal access to contraceptive information. For Dennett, the only solution was to remove all legal restraints on birth control by redefining the obscenity laws. Although Sanger's pragmatic efforts eventually won more adherents than Dennett's legalistic approach, Dennett refused to compromise and instead continued to fight the whole concept of legal obscenity.

Dennett began to openly challenge the obscenity laws in 1922 when the government attempted to suppress a sex education article she had published in 1918. Arguing that access to sex education was an essential prerequisite for a just and enlightened society and any attempts to censor such material violated civil liberties, she defied the ban and continued to circulate the article. Indicted, convicted, and fined in 1929, Dennett was determined to fight the decision. With the aid of counsel provided by the American Civil Liberties Union, an appeal was mounted, and in 1930, the conviction was overturned.

While committed to women's rights, Mary Ware Dennett believed that advancing the position of women in the United States depended on protecting the First Amendment rights of both women and men to freedom of speech and expression. In her efforts to challenge the definition of legal obscenity, she became one of the nation's most effective defenders of civil liberties. *(See also: Birth Control; National American Woman Suffrage Association; Obscenity; Sanger, Margaret Louise; Voluntary Parenthood League)*

—Esther Katz

Further Reading

Chen, Constance M. *"The Sex Side of Life": Mary Ware Dennett's Pioneering Battle for Birth Control and Sex Education.* New York: The New Press, 1996.

Dennett, Mary Ware. *Birth Control Laws: Shall We Keep Them, Change Them, or Abolish Them?* New York: F. H. Hitchcock, 1926.

———. *The Prosecution of Mary Ware Dennett for Obscenity.* Pamphlet. New York: American Civil Liberties Union, 1929.

———. *The Sex Education of Children: A Book for Parents.* New York: Vanguard, 1931.

———. *The Sex Side of Life.* New York: Mary Ware Dennett, 1919.

———. *The Stupidity of US Humans.* New York: Voluntary Parenthood League, n.d.

———. *Who's Obscene?* New York: Vanguard, 1930.

Dienes, Thomas. *Law, Politics, and Birth Control.* Urbana: University of Illinois Press, 1972.

Garrow, David J. *Liberty and Sexuality: The Right to Privacy and the Making of* Roe v. Wade, *1923–1973.* New York: Macmillan, 1994.

Gordon, Linda. *Woman's Body, Woman's Right: A Social History of Birth Control in America.* New York: Grossman, 1976.

Sanger, Margaret. *An Autobiography.* New York: Norton, 1938.

ᔰ Denny, Dorothy (Detzer)
(1893–1981)

Dorothy Denny, executive secretary of the U.S. Section of the Women's International League for Peace and Freedom (WILPF) from 1924 to 1946, was an uncompromising pacifist who led the WILPF to national prominence within the interwar peace movement. Highly respected as an astute political lobbyist, she almost single-handedly initiated the congressional investigation of the munitions industry in the mid-1930s.

Born and raised in Fort Wayne, Indiana, Denny had the middle-class background typical of the woman interwar peace activist. Shocked by the outbreak of World War I although supportive of American involvement, she volunteered with the American Friends Service Committee to alleviate postwar famine in Austria and Russia.

Figure 16. Depression Era
During the Great Depression, unemployment led to violent protests across the country. Here, men and women are shown confronting police in front of the New York City Department of Public Welfare. Used by permission of UPI/Corbis-Bettmann.

Committed to the WILPF's philosophy that there can be no lasting or just peace without freedom and no freedom without peace, Denny played a prominent role in the peace movement's effort to avert war between the United States and Central America in the mid-1920s. Denny and the WILPF supported the Kellogg-Briand Pact (1928), which outlawed war, advocated international disarmament and the congressional debates over neutrality legislation in the 1930s, and attempted to prevent American involvement in World War II.

An unswerving proponent of democracy as both means and end, Denny personified the WILPF's belief that war would bring fascism to America. Convinced by the war's end that such fears were justified by events, Denny resigned from the WILPF in 1946; her role as peace activist died when she lost her faith in democracy.

As was true of a growing number of women in the interwar period, Denny, although opposed to the Equal Rights Amendment, was primarily a "career woman"; not until 1954 did she marry her longtime friend, journalist Ludwell Denny. Although no longer a political activist, Denny regained her faith in the United States as a democracy when outraged public opinion brought an end to American involvement in Vietnam and the downfall of Richard Nixon in the Watergate scandal. *(See also: Pacifism and the Peace Movement; Women's International League for Peace and Freedom)*

—**Carrie Foster**

Further Reading

Bussey, Gertrude, and Margaret Tims. *Pioneers for Peace. Women's International League for Peace and Freedom, 1915–1965.* London: Allen & Unwin, 1965. Reprint, London: WILPF British Section, 1980.

Detzer, Dorothy. *Appointment on the Hill.* New York: Henry Holt, 1948.

Dorothy Detzer Denny Papers. Women's International League for Peace and Freedom Papers. Swarthmore College Peace Collection, Swarthmore, PA.

Foster, Carrie. *The Women and the Warriors: The U.S. Section of the WILPF, 1915–1945.* Syracuse, NY: Syracuse University Press, 1994.

Women's International League for Peace and Freedom Papers. University of Colorado, Boulder, CO.

☙ Depression Era (1929–1941)

The Depression era extended from the infamous Crash of 1929 (October 29, 1929) to the Japanese bombing of Pearl Harbor (December 7, 1941). The abrupt end of the apparent prosperity of the 1920s ushered in the Great Depression, characterized by the economic ruin and the displacement of one-fourth of the workers of the United States. The election of Franklin Delano Roosevelt in 1932 launched the New Deal with its emphasis on "Relief, Reform, and Recovery." The entry of the United States into World War II marked the end of the era, if not of complete economic recovery. For more than a decade, women struggled with the national problems as well as their gender-specific experiences.

The major impact of the Depression on women was their increased participation in the paid labor force without a concomitant accommodation of their sex roles, whether they were single and self-supporting or wives, widows, and mothers. Meanwhile, feminism lost its mainstream support as a national movement focused on the equality of women. Although working mostly in temporary or part-time jobs, married women increased their participation in the labor force from 29 percent of employed women in 1930 to 35 percent in 1940. Throughout the Depression, women who worked in sex-segregated occupations within the tertiary sector of the economy were less affected than men whose jobs had been concentrated in heavy industry. While women's presence in clerical and sales positions increased during the decade, by 1938 one-fifth of the female workforce was still unemployed. Professional women—academics, lawyers, nurses, physicians, librarians, social workers, and public school teachers—fared worst, losing ground that had been gained in the 1920s and that was not recovered even during or after World War II.

"Working" wives were targets of exclusionary employment regulations, policies, and legislation such as Section 213 of the National Economy Act, following which married women constituted three-fourths of those dismissed by the federal government. During the Depression, policymakers and the public debated whether the wages of wives were crucial to the economic survival of their families or merely constituted supplemental or discretionary income for those families. In the 1930s, the majority of adult women provided unpaid domestic labor within their families; the drudgery of household chores intensified as homemakers honed their home industry and household management skills and practiced frugality. Economic difficulties produced a drop in both the number of marriages and the birthrate during the decade. Support for the birth control movement grew as both men and women advocated the practice of effective contraception.

Social feminism forged within the suffrage and reform movements of the Progressive Era reemerged in the 1930s. The presence of Eleanor Roosevelt, Frances Perkins, Molly Dewson, and other social feminists among the New Dealers revealed the continued effectiveness of a well-informed and influential network of women activists. Many of these women held significant offices in both the federal government and within the Democratic Party. However, these women functioned more as role models than as leaders of a national feminist movement; their maturity as well as changes in the political climate limited the period of their renewed public service, and their network expired as these women retired from public life. Despite the significant contribution of their expertise in social welfare to the formulation of the New Deal, their presence in administrative offices and their influence in politics declined as opposition to New Deal policies increased after 1936.

Isolationism in the face of turmoil abroad—especially the rise of fascism and armed conflict of World War II—promoted among the American public an uncritical defense of the status quo in patriarchal society, established politics, and capitalism. This political climate lessened the economic status of women as well as supported and reinforced the gender system with its sex segregation in the workforce. Although women were relegated to low-status, low-paying jobs and often unsafe working conditions, and although they remained subject to layoffs and periodic unemployment, their numbers in the workforce continued to increase. *(See also: Feminism; Housework; New Deal; Sex-Gender System; Sexual Division of Labor; Social Feminism; Wages)*

—Angela M. Howard

Further Reading

Blackwelder, Julia Kirk. *Women of the Depression: Caste and Culture in San Antonio, 1929–1939.* College Station: Texas A&M University Press, 1984.

Loader, Joan. "Women on the Left, 1906–1941: Bibliography of Primary Sources," *University of Michigan Papers in Women's Studies* 2 (February 1974): 9-82.

Orozco, Cynthia E. "Origins of the League of United Latin American Citizens (LULAC) and the Mexican American Civil Rights Movement in Texas with an Analysis of Women's Political Participation in a Gendered Context, 1910–1929." Ph.D. diss., University of California at Los Angeles, 1992.

Scharf, Lois. *To Work and to Wed: Female Employment, Feminism, and the Great Depression.* Westport, CT: Greenwood, 1980.

Ware, Susan. *Beyond Suffrage: Women in the New Deal.* Cambridge, MA: Harvard University Press, 1981.

———. *Holding Their Own: American Women in the 1930s.* Boston: Twayne, 1982.

Westin, Jane. *Making Do: How Women Survived the 1930's.* Chicago: Follett, 1976.

❧ Derivative Citizenship and Naturalization

People interested in genealogy and tracing family history in the United States soon find that their most challenging problem is finding information on the maternal side of ancestry because of the derivative citizenship conferred on wives when their husbands become naturalized citizens.

The U.S. government originally extended preferential treatment to married women and minor children in the naturalization process through derivative citizenship in which wives and minor children of naturalized males became citizens automatically when the husband or father became a citizen. The congressional statutes governing derivative citizenship have changed over time. Minor children were handled much the same way as were wives when their parents became citizens. While married women were not denied the right to follow the same legal procedures as did men and single women in becoming naturalized citizens, they were simply not required to do so by the local courts then handling naturalization.

Minor children received derivative citizenship when their parents became citizens since the enactment of the Naturalization Act of March 26, 1790, which states that "the children of such persons so naturalized, dwelling within the United States, being under the age of twenty-one years at the time of such naturalization, shall also be considered as citizens of the United States," although there was no specific reference in the law between 1790 and 1855 covering this custom of granting derivative citizenship to the wife of a naturalized husband. Then an act of February 10, 1855, stated that "any woman who might lawfully be naturalized under the existing laws, who marries, or who shall be married to a citizen of the United States, shall be deemed and taken to be a citizen." Biographical information on minors and spouses was rarely listed on declaration of intentions and petitions of naturalization before an act of September 27, 1906, which mandated inclusion of the wife's name, age, birth date and place; marriage date and place; and the names of minor children with their birth dates and birthplaces. At no time since the Naturalization Act of 1790 was a certificate of citizenship authorized to be given to the wife or minor children of the person who had been naturalized, even though they held derivative citizenship. However, an act of March 2, 1929, stated that "any individual over twenty-one years of age who claimed to have derived U.S. citizenship through the naturalization of a parent, or a husband, may make application to the Commissioner of Naturalization for a Certificate of Citizenship." However, the Cable Act of 1922 responded to the enfranchisement of women by the Nineteenth Amendment, passed on September 22, 1922; this act (H.R. Bill 12022) required a married woman to be naturalized as an individual citizen, which placed women on a more equal basis with men in the naturalization process. There were a few exceptions in the law enacted by the Cable Act that favored married women over single women and men in the naturaliza-

tion process. No declaration of intent to be a citizen was required as it was with single women and men. In lieu of the five-year period of residence within the United States and the one-year period of residence within the state or territory where the naturalization court is held required for single women and men, a married woman only had to have at least one year of residency immediately preceding the filing of the petition for naturalization.

Previous special provisions for the naturalization of women during the nineteenth century included (a) an act of March 26, 1804, that allowed widows and minor children of a deceased applicant who had filed his declaration of intention for citizenship but had died before the naturalization proceedings to be declared citizens without taking the oath prescribed by law and (b) an act of February 24, 1811, that required no filing of a declaration of intention by the wife and minor children of an alien who had filed his declaration of intention if after that time he became insane and if she filed a homestead entry. These and later laws permitted citizenship automatically without filing a declaration of intention on the wife or minor children's behalf.

At the beginning of the twentieth century, the naturalization statutes reflected the concern regarding "race suicide." Women lost their citizenship by marrying a foreigner under an act of March 2, 1907, which stated "that any American woman who married a foreigner shall take the nationality of her husband." The Cable Act repealed this 1907 act by stating that a woman citizen of the United States shall not cease to be a citizen by reason of her marriage (to a foreigner) after the passage of this act, unless she makes a formal renunciation of her citizenship. However, the Cable Act did decree that she would lose her citizenship if she married an alien who was ineligible to be a citizen of the United States, nor was a woman allowed to be naturalized during marriage to an alien ineligible for citizenship. Although in 1931 Congress repealed this provision of the Cable Act because these restrictions did not apply to men, citizenship was not restored to women who married a foreigner prior to September 22, 1922. To regain citizenship, they had to file a petition for citizenship, provide proof and witnesses to the facts of their petition and character, take an oath of allegiance, and receive a certificate of naturalization. However, an act of June 25, 1936, allowed such women to regain their citizenship by taking the oath of allegiance to the United States and filing a form proving native-born status before losing citizenship by marriage to a foreigner or by proving that the marriage had ended. If the marriage of an American woman and a foreigner terminated between March 2, 1907, and September 22, 1922, the woman could regain her citizenship by registering within one year, if she lived abroad, or by residence in the United States. This act also provided the options for any foreign woman who acquired U.S. citizenship by marriage during this period.

Women and children were usually not mentioned in either early naturalization or census records. Not until the 1850 census was the name of every free person listed, along with age, sex, and other information. Between 1790 and 1840, census records listed only the head of the household, usually the man of the family. A woman was listed only if she were the head of the family as a widow, divorcee, or a single adult living alone or with children. The 1820 and 1830 census indicated how many people in the household were "foreigners not naturalized" but did not indicate individual names until the 1900 census began to list whether each person was "naturalized or alien." *(See also: Immigration; Race Suicide)*

—**Charles G. Howard**

Further Reading

Citizenship and Naturalization of Married Women: Statutes at Large 42 (1922), 1926.

Newman, John J. *American Naturalization Processes and Procedures, 1790–1985.* Indianapolis, IN: Indiana Historical Society, 1985.

Udell, Gilman G., comp. *Naturalization Laws.* Washington, DC: Government Printing Office, 1972.

❧ Deutsch, Helene (1884–1982)

Helene Deutsch was born in Przemysl, Galicia (Poland), which at that time belonged to the Austro-Hungarian Empire. Her father, a lawyer, encouraged his daughter's education, and by the time she was an adolescent, she was dedicated to revolutionary ideology, including equal rights for women.

In 1907, she was admitted to the University of Vienna Medical School, an accomplishment almost unheard of in those days. She became interested in the nascent field of psychiatry, but was initially frustrated in her attempts to obtain a clinical position by laws that limited women's participation in medical practice. However, the outbreak of World War I allowed her the opportunity to work as a "civilian war doctor" in a prestigious psychiatric clinic in Vienna. After the war, she entered into analysis with Sigmund Freud and became a convert to the psychoanalytic approach and a loyal disciple of Freud. She subsequently devoted her career to the clarification of psychoanalytic concepts and to the rigorous training of psychoanalysts, becoming one of the original founders of the Vienna Psychoanalytic Institute in 1925.

Her dedication to psychoanalytic principles soon prompted Deutsch to attempt to revise the image of women propounded by traditional Freudian thought. She devoted over fifty years of her life to the development of a psychoanalytic explanation of normal and neurotic female behavior. Her first approach to the definition of a female personality concerned the resolution of penis envy. In a discussion paper titled "The Psychology of Women in Relation to the Functions of Reproduction," written in 1924, she reinforced the supremacy of the penis over the clitoris as an organ of power and pleasure and outlined the theory of women's "masochistic subjugation to the penis" (Fleiss).

Deutsch's analysis of the female psyche was detailed in her now-classic publication, *The Psychology of Women* (1944). In this two-volume text, based on a series of discussion papers she wrote between 1925 and 1931, Deutsch details the psychological development of women from birth to maturity. Central to this development are themes of passivity, masochism, and narcissism. In keeping with traditional psychoanalytic thinking, Deutsch believed that a child's relationship with her parents, and in particular her resolution of the Oedipal conflict, determined adult personality structure. Following this line of thought, it seemed to Deutsch that woman's personality was strongly affected by her relationship with her mother, to whom she turned after the psychic rejection of the Oedipal conflict. The Oedipal conflict, as identified by Freud, focused on the rivalry of the daughter with the mother for the father's affection. In a conceptualization that anticipated feminist thought by some thirty years, Deutsch maintained that woman's dependency was a direct outgrowth of the overly dependent relationship with her mother that could result at this time. Likewise, woman's dependent relationship with men, in adulthood, stemmed from this learned dependency. Deutsch also explained that this excessive dependency created intense anger, at both the mother and the lover, that the woman strove to contain. As a result of this repressed rage, the woman was constantly in danger of developing neurotic character traits. This line of thought is very similar to that of Nancy Chodorow and other feminist psychologists who are defining a contemporary psychology of women.

Unfortunately, this feminist aspect of Deutsch's work has been overshadowed by other aspects of her depiction of female personality. Her inability to turn away from a Freudian framework for analysis led Deutsch to describe women as passive, masochistic creatures who expected, and indeed derived pleasure from, psychological pain. She cited rape fantasies, the more passive involvement of women in sexual intercourse (by which she meant being the recipient of the male's energy), the loss of self often evident in women's love relationships, and childbirth as clear examples of woman's psychic need for submission and pain. Moreover, she described women as being "narcissistically involved," by which she meant that they were capable of becoming fixated on their own needs to the extent of selfish self-absorption. This complex and unflattering picture of women's psyche has become accepted in classical psychoanalytic thought.

For most women psychologists and psychiatrists, the work of Helene Deutsch is problematic. Although toward the end of her life she softened her approach to woman's psychic structure and integrated into her therapy with women approaches for overcoming dependency, passivity, and masochism, her ideas about the psychoanalytic development of women have been perceived as perpetuating the androcentric approach toward women that has been prevalent in the human sciences.

Helene Deutsch's autobiography (1973) and a recent feminist reconstruction of her work (Webster, 1985) provide us with insight into how and why her thinking developed as it did. Deutsch was extremely attached to her father and devoted much early energy to catching and keeping his attention. She felt strong rivalry with her brother and two sisters for her father's affection. Her desire to be named as her father's heir, over her brother, illustrates the depth of this feeling. That this desire was realized illustrates Helene's proficiency. This strong, emotionally dependent relationship resurfaced in Deutsch's association with Sigmund Freud. Her unquestioning devotion to Freudian concepts, in the face of mounting experiential evidence of their inappropriateness for women, caused her to devise a theoretical stance toward women that was in direct contradiction to her own life and work. She did not see herself as passive, masochistic, narcissistic, or dependent, yet she allowed herself to describe all other women in those terms. She worked all her life and combined the roles of wife and mother with that of psychiatrist. She dedicated many years to the training of analysts, especially after coming to the United States in 1935 to help found the Boston Psychiatric Institute. She led a long and very productive life, dying at the age of ninety-seven.

In sum, Helene Deutsch is a transitional woman for feminist psychology. By its example, her life shows the way in which women can be strong, productive members of society. But her written work, circumscribed by an outmoded, androcentric philosophy, provides us with a model of women's psychology against which contemporary feminist psychologists rebel. (See also: Freudianism; Psychiatry; Psychology)

—Teresa Peck

Further Reading

Chodorow, Nancy. The Reproduction of Mothering. Berkeley: University of California Press, 1978.
Deutsch, Helene. Confrontations with Myself. New York: Norton, 1973.
———. The Psychology of Women. New York: Grune & Stratton, 1944.
Fleiss, Robert. The Psychoanalytic Reader: An Anthology of Essential Papers and Critical Introductions. New York: International University Press, 1969.
Roazen, Paul. Helene Deutsch: A Psychoanalyst's Life. New York: Simon & Schuster, 1985.
Sayers, Janet. Mothers of Psychoanalysis: Helene Deutsch, Karen Horney, Anna Freud, and Melanie Klein. New York: Norton, 1993.
Webster, Brenda. "Helene Deutsch: A New Look," Signs: A Journal of Women in Culture and Society 10 (1985): 553-71.

❧ Dewson, Mary Williams (Molly)
(1874–1962)

Molly Dewson graduated from Wellesley in 1897. She never married; her partner, friend, and companion for 52 years was Polly Porter, whose family fortune from International Harvester enabled both women to volunteer in areas that appealed to them rather than face the necessity of working for a living.

Dewson worked diligently to secure passage of the Nineteenth Amendment. She always chose to reform from within using democratic principals and used the new political activism of the twentieth century to promote progressive social and labor legislation such as the minimum wage, child labor laws, and Social Security and to empower women in public life. She assisted Felix Frankfurter in preparing economic briefs to secure the minimum wage. In 1937, President Roosevelt appointed her to the newly formed three-member Social Security Board.

Never seeking elected political office, Dewson worked through women's networks such as the Consumers' League and the League of Women Voters to promote the access of newly enfranchised women to decision making. Eleanor Roosevelt first involved Dewson in the Democratic Party by encouraging her to work in the presidential campaign of Al Smith in 1928. From this point until 1940, she was involved in each Roosevelt political campaign, becoming director of the Women's Division of the Democratic National Committee during FDR's first administration.

In the presidential campaign of 1936, she was instrumental in bringing parity to women on the Democratic platform committee. Her "Reporter Plan" encouraged women all over the country to join the Democratic Party and to gain and share information on political issues. Her "Rainbow Fliers," one-page, single-issue informational pamphlets in different colors written by and for women and distributed door to door, were used with great success to focus on the individual voter in building a grassroots organization.

Dewson's lifelong friendship with Franklin and Eleanor Roosevelt and her ability to work effectively with both males and females made her one of the most powerful women in politics during the first half of the century. She used her powers to promote women such as Frances Perkins to the cabinet, Ruth Bryan Owen to an ambassadorship, and Florence Allen to the Circuit Court of Appeals. Using her gender and her age as assets rather than liabilities, she was an inspiration to women of her time and the future. In 1954, Eleanor Roosevelt and Lorena Hickok dedicated their book Ladies of Courage to Molly Dewson. (See also: Democratic Party; League of Women Voters; Minimum Wage Laws; National Consumers' League; National Women's Trade Union League; Networking; New Deal; Nineteenth Amendment to the U.S. Constitution; Politics; Roosevelt, Eleanor; Social Security Act of 1935; Suffrage)

—Tamerin Mitchell Hayward

Further Reading

Cook, Blanche Wiesen. Eleanor Roosevelt, Vol. I, 1884–1933. New York: Viking, 1992.
Dewson, Mary W. "An Aid to the End." Unpublished but written in 1949. Dewson papers. Schlesinger Library of Radcliffe College, Cambridge, MA.
Ware, Susan. Partner and I: Molly Dewson, Feminism, and New Deal Politics. New Haven, CT: Yale University Press, 1987.

❧ Diaz, Abby Morton (1821–1904)

Social reformer, woman's rights activist, metaphysical healer, and author, Abby Morton Diaz was born in Plymouth, Massachusetts. Ichabod Morton, an antislavery, temperance, and educational reformer, instilled in his only daughter a commitment to reform that was to last throughout her long and exceptionally active life. Before the age of ten, she had become secretary of the Juvenile Anti-Slavery Society. In 1843, her father, an admirer of abolitionist and transcendentalist Theodore Parker, moved his family for a short time to Brook Farm, a utopian community founded in 1841. The community's precarious finances quickly convinced the thrifty shipbuilder to reverse his decision, but his daughter remained at the farm to teach in its infant school until the community folded in 1847.

While at Brook Farm in 1845, she married Manuel A. Diaz, a Cuban who probably came to the farm for tutoring. The marriage was short-lived but left her with two sons whom she supported by teaching, running a singing school out of her father's home in Plymouth, conducting dance classes, and occasionally hiring herself out as a housekeeper and nurse. She next tried her hand at writing for a juvenile audience, publishing her first short story in 1861. Cheerful and lively in person as well as on paper, she soon attracted a broad readership with tales of youthful adventure and character development, advice on "domestic art" and female self-improvement, and musings on self-culture through "spiritual healing." Her better-known works are *The William Henry Letters* (1870), *Lucy Maria* (1874), *Polly Cologne* (1881), *Domestic Problems* (1884), *Bybury to Beacon Street* (1887), *Only a Flock of Women* (1893), and *The Religious Training of Children* (1895).

Diaz was one of the earliest members of Edward Bellamy's Nationalist movement of the late 1880s, which proposed to ameliorate class antagonism through state socialism. She worked on behalf of woman's rights as president of the Belmont (Massachusetts) Woman's Suffrage League and as a founder and leader of the Woman's Educational and Industrial Union, an organization committed to self-improvement and economic advancement for women of all classes. She was also an enthusiastic devotee of new thought, which anticipated the mixture of gnosticism, mysticism, and occultism of the late-twentieth-century New Age spirituality movement, and a strong advocate of the practice of mental healing.

Abby Morton Diaz spent the last twenty years of her life in Belmont, where she made a home for three of her grandchildren. She died of pneumonia at the age of eighty-two. *(See also: Socialism; Suffrage; Utopian Communities; Women Writers)*

—Catherine Tumber

Further Reading

Abby Morton Diaz Papers. Sophia Smith Collection. Smith College, Northampton, MA.

Blackwell, Alice Stone. "The Life Work of Mrs. Abby Morton Diaz," *Woman's Journal* 33 (June 13, 1903): 188-89.
———. "Mrs. Abby Morton Diaz," *Woman's Journal* 34 (April 9, 1904): 113, 116-17.

❧ Dickinson, Emily (1830–1886)

Emily Dickinson is a major American poet who was not acknowledged during her own lifetime. Her first poem was published when she was twenty-two years old, with a title she had not chosen herself: "A Valentine." Her second poem was published in 1861, when she was thirty-one, under the title "May Wine," but as with most of her poetry that carried no title, we know it by its first line: "I taste a liquor never brewed." During her lifetime, only five other poems were printed, the last in 1878 in an anthology titled *A Masque of Poets*, which also included a previously unpublished poem by Henry David Thoreau. Her image as a literary as well as social recluse had been encouraged by early devotees but does not entirely match the Dickinson of her own correspondence to family and close friends. Her letters reveal earnest efforts to win the favor of the powerful editor of the *Atlantic Monthly*, Thomas Wentworth Higginson. The coyness of tone in the letters to Higginson is deliberate and must be read against the societal pressures of the times for women in the literary hierarchy.

Because Dickinson refused to "know her place," she created her own place and space with the power of a visionary and challenger to accepted mores for women of her time. There is at once a mystic spirituality and radical sociology in her poetry with significant implications for feminists as creative forces for change.

She lived her life in her father's house in Amherst, Massachusetts, and with an intriguing argument concerning agoraphobia we may be able to understand her increasing retreat from the world as not of her own choosing. Whatever the cause, restricting the sphere of her physical environment to a smaller and smaller diameter enhanced the intensity and expanded the range of her vision. Nature, love, passion, death, and immortality are traditionally discussed as her themes, but more relevant to recent feminist reexaminations are themes of empowerment, self-creation, and transcendence.

Her vibrant experimentation with metaphor and imagery is set against the counterpoint of traditional American hymnal meters and a language linking sexuality and suffering, thus creating a tension between visual and sound imagery, between physical and spiritual energy, stressing that all is far more complex than appears on the surface of the world. "My mind to me a kingdom is," are her own words to express this dynamic vision.

While biographers and critics continue to debate the enigmatic puzzle pieces of her life—her not-so-secret loves and family disputes—readers have never let the academic wars stand in the way of empathy with her tragic vision, as it has been called by an editor of her letters and poems. Likened by one critic to Shakespeare's timely appearance in a period of historic crisis, her presence and voice are harbingers in the nineteenth century of those to come after her in a succession of strong women as poets in the twentieth century. In her own century in both Britain and the United States, women were more likely to be tolerated as "scribblers" of prose than poetry.

Rather than as a frail or self-pitying victim, eccentric dissenter in her household, or passive maid spurned, the strongest and yet perhaps the most controversial view of her is simply as a poet creating her own immortality: her poetry. *(See also: Women Writers)*

—Carol Lee Saffioti-Hughes

Further Reading

Bennett, Paula. *My Life, a Loaded Gun: Dickinson, Plath, Rich, and Female Creativity.* Urbana: University of Illinois Press, 1990.

Boswell, Jeanetta. *Emily Dickinson: A Bibliography of Secondary Sources, with Selective Annotations, 1890 through 1987.* Jefferson, NC: McFarland, 1989.

Dandurand, Karen. *Dickinson Scholarship: An Annotated Bibliography, 1969–1985.* New York: Garland, 1988.

Dickinson, Emily. *Selected Letters.* Edited by Thomas H. Johnson. Cambridge, MA: Belknap, 1985.

Dobson, Joanne. *Dickinson and the Strategies of Reticence: The Woman Writer in Nineteenth-Century America.* Bloomington: Indiana University Press, 1989.

Doriana, Beth Maclay. *Emily Dickinson: Daughter of Prophecy.* Amherst: University of Massachusetts Press, 1995.

Erkkila, Betsy. *The Wicked Sisters: Women Poets, Literary History, and Discord.* New York: Oxford University Press, 1992.

Farr, Judith. *Emily Dickinson: A Collection of Critical Essays.* Englewood Cliffs, NJ: Prentice Hall, 1995.

———. *The Passion of Emily Dickinson.* Cambridge, MA: Harvard University Press, 1992.

Garbowsky, Maryanne M. *The House without the Door: A Study of Emily Dickinson and the Illness of Agoraphobia.* Rutherford, NJ: Farleigh Dickinson University Press, 1989.

Hart, Ellen Louise. *The Encoding of Homoerotic Desire: Emily Dickinson's Letters and Poems to Susan Dickinson, 1850–1886.* Santa Cruz: University of California Press, 1991.

Juhasz, Suzanne. *Cosmic Power in Emily Dickinson.* Austin: University of Texas Press, 1993.

Kirkby, Joan. *Emily Dickinson.* New York: St. Martin's, 1991.

Loeffelholz, Mary. *Dickinson and the Boundaries of Feminist Theory.* Urbana: University of Illinois Press, 1991.

Martin, Wendy. *An American Triptych: Anne Bradstreet, Emily Dickinson, and Adrienne Rich.* Chapel Hill: University of North Carolina Press, 1984.

Sewall, Richard Benson. *The Life of Emily Dickinson.* Cambridge, MA: Harvard University Press, 1994.

Shurr, William, ed. *The Marriage of Emily Dickinson: A Study of the Fascicles.* Lexington: University of Kentucky Press, 1983.

Shurr, William, with Anna Dunlap and Emily Grey Shurr. *New Poems of Emily Dickinson.* Chapel Hill: University of North Carolina Press, 1993.

Waugh, Dorothy. *Emily Dickinson Briefly.* New York: Vantage, 1990.

Wright, Sue Lanier. *The Wife without the Sign: Emily Dickinson's Love Stories.* Beaumont, TX: Lamar University Press, 1985.

DiFranco, Ani (b. 1970)

Ani DiFranco is a contemporary singer-songwriter who has formed her own company, Righteous Babe Records, to maintain artistic and financial control over her music. DiFranco set off on her own path from a very early age. Having declared herself an emancipated minor when her parents divorced, she was writing songs by the time she was fifteen. She graduated from the Visual and Performing Arts High School in her hometown of Buffalo, New York, at sixteen.

DiFranco started her career in the tradition of the folk singer, touring the country and playing coffeehouses, bars, and college campuses. She developed a fiercely loyal following among a widely diverse group of young people, and touring, a rarity in contemporary music, paid off with ever-increasing word of mouth and an increased demand for recordings of her work. Resisting the approaches of major record companies, DiFranco formed Righteous Babe Records, based in her hometown of Buffalo, New York, in 1990. She oversees virtually every aspect of the business and has insisted on using local vendors whenever she can. She has released over a dozen compact discs, including two in 1999, *Up Up Up Up Up Up* and *To the Teeth*. With the barest minimum of radio airplay, DiFranco has sold well over one million copies of her entire catalog.

While her distinct do-it-yourself approach to the business aspect has garnered her much attention and admiration, DiFranco's artistry is equally original and is crucial to her appeal. Her music juxtaposes folk instrumentation with the energy of punk rock, and her songs are a torrent of attitude, politics, introspection, and humor. With her body piercings, tattoos, wildly hued hair, and self-avowed bisexuality, DiFranco formed a hard-core audience largely made up of young women. As she approaches her thirties, her musical direction is becoming more diverse and at times more commercial; yet the intensity of her following has not abated as it has increased in size.

In 1997, she released a two-disc compilation of live recordings titled *Living in Clip.* It quickly became one of her best-sellers and widened her audience by exposing listeners who had not seen her perform to the dynamism of her concerts. An extensive tour with legendary troubadour Bob Dylan in that same year brought her to the attention of an entirely new audience that embraced her neofolk sensibilities.

Whether DiFranco will influence other artists, particularly women artists, is unclear at this point. The pitfalls of being a political icon are evident in her recent career, as her early fans have bemoaned both her marriage and the use of one of her songs, *32 Flavors,* in a television spot for the National Football League. Yet, she seems poised to bring her singular artistic vision to a wider audience and is likely to be one of the most important contemporary musicians, irrespective of gender, of her generation. *(See also: Music; Popular Vocalists)*

—Peter Labella

☙ Diggs, Annie LePorte (1848–1916)

Annie Diggs, social reformer, journalist, and Populist politician, was born in London, Ontario. She moved to Lawrence, Kansas, in 1873, marrying Alvin S. Diggs a few months later; the couple had three children. Diggs's interest in reform began with her involvement in and writings about woman suffrage and temperance in the 1870s. Diggs and her husband edited the *Kansas Liberal* until she began writing weekly columns for the *Lawrence Journal*. By the late 1880s, Diggs had become increasingly concerned with the economic problems of farmers and began supporting the National Farmers' Alliance.

As an associate editor of the *Alliance Advocate,* a Topeka newspaper with wide circulation in the plains states, Diggs gained a reputation as a spokesperson for agricultural reform and was asked in 1890 to campaign for the newly formed Populist Party in Kansas. Diggs's influence among Populists increased due to her organizing and lobbying efforts at national conventions of the National Farmers' Alliance and at the nominating convention of the Populist Party in 1892. During the presidential campaigns of 1892 and 1896, Diggs toured the country extensively, supporting James Weaver, the Populist presidential candidate. She moved to Washington, D.C., became the Washington correspondent for the *Alliance Advocate,* and was a frequent congressional lobbyist for woman suffrage, temperance, the alliance, and the Populist Party. In 1896, she served on the Populist National Committee. She also served alternately as vice president and president of the Kansas Equal Suffrage Association.

A pragmatic politician, Diggs supported the Populist Party despite its failure on a national level to include woman suffrage or temperance in its platform. As late as 1900, she was still supporting the fusion of the Democratic Party and the Populist Party rather than an independent Populist Party, believing as many Populists did that a fusion party would have a better chance of winning elections. In 1898, she was appointed Kansas State Librarian as a reward for helping elect a Populist-Democratic administration. By 1902, Diggs had become discouraged with fusion politics and began endorsing Eugene Debs and the Socialist Party. In 1904, Diggs moved to New York City, worked with a civic reform bureau, and continued writing. Her books include *The Story of Jerry Simpson* (1908) and *Bedrock* (1912). She left New York in 1912 to live with her son in Detroit, where she died in 1916. *(See also: Journalism; National Farmers' Alliance; Populist Party; Suffrage in the American West)*

—MaryJo Wagner

Further Reading

Barr, Elizabeth N. "The Populist Uprising." In *A Standard History of Kansas and the Kansans,* edited by William Connelley. Vol. 2, 1115-95. Chicago: Lewis, 1918.

Kansas Scrapbooks, Biog. D. Kansas State Historical Society, Topeka.

Weddle, Connie Andes. "The Platform and the Pen: The Reform Activities of Annie L. Diggs." Master's thesis. Wichita State University, Wichita, KS, 1979.

☙ Dilling, Elizabeth Eloise (Kirkpatrick) (1894–1966)

Elizabeth Dilling, author and lecturer, crusaded against Communism and for conservative causes in the 1930s, 1940s, and 1950s. She published the *Elizabeth Dilling Bulletin* monthly, wrote numerous tracts, and wrote and published four books: *The Red Network: A Who's Who and Handbook of Radicalism for Patriots* (1934), *The Roosevelt Red Record* (1936), *The Octopus* (1940), and *The Plot against Christianity* (1952). A tireless researcher and an inveterate opponent of President Franklin D. Roosevelt, she was an isolationist and a foe of foreign aid.

Born in Chicago in 1894, she graduated from Starrett High School for Girls there, studied harp at the University of Chicago, and briefly was a concert harpist before marrying Albert Wallwick Dilling, a Chicago attorney and engineer, in 1918. They had a son Kirkpatrick and a daughter Elizabeth Jane.

Dilling's life changed after she visited the Soviet Union with her husband in 1931 and was appalled by conditions there under Communism. When she returned to America, she lectured about Communism and showed home movies she had made in Russia. She studied Communism intensively and collected a large library of books about and against Communism. Her first book *The Red Network* was a collection of summaries of the associations of some thirteen hundred individuals and groups she labeled as pro-Communist.

Dilling opposed American participation in World War II before Pearl Harbor. In 1941, she led a group of mothers to Washington to lobby against the Lend-Lease Bill. She was arrested several times for demonstrating at the Capitol and the Senate Office Building. Her opposition to the foreign policies of the Roosevelt administration led to her indictment for sedition in 1942, 1943, and 1944, along with other isolationists, but the trial ended without a verdict in 1944 when the presiding judge died.

After World War II, Dilling crusaded against the United Nations, the Bricker Amendment (a proposed amendment to limit executive authority in foreign policy), and recognition of Red China. She also opposed racial desegregation and wrote extensively on alleged Jewish support of Communism. Allied with a network of ultra-Right activists, she worked against leftist influence in the Democratic and Republican parties and campaigned for minor party candidates for the presidency and lesser offices.

Dilling divorced Albert Wallwick Dilling in 1943 and in 1948 married Jeremiah Stokes, a Salt Lake City attorney, Mormon elder, and anticommunist crusader. Stokes died in 1954.

Dilling was one of the most prominent anticommunist women in the nation for nearly forty years. Her newsletter had only a few thousand subscribers, but her books were read by millions and used as references by some government agencies. A controversial woman, she provoked substantial opposition. She made little money from her crusades and was supported by her husbands and by a modest inheritance. She died in Chicago in 1966. *(See also: Communist Party; Right-Wing Political Movements)*

—**Glen Jeansonne**

Further Reading
Dilling, Elizabeth. *The Red Network.* Chicago: Elizabeth Dilling, 1934.
Dilling Newsletter, 1942–1966.

❧ Displaced Homemakers

Displaced homemakers is a term coined in the 1970s to describe women who have worked in the home a substantial number of years providing unpaid household services for family members, are not participating in the paid labor force, are displaced by divorce or the death of a spouse or loss of public assistance, and would have or have had difficulty securing employment. Because of the drastic rise in the divorce rate since 1960, these women have become a growing and important group in our society who need education or job training to improve their skills and confidence in their efforts to support themselves. Despite women's greater participation in the labor force, the number of displaced homemakers rose drastically during the 1980s, with a greater proportion living in poverty in 1990 than in 1980. Demographic data suggest that this phenomenon will continue for the foreseeable future. Many programs at both the federal and local level have been established to provide these women with needed services. Money for this purpose became available with the beginning of the Comprehensive Employment and Training Act (CETA) program in 1973 and has continued in various programs from the federal government, which in turn awards grants to local agencies and programs to help the women acquire skills and recognize, appreciate, and market those skills they have gained during their years as homemakers.

As more women find it increasingly imperative to enter and remain in the paid workforce, programs such as the Job Training Partnership Act of 1982 (JTPA) have succeeded 1973's CETA, and large cities such as Los Angeles find themselves reallocating funding that previously went to CETA toward more modern job training programs like JTPA. Debates continue across the nation, however, about whether job training is an appropriate government role, and recent welfare reform programs do not support job training but insist on "work first." Funding for displaced worker programs was eliminated by Congress in 1977. *(See also: Divorce; Housework; Welfare Reform)*

—**Anne Statham**

Further Reading
André, Rae. *Homemakers: The Forgotten Workers.* Chicago: University of Chicago Press, 1981.
U.S. Department of Education. *Services to Displaced Homemakers.* Washington, DC: USDE Office of Vocational and Adult Education, 1981.
York, Dwight, and Fran Johnson. *The Displaced Homemaker Program in Wisconsin.* Madison: Wisconsin Technical College System, 1996.

❧ Divorce

In England the ecclesiastical courts had jurisdiction over marriage and applied canon law, which made a valid marriage indissoluble. A true divorce, *divortium a vinculo matrimonii,* which was absolute and allowed remarriage, was never granted unless the marriage was *void ab initio* because of defects such as consanguinity, bigamy, or sexual incapacity. This absolute divorce bastardized the children of the void marriage and ended all support obligations of the husband for the wife. Late in the seventeenth century, the House of Lords began to grant a very limited number of absolute legislative divorces.

Divortium a mensa et thoro, separation from bed and board, could be granted for adultery, desertion, or cruelty. All the legal obligations of the marriage, except cohabitation, continued, and the parties could not remarry. The husband could be ordered to provide support in the form of alimony (payments in cash) to the innocent wife who obtained this decree. The children of the marriage remained legitimate.

In America, the southern colonies followed the English practice, but New England courts and legislatures sometimes granted divorces. The Puritan reformers viewed marriage as a civil contract that could be dissolved if one of the spouses breached the terms of the covenant through adultery, long absence, incest, or irremediable cruelty. That influence was reflected in Connecticut and Massachusetts, the only colonies to enact statutes allowing absolute divorce and to enforce them regularly. The more conservative Pennsylvania statute of 1705 provided for annulments on the grounds of consanguinity and affinity, and permitted separations from bed and board where adultery, bigamy, buggery, or sodomy was shown. In those colonies that had equity courts, as in England, private contracts to live apart and divide property were enforceable if they took the form of a postnuptial trust involving a third party.

After the American Revolution, many states passed divorce laws. By 1800, every New England state had a divorce law, as did New York, New Jersey, and Tennessee. The southern states, however, continued their more conservative policies.

In America, absolute divorce usually meant a division of the property, with the woman receiving one-third to one-half of the estate owned during the marriage. In a separation, husbands retained control of the marital property but were obligated to make monetary payments to innocent wives.

Pennsylvania, however, was the only state that continued the English practice of disallowing any alimony in cases of absolute divorce. The New England states were more willing to grant absolute divorce but less willing to enforce women's property rights during marriage through devices such as separate estates. Conversely, states such as New York and South Carolina, which were conservative about granting absolute divorces, strongly enforced private separation agreements according to equitable principles of law.

From 1850 to 1870, although divorce laws varied, many states enacted fairly liberal laws, such as the Connecticut statute that authorized divorce for any misconduct that permanently destroyed the happiness of the petitioner and defeated the purposes of the marriage relation. After 1870, however, moralists such as Horace Greeley, editor of the *New York Tribune,* and Theodore D. Woolsey, president of Yale University and founder of the New England Divorce Reform League, attacked permissive divorce with increasing force. In 1882, Connecticut repealed its permissive statute.

Despite the tightening of the law, the divorce rate continued to rise. Some unhappy spouses took advantage of "divorce colonies" where they could obtain migratory divorces by satisfying short-residency and liberal-grounds requirements. Other states followed Indiana, which before the 1870s was one of the first divorce colonies. A series of Supreme Court decisions delineated the circumstances under which one state had to recognize a migratory divorce obtained in one of its sister states. The Court developed the idea of the "divisible divorce," in which a state may have the power to dissolve the marital union but not to determine other issues such as support.

Until 1966, New York State retained its very conservative statute that permitted divorce only for adultery, thus producing in-state divorce mills that collusively manufactured evidence to satisfy a court. In effect, New Yorkers, if they had the money and the stomach for it, could obtain divorces by mutual consent.

In 1970, California began what has been called "the divorce revolution" by enacting the first completely no-fault divorce law in the Western world. The term *no fault* indicated that no grounds needed to be established to allow legal dissolution of the union. Since then, every state has enacted some form of no-fault divorce, which allows divorce on the unilateral demand of just one party to the marriage. Although this conclusion has its critics, the evidence suggests that unilateral divorce law results in significantly lower alimony and child support payments to women who have lost the bargaining leverage of the power to block or at least to delay the divorce.

Even before the no-fault revolution, only a minority of divorced women received alimony. In recent years the trend is toward division of the marital property at the time of divorce, rather than the award of continuing support payments in the form of alimony.

Custody rights remain the other significant issue in divorce disputes. In England and early America, fathers possessed a paramount claim to the guardianship and custody of their children during marriage and in the event of divorce. In nineteenth-century America, courts modified this doctrine by asserting their right to select a different guardian in the best interests of the child. Using the doctrine of *parens patriae* and the procedure of the writ of habeas corpus, courts claimed the right to make custodial dispensations. Nineteenth-century activists considered maternal custody rights a central issue of the woman's rights movement. Around mid-century, state legislatures codified the judicial inroads on paternal power, and the courts thereafter defined the limits of maternal rights.

By 1860, New Jersey codified the "tender years" doctrine, which decreed that infants, children below puberty, and youngsters afflicted with health ailments be placed in a mother's care unless she was unworthy. Rather than formally granting women equal custody and guardianship rights, by 1900, most statutes instead vested judges with the discretion to place children.

Modern statutes typically direct placement based on the sex-neutral standard of the best interests of the child. Although the tender-years maternal preference may retain some customary force, courts have ruled that it constitutes prohibited sex discrimination. Statutes in a number of states now incorporate a preference for joint custody. Some observers argue that a "primary caretaker" presumption, adopted in West Virginia in 1981, offers the best hope of promoting stability for children and ensuring that a custody challenge will not be used as a bargaining chip to reduce support payments and property settlements.

All fifty U.S. states currently allow no-fault divorce, which some blame for the escalating divorce rates. Recent trends in legislation indicate concern for the institution of marriage by making access to divorce more difficult. *(See also: Equity Courts; Marriage)*

—**Laura Oren**

Further Reading

Blake, Nelson Manfred. *The Road to Reno: A History of Divorce in the United States.* Westport, CT: Greenwood, 1962.

Chused, Richard. *Private Acts in Public Places: A Social History of Divorce in the Formative Era of American Family Law.* Philadelphia: University of Pennsylvania Press, 1994.

Cott, Nancy. "Divorce and the Changing Status of Women in Eighteenth-Century America," *William and Mary Quarterly* 33 (October 1976): 587-614.

Grossberg, Michael. "Who Gets the Child? Custody, Guardianship, and the Rise of a Judicial Patriarchy in Nineteenth-Century America," *Feminist Studies* 9 (1983): 235-60.

O'Neill, William L. *Divorce in the Progressive Era.* New Haven, CT: Yale University Press, 1967.

Riley, Glenda. *Divorce: An American Tradition.* New York: Oxford University Press, 1991.

Seppa, Nathan. "Should States Keep Families Tied Together?" *American Psychology Association Monitor* (June 1996). Available at http://www.apa.org/monitor/jun96/divorce.html

Smith, Merril D. *Breaking the Bonds: Marital Discord in Pennsylvania.* New York: New York University Press, 1991.

Weitzman, Lenore J. *The Divorce Revolution: The Unexpected Social and Economic Consequences for Women and Children in America.* New York: Free Press, 1985.

Wright, Carroll D., ed. *A Report of Marriage and Divorce in the United States, 1867–1886.* Washington, DC: Government Printing Office, 1889.

ᔕ Dix, Dorothea Lynde (1802–1887)

Dorothea Dix, humanitarian and reformer, crusaded for improved treatment of the mentally ill. Born in Hampden on the Maine frontier, she started a dame school for young girls in Boston in 1821 and authored a children's textbook, *Conversations on Common Things,* published in 1824.

How she became interested in the plight of the unbalanced is unclear, although she was aware of the reforms of Philippe Pinel of Paris and Henry Tuke of York, England. In 1841, she surveyed prison and jail conditions throughout Massachusetts, recording her observations of chained inmates living amid squalor. Dix sought the segregation of the insane and the idiotic from criminals. In January 1843, with the aid of Horace Mann and Charles Sumner, she petitioned the state legislature, which then authorized the construction of additional buildings at the state hospital at Worcester. Dix then focused on conditions in other states, including New Jersey and Rhode Island, where she persuaded state legislatures to fund the establishment of mental hospitals.

In June 1848, she petitioned Congress for passage of a land grant bill. The proceeds from the sale of 5 million acres of public land were to benefit the indigent insane, but Congress deferred the bill and allowed it to die. Dix tried again with a proposal to sell 12.5 million acres of public land, the proceeds from which would go to the indigent insane and the deaf, dumb, and blind. The House and Senate passed a modified version of her proposal, but it was vetoed by President Franklin Pierce in March 1854.

Dix sailed to Liverpool, England, the following September and continued her crusade, securing a royal investigation of asylums in Scotland. In January 1856, she met with Pope Pius IX, who made an unannounced visit to an asylum she had reported to him. Dix then toured hospitals and prisons throughout Europe, from Constantinople to Sweden, and returned to the United States in September 1856.

After serving in the Civil War as superintendent of female nurses, she resumed her investigation of jails, poorhouses, and mental institutions throughout the United States in 1867. She spent the next fifteen years surveying hospital conditions and engaging in charitable activities. On her last major tour in 1881, she visited mental hospitals in Virginia, North Carolina, Georgia, and Florida. Dix is buried in Mount Auburn Cemetery near Boston. *(See also: Nursing; Prison Reform)*

—**Casey Edward Greene**

Further Reading

Colman, Penny. *Breaking the Chains: The Crusade of Dorothea Lynde Dix.* White Hall, VA: Shoe Tree Press, 1992.

Conway, Jill Ker. "Utopian Dream or Dystopian Nightmare? Nineteenth-Century Feminist Ideas about Equality," *Proceedings of the American Antiquarian Society: A Journal of American History and Culture Through 1876–96* (1986): 285-94.

Dix, Dorothea L. *On Behalf of the Insane Poor: Selected Reports, 1843–1852.* 1843. Reprint, Salem, NH: Ayer, 1971.

———. *Remarks on Prison and Prison Discipline in the United States: With Introduction and Index Added,* 2d ed. Introduction by Leonard D. Savitz. 1845. Reprint, Montclair, NJ: Smith, Patterson, 1984.

Gollaher, David. *A Voice for the Mad: The Life of Dorothea Dix.* New York: Free Press, 1994.

Malone, Mary. *Dorothea L. Dix: Hospital Founder.* 1968. Reprint, New York: Chelsea House, 1991.

Marshall, Helen E. *Dorothea Dix: Forgotten Samaritan.* Chapel Hill: University of North Carolina Press, 1937. Reprint, New York: Russell & Russell, 1967.

Snyder, Charles M. *The Lady and the President: The Letters of Dorothea Dix and Millard Fillmore.* Lexington: University Press of Kentucky, 1975.

Tiffany, Francis. *Life of Dorothea Lynde Dix.* 1891. Reprint, Salem, MA: Higginson, 1992.

ᔕ Domestic Feminism

Domestic feminism is a term used by contemporary historians to refer to the post-Civil War conservative philosophy and activities of nineteenth-century middle-class advocates of improving women's education and employment opportunities without challenging the concept of a discreet "woman's sphere" to which women were to be confined. This extension of autonomy for women within the family accompanied the gradual enlargement of the social territory assigned to the domestic sphere during the nineteenth century. The proponents of domestic feminism accepted patriarchy and the Victorian gender system as natural, God-given, and appropriate yet worked within the domestic sphere to expand its limits to include women's conditional entry into the public sphere on the basis of necessity and propriety.

Using a dynamic definition of the cult of true womanhood to justify improvements in women's social and economic conditions, antebellum conservatives and liberal feminists urged and supported the creation of institutions of education to ensure women's proper preparation for their domestic maternal duty to rear and teach children. Liberally defining woman's work enabled the postwar proponents of the cult of domesticity to designate emerging industrial and clerical occupations of the mid-nineteenth century as extensions of woman's sphere, thus paving the way for women's entry into paid employment beyond sewing, teaching, and writing. Eschewing an emphasis on women's legal and political rights, domestic feminists did support reforms in married women's property rights as appropriate protections of woman's sphere.

After the Civil War, domestic feminism continued to expand woman's sphere. Consolidating previous gains that now provided basic educational, employment, and civic opportunity for women, domestic feminism harnessed the restless energy of a generation of educated young women by focusing their attention on their womanly duty to others. The women's club movement provided a respectable forum for married women to gather, develop their intellectual interests, and address community needs for improvement in late Victorian industrial and urban society. Applying their domestic values, the generation of recently college-graduated women, whose social housekeeping developed into the profession of social work, contributed to the achievements of the Progressive Era.

Although frequently their goals paralleled those of contemporary feminists, domestic feminists disavowed any support or approval of attempts to achieve equality of the sexes as degrading to woman's spiritual and moral superiority over men. Thus, domestic feminism was an expedient for improving women's conditions in a piecemeal fashion because it avoided the issue of woman's right to self-definition of herself or of her goals. The legacy of domestic feminism into the twentieth century was not addressed until after World War II. In the 1960s, the modern women's movement challenged the gender system that relegated women to "separate but equal" status within the human race. *(See also: Cult of True Womanhood; Married Women's Property Acts)*

—**Angela M. Howard**

Further Reading

Norton, Mary Beth. "The Paradox of 'Woman's Sphere.'" In *Women of America: A History,* edited by Carol Ruth Berkin and Mary Beth Norton, 139-49. Dallas, TX: Houghton Mifflin, 1979.

Smith, Daniel Scott. "Family Limitation, Social Control, and Domestic Feminism in Victorian America." In *A Heritage of Her Own: Toward a New Social History of American Women,* edited by Nancy F. Cott and Elizabeth H. Pleck, 222-45. New York: Touchstone/Simon & Schuster, 1979.

⮳ Domestic Literature in the United States

Domestic literature in the United States (1822–c. 1870) was predominantly fiction (but included poetry and the personal essay) that focused on the domestic setting and valorized woman's role in the home and community.

Personal essays on domestic subjects were often the first publications of novice women writers. In a variety of contests, regional and national magazines with predominantly women subscribers encouraged contributions focused on domestic life. Publishers promoted women writers in terms of their domestic roles—for example, Harriet Beecher Stowe's introduction in the role of young wife and mother. Poets, essayists, and novelists published in magazines as well as books, and many magazines' fortunes depended on the serialization of popular domestic novels.

Domestic literature frequently is equated with the popular domestic novel, a genre dating from the 1820s with Catharine Maria Sedgwick's publication of *A New England Tale* (1822), *Redwood* (1824), and *Hope Leslie* (1827). From Sedgwick's first rocketing sales, domestic novelists individually and collectively were among the best-selling American writers of their period—dominating popular American fiction in the 1850s and 1860s. The list of domestic novelists and novels is long. Among the most prolific authors and popular works were Augusta Jane Evans, *Beulah* (1859), *St. Elmo* (1867); Mrs. E.D.E.N. Southworth, *Retribution* (1849), *The Hidden Hand* (1859, 1889); Harriet Beecher Stowe, *The Minister's Wooing* (1859), *My Wife and I* (1871); Susan Warner, *The Wide, Wide World* (1851), *Queechy* (1852); and Sara Payson Willis Parton (Fanny Fern), *Ruth Hall* (1855).

Domestic novelists traditionally have been seen as anomalies: public, professional, breadwinning women who wrote of private, domestic, dependent lives. But while dependent domesticity is often the starting point and conclusion of these novels, most plots feature significant episodes of independent and even professional roles. A comfortable home, domestic life based on love between equal partners, happy children, and a stable community of strong Christian values are ultimate goals, but being dependent on others' health, wealth, and goodwill is shown to be a risky means of gaining or continuing such values. As many of the authors stepped out of strictly domestic roles and supported themselves and their families, so in the novels the positive values of home and hearth were most often secured by those who deserved them and worked for them. Rather than promoting dependency or self-sacrifice, the novels supported determination, independence, and enlargement of the traditional "domestic sphere."

While domestic essays promoted scientific homemaking and domestic economy, the novels associated domestic restrictions and drudgery with bleak, unattractive, or even vile characters—not with the successful protagonists whose strengths were in values and imagination.

Rather than endorsing limited cultural and domestic roles for women, the novels showed characters overcoming their own socialization and the restrictions of a narrow worldview to achieve independence, vision, and accomplishment for themselves—as well as a satisfying domestic life. Some feminist scholars' close readings of individual texts catalog rebellion against restriction and authority, self-assertion, independent worth, and professional competence. While both conformity and rebellion vary between works and throughout the period, most scholars agree that by the late 1860s the genre had run its course and that the later works are more conservative than their predecessors.

Traditional American literary history, which uses a dichotomy between popular and high culture, dismissed domestic authors and texts as simplistic and conformist, mindless upholders of traditional social values, religion, and morality. While this view lost favor in the 1950s, it continues to reappear. Feminist literary critics and historians, however, have firmly established the richness and conflict in these texts and in their authors' lives—as well as confirming the works' significance as historical sources in American women's history. *(See also: Domestic Feminism; Feminist Literary Criticism; Magazines; Stowe, Harriet Beecher; Women Writers)*

—Carol Klimick Cyganowski

Further Reading

Baym, Nina. *Woman's Fiction: A Guide to Novels by and about Women in America, 1820–1870.* Ithaca, NY: Cornell University Press, 1978.

Garrison, Dee. "Immoral Fiction in the Late Victorian Library," *American Quarterly* 28 (Spring 1976): 71-89.

Kelley, Mary. *Private Woman, Public Stage: Literary Domesticity in Nineteenth-Century America.* New York: Oxford University Press, 1984.

Papashvily, Helen Waite. *All the Happy Endings: A Study of the Domestic Novel in America, the Women Who Wrote It, the Women Who Read It, in the Nineteenth Century.* New York: Harper, 1956.

☙ *Domestic Manners of the Americans*

Domestic Manners of the Americans (1832) by Frances Milton Trollope (1779–1863) was a satire of the American people and their institutions based on Trollope's controversial journal from her travels in the United States from 1827 to 1831. Having been faced with her family's bankruptcy, the fifty-three-year-old British author journeyed to America on November 4, 1827, with three of her five children, two domestics, and an artist friend. Hoping for personal enrichment as well as financial gain, she first visited the experimental community of Frances Wright in Nashoba, Tennessee, and then undertook a series of imaginative, although unsuccessful, business ventures in Cincinnati. Before returning to England in July 1831, she toured selected cities of the East Coast, and from notes taken during her stay in America, she developed the manuscript that launched her literary career.

Domestic Manners focused on what Mrs. Trollope perceived to be a serious fault of American society: the inferior social position of American women. Much popular and critical response to this work in America and abroad ensured a wide audience for Mrs. Trollope's subsequent work, which consisted of five more travel journals describing various European countries, two long narrative poems, several anti-evangelical verse dramas, and thirty-four novels, four of which use American characters and settings. In most of her work, Frances Trollope championed the strong, independent woman for whom marriage was only one career option, and she also addressed problems of social concern: the British Poor Laws, English factory working conditions, the plight of unwed mothers and orphans, and particularly the

rights and privileges of women. Her second American novel, *The Life and Adventures of Jonathan Jefferson Whitlaw; or, Scenes on the Mississippi* (1836), denounced the cruelties of the American slave system.

Mrs. Trollope retired in May 1850 to the family villa in Florence, Italy, and published her last novel in 1856. Her amazing productivity and her success in two popular Victorian genres, the travel journal and the novel, are generally considered to have inspired the work of her more famous son, Anthony Trollope. *(See also: European Influences; Nashoba; Women Writers)*

—Marilyn Demarest Button

Further Reading

Bethke, Frederick John. *Three Victorian Travel Writers: A Bibliography of Criticism.* Boston: G. K. Hall, 1977.

Button, Marilyn D. "American Women in the Works of Frances Milton Trollope and Anthony Trollope." Ph.D. diss. University of Delaware, 1985.

Heineman, Helen. *Frances Trollope.* Boston: Twayne, 1984.

———. *Mrs. Trollope: The Triumphant Feminine in the Nineteenth Century.* Athens: Ohio University Press, 1979.

Kissel, Susan. *In Common Cause: The "Conservative" Frances Trollope and the "Radical" Frances Wright.* Bowling Green, OH: Bowling Green State University Popular Press, 1993.

Trollope, Frances Milton. *Domestic Manners of the Americans.* London: Whittaker, Treacher, 1932. Reprint, Donald A. Smalley, ed. New York: Knopf, 1949.

———. *The Life and Adventures of Jonathan Jefferson Whitlaw; or, Scenes on the Mississippi.* London: Bentley, 1836.

☙ Domestic Service

Considered a traditional "woman's job," domestic service offered one of the earliest paid employments for working-class women. Although limited and excessively exploitative, domestic service positions for young women were readily available and required no special training or job skill in the United States. Domestic service in North America seldom offered the status of a hierarchical profession of lifetime service found in England and Europe.

In British North America during the colonial period, possibly half of the female colonists were unmarried women between eighteen and twenty-five years old who had secured their passage to the New World as indentured servants under a seven-year contract. Especially in the southern colonies, these unmarried women composed a pool of future wives for the men, who were the majority of colonists, since almost all indentured women married after their contract term expired. In addition to their passage, female indentured servants were to receive a small wage and clothing at the termination of their contract, which was often extended for violations. Chief among the severely punished violations were running away and pregnancy, for indentured women were barred from marriage while under contract. All colonial women performed crucial household chores in addition

Figure 17. Domestic Service
Two domestic servants depicted scrubbing the house with Ivory soap, which was introduced in 1879 by Proctor & Gamble. Used by permission of Corbis.

to the agricultural work required to establish a farm or plantation. As settlement progressed, the labor of indentured women increasingly centered on the household functions of domestic service. Gradually, as the slavery codes evolved, slave women were denied both the legal protection of the indentured status and its limited term of servitude.

In the United States after the eighteenth century, domestic service attracted women who had become displaced from the domestic sphere owing either to industrialization and urbanization or to immigration. Throughout the nineteenth and into the early twentieth century, room and board were included in the domestic service situation; for young single women, being able to live in the homes of their employers was supposed to compensate for the meager wage, interminable hours of drudgery, and absence of privacy that characterized life in domestic service. In the United States, both single and married black and immigrant women had few other employment options during the nineteenth century, while urban middle-class households required and could still afford at least one servant. Black and immigrant Irish women constituted a significant proportion of domestic servants, the number of which doubled between the Civil War and the turn of the century. Despite the romantic myth of the housemaid's social mobility through exosure to middle-class mores, which would enable her eventually to marry well, domestic service more often brought seduction and abandonment, and a decline into prostitution.

By the twentieth century, the increase in opportunities for women's employment offered positions with more sta-

tus, mobility, and autonomy for women workers, while the disadvantages of domestic service remained relatively constant. Consequently, the number of willing domestic workers dwindled as advanced technology in household appliances, the smaller urban household, and the more limited middle-class income all combined to render domestic servants, especially those "living in," a luxury for the wealthy. Limited job options persisted for disadvantaged and unskilled black women In the North and South, who continued to supply domestic service for urban and suburban middle-class households from the 1920s through the 1960s. The dramatic increase in married women's participation in the paid labor force in the 1970s and 1980s created among middle-class "working wives" an urgent demand for domestic service, which was increasingly supplied by first- and second-generation immigrants from Mexico and Central America. In the 1970s, some women entrepreneurs established professional home-cleaning services, but few of these businesses survived because of the general reluctance to pay women adequately for services in the marketplace that are obligatory but unremunerated for women in their family and households.

Domestic service as a woman's job most clearly represents the origin and the persistence of wage discrimination against women within the gender system, due to its expectation that women will provide lifetime unpaid household service to their families. The wages and the status of domestic service have continued to be low and therefore to attract only unskilled women workers for whom few job alternatives exist. *(See also: African American Domestic Workers; Housework; Sex-Gender System; Women's Work: Nineteenth Century)*

—**Angela M. Howard**

Further Reading

Carr, Lois Green, and Lorena S. Walsh. "The Planter's Wife: The Experience of White Women in Seventeenth-Century Maryland." In *The Private Side of American History: Readings in Everyday Life,* edited by Gary B. Nash. Vol. 1, 3d ed., 67-94. New York: Harcourt Brace Jovanovich, 1975.

Lasser, Carol. "The Domestic Balance of Power: Relations between Mistress and Maid in Nineteenth-Century New England," *Labor History* 28 (1987): 5-22.

Palmer, Phyllis. *Domesticity and Dirt: Housewives and Domestic Servants in the United States, 1920–1945.* Philadelphia: Temple University Press, 1989.

Tinsman, Heidi. "The Indispensable Services of Sisters: Considering Domestic Service in United States and Latin American Studies," *Journal of Women's History* 4 (1992): 37-59.

VanRaaphorst, Donna L. *Union Maids Not Wanted: Organizing Domestic Workers, 1870–1940.* New York: Praeger, 1988.

Doolittle, Hilda (1886–1961)

Hilda Doolittle, commonly known as H. D., was the catalyst for the imagist movement in American poetry. Her short, free-verse imagist poems, first published in *Poetry* in 1916 under the pseudonym "H. D., Imagiste," were modeled on fragments of classical Greek verse and derived their power from a juxtaposition of images rather than from words alone. Concerned mainly with natural images, they embodied the qualities of imagism that Ezra Pound later identified as direct treatment of the subject, concise diction, and musical rather than strictly metrical rhythms.

H. D.'s artistry and her search for a feminine and artistic identity resulted from a rich but unconventional life. Especially important to H. D. were the Moravian traditions of her mother's family, inspiring her attraction to images, myth, the occult, numerology, tarot, and psychoanalysis. Other events that figured prominently in her life and work were her temporary engagement but lifelong attachment to Ezra Pound, her brief marriage to the English poet Richard Aldington, her sustained companionship with Winifred Ellerman (commonly known as Bryher), several breakdowns, and psychoanalysis by Sigmund Freud.

While H. D. is primarily known for the short, controlled, and intense imagistic poems that she wrote at the beginning of her career, critics have rediscovered the long poetic narratives and autobiographical novels she devoted the rest of her life to writing, works informed by her personal experiences. In them, H. D. had a dual purpose—to bring meaning to a world torn apart by two world wars and to find her feminine and artistic identity in a masculine culture. She accomplishes this by intertwining layers of historical and personal experience with myths and legends and images of war from Trojan times to the present to create a timeless, spiritual structure that is more manageable and more meaningful to her than the chaotic present. Especially noteworthy among her longer works are the poetic trilogy *The Walls Do Not Fall* (1944), *Tribute to Angels* (1945), and *The Flowering of the Rod* (1946), as well as *Helen in Egypt* (1961) and the prose *HERmione* (1981). Many notes and full-length works remain unpublished. *(See also: Women Writers)*

—**Kenneth E. Gadomski**

Further Reading

DuPlessis, Rachel Blau. *H. D.: The Career of That Struggle*. Brighton, England: Harvester, 1986.

Friedman, Susan Stanford. *Penelope's Web: Gender, Modernity, H. D.'s Fiction*. Cambridge, UK: Cambridge University Press, 1990.

King, Michael, ed. *H. D.: Woman and Poet*. Orono, ME: National Poetry Foundation, 1986.

∽ Douglas, Helen Mary (Gahagan) (1900–1980)

Helen Gahagan Douglas enjoyed auspicious success in three separate careers during her lifetime. At twenty-two, she was a Broadway star. In 1931, she married Melvyn Douglas, her leading man in *Tonight or Never*. Their fifty-year marriage produced two children. She gave up the stage at the height of her success to sing opera, touring successfully in Europe before the anti-Semitism she witnessed in Germany and Austria convinced her to cancel her remaining contracts. When her husband's film career took them to

California, both of the Douglases became involved in local issues such as the mistreatment of the migrant population and the misuse of California's resources.

In 1940, Douglas became Democratic National Committeewoman, and in 1944, she was elected to Congress from California's fourteenth district. Reelected in 1946 and 1948, she served ably on the Foreign Affairs Committee and was appointed as alternate to the U.N. General Assembly by President Truman. An advocate of arms control and international control of nuclear energy, she fought any legislation—such as the House Un-American Activities Committee and the McCarran-Woods acts, which sought restrictions on communists and immigrants—that endangered civil liberties. Her liberal ideals brought her the respect and friendship of Eleanor Roosevelt, Walter Reuther, Henry Wallace, and William O. Douglas.

In 1950, Douglas became a candidate for the Senate, campaigning on the same liberal issues she had always espoused. Her Democratic opponent, Manchester Boddy, and later her Republican opponent, Richard Nixon, used smear tactics, equating liberalism with communism. The Nixon forces printed 550,000 "pink sheets" that claimed Douglas's congressional voting record was identical to the Communist Party line. The onset of the Korean War probably doomed her campaign, already plagued by the opposition of wealthy oil, lumbering, and agricultural groups whose power she sought to limit. The Catholic Church and the major California newspapers also worked to foil her campaign.

After her defeat, Douglas moved back to the East Coast and retired from politics, although she continued to support liberal causes and candidates. She traveled to South America, Russia, and Israel and lectured about the conditions she found there. She maintained a dignified silence regarding the unfounded accusations raised in the 1950 Senate race. Even after the revelations of Watergate, she expressed only sorrow.

Helen Gahagan Douglas died of cancer June 28, 1980, at the age of seventy-nine. *(See also: Democratic Party; Politics)*

—**Tamerin Mitchell Hayward**

Further Reading

Douglas, Helen Gahagan. *A Full Life*. Garden City, NY: Doubleday, 1982.

O'Connor, Colleen Marie. "Through the Valley of Darkness: Helen Gahagan Douglas' Congressional Years." Ph.D. diss. University of California at San Diego, 1982.

Scobie, Ingrid Winther. *Center Stage: Helen Gahagan Douglas—A Life, 1900–1980*. New York: Oxford University Press, 1992.

∽ Douglass, Frederick (1818–1895)

Frederick Douglass was a slave, abolitionist, orator, diplomat, and strong advocate of women's rights. Douglass's formal involvement in the woman's rights movement began in 1848 when he spoke at the Seneca Falls Convention in favor of Elizabeth C. Douglass's resolution advocating female suffrage. His support was largely responsible for its adoption. Douglass was an important presence at most woman's rights conventions during the 1850s; he worked to open government and professional positions to women and to repeal discriminatory property laws. Douglass also shared the goals of the temperance movement and supported Susan B. Anthony in her campaign against capital punishment.

Douglass owed much to the efforts of women in his personal and professional life. For example, his freedom from slavery was purchased by two British antislavery women in 1846; his first paper, the *North Star*, was established and maintained by funds raised by English and American antislavery women; and British abolitionist Julia Griffith was largely responsible for the paper's uninterrupted publication. Not surprisingly, Douglass's newspapers consistently supported the woman's rights movement and provided reliable information about the movement's activities.

During the Civil War, Douglass's interests were redirected to freeing the slaves, recruiting black soldiers, and outlining his vision for postwar society. When woman's rights agitation resumed after the war, Douglass broke with leading feminists over the issue of suffrage. He believed that black male suffrage should take precedence over female suffrage and should be sought separately. In contrast, leading feminists opposed any new suffrage laws that excluded women. Once the Fifteenth Amendment was ratified, however, his relationship with the woman's rights movement was restored. At the National Woman Suffrage Association in 1876, Douglass expressed regret for their disagreements but affirmed his commitment to the cause.

By 1885, Douglass had recommitted his life to obtaining female suffrage and full freedom for blacks. He died on February 20, 1895, after attending the National Council of Women in Washington and was identified by newspapers as a "friend and champion of women." While southern feminists worried that female suffrage would be damaged by Douglass's affiliation with their cause, northern feminists honored him as "the most conspicuous advocate of our rights." *(See also: Anthony, Susan B.; Civil War; Equal Rights Association; Seneca Falls Convention; Stanton, Elizabeth Cady; Woman's Rights Conventions)*

—**Marilyn Demarest Button**

Further Reading

Douglass, Frederick. *Frederick Douglass on Women's Rights*, edited by Philip S. Foner. Westport, CT: Greenwood, 1976.

Foner, Philip S. *Frederick Douglass*. New York: Citadel, 1964.

Quarles, Benjamin. *Frederick Douglass*. New York: Atheneum, 1968.

∾ Dower

As in England, common law in America provided that a man had to leave his wife a dower, or a life interest in one-third of his real estate and one-third of his personal property. The purpose of dower was to prevent the widow from becoming a public charge. If the man did not provide for his wife in his will, the widow could contest the will in court. If the man died without leaving a will, the court would see that she received her "thirds." Life interest in part of an estate meant she could not sell it nor significantly change it because it had to be passed on to future heirs, usually her children, at her death. Some wills stipulated that if a woman remarried, she would lose the accommodations her husband had provided for her.

Some colonies were liberal in the provision for dower. A study of seventeenth-century Maryland shows that one-fifth of the men who had children left all their wealth to their wives, trusting the women to see that the children received fair portions. Only a few of the Maryland men indicated that the estates were only for use during their wives' widowhood or until children came of age. When men did not leave a life estate, they often gave land outright or more than a dower third of their movable property.

After the Revolution, courts and legislatures increasingly encroached on the sacred "widow's thirds." A North Carolina statute included revision of dower rights in the general statute that revised the system of descents. In Pennsylvania, dower was not guaranteed to women when husbands died in debt. Eventually, with the passage of married women's property acts in the mid-nineteenth century, women gained significant control of their property, including inheritances. *(See also: Common Law; Married Women's Property Acts)*

—**Barbara E. Lacey**

Further Reading

Carr, Lois Green, and Lorena S. Walsh. "The Planter's Wife: The Experience of White Women in Seventeenth-Century Maryland," *William and Mary Quarterly*, 3d ser., 34 (October 1977): 542-71.

Hoffman, Ronald, and Peter J. Albert, eds. *Women in the Age of the American Revolution*. Charlottesville: University Press of Virginia, 1989.

∾ Draper, Margaret Green (1727–1807)

Margaret Draper published the *Massachusetts Gazette and Boston News-Letter* from 1754 to 1776 and was one of the most successful female printers in the eighteenth century.

Prior to 1800, American women seldom worked outside the home. Their primary roles were as housewives and mothers. Some, however, had to work in the public arena to survive. Women functioned as dressmakers, taverners, and shopkeepers. Several women also published newspapers. In fact, seventeen women printed newspapers prior to the adoption of the Constitution. Some women became printers to help relatives, but most of them were forced into a new profession because of a husband's death. Most left the business when a son or other male relative became old enough to take charge. Female entrance into the printing fraternity was primarily a matter of necessity, and even the women who succeeded as printers did not remain in the business for long.

Draper's publishing career mirrored the general stereotype. The granddaughter of one printer and the wife of another, she spent most of her life in and around the publishing business. Born in 1727, she married Richard Draper in 1750, and following the death of her husband twenty-four years later, she published the paper with her husband's partner John Boyle. The partnership ended in late 1774, primarily because Boyle supported the American position in the conflict with Great Britain, while Draper was a staunch Loyalist, using her paper to aid the British cause. After Boyle's departure, she managed the paper alone for several months. In October 1775, she formed a partnership with John Howe, and they continued to publish until the British evacuated Boston in March 1776. Expecting ill treatment from the Americans, Draper left with the British Army, going first to Halifax, Nova Scotia, and then to England. The Americans seized her property in Boston in 1783, but the British government rewarded her for her loyalty by granting her a lifetime pension. She died in London early in 1807.

Margaret Draper's loyalty to Britain guided her throughout her brief, successful printing career. Her staunch refusal to support the popular patriot cause in the Revolution, even in the face of severe public ridicule and criticism, indicates her strength of character. Refusing to take the easy route to end her troubles, she took a public stand for what she believed in. She just happened to be on the losing side. *(See also: American Revolutionary Era; Business; Journalism)*

—Carol Sue Humphrey

Further Reading

Avery, Donald R. "Draper, Margaret Green." In *Biographical Dictionary of American Journalism,* edited by Joseph P. McKerns, 192-93. New York: Greenwood, 1989.

Brigham, Clarence S. "Women Newspaper Publishers." In *Journals and Journeymen: A Contribution to the History of Early American Newspapers,* pp. 71-79. Philadelphia: University of Pennsylvania Press, 1950.

Henry, Susan. "Margaret Draper: Colonial Printer Who Challenged the Patriots," *Journalism History* 1 (1974): 141-44.

Hudak, Leona M. *Early American Women Printers and Publishers, 1639–1820.* Metuchen, NJ: Scarecrow, 1978.

Kiessel, William C. "The Green Family: A Dynasty of Printers," *New England Genealogical Register* 104 (April 1950): 81-93.

Oldham, Ellen M. "Early Women Printers of America: Margaret Draper, The Loyalist," *Boston Public Library Quarterly* 10 (July 1958): 141-46.

∾ Dreier, Katherine Sophie
(1877–1952)

Katherine Dreier devoted herself to the cause of modern art. Born in Brooklyn, New York, Dreier had a private art tutor at age twelve, and from 1895 to 1897, she studied at the Brooklyn Art School. Her German parents also instilled

in her a commitment to social reform, and Dreier was an officer of many organizations dedicated to these goals.

While she pursued social reforms, Dreier continued to study art at the Pratt Institute in 1900. Two years later, she traveled to Europe, where she studied traditional art. After returning to New York, she became a private pupil of Walter Shirlaw, who introduced her to modernist theory. Dreier met Ralph Collin and Gustav Britsch, as well as the avant-garde artists at the home of Gertrude and Leo Stein, during later trips to Europe. She held her first exhibition in London at the Dore Galleries, with later exhibitions in influential European cities. Americans first witnessed Dreier's work at the Armory Show in 1913, and solo shows followed.

Dreier founded the Cooperative Mural Workshops, an art school and workshop devoted to the notion of artistic freedom. She subsequently helped organize the Society of Independent Artists in 1916. She met artist Marcel Duchamp and surrealist artist Man Ray in New York, and in 1920 these three produced the *Société Anonyme,* America's first museum of Modern art. The *Société Anonyme* introduced more than seventy important modern artists to the American public, including Kandinsky, Klee, and Mondrian. When Duchamp left the United States for France, Dreier took sole responsibility for the *Société Anonyme's* activities, lecturing, sponsoring symposia, and writing publications about Modern art. The *Société Anonyme's* traveling exhibits gave those outside New York an opportunity to view the new art.

When the stock market crashed in 1929, Dreier could no longer fund the *Société.* She moved to Connecticut and began painting nonobjectively, using organic shapes, geometric forms, and muted colors. Her paintings were included in two of the Museum of Modern Art's exhibitions, in 1936 and 1939. In 1941, Dreier and Duchamp donated the *Société Anonyme's* collection of 616 works of art to Yale University, and Dreier coauthored the catalog with Yale professor George Heard Hamilton. After her death, she left over two hundred works of art to Yale University, the Museum of Modern Art, the Guggenheim Museum, the Phillips Collection, and the American University. *(See also: Art; Social Feminism; Suffrage)*

—Cynthia Lynn Gould

Adapted for the second edition by Marian J. Hollinger.

Further Reading

Bohan, Ruth L. *The Société Anonyme's Brooklyn Exhibition: Katherine Dreier and Modernism in America.* Ann Arbor, MI: UMI Research Press, 1980.

Galassi, Susan Grace. "Crusader for Modernism," *Art News* 83 (September 1984): 92-97.

The Société Anonyme and the Dreier Bequest at Yale University: A Catalogue Raisonné. New Haven, CT: Yale University Press, 1984.

Three Lectures in Modern Art: "Intrinsic Significance" in Modern Art. Port Washington, NY: Kennikat, 1971.

Tufts, Eleanor. *American Women Artists 1830–1930.* Washington, DC: National Museum of Women in the Arts, 1987.

⮵ Dress Reform: Nineteenth Century

Dress reform emerged as a response to the restrictive and cumbersome fashions for nineteenth-century women, whose layers of heavy petticoats, constraining corsets, and long, dragging skirts represented, in the eyes of dress reformers, "badges of degradation." In the 1850s, reformers championed a new costume, which featured a dress reaching just below the knee and a pair of trousers. The new costume, known by many names, was most frequently called "the reform dress" and was modeled on the costume of Moslem women. Women at the Oneida Community, a religious commune in New York State, adopted the costume in 1849, and female visitors to the health resorts run by water cure practitioners often wore it to participate in the healing program of exercise that was part of the water cure regimen. Water cure was a popular mid-nineteenth-century health system that emphasized preventive medicine, a spare and bland diet, regular exercise, and various applications of water as a cure for disease.

Elizabeth Smith Miller was the first woman in the United States to adopt the reform dress for everyday use, and in 1851, she introduced it to her cousin Elizabeth Cady Stanton and Stanton's friend Amelia Bloomer, who advocated it in her journal, the *Lily*. Several other women's rights activists adopted the new style, and when Amelia Bloomer, in response to readers' requests, published a woodcut of herself in the reform dress, it quickly became known as the "Bloomer costume" and became indelibly associated in the public mind with women's rights.

The women's rights leaders rejoiced in the freedom afforded by the new costume, but they were stunned by the fierce ridicule it generated. Fearing that the furor over the reform dress would eclipse the other elements of their struggle for social and political equality, most women's rights activists abandoned the new costume after a few years.

The cause of dress reform was carried on after 1856 by a group of reformers who had close ties with the water cure movement. They supported each other at annual meetings of the Dress Reform Association and through two reform- and health-oriented magazines: *The Sibyl, A Review of the Tastes, Errors, and Fashions of Society,* edited by Lydia Sayer Hasbrouck of Middletown, New York, and *The Laws of Life and Woman's Health Journal,* edited by Harriet Austin and James Jackson of "Our Home" Water-Cure in Dansville, New York. Unlike the women's rights leaders, the members of the dress reform movement believed that women should transform their own lives before attempting to change social institutions. They were convinced that if a few intrepid reformers dressed "fitly for the whole battle of life," others would soon follow their example.

The Dress Reform Association died in 1865, and despite efforts to revive it, the movement languished until 1874, when members of the Boston Woman's Club, led by Aba Woolson, initiated a more moderate effort to improve women's clothing. Woolson believed that the "Bloomer" episode had demonstrated the impossibility of radical dress reform, and the new reformers concentrated instead on reforming the style of undergarments.

Trousers for women reappeared, however, in 1893 at a dress reform session at the World's Congress of Representative Women in Chicago. The National Council of Women presented three costumes they thought would be appropriate for walking comfortably at the World's Fair to be held in Chicago later that year. Two of the costumes featured divided skirts, and the third was a knee-length exercise suit similar to gymnasium costumes. All three received harsh criticism from the local press and were not exhibited at the World's Fair. *(See also: Bloomer, Amelia Jenks; Corset; Utopian Communities; Water Cure; World's Columbian Exposition)*

—Amy Kesselman

Further Reading

Cayleff, Susan E. *Wash and Be Healed: The Water Cure Movement and Women's Health.* Philadelphia: Temple University Press, 1987.

Donegan, Jane. *Hydropathic Highway to Health: Women and Water Cure in Ante-Bellum America.* Westport, CT: Greenwood, 1986.

Henshaw, Betty. "The Bloomer Costume." Master's thesis, University of Colorado, 1955.

Kesselman, Amy. "The 'Freedom Suit': Feminism and Dress Reform in the United States, 1848–1875," *Gender & Society* 5 (December 1991): 495-510.

———. "Lydia Sayer Hasbrouck and *The Sibyl,*" *Orange County Historical Journal* 14 (November 1985): 39-44.

———. "Mary Tillotson." In *Past and Promise, Lives of New Jersey Women,* edited by Joan Burnstyn, 198-99. Metuchen, NJ: Scarecrow, 1990.

Leach, William. *True Love and Perfect Union: The Feminist Reform of Sex and Society.* New York: Basic Books, 1980.

Weimann, Jeanne Madeline. "Fashion and the Fair," *Chicago History* 12 (Spring 1983): 48-56.

⮵ Duncan, Isadora (1878–1927)

Dancer, revolutionist, and defender of the poetic spirit, Isadora Duncan is considered one of the most important forerunners of modern dance. A free spirit whose legendary exploits have sometimes overshadowed her artistic achievements, Duncan viewed dance as a lever of human emancipation. She was a liberating influence on costume, women's moral standards, and education, invoking a widespread acceptance of the dance as physically healthy and intellectually respectable. An early champion of the struggle for women's rights, she maintained, "If my art is symbolic of any one thing, it is symbolic of the freedom of woman and her emancipation." An enduring influence on twentieth-century culture, she had a natural and expressive approach to the dance, which lifted it from the realm of entertainment to that of art.

Born in San Francisco, Duncan and her siblings were raised in poverty by their mother, who nevertheless instilled

Although militantly opposed to schools, systems, and doctrine of any kind, Duncan founded schools of the dance in Germany, France, and Russia. Rather than developing a standardized system of movement, however, she attempted to inspire in her students a receptivity to the natural impulse she herself felt in her dance: an impulse that she believed originated in the solar plexus, the soul's habitat. Duncan was interested in discovering a basic dance, biological in origin and spiritual in impulse, one in which she would find the universal impulse toward movement.

Duncan's private life was as unconventional as her professional career. She bore three children out of wedlock—one died shortly after birth and two others drowned in a tragic car accident. Although violently opposed to the institution of marriage, in 1922 she married Russian poet Sergei Essenin, a man twenty years her junior, and became a Soviet citizen. In 1924, her husband committed suicide, and in 1927, she herself was killed in a tragic accident when her scarf became entangled in the rear spokes of an automobile wheel and strangled her.

For Isadora Duncan, dance was synonymous with life: "To dance is to live." Intensely personal in nature, her art reflected passion, integrity, and vision that has been impossible to recapture. She left a legacy of beauty and truth as expressed in her art, and her spirit continues to influence the dance in America today. *(See also: Dance)*

—**Cecelia A. Albert**

Further Reading

Blair, Frederika. *Isadora: Portrait of the Artist as a Woman.* New York: McGraw-Hill, 1986.
Duncan, Isadora. *Isadora Speaks.* Edited, with an introduction by Franklin Rosemont. San Francisco: City Lights Books, 1981.
———. *My Life.* New York: Horace Liveright, 1927.
Loewenthal, Lillian. *The Search for Isadora.* Pennington, NJ: Princeton Book Club, 1993.
Terry, Walter. *Isadora Duncan: Her Life, Her Art, Her Legacy.* New York: Dodd, Mead, 1963, 1984.

Figure 18. Isadora Duncan
Isadora Duncan performing *Aulis* in a costume inspired by the apparel of the ancient Greeks. Used by permission of Corbis-Bettmann.

in her children a great and abiding love for the arts. In addition to developing a tremendous sensitivity to music, Duncan was profoundly moved by nature. Using nature as her teacher, she approached the dance with a naturalness and freedom of expression characterized by an emotional intensity previously unknown to the world of dance.

Beginning her career first as a showgirl in Chicago, then as a salon dancer in New York, Duncan soon left the United States for London, then Paris, where she toured with a dance company organized by Loie Fuller. She was profoundly influenced by Greek civilization and culture, and her costumes, often classical tunics, further reflected the influence this civilization had on her. Having a natural sympathy for those attempting to overthrow established order, she composed dances using political and social themes of the day. The music to one of her most successful dances, *La Marseillaise* (1915), was to become the French national anthem, and her dance *Marche Slave* (1917) symbolized the Russian peasants' struggle for freedom.

· Duniway, Abigail Jane Scott (1834–1915)

Abigail Duniway, a suffrage leader in the Northwest, was born the second daughter in Ann and John Scott's family of nine on a farm outside Groveland, Illinois. Seventeen-year-old Duniway lost her mother to cholera on the trek to Oregon in 1852. After teaching one year near Eola, Oregon, she married Benjamin C. Duniway and returned to the extreme drudgery of the farm. In 1857, the Duniways moved to a new farm near Lafayette, but in 1862, they lost this farm because her husband endorsed notes for a friend against Duniway's wishes. Following their move to town, her husband was permanently disabled, and she supported her family by running a boarding school. In 1866, she moved to Albany, where she taught in a private school for a year and operated her own millinery and notions shop for five years. During this period, Duniway became aware of the various injustices, facilitated by laws, that all women had to endure. Her invalid husband encouraged her to work for suffrage as the best means to change unjust laws.

Thus in 1871, Duniway moved to Portland and, with her five sons and one daughter, established a weekly newspaper, the *New Northwest,* to further the cause of women's rights. Her only experience in publishing prior to this was as the author of the novel *Captain Gray's Company.* That same year, she managed Susan B. Anthony's speaking tour in the Pacific Northwest and realized her own speaking ability, which she relentlessly pursued to further the suffrage movement. In 1873, Duniway led in founding the Oregon Equal Suffrage Association and was elected its president. During this period, she attended Oregon's legislative sessions, presented petitions, lobbied, and at times spoke from the floor. Duniway's tireless work was important in obtaining suffrage rights in Washington Territory in 1883, in Idaho in 1896, and in Oregon in 1912. Although she denounced the policies and methods of the National Woman Suffrage Association as a hindrance, she served as its vice president in 1884 and was welcomed at its conventions. In recognition of her years of service, she was given major credit for suffrage's being achieved in Oregon in 1912. She authored Oregon's suffrage proclamation, signed it along with the governor, and became Oregon's first registered woman voter. *(See also: Journalism; Migration and Frontier Women; Suffrage in the American West)*

—**Diana Dingess Retzlaff**

Further Reading

Duniway, Abigail Scott. *Captain Gray's Company.* Portland, OR: S. J. McCormick, 1859.

———. *Path Breaking: An Autobiographical History of the Equal Suffrage Movement in Pacific Coast States,* 2d ed. 1914. Reprint, New York: Schocken, 1971.

Gordon, Ann D. "The Political Is the Personal: Two Autobiographies of Woman Suffragists." In *American Women's Autobiography: Fea(s)ts of Memory,* edited by Margo Culley, 111-27. Madison: University of Wisconsin Press, 1992.

Moynihan, Ruth B. *Rebel for Rights: Abigail Scott Duniway.* New Haven, CT: Yale University Press, 1983.

Smith, Helen K., and Harriet L. Smith. *The Presumptuous Dreamers: A Sociological History of the Life and Times of Abigail Scott Duniway, 1877–1912.* Lake Oswego, OR: Smith, Smith, & Smith, 1992.

🐟 Dyer, Mary (?–1660)

Mary Dyer, a Quaker martyr, was born in England although no record remains of her early years. With her husband, William Dyer, a milliner and a prominent Puritan, she emigrated to the Massachusetts Bay Colony in 1635, received membership in the Boston church in December of that year, and soon thereafter gained public recognition as a supporter of Anne Hutchinson, leader of the opposition to Puritan orthodoxy. In 1637, Dyer gave birth to a severely malformed stillborn baby, an event that John Winthrop described as divine retribution for her involvement with Hutchinson. Winthrop's chastisement seems to have had little effect on Dyer, however, for when Hutchinson was excommunicated in 1638, Dyer rose and walked out of the church by her side. Later, the Dyers were themselves banished from the Bay Colony and moved to Rhode Island with their five sons.

In 1652, Dyer returned to England, where, during her five-year stay, she became an adherent of the Quaker faith. Returning to the colonies in 1657, she encountered new laws enacted by the Massachusetts General Court against Quakers, and less than two years after her return, she became the victim of this legislation. Learning of the imprisonment of two English Friends, William Robinson and Marmaduke Stephenson, Dyer visited the jail and was arrested, banished from the colony, and threatened with death if she returned. One month later, they returned to Massachusetts with several other Quakers to test the law. The group was again imprisoned, and three Friends—Robinson, Stephenson, and Dyer—were selected by the authorities for sentencing. Receiving the death sentence from Governor John Endecott, the three went to the gallows amid a large procession of armed militia. Dyer, arms and legs bound to her body and the noose already around her neck, received a last-minute pardon and was again banished to Rhode Island. In 1660, she returned to Boston, and Endecott again sentenced her to death. This time no pardon was issued, and Mary Dyer was hanged.

The south lawn of the Boston State House is the site of a seven-foot bronze statue of Mary Dyer, sculpted by Sylvia Judson and erected in 1959. The statue depicts a seated woman in seventeenth-century plain-style dress, her head bowed slightly; the inscription reads "Witness for Religious Freedom." *(See also: Hutchinson, Anne Marbury; Society of Friends)*

—**Cristine M. Levenduski**

Further Reading

Bacon, Margaret Hope. *Mothers of Feminism: The Story of Quaker Women in America.* San Francisco: Harper & Row, 1986.

Battis, Emery. *Saints and Sectaries: Anne Hutchinson and the Antinomian Controversy in the Massachusetts Bay Colony.* Chapel Hill: University of North Carolina Press, 1962.

Erickson, Kai T. *Wayward Puritans: A Study in the Sociology of Deviance,* pp. 107-36. New York: John Wiley, 1966.

ᴇᴠ Eakins, Susan Hannah (MacDowell) (1851–1938)

Susan Eakins was a realist painter and photographer whose artistic career was overshadowed by that of her husband, artist Thomas Eakins. Daughter of an engraver, she enrolled in the Pennsylvania Academy of Fine Arts in 1876, where she studied under Thomas Eakins and earned the first Mary Smith Prize for the best painting submitted to the academy by a woman. She was a strong proponent of study from the nude, a discipline advocated by Thomas Eakins and opened for the first time to women artists in 1877, in large part due to her advocacy.

She was noted for strong draftsmanship and composition and was regarded as a skilled artist by a variety of colleagues. Thomas Eakins deemed her the finest female artist of the century, and artist-contemporary William Sartain billed her "an artist of talent." Nonetheless, she virtually abandoned her career in 1884 when she married Thomas Eakins, thereafter dedicating her life to advancing her husband's career. During her married years, she is believed to have maintained a separate studio; however, she rarely did more than sketches, instead serving as agent, hostess, secretary, clerk, and cataloger for her husband. After her husband's death, Eakins was responsible for spearheading a show in Philadelphia on Thomas Eakins and his followers. She also took up painting once again. Nevertheless, little is known today of either the quantity or whereabouts of her works. Experts surmise that many of her works, including many photographs, are erroneously attributed to her husband.

A renewed interest in Susan Eakins resulted in the first major exhibition of her work at the Pennsylvania Academy of Fine Arts in 1973, followed four years later by a solo show at North Cross School, Roanoke, Virginia. *(See also: Art; Photography)*

—Anne deHayden Neal

Further Reading

Casteras, Susan. "Mr. & Mrs. Eakins: Two Painters, One Reputation," *Harper's Magazine* 255 (October 1977): 69–71.

Rubenstein, Charlotte Streifer. *American Women Artists from Early Indian Times to the Present.* Boston: G. K. Hall, 1982.

Tufts, E. *American Women Artists: 1830–1930.* Exhibition catalog. Washington, DC: National Museum of Women in the Arts, 1987.

ᴇᴠ Earhart, Amelia (1897–1937)

Amelia Earhart was an American aviator who, among her many accomplishments, helped establish the need and the justification for commercial transport, as well as establishing women's capability and proficiency as pilots. She could write of her own flight experience in simple, direct terms that, to this day, speak to both the layperson and the experienced flier.

Her world records are many. In 1922, she set her first world record—in her own plane, a Kinner Canary—for the highest altitude flown by a woman. However, her most significant achievements were in setting world-class records, such as, in 1935, making the first solo flight from Hawaii to the U.S. mainland. Dissatisfied with being only a passenger on her first transatlantic flight in 1928, one year after Lindbergh's historic flight, she flew it alone in 1932. She was also the first woman to fly from the Atlantic to the Pacific and back again, as part of her "vagabond" tour for fun after her first transatlantic trip.

In her varied career, Earhart was aviation editor for *Cosmopolitan* from 1928 to 1930, a post created for her. She was an executive of Ludington Airways from 1930 to 1931 and vice president of National Airways, Inc. Her international acclaim included being made a Chevalier of the French Legion of Honor and receiving a medal from the National Geographic Society in 1932; she served on the Guggenheim Commission on Aeronautical Education and, later, as the director of the Institute for Professional Relations for Women at Purdue University. She was a member of the National Aeronautic Association (NAA), the National Woman's Party, and the Society of Woman Geographers. In 1932, she was also the first woman to receive the Distinguished Flying Cross.

In her own time, she was heralded as the symbol of the "new womanhood"; she supported her fellow fliers, often recognizing achievements that would otherwise have gone unnoticed. She was the first woman elected as an officer in a chapter of NAA, and she was a charter member of the first association of female pilots, the Ninety-Nines, a group in existence to this day.

Born in Kansas at the turn of the century, Earhart took an early interest in mechanical things that led her in a natural progression from cars to planes. She attended Hyde Park High School in Chicago, the Ogontz School for Girls in

Rydal, Pennsylvania, and later, Columbia University. While she served in the more traditional duties of volunteer nurse in World War I and settlement house worker at Denison House in Boston, these occupations all seem to fade in the background of her drive and determination to learn to fly, which she did, from an early woman flier, Neta Snook.

She aspired to fly the globe, setting out twice to do so, noting in 1937 that there was "one more flight left in my system." Prophetic or no, the words haunt those who continue to piece together the last years and the events of those years. In March 1937, she set out with a navigator to attempt the flight westbound, landed in Hawaii, and due to an accident, was forced to ship the Lockheed Electra back for repairs to the mainland. Her second attempt was eastbound from Florida, passing over Europe, southern Asia, Australia, and the Pacific Islands. She stopped for refueling at Lae, New Guinea, and was lost on July 2, 1937, on her way to the next refueling stop on tiny Howland Island. Several recent feminist biographers have attempted to, as Susan Ware puts it, rescue her from "the clutches of the cult of her disappearance," and balance the tempting speculation over her role in her last mission with the strong drive and determination she had to fit no mold, to meet no predetermined expectations. Although some question her feminist status by later twentieth-century definitions, she clearly continues to inspire generations of both women and men as a major symbol of popular culture and as a primary role model representing adventure, determination, and questing.

A maverick in so many ways, including writing her own marriage ceremony to acknowledge her need to establish her own terms when she married publisher George Putnam, she was determined to make a woman emerging from the cockpit a regular sight. She leaves us wondering what progress she would have noted for others and what achievements she herself would have made in the fields of civil and commercial aviation by the last quarter of the twentieth century had she lived. *(See also: Aviation; Ninety-Nines, Inc.)*

—**Carol Lee Saffioti-Hughes**

Further Reading

Amelia Earhart. In the PBS series *American Experience: Women in American History.* Clinton, NJ: Shanachie, 1993. Video.

Bachus, Jean L., ed. *Letters from Amelia: An Intimate Portrait of Amelia Earhart.* Boston: Beacon, 1982.

Earhart, Amelia. *The Fun of It.* 1932, Reprint, Chicago: Academy, 1977.

————. *Twenty Hours Forty Minutes: Our Flight in the Friendship.* New York: Putnam, 1928.

Kerby, Mona. *Amelia Earhart: Courage in the Sky.* New York: Viking, 1990.

Rich, Doris. *Amelia Earhart: A Biography.* Washington, DC: Smithsonian Institution, 1989.

Wade, Mary Dodson. *Amelia Earhart: Flying for Adventure.* Brookfield, CT: Millbrook, 1992. [Although a book for young readers, this book contains photos not previously published and excellent maps, chronologies, etc.]

Ware, Susan. *Still Missing: Amelia Earhart and the Search for Modern Feminism.* New York: Norton, 1993.

❧ Early American Era (1607–1765)

From the earliest colonial settlement to the American Revolution, immigrants to the North American continent attempted to re-create English society in a "new" world. They brought experimental religions, mercantilist ideology, representative governments, and household economies. At the same time, they also disrupted the existing ecological system and Native American culture and forced the transportation of millions of Africans with the development of the institution of slavery. Women during this era lived within a patriarchal system that did little to promote their autonomy or intelligence. Any woman not fulfilling the role of wife and mother was defeminized and marginalized.

In the earliest days of settlement, most white women migrated to the colonies either as spouses or indentured servants. While women may have worked as milliners or midwives, for example, to contribute to the family income, they had little legal or economic identity separate from their husbands or fathers. Married women seldom controlled their own property, and widows were entitled to only one-third of their deceased husband's property. In New England under the strict dogma of the Puritan church, any act of female independence could bring down the wrath of God, and women who were outspoken or financially independent were often accused of witchcraft or banished from the colony. The first few generations of women in the South enjoyed a moderate amount of freedom in choosing husbands because of the low ratio of women to men.

African women arrived in the American colonies in small numbers at first, often as indentured servants. By 1700, however, slavery had become institutionalized, and gender ratios among the black population began to stabilize by mid-century. To control the slaves, masters encouraged informal slave marriages, even if they did not legally recognize such unions. Since the slave population of most plantations was small, marriages between slaves of different owners were allowed, thus permitting some degree of mobility as slave husbands and wives visited one another. Slave society became matrifocal as women became the center of real and fictive kin networks. Slave women, like female indentured servants, suffered many abuses, including rape, and female slaves were expected to perform heavy physical labor that no white woman would be permitted to do. Only within the slave quarters did gender roles emerge among the slaves.

Native American women were marginalized by both the dominant and their own communities. Before contact, most Native American nations were matrilineal and matrifocal, and Indian women had political power as advisers. White men, however, refused to recognize female authority in Native American governments. In response to this external pressure, Native American culture became more patriarchal, although Indian women retained more power within their nations than white or black women did within colonial society.

While colonial America was sometimes seen as an age of liberation for women because of the significance of their contributions to the preindustrial household economy, the period was, in fact, one in which women of all races had little or no personal identity, autonomy, or power. By the time of the American Revolution, some elite women openly chafed against these restraints and attempted to exert some public influence. *(See also: Black Women; Dower; Married Women's Property Acts; Native American Women; Salem Witch Trials; Slavery)*

—Leigh Fought

Further Reading

Kerber, Linda K. *Women of the Republic: Intellect and Ideology in Revolutionary America.* Chapel Hill: University of North Carolina Press, 1980.

Koehler, Lyle. *A Search for Power: The "Weaker Sex" in 17th Century New England.* Urbana: University of Illinois Press, 1980.

Kulikoff, Allan. *Tobacco and Slaves: The Development of Southern Cultures in the Chesapeake, 1680–1800.* Chapel Hill: University of North Carolina Press, 1986.

Norton, Mary Beth. *Liberty's Daughters: The Revolutionary Experience of American Women, 1750–1800.* Boston: Little, Brown, 1980.

Spurill, Julia Cherry. *Women's Life and Work in the Southern Colonies.* Chapel Hill: University of North Carolina Press, 1938.

Ulrich, Laurel Thatcher. *Good Wives: Image and Reality in the Lives of Women in Northern New England, 1650–1750.* New York: Vantage, 1982.

❧ Eastman, Crystal (1881–1928)

Journalist, social worker, lawyer, socialist, and feminist, Crystal Eastman was born near Seneca Lake, New York. Influenced by her mother, Annis Ford Eastman, a minister and orator, and by the intellectual fervor of New York's Greenwich Village, Eastman was at the vanguard of women's and worker's movements throughout the first decades of the twentieth century.

After graduating from Vassar, Eastman worked in settlement houses while pursuing an M.A. from Columbia and a law degree from New York University. In 1909, Eastman was appointed to the Employment Liability Commission and drafted New York's first workman's compensation law. In 1911, Eastman converted to socialism, arguing that only a "revolution" would truly reform workers' conditions.

When war broke out in Europe, Eastman joined other suffrage leaders, social workers, and socialists in founding the modern peace movement. She served as the secretary of the American Union Against Militarism and as chairperson of the New York chapter of the Woman's Peace Party, editing its controversial newsletter, *The Four Lights*. After the United States entered the war, Eastman and Roger Baldwin unsuccessfully urged the American Union Against Militarism to defend the rights of conscientious objectors. Eastman and Baldwin left that organization to form the Civil Liberties Bureau, the precursor to the American Civil Liberties Union.

Eastman's wartime experiences continued to push her politics to the left. With her brother Max Eastman, between 1918 and 1922, Eastman published *The Liberator,* a socialist magazine loosely patterned after *The Masses.* In 1919, under the auspices of the New York Woman's Peace Party, Eastman organized the First Feminist Conference to bring women from around the world together to discuss women's issues.

Eastman's unconventional personal life, her unflagging commitment to civil liberties and pacifism as well as her agitation for birth control and women's sexual freedom, alienated her from more conservative members of women's and socialist organizations. Always a prolific writer and tireless organizer, Eastman found it increasingly difficult to find work after 1920 due in part to the nation's growing intolerance of socialism. Frustrated and in failing health, Eastman spent her last years traveling between England and the United States. She died in 1928 of nephritis. *(See also: Civil Liberties Movement during World War I; Socialism; Woman's Peace Party)*

—Kathleen Kennedy

Further Reading

American Union Against Militarism papers. Swarthmore College Peace Collection. Swarthmore, PA.

Cook, Blanche Wiesen, ed. *Crystal Eastman on Women and Revolution.* New York: Oxford University Press, 1978.

———. "Female Support Networks and Political Activism: Lillian Wald, Crystal Eastman, and Emma Goldman," *Chrysalis* 3 (1977): 43-61.

Law, Sylvia A. "Crystal Eastman: New York University Graduate," *New York Law Review* 66 (December 1991): 1963-95.

Marchard, Ronald C. *The American Peace Movement and Social Reform.* Princeton, NJ: Princeton University Press, 1972.

Woman's Peace Party papers. Swarthmore College Peace Collection. Swarthmore, PA. Microfilm.

❧ Eating Disorders

Each year, millions of people in America, mostly women, develop serious and sometimes life-threatening eating disorders. Anorexia, bulimia, and obesity are most frequently reported. While none of these disorders is new, there has been a recent surge in professional and public concern about eating disorders leading to the publication of innumerable books on the topic. However, a great deal of confusion in the definition of anorexia nervosa, bulimia nervosa, and related disorders continues to exist. Anorexia and bulimia occur primarily in young girls and women, in whites more than in any other race, and in the socioeconomically affluent. These disorders do occur in males much less frequently than in females, but the number of males developing eating disorders is on the rise. Six of ten high school girls and one of four high school boys are dieting.

The anorectic behavior usually begins in adolescence with a desire to control the redistribution of body fat that occurs naturally during puberty. A psychosocial disease, anorexia is characterized mainly by severe, self-imposed starvation and its accompanied psychic and biochemical changes that can lead to death. The anorectic has a distorted body image, being extremely thin while viewing herself as fat and being obsessed with the subject of food. Some anorexics are also bulimic.

Bulimics, most often young women, typically binge, consuming enormous amounts of food followed by purging the body through self-induced vomiting, the use of laxatives or emetics, and exercising. They appear normal physically, but this is a facade as many medical problems are brewing from the constant binging and purging. These periods of overeating, most always conducted in secret and followed by vomiting, may occur occasionally or up to several times a day. Along with a distorted body image, anorexics and bulimics share common obsessions with weight, food, exercise, and a morbid fear of being fat.

Today's current cultural preoccupation with slenderness in women has played a fundamental role in the increased incidence of eating disorders. Both anorexia and bulimia are considered psychiatric disorders that are as poorly understood as other mental illnesses and respond slowly to treatment. People suffering from these disorders are usually out of touch with their feelings, using food or deprivation to control their underlying feelings of anxiety and depression.

Eating disorders are as rampant as they are complex. One percent of adolescent girls develops anorexia. Another 2 to 3 percent develop bulimia. An estimated 10 percent of teenagers and college students (over 90 percent of them female) struggle with eating disorders. Female athletes are also highly prone to develop eating disorders, with as many as 13 to 22 percent of select groups of runners and dancers severely restricting their diets. One California study reported that one-third of nine-year-old girls and nearly one-half to two-thirds of ten-year-old girls restricted their food intake due to fear of becoming fat.

Obesity is caused by compulsive overeating and, along with anorexia, is the most obvious of the three eating disorders. Although there are plenty of obese men, fat seems more a female than a male problem. Although a quarter of the American population is overweight—defined as 20 percent over ideal weight—35 percent of all women are overweight. Unlike anorexia and bulimia, obesity affects all income levels. Genetic factors related to body size may influence obesity; some studies suggest that there are individual differences in how people metabolize and store food. *(See also: Athletics/Sports)*

—**Sandra Riese**

Further Reading

Abraham, Suzanne. *Eating Disorders: The Facts.* Oxford, UK: Oxford University Press, 1987.

Foley, Denise, and Eileen Nechas. *Women's Encyclopedia of Health and Emotional Healing,* pp. 159-63, 338-44. Emmaus, PA: Rodale, 1993.

Hsu, L. K. George. *Eating Disorders.* New York: Guilford, 1990.

Marx, Russell. *It's Not Your Fault.* New York: Villard, 1991.

Orbach, Susie. *Fat Is a Feminist Issue.* New York: Berkeley, 1979.

———. *Fat Is a Feminist Issue II: A Program to Conquer Compulsive Eating.* New York: Berkeley, 1982.

Zerbe, Kathryn J. *The Body Betrayed: Women, Eating Disorders and Treatment.* Washington, DC: American Psychiatric Press, 1993.

⮑ Eddy, Mary Baker (1821–1910)

The founder of Christian Science, Mary Baker Eddy was born in Bow, New Hampshire, the youngest of Mark and Abigail Baker's six children. This remarkably powerful religious leader was frail and sickly as a child and spent a great deal of her youth struggling with chronic back pain and emotional distress. As a result, she attended school irregularly; her formal education was limited, she claimed, to what she learned from tutoring by her older brother.

Eddy's life can be seen as a continual search for health amid a tumultuous series of relationships. Her first husband, George Washington Glover, died shortly after the couple moved to North Carolina, leaving Eddy pregnant, emotionally distraught, and penniless. Her parents took care of her during a period of emotional collapse; her son, George, was raised by another woman and never lived with his mother. In 1853, Eddy married Daniel Patterson, who traveled extensively and left her alone for long stretches. Loneliness and recurrent back pain contributed to hysterical episodes when her husband was around and, as a result of customary medical practice, to a morphine addiction that plagued her all her life.

Eddy intensified her search for health during this period and found some relief in the doctrines of Phineas Parkhurst Quimby, who used a form of hypnotism (Mesmerism) to heal people. She went to Portland, Maine, after reading about his cures, was touched by him, and was suddenly well, able to walk up the stairs of the town hall. When Quimby died in 1866, she was desolate. Consulting friends, she left her husband and took up the reins of Quimby's movement, moving to Lynn, Massachusetts. A dramatic episode confirmed for her that she should begin a new religious movement. When she arrived in Lynn, she fell on the ice and, according to her memoirs, almost died. On the third day, reading the gospel story of the raising of Jairus's daughter, she rose from her bed and was healed. Christian Science, the name chosen for this new religious movement, was formally chartered in 1879. Mary Baker Eddy, now married to her third husband, Asa Gilbert Eddy, dedicated the rest of her life to study of the relationship between disease and mental health.

Eddy's strong personality and enormous persuasive power soon drew students (primarily female) to her home in Lynn. From there, the movement grew and moved to Boston in 1881. The first edition of *Science and Health,* explaining Eddy's teachings, was published in 1875. This book went through 382 editions, and was continually revised by Eddy. She exerted strong control over her church, which continued to grow despite frequent fallings-out between her and her followers.

During the final years of her life, Mary Baker Eddy became a recluse. Her constant pain, together with her dread of "malicious animal magnetism"—the hostile spiritual energy she felt her enemies had directed at her—contributed to her isolation. She died in her home of pneumonia at the age of eighty-nine. *(See also: Christianity; Mesmerism; Religion)*

—Maria E. Erling

Further Reading

Cather, Willa, and Georgine Milmine. *The Life of Mary Baker Eddy and the History of Christian Science.* New York: Doubleday, 1909. Reprint, Lincoln: University of Nebraska Press, 1993.

Eddy, Mary Baker. *Science and Health.* Boston: Christian Science, 1875.

———. *Science and Health; With a Key to the Scriptures.* Boston: First Church of Christ, Scientist, 1875.

Gill, Gillian. *Mary Baker Eddy,* Radcliffe Biography Series. Reading, MA: Perseus, 1998.

Peel, Robert. *Mary Baker Eddy: The Years of Authority.* New York: Holt, Rinehart & Winston, 1977.

———. *Mary Baker Eddy: The Years of Discovery.* New York: Holt, Rinehart & Winston, 1966.

———. *Mary Baker Eddy: The Years of Trial.* New York: Holt, Rinehart & Winston, 1971.

Education

Women's educational history demonstrates the dual claims of family and school and the tension between the two institutions. In the colonial era, household needs defined women's lives and their education. The growing importance of schools in the nineteenth and twentieth centuries and the gradual access that women won to primary, secondary, and higher education reflect economic change, women's shifting roles within the home, and consciousness among women themselves that schools provided intellectual stimulation, vocational opportunities, companionship, and perhaps alternatives to domesticity. But access to schools did not end the family's influence or claim. Battles over the curriculum—Should women study the liberal or the domestic arts? Would their health break down if they studied the same subjects as men?—reflected the fears and concerns of many Americans that educated women would subordinate or reject family life. And schooling inevitably raised questions about women's relationship to the family. Should they simply return, minds and spirits enriched, to domestic concerns? Or did formal education mark the beginning of a new life? For women outside the white middle class, access to good schooling remains problematic today, and for all women, the relationship between curriculum and vocation, work and family, is complex.

Before the American Revolution, education for both sexes took place within the household economy, linked to the future occupations of children. Boys' possibilities varied according to the means and wishes of their fathers and their own abilities and inclinations. Girls, however, had but one destiny: to marry and raise children. Primarily from their mothers, girls of the colonial era learned to cook, weave, sew, clean, and care for children while assisting or directing the household's economic enterprises. Daughters of the urban merchant class or of wealthy southern planters often had tutors or attended finishing schools, where they studied additional topics and acquired skills appropriate for young women of their social class—for example, dancing, drawing, music, French, and decorative needlework. Some town dwellers attended the "dame schools" of poor but genteel women who themselves had little or no formal education. The better of these schools offered a curriculum that included the alphabet, writing, reading, and arithmetic as well as needlework.

Protestantism provided a spiritual rationale for colonial girls to learn reading and writing: Only thus could they study the Scriptures, prepare for conversion, and work for salvation. Girls learned to read from parents or tutors or possibly at impromptu local "adventure schools" run by older women in the community. However, their exclusion from schools and apprenticeships meant that they had a significantly lower literacy rate than young men, particularly for learning to write.

Some women, born into families of wealth, distinction, or public spirit, read and studied with their brothers' tutors, or craved the opportunity to do so. Catholic orders of sisters established convent schools for girls in Florida, Louisiana, and elsewhere, while Christian missionaries of all sects and both genders sought to educate Native American girls in European customs and culture. By the end of the eighteenth century, American writers such as Judith Sargent Murray and Charles Brockden Brown, influenced by the work of British feminist Mary Wollstonecraft, argued that women needed to be educated for self-support and to fulfill their duties as mothers. The American Revolution intensified these concerns: Were women qualified to raise their children with the citizenship ideals suitable for a republic? Early in the nineteenth century, in response to these concerns, academies and primary schools began admitting white girls. The ideology of republican motherhood, linking domesticity to patriotism, set a pattern for the relationship between women and schooling: Access came more easily when proponents argued that female education would enhance performance of domestic roles, whether traditional or newly defined.

In the nineteenth century, industrialization and urbanization eroded the household economy. Daughters had less to occupy them before marriage and, after marriage, increasingly found themselves isolated in their homes while men worked for wages elsewhere. No longer household producers, women's chief domestic tasks became housekeeping and mothering. During the antebellum era, religious leaders, novelists, educators, and publicists, male and female, promoted and sentimentalized women's role in the home. This "cult of domesticity," confining though it was, opened new educational opportunities for women. Academies, normal

Figure 19. Freedmen's Bureau
Money from the federally funded Freedmen's Bureau went to basic literacy programs as well as to African American schools and universities. Used by permission of Corbis-Bettmann.

schools, a small number of coeducational public high schools, and even some colleges were established for or admitted females, on the ground that women needed advanced education to perform their duties. Furthermore, educators and journalists such as Horace Mann, Catharine Beecher, Emma Willard, Mary Lyon, and Sarah Josepha Hale argued that women's innately nurturing and spiritual qualities made them the repositories of important social values at a time when men had abandoned religion and culture in pursuit of wealth. Teaching became an unmarried woman's profession in the mid-nineteenth century partly because it was viewed as an extension of mothering and partly because women could be paid less than men. Although the Declaration of Sentiments issued in 1848 by the women's rights convention at Seneca Falls, New York, specifically mentioned lack of schooling as a grievance, most women's educators vehemently denied any connections to feminism. They insisted, instead, that women's education led only to happier homes and cultivated motherhood.

Barred by law from formal education before Emancipation, freed black women in the South attended elementary schools established by the Freedmen's Bureau and by various missionary societies after the Civil War. At the turn of the century, the newly reconstituted state governments took over most of these schools, administering them as segregated institutions until the 1960s and beyond. Southern states established some segregated public higher education for blacks, but missionaries, northern philanthropists, and African American communities worked together, making available a higher quality and wider range of institutions. At these institutes, normal schools, and colleges, black women studied the liberal arts, education, nursing, social work, home economics, and agriculture. Through relying heavily on white faculty and being conservative in their social philosophy, such schools created a black middle class. With the exception of Spelman College in Atlanta and Bennett College and Scotia Seminary in North Carolina, black schools and colleges were coeducational. In the North, black children had attended segregated elementary schools since the early nineteenth century, when northern states freed their slaves. While some whites argued for integrated schooling, attempts to provide even segregated higher education for blacks met with violence. A few black men and women attended places such as Oberlin and Bowdoin Colleges before the Civil War; in the late nineteenth century, small numbers of blacks attended northern universities and colleges.

Between 1860 and 1890, many new state universities and a number of private institutions offered access to women students, while women's colleges were established, mostly in the East and the South. Although public debate raged throughout this period about the desirability of a woman's obtaining a "man's" education, parents and daughters looked to the B.A. degree as a means of self-support, of providing entry into a specific occupation, or of satisfying deeply felt needs for self-improvement and intellectual stimulation. Although educators and other writers continued to rationalize women's higher education as enhancing domesticity, a significant number of the first generation of college women (1870–1890) never married at all; those who did had small families. Some graduates distinguished themselves in education and literature, while others entered medicine, academics, science, law, and founded the social work profession. In the 1890s, graduate education became available to American women at state universities and at private institutions such as Chicago, Stanford, and Yale. Those following the more traditional life pattern of marriage and child rearing or staying home to care for parents often engaged in a wide range of civic, cultural, intellectual, and reform activities.

During the Progressive Era (1890–1920), numbers of women attending college grew until, in 1920, they constituted 47.3 percent of all undergraduates. Beginning in the 1910s and 1920s, some colleges instituted quotas for women students and/or Jewish and Catholic students. These did not disappear until after World War II, and in some cases, not until the 1970s. Those fearing careerism and low birthrates among college women argued for domestic science courses. In addition, some social reformers and feminists felt that the chief task lying ahead for educated women was the rationalization of housekeeping and the reformation of home, family, and community; to these ends they, too, promoted a home economics curriculum. Although women's liberal arts colleges rarely instituted such courses, state and private universities and black colleges frequently did so. It should be noted, however, that home economics majors normally expected their studies to lead to careers in nutrition, chemistry, institutional management, or home economics education; few women students regarded them as preparation for domestic life. Settlement workers in urban areas taught home economics courses to immigrant women, hoping to instill standards of middle-class American housekeeping. Similarly, the government and missionary societies set up boarding schools in the West, removing Native American girls from their families to teach them middle-class domesticity. As the twentieth-century high school became a mass institution, attended by more girls than boys, proponents of vocational and life adjustment education made sure that public schools offered home economics.

Tension between family and school continued to characterize American women's education in the mid-twentieth century. While women went to elementary and secondary schools in numbers matching or exceeding men, their attendance at college, graduate, and professional schools and their entry into prestigious and remunerative careers did not match the achievements nor the promise of the presuffrage era. By the 1930s, marriage and childbearing patterns of women college graduates resembled those of noncollege women in the general population. Many factors contributed to the fact that schooling, even advanced education, had little effect on women's social roles. The national crises of economic depression and war led to a reaffirmation of domesticity, when Americans turned to home and family as sources of social stability. Specific occupations and professions continued to bar women from obtaining the necessary training or from advancement. And finally, social science research on gender and on sexuality confirmed that the only "normal" women were heterosexual and married—mothers who shopped wisely, helped their husbands' careers, and encouraged their children's social activities.

Since the 1960s, in the context of the modern feminist movement, schooling has become a key factor in determining the course of women's lives. Women outnumber men in undergraduate education and have entered professional and graduate schools in record numbers. Formerly single-sex schools, including private high schools, colleges, service academies, and Catholic colleges, have become coeducational. Older women, with grown families, have reentered school. Curricular sexism, from elementary school textbooks to scholarly monographs, has come under attack. Women's studies research examines the nature and structure of gender roles. Legislation and judicial decisions have asserted women's rights to educational access, equal treatment within schools, and freedom from sexual harassment. Yet the classic tension remains. In 1992, however, the American Association of University Women (AAUW) published its report "How Schools Shortchange Girls," which observed that females are more likely to be ignored in the classroom than boys, that reports of sexual harassment are on the rise, and that females are increasingly less likely to pursue studies in science. Although awareness of sex discrimination has been raised, much needs to be done before this translates into truly equal learning environments in the schools. *(See also: American Association of University Women; Coeducation; Female Academies; Higher Education; Higher Education for Southern Women; Home Economics; Republican Motherhood; Women's Studies)*

—**Lynn D. Gordon**

Further Reading

Cuthbert, Marion V. *Education and Marginality: The Negro Woman College Graduate.* Ph.D. diss., Columbia University, 1942. Reprint, New York: Garland, 1987.

Fass, Paula S. *Outside In: Minorities and the Transformation of American Education.* New York: Oxford University Press, 1989.

Friedan, Betty. *The Feminine Mystique.* New York: Norton, 1963.

Gordon, Lynn D. *Gender and Higher Education in the Progressive Era.* New Haven, CT: Yale University Press, 1990.

———. "Race, Class, and the Bonds of Womanhood at Spelman Seminary," *History of Higher Education Annual 9* (1990): 7-32.

Holland, Dorothy, and Margaret Eisenhart. *Educated in Romance: Women, Achievement, and College Culture.* Chicago: University of Chicago Press, 1990.

Horowitz, Helen Lefkowitz. *Alma Mater: Design and Experience in the Women's Colleges from their Nineteenth-Century Beginnings to the 1950s.* New York: Knopf, 1984.

Kerber, Linda K. *Women of the Republic.* Chapel Hill: University of North Carolina Press, 1980.

Komarrovsky, Mirra. *Women in College.* New York: Basic Books, 1985.

Rossiter, Margaret. *Women Scientists in America.* Baltimore: Johns Hopkins University Press, 1982.

Rury, John. *Education and Women's Work: Female Schooling and Division of Labor in Urban America.* Albany: State University of New York Press, 1991.

Sklar, Kathryn Kish. *Catharine Beecher.* New Haven, CT: Yale University Press, 1973.

Solomon, Barbara Miller. *In the Company of Educated Women.* New Haven, CT: Yale University Press, 1985.

Woody, Thomas. *A History of Women's Education in the U.S.,* 2 vols. New York: Science Press, 1929.

❧ Elizabethton, Tennessee, Strike of 1929

The Elizabethton, Tennessee, Strike of 1929 was a pivotal event in southern women's labor history. It began on March 12 when workers in the German-owned American Glazstoff and American Bembers rayon plants walked off their jobs in protest against low wages and formed a local of the United Textile Workers (UTW-AFL). The conflict engulfed the whole county and set off a wave of strikes throughout the southern textile industry, signaling the beginning of an era of labor turbulence that peaked in the 1930s but lasted until after World War II.

Women, most of whom were farmers' daughters who commuted to work from their hillside homes, made up approximately 37 percent of the town's 3,200 rayon workers. These women played highly visible roles in the conflict, marching through the streets draped in American flags, blocking mountain roads, and teasing and cursing the guardsmen. When arrested and brought to trial, they neither denied their actions nor curbed their provocations.

Opponents equated women's militancy with sexual misbehavior. But this attempt to discredit the strike with insinuations of promiscuity or prostitution had little effect on the union's rural supporters, who subscribed to a sexual ethic at odds with the values of the companies' backers among the town's middle class. Female strikers adapted rural customs of premarital sex, cohabitation, and early marriage to the new erotic opportunities of working-class life. The townspeople, by contrast, sought to define themselves through privacy, domesticity, and female chastity. Expressing those differences through dress and gesture, the women of Elizabethton devised a highly effective gender- and class-based protest style.

They also symbolized, through their actions, a transitional moment in the history of the southern mountains. On the one hand, their activities harked back to preindustrial rebellions that mobilized heterogeneous coalitions of the poor, relied on crowd action, and provided ample opportunity for female participation. On the other hand, young women were bellwethers of modernity; dressed in the latest store-bought fashions and reveling in new forms of commercialized pleasure, they signaled their identity as "new women" of the 1920s and laid claim to the material promise of post-World War I American life.

Neither militancy nor solidarity, however, could make up for the weakness of the UTW or prevail against the combined power of the corporations and the state. On May 26, six weeks after the first walkout, the union negotiated a settlement that made virtually no concessions to the workers and did nothing to prevent the blacklisting of strike leaders. The Elizabethton strike nevertheless had significant consequences. The parent companies recalled an unpopular manager, installed plant council and welfare systems, and raised wages. Oral history interviews, moreover, reveal that for some participants there were other, less tangible rewards: a feeling of empowerment and a belief that they had made history and that subsequent generations benefited from what they had done. *(See also: American Federation of Labor; New Woman; Textiles: North and South; Unions)*

—Jacquelyn Dowd Hall

Further Reading

Hall, Jacquelyn Dowd. "Disorderly Women: Gender and Labor Militancy in the Appalachian South," *Journal of American History* 73 (September 1986): 354-82.

Hall, Jacquelyn Dowd, James Leloudis, Robert Korstad, Mary Murphy, Lu Ann Jones, and Christopher B. Daly. *Like a Family: The Making of a Southern Cotton Mill World.* Chapel Hill: University of North Carolina Press, 1987.

Hodges, James. "Challenge to the New South: The Great Strike in Elizabethton, Tennessee, 1929," *Tennessee Historical Quarterly* 23 (December 1964): 343-57.

Holly, John F. "Elizabethton, Tennessee: A Case Study of Industrialization." Ph.D. diss., Clark University, 1949.

Tippett, Tom. *When Southern Labor Stirs.* New York: Jonathan Cape & Harrison Smith, 1931.

❧ Emery, Sarah Elizabeth Van de Vort (1838–1895)

Sarah Van de Vort Emery was born in Phelps, New York, and supported third-party politics as a writer, speaker, and campaigner in Michigan, where she had moved in 1866 to teach school. In 1869, she married Wesley Emery, a widower with a three-year-old, who shared her concern for economic and social reform. The Emerys' one daughter, Effie, who died in childhood, was born in 1874.

Emery was a state delegate and speaker to the conventions of the national Greenback Party, the Union Labor Party, the National Farmers' Alliance, and the Populist Party. She was also active in the Knights of Labor and the Woman's Christian Temperance Union. She spent fifteen years as the superintendent of the Lansing Universalist Sunday School and worked for woman suffrage. In 1886, she argued for woman suffrage at both the Democratic Party and Prohibition Party state conventions. Five years later, she campaigned for municipal suffrage before a state legislative committee.

Emery was best known among her contemporaries by her writing. She edited *Cornerstone,* a reform newspaper with a focus on woman suffrage, and wrote two popular economic tracts—*Seven Financial Conspiracies Which Have Enslaved the American People* and *Imperialism in America.* Emery was also an associate editor for the *New Forum,* a national Populist Party newspaper. Wesley Emery published his wife's newspaper and books. *Seven Financial Conspiracies,* first published in 1887, was reprinted in 1888, revised in 1891 and 1892, and reprinted again in 1894. It sold 400,000 copies, was translated into several languages, and was used extensively in Populist congressional and presidential campaigns. The book explained the financial legislation following the Civil War and argued that this legislation had ruined farmers and laborers alike while increasing the wealth of bankers and politicians. Poor health forced Emery to retire from lecturing and writing. She died of cancer at the age of fifty-seven in 1895. *(See also: National Farmers' Alliance; Populist Party)*

—MaryJo Wagner

Further Reading

Adams, Pauline, and Emma S. Thornton. *A Populist Assault: Sarah E. Van De Vort Emery on American Democracy, 1862–1895.* Bowling Green, OH: Bowling Green State University Popular Press, 1982.

Bliss, William D. P., ed. *Encyclopedia of Social Reform.* New York: Funk & Wagnalls, 1897.

Diggs, Annie L. "Women in the Alliance Movement," *Arena* 6 (July 1892): 161-79.

Ostler, Jeffrey. "The Rhetoric of Conspiracy and the Formation of Kansas Populism," *Agricultural History* 69 (Winter 1995): 1-27.

☙ Episcopal Women

The Episcopal Church separated from the Church of England in 1789, producing an American denomination that combined Catholic liturgical practices with a Protestant emphasis on text and conscience. Episcopal women such as Mary Simkhovitch, an early director of Greenwich House Settlement in New York City; Frances Perkins, Secretary of Labor; and Eleanor Roosevelt are known for their inner independence, which flourished within a church whose polity and sacramental leadership remained thoroughly patriarchal until the 1970s.

During the 1800s, women joined prayer and mothers' societies as well as charitable associations (often interdenominational) to promote education, evangelism, and philanthropy. In addition, many a local church depended on its own female organization—for example, the Ladies' Circle of Industry, Immanuel Church, Bellows Falls, Vermont—for funds to repair the roof and provide community benevolence.

In 1872, local parish "women's societies" associated in a national Woman's Auxiliary through the vision and leadership of Mary Emery Twing and Julia Chester Emery. It coordinated the major provision of money and supplies for foreign and domestic missions and in 1889 created a separate fund for new projects, the United Thank Offering. But female participation in the church's national structure remained separate, with women meeting in their own triennial gatherings alongside the General Convention involving bishops, clergy, and laymen.

Episcopal women such as Sarah Josepha Hale and Emma Willard promoted religion in their public writings, as did Alice B. Haven in her Sunday school stories and Dorothy Ann Thrupp in her 1835 hymn, "Savior, Like a Shepherd Lead Us." Drawn by its liturgical Protestantism, Harriet Beecher Stowe became an Episcopalian in mid-life. Later in the century, small, special-purpose organizations such as the Church Periodical Club, Daughters of the King, Girls Friendly Society, and sisterhoods emerged; the role of deaconness was officially recognized in 1889. The first "traditional" religious order, followed by many others, was the Community of St. Mary in Austin, Texas.

Individual Episcopalians expressed their spirituality as mothers and wives, career volunteers, educators, and professional service workers. In the twentieth century, training schools for directors of religious education, deaconesses, and missionaries prefigured the opening of seminary education to women in the 1960s. Because of many women's extensive experience on civic commissions and as trustees or as professionals, lay leadership in local churches expanded with the women's movement. Women were finally seated as deputies in the General Convention of 1970.

The Episcopal Church Women, the contemporary version of the Woman's Auxiliary, gradually came to support ordination for their sisters. New, single-issue groups for specific advocacy evolved in the 1970s and 1980s: ABIL (Asian, Black, Indian-Indigenous, and Latina Women of the Episcopal Church), the Episcopal Women's Caucus (women's ordination and equal participation), the Episcopal Women's History Project, and Integrity (homosexual and lesbian issues). The one organization found in every parish, the Altar Guild, is usually all female.

In 1974, fifteen women were made priests in an "irregular ordination." Subsequent canon law change in 1976 generated some resistance, but approximately two thousand women have since become ordained leaders. One-quarter are parish rectors or vicars, the rest chaplains, teachers, and assistants. When an African American, Barbara Harris, was consecrated suffragan bishop in Boston in 1989, the ultimate institutional barrier fell. Since then, eight dioceses have elected women bishops; in 1994, Martha Horne became the first woman Dean of an Episcopal Seminary (Virginia). The triennially convened policy-making body of the denomination, the General Convention, now has a laywoman as elected head of its House of Deputies, and the House of Bishops has its first woman secretary, the Right Reverend Mary Adelia McLeod, Bishop of Vermont. A late twentieth-century overview of Episcopal women's history documents a changed horizon for the twenty-first century. *(See also: Benevolence; Christianity; Religion)*

—**Joanna Bowen Gillespie**

Further Reading

Darling, Pamela W. *New Wine: The Story of Women Transforming Leadership and Power in the Episcopal Church.* Cambridge, MA: Cowley, 1994.

Deaconess Papers Collection, St. Mary Community. National Archives of the Episcopal Church. Episcopal Theological Seminary of the Southwest, Austin, TX.

Donovan, Mary S. *A Different Call: Women's Ministries in the Episcopal Church, 1850–1920.* Wilton, CT: Morehouse Barlow, 1986.

———. *Women Priests in the Episcopal Church: Experience of the First Decade.* Cincinnati, OH: Forward Movement Publications, 1988.

Fulk, Anne Bass. *A Short History of the Triennial Meetings of the Women of the Episcopal.* Little Rock, AR: Democrat Printing and Lithographing, 1985.

Gillespie, Joanna B. *Women Speak of God, Congregations and Change.* Valley Forge, PA: Trinity Press International, 1995.

Gundersen, Joan R. "The Non-Institutional Church: The Religious Role of Women in Eighteenth-Century Virginia," *Historical Magazine of the Protestant Episcopal Church* 51 (December 1982): 347-57.

———. "Parallel Churches? Women and the Episcopal Church, 1850–1980," *Mid-America* 69 (April/July 1987): 88-97.

Prelinger, Catherine M., ed. *Episcopal Women: Gender, Spirituality, and Commitment in an American Mainline Denomination.* New York: Oxford University Press, 1992.

❧ Equal Employment Opportunity Commission (EEOC)

The Equal Employment Opportunity Commission (EEOC) enforces Title VII of the Civil Rights Act of 1964, which prohibits discrimination in employment on the basis of race, color, religion, national origin, or sex. Adding sex to the bill was actually a ploy by an opponent, Virginia representative Howard W. Smith, who hoped it would help defeat the proposed bill. Michigan representative Martha Griffiths championed the change, however, and it remained in the act when it became law. The EEOC, composed of five members appointed by the president with Senate approval, at first had only the power to investigate and persuade as it attempted to settle disputes arising from allegations of discrimination.

Several minority groups sought to make use of the limited enforcement resources allocated to the EEOC, with the net result that the commission generally ignored the inclusion of the word *sex* in Title VII. The National Organization for Women (NOW) was formed in 1966 partly to pressure the EEOC to pay more attention to women. In 1967, Executive Order 11375 extended Title VII to prohibit discrimination by holders of federal contracts, who then employed about one-third of the labor force in the United States. And by 1969, court decisions finding protective state laws that limited the number of hours a woman could work per week or the weight she could lift on the job to be illegal under Title VII nudged the EEOC into declaring all such state legislation invalid. Finally, in 1972, the EEOC acquired some real teeth against discrimination when it was given the option of taking violators to court.

The EEOC has effected some important settlements, resulting in substantial gains for women; in 1973, for example, an out-of-court settlement between the American Telegraph and Telephone Company and the government resulted in over $38 million in back pay (of an estimated $3.5 billion owed) awarded to women employees who were the victims of job discrimination. In 1998, Mitsubishi Motors Corporation settled a class action lawsuit brought by the EEOC, agreeing to pay $34 million, the highest dollar amount ever granted in a sexual harassment settlement.

There is little question, however, that the inclusion of sex in Title VII has laid the groundwork for what can be profoundly significant changes in the employment structure in favor of women. Especially in the private sector, the twentieth-century American workplace saw many positive effects of the EEOC's intervention. The agency's own reputation, however, was dealt a serious blow in 1991 when law professor Anita Hill testified before the Senate that, while an employee at the EEOC, her supervisor, Clarence Thomas, had sexually harassed her.

Although the EEOC represents a national endorsement of equal opportunity in both private and public employment, from the beginning, it has been short of both funds and staff and only occasionally interested in the plight of women. Under the Reagan administration, the EEOC's effectiveness was crippled by its drastically cut budget and by the appointment of commissioners who proved hostile to the congressionally defined purpose of the commission. In the mid-1990s, Republican congressional leaders maintained a constant opposition to funding for the EEOC to limit its authority to use testers to gather data on discriminatory housing and hiring practices. By restricting allocations to bring the outstanding 6,500 cases in progress to closure, Congress barred the agency's ability to undertake new cases. Simultaneously, Supreme Court decisions such as *Adarand v. Pena* (1995) developed the increasingly stringent requirement that governmental agencies such as the EEOC must establish compelling governmental interest to redress proven instances of past discrimination in federal agencies' antidiscrimination policies.

Even while enjoying many of the benefits of prior EEOC influence that has changed the culture of the American workplace, women and men in the 1990s have seen the

EEOC suffer in its ability to handle complaints. Recent studies of the EEOC's effectiveness have resulted in harsh criticism of the agency, which receives in excess of 100,000 complaints each year and is ill staffed to investigate each one. Forced to eliminate a majority of cases with a swift and impersonal process of elimination, the EEOC has acquired the reputation of an ineffective bureaucracy. Critics call for a 21st-century EEOC overhaul that would include better caseload management and an increase in agency resources.

The EEOC's 1997 to 2002 strategic plan acknowledges the agency's past difficulties and seeks to improve its effectiveness and repair its relationships with state and local agencies. The agency is in the process of reviewing its complaint operations. The 1999 annual performance plan outlines specific objectives for achieving the agency's two general goals: (a) to promote equal opportunity in employment by enforcing the federal civil rights employment laws through administrative and judicial action and (b) to promote equal opportunity in employment by enforcing the federal civil rights employment laws through education and technical assistance. Future performance evaluations will reveal whether the EEOC will effectuate changes and regain its former strength as an agent of positive societal change. *(See also: Civil Rights Act of 1964; National Organization for Women)*

—**Megan E. Hayes**

Further Reading

Adarand v. Pena, 115 S.Ct. 2097 (1995).
Bergmann, Barbara R. *The Economic Emergence of Women.* New York: Basic Books, 1986.
Freeman, Jo. *The Politics of Women's Liberation,* pp. 177-90. New York: David McKay, 1975.
Hill, Anita. *Speaking Truth to Power.* New York: Doubleday, 1997.
Kahn, Wendy, and Joy Ann Grune. "Pay Equity: Beyond Equal Pay for Equal Work." In *Women, Power and Policy,* edited by Ellen Boneparth, 75-89. New York: Pergamon, 1982.
Power, Marilyn. "Falling through the Safety Net: Women, Economic Crisis, and Reaganomics," *Feminist Studies* 10 (1984): 31-58.
http://www.eeoc.gov [EEOC Website]
http://www.feminist.org [The Feminist Majority Online]

∾ Equality Day

Equality Day commemorates the date of the ratification of the Nineteenth Amendment on August 26, 1920. Although there is no national holiday to memorialize the passage of woman suffrage, Equality Day has been celebrated informally by various women's groups at the national, state, and local chapter level since the 1920s. After 1972, Equality Day was used by the National Organization for Women, the American Association of University Women, and other national women's organizations as a symbolic occasion around which to rally support for contemporary women's issues, especially the effort to ratify the Equal Rights Amendment, as well as to pay homage to the suffragists whose long struggle won women the vote. *(See also: Equal*

Rights Amendment; Nineteenth Amendment to the U.S. Constitution; Suffrage)

—**Angela M. Howard**

Further Reading

Eisler, Riane Tennenhaus. *The Equal Rights Handbook.* New York: Avon, 1978.
Whitney, Sharon. *The Equal Rights Amendment: The History and the Movement.* New York: Watts, 1984.

∾ Equal Pay Act of 1963

The Equal Pay Act of 1963 (29 U.S.C. 201 et seq.) was a result of the recommendations of President John F. Kennedy's Commission on the Status of Women. The first national legislation for women's employment since the Progressive Era, this law requires employers to pay their male and female employees the same wages when both men and women perform jobs that entail equal skill, effort, and responsibility and that are carried out under similar working conditions. In addition, it prohibits labor unions from causing or trying to cause an employer to violate this law, and it forbids employers to lower the wages of one sex in order to come into compliance with the law. There are, however, exceptions to the equal-pay requirement; that is, employers may justifiably pay their male and female employees different wages if those wages are determined by (a) a seniority system, (b) a merit system, (c) "a system which measures earnings by quantity or quality of production," or (d) "a differential based on any other factor other than sex."

Because the Equal Pay Act is an amendment to the Fair Labor Standards Act of 1938, the U.S. Labor Department is responsible for its enforcement. Department officials are charged with making routine checks for violations and with investigating individual complaints against specific employers. Although there has been some success under the act in recovering wages for underpaid female employees, several factors have worked against its serving as an effective means of closing the male-female wage gap. One problem stems from the wording of the law itself. In providing a limited but complex definition of wage discrimination, the act allows the courts to arrive at varying, and frequently contradictory, assessments of what constitutes equal skill, effort, and responsibility.

In addition, the Equal Pay Act does not directly address the problem of occupational sex segregation in which men and women are concentrated in different jobs typically labeled "men's work" and "women's work." Because traditional female occupations historically have been undervalued in the United States, women who hold such positions are generally paid less than men, even when their jobs require higher qualifications and entail greater responsibilities. In the 1970s, women acted to rectify this problem by bringing comparable-worth suits against their employers. Comparable worth, later termed *sex equity,* extends the principle of

Figure 20. ERA
A family of four generations participates in an Illinois rally for the ratification of the Equal Rights Amendment. Used by permission of Corbis-Bettmann.

"equal pay for equal work" by requiring equal pay for jobs of similar value. In 1985, women workers won comparable-worth suits in six states, indicating the potential of this concept as an important supplement to Equal Pay Act litigation. However, hostility to the concept from the New Right and conservatives generally and from the Reagan administration particularly obstructed its application at the federal level. *(See also: President's Commission on the Status of Women; Sex Equity/Comparable Worth; Sexual Division of Labor; Wages; Women's Work: Nineteenth Century)*

—**Claire M. Renzetti**

Further Reading

England, P. *Comparable Worth: Theories and Evidence.* New York: Aldine de Gruyter, 1992.

Jacobs, J. A., ed., *Gender Inequality at Work.* Thousand Oaks, CA: Sage, 1995.

Lindgren, J. R., and N. Traub. *The Law of Sexual Discrimination.* Minneapolis, MN: West, 1993.

Rhoads, S. E. *Incomparable Worth.* New York: Cambridge University Press, 1994.

ஓ Equal Rights Amendment (ERA)

The struggle to ensure women's equality under the supreme law of the land through a federal amendment to the U.S. Constitution began soon after the ratification of the Nineteenth Amendment, which gave women the vote. The name Equal Rights Amendment (ERA) was first used in the 1870s on the first federal woman suffrage bill, which was voted down in 1878. Alice Paul, leader of the National Woman's Party, lobbied Congress in 1923 for an equal rights amendment to eradicate discrimination on the basis of sex in existing federal, state, and local laws. Paul's originally proposed amendment read, "Men and women shall have equal rights throughout the United States and every place to its jurisdiction." Nineteen subsequent Congresses refused to send this amendment to the states for ratification.

During the 1920s, former suffragists and social feminists opposed the concept of an equal rights amendment, on the grounds that women's equality under the law would have threatened the pre-World War I special-protection legislation that had been gained for women workers during the Progressive Era. Nor did the ERA receive attention or significant support during the New Deal or World War II eras. The undaunted Alice Paul and the National Woman's Party persevered. Finally, in 1967, the National Organization for Women responded to Paul's persuasion with an endorsement of a federal Equal Rights Amendment, thus initiating a renewed campaign invigorated by the support of the modern women's rights movement.

In 1972, the momentum of the civil rights movement and the astute politicking of Michigan representative Martha Griffiths and others induced Congress to approve an equal rights amendment, which was then sent to the states with a seven-year deadline for ratification. Also known as the Alice Paul Amendment, the ERA now read, "Equality of Rights shall not be denied or abridged by the United States or any state on account of sex." The economic impact of an increased number of single and married women in the paid labor force made visible the economic discrimination against women, while the issues of equality and justice that had been raised by the political reform movements of the 1960s heightened public awareness of the shameful lack of legal, social, political, and economic rights for American women.

By 1973, thirty of the thirty-eight states needed to ratify this Equal Rights Amendment had done so. However, by the mid-1970s, no new states had entered the ratified column and the opposition to the ERA had organized and gathered strength. The success of the International Women's Year national conference in Houston in 1977 focused mainstream support for a national agenda to address women's issues: Its National Plan of Action included support of ERA ratification.

The ERA, however, still lacked three of the required thirty-eight states, and the opposition, although a minority, had been successful in raising doubts about the legal and social consequences of the ERA. The general support of the ERA influenced Congress to grant an unprecedented extension of the original ratification deadline to June 30, 1982. But by the mid-1980s, the instability of the post-Vietnam economy fueled a resurgence of political fundamentalism reminiscent of the conservative political backlash of the 1920s. Ultimately, a handful of state legislators in only three or four states, representing a minority opinion within their own states as well as a minority opinion within the nation, thwarted the ratification of the ERA by the June 1982 deadline.

The ERA has been reintroduced into the U.S. House of Representatives annually and unsuccessfully since November 1983. By the mid-1990s, the National Organization for Women began to apply the information it had gathered on the impact of state ERAs and proposed expanding the concept of constitutional equality to specify inclusion of constitutional protection beyond the categories of sex and gender, to race, ethnicity, national origin, and color as well as sexual orientation, marital status, indigence, age, and disability. This document, developed at the 1995 National NOW Conference, became the working draft of the Constitutional Equality Amendment (CEA). *(See also: Antifeminism; National Woman's Party; Paul, Alice; Right-Wing Political Movements; Schlafly, Phyllis MacAlpin; Social Feminism; Women's Rights Movements: Nineteenth and Twentieth Centuries)*

—**Angela M. Howard**

Further Reading
Becker, Susan D. *The Origins of the Equal Rights Amendment.* Westport, CT: Greenwood, 1982.

Eisler, Riane Tennenhaus. *The Equal Rights Handbook: What ERA Means to Your Life, Your Rights, and the Future.* New York: Avon, 1978.

Gager, Nancy, ed. *Women's Rights Almanac.* New York: Harper Colophon, 1974.

Mathews, Donald G., and Jane S. DeHart. *Sex, Gender, and the Politics of ERA: A State and the Nation.* New York: Oxford University Press, 1992.

Steiner, Gilbert Y. *Constitutional Inequality: The Political Fortunes of the Equal Rights Amendment.* Washington, DC: Brookings Institution, 1985.

Whitney, Sharon. *The Equal Rights Amendment: The History and the Movement.* New York: Franklin Watts, 1984.

Equal Rights Association

In January 1866, Elizabeth Cady Stanton and Susan B. Anthony proposed a union of the American Anti-Slavery Society and their Women's Rights Society under the name Equal Rights Association. The intended objective of the organization was to work for the citizenship of both women and Negro men. Although this union had the approval of a number of influential leaders—including Horace Greeley, Theodore Tilton, Charles Sumner, and Thaddeus Stevens—the president of the Anti-Slavery Society, Wendell Phillips,

was cool to the idea, and as a consequence, at its May 1866 annual convention, the society did not take action on the resolution. However, the Women's Rights Society, at its annual convention in May 1866, did unanimously adopt a change in its name to the Equal Rights Association.

For the next three years, members of the association argued bitterly among themselves over their goals and tactics. During this time, certain factions within the association assailed Stanton and Anthony for threatening to rob the "Negro of his hour" by their impolitic linking of woman's and Negros' rights. At the third annual convention, in 1869, abolitionist and woman's rights advocate Ernestine Rose stated that one-half of the objective of the Equal Rights Association had been achieved with the ratification of the Fourteenth Amendment and congressional approval of the Fifteenth Amendment. Therefore, she proposed that the name of the organization be changed to the National Woman Suffrage Association. Other delegates promptly protested that this motion was out of order. Stanton, as presiding officer, agreed that the constitutional bylaws did not allow such a name change without a three-month notice. Immediately following the meeting, however, Stanton and Anthony—feeling that the male leadership in the association had betrayed women's interests—organized the National Woman Suffrage Association for women only. Several months later, the more conservative women within the Equal Rights Association organized the rival American Woman Suffrage Association. Thus, the Equal Rights Association served as a transitional organization for the woman's rights movement, as its supporters transferred their focus from the issues of abolition to a primary concern for woman suffrage. *(See also: American Woman Suffrage Association; Anthony, Susan B.; National Woman Suffrage Association; Stanton, Elizabeth Cady; Suffrage)*

—**Terry D. Bilhartz**

Further Reading
Du Bois, Ellen. *Feminism and Suffrage: The Emergence of an Independent Women's Movement in America, 1848–1869.* Ithaca, NY: Cornell University Press, 1978.

Harper, Ida Husted. *The Life and Work of Susan B. Anthony,* 3 vols. Indianapolis, IN: Bowen-Merrill, 1898–1908. Reprint, Salem, NH: Ayer, 1983.

Stanton, Elizabeth Cady, Susan B. Anthony, and Matilda Joslyn Gage, eds. *The History of Woman Suffrage.* Vol. 2. Rochester, NY: n.p., 1881.

Equity Courts

In early America, legal restrictions on women were often mitigated by equity courts, which used common sense rather than common law in making judgments. Equity jurisprudence recognized and enforced antenuptial agreements, or marriage settlements, which circumvented coverture and preserved for a woman some control over the property she brought to a marriage. It also allowed her to bequeath her property as she wished. However, few women took advantage of marriage settlements, which were seen as a device for the wealthy or as evidence of distrust. The influence of equity courts eroded slowly and sporadically during the early nineteenth century and was superseded after the 1840s by state married women's property acts that codified an expanding definition of married women's legal rights. *(See also: Antenuptial Agreements; Common Law; Coverture; Married Women's Property Acts)*

—**Barbara E. Lacey**

Further Reading

Norton, Mary Beth. "The Evolution of White Women's Experience in Early America," *American Historical Review* 89 (June 1984): 593-619.

～ Erdrich, Louise (b. 1954)

Born on June 7 to Ralph Louis and Rita Joanne (Gourneau) Erdrich in Little Falls, Minnesota, Louise Erdrich was raised in Wahpeton, North Dakota. Of mixed blood (her father was German-American and her mother was Turtle Mountain Chippewa), she spent a good deal of her childhood visiting her mother's family on the reservation. Erdrich received a B.A. from Dartmouth College in English and creative writing in 1976. While a student, she was awarded the Academy of American Poets Prize (1975). After serving as a visiting poet and teacher for the North Dakota Arts Council, she received a fellowship to Johns Hopkins University, where she received an M.A. degree in the Writing Program in 1979. Before becoming a visiting fellow at Dartmouth College in 1981, Erdrich was an editor of *The Circle,* a Native American newspaper published in Boston, and was a textbook writer for Charles Merrill Company. She married Michael Dorris, then chair of the Department of Native American Studies at Dartmouth, in 1981.

Erdrich started as a poet, then became a short-story writer and novelist. Her poems and short stories have appeared in numerous magazines and journals. With the help of her husband, she turned a collection of short stories into her first novel, *Love Medicine,* in 1984. Erdrich and Dorris enjoyed a unique collaborative effort: Until his suicide on April 11, 1997, they wrote together on every work, choosing which should be published under her name and which should be published under his according to their own personal criteria. Not until the publication of *The Crown of Columbus* (1991) did they publish a book using both of their names. Native American oral tradition and storytelling are major influences on her writing, but Native Americans and their culture are not the only topics on which she writes. Being of mixed blood, Erdrich sees with two eyes, and she writes from both of these perspectives.

Erdrich has been the recipient of many awards, including the Nelson Algren Fiction Award (1982), a National Endowment for the Arts Fellowship (1982), the Pushcart Prize (1983), the National Magazine Award for Fiction (1983), the PEN Syndication Fiction Project (1983 and 1984), the National Book Critics Circle Award for Best Work of Fiction (1984 and 1985), the Sue Kaufman Prize for Best Fiction from the American Academy and Institute of Arts and Letters (1984), a Guggenheim fellowship (1985), the *Los Angeles Times* Award for Fiction (1985), the American Book Award from the Before Columbus Foundation (1985), the O. Henry Prize (1987), and the Western Literary Association Award (1992).

She currently devotes her time to writing, raising her family, and advocating social causes. *(See also: Native American Women; Native American Women's Literature; Women Writers)*

—**Susan L. Rockwell**

Further Reading

Chavkin, Allan, and Nancy Feyl Chavkin. *Conversations with Louise Erdrich and Michael Dorris.* Jackson: University of Mississippi Press, 1994.

Erdrich, Louise. *The Antelope Wife.* New York: HarperFlamingo, 1998.

———. *Baptism of Desire.* New York: Harper & Row, 1989.

———. *The Beet Queen.* New York: Henry Holt, 1986.

———. *The Bingo Palace.* New York: HarperCollins, 1994.

———. *The Blue Jay's Dance: A Birth Year.* New York: HarperCollins, 1995.

———. *Imagination.* Westerville, OH: Charles Merrill, 1981.

———. *Jacklight.* New York: Holt, Rinehart & Winston, 1984.

———. *Love Medicine.* New York: Holt, Rinehart & Winston, 1984.

———. *Love Medicine.* Expanded novel. New York: Henry Holt, 1993.

———. *Tracks.* New York: Henry Holt, 1988.

Erdrich, Louise, and Michael Dorris. *The Crown of Columbus.* New York: HarperCollins, 1991.

———. *Route Two.* Northridge, CA: Lord John, 1991.

～ *Essence* (1969–)

Essence is a popular monthly magazine for black American women. Following the format of other popular women's magazines, *Essence* provides its several million readers with information on health, career, fashion and beauty, love and relationships, business and finance, and current affairs. The works of black poets and writers are regularly featured, in the tradition of other mass market black magazines such as *Negro Digest* (1942–), now titled *Black World,* and *Ebony* (1945–). The monthly readership of *Essence* is estimated at almost 5.1 million. The success of *Essence* in the competition for the black woman's market has helped move *Ebony* from its earlier preoccupation with "sex and sensation" to a more positive image of black women. While all of these mainstream black magazines remain quite traditional in their depiction of women, they do provide an important outlet for black artists and writers. They also allow black businesses to reach the black community. *(See also: Beauty Industry; Black Women; Magazines)*

—**Patricia Haire**

—**Lisa Sirmons Edwards**

Further Reading
Essence: 25 Years Celebrating Black Women, edited by Patricia M. Hinds. New York: Harry N. Abrams, 1995.
Greenburg, Jonathan, "It's a Miracle," *Forbes* 130 (December 20, 1982): 104-10.
Rottenberg, Dan. "Atop the *Ebony* Empire," *United Magazine* 30 (January 1985): 39-40, 84.

Ethnicity and Gender Roles

Historically, the experiences of women have differed dramatically among the many ethnic and racial groups that compose American society. Economic conditions, societal discrimination, and ethnic cultural values have all affected gender roles. The circumstances that led immigrants to leave their native lands for America included poverty, forced removal through enslavement or deportation, political turmoil, and religious intolerance. These circumstances profoundly influenced the conditions under which women adapted to life in the United States and the roles that they would play in American society.

For example, the intense poverty of nineteenth-century Ireland sent many single Irish women off to America in search of employment. Domestic service and factory employment were common occupations of single women in Ireland, and consequently, many Irish immigrants pursued such occupations in the United States. Poverty in Ireland had forced both men and women to postpone marriage or not to marry at all, and these patterns persisted in America and encouraged Irish-American girls to pursue careers in fields such as teaching and nursing.

Ethnic and racial discrimination has touched the lives of most immigrant groups in the United States, but no group has suffered more discrimination than black immigrants and their descendants. Brought to this country in slavery, black immigrant women and their children were compelled to assume roles in domestic and agricultural labor. Their legal status under slavery prevented black women from assuming the full responsibilities of marriage and motherhood and kept their daily lives under an owner's control. Discrimination after Emancipation made it necessary for black wives, mothers, and family heads to remain in the labor force when most other American women remained in the home.

For all ethnic groups, distinctive family values have influenced the roles that women as well as men have played within the family and in society. Italian and Hispanic immigrants, for example, have cherished the importance of mothers being at home full-time. On the other hand, economic necessity often forced these same mothers to earn wages. More than other women, Italian and Hispanic wives chose to earn wages through industrial homework, employment that allowed them to remain at home but forced them to accept the lowest of wages. Similarly, cultural values of ethnic groups encouraged or discouraged the education of women, encouraged women to respect or to challenge authority, discouraged or encouraged family planning, and

influenced women in other ways that determined when and whom they would marry and the economic roles that they would assume as daughters, wives, or mothers. *(See also: Asian American Women; Black Women; Chicana; Immigration; Jewish Women)*

—**Julia Kirk Blackwelder**

Further Reading
Blackwelder, Julia Kirk. *Now Hiring: The Feminization of Work in the United States, 1900–1995.* College Station: Texas A&M University Press, 1997.
———. *Women of the Depression: Caste and Culture in San Antonio, 1929–1939.* College Station: Texas A&M University Press, 1984.
Ewen, Elizabeth. *Immigrant Women in the Land of Dollars: Life and Culture on the Lower East Side, 1890–1925.* New York: Monthly Review, 1985.
Gabaccia, Donna R. *From the Other Side: Women, Gender, and Immigrant Life in the U.S., 1820–1990.* Bloomington: Indiana University Press, 1994.
Harzig, Christiane et al., eds. *Peasant Maids, City Women: From the European Countryside to Urban America.* Ithaca, NY: Cornell University Press, 1997.
Kessler-Harris, Alice. *Out to Work: A History of Wage-Earning Women in the United States.* New York: Oxford University Press, 1982.
McAdoo, Harriette Pipes. *Black Families.* Thousand Oaks, CA: Sage, 1997.
Mindel, Charles H., Robert W. Habenstein, and Roosevelt Wright, Jr. *Ethnic Families in America: Patterns and Variations.* Englewood Cliffs, NJ: Prentice Hall, 1998.
Pozzetta, George E., ed. *Ethnicity and Gender: The Immigrant Woman.* New York: Garland, 1991.

European Influences

The development of women's literature and feminism in the United States has been influenced by European sources from the seventeenth to the twentieth centuries. Works by Aphra Behn, Fanny Burney, Eliza Carter, Jane Austen, the Brontë sisters, and George Eliot inspired the early generations of American women writers. The women whose writings articulated the development of feminist theory in the United States since the Revolution drew on the works and words of Mary Wollstonecraft, John Stuart Mill, Auguste Comte, Ellen Key, Virginia Woolf, and Simone de Beauvoir, among others.

English and French women authors especially served as role models for the "scribbling women" in early nineteenth-century America. Sarah Josepha Hale and Lydia Maria Child drew inspiration to become writers from Mrs. Ann Radcliffe's eighteenth-century gothic novel *The Mysteries of Udolpho* (1794), and later women authors such as Louisa May Alcott, Kate Chopin, and Charlotte Perkins Gilman reassessed women's role in the tradition of George Sand's *Indiana* (1831). Struggling intellectuals such as Margaret Fuller were encouraged by the heroine of Madame de Staäl's *Corinne* (1807) to apply their analytical and scholarly powers. American feminists such as Elizabeth Cady Stanton were influenced by Wollstonecraft's arguments in her *Vindication of the Rights of Woman* (1792), as twentieth-century feminists have been called to introspection and action by the powerful and moving image of Shakespeare's sister in Woolf's *A Room of One's Own* (1929) and challenged to re-evaluate their female identity as "the other" by de Beauvoir's *The Second Sex* (1949).

Although the non-American sources that have had an impact on women's literature and feminist theory are too numerous for inclusion in this entry, the works of Wollstonecraft, de Staäl, John Stuart Mill, Woolf, and de Beauvoir outlined here have become standard references in the literature of American women's history and merit special attention.

While Mrs. Radcliffe's *Mysteries of Udolpho* redefined the gothic novel as one centered on a heroine who ultimately triumphs over danger and betrayal, Madame de Staäl's *Corinne* (1807) created a new kind of heroine, the woman genius, who served as a role model for many antebellum women writers as they established their rightful place among the literati of Victorian America. An often expurgated version of the life and works of the author herself validated the careers of these women writers and further increased de Staäl's reputation among nineteenth-century American women writers.

Of mixed heritage, de Staäl's heroine Corinne is a Florentine improvisator who draws adoring crowds to her recitals. A brilliant speaker, she also possesses abundant wisdom. Yet all of her brilliance fades away when she falls in love with a man who ultimately jilts her. Love topples this genius and in so doing sets up the prototypical plight of the great woman. Indeed, *Corinne* formed feminist ideas about human relationships for decades thereafter; it also provided inspiration for women who aspired to similar genius in the United States. Margaret Fuller, for one, tried to follow de Staäl's lead, as did Anna Jameson in Great Britain.

De Staäl (1766–1817) was the daughter of Jacques Necker, famous banker and minister during the French Revolution, and the former Suzanne Curchod, who conducted a successful literary salon and claimed to have educated her only child, Germaine, "like a boy." Married to Swedish diplomat Staäl-Holstein at an early age, de Sta,l favored the French revolutionary cause until it grew too radical but remained nonetheless an advocate of reform and liberty. Exiled by Napoleon at the height of his power, she traveled to the German states, to Italy, and through the Hapsburg Empire in search of roots and inspiration. In fact, she found both, although Paris remained her desideratum. Travels inspired her greatest works, *Corinne* and *De l'Allemagne* (1813), which changed the course of European cultural life, while her lucid *Considerations on the French Revolution* (1818) gave one of the first clear accounts of that event.

While de Staäl's romantic fiction offered inspiration to individual women in their search for artistic identity, the political and feminist commentary of Wollstonecraft, Mill, Woolf, and de Beauvoir informed and challenged American feminists in their development of feminist theory and feminist literary criticism. In *A Vindication of the Rights of Woman* (1792), Mary Wollstonecraft (1759–1797) argued that women's intellectual and moral deficiencies were a result of unequal education. If women were educated and acknowledged to have an independent existence as moral beings, Wollstonecraft claimed, they would be capable of attaining the level of virtue requisite for participation in the duties of the state. Most contemporary liberal theorists saw civic virtue as an exclusively male quality; Wollstonecraft, however, envisioned a society in which rational mothers, too, could be admitted to an identity in the eyes of the state.

Wollstonecraft applied the Enlightenment tenets of liberal individualism popular among her circle of British and Parisian intellectuals to the problems of middle-class womanhood. Although her stated goal in *A Vindication* was to help women gain power over themselves, she framed both the content and form of her argument for the educated male reader. She asked men to break women's chains of dependence, promising that as women became more rational and virtuous, they would make better companions as wives, daughters, and mothers.

Her career as a liberal theorist began in 1790 with *A Vindication of the Rights of Man,* the first published response to Edmund Burke's classic statement of political conservatism, *Reflections on the Revolution in France* (1790). While Wollstonecraft had written *Thoughts on the Education of Daughters* in 1787, her best-known work remains *A Vindication of the Rights of Woman.*

Wollstonecraft traveled to revolutionary France in 1792. After being jilted by her American lover, she returned to London with her daughter and began a friendship with philosopher William Godwin, who soon became her lover and critic. They married after discovering Wollstonecraft was pregnant, but maintained separate residences. Wollstonecraft died of childbed fever in 1797 following the birth of their daughter, Mary Godwin. In a fit of impassioned grief, Godwin published all of Wollstonecraft's letters (including those to her first lover) and several unfinished works. The response to these revelations was swift and vicious. In the United States, some reprints of *A Vindication of the Rights of Woman* were prefaced with condemnations of Wollstonecraft's sexual misconduct.

Despite the immediate furor on its publication, *A Vindication* was largely forgotten until rediscovered in the 1840s by the American and European women's movements. Advocates of education and legal rights for women (including Margaret Fuller, Lucretia Mott, and Elizabeth Cady Stanton) who were influenced by Wollstonecraft's equal rights doctrine were careful to dissociate themselves from the sexual radicalism with which her name had become synonymous. Only Frances Wright combined Wollstonecraft's Enlightenment egalitarianism with sexual radicalism.

Modern feminists have admired Wollstonecraft for both her personal life and the strong-worded demands of her *Vindication* but have been less comfortable with the emotional vulnerability revealed in her letters and sentimental novels. The reissue of these other works has rejuvenated scholarship on the woman who, for nearly two hundred years, has been seen as a pioneer by liberal feminists in England and the United States.

British philosopher and politician John Stuart Mill (1806–1873) withheld the publication of his essay *The Subjection of Women* until after his unsuccessful attempt to include woman suffrage in the British Reform Bill of 1867, although it had been written in 1861 following the death of Harriet Taylor (1807–1858), his colleague in the cause of human liberty, as well as his wife.

Mill was a feminist particularly active on behalf of the nineteenth-century women's movement. Raised in the utilitarian creed by his father, James Mill, he came to believe, with the founder of utilitarianism, Jeremy Bentham, that the full measure of social happiness would not be realized without the happiness of women. At the age of seventeen, Mill had been detained by the London constabulary for distributing birth control information. The utilitarian influence ultimately took second place to that of Harriet Taylor, with whom Mill maintained an intimate friendship; they married in 1851 after the death of her first husband. Taylor had published in the *Monthly Repository,* and she and Mill wrote essays for one another, particularly on the relationship of women and men. Mill's subsequent essay on "The Enfranchisement of Women" was largely derived from her ideas. Mill acknowledged that *The Subjection of Women* was the result of conversations and work with Taylor and her daughter, Helen.

After his wife's death from tuberculosis, the heartbroken Mill worked mightily, if unsuccessfully, as a member of Parliament to add woman's suffrage to the Reform Bill of 1867. Mill proceeded to support measures giving women control of their property and testified for repeal of the Contagious Diseases Acts, which allowed the forcible examination of women for venereal disease.

His most lasting contribution to the cause of women, however, was *The Subjection of Women,* which was translated into many languages and which exerted international influence on the intellectual discussion of the woman question. In it, Mill shows the regressive condition of women, how similar it is to slavery, and how cruelly the much-vaunted social unit of the family treats its female members. Unlike his wife, he favored the conventional division of labor on which separate-spheres ideology rested. Nonetheless, Mill's rational but convincing arguments against the unequal legal and educational status of women particularly touched the reforming temper of the times and inspired the woman's movement everywhere.

American suffragists of the nineteenth century used the arguments of Wollstonecraft and Mill as they pursued the woman vote, which by the turn of the twentieth century had become the sole feminist goal of their organized movement. Their achievement of the Nineteenth Amendment, however, did not fundamentally address or challenge the legal, economic, or social subordination of women. In the twentieth century, Woolf's *A Room of One's Own* and de Beauvoir's *The Second Sex* emerged as the major European works that assisted American women in their efforts to define the feminist issues of the twentieth century.

A Room of One's Own (1929) by English author and critic Virginia Woolf (1882–1941) is based on speeches delivered at two British women's colleges after World War I. As an essay, *A Room of One's Own* rivals *A Vindication of the Rights of Woman* in its profound contribution to feminist writing and commentary and is consistently included in lists of benchmark works of feminist critical theory, usually in tandem with Woolf's *Three Guineas* (1938). Woolf confronts directly the problems encountered by women artists and writers, arguing that a woman artist lacks not only money and freedom but also the sanction of her society that is so essential to her achievement of success and influence.

Woolf was born Virginia Stephen in London and took her own life when, fearing the onset of incurable madness, she drowned herself in the Ouse River, Lewes, Sussex, in 1941. Until the mid-1970s, she had typically been studied in courses on modern British fiction, where her contributions to modernism—although sometimes grudgingly acknowledged—earned her the designation "the greatest woman novelist of the twentieth century." Since then, however, the feminist aspects of her writing have come under scrutiny. Not surprisingly, critics have discovered that the various Victorian and "modern" images of women emerge, assert themselves, and challenge one another in her works.

Although Woolf's voluminous and influential writings include critical treatises, autobiographical essays, short stories, novels, and experimental prose fiction, the American public recognizes her most readily, perhaps, as the woman in the enigmatic title of Edward Albee's play, *Who's Afraid of Virginia Woolf?* (1962). Woolf never visited the United States and, in fact, retained a condescending attitude toward Americans all her life; nonetheless, her influence on American as well as British feminist writers has been substantial. American critics Jane Marcus and Elaine Showalter, for example, have added their voices to the debate about Woolf's contribution to the women's movement. Woolf did most of her writing at the height of the early British version of that movement, during the first three decades of the twentieth century.

Woolf was not convinced, as many of her contemporaries were, that political power for women, in and of itself, would guarantee their equality with men. She was most concerned with the psychological and economic underpinnings of masculine "superiority." In particular, she sought in her works to assess the consequences to society of the repressed anger in women who acquiesced to masculine power. Two of her most widely studied novels, *Mrs. Dalloway* (1925) and *To the Lighthouse* (1927), reveal Woolf's concern about the systematic though subtle discounting of women's work (and therefore worth) in a patriarchal society. The psychological consequences—both to the individual woman and to society—of women's maintenance of patriarchal conventions is a theme that surfaces in the works of American writers such as poet Adrienne Rich. In the collection *Snapshots of a Daughter-in-Law,* Rich examines the self-disgust and resentment experienced by a woman in a society where she must remain subordinate to men. It is an issue now debated pervasively in American feminist writing, and therefore, Woolf's influence significantly transcends the specious bounds of modern British fiction that originally restrained it.

The Second Sex (1949), Simone de Beauvoir's masterful analysis of "womanhood," begins with the premise that no book about manhood would ever be written because men's experience is taken to be so normative or absolute that it hardly needs talking about. By contrast, women appear different, other, and in need of repeated explanation. Each person acquires and creates self-definition, *The Second Sex* argues, in terms of engaging and coming to terms with "others" in society. Whereas this confrontation with individual others occurs on a personal basis, general categories of otherness, such as blacks, Jews, and women, exist. Oddly enough, while blacks and Jews struggle to escape this otherness, women in fact acquiesce to its terms as they have been arranged by male culture. As the "eternal female," woman thus surrenders her subjectivity and freedom. Rootedness in nature or "immanence" becomes woman's fate once this decision is made, instead of the quest for "transcendence."

The Second Sex provides a rich panorama of women's lives as viewed by scientists, Freudians, and Marxists, as well as by poets and artists across the centuries. Furthermore, it examines the world of the daughter, mother, lesbian, and many other varieties of womanhood. Indicating the difficulties facing the "independent woman," de Beauvoir viewed economic struggle as preliminary to freedom. But the final step involved psychologically escaping self-conceptualization as exclusively an "other." Although *The Second Sex* does not present de Beauvoir's final word on the subject of feminism, it eschews organizing in favor of individual recognition and action.

The Second Sex sold twenty thousand copies almost immediately after its publication in France because readers assumed it to be the work of Jean-Paul Sartre, leading existentialist and de Beauvoir's companion. In 1953, H. M. Parshley, professor of zoology at Smith College, translated the work into English, severely expurgating it. Nonetheless, it had an early impact in the United States and in particular helped inspire Betty Friedan's *The Feminine Mystique* (1963). From then on, the new women's movement recognized *The Second Sex* as a classic statement and an innovative analysis of women's cultural and psychological predicament.

Its author, Simone de Beauvoir (1908–1986), was a French author, philosopher, and activist. Born into a middle-class Parisian family, de Beauvoir thought seriously of a career after her father's financial ruin in World War I. She entered the Sorbonne in the mid-1920s and received her *agrégation* (teaching diploma) in 1927. While there, she met and fell in love with philosopher Jean-Paul Sartre, beginning a lifelong companionship that de Beauvoir refused to legitimate in marriage. Meanwhile, after pursuing a teaching career, she turned all her energies to writing in the 1940s. Her first novel, *L'Invitée/She Came to Stay,* appeared in 1943;

many more followed. From this time on, de Beauvoir and Sartre were at the center of an important radical circle of intellectuals.

In novels, memoirs, and philosophic writings, de Beauvoir developed the existentialist ideas for which she and Sartre were so well-known. Her pathbreaking *Le deuxième sexe/ The Second Sex* continued that philosophical line into the study of women and formed the basis for reconstructing feminist ideas and for rebuilding the women's movement of the 1960s and later. Despite her disclaimer at the close of *The Second Sex* that her book made activism unnecessary, de Beauvoir continued her writing as well as her activism. Her masterpieces include *Les Mandarins* (1954) and several volumes of memoirs.

De Beauvoir's life reflected the feminist axiom, "The personal is political." With the student uprisings of the late 1960s, the Vietnam War, and the rebirth of feminism, de Beauvoir finally realized the need for public political involvement. From then on, often with Sartre, she participated in numerous demonstrations, petitioning movements, and other radical endeavors. In 1971, she shocked the French public when, along with other prominent women, she signed a declaration that she had had an abortion. Later she cofounded the periodical *Questions Feministes/Feminist Questions.* These were but the highlights of a life focusing on writing and activism. De Beauvoir's death in April 1986 brought international recognition of her seminal role in contemporary feminist philosophy as well as in its organizational successes.

The Second Sex and the introduction of deconstruction as a tool for feminist literary criticism have established a significant French influence on American feminist theory since the 1960s. British influence on that theory has continued with writers such as Germaine Greer in *The Female Eunuch* (1972) and the feminist literary works of writers such as Doris Lessing. Marxist thought, Freudianism, and postmodern literary theory also were powerful influences among feminist scholars in academe. *(See also: Deconstruction; Feminism; Feminist Literary Criticism; Friedan, Betty; Prescriptive Literature; Rationalism; Rich, Adrienne; Suffrage; Socialism; Women Writers; Women's Rights Movements: Nineteenth and Twentieth Centuries)*

—Kathleen Mary Brown
—Melinda Dunker
—Mary Lowe-Evans
—Bonnie G. Smith
—Angela M. Howard

Further Reading

Bair, Deirdre. *Simone de Beauvoir: A Biography.* New York: Summit, 1990.

Borghi, Liana. *Dialogue in Utopia: Manners, Purpose and Structure in Three Feminist Works of the 1790s.* Pisa, Italy: ETS, 1984.

Carlisle, Janice. *John Stuart Mill and the Writing of Character.* Athens: University of Georgia Press, 1991.

de Beauvoir, Simone. *The Second Sex.* Translated by H. M. Parshley. New York: Knopf, 1953.

Gutwirth, Madelyn. *Madame de Staäl, Novelist*. Urbana: University of Illinois Press, 1978.

Lorch, Jennifer. *Mary Wollstonecraft: The Making of a Radical Feminist*. New York: St. Martin's, 1990.

Mephani, John. *Virginia Woolf: A Literary Life*. New York: St. Martin's, 1991.

Mill, John Stuart. *The Subjection of Women*. London: Longmans, 1869.

Moers, Ellen. *Literary Women*. Garden City, NY: Doubleday, 1976.

Showalter, Elaine. *A Literature of Their Own: British Women Novelists from Brontë to Lessing*. Rev. ed. London: Virago, 1982.

Tomalin, Claire. *The Life and Death of Mary Wollstonecraft*. London: Penguin, 1992.

Warhol, Robyn R., and Diane Price Herndl. *Feminisms: An Anthology of Literary Theory and Criticism*. New Brunswick, NJ: Rutgers University Press, 1991.

Wollstonecraft, Mary. *A Vindication of the Rights of Woman*. London: Scott, 1792. Reprint, New York: E. P. Dutton, 1929, 1974.

Woolf, Virginia. *A Room of One's Own*. London: Hogarth, 1931.

∽ Ewald, Emmy Carlson (1857–1946)

The best-known Swedish-American woman of her generation, Emmy Ewald worked primarily within the Swedish Lutheran denomination, the Augustana Synod, where she organized the Women's Missionary Society in 1892. She used this base of support to promote women's rights and joined in the national struggle for woman suffrage when she addressed the U.S. Congress in 1902, representing the Swedish women of America.

Ewald was well positioned to become a leader and activist. Her father, the Reverend Erland Carlson, served as pastor of Chicago's largest Swedish Church during the period of heavy Swedish immigration, and parsonage life showed her how the church could respond to social needs. She was educated at premier women's schools in Sweden and in America, studying for three years at the Fryksell Academy in Sweden, then attending Rockford College, where she met classmates Jane Addams and Charlotte McCoughlin. Again in Chicago, she married her father's successor, a celebrated pulpit orator the Reverend Carl Ewald, and took over the role of pastor's wife from her mother. Ewald's own oratorical skills are revealed by the attendance at her weekly Sunday School class—over three hundred.

In 1892, Ewald was invited to convene the Lutheran women at the Women's Congress to be held the next year during the World Parliament of Religions in Chicago. While at the Women's Congress, she was elected to chair the International Congress of Lutheran Women, representing the Lutheran women of Denmark, Germany, Norway, Sweden, and the United States. It became clear to her at these meetings that Lutheran women needed to be more efficiently organized.

Ewald formed the Women's Missionary Society by convincing reluctant pastors to support the venture. Wresting control of society finances from the synod's clergy-led For-

eign Mission Board in 1907 enabled the women to use money raised within their congregations as the society determined. Under Ewald's leadership, the society raised money for seventy-nine hospitals and schools, located in India, China, Palestine, America, and Africa. The society's financial clout gave Ewald leverage within the synod but no formal authority, leaving her, as her friend Charlotte Odman put it, "to blaze her own trail through the wilderness of ecclesiastical red tape and feminine prejudice." Ewald's apocryphal slogan, "The Pastors Are Against Us!" hints at tension in Swedish congregations, and Ewald found ways to put this energy to creative use. When meeting challenges, she did not give up. "Take the D. E. I. out of Depression," she urged, and you can "Press on." *(See also: Christianity; Religion)*

—**Maria E. Erling**

Further Reading

Augustana Women's Missionary Society Archives. Evangelical Lutheran Church in America, Chicago, Illinois.

Telleen, Jane. " 'Yours in the Master's Service': Emmy Evald and the Woman's Missionary Society of the Augustana Lutheran Church, 1892–1942," *Swedish Pioneer Historical Quarterly* 30 (July 1979): 183-95.

These Fifty Years. Chicago: Women's Missionary Society of the Augustana Synod, 1942.

∽ Extramarital Sex

Sex outside of marriage was once considered a male prerogative, but recent studies indicate a waning of the double standard with estimates that roughly half of both husbands and wives violate the Seventh Commandment. Historically, the practice existed in colonial America and continued into the modern world. In 1631, Massachusetts enacted the death penalty for adultery, defined as sexual relations between a man and a married woman. Most other colonies followed suit in punishing extramarital sex, although enforcement remained minimal in most instances. After 1660, New England courts usually imposed fines on convicted adulterers, along with public whipping or the wearing of the letters AD on a garment or burned onto the forehead. Over half the seventeenth-century divorce cases in New England cited adultery as a cause. In the antebellum South, extramarital sexual relations between owners and slaves were common and usually involved white men with black women. Divorce records also indicate that in some cases white women consorted with black men despite enormous social pressures and the possibility of horrible punishments.

Historically, there has been a high degree of tolerance for most males indulging in extramarital relations if they kept their liaisons quiet. Women have generally been more harshly condemned than men for sex outside of marriage. Alfred Kinsey's research in the 1930s and 1940s revealed that half of the males he surveyed had committed adultery while only 25 percent of the women in his sample admitted to sex outside of marriage. Since the 1950s, the percentage of women admitting to extramarital sexual relations has increased to a percentage roughly equal to that for men.

While lip service to the concept of marital fidelity continued after 1970, the popular culture reflected a more relaxed attitude toward men's if not women's participation in extramarital sex. By the late 1990s, although the concept of shame in this regard had been greatly diminished, public exposure of extramarital sexual activity remained a possible catalyst for political if not private scandal. *(See also: Marriage; New Morality; Woodhull, Victoria Claflin)*

—**William G. Shade**
—**Angela M. Howard**

Further Reading

D'Emilio, John, and Estelle Freedman. *Intimate Matters: A History of Sexuality in America.* New York: Harper & Row, 1988.

Gay, Peter. *The Education of the Senses.* New York: Oxford University Press, 1983.

Hunt, Morton. *Sexual Behavior in the 1970s.* New York: Dell, 1974.

Smith, Daniel Scott, and Michael S. Hindus. "Premarital Pregnancy in America, 1640–1971: An Overview and Interpretation," *Journal of Interdisciplinary History* 5 (Spring 1978): 537-70.

Fair Labor Standards Act (1938)

The Fair Labor Standards Act of 1938 was the first piece of federal legislation to provide wage and hour protection for both women and men workers in the United States. The act guaranteed the following to wage workers in industries involved in interstate commerce: (a) a minimum wage of 25 cents an hour, rising over seven years to 40 cents; (b) no wage differentials on grounds of age or sex; (c) a maximum workweek of forty-four hours, reducing to forty over three years; (d) overtime pay for additional hours worked; and (e) an end to child labor (the employment of persons under sixteen). The act was held constitutional by the Supreme Court in *United States v. Darby* (1941).

Frances Perkins, secretary of labor in the Roosevelt administration, was responsible for formulating the law and winning the acquiescence of organized labor. Opposition came from some industrial and employers' organizations and from southern states where labor conditions lagged; it was met by allowing certain exceptions and special terms in the coverage of the act. Passed just a year after its introduction to Congress, the act achieved several goals long associated with women's organizations, but it had mixed results for women workers, and it significantly changed the nature of sex discrimination within the labor market.

Previous wage and hour restrictions were state controlled, restricted to women, and protected only an estimated 12 percent of adult female workers. The new act covered 57 percent of women workers and 39 percent of men workers. On the other hand, some of the occupations excluded from its coverage were major employers of the poorest women: domestic service, in which 97 percent of the workers were women and 52 percent black; agriculture, which employed many women seasonally in the fields; and many small retail and service employments not involved in interstate commerce. Moreover, Perkins's attempt to include in the act a ban on homework, a major mode of exploitation of women, was vetoed by legal advisers who feared it would imperil the entire act in the courts.

Thus, de jure, the act ended the explicit discrimination that had singled out women workers for separate treatment on the invidious argument that they were the weaker sex as well as "the mothers of the race." It therefore opened the way to the reunifying of the women's movement, split for two decades over whether protective laws for women helped by improving their conditions or hindered by contradicting the idea of equality embodied in the proposal for an equal rights amendment. But de facto, the act introduced a different discrimination by focusing on the national and industrial economy in which, given the existing sex-segregated labor market, the workforce was largely male. Subsequent amendments to the act have helped to rectify this situation, notably by the inclusion in 1973 of domestic labor in its minimum wage clause.

In 1996, President William Clinton signed into law a congressional bill that increased minimum wage from $4.25 to $5.15 per hour, in two stages over two years' time. Afterward, the president proposed implementation of another incremental minimum wage increase that would raise the minimum wage to $6.15 per hour by the year 2000. *(See also: New Deal; Perkins, Frances; Protective Legislation; Wages)*

—**Vivien Hart**

Further Reading

Bureau of National Affairs. *Equal Pay for Equal Work: Federal Equal Pay Law of 1963.* Washington, DC: BNA, 1963.

Frances Perkins Papers. Schlesinger Library. Radcliffe College, Cambridge, MA.

Legislative History of the Fair Labor Standards Amendment of 1974, Public Law 93-259. Washington, DC: Government Printing Office, 1976.

Mettler, Suzanne. *Dividing Citizens: Gender and Federalism in New Deal Public Policy.* Ithaca, NY: Cornell University Press, 1998.

United States v. Darby, 312 U.S. 100 (1941).

U.S. Department of Labor, Records, 1933–1945. National Archives, Washington, DC.

Family and Medical Leave Act (1993)

The Family and Medical Leave Act of 1993 entitles workers to twelve workweeks of unpaid leave during any twelve-month period for reasons including (a) child care following birth or adoption; (b) care for a spouse, child, or parent with a serious health condition; and (c) recuperation from an employee's own serious health condition. To be eligible for leave under the act, an employee must have worked for an employer for at least twelve months preceding the leave and for at least 1,250 hours during the year, and the employer must employ at least fifty persons. The law aims to balance the needs of family caregivers with the needs of the workplace.

Several related laws were introduced in the 1980s but were ultimately vetoed owing to the expectation of undue financial and administrative burden on businesses. On February 5, 1993, the act became the first major piece of legislation signed by President William Clinton. The U.S. Department of Labor, responsible for carrying out the law, published the final regulations implementing the act on January 6, 1995.

Congressional supporters argued that the act promotes family stability and economic security and thus promotes national interests. The Senate report accompanying the act noted that 74 percent of women aged 25 to 54 work outside the home; single parents accounted for 27 percent of all family groups with children under 18 years old in 1988, more than twice the 1970 proportion; and 20 to 25 percent of American workers have some caregiving responsibility for an older relative. The Senate report stated, "With men and women alike as wage earners, the crucial unpaid caretaking services traditionally performed by wives—care of young children, ill family members, aging parents—has become increasingly difficult for families to fulfill. . . . With the exception of the United States, virtually every industrialized country, as well as many Third World countries, have national [family leave] policies."

The law responds to the fact that while women have aspired to achieve more in the workplace and families have relied more on women's wages, expectations for females in caregiving roles have not changed. A lack of job protection formerly left many women with a choice between caregiving and employment. Although feminists fought for family leave legislation for several years, its final accomplishments are modest. For low-wage earners, the benefits of the law may be small because leave is unpaid. Proposals have been made to broaden the law to cover businesses with more than 25 workers, compared with 50 under the 1993 law, and to allow for additional leave for medical visits and parent/teacher conferences. (See also: Female-Headed Households; Sexual Division of Labor)

—Anne Hudson Bolin

Further Reading

England, Suzanne E. "Family Leave and Gender Justice," *Affilia* 5 (1990): 8-24.

England, Suzanne E., and Beatrice T. Naulleau. "Women, Work and Elder Care: The Family and Medical Leave Debate," *Women and Politics* 11 (1991): 91-107.

Family and Medical Leave Act of 1993. Public Law 103-3, 107 Stat. 6 (1993).

Marcus, Richard L. *Family and Medical Leave Policies and Procedures.* New York: John Wiley, 1994.

Rigler, Jane. "Analysis and Understanding of the Family and Medical Leave Act of 1993," *Case Western Reserve Law Review* 45 (1995): 457-505.

⟳ Family Violence

Although family violence has a long history, extensive research on it is primarily a phenomenon of the past two to three decades. The social response to family violence has also changed during this time. By the 1990s, police were responding routinely to assault calls, battered women's shelters offered sanctuary in most metropolitan areas, and a court system of mandated treatment groups for batterers and survivors had become commonplace. Since the 1970s, the demands of the women's movement have influenced the professional development of policymakers, media experts, historians, mental health practitioners, and others with authority and responsibility for the protecting the rights and the physical safety of women and children.

Advocates and scholars for the women's movement were responsible in great part for defining the discrepancy between laws and actual policy, such as that between laws against wife assault and the legal policy of not interfering with the male prerogative inherent in the traditional patriarchal institution of the family. They identified wife assault as a social problem of considerable magnitude and incidence and brought public attention to the criminal justice system's failure to respond to its emergency status.

In her book *Domestic Tyranny* (1987), Professor Elizabeth Pleck described the socio-legal process to control family violence prior to current trends. According to Pleck, family violence policies were first implemented by the Puritans, who had laws against wife beating and "unnatural severity" toward children in the colony of Massachusetts between 1640 and 1680, while in non-Puritan society at that time, wife beating was punished informally. For example, in Boston in 1707, nine men tore the clothes off a neighbor and flogged him for having beaten his wife (p. 33).

Pleck (1987) and others argue that the history of the criminalization of family violence reflected widespread social attitudes about the family itself. For example, during eras when views of the rights and privileges of the family as protected from government interference prevailed, interest in criminalizing family violence waned. However, when family violence is seen as threatening not only family members but the social order itself, public support for criminalization of the violence becomes paramount. During some periods, idealization of the family results in a reluctance to criminalize family violence; mainstream opinion affirms that, because parents have the right to physically discipline children and a husband has the right to have sexual access to his wife, "nagging" women or disobedient children provoke the beatings they receive, wives and children need a male economic provider, and the law should not disrupt this basic and traditional pattern of men's financial support of their families except in extreme circumstances.

As the eighteenth century progressed, legal thinkers began to distinguish between public and private behavior. The family came to be considered a private institution beyond the purview of legislative and legal action. Thus, husbands might be punished for permanent injuries inflicted upon family members, but the law often treated wife assaults as significant only if they were lethal, and police and law officials were often barred from intervening in abusive family relationships. However, by the turn of the nineteenth century, female advocates of temperance helped pass laws giving tort protection to the wives and children of drunkards. Since many of these men also abused their families, these laws often benefited victims of abuse within the family unit. During the Progressive Era and the first quarter of the twentieth century, however, the perception of family violence as a serious crime waned once again. With the creation of family courts and social casework, criminal justice system sanctions against family crime came to be viewed by many as inhumane and somewhat outmoded. Instead, there seemed to be a shift toward family privacy and freedom from societal interference; according to many historians, causal analysis of family violence became too narrow and solutions and aid remained too limited. Mothers and children had access to few options that might have enabled them to escape abusive relationships. Without resources—economic, occupational, or social—women were less likely to leave the batterer. Research in the social sciences has revealed that women are more likely to stay with men who batter them if the women are poor, unemployed, have low-paying jobs, have only a high school education or less, and/or receive negative responses from staff of social service agencies to whom they turn for assistance.

Family violence can be discussed through shifts in the politics of the family and in the power issues between the roles of husbands and wives, parents and children, and males and females, along with cultural norms and lack of social service support for the battered in general. Three factors seem to remain true for violent families. First, Americans are more likely to be killed or physically assaulted in their homes by other family members than anywhere else or by anyone else in our society (Gelles and Cornell). Second, a propensity for family violence is transmitted from one generation to the next, according to a substantial body of research. One study concludes that among adults who were abused as children, more than one-fifth later abuse their own children (Straus, Gelles, and Steinmetz). And third, people who were physically abused or neglected as children are twice as likely to be arrested for a violent offense (Widom).

Sanctions are also powerful messages about cultural ideals that have functioned against survivors. They further serve the culture by controlling behavior. External sanctions refer to law authorities, police, courts, clergy, and mental health professionals. The fact of the lack of prosecution overall for batterers through the criminal justice system supports the conclusion that prosecution, for instance, has not been a positive sanction for most battered women. This is especially troubling in light of the emergence of new studies that demonstrate the effectiveness of vigorous prosecution in reducing or stopping the violence. Finally, internal sanctions play a part. Research has shown that women will be more devoted to preserving the relationship even through the stress of violence. They also at times take responsibility for the abuse (Gilligan).

Because earlier interpretations of family violence invoked mechanisms that blamed the victim through theories such as "female masochism" and "passivity," feminists and women's advocates demanded that research combine with common sense to reflect clearly the correlation between availability of options and the likelihood that women will stay in the battering relationship. In the 1970s, the work of activists in the women's movement brought public attention to wife assault, marital rape, and sexual abuse of children. In the 1990s, widespread media focus on the issues of family violence promoted public acceptance research that shifted from a focus on the battered wife syndrome to the better question of why men batter. Feminist scholars and researchers noted the power of the shelter movement to demand systemic political change and to support greater options and sanctions for women, children, and the elderly (Widom). (See also: Marital Rape; Social Purity Movement)

—Leslye King Mize

Further Reading

Barnett, Ola, Cindy L. Miller-Perrin, and Robin D. Perrin. *Family Violence across the Lifespan: An Introduction.* Thousand Oaks CA: Sage, 1997.

Gelles, Richard, and Claire Pedrick Cornell. *Intimate Violence in Families,* 3d ed. Thousand Oaks, CA: Sage, 1997.

Gilligan, Carol. *In a Different Voice: Psychological Theory and Women's Development.* Cambridge, MA: Harvard University Press, 1982.

Gordon, Linda. *Heroes of Their Own Lives: The Politics and History of Family Violence: Boston, 1880–1960.* New York: Viking, 1988.

Lewis, Helen B. *Psychic War in Men and Women.* New York: New York University Press, 1976.

Pleck, Elizabeth. *Domestic Tyranny: The Making of Social Policy against Family Violence from Colonial Times to the Present.* New York: Oxford University Press, 1987.

Schechter, Susan. *Women and Male Violence.* Boston: South End Press, 1982.

Straus, Murray A., Richard J. Gelles, and Suzanne K. Steinmetz. *Behind Closed Doors: Violence in the American Family.* Garden City, NY: Doubleday, 1980.

Swift, Carolyn F. *Women and Violence: Breaking the Connection.* Wellesley, MA: Wellesley College, Stone Center for Developmental Services and Studies, 1987.

Widom, C. "The Cycle of Violence," *Science* 244 (1989): 160-66.

✿ Farley, Harriet (1813–1907)

Operative in the Lowell textile mills, teacher, writer, and editor of the *Lowell Offering* (1842–1845), Harriet Farley was a strong proponent of the intellectual and artistic capabilities of the Lowell mill workers. Dedicated to removing the social stigma of factory work, Farley offered an image of Lowell operatives' active cultural life and leisure time for educational pursuits.

The daughter of a New Hampshire clergyman, Farley was primarily self-educated. She worked as a teacher before coming to the mills, married in 1854, and moved to New York City; she had one child.

Farley's *Offering* countered readers' image of physical labor with emphasis on mill workers' talents and programs for cultural enrichment. Farley was criticized for keeping the *Offering* out of the fray when the mills' paternal benevolence changed to squeezing workers for increased productivity on lower wages. She ignored the Female Labor Reform Association's organizing in the mills ca. 1842 to 1845. In a local labor paper, Sarah Bagley, a former *Offering* contributor, accused Farley of promoting the interests of the mill owners rather than the mill operatives. While changing conditions belied the *Offering*'s vision of workers devoting leisure to intellectual pursuits, Farley staunchly maintained her focus on self-improvement.

Not only Farley herself but also many other contributors went on to publish books, articles, poems, and stories after and outside the *Offering*. Farley continued to attract attention with collections of her own writings: *Shells from the Strand of the Sea of Genius* (1847) and *Happy Nights at Hazel Nook* (1852). (*See also: Lowell Mill Girls;* Lowell Offering; Voice of Industry)

—**Carol Klimick Cyganowski**

Further Reading

Adickes, Sandra. "Mind among the Spindles: An Examination of Some of the Journals, Newspapers, and Memoirs of the Lowell Female Operatives," *Women's Studies* 1 (1973): 279-87.

Foner, Philip S., ed. *The Factory Girls: A Collection of Writings on Life and Struggles in the New England Factories of the 1840's, by the Factory Girls Themselves, and the Story, in Their Own Words, of the First Trade Unions of Women Workers in the United States.* Urbana: University of Illinois Press, 1977.

Josephson, Hannah. *Golden Threads: New England's Millgirls and Magnates.* New York: Duell, Sloan & Pearce, 1949.

Robinson, Harriet Hanson. *Loom and Spindle, or Life among the Early Mill Girls. With a Sketch of "The Lowell Offering" and Some of Its Contributors.* New York: T. Y. Crowell, 1898. Reprint, Kailua, Hawaii: Press Pacifica, 1976.

◈ Farmer, Sarah Jane (1847–1916)

Founder of the American Bahá'í movement, Sarah Farmer was born in Eliot, Maine, the only surviving child of Moses G. Farmer and Hannah Shipleigh Tobey Farmer. Inspired by a visit to the World Parliament of Religions in Chicago in 1893, Farmer persuaded her copartners in a local summer resort to turn the enterprise into a summer school devoted to the study of philosophy, religion, art, mental healing, contemporary social problems, and comparative religion. The Greenacre Summer Conferences opened in the summer of 1894. In its first few years, the institute acted as a successor to the Concord School of Philosophy, with Franklin Sanborn, the last of the transcendentalists, and his associate Charles Malloy taking active roles. Until the mid-1900s, the school attracted a large number of literary and reform luminaries, particularly from the Boston area.

In 1900, overwork, financial difficulty, and early signs of mental illness (caused in part by arteriosclerosis) forced Farmer to bring the school's activities to a minimum. To recuperate, she spent the year on a cruise of the Mediterranean. While traveling in Persia, she met Abdu'l-Bahá', leader of Bahá'í, who was in prison for his religious and political beliefs. Instantly converted, Sarah believed she had found in Bahá'í a spiritual home for her conviction that the world's great religions shared universal characteristics. After her return to Greenacre in 1901, she gave priority to the institute's Monsalvat School of Comparative Religion and personally espoused the "Persian revelation." These changes caused rifts between the original conferees and the followers of Ba'hai. By 1913, Bahá'ís achieved a majority on the board of directors; in 1928, Greenacre formally became an institute of the Bahá'í National Spiritual Assembly, a status it has maintained to the present.

Amid mounting sectarian rivalries, so contrary to her original vision of Greenacre, Farmer's mental health slowly deteriorated. By 1910, she was committed to an insane asylum in nearby Portsmouth, where she died of heart failure in 1916. While it is unclear whether she intended Greenacre to become an official center of Bahá'í activity, Bahá'í rightfully claim her as a leading force in the early days of their movement. (*See also: Religion*)

—**Catherine Tumber**

Further Reading

Atkinson, Robert. "Bahá'í's American Beginnings in Maine," *East/West* 17 (December 1977): 78-80.

Cameron, Kenneth Walter, ed. *Transcendentalists in Transition.* Hartford, CT: Transcendental Books, 1980.

Ingersoll, Anna Josephine. *Greenacre on the Piscataqua.* New York: Alliance, 1900.

Remy, Charles Mason. "Reminiscences of the Summer School, Greenacre, Eliot, Maine." Unpublished manuscript. Remy Family Records. Dartmouth College, Dartmouth, NH.

Tumber, Catherine. "A Politics of the Higher Self: Feminism, Progressivism, and Psychotherapeutics, 1875–1919," chap. 4. Ph.D. diss., University of Rochester, 1992.

◈ Farnham, Eliza Wood Burham (1815–1864)

Eliza Farnham believed firmly in both women's moral superiority and prison reform. An author, teacher, prison matron, and phrenologist, she applied environmentalist theories to both the rehabilitation of women prisoners and to questions of women's rights.

Raised by a "bad-tempered nagging aunt" after her mother's death, Farnham was largely self-educated. At twenty, she left her home in Rensselaerville, New York, for Illinois, where she married Thomas Jefferson Farnham. The couple returned east in 1840, where Farnham wrote *Life in Prairie Land* (1846), a book about her experiences in Illinois, as well as an article arguing against political rights for women. From 1844 to 1848, Farnham served as matron of the women's prison at Sing Sing. She attempted to reform the facility along principles based on phrenology (the deduction of character from the study of bumps on the head). Believing that criminals were not fully responsible for their crimes, she attempted to alter their environment so as to encourage their best instincts. She introduced educational programs, allowed women prisoners to interact, and brightened up the gloomy prison with lamps, flowers, and music. A series of personal and political conflicts eventually forced her out.

Farnham moved to Boston to aid Samuel Gridley Howe in his work with the blind. After her husband's death, she traveled to California with a group of other women in an endeavor designed to civilize men participating in the Gold Rush. Following a second marriage to William Fitzpatrick, the death of a child, and a divorce, she returned to New York in the mid-1850s to study medicine and encourage other women to continue her civilizing missions to California. Farnham moved about for the remainder of her life, working as a matron at the Stockton Insane Asylum in 1861, tending the wounded at Gettysburg in 1863, and publishing both a slightly fictionalized autobiography, *Eliza Woodson; Or, the Early Days of One of the World's Workers* in 1864 and the posthumous classic *Woman and Her Era* in 1865.

Farnham's feminism was a contradictory blend of beliefs and practices that borrowed heavily from evolutionary theories and a belief in women's moral superiority. In *Woman and Her Era,* which anticipated the coming civilization of the world by female principles, she expressed her belief that women were more advanced than men because "woman's organism is more complex and her totality of function larger." While male sexuality was "corporeal," the sexual nature of women was more "spiritual or super-sensual," just as their intellectual powers were more refined and their maternal nature suited them to social reform. Although Farnham wrote against suffrage, she believed firmly in women's ability and duty to advance civilization, and she anticipated the day when this would be realized. *(See also: Prison Reform; Women's Prisons)*

—Miriam Reumann
—William G. Shade

Further Reading

Farnham, Eliza W. *Woman and Her Era.* New York: C. M. Plumb, 1865.

Freedman, Estelle. *Their Sisters' Keepers: Women's Prison Reform in America, 1830–1930.* Ann Arbor: University of Michigan Press, 1980.

Riegel, Robert E. *American Feminists.* Lawrence: University Press of Kansas, 1963.

❧ Farrand, Beatrix Jones (1872–1959)

Beatrix Farrand was one of the foremost landscape designers after World War I and the only woman founder of the American Society of Landscape Architects in 1899.

A niece of Edith Wharton, she was raised in privileged circles in New York City. She commenced study in horticulture under family friend Charles Sprague Sargent, head of the Arnold Arboretum, in 1892 and then traveled abroad. After her return to the states, and with the financial assistance of her aunt, Farrand opened her own landscape practice, which spanned over 50 years.

During those years, Farrand's work involved both public and private commissions, including the Abby Aldrich Rockefeller garden in Seal Harbor, the residences of Gerrish H. Milliken and Mrs. Henry Cabot Lodge, the Ethel Walker School, the Pierpont Morgan Library, and the Santa Barbara Botanic Garden. While much of her work has been modified or obliterated by time, her efforts are well preserved at Dumbarton Oaks, the Washington, D.C., estate of Mildred and Robert Woods Bliss, owned and operated by Harvard University as the Dumbarton Oaks Research Library and Collection. Farrand served as landscape gardener for the property from 1921 to 1947 and there undertook to translate the Italian garden tradition so beloved by her aunt to the American landscape. Dumbarton Oaks today covers 16 acres and ranges in style from formal Italian terraced gardens with garden sculpture designed by Farrand to Jekyll-inspired perennial beds and naturalistic plantings. It is considered one of the finest gardens in America. Farrand's friend and patron Mildred Bliss described her work as never imposing "on the land an arbitrary concept." Farrand "listened," said Bliss, "to the light and wind and grade of each area under study."

Farrand also served as landscape architect to a number of colleges and universities, including Yale, Princeton, Oberlin, Vassar, Hamilton, and the University of Chicago. While she undertook many projects on campuses, she found such landscaping to be trying. Her efforts often met with disagreement, and at Princeton and Yale she became known—behind her back—as the "bush-woman." Notwithstanding, as campus designer, she developed a philosophy that she put to work: unobstructed walkways, broad greenswards, and the establishment of nurseries for experimentation and economical development of plants. "A campus is a place for trees and grass, and nothing more," she noted in a report to Oberlin College dated 1939.

In the years before her death, Farrand dedicated much time and effort to the family property, Reef Point Garden in Bar Harbor, Maine. Hoping to endow it as a place of learning and experimentation, she was unable to raise sufficient funds to ensure its long-term security. As a consequence, she gave her extensive papers to the University of California,

Berkeley, where they reside today. *(See also: Business; Wharton, Edith; Women's Work: Nineteenth Century)*

—Anne deHayden Neal

Further Reading

Balmori, Diana et al. *Beatrix Farrand's American Landscapes—Her Gardens & Campuses.* Sagaponeck, NY: Sagapress, 1985.

Beatrix Farrand's Plant Book for Dumbarton Oaks. Edited by Diane Kostial McGuire. Washington, DC: Dumbarton Oaks, 1980.

Beatrix Jones Farrand: Fifty Years of American Landscape Architecture. Washington, DC: Dumbarton Oaks, 1982.

Beatrix Jones Farrand Document Collection. University of California, Berkeley.

Brochure. Dumbarton Oaks Gardens, Washington, DC.

⚘ Fauset, Jessie Redmon (1882–1961)

Author and literary editor from 1919 to 1926 of *The Crisis: A Record of the Darker Races* published by the National Association for the Advancement of Colored People, Jessie Fauset was a major figure of the Harlem Renaissance. She was born in Camden, New Jersey in 1882; her father, Redmon Fauset, was an African Methodist Episcopal minister. A bright student, Fauset attended Philadelphia's High School for Girls and intended to continue her studies at Bryn Mawr but was denied admission on the basis of her race. She entered Cornell and graduated Phi Beta Kappa in 1905. She received her M.A. from the University of Pennsylvania.

In addition to her role on *The Crisis,* where she was able to encourage the works of many gifted young writers, such as Langston Hughes, Fauset was a major contributor to *Brownies' Book,* a publication for black children. She also wrote essays and poetry. During her life, Fauset published four novels: *There Is Confusion* (1924), *Plum Bun* (1929), *The Chinaberry Tree* (1931), and *Comedy: American Style* (1933). These novels generally dealt with the black middle class, and her protagonists were often mulattoes. Fauset often depicted marriage as a woman's ultimate fulfillment. Although Fauset's novels are stylistically flawed, they were well received at the time. Critic Stanley Braithwaite compared her favorably with other major female literary figures.

For unknown reasons, Fauset left *The Crisis* in 1926. She taught high school in New York City from 1927 until 1944. Her works faded into obscurity, and she died in Philadelphia in 1961. *(See also: Black Women; Women Writers)*

—Rose Kolbasnik Callahan

Further Reading

Sylvander, Carolyn Wedin. *Jessie Redmon Fauset: Black American Writer.* Troy, NY: Whitston, 1981.

⚘ Feder, Sadie Ingalls (1890–?)

Sadie Ingalls Feder served her tribe as politician, historian, and linguist. Born in 1890 near Stroud, Oklahoma, her Indian name was Pon naw pique, and she was a member of the Bear Clan. Horace and Mattie Ingalls, her parents, were full blood Sac and Fox; they all spoke their language fluently.

As a student at the Sac and Fox Mission School, she excelled in all subjects. Her talents got the attention of famed Sac and Fox ethnologist Dr. William Jones, who recruited her to attend the Carlisle Indian School in Pennsylvania. While a student there in 1912, she helped record a Sac and Fox syllabary and stories for Smithsonian linguists. The handwritten language materials continue to be used by researchers at the National Anthropological Archives of the Smithsonian Institution.

When she returned to Oklahoma from Carlisle, she immediately became active in her tribe's government and became known as an activist with progressive ideas about community issues. She was only thirty-four when she was elected to the Sac and Fox Business Committee in 1924. She was returned to that position for five terms and served as secretary for several two-year terms.

Political activist Feder was also a writer and historian who spent parts of several years researching Sac and Fox history in libraries and museums in the Great Lakes region. From this research and her general interest in preservation of culture, she wrote regular columns and articles for publications in Oklahoma and elsewhere. Feder's short history of her tribe's movement from the Great Lakes, "Migration of the Sauk and Fox Indians to the Southland—Promised Land—Oklahoma," was published in several magazines and in the Black Hawk State Park pow wow program in Rock Island, Illinois, in 1977.

She is remembered today by friends, family, and tribesmen as the first activist woman of the Sac and Fox Tribe. Relatives proudly say they are like their "Aunt Sadie" who spoke up and did what was right. *(See also: Native American Women)*

—Jan Vassar

Further Reading

Feder, Sadie. "Migration of the Sauk and Fox Indians to the Southland—Promised Land—Oklahoma." Rock Island, IL: Black Hawk State Park Pow Wow Program, 1977.

Mueller, Kerstin. "The Changing Role of Algonkian Women—A Study on the Contemporary Sac and Fox of Oklahoma." Master's thesis, University of Tulsa, 1991.

Rideout, Henry M. *William Jones: Indian, Cowboy, American Scholar, and Anthropologist in the Field.* New York: Frederick A. Stokes, 1912.

Sac and Fox National Public Library archives. Stroud, Oklahoma.

Snow, Jerry E. "Sac and Fox Tribal Government from 1885 through Reorganization under the Oklahoma Indian Welfare Act in 1937." Master's thesis, University of Oklahoma, 1970.

Stroud Messenger (Stroud, Oklahoma). July 30, 1932; August 12, 1932; August 31, 1934; September 6, 1935.

✒ Female Academies

Female academies (also often called "seminaries") were secondary schools for young women that appeared in greatest numbers in the years between 1820 and 1860. This period is sometimes referred to as the "age of the academy" in the history of American education, simply because of the large number of independent secondary schools for students of both sexes established at that time.

The earliest academies were all male, but many—perhaps most—academies in the antebellum period were coeducational or offered separate courses of study for both boys and girls. The appearance of female academies was a significant development in the history of women's education, however, for it signaled the rise of a new appreciation for women's intellectual powers. The female academies also presented important career alternatives for women interested in a life of intellectual growth and public service; they offered women the opportunity of becoming professional educators and afforded them public visibility as educational reformers. Of course, the female academies represented a valuable resource to thousands of young women whose opportunities for advanced education would have been quite narrow had these schools not existed. The movement of women into higher education in the latter nineteenth century probably would not have been possible without the earlier efforts of educators in female academies to prove that young women were indeed capable of intellectual accomplishment.

Female academies were founded in the eighteenth century as a tangible result of the patriotic post-Revolutionary concept of republican motherhood, which refined and adapted the definition of American womanhood to the needs of the new nation. The Young Ladies Academy of Philadelphia was established by socially prominent and educated men, with a curriculum that paralleled that of a college preparatory school for boys. This academy served as a prototype for the secular girls' schools of the early national period. However, the female academy movement is generally recognized as having started with the establishment of Emma Willard's Troy (New York) Female Seminary in 1821. This school was designed to provide young women with an education generally equivalent to that given boys, at least as regarded standards of intellectual accomplishment. Willard and other women educators were critical of girls' "finishing" schools, which taught little more than embroidery, table manners, music appreciation, and perhaps a smattering of foreign language. Accordingly, the Troy Female Seminary offered courses in history, the sciences, and literature, as well as studies traditionally deemed important for young ladies. Willard and other women educators argued that women needed to study subjects such as these to educate their children (and especially their sons) better for the responsibilities of citizenship in the new republican social and political order. Following Willard's lead, dozens of other women dedicated themselves to careers as educators and founded their own academies. Among the most prominent were Zilpah Grant (Ipswich Academy), Catharine Beecher (Hartford Academy), and Mary Lyon (Mount Holyoke Seminary). Although many of these schools closed after a relatively short time (often because a founder moved on to new interests), their very existence was an affirmation of female intellectual accomplishment in an age when female abilities were often subject to denigration.

It is difficult to gauge the overall effect of the female academy movement on the course of women's history in the United States. Historian Anne Firor Scott has argued, for example, that Troy Female Seminary alumnae composed a national network of early advocates for feminist reform. Although more study is needed, it is likely that other female academies exerted a similar influence. For thousands of women in the early to mid-nineteenth century, the female academy may have been an enlightening—and in certain ways a liberating—experience and one that subsequent generations of women could build on. *(See also: Beecher, Catharine; Education; Higher Education; Mount Holyoke Seminary; Republican Motherhood; Rush, Benjamin and "Thoughts on Female Education"; Troy Female Seminary; Young Ladies Academy of Philadelphia)*

—John L. Rury

Further Reading

Scott, Anne Firor. *Making the Invisible Woman Visible.* Urbana: University of Illinois Press, 1981.
Solomon, Barbara. *In the Company of Educated Women: A History of Women and Higher Education in America.* New Haven, CT: Yale University Press, 1986.

✒ Female Genital Mutilation (FGM)

Female genital mutilation (FGM) is the term used by the World Health Organization and individuals who are committed to the eradication of the practice to refer to female circumcision. The four forms of female circumcision are defined as (a) *ritualistic circumcision:* the clitoris is merely nicked, causing bleeding but little mutilation or long-term damage; (b) *sunna:* the prepuce is removed—the gland and body of the clitoris remain intact, but the procedure may include the removal of the tip of the clitoris; the absence of the prepuce causes intense pain during sexual intercourse; (c) *excision or clitoridectomy:* the clitoris is removed and, often, parts of the labia minora; (d) *infibulation or pharonic:* almost all of the female genitalia is removed, including the clitoris and labia minora; most of the labia majora is removed with the remaining edges sewn together; the entire area is closed, leaving only a small opening (the size of a match head) to allow for the passing of urine and menstrual fluid.

Some of the recent scholarship on West Africa has urged applying the term *female circumcision* to this practice and has challenged critics to consider the importance of its cultural context in developing an informed understanding of the practice. However, the World Health Organization holds the position that female circumcision is mutilation and should be abolished. The subject is debated in political arenas and academic circles within the question of cultural relativism versus human rights. Those who maintain that female circumcision is a violation of human rights see this debate as useful in its contribution to understanding that because of the vast complexity and nature of the practice, only a plan for eradication that considers how culturally ingrained this tradition is in the societies where it is practiced will succeed.

Scholars estimate that FGM has been practiced for at least 2,500 years, probably originating in the upper classes before becoming pervasive throughout all classes. Justifications of the practice include the beliefs that female genital mutilation will prevent promiscuity in women, that the clitoris is a masculine organ and will grow until it hangs between the legs if not removed, and that the operation ensures cleanliness and purity. Attenuating sexual desire in young girls and women and ensuring their virginity are among the main justifications for excision and infibulation today.

FGM jeopardizes the lives of girls and women. Many die from hemorrhage, infections, shock from pain and blood loss, urine detention due to occlusion, and damage done to other organs. Those who live suffer numerous ill effects to their health, including chronic urinary infections, vaginal stones, vulval adhesions, and infections of the reproductive system.

Once a woman has been infibulated, she must be opened before sexual intercourse or childbirth. In areas where husbands are often absent, women are closed while their husbands are away and opened on their husbands' return. After giving birth, an infibulated woman will be sewn closed again. Circumcision, a prerequisite for marriage—the only option for respectable women—becomes an initiation to a lifetime of torture in which a woman's genitals are cut, sewn, and cut again and again throughout the remainder of her life. *(See also: Female Sexuality; Gynecology)*

—**Elizabeth Fields**

Further Reading

Boddy, Janice. "Violence Embodied? Circumcision, Gender Politics, and Cultural Aesthetics." In *Rethinking Violence against Women,* edited by Rebecca Emerson Dobash and Russell P. Dobash, 77-110. Thousand Oaks, CA: Sage, 1998.

Daly Mary. *Gyn/Ecology: The Metaethics of Radical Feminism.* Boston: Beacon, 1990.

Fire Eyes. Produced, Written, and Directed by Soraya Mire. Sunset, 1993.

Gruenbaum, Ellen. "The Movement against Clitoridectomy and Infibulation in Sudan: Public Health Policy and the Women's Movement." In *Gender in Cross-Cultural Perspective,* edited by Caroline B. Brettell and Carolyn Sargent, 411-23. Englewood Cliffs, NJ: Prentice Hall, 1993.

Kwaak, Anke van der. "Female Gender Identity: A Questionable Alliance?" *Social Science & Medicine* 35 (1992): 777-87.

Lightfoot-Klein, Hanny. "The Sexual Experience and Marital Adjustment of Genitally Circumcised Females in the Sudan," *Journal of Sex Research* 26 (1989): 375-92.

Slack, Alison T. "Female Circumcision: A Critical Appraisal," *Human Rights Quarterly* 10 (1988): 437-86.

Thiam, Awa. "Women's Fight for the Abolition of Sexual Mutilation," *International Social Science Journal* 35 (1983): 747-56.

ᵬ Female-Headed Households

A female family head is a woman who maintains a domicile and who may or may not have dependents. From the colonial period to the present, the majority of American families have been headed by males, but the proportion of households headed by women has increased gradually over time. In the early twentieth century, female headship increased more rapidly than previously, and after World War II the rate of growth in female-household headship rose sharply. In 1890, women headed approximately fourteen of one hundred American households, but by 1990, the figure had risen to twenty-eight.

Throughout the eighteenth and nineteenth centuries, widowing was the most common cause of female headship, but in the twentieth century, new trends developed as single women began to establish separate households and as divorce rates rose. Rapidly increasing divorce rates in the 1960s and 1970s were the principal cause of the great increase in female headship during those years. As divorce rates stabilized in the 1980s, so too did the proportion of households that women headed.

The long-term rise in female headship indicates an increase in independence and autonomy among women, but it also reflects the rise in marital instability and the effects of increased life expectancy. Despite the rise in divorce rates, the principal cause of family headship among young mothers, the proportion of female household heads over the age of fifty-five has also risen in the twentieth century. Female headship among separated, divorced, and widowed women has always been associated with poverty. As the share of women living alone or heading families has grown, the relative poverty of these women and their children has also increased. In 1994, almost half of all American children who were poor lived in female-headed households. *(See also: Demography; Divorce)*

—**Julia Kirk Blackwelder**

Further Reading

Blackwelder, Julia Kirk. *Now Hiring: The Feminization of Work in the United States, 1900–1995.* College Station: Texas A&M University Press, 1997.

Jones, Jacqueline. *Labor of Love, Labor of Sorrow: Black Women, Work, and the Family from Slavery to the Present.* New York: Basic Books, 1985.

Kate, Nancy Ten. "Kaleidoscope: Two Careers, One Marriage," *American Demographics* 20 (April 1998): 28.

Ross, Heather L., and Isabel Sawhill, with the assistance of Anita R. MacIntosh. *Time of Transition: The Growth of Families Headed by Women.* Washington, DC: Urban Institute, 1975.

U.S. Bureau of the Census. *Historical Statistics of the United States, Colonial Times to 1970.* Bicentennial ed., Part 1. Table A, 320-49, p. 42. Washington, DC: Government Printing Office, 1975.

———. *U.S. Census of Population: 1980.* U.S. Summary, Vol. 1. Table 121, p. 93. Washington, DC: Government Printing Office, 1981.

Wellstone, Paul. "If Poverty Is the Question . . . , " *Nation* 264 (April 14, 1997): 15-18.

~ Female Sexuality

Female sexuality has always been shaped by historical forces, as well as by factors such as age, race, orientation, and the recurring tension between "pleasure and danger," sexual empowerment, and threat that many women have experienced. Historians of sexuality need to examine not only sexual experiences and behavior, which can be difficult to measure, but also ideologies, systems of power, and the rhetorical meanings of sexuality over time.

In many cultural traditions, female sexuality has been carefully guarded, and "impure" women have been treated harshly. An underlying duality in which women were seen as either hypersexual or uninterested in sex has shaped many theories about women. In the United States, African American, Latina, and Native American women have recurrently been stereotyped as sexually rapacious, and these beliefs have played a major role in their sexual oppression. In the nineteenth century, many upper-class white women negotiated the ideology of women's "passionlessness," a belief in their purity that was both imposed on women by medical writers and moralists and embraced by some women who sought to avoid a coercive male sexuality. During the nineteenth and early twentieth centuries, an ideology of sexual restraint and fear of sexual excess coexisted with a new world of commercial sexual pleasures, access to which varied according to gender and class. The twentieth century has seen the rise (and, some argue, the fall) of an ideology of sexual liberalism, which encompasses the encouragement and expansion of sexual pleasure within certain constraints (such as heterosexual marriage), qualified acceptance of homosexuality, and some blurring of the heterosexual/homosexual binary. The idea that sexuality is a crucial aspect of personal identity has become widely accepted, and Americans continue to debate the effects of the commercialization of sexuality.

Feminists have long disagreed about what female sexuality is or should be. Some nineteenth-century feminists regarded women as less sensual and more morally elevated than men, while others argued for women's entitlement to enjoy sexual pleasure in safety. More recent battles such as feminist debates over pornography and S/M have seen these themes recur. Sexuality has often been understood as an essential, biological capacity or urge, one that varies according to the repression or liberation of an individual or her society. A history of sexuality insists instead that sexuality varies widely across cultures and times. Ideas about female sexuality have shaped, and continue to shape, political and social movements for women's rights as well as other ideological battles. *(See also: Extramarital Sex; Kinsey Report; Lesbianism)*

—Miriam Reumann

Further Reading
Carby, Hazel. " 'It Just Be's dat Way Sometime': The Sexual Politics of Women's Blues." In *Unequal Sisters: A Reader in U.S. Women's History,* edited by Ellen Carol DuBois and Vicki Ruiz, 238-49. New York: Routledge, 1990.

Cott, Nancy F. "Passionlessness: An Interpretation of Victorian Sexual Ideology, 1790–1850." In *A Heritage of Her Own,* edited by Nancy F. Cott and Elizabeth Pleck, 162-81. New York: Simon & Schuster, 1979.

Davis, Katherine B. *Factors in the Sex Life of Twenty-Two Hundred Women.* New York: Harper, 1929.

D'Emilio, John, and Estelle Freedman. *Intimate Matters: A History of Sexuality in America,* 2d ed. Chicago: University of Chicago Press, 1997.

Kinsey, Alfred et al. *Sexual Behavior in the Human Female.* Philadelphia: W. B. Saunders, 1953.

Peiss, Kathy, and Christina Simmons. *Passion and Power: Sexuality in History.* Philadelphia: Temple University Press, 1988.

Smith-Rosenberg, Carroll. *Disorderly Conduct: Visions of Gender in Victorian America.* New York: Knopf, 1985.

Snitow, Ann, Christine Stansell, and Sharon Thompson, eds. *Powers of Desire: The Politics of Sexuality.* New York: Monthly Review Press, 1983.

Vance, Carole, ed. *Pleasure and Danger: Exploring Female Sexuality.* New York: Routledge, 1984.

~ Feme Covert

Feme covert is a legal term describing a married woman whose rights were restricted in early America by the common law concept of coverture. The woman and her husband became one will at the time of marriage, and the will was that of the husband. Her property, inheritance, and wages belonged to the husband, although the wife was protected in her right to dower and her right to veto any sale of family property. There were regional variations in the legal status of the *feme covert;* for example, married women enjoyed more independence in the Chesapeake colonies than they did in New England, particularly with respect to dower. Equity courts gave women some recourse from the restrictions of coverture. *(See also: Coverture; Common Law; Dower; Equity Courts; Feme Sol)*

—Barbara E. Lacey

Further Reading
Kerber, Linda K. *Women of the Republic: Intellect and Ideology in Revolutionary America.* Chapel Hill: University of North Carolina Press, 1980.

Norton, Mary Beth. *Liberty's Daughters: The Revolutionary Experience of American Women, 1750–1800.* Boston: Little, Brown, 1980.

~ *Feme Sol*

Feme sol is a legal term describing a single or widowed woman in early America who was legally free from the male control established in marriage under the concept of coverture. A *feme sol* could own property, enter into contracts, bequeath possessions, and serve as a legal guardian or administrator of an estate, although she had few political rights. A married woman could gain *feme sol* trader status on petition to the legislature if she could show that a husband was away for long periods of time, at sea or at war, and if the husband approved.

Few colonial women chose *feme sol* status deliberately. It was universally expected that a woman would marry, and there was little opportunity for financial support outside of marriage. However, of the tiny percentage of women who experienced personal autonomy, some came to develop conceptions of the self that differed from those of their married contemporaries.

The incremental success of nineteenth-century reform of state statutes that governed married women's property rights gradually rendered less significant the distinction between *feme sol* and *feme covert*. However, even in the late twentieth century, single women retained more legal autonomy than their married counterparts. *(See also: Coverture;* Feme Covert; *Married Women's Property Acts)*

—**Barbara E. Lacey**

Further Reading

Chambers-Schiller, Lee Virginia. *Liberty, A Better Husband: Single Women in America: The Generations of 1780–1840.* New Haven, CT: Yale University Press, 1984.

Lebsock, Suzanne. *The Free Women of Petersburg: Status and Culture in a Southern Town, 1784–1860.* New York: Norton, 1984.

~ Feminism

Feminism is a term used to describe collectively the historical movement for women's equality and (human) liberty within the nineteenth-century woman movement as well as the twentieth-century women's movement in the United States. *Feminism* was originally a French term that referred to the nineteenth-century American woman's movement, but it has since proved a useful term to designate the diverse goals and groups involved in the pursuit of the advancement of women's position in American society.

The phrase *woman movement* was deemed adequate by nineteenth-century women's rights advocates to encompass the contemporary pluralistic activities of reform-minded women and men who worked for women's advancement, although not necessarily for women's equality. Unlike feminism, however, *woman movement* defies application as an adjective, which explains the popularity of *feminism* as the generic term preferred by twentieth-century women's historians to connote in either century the wide range of strategies and tactics, theories, and goals or efforts to improve conditions for women. Regarding the use of *woman movement* versus *women's movement,* generally, women's historians observe the historically contemporary usage of *woman* in the generic sense—as in "the *woman* question" and the woman suffrage movement—when referring to the issues, events, and groups that date to the nineteenth century specifically; however, women's historians customarily use the plural possessive form *women's* as indicative of the twentieth-century historical context.

At the turn of the century, the term *feminist* was applied narrowly to those women's rights advocates who espoused women's gender-unique nature and mystical maternal potential rather than to designate those who emphasized their gender-neutral humanity and their similarity to men. By the latter half of the twentieth century, feminist became popular as the appropriate modifier term to connote advocacy of increased women's rights. American feminists challenged all aspects of the Victorian definition of woman that simultaneously degraded and elevated her. Collectively, their efforts focused on agitation and propaganda on behalf of all the sex, while individually they seized on new opportunities for women to realize personal advantage.

This pattern impelled feminists' participation in the mainstream reform movements of both the nineteenth and twentieth centuries, whether abolition, temperance, or other moral reform movements of the nineteenth century or progressivism, pacifism, or civil rights of the twentieth. Feminism followed the fate of other reform movements during the 1920s; its visibility and impact ebbed until the New Dealers recruited its leaders to assist in the modification of national policies in the wake of the Great Depression. In a restricted fashion, the national emergency of World War II opened doors for women as patriotic citizens that were closed with the onset of demobilization. However, those temporary opportunities in education and employment, again coupled with significant changes in the national economy, fostered women's resurgence as a presence in the civil rights and New Left movements of the 1950s and 1960s. Again, the women reformers confronted gender discrimination and responded by applying the egalitarian democratic philosophies of those movements to women's role and participation in contemporary society.

Thus, in the wake of the modern women's movement since the 1960s, feminism has become the designated term for activities and issues connected with the entire spectrum of the struggle for improvement of women's conditions in society. Within women's studies scholarship of the late 1980s, however, the term feminism was less commonly employed to designate a variety of doctrines, organized movements, theories, and assertions regarding women as a discrete group with a gender-specific history; the definition of feminist activities became more precise and required an explicit challenge to the gender system. *(See also: Deconstruc-*

tion; Domestic Feminism; Patriarchy; Rationalism; Social Feminism; Socialism; Socialist Feminism; Suffrage; Women's Rights Movements: Nineteenth and Twentieth Centuries)

—Angela M. Howard

Further Reading

Cott, Nancy F. *The Grounding of Modern Feminism*. New Haven, CT: Yale University Press, 1988.

Gordon, Linda. *Woman's Body, Woman's Right: A Social History of Birth Control in America*. New York: Penquin, 1977.

Lerner, Gerda. *The Creation of Feminist Consciousness from the Middle Ages to 1870*. New York: Oxford University Press, 1993.

———. *The Creation of Patriarchy*. New York: Oxford University Press, 1986.

Mankiller, Wilma, Gwendolyn Mink, Marysa Navarro, Barbara Smith, and Gloria Steinem, eds. *The Reader's Companion to U.S. Women's History*. Boston: Houghton Mifflin, 1998.

Schneir, Miriam, ed. *Feminism: The Essential Historical Writings*. New York: Vintage, 1972, 1994.

———, ed. *Feminism in Our Time: The Essential Writings, World War II to the Present*. New York: Vintage, 1994.

➣ Feminist Literary Criticism

Feminist literary criticism grew from and with the women's movement. Often focusing on Virginia Woolf's *A Room of One's Own* (1929) as an originating text, from such germinal works as Mary Ellmann's *Thinking about Women* (1968), a feminist literary criticism has considered gender as a fundamental basis for literary analysis and looked to the unique legacies, conditions, topics, and aesthetics of women's writing. In rising from the women's movement, early feminist criticism took its strength from activism and some of its theoretical politics from Marxism, and it led to writing collectives and to the development of women's periodicals and presses, such as the Feminist Press.

As an academic enterprise, feminist literary criticism began in the 1960s in a multipronged effort: to identify the sexism and misogyny in standard literary criticism and in the traditional canon, to provide a feminist critique of canonical male literature, to catalog images and stereotypes of women in conventional literature, and to recover and reclaim "lost" women writers and their texts. This effort produced courses and texts often addressing the oppression of women and sometimes called forth a prescriptive criticism "that attempts to set standards for literature that is 'good' from a feminist viewpoint" (Register 2).

Elaine Showalter in 1979 distinguished "distinct varieties" of feminist criticism: the feminist critique "concerned with woman as reader . . . in which the hypothesis of a female reader changes our apprehension of a given text, awakening us to the significance of its sexual codes" and gynocritics "concerned with the woman as writer . . . the history, themes, genres and structures of literature by women . . . the psychodynamics of female creativity" (128). Gynocritics has evolved in a wide-ranging critical effort, including literary and publishing history; biography, genre, linguistic, and semiotic study; and explication of particular works and careers—a criticism that Annette Kolodny has described as "recognizing the particular achievements of woman-as-author and their applicability in conscientiously decoding woman-as-sign" (185).

Lesbian literary criticism, ignored by the heterosexism of many early feminist texts, developed in periodicals such as *The Ladder* and *Sinister Wisdom*. The first volumes outlining a lesbian literary tradition were Jane Rule's *Lesbian Images* (1975) and Lillian Faderman's *Surpassing the Love of Men* (1980), advancing the literary culture of women-centered women. Adrienne Rich's germinal essay in *Signs*, "Compulsory Heterosexuality and Lesbian Existence," and Bonnie Zimmerman's *Feminist Studies* "What Has Never Been: An Overview of Lesbian Feminist Literary Criticism" established the distinctive perspective of lesbian criticism.

Black feminist criticism has developed into a cultural, contextual approach to the lives and works of black women writers and to explicating a black feminist aesthetic—looking for commonalities of theme, image, myth, and language. Alice Walker's *In Search of Our Mother's Gardens* answered her "desperate need to know and assimilate the experiences of earlier black women writers." Barbara Smith, in her germinal *Conditions: Two* essay "Toward a Black Feminist Criticism," laid out the injustices of inattention, racist, and sexist criticism of black women writers, calling forth the strength of distinctively black feminist analyses that would allow their books "to be real and remembered."

Recent work centering on Hispanic, Asian American, Italian American, and Polish American women writers develops the unique backgrounds and conditions of each group, complicating and enriching the analysis of women as subjects and agents, inscribing their personal histories and cultural identities.

Led by French literary feminists, feminist literary criticism since the mid-1970s has encompassed psychoanalytic, poststructuralist, deconstructionist, postmodernist, and postcolonial theory, applying male theorists to examine the feminine. In querying representation and valorizing the reader over the author, these theoretical positions interrogate discourse and ideology from the established perspectives of European cultural criticism.

Rather than promulgating a consistent school, feminist literary criticism as it has developed uses and adapts a range of methods and theoretical positions to generate new paradigms grounded in women's experience—focusing on woman as reader, as writer, and as sign. Fear of essentializing the concept of woman, of failing to include and understand differences between women, of reifying feminist reading of women's literature, or even of promulgating a countercanon of women's literature has kept feminist critics focused on the multiplicity of women's experiences and articulations. Expanding on considering the valences of race, ethnicity, sexual orientation, and class, cultural studies and postcolonial theory address the complexities of interaction between identity and ideology. *(See also: Deconstruction; Feminism; Women Writers; Women's Liberation Movement)*

—**Carol Klimick Cyganowski**

Further Reading

Benstock, Shari. *Feminist Issues in Literary Scholarship.* Bloomington: Indiana University Press, 1987.

Donaldson, Laura E. *Decolonizing Feminisms: Race, Gender, and Empire-Building.* Chapel Hill: University of North Carolina Press, 1996.

Eagleton, Mary. *Feminist Literary Theory: A Reader.* New York: Basil Blackwell, 1986.

Faderman, Lillian. *Surpassing the Love of Men: Love between Women from the Renaissance to the Present.* New York: Morrow, 1981.

Jardine, Alicia A. *Gynesis: Configurations of Women and Modernity.* Ithaca, NY: Cornell University Press, 1985.

Kolodny, Annette. "Dancing through the Minefield: Some Observations on the Theory, Practice and Politics of a Feminist Literary Criticism." In *Feminist Literary Theory: A Reader,* edited by Mary Eagleton, 184-88. New York: Basil Blackwell, 1986.

Moi, Toril. *Sexual/Textual Politics.* New York: Methuen, 1985.

Register, Cheri. "American Feminist Literary Criticism: A Bibliographical Introduction." In *Feminist Literary Criticism: Explorations in Theory,* edited by Josephine Donovan, 1-28. Lexington: University Press of Kentucky, 1975.

Rich, Adrienne. "Compulsory Heterosexuality and Lesbian Existence," *Signs* 5 (1980): 631-66.

Rule, Jane. *Lesbian Images.* Garden City, NY: Doubleday.

Showalter, Elaine. "Toward a Feminist Poetics." In *The New Feminist Criticism: Essays on Women, Literature and Theory,* pp. 125-43. New York: Pantheon, 1985.

Smith, Barbara. "Toward a Black Feminist Criticism," *Conditions: Two* 1 (October 1977).

Walker, Alice. *In Search of Our Mother's Gardens.* San Diego, CA: Harcourt Brace Jovanovich, 1983.

Zimmerman, Bonnie. "What Has Never Been: An Overview of Lesbian Feminist Literary Criticism," *Feminist Studies* 7 (1981): 451-75.

❧ Ferber, Edna (1885–1968)

Edna Ferber was a prolific journalist, novelist, short-story writer, and playwright whose works portray the American experience and whose fiction often depicts strong women characters.

Daughter of a Hungarian-born small businessman, she often reflected the pattern of her own family life in her literary works. Her father's inability to make a success of any of his various businesses and his eventual blindness led to his wife's taking control of the family finances. This theme of the strong woman who courageously faces adversity and achieves success is seen in a number of Ferber's works, most notably in her Emma McChesney short stories and the novels *So Big* and *Cimarron.*

Emma McChesney, a spunky divorced woman who sells Feather Loom petticoats to support her son, is the character that made Ferber a popular success. More than twenty stories based on this character were published between 1911 and 1915, and when Ferber was covering the 1912 Demo-cratic National Convention, Theodore Roosevelt reportedly asked her when Emma McChesney was going to marry.

Marriage, however, does not appear in Ferber's novels as a deus ex machina for her female protagonists. Rather, in *So Big,* a woman who is widowed receives only a debt-ridden farm as a legacy. However, due to her unceasing effort and strength of mind, she reverses the ineptitude that characterized her husband's management and makes the farm prosper. In *Cimarron,* the wife is the practical, hard-working half of the couple.

Ferber was a great popular success and a prolific writer. She wrote fourteen novels, ten collections of short stories, and nine plays (some in collaboration). *So Big* received a Pulitzer Prize in 1924; many of her works were turned into movies (e.g., *Show Boat, Cimarron,* and *Giant*); some of her plays also enjoyed successful runs on Broadway. Although not generally regarded highly by literary critics, Ferber is an interesting and important writer, especially in her portrayal of women, her sensitivity to the values of the land, and her interest in the social and cultural life of the working classes. *(See also: Journalism; Women Writers)*

—**Mabel Benson DuPriest**

Further Reading

Brenni, V. J., and B. L. Spencer. "Edna Ferber: A Selected Bibliography," *Bulletin of Bibliography* 22 (1958): 152-56.

Gilbert, Julie Goldsmith. *Ferber: A Biography.* Garden City, NY: Doubleday, 1978.

❧ Ferraro, Geraldine (b. 1935)

In 1984, Geraldine Ferraro became the first woman to be the vice presidential candidate of a major political party in the United States. Ferraro was born in Newburgh, New York, to Dominick and Antonetta (Corrieri) Ferraro. Her father was a restaurateur and dime-store owner who died when she was only eight years old. Her mother then moved to the Bronx and supported the family in part by crocheting beads on dresses. Partly because of the sacrifices of her mother and partly due to her own hard work, Ferraro was able to graduate from Marymount College, Tarrytown, New York, in 1956.

She then began a career as a second-grade teacher in the New York City public school system and began attending law school classes at night at Fordham University. In 1960, she married John Zaccaro, a real estate broker, and they eventually raised a family of three children. That same year, she graduated from Fordham's law school. She was admitted to the New York Bar in 1961. Between 1961 and 1974, Ferraro stayed in private practice. In 1974, she became an assistant district attorney for Queens County, New York, handling many child abuse, domestic violence, and rape cases. These experiences between 1974 and 1978 turned her from a self-confessed "small-*c* conservative to a liberal."

Active in local Democratic Party politics, Ferraro ran successfully for the U.S. House of Representatives in 1978, representing the Ninth District (Queens). One of fewer than two dozen congresswomen, Ferraro was reelected for two additional terms in the House. Respected by her colleagues and the House Democratic leadership, she served on the House Public Works Committee, the Democratic Steering and Policy Committee, and in 1983, the powerful Budget Committee. Her stature as a politician was further enhanced when she was named secretary of the House Democratic Caucus. Ferraro's voting record was generally mainstream liberal Democratic. This took considerable political courage, for she represented an often conservative, ethnic, blue-collar district. She did placate her more conservative constituents on one occasion by voting against mandatory busing for school integration. Ferraro's support for the right to choice on abortion also took a great deal of courage and soul-searching for her as a Roman Catholic.

In July 1984, her name became a household word in the United States when Democratic presidential nominee Walter Mondale named her as his vice presidential running mate. Her nomination sparked widespread jubilation among women and sympathetic men—another barrier had been shattered. As Ferraro noted in her acceptance speech to the Democratic National Convention, "By choosing a woman to run for our nation's second highest office, you send a powerful signal to all Americans. There are no doors we cannot unlock."

Despite the harsh glare of public scrutiny, Ferraro ran a spirited and vigorous campaign. She impressed many people with her command of the issues and her ability as a public speaker. Nevertheless, despite her abilities as a campaigner, there was little that could be done to overcome the incredible popularity of Ronald Reagan. Geraldine Ferraro returned to private life and completed her campaign memoirs in 1985. She ran unsuccessfully for the U.S. Senate in 1992. *(See also: Democratic Party; Gender Gap; Politics)*

—**Jonathan W. Zophy**

Further Reading

Adams, James R. "The Lost Honor of Geraldine Ferraro," *Commentary* 81 (January 1986): 34-38.

Ferraro, Geraldine. *Ferraro: My Story.* New York: Bantam, 1985.

Thomas, Evan. " 'Just One of the Guys' and Quite a Bit More," *Time* 124 (July 23, 1984): 18-20, 33.

ᕔ Fertility

With the exception of short-term fluctuations, the birthrate in America has declined consistently from the colonial period to the present. From the seventeenth century until the early nineteenth century, it was very high in comparison with that of other Western societies. For these years, average "completed fertility" was about eight children for every married woman in America. Although demographers variously date the beginning of the modern fertility decline between 1770 and 1830, there is general agreement that the late nineteenth century was a period of sharp decline.

Among women who had completed their childbearing by 1910, the average number of children born to each was 5.4. Since 1910, completed fertility has declined to between two and three children per "ever-married" woman. A noticeable but temporary "boom" in fertility occurred between 1947 and 1964, with the birthrate reaching a twentieth-century high of 25.3 births per 1,000 women between the ages of fifteen to forty-five years in 1957. But these rates were still considerably below the estimated 65 to 77 births per 1,000 women in the late nineteenth century. Fertility in the United States has declined since 1964.

Important differences in fertility exist between regions and among ethnic or racial groups in the United States. Fertility has consistently been higher in rural than in urban areas, and immigrant women and nonwhite women have generally had higher fertility than native-born white women. During the years of Negro slavery, black women had consistently higher fertility than white women, but black fertility rates declined gradually after emancipation, and during the 1930s, the black fertility rate dropped below that of whites. Overall fertility declined by 1995 to 656 births for every 1,000 women of childbearing age. Through the 1990s, Hispanic women experienced the highest fertility followed by non-Hispanic black women and non-Hispanic white women, with Asian-American women maintaining the lowest fertility. *(See also: Baby Boom; Demography)*

—**Julia Kirk Blackwelder**

Further Reading

Grabill, Wilson H., Clyde V. Kiser, and Pascal K. Whelpton. *The Fertility of American Women.* New York: John Wiley, 1958.

Schapiro, Morton Owen. *Filling Up America: An Economic-Demographic Model of Population Growth and Distribution in the Nineteenth-Century United States.* Greenwich, CT: JAI, 1986.

Taeuber, Conrad, and Irene Taeuber. *The Changing Population of the United States.* New York: John Wiley, 1958.

U.S. Bureau of the Census. *Historical Statistics of the United States, Colonial Times to the Present.* Part 1, Bicentennial ed. Washington, DC: Government Printing Office, 1975.

———. *Statistical Abstract of the United States.* Washington, DC: U.S. Department of Commerce, 1997.

Van Horn, Susan Housholder. *Women, Work, and Fertility, 1900–1986.* New York: New York University Press, 1988.

ᕔ Finnigan, Annette (1871–1940)

State and local suffrage leader, Annette Finnigan founded the Houston Equal Suffrage League of Houston, Texas, in February 1903. Annette Finnigan and her sisters Katherine (Daisy) Finnigan Anderson (1867–1951) and Elizabeth (Bessie) Finnigan Fain (unknown) hosted educational social events and tea parties during the first stage of the local suffrage movement between 1903 and 1905.

In 1904, as state president of the first Texas Woman Suffrage Association (founded 1903), Finnigan tried to establish suffrage organizations in LaPorte, Beaumont, San

Antonio, and Austin. Only the effort in LaPorte was successful. She returned to New York in 1905. Without her leadership, the local Houston and state suffrage campaigns languished until 1913 when she returned to Houston and reactivated the local organization under a new name—Houston Women's Political Union (HWPU). During the second phase of the local suffrage effort from 1913 to 1916, the HWPU hosted weekly teas in public facilities, and its members often belonged to more than one woman's club. Finnigan was reelected president at the Fourth Annual Texas Equal Suffrage Association (TESA) convention in April 1914. She directed letter-writing campaigns to lobby for suffrage support from Texas state senators and representatives and addressed the special session of the lower Texas house in September 1914. In January 1915, she led a petition campaign to persuade businessmen and professionals to support woman suffrage in Texas. The suffragists delivered the petitions to the Texas legislature in Austin during the February 1915 session. Annette Finnigan registered as a lobbyist at the Texas state capital. During the summer of 1916, she polled senators and representatives on their position regarding woman suffrage.

By the fifth annual state suffrage convention of the Texas Equal Suffrage Association in Galveston in May 1915, Finnigan had resigned and was succeeded by Minnie Fisher Cunningham (1882–1964) as president of TESA. Cunningham led the final phase of the Texas state suffrage effort.

In 1916, Annette Finnigan, who had assumed leadership of her father's business after his death in 1909, suffered a stroke and moved back to New York. After her recovery, she traveled abroad and purchased many valuable collections, which she later donated to the Houston Museum of Fine Arts. She also purchased a seventeen-acre plot for a Houston city park.

Finnigan died in July 1940. Her efforts for the suffrage cause were vital to the success of the local suffrage organization, which contributed significantly to the state effort. The strong leadership of Annette Finnigan in the early phases of the Houston and Texas suffrage campaigns established the political support that enabled Texas to become the first southern state to ratify the Nineteenth Amendment. (See also: Suffrage; Suffrage in the South)

—Paula Williams Webber

Further Reading

Annette Finnigan file. Houston Metropolitan Research Center, Houston Public Library, Houston, TX.

Chapman, Betty T. "Annette Finnigan: Building an Enlightened Community in Houston." Paper presented at Texas State Historical Association Annual Meeting, Lubbock, TX, March 1989.

Hunter, Helen, Denise Nosal, and Mary Gillette, eds. *Houston Women from Suffrage to City Hall.* Houston, TX: D. Armstrong, 1987.

Webber, Paula Williams. "The Early Houston Woman Suffrage Movement, 1903–1917." Master's thesis. University of Houston–Clear Lake, 1995.

☙ Fiorenza, Elisabeth Schussler
(b. 1938)

Elisabeth Fiorenza is a biblical studies scholar whose work has significantly defined feminist critical interpretation of the New Testament for over a decade. Her groundbreaking work *In Memory of Her* (1983) attempted a reconstruction of traditional historical accounts of early Christian origins in light of the role and importance of women in the early Jesus movement. The result was a thoroughgoing reevaluation and critique of traditional biblical scholarship as it had existed up to that time and the beginning of a systematic feminist methodology concerning biblical texts that resulted in the discipline of feminist interpretive theory. *In Memory of Her* gave hermeneutical, methodological, and theological framework to the work already begun by Elaine Pagels (b. 1943) and others on early canonical and noncanonical materials that illumine and, conversely, subvert women's prominence and significance in early Christianity.

Fiorenza followed *In Memory of Her* immediately with *Bread Not Stone* (1984) and, later, *But She Said* (1992) and *Discipleship of Equals* (1993). These three works extend and amplify the project of feminist critique and reconstruction not only of biblical texts and the traditional historical/critical analysis that has accompanied them but also of the enterprise of feminist interpretation, inasmuch as it can limit itself to and even reimplicate itself into patriarchal modes of analysis and hermeneutical assumptions. Fiorenza locates the center for the feminist interpretive task not in the patriarchal church but in the *ekklesia* of women, or women-church as a discipleship of equals "that can make present the *basileia,* the alternative world of justice and well-being intended by the life-giving power of G-d, as reality and vision in the midst of the death-dealing powers of patriarchal oppression and dehumanization."

Fiorenza's latest work is an attempt to reformulate traditional Christology. *Jesus: Miriam's Child, Sophia's Prophet* (1994) is an imaginative work that exploits strands of early Jesus traditions that understand him as standing in a long line of messengers and prophets sent by Divine Wisdom, or Sophia, to announce good news to the downtrodden. *Basileia* figures prominently here as in earlier works as Fiorenza tries to offer a liberating, open-ended approach to Christology that does not close down the "road to Galilee" for feminists. Finally, Fiorenza has edited a two-volume work titled *Searching the Scriptures* (1993) that seeks to give a comprehensive overview of the various methodologies, theoretical frameworks, theological and philosophical assumptions employed by feminist interpreters of biblical texts by providing provocative examples of feminist analysis of selected biblical and quasi-biblical texts. The larger task of the volumes is to introduce and educate readers into a different mode of analysis and "sociohistorical and theo-ethical imagination" than is traditionally used in biblical criticism. (See also: Christianity; Religion; Theologians)

—B. Jill Carroll

Further Reading
Fiorenza, Elisabeth Schussler. *Bread Not Stone: The Challenge of Feminist Biblical Interpretation.* Boston: Beacon, 1984.
———. *But She Said: Feminist Practices of Biblical Interpretation.* Boston: Beacon, 1984.
———. *Discipleship of Equals: A Critical Feminist Ekklesia-ology of Liberation.* New York: Crossroad, 1993.
———, ed. *Feminist Theology in Different Contexts.* Maryknoll, NY: Orbis, 1997.
———. *In Memory of Her: A Feminist Theological Reconstruction of Christian Origins.* New York: Crossroad, 1983.
———. *Jesus: Miriam's Child, Sophia's Prophet—Critical Issues in Feminist Christology.* New York: Continuum, 1994.
———, ed. *The Power of Naming: A Concilium Reader in Feminist Liberation Theology.* Maryknoll, NY: Orbis, 1996.
———, ed. *Searching the Scriptures,* 2 vols. New York: Crossroad, 1993.

ᴥ Fisher, Welthy Honsinger
(1879–1980)

Missionary educator and pioneer literacy leader in China and India, Welthy Fisher was headmistress of the Baldwin School (Bao-lin) in Nanchang, China, from 1906 to 1917. As the foremost Methodist woman speaker of her time, she wrote and spoke widely throughout the United States, urging women's active participation in antiwar and social reform work. Membership in the Committee for Peaceful Alternatives put her on Senator Joseph McCarthy's list of suspected subversives during the 1950s.

An ordained deacon in the Methodist Church, Fisher was licensed to preach, baptize, and marry. She declined the invitation to become an elder, unwilling to subject herself to control by the ecclesiastical bureaucracy. She advocated women's rights in the Christian Church in the United States, China, and India, where she lived many years as the wife and widow of the U.S. Methodist Bishop to India, Frederick Bohn Fisher. She was a critic of U.S. missionaries' collusion with other Westerners' exploitation of indigenous people in colonial India, China, and Africa. She urged Christian churches to learn from Asian cultures, warning "I dare not take a white-faced or European interpretation of Christ."

Fisher expanded her network of friends far beyond the missionary communities. When living in the United States, she frequently spoke at the Christian Retreat for Black Women. During World War II, she actively supported the Chinese Industrial Cooperatives. In India, she addressed the Indian National Council of Women, supported the All India Women's Conference, and frequently participated in Mahatma Gandhi's daily meditation. From Gandhi, poet Rabindraneth Tagore, and other Indian, Chinese, and Western leaders, she gained a deep commitment to village education and industries.

In 1952, at the age of seventy-three, Fisher initiated her major life's project, Literacy House, a precedent-setting adult education program in four hundred Indian villages. Working closely with the villagers, she and her staff of Indian and Western educators developed educational puppetry, which used traditional Indian epic narratives to teach villagers agriculture and other topics of their choosing. She tried to avoid "spiritual imperialism" by building an interfaith house of prayer and hiring a staff of diverse religious backgrounds.

Fisher received many awards and honorary degrees in the United States, India, Canada, the Philippines, and the United Nations, including the Ramon Magaysay "Asian Peace Prize." The government of India issued a commemorative postage stamp in her honor. To the staff and trainees at Literacy House, she was "Mataji," "Respected Mother." *(See also: Christianity; Pacifism and the Peace Movement; Social Reform)*

—Marjorie King

Further Reading
Fisher, Welthy Honsinger. *Beyond the Moongate: Being a Diary of Ten Years in the Interior of the Middle Kingdom.* New York: Abingdon, 1924.
———. *To Light a Candle.* New York: McGraw-Hill, 1962.
Kelly, Colleen Adele. "The Educational Philosophy of Welthy Honsinger Fisher in China and India, 1906–1980: An Intellectual Biography." Ph.D. diss., University of Connecticut, 1983.
Klaitz, Linda. "An Examination of the Oral Biographies of Eight Exceptional Women." Ph.D. diss., Columbia University, 1978.
Swenson, Sally. *Welthy Honsinger Fisher: Signals of a Century,* 1989. [Sally Swenson, Stittsville, Ontario, K2S 1B9, Canada]

ᴥ Fitzgerald, Zelda (Sayre) (1900–1948)

Zelda Fitzgerald was born in Montgomery, Alabama, the daughter of Judge Anthony D. Sayre and Minnie Machen, but she left the South in 1920 when she married writer F. Scott Fitzgerald. Because of the immediate popularity of his writing, which embodied the freewheeling yet restless spirit of the era, and because of the Fitzgeralds' considerable good looks and charm, they captured the imagination of the American public during the 1920s and came to be known as "the couple" of the era.

Newspapers reported on their flamboyant lifestyle, on the East Coast and then in Europe, and accounts invariably cast Zelda in a 1920s flapper mold. Scott's writing reinforced this image, as he modeled his free-spirited but spoiled heroines after Zelda. Increasingly, it became difficult for Zelda to separate herself from this fictionalized image and also from her husband's fame. In 1925, shortly after the critically acclaimed publication of Fitzgerald's *Great Gatsby,* the couple joined the American expatriate community in France, where the strain on their marriage due to Scott's success and the accompanying lifestyle, excessively self-indulgent and extravagant, began to tell. Scott found it difficult to write during the last half of the decade, and Zelda showed signs of extreme introversion.

Although Scott and Zelda had collaborated on the writing of some stories and essays during the early 1920s, Zelda received only slight recognition, and this began to bother her. Having failed to achieve acclaim as a writer, she sought to earn recognition as a dancer. But she began to study ballet too late in life (at the age of twenty-eight), and eventually the strain of her obsessive workouts, complicated by the strains in the Fitzgeralds' marriage, began to take both a physical and psychological toll. Zelda suffered her first mental breakdown in France in 1930, and what her doctors diagnosed as schizophrenia kept her in and out of institutions, in Europe and in America, for the rest of her life. Interned on the top floor of the main building of the Ashville (North Carolina) Highland Mental Hospital, she died in 1948 when the structure caught fire.

Although Zelda was unable to pursue her dancing, she did achieve a degree of success both as a writer and a painter. Her autobiographical novel *Save Me the Waltz,* which was published in 1932 and which received limited recognition, is generally regarded today as a work that shows potential but lacks discipline, its imagery evocative but disjointed and overwrought. Zelda's painting (primarily watercolors that she began to execute after the appearance of her novel) employed wild, grotesque images—flowers and human figures almost cartoonlike in their vibrant colors and flat, distorted dimensions. Zelda seemed to derive her greatest artistic rewards from her paintings, which she continued to execute throughout the 1940s until her death. Some of these paintings were exhibited in New York at private galleries and purchased by friends. Zelda's creativity was considerable, but the circumstances of her life made it difficult, if not impossible, for her to find a suitable focus for her genius. *(See also: Flapper)*

—**Linda Patterson Miller**

Further Reading

Bruccoli, Matthew J., ed. *Zelda Fitzgerald: The Collected Writings.* New York: Scribners, 1991.

Bruccoli, Matthew J., and Margaret M. Duggan, eds. *Correspondence of F. Scott Fitzgerald.* New York: Random House, 1980.

Hartnett, Koula Svokos. *Zelda Fitzgerald and the Failure of the American Dream for Women.* New York: Peter Lang, 1991.

Mayfield, Sara. *Exiles from Paradise: Zelda and Scott Fitzgerald.* New York: Delacorte, 1971.

Mellow, James R. *Invented Lives: F. Scott & Zelda Fitzgerald.* Boston: Houghton Mifflin, 1984.

Milford, Nancy. *Zelda.* New York: Harper & Row, 1970.

Wood, Mary Elene. "A Wizard Cultivator, Zelda Fitzgerald, Madness and Body." Center for the Study of Women in Society cassette tape, recorded February 19, 1988, University of Oregon, Eugene.

❧ Flapper

The image of the flapper has become inseparable from the popular perception of the 1920s. Originally, the British term for predebutantes, *flapper* came to designate those young women who flaunted unconventional behavior and dress during and after World War I. The flapper was immortalized in the contemporary literature and media of an era characterized by disillusionment and obsessed with the impact of political fundamentalism. A symbol of the social rebellion of youth in the 1920s, the flapper was glamorized far beyond the actual minority of middle-class educated young women who indulged in the unfettered and scandalously hedonistic lifestyle that centered on publicly smoking cigarettes and drinking illegal alcohol while frequenting the after-hours speakeasies and jazz clubs. As a version of womanhood, the flapper not only expressed the power struggle between the rising city and waning rural heartland but also repudiated the duty, dedication, and civic activism of both domestic feminism and social feminism.

The flapper was a commercialized sex object, but she floated between androgyny and child pornography. Physically, she should look like a sexy boy and intellectually and emotionally be a woman of the world. Thus, the fashionable costume of the flapper emphasized her immediate role as a glamorous playmate for idle, overindulged young men rather than offering a suitable ensemble for her ultimate role as worker, wife, or mother. The marketable image of the flapper had little relevance to the lives of the majority of women who—either as sex-segregated workers or as homemakers-consumers—became the mainstay of the unstable and overheated economy of the 1920s. Therefore, the flapper vanished quickly from both literature and the media after the Crash of '29 brought the Great Depression and the repeal of prohibition. *(See also: Fitzgerald, Zelda; Freudianism; New Woman; Social Feminism)*

—**William G. Shade**
—**Angela M. Howard**

Further Reading

Fass, Paula. *The Beautiful and the Damned: American Youth in the 1920s.* New York: Oxford University Press, 1977.

Yellis, Kenneth. "Prosperity's Child: Some Thoughts on the Flapper," *American Quarterly* 21 (Spring 1969): 44-64.

❧ Flint Auto Workers' Strike

The Flint Auto Workers' Strike in Flint, Michigan, was the most famous of the "sit-down" strikes introduced by the United Auto Workers union. Lasting from December 30, 1936, to February 11, 1937, the strike was a response to pent-up anger over an intolerable speedup on the assembly line and management's refusal to bargain with the union even though the law required it. Settlement of the strike brought about recognition of the United Auto Workers (UAW) by General Motors and a wage increase from thirty to 40 cents an hour to one dollar an hour. Union membership grew from 30,000 to 500,000 because of the success of the strike.

During the strike, sit-downers, all men on order of the union leadership, occupied three Fisher Auto Body Assembly plants, subsidiaries of GM. The sit-down strike was effective because any assault against the workers inside the plant would endanger the expensive machinery. Scabs could not be used, and a solidarity developed among the workers

Figure 21. Flint Auto Workers' Strike
Wives of striking Flint auto workers join female strikers, who were not allowed to join the factory sit-in, and march in the Women's Emergency Brigade. Used by permission of UPI/Corbis-Bettmann.

living in the plant. A network of committees helped with legal defense, food, picketing, transportation, publicity, and other needs. Women played a big part in this outside organization. When the police threatened the workers inside the plants, women established a Women's Emergency Brigade with 350 volunteers who formed a protective picket line between strikers and police. "A new type of woman was born in the strike," a volunteer said. "Women who only yesterday were horrified at unionism, who felt inferior to the task of organizing, speaking, leading, have, as if overnight, become the spearhead in the battle of unionism."

On January 21, 1937, the police shot fourteen people in a conflict that became known as the Battle of Bulls Run. The author Mary Heaton Vorse called it that because the "bulls" (the police) ran. She described the confrontation: "Preparatory to the battle the street had been cleared. The women said, 'Nothing was going to stop us getting food in to our men.' The police were firing point-blank into the crowd that included women. Union sympathizers were retaliating with the only means of defense they had—stones, lumps of coal, steel hinges, milk bottles. That, and their courage, were their only weapons. Yet they held their ground."

In the final crisis of the strike, after the sit-downers occupied the "Chevrolet 4" plant, thousands of workers came to Flint. To avoid the appearance of provocation, organizers declared the mobilization Women's Day, and women's brigades came in from Lansing, Pontiac, Detroit, and Toledo, Ohio. One woman addressed a great picket line from the sound wagon, and as Mary Heaton Vorse wrote, "She told the crowd that the women had gone to union headquarters to wipe their eyes clear from tear gas and would soon be back. 'We don't want any violence; we don't want any trouble. . . . But we are going to protect our husbands.' "

The Flint Auto Strike proved significant to both labor and women's history. The success of the strike strengthened the UAW and the organized labor movement of the 1930s because the publicity bolstered public support for unionization and spurred the passage of the major piece of New Deal labor legislation, the Wagner Act of 1935. The strike also demonstrated the importance to the achievement of the union victory in 1937 of women's support for and within the local union. The drama of women's participation in the strike was captured in the documentary *With Babies and Banners. (See also: Unions; United Auto Workers)*

—**Abby Schmelling**

Further Reading
Boyer, Richard, and Herbert Morais. *Labor's Untold Story.* New York: United Electrical, Radio and Machine Workers of America, 1974.

Brecher, Jeremy. *Strike!* Greenwich, CT: Fawcett, 1974.

Fine, Sidney. *Sit-Down, The General Motors Strike of 1936–37.* Ann Arbor: University of Michigan Press, 1969.

Gray, Lorraine. *With Babies and Banners.* Produced with Ann Bohlen and Lyn Goldfarb. Ho-Ho-Kus, NJ: New Day Films. Film, videocassette. [Available from New Day Films, 22D Hollywood Ave., Ho-Ho-Kus, NJ 07423; phone: 201-652-6590; fax: 201-652-1973]

Vorse, Mary Heaton. *Labor's New Millions.* New York: Modern Age, 1938.

❧ Flisch, Julia Anna (1861–1941)

Teacher, author, and advocate for educational and occupational opportunities for women, Julia Flisch epitomized the "New Woman" of the New South. Born at the beginning of the American Civil War and dying as World War II dominated the globe, her life spanned an era of restricted roles for women and one of expanding opportunities. The child of immigrant parents, Flisch was not a typical daughter of the Old South. Denied admission to the all-male University of Georgia in 1879, Flisch fought for a state-supported college not only to educate women but to prepare them to support themselves. Her battle cry became "Give the girls a chance!" In 1890, Flisch was the spokesperson for Georgia women at the laying of the cornerstone for Georgia Normal and Industrial College, where she served as a faculty member from 1891 to 1905. In 1899, twenty years after denying Flisch admission and twenty years before officially enrolling female students, the University of Georgia awarded Flisch the first honorary degree ever given by the school to a woman. In 1908, Flisch received her master's degree from the University of Wisconsin, where she studied history under Frederick Jackson Turner, Ulrich Bonnell Phillips, and Richard Ely. She taught, until 1926, at the prestigious Tubman School for Girls in Augusta, Georgia. Flisch served as dean of women and professor of history at Augusta Junior College, the first junior college in Georgia, until poor health forced her retirement in 1936.

"Common People of the Old South," a paper Flisch presented at the American Historical Association meeting in 1908, called for a shift of focus in traditional southern history from the planter elite to the "common people," thus foreshadowing the work of Frank Owsley in the 1930s and social historians in the 1960s and 1970s. Flisch also published two novels, *Ashes of Hopes* (1886) and *Old Hurricane* (1926), and numerous articles in magazines and newspapers. Her fictional writings were social histories that allowed Flisch to focus on individuals, particularly women, and their struggle to adapt to socioeconomic conditions.

Flisch was active in the Woman's Christian Temperance Union, the Daughters of the Confederacy, the General Federation of Women's Clubs, and the Equal Suffrage Party. During the 1920s, she spearheaded teachers' movements regarding quality education and equal pay. After her death in 1941, Flisch was lauded as "having done more than any

other person to advance the cause of women's education in Georgia." She paved the way for women to receive quality education and practical vocational training. Throughout her life, Flisch consistently urged that women be allowed opportunities to "work out their own independence" to be of "some active use in the world." She was particularly concerned that the post-Civil War South in its efforts to move into the future should not disregard its female citizens and warned that one day society would be held accountable for the "fruitless lives of so many southern women." In her teaching, her writings, and the life she led, Flisch consistently battled for unrestricted educational and occupational choices for women. *(See also: Higher Education for Southern Women; New Woman; Southern Women's History; Southern Women's Organizations/Leaders)*

—**Robin O. Harris**

Further Reading
Cashin, Edward. *A History of Augusta College.* Augusta, GA: Augusta College Press, 1976.

———. *The Quest: A History of Public Education in Richmond County.* Columbia, SC: R. L. Bryan, 1985.

Hair, William I., James C. Bonner, Edward B. Dawson, and Robert J. Wilson III. *A Centennial History of Georgia College.* Milledgeville: Georgia College, 1989.

Harris, Robin O. "Julia Anna Flisch: Georgia Educator and Feminist." Master's thesis, Georgia College, 1993.

———. "Julia Anna Flisch: New South Advocate for Educational and Occupational Opportunities for Women." Ph.D. diss., Georgia Tech., 1996.

———. " 'To Illustrate the Genius of Southern Womanhood': Julia Flisch and Her Campaign for the Higher Education of Georgia Women," *Georgia Historical Quarterly,* April 1996: 506-31.

Julia A. Flisch Collection. Special Collections, Ina Dillard Russell Library, Georgia College, Milledgeville, GA.

❧ Flynn, Elizabeth Gurley (1890–1964)

A political activist for over fifty years, Elizabeth Gurley Flynn was fondly known as "the Rebel Girl" of the Industrial Workers of the World (IWW). Her mother, Annie Gurley Flynn, was a member of the Knights of Labor and the Irish Feminist Club in New York City; her father, Thomas Flynn, belonged to the Socialist Labor Party and the IWW, a revolutionary organization that worked to radicalize the labor movement in the early twentieth century. Flynn made her first political speech at the age of sixteen, addressing the Harlem Socialist Club on the topic "What Socialism Will Do for Women." The following year, she joined the IWW.

Flynn cut her political teeth in the free-speech fights of 1909 during the IWW campaign to organize labor in the West and soared to national prominence as one of the fiery speakers at the 1912 textile strike in Lawrence, Massachusetts. In 1908, she met and married IWW organizer Jack Jones and bore two children, a premature baby who died shortly after birth and a son, Fred. The marriage lasted only two years, and in Lawrence, she met the anarchist Carlo Tresca, with whom she lived for the next thirteen years.

From 1910 until 1917, Flynn worked ceaselessly to organize workers into the IWW and spoke out forcefully on women's issues. She accepted, however, the IWW philosophy that women's problems could not be separated from the problems of the working class. After 1917, Flynn specialized in labor defense work, supporting the hundreds of radicals arrested and imprisoned during the first Red Scare of 1919. In 1926, exhausted from her efforts on behalf of Sacco and Vanzetti and from her breakup with Tresca, she retired to Portland, Oregon, and spent ten years regaining her physical and emotional health.

Flynn was a founding member of the American Civil Liberties Union (ACLU) in 1920 and served on its board of directors until 1940. In 1937, she joined the Communist Party, and three years later, the ACLU board voted narrowly to expel her for her defiance of a resolution designed to purge members who belonged to "any political organization which supports totalitarian dictatorship." (The resolution, originally intended to exclude fascists, was mostly used against members of the Communist Party.)

Flynn remained in the Communist Party and in 1961 became its first woman chairperson. In 1951, she, along with other party leaders, was prosecuted under the Smith Act, also known as the Alien Registration Act. Convicted in 1953, she served two and a half years in Alderson Prison, Alderson, West Virginia. Elizabeth Gurley Flynn died in Moscow in 1964 on her first visit to the USSR. In 1978, the ACLU posthumously rescinded her expulsion. *(See also: Communist Party; Industrial Workers of the World; Lawrence Strike of 1912)*

—**Mary Murphy**

Further Reading

Baxandall, Rosalyn Fraad, ed. *Words on Fire: The Life and Writing of Elizabeth Gurley Flynn.* New Brunswick, NJ: Rutgers University Press, 1987.

Camp, Helen. *Iron in Her Soul: Elizabeth Gurley Flynn and the American Left.* Pullman: Washington State University Press, 1995.

Flynn, Elizabeth Gurley. *The Rebel Girl: An Autobiography, My First Life.* New York: International Publishers, 1973.

ꝏ Folklore

Folklore means folk learning and includes any and all knowledge transmitted by word of mouth. The term *folklore* therefore encompasses all techniques, arts, and crafts learned by imitation rather than formal instruction. The field encompasses studies of arts, crafts, tools, costumes, customs, beliefs, medicine, recipes, dance, games, gestures, speech, and verbal arts, such as folktales, legends, myths, proverbs, riddles, poetry, and humor. Folklore functions in society to provide education, transmit social norms, support political relations, and provide psychological releases from cultural and social restrictions and taboos. Women's

folklore has been included in studies of fairy tales and folktales, rituals and rites of passage, storytelling, and in brief, most aspects of folklore and folk arts. *(See also: Native American Women; Native American Women's Literature; Quilts)*

—**Mary G. Hodge**

Further Reading

Dorson, Richard M., ed. *Folklore and Folklife: An Introduction.* Chicago: University of Chicago Press, 1982.

———, ed. *Handbook of American Folklore.* Bloomington: Indiana University Press, 1983.

Farrer, Claire R., ed. *Women and Folklore.* Austin: University of Texas Press, 1975.

———, ed. *Women and Folklore: Images and Genres.* Prospect Heights, IL: Waveland, 1986.

Harding, M. Esther. *Women's Mysteries, Ancient and Modern.* New York: Rider, 1955.

Lincoln, Bruce. *Emerging from the Chrysalis: Studies in Rituals of Women's Initiation.* Cambridge, MA: Harvard University Press, 1981.

von Franz, Marie Louise. *Problems of the Feminine in Fairytales.* Irving, TX: Spring, 1972.

Weigel, Marta. *Spiders and Spinsters: Women and Mythology.* Albuquerque: University of New Mexico Press, 1982.

ꝏ Fonda, Jane (b. 1937)

Actor, political activist, and entrepreneur, Jane Fonda is the winner of Academy Awards for *Klute* (1971) and *Coming Home* (1978), as well as a New York Film Critics' Award for *They Shoot Horses, Don't They?* (1969), a Golden Globe for *Coming Home,* and an Emmy for *The Dollmaker* (1984). Fonda has proved to be one of America's most talented actors. She is the daughter of American actor Henry Fonda.

While Fonda's earliest success was on the Broadway stage, she is primarily a film actor. Early films, such as *Barbarella* (1968), directed by her first husband Roger Vadim, established her as a sex symbol. But by the early 1970s, Fonda's increasing interest in politics changed her direction in film.

Fonda was one of the most vocal critics of American involvement in Southeast Asia. Her criticism of American foreign policy led to arrests and antipathy from the film industry and some of her audience. She received the Sour Apple Award from the Hollywood Women's Press Club for presenting a sour image of the industry. In 1972, she outraged many by touring North Vietnam and posing next to an antiaircraft gun.

In the mid-1970s, Fonda's professional life brought her to national attention as a businesswoman. Her first business venture was Indo-China Peace Campaign (IPC), now Fonda Films, a film company. The company produced films such as *Coming Home, The China Syndrome* (1979), and *Nine to Five* (1980). Fonda's second business venture, Workout, Inc., operates fitness studios and produces books, records, videotapes, and clothing. Fonda's workout books are best-sellers, and her first *Jane Fonda's Workout* videotape became the top grossing video of all time.

With her second husband, Congressman Tom Hayden, Fonda formed the Campaign for Economic Democracy. Working with Hayden in the 1980s, Fonda was a vocal critic of nuclear energy, sexual discrimination, and other social justice issues.

In 1989, Fonda announced her decision to divorce Hayden. She then married media mogul Ted Turner and took a hiatus from film work. She published a recipe book, *Cooking for Healthy Living*, in 1996. *(See also: Movie Stars; Vietnam War)*

—Preston Lane

Further Reading
Carroll, Peter N. *Famous in America*. New York: E. P. Dutton, 1985.
Davidson, Bill. *Jane Fonda*. London: Sidgwick & Jackson, 1990.
Guiles, F. L. *Jane Fonda*. New York: Doubleday, 1982.

ᴧ Foote, Mary Hallock (1847–1918)

Popular writer and illustrator, Mary Hallock Foote published thirteen novels, fourteen short stories and story collections, and innumerable illustrations of life on the western frontier. Born in Milton, New York, to an old agrarian Quaker family and educated at the Cooper Institute for Art, Foote had launched a promising career as an artist when she suddenly gave it up to marry Arthur DeWint Foote, a mining engineer from the West.

After the wedding in 1876, her husband took her away from the genteel, established East to the rough-hewn, developing frontier in Colorado. Over the next thirty years, he moved his family from mining camp to mining camp in Colorado, Mexico, Idaho, and California, wherever he could find work. Because her husband's career was less than successful, Foote was forced to write novels so that the bills could be paid and the children could be fed.

Set in various mining and irrigation camps, Foote's novels and tales made a significant contribution to nineteenth-century western realism and local color. Her observations of the character of frontier lands and the people who lived there are important because Foote's perspective was unique: She was writing from the point of view of a moderately wealthy Easterner who was suddenly transplanted to the West, and she was writing from the point of view of a woman, a wife, and a mother.

Many of Foote's novels, including *The Led-Horse Claim* (1882), *The Last Assembly Ball* (1886), *The Chosen Valley* (1892), and *Edith Bonham* (1917), were first published serially in *Scribner's Monthly;* the books were all published by Houghton Mifflin & Co. of Boston. Wallace Stegner's 1971 novel *The Angle of Repose*, which won the Pulitzer Prize, is based on the life of Mary Hallock Foote. *(See also: Migration and Frontier Women; Women Writers)*

—Deborah Dawson Bonde

Further Reading
Johnson, LeeAnn. *Mary Hallock Foote*. Boston: Twayne, 1980.
Maguire, James. *Mary Hallock Foote*. Caldwell, ID: Caxton, 1972.
Paul, Rodman, ed. *A Victorian Gentlewoman in the Far West: Reminiscences of Mary Hallock Foote*. San Marino, CA: Huntington Library, 1972.

ᴧ Forsyth, Jessie (1847–1937)

Temperance organizer and editor, Jessie Forsyth was a leading figure in the Good Templar fraternal temperance society and an advocate of total abstinence, prohibition, and saving children from the evils caused by alcohol. She also advocated woman's suffrage, racial equality, world peace, and the utopian socialism of Edward Bellamy. She was a devout Anglican.

Her life illustrates the internationalism of the temperance movement and its connections with other reform agitations. She was born in London, England, where she joined the Good Templars in 1872, emigrated to Boston in 1874 and to Australia, where her sister lived, in 1911. When her organization, between 1876 and 1887, became divided over rights for blacks, she emerged as a leader in the faction that advocated full rights for peoples of all races. From 1883 to 1887, she edited the monthly *Temperance Brotherhood*. After the reunion of the Good Templars, she served as International Superintendent of Juvenile Templars, 1893–1908 (in the final year the membership in this children's auxiliary approached 240,000), and edited the monthly *International Good Templar* from 1901 to 1908.

Forsyth also served as state president of the Woman's Christian Temperance Union of Western Australia, 1913 to 1916, and as organizing secretary of the Australian National Prohibition League, 1917 to 1918. *(See also: Good Templars; Temperance Movement)*

—David M. Fahey

Further Reading
Fahey, David M., ed. *The Collected Writings of Jessie Forsyth, 1847–1937: The Good Templars and Temperance Reform on Three Continents*. Lewiston, NY: Edwin Mellen, 1988.

ᴧ Foster, Abby Kelley (1811–1887)

Abby Kelley Foster was the unwitting symbol of the women's rights movement of the 1840s. Born in Massachusetts of Irish Quaker parents, Abby Kelley inherited a strong belief in human and sexual equality and in pacifism. The antislavery teachings of William Lloyd Garrison became a major influence, casting her fully in the role of abolitionist. Her marriage to Stephen Foster, an abolitionist and follower of the Quaker-influenced nonresistance, broadened and shaped her activities. Together, the Fosters emphasized the importance of individual independent effort, mistrusting all organizations, including the formal church and political groups. Originally a teacher, Foster became a reformer, a wife, and mother. However, she continued to be an active, freethinking woman, more closely aligned with modern woman than with her peers.

Foster was the first woman to insist on speaking in the public arena and to "mixed" audiences. She steadfastly recognized the urgent need to resolve the antislavery issues and opposed efforts to merge the rights of blacks with the rights of white women and the poor. The validation of Foster's life work was the ratification of the Thirteenth Amendment (1865), which abolished slavery forever in the United States, and ratification of the Fifteenth Amendment (1870), which secured this freedom by giving black men the right to vote. In her zeal to achieve freedom for blacks, Foster provided focus to the movement for the equal rights of women. *(See also: Abolition and the Antislavery Movement; Public Speakers: Nineteenth Century)*

—Beverly Falconer Watkins

Further Reading

Bacon, Margaret Hope. *I Speak for My Slave Sister.* New York: Crowell, 1974.

Foster Papers. American Antiquarian Society. Worcester, MA.

Pease, Jane. "The Freshness of Fanaticism, Abby Kelley Foster, An Essay in Reform." Ph.D. diss., University of Rochester, 1969.

Sterling, Dorothy. *Ahead of Her Time: Abby Kelley and the Politics of Antislavery.* New York: Norton, 1991.

Whitman, Alden. *American Reformers: An H. W. Wilson Biographical Dictionary.* New York: H. W. Wilson, 1985.

Fourteenth Amendment to the U.S. Constitution (1866)

The Fourteenth Amendment to the U.S. Constitution, which enfranchised freedmen, was passed by Congress on June 16, 1866, and ratified by the required three-fourths of the states on July 28, 1868. Proposed by the majority Radical Republicans through their Joint Committee of Fifteen, this amendment followed the Union victory in the Civil War and was proposed as a consequence of the Thirteenth Amendment, which abolished the institution of slavery within the United States. In the Constitution as ratified in 1789, the designation of enfranchisement had been left to the individual states. The Fourteenth Amendment reflected the Unionists' determination to assert the preeminence of federal authority in an area that previously constituted a major "states' right." However, in their concern to ensure the enfranchisement of the freedmen in the recalcitrant southern states, the abolitionist-minded Radical Republicans allowed the specific introduction of gender into the Constitution through the Fourteenth Amendment.

Section 1 of the Fourteenth Amendment provided a formal definition of national citizenship and prohibited a state's right to "abridge the privileges or immunities" of those citizens. Moreover, Section 1 denied to any state the power to "deprive any person of life, liberty, or property, without due

process," a passage now known as the "equal protection" clause. Section 2 asserted congressional protection of the right to vote of "any of the male inhabitants of such state, being twenty-one years of age and citizens of the United States" (except Indians, who were not taxed, and convicts or participants in rebellion), thus introducing the word *male* and the issue of gender into the Constitution. The high court's hostile ruling in *Minor v. Happersett* (1874) ended, for the remainder of the nineteenth century, the suffragists' attempts to win the franchise for women through judicial fiat based on the equal protection clause of the Fourteenth Amendment.

While the definition of citizenship in Section 1 included women and seemingly ensured their equal protection under the law, the gender-specific definition of the franchise in Section 2 made the task of woman suffrage advocates more difficult. The debate over passage of the Fourteenth Amendment initiated a postwar split within the ranks of woman suffrage supporters because it presented a dilemma for a significant proportion of their number who supported women's rights as well as the abolition and antislavery movement. Capitalizing on the unconditional support for the Thirteenth Amendment, antislavery and abolition men and women of both races established the Equal Rights Association in 1866 to pursue both black and woman suffrage. The disastrous and divisive "Kansas Campaign" of 1867, in which separate state referenda on black and woman suffrage were defeated, precipitated the schism within the woman suffrage movement that produced first the National Woman Suffrage Association in 1868 and then the American Woman Suffrage Association in 1869.

In 1871, the flamboyant free love advocate Victoria Woodhull appeared before the House Judicial Committee to present a petition on woman suffrage, arguing that the Fourteenth and Fifteenth amendments guaranteed the political rights of all citizens and that suffrage was a right of citizenship. Although neither Congress nor the federal courts were convinced, many suffragists, including Susan B. Anthony, asserted their right to the franchise by voting in the 1872 federal elections: Anthony was subsequently convicted of "illegal voting," and an 1884 Supreme Court decision, by affirming a state's right to interpret the rights of citizenship, categorically denied women's claim to equal protection as citizens under the Fourteenth Amendment.

After the ratification of the Nineteenth Amendment (1920) granted women the vote, the potential efficacy of the equal protection clause of the Fourteenth Amendment was frequently offered by social feminists as well as conservatives and antifeminists to support their argument that the proposed Equal Rights Amendment was unnecessary and a possible threat to protective legislation. However, the equal protection clause of the Fourteenth Amendment has not been employed effectively as a judicial basis for furthering women's equality under the law in the twentieth century. *(See also: Abolition and the Antislavery Movement; American Woman Suffrage Association; Anthony, Susan B.; Minor*

v. Happersett; *National Woman Suffrage Association; Nineteenth Amendment to the U.S. Constitution; Woodhull, Victoria Claflin)*

—Angela M. Howard

Further Reading
DuBois, Ellen. *Feminism and Suffrage: The Emergence of an Independent Women's Movement in America, 1848–1869.* Ithaca, NY: Cornell University Press, 1978.
Kraditor, Aileen. *The Ideas of the Woman Suffrage Movement, 1890–1920.* Garden City, NY: Anchor/Doubleday, 1971.
Minor v. Happersett, 53 No. 58 and 21 Wallace, 162 (1874).

Free Love

Free love is a nineteenth-century term to describe the opposition of some individuals and groups to legal and clerical marriage, which they believed stifled a naturally loving relationship between women and men. Free-love groups were typically small, sectarian, and usually male dominated and offered intellectual leadership to the later birth control and suffrage movements. Free lovers strongly favored motherhood, but they separated a woman's free choice to bear children from the sexual exclusivity required by the legal institution of marriage. Therefore, the free lovers scandalized mainstream American Victorian society and challenged the very core of the "cult of domesticity." Victoria Woodhull and her sister Tennessee Claflin were two of the more notorious nineteenth-century advocates of free love. Woodhull unreservedly supported each woman's right to decide whether, when, and with whom to become sexually active.

Conservative opponents of the nineteenth-century woman's movement raised the free-love issue to impugn the respectability of the advocates of women's rights. This antifeminist, antisuffragist tactic persisted into the twentieth century, as the specter of the wanton free-lover woman was thrust into discussions of women's rights or an expanded role for women.

In the twentieth century, the free-love issue resurfaced first after World War I and then as a result of the Cold War and the Vietnam War. The so-called Lost Generation expressed its disillusionment with the results of the "War to End All Wars" and its challenge to the political fundamentalism of the Roaring Twenties by applying popularized Freudianism to justify sensual indulgence and immediate gratification. Affluent and college-educated women described as flappers were believed to engage in sexual activity with abandon, now having general if illicit access to contraception devices such as the diaphragm.

As an issue of the so-called new morality of the 1960s, the concept of free love was adopted by the affluent baby boomer generation; the modern application was facilitated by advances in and an availability of contraception (especially "the pill") and reflected more the youth movement's search for an identity distinct from their parents than an issue of the

nascent modern women's rights movement. Reflecting the male-identified youth movement's challenge to authority, these advocates of sexual freedom argued that premarital, extramarital, and communal/group variations of sexual activity offered an expanded experience on an "if it feels good, do it" basis. According to this philosophy, people could indulge and satiate their sensual appetites without personal commitment or lingering obligations.

For women, this concept of free love now required that they acquiesce to sex on male demand or be labeled repressed and bourgeois. Rejecting this sexist application of the concept of free love, feminists of the early 1970s reasserted the Woodhull interpretation, which offered the opportunity for women to define their own sexuality as an aspect of women's autonomy, beyond the strictures of marriage and motherhood. Conservatives labeled feminists free lovers and thus a threat to decency and national survival.

The excesses of the late 1960s and 1970s ultimately proved unsatisfying for men and women. The medical concerns over venereal disease, especially herpes and AIDS, discredited this variety of free love by the 1980s, as the uncertain economic situation refocused the priorities of the baby boomer generation on personal and professional stability. During the 1990s, some segments of the population overtly stood against the concept of free love by embracing more traditional values, such as abstinence before marriage and monogamy. *(See also: AIDS; Antifeminism; Birth Control; Female Sexuality; Flapper; Freudianism; New Morality; Sexual Revolution; Venereal Disease/STDs; Woodhull, Victoria)*

—Barry Arnold

Further Reading
Covitz, Howard. *Oedipal Paradigms in Collision.* Edited by Barry Arnold. New York: Peter Lang, 1997.
D'Emilio, John, and Estelle Freedman. *Intimate Matters: A History of Sexuality in America.* New York: Harper & Row, 1988.
Dunbar, Dirk. *The Balance of Nature's Polarities in New Paradigm Theory.* Edited by Barry Arnold. New York: Peter Lang, 1994.
Stoehr, Taylor. *Free Love in America: A Documentary History.* New York: AMS Press, 1979.
Tipton, Steven. *Getting Saved from the Sixties.* Berkeley: University of California Press, 1982.

Freedmen's Bureau

The Freedmen's Bureau was the popular name for the Bureau of Refugees, Freedmen, and Abandoned Lands. The Freedmen's Bureau Bill, passed in March 1865, established this agency in response to demands by abolitionists, particularly those of Josephine Griffing, who was also a prominent woman's rights activist. President Abraham Lincoln's endorsement of the Freedmen's Bureau was largely due to the influence of Griffing, who organized and solicited volunteers to work in the newly formed bureau.

The Freedmen's Bureau served as a temporary means of assisting newly freed blacks by providing education, food, and shelter and by managing the distribution of abandoned and confiscated Confederate estates. It extended the work begun by the freedmen's aid societies that had formed in Boston, New York, and Philadelphia. These societies, composed of missionaries and abolitionists, were concerned with the welfare and educational needs of the former slaves, and they were responsible for sending supplies and funds for the recruiting and maintenance of teachers for newly freed blacks. The Freedmen's Bureau assisted by establishing a system of record keeping, providing school buildings, and funding the transportation for teachers. At a cost of $3 million, the bureau enabled between 150,000 and 200,000 freedmen to obtain the beginnings of an education.

Women volunteers played a large part in the educational assistance rendered to freed blacks, such that by 1869 one-half of the nine thousand teachers were women. These dedicated teachers endured many hardships and a great deal of intolerance by southerners, but they persisted in this venture and were later referred to as the "tenth crusade." Some of these women stayed on even after the 1870s to continue providing education for freed blacks. The bureau was terminated in 1869. *(See also: Griffing, Josephine; Slavery)*

—**Jean Nettles**

Further Reading
McPherson, James M. *The Struggle for Equality.* Princeton, NJ: Princeton University Press, 1964.
Sorin, Gerald. *Abolitionism.* New York: Praeger, 1972.

～ Freeman, Mary Eleanor Wilkins (1852–1930)

Mary Eleanor Wilkins Freeman was one of the foremost authors in the school of regional local colorists who wrote short stories and novels in the realistic style popular during the late nineteenth and early twentieth century. She drew on the rural New England environment and its strong women, an environment she knew well from her childhood in rural Massachusetts.

Wilkins was educated in the best New England school tradition but found no career plans that suited her. She created an avenue for her talents in writing, as had other well-educated New England women of her day. The publication of her stories in *Harper's Bazaar* in the 1880s brought economic self-sufficiency. *A New England Nun* (1891) described the peculiarities of small-town people and settings as well as the strength of character that upheld many New Englanders, especially women. The author's skill at characterization and the appeal of her strong women figures made her stories popular in her day and have given them a lasting quality. Accepting her "spinsterhood," she enjoyed the fruits of her success by traveling freely and tasting the social life in New York and Boston, which included friendships with many publishers and writers.

Through these contacts, she later met and married Charles M. Freeman in 1902, when she was almost fifty

years old. She continued her writing career with *Six Trees* in 1903; the revenues from earlier works such as *Pembroke* (1894, novel) and *A Humble Romance* (1887, story collection) sustained her well financially. Remaining active into the 1920s, Freeman was one of the most successful of the many female regional local colorists. Marital problems and her husband's death in 1923 were offset by the pleasure of literary rewards and honors, such as her election to the National Institute of Arts and Letters in New York. She died in 1930 at the age of seventy-eight, one of the few writers of the early local-color realistic movement in fiction whose reputation had outlived both the world war and the changed literary tastes of the 1920s. *(See also: Women Writers)*

—**Ellen D. Langill**

Further Reading
Foster, Edward. *Mary E. Wilkins Freeman.* New York: Hendricks House, 1956.
Hamblin, Abigail Ann. *The New England Art of Mary E. Wilkins Freeman.* Amherst, MA: Green Knight, 1966.
Overton, Grant. *The Women Who Make our Novels.* New York: Dodd, Mead, 1918.
Westbrook, Perry D. *Mary Wilkins Freeman.* Rev. ed. New York: Twayne, 1988.

～ Freudianism

Freudianism refers to the psychoanalytic theories of Viennese physician Sigmund Freud (1856–1939), who developed a picture of the human psyche as a conflicted and divided entity, challenging the then-prevailing belief in the individual as autonomous and harmonious. His theory of unconscious areas of psychic experience and of the power of sexual drives beginning in infancy disputed the century-old faith in human rationality. For Freud, the id (sexual force), ego (reality principle), and superego (morality and law) were sections of the psyche competing for energy in a never-ending struggle. Any balance achieved by an individual, moreover, differed according to whether one was male or female.

Since many of Freud's patients were middle-class women, it is hardly surprising that his theories paid them a good deal of attention. For one thing, he totally revised common wisdom that those suffering from hysteria—a psychiatric illness particularly associated with nineteenth-century women—were immoral and of low intelligence. Instead, his *Studies in Hysteria* (1899) maintained that they were usually very intelligent and excessively moral. Indeed, Freudianism blamed many psychological ills on society's extreme repression of women's sexuality. Although this opinion broke with Victorian conventions, other aspects of Freudianism reinforced their assumptions about women. Notably, the Oedipal and Electral moments during which one reached an adult gender identity differed sharply for boys and girls. Boys, recognizing their mother's lack of a penis and their own possession of one, rejected their infantile love for her and identified with their father's power gained from the penis. By contrast, girls did not have to fear castration and so did not have to develop a strong ego to deal with that reality. Instead, they could devote themselves to love of their father rather than repress it and substitute having a baby for having a penis. Freudianism saw feminists as women who failed to accept their castration but, rather, suffered from "penis envy." They sought not love and children, but a masculine identity.

After World War II, Lundberg and Farnham's *Modern Woman: The Lost Sex* (1946) and other journalistic writings popularized these normative aspects of Freudianism. Neurosis and other disorders, these writings maintained, were a result of women's rejecting their femininity. In 1963, Betty Friedan's *Feminine Mystique* took issue with Freudianism, especially the concept of "penis envy" and the attendant stereotyping of sex roles. A culture oriented toward psychological therapy, she argued, was making women who wanted to achieve feel abnormal because of Freud. A decade later, however, Juliet Mitchell's *Psychoanalysis and Feminism* (1974) sought to rehabilitate the doctrine as one that explicitly pointed out the cultural power of the phallus and the resulting power accorded fathers. Other feminist psychologists have attempted to refute even this fundament by postulating breast and womb envy.

The 1990s saw further changes in attitudes toward Freud. Scholars showed the ways in which his theory of seduction by male relatives, especially fathers, as being only a female fantasy had influenced generations of therapists. Feminist therapists like Jessica Benjamin used psychoanalytic theories to analyze men's psychosexual development. In the academy, the theories of Jacques Lacan, sketched for an anglophone audience in Mitchell's 1974 work, became more influential in some feminist theorists' work, even supplanting Freud. *(See also: Deutsch, Helene; Friedan, Betty; Gender Role Socialization; Horney, Karen; Hysteria; Modern Woman: The Lost Sex; Psychiatry; Psychology; Sex-Gender System)*

—**Bonnie G. Smith**

Further Reading

Brennan, Teresa. *The Interpretation of the Flesh: Freud and Femininity.* London: Routledge, 1992.

Elliot, Patricia. *From Mastery to Analysis: Theories of Gender in Psychoanalytic Feminism.* Ithaca, NY: Cornell University Press, 1991.

Grubrich-Simitis, Ilse. *Early Freud and Late Freud: Reading Anew Studies on Hysteria and Moses and Monotheism.* London: Routledge, 1997.

Lacan, Jacques. *Feminine Sexuality: Jacques Lacan and the école freudienne.* Edited by Juliet Mitchell and Jacqueline Rose. Translated by J. Rose. New York: Norton/Pantheon, 1982.

Sayers, Janet. *Mothers of Psychoanalysis: Helene Deutsch, Anna Freud, Melanie Klein.* New York: Norton, 1991.

Slipp, Samuel. *The Freudian Mystique: Freud, Women, and Feminism.* New York: New York University Press, 1993.

ᔕ Friedan, Betty (b. 1921)

Author of *The Feminine Mystique* and a founder of the National Organization for Women (NOW), Betty Friedan was born Betty Naomi Goldstein in Peoria, Illinois. In high school, Friedan founded a literary magazine and was named class valedictorian. Then she traveled east to Smith College, later described by her as "a great marvelous thing." A psychology major, she was editor of the college paper, graduated summa cum laude (1942), and won a research fellowship to Berkeley. A year later, she left Berkeley to work in New York City as a reporter for the labor press. In 1947, she married Carl Friedan.

Less conventional than many of her contemporaries, Friedan returned to work after the birth of her first child. However, she was fired as a result of her second pregnancy and throughout the early 1950s led the life of a suburban housewife, first on Long Island and then in an "eleven-room Victorian house in Rockland County." In 1957, Friedan began to research and write what was to become *The Feminine Mystique* as a reaction to questionnaire answers she had gathered from Smith College classmates. Responding to their unhappiness and her own, she described "the problem that has no name" and detailed the ways in which American society forced women into traditional, unfulfilling, subservient roles.

Published in 1963, *The Feminine Mystique* is often viewed as trumpeting the rebirth of American feminism. It has sold 3 million copies and reached millions more through excerpts in *Ladies' Home Journal, Good Housekeeping, Mademoiselle,* and *McCall's.*

The Feminine Mystique questioned the assumptions underlying the alleged "happiness" of well-educated, middle-class housewives. The book described the problems of women who identified themselves as wives, mothers, and homemakers but never as persons. In developing her argument, Friedan indicted women's magazines for dealing with trivial topics. She portrayed the dilemma of college-educated women who, despite their intellectual interests and worldly inclinations, saw nothing but marriage in their future. The book also roundly condemned the social sciences for supporting the status quo of sexual inequality by embracing Freudian and neo-Freudian models of masculine activity and feminine passivity. Friedan concluded her picture of American social and sexual realities by showing how advertisers goad women into becoming housewife consumers and educational institutions strive to produce well-educated but subservient women. To solve the problems created by a society that pushes women into the background of its political, economic, and social life, the book counsels individual women to say no to the "housewife image" and adopt "a new life plan" based on meaningful activity.

After the publication of *The Feminine Mystique,* Friedan became a lecturer for feminist causes. In 1966, she cofounded the National Organization for Women (NOW) and became its president. NOW's stated goal was to enable women to achieve full equality with men in American society. Its first success was the banning of sex distinctions in employment advertising. In 1970, Friedan helped organize the Women's Strike for Equality, a massive nationwide demonstration on the fiftieth anniversary of the suffrage victory. Seeking to establish mainstream respectability and credibility for NOW, Friedan during this period reflected in her leadership the ambivalence among the organization's professional and middle-class members regarding an open declaration of support for lesbianism and the minority of lesbians within the membership. The ensuing controversy and criticism of her leadership style contributed to her decision to step down as NOW president in 1970. She quickly became involved in organizing feminist enterprises such as the Women's Political Caucus, the National Association to Repeal Abortion Laws, and the First Women's Bank. As a nationally recognized spokeswoman for the modern women's movement, she participated in the cooperative effort of national women's groups to achieve ratification of the Equal Rights Amendment. Entering the academic world, she held appointments at Yale and Temple universities and at Queens College in New York.

In 1981, responding to criticisms that the feminist movement failed to recognize the importance to most women of family and relationships with men, Friedan published *The Second Stage,* in which she condemned the "feminist mystique" that denied "love, nurturance and home," and she called for women and men to transcend the false polarization between feminism and family. As the grande dame of the modern women's movement, she then focused on the life issues of older women in American society, publishing *The Fountain of Age* in 1993. Friedan has spent recent years as a Visiting Distinguished Professor at the University of Southern California, New York University, and George Mason University. She is currently an Adjunct Scholar at the Wilson International Center for Scholars at the Smithsonian Institution and Distinguished Professor of Social Evolution at Mount Vernon College. Her latest book is titled *Beyond Gender: The New Politics of Work and Family* (1997). *(See also: Freudianism; National Organization for Women; Women's Liberation Movement)*

—**Barbara McGowan**

Further Reading

Friedan, Betty. *The Feminine Mystique.* New York: Norton, 1963.

———. *The Fountain of Age.* New York: Simon & Schuster, 1994.

———. *It Changed My Life.* New York: Random House, 1976.

———. *The Second Stage.* New York: Summit, 1981.

Friedan, Betty, and Bridgid O'Farrell, eds. *Beyond Gender: The New Politics of Work and Family.* Washington, DC: Woodrow Wilson Center Press, 1997.

Hennessee, Judith Adler. *Betty Friedan: A Biography.* New York: Random House, 1999.

✺ Friendships

From both historical and contemporary perspectives, friendships reveal a number of characteristics. In the past, two variables prevailed. First, women found support and intimacy with female relations primarily within the realms of family and home. Second, these friendships were encouraged by society as a means of support for women in times of despair and anxiety. In assessing female friendship, historians analyze journals, diaries, correspondence, and autobiographies of American women living during the eighteenth and nineteenth centuries. The "world of women" that institutionalized friendship effectively segregated men and women and allowed women to display a wide latitude of emotions and sexual feelings with their friends. Because of their friendships, women developed a sense of inner security and self-esteem not available to them in the male-dominated world at this time. Women sought this "way of life" because it reinforced their sense of solidarity and moral superiority. By upholding such attributes of "heart" as positive qualities, female friendships asserted that "women were different from but not lesser than—perhaps better than—men." Furthermore, in some cases, such as in the lives of Lillian Wald, Crystal Eastman, and Emma Goldman, the love and support expressed between female friends gave the women the power and energy to engage in political activism.

Contemporary research on women's friendships acknowledges that friendship evolves through conversation and that through dialogue, intimacy and bonding between women occurs, thus often resulting in a blurring of the distinction between family and friend. For the most part, friendships serve a therapeutic function yet occur primarily between equals, women in the same culture, class, life position, and affectional circumstances, which limits the potential for cross-cultural closeness.

On extensive interviews and questionnaires, women indicate that they define themselves in terms of their friendships and that this "personalistic focus" demonstrates their ability to care and to communicate for the purposes of increasing intimacy and avoiding conflict and the dissolution of their relationships. In addition, investigations affirm that women make and change the rules for preservation of friendships and that these friendships can serve as the "site for both conservation and resistance of gendered social structures and processes." *(See also: Boston Marriages; Goldman, Emma; Marriage; Wald, Lillian)*

—**Susan H. Koester**

Further Reading

Cook, Blanche Wiesen. "Female Support Networks and Political Activism: Lillian Wald, Crystal Eastman, Emma Goldman." In *A Heritage of Her Own: Toward a New Social History of American Women,* edited by Nancy F. Cott and Elizabeth H. Pleck, 412-44. New York: Simon & Schuster, 1979.

Cott, Nancy F. *The Bonds of Womanhood: Women's Spheres in New England, 1780–1835*. New Haven, CT: Yale University Press, 1977.

Faderman, Lillian. *Surpassing the Love of Men: Romantic Friendship between Women from the Renaissance to the Present*. New York: William Morrow, 1981.

Johnson, Fern L. "Friendships among Women, Closeness in Dialogue." In *Gendered Relationships*, edited by Julia T. Wood, 79-94. Mountain View, CA: Mayfield, 1996.

Koester, Susan H. "A Cross Cultural Comparison of Friendship between Women." Ph.D. diss., Union Institute, Cincinnati, OH, 1985.

Rubin, Lillian. *Just Friends: The Role of Friendship in Our Lives*. New York: Harper & Row, 1985.

Smith-Rosenberg, Carroll. *Disorderly Conduct: Visions of Gender in Victorian America*. New York: Knopf, 1985.

Sollie, Donna L., and Leigh A. Leslie, eds. *Gender, Families, and Close Relationships*. Thousand Oaks, CA: Sage, 1994.

Fry, Laura Anne (1857–1943)

Laura Fry was an important figure in Cincinnati's "golden age" of art, 1870 to 1890, and played an especially prominent role in the city's emergence as a center of the decorative arts. While still a young girl, Fry made some minor contributions to the "women's wood-carving movement" of the 1870s, a phenomenon nurtured to a large extent by her grandfather, Henry L. Fry, and her father, William H. Fry, both of whom had regional reputations. During the 1880s, she joined the decorating staff at the nationally recognized Rookwood Pottery in Cincinnati and gained a reputation as a leading ceramic artist. Although she maintained constant contact with Cincinnati and would eventually retire there, Fry spent most of the next three decades in West Lafayette, Indiana, as a professor of industrial art at Purdue University.

Fry's career illustrates the degree to which women in the arts had become professionalized by the late nineteenth century. Her identity as an artist was defined by the specific roles (such as student, employee, and teacher) that she performed within a series of hierarchically structured organizations. For example, even though she had learned the basics of wood carving in her family's studio, Fry received formal training in the various decorative arts at the University of Cincinnati's School of Design and, later, in painting at the Art Students League in New York. At Rookwood, she was one member of one department in a business enterprise that increasingly encouraged the efficient production, distribution, and inventory of its pottery wares. Fry was the decorator most closely associated with the fine-spray application of background colors, a technique that helped standardize Rookwood's designs and make them more commercially dependable.

As a professor at Purdue, she shifted her focus from the making of art to the teaching of it. She was regarded by the surrounding community as an art "expert," and in this capacity, she exhibited her work and that of others, spoke on numerous topics, and aided in the establishment of the La-

fayette Art Association in 1909. Thus, Fry devoted her life not only to the practice of the crafts but also to the wider responsibilities and the service ethic of the "professional." *(See also: Art)*

—Bruce R. Kahler

Further Reading

The Ladies, God Bless 'Em: The Women's Art Movement in Cincinnati in the Nineteenth Century. Cincinnati, OH: Cincinnati Art Museum, 1976.

Perry, Mrs. Aaron F. "Decorative Pottery of Cincinnati," *Harper's New Monthly Magazine* 62 (May 1881): 834-45.

Trapp, Kenneth R. "Toward a Correct Taste: Women and the Rise of the Design Reform Movement in Cincinnati, 1875–1880." In *Celebrate Cincinnati Art*, edited by Kenneth R. Trapp, 48-70. Cincinnati, OH: Cincinnati Art Museum, 1982.

Vitz, Robert C. *The Queen and the Arts: Cultural Life in Nineteenth-Century Cincinnati*. Kent, OH: Kent State University Press, 1988.

Fuller, Margaret (1810–1850)

Translator, editor, conversationalist, critic, philosopher, journalist, revolutionary, early socialist, and feminist, Margaret Fuller was one of the most important women of her time, influencing not only her own century but also the twentieth. Gravely misunderstood and misinterpreted by her male and many of her female contemporaries, Fuller has only recently begun to be accorded a more appropriate scholarly approach.

The first child of Timothy and Margaret (Crane) Fuller, Sarah Margaret Fuller enjoyed (and suffered under) a typically masculine education, having studied Latin, Greek, French, Italian, and German by the time she was twenty. This lack of a more carefree childhood was at once one of the many denials of her life and the means to her future livelihood. Up to the time of her father's death in 1835, her life was spent mostly in study in Cambridge, Massachusetts. In 1833, in Groton, Fuller took over her siblings' education, denying herself a trip to Europe with friends.

She pursued acquaintanceships with Ralph Waldo Emerson and Harriet Martineau and in 1836 took up a teaching post at Bronson Alcott's experimental Temple School in Boston. Overexertion led her to take a post in Providence, Rhode Island, until 1839, where she began working on translations of Goethe and on her critical writings. Returning to Boston in 1839 led to her deeper involvement in transcendentalism and the beginnings of her "conversations." These weekly sessions concentrated on a variety of aesthetic topics and were held in fall and spring from 1839 to 1844 for women subscribers only, with the exception of a brief attempt in 1841 to include men as well. In 1840, she founded, with other transcendentalists, the quarterly *Dial*, which she then edited for two years and which continued until 1844 as the mouthpiece of the New England transcendentalists. She was also involved in plans for the utopian

Figure 22. Margaret Fuller
A daguerrotype of Margaret Fuller, transcendentalist and feminist. Used by permission of Corbis.

Brook Farm community, although she did not choose to live there.

In 1845, shortly after publication of her first book, *Summer on the Lakes* (1844), Fuller was offered a job on Horace Greeley's *New York Tribune* as a literary critic. She also extended her 1843 *Dial* essay supporting the need for property rights for women—"The Great Lawsuit: Man *versus* Men. Woman *versus* Women,"—into a second book, *Woman in the Nineteenth Century,* considered the first book by an American that addresses the question of woman's place or "sphere" within society.

Published three years before the first national women's rights convention convened at Seneca Falls, New York, *Woman in the Nineteenth Century* established a precedent for future suffragists by defining and advocating women's rights. Directed specifically to younger contemporary women, it nonetheless emphasized independence for all women. Fuller advocated education and broader horizons for women, equality between the sexes, and legal rights to retain property and protect against abuse. Many of Fuller's readers were shocked by her forthright discussion of marriage and relations between the sexes; others applauded her efforts. *Woman in the Nineteenth Century* was sold out within a week and created a furious debate.

After the publication of *Woman in the Nineteenth Century,* Fuller resided in Greeley's New York house and, concentrating on her critical writings over the following fifteen months, published over two hundred articles on a variety of aesthetic and social topics. At the height of her success, she left the *Tribune* to become Greeley's foreign correspondent.

In 1846, Fuller traveled to England, then on to France and Italy. She met major writers and politicians at each stop. In Italy in 1847, she became involved in the revolutionary drive to unify Italy and with fellow revolutionary Giovanni Angelo, Marchese d'Ossoli. Fuller's activities during the following years are uncertain, but the period does seem to represent a liberation for her, despite the military setbacks of the Italian cause. Fuller became pregnant, which cut off her contacts with most of the Anglo-American community. Angelo Eugene, the son of Fuller and d'Ossoli, was born in May 1848 outside Rome. Soon after his birth, Fuller returned alone to Rome to continue her work for the revolution, running a hospital and carrying supplies. In the summer of 1849, the Roman Republic was defeated, and Fuller and d'Ossoli fled with their child to Florence. Fuller may have married d'Ossoli, perhaps as early as April 1848 or in 1849, which made her more welcome in the expatriate community, and she began her work on a revolutionary history. Despite her very deep ties to Rome and premonitions of disaster, Fuller decided to return to the United States with d'Ossoli and her son in 1850. Their ship, the *Elizabeth,* sank off Fire Island, New York; most biographers agree that of the three, only Fuller's son's body was recovered.

It is safe to say that Sarah Margaret Fuller's life was much too short for her to continue developing her great promise, and this has made the attempts of biographers and literary critics to evaluate her more difficult. We know Fuller today mainly due to *Woman in the Nineteenth Century,* which does little justice to her accomplishments as critic, conversationalist, and translator and as one who contributed a great deal to the advancement of women's liberation. *(See also: Journalism; Seneca Falls Convention; Transcendentalism)*

—**Maureen R. Liston**
Adapted for the second edition by Karen C. Knowles.

Further Reading

Capper, Charles. *Margaret Fuller: An American Romantic Life.* Vol. 1, *The Private Years.* New York: Oxford University Press, 1992.

Dickinson, Donna. *Margaret Fuller: Writing a Woman's Life.* Basingstoke, UK: Macmillan, 1993.

Fuller, Margaret. *The Letters of Margaret Fuller.* Edited by Robert N. Hudspeth, 6 vols. Ithaca, NY: Cornell University Press, 1983–1993.

———. *"These Sad but Glorious Days": Dispatches from Europe, 1846–1850.* Edited by Larry J. Reynolds and Susan Belasco Smith. New Haven, CT: Yale University Press, 1991.

———. *Woman in the Nineteenth Century.* 1845. Reprint, New York: Norton, 1971.

Myerson, Joel, ed. *Critical Essays on Margaret Fuller.* Boston: Hall, 1980.

✐ Gage, Matilda Joslyn (1826–1898)

More radical than the other two members of the suffrage "triumvirate" (Susan B. Anthony and Elizabeth Cady Stanton), Matilda Joslyn Gage was regarded as "one of the most logical, fearless, and scientific writers of her day." Stanton lauded her for "bringing more startling facts to light than any woman I ever knew" through a series of pamphlets, including evidence that a woman invented the cotton gin ("Woman as Inventor," 1870) and planned the military strategy that changed the course of the Civil War ("Who Planned the Tennessee Campaign?" 1880).

An excellent speaker and capable organizer on the local, state, and national levels, Gage held positions in the National Woman Suffrage Association (NWSA) roughly equivalent to those of Anthony. Gage created the NWSA's "Relief from Political Disabilities" campaign in 1878 and ran as an elector-at-large for Belva Lockwood's presidential bid on the Equal Rights Party ticket in 1884. When Gage was prosecuted for exercising school board suffrage in New York state, her 1893 court action became the test case for the constitutionality of state school suffrage. Threatened with arrest three times because of her reform work, Gage responded that the "country owes its existence to disobedience to law."

A prolific writer, Gage edited a suffrage paper, the *National Citizen and Ballot Box,* for four years and penned many of the strongest protests, resolutions, and addresses of the NWSA, including her "Woman's Rights Catechism" (1868). With Stanton, she coauthored the Declaration of Rights of Women (1876), which Gage and Anthony—fully expecting to be arrested—illegally presented at the nation's official centennial celebration that year.

Unable to stop the radical NWSA from merging with the conservative American Woman Suffrage Association in 1889, Gage turned to what she believed was her "grandest, most courageous work": to free woman "from the bondage of the church," which was the "chief means of enslaving woman's conscience and reason." She formed the anti-church National Woman's Liberal Union (1890), contributed to the *Woman's Bible* (1898), and published her magnum opus, *Woman, Church and State* (1893), acclaimed as one of the most important theoretical documents produced by the nineteenth-century woman's movement. Gage made a major contribution to American feminist theory in the latter publication, a persuasive critique of the role of the church and the state in the historic subordination and subjection of women. Specifically, Gage directly challenged the male-identified image of women that mainstream Christianity had promulgated.

Gage's contributions to nineteenth-century woman's rights and American feminism were eclipsed somewhat by the fame of Anthony and Stanton, both of whom she preceded in death. *(See also: Anthony, Susan B.; Christianity; History of Woman Suffrage; National Woman Suffrage Association; Religion; Stanton, Elizabeth Cady; Suffrage)*

—**Sally Roesch Wagner**

Further Reading

Gage Collection. Schlesinger Library. Radcliffe College, Cambridge, MA.

Gage, Matilda Joslyn. *Woman, Church and State.* Edited by Sally Roesch Wagner. Aberdeen, SD: Sky Carrier Press, 1998.

Spender, Dale. *Women of Ideas.* London: Routledge & Kegan Paul, 1982.

✐ Garment Industries

The garment industries included American business enterprises, factories, sweatshops, and family sewing operations involved in the mass production of ready-to-wear clothing. The large-scale manufacture of clothing was made possible by the invention of the sewing machine in 1846, as well as by the development of the textile industry, which, by the 1820s, had established women's presence as workers in the paid labor force that mass-produced wool and cotton cloth. Replaced by immigrants and men in the New England factories by the 1850s on account of declining wages, these women workers gravitated to the garment industry as a paid employment that paralleled traditional "woman's work." The percentage of women employed in the clothing industry rose from 45 percent in 1860 to 56 percent in 1890. Throughout the nineteenth and twentieth centuries, the clothing industry has been one of the ten primary areas of employment for American women workers. But as in other industries, women in the garment trade remained second-class workers in terms of status, wages, and working conditions.

By the late nineteenth century, the garment industry operated on various levels: manufacturers, sweatshops, contractors, and homeworkers. Manufacturers established factories where cloth was cut from patterns. Most clothing production took place in sweatshops generally run by immigrant contractors. Workers recruited and supervised by the contractor were often foreign-born women and children. The contractor paid them and delivered the completed order to the manufacturer. Homeworkers were women who did work at home for a contractor or factory and were paid at a piece rate.

These transient, unskilled workers, generally Jewish or Italian women, worked ten- to fourteen-hour days, seasonally, under poor sanitary and lighting conditions for low wages (from four to seven dollars for a five-and-a-half- to six-day workweek). Women usually rented or bought their sewing machines, needles, and thread; shop owners often charged for the electricity they used. Workers were fined for breaking equipment, being late, and talking. Although garment unions existed before 1900, the Amalgamated Clothing Workers and the International Ladies Garment Workers Union helped effect changes in sweatshop conditions thereafter. The Triangle Shirtwaist fire of 1911, which caused the deaths of 147 workers in New York City, tragically demonstrated the need for better factory conditions, while the Uprising of the Twenty Thousand (1909–1910), a walkout of New York City shirtwaist workers from 500 shops, fostered the growth of unionization.

New Deal legislation attempted to standardize hours and wages throughout America while supporting unionization (i.e., the National Industrial Recovery Act of 1933 and the National Labor Relations Act of 1935). But even before World War I, manufacturers left the mid-Atlantic region for the South to use nonunion labor. The creation of "runaway" shops continued through the 1950s as black females entered the industry.

Sweatshops, often employing illegal aliens and the new immigrants from Latin America and the Far East, still prospered in parts of America during the 1990s. During that decade, several sweatshop scandals within the United States and abroad, involving American clothing companies, came to the public's attention.

A sweatshop in El Monte, California, a blue-collar district east of Los Angeles, used the labor of Thai immigrants who were paid between 60 cents and $1.60 per hour and who worked up to seventeen hours a day. The *New York Times* reported that in Pakistan children as young as six years old work as virtual slaves for pennies an hour in awful conditions stitching soccer balls for Nike and other transnational athletic equipment companies. Wal-Mart's Kathie Lee Collection, a line of clothes endorsed by Kathie Lee Gifford, a morning talk show cohost, was made in Honduras by women and children slaving up to twenty hours a day for about 29 cents an hour. A model who endorsed a line of clothes for Kmart, Kathy Ireland, discovered that her clothing was produced in Brooklyn sweatshops.

As a result of such disclosures, President William Clinton endorsed an apparel industry code of conduct prohibiting child labor and other sweatshop conditions at shoe and clothing factories used by U.S. firms around the globe. This agreement resulted from a task force made up of labor unions, human rights groups, and apparel manufacturers such as L. L. Bean, Nike, and Liz Claiborne. A new association will enforce the agreement, which will be a challenging task.

In 1997, North Olmsted, Ohio, a blue-collar suburb of Cleveland, became the first city in the United States to ban municipal purchases of products made in sweatshops. Another Cleveland suburb, Bedford Heights, subsequently passed an antisweatshop ordinance. Such actions demonstrate the importance of the fight against sweatshop labor in America during the 1990s. *(See also: Fair Labor Standards Act; Industrial Revolution; International Ladies Garment Workers Union; Sewing Machines; Textiles: North and South; Triangle Fire of 1911)*

—**Mary Jane Capozzoli Ingui**

Further Reading

Blewett, Mary H. *The Last Generation.* Amherst: University of Massachusetts Press, 1990.

Dye, Nancy Schrom. *As Equals and as Sisters: Feminism, Unionism, and the Women's Trade Union League of New York.* Columbia: University of Missouri Press, 1980.

Glenn, Susan A. *Daughters of the Shtetl: Life and Labor in the Immigrant Generation.* Ithaca, NY: Cornell University Press, 1990.

Jensen, Joan M., and Sue Davidson, eds. *A Needle, a Bobbin: Women Needleworkers in America.* Philadelphia: Temple University Press, 1984.

Kessler-Harris, Alice. *Out to Work: A History of Wage-Earning Women in the United States.* New York: Oxford University Press, 1982.

Laslett, John, and Mary Tyler. *ILGWU in Los Angeles, 1907–1988.* Santa Fe, NM: Ten Star, 1989.

McCreesh, Carolyn Daniel. *Women in the Campaign to Organize Garment Workers, 1880–1917.* New York: Garland, 1985.

McHugh, Cathy L. *Mill Family: The Labor System in the Southern Cotton Textile Industry, 1880–1915.* New York: Oxford University Press, 1988.

Ross, Andrew, ed. *No Sweat: Fashion, Free Trade and the Rights of Garment Workers.* New York: Verso, 1997.

Tentler, Leslie Woodcock. *Wage-Earning Women: Industrial Work and Family Life in the United States, 1900–1930.* New York: Oxford University Press, 1979.

Tyler, Gus. *Look for the Union Label: A History of the ILGWU.* Armonk, NY: M. E. Sharpe, 1995.

Waldinger, Roger D. *Through the Eye of the Needle: Immigrants and Enterprise in New York Garment Trades.* New York: New York University Press, 1989.

⟋ Garrisonians

Garrisonians were the followers of William Lloyd Garrison (1805–1879), a radical abolitionist. In 1831, he withdrew his earlier support for the colonization of liberated slaves to Africa and established *The Liberator,* a newspaper that pressed the cause of immediate abolition. He was an eccentric individualist who in 1854 publicly burned the Constitution, which he described as a "covenant with death and an agreement with Hell." His uncompromising position on a wide agenda of reforms split the abolition movement. While he supported health reform, the nineteenth-century peace movement, and temperance, Garrison's most divisive positions involved anarchism and women's rights. Late in his life, he moderated his position, but in the 1840s, he opposed voting even for the abolitionist Liberty Party and criticized northern Protestants for hypocrisy in giving even tacit approval to slavery. On the basis of the twin ideas of perfectionism and nonresistance, Garrison called for universal emancipation of all men the world over. However, he insisted that by "universal emancipation" he meant the redemption of "women as well as men from a servile to an equal condition." Female abolitionists such as Abby Kelley Foster and Lydia Maria Child were allied with Garrison. In 1840, at the World Anti-Slavery Convention, when Lucretia Mott, Ann Green Phillips, and Elizabeth Cady Stanton were denied seats on the floor and forced to sit in the gallery, Garrison joined them. Not all women abolitionists were Garrisonians, but he and his followers were more open to feminist activism than the majority of male antislavery leaders. *(See also: Abolition and the Antislavery Movement; Child, Lydia Maria Francis; Foster, Abby Kelley; Stanton, Elizabeth Cady)*

—**William G. Shade**

Further Reading

Hersh, Blanch Glassman. *The Slavery of Sex.* Urbana: University of Illinois Press, 1978.

Kraditor, Aileen S. *Means and Ends in American Abolitionism.* New York: Pantheon, 1969.

Thomas, John L. *The Liberator.* Boston: Houghton Mifflin, 1963.

Yellin, Jean Fagin. *Women & Sisters: The Antislavery Feminists in American Culture.* New Haven, CT: Yale University Press, 1989.

∽ Gastonia Strike

The Gastonia Strike was a Communist-led strike waged by a predominantly female workforce in the textile town of Gastonia, North Carolina. Although largely unsuccessful, the strike spawned a series of novels by women writers who used the incident to introduce women's, and in some cases feminist, issues into the genre of proletarian literature.

The strike at the Loray Mill, which erupted on April 1, 1929, and lasted through the early fall, was the first attempt by the Communist Party to organize southern textile workers. The mill workforce was composed of poor farming families who had journeyed to Gastonia from sharecropping farms and from the surrounding mountains. The strike instilled in the largely female workforce, if briefly, a sense of hope and a willingness to fight for better lives. They endured being arrested, beaten, and assaulted by bayonets on the picket lines. One woman, Ella May Wiggins, who wrote the "ballets" that unified the workers who sang them together during the strike, was shot and killed. Despite their determination, however, the strike was not a success. The mill owners broke the strike and refused to recognize the Communist-led National Textile Workers Union. Because of the strike, women workers no longer had to face night work, but they received no relief from the chronic problems of poverty and disease that plagued them.

The strike had a more profound and beneficial effect on the genre of proletarian literature. It inspired six novels, four by women writers whose works offered an alternative to the strict masculinism being touted by Communist Party literati. All four novels addressed, implicitly or explicitly, the particular problems and conditions that women workers faced. This meant, in the context of Gastonia, the exhausting reality of almost yearly pregnancies. For example, Ella May Wiggins, the murdered songwriter and striker, had nine children. Thus, these women novelists brought to the fore issues and problems to which the Communist Party paid little more than lip service. The most doctrinaire of the novels, Myra Page's *The Gathering Storm,* suggested that these problems could be solved through a Communist revolution. The most compelling and complex of the novels, Fielding Burke's *Call Home the Heart,* presented the Communist-led strike as the setting within which the protagonist struggles between her intellect—the Leftist lessons she learns during the strike—and her heart—the pull of her mountain home and her traditional way of life. *(See also: Communist Party; Textiles: North and South; Women Writers)*

—**Michael Miller Topp**

Further Reading

Burke, Fielding [Olive Tilford Dargan]. *Call Home the Heart.* 1932. Reprint, Old Westbury, NY: Feminist Press, 1983.

Cook, Sylvia Jenkins. *From Tobacco Road to Route 66: The Southern Poor White in Fiction.* Chapel Hill: University of North Carolina Press, 1976.

Lumpkin, Grace. *To Make My Bread.* New York: Macauley, 1932.

Page, Myra. *The Gathering Storm: A Story of the Blackbelt.* New York: International Publishers, 1932.

Shaffer, Robert. "Women and the Communist Party," *Socialist Review* 45 (May-June 1979): 73-118.

Urgo, Joseph. "Proletarian Literature and Feminism: The Gastonia Novels and Feminist Protest," *Minnesota Review* 24 (Spring 1985): 64-84.

Vorse, Mary Heaton. *Strike!* New York: Horace Liveright, 1930.

∽ Gender Gap

Gender gap is a term used to refer to differences in voting patterns between men and women in the 1980s; the term was applied whenever a distinct pattern of women voting in large numbers produced a political effect. The first generations of women voters after enfranchisement in 1920 seemed generally to vote along similar lines with their husbands, fathers, and other males. It was hard to see that women as a group cast their votes differently from men. However, given the vagaries of the secret ballot and early

Figure 23. Gastonia Strike
Five orphaned children at the funeral of their mother, Mrs. Ella May Wiggins, who was killed while on her way to a strikers' rally in South Gastonia. Used by permission of Corbis-Bettmann.

election polls, one must be cautious about the existence or nonexistence of the gender gap prior to the 1980s.

With the growth of the modern women's movement in the late 1960s and 1970s, many politically active women, such as Congresswomen Bella Abzug and Shirley Chisholm as well as feminist Gloria Steinem, predicted that the gender gap would become a potent force to be reckoned with in American politics. Still, the failure of male-dominated legislatures to ratify the Equal Rights Amendment (ERA) and the popularity of Ronald Reagan, an anti-ERA president, seemed to indicate that women were still not identifying their own interests as a voting group. All this began to change during the 1980s as women in increasing numbers began to realize that on some issues they had a different agenda from many men.

The gender gap became most noticeable during the 1982 elections when, according to historian Robert Daniel, fe-

male voters showed "less enthusiasm for conservative candidates than men by a margin of 5 percent." Daniel notes further that exit polls demonstrated that female voters were less supportive of Reagan policies regarding the economy, Social Security, inflation, unemployment, and the military. Former president of the National Organization for Women Ellie Smeal found that on core women's rights issues (ERA, abortion, child care) "women are consistently from 10 to 20 percent more supportive than men."

In 1992, Democrat Ann Richards won election as governor of Texas largely because of crossover votes from Texas Republican women. That same year, more women ran for and were elected to the U.S. Congress than ever before. Gender voting was a major factor in most of those elections.

While American women still do not vote as a bloc, there is no doubt of their potential for power. Women constitute about 53 percent of the voting-age population and are registered in slightly higher numbers than men. As women increase in political self-awareness and power, the gender gap and the need to bridge it has become an even greater reality in American political life. *(See also: Democratic Party; Equal Employment Opportunity Commission; Ethnicity and Gender Roles; Republican Party)*

—Jonathan W. Zophy

Further Reading

Abzug, Bella, with Mim Keller. *Gender Gap: Bella Abzug's Guide to Political Power.* Boston: Houghton Mifflin, 1984.

Costain, Anne. "After Reagan: New Party Attitudes toward Gender," *Annals of the American Academy of Political and Social Science* 515 (1991): 114-25.

Mueller, Carol. "The Gender Gap and Women's Political Influence," *Annals of the American Academy of Political and Social Science* 515 (1991): 23-37.

Smeal, Ellie. *Why and How Women Will Elect the Next President.* New York: Harper & Row, 1984.

～ Gender Roles

Gender roles refer to the set of social expectations pertaining to females and males. Gender roles have been shaped less by the biological and anatomical differences between the sexes than by parental teaching, formal education, religion, and the law, all of which serve to define and reinforce gender roles. From the colonial period to the present day, legal inequalities between the sexes have prevented women from achieving economic and political parity with men. Although America is a pluralistic nation, the teaching of secondary and passive roles for women has characterized religious and secular instruction until very recently. Women's roles have consistently been linked with child care, the nurturing of children and adults, and domestic work, whether or not women's work has been directly connected to home and family.

In the seventeenth century, the social and legal inferiority of women followed from religious and scientific precepts that held women to be morally and physically weak and therefore rightly subject to the superior male. In the eighteenth and the nineteenth centuries, Enlightenment and Romantic philosophers challenged these views. By the mid-nineteenth century, the concept that women were morally inferior had been replaced by the view that women were more capable than men of moral purity but that women were delicate creatures whose ability to bear children was jeopardized by extended rigorous physical or mental activity. In the late nineteenth century, the acceptance of women's moral superiority improved their status within the family, but it also reinforced notions that women's ideal place was in the home while economic trends were drawing increasing numbers of women into paid employment outside the home. The Industrial Revolution created jobs for women. Expanding on traditional notions of women as producers of food and clothing, factories employed women as operatives beginning in the late 1820s. By the time of the Civil War,

women had moved into positions as teachers and as office workers as well. Here, too, women's jobs were defined as extensions of women's nurturing instincts and their contentment with simple, repetitive tasks.

The Seneca Falls (New York) Woman's Rights Convention of 1848 initiated a long campaign to redefine women's roles in society and under the law. The ratification of the Nineteenth Amendment, which secured woman suffrage, ended one phase of the broadening of gender roles in America. During this period, women gained legal authority over their own children, the right to own property, the right to possess their own wages, and the right to participate in the political process.

Such nineteenth-century political and theoretical challenges wrought significant modifications in gender roles, but motherhood remained the central expectation for women's lives. Through the early twentieth century, social norms also prescribed motherhood for all women, but post-World War II economic realities reshaped gender roles as married women increasingly entered the paid labor force out of necessity. The feminist movement, particularly Third Wave feminism, contributed to the refashioning of women's roles, coupling sexual liberation with broader public roles for women. *(See also: Gender Role Socialization; Sex-Gender System)*

—Julia Kirk Blackwelder

Further Reading

Berkin, Carol. *Within the Conjurer's Circle: Women in Colonial America.* Morristown, NJ: Grossmann, 1974.

Faderman, Lillian. *Odd Girls and Twilight Lovers: A History of Lesbian Life in Twentieth-Century America.* New York: Columbia University Press, 1991.

Filene, Peter G. *Him/Her/Self: Sex Roles in Modern America,* 2d ed. Baltimore: Johns Hopkins University Press, 1986.

Hood, Jane C., ed. *Men, Work, and Family.* Newbury Park, CA: Sage, 1993.

Rosenberg, Rosalind. *Divided Lives: American Women in the Twentieth Century.* New York: Hill & Wang, 1992.

Welter, Barbara. "The Cult of True Womanhood, 1820–1860," *American Quarterly* 18 (Summer 1966): 151-74.

～ Gender Role Socialization (Sex Role Socialization)

Gender role socialization is the process by which the members of a society learn its cultural expectations of masculinity and femininity. *Gender* refers to a social process of learning what it means to be a male or female, while *sex* refers to biological differences. Various individuals, groups, and institutions—known as socializing agents—are responsible for this engendering; among the most important are one's family, one's peers, the educational system, the mass media, religion, and language.

Traditionally in the United States, the two genders have been viewed as dichotomous and extremely different; in fact, one refers to the other as the "opposite sex." Gender roles become stereotyped social norms that should not be violated. Females have been socialized to be passive, emotionally nurturant, and inept in solving mathematical and mechanical problems. Males, in contrast, have been socialized to be aggressive, unemotional, competitive, and mathematically and mechanically inclined. Although some observers have argued that these behavioral differences are due at least in part to the biological differences between males and females, this claim receives little support from empirical evidence. Research demonstrates that gender role socialization begins immediately after birth, making it very difficult to determine which, if any, behavioral differences are due to biology and which are the products of social learning. Starting with infancy, differential treatment continues throughout childhood and can be seen not only in parent-child interaction but also in the different toys designed for boys and girls, in the different games they are taught to play, in the living spaces (complete with colors) designed for them, and in the literature written for them. The tremendous variation in gender roles cross-culturally also indicates that they are socially learned rather than biologically driven.

Research also demonstrates that small observed gender differences are in fact exaggerated. As a group, one sex may, on average, have a higher score on a trait (e.g., males and mathematical ability). However, the two sexes are, in fact, much more similar than different, and any individual woman and man are just as likely to have the same skill level as two people of the same sex.

Gender role socialization and our view of the sexes as opposite are both very powerful means of social control, seriously affecting men's and women's personalities and social relationships. Several researchers have documented the detrimental effects of traditional gender role socialization in the United States; men and women have been allowed to develop only parts of themselves instead of their full human potential. Because it is a learned process rather than a biological one, gender roles and their stereotypes can be challenged and changed. One of the primary goals of feminism is to alter the process of gender role socialization so that individuals can develop their unique potentials. (See also: Child Rearing; Gender Roles; Sex-Gender System; Sexism; Sexual Division of Labor)

—Susan C. Turell
—Claire M. Renzetti

Further Reading

Anselmi, D., and A. Law. Questions of Gender: Perspectives and Paradoxes. Boston: McGraw-Hill, 1998.

Basow, S. Gender: Stereotypes and Roles, 3d ed. Pacific Grove, CA: Brooks Cole, 1992.

Doyle, J., and M. Paludi. Sex and Gender: The Human Experience. Madison, WI: Brown & Benchmark, 1995.

Hyde, J. "How Large Are Cognitive Differences?" American Psychologist 36 (1981): 892-901.

Maccoby, E., and C. Jacklin. The Psychology of Sex Differences. Stanford, CA: Stanford University Press, 1974.

Renzetti, Claire M., and Daniel J. Curran. Women, Men, and Society, 4th ed. Boston: Allyn & Bacon, 1994.

⟋ General Federation of Women's Clubs (GFWC)

The General Federation of Women's Clubs became the largest national organization of women in the late nineteenth century, providing middle-class women a crucial social nexus between the domestic values of the cult of true womanhood and the political activism of the woman suffrage movement. In 1889, journalist Jane Cunningham Croly, who had earlier founded the women's club Sorosis, invited other women's literary clubs to help Sorosis celebrate its twenty-first anniversary. By the next year, many of these clubs had joined together to form the federation. Women's literary clubs had flourished in the late 1890s, but Croly believed that these clubs could undertake other activities and apply woman's influence through the strength of the federation, especially in areas of social reform such as expansion of public libraries and betterment of conditions in public schools. Although the GFWC worked for the rights of women workers, it was slow to endorse woman suffrage. While most of the leaders did, the federation itself did not endorse the right of women to vote until 1914.

The GFWC had always had pacifist leanings, and during World War I, the federation supported the Woman's Peace Party. However, when the country joined the war effort, the federation raised money for liberty bonds and supported the Red Cross. After the war, many clubs were disheartened since the problems the war had sought to solve still remained. The federation sought to maintain its commitment to worthwhile projects, supporting Prohibition and joining other women's groups in favoring censorship in the movie industry. The federation was reluctant to support the Equal Rights Amendment. In fact, the GFWC did not support the amendment until 1944, when it sent representatives to the Democratic and Republican national conventions to ask for support for equal rights.

After World War II, the federation was less visible nationally, but it continued to grow. In 1953, there were 15,000 clubs involved. Currently, there are 500,000 members in 11,000 clubs. (See also: Black Women's Clubs; Cult of True Womanhood; Equal Rights Amendment; Woman's Peace Party)

—Judith Pryor

Further Reading

Blair, Karen J. The Clubwoman as Feminist: True Womanhood Redefined, 1868–1914. New York: Holmes & Meier, 1980.

O'Neill, William L. Everyone Was Brave: The Rise and Fall of Feminism in America. Chicago: Quadrangle, 1969.

Wells, Mildred White. Unity in Diversity; The History of the General Federation of Women's Clubs. Washington, DC: General Federation of Women's Clubs, 1953.

Wood, Mary I. The History of the General Federation of Women's Clubs. New York: General Federation of Women's Clubs, 1912.

↝ Geology

In the early years of the nineteenth century, women provided drawings of landscapes and fossils for state geological survey reports. Their early schooling in science and sketching prepared them for this "genteel" work. Among the first such artists was Orra White Hitchcock, whose illustrations appeared in the 1830s and 1840s in publications written by her husband, Edward, the first state geologist of Massachusetts. Later Cecilia Beaux contributed drawings for the four federal surveys, 1867–1879. Early writings in geology, few in number, were for the most part textbooks or personal observations. Amateur fossil and mineral collectors contributed to research. One of the first amateur geologists, Erminnie Adelle Platt Smith (1836–1896), an ethnologist, classified and labeled specimens for European collections and presented a paper on jade at the 1879 American Association for the Advancement of Science meeting.

In the latter nineteenth century, women had the opportunity to pursue formal education in geology. Florence Bascom (1862–1945) received her doctorate from Johns Hopkins University, the first woman to do so. In the 1880s, she introduced the use of microscopic techniques in petrology in the United States. She founded the Department of Geology at Bryn Mawr College, a training ground for most U.S. female geologists well into the 1930s. Among her notable students were Ida Ogilvie (1874–1963), who later established Barnard College's Department of Geology and conducted studies of New York State geology and Alberta glaciology; Anna Isabel Jonas Stose (1881–1974), who worked for the Maryland, Pennsylvania, and Virginia state geological surveys and the U.S. Geological Survey and made an outstanding contribution to the understanding of Appalachian geology; Julia Anna Gardner (1882–1960), who conducted paleontological studies in Texas and southeastern Mexico; and Eleanora Frances Bliss Knopf (1883–1974), whose work at the U.S. Geological Survey led to the reporting of a Pennsylvania deposit of the mineral glaucopane, previously believed to be found only on the Pacific coast.

Early paleontologists associated with museums included Winifred Goldring (1888–1971), whose research at the New York State Museum led to the publication of *The Devonian Crinoids of the State of New York* in 1923. In 1949, she became the first woman president of the Paleontological Society. Billie Untermann (1906–1973) assembled dinosaur skeletons at the Utah Field House of Natural History and later became its director. Angelina Messina (1910–1968) compiled extensive catalogs of foraminifera and ostracoda at the American Museum of Natural History and in 1955 cofounded the journal *Micropaleontology*. Tilly Edinger (1897–1967), born and educated in Germany, published a monumental work on fossil brains while working as an unpaid curator of the Senckenberg Museum's vertebrate collection. In 1940, she arrived at Harvard University and spent the rest of her life at its Museum of Comparative Zoology.

Those women who elected to work for oil companies in the 1920s encountered some hostility from their male colleagues. At that time, micropaleontology was just receiving recognition. Alva Ellison of Humble Oil and Esther Applin of Rio Bravo were among the first to recognize the importance of using microfossils to date formations and predict the likelihood of petroleum deposits. Carlotta Maury (1876–1938) served from 1910 until her death as a consultant for the Royal Dutch Shell Petroleum Division. Elizabeth Florette Fisher (1873–1941), one of the few women field geologists, made extensive surveys in the Texas oil regions. Isabel Bassett Wasson (1896–1994), one of the country's first female petroleum geologists, conducted explorations through remote areas of South America in the 1920s and published the first report on the geology of the Cabin Creek pool, West Virginia.

Mention should be made of those women, some unheralded, whose contributions to geology may be found in the assistance they gave their husbands or relatives. One such is Lou Henry Hoover (1874–1944), wife of President Herbert Hoover. She studied geology at Stanford (1894–1898) and later collaborated with her husband in their 1950 translation of Georgius Agricola's *De Re Metallica* (1556). *(See also: Beaux, Cecilia; Higher Education; Science)*

—**Regina A. Brown**

Further Reading

Aldrich, Michele L. "Women in Geology." In *Women of Science: Righting the Record*, edited by G. Kass-Simon and Patricia Farnes, 42-71. Bloomington: Indiana University Press, 1993.

———. "Women in Paleontology in the United States 1840–1960," *Earth Science History* 1 (1962): 14-22.

Elder, Eleanor S. "Women in Early Geology," *Journal of Geological Education* 30 (November 1982): 287-93.

"Geology and Earth Sciences." In *The History of Women and Science, Health, and Technology: A Bibliographic Guide to the Professions and the Disciplines*, edited by Phyllis Holman Weisbard, 2d ed., 26-28. Madison: University of Wisconsin System Women's Studies Librarian, 1993.

Ogilvie, Marilyn Bailey. *Women in Science: Antiquity through the Nineteenth Century: A Biographical Dictionary with Annotated Bibliography*. Cambridge: MIT Press, 1986.

Rossiter, Margaret W. *Women Scientists in America: Struggles and Strategies to 1940*. Baltimore: Johns Hopkins University Press, 1982.

Siegel, Patricia Joan. *Women in the Scientific Search: An American Bio-Bibliography, 1724-1979*. Metuchen, NJ: Scarecrow, 1985.

↝ Gibson, Althea (b. 1927)

Althea Gibson was the first black invited to play in the American Lawn Tennis Association championships, and in 1957 and 1958 she won both at Wimbledon and at Forest Hills.

Born in Silver, South Carolina, Gibson was raised in Harlem in New York City where she began to play "paddle tennis" on the streets. She entered and won the Department of

Parks Manhattan Girls' Tennis Championship and in 1942 began to receive professional coaching. She dominated the girls' and women's divisions of the black tennis circuit from 1945 to 1958. She received a Bachelor of Science degree in physical education from Florida Agricultural and Mechanical University in Tallahassee in 1953.

After her successes at Wimbledon and Forest Hills, she was named Woman Athlete of the Year in the Associated Press polls of 1957 and 1958 and was elected to the Lawn Tennis Hall of Fame and Tennis Museum in 1971. She won the world professional tennis championship in 1960 and then joined the women's professional golf tour in 1963. She became the athletic commissioner of New Jersey in 1975 and married Sydney Llewellyn in 1983.

Althea Gibson's contributions to the world of tennis will long stand as a monument to talent and determination. Her rise to the top in a sport dominated by white, affluent, "private club" players is an inspiring success story. Unfortunately, Gibson's later years have been marred by serious illness, and she has had financial difficulties because of it. A benefit was held for her in New York City in May 1997, and her friends in Atlanta, Georgia, have sponsored a Website on her behalf. *(See also: Athletics/Sports)*

—**Susan Kinnell**

Further Reading

Althea Gibson: The Champion. [Video documentary, Prod: Carol Clarke; Narr. Maya Angelou; Spons. USTA]. Thunderhead Productions, 1998.

Biracree, Tom. *Althea Gibson.* Los Angeles: Melrose Square, 1990.

Davidson, Sue. Changing the Game: *The Stories of Tennis Champions Alice Marble and Althea Gibson.* Seattle, WA: Seal Press, 1997.

Gibson, Althea. *I Always Wanted to Be Somebody.* New York: Harper & Row, 1958.

http://www.geocities.com/Heartland/Plains/3555 [Friends of Althea Gibson site]

http://www.altheagibson.com

Gilbreth, Lillian Evelyn (Moller)
(1878–1972)

Lillian Gilbreth was a pioneer in the field of scientific management and the principles of motion study, which she formulated with her husband, Frank Gilbreth. They established efficient techniques for saving wasted motion in industry so that the workers could maximize production with minimal exertion. The whole idea was to find the "one best way" to do a job. Believing the home was an important institution, Gilbreth applied the principles of scientific management to achieve efficiency in household tasks. She sought to provide women with shorter, simpler, and easier ways of doing housework to enable them to seek paid employment outside the home.

In 1904, she married efficiency expert Frank Gilbreth and over a period of seventeen years bore twelve children. Widowed in 1924, she nonetheless managed to rear her fam-

ily and send her children to college while she continued to develop efficient techniques for industry and the home. Her son and daughter provided a description of this unusual household in the books *Cheaper by the Dozen* (1948) and *Belles on Their Toes* (1950). Ultimately, many of her techniques were used by the defense industry during World War II.

Gilbreth's academic degrees included a bachelor's (1900) and a master's (1902) in literature, both obtained from the University of California at Berkeley, and a doctorate in industrial psychology from Brown University (1915). Among her more important publications are *Psychology of Management* (1914), *The Home-Maker and Her Job* (1927), and *Management in the Home* (1954).

Lillian Gilbreth was atypical of women during her time; the mother of twelve, she nevertheless pursued a successful career and effectively challenged the myth that a woman's place was in the home. *(See also: Housework; Science)*

—**Michael A. de León**

Further Reading

Gilbreth, Lillian M. "Women in Industry." In *American Women: The Changing Image,* edited by Beverly Benner Cassara, 90-98. Boston: Beacon, 1962.

Spriegel, William R., and Clark E. Myers, eds. *The Writings of the Gilbreths.* Homewood, IL: Irwin, 1953.

Yost, Edna. *American Women of Science.* Philadelphia: Frederick A. Stokes, 1943.

Gilman, Charlotte Perkins
(1860–1935)

Charlotte Perkins Gilman was a Progressive Era feminist and sociologist who wrote major studies of gender and economic relations. Both Gilman's life and writings explore the contradictions between modern logic and American domestic mythology. Gilman was related through her father to Harriet Beecher Stowe and an extended family of preachers and domestic writers, but Frederick Beecher Perkins, a librarian and writer, early left his wife, son, and Charlotte, who subsequently moved nineteen times in eighteen years—fourteen times to different cities. Although strikingly attractive, Gilman disregarded conventional interests such as clothes and flirting in favor of reading and fitness. In May 1884, she married artist Charles Walter Stetson and a year later gave birth to their daughter, Katharine, but marriage and motherhood left Gilman suffering from a "nervous prostration" that only separation and divorce relieved. When Stetson married Gilman's best friend in 1894, Gilman gave them custody of Katharine and maintained good relations with them all thereafter. In 1900, Gilman remarried, this time to her first cousin George Houghton Gilman. During the 1890s, she began lecturing in the United States and Europe. Her literary activity and fame peaked from about 1900 until World War I. Terminally ill in 1935, she wrote, "I have preferred chloroform to cancer" and died by her own hand, an end consistent with her life of determined independence.

Later readers often encounter Gilman first through her fiction, especially her widely anthologized story, "The Yellow Wall-Paper" (1892). This brief but powerful tale, which recalls Gilman's absurd treatment for marital depression through a "rest cure," uses fiction to represent a favorite theme of Gilman's—that women need opportunities to transcend trivial household labor and to perform serious, socially significant work. Gilman's novel *Herland* (1915) also remains interesting for its depiction of a humane, socialist, two-thousand-year-old utopia peopled solely by women, who reproduce through parthenogenesis. *Herland*'s plot turns on an accidental visit by three men and their varying reactions, which are keyed to their preconceptions of women's roles in American society; conversely, the women of Herland ply their visitors with questions that expose the irrational cruelties and distortions of male-dominated society.

Gilman wrote much other fiction, but during her lifetime she was most famous for her writings and lectures advocating reform of women's social status. *Women and Economics* (1898) is a classic of its subject, meriting comparison with Mary Wollstonecraft's *A Vindication of the Rights of Woman* (1792) and Olive Schreiner's *Woman and Labor* (1911). Combining history with the new social sciences of sociology, anthropology, and psychology, *Women and Economics* uses contemporary social Darwinism to make startling comparisons between culture and nature: "We are the only animal species in which the female depends on the male for food, the only animal species in which the sex relation is also the economic relation." Woman's indirect contact with her economic environment has led her to overdevelop sexually, as a female cow "has become a walking milk-machine." According to Gilman, this "sexuo-economic relationship," which prevents humanity's full social development, can be eliminated by no longer restricting women's work to marriage, maternity, and housekeeping, a change to be made possible by professionalizing food preparation and child care. In theory, the modern home would be a kitchenless establishment intended only to provide rest and recreation for the family unit. Although her solutions may appear radical, Gilman does not aim to destroy the family but to help it adapt to modern industrial society, "to reconcile happy work with a happy marriage."

Women and Economics went through seven English-language editions, was translated into seven languages, and gained fame for Gilman in German and English feminist circles. In the next two decades, Gilman developed ideas incipient in her great treatise in other major sociological works. Among them, *The Home: Its Work and Influence* (1903) applied Darwinian evolution to domestic America of the early 1900s, showing that while humans have evolved economically from hunters to farmers and finally to industrialists, the average single-family American home has remained in a state more primitive than that of the rest of society, inhibiting the growth of other institutions and slowing social progress. Gilman again contended that children would thrive

better under the guidance of professionals than under the care of their overworked mothers, whose notions of health, nutrition, and education are outdated.

Much of Gilman's writings appeared in original or revised form in *The Forerunner,* the remarkable monthly magazine combining feminism and socialism that she edited and published from 1909 through 1916. Gilman wrote nearly all the magazine's copy, from its editorials, articles, and theoretical pieces to its short stories and poetry—even its advertisements, which she accepted only for products she could endorse. Gilman's remarkable productivity coincided largely with the Progressive Era and its confidence that reason, logic, and enlightened work habits could effect positive social change; with the catastrophic irrationality of World War I and the rise of hedonism in the 1920s, that attitude and Gilman's work began to decline. In 1923, *His Religion and Hers* deplored the dominion of death in male-dominated religion and advocated woman's life principle as a social bond and moral force. At her death, Gilman left *The Living of Charlotte Perkins Gilman: An Autobiography* with a dedication to her daughter. *(See also: Cult of True Womanhood; Women Writers)*

—**Craig White**

Further Reading

Berkin, Carol Ruth. "Private Woman, Public Woman: The Contradictions of Charlotte Perkins Gilman." In *Women of America: A History,* edited by C. R. Berkin and Mary Beth Norton, 150-76. Boston: Houghton Mifflin, 1979.

Charlotte Perkins Gilman Papers. Schlesinger Library. Radcliffe College, Cambridge, MA.

Gilman, Charlotte Perkins. *Concerning Children.* Boston: Small, Maynard, 1900.

Hill, Mary A. *Charlotte Perkins Gilman: The Making of a Radical Feminist, 1860–1896.* Philadelphia: Temple University Press, 1980.

Lane, Ann J. *To Herland and Beyond: The Life and Work of Charlotte Perkins Gilman.* New York: Pantheon, 1990.

O'Neill, William L. *Everyone Was Brave.* New York: Quadrangle, 1969.

Scharnhorst, Gary. *Charlotte Perkins Gilman.* Boston: Twayne, 1985.

✎ Girl Scouts of America (GSA)

The Girl Scouts of America (GSA) was founded in 1912 by Juliette Gordon Low. An American who spent much of her time in England, Low became acquainted with Sir Robert Baden-Powell, who founded the Boy Scouts, and his sister Agnes Powell, who directed the girls' branch known as the Girl Guides. With the Powells' encouragement, Low started several troops of the Girl Guides, one in Scotland and the rest in London.

On her next trip to the United States, she told an old friend, Nina Pape, that she was going to start a new program for girls all over the world. She enlisted Pape and other friends to start two troops in Savannah, enrolling her niece Daisy Gordon as the first Girl Guide. After the first year, the name was changed to Girl Scouts, partly to match the Boy Scout movement and also because the members thought the name Scouts fit the American pioneer heritage. In 1913, she set up a national headquarters in Washington, D.C., with Edith D. Johnston as the first national secretary. Later, the headquarters was moved to New York.

Low was just as successful at recruiting leaders and building a national organization as she was at starting troops. The movement grew rapidly, partly because there was an interest at this time in an organization for girls. Girls were no longer willing to play the role of decorative and proper young ladies; they wanted to engage in spirited and adventurous activities and to become more self-reliant. Having been raised to play only the role of wife, hostess, and mother, Low was in favor of this expanded role for young girls, but she did not see the Girl Scouts as a feminist organization nor herself as a feminist. In fact, she was publicly opposed to the suffrage movement, and her handbook for the organization proposed a rather conservative role for girls and advised the members not to try to imitate men. The movement also succeeded because of Low's enthusiasm and ability to recruit family members and friends to be a part of this new organization.

The first national council in 1915 elected Low president. Many of the original leaders were leisured middle-class young women eager to find a meaningful activity to fill their time. By 1919, there were troops in every state except Utah and in the territory of Hawaii as well. Although the founders and original leaders of the organization were middle- and upper-class white women, the Girl Scouts organization reached out to girls of all races and economic backgrounds.

Although the organization owed much to the Boy Scouts, which had been founded in 1909, and despite the similarity of names, the Girl Scouts of America leaders did not want it to be a female version of that organization. The Girl Scouts emphasized outdoor activities, encouraged the traditional interests and skills of homemaking and crafts, and inculcated good citizenship in native-born and immigrant girls. The U.S. entry into World War I soon after the founding of the GSA spurred the organization to support the war effort by working with the Red Cross, selling war bonds, and conducting other activities. The wartime emphasis on marching and drills was abandoned after 1920.

Despite changes through the years, the GSA purpose remained to emphasize good citizenship, outdoor activities, and the idea that girls should do something for someone else every day. The organization handbook of the late 1970s reflected the change in women's employment patterns by including a section about career selection that encourages girls to think that any career is appropriate for girls. The largest women's volunteer organization in the world, the Girl Scouts of the U.S.A., as the organization is now called, still uses volunteers as leaders: Only a small percentage of the adults involved are professional workers. Current membership of the Girl Scouts of the U.S.A. is 3.5 million. In October 1996, the National Council of the Girl Scouts of the U.S.A. updated the Girl Scout law to make its language more contemporary. *(See also: Low, Juliette)*

—Judith Pryor

Further Reading

Girl Scouts of America. *How Girls Can Help Their Country.* New York: Girl Scouts of America, 1917.

Girl Scouts of the U.S.A. *Girl Scouts, Its Role in the Lives of American Women of Distinction.* New York: Girl Scouts of the U.S.A., 1991.

———. *Seventy-Five Years of Girl Scouting.* New York: Girl Scouts of the U.S.A., 1986.

———. *Worlds to Explore: Handbook for Brownie and Junior Girl Scouts.* New York: Girl Scouts of the U.S.A., 1977.

Schultz, Gladys, and Daisy Gordon Lawrence. *Lady from Savannah: The Life of Juliette Low.* Philadelphia: J. B. Lippincott, 1958.

Strickland, Charles E. "Juliette Low, the Girl Scouts, and the Role of American Women." In *Woman's Being, Woman's Place: Female Identity and Vocation in American History,* edited by Mary Kelley, 252-64. Boston: G. K. Hall, 1977.

ॐ Goldman, Emma (1869–1940)

Anarchist lecturer and author, Emma Goldman was possibly the most charismatic speaker among women leftists in American history. She embodied anarchism in the United States and campaigned against government and organized religion and on behalf of individualism, civil liberties, sexual freedom, free speech, feminism, birth control, and modern drama. Through her annual lecture tours, "Red Emma" fascinated an American public unresponsive to her basic message. Harassed by the authorities as much for her feminist message of women's absolute equality as for her avowed anarchism, Goldman staunchly confronted the reality and the implications of the "woman question" for radical reform philosophies. Raising the consciousness of women and men on the actual conditions of women, she decried women's sexual exploitation and declared women's right to both sexual autonomy and reproductive freedom of choice.

Born in Kovno, Russia, to a lower-middle-class Jewish family, Goldman emigrated with her family in 1886, settling in Rochester, New York. While working in sweatshops in various eastern cities, she was radicalized by the executions of four anarchist protesters in the aftermath of the Haymarket Affair in 1886 and briefly became a disciple of the anarchist editor Johann Most. She soon established a lifelong association with anarchist Alexander Berkman; in 1892, she served as an accomplice in his attempted assassination of steel company official Henry Clay Frick after the Homestead Strike, in which ten people were killed in clashes between striking steel workers and armed guards hired by the Carnegie Steel Company in Homestead, Pennsylvania. Thereafter, she opposed such individual acts of violence but was persecuted by police and mobs, blamed for the assassination of President William McKinley by the self-styled anarchist Leon Czolgosz, and occasionally jailed for her public remarks.

Goldman edited the monthly *Mother Earth* from 1906 to 1917, and published *Anarchism and Other Essays,* among various works. As an anarchist influenced by the Russian theorist Peter Kropotkin, she believed that all governments were inherently oppressive, and instead of endorsing political methods of promoting revolution—as did Socialists— she favored direct economic action to undermine capitalism. Her goal was individual liberty within a decentralized, collectivist framework of autonomous, loosely organized units.

During World War I, Goldman and Berkman organized the No-Conscription League and were convicted in 1917 for conspiring against the draft. Goldman, already denaturalized by the government's stripping of citizenship from Jacob Kersner, her apolitical ex-husband, was deported with other radicals to the Soviet Union during the First Red Scare of 1919. There, she became one of the first revolutionaries to condemn totalitarianism in the new Soviet system after the Russian Revolution, and for the next two decades, she wandered as a woman without a country. She died in Toronto, Canada, while raising money for the antifascists in Spain's Civil War. *(See also: Civil Liberties Movement During World War I; Woman Question; World War I)*

—**Sally M. Miller**

Further Reading

Drinnon, Richard. *Rebel in Paradise: A Biography of Emma Goldman.* Boston: Beacon, 1961.
Falk, Candace. *Love, Anarchy, and Emma Goldman.* New Brunswick, NJ: Rutgers University Press, 1990.
Goldman, Emma. *Living My Life.* New York: Knopf, 1931.
Wexler, Alice. *Emma Goldman: An Intimate Life.* New York: Pantheon, 1984.
———. *Emma Goldman in Exile: From the Russian Revolution to the Spanish Civil War.* Boston: Beacon, 1989.

❧ Good Templars

Good Templars, a fraternal temperance order founded in New York State in 1851, was superseded by the Independent Order of Good Templars (IOGT), organized in 1852. The order demanded total abstinence from its members and worked for prohibition. Weekly lodge meetings provided the mostly youthful membership with fellowship and recreation in a morally uplifting atmosphere. At the end of 1868, the IOGT claimed more than 500,000 members in North America. In the 1870s, it became a power in Britain and Sweden. By the early 1900s, it had few American members, and many of those few were Scandinavian immigrants.

Nearly a generation before the founding of the Woman's Christian Temperance Union (1874), the IOGT offered women the opportunity to work for temperance and other social reforms. Women were admitted to membership in August 1852 and were made eligible for election to all offices in November. Amelia Bloomer was one of the first women Good Templars.

Although men dominated the IOGT, women served in the Good Templars as officers, organizers, and speakers. Amanda Way headed the Grand Lodge of Indiana in 1867 and 1868, while Martha McClellan Brown led the Grand Lodge of Ohio in 1872. Martha B. O'Donnell was elected to superintend the international children's auxiliary from 1874 to 1878. Jessie Forsyth held the same international office between 1893 and 1908. *(See also: Bloomer, Amelia Jenks; Forsyth, Jessie; Temperance Movement; Way, Amanda M.; Woman's Christian Temperance Union)*

—**David M. Fahey**

Further Reading

Larsen-Ledet, Lars. *Good Templary through a Hundred Years.* Aarhus, Denmark: International Supreme Lodge, 1951.
Peirce, Isaac Newton. *The History of the Independent Order of Good Templars.* Philadelphia: Daughaday & Becker, 1869.
Turnbull, William W. *The Good Templars: A History of the Rise and Progress of the Independent Order of Good Templars, 1851–1901, Jubilee Volume.* Edited by James Yeames. N.P.: IOGT, 1901.

❧ Graham, Martha (1894–1991)

As dancer and choreographer, Martha Graham has left an indelible mark on the arts of the twentieth century. Innovator of a revolutionary dance technique based on the principle of contraction and release of the torso, Graham created dramatic choreography often based on women in history or literature. Creating nearly two hundred dances for herself and her company, she sought to expose the depths of human emotion, defied conventional standards of movement and rhythm, and moved her audience to experience dance as an enormously personal and passionate means of communication.

Born in Allegheny, Pennsylvania, Graham and her family moved in 1908 to Santa Barbara, California, where she grew up. Receiving her first dance instruction at the Cumnock School in Los Angeles, in 1916 she attended a summer session of the Denishawn School, the original modern dance company in the United States, where she subsequently taught and performed as a member of the company from 1919 to 1923. In 1926, she formed her first independent dance company, consisting of herself and three other dancers, and a year later opened her own studio—the Martha Graham School of Contemporary Dance.

Graham's influence on the dance is matched only by her influence on the artists, musicians, poets, sculptors, and stage designers with whom she collaborated. Persons of note include Aaron Copland, composer of the famous score to *Appalachian Spring;* Louis Horst, considered to be the father of modern choreography and the greatest artistic influence in Graham's life; poet Ben Belit; artist sculptor Isamu Noguchi; and light designer Jean Rosenthal.

Figure 24. Martha Graham
Dancer and choreographer Martha Graham broke away from the restrained movements of ballet, creating a style that expressed greater emotion. Used by permission of UPI/Corbis-Bettmann.

Graham's breadth of vision is evidenced most clearly in the range of works she created, including *Primitive Mysteries* (1931), her first unanimously acclaimed masterpiece; *Letter to the World* (1940), inspired by the poetry of Emily Dickinson and one of the most successful marriages of verse and movement ever achieved; *Appalachian Spring* (1944), an enduring signature work; *Clytemnestra* (1958), Graham's first evening-long work, in which she masterfully resolved the tension between the themes of passion and duty; and *Acts of Light* (1981), a joyous celebration and rebirth out of darkness into the light, considered by some to be the most significant creation of her later, nondancing years.

Proclaimed a "national treasure" by President Gerald Ford in 1976, Graham was awarded the Medal of Freedom. Later awards included the Kennedy Center Honors Award in 1979, the Royal Medal of Jordan, the American Dance Festival Award, the Bryn Mawr College M. Carey Thomas Prize awarded to "American women of eminent achievement," the Golden Florin award of Italy, the Knight of the French Legion of Honor, the Grand Vermeil Medal of France, President Reagan's National Medal of Honor, the Japanese Order of the Precious Butterfly with Diamond, and the Council of Fashion Designers of America Lifetime Achievement Award.

Martha Graham was known as a genius, a tempestuous originator, and an unrelenting taskmaster. She sacrificed everything for her art—love, friendship, money—and was no less demanding of her dancers. In the words of Martha Graham, "My dancing . . . is an affirmation of life through movement." *(See also: Dance; Duncan, Isadora)*

—**Cecelia A. Albert**
Adapted for the second edition by Jan Stockman Simonds.

Further Reading

De Mille, Agnes. *Martha: The Life and Works of Martha Graham.* New York: Random House, 1991.

Graham, Martha. *Blood Money: An Autobiography.* New York: Doubleday, 1991.

Morgan, Barbara. *Martha Graham: Sixteen Dances in Photographs.* Dobbs Ferry, NY: Morgan & Morgan, 1980.

Stodelle, Ernestine. *Deep Song: The Dance Story of Martha Graham.* New York: Schirmer, 1984.

Terry, Walter. *Frontiers of the Dance: The Life of Martha Graham.* New York: Crowell, 1975.

∿ Grahamism

Grahamism was a movement initiated by Sylvester Graham (1794–1851), for whom today's cracker is named. The son of a Connecticut clergyman, Graham himself was a Presbyterian minister who began his public career as a temperance lecturer in Philadelphia. During the cholera epidemic of 1832, he broadened his message to emphasize other harmful foods and practices.

During the remainder of his life, he lectured and wrote on diet and hygiene. He opposed the drinking of coffee and tea as well as alcohol, the use of spices, and the eating of meat. The center of his health regimen, laid out in his *Treatise on Bread and Bread Making* (1837), was homemade bread made with coarsely ground flour. He advocated that, aside from changing their diet, people change their lifestyle by opening their homes to fresh air, wearing less restrictive clothing, and bathing regularly. Much of this advice was directed specifically to women. In his *Lecture to Young Men on Chastity* (1834), he warned against sexual indulgence as well. He was an early and extreme Victorian who denounced "venereal indulgence" (sex for pleasure) in marriage as well as "solitary vice" (masturbation). A clean mind and a clean body led to salvation.

His ideas were picked up and disseminated by numerous Grahamites with whom he had little personal connection. In 1837, the American Physiological Society was founded in Boston. This organization published *The Graham Journal of Health and Longevity* and held several health conventions in the late 1830s. Oberlin College turned over its refectory to a Grahamite, and boardinghouses such as that run by Mary

Gove Nichols in Boston followed Grahamite principles. Stores resembling modern health food co-ops sprang up across the country. Although Graham died in 1851 and the health reform movement became fragmented, his influence was embodied in the religious practices of the Seventh Day Adventists, founded by Ellen White, and in the work of John Harvey Kellogg, an opponent of masturbation and the "inventor" of corn flakes. A wide range of women health reformers from Mary Gove Nichols to Amelia Bloomer and Catharine Beecher echoed many of Graham's ideas. *(See also: Beecher, Catharine; Bloomer, Amelia Jenks; Nichols, Mary Gove)*

—**William G. Shade**

Further Reading

Nissenbaum, Stephen. *Sex, Diet and Debility in Jacksonian America: Sylvester Graham and Health Reform.* Westport, CT: Greenwood, 1980.

Sokolow, Jayme. *Eros and Modernization: Sylvester Graham, Health Reform, and the Origins of Victorian Sexuality in America.* Rutherford, NJ: Fairleigh Dickinson University Press, 1983.

～ "Granny" Midwifery

A "granny" midwife is a traditional lay midwife who has received little formal training and who usually serves low-income women. The term is most often associated with black midwives living in the southern region of the United States. However, granny midwives may also be found among whites in Appalachia, Mexican Americans, Native Americans, the Cajuns of southwestern Louisiana, and other impoverished ethnic and regional communities.

During the early years of the twentieth century, granny midwives attended as many as 90 percent of all black births occurring in the southern states. These women usually received a "calling by the Lord" before beginning a lengthy apprenticeship with an older, senior midwife. The typical "granny" was also a married woman who had borne several children.

In the early twentieth century, the black granny midwife subscribed to a noninterventionist approach to childbirth, letting nature take its course. Her chief duty was to comfort the parturient woman during the long and often arduous hours of labor. Basically, it was her responsibility to catch the baby, tie the umbilical cord, and, if necessary, fetch the placenta. She probably encouraged the laboring woman to walk around and may also have offered her herbal teas, wine, or perhaps hard liquor to help ease the birthing pains. To determine the progress of labor, she sometimes examined the cervix. During complicated cases, she might even have found it necessary to turn the fetus. Although the major function of the granny midwife was to care for the laboring woman, she could also be depended on to provide information about prenatal care, food preparation, and child care training. In-

deed, the granny midwife was a highly respected member of her community, and many people turned to her for advice on a variety of medical and social problems.

With the passage of the Sheppard-Towner Maternity and Infancy Protection Act of 1921, federal funds were made available to the states to provide for midwife training and regulation. Many southern states used these funds to establish educational and certification programs for their grannies. In recent years, health departments across the nation have discontinued issuing certificates to granny midwives. Although a few elderly grannies continue to practice, their ranks are rapidly dwindling, and this last generation of granny midwives will soon die out. *(See also: Childbirth; Midwifery; Sheppard-Towner Act of 1921)*

—**Judy Barrett Litoff**

Further Reading

Dougherty, Molly C. "Southern Lay Midwives as Ritual Specialists." In *Women in Ritual and Symbolic Roles,* edited by Judith Hoch-Smith and Anita Spring, 151-64. New York: Plenum, 1978.

Holmes, Linda. "Alabama Granny Midwife," *Journal of the Medical Society of New Jersey* 81 (May 1984): 389-91.

Litoff, Judy Barrett. *The American Midwife Debate: A Sourcebook on Its Modern Origins.* Westport, CT: Greenwood, 1986.

———. *American Midwives, 1860 to the Present.* Westport, CT: Greenwood, 1978.

～ Grant, Zilpah P. (1794–1874)

Zilpah Grant was an important advocate of increased education for girls. Born in South Norfolk, Massachusetts, Grant attended the local school and at the age of fourteen began her career in teaching. Her first position was in the public schools of nearby East Norfolk, where she taught for twelve years.

In 1821, Grant began studying grammar, history, and English literature with Reverend Ralph Emerson, a minister in Norfolk. Emerson's brother had a school for young ladies at Saugus, Massachusetts, and Grant was interested in continuing her studies there. After considerable thought, she took her savings and enrolled in Emerson's school. Here she met Mary Lyon, another reformer and, with the encouragement of Emerson, took over a select school for young ladies at Winsted in 1821. Her success there led to an invitation to direct Adams Female Academy at Derry, New Hampshire. As was characteristic in administering girls' schools, Grant received the building free of charge, but she was responsible for all other expenses. She managed both the business and educational affairs of the school. With the assistance of Mary Lyon, Grant turned it into an influential girl's school.

But in 1828, Grant became dissatisfied with the trustees and moved to the Ipswich Female Seminary. Many of the pupils followed Grant, and here she achieved her greatest success. At Ipswich, Grant found a school with no provisions for boarders; pupils and teachers were scattered throughout the community. Already in 1834, Grant advocated the construction of a facility to house pupils and teachers. The emphasis of the school program was on individual care of the pupils and close supervision by the teachers. Each teacher was required, as the early regulations noted, "to acquaint herself with the health, habits, intellectual improvement, and moral and religious state of every young lady in her section; to attend to the investigation and recitation of a Bible lesson every week; to be the friend and adviser of each; to interest herself in everything that concerned their general improvement."

At Ipswich, the three-year program of study was rigorous and included a variety of courses, such as a three-year course of English studies and Bible instruction, the main subject. "The primary objective of the school seems to be to provide faithful and enlightened teachers; but the course of instruction is such as to prepare the pupil for any destination in life," wrote an observer in 1833. After 1834, the number of pupils was limited to one hundred, as the program focused on the solid training of girls. The teachers trained at Ipswich went west, into Ohio, Indiana, Illinois, Iowa, and Wisconsin, to offer educational opportunities in an expanding America. The demand for these well-schooled teachers was great. In addition, the seminaries built up by Grant made important contributions to the ideal of higher education for females. In 1839, Grant's ill health forced her to withdraw from the direction of Ipswich Seminary. *(See also: Education; Female Academies; Higher Education; Teaching)*

—**Robert G. Waite**

Further Reading

Barnard, Henry. "Female Education: Memoirs of Founders, Promoters, and Teachers of Institutions for Girls and Young Women." *American Journal of Education* 30 (1880). [Special Issue]

Cowles, John P. "Ipswich Female Seminary," *American Journal of Education* 30 (1880): 593.

———. "Miss Zilpah P. Grant—Mrs. William B. Banister," *American Journal of Education* 30 (1880): 611-19.

"Seminary for Female Teachers, at Ipswich, MA" and "Motives to Study in the Ipswich Female Seminary," *American Annals of Education* 3 (February 1833): 69-80.

⁊ Gray Panthers

The Gray Panthers is a group founded by Margaret (Maggie) F. Kuhn and five friends—Eleanor French, Helen Smith, Polly Cuthbertson, Anne Bennett, and Helen Baker—in 1970 as they faced mandatory retirement age. They called together a Consultation of Older and Younger Adults for Social Change. As a result of the consultation, this action group organized to oppose the war in Vietnam, and within one year it had expanded to over 100 members of all ages. In recognition of its dramatic and sometimes radical techniques, the media dubbed it "Gray Panthers." This name was officially adopted in 1972.

At the first White House Conference on Aging in 1971, the Gray Panthers drew public attention to the fact that there were no African American representatives by organizing a "Black House Conference" prior to the official White House Conference. In 1973, the Gray Panthers merged with Retired Professional Action Group, a Ralph Nader affiliate. Together the groups published "Paying through the Ear," a report on hearing health care that led to new legislation and guidelines for control of the hearing aid industry. The organization also persuaded the National Association of Broadcasters to amend the Television Code of Ethics to include "age" along with race and sex, encouraging the media to be more sensitive to ageist stereotyping.

Presently, the Gray Panthers is composed of approximately 40,000 people of all ages who are active in fifty-two networks (chapters) in the United States. An international organization, the Gray Panthers is affiliated with groups in Canada, England, France, Switzerland, and Germany. To keep the membership informed, the organization has a bimonthly newsletter called "The Network."

The principal goal of the Gray Panthers is advocacy for progressive social policy. Its motto is "Age and Youth in Action." Nationally, the organization has several intergenerational task forces that address the following issues: national health care, peace, economic and tax justice, environment, affordable housing, education, and issues of ageism, sexism, and racism.

National issues are addressed by local networks in a number of ways. For example, membership has been mobilized to monitor Housing and Urban Development practices and to provide leadership in local coalitions concerning health care reform. Most networks are involved in activities that promote intergenerational opportunities such as visiting high schools to discuss current affairs or holding picnics to honor young people.

In 1981, Gray Panthers was voted Consultative Status to the Economic and Social Council of the United Nations. It also has representation on the Executive Committee of the American Section of the World Assembly of Aging. Maggie Kuhn remained active in the organization until her death in 1995. *(See also: Kuhn, Margaret E.)*

—**Nancy Johns**

Further Reading

Bronte, Lydia. *The Longevity Factor: The New Reality of Long Careers and How It Can Lead to Richer Lives.* New York: HarperCollins, 1993.

"Gray Power" [editorial], *The Nation* 250 (May 28, 1990): 727-28.

Kuhn, Maggie. *No Stone Unturned: The Life and Times of Maggie Kuhn,* pp. 103-38. New York: Ballantine 1991.

Torres-Gil, Fernando M. *The New Aging: Politics and Change in America.* Westport, CT: Auburn House, 1992.

ॐ Great Awakening

The Great Awakening of the 1740s was the first major religious revival in America. Religious emotionalism spread rapidly under the leadership of ministers Theodore Frelinghuysen, Jonathan Edwards, and George Whitefield, who exhorted their listeners about God's omnipotence, human depravity, and saving grace. Emphasis on the conversion experience as the condition for admission to a church gave a new quest to individuals who felt lost in a communal society undermined by concern for wealth. The frequency of religious conversion among young persons may be seen as an eighteenth-century expression of adolescent crisis, experienced by those coming to adulthood in a new, uncertain world.

While proportionately more men than women joined the church during the revivals, increasing numbers of women joined and continued to form the majority of the membership, a trend known as the "feminization of the church." By the 1760s, 92 percent of the women who became full communicants were single, widowed, or married women unaccompanied by their husbands. Some of these women, diarist Hannah Heaton for example, criticized the established form of religion, while others, such as schoolmistress Sarah Osborn, formed close reciprocal relationships with ministers, establishing a pattern that became more widespread in the nineteenth century.

Study of sermons and the pious poetry of the laity during this period reveals that a definition of the spheres of women and men was beginning to emerge in the mid-eighteenth century. Men were praised for diligence in their vocational calling, while women were lauded for their spiritual gifts. Women attended church regularly, studied Scripture, and testified to extraordinary visions. These accounts were offered by ministers as models of behavior for both sexes. By the nineteenth century, women learned to incorporate their spiritual experiences into secular literature. *(See also: Christianity; Heaton, Hannah; Religion)*

—**Barbara E. Lacey**

Further Reading

Shiels, Richard D. "The Feminization of American Congregationalism, 1730–1835," *American Quarterly* 33 (Spring 1981): 46-62.

Stout, Harry S., and Catherine A. Brekus. "Declension, Gender, and the 'New Religious History.'" In *Belief and Behavior: Essays in the New Religious History,* edited by Philip R. Vandermeer and Robert P. Swierenga, 15-37. New Brunswick, NJ: Rutgers University Press, 1991.

ॐ Greer, Germaine (b. 1939)

Germaine Greer is a feminist theoretician, writer, teacher, scholar, lecturer, television performer, and journalist. A native of Melbourne, Australia, Greer took her B.A. in 1959 from Melbourne University, an M.A. with first-class honors from Sydney University, and a Ph.D. in Renaissance literature from Cambridge University in 1968. A woman of many talents, Greer was teaching at Warwick University while writing for popular magazines and appearing on the British television series *Nice Times*.

While at Warwick, where she taught English literature from 1968 to 1973, she published her international bestseller, *The Female Eunuch* (1970), whose impact on the modern women's movement rivaled that of Betty Friedan's *The Feminine Mystique*. In it, Greer argued that "female sexuality had been masked and deformed" by a sexist society; she called for women to "take possession" of their bodies and glory "in their power." Her bold and provocative statement created a great sensation in the United States and throughout the English-speaking world. She became a media celebrity and one of the most visible feminists of the 1970s, in constant demand on the talk show circuit.

However, despite the pressures of the life of a media celebrity, Greer has never abandoned her academic interests. Indeed, her intellectual horizons have been continually expanding. For example, in 1979, she published a major scholarly work on women painters, *The Obstacle Race*. Between 1979 and 1982, Greer taught for and directed the Center for the Study of Women and Literature at the University of Tulsa. Since then, she has devoted herself to her research and writing projects, which have ranged from *Shakespeare* (1985) to another controversial study titled *Sex and Destiny: The Politics of Human Fertility* (1984). In 1993, she returned to the best-seller lists with *The Change: Women, Aging and Menopause*. Although she now resides almost exclusively in Europe, Greer's writings—both her books and her articles for a host of popular journals here and abroad—continue to exert a great influence in the United States. *(See also: Art; Higher Education; Women's Liberation Movement; Women's Studies)*

—**Jonathan W. Zophy**

Further Reading

Davis, Elizabeth, and Germaine Greer. *Women, Sex, and Desire: Understanding Your Sexuality at Every Stage of Life.* Alameda, CA: Hunter House, 1996.

Greer, Germaine. *The Change: Women, Aging and Menopause.* New York: Knopf, 1993.

———. *Daddy We Hardly Know You.* New York: Knopf, 1990.

———. *The Female Eunuch.* 1970. Reprint, London: Granada, 1980.

———. *The Madwomen's Underclothes: Essays and Occasional Writings.* New York: Grove-Attic, 1989.

———. *The Obstacle Race: Women Painters and Their Work.* New York: Farrar, Straus & Giroux, 1979.

———. *Sex and Destiny: The Politics of Human Fertility.* New York: Harper & Row, 1984.

Plante, David. *Difficult Women: A Memoir of Three.* New York: Atheneum, 1983.

ॐ Griffing, Josephine (1814–1872)

Josephine Griffing was an abolitionist and activist for the early women's movement. A founding member of the Ohio

Woman's Rights Association, Griffing was elected its president in 1853. She arrived in Washington, D.C., in 1863 as the general agent for the National Freedmen's Relief Association of the District of Columbia (1863–1872). The sight of the miserable condition of freed blacks in that city so moved Griffing that she converted her own home into a settlement house and devoted much of her remaining life to helping the former slaves. She was determined that freed men and women should be self-supporting if they were physically able, but she furnished care and medical help for those who were not. Griffing wanted to keep freedmen from being dependent on charity offered by benevolent organizations, so she established sewing and other vocational schools and sought employment and housing for families.

When this responsibility became overwhelming for one individual, she convinced President Abraham Lincoln to support the creation of the Bureau of Refugees, Freedmen and Abandoned Lands. In 1865, she became subassistant commissioner of the Freedmen's Bureau in Washington, D.C., and during the period from 1865 to 1867, she was instrumental in locating jobs and housing for seven thousand blacks in the Washington, D.C., area. In late 1865, the bureau tried to reduce funding, and Griffing spoke out in a series of lectures to gain public support against any such reduction. Griffing constantly lobbied for congressional aid, even attempting to get congressional approval of public works projects to benefit the unemployed.

During the same period, she was also active in the woman's movement. She was the first vice president to the American Equal Rights Association and a corresponding secretary in the National Woman Suffrage Association. She also founded the Universal Franchise Association of the District of Columbia. Despite opposition and instances of mob violence, Griffing lectured and worked tirelessly in support of both causes. *(See also: Freedmen's Bureau; National Woman Suffrage Association)*

—Jean Nettles

Further Reading

McPherson, James M. *The Struggle for Equality.* Princeton, NJ: Princeton University Press, 1964.

∾ Grimké, Angelina Emily (1805–1879)

Angelina Grimké was a southern-born woman raised amid wealth on a plantation in Charleston, South Carolina, but she abhorred the institution of slavery and was a firsthand witness to its cruelties. In 1829, she joined her sister Sarah in Philadelphia and became a member of the Quakers. There, Grimké joined the American Anti-Slavery Society, to which she would devote much of her life. After a letter she had written to the *Gazette,* an abolitionist newspaper, was published, she began her career as a speaker for the society.

Public speaking by a woman in front of an assembly of both men and women was unheard of in the years before the Civil War, and Grimké's speeches drew curious onlookers and also fiery criticism from the clergy and much of the public. An eloquent, emotional speaker, she dramatized her speeches with descriptions of events she had witnessed on the plantation. Using this technique, she effectively illustrated the horrors of slavery to an audience that had no direct, personal contact with slavery.

The Grimké sisters drew large audiences in the North made up of abolitionists, sympathizers, and also women working in the factories of New England. Grimké's pamphlet *An Appeal to the Christian Women in the South* detailed the tragedies of life under slavery and asked the women of the South to influence their husbands and sons to put an end to slavery. The pamphlet was burned in the South, and a warrant was issued for her arrest if she ever returned to South Carolina.

In 1838, Grimké married Theodore Weld, a prominent abolitionist. As Mrs. Weld, she discontinued her lectures and helped administer a school they established in New Jersey. Angelina Grimké was one of the first woman abolitionists in the country and paved the way for others like her to speak out in public against injustice. *(See also: Abolition and the Antislavery Movement; Grimké, Sarah Moore; Public Speakers: Nineteenth Century; Society of Friends)*

—Lynn E. Lipor

Further Reading

Grimké, Angelina Emily. *An Appeal to the Christian Women of the Southern States.* New York: n.p., 1836. Reprint, New York: Arno, 1969.

Lerner, Gerda. *The Grimké Sisters from South Carolina: Rebels against Slavery.* Boston: Houghton Mifflin, 1967.

Weld, Theodore Dwight. *Letters of Theodore Dwight Weld, Angelina Grimké Weld, and Sarah Grimké, 1822–1844.* Edited by Gilbert H. Barnes and Dwight L. Dumond. New York: Da Capo, 1970.

∾ Grimké, Sarah Moore (1792–1873)

Sarah Grimké was an abolitionist and an early supporter of women's rights. Born into an aristocratic, slave-holding family in South Carolina, Grimké became well-known as a public speaker for women's rights as well as the author of *Letters on the Equality of the Sexes and the Condition of Women* (1838).

Grimké spent her childhood in South Carolina and then moved to Philadelphia after the death of her father. She became a Quaker and began studying the Scriptures in anticipation of a ministerial position within the church. Grimké's sister Angelina joined her in Philadelphia, and the two began attending antislavery society meetings. Angelina became a speaker for the abolition movement, and Sarah accompanied her as a chaperone. Soon, Sarah joined her sister in speaking out against the evils of slavery, and the two sisters embarked on speaking tours throughout the Northeast.

Sarah Grimké also began pointing out the similarities between slavery and the oppressive social and legal conditions affecting women's lives. Her pamphlet, *Letters on the Equality of the Sexes,* a collection of fifteen letters addressed to Mary Parker, the president of the Boston Female Anti-Slavery Society, discussed sexual inequality in the United States and demonstrated the historical oppression of women. She argued that women were intellectually, legally, and morally equal to men and rejected ideas of inherent differences between the two sexes. Grimké's knowledge of Scripture assisted her in her repudiation of the clergy who used the Bible to support the institution of slavery as well as the subordinate status of women. She also challenged those who censured the sisters for speaking before mixed audiences, arguing that woman must be allowed to use her God-given talents within both the domestic and public spheres.

Grimké's *Letters on the Equality of the Sexes,* published in both the *New England Spectator* and *The Liberator,* posed the basic questions of human equality that would extend throughout most of the nineteenth century. Her ideas formed the basis of the women's rights and suffrage movements and were inspirational for leaders such as Lucretia Mott, Elizabeth Cady Stanton, and Susan B. Anthony.

After the marriage of Angelina Grimké to Theodore Weld, Sarah Grimké lived with the couple and cared for their children. In her later life, however, she again became active in the women's rights movement. Sarah Grimké died on December 23, 1873, in Boston, Massachusetts. *(See also: Abolition and the Antislavery Movement; Grimké, Angelina Emily; Public Speakers: Nineteenth Century; Society of Friends)*

—Pamela F. Wille
—Lynn E. Lipor

Further Reading

Barnes, Gilbert, and Dwight Dumond, eds. *Letters of Theodore Dwight Weld, Angelina Grimké Weld, and Sarah Grimké, 1822–1844,* 2 vols. New York: Appleton-Century, 1934.

Ceplair, Larry, ed. *The Public Years of Sarah and Angelina Grimké: Selected Writings, 1835–1839.* New York: Columbia University Press, 1989.

Grimké, Sarah Moore. *Letters on the Equality of the Sexes and the Condition of Women.* Boston: Knapp, 1838.

Lerner, Gerda. *The Grimké Sisters from South Carolina: Pioneers for Woman's Rights and Abolition.* New York: Schocken, 1967.

Nies, Judith. "Sarah Moore Grimké." In *Seven Women: Portraits from the American Radical Tradition,* pp. 1-35. New York Viking, 1977.

♠ Griswold v. Connecticut (1965)

In *Griswold v. Connecticut* (1965), the Supreme Court declared unconstitutional a Connecticut statute that made the use of birth control devices illegal and made it a criminal offense for anyone to give information about them or instruction on their use. This decision gave legal foundation to the right of privacy in matters of marital intimacy. The same statute had previously been unsuccessfully challenged before the Supreme Court in *Tileston v. Ullman* (1943).

Estelle Griswold, executive director of the Planned Parenthood League of Connecticut, and Dr. C. Lee Buxton, its medical director and a professor at the Yale Medical School, were convicted under this statute for dispensing birth control information to married persons and were fined $100 each. Their conviction was upheld by two different appeals courts within Connecticut before its review by the U.S. Supreme Court.

Writing for the Court, Justice William O. Douglas viewed the enforcement of this law, which entailed police searching the bedrooms of married couples for evidence of contraceptive use, as an idea that is "repulsive to the notion of privacy surrounding the marriage relationship." Justice Douglas found the greatest strength for this decision in that these were the "intimate relation(s) of husband and wife"; the relationship of marriage was the source of privacy—contraceptives were the extension of the relationship. *Griswold's* heavy emphasis on the privacy of the conjugal bed in a marital relationship was surpassed by *Eisenstadt v. Baird* (1972), in which the Court invalidated a Massachusetts law that made it a felony to give any one other than a married person contraceptives; in this court decision, Justice William J. Brennan argued that the right of privacy inheres in the person and is not limited to certain relationships. *(See also: Birth Control; Comstock Law; Planned Parenthood Federation of America)*

—Sue E. Strickler

Further Reading

Dixon, Robert G., Jr. et al. *The Right of Privacy: A Symposium on the Implications of Griswold vs. Connecticut.* New York: Da Capo, 1965.

Eisenstadt v. Baird, 405 U.S. 438 at 453 (1972).

Goldstein, Leslie Friedman. *Contemporary Cases in Women's Rights.* Madison: University of Wisconsin Press, 1994.

Griswold v. Connecticut, 381 U.S. 479; 85 S. Ct. 1678; 14 L. Ed. 2d 510 (1965).

Guitton, Stephanie, and Peter Irons, eds. *May It Please the Court: Arguments in Abortion.* New York: New Press, 1995.

Rossum, Ralph A., and G. Alan Tarr. *American Constitutional Law.* New York: St. Martin's, 1987.

Tileston v. Ullman, 26 A (2d) 582 (Conn.) (1943).

♠ Gynecology

Gynecology is traditionally thought of by its practitioners as the study and treatment of diseases of the female reproductive organs. A physician who is a gynecologist may often also be an obstetrician, administering care to pregnant women and assisting in the birth process. Gynecology was not a medical specialty until the mid-nineteenth century.

The progress of gynecology was slowed by the moral atmosphere prevalent in the Victorian era. Since most physicians were men, concern for modesty was an issue. The vaginal speculum, although in use, was regarded in some quarters as an indecent instrument.

The Industrial Revolution brought a new set of health problems as cities and factories grew. Health care focused on sickness and disease rather than on the natural occurrence of childbirth. As scientific advances were made during this period, medicine grew along with knowledge of bacteria and X rays.

In the latter nineteenth century, the development and widespread use of anesthesia and antisepsis brought gynecology into its own, predominantly as a surgical specialty. Nonetheless, the field of gynecology and its research held a low status within the medical profession as a whole well into the twentieth century, and most women were attended by general practitioners rather than gynecologists.

The authority of gynecologists, as of most physicians, remained largely unquestioned by their patients until the 1960s. Consciousness-raising among women led to their identification of medical issues with feminist implications, and enlightened consumerism prompted investigatory news reporting and governmental inquiry into the actual quality of medical treatment women received from gynecologists.

Women today continue to shape the treatment issues in gynecology. Surgery has secured gynecology's place as a distinct specialty. Gynecologists perform a variety of surgeries, including the cesarean section, an abdominal and uterine incision to remove the fetus, as a substitute for vaginal delivery. The decline in infant mortality parallels the increase in cesarean births.

In addition to this surgical base, gynecology now addresses issues of birth control, fertility, sexual dysfunction, sexually transmitted diseases, nutrition, cancer prevention and treatment, hormonal changes and imbalances, and problems related to the postmenopausal client.

As health care and the role of women change, so does the specialty. The obstetric-gynecological nurse practitioner is a new specialty focusing on primary care of the healthy pregnant and nonpregnant woman, emphasizing health promotion and maintenance. This master's-prepared nurse practitioner collaborates with the physician and may diagnose and treat common problems. Future trends will continue to evolve along with new or modified forms of health care. *(See also: Childbirth; Lying-In; Midwifery)*

—**Louise M. Kawada**

—**Sandra Riese**

Further Reading

Axelsen, Diana E. "Women as Victims of Medical Experimentation: J. Marion Sims' Surgery on Slave Women, 1845–1849." In *Black Women in United States History,* Vol. 1, ed. Darlene Clark Hine, pp. 51-60. Brooklyn, New York: Carlson, 1990.

Cohen, Susan M., Carole A. Kenner, and Andrea Hollingsworth. *Maternal, Neonatal, and Women's Health Nursing.* Springhouse, PA: Springhouse, 1991.

Danforth, David N., ed. *Obstetrics and Gynecology,* 4th ed. Philadelphia: Harper & Row, 1982.

Morantz-Sanchez, Regina. *Sympathy and Science: Women Physicans in American Medicine.* New York: Oxford University Press, 1985.

Speert, Harold. *Obstetrics and Gynecology in America: A History,* 2d ed. Baltimore: Waverly, 1994.

Hadassah

Hadassah, the Women's Zionist Organization of America, is the largest volunteer women's organization in the United States. In the eighty-two years since its founding, it has operated as Israel's major partner in medical research and development of educational and social programs. Hadassah chapters with 385,000 members in the United States and Puerto Rico raise money for projects in Israel and have aided hundreds of thousands of immigrants.

Hadassah was founded by Henrietta Szold, a Jewish scholar and activist, on February 24, 1912, in New York City, to foster Jewish ideals through education in America and to meet the health needs of the people of Palestine. Within a year, the first Hadassah medical installation in Palestine began operation, and in 1918, the Henrietta Szold Hadassah School of Nursing opened with thirty students. The Rothschild-Hadassah University Hospital opened in 1939 in partnership with Hebrew University, and in 1949, the Hebrew University-Hadassah Medical School was established. The Hadassah Medical Organization's two hospitals and 199 clinics serve Moslems, Christians, and Jews and reach outside of Israel by means of the Hadassah Medical Relief Association, formed in 1983.

Youth Aliyah, Hadassah's relief movement for refugee children, was cofounded in 1934 by Recha Freier and others in Germany and by Henrietta Szold, who became its director in Palestine. This branch of Hadassah has relocated successive waves of children, from Germany and Europe in the 1930s to children from Ethiopia in the 1980s.

Education has been a priority with Hadassah since the days of its founders, who stressed a commitment to Jewish values and Zionism and the creation of a strong bond between the Jewish community here and in Israel. At the national level, the education department produces guides for beginning or advanced students in many areas, including history, literature, Hebrew, and current events. *Hadassah Magazine,* the first Jewish magazine to be nominated for a National Magazine Award, is sent monthly to every member, the largest circulation of any Jewish publication in the United States. Each issue includes articles on Hadassah-related people and projects in Israel and the United States,

book reviews, current affairs, travel, the arts, and a Hebrew lesson. *(See also: Jewish Women)*

—Abby Schmelling
—Barbara Oberlander

Further Reading

Goldreich, Gloria. *The Hadassah Idea,* 4th ed. New York: Hadassah, 1986.

Hadassah Magazine,

Levin, Marlin. *Balm in Gilead: The Story of Hadassah.* New York: Schocken, 1973.

http://www.hadassah.org [Hadassah Website]

Hale, Sarah Josepha (Buell) (1788–1879)

Author and editor of *Godey's Lady's Book and American Ladies' Magazine* (1837–1877) Sarah Josepha Hale was a conservative advocate of increased education and employment opportunities for women. As editor of the major nineteenth-century women's magazine for forty years, Hale became a nationally influential supporter and purveyor of the contemporary antebellum concepts defining womanhood and woman's role; she urged expanding women's educational facilities and curriculum as well as their entry into professions and employments suitable for "ladies" who supported themselves and their families.

Hale's life and career typified that of popular women writers who promulgated the cult of true womanhood in the antebellum United States. Born and reared in New England and self-educated, Hale briefly taught before marrying David Hale in 1813. Hale was widowed at the age of thirty-five, with five young children whom she supported and educated through her writing and editing of women's magazines. Editing her own *American Ladies' Magazine* (1828–1836) established Hale's reputation for producing original and native material before her tenure at *Godey's* ensured her prominence as a social and literary critic for her largely female audience.

Godey's Lady's Book and American Ladies' Magazine was originally published in Philadelphia by Louis A. Godey. Initiated in 1831, *Godey's Lady's Book* offered lavish embellishments (fashion plates, woodcuts, engraved pictures) but only reprinted poetry and prose that Godey shamelessly "cut and pasted" from contemporary fashionable English women's periodicals to accompany the plates and prints. *Godey's* was a flashy women's magazine with no discernible substance when Godey recruited Sarah Josepha Hale to edit it in 1837, thereby bringing Hale's editorial substance to enrich the lavish but heretofore superficial *Lady's Book*.

Hale brought her established agenda of "improving her sex" to the more prosperous and popular monthly. She introduced original poetry, prose, and nonfiction written by American authors, many of whom became the notable (male and female) literati of Victorian America. Hale's most enduring contribution to women's magazines was the development, indeed the perfection, of the standard content format for that genre of periodical: sentimental poetry and unimpeachably correct fiction (written primarily by women and designed to inculcate the traits of true womanhood in readers), instructional but noncontroversial nonfiction (which included patriotic and women's history), and the popular fashion plates and other hallmark "embellishments," supplemented by craft and homemaking arts instructions. At the "back of the book" appeared Hale's monthly editorials, "The Editors' Table"; her literary notices, which featured books by and for women; Godey's own monthly notices to his gentle readers; and merchandise that could be ordered by mail. As a medium of both women's and popular culture, *Godey's* dominated the market during the 1840s and 1850s; however, the Civil War marked the beginning of the magazine's decline until Hale retired in 1877, following Godey's sale of the magazine. As a national institution, *Godey's* survived until the end of the nineteenth century, when its market and its message were supplanted by *The Ladies' Home Journal*.

Although Hale maintained the absolute propriety of *Godey's* contents and concurred with her publisher's dictum that all political references be avoided as inappropriate and outside the domestic limits of woman's sphere, she circumspectly used her editorials to expand the limits of woman's sphere by supporting and urging increased educational and other opportunities for women and to argue that true women required an adequate education to perform their domestic and maternal roles. Although *Godey's* is remembered as a quaint publication that catered to the Victorian Lady of Leisure, under Hale's control, the magazine advanced women's interests in subtle ways.

Hale's major works commemorated women's accomplishments, educated children, and instructed readers in the homemaking arts and patriotic values. *Woman's Record: or, Sketches of All Distinguished Women, from 'the Beginning' till A.D. 1850. Arranged in Four Eras with Selections from Female Writers of Every Age* (1852) was compiled by her to commemorate women's contribution to Western civilization. As an expression of nineteenth-century domestic feminism, this 903-page, exquisitely bound and embellished volume celebrated the achievements and accomplishments of outstanding historical and contemporary women, primarily highlighting women authors and poets.

Hale herself was a representative of the American antebellum eastern seaboard women writers who entered professional writing as a means of supporting themselves and their families; writing thus became an appropriate employment for true women. Hale stated in her introduction her intention that *Woman's Record* should venerate womanhood, thereby reinforcing the respectability of herself and her American contemporaries—all of whom she included within this ambitious collection of "women worthies." *Woman's Record* was a monument to both her nationalism and the gender partisanship of Hale and the Victorian middle-class women for whom she served as the high priestess of the cult of true womanhood.

In her capacity as editor of *Godey's,* her support of certain women's issues, although a part of domestic feminism, translated into significant and effective propaganda among the middle class. Whether Hale led or rode the crest of public opinion on the necessity and propriety of expanding woman's sphere, her use of woman's influence provided a model for consistent if conservative reform that allowed women to breach the public sphere without incurring censure for violating their duty or abandoning their own proper sphere.

As the unimpeachable authority on woman's sphere and a consummate practitioner of woman's influence, Hale in her conservative campaigns publicized and made respectable reform movements to improve women through education and employment opportunities, including their entry into medical and teaching professions. Hale opposed the woman's rights movement but contributed to increased access for women to education and paid employments outside the home. *(See also: Cult of True Womanhood; Domestic Feminism; Magazines; Women Writers)*

—**Angela M. Howard**

Further Reading

Entrikin, Isabelle Webb. *Sarah Josepha Hale and* Godey's Lady's Book. Philadelphia: Lancaster, 1946.

Finley, Ruth. *The Lady of* Godey's. Philadelphia: J. B. Lippincott, 1931.

Godey's Lady's Book. Vols. 14–94. Philadelphia: Louis A Godey, 1837–1877.

Hale, Sarah Josepha. *Woman's Record: or, Sketches of All Distinguished Women, from 'the Beginning' till A.D. 1850. Arranged in Four Eras with Selections from Female Writers of Every Age.* New York: Harper's, 1853.

Okker, Patricia. *Our Sister Editors: Sarah J. Hale and the Traditions of Nineteenth-Century American Women Editors.* Athens: University of Georgia Press, 1995.

Woodward, Helen. *The Lady Persuaders.* New York: Ivanobenski, 1960.

Zophy, Angela Howard. "Sarah Josepha Hale, Matron of Victorian Womanhood." In *For the General Welfare: Essays in Honor of Robert H. Bremner,* edited by Frank Annunziata, Patrick Reagan, and Roy T. Wortman, 61-84. New York: Peter Lang, 1989.

———. "A True Woman's Duty 'To Do Good': Sarah Josepha Hale and Benevolence in Antebellum America." In *The Moment of Decision: Biographical Essays on American Character and Regional Identity*, edited by Randall M. Miller and John R. McKivigan, 155-69. Westport, CT: Greenwood, 1994.

✎ Haley, Margaret A. (1861–1939)

Margaret Haley was business agent for the Chicago Teachers Federation for over forty-one years and leader of the teachers of Chicago in the most vibrant demonstration of teacher power in the early twentieth century. A schoolteacher for twenty years in Chicago's South Side stockyards district, Haley became interested in the Chicago Teachers Federation when she was thirty-eight and the organization was in its first few years of existence. Concerned over a district announcement that teachers would not receive a pay increase, Haley went to the Cook County tax office to find that five city corporations owed the county over $2 million in back taxes. After three years of legal pursuit, a federal court awarded Cook County its back taxes, but the board of education continued to deny teachers their pay raise. Haley then led the teachers in an unprecedented affiliation with the Chicago Federation of Labor, and the next year, the teachers gained their back pay through a scathing decision by a municipal judge.

Her persistence, defiance, and courage earned Margaret Haley the reputation of a woman of leadership in education. In a stunning speech delivered to the National Education Association (NEA) in 1904, Haley urged teachers to pursue the goal of democracy in education and to resist becoming agents of the materialism and consumerism that she thought were taking over the schools. Finally, in 1910, she organized the campaign that made a woman—Ella Flagg Young—the first president of the NEA.

Haley had become so powerful in Chicago politics by 1906 that the new mayor asked her for names to appoint to the city board of education. Haley chose Jane Addams, but the two parted ways on educational policy because Haley's pro-union policies conflicted with Addams's willingness to find compromises, especially at the expense of working teachers. Haley's involvement in local campaigns for a municipal petition process, penny gas, and a municipal ownership gave her a citywide reputation as a power broker. As legislative lobbyist for the Chicago Federation of Labor, Haley remained a close ally and friend of John Fitzpatrick, president of the Chicago Federation of Labor. In 1913, when the governor hesitated to sign the bill for woman's suffrage in the state of Illinois, Haley stood at his desk to make sure he did so.

Haley also gained a national reputation in educational, municipal reform, and suffrage circles in the years between 1903 and 1917. A tireless campaigner, Haley worked actively in the California and Washington suffrage campaigns in 1911 and 1912. In 1915, after an ugly and protracted dispute, Haley's organization was outlawed by a school board

ruling that was upheld by the Illinois Supreme Court in 1917. To keep her organization going, Haley was forced to withdraw her affiliations with trade unions. Unaffiliated and disgraced by a two-year name-calling campaign, the Chicago Teachers Federation and Margaret Haley never recovered from the board attack. When she died on the eve of World War II, thousands of teachers paid their respects to the woman who brought teachers to the trade union movement. (*See also: Consumerism; National Consumers' League; National Education Association; Politics; Progressive Era; Social Feminism; Suffrage; Teaching; Unions; Young, Ella Flagg*)

—Marjorie Murphy

Further Reading

Davis, Allen F. *American Heroine: The Life and Legend of Jane Addams.* New York: Oxford University Press, 1973.

Munro, Petra. "Educators as Activists: Five Women from Chicago," *Social Education* 59 (September 1995): 274-78.

Reid, Robert, ed. *Battleground: The Autobiography of Margaret Haley.* Urbana: University of Illinois Press, 1982.

✎ Hamer, Fannie Lou (1917–1977)

Fannie Lou Hamer, Mississippi civil rights leader, was born October 6, 1917, in Montgomery County, Mississippi, and died March 14, 1977, in Mound Bayou, Mississippi. Born Fannie Lou Townsend, she was the youngest of twenty children and left school in the sixth grade to help support her family by picking cotton. She married Perry Hamer, a tractor driver, in 1944.

At an August 1962 meeting, Hamer volunteered to try to register. Blacks had effectively been denied the vote since Mississippi passed restrictive laws in 1890. Hamer failed to interpret to the registrar's satisfaction a section of the Mississippi constitution, but a few months later, she passed. In the summer of 1963, she was arrested in Winona, Mississippi, on her way home from a voter literacy training session. She was beaten in jail by two prisoners acting under threat of violence from the law officers. An eloquent speaker, Hamer incorporated the beating into speeches she gave around the country about injustices in Mississippi.

At the 1964 Democratic National Convention, Hamer testified in favor of the challenge by the predominantly black Mississippi Freedom Democratic Party against the all-white Mississippi delegation. "If the Freedom Democratic Party is not seated now," she said, "I question America; is this America, the land of the free and the home of the brave where we have to sleep with our telephones off the hooks because our lives be threatened daily because we want to live as decent human beings?" The Freedom Democrats lost that challenge, but the Democratic Party rewrote its rules so that thereafter no delegation that discriminated would be seated.

In 1965, Hamer, Victoria Gray, and Annie Devine challenged the seating of Mississippi's five members of the U.S. House of Representatives. They lost again, but their challenge contributed to passage that year of the Voting Rights Act.

Hamer sued the Sunflower County voter registrar, winning new elections for two small Mississippi Delta towns in 1967. She was a member of the 1968 delegation that challenged the regular Democrats and was seated at the Chicago convention, and she was a delegate to the 1972 Democratic National Convention. She also sued the local school system over the lagging pace of desegregation. She was a founding member of the National Women's Political Caucus, ran unsuccessfully in 1971 for the Mississippi state senate, and operated Freedom Farm, a cooperative venture seeking to increase blacks' economic independence. Ultimately, it failed.

Hamer had a mastectomy in 1976. She died March 14, 1977, and is buried near her home in Ruleville. She helped open the national Democratic Party and Mississippi politics to greater participation by African Americans. *(See also: Black Women; Civil Rights; Democratic Party; National Women's Political Caucus; Politics; Voting Rights)*

—**Kay Mills**

Further Reading

Civil Rights Oral Histories. Oral History Department, Moorland-Spingarn Research Center. Howard University, Washington, DC.

Fannie Lou Hamer Papers. Armistad Research Center. Tulane University, New Orleans.

Hamer, Fannie Lou. "To Praise Our Bridges." In *Mississippi Writers: Reflections of Childhood and Youth,* Vol. 2, edited by Dorothy Abbott, 323-24. Jackson: University Press of Mississippi, 1986.

McLemore, Leslie. "The Mississippi Freedom Democratic Party—A Case Study of Grass-Roots Politics." Ph.D. diss., University of Massachusetts, 1971.

Mills, Kay. *This Little Light of Mine: The Life of Fannie Lou Hamer.* New York: E. P. Dutton, 1999.

Mississippi Freedom Democratic Party files. State Historical Society of Wisconsin, Madison.

Mississippi Oral History Program interviews. University of Southern Mississippi, Hattiesburg.

O'Dell, J. H. "Life in Mississippi: An Interview with Fannie Lou Hamer," *Freedomways* (Second Quarter 1965): 231-32.

Romaine, Anne. "The Mississippi Freedom Democratic Party through August, 1964." Master's thesis, University of Virginia, 1970.

Student Non-Violent Coordinating Committee files, 1959–1972. NYT Microfilming Corp. of America. Microfilm.

Sugarman, Tracy. *Stranger at the Gates.* New York: Hill & Wang, 1966.

Voter Education Project Files, Southern Regional Council Papers, 1944–1968. NYT Microfilming Corp. of America. Microfilm.

⮌ Hamilton, Alice (1869–1970)

Reformer, physician, and toxicologist, Alice Hamilton was the daughter of Montgomery and Gertrude Pond Hamilton. Although born in New York, she was raised on the family compound in Fort Wayne, Indiana. She had a strong relationship with her mother, who encouraged her

four daughters' ambitions. As a child, Hamilton was educated at home with her sisters and cousins and, later, followed family custom by attending Miss Porter's School in Farmington, Connecticut. She studied medicine at the University of Michigan, receiving her M.D. in 1893, and held internships at the Northwestern Hospital for Women and Children in Minneapolis and the New England Hospital for Women and Children in Boston. She then did postgraduate work in bacteriology and pathology at the universities of Michigan, Leipzig, and Munich and at the Johns Hopkins Medical School. In the autumn of 1897, she became a professor of pathology at Chicago's Woman's Medical School of Northwestern University.

Shortly after arriving in Chicago, she fulfilled a lifelong dream and moved to Hull House, a settlement house, where educated young people worked among the poor and advocated social reform. She quickly became a member of the settlement's inner circle. There, she was introduced to the field of industrial medicine. Her investigation of lead poisoning in the modern factory system was a pioneering study and established Hamilton as one of the nation's leading industrial toxicologists. In time, her work in the field earned Hamilton an appointment to Harvard Medical School as assistant professor of industrial medicine, making her the first woman member of the Harvard medical faculty. While teaching, she continued to conduct the field studies that were important to her as a reformer. Her book *Industrial Poisons in the United States* was published in 1925 and quickly established her as one of the world's leading experts in the field. In 1935, she left Harvard and became a consultant in the Department of Labor's Division of Labor Standards. After her professional retirement, Hamilton continued her career as a reformer, heading the National Consumers' League for five years, writing an autobiography, and remaining politically active. The social and political values established in her youth and through her lifelong involvement with Hull House drew her to public service and achievement in the cause of both peace and civil rights. She died in 1970 at the age of 101. *(See also: Higher Education; Hull House; Physicians; Science; Social Feminism)*

—**Rebecca L. Sherrick**

Further Reading

Alice Hamilton Papers. Schlesinger Library. Radcliffe College, Cambridge, MA.

Hamilton, Alice. *Exploring the Dangerous Trades.* Boston: Little, Brown, 1943.

⮌ Hamilton, (Amy) Gordon (1892–1967)

Gordon Hamilton was a distinguished social work educator, consultant, and leading proponent of the diagnostic school of social casework. After graduation from Bryn Mawr, Hamilton, who never used her given name professionally, worked with the American Red Cross in Denver and the New York Charity Organization Society before joining the faculty of the New York School of Social Work (later known as the Columbia University School of Social Work) in 1923. In more than thirty years on the Columbia faculty, she helped establish the doctoral program in social work there and served as associate dean for three years (1952–1955) before her retirement in 1957.

Her best known and most influential work is *Theory and Practice of Social Case Work* (1940, rev. 1951). This work is recognized as the first definitive effort since Mary Richmond's *Social Diagnosis* (1917) to define and examine fully the social casework process. Hamilton also wrote *Medical Social Terminology* (1927), *Social Case Recording* (1936), *Principles of Social Case Recording* (1946), and *Psychotherapy in Child Guidance* (1947). From 1962 until her death, she was editor-in-chief of *Social Work*, the journal of the National Association of Social Workers. (*See also: Higher Education; Social Work*)

—**Roger A. Lohmann**

Further Reading

"Hamilton, Gordon." In *Encyclopedia of Social Work*, 18th ed., edited by Richard Edwards, 2589-90. Silver Spring, MD: National Association of Social Workers, 1995.

Hamilton, Gordon. *Principles of Social Case Recording.* New York: Columbia University Press, 1946.

———. *Psychotherapy in Child Guidance.* New York: Columbia University Press, 1947.

———. *Social Case Recording.* New York: Columbia University Press, 1936.

———. *Theory and Practice of Social Case Work*, 1940. Rev. ed. New York: Columbia University Press, 1951.

Shoshani, Batya S. "Gordon Hamilton: An Investigation of Core Ideas." Ph.D. diss., Columbia University School of Social Work, 1984.

～ Hansberry, Lorraine (1930–1965)

Lorraine Hansberry was the first African American woman to have a play produced on Broadway. *A Raisin in the Sun,* her first play, found popular and critical acclaim and won the New York Drama Critics' Circle Award for the best play of the 1958–1959 season. The Broadway production was also the first for a black director, Lloyd Richards, and marked the beginning of national prominence for players such as Sidney Poitier, Diana Sands, and Claudia McNeil.

Set against Langston Hughes's famous poem, "Montage of a Dream Deferred," *A Raisin* attempted to answer Hughes's question: "What happens to a dream deferred?/Does it dry up/like a raisin in the sun?/Or fester like a sore—/and then run?" Its action generated by the family's receiving the proceeds of a life insurance settlement, the play follows a multigeneration black family, striving for opportunity, as they work through their competing dreams—for education, for a business, for a home of their own. The play concludes with the family's purchase of a house in an all-white neigh-

borhood and with their dignified rejection of the white homeowners association's offer to buy them out.

A native Chicagoan, Hansberry lived through a parallel incident. The daughter of middle-class blacks who democratically sent their daughter to public schools but who also dressed her and taught her in ways that set her off from her peers, Hansberry moved at the age of eight to a middle-class, white neighborhood. Their housing suit (*Hansberry v. Lee*), supported by the National Association for the Advancement of Colored People, went to the Supreme Court, and Hansberry's memories of the time cemented her dedication to civil rights. Hansberry discovered drama at the University of Wisconsin. Early publications in *Freedom* and other periodicals, residence in Greenwich Village in New York, marriage to and later divorce from Robert Nemiroff, and a move to the country draw the outlines of Hansberry's life as she struggled to find her voice and sexual identity and as she struggled against the cancer that killed her.

Much of Hansberry's writing remains unpublished and in fragments. Her other finished plays include *The Drinking Gourd* (1960), a television script on slavery; *The Sign in Sidney Brustein's Window* (1965), originally planned with a female central character but, as finished, centered on a male, urban intellectual; and *Les Blancs* (1970), dealing with an African's return to his community at a time of crisis. Unfinished at Hansberry's death, it was completed by Nemiroff. *Sign* was kept in production by an informal but widespread movement until the day after Hansberry died.

Lorraine Hansberry's popular image rests on the film version of *A Raisin in the Sun*, the musical adaptation *Raisin*, and the biographical compilation and tribute, *To Be Young, Gifted and Black*, created by Nemiroff and others from her scattered writing and interviews—especially the filmed interview, *The Black Experience and the Creation of Drama*, in which Hansberry engagingly discusses her life and work and her views of fellow playwrights.

What Hansberry saw as a lack of dramatic unity in *A Raisin*, a diffused focus on the family rather than on a strong central character, brought distinctive women's voices to her stage. What Hansberry saw as increasing dramatic unity in her later plays was also a movement away from these pluralistic women's voices and roles—movement toward a male playwright's tradition and form.

While traditional critics have occasionally faulted Hansberry's work for sentimentality or melodrama, feminist critics have lamented that her drama remained male centered. Hansberry's sense that the collective voice of *A Raisin* was an artistic weakness seemed to urge her toward finding a more centered vision through a male protagonist, although her notes for both plays after *A Raisin* show her struggling with the possibility of women characters as centers. (*See also: Black Women; Theater and Drama; Women Writers*)

—**Carol Klimick Cyganowski**

Further Reading

The Black Experience and the Creation of Drama. Filmed interview. Princeton, NJ: Films for the Humanities.

Cheney, Anne. *Lorraine Hansberry*. Boston: G. K. Hall, 1984.

Hansberry, Lorraine. *The Collected Last Plays*. Edited by Robert Nemiroff. New York: New American Library, 1983.

———. *A Raisin in the Sun*. New York: New American Library, 1961.

———. *To Be Young, Gifted and Black*. Adapted by Robert Nemiroff. New York: New American Library, 1970.

Wilkerson, Margaret B. "The Dark Vision of Lorraine Hansberry: Excerpts from a Literary Biography," *The Massachusetts Review* 28 (Winter 1987): 642-50.

Harlem Renaissance

African American women played a prominent role in the development of contemporary black culture during the Harlem Renaissance, but they have generally been overlooked or discredited in historical texts. African American artists experienced discrimination and oppression because of their race. African American women artists also faced sex discrimination, not only from whites but from their black male counterparts.

The Harlem Renaissance is the name given to an indefinite period between World War I and the 1930s that saw the rebirth of African American cultural arts and the emergence of what author Alain Locke called the "New Negro," which referred to African American artists who worked to preserve their African heritage while changing racist attitudes.

Some African American women, such as Gladys Bentley, "Ma" Rainey, Bessie Smith, and Ethel Waters, achieved success through performing in Harlem nightclubs and theaters. Jackie "Moms" Mabley, one of the first African American comediennes, developed her act in Harlem's nightclubs and became the Apollo Theater's headliner for thirty years. Marian Anderson, Minto Cato, and Lillian Evanti and other classical singers and musicians gained international recognition traveling abroad, then returned to the United States to perform. Josephine Baker also went to Europe to escape typecasting as a comic and became the renaissance's best-known actress and dancer. Women writers, including Marita Bonner, Nellie Bright, Jessie Redmon Fauset, Zora Neale Hurston, Nella Larson, and Dorothy West, provided a treasury of fiction, folklore, and poetry about the lives of African Americans.

Recently published anthologies and histories of the Harlem Renaissance have focused on the contributions of African American women artists, giving a more complete view of the period. *(See also: Anderson, Marian; Art; Baker, Josephine; Black Women; Fauset, Jessie Redmon; Hurston, Zora Neale; Rainey, Gertrude "Ma"; Smith, Bessie; Waters, Ethel; Women Writers)*

—**Merri Scheibe Edwards**

Further Reading

Cohee, Gail, and Leslie Lewis. *Sisters of the Harlem Renaissance: A Photographic Postcard Series*. Bloomington, IN: Helaine Victoria, 1991.

Harrison, Daphne Duval. *Black Pearls: Blues Queens of the 1920s*. New Brunswick, NJ: Rutgers University Press, 1988.

Honey, Maureen, ed. *Shadowed Dreams: Women's Poetry of the Harlem Renaissance*. New Brunswick, NJ: Rutgers University Press, 1989.

Hull, Gloria T. *Color, Sex, and Poetry: Three Women Writers of the Harlem Renaissance*. Bloomington: Indiana University Press, 1987.

Kellner, Bruce. *The Harlem Renaissance: A Historical Dictionary for the Era*. New York: Methuen, 1987.

Knopf, Marcy, ed. *The Sleeper Wakes: Harlem Renaissance Stories by Women*. Foreword by Nellie Y. McKay. New Brunswick, NJ: Rutgers University Press, 1993.

Lewis, David Levering. *When Harlem Was in Vogue*. New York: Oxford University Press, 1979.

Locke, Alain, ed. *The New Negro*. New York: Atheneum, 1968.

Roses, Lorraine Elena, and Ruth Elizabeth Randolph. *Harlem Renaissance and Beyond: Literary Biographies of 100 Black Women Writers, 1900–1945*. New York: Macmillan, 1990.

The Studio Museum in Harlem. *Harlem Renaissance Art of Black America*. Introduction by Mary Schmidt Campbell. New York: Harry N. Abrams, 1987.

Harnack, Mildred (1902–1943)

Quite possibly the only American tried, condemned, and executed by the Nazis, Mildred Harnack was long considered a heroine by the former German Democratic Republic and the Soviet Union before she was finally acknowledged in 1986 as "a Wisconsin woman who suffered and died for the pursuit of justice and freedom."

Born Mildred Fish in Milwaukee on September 16, 1902, she studied at the University of Wisconsin–Madison, completing a B.A. and an M.A. in English language and literature. Following her 1926 marriage to Dr. Arvid Harnack, a German economist and jurist, she traveled to Germany in 1929, continuing her studies as well as lecturing on and teaching American Studies. After the completion of her dissertation on the development of contemporary American literature, she was awarded her Dr. phil. from the university in Giessen on November 20, 1941.

Even before the Nazi takeover in 1933, both Arvid and Mildred Harnack were involved in antifascist activities, which included spying for the Soviet Union; the group known as the "Rote Kapelle" was the Schulze-Boysen/Harnack organization. One hundred seventeen members of the group, among them the Harnacks, were arrested in August 1942; more than fifty members were executed. Mildred Harnack was found guilty of espionage and of aiding and abetting acts preparative to high treason; on December 14, 1942, she received a six-year prison sentence, which included the loss of her civil rights. This sentence was found unacceptable by Adolf Hitler and Wilhelm Keitel on December 21. The retrial sentenced her to death, and Mildred Harnack was beheaded in Berlin-Ploetzensee on February 14, 1943. *(See also: World War II)*

—**Maureen R. Liston**

Further Reading

Harnack-Fish, Mildred. *Variationen ueber das Thema Amerika: Studien zur Literatur der USA.* Edited by Eberhard Bruening. Berlin: Aufbau Verlag, 1988.

Rote Kapelle: Ein Portrait der Widerstandsgruppe in Fotografien und Selbstzeugnissen. Berlin: Humblot, 1992.

⟡ Harper, Frances Ellen Watkins (1825–1911)

Frances Harper, novelist, poet, journalist, orator, activist for abolition, temperance, and women's rights movements, was born September 24, 1825, to free parents in Baltimore, Maryland. She has been called the best-known African American writer of the nineteenth century, a journalistic "foremother," and an eloquent and persuasive lecturer who achieved a national stature rare for African American women of the period.

Frances Watkins, orphaned at the age of three, was raised by an aunt and uncle, received a classical education in her uncle's school, the William Watkins Academy for Negro Youth, and gained exposure to social reform and abolitionist activities. In 1850, the year of the Fugitive Slave Act, she moved to Ohio, working as a live-in seamstress and housekeeper. She taught at Union Seminary, becoming the first female faculty member, and accepted another position two years later in Little York, Pennsylvania, bringing her into contact with one of the leaders of the Underground Railroad, William Still.

Increasingly politicized during this period due to the increased persecution of African Americans, she became a crusader for the abolitionist movement and started to write poetry, resulting in the publication of her first collection, *Forest Leaves,* around 1854. She moved to Philadelphia, where she contributed to abolitionist newspapers and participated in the Underground Railroad. She became the first female orator on the traveling lecture circuit through support from the Maine Anti-Slavery Society, giving her first speech, "Education and the Elevation of the Colored Race," to an antislavery gathering in New Bedford, Massachusetts, in August 1854.

Human rights for African Americans and women became her central themes in her *Poems on Miscellaneous Subjects* (1854), a best-seller going through several reprintings. By her mid-twenties, Frances Watkins had become a widely read author. When she returned to Philadelphia in 1857, she served as a lecturer for the Pennsylvania Anti-Slavery Society and published another volume of poetry, *Poems.* In 1859, she wrote "The Two Offers" in *Anglo-African Magazine,* reputedly the first short story published by an African American.

Marriage to Fenton Harper, a widower from Cincinnati, on November 22, 1860, brought family priorities. She settled on a farm near Columbus, Ohio, where she raised Harper's three children and their own daughter, Mary, while she continued to write and publish her work in a number of abolitionist newspapers and magazines. Following the death of her husband in 1864, Harper resumed her public lecturing career; published a narrative poem, *Moses: A Story of the Nile* (1869); and became active in women's crusades to improve family life. She worked with black and white women building coalitions. Through the American Woman Suffrage Association, she criticized National Woman Suffrage Association leaders Elizabeth Cady Stanton and Susan B. Anthony for their opposition to black suffrage. Harper traveled extensively through the South, leading to her publication of *Sketches of Southern Life* (1872). Reform interests expanded to include leadership in the Woman's Christian Temperance Union, the Colored Women's Congress, and the National Association of Colored Women.

Her later work included a novel, *Iola Leroy; or, Shadows Uplifted* (1883), a reflection of her views on black women's experiences and racism at the end of the nineteenth century, followed by several collections of poetry: *The Sparrow's Fall and Other Poems* (1894), *Atlanta Offering: Poems* (1895), and *Poems* (1900). Harper died in her beloved Philadelphia on February 20, 1911, following many years of failing health. (*See also: Abolition and the Antislavery Movement; Black Women; Suffrage*)

—**Dorothy C. Salem**

Further Reading

Brown, Hallie Q. *Homespun Heroines and Other Women of Distinction.* Xenia, OH: Aldine, 1926.

Carby, Hazel. *Reconstructing Womanhood.* New York: Oxford University Press, 1987.

Foster, Frances Smith, ed. *A Brighter Coming Day: A Frances Ellen Watkins Harper Reader.* New York: Feminist Press, 1990.

Still, William. *The Underground Railroad.* Philadelphia: Porters & Coates, 1872.

Washington, Mary Helen. *Invented Lives.* New York: Anchor, 1987.

⟡ Hayes, Anna Mae McCabe (b. 1920)

In the history of American wars, the largest group of unsung heroines has been the women of the U.S. Army's Army Nurse Corps. In 1970, one of its members—Anna Mae McCabe Hayes—finally received recognition in the name of her corps when she was promoted to the rank of brigadier general. Army nurses historically have accompanied U.S. combat armies into war zones, helped retrieve wounded soldiers from the battlefields, and treated them as they were transported to safety at field hospitals, where additional nurses and doctors provided the best possible care for their recovery. Established as a civilian corps of the Army in 1901, the Army Nurse Corps was given military status by Congress in 1944. Later, in 1947, it achieved status as a corps of the Regular Army. Born in Buffalo, New York, in 1920 and raised in Allentown, Pennsylvania, Hayes joined the Army Nurse Corps in 1942 and served in the China-Burma-India Theater throughout World War II. During the Korean War, she served at a field hospital near the front lines in Korea (1950–1951), followed by a tour at an Army hospital in Tokyo, Japan (1951–1953), again caring for wounded American soldiers during that war. While stationed at Walter Reed General Hospital (1953–1960), she was private nurse for an American president—Dwight D. Eisenhower. After her Washington, D.C., tour, she was reassigned to Korea as chief nurse of an evacuation hospital. When she returned to the United States, she served as Assistant Chief of the Army Nurse Corps (1963) until 1967 when she was selected to be the Chief of the Army Nurse Corps. In this position, she stimulated nurse recruitment for service during the Vietnam War, intensified training for nurses at all levels, and improved their opportunities to advance in grade. Promoted to brigadier general on June 11, 1970, she retired a year later and received the Distinguished Service Medal. She retired in Arlington, Virginia, where she continues to be active in promoting service in the U.S. Army Nurse Corps. (*See also: Army Nurse Corps; Military Service; Nursing*)

—**Colonel (Ret.) Bettie J. Morden**

Further Reading

Carson, Col. Amelia J. "Biographical Information, BG Anna Mae McCabe Hayes." Carlisle Barracks, PA: Military History Institute, 1983.

Shields, Elizabeth A. "Highlights in the History of the Army Nurse Corps." Washington, DC: U.S. Army Center of Military History, 1981.

❦ Heaton, Hannah (Cook) (1721–1794)

Hannah Heaton wrote one of the few surviving autobiographies by eighteenth-century American women. It records events and reflections from the time of the Great Awakening—an intense and widespread religious revival—to the early years of the Republic.

Born on Long Island, New York, she married Theophilus Heaton, Jr., and, with her husband and their two sons, spent her life on a farm in North Haven, Connecticut. There, she described her spiritual reflections, including her conversion experience, and noted her daily prayers, times of despair, books she read, and omens she saw in dreams. She also revealed the social conditions of her time, portraying tempestuous relationships with her husband, children, neighbors, ministers, and magistrates. She gave an account of political events of the Revolutionary period reported in the newspapers she read and the sermons she heard. She recorded revivals that occurred near the end of her life (the beginnings of the Second Great Awakening), which seemed to announce the millennium. While she composed a deeply religious autobiography, her account foreshadows the romantic sensibility that values a life lived with feeling, sensitivity, and suffering. (*See also: Great Awakening*)

—**Barbara E. Lacey**

Further Reading

Lacey, Barbara E. "The World of Hannah Heaton: The Autobiography of an Eighteenth-Century Connecticut Farm Woman," *William and Mary Quarterly* 3d Ser., 45 (April 1988): 280-304.

❦ Hellman, Lillian (1905–1984)

Dramatist Lillian Hellman was born in New Orleans, the only child of Julia Newhouse and Max Hellman. When she was five, the family moved to New York, and for several years, she lived six months in each of these cities, attending school in both. Her life in the South had a profound influence on her plays, and several people from that time and place found their way into her work.

She attended New York University for two years, following which she was a manuscript reader for a publishing firm, wrote book reviews for the *Herald Tribune,* published a few short stories, and worked as a theatrical agent. At this time, she met Arthur Kober, a playwright whom she married and later divorced, and a number of literary and theatrical figures, including Dashiell Hammett, the novelist and screenwriter who was to become her literary mentor, confidant, and lover until his death in 1961.

Through Hammett's encouragement, she wrote her first play, *The Children's Hour* (1934). It was enormously successful, partly due to its then-shocking theme of lesbianism but also due to its sensitive probing of moral issues, an interest that continued to dominate her personal life and her plays. All of her dramas are explorations into the nature of evil, deriving their great power from fine characterizations, economy of language, and carefully structured plots. Her most famous plays are *The Little Foxes* (1939), whose theme of monstrous egotism and ruthless greed within a single southern family had its roots in the history of her mother's family, the Newhouses; and *Watch on the Rhine* (1941), the story of an anti-Nazi German who sacrifices his personal happiness for the cause of freedom.

While Hellman is frequently celebrated as America's finest woman playwright, she was equally well-known for her involvement in liberal political causes. She was an early and ardent antifascist in the 1930s and a left-wing sympathizer into the 1940s; she was called before the House Un-American Activities Committee in 1952, where her refusal to implicate others (to "name names") led to her famous statement: "I will not cut my conscience to fit this year's fashions." She and Hammett were blacklisted in Hollywood, losing most of their sources of income, and were forced to sell Hardscrabble Farm, the home in New York State where they had spent many of their happiest and most productive years.

At the time of her death in 1984, a new storm of controversy surrounded her. Many critics asserted that much of the biographical "fact" in her memoirs was distortion and invention, most notably in the story "Julia" (*Pentimento* 1973). She began litigation against the writer, Mary McCarthy, who had attacked her as a liar on a national television program, but Hellman died before the case came to trial.

Her memoirs—*An Unfinished Woman* (1969), *Pentimento,* and *Scoundrel Time* (1976)—have achieved nearly as much critical acclaim as her plays. They are filled with rich character studies, serve as a vivid record of an earlier period in our history, and document Hellman's determined battle to win recognition for her art and her principles.

Among the awards Hellman received in her lifetime were the New York Drama Critics' Circle Awards for *Watch on the Rhine* and *Toys in the Attic* (1960), the National Book Award for *An Unfinished Woman,* and Academy Award nominations for her screenplays of *The Little Foxes* and *The North Star* (1943). She received honorary degrees from Douglass, Smith, and Wheaton colleges and Tufts, Brandeis, Yale, and New York universities. *(See also: Theater and Drama; Women Writers)*

—**Bobby Ellen Kimbel**

Further Reading

Adler, Jacob H. *Lillian Hellman.* Austin: University of Texas Press, 1969.

Bryer, Jackson. *Conversations with Lillian Hellman.* Jackson: University of Mississippi Press, 1986.

Falk, Doris V. *Lillian Hellman.* New York: Ungar, 1977.

Hellman, Lillian. *Another Part of the Forest.* New York: Viking, 1947.

————. *The Autumn Garden.* Boston: Little, Brown, 1951.

————. *Candide.* New York: Random House, 1957.

————. *The Children's Hour.* New York: Random House, 1934.

————. *The Little Foxes.* New York: Random House, 1936.

————. *Pentimento: A Book of Portraits.* Boston: Little, Brown, 1973.

————. *Scoundrel Time.* Boston: Little, Brown, 1972.

————. *Toys in the Attic.* New York: Random House, 1960.

————. *An Unfinished Woman.* Boston: Little, Brown, 1969.

————. *Watch on the Rhine.* New York: Random House, 1941.

Newman, Robert P. *The Cold War Romance of Lillian Hellman and John Melby.* Chapel Hill: University of North Carolina Press, 1989.

Townes, Saundra. *Lillian Hellman.* Philadelphia: Chelsea House, 1989.

Wright, William. *Lillian Hellman: The Image, the Woman.* New York: Simon & Schuster, 1986.

➜ Henry Street Settlement

Established on the Lower East Side of New York in 1893 by two nurses, Lillian Wald and Mary Brewster, Henry Street Settlement is one of the best known and most influential settlement houses in the United States. Initially called Nurses' Settlement, it was used by Wald as a base to originate a visiting nurse service designed to provide home nursing care for the poor, who paid whatever they could. Brought into intimate contact with the effects of poverty through home nursing, Wald and others at Henry Street Settlement campaigned for reforms to improve housing and working conditions and to end child labor. Wald was an effective speaker, writer, and lobbyist. Her concerns ex-

tended beyond the poverty of her neighborhood to embrace woman suffrage and pacifism. She also attracted to Henry Street other prominent women, such as reformer Florence Kelley and Lavinia Lloyd Dock, who was instrumental in improving nursing education.

Besides trying to solve the problems of poverty through social reform, Wald also implemented the settlement house idea through educational, cultural, and recreational programs. Among the volunteers at Henry Street were Rita Wallach Morgenthau and Irene and Alice Lewisohn, who in 1915 established the Neighborhood Playhouse there, a project important to the development of little theater. The settlement also operated one of the first playgrounds in New York and pioneered a vocational counseling service in 1920.

When Wald resigned in 1933 due to ill health, Helen Hall replaced her. Hall was the most prominent among the second generation of settlement workers. The former head of Philadelphia's University Settlement and a president of the National Federation of Settlements, Hall continued Wald's emphasis on social reform. Hall served on the advisory committee that constructed the Social Security Act, frequently testified before congressional committees on consumer and welfare issues, and helped to originate Mobilization for Youth, a program that increased social services on the Lower East Side in the early 1960s and became the prototype for the War on Poverty. In 1967, at the age of seventy-five, Hall resigned as head of Henry Street. Since then, the settlement has had a series of male executive directors and has not been as prominent in social reform. *(See also: National Federation of Settlements; Nursing; Settlement House Movement; Social Work; Wald, Lillian)*

—**Judith Ann Trolander**

Further Reading

Daniels, Doris. *Always a Sister: The Feminism of Lillian B. Wald.* New York: Feminist Press, 1989.

Hall, Helen. *Unfinished Business.* New York: Macmillan, 1971.

Trolander, Judith Ann. *Settlement Houses and the Great Depression.* Detroit, MI: Wayne State University Press, 1975.

Wald, Lillian. *The House on Henry Street.* New York: Henry Holt, 1915.

————. *Windows on Henry Street.* Boston: Little, Brown, 1934.

➜ Hepburn, Katharine (b. 1907)

Stage and film actor Katharine Hepburn has enthralled successive generations of audiences and maintained her popularity in an industry that has typically discarded female stars within a decade or so. Her indomitable personality and strong character have won her the respect of her colleagues, along with the admiration of many generations of fans.

She was born in Hartford, Connecticut, the second of six children, to parents renowned for unconventional thinking and activities. Her father, Norval Thomas Hepburn, was a "radical" surgeon interested in social hygiene; her mother,

Katharine Martha Houghton, was an activist in the suffrage and birth control movements and an associate of Emmeline Pankhurst, Charlotte Perkins Gilman, and Margaret Sanger. Throughout her life, Hepburn remained close to her family and her roots, returning to Connecticut to escape the publicity and the tinsel of Hollywood.

Educated at Bryn Mawr College, her mother's alma mater, Hepburn started acting with a Baltimore stock company right after graduation in 1928. Her career was rocky at first, fraught with mixed reviews and several dismissals for insubordination, yet she persevered. Persuaded to do a screen test for RKO, she was spotted by director George Cukor who convinced producer David O. Selznik to offer her a contract. Her first film, *A Bill of Divorcement* (1932), costarring John Barrymore, won her rave reviews and a long-term contract with RKO and was the first in a long series of creative partnerships with Cukor. It also launched a Hollywood career that spanned more than five decades and resulted in four Best Actress Academy Awards (*Morning Glory*, 1933; *Guess Who's Coming to Dinner*, 1967; *The Lion in Winter*, 1968; and *On Golden Pond*, 1981) and eight more nominations (*Alice Adams*, 1935; *The Philadelphia Story*, 1940; *Woman of the Year*, 1942; *The African Queen*, 1951; *Summertime*, 1955; *The Rainmaker*, 1956; *Suddenly Last Summer*, 1959; and *Long Day's Journey into Night*, 1962).

Although her film career was extraordinarily successful, her route was often unconventional. She did not at any time fit the movie star pattern, avoiding Hollywood crowds and entertainments and demanding respect from studio executives who preferred to dictate to their contract players, especially females. When in the late 1930s the Independent Theatre Owners Association labeled her, along with Joan Crawford, Greta Garbo, and Marlene Dietrich, "box office poison," she left California, prepared to return only on her own terms. Philip Barry's play *The Philadelphia Story* made her a Broadway star, and she shrewdly secured the film rights in lieu of salary. Bargaining with MGM over those rights, she took the starring part for herself and chose both her director (Cukor) and costars (Cary Grant, James Stewart). From that point on, Hepburn exerted substantial control over all her films and other projects.

Her personal life was no less distinctive. Her marriage to Philadelphia stockbroker Ludlow Ogden Smith lasted six years (1928–1934), succeeded by intimate relationships with agent Leland Hayward, billionaire aviator Howard Hughes, and director John Ford. Then in 1942, she met costar Spencer Tracy on the set of *Woman of the Year.* Their love affair lasted until his death in 1967 and was Hollywood's best-kept secret until Garson Kanin's *Tracy and Hepburn* became a best-seller in 1970. During that time, Hepburn and Tracy made nine memorable films together, among them the brightest "couple comedies" ever filmed. The energetic Hepburn's longest period of professional inactivity was the last five years of Tracy's life, when she spent much of her time attending to his needs.

Into her eighties, beset with physical problems herself, she continued to act on stage and television and in films and to write books with provocative titles, accepting new challenges whenever they appeared. In a televised interview, Barbara Walters once asked Hepburn how she was able to do so much for so long; she responded with typical directness: "Just *do* it." (See also: Movie Stars; Woman's Film)

—**Frances M. Kavenik**

Further Reading

Dickens, Homer. *The Films of Katharine Hepburn.* New York: Citadel, 1971.

Edwards, Anne. *A Remarkable Woman: A Biography of Katharine Hepburn.* New York: William Morrow, 1985.

Hepburn, Katharine. *The Making of the African Queen, or How I Went to Africa with Bogart, Bacall, and Huston and Almost Lost My Mind.* New York: Knopf, 1987.

———. *Me: Stories of My Life.* New York: Knopf, 1991.

Kanin, Garson. *Tracy and Hepburn: An Intimate Memoir.* New York: Viking, 1970.

Leaming, Barbara. *Katharine Hepburn.* New York: Crown, 1995.

ᐱ Herman, Alexis (b. 1947)

Alexis Herman was sworn in on May 9, 1997, as the secretary of labor under President Clinton. Herman became the twenty-third person to hold the position and the only black woman at that time in the president's cabinet. Herman brought to her appointment many years of political experience with a history of leadership in several areas concerning working people and minority women, including all the issues that affect jobs in America.

Herman was born in Mobile, Alabama, and grew up in the rural south. She attended Edgewood College in Madison, Wisconsin (1965–1967), and Spring Hill College in Mobile (1967) and received her B.S. in 1969 from Xavier University in New Orleans, followed by her graduate study at the University of South Alabama in Mobile in 1970 to 1971. While still a student, Herman worked for Interfaith Ministries and the Catholic Social Services in Mobile and moved on to the Recruitment and Training Program in Mississippi. She was exposed to the problems facing young people beginning their careers as well as the discrimination and disadvantages of minorities and women with limited skills. In 1974, Herman directed a program called the Minority Women Employment Program that she developed to help minority women obtain white-collar, nontraditional jobs. From this background, Herman moved into national politics under President Carter beginning in 1977. Until 1981, she served as the director of the Women's Bureau, Office of the Secretary, U.S. Department of Labor. At only twenty-nine, Herman was the youngest person in history ever to hold this position. She advised President Carter on the economic concerns of women and directed the programs for small businesses.

In 1991, Herman became the deputy chair of the Democratic National Committee and in 1992 served as the chief executive officer of the Democratic National Convention Committee with responsibilities of strategy as well as production. While holding her various positions, Herman traveled the United States speaking on workplace issues, addressing concerns of wages, job safety, child care, and affirmative action. She has written numerous articles about issues facing working people for worker magazines and minority publications.

In the private sector, Herman successfully founded her marketing and management firm of A. M. Herman and Associates, which targets marketing strategies, organizational analysis, and human resources. She has been an active community member involved in many organizations both service and religious, such as the National Council of Negro Women, the U.S. Catholic Conference on Social Justice, and the World Peace Commission, as well as many professional organizations, including the Organization of Economic Cooperation and Development. Her experience in these areas has contributed to her knowledge of working people and minorities and the challenges they face in everyday life.

In 1992, Herman served as the deputy director of the Presidential Transition Office for President Clinton, and in 1994 became assistant to Clinton in the White House Public Liaison Office. Her appointment to the cabinet in 1997 was supported by the AFL-CIO, the American Federation of Teachers, and many other labor-oriented groups. She has supported a higher minimum wage, affirmative action, equal opportunity in education and the workplace, and securing job safety in all areas. Herman's varied experience has led her to the position she now holds and has prepared her for service in leadership capabilities. *(See also: Black Women; Democratic Party; Politics; Women's Bureau)*

—**Debra Preston Hutchins**

Further Reading

AFL-CIO Home Page/Executive Council Page. http://www.aflcio. org/estatements/alexis.htm 1997. [Statement in support of Herman's appointment as secretary of labor]

American Federation of Teachers. http://www.aft.org/pr/pr 122096.htm 1996. [Statement in support of Herman's appointment as secretary of labor]

Biographies of U.S. Government Officials. American Embassy, Stockholm. http://www.usis.usemb.se/cabbio/herman.html 1997 [Biography]

The International Year Book and Statesmen's Who's Who: 1998 45th ed., 916. United Kingdom: Bowker-Saur, 1997.

Notable Black American Women, Book II, edited by Jessie Carney Smith, 287-88. New York: Gale Research, 1996.

～ Hernández, María Latigo
(1893–1986)

María Hernández was a community leader, author, and activist in the areas of education and civil rights, and a feminist. Born in Mexico, she came to the United States in 1910. She met and married Don Pedro Hernández in 1915, and the couple settled in San Antonio, Texas, where they opened a grocery store and bakery. In 1927, they helped found the Orden Caballeros de America, a volunteer group that sought to provide its members with mutual support and protection from illegal deportation and police brutality.

When the League of Latin American Citizens (LULAC) was formed in 1929, the Hernándezes and the San Antonio chapter of La Orden refused to join. LULAC restricted its membership to men over eighteen years of age who were American citizens of Latin ancestry. The couple believed in civic organizations that promoted electoral participation for both sexes and in maintaining Hispanic cultural awareness. They disapproved of the assimilationist attitude of the founders of LULAC and the implications inherent in using English words in the name of the group.

In 1934, the Hernándezes and Eluterio Escobar organized the Liga de Defensa Escolar in San Antonio. This organization advocated improved school facilities, increased educational opportunities, and bilingual programs for Chicano students. La Liga employed rallies and street marches to attract public attention. Known as an excellent orator, María Hernández frequently spoke at rallies and demonstrations.

Her skills as a great communicator led Hernández into a new career. In the 1930s, she hosted "La Voz de las Americas," one of the first Spanish-speaking radio programs in San Antonio. In the 1940s, she authored *México y Los Cuatro Poderes Que Dirigen al Pueblo* (Mexico and the Four Powers That Direct the People) and several articles directed at Mexican nationals. Her work primarily discussed the importance of the family and advocated political activism to improve education and increase civil rights for Mexicans and Mexican Americans.

When the Chicano movement began in the 1960s, Hernández became involved, providing a direct sense of continuity to the Chicano struggle for civil rights in Texas. She was the host of a weekly television program called "La Hora de la Mujer." Despite her advanced age, she helped organize La Raza Unida Party (RUP), and in July 1970, she delivered the keynote speech at the RUP conference in Austin, Texas. Then in 1972, she campaigned extensively for RUP candidates Ramsay Muñoz and Martha Cotera.

Her lifelong political and social involvement made her an important role model and leader in the Mexican American civil rights movement. She believed in the equality of the sexes and family unity and that political activism is everyone's moral responsibility. *(See also:* Chicana; *Politics)*

—**Joyce Ann Kievit**

Further Reading

Cotera, Marta. *Profile of the Mexican American Woman.* Austin, TX: National Education Laboratory, 1976.

Hammerback, John C., Richard J. Jensen, and José Angle Gutierrez. *A War of Words: Chicano Protest in the 1960s and 1970s.* New York: Greenwood, 1985.

Hernández, María L. *México y Los Cuatro Poderes Que Dirigen al Pueblo.* San Antonio, TX: Munguia Printers, 1945.

Lewels, Francisco, Jr. *The Uses of the Media by the Chicano Movement: A Study in Minority Access.* New York: Praeger, 1974.

Muñoz, Carlos. *Youth, Identity, and Power.* New York: Verso, 1989.

San Antonio Express-News. January 11, 1986.

⁊ Heterodoxy

A Greenwich Village woman's organization, 1912 to 1942, Heterodoxy was named and founded by Marie Jenney Howe to give the New Woman of her time a place to voice unorthodox ideas without fear of reprisal. Therefore, no official minutes were recorded, and the club's activities and membership were ascertained only through biographies, personal papers, and scant news clippings.

Through a series of public forums—"Twenty-Five Answers to Antis" (1912) and "What Is Feminism?" (1914)—Heterodoxy transformed its public image from a suffrage support group to a genuinely feminist organization. Almost all the club's members were involved with the National American Woman Suffrage Association in some capacity at various times. The members were independently so active in various reform movements that only a third of them attended any one luncheon meeting.

Names such as Elizabeth Gurley Flynn, Charlotte Perkins Gilman, and Henrietta Rodman are on the list of the club's 105 documented members. Most members were traveled, educated, and financially independent. They were writers, journalists, theatrical artists, educators, and business professionals such as doctors, lawyers, and stockbrokers. Democrats, Republicans, Prohibitionists, Socialists, anarchists, liberals, and radicals were represented among the membership. The members' marital status also varied: Any living arrangement that accommodated the individual involved was acceptable. In its willingness to accept and discuss different points of view, Heterodoxy was the forerunner of what the later modern feminist movement would call consciousness-raising groups.

The one issue that even Heterodites could not discuss intellectually was World War I. Some members left the club following bitter disputes between pacifists and those favoring U.S. involvement. The First Red Scare of 1919 brought persecution to many of the club's members who were socialists. Some were put under surveillance, and others were jailed for various activities. Its chosen paper, *The Masses,* was closed down. Although the club supported its needy members both financially and emotionally, its cause and membership were old and dying. Once suffrage was achieved, few new members joined. High food prices during World War I caused remaining members to abandon their luncheons. Slowly, the club slid into oblivion, holding only memorials for its members. Agnes de Mille is listed as Heterodoxy's last surviving member. *(See also: National American Woman Suffrage Association; New Woman; Woman Question)*

—**Dianna Dingess Retzlaff**

Further Reading

Banner, Lois W. *Women in Modern America: A Brief History.* New York: Harcourt Brace Jovanovich, 1974, 1984.

Dresner, Zita. "Heterodite Humor: Alice Duer Miller and Florence Guy Seabury," *Journal of American Culture* 10 (1987): 33-38.

Loeb, Catherine R., Susan E. Searing, and Esther F. Stineman, with the assistance of Meredith J. Ross. *Women's Studies: A Recommended Core Bibliography, 1980–1985.* Littleton, CO: Libraries Unlimited, 1987.

Schwarz, Judith. *Radical Feminists of Heterodoxy: Greenwich Village 1912–1940.* Lebanon, NH: New Victoria, 1982.

Wittenstein, Kate E. "The Heterodoxy Club and American Feminism, 1912–1930." Ph.D. diss., Boston University, 1989.

⁊ Heterosexism

Heterosexism is the assumption that all people are heterosexual and the resulting negation of the needs, desires, and life experiences of gay men and lesbians. Heterosexuality, especially heterosexual intercourse, is sanctioned, indeed almost sanctified, while homosexuality is criminalized and seen as a perversion, sickness, or abnormality. The persecution of lesbian relationships—and the refusal to take the lesbian feminist view seriously—has untold repercussions on society at large as well as on the women directly affected. Lost are role models of viable egalitarian relationships, not based on predetermined sex roles; a deep and abiding valuing of women's concerns; and new perspectives on how societies not based on aggression and competition can be formed.

Lesbian feminist theorists often see other feminist theorists as suffering from heterosexism: By assuming that all women are straight, heterosexual feminists focus on economic or biological variables in trying to explain women's oppression. They fail to see women's oppression as a sexual oppression, in which women are tied to their oppressors by affection, marriage, and sexual desire and are thus unable to form bonds with other women that would elucidate their common plight. Lesbian feminists argue that straight women expend much time, as well as emotional and physical energy, in trying to understand, placate, and change their oppressors. Exhausted from "polishing their chains" and blamed for all the emotional ills of men and children if they desist, they have little energy left to create positive social changes for women.

Heterosexism can also be seen as a form of institutionalized homophobia. The unions between gay women are not legally recognized: They are at best ignored and at worst seen as reason enough for a person to lose her job, not have equal access to housing, or find it difficult to adopt a child. Heterosexism and homophobia are the mortar holding together the bricks of patriarchal structures and, as such, are inherently political rather than sexual ideologies. *(See also: Homophobia; Lesbian Rights; Lesbianism)*

—**Susan Lee Weeks**

Further Reading

Blumenfeld, Warren, and Diane Raymond. *Looking at Gay and Lesbian Life.* Boston: Beacon, 1993.

Dworkin, Andrea. *Intercourse.* New York: Free Press, 1987.

Jung, Patricia Beattie, and Ralph T. Smith. *Heterosexism: An Ethical Challenge.* Albany: State University of New York Press, 1993.

Mintz, Beth, and Esther D. Rothblum, eds. *Lesbians in Academia: Degrees of Freedom.* New York: Routledge, 1997.

Rich, Adrienne. *Blood, Bread and Poetry, Selected Prose, 1979–85.* New York: Norton, 1986.

Robson, Ruthann. *Sappho Goes to Law School.* New York: Columbia University Press, 1998.

Wittig, Monique. *The Straight Mind and Other Essays.* New York: Harvester Wheatsheaf, 1992.

～ Hewins, Caroline Maria (1846–1926)

Caroline Hewins, librarian, pioneer of library services to children, and librarian of Hartford, Connecticut, for a half century, was one of nine children born to a cultivated middle-class Roxbury, Massachusetts, family. Educated at home or in private schools for the most part, she briefly attended the public Boston Girls' High and Normal School, which brought her into contact with the Boston Athenaeum, a private lending library, and established her lifelong interest in libraries. In 1875, she moved to Hartford, Connecticut, to become librarian of the subscription library at the Young Men's Institute, which became the Hartford Public Library in 1893. Hewins's life and career illustrate the merging of three separate ideas: that books played a major role in the development of the child, that the city or state had a responsibility to provide books for children, and that no child was exempt from the benefits of books and libraries.

Recalling her own childhood, where good books were a part of everyday life, Hewins was shocked at the lack of reading materials for Hartford children. Her efforts to remedy the situation included the publication of lists of recommended titles for the young, distributed to schools and parents; giving papers before child development conferences, book talks, and clubs; and finally in 1904 the opening of the children's room. Her 1882 *Books for the Young: A Guide for Parents and Children* summarizes her views of the place of reading in the development of the child. Hewins targeted the large population of immigrant children as especially in need of library service. Programs and exhibits focused on the holidays and customs of the countries of origin of many of the children as well as on those of their new homeland.

Instrumental in the formation of the Connecticut Public Library Committee in 1893 and its only woman member, Hewins encouraged the development of public libraries throughout the state. She also helped form the Connecticut Library Association in 1891, and she participated in the memorable first meeting of children's librarians at the American Library Association meeting in 1900.

Hewins was active in community affairs, participated in the work of the settlement houses, indeed living at the North Street Settlement for years, and was a supporter of local schools and the museums. *(See also: Children's Library Movement; Librarianship)*

—Suzanne Hildenbrand

Further Reading

Hewins, Caroline M. *Books for the Young.* New York: Leypoldt, 1882.

———. "A Mid-Century Child and Her Books." In *Caroline M. Hewins: Her Book,* edited by Jennie D. Lindquist, 1-76. Boston: Horn Book, 1954.

Jagusch, Sybille A. "First among Equals: Caroline M. Hewins and Anne C. Moore. Foundations of Library Work with Children." Ph.D. diss., University of Maryland–College Park, 1990.

Lindquist, Jennie D. "Caroline M. Hewins and Books for Children." In *Caroline M. Hewins: Her Book,* edited by Jennie D. Lindquist, 79-107. Boston: Horn Book, 1954.

～ Higher Education

The entry of women into higher education, as students and as faculty, is best characterized in the title of Eleanor Flexner's overview of the early part of that history: *A Century of Struggle.* In the nineteenth century, quaint notions limited the access of women to higher education: that learning would cause them brain fever, that it would harm their ability to bear children, that it was an enemy to marriage and the family. The education of women was generally limited to the wealthy classes and to "accomplishments" such as French, fine needlework, and music. Female pioneers of advanced education for women were often only children whose fathers educated them as they might a son.

Emma Willard was an early pioneer who, in 1819, tried to persuade the New York legislature to fund the education of girls at that time beginning to enter the field of teaching. She founded a seminary, funded by the city of Troy (New York), for the education of young women in 1821. Oberlin College was the first institution of advanced learning to educate women and men together, beginning in 1833. Opened in 1865, Vassar was the first college for women that attempted to give as rigorous education to women as men's colleges offered to men, emphasizing physical education in the curriculum to counter claims of the physical incapacities of women who enhanced the life of the mind. Smith, which admitted its first students in 1875, accepted only those women who could pass the same entrance examination as was administered by Harvard. By 1880, a year after women began to receive instruction directly from Harvard faculty, women made up one-third of college students across the country. Bryn Mawr became the first college to offer graduate work to women.

Women's advancement as academics in higher education came slowly also. In 1900, the proportion of doctorates that went to women was 6 percent. This figure rose to 15 to 16 percent in the 1930s but dropped back to 10 percent in 1950, reflecting the post–World War II trend in America to discourage women from pursuing advanced education and careers. Two seminal studies of the employment status of women in academia were published by Jessie Bernard and Helen Astin in the 1960s. Patterns of discrimination were evident, including small numbers of women in the most prestigious universities, lower salaries than men's, slower promotion, lower status, and less likelihood of being part of the administration of the institution. However, the Civil Rights Act of 1964, supplemented by a series of executive orders and laws that followed, began to effect a change in the status of women and minorities, as Title IX of the 1972 Education Amendments to the Higher Education Act began to change the status of women students and employees.

The effects of Title IX created a more hospitable environment in higher education, one in which women flourished. In the next decade or so, women eventually accounted for half the undergraduates in U.S. colleges and universities and claimed half the scholarships and other financial aid available. Women's athletics burgeoned as funds traditionally available only for football, men's basketball, and a few other men's sports were reallocated to include volleyball, women's basketball, and other women's sports.

Allocation of financial aid by gender also came under close scrutiny under the new regulation. Not surprisingly, it was discovered that many privately funded scholarships were available only to men. Although the law allowed single-sex scholarships so long as the overall availability of scholarship funds was evenly distributed among men and women, much reevaluation has taken place over the years since 1972, and there remain few sizable or prestigious scholarship awards limited by gender. Perhaps the clearest embodiment of that change can be seen in the inclusion of women as recipients of the highly prestigious Rhodes Scholarships. These awards, given to new graduates for study at Oxford University in England, were funded by South African Cecil Rhodes in the nineteenth century and intended for young men who had achieved at high levels in academic programs and in the "manly" athletic arts. Women have been increasingly represented among Rhodes winners, however; in the 1998 competition, thirteen women and nineteen men were awarded the fellowship.

In academic programs, the effect of Title IX is more mixed. Certainly, women, who constituted 55.8 percent of all undergraduate enrollments in 1992, are pursuing academic degrees in unprecedented numbers and achieving them in equally satisfying numbers. Moreover, the women's studies programs that began in the 1970s have multiplied and earned stature in colleges and universities nationwide, and research on topics focused on women is prolific in the humanities and social sciences.

The continuing problem, and one that both reflects and contributes to gender inequality in the workforce, is distribution across disciplines. At both the undergraduate and graduate levels, women still prefer the courses of study traditional for women—education, the humanities, and increasingly, the social sciences. And while there is steady movement of women in recent years into the biological sciences, their numbers remain few in the mathematics-based disciplines. Many of the women who are graduate students, postdoctoral scholars, and faculty in American universities in fields such as physics are foreign-born. The American educational system is still failing to prepare or to engage its young women in these nontraditional fields. Thus, while 59.5 percent of U.S. doctorates awarded in 1991–1992 in education went to women, and 47.1 percent in the social sciences, including history and psychology, only 9.6 percent of doctorates in engineering and 13.3 percent in computer sciences went to women in that year.

Finally, among the categories covered by Title IX, there is academic employment. Prior to 1972, percentages of women on faculties of American colleges and universities were small indeed. Even in fields such as English, in which undergraduate populations had been half women for years, faculties were predominately, even solely, male. Under Title IX, as well as under other federal laws, numerous charges of sex discrimination were filed against institutions of higher education in the 1970s and 1980s. Many of these were unsuccessful, as the courts revealed themselves to be extremely reluctant to supersede personnel decisions made through academic processes. Several significant class action suits were successful, however, including the suit of Louise Lamphere against Brown University, and the *Rajender v. University of Minnesota* suit, both of which addressed the propensity of colleges and universities to restrict women to teaching positions in which they were not eligible for tenure or permanent status. The latter suit led to an external administrator's being appointed by the court to monitor all academic personnel decisions at Minnesota for several years.

Percentages of women faculty in the nonscience disciplines have increased greatly, hovering around 35 percent nationwide. However, women continue to lag behind in terms of promotion to tenure, professorships in math and science, and positions held within the elite American colleges and universities. *(See also: Athletics/Sports; Coeducation; Education; Higher Education for Southern Women; Mathematics; Science; "Seven Sisters"; Title IX of the Education Amendments of 1972; Willard, Emma Hart; Women's Studies)*

—**Karen Merritt**
—**Michele Wender Zak**

Further Reading

Astin, Helen S. *The Woman Doctorate in America: Origins, Career and Family.* New York: Russell Sage, 1969.

Bernard, Jessie Shirley. *Academic Women.* University Park: Pennsylvania State University Press, 1964.

Chamberlain, Mariam K., ed. *Women in Academe: Progress and Prospects.* New York: Russell Sage, 1988.

Flexner, Eleanor, and Ellen F. Fitzpatrick. *A Century of Struggle: The Women's Rights Movement in the United States.* Enlarged ed. Cambridge, MA: Belknap, 1996.

McClelland, Averil. *The Education of Women in the United States: A Guide to Theory, Teaching, and Research.* New York: Garland, 1992.

Miller, Barbara Soloman. *In the Company of Educated Women: A History of Women and Higher Education in America.* New Haven, CT: Yale University Press, 1985.

Pearson, Carol S., Donna L. Shavlik, and Judith L. Touchton, eds. *Educating the Majority: Women Challenge Tradition in Higher Education.* New York: American Council on Education, 1989.

ᕕ Higher Education for Southern Women

In the late nineteenth and early twentieth centuries, higher education for southern women was shaped by race and gender in ways unique to the region. Segregated by race—and among whites by sex—higher education was nonetheless a central element for women of both races in their movement from the traditional domestic sphere into more public arenas of clubs, social reform, and paid white-collar work.

For white women, the entrenched ideal of the Southern Lady affected both the timing and format of the development of higher education. More than twenty years after Vassar College opened in 1865, a handful of southern women's colleges were just beginning to offer a standard liberal arts curriculum; by 1911, only 4 of over 140 women's schools were accredited. While coeducation was the dominant mode nationally (coeducational outnumbered single-sex institutions two to one by 1870), sex segregation continued to be the most common form in the South well into the twentieth century.

Education in the antebellum South was primarily the creation of evangelical denominations, which established a plethora of white women's academies and seminaries, many calling themselves colleges. By 1900, however, most were junior colleges at best and often little more than secondary or even finishing schools dedicated to perpetuating the Southern Lady. Women's colleges continued to be plagued by the postwar poverty of the region and the lingering conviction that higher education was neither necessary nor suitable for ladies. Such attitudes, coupled with a paucity of secondary schools, ensured that women were seldom prepared for college work. Thus, generally underendowed women's colleges had to devote significant portions of their meager resources to preparatory departments at the expense of the facilities and faculty needed to meet national norms. By the 1920s, however, conditions had improved, and many schools were able to drop their preparatory departments and became accredited four-year colleges.

Impelled in part by the desperate need for teachers, southern states began establishing normal colleges for women in the 1890s. While such institutions challenged the concept of the Southern Lady by preparing women for employment, the education they offered remained separate and distinct from that for men. State universities were only grad-ually opened to women, usually only as graduates and upper-division transfer students; not until the second half of the twentieth century would many southern state universities, pressured by feminists and the federal government, admit women on the same basis as men.

Higher education for black women was shaped by racism as well as sexism. Educated black women were expected to play a crucial role in racial uplift as mothers and teachers, but when W. E. B. Du Bois spoke of the "talented tenth" who should be educated as leaders of the race, he meant men.

Unlike white institutions, black colleges were predominantly coeducational—only four of seventy-five schools established between 1865 and 1933 were exclusively for women—and vocational. Although the denominational sponsors of black schools in the postwar South sought to provide classical or liberal arts education for future black leaders, their attempts were made more difficult by inadequate funding, lack of local support, and unprepared students, the latter caused by the lack of primary and secondary schools. By the turn of the century, a combination of New South conservatives and northern philanthropists controlled many black schools and had shifted the emphasis to vocational and technical education designed to train a labor force that would both fill the needs of southern industry and not threaten the region's racial order. For women, this meant teacher training and domestic skills. The approximately one-half of black college students who were women were heavily concentrated in institutions emphasizing normal rather than liberal arts or agricultural and mechanical curricula.

More research is needed to determine how black college women's experiences differed from those of either black men or white women or how they responded to or shaped those experiences. What we do know suggests that, like white women, black coeds lived under more strict social controls than men and, compared with whites, were subjected to an even greater emphasis on morality, the latter a response to the slave owner's fantasy of the lasciviousness of black women. The thrust of their education was to create wives, mothers, and teachers who would promote respectability and responsibility of the race and not challenge racial or gender norms of southern society.

In their postcollege lives, black women, who, unlike their white counterparts, generally worked even after marriage, sought to use their training in the great work of racial uplift. As teachers, they played a central role in the development of much needed primary and secondary schools for their race. They also went into nursing and were leaders in civic improvement and social welfare organizations in their communities.

State-supported or privately funded, southern universities and women's colleges remained racially—and to a lesser degree sexually—segregated until the 1960s. They nonetheless provided education that aided women of both races in moving out of the traditional roles of Southern Lady for whites and of domestic or field worker for blacks. However, cultural and economic forces shaped distinct regional patterns that also tended to reduce the challenge to established gender and racial norms implicit in higher education.

In the twentieth century, historically black colleges have offered undergraduate women an increasingly rich and varied liberal arts curriculum, preparing them for participation in a variety of professions. As private, four-year liberal arts institutions for women, Bennett College in Greensboro, North Carolina, and Spelman College in Atlanta, Georgia, have made special contributions to the education of African American women from across the United States. Today, a number of private, liberal arts colleges in the South continue to offer a wide range of educational opportunities for women. Among these institutions is Agnes Scott College in Decatur, Georgia, an independent college founded in 1889 and consistently rated one of the best women's colleges in the country. Its ranking as first among national liberal arts colleges in endowment per student reflects the changing status of higher education for women in the South during the twentieth century. *(See also: Black Women; Education; Higher Education; Southern Lady; Southern Women's History; Spelman College)*

—**Pamela Dean**
—**Diana E. Axelsen**

Further Reading

Anderson, James D. *The Education of Blacks in the South: 1860–1935*. Chapel Hill: University of North Carolina Press, 1988.

Farnham, Christie Anne. *Education of the Southern Belle: Higher Education and Student Socialization in the Antebellum South.* New York: New York University Press, 1994.

Gordon, Lynn D. *Gender and Higher Education in the Progressive Era, 1890–1920*. New Haven, CT: Yale University Press, 1990.

Guy-Sheftall, Beverly. "Black Women and Higher Education: Spelman and Bennett Colleges Revisited," *Journal of Negro Education* 51 (1982): 278-87.

Solomon, Barbara Miller. *In the Company of Educated Women: A History of Women and Higher Education in America*. New Haven, CT: Yale University Press, 1985.

ᕦ Highgate, Edmonia (1844–1870)

Edmonia Highgate was a teacher, lecturer, and fund-raiser who advocated education for blacks during the latter half of the 1800s. In addition, she lectured on the peculiar institution of slavery, temperance, and the suffrage movement. She traveled extensively throughout Canada and the United States raising money and resources for the post-Civil War Freedmen's Association and the American Missionary Association.

Highgate was born in Albany, New York, in 1844. Her parents, Charles and Hannah Highgate, moved their family to Syracuse, New York, following the denial of the Albany school commissioners to admit the Highgate children to the district school. Highgate graduated from Syracuse High School with distinction. Her high school senior thesis was a paper on slavery that, when publicly presented, was very well received. She was certified as a teacher. However, she was not able to obtain a position as a teacher of white children because of her color. Her first teaching position was in Binghamton, New York, where she taught in the "colored" school. She then taught at the mission schools in Norfolk, Virginia, and Darlington, Maryland, run by the American Missionary Association before becoming principal of Frederick Douglass School in New Orleans in 1866.

Noted abolitionists who admired and encouraged Highgate were Reverend Jermain Loguen, Frederick Douglass, Gerrit Smith, and Samuel J. May. They were impressed with her ability as a lecturer and her unfailing dedication to addressing the educational needs of blacks. She was the first of two women to address the all-male National Convention of Colored Citizens of the United States held in Syracuse in 1864. Her commitment to bringing education to former slaves was not without threat to her person and her students. Both were shot at. Highgate taught under deplorable conditions with meager support and resources; one of her schools consisted of a former slave pen. A woman of high ideals, she refused to teach or be a part of a segregated public school system in New Orleans. In protest, as the only woman officer of the Louisiana Education Relief Association, she gave up a highly coveted salary of $1,000 per year rather than be a part of a segregated system. Subsequently, the New Orleans school district adopted and implemented a plan to integrate its schools.

Highgate was plagued with ill health, caused in part by exhaustion from work and the circumstances under which she was forced to live as a black teacher and principal in the South. She died prematurely at the age of twenty-six in Syracuse. *(See also: Black Women; Education; Freedmen's Bureau; Teaching)*

—**Constance H. Timberlake**

Further Reading

American Missionary Association Archives. Amistad Research Center, New Orleans, La. 1864–1865.

"Coroner's Inquest," *Syracuse Journal* (Oct. 19, 1870). Onondaga Historical Society, Syracuse, NY.

Federal Census Bureau. "1850 Census Taken in Albany" (Aug. 16, 1850). New York State Library, Albany, NY.

The Gerrit Smith Papers. Bird Library. Syracuse University, Syracuse, NY, 1869–1870.

Morris, Robert C. "Freedmen's Education." In *Black Women in America: An Historical Encyclopedia*, edited by Carlene Clark Hine, 462-69. New York: Carlson, 1993.

Weisenfeld, Judith. " 'Who Is Sufficient for These Things?' Sara G. Stanley and the American Missionary Association, 1864–1868," *Church History* 60 (1991): 493-507.

Untitled clippings without page numbers on file at the Onondaga Historical Society, Syracuse, NY: *Albany Press* (Albany, NY), Aug. 31, 1870; *Binghamton Standard* (Binghamton, NY), Sept. 5, 1863; *Syracuse Standard*, Dec. 9, 1858.

❧ History of Woman Suffrage
(1881–1922)

When the "triumvirate" of the radical wing of the suffrage movement—Susan B. Anthony, Matilda Joslyn Gage, and Elizabeth Cady Stanton—decided to tell the story of their reform work in 1876, they envisioned writing a short pamphlet in two months. But as the *History of Woman Suffrage* took shape, it grew. Gage and Stanton agreed to "write, collect, select and arrange the material for said history," while the nonwriter Anthony, under the terms of their contract, would arrange for publication. Veteran reform activists from the various states were asked to prepare "a general resume of what has been done, by whom and when," and prominent workers were asked to provide their reminiscences. Much of the submitted material had to be rewritten for clarity; Stanton bemoaned how "dry bones" boring it was.

The project had its share of internal dissent and external criticism. Gage and Stanton disagreed on political interpretation with the more conservative Anthony and were angry when she didn't provide them with a regular financial accounting. Discontented contributors wanted credit for their writing. Lucy Stone of the American Woman Suffrage Association—more conservative than the National Woman Suffrage Association, which the "triumvirate" supported—refused to submit information, with "ceaseless regrets that any 'wing' of the suffragists should attempt to write the history of the other." One newspaper suggested that writing about a cause that had not been won resembled the celebrated book on "Snakes in Iceland": Its subject matter did not exist. Despite the problems, the women proceeded, believing that "those who fight the battle can best give what all readers like to know—the impelling motives to action; the struggle in the face of opposition; the vexation under ridicule; and the despair in success too long deferred." When they finished editing ten years later, the *History* had grown to three volumes, each one thousand pages long, consisting of letters, speeches, petitions, reminiscences, and convention proceedings—all tied together with a brilliant and passionate radical suffragist analysis. As Stanton predicted, these volumes remain the major source for anyone studying "the most momentous reform that has yet been launched on the world—the first organized protest against the injustice which has brooded over the character and destiny of one-half the human race."

Fourteen years later, after Gage had died and Stanton had largely withdrawn from the increasingly conservative suffrage movement, Anthony asked her hand-picked biographer, Ida Husted Harper, to assist in editing the fourth volume of the *History*, picking up where the third volume had left off in 1883. Harper finished the *History* in two more volumes, ending with the passage of the woman suffrage amendment in 1920.

These last three volumes differ fundamentally from the first three. Essentially a bland chronicle of campaign and convention dates from the pen of a professional publicist, Harper's volumes served the needs of a conservative movement denying its radical origins. Her systematic exclusion of references to many important protests, major figures, fundamental theoretical differences, and nonsuffrage feminist organizations create a questionable historical source. Ironically, in her attempt to "clean up" the movement's history and make it respectable, Harper emphasized the work of Anthony and virtually eliminated the contributions of her coeditors Gage and, to a lesser extent, Stanton. *(See also: Anthony, Susan B.; Gage, Matilda Joslyn; Stanton, Elizabeth Cady; Suffrage)*

—Sally Roesch Wagner

Further Reading

Vols. 1 and 2 of *History of Woman Suffrage* (ed. Elizabeth C. Stanton, Matilda J. Gage, and Susan B. Anthony) were published in Rochester, NY in 1881; Vol. 3 in 1886. Susan B. Anthony and Ida Husted Harper published Vol. 4 in Rochester in 1902; Ida Husted Harper, Vols. 5 and 6 in New York in 1922. All six volumes of the *History* were reprinted by Arno and the New York Times Company in 1969.

Harper, Ida Husted. *Life and Work of Susan B. Anthony*, 3 vols. Indianapolis, IN: Bowen-Merrill, 1899, 1908.

Stanton, Theodore, and Harriot Stanton Blatch, eds. *Elizabeth Cady Stanton as Revealed in Her Letters, Diary, and Reminiscences*, 2 vols. New York: Harper, 1922.

Wagner, Sally Roesch, intro. *Woman, Church and State*, by Matilda Joslyn Gage. Chicago: Charles Kerr, 1893. Reprint, Watertown, MA: Persephone, 1980.

❧ Hobby, Oveta Culp (1905–1995)

In an era when most women would have settled for a pleasant life as a wife, mother, and social leader, Oveta Culp Hobby instead devoted her life to public service. In 1941, she responded patriotically to a request from the War Department to move to Washington, D.C., and to organize and run the Women's Interests Section of the Department's Bureau of Public Relations. In that position, she worked to bring about a women's corps of the Army as the United States prepared to enter World War II. After Congress approved the corps in May 1942, she was named to the position of director of the Women's Army Auxiliary Corps and given the title of colonel. During her three-year tenure, the corps received its highly prized full military status in 1943 and was renamed the Women's Army Corps (WAC). Poor health forced her to resign the post as director in 1945. On her departure, she was awarded the Distinguished Service Medal—one of the first women to receive this high military decoration.

She returned to Texas and, after regaining her health, became editor and president of the *Houston Post*. President Dwight D. Eisenhower appointed her (April 11, 1953) Secretary of the Department of Health, Education and Welfare. She was the only woman to serve in President Eisenhower's cabinet. In her new post, she expanded Social Security to

Security to farmers, domestic workers, and the self-employed and improved hospital construction. In 1955, she resigned because of her husband's declining health and returned to Houston.

Oveta Culp was born in Killeen, Texas, January 19, 1905. When her lawyer father was elected to the Texas State Legislature, she accompanied him to Austin as an assistant. Later, she spent a year at Mary Hardin Baylor College in Belton but left to work again beside her father. At the age of twenty-one, she was appointed Legislative Parliamentarian (1926–1931), the first woman to hold that position. In 1931, she married William P. Hobby, former governor of Texas and owner of the *Houston Post*. After her children were born (William Jr. in 1932 and Jessica in 1935), she worked on the newspaper as a writer, editor, and in executive positions. During her husband's illness, she became editor and publisher of the *Houston Post* and took over management of the family's radio and television stations and real estate holdings. Her husband died in 1964.

Throughout her life, Mrs. Hobby received many civic honors for service to her country, state, and city. Her sterling reputation as an active, influential, and highly respected public servant never diminished. She died at the age of 90 on August 16, 1995, at her home in Houston, Texas. *(See also: Journalism; Politics; Women's Army Auxiliary Corps; Women's Army Corps; World War II)*

—**Colonel (Ret.) Bettie J. Morden**

Further Reading

Culp, Oveta. *Mr. Chairman, Parliamentary Procedure for Children*. Oklahoma City: Economy Company, 1936.

Treadwell, Mattie E. *The Women's Army Corps, the United States Army in World War II*. Washington, DC: Department of the Army, 1954.

U.S. Department of Health, Education and Welfare. *A Common Thread of Service: An Historical Guide to HEW*. Washington, DC: Government Printing Office, 1973.

⮌ Hoffman, Malvina Cornell
(1887–1966)

Malvina Hoffman was one of the foremost American sculptors after World War I. Born in New York City, Hoffman attended the Brearley School for Girls as well as the Women's School of Applied Design before taking up sculpture under the tutelage of Herbert Adams, George Grey Barnard, and Gutzon Borglum. In 1910, she traveled to France with a letter of introduction to Auguste Rodin. When her efforts to meet the great sculptor were rebuffed, Hoffman literally camped outside the famous sculptor's door to obtain his attention and, ultimately, his support. It was, indeed, at Rodin's urging that Hoffman returned to the United States from 1911 to 1913 to undertake anatomy and dissection classes at Columbia (New York) College of Physicians and Surgeons. After her return to Paris, Hoffman enrolled at

Colarossi Academy, a private art school, and began once again to obtain weekly criticism of her work from Rodin.

Hoffman was acutely concerned that her technical training and skills had suffered because she was female. Accordingly, she devoted special attention to the fundamentals of sculptural technique, learning to build tools, chase and finish bronze, and accomplish various castings of her works. Hoffman worked in a variety of media, at first sculpting in plaster, then bronze, and then directly in stone. Hoffman's career in large part capitalized on a contemporary fascination with primitivism and anthropology as well as a growing demand from the newly famous for portrait busts. Hoffman's works include portrait busts of English poet John Keats and Polish pianist and statesman Ignace Paderewski, as well as intimate sculptural portrayals of famous ballet stars such as her close friend Anna Pavlova.

Hoffman is most remembered today for her series of 110 bronzes titled *The Races of Man,* on display in the Marshall Field Museum of Natural History, Chicago. Commissioned by the museum to identify and document the major ethnic types throughout the world, Hoffman, along with her husband, traveled the world for two years to locate and model identifiable racial types. In one of her two autobiographies, *Heads and Tales* (1936), Hoffman recounts her colorful experiences.

In 1964, Hoffman received the Gold Medal of Honor from the National Sculpture Society and five honorary degrees. In 1931, she had been made a full member of the National Academy of Design, followed in 1951 by her designation as Chevalier of the French Legion of Honor. She also wrote *Yesterday Is Tomorrow: A Personal History* (1965) and a textbook on sculpture titled *Sculpture Inside and Out* (1939). *(See also: Art)*

—**Anne deHayden Neal**

Further Reading

Armstrong, Tom et al. *200 Years of American Sculpture*. Exhibition catalog. New York: Whitney Museum of American Art, 1976.

Hoffman, M. *Heads and Tales*. New York: Scribner, 1936.

———. *Sculpture Inside and Out*. New York: Norton, 1939.

———. *Yesterday Is Tomorrow: A Personal History*. New York: Crown, 1965.

Rubenstein, Charlotte Streifer. *American Women Artists from Early Indian Times to the Present*. Boston: G. K. Hall, 1982.

Tufts, E. *American Women Artists: 1830–1930*. Exhibition catalog. Washington, DC: National Museum of Women in the Arts, 1987.

⮌ Hoisington, Elizabeth Paschel
(b. 1918)

Elizabeth Hoisington was the first woman to be promoted to brigadier general in the Women's Army Corps (1970) and one of the first two women to achieve general officer rank in any of the military services. (She and Anna Mae Hayes of the Army Nurse Corps were promoted in the same ceremony.)

As the daughter of a West Point graduate and career Army officer, Hoisington had little trouble convincing her parents that enlisting in the Women's Army Auxiliary Corps (WAAC) was the right thing for her. She was born November 3, 1918, in Newton, Kansas. Throughout her childhood, the family moved to posts in the United States and overseas. She graduated (June 1940) from the College of Notre Dame of Maryland in Baltimore. In November 1942, she enlisted in the WAAC (renamed the Women's Army Corps [WAC] in 1943). After several assignments as an enlisted woman, she attended WAC Officer Candidate School and received her commission in May 1943. She served in London, Paris, and Frankfurt during World War II. In 1948, she was executive officer in a WAC battalion in Tokyo (1949–1950). She commanded a WAC unit at Fort Monroe, Virginia (1950–1951), and was a personnel staff officer in the Office of the Director of the Women's Army Corps at the Pentagon (1951–1954). For the next 10 years, she held other staff officer positions. In 1964, she took command of the WAC Center and WAC School at Fort McClellan, Alabama, and in 1966, she was promoted to colonel and assigned as the director of the Women's Army Corps.

As director of the WAC throughout the difficult years of the Vietnam War, she increased the size of the corps by a third and opened many Army schools and jobs to WACs that had been closed to women. In 1967, after Congress removed career restrictions on women officers, she obtained promotions for key officers of her corps. In June 1970, she was promoted to the rank of brigadier general and continued to serve as director of the WAC for one more year. She received the Distinquished Service Medal on her retirement in July 1971. Her rise from private to general—the first in her corps—was a singular achievement in an era when women's leadership abilities were seldom recognized. She retired in Arlington, Virginia, where she continues to serve as a leader of women in her community. *(See also: Military Service; Vietnam War; Women's Army Corps)*

—**Colonel (Ret.) Bettie J. Morden**

Further Reading

Morden, Bettie J. *The Women's Army Corps, 1945–1978.* Washington, DC: Government Printing Office, 1990.

~ Holiday, Billie (Eleanora)
(1915–1959)

Billie Holiday was one of the greatest female vocalists in the history of jazz. Her particular talent was for finding emotional and melodic beauty in the second-rate material she often had to work with. Holiday helped revolutionize jazz singing by being the first singer to realize the microphone's potential for amplifying many vocal subtleties that had previously been inaudible on recordings or before a large audience. She made more than 350 records in her lifetime. Her supple, elegant voice and emotional reticence

Figure 25. Billie Holiday
Portrait of jazz vocalist Billie Holiday during her concert at Carnegie Hall. Used by permission of Florence and Carol Reiff/Corbis-Bettmann.

were best captured when recorded with a small jazz combo or a piano accompaniment.

Her childhood in Baltimore was difficult and violent. Forced to live for a time with her grandparents, she was physically abused and probably raped. In her early teens, she was arrested for prostitution. Holiday had a precocious talent, however, and her singing career advanced quickly.

In 1934, she teamed up with the great saxophonist Lester Young, whose highly original improvisational style influenced her tremendously. Their simultaneous improvising on songs such as "Me, Myself and I" and "A Sailboat in the Moonlight" rate among the finest jazz recordings of the 1930s. Because she refused to alter her unique vocal style, she was allowed to record only second-rate popular and jazz material throughout her early career. Yet she still managed to make brilliant records, especially with Teddy Wilson leading an orchestra composed of some of the leading jazz musicians of the day. In 1937, she performed with the Count Basie band, an all-black group. So as not to appear to be a white singer, Holiday was forced to darken her skin. The following year she toured with the all-white Artie Shaw band and was forced to use service elevators, stay in dingy hotels, and eat separately from the band. The tensions caused by racism were exacerbated by her tempestuous personality, alcoholism, and drug addiction.

Despite the increasing mental and physical troubles that eventually claimed her life at the age of forty-four, Holiday continued to make distinguished music throughout her career. In the 1950s, she toured Europe and the United States with her own orchestra, and she retained her magnetic powers, if not her magnificent voice. Although she never reached a wide audience, Holiday was and is respected by knowledgeable jazz fans and musicians for her spiritual powers of creativity and expression. *(See also: Black Women; Jazz; Music; Popular Vocalists)*

—**Richard Prouty**

Further Reading
Burnett, James. *Billie Holiday.* With selected discography by Tony Middleton. New York: Hippocrene, 1994.
Chilton, John. *Billie's Blues: Billie Holiday's Story, 1933–1959.* New York: Stein & Day, 1975.
Clarke, Donald. *Wishing on the Moon: The Life and Times of Billie Holiday.* New York: Viking, 1994.
O'Meally, Robert G. *Lady Day: The Many Faces of Billie Holiday.* New York: Arcades, 1991.

☙ Holzer, Jenny (b. 1950)

Jenny Holzer is a prominent American artist of the 1980s and 1990s, whose provocative language-based art expresses the diverse and contradictory concerns of contemporary society. Described by Michael Auping as the "cool Eighties executive of psychological inquiry," Holzer successfully trumps the exploitative strategies of modern advertising with socially relevant texts printed on items ranging from T-shirts, posters, and park benches to electronic signs programmed for LED (light-emitting diode) machines that confront the viewer at airports, ballparks, shopping malls, and other visual environments around the world.

Born in 1950 in Gallipolis, Ohio, Holzer attended college at Duke University in Durham, North Carolina, and after one year at the University of Chicago, she completed a degree in fine arts at Ohio University in Athens in 1972. She earned an M.F.A. at the Rhode Island School of Design in 1977 and was accepted into the Whitney Museum's Independent Study Program the same year. Confronted with an intimidating required reading list of classic texts at the Whitney, Holzer created one-line aphorisms to translate "all these great thoughts . . . into a language that was more accessible." This led to Holzer's artistic epiphany, her first series of art texts, the *Truisms* that appeared on posters around Manhattan. "ABUSE OF POWER SHOULD COME AS NO SURPRISE," "MURDER HAS ITS SEXUAL SIDE," and "PEOPLE WHO GO CRAZY ARE TOO SENSITIVE" are well-known examples.

Holzer discovered her signature medium, the electronic signboard, after the 1980 *Times Square Show* organized by the Collaborative Projects artists' group. Invited by the Public Art Fund to install her texts on the Spectracolor board in Times Square, Holzer has since mounted the *Truisms* in surprising contexts: "LACK OF CHARISMA CAN BE FATAL" and "MONEY CREATES TASTE" appeared outside Caesar's Palace in Las Vegas in 1986; "RAISE BOYS AND GIRLS THE SAME WAY" greeted crowds to San Francisco's Candlestick Park in 1987. Holzer's subsequent

text series, *Inflammatory Essays* (1979–1982), *Living* (1980–1982), and *Survival* (1983–1985), convey more urgent messages: "PROTECT ME FROM WHAT I WANT"; "WHAT COUNTRY SHOULD YOU ADOPT IF YOU HATE POOR PEOPLE?" Since the mid-1980s, Holzer's progressively more dramatic installations at New York galleries and museums have involved minimalist-inspired site-specific intentions, in which language and site enhance each other. These include *Under a Rock* at the Barbara Gladstone Gallery (1986); *Laments* at the Dia Art Foundation (1989); *Untitled (Selected Writings)* at the Solomon R. Guggenheim Museum (1989–1990); and *The Venice Installation* (1990), in which Holzer was selected to represent the United States at the internationally acclaimed Venice Biennale.

Holzer stands apart from other language-based artists with her populist approach to art. Whereas Joseph Kosuth and other conceptualists of the 1960s directed viewer response through esoteric word-image strategies, Holzer says she uses language to convey "thoughts and topics that polarize people" to stimulate a wide range of deeply felt personal responses. Mary Jane Jacob, chief curator at the Museum of Contemporary Art in Los Angeles, notes that Holzer's art "hits people deeply, which a lot of work doesn't" because of its humanistic orientation. Whereas much of contemporary art is pessimistic and confirms the emptiness of life, Holzer's "jars you and makes you think—and this gives you hope that emptiness can be overcome." *(See also: Art)*

—**Vivian Atwater**

Further Reading
Auping, Michael. *Jenny Holzer.* New York: Universe, 1992.
Howell, John. "The Message Is the Medium," *Art News* 87 (Summer 1988): 122-27.

☙ Home Economics

Home economics is the name given to an area of academic study that takes the family and problems of domestic life as its subject. Historically, the overwhelming preponderance of students in home economics courses has been women, and home economics has constituted an important aspect of women's education. Home economics educators often trace their lineage to Catharine Beecher, who first advocated making the family and domestic problems a focal point of study in women's education.

Home economics did not gain a distinctive identity as an academic discipline until the early twentieth century, however, when the American Home Economics Association was formed by a group of leading women scientists, scholars, and educators. With the rapid growth of high school enrollments in this period, home economics courses became a standard element of secondary school curricula across the country. At the same time, as larger numbers of women enrolled in colleges and universities, home economics became an important aspect of collegiate curricula as well. By 1919, when home economics was included in the battery of vocational subjects approved for federal support under the Smith-Hughes Act, it had become a central dimension of women's education in the United States, from elementary school through college.

The development of home economics as an established course of study in American schools and colleges was related to a host of developments in social and educational history. The first courses in sewing and cooking appeared in major public school systems as a part of the manual training movement in the latter nineteenth century. In the 1890s, an influential group of educators and scientists, most of them women, began to explore the possibility of defining an area of academic study with problems of families and the home as its focal point. Led by Ellen Richards, a chemist and the first female faculty member at the Massachusetts Institute of Technology, this movement took shape in a series of annual conferences in Lake Placid, New York, and led directly to the founding of the American Home Economics Association.

The rise of home economics was related to Progressive Era anxieties about the role of the family in the emerging urban-industrial society in turn-of-the-century America. Many educated, middle-class observers of American life felt that family life was threatened by the development of vast urban slums, by new patterns of female labor force participation, by child labor, by rising rates of divorce, and by other social problems. Educators and social reformers saw home economics as a means of helping young women to develop the skills and scientific knowledge necessary to cope with the complex problems they would face as homemakers in this new social environment. Home economics also provided career opportunities for thousands of women who were interested in studying these issues, particularly as they related to women. In this regard, the home economics movement also functioned as a very early precursor to women's studies, particularly in colleges and universities. *(See also: American Home Economics Association; Beecher, Catharine; Progressive Era; Smith-Hughes Act of 1917)*

—**John L. Rury**

Further Reading

Powers, Jane Bernard. *The "Girl Question" in Education: Vocational Training for Young Women in the Progressive Era.* London: Falmer, 1992.

Rury, John L. *Education and Women's Work: Female Schooling and the Division of Labor in Urban America, 1870–1930.* Albany: State University of New York Press, 1991.

Solomon, Barbara Miller. *In the Company of Educated Women: A History of Women and Higher Education in America.* New Haven, CT: Yale University Press, 1985.

ᴄᴧ Homemaker's Extension

Educating women to a better way of family living was the original purpose of county Homemaker's Extension clubs. During the 1920s and 1930s, homemaking clubs attained success because women wished to learn better and safer methods of preserving and canning food, cheaper sewing methods, and many more home economical measures. At one time, Homemaker's Extension clubs held the largest membership of any women's club in America. Yet each club became a part of a worldwide extension program. County extension agents, acting through the club, were the go-betweens from colleges to homebound women and among women themselves. Although methods and programs of homemaker's clubs have changed over the years, their purpose of strengthening the family and community life remains the same. Today's members are encouraged to develop skills to meet life's many challenges.

Throughout their history in different states and in different areas, Homemaker's Extension clubs have been known by various names, including Home Bureaus, Home Units, Home Economics clubs, and Home Demonstration clubs. Today, most organizations are called Family and Community Education clubs.

Cooperative extension work originated in 1862 when President Abraham Lincoln signed the Morrill Land Grant Act creating land grant colleges in each state. Land grant colleges taught agriculture and mechanical arts along with other subject matter. In 1914, the Smith-Lever Act provided money for states to establish extension work in agricultural education. However, it took a combination of several pieces of related legislation to initiate county extension service work. One facet of this extension work was conducting practical demonstrations in agriculture and home economics for people not attending college.

Homemaker's Extension clubs especially appealed to rural and small-town women. Urban women joined homemaker's organizations, but not at the same high rate that country women enrolled in club work. These clubs offered an opportunity for country women who were starved for socialization to meet and enjoy the company of their sisters. The Great Depression left many homemakers with no money to spend on themselves and a need to stretch precious few household dollars. A monthly club meeting of learning, gaiety, and joy made for a happier homemaker.

While county extension clubs taught women to improve living standards for their families immediately, they also fostered women's leadership skills. National and state programs encouraged women to lead in their extension groups, churches, and communities on local, state, and national levels. Leadership and education always were, and continue to be, the objective of county extension club work. *(See also: Depression Era; Home Economics; Morrill Land Grant Act; Smith-Lever Act of 1914)*

—**Mary E. Demeny**

Further Reading

Arnold, Eleanor, ed. *Voices of American Homemakers: An Oral History Project of the National Extension Homemakers Council.* Bloomington: Indiana University Press, 1993.

Chastain, Kay, ed. *The Messenger* [Emory, TX] 41 (1993).

⮬ Homeopathy

Homeopathy was one of the most popular of a profusion of medical sects founded in the mid-nineteenth century that offered an alternative to the "heroic" therapeutics of the so-called regular medical establishment. "Regular" physicians of the time employed purging, leeching, bloodletting, sweating, and surgery to effect dramatic changes in the patient's bodily state. The homeopathic maxim was "the less the better." Heavily diluted drugs, often served in sugar cubes, were prescribed on the principle that their curative power was enhanced by a reduction in quantity.

Women were attracted to many of the "irregular" sects, partly due to the less dangerous methods employed and partly to the more equal roles advocated for women in the healing professions. Homeopathic colleges were more willing to accept women students, and homeopathic hospitals were more willing to admit them to practice than were their orthodox competitors. Homeopathic treatment was especially popular among the middle- and upper-class women who were also the prime customers of "regular" physicians. Thus, homeopathy posed a significant threat to orthodox physicians' attempt to regularize and regulate the profession. Nonetheless, most homeopaths were not feminists per se, and leading male practitioners debated the propriety of coeducation and its potential effects on homeopathic medicine's status in the larger society.

Homeopathy, along with many other forms of nineteenth-century therapeutics, declined in the early twentieth century in the face of scientific medicine. In the late twentieth century, however, it has gained favor again among followers of alternative medicine, including many women, and has sparked new debates over the medical efficacy of homeopathy in the United States and abroad. *(See also: Water Cure)*

—**Nancy A. Hewitt**

Further Reading

Barlow, William, and David O. Powell. "Homeopathy and Sexual Equality: The Controversy over Coeducation at Cincinnati's Pulte Medical College, 1873–1879." In *Women and Health in America,* edited by Judith Walzer Leavitt, 422-28. Madison: University of Wisconsin Press, 1984.
Danciger, Elizabeth. *Homeopathy: From Alchemy to Medicine.* New York: Harper & Row, 1988.
Lockie, Andrew, and Nicola Geddes. *The Complete Guide to Homeopathy.* Boston: Houghton Mifflin, 1995.
Stehlin, Isadora. *Homeopathy, Real Medicine or Empty Promises?* Rockville, MD: U.S. Department of Health and Human Services, 1997.

⮬ Homophobia

Homophobia is the irrational fear of homosexuality that results in hatred, fear, and prejudice directed toward lesbians and gay men. Since 1973 homosexuality has not been seen as a deviant behavior by the American Psychiatric Association; however, many otherwise liberal and tolerant people suffer from homophobia, displaying behaviors ranging from open derision toward gays to discomfort at being associated with them. Extreme forms of homophobia are sometimes thought to stem from latent homosexuality in a person who cannot consciously accept being identified with gays. All homophobia is ultimately the fear of loving one's own sex and hating those who do.

The United States is a very homophobic society. One common but mistaken (and arrogant) assumption is the paranoid belief that all homosexuals want to sleep with heterosexuals in the hope of turning them into homosexuals. Functionally, a person is homophobic if he or she

- thinks of all touching and affection by a lesbian friend as a sexual advance,
- thinks that a lesbian is just a woman who couldn't find a man,
- feels repulsed by displays of affection between homosexuals that would be endearing in heterosexuals,
- fails to be supportive when a gay friend is upset about a quarrel or breakup.

Homophobia has many negative effects on lesbian women's lives. Because marriage between lesbians is not legally recognized, there are no spousal rights for partners in long-term, permanent relationships (i.e., insurance benefits, next-of-kin hospital visits, Social Security benefits). There is often little recognition by heterosexual friends of the relationship in social situations, such as inquiry about the partner's health or work or including both women in "couples" functions. Perhaps the most devastating result of homophobia is that the word *lesbian* is often seen as negative and accusatory. It becomes a threat that can be used against someone, a way to divide women, ensuring against their independence from men and their solidarity with one another. *(See also: Heterosexism; Lesbianism)*

—**Susan Lee Weeks**

Further Reading

Berube, Allan. *Coming Out Under Fire: A History of Gay Men and Women in World War II.* New York: Free Press, 1990.
Blumenfeld, Warren J. *Homophobia: How We All Pay the Price.* Boston: Beacon, 1993.
Bunch, Charlotte. *Passionate Politics: Feminist Theory in Action, Essays 1968–1986.* New York: St. Martin's, 1987.
Burch, Beverly. *Other Women: Lesbian/Bisexual Experience and Psychoanalytic Views of Women.* New York: Columbia University Press, 1997.
Dworkin, Andrea. *Letters from a War Zone: Writings 1976–1987.* London: Secker & Wachburg, 1988.
Lorde, Audre. *The Black Unicorn.* New York: Norton, 1978.
Nestle, Joan. *A Fragile Union: New and Selected Writings.* San Francisco: Cleis, 1998.

❧ Hope, Lugenia Burns (1871–1947)

Community organizer and proponent of racial justice Lugenia Hope was a leader in the fight to expose discrimination among women's social reform groups that sprang from the Progressive Movement. Born the last of seven children to Louisa and Ferdinand Burns in Mississippi in 1871, she moved with her family to Chicago following her father's death. As the first and only black member of the Cook County board of King's Daughters, Hope became acquainted with intellectuals from the University of Chicago, worked with Jane Addams, and met black intellectuals such as Paul Laurence Dunbar. At the Chicago Columbian Exposition in 1893, her beauty led to the title of "Genie with the light brown hair." She met John Hope, a theological student at Brown University and a person with whom she could share similar interests in urban reform. They married in 1897 and moved to Nashville, where he taught at Roger Williams University. They became friends with the families of nationally known black business and education leaders, such as John Napier and W. E. B. Du Bois.

Her husband's career in education brought the young couple in 1898 to Atlanta Baptist College (later renamed Morehouse College), where she raised their two sons, Edward Swain and John Jr. She organized the Atlanta Neighborhood Union in 1908. Under the motto "And Thy Neighbor as Thyself," the black women of the community developed lecture courses, fresh-air work, clean-up campaigns, probation and employment services, reading rooms, clubs, classes, and health and recreation campaigns. Applying the techniques of scientific reform, they conducted methodical investigations of schools, sanitation, and vice to improve community life and stimulate community responsibility. In cooperation with professionals in the sociology department at Morehouse College, Hope improved the efficiency and efficacy of black social work by dividing areas into zones, districts, and neighborhoods to determine objective needs of each section. The techniques developed through the Atlanta Neighborhood Union influenced other communities through Hope's position as the director of neighborhood work in the National Association of Colored Women. As an affiliate of the National Urban League, the Neighborhood Union became the model for urban reform recommended by the league.

Hope did not limit her activities to the Atlanta community. During World War I, she served as the director of Hostess House, sponsored by the Young Women's Christian Association (YWCA), at Camp Upton in New York. She hoped that the efforts of blacks during World War I merited improved conditions in postwar America. When worsening race relations followed the war, Hope was instrumental in organizing black women to pressure the YWCA to become more interracial in its policies and leadership and in bringing black women into the interracial antilynching movement through an alliance with Southern Methodist women and the Association of Southern Women for the Prevention of Lynching. After the Neighborhood Union became part of the Community Chest, she served as the first vice president of the Atlanta branch of the NAACP, working to create citizenship schools to increase voting in the black community, strategies that came to fruition during the civil rights movement in the 1950s and 1960s.

Hope survived her husband (d. 1936) by almost a decade. She moved to New York, Chicago, and then to Nashville in the years following his death. Her direct style of social activism ended with her death on August 14, 1947. *(See also: Black Women; National Association of Colored Women; Voluntarism)*

—Dorothy C. Salem

Further Reading
Much of the information about Hope can be found in the Neighborhood Union Papers, Woodruff Library, Atlanta University Center.

Chivers, Walter. "Neighborhood Union: An Effort of Community Organization," *Opportunity* 3 (June 1925): 178-79.

Hall, Jacqueline Dowd. "Revolt against Chivalry: Jessie Daniel Ames and the Women's Campaign against Lynching." Ph.D. diss., Columbia University, 1974.

Johnson, Georgia D. "Frederick Douglass and Paul Laurence Dunbar at the World's Fair," *National Notes* 49 (January-February 1947): 10, 29.

Rouse, Jacqueline. *Lugenia Burns Hope: Black Southern Reformer.* Athens: University of Georgia Press, 1989.

❧ Hopkins, Sarah Winnemucca (1844?–1891)

Sarah Winnemucca Hopkins (also known as Thocmetony, Tos-Me-To-Ne, Shell Flower, Sonometa, Somitone, Sa-Mit-Tau-Nee, White Shell) was born near Humboldt Sink in Nevada, the daughter of Paiute Chief Winnemucca and the granddaughter of Chief Truckee. In the spring of 1847, she went with her family to California. For three years, she attended a Catholic convent school in San Jose, where she gained the speaking and writing skills she used as an interpreter at Camp McDermitt in northern Nevada close to the Oregon border and later at the Malheur Agency, headquarters for the Malheur reservation in Oregon. She was also the personal interpreter and guide for General Oliver O. Howard in the battle against the Bannocks in 1878.

Although Hopkins viewed her mission as a lifelong crusade for justice for her people, she was often duped by the very people she beseeched her people to trust. The Nevada Paiutes were sent to the Yakima Reservation in Washington Territory, and Hopkins's autobiography ends with a plea to readers to urge Congress to restore her people to their land. In 1883, she went East and became the protégée of Elizabeth Palmer Peabody and her sister Mary (Mrs. Horace) Mann. Hopkins was controversial because she had friends among the whites and at times appeared to be contradicting the

Indians' interests, but she always believed she was doing what was best for her people.

She spoke English, Spanish, and three Indian dialects. Her real history is in the legacy she left the Paiute people. Although she failed to restore rights to her people, she left them with an example of how to fight. Since her time, the Paiutes have augmented their reservation by recovering land lost in the 1860s and have won a court order to preserve Pyramid Lake, Nevada. *(See also: Native American Women)*

—Gretchen M. Bataille

Further Reading

Brimlow, George. "The Life of Sarah Winnemucca: The Formative Years," *Oregon Historical Quarterly* 53 (June 1952): 103-34.

Canfield, Gae Whitney. *Sarah Winnemucca of the Northern Paiutes*. Norman: University of Oklahoma Press, 1983.

Gehm, Katherine. *Sarah Winnemucca*. Phoenix, AZ: O'Sullivan, Woodside, 1975.

Hopkins, Sarah Winnemucca. *Life among the Paiutes: Their Wrongs and Claims*. Edited by Mrs. Horace Mann. Boston: Putnam's, 1883.

———. "The Pah-Utes," *The Californian, A Western Monthly Magazine* 6 (1882): 252.

Morrison, Dorothy Nafus. *Chief Sarah: Sarah Winnemucca's Fight for Indian Rights*. New York: Atheneum, 1980.

Ruoff, A. LaVonne Brown. "American Indian Authors, 1774–1899." In *Critical Essays on Native American Literature*, edited by Andrew Wiget, 191-201. Boston: G. K. Hall, 1985.

———. "Nineteenth-Century American Indian Autobiographers: William Apes, George Copway and Sarah Winnemucca." In *Redefining American Literary History*, edited by A. LaVonne Brown Ruoff and Jerry W. Ward, 251-69. New York: Modern Language Association, 1990.

Sands, Kathleen Mullen. "Indian Women's Personal Narratives: Voices Past and Present." In *Fea(s)ts of Memory*, edited by Margo Culley, 268-94. Madison: University of Wisconsin Press, 1991.

Scordato, Ellen. *Sarah Winnemucca: Northern Paiute Writer and Diplomat*. New York: Chelsa House, 1992.

Stewart, Patricia. "Sarah Winnemucca," *Nevada Historical Society Quarterly* 14 (Winter 1971): 23-38.

⨀ Hopper, Admiral Grace Murray
(1906–1992)

Grace Hopper was the most prominent woman computer scientist active in the early days of computing. She worked with the first large-scale U.S. computer, the Harvard Mark I, and is best known for her influence on the development of the programming language Cobol.

Hopper received her B.A. in mathematics and physics from Vassar (1928) and a Ph.D. in mathematics from Yale (1934). After teaching at Vassar for ten years, she served for forty-two years in the U.S. Navy. She strongly promoted the use of computers and developed many military and commercial applications. After retiring from the military, Hopper served as a consultant for the Digital Equipment Corporation.

Figure 26. Grace Murray Hopper
Captain Grace Murray Hopper, whose first love was the Navy, photographed in 1975 in her Navy uniform. Used by permission of UPI/Corbis-Bettmann.

Hopper's lifelong interest in encouraging young computer scientists was memorialized by the creation of the Grace Hopper Award in 1971. This award, sponsored by Univac, a division of Sperry Rand Corporation, is presented each year to computer scientists who have made outstanding contributions before the age of thirty. *(See also: Mathematics; Military Service; Science)*

—Jonell Duda Comerford

Further Reading

Leopold, George. "Beacon for the Future," *Datamation* 32 (1986): 109-10.

Sammet, Jean E. "Farewell to Grace Hopper—End of an Era!" *Communications of the ACM* 30 (October 1987): 815-28.

Zientara, Marguerite. *Women, Technology, and Power.* New York: AMACOM, 1987.

⨀ Horney, Karen (1885–1952)

Psychoanalyst and pioneer in the psychology of women, Karen Horney was born in Hamburg, Germany. She completed her M.D. in 1913 at the University of Berlin. From 1914 to 1918, Horney underwent psychoanalytic training at the Berlin Psychoanalytic Institute. She began private practice in 1919 while serving as a faculty member at the Berlin Institute. Horney immigrated to the United States in 1932 as an associate director of the Chicago Institute for Psychoanalysis. Two years later, she returned to private practice and took a teaching position at the New York Psychoanalytic Institute, which she found excessively Freudian.

Dr. Horney soon broke with the New York Institute and founded the American Institute of Psychoanalysis, which she headed until her death in 1952. While accepting certain aspects of Freud's teaching, she challenged his bias against women and stressed the social rather than the biological determinants of sex differences and "feminine psychology." She discussed this as "status envy" rather than "penis envy." She promulgated these viewpoints in a widely read series of books, including *The Neurotic Personality of Our Time* (1937), *New Ways in Psychoanalysis* (1939), and *Our Inner Conflicts: A Constructive Theory of Neurosis* (1945). Horney went beyond Freud in arguing that the neurotic's basic conflicts are neither innate nor inevitable but arise out of undesirable social situations in childhood and can be prevented. *(See also: Freudianism; Psychiatry; Psychology)*

—**Jonathan W. Zophy**

Further Reading

Horney, Karen. *The Neurotic Personality of Our Time*. New York: Norton, 1937.

———. *New Ways in Psychoanalysis*. New York: Norton, 1939.

———. *Our Inner Conflicts*. New York: Norton, 1945.

Schultz, Duane. *A History of Modern Psychology*. New York: Academic Press, 1975.

Figure 27. Harriet Hosmer
Harriet Hosmer was rare among women sculptors of her time, supporting herself entirely through her art. Used by permission of Corbis-Bettmann.

ᴥ Hosmer, Harriet Goodhue
(1830–1908)

Harriet Hosmer was the first internationally renowned American woman sculptor. Born in Watertown, Massachusetts, she was educated by her physician father; the results of this permissive upbringing with its emphasis on an outdoor life were later balanced at Mrs. Charles Sedgwick's school, where she was also encouraged to develop her interests in sculpting and mechanics. Hosmer also became closely acquainted there with Fanny Kemble, an English actress who would foster Hosmer's career. There were few opportunities to study art in the United States during this period, even fewer for women. Hosmer received technical lessons from Paul Stephenson, after Cornelia Crow and her father, Wayman, arranged for Hosmer to study anatomy in St. Louis, Missouri, with Dr. J. N. McDowell. Hosmer defied Victorian expectations for women by traveling first to St. Louis and, after studying there, then down and up the Mississippi, instead of marrying.

In 1852, Hosmer traveled to Rome (at first accompanied by actress Charlotte Cushman, who recognized and encouraged Hosmer's talent, although she would later travel throughout Europe and between continental Europe, England, and the United States frequently unaccompanied) in search of a teacher. John Gibson, the famous English neoclassical sculptor, took her as his student. Unique as an individual and as an artist, Hosmer quickly gained fame as a sculptress and a presence. Her first commissions date back to 1855. By the end of the Civil War, Hosmer had attained international recognition and completed some of her most important works. Neoclassicism was, however, being replaced by realism, and Hosmer's commissions became fewer. While her base moved from Rome to England, she remained in Europe until around 1900, when she returned to Watertown and her scientific experiments.

Harriet Hosmer remains important today as one of the foremost American neoclassical sculptors; she also designed fountains and gates (mainly for English estates), carried out mechanical experiments, and is renowned for her friendships, especially among women. Her most important statues include *Puck* (1856), *Beatrice Cenci* (1857), and *Zenobia in Chains* (1859). *(See also: Art; Kemble, Fanny)*

—**Maureen R. Liston**

Further Reading

Gerdts, William H. *The White Marmorean Flock: Nineteenth Century American Women Neoclassical Sculptors*. Exhibition catalog. Poughkeepsie, NY: Vassar College Art Gallery, 1972.

Hosmer, Harriet. *Letters and Memories.* Edited by Cornelia Carr. New York: Moffat, Yard, 1912.

Leach, Joseph. *Bright Particular Star: The Life and Times of Charlotte Cushman.* New Haven, CT: Yale University Press, 1970.

Sherwood, Dolly. *Harriet Hosmer, American Sculptor, 1830–1908.* Columbia: University of Missouri Press, 1991.

Thorp, Margaret Farrand. "The White, Marmorean Flock," *New England Quarterly* 32 (June 1959): 147-69.

Housework

Women's unpaid service to the family household represents the fundamental sexual division of labor. The ways in which women cook, clean, launder, and perform a multitude of tasks for their homes sheds light on both the level of technology and the status of women in any culture or era. In the preindustrial period, ending at about the turn of the nineteenth century, housework, although considered "women's work," was done by all household members, including husband and children. Simplicity of life and scarcity of resources made the care of the home only one aspect of a woman's activities; many housework chores, such as the large-scale food preparation of canning or collective spinning and cloth production, were performed by groups of women together. Preindustrial housework was not only arduous but dangerous: for example, to do the laundry, women were exposed to the harmful effects of lye soap and had to lift heavy sodden clothing; many housewives' skirts caught fire as they cooked at the hearth.

With industrialization, housework became the wife's province alone. The husband's duties shifted exclusively to the outside world of work, while children spent longer amounts of time in school, which changed the nature of the home itself. Moreover, women's housework played a hidden role in the economics of industrialization since their unpaid labor subsidized the paid labor of employed men and women. Coupled with urbanization, technological innovations in the form of cast-iron stoves, manufactured cloth, commercially prepared flour, and municipal water altered the housewife's basic tasks, making housework the private enterprise of each woman working alone in her home. As housework became a woman's major responsibility, writers such as Catharine Beecher produced a voluminous literature promoting the cult of domesticity not only to help women learn how to do housework but to celebrate the joys of caring for a home, as well as to raise the esteem of woman in her divinely ordained sphere. By the end of the nineteenth century, secondary schools and women's institutions of higher education included home economics in their curricula to train women in standardized housework skills, to establish that housework now constituted a professional vocation even if it continued to be unpaid when performed by women within their families.

By the twentieth century, housework shifted from an emphasis on production to consumption. As the size of the middle-class household and family decreased, the number of mechanical and electric devices for the home—refrigerator, vacuum cleaner, washing machine, dishwasher—compensated for the loss of domestic servants and actually raised the standard of cleanliness. Goods that during the previous century had been made in the home were now mass produced in factories, thus requiring the housewife to assume responsibility for purchasing these goods for the family's consumption. The invention of the automobile and increased suburbanization added the duties of chauffeuring of the children as well as traveling some distances to stores, thereby expanding the physical boundaries within which the housewife performed her increased role. By the 1950s, housework included the social and psychological services required to rear achieving and well-adjusted children as well as to maintain a well-stocked, harmonious, spotless, and comfortable home. Housework issues facing women in the new millenium involve envisioning economic models that include domestic labor in the economy of the paid workforce and will require extensive scrutiny of the worth and value systems underlying our culture. *(See also: Beecher, Catharine; Consumerism; Home Economics; Industrial Revolution; Sexual Division of Labor; Women's Work: Nineteenth Century)*

—**Hasia R. Diner**

Further Reading

Boydston, Jeanne. *Home and Work: Housework, Wages, and the Ideology of Labor in the Early Republic.* New York: Oxford University Press, 1990.

Cowan, Ruth Schwartz. *More Work for Mother: The Ironies of Household Technology from the Open Hearth to the Microwave.* New York: Basic, 1983.

Davison, Jane. *To Make a House a Home: Four Generations of American Women and the Houses They Lived In.* New York: Random House, 1994.

Matthews, Glenna. *"Just a Housewife": The Rise and Fall of Domesticity in America.* New York: Oxford University Press, 1987.

Oakley, Ann. *Women's Work: The Housewife Past and Present.* New York: Pantheon, 1974.

Ogden, Annegret S. *The Great American Housewife: From Helpmate to Wage Earner, 1776–1986.* Westport, CT: Greenwood, 1986.

Palmer, Phyllis M. *Domesticity and Dirt: Housewives and Domestic Servants in the United States, 1920–1945.* Philadelphia: Temple University Press, 1989.

Sklar, Katharine Kish. *Catharine Beecher: A Study in American Domesticity.* New Haven, CT: Yale University Press, 1973.

Strasser, Susan. *Never Done: A History of American Housework.* New York: Pantheon, 1982.

Howe, Julia Ward (1819–1910)

Julia Ward Howe was born in New York City to Samuel Ward, a prosperous banker, and Julia Cutler Ward, a poet. Howe's mother died when she was five, and she was raised by governesses and educated in private schools. In 1843, she married Samuel Gridley Howe, a well-known social activist and the founder of the first American school for the blind. Together, the Howes edited the abolitionist newspaper *The Commonwealth.*

Howe began writing unsuccessful plays: *Hippolytus* was never produced, and *The World's Own* (1857) was a dismal failure. She had more success as a poet, producing three volumes of verse: *Passion Flowers* (1854), *Words for the Hour* (1857), and *Later Lyrics* (1865).

In 1861, following the Battle of Bull Run, the Howes accompanied a group to Washington, D.C., to observe conditions and morale among soldiers in the Union Army. On November 18, the Howes attended a grand review, which was cut short by attacking Confederate troops. On the way back to their hotel, the group, which included Massachusetts governor John Andrew and James Freeman Clarke, began singing "John Brown's Body," and the soldiers along the road joined in. The next morning, inspired by the song's haunting melody, Julia Ward Howe wrote "The Battle Hymn of the Republic." The poem was published in *Atlantic Monthly* in February 1862, and Howe received five dollars for it. The poem became extremely popular, and people began singing it at public events. On the basis of "The Battle Hymn of the Republic," Howe became the first woman inducted into the American Academy of Arts and Letters.

After the emancipation of the slaves in 1865, Julia Ward Howe was active in the campaigns for women's rights, prison reform, international relations, and sex education. She supported ratification of the Fourteenth Amendment and cofounded the New England Women's Club in 1868. A leader of the more conservative American Woman Suffrage Association, which she helped found in 1869, Howe approved its merger with the National Woman Suffrage Association in 1890. She died in 1910. *(See also: Abolition and the Antislavery Movement; American Woman Suffrage Association; Civil War)*

—**Rose Kolbasnik Callahan**

Further Reading

Clifford, Deborah Pickman. *Mine Eyes Have Seen the Glory.* Boston: Little, Brown, 1978.

Howe, Julia Ward. *Reminiscences, 1819–1899.* Boston: Houghton Mifflin, 1899.

⟡ Hoxie, Vinnie (Ream) (1847–1914)

Sculptor Vinnie Ream Hoxie was the first woman artist awarded a U.S. government commission. Born in Madison, Wisconsin, Hoxie later moved to Washington, D.C., with her family, where she worked as a U.S. postal clerk. Through the intervention of several government officials who were also family friends, she began to pursue her interest in sculpture and obtained access to President Abraham Lincoln for daily sittings in 1864. Because of these sittings, Hoxie was one of the last persons to see the president alive. After Lincoln's assassination, she was selected from a group of nineteen competitors to create a commemorative statue of the president to stand in the Capitol Rotunda.

Hoxie's struggle to win the Lincoln commission typifies the career difficulties of many women artists in nineteenth-century America. Award of the $10,000 commission to eighteen-year-old Hoxie created a major uproar in the nation's capital. Mary Todd Lincoln publicly disavowed the young sculptor, and abolitionist Charles Sumner strongly criticized Hoxie's selection on the grounds that she was too inexperienced to create a statue suitable for the nation's capitol. Many other contemporaries, both male and female, condemned her selection as masterminded by "feminine wiles." Despite opposition, she completed the greater-than-life-size statue of Lincoln in 1871.

During this same period, Hoxie did a series of portrait busts, as well as a variety of neoclassical pieces, many of which are lost today. Several of these works were exhibited at the Philadelphia Centennial Exposition of 1876. In 1875, Hoxie was awarded a $20,000 commission to prepare a full-size bronze of Admiral David G. Farragut from the bronze propeller retrieved from Farragut's flagship.

In 1878, she married then-Lieutenant Richard Leveridge Hoxie. At the apparent urging of her husband, she virtually abandoned sculpture in favor of charitable work and became a well-known hostess. She lived on K Street, overlooking Farragut Square, within view of her own sculpture. Later in life, however, already stricken by a fatal kidney ailment, Hoxie recommenced sculptural activity, completing a full-size statue of Governor Samuel Kirkwood of Iowa for the Capitol and commencing a statue of Sequoya for the state of Oklahoma.

Hoxie is buried in Arlington Cemetery, Arlington, Virginia, where a bronze replica of her neoclassical sculpture *Sappho* stands over her grave. *(See also: Art)*

—**Anne deHayden Neal**

Further Reading

Becker, Carolyn Berry. "Vinnie Ream: Portrait of a Young Sculptor," *Feminist Art Journal* 5 (Fall 1976): 29-31.

Gerdts, William H., Jr. *The White Marmorean Flock: Nineteenth Century American Women Neoclassical Sculptors.* Exhibition catalog. Poughkeepsie, NY: Vassar College Art Gallery, 1972.

Peterson, Karen, and J. J. Wilson. *Women Artists: Recognition and Reappraisal from the Early Middle Ages to the Twentieth Century.* London: Women's Press, 1976.

⟡ Huerta, Dolores (b. 1930)

Dolores Huerta was a labor organizer, lobbyist, chief negotiator, and vice president (1970–1973) for the United Farm Workers (UFW). She was the second child of Alicia and Juan Fernandez, migrant farmworkers. The family settled in Stockton, California, in the 1930s, and there, she graduated from high school in 1947. Later, she attended Stockton Junior College and received an Associate of Arts degree. In 1950, she married Ralph Head, a high school friend. The couple had two children.

Citing cultural and religious differences, the couple divorced in 1953. Huerta then returned to school to pursue her teaching certification at Stockton State College. There, she renewed a friendship with Ventura Huerta, a

Figure 28. Dolores Huerta
Dolores Huerta in prayer for César Chávez at a Mass outside the Monterey, California, County Jail. Chávez was in jail for violating a court injunction prohibiting a lettuce boycott. Used by permission of UPI/Corbis-Bettmann.

young ex-marine she met at a local Hispanic organization. She married him in 1955, and they had five children. During this eight-year marriage, Huerta worked at several clerical jobs, taught school, and joined the Community Service Organization (CSO), an association that sought to increase civic participation in the Spanish-speaking community through registering Hispanic voters and teaching citizenship and naturalization classes.

In 1958, Huerta began to work with the Agricultural Workers Association (AWA), a group of socially conscious citizens dedicated to helping local farmworkers. The next year, the AFL-CIO launched a major effort to organize farmworkers in the Stockton area and hired Huerta as part of the administrative staff. Huerta gained political contacts and valuable experience through this position. In 1959, she returned to the CSO as a paid staff member responsible to the general director of the organization, César Chávez. Huerta worked for the CSO primarily as a legislative representative promoting the interests of workers before the legislature and various state agencies. This position provided considerable exposure, and she received invitations to attend meetings on poverty in Washington, D.C., and an appointment to an AFL-CIO advisory committee.

In 1962, she was cofounder with César Chávez of the Farm Workers Association (FWA), a precursor to the UFW. The goal of the FWA was to improve the economic circumstances of seasonal, migrant workers who traveled and worked in family groups. Huerta researched, designed, and administered many FWA programs, including the death benefit policy, the credit union, and a workers cooperative.

In 1963, Huerta divorced her second husband. The following year, César Chávez convinced her to move to Delano in the San Joaquin Valley to recruit new members to the FWA. In 1966, the FWA became the UFW, and Huerta plunged into every facet of the union—picketing, organizing, traveling, and speaking on behalf of the union. She recruited many dedicated supporters and generated much-needed funds for the union.

Huerta established the UFW's negotiations department, and for several years, she served as the lead negotiator. During her administration, agricultural wages increased, working conditions improved, and benefits expanded. She was known for unusual and unconventional negotiation techniques, such as inviting Teatro Campesino, a pro-farm worker theater group, to perform a skit critical of labor contractors as part of the UFW position in negotiations with the DiGiorgio Fruit Corporation.

Throughout her career, Huerta challenged the conventional restraints placed on women and has become an admired cultural heroine and role model for Chicanas. Huerta's dedication to the UFW has caused her to be arrested over twenty times and injured during some demonstrations. In 1988, she was clubbed by a San Francisco police officer during a demonstration and underwent emergency surgery. After a lengthy recuperation, she gradually returned to the UFW in 1990.

Today, she is married to Richard Chávez, César Chávez's brother. Respecting the tenets of the Roman Catholic Church, she is opposed to birth control and is the mother of eleven children. She currently works out of the UFW headquarters in La Paz, California. *(See also:* Chicana, *United Farm Workers)*

—**Joyce Ann Kievit**

Further Reading

Chavez, Henri. "Unsung Heroine of La Causa," *Regeneracioón 1* (1971): 20-25.

Coburn, Judith. "Dolores Huerta: La Paionaria of the Farmworkers," *Ms. 5* (November 1976): 11-16.

Echaveste, Beatrice, and Dolores Huerta. "In the Shadow of the Eagle: Huerta = A la sombra del aguila: Huerta," *Americas 2001 1* (November-December 1987): 26-30.

Huerta, Dolores. "Dolores Huerta: Un soldado [sic] del movimiento." In *With These Hands: Women Working on the Land,* edited by Joan M. Jensen, 215-20. New York: McGraw-Hill, 1981.

———. "Dolores Huerta Talks about Republicans, César, Children, and Her Home Town." *Regeneración 2* (1975): 20-24.

———. "Reflexions on the UFW Experience," *Center Magazine 18* (July-August 1985): 2-8.

Mercado, Olivia. "Chicanas, Myths and Roles," *Comadre* 1 (Summer 1977): 26-32.

Rose, Margaret Eleanor. "Traditional and Non-traditional Patterns of Female Activism in the United Farm Workers of America, 1962–1980," *Frontiers: A Journal of Women's Studies* 11 (1990): 26-32.

———. "Women in the United Farm Workers: A study of Chicana and Mexicana Participation in a Labor Union, 1950–1980." Ph.D. diss., University of California, Los Angeles, 1988.

Valdez, Luis. "Tribute: Dolores Huerta," *Image* 12 (August 1990): 8-11.

http://latino.sscnet.ucla.edu/women/Huerta/readings.html [Bibliography of readings]

~ Hughan, Jessie Wallace (1875–1955)

Jessie Hughan, pacifist proponent of nonviolent resistance, Fabian socialist, and feminist, was born in Brooklyn, New York, of parents who were prominent citizens of their community and devoted "single taxers," followers of Henry George. Hughan attended Northfield Seminary in Northfield, Massachusetts, the school founded by Dwight L. Moody and famous as one of the first girls' boarding schools in the country. She received her B.A. from Barnard College in 1898 and earned an M.A. and Ph.D. at Columbia University.

While researching her dissertation on American socialism (published in 1911 as *American Socialism of the Present Day*), Hughan became a Socialist herself. As an active Socialist before and during World War I, she was barred from university teaching and became instead a New York public school teacher and administrator. Hughan was an absolute pacifist by 1914. Acting on her principles, she became a charter member of the Christian pacifist Fellowship of Reconciliation (FOR), served on the executive committee of the New York City branch of the Woman's Peace Party, and organized the Anti-Enlistment League (1915–1917) to enroll men and women who opposed enlistment in or support of any international war. During this period, Hughan also worked for woman suffrage under the aegis of the Woman Suffrage Party and ran on the Socialist Party ticket for the offices of lieutenant governor, congresswoman, and U.S. senator (New York State).

After the war, with the cooperation of FOR, the Women's Peace Society (in which she was active), and the Women's Peace Union, she founded the War Resisters League (WRL), which had as its object the enrollment of women and men "who for any reason whatsoever are uncompromisingly opposed to all war" and "have determined to give no support to any war." In the 1920s, Hughan, as executive secretary, worked hard to build up the league and in the 1930s contributed significantly to the success of a number of no-more-war parades. During World War II, Hughan and the WRL supported all conscientious objectors, including those who accepted alternative civilian service. The WRL helped to ensure that by 1942 men serving in Civilian Public Service Camps were paid a nominal amount for their work and were permitted to choose between service in private, church-administered camps or government camps.

Hughan wrote extensively on pacifism, socialism, and world government, both as a scholar and theorist and as a poet. In addition to her published Ph.D. dissertation, her books and pamphlets include *The Facts of Socialism* (1913), *A Study of International Government* (1923), *The Challenge of Mars and Other Verse* (1932), *The Beginnings of War Resistance* (1935), and *Pacifism and Invasion* (1941). Her writings on organized war resistance and nonviolent national defense constitute important contributions to pacifist theory. (*See also: Pacifism and the Peace Movement; Socialism; Woman's Peace Party*)

—**Frances H. Early**

Further Reading

Early, Frances H. "Revolutionary Pacifism and War Resistance: Jessie Wallace Hughan's 'War against War,'" *Peace and Change* 20 (July 1995): 307-28.

Hughan, Jessie Wallace. *American Socialism of the Present Day.* New York: Lane, 1911.

———. *The Beginnings of War Resistance.* New York: City Resisters League, 1935.

———. *The Challenge of Mars and Other Verse.* New York: Correlated Graphic Industries, 1932.

———. *The Facts of Socialism.* New York: Lane, 1913.

———. *Pacifism and Invasion.* New York: War Resisters League, 1942.

———. *A Study of International Government.* New York: Crowell, 1923.

The papers of Jessie Wallace Hughan. Swarthmore College Peace Collection, Swarthmore, PA.

~ Hull House

Hull House was the third settlement house to be established in America. The original residence, on Halsted Street in Chicago, was constructed in 1856 for Charles J. Hull, a philanthropist and realtor. When first built, it was situated in a rural area. By the time it opened as a settlement house, the city had grown so much that it sat in a poor, multiethnic community on the southwest side of Chicago.

Jane Addams, together with Ellen Gates Starr, created and founded Hull House, which they moved into on September 18, 1889. Although Addams assumed the leadership position, she could not have done her part without support from a cadre of other women who not only influenced Hull House but went on to make their own contributions to society. Among these women were Julia Lathrop, Florence Kelley, Grace and Edith Abbott, Sophonisba Breckinridge, and Alice Hamilton, who contributed to the founding of social work as a profession. Mary Smith was a friend and financial backer. Helen Culver, who was Charles Hull's heir, eventually gave the property to Addams. There were many male residents, visitors, and supporters, including intellectuals such as educational theorist John Dewey, historian Charles Beard, and social behavioral thinker George Mead.

Figure 29. Hull House
A worker at Hull House greets an immigrant family. Used by permission of Jane Addams Memorial Collection, Special Collections, the University Library, University of Illinois at Chicago.

The motivation for establishing Hull House was humanitarian, democratic, and Christian. It was considered beneficial to residents and the community that educated young people "settle" among and associate with the poor. In the early years, Hull House sponsored lectures, art exhibits, and other cultural activities that were open to the neighbors. Before long, the settlement house responded to the community needs for day nurseries, sewing classes, a cooperative residence for working women, clubs, citizenship classes, and space in which labor unions could meet. Hull House also became active in working for reforms in child labor, sanitation, and housing conditions.

Hull House lost some of its financial support during World War I because of Jane Addams's unpopular pacifist views and the Red Scare. Following the war, there was a waning of interest in social activism. After Addams's death in 1935, there was a period of leadership confusion and conflict. Consistent leadership was restored from 1943 to 1962. In 1963, however, the Hull House property was taken over by the University of Illinois, which had for years been seeking a site for a Chicago campus. Subsequently, Hull House relocated and adopted decentralized community centers around the city. *(See also: Abbott, Edith; Abbott, Grace; Addams, Jane; Hamilton, Alice; Kelley, Florence; Lathrop, Julia Clifford; Settlement House Movement; Social Work; Starr, Ellen Gates)*

—Roberta G. Sands

Further Reading

Addams, Jane. *Second Twenty Years at Hull-House.* New York: Macmillan, 1930.
———. *Twenty Years at Hull-House.* 1910. Reprint, with autobiographical notes by James Hart. Champaign, IL: University of Illinois Press, 1990.
Bryan, Mary Linn McCree, and Allen F. Davis. *One Hundred Years at Hull-House.* Indianapolis: Indiana University Press, 1990.
Carson, Mina. *Settlement Folk: Social Thought and the American Settlement Movement, 1885–1930.* Chicago: University of Chicago Press, 1990.

Davis, Allen F. *Spearheads for Reform: The Social Settlements and the Progressive Movement, 1890–1914.* New York: Oxford University Press, 1967.

Polacheck, Hilda Satt. *I Came a Stranger: The Story of a Hull-House Girl.* Edited by Dena J. Polacheck Epstein. Urbana: University of Illinois Press, 1989.

ᴥ Hunter College of the City University of New York

Hunter College of the City University of New York was the first college in the United States to provide free education for all women and, until 1964, was the largest women's college in the world. Since its opening in 1870, it has expanded from a teacher training school to a large, coeducational liberal arts college.

Established as a free academy known as the Female Normal and High School, it opened on February 14, 1870. Its purpose was to provide free higher education for women so as to afford the city "a constant supply of trained and competent teachers." In keeping with this role, the college adopted the motto *Mihi Cura Futuri* ("Mine Is the Care of the Future"). Two months after the school's inception, its name was changed to the Normal College of the City of New York, although it granted no degrees at that time.

Its principal founder and first president was Irish-born Thomas Hunter, who insisted that the school admit blacks and whites on equal terms, even though New York in that period was still maintaining separate elementary schools. President Hunter also advocated a liberal arts education along with professional training. In 1914, to honor the founder-president, the college was renamed Hunter College of the City of New York.

Its first class consisted of 1,095 young women who were officially called "teacher-pupils." After completing five months of professional teacher training, they took their places as teachers in the city's elementary schools. By 1879, the curriculum was extended to four years, and in 1888, Hunter became the first tuition-free college in the country to grant degrees. At the turn of the century, Hunter was no longer a college serving solely as a professional school for prospective teachers but had a broad liberal arts curriculum. In 1961, the college, together with City, Brooklyn, and Queens colleges, united to become the City University of New York with the power to grant doctoral degrees. In size, the City University is second only to the University of California and is the largest system of municipal education in the United States. After nearly a century of service as an exclusively women's college, Hunter became coeducational in 1964, although at the beginning of the 21st century, women still made up about three-fourths of the student body. Notable alumni include Bella Abzug, Bess Meyerson, and Sylvia Porter. *(See also: Education; Higher Education)*

—**Ruth Jacknow Markowitz**

Further Reading
Hunter College Bulletin.
Hunter College Wisterian.
Patterson, Samuel White. *Hunter College: Eighty-Five Years of Service.* New York: Lantern, 1955.
Shuster, George N. *The Ground I Walked On: Reflections of a College President.* New York: Farrar, Straus & Giroux, 1961.
Stern, Elizabeth Vera Loeb. "1870–1970: A History of Hunter's Splendid Century," *Hunter College Alumni Quarterly* 78 (Winter 1970): 13-21.

ᴥ Hurston, Zora Neale (c. 1901–1960)

Zora Neale Hurston was the author of five novels, numerous short stories, various articles and plays, an autobiography, and a collection of folktales. Between 1920 and 1950, she was the most prolific African American woman writer in America. Aside from her interest in writing, she has been highly regarded for her anthropological studies, focusing primarily on the language and lore of her people. A proud daughter of black culture in the rural South and a participant in the Harlem Renaissance, she committed herself to the preservation of her heritage; she was one of the leaders in bringing the experiences of the common black masses to the attention of the literary world.

As a black woman writer during the Harlem Renaissance, Hurston was ahead of her time. Rather than limit herself to the themes and characters of her male counterparts in the literary world, Hurston wrote not only about the freedom of blacks but also about the specific issues and feelings related to the freedom of black women. The needs, thoughts, and words of black women—never stereotyped—were communicated in a style that established Hurston as the first in a continuing series of black North American women writers to give voice to black women's experiences.

Because she was a social and political nonconformist, Hurston's literary place in history has often been overshadowed by the controversy that surrounded her as a person. She was forceful, defying traditional roles with open rebellion. Personally, she demanded equality; the characters of her novels and stories became an extension of her own private demands. The current interest and respect given to her work provides a belated awareness of the universality of her voice of integrity in the face of oppression. *(See also: Black Women; Harlem Renaissance; Women Writers)*

—**Joanne S. Richmond**
—**Merri Scheibe Edwards**

Further Reading
Brown, Rosellen. "Writers under a Double Disadvantage," *New York Times Book Review* 23 (January 23, 1984): 15.
Cannon, Katie Geneva. "Resources for a Constructive Ethic in the Life and Work of Zora Neale Hurston," *Journal of Feminist Studies in Religion* 1 (1975): 37-51.
Evans, Marie. *Black Women Writers (1930–1980).* Garden City, NY: Anchor, 1984.
Hemenway, Robert. *Zora Neale Hurston, A Literary Biography.* Urbana: University of Illinois Press, 1980.

Hurston, Zora Neale. *Dust Tracks on a Road, An Autobiography.* Philadelphia: J. B. Lippincott, 1937. Reprint, Urbana: University of Illinois Press, 1984.

——. *Their Eyes Were Watching God.* Foreword by Sherley Anne Williams. Urbana: University of Illinois Press, 1978.

Walker, Alice, ed. *I Love Myself When I Am Laughing . . . And Then Again When I Am Looking Mean and Impressive.* Introduction by Mary Helen Washington. New York: Feminist Press, 1979.

∝ Hutchinson, Anne Marbury
(1591–1643)

Anne Hutchinson, leader of the opposition party to Puritan orthodoxy in seventeenth-century Massachusetts, was the eldest daughter of Francis Marbury, an Anglican cleric, and his second wife, Bridget Dryden. Owing to her mother's tutelage, Hutchinson became a skilled nurse and midwife, while her father, censured and without clerical responsibilities during her early years in Alfred, Lincolnshire, took charge of her education, providing her with detailed knowledge of doctrinal issues and a willingness to question established authority. In 1612, she married William Hutchinson, a merchant, and began to assume the prominent role that his successful business required.

The Hutchinsons became followers of John Cotton, an Anglican minister with Puritan leanings, who emphasized a "covenant of grace" and an inward awareness of one's spiritual salvation, rather than a "covenant of works," in which one's ability to lead a sanctified life was seen as a sign of election. When Cotton went to the Massachusetts Bay Colony, the Hutchinsons followed.

Arriving in New England in September 1634 aboard the *Griffin,* Hutchinson found a community alert to any signs of strife or challenges to its orthodoxy, and the twice-weekly meetings that Hutchinson held in her home came to be seen as such a challenge. In the beginning, the meetings consisted of Hutchinson's recitations of sermons for those women unable to attend the weekly lecture or worship service, but gradually they moved toward exegesis and commentary on the sermons, and prominent members of the community, men as well as women, began to gather in her home. When Hutchinson denounced all Boston clergymen, with the exception of Cotton and John Wheelwright, her husband's brother-in-law, for preaching a covenant of works rather than a covenant of grace, the political content of her meetings became clear.

The issue was much more than a point of dogmatic dispute. By challenging clerical authority, she was striking at the primary supports of the entire Puritan system. In November 1637, Anne Hutchinson stood trial, charged with having "troubled the peace of the commonwealth" through actions "not fitting for [her] sex." The magistrates found her guilty and banished her from Massachusetts.

The Hutchinson family moved to Rhode Island. When her husband died in 1642, Hutchinson and those of her fifteen children still at home moved to New Netherlands—a Dutch colonial territory later divided into New York and New Jersey—where she and all but one of her children were killed in 1643 in a war between the Dutch settlers and the Indians. *(See also: Christianity; Religion)*

—Cristine M. Levenduski

Further Reading

Battis, Emery. *Saints and Sectaries: Anne Hutchinson and the Antinomian Controversy in the Massachusetts Bay Colony.* Chapel Hill: University of North Carolina Press, 1962.

Hutchinson, Thomas. *The History of the Colony and Province of Massachusetts Bay.* Edited by Lawrence Shaw Mayo. Cambridge, MA: Harvard University Press, 1936.

Lang, Amy Schranger. *Prophetic Women: Anne Hutchinson and the Problem of Dissent in the Literature of New England.* Berkeley: University of California Press, 1987.

Williams, Selma. *Divine Rebel: The Life of Anne Marbury Hutchinson.* New York: Holt, Rinehart & Winston, 1981.

∝ Hyatt, Anna Vaughn (Huntington)
(1876–1973)

Sculptor Anna Vaughn Hyatt gained international recognition for her accurately executed animal sculptures. Hyatt became an expert in animal anatomy and behavior through careful observation of animals, both at zoos and at her family's farm, where she spent summers as a child. She began sculpting at the age of nineteen after finding she enjoyed assisting her sculptor sister Harriet Hyatt (Mayor). Hyatt studied in Boston and at the Art Students League in New York. In 1900, she had her first solo exhibit at the Boston Art Club, where she showed forty animal figures, all portrayed with vigor and power.

In 1907, Hyatt spent a year in France, executing a large jaguar sculpture that was shown at the Paris Salon Exhibition that year. She later dropped all commissions to devote her time to an equestrian statue of Joan of Arc. Her model won honorable mention in the Paris Salon of 1910, and New York City commissioned her to execute the monument in bronze. The sculpture stands on Riverside Drive, and replicas appear elsewhere in the United States and France. The government of France made her a Chevalier of the Legion of Honor for this piece.

Among her many other awards were the Saltus Medal from the National Academy of Design in 1922 for *Diana and the Chase,* the Grand Cross of Alfonso XII for *El Cid Campeador* (Seville, Spain, 1927), and gold medals from the American Academy of Arts and Letters and the National Sculpture Society. Her works are in the collections of over two hundred museums.

At the age of forty-seven, Anna Hyatt married poet and philanthropist Archer M. Huntington. They established Brookgreen Gardens in South Carolina, which exhibits works by Hyatt and over 150 other artists. Anna Hyatt Huntington completed the last of seven equestrian statues at the age of ninety and left works in progress when she died at ninety-seven. *(See also: Art)*

—Anne L. Clare

Further Reading

Brookgreen Journal. (Brookgreen Gardens, SC) 15 (1985).

Evans, Cerinda W. *Anna Hyatt Huntington.* Newport News, VA: Mariners Museum, 1965.

McHenry, Robert, ed. *Liberty's Women.* Springfield, MA: Merriam, 1980.

Hysteria

Hysteria is a psychiatric illness particularly associated with nineteenth-century women. Common enough even earlier, the disease reached a peak in the half century before World War I. Hysterics suffered fits, tics, fainting spells, and paralysis of limbs and often experienced long periods of invalidism. Doctors diagnosed a variety of sometimes mortal illnesses as hysteria, so dominant had it become in the medical literature. Until recently, historians assumed hysteria to be a disease predominantly affecting the middle class, but in fact, there were as many and sometimes more victims among working-class women. Treatment involved electrotherapy, hypnosis, and especially the famous rest cure devised by S. Weir Mitchell, whose patients were encouraged to stay in bed for weeks on end and to gain thirty or forty pounds. Since anorexia was another manifestation of hysteria, the cure sometimes worked.

Sigmund Freud revolutionized the understanding of hysteria when he attributed its origins in part to the sexual repression of women and their attendant hypermoralism. Once divorced from physical causes and from explanations grounded in sufferers' inferior intelligence or immorality, the disease received a psychological rather than a medical treatment. Indeed, from being a major malady across North America and Europe, hysteria declined in frequency. Moreover, after World War I, it came to afflict those in the countryside who were remote from psychological discourse.

Among famous hysterics or invalids during this period, Alice James, sister of renowned intellectuals Henry and William James, has received careful study, while feminist Charlotte Perkins Gilman has left her account of the rest cure. Some victims of the Salem witch trials centuries before are also believed to have suffered hysterical symptoms. Recently, the theorist Elaine Showalter has posited that Gulf War syndrome, Epstein Barr syndrome, chronic fatigue syndrome, and other illnesses are modern epidemics of hysteria. *(See also: Freudianism; Gilman, Charlotte Perkins; James, Alice; Salem Witch Trials)*

—**Bonnie G. Smith**

Further Reading

Bernheimer, Charles, and Claire Kahane, eds. *In Dora's Case: Freud-Hysteria-Feminism.* New York: Columbia University Press, 1985.

Ehrenreich, Barbara, and Dierdre English. *For Her Own Good: 150 Years of Experts' Advice to Women.* New York: Doubleday, 1978.

Lunbeck, Elizabeth. *The Psychiatric Persuasion.* Princeton, NJ: Princeton University Press, 1994.

Shorter, Edward. "Paralysis: The Rise and Fall of a 'Hysterical' Symptom," *Journal of Social History* 19 (Spring 1986): 549-82.

Showalter, Elaine. *The Female Malady.* New York: Pantheon, 1985.

———. *Hystories: Hysterical Epidemics and Modern Culture.* New York: Columbia University Press, 1997.

Smith-Rosenberg, Carroll. "The Hysterical Woman: Sex Roles and Role Conflict in Nineteenth Century America." In *Disorderly Conduct: Visions of Gender in Victorian America,* edited by Carroll Smith-Rosenberg, 197-217. New York: Oxford University Press, 1985.

Strouse, Jean. *Alice James: A Biography.* Boston: Houghton Mifflin, 1980.

Immigrant Midwifery

During the latter decades of the nineteenth century, it appeared that American midwifery would soon become obsolete. The growth of medical professionalism and the advancement of obstetrics as a recognized medical specialty seemed to ensure that the midwife would be displaced by the physician. However, the arrival of millions of immigrants from Eastern and Southern Europe onto American shores between 1880 and 1920 brought a new visibility to the midwife. Midwifery was a long-established and highly respected profession throughout Europe, and most European midwives held distinguished positions within their communities. When immigrant women arrived in America, they continued to employ midwives. In fact, by the early decades of the twentieth century, many cities and towns of the urban Northeast and Midwest, where immigrants most often settled, had begun to experience an unexpected revival of midwifery.

Most immigrant midwives were mature, married women with children. Some had earned diplomas from European midwifery schools before coming to America, while others were empirically trained. A minority of immigrant midwives received training at one of the few well-recognized midwifery schools established in the United States, such as New York City's Bellevue School for Midwives. Although opponents of midwifery often characterized these women as ignorant, incompetent, and dirty, most immigrant midwives were intelligent, literate women who were concerned with aseptic techniques and whose maternal and infant mortality rates were equal to or better than those of local physicians.

Recently arrived immigrants sought out midwives for a variety of reasons. Midwives spoke the same language and shared similar traditions and customs with the parturient women whom they served. Immigrant contempt for men in the birthing room also contributed to the popularity of midwives. Furthermore, the midwife generally charged less than the physician, and she also allowed for the informal arrangement of payment in kind. Immigrant midwives rarely joined together to form professional midwifery associations. Because they usually worked independently of each other, they were ill equipped to help frame training and regulatory legislation or to respond to the charges that they were ignorant and dirty.

The halting of immigration from Eastern and Southern Europe in the early 1920s, coupled with the enactment of more stringent state regulatory measures, resulted in a significant decline in the number of immigrant midwives. In addition, second- and third-generation immigrant women were beginning to express a preference for the "American way" of physician-managed childbirth. By the 1930s, the immigrant midwife, who had been the predominant birth attendant among ethnic communities three decades earlier, was becoming less commonplace and would eventually disappear from the American setting. *(See also: Childbirth; "Granny" Midwifery; Immigration; Midwifery)*

—**Judy Barrett Litoff**

Further Reading

Declercq, Eugene. "The Nature and Style of Practice of Immigrant Midwives in Early Twentieth Century Massachusetts," *Journal of Social History* 19 (Fall 1985): 113-29.

Declercq, Eugene, and Richard Lacroix. "The Immigrant Midwives of Lawrence: The Conflict between Law and Culture in Early Twentieth-Century Massachusetts," *Bulletin of the History of Medicine* 59 (1985): 232-46.

Litoff, Judy Barrett. *The American Midwife Debate: A Sourcebook on Its Modern Origins.* Westport, CT: Greenwood, 1986.

———. *American Midwives, 1860 to the Present.* Westport, CT: Greenwood, 1978.

Immigrant Protective League (IPL)

The Immigrant Protective League (IPL) evolved out of a committee formed by the Women's Trade Union League at its 1908 convention to deal with the peculiar problems faced by immigrant women traveling alone. The committee discovered that each year about 20 percent of such travelers leaving Ellis Island for Chicago failed to arrive at the proper address and that many of them were steered by unscrupulous cabbies, baggage express men, and policemen to saloons and brothels. It recommended the creation of a permanent agency to register single immigrant women at the port of entry and to assist them to their ultimate destination. The initial impetus for the league's formation was provided by Jane Addams and Sophonisba Breckenridge, with the latter serving as temporary director for several months. The directorship was eventually assumed by Grace

Abbott, who served in that capacity for the duration of the league's most active years.

The IPL was funded by private philanthropy and had close ties to Hull House, the Chicago Commons, the Chicago School of Civics and Philanthropy, and the Women's Trade Union League. Besides Addams, Breckenridge, and Abbott, it also numbered in its ranks Julia Lathrop, Mary McDowell, Agnes Nestor, and Margaret Dreier Robins. Its board of directors included male luminaries such as philanthropist Julius Rosenwald, juvenile court judge Julian Mack, and legal scholar Ernst Freund. Its members were mostly professionals, businessmen, and civic leaders who were predominantly old stock, Protestant, well educated, and affluent. They agreed with the fundamental tenets of American society, wanted these extended to newcomers, concentrated on concrete practical solutions, and proposed no radical reconstruction of the socioeconomic or political order. Most of the staff members were social workers and other professionals who sought to bring to bear the values and methods of their various disciplines. The primary goal was to facilitate the assimilation of immigrants while preserving many of the "gifts" and "contributions" that the newcomers added to the American cultural mix. The league aimed to make immigrants self-sustaining: employed at useful, remunerative labor; exercising their full citizenship rights; gaining access to opportunity; and supporting their children in the educational system. Its members believed that the immigrants' problems were due to their temporarily debased status in American society rather than innate inferiority. The IPL hired only bilingual staff members, challenged the ethnic biases of the Dillingham Immigration Commission, and opposed the literacy test required by immigration restriction laws of the period, believing that acculturation would come naturally.

Much of the league's work involved the provision of direct services to immigrants. IPL workers met immigrants at train stations, found lost luggage, arranged accommodations for those who were stranded, delivered others to the correct address, found temporary employment, provided translators, or arranged for continuing passage. They protected the new arrivals from exploitative actions by ticket brokers, steamship and railroad companies, employment agencies, taxi drivers, and baggage express men. The IPL also served as an advocate of the newer immigrant groups, representing their interests in court, before government regulatory commissions, and with municipal and state agencies. It lobbied for laws to police private employment offices, to regulate immigrant banks, and to increase state and federal responsibility for the welfare of immigrants. In 1913, the league was largely instrumental in the passage of a federal law requiring Immigration and Naturalization Service inspectors in railroad stations and at ports of entry. Its staff conducted important studies of immigrant employment and of the status of women and children.

In 1918, the State of Illinois created the Immigrant's Commission with Abbott as director, thereby virtually subsuming the IPL. The commission produced important studies, on the educational needs of immigrants in Illinois and on the status of immigrant coal miners. The former led to the institution of adult education programs and a significant reduction in immigrant illiteracy. Abbott's work with the IPL largely provided the basis for her influential work *The Immigrant and the Community*.

From 1917 on, the league's direct service work was significantly reduced, as World War I and immigration restriction drastically curtailed the number of newcomers. Its work became largely legal and technical rather than social in nature. In 1958, the IPL changed its name to the Immigrants Service League, and in 1967, it became an administrative arm of the Traveler's Aid Society of Metropolitan Chicago. *(See also: Abbott, Grace; Hull House; Immigration; National Women's Trade Union League)*

—**John D. Buenker**

Further Reading

Buroker, Robert L. "From Voluntary Association to Welfare State: The Illinois Immigrant's Protective League, 1908–1926," *Journal of American History* 58 (December 1971): 643-60.

Costin, Lela. *Two Sisters for Social Justice: A Biography of Grace and Edith Abbott*. Urbana: University of Illinois Press, 1983.

Diner, Steven J. *A City and Its Universities: Public Policy in Chicago, 1892–1919*. Chapel Hill: University of North Carolina, 1980.

Leonard, Henry B. "The Immigrants Protective League of Chicago, 1908–1921," *Journal of the Illinois State Historical Society* 66 (1973): 271-84.

~ Immigration

Immigration represents a significant yet largely neglected aspect of women's history in the United States. The migration of over 50 million people from Europe, Asia, and the Western Hemisphere to America has been analyzed primarily from the point of view of the male experience. Historians who have attempted to analyze the experience of women migrants have tended to create a collective category, "immigrant women," ignoring cultural and social variations.

The characteristics of the immigrant group, in terms of gender, as well as age, marital status, and class reflects both the nature of the sending society and the structure of opportunity in the United States. Generally, however, historians of immigration have placed more emphasis on the former than the latter. They have emphasized, for women, that immigration tends to be highest from such places that allow greater levels of female autonomy and where opportunities for both marriage and employment have declined.

The processes of female migration, modes and rates of adaptation to life in the United States, and patterns of retention of traditional ways varied historically from group to group. Particularly noteworthy were the differences in male-female ratio from one immigrant group to the next. Among several of the Western European immigrant groups of the mid-nineteenth century, such as the Germans and the

Figure 30. Immigration

Maria Balazova, 79, shown at LaGuardia Airport on her arrival from her native Prague, Czechoslovakia, en route to Chicago to join a daughter. She spoke no English and wore a card reading "I look for Mr. Marshal"—someone who was supposed to meet her. Used by permission of UPI/Corbis-Bettmann.

1924 with the passage of the National Origins Act. The relatively light level of immigration that occurred between 1924 and the late 1960s saw a higher percentage of women than the previous decades, reflecting a process by which male immigrants who had come on their own earlier and had become American citizens called for wives from back home.

A new era in the history of immigration and in the history of immigrant women began in 1965. The 1965 law, passed in the era of expanded civil rights, removed the nationality-based quotas of the 1924 legislation. In place of these quotas, the new legislation gave preference to immigrants with family members already in the United States and for certain occupational categories.

In this new phase of immigration, the ratio between men and women has changed, and since 1968 when the law went into effect, women outnumber men as immigrants from all of Central and South America, the Caribbean, South East Asia, and Europe. The only places that send primarily male immigrants are African and Islamic countries. Not only have the number and proportion of women immigrants risen, but women are now likely to be the first family member to venture to the United States. Women have become the "pioneers" in the immigration process, coming to America, securing employment, establishing communal networks, and then bringing over other family members.

The post-1965 immigration has been geared toward the service sector of the U.S. economy. As such, it has focused heavily on traditionally female employment, as opposed to earlier immigrations drawn by heavy industry, defined as "men's work." In addition, as educational opportunities for women have risen around the world, women with professional skills have flooded into the United States. For example, many women in the Philippines and Jamaica are trained nurses, and they have come to the United States in large numbers. Their arrival has in part compensated for a drop in the number of American women who have opted for this field. Indeed, in 1989, Congress passed the Immigration Nurses Act to ensure that these professional women will continue to immigrate to the United States. *(See also: Asian American Women; Black Women; Chicana; Hull House; Immigrant Midwifery; Immigrant Protective League; Jewish Women; Settlement House Movement)*

—**Hasia R. Diner**

Scandinavians, men and women migrated in roughly equal numbers, although single people predominated. Jewish men and women from Eastern Europe in the years between 1881 and 1924 came to the United States at the same rate, with married couples being just as numerous as single people of either gender. The Irish, whose migration began in massive numbers in the 1840s and continued through the last decades of the nineteenth century, were the only group in which women outnumbered male migrants. Owing to landholding patterns in Ireland that prevented most men and women from marrying and the acute shortage of domestic servants in the United States, Irish women found themselves more "pulled" to America than were their brothers. Among other groups, such as the Italians, the Greeks, and the Chinese, male migrants far outnumbered women. The paucity of female immigrants reflects the relative impermanence of at least the initial migration from these countries, and as more women from Italy, Greece, and China did arrive in the United States, the process of permanent ethnic community building began in earnest.

Unrestricted and relatively unregulated immigration (from outside of the Western Hemisphere) to the United States (with certain notable exceptions such as the exclusion of the Chinese in 1882 and the Japanese in 1905) ended in

Further Reading

Bodnar, John E. "Socialization and Adaptation: Immigrant Families in Scranton, 1880–1890," *Pennsylvania History* 43 (1976): 147-62.

Diner, Hasia R. *Erin's Daughters in America: Irish Immigrant Women in the Nineteenth Century.* Baltimore: Johns Hopkins University Press, 1983.

Gabaccia, Donna R. *From the Other Side: Women, Gender, and Immigrant Life in the United States, 1820–1990.* Bloomington: Indiana University Press, 1994.

———. *Immigrant Women in the United States: A Selectively Annotated Multidisciplinary Bibliography.* New York: Greenwood, 1989.

———. *Seeking Common Ground: Multidisciplinary Studies of Immigrant Women in the United States.* Westport, CT: Greenwood, 1992.

Lamphere, Louise. *From Working Daughters to Working Mothers: Immigrant Women in a New England Industrial Community.* Ithaca, NY: Cornell University Press, 1987.

Seller, Maxine. "Beyond the Stereotype: A New Look at the Immigrant Woman, 1880–1924," *Journal of Ethnic Studies* 3 (1975): 59–70.

Smith, Judith E. *Family Connections: A History of Italian and Jewish Immigrant Lives in Providence, Rhode Island, 1900–1940.* Albany: State University of New York Press, 1985.

Yans-McLaughlin, Virginia. *Family and Community: Italian Immigrants in Buffalo, 1880–1930.* Ithaca, NY: Cornell University Press, 1977.

ᔕ Incidents in the Life of a Slave Girl
(1861)

Incidents in the Life of a Slave Girl was an autobiography, published under the pseudonym Linda Brent, recording the horrors of life under slavery for Harriet Brent Jacobs. Born into slavery in 1818, Jacobs was bequeathed at the age of thirteen to a child of five whose father, called Dr. Flint in the book, became her master. Without the protection of her parents, who were deceased, Jacobs faced the sexual advances of Flint and the jealous rage of his wife. Only the fact that she and her younger brother lived in Flint's hometown and that the master felt some concern for his local reputation protected Jacobs from violent assault. It did not save her from Flint's domination in other ways, however.

At the age of twenty-one, Jacobs escaped to her grandmother's house a few miles away and hid there for seven years. Finally, she made her way to Philadelphia, where she found work as a domestic servant in the Nathaniel P. Willis family and a home in the antislavery cause. Her brother John escaped about the same time, 1841, and became an antislavery lecturer. Harriet joined John in Rochester, New York, in 1849–1850 and worked with the Western New York Anti-Slavery Society, whose members included abolitionists Frederick Douglass and Amy Post. Jacobs returned to the Willis family's employ from 1850 to 1861, continuing to confide in Amy Post through letters. A feminist as well as an abolitionist, Post was particularly concerned with the plight of slave women and encouraged Jacobs to write the story of her life.

Often exhausted from household chores, responsible for the care of a son and daughter brought out of slavery, insecure in her literary abilities, and rebuffed by abolitionist writer Harriet Beecher Stowe, Jacobs finally completed her autobiography with the encouragement of Post and abolitionist William C. Nell. In 1861, *Incidents* was finally published with the aid of and an introduction by Lydia Maria Child and an afterword by Post. Its publication, coinciding with the opening campaigns of the Civil War, never aroused the attention of the public as earlier slave histories had done. Long believed to be a fictionalized account penned by a white abolitionist, *Incidents* only recently came to be recognized as an important and authentic source of information about black women's lives under slavery. *(See also: Abolition and the Antislavery Movement; Child, Lydia Maria Francis; Douglass, Frederick; Slavery)*

—**Nancy A. Hewitt**

Further Reading

Amy and Isaac Post Family Papers. University of Rochester, Rochester, NY.

Doriana, Beth Maclay. "Black Womanhood in Nineteenth-Century America: Subversion and Self-Construction in Two Women's Autobiographies," *American Quarterly* 43 (1991): 199–222.

Jacobs, Harriet Brent. *Incidents in the Life of a Slave Girl.* Edited by Jean Fagan Yellin. Cambridge, MA: Harvard University Press, 1986.

ᔕ Indian Child Welfare Act of 1978

In 1978, the U.S. Congress enacted the Indian Child Welfare Act (ICWA), preventing the inappropriate removal of Indian children from their families and placing Indian children in homes reflecting Indian cultural values. After a congressional review found that 85 percent of Indian children removed from their homes were being placed in non-Indian homes, this act established a federal policy whereby an Indian child should remain, when at all possible, with the Indian community. In addition, a large majority of Indian children were being removed from their families on vague grounds that showed no comprehension of the dynamics of Indian family life. Thus, the ICWA also narrows the grounds for which a child can be removed from its home, stating that poverty, inadequate housing, alcohol abuse, or nonconforming social behavior does not constitute evidence for removal of an Indian child.

The primary purpose of the act is to legislate Indian child custody proceedings, including foster care placement, termination of parental rights, preadoptive placement, and adoptive placement. Under the act, Indian child custody proceedings are under the jurisdiction of the tribe, and a state court must send such custody cases to tribal court. If placement of an Indian child is made without the consent of a tribal court, such placements can be invalidated. Preference for placement of children in foster care goes to (a) members of the child's extended family, (b) a foster home licensed by the child's tribe, (c) an Indian foster home, and (d) an institution approved by the tribe or run by an Indian organization. Preference for adoption of children goes to (a) member of the child's extended family, (b) other members of the tribe, and (c) other Indian families. Extended family does include non-Indian family members as well as Indians, for the act protects the constitutional rights of all family members who are biologically related to the child. In addition, the preference section of the act does not preclude non-Indian families from adopting Indian children if the tribe feels it is in the best interest of the child.

The act protects only children who are members of an Indian tribe or who are eligible for membership in a tribe. The ICWA also states that the domicile of an illegitimate child is that of its mother, explicitly excluding an unwed father unless the father has established paternity. The ICWA places emphasis on the tribe's right to have Indian children remain within its social and cultural structure and establishes the tribe's right to decide what is in the best interest of its children. The U.S. Supreme Court upheld the act in *Mississippi Band of Choctaw Indians v. Holyfield* (1989), and one of the Court's basic findings was that if the parents reside on the reservation, the rights of the tribe take precedence over the rights of the parents when determining custody of the children. *(See also: Native American Women)*

—**Susan L. Rockwell**

Further Reading

American Indian Training Program, Inc. *Suggested Strategies for Successful Implementation of the Indian Child Welfare Act of 1978: A Preliminary Review*. Oakland, CA: American Indian Training Program, 1979.

Dorsay, Craig J. *The Indian Child Welfare Act and Laws Affecting Indian Juveniles*. Window Rock, AZ: Native American Rights Fund, 1984.

Dorsay, Craig J., Steven C. Moore, and Thomas J. Van Norman. *1992 Update to the Indian Child Welfare Act and Laws Affecting Indian Juveniles Manual*. Boulder, CO: Indian Law Support Center, 1992.

Mississippi Band of Choctaw Indians v. Holyfield, 490 U.S. 30, 104 L.Ed.2d 29, 109 S.Ct. 1597 (1989).

National American Indian Court Judges Association. *Handbook: Indian Child Welfare Act*. Washington, DC: National American Indian Court Judges Association, 1980.

Tellinghuisen, Roger A. "The Indian Child Welfare Act of 1978: A Practical Guide with [Limited] Commentary," *South Dakota Law Review* 34 (1989): 660-99.

ᴧ Industrial Revolution

Industrial revolution is the term used to describe a society's rapid transformation from an agrarian to industrial base. Specifically, it refers to the period in late-eighteenth-century and early-nineteenth-century England when dramatic social and economic change occurred because of the development of mechanical means of textile production in factories. Because of the accompanying increase in both the number and the size of factories that made large-scale production possible, all segments of the population, workers and consumers alike, were affected. By the mid-eighteenth century, the invention of the flying shuttle and spinning jenny had significantly increased the volume of textiles produced by spinning and weaving. The further development of the mule jenny, water frame, and eventually, the mechanical loom sparked the imagination of would-be entrepreneurs to place these latter machines in factories where steam engines provided a nonhuman source of power. Simultaneously, changes in the production of iron began transforming metallurgy as well. None of these technological innovations would have changed production, however, without a prior agricultural revolution on the land in which many self-sufficient farms succumbed to absorption into large agricultural holdings that functioned as capitalist enterprises. These developments drove people to search for work, thus creating a labor supply. In creating landless day laborers, the agricultural revolution also created a pool of consumers. Finally, an emerging middle class born of cottage industry and growing trade created an entrepreneurial class ripe for industrial adventures.

Samuel Slater set up the first textile mill in the United States in 1791. Like many European industrialists, he hired whole families, who worked as teams, with tasks allocated in accord with traditional divisions of labor. In the 1820s, entrepreneurs in Lowell, Massachusetts, developed another model, employing female labor almost exclusively. Underemployed daughters from New England farms moved into Lowell's boardinghouses and from there joined the industrial workforce. Initially, such industrial employment provided a happy alternative to other possibilities for work such as domestic service, school teaching, and farmwork. For one thing, it was "socialized," that is, accomplished with large numbers of people. For another, wages were higher than could be obtained in other forms of employment. These beneficial conditions in fact remained constant, if compared with alternatives.

The next stage in the Industrial Revolution—that occurring in metallurgy and transport—affected women's work much less. In the United States, the initial phase of the Industrial Revolution, which was associated with the rise of the textile industry, gave way to the post-Civil War expansion into steel, railways, and chemical production. After the turn of the twentieth century, these industries were superseded by automobile, airplane, and other durable-goods production until the 1950s brought the development of the computer and, in its wake, related so-called high-tech industries.

Women in the antebellum industrial sector had prevailed in textiles above all else. Moreover, although factory work did employ many females, women in the nineteenth-century paid labor force were more likely to work in domestic service, the "needle trades," and other nonindustrialized sectors. As an aspect of the post-Industrial Era, the rise of the service or tertiary sector reflected the greatest increase in women's employment. Thus, although the Industrial Revolution changed familial relations, patterns of work, and patterns of opportunity, women's work lives continued to be variegated and not necessarily "industrialized." *(See also: Lowell Mill Girls; Textiles: North and South; Unions; Urbanization; Women's Work: Nineteenth Century)*

—**Bonnie G. Smith**

Further Reading

Blewett, Mary. *Men, Women and Work: Class, Gender, and Protest in the New England Shoe Industry*. Urbana: University of Illinois Press, 1988.

Dublin, Thomas. *Transforming Women's Work: New England Lives in the Industrial Revolution.* Ithaca, NY: Cornell University Press, 1994.

Hall, Jacquelyn Dowd. *Like a Family: The Making of a Southern Cotton Mill World.* Chapel Hill: University of North Carolina Press, 1987.

Kessler-Harris, Alice. *Out to Work: A History of Wage-Earning Women in the United States.* New York: Oxford University Press, 1982.

Rendall, Jane. *Women in an Industrializing Society: England 1750–1880.* Oxford: Basil Blackwell, 1991.

Trebilcock, Clive. *The Industrialization of the Continental Powers, 1780–1914.* London: Longman, 1981.

⁊ Industrial Workers of the World (IWW)

Founded on June 27, 1905, the Industrial Workers of the World (IWW) advocated the creation of a worker-controlled system of industrial democracy. The Wobblies, as members were known, were most successful in the American West, where they concentrated on organizing the transient male workers of the agriculture, mining, and lumber industries. They also achieved considerable success in the East, mobilizing textile workers. The famous "Bread and Roses" strike in Lawrence, Massachusetts, in 1912, was organized by the IWW. The Wobblies gave the American labor movement some of its most dramatic characters and martyrs, including Elizabeth Gurley Flynn, Big Bill Haywood, Frank Little, and Joe Hill.

The IWW made several attempts to organize women, employing Matilda Rabinowitz to unionize textile workers in New York and the South and forming locals of domestic workers in Chicago, Salt Lake City, Denver, and Seattle. More than any other early twentieth-century labor or radical organization, the IWW advocated equality for women. It lowered initiation fees and dues in recognition of that fact that women earned less than men; it demanded equal pay for equal work; and it supported the birth control movement. Yet the IWW was a creature of its times and as such was limited by the sexual ideology of the early twentieth century. Women, in Wobblies' eyes, were chaste, moral, and essentially domestic. While Wobblies recognized the need to organize women who were in the labor force, they strove for a society in which men would earn enough to support a family and allow wives to remain in their rightful place—the home. When IWW representative Jane Street organized domestic workers in Denver, she received little support from male Wobblies, who felt that the women's local existed only to provide them with girlfriends. Street discouraged a friend from undertaking a similar effort, warning her that "sex can come rushing into your office like a great hurricane and blow all the papers of industrialism out of the window."

While small numbers of Wobblies continued to agitate in the 1920s, the ranks of the organization were decimated by the savage repression of the Left during and after World War I. Today, only a skeleton of the organization remains.

Figure 31. Industrial Workers of the World
Carolina A. Low, a Chicago attorney, represented the Industrial Workers of the World in court. Used by permission of Corbis-Bettmann.

(See also: Flynn, Elizabeth Gurley; Lawrence Strike of 1912; Unions)

—**Mary Murphy**

Further Reading

Bird, Stewart, Dan Georgakas, and Deborah Shaffer. *Solidarity Forever: An Oral History of the I.W.W.* Chicago: Lake View, 1985.

Schofield, Ann. "Rebel Girls and Union Maids: The Woman Question in the Journals of the A.F.L. and I.W.W., 1905–1920," *Feminist Studies* 9 (Summer 1983): 335-58.

Tax, Meredith. *The Rising of the Women: Feminist Solidarity and Class Consciousness, 1880–1917.* New York: Monthly Review, 1980.

❧ Institute for Colored Youth

The Institute for Colored Youth (now Cheyney University, Cheyney, Pennsylvania) in Philadelphia was established in 1837 through a legacy designated for training black youth for the teaching profession. The institute was one of a handful of nineteenth-century schools offering qualified blacks an opportunity for rigorous preparatory, high school, and normal school education from an all-black faculty. Graduates with degrees from the institute were in high demand for teaching and administrative positions in the growing black school systems both in the North and South.

Educated, activist women such as Grace Mapps and her daughter Sarah Mapps Douglass taught at the institute during its formative years. Fanny Jackson Coppin, a former slave, was hired in 1865 to teach Latin, Greek, and higher mathematics and to serve as principal of the girls' department. During her thirty-five-year tenure, which included many years as principal, she introduced innovative pedagogical methods, raised educational standards, and expanded the institute's role in the black community. Her awareness of the need for blacks to have steady employment prompted her to organize an industrial skills department at the institute in 1882. This nondegree training program eventually offered a wide variety of courses, including carpentry, bricklaying, millinery, tailoring, and dressmaking. Because it was one of Philadelphia's few industrial training schools for blacks, the institute's enrollment swelled to the point that, by the turn of the century, the school's focus had shifted from teacher training to vocational skills education.

Fanny Jackson Coppin viewed the institute as playing an integral role in improving the economic and social conditions in the black community. To this end, the institute offered night classes, sponsored lecture series, opened a dormitory for girls, and had a library. In 1903, the institute held its final classes in Philadelphia, as the move to the new suburban campus in Cheyney, Pennsylvania, had been completed. *(See also: Bethune, Mary McLeod; Black Women; Crandall, Prudence; Education)*

—**Cynthia Jeffress Little**

Further Reading

Institute for Colored Youth. Annual Reports, 1837–1912. Historical Society of Pennsylvania, Philadelphia.

Perkins, Linda M. *Fanny Jackson Coppin and the Institute for Colored Youth, 1837–1902.* New York: Garland, 1987.

Silcox, Harry. "The Search by Blacks for Employment Opportunity: Industrial Education in Philadelphia," *Pennsylvania Heritage* 4 (December 1977): 38-43.

❧ International Campaign to Ban Landmines (ICBL)

Horrified by the destructive force of land mines, Jody Williams of Putney, Vermont, organized the International Campaign to Ban Landmines (ICBL) in 1991. After six years of campaigning in conjunction with more than 1,000 organizations and millions of people around the world, including the late Princess Diana, the ICBL impelled world leaders to sign a treaty banning land mines. The ICBL adopted a two-part campaign to educate humanity about land mines and convince governments to eliminate the weapon. In December 1997, Williams and the ICBL earned equal honors as corecipients of the Nobel Peace Prize. "Land mines" said Williams in her acceptance speech, "cannot tell the difference between a soldier or a civilian, a woman, a child, a grandmother going out to collect firewood to make the family meal."

In his 1895 will, the inventor of dynamite Alfred Nobel ordered establishment of a foundation to honor the best work annually in chemistry, literature, medicine, physics, and peace. Nobel stipulated that the peace prize go to "the person who shall have done the most or the best work for fraternity between the nations, for the abolition of standing armies and for the holding and promotion of peace congresses." Norwegian Secretary of State Jan Egeland stated that the ICBL came closest to what Nobel wished to reward than any recipient in memory. Ironically, Nobel's invention, dynamite, creates the explosive force inside land mines.

Nobel Peace Prize laureate Jody Williams called for a partnership between campaigning groups and governments to create a new superpower capable of banishing land mines. In 1997, an estimated 100 million land mines remained buried in sixty countries worldwide. These mines kill or maim 26,000 people every year, or one person every twenty minutes. Civilians constitute approximately 80 percent of land mine victims; of those, children make up 75 percent. Almost all deaths and dismemberments caused by land mines take place after fighting ends.

Although she gratefully accepted the peace prize, Williams stated that ratification of the Ottawa treaty outlawing land mines remained the prize her group sought most. On December 4, 1997, one week before the Nobel ceremony, 122 nations signed that treaty. However, forty more nations must ratify this treaty for it to bind nations under international law. Notable holdouts to the treaty— the United States, Russia, and China—remain unconvinced by the ICBL's work. ICBL spokesperson Rae McGrathe chided holdouts as intransigent and uncaring nations who failed humanity. The Nobel Committee awarded the peace prize to the ICBL to demonstrate support for ICBL efforts and to increase pressure on nations to ratify the Ottawa treaty.

Honoring the ICBL with the Nobel prize recognized and encouraged the type of grassroots organizational pressure that Williams's campaign represents. Beyond ratification of the Ottawa treaty, Williams drafted a plan for promoting rapid enforcement, universal monitoring, mine clearance, and victim assistance. Jody Williams and the ICBL form the latest chapter in a long history of women peace activists, including Jane Addams. *(See also: Pacifism and the Peace Movement)*

—**Sasha Ranaé Adams Tarrant**

Further Reading

Cahill, Kevin M., ed. *Clearing the Fields: Solutions to the Global Land Mines Crisis.* New York: Basic Books, 1995.

International Campaigning to Ban Landmines. Available on-line from Vietnam Veterans of America Foundation at http://www. vvaf.org/landmine.html

"Landmine Campaigner Gets Peace Prize." Available on-line from BBC News at http://news.bbc.co.uk/hi/english/world/newsid %5F38000/38427.stm

The Nobel Prize Internet Archive. International Campaign to Ban Landmines. Available on-line at http://nobelprizes.com/nobel/ peace/1997a.html

Nytt fra Norge for the Ministry of Foreign Affairs. The Nobel Peace Prize to Jody Williams and the International Campaign to Ban Landmines. Available on-line from ODIN Ministry of Foreign Affairs at http://odin.dep.no/html/nofovalt/depter/ud/ nornytt/unn-171e.html (October 1997).

ᴧ International Kindergarten Union (IKU)

An association of women organized by Sarah Stewart at Saratoga Springs, New York, in 1892, the International Kindergarten Union (IKU) was intended to showcase the idea of, consolidate the interests in, and build the momentum for establishing kindergarten work as a profession. The charter membership of the IKU consisted of thirty prominent kindergartners whose initial task was to oversee the preparation of an exhibit for the World's Fair in Chicago in 1893. While this presentation was successful from the standpoint of providing publicity, it was also problematic for the would-be profession because it served as a catalyst for the entrenchment of competing conceptions of the purpose and nature of kindergartening. For the next two decades, the IKU served as a forum for an ideological battle between conservative and liberal factions, as each group sought control of the theory and the practice that would define the aspiring profession.

The conservatives' platform centered on promoting the validity of the philosophy espoused by Friedrich Froebel, the German educator who founded the kindergarten system—namely, that the understanding and training of the divine maternal instinct was imperative for appropriate child nurture. These kindergartners claimed the right of professional status on the basis of thirty years of success of Froebelian methodology in American kindergartens, the demonstrated need of specialized training for kindergarten work, and an elevated sense of woman's mission.

The liberals' view pivoted on the utility of scientific knowledge as the guarantor of a profession of child nurture. These kindergartners sought to realign the traditional system with the new insights provided by the scientific study of the child. They assumed that by focusing on the extensive knowledge necessary to understand the intricate nature and needs of the child, the kindergarten could logically claim professional status. If they could ally themselves with other progressive reforms that had a scientific base, they felt that

kindergartners could build a coalition of public support sufficient to realize their professional goals.

Unable to resolve their ideological differences, the two factions could only agree to disagree. In the vacuum of effective leadership for the would-be profession, the kindergarten became redefined by its existence in the public schools. By the time the IKU merged with the National Council of Primary Education to form the Association of Childhood Education International in 1931, kindergartners had assumed the role of teachers and been absorbed into the grade system of the schools. *(See also: Blow, Susan Elizabeth; Education; Teaching)*

—Catherine Cosgrove

Further Reading

Haven, Caroline, Annie Laws, and Bertha Payne. "The International Kindergarten Union," *Kindergarten Review* 18 (June 1908): 634-43.

Hill, Patty Smith. *Kindergarten.* Washington, DC: Association for Childhood Education International, 1942.

Vandewalker, Nina. *Kindergarten in American Education.* New York: Macmillan, 1908.

ᴧ International Ladies Garment Workers Union (ILGWU)

The International Ladies Garment Workers Union (ILGWU) was the one union formed with a significant female membership in the late-nineteenth and early-twentieth centuries. Traditionally, this industry had proved extremely difficult to organize, mostly because the ladies' garment industry operated largely on a contract basis, with workers scattered in shops throughout urban areas, isolated from each other in a way other industrial workers, concentrated in the large factories and workshops, were not. Through the 1890s, early efforts to organize the garment workers had failed; however, in 1900, the situation changed. In March of that year, the New York local of the United Brotherhood of Cloak Makers in New York called for the formation of a national union to promulgate a national union label and effectively resist injunctions against striking garment workers. All workers in the manufacturing of ladies' garments were, subsequently, invited to a conference in New York City on June 3, 1900. On that day, delegates from New York, Brooklyn, Philadelphia, Newark, and Baltimore, representing two thousand workers, met, and later that month, the American Federation of Labor (AFL) issued a charter to their new union, the International Ladies Garment Workers Union.

The founders of the ILGWU were socialist; however, they discouraged strikes and favored instead the effective use of the boycott and sought to create popular support for the new union label. Unlike other AFL unions, the ILGWU was in no position to overlook women workers because women dominated the ladies' garment industry workforce. Nonetheless, men occupied all positions of leadership within the union, feeling, as most labor leaders did, that women were not capable of competent work within the union hierarchy and that this inability to function on a par with men was only exacerbated by women's preoccupation with marriage. As evidence of the strength of this bias against women, one may note that only one woman during this time, Fannia Cohn, sat on the ILGWU executive board, from 1916 through 1918.

The ILGWU became a union of some significance when, in 1909, the New York City ladies' shirtwaist makers went on strike. This strike of twenty thousand workers, 80 percent of whom were women (75 percent of whom were aged twenty-five or younger), is today known as the Great Uprising, and when it ended, more women had been organized than had ever been unionized before in the United States. In New York City shops alone, over thirty thousand women were unionized by the ILGWU.

In 1913, the ILGWU approved the "Protocol in the Dress and Waist Industry," which formalized division of labor and wages by gender within the garment industry. All skilled and higher-paying jobs were thus reserved for male workers, so much so that the lowest-paid male earned more wages than the highest-paid female worker. This occurred even though women made up half the ILGWU membership, illustrating the poor position to which women were relegated within the union.

By 1930, the ILGWU had lost much of its former status and influence and was on the verge of folding. Within a short span, however, a reversal occurred that placed the ILGWU once again in the ranks of America's more powerful unions. In the mid-1930s, the ILGWU staged a series of extremely effective strikes, paving the way for reduced hours and increasing wages by as much as 50 percent in some cases. In addition, ILGWU membership soared once again. By 1940, membership was up 300 percent from a decade before. Of the then 800,000 members, 75 percent were women, including for the first time substantial numbers of black, Hispanic, and Asian workers. Despite these advances, only one of twenty-four members of the ILGWU executive board was female, and the union continued to sign contracts permitting unequal pay for men and women. *(See also: American Federation of Labor; Garment Industries; National Consumers' League; Shirtwaist Makers Strike of 1909; Unions)*

—**Maureen Anna Harp**

Further Reading

Foner, Philip S. *Women and the American Labor Movement: From Colonial Times to the Eve of World War One.* New York: Free Press, 1979.

———. *Women and the American Labor Movement: From World War One to the Present.* New York: Free Press, 1980.

Levine, Louis. *The Women's Garment Workers.* New York: B. W. Huebsch, 1924.

McCreesh, Carolyn D. *Women in the Campaign to Organize Garment Workers, 1880–1917.* New York: Garland, 1985.

Tyler, Gus. *Look for the Union Label: A History of the International Ladies Garment Workers' Union.* Armonk, NY: Sharpe, 1995.

Willet, Mabel Hured. *The Employment of Women in the Clothing Trade.* New York: Columbia University Press, 1902.

✎ International Women's Day, March 8

Received tradition has been that International Women's Day (March 8) was initially inspired by a New York City demonstration on March 8, 1857, of women garment and textile workers who were protesting low wages, the twelve-hour workday, and uncompensated increased workloads. Although their march was brutally broken up by the police, they repeated their call for improved working conditions and equal pay for all working women as they formed their own union in March 1860. A subsequent demonstration of thousands of women workers in the "needle trades" on March 8, 1908, called for child-labor protection legislation and woman suffrage in addition to their long-standing demands. Two years later, Clara Zetkin, a German labor leader, proposed that an International Women's Day be established on March 8 to commemorate the historic struggle to improve women's lives. International Women's Day, observed in Socialist countries during the following sixty years, began to be celebrated in the United States in 1967 by various women's groups, and as a result of the consciousness-raising of the women's liberation movement, International Women's Day commemorative events occurred in most major American cities after 1970.

In 1977, the schools in Sonoma County, California, designated March as Women's History Month as a means of raising awareness of women's history and encouraging its integration into the public and postsecondary curriculum. The development of the National Women's History Project in Santa Rosa, California, in 1980 provided a national clearinghouse for information on International Women's Day as the focal point for the celebration of Women's History Month. Since 1981, Congress has annually passed a National Women's History Week proclamation for the week surrounding March 8. *(See also: International Ladies Garment Workers Union; National Women's History Project)*

—**Angela M. Howard**

Further Reading

Stites, Richard. *The Women's Liberation Movement in Russia: Feminism, Nihilism, and Bolshevism, 1860–1930.* Princeton, NJ: Princeton University Press, 1978.

Women's History Resources: Resources Catalogue for 1984. Santa Rosa, CA: National Women's History Project, 1984.

✎ International Women's Year (IWY) Conference of 1977

The International Women's Year (IWY) Conference of 1977 was held in Houston, Texas, from November 18 to 21. The conference was attended by two thousand delegates and twenty thousand guests from all over the world. According to feminist Gloria Steinem, Congresswoman Bella Abzug was the "main author of the idea for the conference and the presiding officer of its commissioners."

The delegates heard speeches by many of the superstars of the women's movement and adopted a twenty-six-plank "National Plan of Action," presented to President Jimmy Carter on March 22, 1978, as part of the official report of the conference, titled *The Spirit of Houston*. The plan included specific recommendations for national policies on issues such as child abuse, child care, disabled women, education, employment, the Equal Rights Amendment, health, homemakers, insurance, minority women, older women, rape, reproductive freedom, rural women, and poverty. Its concerns were global in scope and provided a document that could well serve as a blueprint for governmental action, especially since many of its suggested reforms have still not been implemented.

The event drew widespread media attention and in some ways served as a 1970s counterpoint to the 1848 women's rights convention in Seneca Falls, New York. The Houston conference served as a landmark event in the history of the women's movement in the United States if only for the many ways in which it served to inspire several generations of women and supportive men. *(See also: Abzug, Bella Savitsky; Steinem, Gloria)*

—**Jonathan W. Zophy**

Further Reading

Bird, Caroline et al. *What Women Want: From the Official Report to the President, the Congress and the People of the United States.* New York: Simon & Schuster, 1979.

⮞ Internet Resources

In the 1990s, it became possible for everyone, from school children to researchers and others who simply enjoy history, to view facsimiles of primary source documents and tour specially mounted exhibits on the Internet. In addition, the Internet provides an abundance of background information and connections to the catalogs of hundreds of American libraries and archives. Among the many projects and sites are scores that offer useful resources in American women's history.

It is often difficult to know where to look for archival resources on women. Jill U. Jackson, Archivist of the Archives for Research on Women and Gender at the University of Texas at San Antonio, has addressed this situation by maintaining "Uncovering Women's History in Archival Collections" (http://www.lib.utsa.edu/Archives/links.htm), a useful state-by-state guide to Web pages from archives, libraries, and other repositories with significant holdings by or about women. Jackson includes links to wholly women-focused endeavors, such as the General Federation of Women's Clubs Women's History and Resource Center in Washington, D.C., the Arthur and Elizabeth Schlesinger Library on

the History of Women in America at Radcliffe College, the Sophia Smith Collection at Smith College, and the June L. Mazer Lesbian Collection in Los Angeles. She also links to more general-purpose repositories that contain significant holdings on women, such as the Wayne State University Archives of Labor and Urban Affairs, and numerous state and university collections. On their sites, many of the repositories include exhibits, subject guides, and finding aids for individual manuscript collections.

Two massive American history digitization projects contain useful source material on women. As part of its American Memory Project (http://memory.loc.gov/ammem/), the Rare Books and Special Collections Division of the Library of Congress digitized more than 150 representative pamphlets, letters, and other artifacts from its vast National American Woman Suffrage Association Collection (1848–1921), originally donated by longtime National American Woman Suffrage Association president Carrie Chapman Catt. The Prints and Photographs Division of the library created a partner exhibit of thirty-eight suffrage campaign photographs, cartoons, and portraits. Catharine E. Beecher's *Educational Reminiscences and Suggestions* (1874) and Virginia Penny's *The Employments of Women* (1863) are two of the many books made available through the Making of America Project at the University of Michigan (http://www.umdl.umich.edu/moa/). Because the Library of Congress and University of Michigan sites and others offering whole works in electronic form may be searched for words occurring anywhere in the full texts, researchers can zero in on descriptions of customs, events, and people, study word usage, trace the progress of an idea, and undoubtedly see connections never before discernible.

One doesn't have to be an august body, however, to create an excellent historical Web resource. University of Virginia Master's degree student Mary Halnon put together comments about women made by eighteen European travelers to America between 1820 and 1842, filling out the picture of American women presented by the most well-known visitor of the time, Alexis de Tocqueville (http://xroads.virginia.edu/HYPER/DETOC/FEM/home.htm). In 1991, history lover Irene Stuber began publishing a weekly electronic newsletter, *Women of Achievement and Herstory,* replete with vignettes, anniversaries, and quotations from women. By 1998, her information was being assembled into a 366-episode daybook on the Women's Internet Information Network site (http://www.undelete.org), which features an exhibit of photographs from a private collection as well as public sources.

In 1998, the National Women's History Project (http://nwhp.org) invited Web visitors to celebrate the 150th anniversary of the women's rights movement on a site "Living the Legacy: The Women's Rights Movement, 1948–1998" (http://www.legacy98.org/), which summarized the history of the movement and suggested ways to commemorate the anniversary. More detailed information on recent feminist history is available in *The Feminist Chronicles, 1953–1993* (http://www.feminist.org/research/chronicles/chronicl. html), the online version of a 1993 book by Toni Carabillo, Judith Meuli, and June Bundy Csida, and within documents from the women's liberation movement assembled by the Duke University Rare Book, Manuscript and Special Collections Library Digital Scriptorium Project: (http://scriptorium.lib. duke.edu).

Women's lives in the Civil War era are also well covered by Internet resources, thanks in large measure to the Scriptorium site. Visitors can examine scanned pages or read transcriptions of diaries, letters, and memoirs of former slaves Elizabeth Johnson Harris, Hannah Valentine, and others; an 1864 diary of a sixteen-year-old Tennessean; and the papers of two Confederate spies, Rose O'Neal Greenhow and Sarah E. Thompson. Ginny Daley, Duke Women's Studies Bibliographer and Archivist, also compiled a set of links to other Civil War Websites on women (http://scriptorium. lib.duke.edu/women/cwdocs.html). The mid-nineteenth century is also represented in two sites reproducing illustrations and text from *Godey's Lady's Book,* a popular women's magazine of the time. Roger Carrie's site (http://www. history.rochester.edu/godeys) contains sample issues. A site maintained by Hope Greenberg contains portions of the magazine and commentary on it (http://www.edu:80/~hag/ godey/index. html).

Several women significant in American history have entire Websites devoted to them. An online exhibit from the Emma Goldman Papers Project describes her concerns with free speech, reproductive rights, and pacifism, offering viewers a glimpse into the thousands of documents that are her legacy (http://sunsite.berkeley.edu/Goldman/Exhibition/). Likewise, the Margaret Sanger Papers Project provides a digital image of a pamphlet used by Sanger to promote birth control, in addition to a detailed description of the project (http://www.nyu.edu/projects/sanger/). The University of Kansas Clendening Medical Library site exhibits Florence Nightingale letters from the library's collection (http://clendening.kumc.edu/florence).

The Internet also offers the opportunity to create entirely new virtual archives. For example, a major objective of the Jewish Women's Archive (http://www.jwa.org/), established in 1995, is to build a searchable online directory of all archival and library material related to Jewish women in America, regardless of where the items are held physically. The Jewish Women's Archive site also includes biographical exhibits on several American Jewish women, including Rebecca Gratz, Lillian Wald, and Molly Picon.

The availability of such resources and those many more that are sure to appear are changing how people study and teach history. They should be celebrated and used. *(See also: Archives and Sources; Civil War; Goldman, Emma; National American Woman Suffrage Association; National Women's History Project; Sanger, Margaret Louise)*

—**Phyllis Holman Weisbard**

Internet Sources

American Memory Project, Library of Congress: http://memory. loc.gov/ammem/

Civil War Women: Primary Sources on the Internet, by Ginny Daley: http://scriptorium.lib.duke.edu/women/cwdocs.html

Digital Scriptorium, Rare Book, Manuscript, and Special Collections Library, Duke University: http://scriptorium.lib.duke. edu/wlm

Emma Goldman Papers Project, online exhibit: http://sunsite. berkeley.edu/Goldman/Exhibition

The Feminist Chronicles, 1953–1993: http://www.feminist.org/ research/chronicles/chronicl.html

Florence Nightingale letters, University of Kansas Clendening Medical Library site: http://clendening.kumc.edu/florence

Godey's Lady's Book sample issues, site by Roger Corrie: http:// www.history.rochester.edu/godeys

Godey's Lady's Book (portions and commentary), site by Hope Greenberg: http://www.uvm.edu:80/~hag/godey/index.html

Jewish Women's Archive: http://www.jwa.org

Living the Legacy: The Women's Rights Movement, 1948–1998: http://www.legacy98.org

Making of America Project, University of Michigan: http://www. umdl.umich.edu/moa/

Margaret Sanger Papers Project: http://www.nyu.edu/projects/ sanger/

National Women's History Project: http://www.nwhp.org

Uncovering Women's History in Archival Collections, by Jill U. Jackson: http://www.lib.utsa.edu/Archives/links.htm

Women in America: 1820–1842, by Mary Halnon: http://xroads. virginia.edu/~HYPER/DETOC/FEM/home.htm

Women's Internet Information Network, including *Women of Achievement,* by Irene Stuber: http://www.undelete.org

Jackson, Helen Maria (Fiske) Hunt (1830–1885)

Helen Hunt Jackson was a prolific poet, novelist, and Indian rights activist. Born in Amherst, Massachusetts, she was the second of four children born to Deborah Waterman (Vinal), homemaker and writer, and Nathan Welby Fiske, a professor. Strong willed and feisty, by the age of twenty, Jackson found herself the most sought-after and attended woman at social functions. One gentleman described her as "more alive than any one else I ever knew." At a ball given by the governor of New York, she met her first husband, Lieutenant Edward Bissell Hunt, an Army engineer. The marriage, however, was fraught with tragedy. Jackson bore two sons—one who died in infancy and the other at nine years of age. Two years before the death of her second son, in 1863, her husband was killed in an engineering accident.

Jackson's intense grief led to the birth of her literary career. She wrote and published hundreds of articles and poems for a variety of East Coast newspapers. An astute businesswoman, Jackson sold her work to the highest bidder. Shunning personal celebrity, she adopted various pseudonyms, such as "H. H.," "Rip Van Winkle," "Saxe Holm," and "No-Name." Much of her writing was descriptive travelogues drawn from her European and Southern California travels with Sarah Woolsey, Jackson's longtime female companion. Repeated illness, however, forced Jackson to relocate to Colorado Springs, Colorado, where she met and married in 1875 William Sharpless Jackson, a Quaker banker.

On a visit to Boston in 1879, Jackson heard an elegant oratory by the Ponca leader Standing Bear and "Bright Eyes" (Susette LaFlesche Tibbles) that would change her life. They told of the breaking of treaties and the forced removal of the Poncas to the Indian Territory in Oklahoma by the U.S. Army. Jackson diligently researched government Indian policy and authored *A Century of Dishonor* (1881), an angry reproach of the federal government for its management of Indian affairs. The following year, Jackson received a commission from the Interior Department to document the needs of the Mission Indians of southern and coastal California.

Disillusioned by the government's lack of response after *Dishonor*, she attempted to publish her findings on the Mission Indians as a protest novel. *Ramona* (1884), however, became the nineteenth century's best-selling romance novel. Satisfied with her mission, she returned to her home in Colorado.

Jackson died of cancer in 1885 at the age of fifty-four. Her life is testimony to an unbounded and independent spirit whose zest knew no bounds. *(See also: Native American Women; Women Writers)*

—Roberta A. Hobson

Further Reading

Related Media: A yearly stage production of *Ramona* in Hemet, California.

Banning, Evelyn I. *Helen Hunt Jackson.* New York: Vanguard, 1973.

Jackson, Helen Hunt. *A Century of Dishonor: A Sketch of the United States Government's Dealings with Some of the Indian Tribes.* 1882. Reprint, Minneapolis, MN: Ross & Haines, 1964.

———. *Ramona.* 1884. Reprint, Boston: Little, Brown, 1939.

Mathes, Valerie Sherer. *Helen Hunt Jackson and Her Indian Reform Legacy,* 1st ed., American Studies Series. Edited by William H. Goetzmann. Austin: University of Texas Press, 1990.

Odell, Ruth. *Helen Hunt Jackson (H. H.).* New York: Appleton-Century, 1939.

James, Alice (1848–1892)

Alice James was a great American family's youngest and only female child, whose diary and letters have stimulated considerable interest in her unique life and brilliant mind. Her independently wealthy father, the metaphysician Henry James, Sr., affectionately indulged his children with eccentric educations in Boston, New York, and Europe. Her eldest brothers, the philosopher-psychologist William James and the novelist Henry James, fashioned public careers that rank them among the most distinguished men of letters in United States. Such vocations, however, were not widely available for young women of Alice James's class, which constrained her to create a private career that to later readers appears as both a case study of nineteenth-century female invalidism and a testament to intellectual originality.

Although James appears to have been a vigorous and sociable child, in her passage into adulthood, she became susceptible to suicidal depression and fits of fainting and nervous paralysis, which doctors euphemistically diagnosed as "nervous hyperaesthesia" and "hysteria." How much her illness derived from physical or psychosomatic causes may be inferred from her own account: "Owing to muscular circumstances my youth was not of the most ardent, but I had to peg away pretty hard between 12 and 24, 'killing myself,' as one calls it—absorbing into the bone that the better part is to clothe oneself in neutral tints, walk by still waters, and possess one's soul in silence." Her suffering sometimes abated: After her mother's death, she carefully attended her father, but after his death, she moved with her lifelong companion Katherine Loring to England, where at last she died of breast cancer at the age of 43.

If such a record of her experience were all that later readers knew of Alice James, her name might appear only as a footnote to those of her kinsmen. Three years before she died, however, she wrote inside a scholastic notebook, "I think that if I get into the habit of writing a bit about what happens, or rather doesn't happen, I may lose a little of the sense of loneliness and desolation which abides with me." The text that emerges is altogether remarkable. Besides providing a pitilessly realistic documentary of an invalid's daily battles with gossiping nurses and insensitive visitors, *The Diary of Alice James* brims with humorous and critical observations on English and American manners, pungent commentary on Parliamentary debates concerning her ancestral Ireland, and shimmering reminiscences that reveal the family genius.

Yet Alice James's peculiar career continues to appear as an affair with death. The entry reporting her doctor's "uncompromising verdict" on the lump in her breast opens, "To him who waits, all things come!" A month before dying, she dictates to Loring, "I have been dead so long and it has been simply such a grim shoving of the hours behind me . . . since that hideous summer . . . when I went down to the deep sea, its dark waters closed over me and I knew neither hope nor peace." *The Diary of Alice James* memorializes American women's perversely constricted past even as it frustrates any attempt to reduce that past to a simplistic category. *(See also: Hysteria; Women Writers)*

—**Craig White**

Further Reading

Edel, Leon, ed. *The Diary of Alice James.* 1934. Reprint, New York: Penguin, 1964.

Kahane, Claire. "The Aesthetic Politics of Rage," *LIT* 3 (1991): 19-31.

Lewis, R. W. B. *The Jameses: A Family Narrative.* New York: Farrar, Straus & Giroux, 1991.

Saracino, Maria Antonietta. "Alice James and Italy." In *The Sweetest Impression of Life: The James Family and Italy,* edited by James W. Tuttleton and Agostino Lombardo, 149-61. New York: New York University Press, 1990.

Strouse, Jean. *Alice James: A Biography.* Boston: Houghton Mifflin, 1980.

———. "Alice James: A Family Romance." In *Psychoanalytic Studies of Biography,* edited by George Maraitis and George H. Pollock, 63-83. Madison, CT: International University Press, 1987.

Strout, Cushing. "Mr. James's Daughter and Shakespeare's Sister: A Review-Essay on Jean Strouse's *Alice James: A Biography,*" *Henry James Review* 3 (Fall 1981): 59-63.

Walker, Nancy. " 'Wider Than the Sky': Public Presence and Private Self in Dickinson, James, and Woolf." In *The Private Self: Theory and Practice of Women's Autobiographical Writings,* edited by Shari Benstock, 272-303. Chapel Hill: University of North Carolina Press, 1988.

Yeazell, Ruth. *The Death and Letters of Alice James: Selected Correspondence Edited, with a Biographical Essay.* Berkeley: University of California Press, 1981.

✍ Jane Club

Founded in 1891 as part of the Hull House settlement endeavor in Chicago's Halsted Street neighborhood, the Jane Club was conceived as a cooperative housing arrangement for young working women, intended to provide inexpensive living arrangements to protect the women against eviction and homelessness in the event of loss of income resulting from layoffs or strikes. The latter aspect was uppermost in the mind of Mary Kenney, under whose leadership the housing cooperative took shape. Kenney was at the time a twenty-seven-year-old Irish immigrant and labor organizer, and historian Allen F. Davis has referred to her as one of the people whose influence transformed Jane Addams from a Christian philanthropist to a social reformer. Addams initially invited Kenney to visit Hull House after learning of her role in organizing the first bookbinders' union for women in Chicago. Kenney went reluctantly, suspecting that Addams and the other Hull House residents "were all rich and not friends of the workers." She changed her mind after meeting Addams, who won over the younger woman when she put the facilities of Hull House, in particular its parlor ("different from anything I had ever seen before"), at Kenney's disposal for meetings of union women.

Kenney realized that women workers were in a vulnerable position during labor-organizing efforts and disputes, since their fear of being unable to meet room and board expenses in the event of lost work and wages would often lead them to capitulate to employer demands. During the course of a strike meeting at Hull House, according to Jane Addams, one young woman stated, "Wouldn't it be fine if we had a boarding-club of our own, and then we could stand by each other in a time like this?"

Accordingly, in May 1891, Hull House paid the first month's rent and supplied furnishings for two vacant apartments in a tenement on Ewing Street, near Halsted. Fifteen women, plus a cook and "general worker," moved in. Residents organized themselves as the "Jane Club" and voted to pay three dollars per week to cover room, board, and service. Within three years, the club had grown to fifty members, occupying all six apartments in the tenement. Reflecting and accepting the contemporary racism of progressive America, the club was racially segregated.

As with all Hull House undertakings, a philosophical approach guided the development of the Jane Club. According to Addams, the first little group of members met together, read "Cooperation" and "Diligence" aloud from Beatrice Potter's book, *The Co-Operative Movement in Great Britain,* and "discussed all the difficulties and fascinations of such an undertaking." The Jane Club concept, that of providing inexpensive lodgings to women to allow them to save their money, echoes earlier communal undertakings in Europe, such as the *béates* in seventeenth-century France: pious widows or spinsters who ran dormitories for female lace makers, allowing the young women to pool their earnings for food and materials and thus save money for their dowries. The Jane Club was part and parcel of the interest in communal living arrangements expressed by turn-of-the-century feminists such as Charlotte Perkins Gilman and also finds parallels in the ideas that shaped the formation of women's colleges in the nineteenth century, with attention given to the implications of living as a community of women. In keeping with the spirit of Hull House, however, the Jane Club was democratic in structure. Members elected officers and determined duties and regulations. The club, following the initial contribution from Hull House, was financially self-sustaining.

In 1898, a benefactor donated $15,000 to build a new facility for the Jane Club. The club continued as a residence for working women until 1938 with the arrival, following Addams's death, of a new head resident at Hull House. In that year, Charlotte E. Carr came from New York to lead the foundation. During her tempestuous five years as head of Hull House, she was determined to reinvigorate the foundation with the spirit of its first twenty years. Carr complained that Hull House was in danger of becoming a museum, a monument to past achievements rather than an institution facing the challenges of the mid-twentieth century. The Jane Club, in her opinion, belonged to a past era. According to Allen Davis, "Charlotte Carr put carpenters to work inside the ancient buildings of Hull House, and classrooms took shape in such holy relics as the Jane Club. Founded by Miss Addams as a cooperative home for working women who were dispossessed when they went out on strike, the Jane Club had become just a good cheap place to live." *(See also: Addams, Jane; Hull House; O'Sullivan, Mary Kenney)*

—**Laura Gellott**

Further Reading

Addams, Jane. *Twenty Years at Hull-House.* New York: Macmillan, 1910.

Davis, Allen F. *American Heroine: The Life and Legend of Jane Addams.* New York: Oxford University Press, 1973.

Davis, Allen F., and Mary Lynn McCree, eds. *Eighty Years at Hull-House.* Chicago: Quadrangle, 1969.

———. *Hull-House Maps and Papers.* New York: Arno, 1970.

Elshtain, Jean Bethke. "A Return to Hull-House: Reflections on Jane Addams." In *Power Trips and Other Journeys: Essays in Feminism as Civic Discourse,* pp. 3-12. Madison: University of Wisconsin Press, 1990.

Linn, James Weber. *Jane Addams: A Biography.* 1935. Reprint, New York: Greenwood, 1968.

Phipott, Thomas. *The Slum and the Ghetto: Neighborhood Deterioration and Middle Class Reform, Chicago, 1880–1930.* New York: Oxford University Press, 1978.

Sklar, Kathryn Kish. "Hull House in the 1890s: A Community of Women Reformers," *Signs* 10 (Summer 1985): 658-77.

Webb, Beatrice Potter. *The Co-Operative Movement in Great Britain.* London: F. Sonnenschein & c [sic], 1891.

ॐ Japanese Relocation Camps: World War II

After the bombing of Pearl Harbor, war hysteria and racism were combined with the economic jealousies of non-Japanese California agricultural interests to pressure the federal government to take action against the resident Japanese and Japanese-Americans living on the West Coast. On February 19, 1942, by Executive Order 9066 President Roosevelt called for the exclusion of all persons of Japanese ancestry from the newly created Military Area 1 (western portions of Washington, Oregon, and California). The forced removal and internment in relocation camps of Issei, Japanese living in America, and Nisei, Americans of Japanese descent, began under the auspices of the War Relocation Authority, headed briefly by Milton Eisenhower and then by Dillon Myer.

The removal of families and individuals to fifteen temporary assembly centers such as race tracks and fairgrounds and then to hastily constructed relocation camps on federally owned wasteland was conducted by the Army with only a few days' warning. This brought particular hardship to the Issei women whose main responsibility was the home and the care of children and elderly family members. How could the family be maintained with no privacy when all bathing, laundry, and eating was communal and with the few personal possessions that each family was allowed to carry with them? These older women had either been restricted to domestic labor, if widowhood forced them to work outside their homes, or were cloistered in the segregated Issei communities of the West Coast in traditional women's roles. Neither experience prepared them for life in the internment camps where their husbands grew sullen and their children were either ashamed of their Japanese heritage or resentful of their American citizenship for its failure to protect them from such discrimination.

The Nisei women were already accustomed to the discrimination of the world outside their communities when they sought education or employment. In their homes, however, they were encouraged to remain traditional Japanese girls to be faithful to the family and eligible for marriage. For these women, the added pressure of the internment camps confirmed their status as second- or even third-class citizens.

Alan Parker's 1990 film, *Come See the Paradise,* shows these problems quite well.

The creation of the 442nd all-Nisei combat team provided an escape from the camps for approximately 2,500 Nisei men, while a few Nisei women joined the Women's Army Corps. A more common escape for Nisei women who did not have children or elderly family members to care for was to accept voluntary relocation to areas away from the West Coast where they were often helped to find employment by their church affiliations or family friends. To some of these young women, the opportunity to function in a society that did not see them as the object of racial discrimination (less common away from the West Coast) or as the enemy was an enlightening experience. Few would return to their homes on a permanent basis after the war.

When the exclusion order was rescinded on December 17, 1944, over half the original 110,000 evacuees were still living in the camps. Eventually 57,000 returned to the West Coast to find that 80 percent of their personal possessions had been stolen and much of their property had been illegally resold by those entrusted with it or confiscated under a law passed by the state of California. These losses combined with lost earnings were estimated at more than $2.5 billion. In 1988, federal legislation to pay compensation of $20,000 to each survivor of the internment camps was passed. When actual payment was begun in 1990, half of those eligible were already deceased. *(See also: Asian American Women; World War II)*

—**Tamerin Mitchell Hayward**

Further Reading

Daniels, Roger, Sandra C. Taylor, and Harry Kitano, eds. *Japanese Americans: From Relocation to Redress.* Rev. ed. Seattle: University of Washington Press, 1991.

Houston, Jeanne Wakatsuke, and James D. Houston. *Farewell to Manzanar.* Boston: Houghton Mifflin, 1973.

Myer, Dillon S. *Uprooted Americans: The Japanese Americans and the War Relocation Authority during World War II.* Tucson: University of Arizona Press, 1971.

Parker, Alan. *Come See the Paradise.* Produced by Robert F. Colseberry. Beverly Hills, CA: Fox Video, 1990. Videocassette.

Sone, Monica. *Nisei Daughter.* 1953. Reprint, Seattle: University of Washington Press, 1979.

Weglyn, Michi. *Years of Infamy: The Untold Story of America's Concentration Camps.* New York: William Morrow, 1976.

∞ Jazz

Aside from the human voice, the piano is arguably the only instrument with which women have made a significant impact on the music frequently termed America's only native art. In the 1920s, Lil Hardin Armstrong, a competent composer as well as pianist, came to the public's attention largely through her association with her far more famous husband, Louis. During the 1930s and 1940s, another composer-pianist, Mary Lou Williams, became recognized as a leading exponent of the modern idiom called "bebop."

The 1950s saw the emergence of numerous prominent keyboard stylists, two of whom remained powerful influences on the music of the 1990s: British-born Marian McPartland is not only a prodigious player but popular host of a regular jazz program on National Public Radio; Toshiko Akiyoshi, a Japanese expatriate, is pianist, co-leader, and exclusive composer-arranger of a big band many critics acclaim the finest large jazz ensemble of the 1980s and 1990s. A later generation of pianist-composers whose music frequently expresses elements of the avant-garde includes Alice Coltrane, Carla Bley, and JoAnne Brackeen. The 1990s have been witness to the emergence of fresh, underpublicized talent, most notably jazz pianists Geri Allen, Myra Melford, and Marilyn Crispell.

Until the 1980s, the only woman to achieve fame on a jazz instrument other than the piano was trombonist-composer Melba Liston. With the increasing emphasis on women in the arts and the challenging of gender stereotypes in music, jazz is beginning to attract greater numbers of women reed, brass, percussion, and bass players. Throughout the 1990s, two women frequently appeared among the poll winners in the woodwind category: soprano saxophonists Jane Ira Bloom and Jane Bunnett.

While women have had to struggle for acceptance in instrumental jazz by proving they can "sound" like their male counterparts, they are under no such strictures as vocalists; in that area, in fact, they have exerted a greater influence on the music than have men. Bessie Smith, the "Empress of the Blues," virtually popularized the blues form single-handedly while achieving fame second only to Louis Armstrong's. During the "Swing Era" that followed, Billie Holiday gained international recognition as the outstanding interpreter of American popular song. Although Holiday's life ended tragically and abruptly, several of her contemporaries remained active, vital contributors into the late 1980s. For over three decades, Ella Fitzgerald, Sarah Vaughan, and Carmen McRae were the perennial first, second, and third choices of fans and critics alike in virtually every jazz poll. In the 1990s, the most noteworthy "keepers of the flame" were veterans Betty Carter, Abbey Lincoln, Shirley Horn, and Nancy Wilson. All of the foregoing are experts at "scat," "vocalese," and highly improvisatory approaches to melody in which the human voice takes on the characteristics of a horn. Paradoxically, then, women have gained mass acceptance as jazz instrumentalists, if under the guise of being vocalists.

As jazz gives ground to current pop styles, younger jazz vocalists have had to employ eclectic styles to gain widespread acceptance, although a few, such as Cassandra Wilson, have done so while remaining firmly planted within the jazz tradition. Primarily a creative rather than a commercial music, jazz has been a major inspiration for numerous popular stylists, from Diana Ross to Natalie Cole. In the area of vocal music, at least, jazz has provided undeniable opportunities for all women, regardless of race. *(See also: Holiday, Billie; Popular Vocalists; Smith, Bessie)*

—**Samuel L. Chell**

Further Reading

Feather, Leonard. *The Book of Jazz.* New York: Dell, 1976.

Gourse, Leslie. *Madam Jazz: Contemporary Women Instrumentalists.* New York: Oxford University Press, 1995.

Leder, Jan. *Women in Jazz: A Discography.* Westport, CT: Greenwood, 1985.

Placksin, Sally. *American Women in Jazz: 1900 to the Present.* New York: Wideview, 1982.

~ Jewett, Sarah Orne (1849–1909)

Sarah Orne Jewett was a writer of exquisite, realistic fiction depicting the lives and friendships of women in nineteenth-century New England. Born in South Berwick, Maine, Jewett learned her region's landscape, speech, and folkways by accompanying her father, a country doctor, to farms and fishing villages. After graduating from Berwick Academy in 1865, she considered becoming a physician before choosing to write—a decision she revisited in *A Country Doctor* (1884).

Although Jewett was reared in comfortable conditions, the Maine of her youth was marked by declining ports and deserted farms. Many men moved west to seek new opportunity, and her works often represent a largely female population (often seen and overheard by a visitor) who enliven their surroundings by sharing visits and remembrances of earlier times when shipping trade with the West Indies brought wealth and exotic strangers.

Inspired by Harriet Beecher Stowe's fiction about old New England, Jewett at the age of nineteen published her first sketch of the Maine region in the prestigious *Atlantic Monthly.* Her early pieces were collected in *Deephaven* (1877), and in the next decades, she published several volumes of fiction, whose delicate yet lifelike art culminated in *The Country of the Pointed Firs* (1896), in which the odd and gentle characters of a Maine seaport relate their lives in tones of humor, frustration, and nostalgia.

Jewett's finest work unites place, people, and moment in an evanescent beauty that was admired internationally in her own time. Literary history often classifies her as a leading practitioner of New England's "local color" or "regional" movement, along with Mary Wilkins Freeman, Alice Brown, and Rose Terry Cooke. In the twentieth century, Jewett inspired the work of Kate Chopin and Willa Cather. Cather dedicated her novel *O Pioneers!* (1913) to Jewett, collected and edited Jewett's *Best Stories* in 1925 (reissued as *The Country of the Pointed Firs and Other Stories,* 1955), and featured portraits of Jewett and her companion Annie Fields in *Not under Forty* (1936).

In 1901, Bowdoin College granted a Doctorate of Letters to Jewett, the first American woman to receive such an honor. Her Boston home with Fields, the widow of the publisher James T. Fields, was a literary and social center. In 1909, Jewett died at her family home in South Berwick. Fields edited her *Letters* in 1911, and her *Verses* appeared posthumously in 1916. Stories such as "The White Heron," "The Town Poor," and "The Foreigner" continue to be widely anthologized, introducing readers to the old world of New England and the woman's voice in which it lives. *(See also: Friendships; Women Writers)*

—Craig White

Further Reading

Cary, Richard, ed. *Sarah Orne Jewett.* New York: Twayne, 1962.

———. *Sarah Orne Jewett: Letters.* Enlarged and rev. ed. Waterville, ME: Colby College Press, 1967.

Donovan, Josephine. *New England Local Color Literature: A Woman's Tradition.* New York: Ungar, 1983.

Eicheberger, Clayton. "Sarah Orne Jewett (1849–1909): Critical Bibliography of Secondary Comment," *American Literary Realism, 1897–1910* 2 (1969): 189-262.

Frost, John Eldridge. "Sarah Orne Jewett Bibliography: 1949–1963," *Colby Library Quarterly Series* 6 (June 1964): 405-17.

Matthiessen, F. O. *Sarah Orne Jewett.* Boston: Houghton Mifflin, 1920.

Nagel, Gwen L. *Critical Essays on Sarah Orne Jewett.* Boston: G. K. Hall, 1984.

Sherman, Sarah Way. *Sarah Orne Jewett, An American Persephone.* Hanover, NH: University Press of New England, 1989.

Weber, Clara Carter, and Carl J. Weber. *A Bibliography of the Published Writings of Sarah Orne Jewett.* Waterville, ME: Colby College Press, 1949.

~ Jewish Women

The first Jewish women to arrive in the United States in significant numbers came from Germany in the 1840s, preceded by a few thousand Sephardic Jewish men and women whose ancestors had lived in Spain ("Sepharad") and Portugal until the Jews were expelled from the Iberian peninsula at the end of the fifteenth century. Many of the Sephardic Jews in the United States intermarried with Christians, before the arrival of the wave of German Jews. German Jews settled on the East Coast and in Cincinnati, Milwaukee, and other midwestern cities. They were generally adherents of the Reform branch of Judaism, which they brought with them from Germany.

The German Jewish community was a prosperous one, and wives and unmarried women engaged in communal and charitable work. Prominent among them was Rebecca Kohut (1864–1951), founder of a school for girls and president of the New York Section of the National Council of Jewish Women (NCJW), a socially conscious philanthropic organization. NCJW is the ongoing legacy of the First Congress of Jewish Women (1893), organized by another important German Jewish woman, Hannah Greenebaum Solomon (1858–1942). One of the speakers at the congress was Henrietta Szold (1860–1945), daughter of a Baltimore rabbi and the first woman allowed to attend classes at the Jewish Theological Seminary of America. Henrietta Szold toiled underappreciated for years as literary secretary of the Jewish Publication Society, editor of the *American Jewish Yearbook,* and translator into English of the works of German Jewish scholars Heinrich Graetz and Louis Ginzberg.

Not until she took up the cause of improving medical care and conditions in Palestine by founding another Jewish women's organization, Hadassah, in 1912, did her talents really flower. In 1993, Hadassah had a membership of 385,000 women.

The largest wave of Jewish immigration dates from the 1880s when Russian and Polish Jews began seeking religious freedom and improvement in their impoverished condition. Almost 2 million had arrived in the United States by 1915, settling mainly on the East Coast and overwhelming the German-Jewish benevolent societies. Many Jewish immigrant women traveled alone or with small children. They were met at Ellis Island Immigration Center by Yiddish-speaking workers supervised by the NCJW, who counseled the women about housing, employment, and locating their relatives. Unmarried Jewish women found work in sweatshop factories in the garment industry. Married women augmented meager family resources by taking in laundry, boarders, or garment piecework they could produce at home.

Jewish women dominated the ladies garment industry. Many became union activists and strike leaders. The shirtwaist makers strike (1909–1910) was spurred on by stirring words addressed to strikers in Yiddish by Clara Lemlich on November 22, 1909: "I am a working girl, one of those who are on strike against intolerable conditions. I am tired of listening to speakers who talk in general terms. What we are here for is to decide whether we shall or shall not strike. I offer a resolution that a general strike be declared NOW" (Baum, Hyman, and Michel 142). Rose Schneiderman (1882–1972) rose through the ranks of the United Cloth Hat and Cap Makers Union to serve on the executive board of the union. She later became a professional unionist with the Women's Trade Union League.

Eastern European Jews generally arrived in America upholding the body of Jewish law and observance, or "orthodox," but they and their descendants also came to make up the majority of the Conservative movement, founded by German Jews searching for a more traditional path than that taken by Reform. None of the movements then encouraged the participation of women in liturgical life or serious Jewish study, both hallmarks of honor for male Jews, but each movement has made strides in the past two decades. The first such gesture actually came earlier, in 1922, when Mordecai Kaplan, at that time a professor at the Jewish Theological Seminary of the Conservative movement, devised and conducted the first public Bat Mitzvah ceremony for his daughter Judith. Until then, the age of assumption of religious obligations had been marked only by boys, with a Bar Mitzvah at the age of thirteen. This ceremony is now given for Reform, Conservative, and Reconstructionist (the movement spawned by Kaplan's thought) girls. Many Orthodox families take note of their daughter's coming-of-age, too, by having a festive meal at which the daughter delivers a talk demonstrating her learning of Jewish texts.

Reform Judaism was the first to ordain a woman rabbi, accepting Sally Priesand (b. 1946) into the rabbinate in 1972. The Reconstructionist Rabbinical College admitted women from its first class of rabbinical students in 1968, with Sandy Sasso (b. 1947) the first woman to complete the requirements for ordination in 1974. The Conservative movement agreed to accept women rabbinical students at the Jewish Theological Seminary in 1983, ordaining Amy Eilberg (b. 1954) in 1985. An increasing number of Orthodox women form women's communal prayer groups and participate in the study of the Talmud and other traditional Jewish texts.

From early on, Jewish women have been a significant presence in the leadership and ranks of the women's rights movement. Betty Friedan (b. 1921), Bella Abzug (1920–1998), Letty Cottin Pogrebin (b. 1939), and other editors of *Ms.* magazine are examples of some of the many Jewish women leaders of the modern women's movement. Their relationships and their Jewishness are explored in *The Telling,* a 1993 book by E. M. Broner. Today, American Jewish women's history courses are taught at several universities, and books and articles on the subject are published by academic presses and journals. Jewish women's issues are discussed in numerous women's periodicals, especially in *Lilith* (founded in 1976) and *Bridges* (founded in 1990). Jewish women have also taken to the Internet, with several Websites devoted to their activities and interests. *(See also: Abzug, Bella Savitsky; Friedan, Betty; Hadassah; National Women's Trade Union League; Politics; Schneiderman, Rose; Shirtwaist Makers Strike of 1909; Synagogue Sisterhoods)*

—**Phyllis Holman Weisbard**

Further Reading

Baum, Charlotte, Paula Hyman, and Sonya Michel. *The Jewish Woman in America.* New York: New American Library, 1975.

Bridges, 1990–present in print. Sample articles available at http://www.pond.net/ckinberg/bridges/

Broner, E. M. *The Telling: The Story of a Group of Jewish Women Who Journey to Spirituality through Community and Ceremony.* San Francisco: Harper, 1993.

Fishman, Sylvia Barack. *A Breath of Life: Feminism in the American Jewish Community.* New York: Free Press, 1993.

Hyman, Paula E., and Deborah Dash Moore, eds. *Jewish Women in America: An Historical Encyclopedia,* 2 vols. New York: Routledge, 1997.

Lilith Magazine, 1976–present in print. Sample articles available at http://www.lilithmag.com

Marcus, Jacob Rader. *The American Jewish Woman: A Documentary History.* New York: KTAV, 1981.

Pogrebin, Letty Cottin. *Deborah, Golda, and Me: Being Jewish and Female in America.* New York: Simon & Schuster, 1991.

Rogow, Faith. *Gone to Another Meeting: The National Council of Jewish Women, 1893–1993.* Tuscaloosa: University of Alabama Press, 1993.

Weinberg, Sydney Stahl. *The World of Our Mothers: The Lives of Jewish Immigrant Women.* Chapel Hill: University of North Carolina Press, 1988.

http://www.jwa.org [Jewish Women's Archive]

Johnston, Frances Benjamin (1864–1952)

Frances Benjamin Johnston was probably the best-known professional woman photographer in turn-of-the-century America. Throughout a long career, Johnston specialized in photo-stories for popular magazines, architectural photography, and portraiture. Known for her artistry as well as for her energy and enthusiasm, she consistently promoted photography as a viable profession for women.

Many aspects of Johnston's life and career bear similarities to the experiences of other professional women of the late nineteenth century. The women were from the middle class, many never married, and most were educated. The only child of a well-to-do family, Johnston grew up in Washington, D.C., and after graduating from Notre Dame Convent, she studied painting in Paris. Her parents encouraged and supported her artistic, business, and photographic pursuits.

By the late 1880s, Johnston embarked on a serious career as a professional photographer by doing photo assignments for popular magazines such as *Demorest's Family Magazine, Frank Leslie's,* and *Ladies Home Journal.* She produced photographs and stories on a wide range of subjects—coal miners in Pennsylvania, women factory workers in Massachusetts, cadets at Annapolis, the beauty of Yellowstone Park. In 1895, she opened her own up-to-date public studio built onto the rear of her parents' V Street home. As a well-known Washingtonian, Johnston photographed many among the elite of that city. She wrote about and photographed Presidents Harrison, Cleveland, McKinley, Roosevelt, and Taft, as well as many other government officials and national celebrities. Of particular interest are her photographs of well-known Washington women, including Alice Roosevelt, Ida McKinley, and Lillian Paunceforte. Her series of photographs taken in 1899 and 1900 depicting life at the Hampton Institute—a training school for black youth in Hampton, Virginia—has gained special recognition. First shown at the Paris Exposition of 1900, these evocative photographs were exhibited at the Museum of Modern Art in 1966.

Johnston always demonstrated an interest in women and their lives and was the center of an informal network of female amateur and professional photographers. In the late 1880s, women from all over the United States wrote to Johnston asking for her advice and support of their photographic efforts. In addition, Johnston made a unique contribution to the history of photography by organizing an exhibition of the work of twenty-eight American women photographers for the International Photographic Congress of the Paris Exposition in 1900. She herself served as a delegate to that exposition. *(See also: Photography)*

—C. Jane Gover

Further Reading

Daniel, Pete, and Raymond Smock. *A Talent for Detail.* New York: Harmony, 1974.

Glen, Constance W., and Leland Rice. *Frances Benjamin Johnston: Women of Class and Station.* Long Beach: California State University Press, 1979.

Gover, C. Jane. *The Positive Image: Women Photographers in Turn of the Century America.* Albany: State University of New York Press, 1987.

Quitslund, Toby. "Her Feminine Colleagues—Photographs and Letters Collected by Frances Benjamin Johnston in 1900." In *Women Artists in Washington Collections,* edited by Josephine Withers, 97-109. College Park: University of Maryland Art Gallery and Women's Caucus for the Arts, 1979.

Tucker, Ann. *The Woman's Eye.* New York: Random House, 1973.

Johnston, Henrietta (Deering) (c. 1670–1728/9)

Henrietta Deering Johnston was a pioneer both in America and in the field of pastel portraiture. Pastel painting (the practice of applying dry pigments onto a ground, using only the binder necessary to hold the pigments in a crayon shape) was approaching its finest development in Europe at the same time Henrietta Johnston was putting the medium to use for the support of her family in the New World. It is thought that she was born in Ireland and married in 1704 or 1705 in Dublin to the Reverend Gideon Johnston, an impecunious minister of the Church of England. He was assigned to the Carolinas and the Bahamas, and they moved to what was to become known as Charleston, South Carolina. Their arrival and tenure in the New World were marked by episodes of bureaucratic misunderstandings relating to his employment, illness, misadventures on the high seas, Indian wars, and other tragedies.

The needs of their extended family and retinue were often met by her efforts at portraiture using pastel crayons, an art she may have learned in Ireland. The economic necessity to exploit her talent and the scarcity of art supplies may have limited her aesthetic exploits in this new medium. Her small portraits are of single figures, simply arranged. They are treasured by their owners, many of whom are descendants of the original subjects, for their charm and historical importance. Johnston is known to have worked in the Carolinas and in New York. After her husband died at sea in 1716, it may be supposed that Johnston lived out her days bartering art for sustenance, for she received no pension. *(See also: Art)*

—Susan Kellogg Portney

Further Reading

Willis, Euola. "The First Woman Painter in America," *Studio* 87 (July 1927): 13-20.

Jones, "Mother" (1836?–1930)

Labor organizer and agitator, "Mother" Jones was a unique figure in the American labor movement. For decades, she organized miners and was involved in all the famous labor upheavals of her era. A fiery speaker, she used the rhetoric of socialism in pursuit of social justice for workers but was beholden to no ideology or party.

Biographical details of her life, even her year of birth, are obscured by tales of a white-haired, petite woman tramping from one mining camp to another. Born Mary Harris in Cork, Ireland, she emigrated with her family to the United States, taught school, and became a dressmaker. After losing her husband, George Jones of the Iron Molders' Union, and her four young children to yellow fever in 1867 in Memphis, she operated a dressmaking business. When it was destroyed in the Chicago fire of 1871, she was drawn to the Knights of Labor and became a full-time organizer without a permanent home.

She worked for the United Mine Workers (UMW) and was also a founding member of the Social Democratic Party and the Industrial Workers of the World but remained aloof from all party activities. From 1900 to 1920, she organized among bituminous and anthracite miners in West Virginia and Pennsylvania; miners in Colorado, Arizona, Michigan, and Minnesota; garment strikers in New York; and steel strikers in Pennsylvania. She was adept at winning media attention for her causes, whether through her arrests or testimony before congressional investigating committees or through leading marches of strikers' wives or of working children to the Oyster Bay, New York, home of President Theodore Roosevelt.

Sometime friend of Terence Powderly of the Knights of Labor and of John Mitchell and John L. Lewis of the UMW, she was an outspoken individualist who could irritate both labor colleagues and management foes, while her ideological eccentricities annoyed socialists and suffragists alike. Her purported one hundredth birthday saw her celebrated by all sides as an American legend. *(See also: Industrial Workers of the World; Knights of Labor; Unions; United Mine Workers of America)*

—**Sally M. Miller**

Further Reading

Fetherling, Dale. *Mother Jones: The Miners' Angel.* Carbondale: Southern Illinois University Press, 1974.
Foner, Philip S., ed. *Mother Jones Speaks: Collected Writings and Speeches.* New York: Anchor Foundation, 1983.
Jones, Mary Harris. *The Autobiography of Mother Jones.* Chicago: Charles Kerr, 1925.

⮌ Jones, Virginia Lacy (1912–1984)

Virginia Lacy Jones was a black librarian and library educator whose distinguished career, although it began inauspiciously in the segregated and underfunded libraries of the South, contributed enormously to American librarianship. Jones studied librarianship first at Hampton Institute and later at the University of Illinois and eventually became, in 1945, the second black to receive a doctorate from the

Graduate Library School at the University of Chicago. (Dr. Eliza Gleason, 1940, was the first.) During her thirty-six years as dean of the Atlanta University School of Library Service, more than fifteen hundred black librarians were educated there, more than at any other school in the country. Jones was an energetic fund-raiser, and numerous conferences and in-service training programs were held in an effort to upgrade library service to black schools, colleges, and communities.

Jones's numerous awards and honors included the presidency of the Association of American Library Schools in 1967, receipt of the Melvil Dewey Award for professional achievement of high order in 1973, and an honorary doctorate from the University of Michigan in 1979.

A prolific writer, her "A Dean's Career" presents an unforgettable picture of black student life at the University of Illinois in the 1930s. She also contributed to the *Proceedings of the Governor's Conference on Georgia Libraries and Information Services* (1976), *Proceedings of Two Symposia Sponsored in Honor of Louis Round Wilson's 100th Birthday* (1976), and *Dictionary of American Library Biography* (1978), among other publications. *(See also: Black Women; Higher Education; Librarianship)*

—**Suzanne Hildenbrand**

Further Reading

Jones, Virginia Lacy. "A Dean's Career." In *The Black Librarian in America,* edited by E. J. Josey. Metuchen, NJ: Scarecrow, 1970.
———. *Reminiscences in Librarianship and Library Education.* Ann Arbor: University of Michigan Press, 1979.
Jordan, Casper LeRoy. "The Multifaceted Career of Virginia Lacy Jones." In *The Black Librarian in America Revisited,* edited by E. J. Josey, 75-83. Metuchen, NJ: Scarecrow, 1994.

⮌ Jong, Erica (Mann) (b. 1942)

Erica Jong is an author best known for her bold, controversial novels that explore social and sexual relationships from a feminist perspective.

After receiving a master's degree from Columbia University, teaching English both in the United States and abroad, publishing two volumes of poems, and being honored with poetry awards, Jong was propelled to international recognition in 1973 with her first novel, *Fear of Flying,* which became a sexual metaphor for a generation. Her first bestseller, the book sold over 12.5 million copies worldwide. The bawdy, confessional novel was published while she was married to psychiatrist Allan Jong, from whom she was divorced in 1975. Keeping "Jong" as her publishing name, in 1977 she published a second novel, *How to Save Your Own Life,* which carried forward the psychological observations of her memoir-style fiction. That same year, she married Jonathan Fast, from whom she was divorced in 1982 and with whom she has one daughter, Molly. In her 1984 novel, *Parachutes & Kisses,* she revisited the style of this early fiction in a protagonist's search for self.

Jong has been a prolific author and researcher, often combining these skills, perhaps most prominently in her 1980 novel, *Fanny, Being the True History of the Adventures of Fanny Hackabout-Jones,* written in the picaresque style of eighteenth-century English novelists. She often blends genres, as in the prose and poetry of *Witches* (1981). Her other novels include two released as audio recordings, most successfully, *Any Woman's Blues* (1990). Her "unauthorized autobiography," *Fear of Fifty* (1994), was followed in 1997 by *Inventing Memory: A Novel of Mothers and Daughters* and in 1998 by *What Do Women Want? Bread, Roses, Sex, Power.*

Poetry, her true literary love, spans her publishing career and includes poems published individually in poetry journals and popular magazines, as well as in volumes such as *Here Comes & Other Poems* (1975; originally published as *Fruits & Vegetables,* 1971), *Half-Lives* (1973), *Loveroot* (1975), *At the Edge of the Body* (1979), and *Ordinary Miracles* (1983). *Becoming Light* (1991), an imposing compilation of new and previously published poetry, draws from her varied phases of both free and formal verse.

Compelled to explore what it means to be Jewish and to be female—and, most recently, what it means to age—in American culture, Jong's writing mixes sophisticated literary allusions with an earthy, and often erotic, popular style. *(See also: Women Writers)*

—**Therese L. Lueck**

Further Reading

Jong, Erica. *Becoming Light: Poems New and Selected.* New York: HarperCollins, 1991.
———. *Fear of Fifty: A Midlife Memoir.* New York: HarperCollins, 1994.
———. *Fear of Flying.* New York: Holt, Rinehart & Winston, 1973.
———. "Introduction." In *Three Eighteenth-Century Novels,* v-xi. New York: New American Library, 1982.
———. *Inventing Memory: A Novel of Mothers and Daughters.* New York: HarperCollins, 1997.
———. *What Do Women Want? Bread, Roses, Sex, Power.* New York: HarperCollins, 1998.
Mantell, Suzanne. "Jong Casts Gleeful Eye on Sea Changes in Midlife," *Publishers Weekly* 241 (June 13, 1994): 22, 24.

∞ Jordan, Barbara (Charline)
(1936–1996)

An attorney who served in the House of Representatives from 1972 to 1978, Barbara Jordan was the first African American and first woman to serve in Congress since Reconstruction and an outspoken defender of the Constitution. An assertive member of the Texas state senate from 1966 to 1972, she was instrumental in the passage of an improved workmen's compensation act and the state's first minimum wage law. In the final year before her death, she also chaired the Commission on Immigration Reform.

Jordan was born in Houston, Texas, and grew up in the segregated community of the Fourth Ward. After graduating

Figure 32. Barbara Jordan
Congresswoman Barbara Jordan was a commanding and persuasive speaker. She played an instrumental role in the House Judiciary Committee's impeachment hearings in 1974 and delivered the keynote speech at the Democratic Convention of 1976. Used by permission of UPI/Corbis-Bettmann.

magna cum laude from Texas Southern University, she attended the law school at Boston University, receiving her degree in 1959. She returned to private practice in Houston, then began her public career as the first black senator in the Texas legislature and, later, in Congress.

Always dedicated to the idea of justice, Jordan became a member of the House Judiciary Committee. She distinguished herself during the committee's hearings on the Watergate affair, which revealed widespread corruption in the administration of President Richard M. Nixon and led to his resignation in 1974. Although only a freshman legislator at the time, Jordan proved to be one of the most articulate and thoughtful members of the committee, condemning the affair as a perversion of the Constitution. Ever optimistic, however, she concluded that the whole process surrounding the Watergate scandal was a "cleansing experience" for American politics.

Committed to civil rights, the welfare of the underprivileged, and the environment, she sponsored key legislation in these areas during her three terms in Congress. A strong opponent of increased military expenditures, Jordan consistently voted to curb military involvement in Southeast Asia and voted to override President Nixon's veto of the War Powers Bill limiting presidential war-making authority.

In 1979, after her retirement from Congress, Jordan joined the faculty of the Lyndon B. Johnson School of Public Affairs at the University of Texas in Austin. In 1994, she received the Presidential Medal of Freedom, the highest civilian honor. Jordan returned to public life, at the request of President Bill Clinton, to head the Commission on Immigration Reform. She strongly opposed proposals to deny citizenship to the children of illegal immigrants, hoping to keep open the doors of liberty to all.

A victim of multiple sclerosis, Jordan remained in a wheelchair for much of her adult life. She died on January 17, 1996, from viral pneumonia, a complication of leukemia. Over 1,500 people attended her funeral in Houston, with President Clinton eloquently addressing the crowd: "Barbara Jordan's life was a monument to the three great threads that run constantly throughout the fabric of American history—our love of liberty, our belief in progress, our search for common ground. Wherever she could and whenever she stood to speak, she jolted the nation's attention with her artful and articulate defense of the Constitution, the American Dream, and the common heritage and destiny we share, whether we like it or not. . . . Barbara's magnificent voice is silenced. But she left the vivid air signed in her honor." *(See also: Black Women; Democratic Party; Politics)*

—Sue E. Strickler
—Leigh Fought

Further Reading

Bryant, Ira Babington. *Barbara Charline Jordan: From the Ghetto to the Capitol.* Houston, TX: D. Armstrong, 1977.
Christian Science Monitor (March 18, 1974): 6.
Hearon, Shelby, and Barbara Jordan. *Barbara Jordan: A Self-Portrait.* Garden City, NY: Doubleday, 1979.
Margolies-Mezvinsky, Marjorie. *A Woman's Place: The Freshmen Who Changed the Face of Congress.* New York: Crown, 1994.
Robinson, Louie. "Women Lawmakers on the Move," *Ebony* 27 (October 1972): 48-56.
Smith, Jessie Carney, ed. *Epic Lives: One Hundred Black Women Who Made a Difference.* Detroit, MI: Visible Ink Press, 1993.
The Washington Post (October 22, 1972): K1.
http://www.whitehouse.gov/uri-res/12R?urn:pdf//oma.eop.gov.us/1996/1/21/1.text.1 [Remarks by President Bill Clinton at funeral service]

ॐ Journalism

Although not always recognized, women have been involved in American journalism from its earliest beginnings. Women have served as printers, publishers, editors, and reporters from the early eighteenth century to the present.

Prior to the adoption of the Constitution in 1787, at least seventeen women served as newspaper printers in America.

Generally, they assumed the job when their husbands were unable to continue because of imprisonment, illness, or death. Many women kept the business going until their sons were old enough to assume control. Most of them then returned to the home. Thus, women's involvement in journalism in the eighteenth century came primarily out of necessity and ended when the need no longer existed.

In the nineteenth century, more jobs opened up for women. As a result, more took jobs to supplement the family income. Female editors, publishers, and owners became more common and accepted. Ann Royall (1769–1864) published *The Huntress* in Washington, D.C., from 1836 to 1854, supporting Andrew Jackson, free public education, free speech, and justice for the downtrodden. She reportedly had to sit on the clothes of President John Quincy Adams on a riverbank where he was swimming before he would grant her an interview. Jane Grey Swisshelm, editor of the Pittsburgh antislavery sheet *Saturday Visiter,* became the first woman to sit in the congressional press gallery in 1850. Women also succeeded as magazine editors, the most famous being Sarah Josepha Hale, editor of *Godey's Lady's Book* from 1836 to 1877. Although the Civil War opened up more opportunities for women in journalism, the Capitol press galleries barred them as more women came to Washington as correspondents.

In 1870, only 35 of 5,286 journalists listed in the U.S. census were women, but by 1900, there were 2,193 women among the 30,098 journalists cited. Increasingly, newspapers and magazines had female columnists who provided the woman's perspective on a variety of topics and issues. This change was partially due to newspaper editors' efforts to increase circulation. In the early half of the nineteenth century, most women read only books and magazines; however, newspaper editors wanted to attract women readers. Early women journalists such as Jennie June (1829–1901), the first woman to write daily for a newspaper, helped develop women's pages. At first, newspaper women wrote about domestic life, food, and fashion, often from their homes. Gradually, women began working from the newsrooms, covering the same range of topics as the men. Women's pages appeared in the *Philadelphia Ledger* and the *New York Times* in the 1890s.

The antebellum desire for reform sweeping the country brought women into journalism and was fired by women journalists. Women were often editors of abolitionist and suffragist papers, such as *Revolution.* Editors hired women for stunt writing and often used their sex to sensationalize the dangers of undercover investigation and to titillate readers. Competing men, writing in the same highly emotional style, called these women "Sob Sisters." Annie Laurie (1863–1936), who covered the Galveston tidal wave in 1900 and the San Francisco earthquake in 1906 with first-person, tear-jerking accounts, hated this label. She thought of herself simply as a practical, all-around newspaper woman. The last half of the century witnessed several famous female reporters, including Elizabeth Cochrane

Seaman ("Nellie Bly") (1865–1922) of the *New York World,* Sally Joy ("Penelope Penfeather") (1852–1910) of the *Boston Herald,* and Ida Tarbell (1857–1944) of *McClure's,* one of the original "muckrakers." From Margaret Fuller (1810–1850), who wrote of women's rights and duties and produced caustic literary criticism, to Dorothy Dix (1861–1951) and her widely reprinted advice columns, to Ida Bell Wells-Barnett (1862–1931), who fought for racial pride and against lynchings in her writing, early newspaperwomen opened the way for women reporters and helped open doors for women in ever-expanding job fields.

Slow, steady gains were made in the early twentieth century, with more women working in most areas of journalism. Beginning in the 1930s, women served as foreign correspondents for several American newspapers and news services. Anne O'Hare McCormick (1880–1954) won a Pulitzer Prize in 1937 for her European reporting for the *New York Times* News Service. One of her first stories was a 1921 profile of unknown Benito Mussolini, in which she predicted that he would one day master Italy. During World War II, women served as correspondents in several theaters of war, primarily in Europe. Margaret Bourke-White (1904–1971) served in Europe as a photographer for *Time* and *Life.* Leah Burdette (1900–1942), correspondent for *PM,* lost her life in Iran. Marguerite Higgins (1920–1966) of the *New York Herald Tribune* served in Europe during the 1940s and became Berlin bureau chief after the war ended.

Since World War II, women have become increasingly involved in all areas of American journalism. The women's rights movement of the 1960s and 1970s helped many women advance into new areas. By the 1990s, women were serving as sports reporters and editorial columnists, as newspaper publishers and White House correspondents, as copy editors and television anchorpersons. Barbara Walters, Katie Couric, and Jane Pauley had become household words. From 1995 to 1998, women won nearly a dozen Pulitzer Prizes, often in job categories that once were closed to them, such as spot news photography and beat reporting. *(See also: "Bly, Nellie"; Bourke-White, Margaret; Bryant, Louise; Cary, Mary Ann Shadd; Day, Dorothy; Diggs, Annie LePorte; Draper, Margaret Green; Duniway, Abigail Jane Scott; Ferber, Edna; Fuller, Margaret; Hale, Sarah Josepha; Magazines; O'Hare, Kate Richards; Ramírez, Sara Estella; Revolution; Spanish Civil War; Tarbell, Ida; Thompson, Dorothy; Valesh, Eva McDonald; Wells-Barnett, Ida B.)*

—**Terri Evert Karsten**
—**Carol Sue Humphrey**

Further Reading

Beasley, Maurine Hoffman. *Taking Their Place: A Documentary History of Women and Journalism.* Washington, DC: American University Press, 1993.

Beasley, Maurine Hoffman, and Sheila Gibbons. *Women in Media: A Documentary Source Book.* Washington, DC: Women's Institute for Freedom of the Press, 1977.

Belford, Barbara. *Brilliant Bylines.* New York: Columbia University Press, 1986.

Braden, Maria. *She Said What? Interviews with Women Newspaper Columnists.* Lexington: University of Kentucky Press, 1993.

Emery, Edwin, and Michael Emery. *The Press and America: An Interpretive History of the Mass Media,* 7th ed. Englewood Cliffs, NJ: Prentice Hall, 1991.

Folkerts, Jean, and Dwight L. Teeter, Jr. *Voices of a Nation: A History of Media in the United States,* 2d ed. New York: Macmillan, 1993.

Robertson, Nan. *The Girls in the Balcony: Women, Men, and the New York Times.* New York: Random House, 1992.

Sloan, William David, James G. Stovall, and James D. Startt. *The Media in America: A History,* 2d ed. Scottsdale, AZ: Publishing Horizons, 1993.

Kahn, Florence Prag (1866–1948)

Florence Kahn served as Republican representative to Congress from San Francisco's Fourth District from 1925 to 1936. Like many daughters of her generation, Kahn was forced to give up dreams of becoming a lawyer to support her Polish Jewish immigrant parents. After graduating from the University of California at Berkeley in 1887, she taught high school English until 1899, when she married Congressman Julius Kahn. Julius built his political reputation on support for military preparedness. When elected to fill the seat vacated at his death, Florence continued to support that policy.

Unlike many women of her day who "inherited" offices from their husbands, Kahn quickly forged an independent political identity largely based on her quick wit. When asked if she favored birth control, she answered, "I will if you make it retroactive." Kahn rejected the notion of a distinct feminine contribution and did not concentrate on "women's issues." She opposed female politicians who promoted pacifism as the political expression of women's "naturally" superior nurturing capabilities.

While in office, Kahn supported increasing the size of the military, even when such increases were opposed by President Calvin Coolidge, a Republican. She also sponsored a bill to create military pensions for nurses, arguing for it not as a feminist issue but as practical legislation necessary to attract nurses away from higher-paying, less dangerous, private sector jobs. In April 1929, Kahn was honored by being appointed Speaker of the House to chair a debate on the military budget. One likely reason behind Kahn's pro-military stance was that as an anti-Zionist she saw the United States as the only place in the world where Jews could live safely, and she believed military might was the only means of ensuring that security. Kahn also promoted the interests of the Federal Bureau of Investigation so successfully that J. Edgar Hoover dubbed her "the mother of the FBI." In contrast to most feminists of her day, Kahn opposed Prohibition and motion picture censorship, considering the first unenforceable and the second an impediment to the growing movie industry in California.

Before Kahn was defeated by Roosevelt's Democratic landslide in 1936, she managed to attract much federal construction to San Francisco, including the San Francisco-Oakland Bay Bridge. After her defeat, Kahn remained active in the Republican Party. She was a member of the American Association of University Women, Temple Emanu-El (San Francisco-Reform), Woman's City Club (San Francisco), and the Congressional Club. She was also a member of Hadassah and the National Council of Jewish Women, but since she opposed much of what these organizations worked for, she probably joined them because it seemed the proper thing to do as an upper-class, prominent Jewish woman. *(See also: Hadassah; Jewish Women; Politics; Republican Party; Right-Wing Political Movements)*

—**Faith Rogow**

Further Reading

"Kahn, Florence Prag." Nearprint Box, Bos 2282. American Jewish Archives, Cincinnati, OH.

Keyes, Frances Parkinson. "The Lady from California," *Delineator* 118 (February 1931): 14 ff.

Käsebier, Gertrude Stanton (1852–1934)

Gertrude Käsebier established an impressive reputation as an art photographer in the late nineteenth century. She was included in Alfred Stieglitz's famed Photo-Secession, founded in 1902 to promote the art of photography, and was well-known for her portraiture and her soft-focus, impressionistic images of women and children.

Born in Leadville, Colorado, and brought up in the East, Käsebier attended a girls' seminary in Bethlehem, Pennsylvania. In 1873, she married Edward Käsebier, a German businessman, and then after several years of attending to the traditional roles of wife and mother, she changed the pattern of her life. In 1888, when her children were nearly grown, Käsebier enrolled at Brooklyn's Pratt Institute to study painting. She also spent two summers in France as a student of academic painter Frank Vincent Dumond. During this period, Käsebier was discouraged by her art teachers from taking up photography; by 1893, however, she had committed herself to the controversial new medium. She gained practical experience in the field by apprenticing herself to a Brooklyn portrait photographer, Samuel Lifshey.

Close to forty years old, married, and the mother of three teenage children, Käsebier opened a portrait studio in New York City in 1897. Fame and recognition came quickly because of her innovative approach to portraiture, which emphasized simple principles of design, dramatic lighting, and natural settings. She rejected the banal techniques of commercial portraiture that depended on theatrical props, unimaginative lighting, and stiff, conventional poses.

Most of Käsebier's photographs were done in the pictorial tradition popular among art photographers of the late nineteenth and early twentieth century. Typically, a pictorialist photograph was impressionistic in style—hazy, moody landscapes. In her pictorial work, Käsebier frequently favored the mother and child theme, but she often used it to comment on the status of women, such as the disadvantages of marriage. She remained committed to pictorialism throughout her career. In 1916, Käsebier and photographers Clarence White and Alvin Langdon Coburn organized the Pictorial Photographers of America.

Käsebier's relationship with photographer and art patron Alfred Stieglitz was very significant to her career. Stieglitz published her work in his journal *Camera Notes* (1897–1902) and in 1903 featured Käsebier's images as the first issue dedicated to the work of one photographer in the renowned journal *Camera Work*. Also, Stieglitz often exhibited Käsebier's photographs at the New York Camera Club and at his "291" gallery. *(See also: Art; Photography)*

—**C. Jane Gover**

Further Reading

Gover, C. Jane. *The Positive Image: Women Photographers in Turn of the Century America.* Albany: State University of New York Press, 1987.

Homer, William Innes. *A Pictorial Heritage: The Photographs of Gertrude Käsebier.* Wilmington: Delaware Art Museum and the University of Delaware, 1979.

Michaels, Barbara L. *Gertrude Käsebier: The Photographer and Her Photographs.* New York: Abrams, 1992.

Tucker, Ann. *The Woman's Eye.* New York: Random House, 1973.

Keller, Helen (1880–1968)

Helen Keller's struggle to overcome the severe limitations of deafness and blindness inspired many and was captured by the Pulitzer Prize-winning drama *The Miracle Worker*. She was born in Tuscumbia, Alabama, with normal vision and hearing. A mysterious ailment—speculation has centered on scarlet fever or meningitis—struck her as she approached her second birthday, leaving her deaf, blind, and functionally mute. At that time, so great was the shame associated with disabilities that those suffering them were often institutionalized for life.

The Kellers traveled widely seeking a medical remedy. In 1886, they met with Alexander Graham Bell, who suggested that the Kellers contact the director of the Perkins Institution in Boston, Massachusetts. The director recommended that a recent star graduate, Anne Sullivan, might make a suitable governess and teacher for Helen.

Sullivan, a highly driven and fiery woman, arrived in Alabama in 1887 and devoted herself to getting through to the seven-year-old child. Helen had become increasingly wild, and occasionally violent, as her frustration over her inability to communicate mounted. After only a month, a breakthrough occurred in which Helen rediscovered the mystery of language. Sullivan hand-spelled W-A-T-E-R in one of the child's hands, as the other was placed under the spout of a well pump. The acquisition of language prompted Helen's personality to emerge in full flower, which in turn led to Sullivan's reporting back to Bell the extent of the child's transformation. Understanding the implications of the results of this extraordinary teacher-pupil relationship, Bell emerged as a major force in establishing Helen Keller as a celebrity.

Much has been written about the symbiotic relationship between Helen Keller and Annie Sullivan. Some felt that the relationship was unhealthy—that Sullivan was overworking Helen and using her for self-promotion. Various attempts were made to separate them, but the bond endured.

As she attained adulthood, Helen Keller authored several accounts of her life that became best-sellers and increased her renown, including *The Story of My Life* (1904) and *The World I Live In* (1908). Gaining in confidence, she became a more forceful political voice, advocating for woman suffrage and supporting the International Workers of the World.

After Sullivan's death in 1936, Helen Keller continued her near-constant touring and fund-raising for various foundations, especially the American Foundation for the Blind. She also kept up her writing, including a memoir of her life with Sullivan, entitled *Teacher* (1955). In 1964, in recognition of her lifetime as a symbol of the indomitability of the human spirit, she was awarded the Presidential Medal of Freedom. In 1965, she was elected to the Women's Hall of Fame. Keller died at her home on June 1, 1968. *(See also: Education; Friendships; Mentor/Protégée Relationships; National Women's Hall of Fame)*

—**Peter Labella**

Further Reading

Herrmann, Dorothy. *Helen Keller: A Life.* New York: Knopf, 1998.

Lash, Joseph. *Helen and Teacher: The Story of Helen Keller and Anne Sullivan Macy.* New York: Delacorte/Seymour Lawrence, 1980.

Keller, Helen. *The Story of My Life.* New York: Grosset & Dunlap, 1904.

Kelley, Florence (1859–1932)

Florence Kelley was a leader in the effort to enact protective labor legislation for American workers. She was born in Philadelphia, the youngest surviving daughter of William and Caroline Bonsall Kelley, and was raised in a family rich with a tradition of public service. Her father, for instance, was a longtime member of the House of Representatives and a Republican organizer. Kelley was especially close to him and wanted to follow his example. With his support, she earned a bachelor's degree in 1882 from Cornell University. She then undertook a tour of Europe before settling in Zurich to study at the University of Zurich, one of the few to accept women. There she met and married a young Russian medical student, a union that lasted seven years and produced three children. In 1891, Kelley and the children went to Illinois, where she obtained a divorce and became a resident of Chicago's Hull House settlement.

From that vantage point, she began her investigation of the factory system. She studied the sweatshops of the garment industry, surveyed city slums, earned a law degree, and served as chief factory inspector for the state of Illinois. Largely as a result of her work, the Illinois General Assembly passed an act limiting women's work hours, banning child labor, and controlling the sweatshops. In 1899, Kelley and her family returned to New York, where she lived at Lillian Wald's Henry Street Settlement and became the executive secretary of the National Consumers' League, a position she held for the remainder of her life. The league attempted to use customer pressure to ensure that products be manufactured and marketed under proper conditions.

That was only one of the ways Kelley encouraged industrial reform. She was also an avid speaker on the subject, outlining her objectives in *Some Ethical Gains through Legislation,* published in 1905. Together with league cohort Josephine Goldmark, Kelley persuaded attorney Louis Brandeis to use medical and sociological data in his Supreme Court defense of an Oregon ten-hour law for woman laborers. The famous "Brandeis brief" of 1914 revolutionized the use of such evidence in the American judicial system. Beyond her work at the league, Kelley championed woman suffrage, opposed World War I, and helped organize the National Association for the Advancement of Colored People. In the final years of her life until her death in 1932, she struggled to preserve earlier legislative gains. *(See also: Hull House; National Consumers' League; Social Feminism; Wages)*

—**Rebecca L. Sherrick**

Further Reading

Blumberg, Dorothy Rose. *Florence Kelley: The Making of a Social Pioneer.* New York: A. M. Kelly, 1966.

∿ Kellie, Luna Elizabeth Sanford (1857–1940)

State secretary of the Nebraska Farmers' Alliance, journalist, and Nebraska pioneer, Luna Kellie was born in Pipestone, Minnesota, moving with her family to Madison, Wisconsin, and then to Rockford, Illinois. In 1874, she married James Thompson Kellie. Two years later, her father, two brothers, and husband moved to Adams County, Nebraska, to homestead. Kellie followed a few months later. In addition to homesteading, the Kellies raised eleven children, operated a grocery store for a short time, and participated locally in reform politics. When the first homestead failed, the Kellies took over her father's timber claim and turned it into a successful orchard.

After being active briefly in county politics, Kellie attended the Nebraska Farmers' Alliance convention in 1894 and was elected state secretary. Her duties consisted of keeping the records of the alliance, lecturing for the alliance in surrounding counties, and writing for *Wealthmakers,* a reform newspaper in Lincoln. A year later, having decided that the *Wealthmakers* was not sufficiently radical, she bought a used printing press and began, with the help of her oldest daughter, Jessie, to publish the *Nebraska Farmers' Alliance and Industrial Union.*

As the Nebraska Farmers' Alliance waned and the Populist Party lost the 1896 election, Kellie changed the name of the newspaper to *Prairie Home,* hoping to gain more subscriptions. Still clinging to the hope that the Populists could alleviate the economic crisis of farmers, Kellie and her husband, members of the National Reform Press Association, attended the 1900 National Populist Convention in Cincinnati as delegates. Soon after this convention, Kellie became discouraged with the lack of economic reform, sold the newspaper, and resigned from the alliance. Her husband died in 1918.

Kellie continued managing the orchard and again operated a small grocery store. She also wrote two sets of memoirs. The first detailed her involvement with the Farmers' Alliance, its financial difficulties, and the factions within the organization. The second described the Kellies' early homesteading years. During the Great Depression, Kellie lost the homestead and moved back and forth between Arizona and Nebraska. In the Arizona desert north of Tucson, she attempted homesteading a second time, but failing health prevented her from obtaining a permanent deed to her claim. She died in Phoenix on March 4, 1940. *(See also: Journalism; Migration and Frontier Women; National Farmers' Alliance; Populist Party)*

—**MaryJo Wagner**

Further Reading

Baaken, Douglas A. "Luna E. Kellie and the Farmers' Alliance," *Nebraska History* 50 (1969): 185-205.

Kellie, Luna E. *The Farmers' Alliance in Nebraska.* Lincoln: Nebraska State Historical Society, 1926.

———. *Memoirs.* Lincoln: Nebraska State Historical Society, ca. 1918.

Wagner, MaryJo. "Prairie Populists: Luna Kellie and Mary Elizabeth Lease." In *Northwest Women's Heritage,* edited by Karen Blair, 200-10. Seattle, WA: Northwest Center for Research on Women, 1984.

∿ Kemble, Fanny (1809–1893)

Fanny Kemble was born in London into one of the great English theatrical families. When she made her own stage debut in 1829, she became an overnight sensation, her success rivaling that of her recently retired aunt, Sarah Siddons.

During an American tour, she fell in love with Philadelphian Pierce Butler. When they married in June 1834, she gave up the stage and settled into his Pennsylvania home. But Butler's vast estates in Georgia and his slaveholding soon became a source of conflict for the couple. Also, although Kemble had abandoned her acting career, she wanted to resume her writing. Her frank and vivid travel account of her American tour had been promised to a publisher before her engagement. Although Butler forbade her to pursue this project, she prepared the manuscript for publication, and when the journal appeared in 1835, it caused further disharmony. After years of marital discord, bitterness, and several separations, the couple divorced in 1849 due to irreconcilable differences. Butler was granted complete custody of their two daughters, while Kemble returned to England to resume her stage career. Although she was unable to regain her former popularity (and to maintain the pace), Kemble gathered a new following through her Shakespearean readings, her occasional benefit performances, and her many publications.

Her *Journal of Residence on a Georgian Plantation*, written in the winter of 1838–1839 while living on Butler's Sea Islands estates, was a British best-seller when it appeared in 1863. In addition, Kemble's harsh portrait of slavery served to dampen English enthusiasm for support of the Confederacy. Her volume had considerable impact in its day and remains an important primary source for scholars. Her talent for fiction (she published three plays, three volumes of poetry, and even a novel—at the age of eighty) was surpassed by her talent for living; her witty and engaging memoirs (*Records of Girlhood*, 3 vols.; *Records of Later Life*; and *Further Records*, 2 vols.) display impressive gifts. She lived in Italy for several years, acquainting herself with American artists in exile, including Harriet Hosmer and Henry James. She made annual treks to Switzerland to mountain climb and revisit friends, and wrote a humorous tale, *The Adventures of Mr. John Timothy Homespun in Switzerland* (also published when she was eighty).

She spent her later years in the country of her birth, but her involvement in American abolitionist and literary circles during the middle decades of the nineteenth century places her firmly at the center of New England culture and reform during its antebellum flowering. She was especially fond of her elder daughter's only son Owen Wister, who went on to become a popular novelist, author of *The Virginian*. Kemble's strong will, eccentricity, and generosity were all lauded by those who knew her. And the writing she left behind gives valuable insights into the attitudes and experiences of women during the nineteenth century. *(See also: Abolition and the Antislavery Movement; Civil War; Slavery)*

—**Catherine Clinton**

Further Reading

Furnas, J. C. *Fanny Kemble: Leading Lady of the Nineteenth-Century Stage: A Biography.* New York: Dial, 1982.

Kemble, Fanny. *Fanny Kemble: The American Journals.* Compiled and edited by Elizabeth Mavor. London: Weidenfeld & Nicolson, 1990.
———. *Further Records.* New York: Henry Holt, 1890.
———. *Journal.* Philadelphia: Carey, Lea & Blanchard, 1835.
———. *Journal of Residence on a Georgian Plantation.* Edited by John A. Scott. Athens: University of Georgia Press, 1985.
———. *Records of Girlhood.* New York: Henry Holt, 1879.
———. *Records of Later Life.* New York: Henry Holt, 1882.
Marshall, Dorothy. *Fanny Kemble.* London: Weidenfeld & Nicholson, 1977.
Wister, Fanny Kemble. *Fanny: The American Kemble.* Tallahassee, FL: South Pass, 1972.

⤳ Keyserling, Mary Dublin (b. 1910)

A London School of Economics and Columbia University-trained economist, Mary Keyserling served in three presidential administrations. Her last federal position was as President Lyndon Johnson's appointee to head the Women's Bureau, U.S. Department of Labor, a position she held from 1964 to 1969.

Keyserling advocated public policies to improve the status of working women throughout her career. As executive director of the National Consumers' League from 1938 to 1941, she presided over the league's advocacy for improvement of state minimum wage laws for women, for maintaining provisions of the National Labor Act, and for enactment of national health insurance. During World War II, while assisting Eleanor Roosevelt in the Office of Civilian Defense, Keyserling helped to develop national policies aimed at working women. During the 1950s, she and her husband Leon Keyserling founded the Conference on Economic Progress, a think tank promoting national economic planning. In addition to her research work, Keyserling remained active in the Democratic Party as a member of the Woman's National Democratic Club and as the only female member of the Democratic Platform Committee. From 1961 to 1963, she served on the President's Commission on the State of Women's Protective Labor Legislation Committee.

As director of the Women's Bureau, Keyserling actively promoted the formation of governors' commissions on the status of women and maintained the institutions created by the President's Commission on the Status of Women: the Citizens' Advisory Council on the Status of Women and the Interdepartmental Committee on the Status of Women, serving as vice chair of the latter. Through these institutions, Keyserling worked to ensure that Johnson's War on Poverty programs met the interests of women and girls.

Keyserling resumed her work with the Conference on Economic Progress after her government service. In the 1970s, she directed research and wrote reports on child care. *(See also: Democratic Party; National Consumers' League; President's Commission on the Status of Women; Women's Bureau)*

—**Kathleen Laughlin**

Further Reading

Harrison, Cynthia. *On Account of Sex: The Politics of Women's Issues, 1945–1968*. Berkeley: University of California Press, 1988.

⨯ King, Billie Jean (b. 1943)

One of the world's greatest and best-known tennis players, Billie Jean King played a monumental role in establishing women's tennis as a major sport. King accomplished this not only through her prowess on the court but with her unflagging efforts as an organizer and promoter of the sport.

In 1961, at the age of eighteen, she became the youngest player to win at Wimbledon (a doubles title). During the next twelve years, she went on to win a record number of Wimbledon titles—twenty in all—in singles, doubles, and mixed doubles. During those years, she also won titles at Forest Hills, the U.S. Open, and the French Open. She captured the Virginia Slims singles title from 1970 to 1977. It was not just her victories that won the world's attention but the way she played the game. Her quick, aggressive moves on the court drew a large audience to women's tennis, a game that had previously been dismissed as slow and uninteresting.

That women players were grossly underpaid compared with their male counterparts (even though women were beginning to draw large crowds) led King to spearhead the formation of the Women's Tennis Association in 1973. The group was a "union" that gave the women the power to bargain for the same advantages the men enjoyed. She and other women professionals also agreed to appear in the high-paying Virginia Slims tournaments organized by Gladys Heldman, a move that forced increases in prize money for women throughout the sport. In 1973, King increased the stature of women in the sport by thrashing her male challenger, Bobby Riggs, in a much-publicized match.

In the late 1980s, King became involved in promoting Team Tennis, which comprises teams of men and women playing singles, doubles, and mixed doubles and gives exposure to some of the best but lesser-known players in the sport. She is also the author of several books on playing tennis and an autobiography.

King's efforts to create a place for women to compete in sports have not been limited to tennis. In 1974, she and husband Larry King founded *WomenSports,* a magazine now published by the Women's Sports Federation as *Women's Sports and Fitness.* She further expanded the place of women in sports by serving as a broadcaster for ABC from 1975 to 1978. The honors King has gathered attest to her visibility as a great sportswoman and strong example for other women: She was named Sportswoman of the Year by *Sports Illustrated* in 1972, Woman Athlete of the Year by the Associated Press in 1967 and 1973, and Woman of the Year by *Time* in 1976.

In addition to the strides she has made for women's professional tennis, King must be credited with helping to create

Figure 33. Billie Jean King
Billie Jean King crushed Bobby Riggs in the so-called Battle of the Sexes, which boosted the popularity of women's tennis and set a record for the largest purse offered. Used by permission of UPI/Corbis-Bettmann.

a place for all women's sports in this century. King's career paralleled the rise of the modern women's movement, of which she was a part: The athlete's publicized experience with the two most controversial issues of the 1970s, abortion and lesbianism, provoked public furor. However, she confronted and survived the adverse publicity and continued to work for the advancement and improvement of women's tennis. In recent years, King has been active in WORLD TEAMTENNIS, the only professional coed team sport in the United States. Cofounded by King, the organization provides a format in which world-class male and female players compete for the same team in singles, doubles, and mixed doubles. *(See also: Athletics/Sports; Gibson, Althea)*

—**Carol Ann Sadtler**

Further Reading

Collins, Bud. "Billie Jean King Evens the Score," *Ms.* 11 (July 1973): 39-43, 101-2.

King, Billie Jean, with Frank Deford. *Billie Jean.* New York: Viking, 1982.

⨯ King, Coretta Scott (b. 1927)

Civil rights crusader and spokesperson, Coretta Scott King first came into the public view as the wife of Martin Luther King, Jr., but after his death in 1968, she established her own place within the leadership of the civil rights movement.

King was born in Marion, Alabama, on April 27, 1927. She graduated from Antioch College in 1951 and went on to study music and singing at the New England Conservatory of Music in Boston. She received a bachelor's degree in 1954 and a doctorate in music in 1971. She married Martin Luther King, Jr., on June 18, 1953, in Marion, Alabama, and they moved to Montgomery the following year. There, Dr. King was pastor of the Dexter Avenue Baptist Church, and Coretta assumed all of the roles and duties of the pastor's wife. From 1955 to 1963, she became the mother of two daughters and two sons. On December 5, 1956, she gave a concert in New York City to celebrate the first anniversary of the bus boycott initiated by blacks in Montgomery to protest racist policies and treatment. She subsequently gave over thirty concerts in the United States and Europe to benefit the Southern Christian Leadership Conference (SCLC).

In 1968, King was voted Woman of the Year and Most Admired Woman by college students across the country. In March 1969, she become the first woman to speak from the pulpit during a regularly scheduled service at St. Paul's Cathedral in London. She wrote a book titled *My Life with Martin Luther King, Jr.* in 1969 and has been active in the SCLC. She has organized antinuclear lobbies and anti-Vietnam protests, and in April 1998 (the anniversary of Martin Luther King, Jr.'s death), she formally requested the formation of a Presidential Commission to determine the truth behind her husband's assassination. She has been honored over the past 25 years by the Coretta Scott King Award, given annually by the American Library Association to outstanding African American authors and artists.

Although she has now relinquished the day-to-day running of the Martin Luther King, Jr. Center for Social Change in Atlanta to her son, Dexter King, she maintains an active interest in the activities of the center. In addition, she is a respected speaker on topics such as civil rights, women's rights, and gay and lesbian rights. *(See also: Black Women; Civil Rights; Southern Christian Leadership Conference)*

—**Susan Kinnell**

Further Reading

Henry, Sondra, and Emily Taitz. *Coretta Scott King: Keeper of the Dream.* Hillside, NJ: Enslow, 1992.

Medearis, Angela Shelf, and Anna Rich. *Dare to Dream: Coretta Scott King and the Civil Rights Movement.* New York: Lodestar, 1994. [Young adult title]

Patterson, Lillie. *Coretta Scott King.* Champaign, IL: Garrard, 1977.

Rhodes, Lisa Renee. *Coretta Scott King (Black Americans of Achievement).* Brommall, PA: Chelsea House, 1998. [Young adult title]

Taylor, Paula. *Coretta King, A Woman of Peace.* Mankato, MN: Creative Education, 1974.

Turk, Ruth. *Coretta Scott King: Fighter for Justice.* Boston: Branden, 1997.

Vivian, Octavia. *Coretta: The Story of Mrs. Martin Luther King, Jr.* Philadelphia: Fortress, 1970.

http://www.triadntr.net/rdavis/mlkwife.htm [a brief biography]

http://www.williamcoupon.com/PLACES/coretta.html [a recent portrait]

http://pathfinder.com/photo/essay/african/cap36.htm [a 1969 portrait]

⌒ Kingston, Maxine Hong (b. 1940)

Author of *The Woman Warrior* and *China Men,* Maxine Hong Kingston explored a new dimension in women's quest for identity. The two books form her autobiography. Written from the perspective of a young Chinese American girl struggling to grow beyond the confining limits of both Chinese and U.S. traditions, particularly misogyny, *The Woman Warrior* intermingles childhood memories with mythic stories and ironic humor to reveal the paradoxic experiences of women in Kingston's family. *China Men* uses similar means to describe the efforts of the men of her family to become a "founding generation" in the "Gold Mountain"—America. Together, the two books reveal the painful struggle of a young girl caught between two cultures who finally emerges healthy when she rejects old family myths for stories of her own creation. *The Woman Warrior* won the 1976 National Book Critics Circle Award, and *China Men* won the 1980 American Book Award.

With the assistance of eleven scholarships, Kingston graduated with a bachelor's degree from the University of California at Berkeley in 1962 and obtained a teaching certificate. She married Earll Kingston, and they lived in Hawaii where she taught English and creative writing while working on her autobiography as a way to establish her identity as both Chinese and American. Her books are touchstones for women who have fought the constraints of a foreign culture; they are particularly significant literary examples of "ethnic" women's efforts to eschew misogynist cultural myths in favor of self-created and self-affirming new myths. In 1989, Kingston published a novel, *Tripmaster Monkey: His Fake Book.* In 1990, Kingston was featured in a Modern Educational Video Network film series titled *America: A Cultural Mosaic,* in which she commented on her life and works. In 1998, she published *Conversations with Maxine Hong Kingston* as part of a Literary Conversations series. *(See also: Asian American Women; Women Writers)*

—**Nancy Baker Jones**
—**Anne Elizabeth Cooperman**

Further Reading

Islas, Arturo. "Maxine Hong Kingston." In *Women Writers of the West Coast: Speaking of Their Lives and Careers,* edited by Marilyn Yalom, 11-19. Santa Barbara: Capra, 1983.

Kingston, Maxine Hong. *China Men.* New York: Knopf, 1980.

———. *Conversations with Maxine Hong Kingston.* Jackson: University Press of Mississippi, 1998.

———. *Maxine Hong Kingston,* audiovisual narrated by B. D. Wong. New York: Modern Educational Video Network, 1990.

———. *Tripmaster Monkey: His Fake Book.* New York: Knopf, 1989.

———. *The Woman Warrior: Memoirs of a Girlhood among Ghosts.* New York: Knopf, 1976.

Thompson, Phyllis Hoge. "This Is the Story I Heard: A Conversation with Maxine Hong Kingston and Earll Kingston," *Biography* 6 (1983): 1-12.

http://www.gale.com/gale/cwh/kingsto.html

Kinsey Report

The Kinsey Report refers to two best-selling studies by American zoologist Alfred C. Kinsey, who sought to apply scientific methodology to human sexual behavior. His statistical analysis of interviewees' sexual practices and beliefs exposed a wide gulf between postwar Americans' sexual ideologies and their actual behavior.

Sexual Behavior in the Human Male (1948), with its revelation that nearly all American men were sexually active outside of marriage, was greeted with an outpouring of criticism and alarm. *Sexual Behavior in the Human Female* (1953) soon reported that of a sample of 5,940 white women, 75 percent had masturbated, 50 percent had had premarital and 26 percent extramarital sex, and nearly 20 percent had been involved in lesbian relationships. Responses to this volume were even more heated than to the first. Many critics saw it as a slur on American womanhood, and the Rockefeller Foundation eliminated Kinsey's funding in 1954.

Kinsey based his conclusions on behavior rather than religious doctrine or psychoanalytic theories of sexuality. He refused to label any sexual behavior as "abnormal" or "unnatural," argued against existing sex laws, and created a 7-point scale ranging between exclusive heterosexuality and homosexuality, emphasizing that most Americans fall between extremes. Attacked variously as inaccurate, immoral, and dangerous, the reports also elicited positive comments from many who saw them as signaling an end to repression and an era of new scientific enlightenment. These views, along with all possible opinions in between, were debated exhaustively in the popular and scientific press. Although the reports were based solely on interviews with whites, they remain the largest and most comprehensive sex survey ever conducted. *(See also: Female Sexuality; Heterosexism; Lesbianism; Masturbation; Orgasm, Female)*

—Miriam Reumann
—William G. Shade

Further Reading

Himelhoch, Jerome, and Sylvia Fleiss Fava, eds. *Sexual Behavior in American Society: An Appraisal of the First Two Kinsey Reports.* Edited for the Society for the Study of Social Problems. New York: Norton, 1955.

Irvine, Janice. *Disorders of Desire: Sex and Gender in Modern American Sexology.* Philadelphia: Temple University Press, 1990.

Jones, James H. *Alfred C. Kinsey: A Public/Private Life.* New York: Norton, 1997.

Kinsey, Alfred et al. *Sexual Behavior in the Human Female.* Philadelphia: W. B. Saunders, 1953.

Morantz, Regina Markell. "The Scientist as Sex Crusader: Alfred Kinsey and American Culture," *American Quarterly* 29 (Winter 1979): 563-89.

Robinson, Paul. *The Modernization of Sex: Havelock Ellis, Alfred Kinsey, William Masters, and Virginia Johnson.* New York: Harper & Row, 1976.

Kirby, Charlotte Ives Cobb Godbe (1836–1908)

Charlotte Kirby was a feminist, Mormon, and woman suffragist leader in the nineteenth-century American West. She became associated with the Mormons as a child, when her mother, a member of the prominent Bostonian Adams family, abandoned her husband and five of her children to become Brigham Young's fifth wife. When Augusta Adams Cobb went West to join the Mormon leader, she took six-year-old Charlotte and an infant who later died. Thus Kirby was raised in Utah in Brigham Young's "Lion House" as one of his daughters and was given by him in polygamous marriage as the fourth wife of a prosperous and liberal Mormon.

Many years later, Kirby would attribute her interest in woman suffrage to her mother, who had been an acquaintance of suffragist Lucy Stone in Boston. Kirby attributed the commencement of woman suffrage in Utah to her mother and reported that it had been her mother's deathbed wish that her daughter continue the work she had begun.

For three decades, from 1869, when the discussion of women's rights first began in Territorial Utah, until 1896, when the state of Utah was created with a clause in its constitution enfranchising women, Kirby was spokesperson for woman suffrage in Utah and at national suffrage meetings. Arguing that one's sex should not "prevent the full and free expression of intelligence," she repeatedly called for women around the world, regardless of religious or political affiliations, to unite to promote the well-being of all women. "The rights of all, as women, must be respected," she said; then she went on to urge women "to stand by each other, setting aside trifling differences and all work unitedly for the good of the whole."

Kirby gave speeches promoting woman suffrage and temperance in Boston, Washington, D.C., and Utah, and she was an officer of the earliest suffrage organization in Utah. Remaining a member of the Church of Jesus Christ of Latter-Day Saints, she divorced William S. Godbe, who had been excommunicated from the church for his liberal views. Five years later, in 1884, she married a wealthy, non-Mormon mining man, John Kirby, who was twenty years younger. *(See also: Migration and Frontier Women; Mormonism; Suffrage in the American West)*

—Beverly Beeton

Further Reading

Beeton, Beverly. *Women Vote in the West: The Woman Suffrage Movement, 1869–1896.* New York: Garland, 1986.

Cable, Mary. "She Who Shall Be Nameless," *American Heritage* 16 (February 1965): 50-55.

Knights of Labor

The Noble Order of the Knights of Labor was established as a secret society in 1869 by nine Philadelphia garment cutters under the leadership of Uriah S. Stephens. The society's basic premise was that since all workers had common interests, all workers should belong to a common society. Membership was open to all those who "toiled" and excluded only professional gamblers, lawyers, bankers, and liquor dealers. While the founders mentioned the inclusion of women, membership was not initially open to women because of the assumption that they could not keep secrets and thus would be a liability to a secret society. On this basis, women were excluded from the Knights of Labor for over a decade; when secrecy was discouraged, the rationale against women collapsed.

The Knights of Labor was organized on the basis of local assemblies. These assemblies could consist of workers from one particular trade or simply all the workers in a given locality, regardless of occupation. A general assembly presided over the entire organization. At the first national convention (1878), the impact of unskilled female laborers on the wages of men was discussed. To safeguard the wages of male workers, the Knights included in their constitution a provision stating that the goal of the organization was to secure "for both sexes equal pay for equal work." Nonetheless, no provision was made at this time for female membership.

In 1881, shoe workers of Local Assembly 64 (Philadelphia) refused a wage cut, and nonunion female workers were brought in to work in their place at a 30 to 60 percent reduction in wages. Under the leadership of Mary Strikling, the women went on strike, and the local Knights' organizer inducted the women into the Knights of Labor, thereby paving the way for the entrance of other female assemblies. By 1886, there were 121 such women's assemblies in the Knights of Labor.

Women were included in both mixed and trade assemblies, and while figures on exact female membership vary considerably, when the Knights' membership was at a high point (1886), women constituted approximately 9 percent of the total membership (approximately fifty thousand). There were assemblies for black female domestic workers in four cities (Washington, D.C.; Wilmington, North Carolina; Norfolk, Virginia; and Philadelphia). In addition, the Knights became the first American labor organization to establish a Department of Women's Work, which concentrated on the status and needs of female workers.

The Knights of Labor, although initially closed to women, in its time did more to open its doors to women and their labor problems than any previous labor organization had done. In theory, at least, the Knights placed women and men workers on an equal footing; in reality, the Knights did little to give women an equal voice, status, or influence within the organizational structure. It did not alter the condition of the American working woman but did provide training and experience for women in a labor organization setting, which would be of value to future movements on behalf of women workers.

By 1890, the Knights of Labor began a decline that was not reversed, and so it faded from the American labor scene. (See also: Unions; Women's Work: Nineteenth Century)

—**Maureen Anna Harp**

Further Reading

Dubofsky, Melvyn. *Industrialism and the American Worker.* Arlington Heights, IL: AHM, 1975.

Foner, Philip S. *Women and the American Labor Movement: From Colonial Times to the Eve of World War One.* New York: Free Press, 1979.

Leeder, Elaine J. *The Gentle General: Rose Pesotta, Anarchist and Labor Organizer.* Albany: State University of New York Press, 1993.

Levine, Susan. *Labor's True Woman.* Philadelphia: Temple University Press, 1984.

Montgomery, David. *Beyond Equality.* New York: Knopf, 1975.

———. *Workers' Control in America: Studies in the History of Work, Technology, and Labor Struggles.* Cambridge, UK: Cambridge University Press, 1979.

⮭ Korean War (1950–1953)

At the conclusion of World War II, Korea was divided at the 38th parallel into two zones, one occupied by the United States and the other by the Soviet Union. The United States informed the Soviets that it wanted the United Nations to make the arrangements for reuniting Korea and securing its independence. The Soviets and their North Korean allies refused to cooperate with the United Nations; instead, in February 1948, they established the Democratic People's Republic of Korea. In July, U.N.-sponsored measures resulted in the creation of the Republic of Korea based in the South. Both governments claimed jurisdiction over all of Korea and announced their intention to achieve unification by force if necessary.

On June 25, 1950, the North Korean Army, trained and armed by the Soviets, attacked over the 38th parallel with about 100,000 troops. On June 26, President Harry Truman ordered the U.S. Air Force and Navy to support the South Korean forces. The next day, the U.N. Security Council called on the U.N. membership to help the South Koreans "repel the armed attack and to restore international peace and security to the area." The United States was joined by U.N. contingents from fifteen other countries.

The United States eventually put 1.6 million servicemen and women into the undeclared war. While the exact number of women serving in the conflict went undocumented, their presence in Korea was the result of the Women's Armed Forces Integration Act of 1948, which gave women the prospect of a career in the military. Although denied combat status, women served in Korea in nursing, health services, and administrative fields. The use of mobile Army hospitals and numerous helicopter evacuations of casualties meant that there were many real-life counterparts to the fic-

Higgins, Marguerite. *War in Korea: The Report of a Woman Combat Correspondent.* New York: Doubleday, 1951.
Holm, Jean. *Women in the Military: An Unfinished Revolution.* Novato, CA: Presidio, 1992.
Rees, David. *Korea: The Unlimited War.* New York: St. Martin's, 1964.

⚬ Krasner, Lee (1908–1984)

Lee Krasner was a leading member of the group of American painters known as the New York School or abstract expressionists. It took many years, however, for her to receive this recognition, because her work was overshadowed by that of her husband, Jackson Pollock.

She was born in Brooklyn, New York, a child of Russian-Jewish immigrants. Her training as an artist at the Woman's Art School of Cooper Union and the National Academy of Design was traditionally classical in its emphasis on drawing, design, and Old Master techniques. Her interest in modern painting started when the Museum of Modern Art was opened in New York City in 1929. A first encounter with the works of Cezanne immediately affected her own work. Graduating during the early years of the Great Depression, she joined the Federal Art Project of the Works Progress Administration and was assigned to the mural division. From 1937 to 1940, she attended the classes of Hans Hofmann, who introduced his students to the twentieth-century avant-garde, especially Picasso, Matisse, and Mondrian. Soon, her personal style evolved in the direction of Cubist abstraction.

By 1941, Krasner had exhibited in several important shows and was well respected by her peers. In January 1942, she participated in an exhibition of French and American contemporary artists, including Jackson Pollock, whose innovative work intrigued and excited her. She became his enthusiastic champion, and in 1945, his wife. In their studio in eastern Long Island, Pollack used the barn to pour paint on huge, unstretched canvases, while Krasner worked in the house creating small, calligraphic abstractions. In some of these, she used a drip technique similar to Pollack's. During the early 1950s, her style changed. She made large collages, many of which were composed of fragments of earlier, discarded works. Shown in 1955, these collages were acclaimed by the critic Clement Greenberg as one of the great exhibitions of the decade.

In August 1956, Krasner's first trip to Europe was cut short by the news of Pollock's death in an automobile accident. Returning home as the widow of one of the most important painters of the period, she became the executrix of his legacy but continued with her own art. In the nearly thirty years following this tragedy, she produced paintings and collages in a variety of styles: large-scale, curvilinear action paintings; huge, somber black and umber paintings called "Night Journeys"; small, delicate, impressionistic works; hard-edged, linear collage-paintings; and works related to color-field painting. During these years, Krasner

Figure 34. Korean War
Navy WAVE scientists from Berkeley study the effects of combat on Korean war infantrymen. Used by permission of UPI/Corbis-Bettmann.

tional "Major Margaret Hoolihan" of the motion picture and television series *M*A*S*H*. Furthermore, women served in the U.S. military civilian workforce, with the Red Cross and with USO entertainment groups. Marguerite Higgins of the *New York Herald Tribune* covered the war as a combat correspondent almost from the inception of the "police action."

Despite the arrival of regular Army units from mainland China to reinforce the North Korean troops, the U.N. forces were able to hold onto the south of Korea. Finally, on July 27, 1953, an armistice was signed. The United States suffered 54,246 deaths and 103,284 wounded, and 4,675 Americans were captured. The Korean War cost the United States a great deal of suffering and around $40 billion. Korea remains a divided country today, and democratic reforms have still not been fully implemented even in South Korea. Women played an even larger role in the next American land war in Asia, the Vietnam War. *(See also: Journalism; Military Service; Nursing; Vietnam War)*

—Jonathan W. Zophy

Further Reading

Heller, Francis, comp. *The Korean War: A 25-Year Perspective.* Lawrence: Regents Press of Kansas, 1977.

exhibited regularly in solo or group shows in New York City, other parts of this country, and abroad. A large retrospective, organized by the critic Barbara Rose, opened at the Houston Museum of Fine Arts on October 27, 1983—the artist's 75th birthday. The exhibit traveled to the San Francisco Museum of Modern Art, New York Museum of Modern Art, and the Georges Pompidou Center in Paris. Soon after this acclamation of her life's work, Lee Krasner died in New York City on June 20, 1984. *(See also: Art)*

—**Joan Jacks Silverman**

Further Reading

Hobbs, Robert. *Modern Masters: Lee Krasner.* New York: Abbeville, 1993.

Landau, Ellen G. "Lee Krasner: A Study of Her Early Career (1926–1949)." Ph.D. diss., University of Delaware, 1981.

———. "Lee Krasner's Past Continuous," *Artnews* 83 (February 1984): 68-76.

Munroe, Eleanor. *Originals: American Woman Artists.* New York: Simon & Schuster, 1979.

Robertson, Bryan, and B. H. Friedman. *Lee Krasner: Paintings, Drawings and Collages.* London: Whitechapel Art Gallery, 1965.

Rose, Barbara. *Lee Krasner: A Retrospective.* Houston, TX: Museum of Fine Arts; New York: Museum of Modern Art, 1983.

Rubenstein, Charlotte Streifer. *American Women Artists.* New York: Avon, 1982.

Tucker, Marcia. *Lee Krasner: Large Paintings.* New York: Whitney Museum of American Art, 1974.

❧ Krawczyk, Monica (1887–1954)

Teacher, social worker, and author of about thirty works, Monica Krawczyk was the most important Polish American woman author during the first half of the twentieth century. Raised in Winona, Minnesota, this first-generation American-born child of Polish immigrants had two goals: writing short fiction about her ethnic traditions and disseminating information about the culture of her parents' mother country.

Krawczyk worked with Jane Addams at Hull House in Chicago before moving back to Minnesota, where as a social worker in the Minneapolis public schools, she taught immigrants English and helped them find employment. One summer, she posed as a menial worker to expose the unsanitary conditions that newly arrived migrants faced and was successful in obtaining much-needed reform. In 1915, Krawczyk married a Polish newcomer, and the eldest of their three children became a doctor, fulfilling the American dream of upward mobility. Despite family duties, she published articles on innovative teaching techniques for exceptional children, gave lectures, organized a Polish Society at the University of Minnesota, and established the Polanie Club there, still active today.

In addition to promoting Polish pride at the state level, Krawczyk was actively involved in the Kosciuszko Foundation, the Polish-American Historical Society, and the Polish Museum. These contacts provided material for her realistic depictions of first- and second-generation family life in her thinly disguised narrative sketches. Krawczyk's short stories appeared in *Woman's Day* and *Good Housekeeping* during the second and third decades of the twentieth century. One work, "Luxuries," was given honorable mention recognition by *Minnesota Quarterly,* and another story, "No Man Alone," was chosen from over five thousand entrants in a contest sponsored by *Country Home* magazine for the best narrative about farm life during the 1930s and awarded $1,000. A third tale, "My Man," was listed in the "Index of Distinctive Short Stories" of E. J. O'Brien's *Best Short Stories for 1934.* Krawczyk's unpublished novel, *Not for Bread Alone,* explored the adjustment techniques of Polish immigrants to the United States. She published *If the Branch Blossoms and Other Stories,* a collection of twelve works, in 1950.

Krawczyk's short stories depicted immigrant family life insightfully, especially the demanding role of women, but also re-created Polish customs and ceremonies that flowed into the mainstream of American life. These lifelong efforts were recognized by the Polish government when she received the national honor of the Polania Restituta. Ironically, Krawczyk died without traveling to Poland whose traditions she helped preserve by recording with loving skill the transformation of that Polish culture in the United States. *(See also: Hull House; Immigration; Social Work; Women Writers)*

—**Edith Blicksilver**

Further Reading

Blicksilver, Edith. "Chronicler of Polish-American Life," *MELUS: Journal of the Society for the Study of the Multi-Ethnic Literature of the United States* 7 (Fall 1980): 13-20.

———. "Monica Krawczyk's Polish Pride," *Turn-of-the-Century Women* 1 (Winter 1984): 42-44.

Krawczyk, Monica. "For Dimes and Quarters." In *The Ethnic American Woman: Problems, Protests, Lifestyle,* edited by Edith Blicksilver, 118-25. Dubuque, IA: Kendall/Hunt, 1978.

———. *If the Branch Blossoms and Other Stories.* Minneapolis, MN: Polanie, 1950.

❧ Kreps, Juanita Morris (b. 1921)

Juanita Kreps, economist, was not only the first woman to be secretary of commerce but also the first woman to serve as director of the New York Stock Exchange. In fact, she is a veteran of eleven corporate boards; she claims, "Having women there is a consciousness-raising experience for men even though we rarely come down on issues differently because we are women." In addition to corporate boards, she works with organizations such as the Women's Research and Education Institute to investigate issues involving women in the workplace and the compensation they receive.

Because of her broad experience in administrative roles and directorships in conjunction with her academic career, President Carter became interested in Kreps when he was searching for the best-qualified woman to serve in his administration. When Carter told her about the role he envisioned for the Department of Commerce, which would include a concern for consumer issues, she accepted the position, taking office on January 23, 1977.

Juanita Morris was born in Lynch, Kentucky, a coal-mining community where her father was a mine operator. She attended Berea College, a work-study school that catered to students with limited financial support. Kreps then went on to Duke University, earning her Ph.D. in 1948. Early in her career, she assumed short-term academic positions, and in 1955, when she was ready to enter the workforce on a full-time basis, she was only able to secure a post as a part-time visiting lecturer at Duke. She advanced in academic rank and in 1971 was named James B. Duke Professor of Economics; later, she became vice president of Duke University. After cabinet service, Kreps did not return to administration at Duke, but she holds the rank of Emeritus Professor.

Her research focused on women's employment within the context of the changing demographics of the workforce. Kreps addressed such issues in *Sex, Age and Work* (1975) as well as in *Sex in the Marketplace: American Women at Work* (1971). In 1975, she organized a major conference on "Women and the American Economy" that developed policy regarding young women's knowledge about work in the marketplace and public education for preschoolers. She also encouraged the formation of the President's Interagency Task Force on Women Business Owners in 1977. In the Clinton administration, Kreps was named to the Commission for the Future of Worker-Management Relations in an attempt to balance the labor advocates.

Committed to equality, Kreps acted as a role model for her own daughters as well as for women, who now work at all ages, make greater investment in their human capital, and remain in the workplace for greater periods of time, regardless of marriage or childbearing. *(See also: Democratic Party; Politics)*

—**Patricia M. Duetsch**

Further Reading

Lamson, Peggy. *In the Vanguard.* Boston: Houghton Mifflin, 1979.

Stineman, Esther. *American Political Women,* pp. 95-98. Littleton, CO: Libraries Unlimited, 1980.

Tifft, Susan E. "Board Gains," *Working Women* 19 (February 1994): 36-38.

࿆ Kuhn, Margaret E. (Maggie)
(1905–1995)

An activist and advocate for peace and justice at home and around the world, Maggie Kuhn and five friends—Eleanor French, Helen Smith, Polly Cuthbertson, Anne Bennett, and Helen Baker—founded the Gray Panthers when they faced mandatory retirement in 1970. The Gray Panther organization embodies Kuhn's unique philosophy of old and young working together, linking the historical perspective of the old with the energy and new ideas of the young, to eradicate ageism and bring about peace and social justice.

In 1927, Kuhn began her professional life in Cleveland with the Young Women's Christian Association (YWCA), worked in Philadelphia, and moved on to the national staff in New York. During World War II, she initiated programs of support and education for women working in war-related industries. In 1946, she worked for the General Alliance of Unitarian Women in Boston. She was named associate secretary in 1950 for the Office of Church and Society of the United Presbyterian Church and later became Program Coordinator in the Division of Church and Race. In these roles, she worked within the church for the empowerment of women and for their acceptance in leadership roles in the church and in society.

Kuhn served on the boards of many organizations, including the National Committee for Responsive Philanthropy, the National Shared Housing Resource Center, the Points of Light Foundation, the Pension Rights Center, the National Senior Citizens Law Center, the Center for Intergenerational Learning, the Independence Public Media, the Earth Trust, and Madre.

Kuhn received her B.A. from the Flora Stone Mather College of Case Western Reserve University in Cleveland and did graduate work in community organization at Temple University and sociology and ethics at the University of Southern California, the University of Hawaii, San Francisco Theological Seminary, and LaSalle College. She received many honorary doctorates.

Among the many awards given to Kuhn were the Humanist of the Year by the American Humanist Association, the National Freedom Award of Roosevelt University in Chicago, the National Award of the American Speech and Hearing Society, the Unitarian Women's Annual Award for Ministries to Women, the 1977 Annual Peaceseeker Award of the United Presbyterian Peace Fellowship, the Gimbel Award, the Presidential Citation of the American Public Health Association, and the keys to sixteen cities. In 1978, she was named by *World Almanac* one of the "Twenty-five Most Influential Women in America" for her unique combination of humanitarianism, social criticism, and leadership. *Ladies Home Journal* named her as one of "America's 100 Most Important Women" in the October 1983 issue, and she was profiled as one of the "Fifty Faces of Feminism" in the July/August 1994 issue of *Ms.* magazine.

Kuhn authored four books: *Maggie Kuhn on Aging, You Can't Be Human Alone, Let's Get Out There and Do Something about Injustice,* and *No Stone Unturned: The Life and Times of Maggie Kuhn.* She was the subject of two documentary films: *Aging in America* and *Maggie Kuhn: Wrinkled Radical. (See also: Gray Panthers)*

—**Nancy Johns**

Further Reading

Halamandaris, Val J. "Compassionate Revolutionary: A Tribute to Maggie Kuhn," *Caring* 5 (February 1986): 34-39.

Kuhn, Maggie. *No Stone Unturned: The Life and Times of Maggie Kuhn.* New York: Ballantine, 1991.

Ladies Association of Philadelphia

Informally known as George Washington's sewing circle, the Ladies Association of Philadelphia was an organization engaged in women's relief work during the American Revolution. It was organized in 1780 by Esther De Berdt Reed, a British-born daughter of a colonial merchant, to donate clothing and supplies to colonial patriots as an "offering of the Ladies." A broadside asking women to contribute to the public cause generated such a great response that the idea spread nationally. The membership of the association included wives of prominent revolutionary politicians and military officers such as Martha Wayles Jefferson and Mrs. Robert Morris. They collected $300,000 in Continental money ($7,500 specie) from Pennsylvania alone, which George Washington requested be used for linen shirts for his soldiers. The ladies delivered 2,005 linen shirts to the soldiers of the Revolution; each shirt bore the name of the lady who made it.

After Reed died in 1780, Sarah Franklin Bache, daughter of Benjamin Franklin, continued the project. *(See also: American Revolutionary Era)*

—**Ginger Rae Allee**

Further Reading

Adelman, Joseph. *Famous Women,* p. 87. New York: Lonow, 1926.

Bruce, H. Addington. *Women in the Making of America,* pp. 87, 106-08. Rev. ed. Boston: Little, Brown, 1928.

Ellet, Elizabeth F. *The Women of the American Revolution,* Vol. 1, pp. 332-43. New York: Baker & Scribner, 1848. Reprint, New York: Arno, 1974.

Green, Henry Clinton, and Mary Wolcott Green. *The Pioneer Mothers of America,* Vol. 2, p. 14; Vol. 3, pp. 144-52, 179-92, 279-80. New York: Putnam, 1912. [portrait]

Leonard, Eugene Andruss, Sophia Drinker, and Miriam Young Holden. *The American Women in Colonial and Revolutionary Times, 1765–1800,* pp. 112, 120-21. Philadelphia: University of Pennsylvania Press, 1962.

Logan, Mary Simmerson. *The Part Taken by Women in American History,* pp. 150-52, 202. 1912. Reprint, New York: Arno, 1972.

Norton, Mary Beth. *Liberty's Daughters,* pp. 178-94. Boston: Little, Brown, 1980.

Ladies Magazine and Repository of Entertaining Knowledge
(1792–1793)

Published biannually by William Gibbons in Philadelphia, *Ladies Magazine and Repository of Entertaining Knowledge* contained reviews of contemporary literature, essays, travelogues, and poetry. This bold experiment marked the debut of women's magazines. Entries that focused on the importance of women's intellectual growth distinguished the provocative and innovative *Ladies Magazine* from contemporaneous popular women's literature, which was primarily either romantic escapist pap or religious prescriptive tracts. The editorial policy of the magazine proposed to "inspire the Female mind with love of religion, of patience, of prudence, and fortitude."

In an attempt to preserve the "fairer sex," general guidelines for appropriate reading material were set by men such as lexicographer Noah Webster and reformer Dr. Benjamin Rush. While their opinions differed concerning the appropriate degree of edification, both argued in favor of female learning only insofar as it enabled women to understand and uphold the new Republican ideals. In an attempt to broaden this definition, *Ladies Magazine* included comprehensive works to elucidate female intellectuality—for example, excerpts from Mary Wollstonecraft's *A Vindication of the Rights of Woman* (1792). More subtle works also conveyed the rights and responsibilities of women as equal to those of men. One essay, "On Love," professed that the institution of marriage was a mutual venture between woman and man. As a contemporary voice, *Ladies Magazine* elevated women's reading material ideologically and culturally to a position of equality with that of men's. *(See also: European Influences; Magazines; Republican Motherhood; Rush, Benjamin and "Thoughts on Female Education")*

—**Robin S. Taylor**

Further Reading

Cott, Nancy F. *The Bonds of Womanhood.* New Haven, CT: Yale University Press, 1977.

Kerber, Linda. "Daughters of Columbia: Educating Women for the Republic, 1787–1805." In *Our American Sisters: Women in American Life and Thought,* edited by Jean E. Friedman and William G. Shade, 137-53. Lexington, MA: Heath, 1982.

~ LaFlesche Picotte, Susan
(1865–1915)

Susan Picotte LaFlesche was the first American Indian woman physician. She was the daughter of Iron Eye, the last federally recognized chief of the Omaha tribe, and his wife Mary Gale, a daughter of a U.S. Army physician and a full-blooded Omaha mother.

LaFlesche attended the Presbyterian mission school on the Omaha Reservation until 1879, when she and her sister Marguerite entered the Institution for Young Ladies in Elizabeth, New Jersey. In 1882, they returned to the reservation and taught school. In 1884, the sisters entered Hampton Normal and Agricultural Institute in Hampton, Virginia. Two years later, Susan LaFlesche graduated as salutatorian of her class.

In October 1886, LaFlesche entered the Woman's Medical College of Pennsylvania in Philadelphia. Her tuition was paid through a grant by the federal government and a scholarship by the Connecticut Indian Association. She graduated in 1889 at the head of her class and served her internship at Philadelphia's Woman's Hospital.

Returning to her reservation in late 1889, she was appointed the physician for the government boarding school. By 1890, she became the appointed physician for the Omaha agency. The work was extremely difficult, treating all the residents scattered over the 1,350 square mile reservation. In 1893, she resigned her position due to ill health.

In 1894, she announced she would marry Henry Picotte, a Sioux Indian. They had two sons, Pierre and Caryl. She and her husband moved to the nearby town of Bancroft, Nebraska, where she practiced medicine on both whites and Indians. She became an advocate of temperance, helped found a local hospital, and became an activist for Native American rights. In 1905, her husband died due to alcoholism.

Shortly after her husband's death, the Presbyterian Board of Home Missions appointed her as the missionary to her tribe, the first Indian ever to hold that position. The board provided her with a house and a modest income to work out of the Blackbird Hills Presbyterian Church as a teacher, field-worker, minister, and physician. She became a role model for many young Omahas and remained at this post until her death at the age of fifty, probably due to cancer.

Although LaFlesche revered her Indian ancestry, she embraced assimilation, believing the tribal tie was an obstacle to "progress." She advocated allotment of lands and education in the white man's schools as the only way for her people to succeed in America. To Indian reformers of her generation, her life was a testimony to the benefits of acculturation. *(See also: Native American Women; Physicians; Woman's Medical College of Pennsylvania)*

—Joyce Ann Kievit

Further Reading

Herzog, Kristin. "The LaFlesche Family: Native American Spirituality, Calvinism, and Presbyterian Missions," *American Presbyterians* 65 (1987): 222-32.

Mathes, Valerie Sherer. "Dr. Susan LaFlesche Picotte: The Reformed and the Reformer." In *Indian Lives,* edited by L. G. Moses and Raymond Wilson, 61-90. Albuquerque: University of New Mexico Press, 1985.

———. "Susan LaFlesche Picotte: Nebraska's Indian Physician, 1865–1915," *Nebraska History* 63 (1982): 502-30.

~ Language and Linguistics

Although contemporary U.S. feminists since about 1970 have paid close attention to language about the sexes as well as sex differences in the use of language, few attempts have been made to place this inquiry in the context of American women's history. In fact, however, leading nineteenth-century feminists, notably Elizabeth Cady Stanton and Susan B. Anthony, did concern themselves with linguistic issues such as women's authority to speak in public, the married woman's right to her own name, the possibility of feminine imagery for God, and the legal interpretation of *person, man,* and *he.* For example, after the Civil War, many suffragists objected strenuously to the wording of the Fourteenth Amendment, which for the first time inserted the word *male* into the Constitution, and they noted the irony of laws that imposed criminal penalties on women while denying them civil rights. This analysis led to lawsuits such as *United States v. Susan B. Anthony* (1873) and *Minor v. Happersett* (1874), which challenged the courts to establish a consistent interpretation of "generic" legal language. Near the turn of the century, Stanton's *Woman's Bible* incorporated religious and legal linguistic arguments into a radical feminist critique. Not long afterward, Henry James penned a vicious attack on the "degenerate" speech of American women, blaming feminism for the breakdown of linguistic standards of social class. Exactly the opposite view was held by the very influential feminist writer Charlotte Perkins Gilman, who believed that improvements in language would accompany a socialist-feminist transformation of society.

The first decades of the twentieth century saw the establishment of linguistics as a unified discipline. Researchers in the new field observed male and female speech in different cultures and contributed a feminist perspective to lexicography; however, a feminist historiography of linguistics has yet to be written. In 1946, Mary R. Beard devoted an entire chapter of *Woman as Force in History* to documenting the still troublesome ambiguity of masculine generic usage.

As the twentieth century drew to a close, contentious attention to sexist language existed on many fronts. Touching on the concerns of Elizabeth Cady Stanton and Susan B. Anthony, biblical scholars continue to debate the standard biblical wording that excludes women, and although a gender-revised version of the Bible was published in England, the effort has not yet gotten far in the United States. In the secular community, much progress in nonsexist language has been made, and debate has shifted from contention about whether or not biased language is damaging and avoidable to discovering the most natural, least contrived methods of communicating inclusion of both sexes. This shift in focus, however, is not without controversy, and changing sexist language continues to involve researchers and scholars in many disciplines. Finally, electronic communication offers a new field of concern and debate as control issues involve politicians, lawmakers, and educators.

One difficulty of historical research on women in language is that feminist historians and linguists alike have shown little interest in crossing each other's disciplinary boundaries. As a result, there is little direct knowledge of what women in general (and feminists in particular) have been saying about language and the sexes throughout most of American history. *(See also: Beard, Mary; Deconstruction; Minor v. Happersett; Stanton, Elizabeth Cady)*

—**Lou Ann Matossian**
—**Celia Esplugas**

Further Reading

Barron, Dennis. *Grammar and Gender.* New Haven, CT: Yale University Press, 1986.

Hall, Kira, and Mary Bucholtz, eds. *Gender Articulated: Language and the Socially Constructed Self.* New York: Routledge, 1996.

Kramarae, Cheris, and Paula A. Treichler. *A Feminist Dictionary.* London: Pandora, 1985.

Livia, Anna, and Kira Hall, eds. *Queerly Phrased: Language, Gender and Sexuality.* New York: Oxford University Press, 1997.

Miller, Casey, and Kate Swift. *Handbook of Nonsexist Writing: For Writers, Editors, and Speakers,* 2d ed. New York: Harper Collins, 1992.

———. *Words and Women: New Language in New Times.* New York: HarperCollins, 1991.

Minor v. Happersett, 53 No. 58 and 21 Wallace, 162 (1874).

Penfield, Joyce. *Women and Language in Transition.* Albany: State University of New York Press, 1987.

Perry, Linda, Lynn Turner, and Helen Sterk. *Constructing and Reconstructing Gender: The Links among Communication, Language and Gender.* Albany: State University of New York Press, 1992.

Thorne, Barrie, Cheris Kramarae, and Nancy Henley, eds. *Language, Gender, and Society.* Rowley, MA: Newbury House, 1983.

United States v. Susan B. Anthony, 11 Blatch. C. C. 202 (1873).

☙ Lanham Act (1943)

The application of this act (Lanham Act of 1943, 54 Stat. 1125) for the construction of wartime facilities to build day care centers and to support their operating costs exemplified the ambivalent response of the federal government to married women in the workforce and to working mothers' need of child care services for their young children during World War II. In response to the inability of local governments to provide these facilities for women working in the defense industries, the Lanham Act allocated federal funds through a complicated system that involved seven federal agencies.

Although the U.S. Children's Bureau championed the cause of the working mother's need for adequate child care

services, ultimately, control of the development of day care facilities was achieved by those within the Roosevelt administration who accepted married women into the labor force only as an emergency wartime measure. Thus, by 1944, day care centers serviced a mere 10 percent of the children of working mothers. Without adequate child care, the working mother retained the pre-World War II sense that her primary obligation was to care for her children in her home, while she was barraged with the relentless propaganda of the Office of War Information, which exhorted her to do her patriotic duty in the workforce. *(See also: Child Rearing; Day Care; United States Children's Bureau; World War II)*

—**Angela M. Howard**

Further Reading

Rupp, Leila M. *Mobilizing Women for War: German and American Propaganda, 1939–1945.* Princeton, NJ: Princeton University Press, 1978.

☙ Larcom, Lucy (1824–1893)

Teacher, editor, lecturer, and poet, Lucy Larcom achieved a national reputation in the late 1850s that lasted to her death and beyond. Poems and articles appeared in newspapers and magazines, and four collections of her poems were published in her lifetime. Although primarily a poet, her best, and best-known, work is her partial autobiography, *A New England Girlhood* (1889).

She was born in Beverly, Massachusetts, to a large but comfortably situated family; her father's death when she was six sent her mother to Lowell, Massachusetts, as a mill boardinghouse keeper. From the age of ten to twenty-one, Larcom worked in the Lowell mills; taking advantage of the opportunities available to the much-publicized mill girls, she developed her passionate desire to read and learn, and she also developed the independence characteristic of the mill girls. In 1846, she went to the West (then Illinois) to teach in a district school; she was able to get the formal education she longed for in an excellent academy there. She was engaged, but the sight of her brilliant sister's talents lost in the drudgery of a prairie marriage turned her away from that commitment. Her contributions to the *Lowell Offering* attracted the attention of John Greenleaf Whittier, who published her poems in *National Era.*

In 1852, she returned to Massachusetts, and two years later began to teach at Wheaton Female Seminary. Her first book, *Similitudes, from the Ocean and Prairie* (1853) was a collection of moral-religious stories aimed at children; it was pushed into print by Whittier, who had adopted her as his protégée. During her nine years at Wheaton, she published three similar books and many poems, but she suffered psychosomatic illnesses as a result of conflict between her need for security (which the teaching she disliked gave her) and her desire to be free of restrictions and to write. National fame came suddenly in 1858 with a poem called "Hannah Binding Shoes": It was set to music, inspired paintings, was frequently anthologized, and, ironically, since she did not much like it, followed her all her life. In 1861, her "The Rose Enthroned" appeared in *Atlantic Monthly;* this literary effort to reconcile Christianity and Darwinism and the Civil War brought notice from James T. Fields.

She left Wheaton in 1863 and became an editor of a new magazine for children, *Our Young Folks.* Her first collection, called *Poems,* was published in 1868; two years earlier, she had done an anthology of inspirational passages called *Breathings from the Better Life.* When the magazine was sold in 1873, she determined to support herself as a freelance writer and lecturer, managing to earn enough money to live, in a modest way, the life she wanted. Her publications in the 1870s included *An Idyl of Work,* a blank-verse story of the Lowell mill girls; *Childhood Songs,* a collection of her poems for children; and five anthologies. Three of these were collaborations in which she did the work and Whittier took the credit. In the 1880s, she published *Wild Roses of Cape Ann,* mostly local-color poems, and Houghton Mifflin's Household Edition, *Lucy Larcom's Works* (1884). Her autobiography, *A New England Girlhood* (1889), was a critical success. In the last years of her life, she wrote three religious books that sold well.

Most of Larcom's poems begin with richly textured descriptions of the natural world, then move to a moral or religious insight. Much of her work is topical and autobiographical; it reflected her own experience and thinking. None of her poetry is particularly original, but her descriptions of nature still make pleasant reading. A deeply religious woman, she struggled painfully from the Puritanism into which she was born to a kind of Christian transcendentalism that informs much of her work. She avoided the controversial women's rights movement; she agreed with those who glorified woman as the light of the home, although several of her poems indicate that she was aware of womn's problems, and certainly her own life choices contradicted her stated position. Both her work and her public behavior stayed safely within the norms of the nineteenth-century American literary establishment. *(See also: Lowell Mill Girls; Lowell Offering; Transcendentalism; Women Writers)*

—**Shirley Marchalonis**

Further Reading

Addison, Daniel Dulany. *The Life, Letters and Diary of Lucy Larcom.* Boston: Houghton Mifflin, 1894. [unreliable biography]

Larcom, Lucy. *A New England Girlhood.* Boston: Houghton Mifflin, 1889. Reprint, Boston: Northeastern University Press, 1985.

Marchalonis, Shirley. *The Worlds of Lucy Larcom, 1824–1893.* Athens: University of Georgia Press, 1989.

⋄ Late Twentieth-Century Feminism

During the last two decades of the twentieth century, women scored significant victories in politics, education, and the economy but also suffered setbacks, including the defeat of the Equal Rights Amendment. The defeat of the ERA demoralized feminists. The campaign for ratification had polarized the nation's women and ignited a backlash against equality for women. In this climate, many grassroots feminist organizations withered, but major organizations such as the National Organization for Women and the National Abortion Rights Action League remained strong and carried out focused efforts to protect and advance women's rights through legislation and litigation. The ERA campaign had brought women on both sides of the issue to national prominence. Women from both major political parties achieved unprecedented success in winning elective offices at local, state, and federal levels in the wake of the ERA defeat. Presidents Ronald Reagan and Bill Clinton appointed, respectively, Sandra Day O'Connor and Ruth Bader Ginsberg as the first female justices to serve on the U.S. Supreme Court.

Women enjoyed considerable upward occupational mobility after 1980, and three-fifths of all women participated in the labor force in the 1990s. During the 1980s, women earned more baccalaureate and master's degrees than did men, and women increased their representation among the holders of law, medical, and other advanced degrees. Affirmative action policies aided in women's educational and employment advances, and throughout the 1980s and 1990s, federal courts disallowed some corporate affirmative action plans but upheld others. California's revocation of affirmative action in higher education in 1995 and the 1996 fifth-district federal circuit court ruling against the University of Texas Law School's admission policies in the *Hopwood* case (*Hopwood v. State of Texas,* 1994) signaled a decline in public support for affirmative action.

The gender gap in wages, an ever-present facet of the American labor market, narrowed considerably in the 1980s and 1990s as women improved their wages relative to men in the same or similar occupations, but women's progress was partly illusory. Real incomes in the United States did not improve over these two decades as recessions and industrial reorganizations repeatedly afflicted working Americans with layoffs, job terminations, and wage stagnation. Furthermore, not all women shared in the occupational progress of the 1980s and 1990s. African American and Hispanic women remained disproportionately locked in minimum wage jobs and burdened by unemployment, while female college graduates, especially white women, marched up the earnings ladder. The industrial sweatshop, which had nearly disappeared by the end of World War II, reappeared as the century wore on. Especially in the Northeast, the Southwest, and the West, sweatshops reappeared and employed immigrant Asian and Hispanic women at wages far below the legal minimum. Unable to read or speak English and fearful of deportation, thousands of garment workers of the 1990s became virtual prisoners of their employers.

Significant changes in the life cycle and family lives of women occurred as the end of the century approached.

Fertility reached an all-time low despite continuing increases in teenage childbearing (largely accounted for by rising white teenage fertility). Women's age at first marriage rose through the 1990s, and the share of women who never married or never bore children also increased. Mothers of all races and classes faced increasing responsibilities as the share of families headed by women continued to rise. In the last decade of the century, welfare policy emerged as a major political issue in the nation. Conservative legislators strove to reduce welfare funding and to terminate welfare benefits to families in which mothers neither earned wages nor pursued job training. Single mothers living in poverty faced cuts in public assistance for their children at the same time that the real value of the minimum wage declined.

During the efforts to secure the Equal Rights Amendment, feminists had laid aside their differences on other issues. With the ERA's defeat, the many different perspectives and concerns that had characterized second-wave feminism again came to the fore. Feminists of the 1970s had made progress in bettering employment conditions, in fighting sexual harassment, in advancing gay rights, and in protecting abortion rights, but these agendas and others stood unfinished at the end of the decade. In addition to these concerns, feminists worked to protect welfare programs, fought for the enforcement of fathers' child support obligations, worked to prosecute perpetrators of domestic violence, and supported women's bids to gain equality in education. Women of differing political perspectives worked together to discourage sexual harassment in the workplace and domestic violence on the home front, but the issue of abortion rights continued to divide female activists. Partly because women openly supported more single-issue agendas and worked for continuity or change in more areas than ever before, the 1990s brought women to an unprecedented level of public leadership. *(See also: Abortion; Affirmative Action; Equal Rights Amendment; Female-Headed Households; Feminism; Fertility; Gender Gap; National Organization for Women; United States Supreme Court)*

—**Julia Kirk Blackwelder**

Further Reading

AAUW Educational Foundation. *How Schools Shortchange Women: The AAUW Report: A Study of Major Findings on Girls and Education.* Washington, DC: National Education Association and AAUW Education Foundation, 1992.

Edelman, Marian Wright. *Families in Peril: An Agenda for Social Change.* Cambridge, MA: Harvard University Press, 1987.

Giannaros, Martin, and Demetrios Giannaros. "Would a Higher Minimum Wage Help Poor Families Headed by Women?" *Monthly Labor Review* 113 (August 1990): 30-34.

Goldin, Claudia. *Understanding the Gender Gap: An Economic History of American Women.* New York: Oxford University Press, 1990.

Hopwood v. State of Texas, 861 F. Supp. 551 W.D. Tex. (1994).

Horrigan, Michael W., and James P. Markey. "Recent Gains in Women's Earnings: Better Pay or Longer Hours?" *Monthly Labor Review* 113 (July 1990): 11-16.

Rubin, Lillian B. *Worlds of Pain: Life in the Working-Class Family.* New York: Basic Books, 1992.

Whittier, Nancy. *Feminist Generations: The Persistence of the Radical Women's Movement.* Philadelphia: Temple University Press, 1995.

Willie, Charles Vert. *Black and White Families: A Study in Complementarity.* Bayside, NY: General Hall, 1985.

⌒ Lathrop, Julia Clifford (1858–1932)

Julia Lathrop, social reformer, was born in Rockford, Illinois, the eldest of William and Sarah Potter Lathrop's five children. The family had a long tradition of public activism. William was a leader in the Republican Party and served first in the state general assembly and later in Congress, while Sarah was an ardent advocate of woman suffrage. Lathrop received her bachelor's degree in 1880 from Vassar College and then returned home to read law in her father's office. In 1890, she moved to Chicago's Hull House, the third "settlement house" established in America in a movement that encouraged educated young people to "settle" and work among the poor. She quickly became a member of the settlement's inner circle. There, she launched a reform career that spanned more than forty years and eventually carried her to a post in Washington.

At Hull House, Lathrop worked in a variety of capacities. She volunteered to be a county agent investigating the neighborhood's relief applicants. Next, she joined the Illinois Board of Charities, an assignment that she filled by visiting all of the state's county farms and almshouses, institutions that provided minimal shelter for the poor. In subsequent years, she traveled to Europe to explore treatment of the insane, helped found the Chicago School of Civics and Philanthropy, participated in the juvenile court movement, and established the Illinois Immigrants' Protective League.

In 1912, President William Howard Taft appointed Lathrop the first director of the newly established U.S. Children's Bureau. Under her leadership, the agency undertook studies of maternal and infant mortality, nutrition, juvenile delinquency, juvenile courts, illegitimacy, mental defectives, child labor, and mothers' pensions. The bureau was also responsible for enforcement of the nation's first child labor law, passed by Congress in 1916. Lathrop served in Washington until 1921, when she resigned and was replaced by Grace Abbott, another Hull House veteran.

Lathrop returned to Rockford to live with her sister, but even in retirement, she remained active; she was president of the Illinois League of Women Voters from 1922 to 1924 and served on a presidential commission to study conditions at New York's Ellis Island center for immigration. In 1925, she became an advisory member of the Child Welfare Committee of the League of Nations. Lathrop died in Rockford in 1932 following surgery. *(See also: Hull House; Immigrant Protective League; Sheppard-Towner Act; United States Children's Bureau)*

—**Rebecca L. Sherrick**

Further Reading
Julia Lathrop Papers. Rockford College, Rockford, IL.
Addams, Jane. *My Friend, Julia Lathrop.* New York: Macmillan, 1935.

♨ Law Enforcement

The first efforts to bring women into law enforcement date from the mid-1800s. In 1845, the American Female Reform Society of New York City advocated the employment of matrons in local jails, and matrons were hired to deal with the arrested women and juveniles. Other reform groups, such as the Woman's Christian Temperance Union, also called for matrons, and by 1900, most major cities had adopted their use.

The first woman with police duties was Mrs. Lola Baldwin, appointed to the Portland, Oregon, police department in 1905. She was assigned to "child protection" work during that summer's world's fair. The 1910 appointment of Mrs. Alice Stebbins Wells to the Los Angeles police department marked the beginning of a vigorous and organized movement. She led the campaign to get cities to hire women police, and in 1915, she organized the International Association of Policewomen. The movement gained strength, and over the next fifteen years, more than 140 cities hired women police officers. Their responsibilities, however, remained much the same—dealing with juveniles and females, counseling and protecting them, and serving essentially as social workers. After the mid-1920s, however, few additional cities had added women to their police forces. The crime prevention model of police work that aided the policewomen's movement was relegated to a position of minor importance, supplanted in the late 1920s and 1930s by the crime fighter model of policing. But no new concept of women police emerged to fit this emphasis, and the movement stagnated for the next three decades.

In 1968, Indianapolis opened new opportunities with the appointment of two women officers to patrol duty, and in the 1970s, the use of women police again expanded and attracted much attention. Since then, women have been involved in a broader range of police work. One indication of the expanding role is that the term *policeman* has given way to *police officer* as women once again enter the law enforcement profession and expand their role in it. Women have made progress in the field of law enforcement, but it continues to be a male-dominated profession. In 1998, Department of Justice data reported that as of 1996, women held 14 percent of 74,500 full-time fed eral officer positions. The twenty-first century promises to bring about alternative forms of conflict resolution centered around grassroots efforts to protect urban neighborhoods from violent crime. *(See also: Legal Profession)*

—**Robert G. Waite**

Further Reading
Horne, Peter. *Women in Law Enforcement.* Springfield, IL: Charles C Thomas, 1980.
Owings, Chloe. *Women Police: A Study of the Development and Status of the Women Police Movement.* 1925. Reprint, Montclair, NJ: Patterson Smith, 1969.
Walker, Samuel. *A Critical History of Police Reform.* Lexington, MA: Heath, 1977.

♨ Lawrence Strike (1912)

The Lawrence Strike of 1912 was the most publicized strike prior to World War I; 23,000 textile workers challenged powerful corporations and won. The strikers were largely foreign-born and unskilled workers, more than half of whom were women and children.

By 1912, the city of Lawrence, Massachusetts, was a one-industry town, with twelve wool and cotton mills supporting 32,000 textile operatives and 60,000 more dependent on them for their daily bread. Foul tenements, poor diets, and lack of warm clothing created a living hell. In view of the low wages, entire families had to work in the mills. Lodgers and boarders were an economic necessity for the majority of immigrant households, increasing the burden of work for the woman of the house, particularly when she too worked in the mill. Lawrence held the distinction of having one of the highest mortality rates of all industrial cities in the nation. In 1910, of the 1,524 deaths in Lawrence, almost half were children under six years old. A medical examiner concluded that thirty-six of every one hundred men and women who worked in the mills died before they were twenty-five years old.

The strike resulted from a new policy that reduced the workweek for women and children from fifty-six hours to fifty-four, provoking widespread anxiety. The reduction of the workweek, with the corresponding reduction in already starvation-level wages, brought past injustices and miseries exploding to the surface.

On January 11, 1912, a cold, bleak Thursday, the Battle of Lawrence began. Spontaneously, as the pay envelopes were passed out, the Polish weavers, mostly women, began shouting "not enough pay," then sat at their machines, refusing to work. They left the mill, calling for a demonstration and vowing not to return to work until their pay envelopes were increased by the amount deducted, 32 cents, or "four loaves of bread."

Within a week, 23,000 workers joined the protest. The Industrial Workers of the World, the IWW, inspired and molded the strikers into an effective fighting unit and organized the first large-scale picketing in New England. Four days after the uprising began, the IWW directed it into a bona fide strike with mass picketing in front of all mills, twenty-four hours a day. Believing they would be handled less brutally than the men by police and state militia, women voluntarily placed themselves at the forefront of the picket lines and held their ground despite police policy that female strikers be beat about the breasts and arms while men be beat about the head. The strikers chanted, "We Want Bread, and Roses Too" and "Better to Starve Fighting Than to Starve Working."

One month after the strike began, IWW organizer Elizabeth Gurley Flynn launched the "Children's Crusade," a plan to lighten the relief burden and gain publicity for the strikers by placing strikers' children in foster homes in other cities. Every one of the children, according to physicians who examined them, suffered from malnutrition. The exodus of children created national attention and sympathy for the strikers. Police tried to prevent the children from leaving Lawrence, brutally beating and arresting fifteen children and eight women, which horrified the public and created a demand for a congressional investigation into the strike. With the public and press now in support of the strikers, the mill owners were forced to negotiate.

The women of Lawrence dispelled two myths that had historically excluded women from the organized labor movement. First, they were not "temporary," working for "pin money," but workers whose wages were necessary for family survival. Second, women proved themselves capable of leadership and of acting in roles beyond those traditionally relegated to them. *(See also: Flynn, Elizabeth Gurley; Industrial Workers of the World; Textiles: North and South)*

—**Sandra J. Weidner**
Adapted for the second edition by Robert G. Waite.

Further Reading

Brooks, Thomas R. *Toil and Trouble: A History of American Labor.* New York: Delacorte, 1964.

Cahn, William. *Lawrence, 1912: The Bread and Roses Strike.* New York: Pilgrim, 1980.

Dubofsky, Melvyn. *We Shall Be All: A History of the IWW.* Chicago: Quadrangle, 1969.

Foner, Philip S. *History of the Labor Movement in the U.S.* Vol. 4, *The IWW, 1905–1917.* New York: International Publishers, 1965, 1972.

———. *Women and the American Labor Movement, from the First Trade Unions to the Present.* New York: Macmillan, 1979.

Yellen, Samuel. *American Labor Struggles.* New York: Harcourt Brace, 1936.

⌒ Lazarus, Emma (1849–1887)

Jewish American poet, translator, and essayist, Emma Lazarus is best known for her 1883 poem "The New Colossus," which was inscribed on the pedestal of the Statue of Liberty in 1903. Lazarus was the member of a wealthy New York family, descendants of Sephardic and Ashkenazi Jews. A child prodigy, she was privately educated and became proficient in several languages, gaining a wide knowledge of American literature and the work of medieval Hebrew poets. Although her parents encouraged her writing, she was aware of the difficulties facing women who attempted to be taken seriously in the profession. She expressed this consciousness of imposed limitations in an early sonnet, "Echoes":

> Late-born and woman-souled I dare not hope . . .
> the might of manly, modern passion shall alight
> Upon my Muse's lips, nor may I cope
> (Who veiled and screened by womanhood must
>   grope).

The publication of *Poems and Translations by Emma Lazarus* in 1866, when she was seventeen, brought her praise from Ralph Waldo Emerson, who became one in a series of male mentors. Her published work in the following decade was classical and romantic in style. In the early 1880s, she became an activist in providing relief to Jewish refugees fleeing from pogroms in Russia. Her firsthand knowledge of their persecution brought an increased militancy and power to her poetry, expressed in her critically acclaimed *Songs of a Semite* (1882). She was further influenced by the egalitarian ideas of Henry George and William Morris, and by the writings of George Eliot and Walt Whitman. Her work became infused with a deeply historical analysis of her Jewish heritage; a proud identification with women, exemplified in her personification of values such as freedom, heroism, and labor in female form; and the articulation of the experiences of the oppressed.

As a writer for *Critic, Century, American Hebrew,* and other magazines, she influenced public debate over issues such as political repression, poverty, and Jewish nationalism. She died of cancer at the age of thirty-eight. *By the Waters of Babylon* (1887), a collection of prose poems that demonstrate her break from the conventional forms of her early work, was her last publication. *(See also: Jewish Women)*

—**Barbara Bair**

Further Reading

Jacob, H. E. *The World of Emma Lazarus.* New York: Schocken, 1949.

Lichtenstein, Diane Marilyn. *Writing Their Nations: The Tradition of Nineteenth-Century American Jewish Women Writers,* pp. 36–59. Bloomington: Indiana University Press, 1992.

Merriam, Eve. *Emma Lazarus: Woman with a Torch.* New York: Citadel, 1956.

Schappes, Morris, ed. *Emma Lazarus: Selections from Her Poetry and Prose.* New York: Cooperative Book League, 1944.

Vogel, Dan. *Emma Lazarus.* Boston: G. K. Hall, 1980.

⌒ League of Women Voters

The League of Women Voters was a direct outgrowth of the National American Woman Suffrage Association (NAWSA), which had led the successful campaign for women's right to vote in the decades preceding 1920. In 1919, NAWSA President Carrie Chapman Catt proposed a league of women voters on the eve of the successful ratification of the Nineteenth Amendment, which federally enfranchised women. At the NAWSA convention in St. Louis on March 24, 1919, Catt announced, "Let us then raise up a league of women voters . . . a league that shall be non-partisan and nonsectarian in nature." Catt called for the league to adopt three distinct aims: first, to secure a final enfranchisement of women in every state; second, to remove remaining legal discriminations against women; and third, to make democracy safe enough to provide for world security. In February 1920, the NAWSA was officially dissolved, and the organization proceeded under the name the League of Women Voters.

Following the adoption of the Nineteenth Amendment with Tennessee's ratification on August 26, 1920, the league turned its focus to issues concerning good citizenship, peace, child welfare, effective government, and the status of women. Two of the league's early successes came in 1922 with the passage of the Cable Citizenship Act guaranteeing independent citizenship for married women and the Sheppard-Towner Act protecting mothers and newborns. In 1924, the league launched its first of many "Get Out the Vote" campaigns, which was not only a crusade for voter participation but for voter education as well. The slogan in 1928 became "Democracy Is a Bandwagon and There Are too Many Empty Seats." A significant victory came in the same year as the league helped to win jury membership for women.

In succeeding years, the league continued its drive for an educated electorate by establishing its own research facilities nationwide and by publishing *The National Voter* magazine from its headquarters in Washington, D.C. On its seventy-fifth anniversary in 1995, the league had five hundred chapters in all fifty states, organized at the grassroots level—a nonpartisan, multi-issue, activist network. The league serves as a successful lobbying group for tax reform, clean water, arms control, and the "superfund" for toxic cleanup. Most visible are the league's televised debates between presidential, congressional, state, and local candidates for public office. *(See also: Catt, Carrie Chapman; National American Woman Suffrage Association; Sheppard-Towner Act of 1921)*

—Ellen D. Langill

Further Reading

Lemons, J. Stanley. *The Woman Citizen: Social Feminism in the 1920s.* Urbana: University of Illinois Press, 1973.

"On the Road to Reform, The League's Place in History," *National Voter* 35 (November/December 1986). [Special Issue]

Young, Louise. *In the Public Interest: The League of Women Voters, 1920–1970.* Westport, CT: Greenwood, 1989.

◆ Lease, Mary Elizabeth Clyens
(1850–1933)

Born in Ridgway, Pennsylvania, Mary Elizabeth Lease was an orator for the Farmers' Alliance and Populist Party. In 1870, she moved to Kansas to teach school, and three years later she married Charles L. Lease, a pharmacist. The couple had four children. The family farmed in Kansas and then in Texas until 1883, when they returned to Wichita,

Kansas, where Lease's husband resumed working as a pharmacist. Lease spoke for the Irish National League and the Union Labor Party, edited the *Union Labor Press,* joined the Knights of Labor, and was elected "master workman" for Kansas. She also cofounded the *Colorado Workman,* joined the Farmers' Alliance and the Woman's Christian Temperance Union, and wrote several articles on women's rights. Lease served briefly as president of the Wichita Equal Suffrage Association and ran for superintendent of schools in Sedgewick, Kansas.

In 1890, Lease joined a speakers' bureau whose focus was the defeat of Senator John J. Ingalls of Kansas, because he had not supported the demands of the Kansas Farmers' Alliance. For seven months, Lease campaigned against Ingalls, traveling to sixteen counties and some fifty towns and cities, making approximately 160 speeches during the summer. With the defeat of Ingalls and the advent of the Populist Party, Lease gained notoriety. From 1890 to 1894, she worked for the Populists, speaking to hundreds of groups of farmers in states as far away as Oregon and Washington and attending Populist conventions. She was rewarded for this work by an appointment as the first woman president of the Kansas State Board of Charities and Corrections. By 1893, because of quarrels with the Populist administration, Lease began supporting the Republican Party and ceased advocating woman suffrage and temperance. This ended her political effectiveness and her career as an orator.

She moved to New York in 1896 after arguing against the nomination of William Jennings Bryan at the St. Louis Populist convention. In New York, Lease once more supported woman suffrage and temperance. She divorced her husband in 1902 and filed for bankruptcy. Her later activities included lecturing for the adult education program of the New York City Board of Education and serving as president of the National Society for Birth Control. She died in New York in 1933. *(See also: National Farmers' Alliance; Populist Party)*

—MaryJo Wagner

Further Reading

Blumberg, Dorothy. "Mary Elizabeth Lease: Populist Campaigner." Unpublished manuscript, Berkshire Women's History Conference, 1974.

Lease, Mary Elizabeth [James Arnold]. *M. E. Lease.* Topeka: Kansas State Historical Society, n.d.

Livermore, A. L. "Mary Elizabeth Lease: The Foremost Woman Politician of the Times," *Metropolitan Magazine* 14 (November 1896): 263-66.

Wagner, MaryJo. "Prairie Populists: Luna Kellie and Mary Elizabeth Lease." In *Northwest Women's Heritage,* edited by Karen Blair, 200-10. Seattle: Northwest Center for Research on Women, 1984.

◆ Lee, Mother Ann (1736–1784)

Mother Ann Lee was the founder and leader of the Shakers, a Protestant, celibate, and communitarian sect known for its female participation and leadership. Her followers viewed Lee as the female embodiment of Christ and the maternal component of a Mother/Father God.

Born to a working-class family in Manchester, England, Lee was sent out, like many girls of her class and time, to work in the textile mills. Thus, she lacked any schooling and remained illiterate. Throughout her life, Lee exhibited signs of religious mysticism. In 1758, she joined John and Jane Wardley's sect of Shaking Quakers. The Wardleys advocated celibacy and public confession of sin. Ann Lee, a talented woman with a charismatic personality, soon rose to a position of religious leadership within the sect.

Although she felt a physical and spiritual repugnance toward marriage, Lee was persuaded to marry Abraham Stanley. Four difficult childbirths and the deaths of all four children may have contributed to Lee's conviction that lust was the root of all evil. Imprisoned in 1770 for Sabbath breaking, Lee experienced visions in which it was revealed to her that lustful sexual intercourse was the primary impediment to human perfection and that she, as the conduit for Christ's second appearance on earth, was to spread this message.

In 1774, Ann Lee and a small band sailed for America. Taking advantage of religious revivals in New York and New England, Lee and her followers spread the message of Christ's reappearance in female form. These early Shakers suffered physical persecution. They were charged with being British spies, blasphemers, and dangerous disrupters of the community. In 1784, Lee died as a result of injuries probably sustained at the hands of a mob.

Although Ann Lee served as a spiritual guide and role model for many women who joined the Shakers, she believed men should remain as heads of traditional families and often counseled women to remain with their husbands. It was not until several years after her death that the Shaker tradition of dual male and female leadership and representation was put into practice. Belief in Lee as an embodiment of God's spirit in female form, however, served later generations of Shakers with a theological basis for their espousal of equal rights for women. *(See also: Christianity; Religion; Shakers)*

—Wendy E. Chmielewski

Further Reading

Andrews, Edward Deming. *The People Called Shakers.* New York: Dover, 1963.

Bishop, Rufus, and Seth Y. Wells, eds. *Testimonies of the Life, Character, Revelations, and Doctrines of Our Ever Blessed Mother Ann Lee, and the Elders with Her.* Hancock, MA: J. Tallcott & J. Deming, 1816.

Campion, Nardi Reed. *Ann the Word: The Life of Mother Ann Lee.* Boston: Little, Brown, 1976.

Garrett, Clarke. *Spirit Possession and Popular Religion: From the Camisards to the Shakers.* Baltimore: Johns Hopkins University Press, 1987.

Humez, Jean M. " 'Ye Are My Epistles': The Construction of Ann Lee Imagery in Early Shaker Sacred Literature," *Journal of Feminist Studies in Religion* 8 (Spring 1992): 83-103.

⚬ Legal Profession

Since the nineteenth century, women struggled to gain admission to and then advancement in the legal profession in the United States. Regardless of their training, women wishing to practice law had to apply to their state supreme court for a license to argue cases in courts from which they were barred because of gender. Initially barred from attending all-male law schools and denied opportunities for internships with licensed attorneys, some women began to challenge their exclusion from the legal profession as the nineteenth-century woman's rights movement developed.

Barriers began to crumble when in 1869 Arabella Babb Mansfield applied for admission to the Iowa bar. A sympathetic judge issued an order allowing Mansfield to take the bar examination, which she passed with high honors. Despite passing the Iowa bar, she never practiced law; instead, Mansfield chose a teaching career and taught at Iowa Wesleyan and later at DePaul University.

In 1870, Myra Bradwell issued a similar challenge to the Illinois bar. She had studied law with her husband and was the founder and editor of the very successful *Chicago Legal News.* Her petition to be admitted to the Illinois bar was denied on the grounds that married women could not make contracts and "that it belonged to men to make, apply and execute the laws." Bradwell then appealed to the U.S. Supreme Court, which rejected her appeal. Fortunately, the Illinois legislature settled the matter in 1871 by passing legislation that specified that "no person shall be precluded or debarred from any occupation, profession or employment (except military) on account of sex."

In 1871, Phoebe Couzins became the first woman to receive a formal law degree from an American university. Couzins graduated from Washington University in St. Louis and went on to become a leading figure in the woman suffrage movement. Charlotte E. Ray was the first black woman to qualify as a lawyer when she graduated from Howard University Law School. Former abolitionist and teacher Mary Ann Shadd Cary was another legal pioneer when she graduated from Howard University Law School in 1883 at the age of sixty-three. Belva Lockwood became the first woman lawyer to practice law before the Supreme Court, in 1879.

The legal profession continued to be dominated by men, and by 1910, there were still only fifteen hundred female attorneys, most of whom were excluded from courtroom practice once licensed. Most women attorneys worked for government agencies, legal journals, and women's organizations. Few women were law school professors. Indeed, as late as 1968, only 1.6 percent of the nation's law school professors were women, and until the 1980s, most law clerks were male.

With the advent of the modern women's movement all of this began to change. In 1970, the Association of American Law Schools became one of the first national academic associations to prohibit sex discrimination in admissions, employment, and placement at member schools. The percentages of women in law schools rose from 3.6 percent in 1961 to 12 percent in 1972. As of 1981, 14 percent of the nation's judges and lawyers were women. In that same year, Sandra Day O'Connor became the first woman to sit on the Supreme Court. In 1993, she was joined by Ruth Bader Ginsberg. Also in 1993, Janet Reno was appointed U.S. Attorney General, the first woman to hold that position. Women now constitute more than a third of law school graduates. A 1998 U.S. Census Bureau press release reported that the number of female attorneys in the United States rose from 15 percent in 1983 to 30 percent in 1996.

Women also enter the legal profession as clerks and paralegals. Paralegals, or legal assistants, assist attorneys in the administration of a wide variety of legal matters. They perform the same duties as attorneys except setting fees, giving advice, signing up new clients, and trying a case in court. Of the forty thousand paralegals employed in the United States in the 1980s, about 80 percent were women. However, increased reliance on paralegals places these women in jobs that require similar skills but pay considerably less than lawyers earn. Even women attorneys generally do not make as much money as their male counterparts and are still often encouraged to enter into "women specialties," such as family law and real estate. A 1996 report from the U.S. Department of Labor's Glass Ceiling Commission described women as making up only 11 percent of partners in law firms. Despite continued resistance within the male-dominated profession, women continue to establish themselves as active and significant members of the legal profession at all levels. *(See also: Abzug, Bella Savitsky; Cary, Mary Ann Shadd; Ferraro, Geraldine; Jordan, Barbara; Lockwood, Belva Ann Bennet McNall; Lytle, Lutie; Schlafly, Phyllis MacAlpin)*

—**Richard Prouty**
—**Jonathan W. Zophy**

Further Reading

DeCrow, Karen. *Sexist Justice.* New York: Vintage, 1975.
Esser, John, and Sherry Sullivan. *Women in the Law: A Bibliography.* Madison: University of Wisconsin Law Center, 1994.
Feinman, Clarice. *Women in the Criminal Justice System.* Westport, CT: Praeger, 1994.
Harris, Barbara. *Beyond Her Sphere: Women and the Professions in America.* Westport, CT: Greenwood, 1978.
Kanowitz, Leo. *Women and the Law.* Albuquerque: University of New Mexico Press, 1975.
Roberts, Marilyn, and David Rhein. *Women in the Judiciary.* Washington, DC: National Center for Court Studies, 1983.
White, Matthew. *The History of American Law.* New York: Random House, 1985.

ᴥ Lentfoehr, Sister Mary Therese (1902–1981)

Salvatorian sister, poet, author, and lecturer, Sister Mary Therese Lentfoehr was born Florence Mae Brooks Lentfoehr in Oconto Falls, Wisconsin, the daughter of George and Florence (Brooks) Lentfoehr. She entered the Sisters of the Divine Savior at Milwaukee in 1923, receiving the name "Mary Therese," and graduated from Marquette University with a B.A. (English) in 1933 and an M.A. (philosophy) in 1938. She was also a graduate of St. Joseph's Conservatory of Music (1928) and the Wisconsin Conservatory of Music. Sister Therese served on the faculties of St. Mary's Convent High School, Divine Savior Junior College, Marquette University, Georgetown University, Fordham University, Mount St. Paul College, and Dominican College of Racine, Wisconsin. Her poetry appeared in the *American Mercury, Saturday Review,* the *New York Times,* and the *New York Herald-Tribune.* Her first collection of poems, *Now There Is Beauty,* was published in 1940, followed by *Give Joan a Sword* in 1944.

Her edited anthology of poems to the Blessed Virgin, *I Sing of a Maiden* (1947), attracted a favorable review from the Trappist poet and author Thomas Merton. He later sent her a manuscript copy of his classic *Seven Storey Mountain* and began a friendship that lasted until his death in 1968. Over the years, she received numerous manuscripts and drafts of his prose and poetry, autographed first editions, and assorted memorabilia. She also assisted him in preparing *Monastic Orientation Notes* for his classes with young monks, and transcribed numerous manuscripts (including *Sign of Jonas*) from his holograph journals. Her close association with Merton gave her one of the largest collections of the monk's manuscripts (now housed at Columbia University) and made her one of the leading Merton experts in America. After his death, Sister Therese wrote and lectured extensively on his work. Her last work was a commentary on his poetry titled *Words and Silence* (1979). *(See also: Christianity; Religion; Women Writers)*

—**Steven M. Avella**

Further Reading

Lentfoehr, Therese. *Marianne Moore.* Grand Rapids, MI: Eerdmans, 1960.
———. *Moments in Ostia.* New York: Doubleday, 1959.
Shekleton, Margaret. *Bending in Season: History of the North American Province of the Sisters of the Divine Savior, 1895 to 1985.* Milwaukee, WI: Sisters of the Divine Savior, 1985.

ᴥ Leonard, Clara Temple (1828–1904)

Clara Temple Leonard was an influential advocate of women's prison reform and child welfare measures in nineteenth-century Massachusetts. Born in Greenfield, Massachusetts, she trained as a teacher. Her involvement in women's prison issues began in the mid-1860s when a church rector asked her to be a substitute teacher for the weekly Sunday school service held for women prisoners in the county jail. She taught there for the next nine years, leading the female inmates in hymns, prayers, and Bible reading.

In February 1865, Leonard organized the Home for Friendless Women and Children, a shelter for the needy or those recently released from prison, and remained active with this organization until 1876. She also worked with the Dedham Home for Discharged Female Prisoners. Increasingly, the subject of women in prison absorbed her attention, as she and other representatives from these organizations visited female prisoners throughout the state. The conditions they found were abysmal. At Leonard's urging, a public meeting, presided over by the governor, was held in Boston on November 27, 1869. The objective, she wrote, was "the ladies' desire to call attention to the necessity of a separate prison for women, with a separate reformatory or workhouse for confined inebriates, and of the State taking charge of young girls who have no legal guardians. Reformation is the prime objective, and to this end instruction, secular and religious, is essential." A petition calling for "the establishment of separate prisons for women, under female supervision," was presented to the state legislature.

Members of a commission established in 1870 toured and inspected county prisons. An important result of their efforts was the identification of Greenfield jail as a separate prison for women. Leonard led this drive by organizing a statewide campaign in 1873. As a result of its efforts, the legislature passed a bill on June 30, 1874, appropriating $300,000 to build a separate facility for women. This prison, at Sherborn, opened on November 1, 1877, and, as the superintendent wrote, "every effort [was] put forth to teach the women how to work, how to read and write, and how to apply themselves industriously to their given tasks."

Leonard now turned her energies toward children's issues and the care of the insane. In 1878, she helped establish the Hampden County Children's Aid Association, an organization that helped impoverished children and monitored the conditions of children placed out as apprentice workers. In June 1880, Leonard was appointed the only female member of the Massachusetts Board of Health, Lunacy and Charity. Her interests were almshouses, which provided refuge for the poor, and insane asylums, and she traveled extensively throughout the state visiting them. In 1882, she advocated the appointment of women physicians to the staff of each hospital, a measure adopted by the board. Her activities slowed, however, because of illness, and although constantly appealed to as an expert on charitable matters, Leonard stayed largely out of public work. *(See also: Criminals; Prison Reform; Women's Prisons)*

—**Robert G. Waite**

Further Reading

Leonard, Katherine H. *Clara Temple Leonard, 1828–1904. A Memoir of Her Life.* Springfield, MA: Loring-Axtell, 1908.

Pettigrove, Frederick G. *An Account of the Prisons of Massachusetts.* Boston: Wright & Potter, 1904.

∽ Lesbianism

Lesbianism generally refers to women maintaining primary sexual and emotional attachments to other women. In her groundbreaking article, "Compulsory Heterosexuality and Lesbian Existence," Adrienne Rich, however, makes a distinction between "lesbian existence" and "lesbian continuum" and rejects the word *lesbianism* as "clinical and limiting." In Rich's terms, *lesbian existence* refers to the historical and present lives of women who have broken the sexual and social taboos of "compulsory heterosexuality." *Lesbian continuum* is intended to include a wider range of woman-identified experience, including attachments to women and resistance to patriarchy, not necessarily sexual in nature.

Rich's formulations are not universally accepted, but the inclusion of lesbianism as a category for discussion and inquiry, and the analysis of "compulsory heterosexuality" as an institutional force that affects all women, has had important implications for scholarship on women. Discussions of the lesbian relationships and female support networks shared by nineteenth-century white middle-class women, among women reformers and writers, and in black and working-class communities have served to illuminate the heterosexist bias of much scholarship and to provide a new context for interpreting women's experiences.

In the twentieth century, a basic shift in the perception of contemporary as well as of Victorian female friendships occurred. Until the 1960s, lesbian relationships were unacknowledged or denied outright to avoid social stigma and harassment, as depicted in Lillian Hellman's *The Children's Hour,* for example. In the wake of the modern women's movement, lesbian women asserted a positive self-conscious definition of themselves and their lifestyle, establishing lesbian communities and support groups. These woman-identified women, some separatist and some not, demonstrated a willingness to define themselves by their sexual preference to their families, co-workers, and society at large and to demand equality of rights. *(See also: Boston Marriages; Friendships; Homophobia; Lesbian Rights; Lesbian Separatism)*

—**Mary Battenfeld**

Further Reading

D'Emilio, John. *Sexual Politics, Sexual Communities: The Making of a Homosexual Minority in the U.S., 1940–1970.* Chicago: University of Chicago Press, 1983.

Faderman, Lillian. *Surpassing the Love of Men: Love between Women from the Renaissance to the Present.* New York: Morrow, 1981.

Rich, Adrienne. "Compulsory Heterosexuality and Lesbian Existence," *Signs* 5 (1980): 631-60.

Shugar, Dana R. *Separatism and Women's Community.* Lincoln: University of Nebraska Press, 1995.

◈ Lesbian Rights

Lesbian rights refers to the struggle for social and legal tolerance of lesbians as well as protection of their full civil rights, including freedom from discrimination in employment, housing, and child custody decisions. In the nineteenth century, lesbians were unlikely to avow publicly their sexual preference or to work openly for legal reform to ensure specific lesbian rights. Direct confrontation of the issue of lesbian rights emerged from the gay and women's liberation movements of the 1960s. Out of these movements came a consciousness of the specific forms of discrimination and oppression encountered by lesbians in their personal and public lives. The momentum of political action to address these issues resulted in cooperative efforts to establish as one of the political priorities of the modern women's movement the right of women to make individual choices in all areas of their lives, including sexual preference.

Although the lesbian-feminist movement may have developed out of women's rights organizations, leaders of liberal groups such as the National Organization for Women (NOW) were not always supportive of lesbian rights. But by the 1977 International Women's Year Conference in Houston, Betty Friedan, who had earlier described lesbians as "the lavender menace," defended the right to choose one's own sexual preference, noting that "we must protect women who are lesbians in their own civil rights." The natural rights ideology on which liberal feminism was based, as well as a need to heal the gay/straight split developing in the women's movement, led to at least tentative support for lesbian rights among mainstream feminists.

In the 1980s, lesbians were still subject to economic, legal, and social discrimination. The lesbian rights movement, consisting of autonomous lesbian-feminist organizations supported by feminist, gay male, and civil libertarian groups, continues to challenge such discrimination at the local and state level, as well as issue by issue. The agenda for lesbian rights has been articulated and pursued at the national level most prominently by the National Gay and Lesbian Task Force and the Lambda Legal Defense Fund.

In the landmark decision *Baehr v. Lewin* (1993), the Hawaii State Supreme Court ruled that the state's refusal to grant marriage licenses to three same-sex couples appeared to violate the state's constitutional guarantee of equal protection. In December 1996, a trial court in Hawaii ruled that civil marriage law cannot discriminate against lesbian and gay couples *(Baehr v. Miike)*. The decision was stayed pending appeal, but in November 1998, the voters authorized a constitutional amendment restricting marriage to men and women. In December 1999, the State Supreme Court decided that this amendment had made the case moot. Nonetheless, also in December 1999, the Vermont Supreme Court in *Baker v. State of Vermont* ruled that same sex couples are entitled to all of the benefits and protections the law offers to married couples. In April 2000, Vermont passed legislation that sanctioned the civil unions of same-sex couples, extending to them the same rights and benefits available to spouses in a marriage. While the legal and legislative battles rage across the United States, the ultimate goal of lesbian rights is not only legal but also cultural acceptance of this alternative lifestyle and sexual orientation. *(See also: Daughters of Bilitis; Heterosexism; Homophobia; International Women's Year Conference; Lesbianism; Radicalesbians)*

—Mary Battenfeld
Updated for the second edition by Diana E. Axelsen.

Further Reading

Baehr v. Lewin, 74 Haw. 530 (1993).
Baehr v. Miike, 80 Haw. 341 P. 2d 112, 1996.
D'Emilio, John. *Sexual Politics, Sexual Communities: The Making of a Homosexual Minority in the U.S., 1940–1970.* Chicago: University of Chicago Press, 1983.
http://members.tripod.com/~MPHAWAII/VermontApr25.htm [Marriage Project Hawaii website]
http://www.hawaii.gov/lrb/pref.html [State of Hawaii Report of the Commission on Sexual Orientation and the Law, 1995]
http://www.indiana.edu/glbtpol/ [Gay and Lesbian Politics: Web and Internet resources]

◈ Lesbian Separatism

As a form of resistance, lesbian separatism is an appeal to women to cease to participate in all the institutions of patriarchy, including heterosexuality, the family, economy, church, and state. Understanding the difficulty of complete withdrawal from patriarchal society, proponents of separatism suggest that women, as much as they are capable of doing, live as woman-identified women who reserve their resources for themselves and other woman-identified women and refrain from supporting the patriarchy in every way, shape, and form possible. The practice of lesbian separatism, depending somewhat on how the word *lesbian* is defined, may range from activities such as organizing and attending consciousness-raising groups, supporting women-owned businesses, voting for women politicians, living as a female homophile-homosexual, or living in all-women communities. In short, the idea is to recognize that the very concept of woman within the patriarchy has been defined by the predominant culture and that women must create space or room of their own, free from this influence, for women to discover and define for themselves who and what they are and will become individually and collectively. *(See also: Homophobia; Lesbian Rights; Lesbianism; Radical Feminism)*

—Elizabeth Fields

Further Reading

Daly, Mary. *Beyond God the Father: Toward a Philosophy of Women's Liberation.* Boston: Beacon, 1973.
———. *Gyn/Ecology: The Metaethics of Radical Feminism.* Boston: Beacon, 1978.
———. *Pure Lust: Elemental Feminist Philosophy.* Boston: Beacon, 1984.

———. *Websters' First New Intergalactic Wickedary of the English Language.* Conjured in Cahoots with Jane Caputi. 1977. Reprint, Boston: Beacon, 1987.

French, Merilyn. "To Be and Be Seen: The Politics of Reality." In *Feminism and Philosophy: Essential Readings in Theory, Reinterpretation and Application,* edited by Nancy Tuana and Rosemary Tong, 162-74. Boulder, CO: Westview, 1995.

Grahn, Judy. *Another Mother Tongue: Gay Words, Gay Worlds.* Boston: Beacon, 1984.

Johnson, Sonia. *Wildfire: Igniting the She/volution.* Albuquerque, NM: Wildfire Books, 1989.

Tong, Rosemarie. *Feminist Thought: A Comprehensive Introduction.* Boulder, CO: Westview, 1989.

Woolf, Virginia. *A Room of One's Own.* London: Harcourt Brace, 1929.

∞ Lewis, Edmonia (1843/45 to post-1911)

A successful American sculptor who was a member of the expatriate community in Italy, Edmonia Lewis was the first minority artist to be nationally and internationally acknowledged.

Lewis's biographical data still remain vague, partially due to her own inaccuracies. It seems accepted that Mary Edmonia "Wildfire" Lewis was the daughter of a black father and a Chippewa mother who reportedly died when Wildfire was about three; she may or may not have been orphaned. It seems she spent her childhood with her mother's tribe until, in the 1850s, her brother Sunrise encouraged her financially and otherwise to attend school and later to enroll in Oberlin College, Ohio (preparatory, 1859; college 1860–1862 or 1863). Here, Lewis began drawing. After a scandal in which she was accused and acquitted of the attempted poisoning of two white women students (and perhaps also of stealing art supplies), Lewis left Oberlin for Boston, where, with support from abolitionists, she began her career as a sculptor.

The sales of plaster copies of Lewis's bust of the dead commander of the first black regiment in the Civil War, Bostonian Colonel Robert Gould Shaw, and of her medallion of John Brown financed a trip to England, France, and Italy, where she finally settled in Rome in 1865, joining a growing community of American women expatriates. Concentrating on her art, Lewis began carving marble figures without further formal instruction. The predominant style was neoclassical, but Lewis also experimented, especially in her frequent choice of black and Indian themes. In 1869, she returned to the United States to sell and to exhibit her work, the first of many subsequent visits. She may have married a Philadelphian, Dr. Peck, around 1869. Very little is known about Lewis after about 1883. She was known to have been living in Rome in 1911, but no record of her death has been found.

Critical reception of Lewis's sculpture is varied. She is indubitably an important personage in women's history. Among the more important of her located sculptures are *Forever Free* (c. 1867), *Hagar in the Wilderness* (1868), and *Old Arrow Maker (and His Daughter)* (1872). *(See also: Art; Native American Women)*

—**Maureen R. Liston**

Further Reading

Hartigan, Lynda Roscoe. "Edmonia Lewis." In *Sharing Traditions: Five Black Artists in Nineteenth-Century America,* pp. 85-98. Washington, DC: Smithsonian Institution, 1985.

∞ Librarianship

Librarianship became a female-intensive occupation during the last quarter of the nineteenth century at the same time that libraries expanded in number, size, and services offered and that librarianship professionalized. While it is difficult to establish cause-and-effect relationships, it is also difficult to imagine this transition to modern library service without the availability of a large pool of well-educated but underpaid women workers. Financial support for libraries lagged badly, but educated women, with few employment opportunities elsewhere, and supported by the view that library work was suited to their nature, entered librarianship in great numbers.

The 1900 census (figures for librarians are not available for earlier dates) reported that approximately three of every four librarians was a woman, while by 1920, almost nine of every ten librarians was a woman. The present ratio is approximately four of five. The number of American public libraries tripled between 1876 and 1900, and by 1923 they had more than doubled again; school and academic libraries underwent comparable increases. Library education, fostering professional standards, developed in this period with the establishment of the schools in the New York State Library in 1889 and at the University of Illinois in 1893. More Americans than ever had access to libraries by 1900, and these libraries offered more services, usually delivered by a woman librarian.

Library services pioneered by women emphasized client services, while earlier libraries had emphasized collection services, often merely custodial duties. Women librarians pioneered outreach to new groups of patrons, including children, immigrants, college students, and settlers in frontier regions.

The origins of services to children, described elsewhere in this work, began in 1877 in the Pawtucket (Rhode Island) Public Library under the auspices of Minerva Sanders (1837–1912). Special training programs were soon developed for children's librarians, and the service became one of the great successes of American librarianship. Yet its practitioners have endured low status and salaries in the profession.

Americanization of the waves of immigrants, increasingly from Eastern and Southern Europe, was assisted by library programs that reached out to them with collections at work sites and in the new neighborhood branches. In addition, books were purchased in many of the languages of the newcomers. Anne Carroll Moore (1871–1961), a pioneer in children's services, held programs featuring tales, songs, and dances from the countries of origin represented among neighborhood children. Edith Guerrier (1870–1958) of the Boston Public Library founded the Saturday Evening Girls

Club in the North End to reach out to the daughters of Italian and Jewish immigrant families.

While many had recognized the need for assistance for students (and faculty) in the use of the collection, it remained for a woman librarian named Isadore Mudge (1875–1957) to develop a modern academic reference department. Working at the Low Memorial Library at Columbia University, Mudge assembled from various sites in the library a core reference collection and saw that it was staffed with professionals capable of answering complex bibliographic questions. While the questions were less complex at the Oregon State Agricultural College at Corvallis, Angeline Kidder (1857–1920) pioneered instruction in the use of the library to college students, many of whom had no previous experience with libraries.

A final example of pioneering client-oriented services is the work of circuit-riding librarians in the western territories and states. Often alone and on horseback, with saddlebags full of books and perhaps carrying a firearm, these women brought library service to isolated communities. Working closely with community people, they understood the needs of their users better than the distant library leaders who produced lists of "best books" that few on the frontier were interested in reading. Oregon State Library Commission secretary Cornelia Marvin (1873–1957) assailed these lists as elitist and not what the "untrained readers" in remote Oregon communities needed and replaced them with ones of her own making.

But contributions of this sort did not much advance individual library women into leadership roles. For a pattern had been early established that still persists. Melvil Dewey (1851–1931) in 1883 both urged the "college-bred" woman to choose librarianship as a career and warned that women could not expect to run libraries because administration was work better suited to men. Thus, he laid the basis of what came to be called the dual career structure, so common in female-intensive occupations, with men holding a disproportionate share of the top-paying posts, in administration or in prestigious specialties.

Among the most prestigious specialties today is library automation or information science. The latter, described by one wit as "library science for boys," does promise once again to entrench men in the top positions. The little research available on this, however, is inconclusive.

Black Librarians

The historiography of black women in development of librarianship from 1900 to 1945 represents a field ripe for research. Within the constraints of segregated southern society, pioneering black women struggled to obtain libraries for blacks, to establish appropriate collections featuring black culture and history, to develop professional education and standards for service to black communities; in the process, they themselves led an effort to promote racial justice and end segregation. In several areas, black women

librarians developed techniques that set models for American librarianship.

Pioneers such as Susan Dart Butler (1888–1959) and Mollie Huston Lee (b. 1907) struggled to establish libraries to serve black communities. In 1927, Butler opened a library in Charleston, South Carolina, that was privately supported and consisted of books from her deceased father's library and donated items. Lee, a librarian at Shaw University in Raleigh, North Carolina, from 1930 to 1935, together with other black civic leaders organized a "public" library largely supported by private contributions. Lee and Howard University librarian and archivist Dorothy Porter (1905–1995) both recognized the need to develop black-centered collections, and their collections became invaluable resources. The early guides and bibliographies they produced were forerunners of publications that were to be useful in developing black collections in all American libraries.

Another innovator whose work proved to be of value outside her own community was Sadie Peterson Delaney (1889–1959) who, while serving as a librarian with the Veterans Administration hospital in Tuskegee, Alabama, developed bibliotherapy techniques that have been widely copied.

It was difficult for blacks to obtain education for librarianship in the South, and the first formal training program was opened at Hampton Institute in 1925, closing in 1939. In 1941, Atlanta University's School of Library Service was opened, headed by Dr. Eliza Gleason (b. 1909), the first black library science Ph.D., with Virginia Lacy (later Jones, 1912–1984), who became the second black to receive a doctorate in library science, on the staff. Also in 1941, North Carolina Central College for Negroes (today North Carolina Central University) in Durham opened its School of Library Science.

In addition to fighting for better education for blacks, many black women librarians in this period took more direct measures against injustice. Ruby Stutts Lyells, the first black professional librarian in Mississippi, for example, was an active member of the National Association for the Advancement of Colored People, participating in sit-ins in the 1930s.

The civil rights movement and the modern women's movement of the 1960s raised issues of the impact of both racism and sexism on librarianship as a woman's profession. As a result of the feminist movement, groups within the American Library Association worked to publicize discrimination against women in the profession. At first, their concerns were mainly inequalities in library employment, but they were also concerned with career opportunities and nepotism within the profession and have renewed their commitment to attack inequalities, of race or gender, through career development and support of pay equity. (See also: Black Women; Children's Library Movement; Higher Education for Southern Women; Women's Work: Nineteenth Century)

—Suzanne Hildenbrand
—Judith Pryor

Further Reading

Gleason, Eliza. *The Southern Negro and the Public Library.* Chicago: University of Chicago Press, 1941.

Gubert, Betty K. "Sadie Peterson Delaney: Pioneer Bibliotherapist," *American Libraries* 24 (February 1993): 124-29.

Heim, Kathleen M. "The Demographic and Economic Status of Librarians in the 1970s, with Special References to Women." In *Advances in Librarianship,* edited by Wesley Simonton, 1-45. New York: Academic Press, 1982.

Hildenbrand, Suzanne, ed. *Reclaiming the American Library Past: Writing the Women In.* Norwood, NJ: Ablex, 1996.

Josey, E. J. *The Black Librarian in America, Revisited.* Metuchen, NJ: Scarecrow, 1994.

Josey, E. J., and Ann Allen Shockley, comps. and eds. *Handbook of Black Librarianship.* Littleton, CO: Libraries Unlimited, 1970.

Passet, Joanne E. *Cultural Crusaders: Women Librarians in the American West, 1900–1917.* Albuquerque: University of New Mexico Press, 1994.

Phinazee, Annette, ed. *The Black Librarian in the Southeast: Reminiscences, Activities, Challenges.* Durham: North Carolina Central University Press, 1980.

Reuter, Monika. "The Influence of Technology on Women Librarians' and Library Assistants' Work Experience." Ph.D. diss., State University of New York at Albany, 1991.

Van Slyck, Abigail. *Free to All: Carnegie Libraries and American Culture: 1890–1920.* Chicago: University of Chicago Press, 1995.

Weibel, Kathleen, and Kathleen M. Heim, eds. Assisted by Dianne J. Ellsworth. *The Role of Women in Librarianship, 1876–1976: The Entry, Advancement, and Struggle for Equalization in One Profession.* Phoenix: Oryx, 1979.

Women of Color in Librarianship: An Oral History. Chicago: American Library Association, 1999.

✑ Linden Hall Seminary

Linden Hall Seminary grew out of a girl's day school established by the Moravians, the Church of the Brethren, in Lititz, Pennsylvania, on January 2, 1764. After the community struggled for two years offering instruction for boys in the morning and girls in the afternoon, a day school for girls was begun on August 21, 1766. Two sisters from the church taught the ten pupils. Although it was called a day school, pupils from distant Moravian congregations were boarded at the site. Enrollment grew, reaching fifteen by 1768, and a new building opened on November 14, 1769.

The years of the American Revolution were hard on the school; its boarding pupils were sent home, and part of the facility was used as a military hospital. After the war, the school prospered, and by 1790, a dozen girls were again enrolled. It was reorganized as the Lititz Boarding School, and applications grew rapidly. As a teacher wrote in 1799, "We cannot increase our numbers for want of teachers, every one must wait for a vacancy." A resolution passed by the church called for a maximum of forty boarding pupils, but the renovation of the new building enabled enrollment to grow. By 1804, seventeen day pupils and fifty-two boarders attended the school. The number of pupils rose, reaching more than one hundred in 1838. The school gained a charter from the state of Pennsylvania in 1863 as Linden Hall Seminary. A

postsecondary department developed into a junior college, known since 1935 as Linden Hall Junior College and School for Girls. *(See also: Education; Female Academies; Moravian Seminary for Young Females)*

—**Robert G. Waite**

Further Reading

Haller, Mabel. "Early Moravian Education in Pennsylvania," *Transactions of the Moravian Historical Society* 15 (1953): 1-397.

Wiltzel, Louisa A. "Linden Hall Seminary." In *Historical and Pictorial Lititz,* edited by John G. Zook, 24-31. Lititz, PA: Express Printing Company, 1905.

Woody, Thomas. *A History of Women's Education in the United States.* 1929. Reprint, New York: Octagon, 1966.

✑ Litchfield Academy

Litchfield Academy was a school for women run by Sarah Pierce (1767–1852) in Litchfield, Connecticut. Pierce began the school in 1792 with one pupil in her dining room. The school expanded to include permanent buildings as well as full-time instructors, male and female. In 1827, the school became the Litchfield Female Academy. Women from as far away as Georgia and the West Indies attended Litchfield Academy, which provided upper- to middle-class young women from rural as well as urban areas with an education their mothers were denied before the concept of Republican Motherhood and the availability of academies.

Unlike adventure schools of the pre-Revolutionary period, Litchfield Academy, like other academies, instructed female students in academics such as history, geography, and arithmetic as well as in "accomplishments" such as dancing, music, French, painting, and needlework. Pierce also saw that the young women were instructed in the virtues of Republican Motherhood, which emphasized the patriotic duty of young women to educate themselves. Pierce was adamant that the students at Litchfield acquire a quality education. She called the students "scholars," awarded prizes for academic achievement, and claimed to cultivate in her students "memory, imagination, and reason." One such scholar was Harriet Beecher Stowe (1811–1896).

Pierce also wrote plays to be acted by the school that incorporated strong female characters who taught moral lessons as well as the values of Republican Motherhood. Furthermore, the students at Litchfield studied feminism. Mary Wollstonecraft's *A Vindication of the Rights of Women* (1792) was on the reading list as early as 1814, and the students often declared a desire for political participation. Moreover, in the 1830s, more than ten years before Elizabeth Cady Stanton's *Declaration of Sentiments,* Pierce wrote a "Ladies' Declaration of Independence" in celebration of the July 4th holiday. In the document, she remarked on the unfulfilled promises of the Revolution in regard to women, using language such as "We hold these truths to be self-evident. That all *mankind* are created equal."

Litchfield Academy, like other female academies that developed in the 1790s around the country, represented a transition for women's education from finishing schools to the development of universities for women. Furthermore, the education prepared them to be "better mothers" and for a career increasingly open to women in the mid-nineteenth century, teaching. *(See also: Education; European Influences; Female Academies; Republican Motherhood; Stowe, Harriet Beecher; Teaching)*

—**Monica L. Everett**

Further Reading

Buel, Elizabeth Barney, ed. *Chronicles of a Pioneer School from 1792 to 1833: The History of Miss Sarah Pierce and Her Litchfield School.* Compiled by Emily Noyes Vanderpoel. Boston: University Press, 1903.

Kerber, Linda, and Jane Sherron DeHart. *Women's America: Refocusing the Past.* New York: Oxford University Press, 1991.

Norton, Mary Beth. *Liberty's Daughters: The Revolutionary Experience of American Women, 1750–1800.* Glenview, IL: Scott, Foresman, 1980.

✎ Livermore, Mary Ashton (Rice) (1820–1905)

Reformer and woman's rights leader, Mary Livermore earned national acclaim for her work on behalf of Civil War soldiers. An agent of the Northwestern Department of the U.S. Sanitary Commission, she was skilled at cutting through red tape to secure needed supplies for the troops. While on an inspection tour of hospitals and camps along the Mississippi River, Livermore and her co-worker Jane Hoge found early symptoms of scurvy near Vicksburg, Mississippi. The two women traveled north, and after making repeated appeals for help, secured huge quantities of potatoes and onions to feed the troops.

In addition to her hospital inspection tours, Livermore traveled extensively to northern towns encouraging women to set up soldier's aid societies. In 1863, along with Jane Hoge, she organized the Northwestern Sanitary Fair in Chicago. In her autobiography, she would later recall that the fair was "pre-eminently an enterprise of women, receiving no assistance from men in its early beginnings" (*My Story* 412). Netting close to $100,000 for the troops, this fair became a model for subsequent fund-raisers. Its success gave northern women a sense of pride and accomplishment.

. Born and educated in Boston, Livermore became active in the abolition movement as a young woman after serving as governess to a slave-owning Virginia family. Marriage to Daniel P. Livermore, a Universalist minister, led her to settle in Chicago. Together, the Livermores edited a reform newspaper. After the war, she joined the lyceum circuit as a speaker to local reading and self-improvement groups, giving popular orations on topics such as "Women of the War" and "What Shall We Do with Our Daughters?" She published her wartime reminiscences, *My Story of the War,* in 1887, and later wrote *The Story of My Life* (1897).

Livermore was an active participant in the late-nineteenth-century temperance and woman's suffrage movements. She joined with Lucy Stone, Henry Ward Beecher, and others in founding the American Woman Suffrage Association, serving as editor of the organization's Boston-based newspaper, *Woman's Journal,* and later as its president. During her lengthy public career Mary Livermore was one of the most eminent and influential nineteenth-century feminists. *(See also: American Woman Suffrage Association; Civil War; United States Sanitary Commission; Woman's Journal)*

—**Wendy Hamand Venet**

Further Reading

Livermore, Mary A. *My Story of the War.* Hartford, CT: A. D. Worthington, 1889.

———. *The Story of My Life.* Hartford, CT: A. D. Worthington, 1899.

Matthews, Glenna. *The Rise of Public Woman: Woman's Power and Woman's Place in the United States, 1630–1970.* New York: Oxford University Press, 1992.

Stanton, Elizabeth Cady, Susan B. Anthony, and Matilda J. Gage. *History of Woman Suffrage,* 6 vols. Rochester, NY: Charles Mann, 1886.

✎ Lockwood, Belva Ann Bennett McNall (1830–1917)

Belva Lockwood became in 1879 the first woman attorney to practice before the U.S. Supreme Court. The honor was not easily won. Several law schools to which Lockwood applied refused to accept women; and after completing her course of study, she had to demand of the school's ex-officio president that her diploma be awarded. Barred from pleading cases before the federal Court of Claims and the Supreme Court, Lockwood successfully lobbied Congress for legislation admitting women lawyers to the nation's highest courts. She later bravely demonstrated her commitment to equality for all by championing the first southern black lawyer to argue before the Supreme Court.

Lockwood began her career as a teacher in western New York, was married to a farmer in 1848 and widowed in 1853, resumed teaching, and moved to Washington, D.C., in 1866, where she opened a private school and remarried. After obtaining her law degree at the age of forty-three, she made her reputation by specializing in claims against the federal government. In 1906, she won a historic $5 million settlement for the Eastern Cherokees.

A staunch supporter of women's rights and universal suffrage, Lockwood lectured widely and worked tirelessly for legal reforms. In 1884 and 1888, she ran for the presidency of the United States on the National Equal Rights Party ticket. Her campaign, although mocked by the general public and opposed by Susan B. Anthony and other prominent suffragists, called voters' attention to the pressing issues of suffrage, temperance, and peace. In the late 1880s,

Lockwood turned her efforts toward world affairs, assuming leadership posts in the Universal Peace Union and advocating arbitration as a solution to international conflict. *(See also: Legal Profession; Politics; Suffrage)*

—**Susan E. Searing**

Further Reading

Sterne, Madeleine B, *We the Women: Career Firsts of Nineteenth-Century America.* New York: Lenox Hill, 1962. [Includes extensive information on primary sources]

❧ Longworth, Alice Roosevelt (1884–1980)

Alice Roosevelt Longworth was the daughter of Theodore Roosevelt and Alice (Lee) Roosevelt, whose families were prominent in New York and Boston. Alice's mother died at the time of her birth, and she was raised by a paternal aunt, but she was always close to her father and rejoined the family circle after her father's second marriage. As Theodore Roosevelt's star rose in the political firmament, so did that of "Princess Alice," who reflected her father's popularity. Alice was highly intelligent, fiercely independent, and much attracted to public notice. Like her father, she was endowed with enormous energy. Because she was a maverick, active politics had no place for her, and she had no time for conventional politics. Society had a stronger appeal, and in this sense, she was very much part of her environment: chic New York and fashionable Back Bay.

In 1906, she married Nicholas Longworth, a member of Congress from a prominent Cincinnati family. The Longworth connection gained her access to the councils of the Republican Party after her father's death, and her husband rose to be Speaker of the House of Representatives. With her husband's death in 1931, she came into her own: a member of the board of councilors of the Women's Division of the Republican Party (1932), a delegate to the Republican National Convention (1936), and a member of the America First Committee (1940). Meanwhile, she became an immensely quotable critic of both President Franklin Roosevelt, a distant kinsman, and his wife, Eleanor, her first cousin, but her writings in general were negative, and she made little if any positive contribution to American politics or government.

With advancing age, she became a grand dame of Washington society, lionized by the press, the guest of presidents, and the mother hen of the capital coop. In this latter role, she took on a glow; even New Dealers forgave her blind opposition to Franklin and Eleanor, and for the last two decades of her life, she was treated like a national institution. *(See also: Republican Party; Roosevelt, Eleanor)*

—**David H. Burton**

Further Reading

Collier, Peter, with David Horowitz. *The Roosevelts: An American Saga.* New York: Simon & Schuster, 1994.

Curtis, Sandra R. *Alice and Eleanor: A Contrast in Style and Purpose.* Bowling Green, OH: Bowling Green State University Popular Press, 1994.

Felsenthal, Carol. *Princess Alice: The Life and Times of Alice Roosevelt Longworth.* New York: St. Martin's, 1988.

Longworth, Alice Roosevelt. *Crowded Hours.* 1933. Reprint, New York: Arno, 1980.

———. *Mrs. L. Conversations with Alice Roosevelt Longworth.* Garden City, NY: Doubleday, 1981.

Rozek, Stacy Ann. "Alice Roosevelt Longworth: Life in a Public Crucible." Ph.D. diss., University of Texas at Austin, 1992.

❧ Loom

The loom has been used to weave fabric since ancient times, and its use did not change dramatically until the eighteenth century. In 1733, John Kay developed the automatically operated fly shuttle, and in 1785, Edmund Cartwright invented the power loom. These advances were followed by the Jacquard attachment, which used perforated cards to aid in the control of warp threads. All of these inventions greatly increased the productivity of the loom and contributed in no small part to the industrialization of the process of weaving.

The significance of the loom for women in the United States is considerable and begins in the New England mill towns of the early nineteenth century. During the 1820s and 1830s, textile mills sprang up across New England wherever there was the prerequisite water supply. Employment in such mills was considered an excellent opportunity for young, unmarried women to earn money. Francis Cabot Lowell pioneered the American textile industry by promoting the idea of women factory workers in the mills.

Young single women were the best candidates for this work since they were already skilled in cloth making; men were needed for farmwork, and married women had domestic responsibilities. Mill operators demanded twelve to thirteen hours a day on the loom from these young women and required at least a one-year commitment to the mill. There was no shortage of women to fill the ranks of loom workers. Typically, these women were trying to earn money of their own before marriage or sought to escape the narrow confines of their family life and secure some measure of personal independence. The mill workers generally earned $1.25 per week for board and a salary of 55 cents per week, which could be supplemented by doing extra piecework. In the 1830s, this was considered the best wages a woman could hope to earn in the American economy.

In the mill towns, women were housed in dormitories and were closely supervised. The workday typically began at 5:00 a.m. and continued until dusk, with two half-hour breaks for meals. Girls, sometimes aged ten and under, were "doffers," replacing used bobbins; teenagers and adults worked as spinners and weavers directly on the looms. Early on, women were not pushed severely on the job, since most of them were "Yankee" women, and the public had to be shown that work in the mills would not destroy the moral fiber or physical health of New England's future mothers. As the worker pool began to change, especially after the 1840s, when mass Irish immigration brought many Irish immigrant women to the mills and as the mills themselves began to expand, less attention was paid to the working and living conditions of these women. Work at the loom thus became less appealing, less lucrative, and considerably more difficult for the women who were employed in the textile industry. Women were eventually required to attend more than one loom (sometimes as many as four) single-handedly.

Meanwhile, new advances in the loom technology (specifically the crank-driven loom) speeded up production but also increased noise, heat, and the dangerous accumulation of lint within the mills. As production went up, wages fell, and the "premium system" was introduced whereby employers could get still more work out of the loom operators by offering bonuses for productivity. By 1840, women could be fired from loom work for any number of violations, including hysteria, exhibiting overcautiousness, impudent behavior, or disobedience. Women protested such developments and staged periodic walkouts to combat the abuses inherent in mill work by 1850. *(See also: Industrial Revolution; Lowell Mill Girls; Textiles: North and South)*

—**Maureen Anna Harp**

Further Reading

Abbott, Edith. *Women in Industry: A Study in American Economic History.* New York: Appleton, 1919.

Baker, Elizabeth Faulkner. *Technology and Women's Work in America.* New York: Columbia University Press, 1959.

Butler, Elizabeth Beardsley. *Women and the Trades.* New York: Charities Publication Committee, 1909.

Dublin, Thomas. *Women at Work: The Transformation of Work and Community in Lowell, Massachusetts.* New York: Columbia University Press, 1981.

Manning, Caroline. *The Immigrant Woman and Her Job.* New York: Arno, 1970.

Robinson, Harriet Hanson. *Loom and Spindle, or Life among the Early Mill Girls. With a Sketch of "The Lowell Offering" and Some of Its Contributors.* New York: T. Y. Crowell, 1898. Reprint, Kailua, Hawaii: Press Pacifica, 1976.

Lorde, Audre (1934–1992)

Audre Lorde was a poet, essayist, lecturer, and author of several books, including *The First Cities; Sister Outsider: Essays and Speeches; Between Ourselves; The Cancer Journals; The Black Unicorn; Zami, A New Spelling of My Name;* and *The Marvelous Arithmetics of Distance.* Lorde was an African American lesbian feminist who wrote and spoke in ways that give voice to the similarities and differences of all people, particularly women. Her perspectives on myriad sexual and social justice issues enable the people of her audience to reconsider the connections she says exist inside themselves, connections between thinking and feeling. When realized, these internal connections carry people into new relationships with one another, breaking down the barriers that pervade twentieth-century society.

The mother of two, Lorde found her life dramatically altered by the discovery that she had cancer. She wrote openly about her encounter with the possibility of death and her new freedom as a result of her struggle, the freedom being a fruit of her subsequent wholeness. She died in November 1992, after battling the disease for fourteen years.

As a teacher, Lorde instructed her students to claim every aspect of themselves and encouraged them to discover the power of a spirited wholeness, knowing that in silence there is no growth, in suppression there is no personal satisfaction. The intensity of her honesty seems intimidating at times; yet it is her honesty, her self-respect, and her courage that have profoundly affected the relationships and lives of her readers and students. *(See also: Black Women; Lesbianism; Women Writers)*

—**Joanne S. Richmond**
—**Merri Scheibe Edwards**

Further Reading

Koolish, Lynda. "This Is Who She Is to Me." In *Between Women,* edited by Carol Ascher, Louise DeSalvo, and Sara Ruddick, 113-36. Boston: Beacon, 1984.

Lorde, Audre. *Between Ourselves.* Point Reyes, CA: Eidolon Editions, 1976.

———. *The Black Unicorn.* New York: Norton, 1978.

———. *The Cancer Journals.* Argyle, NY: Spinsters Ink, 1980.

———. *The First Cities.* New York: Poets Press, 1968.

———. *The Marvelous Arithmetics of Distance: Poems, 1987–1992.* New York: Norton, 1993.

———. *Sister Outsider: Essays and Speeches.* Introduction by Nancy Bereano. Trumansburg, NY: Crossing, 1984.

———. *Zami, A New Spelling of My Name.* Watertown, MA: Persephone, 1982.

Low, Juliette (1860–1927)

The founder of the Girl Scouts in America, Juliette Low was born in Chicago, Illinois. Christened Juliette Magill Kinzie for her grandmother, she was always called Daisy by family and close friends. On her mother's side, she was descended from a well-known family influential in the founding of Chicago. Her father's family was prominent in Savannah, Georgia, where her grandfather was mayor for many years, and Low always considered herself a southerner. She was educated at several private boarding schools, first in Savannah, then at Stuart Hall and Edge Hall in Virginia, and finally at Madame Charbonnier's school in New York. Low excelled in languages and history, but her first love was art.

Her schooling and her family training prepared her for the role expected of most well-to-do young women of her time—wife and mother. In 1882, after her social debut in Savannah, Low made her first trip to Europe and met her future husband William Mackey Low, who was from a wealthy English family with business interests in Savannah.

Apparently fearing disapproval from her parents, she kept the nature of their relationship a secret but finally gained family approval and married in 1894. The marriage proved to be very unhappy, and the Lows were in the middle of divorce proceedings in 1905 when he died. Although he had apparently meant to leave her very little in his will, Low inherited enough money to ensure a comfortable life. For several years after the death of her husband, Low led a very social existence, traveling back and forth between Savannah and Europe and studying sculpture, at which she was quite talented. Although her life was full of activity, she was depressed and unfulfilled: She thought she had failed as a wife and regretted never having had children.

In 1908, she met Sir Robert Baden-Powell, a well-known English general who had recently founded the Boy Scouts and whose sister Agnes headed the girls' branch, the Girl Guides. Low was quite taken with the idea of an organization for young girls and soon formed a troop near her country estate in Scotland. In 1912, she started the first Girl Guide troop in the United States in Savannah. During its first year, the name was changed to Girl Scouts to match that of the organization for American boys, the Boy Scouts. Low spent the rest of her life working with the organization, giving her a purpose in life and the children she had always wanted. Much of the early success of the Girl Scouts can be attributed to Low's hard work, friendships, and contacts. After several years of active involvement with the Girl Scouts, she resigned the presidency, turned control over to the National Girl Scout Board, and confined her active involvement to her work as U.S. representative to the International Council of Girl Guides and Girl Scouts.

Enthusiastic by nature, she was often able to convince women to assist in the organization through her charm and strong personality. She had a great sense of fun and was known in Savannah as a person who would try anything. Stories of her escapades sometimes made her seem somewhat eccentric, but she was also thoughtful, kind, and a favorite among members of her large family. Low was also known as an entertaining conversationalist, a skill she developed partly to cover up the fact that she had suffered from a rather severe hearing loss since adolescence and often did not hear what others were saying. Low died in Savannah after a battle with cancer that she managed to keep secret from family and friends until near the end. *(See also: Girl Scouts of America)*

—**Judith Pryor**

Further Reading

Schultz, Gladys, and Daisy Gordon Lawrence. *Lady from Savannah: The Life of Juliette Low.* Philadelphia: J. B. Lippincott, 1958.

Strickland, Charles E. "Juliette Low, the Girl Scouts, and the Role of American Women." In *Woman's Being, Woman's Place: Female Identity and Vocation in American History,* edited by Mary Kelley, 252-64. Boston: G. K. Hall, 1977.

⤳ Lowell Female Industrial Reform and Mutual Aid Society (LFIRMAS)

The Lowell Female Industrial Reform and Mutual Aid Society (LFIRMAS) was a transformation in January 1847 of an earlier organization of the Lowell mill girls, the Lowell Female Labor Reform Association (LFLRA).

Organized in 1845 by native-born female operatives in the Lowell mills, the Female Labor Reform Association was one of the earliest permanent women's labor organizations in the United States. Under the leadership of Sarah Bagley, the LFLRA circulated petitions, dispatched organizers throughout New England, published a labor weekly, *The Voice of Industry,* and testified before legislative committees. By the late 1840s, expansion and mechanization of production as well as the introduction of low-paid immigrant labor transformed and degraded mill work, eroding the basis of labor organization and turning unmarried native-born women to alternative occupations.

A new organization of female operatives in the Lowell textile mills, the Lowell Female Industrial Reform and Mutual Aid Society, was formed during the 1840s and was less reformist than the original organization. Little is known of its activities except for weekly announcements in *The Voice of Industry.* The LFIRMAS stressed care of the poor and the ill as well as the women's individual rights as workers. By the 1850s, many of the native-born women had been replaced by Irish immigrant girls who were less likely to organize and who were willing to work long hours under speedup conditions for a noncommensurate wage. Although petitions continued to be sent regularly to the state legislature, the era of the Lowell Female Industrial Reform and Mutual Aid Society indicated that the high hopeful days of the labor reform movement of the 1840s were over. *(See also: Bagley, Sarah G.; Loom; Lowell Mill Girls;* Voice of Industry)

—**Joyce Follet**
—**Virginia Beattie Mattes**

Further Reading

Dublin, Thomas. *Women at Work: The Transformation of Work and Community in Lowell, Massachusetts, 1826–1860.* New York: Columbia University Press, 1979.

Early, Frances H. "A Reappraisal of the New England Labour-Reform Movement of the 1840s: The Lowell Female Labor Reform Association and the New England Workingmen's Association," *Histoire Sociale* (Canada) 13 (1980): 33-54.

Josephson, Hannah. *The Golden Threads: New England's Mill Girls and Magnates.* New York: Duell, Sloan & Pearce, 1949.

Robinson, Harriet Hanson. *Loom and Spindle, or Life among the Early Mill Girls. With a Sketch of "The Lowell Offering" and Some of Its Contributors.* New York: T. Y. Crowell, 1898. Reprint, Kailua, Hawaii: Press Pacifica, 1976.

Voice of Industry, 1845–1848.

Ware, Caroline F. *The Early New England Cotton Manufacture: A Study in Industrial Beginnings.* Boston: Houghton Mifflin, 1931.

⨍ Lowell Mill Girls

The Lowell mill girls constituted the first large-scale involvement of women in a factory system in the United States beginning in the 1830s and are therefore an integral part of women's history. In this early period, labor was in short supply due to westward expansion, a largely rural population, and the stigma attached to factory work. The Lowell, Massachusetts, mill owners were ingenious in planning a system with all facets of cloth manufacture under one roof and also in solving their labor problem by recruiting young New England farm girls of the same stock as themselves. The well-supervised, adjacent boarding houses for the girls, a lending library, a lyceum lecture series, diverse churches, wages paid in cash, and a bank for saving all appealed to these pious and thrifty girls. The socialization, independence, and "esprit de corps" derived from their respectable adventure in Lowell heightened their awareness of their abilities and resulted in "Improvement Circles" and a flowering of creativity in their poems and articles for *Lowell Offering,* a periodical created to demonstrate the intellectual capabilities of the mill girls.

Lowell became a world-famous town in the early nineteenth century, not only because of its efficient mill operations in juxtaposition to the Rhode Island and English systems—where makeshift villages sprang up near the mills and whole families existed on the meager wages of children—but also because of the uncommon mill girls. The hardworking Lowell mill girls with their thirst for education and culture attracted the attention of notable foreign visitors such as Charles Dickens and Harriet Martineau, as well as congressmen, senators, and three presidents of the United States, and elicited the praise of native-born Nathaniel Hawthorne.

The Lowell mills were located on the border of the states of Massachusetts and New Hampshire at the juncture of the Concord and Merrimack rivers, where the thirty-foot Pawtucket Falls provided ample power. Construction of the mills began in 1822. The first Lowell mill had its genesis in the Waltham, Massachusetts, mill, established by the Boston Manufacturing Company in 1813. The Waltham or boardinghouse concept was the ingenious idea of Francis Cabot Lowell, an exporter turned entrepreneur, who wished to avoid the deteriorating conditions of the Rhode Island and English systems. At Waltham, and later at Lowell, young women worked on the roving and spinning frames, drawing in the warps and tending the looms. Men worked mainly as overseers, machinists, or mechanics or in occupations such as calico printing, which required a specific skill.

The Lowell mills prospered in the early years, not only because of their efficient operations, abundant power from Pawtucket Falls, and adequate capital from risk-taking investors, but also because of a ready source of labor. Unlike the working-class mill girls in Rhode Island and England, many of the Lowell girls wished to further their brothers' higher education or to augment family income. Their motivation was not only financial independence but also educational opportunities.

The Lowell idyll began to unravel in the mid-1830s, when increased competition in the textile industry brought decreased wages, loom speedups, additional looms per worker, and less time for intellectual pursuits even before the panic of 1837, which brought on a national economic depression. Unsuccessful strikes initiated by female operatives in 1834 and 1836 reflected the concerted efforts of the mill women to instill a group consciousness and indicated a level of cooperation and determination that eventually propelled them to testify before the state legislature for a ten-hour day.

The first Lowell strike occurred after an announcement in February 1834 that wages paid in some departments would be cut by 15 percent. According to the February 20, 1834 *Boston Transcript,* the female operatives who were mainly affected by this cut held several meetings and decided to strike and "make a run" on the factory savings bank. The young woman leading the revolt was thereupon dismissed by the mill agent, but after leaving the mill, she led some eight hundred mill girls in procession around the town. They issued the "Lowell Proclamation," which stated they would not return to work until their wage cuts had been restored. The *Boston Transcript* indicated that the marchers were looked on with amusement. They walked out on a Saturday, attended church on Sunday, and on Monday all returned to work except those who had gone home to their families. The wage cuts took effect on March 1, 1834, with no further opposition.

The next strike had different causes and results. In 1836, the mill girls' average salary consisted of $2.00 per week plus board. By arrangement with the corporation, a board fee of $1.25 was taken out of each worker's total pay of $3.25 at the counting houses. Because of a sharp rise in the cost of living, the boardinghouse keepers could barely make ends meet. The corporation therefore lowered the rent charged housekeepers for the company-owned houses by 12.5 cents per boarder and correspondingly increased the amount deducted from the girls' wages by the same amount. This resulted in a 6 percent wage cut, and the girls went on strike. During this monthlong strike, they were evicted from the boarding houses and had no funds for their livelihood. They returned either to the mill or their farm homes.

A decade later, in the spring of 1846, one of the Lowell mills announced that the weavers would be required to tend four looms instead of three and that wages would be reduced one cent per piece. A meeting of the Lowell Female Labor Reform Association (LFLRA), a short-lived union organized by the workers in 1845, resulted in a pledge that an increased workload would not be accepted without a corresponding increase in wages. Virtually all of the women weavers signed the pledge and stuck to it. The speedup was canceled. The LFLRA had succeeded in directing the female operatives from fruitless strikes to an alternative tactic. This isolated incident involved the women weavers at only one mill, but it foreshadowed the organizing efforts, fortitude, and persistence of the early labor feminists, which ultimately earned them a ten-hour day in 1874.

The New England mill girls were eventually replaced in the mid-1840s by Irish immigrants who were willing to work for lower wages, but not before they tirelessly and valiantly fought for a ten-hour day under the leadership of Sarah Bagley and other LFLRA members, whose motto was "Try Again." Sarah Bagley's incendiary speeches and articles, published in *The Voice of Industry*, a labor weekly, as well as articles of other mill girls, lifted the Lowell girls out of women's sphere of silence.

The flowering of the Waltham experiment in Lowell, with its benevolent paternalism, did not make a lasting contribution to labor. However, the extraordinary Lowell mill girls' thirst for knowledge and culture and their subsequent battle for the ten-hour day earned them a permanent place in social and labor history. *(See also: Bagley, Sarah G.; Industrial Revolution; Loom; Lowell Female Industrial Reform and Mutual Aid Society;* Lowell Offering; *Textiles: North and South;* Voice of Industry)*

—**Virginia Beattie Mattes**

Further Reading

Adickes, Sandra. "Mind among the Spindles: An Examination of Some of the Journals, Newspapers, and Memoirs of the Lowell Female Operatives," *Women's Studies* 1 (1973): 279-87.

Dublin, Thomas. *Women at Work, The Transformation of Work and Community in Lowell, Massachusetts, 1826–1860*. New York: Columbia University Press, 1979.

Eisler, Benita, ed. *The Lowell Offering: Writings by New England Mill Women (1840–1845)*. Philadelphia: J. B. Lippincott, 1977.

Josephson, Hannah. *The Golden Threads, New England's Mill Girls and Magnates*. New York: Duell, Sloan & Pearce, 1949.

Papachristou, Judith. *Women Together: A History in Documents of the Women's Movement in the U.S.* New York: Knopf, 1976.

Robinson, Harriet Hanson. *Loom and Spindle, or Life among the Early Mill Girls. With a Sketch of "The Lowell Offering" and Some of Its Contributors*. New York: T. Y. Crowell, 1898. Reprint, Kailua, Hawaii: Press Pacifica, 1976.

Selden, Bernice. *The Mill Girls: Lucy Larcom, Harriet Hanson Robinson, Sarah G. Bagley*. New York: Atheneum, 1983.

Thompson, Agnes L. "New England Mill Girls," *New England Galaxy* 16 (1974): 43-49.

Ware, Caroline. *The Early New England Cotton Manufacture: A Study in Industrial Beginnings*. Boston: Houghton Mifflin, 1931.

Wright, Helena. "The Uncommon Mill Girls of Lowell," *History Today* 23 (1973): 10-19.

⁓ *Lowell Offering* (1840–1845)

Lowell Offering was a periodical written by women operatives in the Lowell textile mills. Developed from modest collections of writings from workers' self-improvement societies, the *Offering* became an ambitious testimonial to the capacities of young Yankee women who left their homes to

Figure 35. Lowell Offering
The Lowell factory was considered a model for its protection of its workers and its refusal to exploit children. Here is depicted a newspaper created by the Lowell factory workers. Used by permission of UPI/Corbis-Bettmann.

work in the mills and live in the boardinghouses established by their paternalistic employers.

Edited by A. C. Thomas (1840–1842) and Harriet Farley (1842–1845), a mill worker, the *Offering* contained a diverse range of poems, essays on scientific and moral subjects, translations, and stories. Farley saw her principal purpose as showing factory laborers equal to young women anywhere in terms of intellectual accomplishments. The *Offering* was read by mill operatives, although perhaps less by them than by the inhabitants of surrounding communities and by a national and international audience interested in Lowell as a social experiment and in the *Offering* as a unique phenomenon. While some early readers questioned whether writing of competence and dignity could be the work of mill girls, such cultural bastions as the *North American Review* eventually gave the periodical a stamp of interested, if condescending, approval. A selection of *Offering* contributions appeared in book form as *Mind amongst the Spindles* (1844).

As economic pressure on the mills increased in the 1840s, the owners abandoned benevolent paternalism, reducing wages and forcing increased production. The Lowell Female Labor Reform Association's attempts to organize the mills brought Farley into conflict with those who wanted the *Offering* to represent the interests of mill operatives. Farley refused to let the *Offering* include any discussion of current conditions in the mills. Subscriptions declined, and the *Lowell Offering* ceased publication in 1845.

The magazine was resurrected as the *New England Offering* (1847–1850), which retained the general character of the original periodical but expanded its contributors beyond the Lowell workers. *(See also: Farley, Harriet; Lowell Mill Girls)*

—**Carol Klimick Cyganowski**

Further Reading

Adickes, Sandra. "Mind among the Spindles: An Examination of Some of the Journals, Newspapers, and Memoirs of the Lowell Female Operatives," *Women's Studies* 1 (1973): 279-87.

Eisler, Benita, ed. *The Lowell Offering: Writings by New England Mill Women (1840–1845)*. Philadelphia: J. B. Lippincott, 1977.

Robinson, Harriet Hanson. *Loom and Spindle, or Life among the Early Mill Girls. With a Sketch of "The Lowell Offering" and Some of Its Contributors*. New York: Crowell, 1898. Reprint, Kailua, Hawaii: Press Pacifica, 1976.

❧ Luhan, Mabel Dodge (1879–1962)

Writer, patron of the arts, and political activist, Mabel Dodge Luhan was a woman ahead of her time who inspired and gathered around her artists and writers both in Europe and in America and who had an eye for artistic trends. In Florence, Italy, from 1904 to 1912 she helped her architect husband, Edwin S. Dodge, renovate Villa Curonia, where an international group of literati (including André Gide and Gertrude Stein) gathered to discuss matters of art and life. After she had moved to New York City late in 1912, partly as a way of separating from her husband (whom she divorced in 1916), she again attracted the avant-garde to her Greenwich Village apartment for weekly sessions. These sessions were more formal and more politically oriented than those in Florence, as Luhan and her cohorts became involved in workers' rights. In particular, she suggested and helped organize the Patterson Strike Pageant held on June 7, 1913, at Madison Square Garden and designed to dramatize the plight of immigrant silk workers in New Jersey. The event was considered a theatrical success, with over fifteen thousand in attendance, although it did not resolve worker/owner tensions. In the same year, she helped arrange the Armory Show in New York, which introduced many Americans to modernist art and which revolutionized the art world in America thereafter.

Following her marriage to painter Lawrence Sterne in 1917, Luhan moved with him to Taos, New Mexico, where she remained until her death. Once again, art and politics commingled as she embraced Indian causes, particularly the Pueblo Indians' eleven-year struggle to maintain their land and traditions. Helping to reactivate the Pueblos' Council of All the New Mexico Pueblos, she played a crucial role in preventing the Bursam Bill (which had then passed in the U.S. Senate) from becoming law. This bill, if enacted, would have allowed for the transfer of Indian land to squatters, while it would also have prohibited Indian religious activities. Her marriage to an Indian, Antonio Lujan (she spelled it with an h), in 1923, following her divorce from Sterne, reflected her intimate involvement with Pueblo life.

Luhan's several marriages (including her first marriage in 1900 to Karl Kellog Evans, who died in a hunting accident shortly thereafter), as well as her several affairs, attest to her restlessness as well as her vitality, which became legendary. Those luminaries who were drawn to her in New York and then in Taos included Marsden Hartley, Jo Davidson, Max Eastman, Carl Van Vechten, Robinson Jeffers, Thorton Wilder, D. H. Lawrence, and Georgia O'Keeffe. Admirers of Luhan saw her as an exciting listener who generated new ideas in others, and they also recognized her own considerable talent as a writer, particularly as an informal "historian" of twentieth-century cultural and political life. Her works include her *Intimate Memoirs* (four volumes, 1933–1937) and accounts of Taos life, including *Lorenzo in Taos* (about D. H. Lawrence, 1932), *Winter in Taos* (1935), and *Taos and Its Artists* (1947). Luhan appreciated the gentler life of Taos although, even there, she continued to battle the depression that plagued her throughout her life. Her writing helped her counteract this depression and also reveals how Luhan, a complicated individual who creatively resisted the status quo, inspired and sometimes coalesced the cultural and social leaders of her day. *(See also: Art; O'Keeffe, Georgia; Women Writers)*

—**Linda Patterson Miller**

Further Reading

Hahn, Emily. *Mabel: A Biography of Mabel Dodge Luhan*. Boston: Houghton Mifflin, 1977.

Luhan Collection. Beinecke Rare Book and Manuscript Library. Yale University, New Haven, CT.

Luhan, Mabel Dodge. *Intimate Memories*, 4 vols. New York: Harcourt Brace, 1933–1937.

Sterne, Maurice. *Shadow and Light: The Life, Friends and Opinions of Maurice Stern*. New York: Harcourt Brace, 1965.

❧ Lupino, Ida (1918–1995)

Ida Lupino, film actress and director, bristled at the label "feminist director" in her lifetime. Yet as the only woman to direct a sizable body of work in the American commercial cinema during the 1950s, and as an innovative director of dozens of television series episodes and pilots, she is at least a major role model of her time for women seeking access to the film and television industries. Her work shows her to have been a reflective interrogator of American women's issues as well.

Lupino was born in England in 1918, the scion of a famous acting family. After an education at the Royal Academy of Dramatic Art, she was brought to Hollywood in 1933 as an ingenue. After critical acclaim in several roles at Paramount from 1934 to 1939, she was under contract to Warner Brothers as an actress from 1939 to 1947. At Warners, a studio that was consciously tailoring its product to female audiences, Lupino, along with Bette Davis, Olivia de Havilland, and Joan Crawford, starred in period and contemporary melodramas of women in crisis. Her best films as an actress during this time (*The Light That Failed*, 1940; *They Drive by Night*, 1940; *High Sierra*, 1941; *The Hard Way*, 1943; and *The Man I Love*, 1947) consistently showed a tough, sympathetic woman in conflict with restrictive social norms. Altogether, she starred in over fifty films through 1982.

Considered one of Hollywood's best actresses by critics and the public, she found the life of a contract player constricting, and in 1949, she formed The Filmmakers, an independent production company with her then-husband Collier Young. From 1949 to 1954, she wrote, directed, acted in, and/or produced several films under The Filmmakers banner. In 1959, she turned to television, directing episodes of *Alfred Hitchcock Presents; Thriller; The Twilight Zone; Have Gun, Will Travel; The Untouchables*, and over twenty others. Ironically, her speciality as a television director was "action" episodes, but she was recognized as one of the television industry's best all-around talents.

Ida Lupino's seven productions for The Filmmakers show her to have been very much a feminist artist. The topics of her films—illegitimacy in *Not Wanted* (1949), rape in *The Outrage* (1950)—were remarkable enough. Yet works such as *Hard, Fast, and Beautiful* (1951), *The Bigamist* (1953), and *The Hitchhiker* (1953) also show a powerful critique of postwar consumerism and home/career confrontations. "You're up to your eyes in I.O.U's!" the psychotic killer in *The Hitchhiker* mockingly says to his middle-class captives, and he is right, for characters in Lupino's films feel the tension between family and economics far more deeply and more subtly than in works of other directors of the period. As critic Ronnie Scheib has said, "The 'problem' for Lupino's characters is not how to reintegrate them back into the mainstream; the 'problem' is the shallowness of the mainstream and the void it projects around them—the essential passivity of ready-made lives."

Full of expressionistic, passionate characters giving cynical opinions about social mores and the economic aspects of intimate relationships, Lupino's films use narrative modes typified by a cold, objective viewpoint on characters. This stylistic coolness avoided traditional Hollywood empathetic devices that encouraged identification with individual suffering characters. Indeed, characters who are nominally criminals in films such as *The Bigamist* and *The Hitchhiker* are also portrayed as victims of American society's most in-

sidious ideological norms. These modernist tendencies in style and Lupino's ambivalence toward social order were a combination calculated to alienate contemporary critics. In response, Lupino carefully refused publicly to identify herself as the feminist she demonstrably was.

Lupino's case as an auteur was first championed by the *Cahiers du Cinema* group of critics in the 1950s, which included the young François Truffaut and Jean-Luc Godard. However, it was the group of feminist critics loosely associated with the British Film Institute and *Screen* magazine during the 1970s who first prized Lupino's work as distinctively feminist. Her vision of the tragic self-loathing involved in contemporary women's identity, these critics recognized, is often repulsive in its aspect but also presents a clear critique of the conditions of oppression. *(See also: Movie Stars; Woman's Film)*

—**Kevin Jack Hagopian**

Further Reading

Acker, Ally. *Reel Women: Pioneers of the Cinema, 1896 to the Present*, pp. 74–78. New York: Continuum, 1991.

Johnston, Claire, ed. *Notes on Women's Cinema*. London: Society for Education in Film and Television, n.d.

Lupino, Ida. "Me, Mother Directress." In *Hollywood Directors: 1941–1976*, edited by Richard Koszarski, 371–77. New York: Oxford University Press, 1977.

———. "New Faces in New Places," *Films in Review* 1 (1950): 17–19.

Scheib, Ronnie. "Ida Lupino: Auteuress," *Film Comment* 16 (January–February 1980): 54–64.

Stewart, Lucy. *Ida Lupino as Film Director*. Salem, NH: Ayer, 1980.

Weiner, Debra. "Interview with Ida Lupino." In *Women and the Cinema*, edited by Karyn Kay and Gerald Peary, 169–78. New York: E. P. Dutton, 1977.

∿ Lusk, Georgia Lee (Witt) (1893–1971)

Educator and politician, Georgia Lusk was the first woman from New Mexico to serve in the U.S. Congress.

Born on a ranch in New Mexico Territory, Lusk attended New Mexico State Teachers College (now Western New Mexico University). While teaching school, she married rancher Dolph Lusk, quit her job, and subsequently had three sons. Her husband died of a heart attack in 1919 when Lusk was only twenty-six, necessitating her reentry into the field of education. A desire to be an educational administrator led Lusk into the political arena, and she was elected superintendent of Lea County schools in 1924 and 1926. Her first statewide campaign in 1928 for the post of superintendent of public instruction was unsuccessful; a Democrat, Lusk lost in the landslide victory of President Herbert Hoover, a Republican.

Subsequently, Lusk won election to the state's top education post six times between 1930 and 1956, serving three four-year stints in that position: 1931 to 1935, 1943 to 1947, and 1955 to 1959. She is generally credited with upgrading the quality of New Mexico's underfunded

Depression-era schools. Lusk also pushed for tougher science and mathematics requirements for high school graduates in the wake of concern over the launching of the satellite "Sputnik" by the Soviet Union in 1957.

In 1946, Lusk captured one of New Mexico's two at-large seats in the U.S. House of Representatives. As a congresswoman, she advocated federal aid to education and benefits for veterans. (Her three sons all served in World War II, and the oldest, Virgil, was killed in a military plane crash.) Lusk was defeated for reelection to Congress in 1948, but was appointed to the War Claims Commission in 1949 by President Harry Truman. She served four years in this post, processing the reparation claims of Americans who had been prisoners of war or civilian internees during World War II.

Lusk retired from politics in 1959, when her last term as superintendent of public instruction ended. The acumen she exhibited during her thirty-five-year political career, which included victories in seven statewide campaigns, won Lusk the sobriquet of "the first lady of New Mexico politics." *(See also: Democratic Party; Education; Politics)*

—**Roger D. Hardaway**

Further Reading

Hardaway, Roger D. "Georgia Lusk of New Mexico: A Political Biography." Master's thesis, New Mexico State University, 1979.

———. "New Mexico Elects a Congresswoman," *Red River Valley Historical Review* 4 (Fall 1979): 75-89.

⁊ Lutheran Women

A discussion of Lutheran women and their contributions to Lutheranism in North America must begin with a brief discussion of Lutheranism's status as an immigrant church and the relatively late assimilation of most of its members into American culture. By the late nineteenth century, primarily due to massive immigration, Lutherans composed one of the largest groups of Protestants in the United States. However, because of numerous ethnic, linguistic, cultural, and theological differences, Lutherans remained institutionally fractured until the later twentieth century. At one point in the late nineteenth century, there were 66 different Lutheran denominations in this country. And by 1900, 80 percent of all U.S. Lutherans were still using one of 29 different languages in their worship. Thus, it is not surprising that there is relatively little research on women and women's church groups in earlier American Lutheranism and that most of the research focuses on just one or two larger linguistic groups. Despite these limitations, however, it is possible to make a few generalizations about the contributions of American Lutheran women to the work of their church.

American Lutheran women have long sought to serve their church in a variety of ways. They brought some models of service, such as deaconess work, with them from Europe. They formed other organizations, such as local congrega-

tional women's groups, in response to America's climate of reform and volunteerism. In both cases, to more fully serve the church's mission, Lutheran women have displayed a clear impulse toward further organization and institutionalization of their forms of service.

Deaconess service gave Lutheran women one of their earliest institutionalized opportunities to work as church professionals. Their primary activities were ameliorative, such as staffing orphanages and hospitals, but deaconesses also served as schoolteachers and lay parish workers. The opportunity for deaconess service is still available to Lutheran women.

The most common form of institutionalized service has been in the form of women's auxiliaries, although rarely has women's service been merely auxiliary to the church's work. Rather, it has often been central, taking the form of financial support for home and foreign missions, for higher education, and for the training of clergy, among other things. By the late nineteenth century, many if not most Lutheran congregations had organized women's groups. As the process of merger gathered many small Lutheran groups into larger denominations in the late twentieth century, local women's societies gradually joined together to form churchwide federations. Although the formation of these federations sometimes met some initial resistance, over time, women's federations gained a secure footing in most Lutheran denominations. Their unity gave them some financial and political clout and enabled women to make important contributions to the life of the church, such as providing the bulk of support for various foreign mission stations and even serving as missionaries themselves.

In the later twentieth century, Lutheran women's groups continued to exert significant influence in the church in a wide variety of ways. Three ways deserve special comment. First, these groups provided Lutheran women with a training ground in which to develop leadership skills in the church. Second, particularly through their various churchwide publications, these groups gave Lutheran women a forum in which to grapple with the insights and implications of feminism for their own faith. Finally and most notably, the churchwide women's organizations of the American Lutheran Church (American Lutheran Church Women, or ALCW) and the Lutheran Church in America (Lutheran Church Women, or LCW) provided their churches with skilled women leaders, gentle agitation, and needed momentum in the deliberations of the late 1960s about women's ordination. Some of the credit for the decisions of the American Lutheran Church (ALC) and Lutheran Church of America (LCA) to begin ordaining women in 1970 must be given to the numerous laywomen who both supported and staffed their churches' women's organization.

In 1988, three major Lutheran groups in the United States, the ALC, the LCA, and the Association of Evangelical Lutheran Churches (AELC) merged to form the Evangelical Lutheran Church in America (ELCA). The ELCA and the Lutheran Church—Missouri Synod (LCMS) are the two largest Lutheran bodies in the United States. Although the question of women's ordination has arisen at various times in the LCMS, that church has continued to assert that to ordain women would violate the mandates of Scripture and thus does not ordain women into Word and Sacrament ministry.

Following the tradition of its predecessor churches, the ELCA does ordain women into the ministry of Word and Sacrament. In 1987, women composed about 35 percent of each graduating class at Lutheran seminaries. Ten years later, that figure had risen to 44 percent. In 1997, there were 1,191 ordained women on the ELCA clergy roster of a total of 17,316 ordained pastors. Both lay and ordained women are active leaders in almost every aspect of ELCA church life, from serving in positions in the national church offices and other Lutheran agencies, to teaching at Lutheran seminaries and serving as bishops in various regions of the church. *(See also: Christianity; Immigration; Religion)*

—Cynthia Jurisson

Further Reading

Albers, James W. "Perspectives on the History of Women in the Lutheran Church—Missouri Synod during the Nineteenth Century," *Lutheran Historical Conference: Essays and Reports* 9 (1982): 137-83.

Commission for Women. Evangelical Lutheran Church in America. *A Cloud of Witnesses: Celebrating Lutheran Women's History.* Chicago: The Commission, 1990. [Single copies available from the ELCA Resource Center at 1-800-NET-ELCA]

DeBerg, Betty, with Elizabeth Sherman. *Women and Women's Issues in Northern American Lutheranism: A Bibliography.* Chicago: Commission for Women of the ELCA and Augsburg Fortress, 1992.

Grindal, Gracia. "Getting Women Ordained." In *Called and Ordained: Lutheran Perspectives on the Office of the Ministry,* edited by Todd Nichol and Mark Kolden, 161-79. Minneapolis, MN: Fortress, 1990.

Lagerquist, L. DeAne. *From Our Mother's Arms: A History of Women in the American Lutheran Church.* Minneapolis, MN: Augsburg, 1987.

———. *In America the Men Milk the Cows: Factors of Gender, Ethnicity and Religion in the Americanization of Norwegian-American Women.* Brooklyn: Carlson, 1990.

Nelson, Clifford E. *The Lutherans in North America.* Philadelphia: Fortress, 1980.

http://www.elca.org [Evangelical Lutheran Church in America Website]

❧ Lying-In

Lying-in was a term used in early America to refer both to childbirth and to the period of recuperation that followed. The period of confinement implied by the term began with the onset of labor and ended when the new mother resumed her household duties. Depending on what help was available to her and what her household responsibilities encompassed, a woman in the seventeenth and eighteenth centuries might be lying-in for as long as six weeks. Immediately after the child's birth, the mother would be bathed and "brought to bed," that is, moved into her bed, where

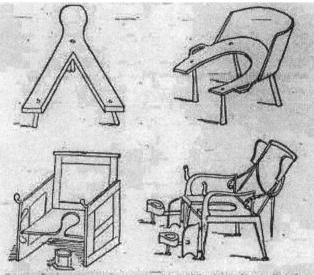

Figure 36. Lying-In
The obstetrics chair went through many stages, ranging from the primitive to those resembling the modern-day gynecologist's chair. Used by permission of Corbis-Bettmann.

she would be kept well covered and quiet for a few days. After three to six days, she would be allowed to sit up briefly. In the eighteenth century, among those with sufficient means, this period included "sitting up" visits by friends and well-wishers. Such visits typically included presents as well as exchanges of gossip and information about other births and other friends and relatives. By the time a new mother was ready for a walk or a ride in the open air, her confinement, her lying-in, had come to a close.

The notion of childbirth as a period of confinement that included recuperation and adjustment is reflected in the names given the institutions that arose in the nineteenth century to accommodate those women giving birth who were bereft of support or care. The New York Asylum for Lying-In Women and the Lying-In Ward of the Pennsylvania Hospital in Philadelphia were two such institutions established early in the nineteenth century. Each acknowledged and provided for the social and familial/relational needs of women at childbirth, both those that preceded the birth and those that followed it. By the end of the nineteenth century and increasingly in the twentieth, however, the focus of childbirth in hospital lying-in wards was very medical. Each expectant mother was of interest principally during the delivery phase of her childbirth. As soon after giving birth as possible, the new mother was sent home. Rest and recuperation came at home if at all. The New York Asylum for Lying-In Women tried to maintain its tradition of caring for women during lying-in, but medical and financial exigencies forced it to merge in 1899 with a more medically oriented institution, the New York Infant Asylum. The concept of lying-in disappeared. *(See also: Childbirth; Midwifery)*

—**Janet Carlisle Bogdan**

Further Reading

Bogdan, Janet Carlisle. "Aggressive Intervention and Mortality." In *The American Way of Birth*, edited by Pamela Eakins, 60-98. Philadelphia: Temple University Press, 1987.

———. "Care or Cure? Childbirth Practices in Nineteenth Century America," *Feminist Studies* 4 (1978): 92-99.

———. "Childbirth in America, 1659–1990." In *Women, Health, and Medicine in America: A Historical Handbook,* edited by Rima D. Apple, 101-20. New York: Garland, 1990.

———. "Losing Childbirth: The Erosion of Women's Knowledge about and Control over Childbirth, 1659–1900." In *Changing Education: Women as Radicals and Conservators,* edited by Joyce Antler and Sari Knopp Biklen, 83-191. Albany: State University of New York Press, 1990.

Scholten, Catherine. *Childbearing in American Society, 1650–1850.* New York: New York University Press, 1986.

Wertz, Richard, and Dorothy Wertz. *Lying-In.* 1977. Reprint, New Haven, CT: Yale University Press, 1989.

Lyons, Maritcha Remond
(1848–1929)

Maritcha Lyons was born in New York City, the daughter of Albro and Mary Marshall Lyons who operated a Colored Sailors' Home and Clothing Store and were active in the Underground Railroad. They frequently housed runaway slaves in their home. Following the Draft Riots of 1863, in which many homes and businesses were burned, Lyons's family moved to Rhode Island, where mother and daughter successfully petitioned the governor and legislature to repeal a school segregation law. Lyons thus became the first black to graduate from Providence High School. Between 1870 and 1880, she studied languages and music at Brooklyn Institute.

Lyons began teaching at Brooklyn's Colored School No. 1 in 1869. When the school systems merged in 1887, Colored Schools Nos. 1, 2, and 3 became Public Schools 67, 68, and 69. In 1893, Public School 68 in the black community of Weeksville was consolidated with Public School 83, a white school at Bergen and Schenectady Avenues. Lyons was assigned to Public School 83 as assistant principal in 1893 and appointed principal in 1898.

In 1892, Lyons and Victoria Matthews sponsored a testimonial for Ida B. Wells, the antilynching crusader. The same year, Lyons and Matthews were cofounders of the Woman's Loyal Union of New York City and Brooklyn. Lyons was also a member of the Brooklyn Literary Union, the Equal Suffrage League, and the Auxilium Club. Her address to the American Negro Academy in 1898 on "Afro-American Literature" was the first speech by a woman to be delivered before the all-male organization.

Lyons, Sarah Garnet, and other New York women supported the Niagara Movement, a forerunner of the National Association of Colored People (NAACP). Lyons was elected to the General Committee of the NAACP. As a member of the Press Committee, she spoke to women's clubs and organizations to increase the membership of the NAACP. She was a charter member of the Brooklyn Branch of the NAACP.

For forty-eight years, Maritcha Lyons was a teacher and grammar school principal. She retired in 1918 and died of pneumonia and kidney failure on January 28, 1929. *(See also: Black Women's Clubs; Education; National Association of Colored People; Wells-Barnett, Ida B.)*

—**Floris Barnett Cash**

Further Reading

"Along the Color Line," *The Crisis Magazine* 36 (April 1929): 127.

Cash, Floris Barnett. *Black Women of Brooklyn: Seventeenth Century to the Present.* New York: Brooklyn Historical Society, 1985.

Mather, Frank Lincoln. *Who's Who of the Colored Race: A General Biographical Dictionary.* Vol. I, 1915; Memento ed., p. 182. Detroit, MI: Gale Research, 1976.

Moss, Alfred, Jr. *The American Negro Academy: Voice of the Talented Tenth.* Baton Rouge: Louisiana State University Press, 1981.

Salem, Dorothy. *To Better Our World: Black Women in Organized Reform, 1890–1920.* New York: Carlson, 1990.

Lytle, Lutie (c. 1871–?)

Born in Topeka, Kansas, Lutie Lytle became one of the first black women in the United States to practice law and allegedly the first to receive full accreditation. As a teenager, she worked as a compositor in a printing office in Topeka, where she had access to newspaper exchanges from which she first learned about Kansas and national politics. In 1896, her father, John R. Lytle, a Topeka barber, ran successfully for the post of assistant city jailer and received the nomination for register of deeds from the Populist Party in 1897. Lytle herself campaigned for the Populist Party and was rewarded with a patronage job as assistant enrolling clerk in 1894, the only black woman to receive such a position from the Populist Party.

A year after her appointment by the Populists, Lytle enrolled in Central Tennessee Law College of Nashville, receiving a law degree and admission to the Tennessee Bar in 1897. She lived in Topeka for a short time after receiving her degree and then returned to her alma mater to teach law. After her marriage, Lytle and her husband moved to New Paltz, New York, where she continued to practice law. *(See also: Black Women; Legal Profession; Politics; Populist Party)*

—**MaryJo Wagner**

Further Reading

Colored Citizen (Topeka, Kansas), October 7, 1897.

Historical Preservation in Kansas: Black Historic Sites, p. 31. Topeka: Kansas State Historical Society, 1977.

Topeka (Kansas) *Capital,* September 15, 1897.

Topeka (Kansas) *State Ledger,* January 11, 1895.

➴ Magazines

As early as the late eighteenth century, popular periodicals were being published for an eager, if limited, audience of literate and leisured women readers in England and British North America. After the American Revolution, such magazines were published in the United States. Nineteenth-century American women's magazines were designed both to amuse and to instruct the True Woman in the ideal middle-class American home. As they defined and refined the proper role of women, these specialized periodicals also molded public opinion on women's issues. The publishers and editors of mainstream Victorian women's magazines offered their readers a conservative perspective that became known as domestic feminism, which wholeheartedly nurtured and supported the cult of domesticity and its attendant consumerism. Throughout the twentieth century, American women's magazines increasingly adjusted their focus on the suburban consumer/homemaker to reflect contemporary changes wrought in her life by the urbanization and industrialization of American society. By the end of the twentieth century, both new and established women's magazines attempted to court not only traditional homemakers but "working wives" and single employed women.

Early American magazines for women focused almost exclusively on fashion and sentimental escape fiction rather than on factual information and education. Most of their contents were plagiarized from English women's magazines, and therefore their contents reflected the social attitudes and behavior of the upper class of England rather than the republican middle class of the new nation. Within this literate middle class, women especially read and subscribed to American women's magazines that increasingly featured native authors and original material as they focused on the developing concept of a separate woman's sphere.

After the American Revolution, the contents of these magazines reflected the alteration of women's role in the family from their chattel status within the strict authoritarian patriarchal model of the preindustrial era to a slightly higher status as a result of the more companionate marriage that began to characterize the marital relationships of the nuclear family of the nineteenth century. Especially in the early New England women's magazines, a patriotic and domestic image of "republican motherhood" prepared the way for the true womanhood of the Victorian era. Usually, these early periodicals were religious in orientation and were edited by ministers or other pious men.

In the antebellum period of Victorian America, many monthly periodicals vied for the faithful readership of women who were a generation removed from the republican mother of the rural preindustrial extended family. The role of these urban middle-class, native-born white women within the smaller urban family required modification and adjustment to the new circumstance that rendered women economic dependents of wage-earning men. No longer coworkers or producers of crucial household goods and services, women were now consumers and household managers. American women's magazines spoke to and for these women, providing them with both entertainment and instruction in their new role as True Women. Moreover, women's magazines fostered the new genteel occupations of editor and contributing author for destitute ladies. Philadelphia and New York became the centers of publishing for women's magazines by the mid-nineteenth century.

Godey's Lady's Book, published by Louis A. Godey of Philadelphia, became the premier American Victorian women's magazine by the 1840s and 1850s, and it set the standard for all popular women's magazines of the era, as well as of the next century. Sarah Josepha Hale, its editor of forty years, brought a content format that she had perfected while editing her *American Ladies' Magazine* in Boston from 1828 to 1836. This fortified the memorable Godey's fashion plates, woodcuts, and other lavish "embellishments" with fiction, features, poetry and prose, household "how-to" articles, and crafts instructions. Hale also brought a commitment to improve her women readers through her editorial support of educational and employment advances for women. *Godey's* peaked as a literary magazine in the 1850s but lingered on until the last decade of the nineteenth century, coasting as it were on the indisputable reputation it earned under Hale's editorship as an impeccable source of entertainment and instruction for ladies. The Civil War marked the beginning of *Godey's* decline. By the turn of the century, Edward Bok's *Ladies' Home Journal* was the leading American women's magazine. Adhering for the most part to the format established by *Godey's,* the *Journal* and its contemporaries cautiously integrated aspects of the New

Woman into the twentieth-century cult of domesticity that spanned the 1920s and survived both the Great Depression and World War II. *Godey's* editorial policy of an exclusively domestic and apolitical focus of American women's magazines persisted through the 1960s. Not until the mainstream women's magazines banded together to support the ratification of the Equal Rights Amendment in the late 1970s did women's magazines directly broach a national political issue.

During the 1950s, women's magazines presented the ideal lifestyle for the suburban housewife and relentlessly fortified the compulsory domesticity and femininity of the feminine mystique. Under the editorship of Helen Gurley Brown, *Cosmopolitan* by the mid-1960s was approaching a candor regarding sex and marriage that would have scandalized Hale and Bok but that reflected the impact on women's role and behavior of the so-called sexual revolution and of women's emerging economic independence through their increased participation in the workforce. In 1972, *Ms.* magazine became the first frankly feminist mainstream women's magazine. It wooed the professional woman as well as the traditional homemaker with a raised consciousness. The product of feminist writers and editors such as Gloria Steinem, *Ms.* addressed a politically active and astute readership during its first decade. However, with the failure of the ERA ratification drive and the waning of the women's movement, even *Ms.* increasingly began to focus on personal relationships and family issues by the 1980s; it was purchased by a commercial corporation in the late 1980s. Not unlike feminist magazines such as *Una* and *Revolution* in the nineteenth century, a few magazines that focused on lesbian and radical feminist issues depended on a discrete feminist readership; while these had flourished during the early 1970s, they were struggling for survival by the 1980s.

By the 1970s, American magazines in general altered their emphasis to appeal to the reading taste of the maturing baby boomers or "Yuppies" (young urban upwardly mobile professionals). This generation, which followed the counterculture of the politically active youth of the 1960s, became known as the "me generation." Women's magazines, too, reflected the contemporary obsession with self. Although acknowledging that women's lives were being affected by the austere economic situation as well as by the additional career and lifestyle choices available to them by the 1980s, magazines such as *Family Circle* and *Woman's Day* still defined womanhood for their readers in terms of the cult of domesticity. Mainstream women's magazines broached many unpleasant issues that had previously been editorially taboo—rape, divorce, spouse abuse, alcohol and drug abuse—but their primary focus continued to be women's home duties and family relationships.

By the 1990s, the women's magazines that had weathered the turbulence of the 1980s were joined by a new breed of target market magazines trying to reinterpret the standard format of topics and emphasis of women's magazines to lure various segments of the single-issue readership within the mass market. *Ms.* magazine, after a near demise, reemerged as an advertising-free publication and celebrated its 25th anniversary as a magazine devoted to contemporary mainstream feminist issues of concern to women generally. Some new titles entered as competitors to the long-standing standard monthly publications; these trendy magazines targeted the aging baby boomers among women readers, the new athleticism among younger women, or other specific audiences of employed and professional women, careerists as well as those who were juggling the demands of work and home duties. The established women's magazines continued to adjust their standard format to maintain a contemporary relevance to the changing lifestyles of adult women as well as to younger women and girls. *(See also: Cult of True Womanhood; Domestic Literature in the United States; Ms. Magazine; New Woman;* Revolution; Una*)*

—**Angela M. Howard**

Further Reading

Douglas, Ann. *The Feminization of American Culture.* New York: Knopf, 1977.

Meyerowitz, Joanne. "Beyond the Feminist Mystique: A Reassessment of Postwar Mass Culture, 1946–1948," *Journal of American History* 79 (1994): 1455-82.

Mott, Frank. *A History of American Women's Magazines,* 2 vols. New York: Appleton, 1930.

Stearns, Bertha M. "Before *Godey's,*" *American Literature* 21 (1930): 248-55.

Woodward, Helen Beal. *The Lady Persuaders.* New York: Ivan Obolensky, 1960.

Zuckman, Mary Ellen, comp. *Sources on the History of Women's Magazines, 1792–1960: An Annotated Bibliography.* Westport, CT: Greenwood, 1991.

⤜ Malkiel, Theresa Serber (1874–1949)

Trade union organizer and socialist activist Theresa Malkiel migrated to New York from Bar, Russia, in 1891. She immediately went to work in the city's garment industry, developing a commitment to unionism. She joined the Russian Workingmen's Club in 1892, helped found the Woman's Infant Cloak Maker's Union, and served as its president as well as its representative to the Knights of Labor. Although she left the labor force after her marriage to lawyer Leon Malkiel in 1900, she maintained a high profile in the labor movement. An early member of the New York Women's Trade Union League, she played an active role in the garment industry's labor struggles from 1909 to 1911. This strike provided the backdrop for her novel, *Diary of a Shirtwaist Striker* (1910).

Diary of a Shirtwaist Striker depicts labor struggles in the garment industry of the early twentieth century in fictional terms. Unlike Malkiel, a Jewish immigrant from Russia, the heroine of this didactic novel, Mary, is a middle-class American woman, presented at first as a timid, callow girl who works in a garment factory only for "pin money" and who cannot share the experiences or goals of the other workers, mostly poor immigrant women, laboring for their livelihood. She believes herself better than they. In the course of the novel, however, Mary's consciousness changes, and she comes to support a strike in the factory, despite the objections of her father and her fiancé. She surfaces as a leader of the strike, finds herself on a picket line, and gets arrested. Her time in a workhouse causes her to understand the problems beyond those of a single shop, and she sees the need for broad changes in society. She becomes a Socialist. Mary also recognizes that women workers have special needs and must have the vote.

Malkiel's socialism began shortly after her migration from Russia. Although she belonged first to the Socialist Labor Party, she associated with the Socialist Party of America (SPA), within which she consistently drew members' attention to the links between feminism and socialism. Her goal of fusing socialism and feminism led her in 1907 to found the Women's Progressive Society of Yonkers (New York), which she hoped would give Socialist women a chance to exert the leadership that, she believed, the SPA consistently denied them. She chided the party for refusing to recognize the significance of the "woman question" and for failing to see that feminism and socialism shared visions. She articulated the organic connection between feminist and socialist goals in two 1915 pamphlets, *Woman of Yesterday and Today* and *Woman and Freedom.* She also contributed to socialist publications such as *Socialist Woman* and *Progressive Woman* as well as to *Call* and *Jewish Daily Forward,* a Yiddish newspaper for which she edited a special woman's column.

In the years immediately following World War I, Malkiel remained in the Socialist Party and ran for the New York State Assembly in 1920 on its ticket. This represented Malkiel's last involvement with socialism. She shifted her attention in the 1920s and 1930s to promoting women's education, with special emphasis on the needs of immigrant women. *(See also: Garment Industries; Jewish Women; Shirtwaist Makers Strike of 1909; Socialist Party of America; "Woman Question")*

—**Hasia R. Diner**

Further Reading

Blake, Fay M. *The Strike in the American Novel.* Metuchen, NJ: Scarecrow, 1972.

Buhle, Mari Jo. *Women and American Socialism, 1870–1920.* Urbana: University of Illinois Press, 1981.

Glenn, Susan A. *Daughters of the Shtetl: Life and Labor in the Immigrant Generation.* Ithaca, NY: Cornell University Press, 1990.

Malkiel, Theresa. *Diary of a Shirtwaist Striker.* New York: Co-operative Press, 1910.

———. *Woman and Freedom.* New York: Co-operative Press, 1915.

———. *Woman of Yesterday and Today.* New York: Co-operative Press, 1915.

Miller, Sally M. "From Sweatshop Worker to Labor Leader: Theresa Malkiel, a Case Study," *American Jewish History* 68 (December 1978): 189-205.

Weinberg, Sydney S. *The World of Our Mothers: The Lives of Jewish Immigrant Women.* Chapel Hill: University of North Carolina Press, 1988.

~ Malone, Annie Turnbo (c. 1868–1957)

Annie Turnbo Malone, black businesswoman, manufacturer, and philanthropist, dreamed of making products to enhance the beauty of black women. She experimented with chemistry in high school and developed a scalp treatment solution to grow and straighten hair. A native of Illinois, Malone started a business in Lovejoy, Illinois, and moved to St. Louis, Missouri, in 1902. Four years later, she patented her products under the trade name Poro. By 1914, Malone owned the largest black enterprise in St. Louis. Her business, called Poro College, consisted of a factory and store for hair and cosmetic products, hairdressing school, dormitory, and business office, plus a large auditorium and dining room that served as a community center for religious, fraternal, civic, and social organizations.

In addition to her business responsibilities, Malone was active in Colored Women's Federated Clubs of St. Louis, the National Negro Business League, the St. Louis Community Council, and the Commission on Inter-Racial Cooperation. Because of her interest in young people, especially women, she gave generous financial assistance to the St. Louis Maternity Hospital, St. Louis Children's Hospital, the Young Men's Christian Association (YMCA), the St. James AME Church, and the St. Louis Colored Orphans' Home. She served as board president of the latter from 1919 until 1943, and the home was named for her in 1946.

In 1930, Malone moved to Chicago, where she purchased a complete city block. By this time, she was considered one of the world's wealthiest black women. Poro College, built on a foundation of black women's commitment to honor, industry, and generosity, established branch offices in principal cities throughout the United States. Always interested in education, Malone made large financial contributions to Howard University, Washington, D.C., and Wilberforce University, Ohio. Both institutions, among several others, conferred honorary degrees on her.

Malone's life provided an inspiration to young people, particularly women. She typified the traditional spirit of American business, rising from meager circumstances to a position of affluence through remarkable executive power and business acumen. *(See also: Beauty Industry; Black Women; Business)*

—**Mary K. Dains**

Further Reading

Dains, Mary K. "Annie Turnbo Malone." In *Show Me Missouri Women, Selected Biographies.* Vol. I, edited by Mary K. Dains, 81. Kirksville, MO: Thomas Jefferson University Press, 1989.

"Missouri Women in History," *Missouri Historical Review* 67 (July 1973): inside back cover.

🐾 Mankiller, Wilma Pearl (b. 1945)

Wilma Mankiller was the first woman elected principal chief of the Cherokee Nation of Oklahoma. She was the sixth of eleven children born to a full-blooded Cherokee father and a Dutch-Irish mother in the small rural community of Rocky Mountain, Oklahoma. Her family name refers to an ancestor who had the title of "mankiller," meaning someone responsible for the security of the village.

In 1956, her family was relocated to San Francisco, California, as part of a federal program to mainstream and urbanize rural Indians. There, the Mankillers were introduced to urban poverty and violence. Her family became active in the American Indian Center in San Francisco and found the organization a safe haven where they met other Indian relocatees.

In 1963, Wilma Mankiller graduated from high school and five months later married Hector Hugo Olaya de Bardi. They had two children, Felicia in 1964 and Gina in 1966. In the late 1960s, she decided to go to college and major in social work.

By 1969, a new era of Indian militancy began when a small group of Native Americans seized Alcatraz Island. This event politicized Mankiller, and she became involved in fund-raising activities for the native people who remained on the island for nineteen months. As her activism increased, her marriage soured. In 1974, she divorced de Bardi. To support herself and her daughters, she took a job with the Urban Indian Resource Center and continued to do volunteer work for the American Indian Center.

In 1977, Mankiller returned to Oklahoma with her daughters. A few months later, she began working for the Cherokee Nation as an economic stimulus coordinator. She had considerable skill in writing grant proposals, and by 1979, she became a program development specialist. That same year, she returned to school to finish her bachelor's degree in social work. She also began graduate work in community planning at the University of Arkansas at Fayetteville.

In November 1979, she was involved in an auto accident in which her face and right leg were crushed and her left leg and both ankles were broken. While recovering from the accident, she was diagnosed with myasthenia gravis, which required surgery to remove her thymus. She was unable to return to her post with the Cherokee Nation until January 1981. Later that year, she helped found the Cherokee Nation Community Development Department and then became its director.

In 1983, Mankiller agreed to run with Principal Chief Ross Swimmer as his deputy chief in the next election. She assumed office in August 1983. Two years later, Swimmer became director of the Bureau of Indian Affairs (BIA); Mankiller finished the remainder of his four-year term and was subsequently elected to the office of Principal Chief in 1987 and again in 1991.

She has a service-oriented approach to leadership. Under her direction, the Cherokee Nation experienced economic growth, improved health care, and increased political au-

tonomy. The nation now administers funds formerly controlled by the BIA. Mankiller was *Ms.* Magazine Woman of the Year in 1987 and has honorary degrees from several Ivy League colleges. In 1993, she was inducted into the National Women's Hall of Fame in Seneca Falls, New York, and she has also received the Humanitarian Award from the Ford Foundation and the Distinguished Leadership Award of the Harvard Foundation. She was inducted into the International Women's Hall of Fame in 1992. She currently lives in Mankiller Flats, Oklahoma, with her husband Charlie Soap, a full-blooded Cherokee whom she married in 1986. *(See also: Native American Women; Politics)*

—Joyce Ann Kievit

Further Reading

Griffin, Connie. "Relearning to Trust Ourselves: An Interview with Chief Wilma Mankiller, Tahlequa, Oklahoma," *Women of Power* 7 (Summer 1987): 38-40, 72-74.

Mankiller, Wilma, Gwendolyn Mink, Marysa Navarro, Barbara Smith, and Gloria Steinem, eds. *The Reader's Companion to U.S. Women's History.* New York: Houghton Mifflin, 1998.

Mankiller, Wilma Pearl, and Michael Wallis. *Mankiller: A Chief and Her People.* New York: St. Martin's, 1993.

Verhovek, Sam Howe. "At Work with Chief Wilma Mankiller: The Name Is the Most and the Least of Her," *New York Times* 4 (November 1993): 1(C).

Wallis, Michael. "Hail to the Chief: Wilma Mankiller Is the First Woman to Be Elected Cherokee Nation Chief," *Phillip Morris Magazine* (October 1989): 37-39.

Whittlemore, Hank. "She Leads a Nation," *Parade Magazine* (18 August 1991): 4-5.

🐾 Marine Corps, Women's Reserve

The Marines may be the first service to land on beaches, but they were the last service to create a women's corps, reluctantly, in February 1943. Unlike the other services (WAAC, WAVES, SPARS), the Marine Corps did not give their women's corps a nickname; they were marines, or at least, women marines.

The marines report to the Navy during war, and during World War I, the Navy found a loophole in the law and recruited women to serve as telephone operators and clericals. By the war's end, 11,275 yeomen (F), women typists and telephone operators, had served commendably with the Navy and the Marine Corps. More than one hundred women Marine Corps veterans of World War I were still attending annual meetings in the late 1980s.

During World War II, women marines prided themselves in taking over stateside work so that the men could fight. At Cherry Point, North Carolina, by August 1944, all the airplane instructors for beginning pilots were women marines. At this base, women marines took almost complete charge of the photography department and film library, did 90 percent of the parachute packing, and conducted 80 percent of the landing-field control tower operations. Women marines made up from one-third to one-half of the post troops at representative Marine Corps posts and stations. Some

Figure 37. Marine Corps
The Marines were the last of the armed services to create a women's corps. These women, photographed at Hunter College in 1943, were among the first members. Used by permission of UPI/Corbis-Bettmann.

women handled mail, others the radios and the storerooms, while still others trained pilots or were mechanics. At the war's peak, 17,600 women served in the Marines Corps; in all, 23,000 served during World War II.

Women joined the Marines Corps for different reasons. While the overwhelming majority cited patriotism first, over a quarter cited escape from a difficult job or family situation as the next most important reason. Ruth Chenery Streeter became the first director of women marines during this period. A Bryn Mawr alumna, she had experience in civic activities such as public health and welfare unemployment, relief, and old-age assistance in her home state of New Jersey.

With the passage of the Women's Armed Services Integration Act in June 1948, the Women's Reserve was made a permanent part of the Marines Corps. In 1976, women began attending the U.S. Naval Academy at Annapolis, Maryland, and in 1978, the Women's Reserves were abolished and women were integrated into the service. Women in the Marine Corps are blocked by Navy regulations from hold-

ing combat positions, which limits their chances for promotion in the Marine Corps and Navy. Current debate centers around the definition of combat jobs and whether Congress should abolish these restrictions and draft women. *(See also: Military Service)*

—**D'Ann Campbell**

Further Reading

Campbell, D'Ann. *Women at War with America: Private Lives in a Patriotic Era.* Cambridge, MA: Harvard University Press, 1984.

Chapline, Neal. *Molly's Boots.* Detroit, MI: Harlo, 1983.

Hewit, Linda L., Capt., USMCR. *Women Marines in World War I.* Washington, DC: History and Museums Division, Headquarters U.S. Marine Corps, 1974.

Meid, Pat, Lt. Col., USMCR. *Marine Corps Women's Reserve in World War II.* Washington DC: Historical Branch, C-3 Division, Headquarters, U.S. Marine Corps, 1968.

Mitchell, Frances Robinson. *Experiencing the Depression of World War II.* Orono, ME: Bear Paw, 1989.

Soderbergh, Peter A. *Women Marines: The World War II Era.* Westport, CT: Praeger/Greenwood, 1992.

Streeter, Ruth Chenery. "History of the Marine Corps Women's Reserve: A Critical Analysis of Its Development and Operation, 1943–1945." Schlesinger Library, Radcliffe College, Cambridge, MA.

———. "Recollections with Ruth Chenery Streeter." Oral History Program, The Naval Institute, 1972. Schlesinger Library, Radcliffe College, Cambridge, MA.

Stremlow, Mary V., Col., USMCR. *A History of Women Marines 1946–1977.* Washington, DC: History and Museums Division, Headquarters U.S. Marine Corps, 1982.

White, Barbara A. *Lady Leatherneck.* New York: Dodd, Mead, 1945.

⚓ Marital Rape

Marital rape (spousal rape) is forced sexual intercourse and/or other forced sexual intimacy between persons married to one another. Research indicates that 14 percent of women report that this has happened to them during previous or current marriages.

Historically, forced sex between spouses has not been recognized as a crime. Traditionally, holding the status of "husband" to the victim was a defense to the crime. However, over the past two decades, numerous states have begun to modify their sexual assault laws to omit or limit this defense and recognize a wife's legal entitlement to refuse sex.

The spousal exemption is a carryover from early family law, which defined a married woman and her children as the property of her husband. A man had complete control over his wife. Legally, he could beat her, and he could force sex on her without being charged with rape, the rationale being that he could not "steal" what he already "owned." Gradually, states' laws have changed to limit this protection. If not omitted altogether, many states now protect women who are legally separated or not currently living with their spouse.

Those who have opposed the enactment of marital rape laws maintain that such laws may spark an onslaught of fabricated charges. As with sexual assault between persons not married to one another, the faulty assumption underlying this argument is that women, by and large, might use rape charges for revenge. In states that have marital rape laws, however, there has not been a flood of cases. Wives themselves have difficulty defining their husbands' sexual assaults as rape, and in those cases that have been successfully prosecuted, the husbands typically have had a history of violent and abusive behavior. It is still extremely difficult for women to be taken seriously by law enforcement in marital rape cases; consequently, prosecution of and convictions in such cases are rare, even with marital rape laws. Even more rare is the recognition of the sexual and physical violence that occurs in lesbian and gay male relationships, of which there is increasing evidence.

Importantly, recent research indicates that marital rape has a more traumatic effect on victims than rape between strangers. This is because marital rape victims not only experience "rape trauma syndrome" but are also more vulnerable than victims raped by strangers. Their assailant is someone they've intimately trusted and with whom they live; often, they are subjected to multiple rapes. Yet in some states, marital rape victims receive no legal protection or recourse. Instead, the laws protect abusive husbands from prosecution. It is likely, therefore, that until the laws are changed, marital rape will continue to be a common form of sexual assault. By 1996, seventeen states and Washington, D.C., had abolished the marital rape exemption altogether, and by 1999, all fifty states had added statutes to address the issue. *(See also: Acquaintance/Date Rape; Common Law; Family Violence; Marriage; Rape/Sexual Assault)*

—Claire M. Renzetti
—Susan C. Turell

Further Reading

Bergen, Raquel Kennedy. *Wife Rape: Understanding the Response of Survivors and Service Providers.* Thousand Oaks, CA: Sage, 1996.

Finkelhor, David, and Kristi Yllö. *License to Rape: Sexual Abuse of Wives.* New York: Holt, Rinehart & Winston, 1985.

Goldberg-Ambrose, C. "Unfinished Business in Rape Law Reform," *Journal of Social Issues* 48 (1992): 173-86.

Jasinski, S., and L. Williams, eds. *Partner Violence: A Comprehensive Review of Twenty Years of Research.* Thousand Oaks, CA: Sage, 1998.

Russell, Diana E. H. *Rape in Marriage.* New York: Collier, 1982.

Ryan, R. "The Sex Right: A Legal History of the Marital Rape Exemption," *Law and Social Inquiry* 20 (1996): 941-99.

⚓ Marriage

In his *Commentaries on the Laws of England* (1765), William Blackstone, the most popular theoretician of English common law, explained the legal consequences of marriage. In principle, a man and woman entered marriage on an equal basis, based on their mutual consent, as in any other civil contract. Once married, however, the status of marriage carried its own legal consequences: "By marriage, the husband and wife are one person in law; that is, the very being or legal existence of the woman is suspended during the marriage." This legal fiction of marital unity, and the married woman's condition of coverture during marriage, shaped the legal rights of American married women from the colonial period, and its influence persisted through the twentieth century.

This unity of person meant that in common law the husband could not grant anything to his wife during the marriage or enter into an agreement with her, "for the grant would presuppose her separate existence." To enter an agreement with her would be only to agree with himself. A wife, however, could represent her husband as an agent, because that did not imply a separation of herself from him. The husband was bound to supply "necessaries" to his wife. If he failed to do so, the wife could buy them on credit, and if they were truly necessities, the husband would be responsible for the debt. The wife could not sue or be sued in her own name; the husband had to be joined to the suit. Except where a criminal offense was directed against the person of the wife herself, husband and wife were not allowed to testify for or against each other because of the fiction of marital unity.

After marriage, the husband controlled all of his wife's personal property and also had extensive powers over her real property. The law, however, assumed that a woman was under the compulsion of her husband and did not allow him to convey her real property without her consent. At her death, the wife's real property returned to her parents' family, unless there was a child. In that case, the husband became a "tenant by the curtesy"; that is, he owned an interest in his wife's estate for his lifetime. The most important property right of women under common law was dower, a share of the real property owned by husbands during marriage that was designated for the support of widows. A husband could not sell or mortgage his property and deny his wife her dower interest without her agreement to the transaction.

Variations among the colonies, and then the states, and differences between social classes and between free and nonfree people complicated this simplified picture. There were no legal consequences of marriage for slave women, because American law, except briefly in Louisiana, did not recognize the validity of slave marriages. The rules developed for property were of little relevance to poor women.

Regional differences in laws affecting women's property rights characterized the late-colonial and early-national periods. For example, in states such as New York and South Carolina, there were separate courts of chancery, which developed a body of law allowing married women, *feme coverts,* to own separate property. In Connecticut and Massachusetts, however, where there were no separate equity courts and the Puritan view of the family influenced jurists, courts were very slow to recognize women's separate estates. Regional differences were reflected as well in (a) treatment of the procedures for conveyances by married women; (b) the development of the *feme sole* trader laws, which gave some married women the right to conduct their own businesses as if they were single; (c) changes to the dower and inheritance provisions affecting widows; and (d) the law of divorce. Despite regional variations and some setbacks, there was a steady development toward increased legal autonomy for women in the early national period.

The Married Women's Property Acts of the mid-nineteenth century continued this development of increased legal autonomy in the ownership and control of property. Twenty-nine states had passed some form of married women's property law by 1865. These acts often owed their existence to influences other than the organized woman's rights movement that developed after 1848. The most radical of these statutes, New York's Earnings Act of 1860, initially also equalized the intestate succession rights of husbands and wives and their rights to be guardian of any children of the marriage. The legislature, however, soon diluted these bold measures.

In the late twentieth century, some of the Blackstonian principles of marital unity lingered despite the political emancipation of women in 1920 and the passage of a number of state equal rights amendments more recently. For example, interspousal tort immunities, which prohibit one spouse from suing another for an injury, and the marital exception from rape laws both reflect the Blackstonian unity. Although the trend is clearly to reject these legal doctrines, they are by no means defunct everywhere. On the other hand, many states have enacted the Uniform Premarital Agreement Act, which permits husbands and wives to determine many of the consequences of the legal status of marriage through their own agreement or contract. This increased legal autonomy does not represent a clear-cut gain for women. An agreement, made before marriage but enforced years later, to waive some of the protections that the law provides can be devastating to women who still suffer economic and social disadvantages and who more often than not have primary responsibility for children. Despite significant changes, however, marriage still retains its character as a legal status rather than an ordinary civil contract.

The legal changes in the meaning of marriage have been accompanied by profound social and demographic changes. Whereas according to data from the U.S. Bureau of the Census in 1970, 40 percent of households consisted of married couples with their own children under the age of eighteen, during the next two decades the percentage of nuclear families declined: to 31 percent by 1980 and 26 percent by 1990. By 1993, the overwhelming majority (75 percent) of these nuclear families were dual-earner households. Even so, married women continued to perform a disproportionate share of the household work.

As the meaning of marriage changed within the institution, same-sex couples challenged their exclusion from the benefits and obligations of marriage. The Hawaii Supreme Court ruled in 1993 that limiting marriage to a man and a woman was presumptively unconstitutional under the state's own equal rights amendment. Subsequently, in 1996, Congress enacted the Defense of Marriage Act (DOMA) designed to undermine the impact of any final ruling in Hawaii. The DOMA statute denies federal benefits to same-sex marriages and permits other states to refuse to recognize a same-sex marriage that is lawful in another state. Many states passed laws expressly prohibiting same-sex marriage. In Hawaii and other states, judicial moves toward recognizing same-sex marriage were countered with referenda designed to change state constitutions to avert that result. The recognition of same-sex marriage in even one state, however, necessarily must change even further the meaning of marriage, premised as it always has been on the law of husband and wife. *(See also: Coverture; Divorce; Dower; Equity Courts; Feme Covert; Feme Sol; Married Women's Property Acts)*

—Laura Oren

Further Reading

Basch, Norma. *In the Eyes of the Law: Women, Marriage, and Property in Nineteenth-Century New York.* Ithaca, NY: Cornell University Press, 1982.

Blackstone, William. *Commentaries on the Laws of England, Book I. A Facsimile of the First Edition of 1765–1769.* Introduction by Stanley N. Katz. Chicago: University of Chicago Press, 1979.

Burnham, Margaret. "An Impossible Marriage: Slave Law and Family Law," *Law and Inequality* 5 (July 1978): 187-225.

Eskridge, William N., Jr. "A History of Same-Sex Marriage," *Virginia Law Review* 79 (October 1993): 1419-1513.

Kurz, Demie. *For Richer, For Poorer: Women Confront Divorce.* New York: Routledge, 1995.

Narrett, David E. *Inheritance and Family Life in Colonial New York.* Ithaca, NY: Cornell University Press, 1992.

Reeve, Tapping. *The Law of Baron and Femme, of Parent and Child, Guardian and Ward, Master and Servant, and of the Powers of Courts of Chancery; with an essay on the Terms Heir, Heirs, and Heirs of the Body,* 2d ed. Burlington, VT: Chauncey Goodrich, 1846.

Salmon, Marylynn. *Women and the Law of Property in Early America.* Chapel Hill: University of North Carolina Press, 1986.

❧ Marriage Education Movement

The marriage education movement, which flourished on American college and university campuses from the 1930s through the mid-1960s, attempted to provide American youths with a "practical" education in courtship, marriage, and family life in order to produce more "wholesome" and functional patterns of behavior. The social scientists who were scholars and educators in the field of family life worried that parents could no longer be adequate sources of information and authority for their children. Hoping to establish a new source of authority in keeping with the modern age, marriage educators sought to bring youth's experience in courtship and marriage under the authority of experts who could provide youths with answers and models of appropriate behavior based solidly on scientific research.

By the late 1950s, approximately twelve hundred U.S. colleges and universities—of the full range of academic statuses—offered "self-help" marriage courses. Approving articles describing the content and expected results of marriage courses ran in magazines and newspapers, including *Mademoiselle, Woman's Home Companion,* and the *New York Times.* The scholar-educators who taught marriage courses and wrote marriage texts frequently doubled as columnists for such magazines, thus reaching a large audience with their advice.

While the marriage education movement was a sincere attempt to address the problems of educating youth in modern society, it had, in retrospect, many faults. "Scientific" conclusions were usually derived from studies of middle-class college students, and descriptive data were translated into prescriptive norms. "Normal" behavior was advocated as correct, thus reinforcing a status quo in which women's roles were highly restricted. The movement's reliance on experts denied the legitimacy of individual experience. And finally, the movement as a whole was extremely concerned with buttressing what individual scholars defined as the "timeless" and "traditional" differences between the sexes. While only a very small percentage of Americans ever took a marriage course, the movement's emphasis on expert planning and scientifically determined facts had an important impact on social policy and on the way Americans thought about courtship and relations between the sexes. *(See also: Gender Role Socialization; Higher Education; Magazines; Marriage)*

—Beth L. Bailey

Further Reading

Bailey, Beth L. "Scientific Truth . . . and Love: The Marriage Education Movement in the United States," *Journal of Social History* 20 (Summer 1987): 711-32.

❧ Marriage Manuals

Marriage manuals, which have traditionally offered advice to heterosexual couples contemplating or embarking on marriage, have long served as a major source of popular information about sex. A form of prescriptive literature, marriage manuals mirror dominant ideas about gender and sexuality in their recommendations to the young.

Seventeenth- and eighteenth-century manuals such as the British *Aristotle's Masterpiece* emphasized the connection between sexual pleasure and procreation. Nineteenth-century manuals, which instead highlighted information about health, physiology, and hygiene, also featured advice on the proper running of a household and prescribed specific roles for husband and wife. In the twentieth century, marriage manuals increasingly identified sex as the central concern of marriage, with many including discussions of sexual positions, orgasm, and even birth control, as well as advice on making marriage harmonious. Theodore H. Van de Velde's *Ideal Marriage: Its Physiology and Technique* (1926) exemplified the modern marriage manual in its prescription of companionate marriage and advocacy of foreplay and simultaneous orgasm. Manuals increasingly counseled couples to concentrate on women's sexual satisfaction, and by mid-century, a wide range of guides by authors including Frank Caprio and Abraham and Hannah Stone were extremely popular. In the 1960s, sex manuals such as *The Joy of Sex* offered tips on sexual variations and often embraced a philosophy of sexual liberalism and divorced sex from marriage. Today, sexual advice literature and guides to marriage and relationships reflect a wide range of different viewpoints: Specific audiences targeted include women, teens, fundamentalists, and gays and lesbians.

Marriage manuals have always offered information on an era's views of sex and marriage. As with all prescriptive literature, it is difficult to guess how people read and used the suggestions of marriage manuals. In general, such works identified sex with a heterosexual couple, saw female sexuality as more problematic than male sexuality, and depicted sexuality both as a "natural" behavior and as a realm of ignorance about which readers needed to be educated. *(See also: Female Sexuality; Marriage; Prescriptive Literature; Sexual Revolution)*

—**Miriam Reumann**

Further Reading

Altman, Meryl. "Everything They Always Wanted You to Know: The Ideology of Popular Sex Literature." In *Pleasure and Danger,* edited by Carole Vance, 115-30. New York: Routledge, 1984.

D'Emilio, John, and Estelle Freedman. *Intimate Matters: A History of Sexuality in America,* 2d ed. Chicago: University of Chicago Press, 1997.

Gordon, Michael. "From Unfortunate Necessity to a Cult of Mutual Orgasm: Sex in American Marital Education Literature, 1830–1940." In *The Sociology of Sex,* edited by James M. Henslin and Edward Sagarin, 53-77. New York: Schocken, 1978.

Irvine, Janice. *Disorders of Desire: Sex and Gender in Modern American Sexology.* Philadelphia: Temple University Press, 1990.

∾ Married Women's Property Acts

The common law traditions derived from English practice made a husband and wife economically inseparable. A woman's property became that of her husband, and her earnings were his as well. The harsh realities implied by these traditions were softened by the concept of equity as practiced in England and as widely applied in the British North American colonies. Because of the concept of equity, prenuptial agreements were upheld in colonial courts. Few colonial women seemed to have taken advantage of such agreements, and those that were used were developed out of the need for insurance on a woman's income in the event of the death of a spouse rather than out of a sense of a woman's independence with regard to her property. Prenuptial agreements were more commonplace among widows who remarried than among women marrying for the first time.

Gradually, states ratified these equity developments. Massachusetts allowed women deserted by their husbands to sell property under legislation of 1787; Maine extended the concept to allow women to control property after desertion. In the 1830s, several states debated statutes that would have confirmed the property rights of women. The New York legislature considered such a statute in 1836. The first state to pass married women's property legislation was Mississippi in 1839. The law was ambiguously worded and designed to protect the rights of women to sell or dispose of slaves that they had brought to the marriage. Michigan, New York, and Pennsylvania passed married women's property

legislation in the 1840s, and in the 1850s, several other states enacted parallel statutes.

Notwithstanding the growing advocacy for women's rights in the mid-nineteenth century, these laws developed from different motives—namely, the desire to protect a family's inheritance. Fathers did not want irresponsible sons-in-law disposing of property that came as part of the marriage. The laws, in effect, ratified long-standing equity decisions and extended those decisions to those who previously could not afford to take or did not take advantage of prenuptial agreements. Even with this motivation, the laws had the effect of separating married men and women under the law. That trend would prove irreversible and open the legal door for further development of independent women's rights in the latter nineteenth century. *(See also: Antenuptial Agreements; Marriage)*

—**Thomas F. Armstrong**

Further Reading

Basch, Norma. *In the Eyes of the Law: Women, Marriage and Property in Nineteenth Century New York.* Ithaca, NY: Cornell University Press, 1982.

Norton, Mary Beth. *Liberty's Daughters: The Revolutionary Experience of American Women, 1750–1800.* Ithaca, NY: Cornell University Press, 1996.

Salmon, Marylynn. "Republican Sentiment, Economic Change and the Property Rights of Women in American Law." In *Women in the Age of the American Revolution,* edited by Ronald Hoffman and Peter J. Albert, 447-75. Charlottesville, VA: U.S. Capitol Historical Society/University Press of Virginia, 1989.

———. *Women and the Law of Property in Early America.* Chapel Hill: University of North Carolina Press, 1986.

∾ Martinez, Maria Montoya
(c. 1881–1980)

If the United States honored its artists and craftspeople as does Japan, Maria Martinez would have been declared a "national treasure."

Along with her husband, Julian, she reconstructed pots similar in design and form to the ancient shards excavated by Dr. Edward Hewitt from the plateau at Pajarito near the San Ildefonso pueblo in the Rio Grande Valley of New Mexico. In performing this task, Martinez, a Pueblo Indian, worked with reverence and sensitivity in recreating the work of her ancestors. She hand-turned the classic pottery shapes on a disk made from a gourd, skillfully copying and then adapting the ancient shapes. She then polished the surfaces with a smooth round river stone. With the encouragement of Dr. Hewitt of the Museum of New Mexico's Anthropology and Archaeology Department, the Martinezes developed a way of painting decorations in dull, velvety black on the polished pottery before firing. Using this technique, Julian painted elegant designs based on old Indian motifs, which he often modified with his own artistry. To achieve the black color, Maria then stacked the pieces in the kiln, surrounded them

Figure 38. Maria Martinez

Maria Martinez, shown here with her husband, Julian, is recognized as one of the world's great potters. Used by permission of UPI/Corbis-Bettmann.

with dried cow manure, and fired them until all the carbon was reduced. They emerged with the familiar silvery black sheen.

After her husband's death, Martinez continued to work with her sons, Popovi Da and Adam, and her daughter-in-law, Santana; she also enlarged the pottery community at San Ildefonso by teaching the craft to relatives and other residents. After her own death in her late nineties, her work was continued by her great-granddaughter, Barbara Gonzales, as well as by Santana, Blue Corn, and others of the extended village family.

During her long career, Martinez was an honored figure, not only in her own pueblo but throughout the art world. She was awarded honorary doctorates by the University of New Mexico and the University of Colorado, which recognized her as one of the world's great potters. Such masters as Bernard Leach and Shoji Hamada came to San Ildefonso to work with and receive inspiration from her. She demonstrated her pottery at almost every important world's fair since 1904. As a further tribute, she was asked to lay the cornerstone in Rockefeller Center in New York.

For all her worldly acclaim, she most enjoyed her own native village community, where she shared the life of her people. *(See also: Art; Native American Women)*

—**Evelyn G. Katz**

Further Reading

Chapman, Kenneth M. *The Pottery of San Ildefonso Pueblo.* Albuquerque: University of New Mexico Press, 1970.

Hyde, Hazel. *Maria Making Pottery.* Santa Fe: Sunstone, 1973.

Kreischer, Elsie Karr. *Maria Montoya Martinez, Master Potter.* Gretna, LA: Pelican, 1995.

Marriott, Alice. *Maria: Potter of San Ildefonso.* Norman: University of Oklahoma Press, 1948.

Peterson, Susan (Susan Harnly). *The Living Tradition of Maria Martinez.* Tokyo: Kodansha International, 1989.

⌘ Mary Baldwin School

Long known as the Augusta Female Seminary, the Mary Baldwin School was one of the most famous of the many early-nineteenth-century schools for girls. Located in Staunton, Virginia, it dates from 1842, when the Reverend Rufus W. Bailey came to the community seeking a location for a girls' school. Bailey gained support of the local Presbyterian congregation, and he suggested establishing a high-grade seminary there. In August 1842, Bailey prepared a "Plan or Constitution of the Augusta Female Seminary," which identified the objective of the school as providing a "thorough literary and Christian education to the female youths of this portion of our country." The community backed the project, and the school opened in the fall of 1842 with Bailey serving as the principal. Within two years, the school had enrolled fifty-seven pupils and was a success, but in 1848, Bailey resigned his position, and several other principals followed in rapid succession.

Mary Baldwin took over in 1863 during the Civil War. Baldwin had grown up in Staunton and had long been interested in education. Earlier, she had opened a charity school there, providing free education to the needy. As the new principal, Baldwin took over at a difficult time. The school remained open throughout the war, with eighty pupils enrolled by 1863. By the end of the decade, the number had risen to 137 and continued to rise as pupils came from throughout the South. The success of Baldwin in building the size and reputation of the school led the trustees to change its name in December 1895 to Mary Baldwin Seminary in recognition of "the valuable services and unparalleled success of the Principal." After her death on July 1, 1897, the school received the bulk of her estate, which provided a sizable endowment for the institution.

By 1899, the school had enrolled two hundred pupils and was growing steadily. The seminary's name was changed to Mary Baldwin Junior College in 1916, and it became a four-year college in 1923. The name was then changed to Mary Baldwin College, and today it is the nation's oldest Presbyterian women's college. *(See also: Education; Female Academies)*

—**Robert G. Waite**

Further Reading

Waddell, Joseph A. *History of Mary Baldwin Seminary.* Staunton, VA: Augusta Printing Company, 1905.

Watters, Mary. *The History of the Mary Baldwin College, 1842–1942.* Staunton, VA: Mary Baldwin College, 1942.

Woody, Thomas. *A History of Women's Education in the United States.* Vol. 1. New York: Science Press, 1929.

⌘ Mass Communication Media

The mass media have been the object of feminist criticism since the nineteenth century, when women founded dozens of their own newspapers in response to the news coverage by mass circulation newspapers. The current phase of the U.S. women's movement could be said to have been spurred into being in the early 1960s by the content of the news and entertainment media. Betty Friedan's *The Feminine Mystique,* published in 1963, and the National Organization for Women (NOW), founded in 1966, exposed the myth advanced by the mass media that women were content with their home, family, and work lives.

Women's representation in advertising and entertainment content and their invisibility in news content, along with their underrepresentation and exploitation in employment within media industries, have been areas of primary concern to feminist activists and scholars. Dominant forms of media have generally excluded alternate stories and explanations by and about women and have undoubtedly had a hand in shaping the direction of the women's movement itself and the perception of it by the public. Feminist scholars have countered this representation by uncovering women's long, neglected history as publishers, filmmakers, writers, and speakers of their own forms of communication, clearly significant to the success of women's reform efforts at various times in history.

Feminist communication theory has passed through several phases of understanding women's relationship to the mass media. Questions about representation have grown more complex from the earliest concerns about "images," which assumed that without significant changes in media structure women could be presented more realistically, an optimism that has not been borne out. Also, scholars turned their attention to women's reception of media content, discovering that women have complex interpretations of media texts and their own involvement with women's genres, such as romance novels and soap operas.

Feminist communication scholars view new communication technologies with both caution and optimism. With the potential for providing more sources of information and more opportunities to speak, computer technology could break the mass media's monopolistic hold on public information and entertainment. On the other hand, evidence being gathered suggests that women are finding inequities in access, training, and treatment on-line, repeating patterns found in earlier forms of media. *(See also: Friedan, Betty; Magazines; National Organization for Women; Popular Culture; Soap Operas)*

—**Lana F. Rakow**

Further Reading

Creedon, Pamela J., ed. *Women in Mass Communication,* 2d ed. Newbury Park, CA: Sage, 1993.

Dines, Gail, and Jean M. Humez, eds. *Gender, Race and Class in Media.* Thousand Oaks, CA: Sage, 1995.

Taylor, H. Jeanie, Cheris Kramarae, and Maureen Ebben, eds. *Women, Information Technology, and Scholarship.* Urbana, IL: Center for Advanced Study, 1993.

van Zoonen, Liesbet. *Feminist Media Studies.* London: Sage, 1994.

❧ Masturbation

Masturbation, or sexual self-stimulation, is most commonly practiced by touching the genitals but can include the use of objects, fantasy, or other methods. Taboo in many Western religious traditions, masturbation is one of the most commonly practiced and the most policed sexual activities.

Early prohibitions against masturbation applied primarily to men, since the practice was seen as inhibiting procreation. By the eighteenth century, arguments against masturbation focused as much on its alleged emotional and physical damage as on moral transgression. Medical literature often warned that masturbation depleted energy and could lead to physical ruin and insanity. Antimasturbation hysteria peaked in the nineteenth century, when all manner of medical practitioners, from orthodox physicians to health curists and sectarians, advocated the use of mechanical restraints, medications, and even surgery to prevent or cure "self-abuse." Authorities identified the habitual masturbator as a weak man or a dangerously excitable woman. Such warnings pathologized masturbating women but also recognized them as sexual subjects.

American sex surveys have consistently revealed that virtually all women masturbate. Kinsey (1953) observed that masturbation was the most reliable route to orgasm for women, as did Masters and Johnson (1966). The resurgent feminist movement of the 1960s and 1970s rediscovered masturbation, with some feminists advocating it as the only sexual outlet women needed, to reduce dependence on men. Other feminists held workshops on masturbation techniques. Today, feminist health activists continue to recommend masturbation as a way for women to explore their sexuality and attain sexual self-sufficiency, a view seconded by many sex therapists. *(See also: Female Sexuality; Kinsey Report; Orgasm, Female)*

—**Miriam Reumann**
—**William G. Shade**

Further Reading

D'Emilio, John, and Estelle B. Freedman. *Intimate Matters: A History of Sexuality in America,* 2d ed. Chicago: University of Chicago Press, 1997.

Englehardt, H. Tristram, Jr. "The Disease of Masturbation: Values and the Concept of Disease." In *Sickness and Health in America: Readings in the History of Medicine and Public Health,* edited by Judith W. Leavitt and Ronald Numbers, 15-23. Madison: University of Wisconsin Press, 1978.

Koedt, Anne. "The Myth of the Vaginal Orgasm," In *Radical Feminism,* edited by Anne Koedt et al., 198-207. New York: Quadrangle, 1973.

❧ Mathematics

Women in mathematics have faced unusually strong barriers to achievement but have, nevertheless, made outstanding contributions to the field. For a long time, many

American universities would not admit women to their graduate programs. Princeton, for example, did not admit women to its graduate math program until the late 1960s. Winifred Edgerton was the first American woman to receive a Ph.D. in mathematics when she graduated from Columbia University in 1886. Only 230 American women received Ph.D.s in mathematics prior to 1940. Women with doctorates in mathematics often had a difficult time finding employment, especially at top-ranked research universities. In 1970, not a single woman had tenure at any of the top five math departments.

The life and career of Christine Ladd-Franklin (1847–1930) illustrates some of the problems faced by women in mathematics. Ladd-Franklin was an 1869 graduate of Vassar, who went on to four years of graduate study at Johns Hopkins University. She completed her doctoral dissertation in mathematics in 1882 and had the dissertation published to scholarly acclaim. However, the university refused to grant doctorates to women, so Ladd-Franklin left Johns Hopkins without receiving her Ph.D. She married, had two children, and continued to work in the field of symbolic logic. In 1887, Ladd-Franklin published the first of many papers in the field of physiological optics, a subject she devoted the next thirty-seven years of her life to, along with a developing interest in psychology. She also taught logic and psychology at Johns Hopkins and Columbia. Her interests extended to the status of women in society generally, and she wrote a number of pieces for newspapers and magazines on women's issues. Finally, in 1925, Johns Hopkins granted her the Ph.D. in mathematics that she had earned forty-four years earlier.

Despite the obstacles faced by Christine Ladd-Franklin and other women mathematicians, more women are choosing mathematics as a career. Women composed 43 percent of undergraduate mathematics majors and 27 percent of mathematics doctorates, a record high, in 1993. Unfortunately, this pattern of a significant drop in women from undergraduate to graduate studies continues into the job market. Women make up only 13 percent of doctoral mathematics faculty, 10 percent of tenured doctoral mathematics faculty, and less than 5 percent of tenured faculty at the most prestigious mathematics departments.

To encourage the entry of women into mathematical fields and to promote the equal treatment of women in the mathematical community, the Association for Women in Mathematics (AWM) was founded in 1971. The association has established a speakers' bureau of women available for presentations to audiences ranging from high school students to research mathematicians, offers a variety of publications on careers for women in mathematics, and maintains a Website that includes biographies of women mathematicians (http://www.awm-math.org). The North Central Regional Educational Laboratory, in cooperation with the Regional Educational Laboratory network, also maintains a Website with contact information on organizations addressing equity and education in mathematics (http://www.ncrel.org).

Still, a disproportionate number of girls and women leave school without the mathematical skills they need in today's world. To address this issue, the National Council of Teachers of Mathematics (NCTM) established a task force to promote equity and excellence in mathematics for students. In its 1989 publication, *Curriculum and Evaluation Standards for School Mathematics,* the NCTM charged the Commission of Standards for School Mathematics to create a coherent definition of what it means to be mathematically literate and to develop a set of standards by which to implement and evaluate programs aimed at mathematics education reform. Portions of the Goals 2000: Educate America Act (1994, P.L. 103-227, 108 Stat. 125) also called for reform in mathematics education that would enable all students to master a significant core of mathematics. A number of regional and national consortia and clearinghouses are active today in fostering programs that will provide equal access for all students to meaningful mathematics learning and achievement. *(See also: Association for Women in Mathematics; Noether, Emmy; Robinson, Julia Bowman; Science)*

—**Jonell Duda Comerford**
—**Jonathan W. Zophy**

Further Reading

Cuevas, G., and M. Driscoll, eds. *Reaching All Students with Mathematics.* Reston, VA: National Council of Teachers of Mathematics, 1993.

Fulton, John D. "1993 Annual AMS-IMS-MAA Survey," *Notices of the American Mathematical Society* 41, no. 6 (July/August 1994): 598-606.

Green, Judy, and Jeanne La Duke. "Women in the American Mathematics Community: The Pre-1940s Ph.D.'s," *The Mathematical Intelligencer* 9 (1987): 11-21.

Grindstein, Louise, and Paul Campbell, eds. *Women of Mathematics: A Biobibliographic Sourcebook.* Westport, CT: Greenwood, 1987.

National Council for Teachers of Mathematics. *Curriculum and Evaluation Standards for School Mathematics.* Reston, VA: National Council for Teachers of Mathematics, 1989.

Perl, Teri. *Math Equals: Biographies of Women Mathematicians.* Menlo Park, CA: Addison-Wesley, 1978.

❧ Matriarchy

Matriarchy is a hypothetical cultural form in which gender dominance is constructed in such a way that women maintain a greater control over the distribution and use of culturally sanctioned power than do men. To date, no true matriarchies have yet been conclusively documented in historical or contemporary cultures, although in some societies, such as the matrilineal Iroquois, in which women exercised a considerable degree of leadership as mothers, approximately equal quantities of power existed between the genders.

Recently, poor African American families, which are often female-headed, have been depicted as a matriarchal system. Theorists who assert that these families are matriarchies also often imply that this familial structure contributes to these families' lack of resources among urban blacks in the United States. More critical analysis of this phenomenon reveals that these "matriarchies" (more properly, "female-headed households" or "female-headed kin networks") can actually help the urban poor survive but that men still have a greater amount of power (i.e., white males remain in control of economic resources within the greater society).

During the nineteenth century, several theorists argued that human cultures evolved from a period of primitive anarchy in which women ruled but that, over time, this authority was transferred to men, either by women voluntarily giving up their power or by men taking power away from them. Most notable amongst these theorists were J. J. Bachofen, whose *Das Mutterrecht/Mother Law* was first published in 1861, and Lewis Henry Morgan, whose *Ancient Society* was published in 1877. Since then, most anthropologists have dismissed these theories.

Myths of matriarchy have often been used to validate male dominance by claiming that men were forced to take control away from women for various reasons. These myths come in at least two forms: (a) one in which women are presented as inept bunglers and (b) another in which women are presented as dangerous creatures who use their evil sorceries to destroy men. In the first myth, women's bungling in their control of society endangered the survival of the community as a whole; thus, men were forced into taking power away from women to save the community.

The second myth of matriarchy holds that women were originally in control but that they misused their powers, both secular and magical, to dominate men ruthlessly. Men, to protect themselves, were "forced" to wrest power from women to save themselves. Tales of such mythic battles of the sexes can be found in many cultures, including those of certain South American Indians, the aboriginal peoples of Australia, and in the various myths of Amazon warriors. *(See also: Female-headed Households; Matriliny; Sex-Gender System)*

—Steven Mandeville-Gamble

Further Reading
Bachofen, J. J. *Das Mutterrecht*. Stuttgart, Germany: Krais & Hoffman, 1861.
Stack, Carol B. *All Our Kin*. New York: Harper, 1970.
Tiffany, Sharon W., and Kathleen J. Adams. *The Wild Woman: An Inquiry into the Anthropology of an Idea*. Cambridge, MA: Schenkman, 1985.

∞ Matriliny

Matriliny refers to descent systems in which descent is traced through the mother. In matrilineal societies, children inherit their wealth, prestige, clan, or lineage membership from their mother's kin group, although in most of these societies, the mother's brother (i.e., the maternal uncle) controls these resources. Thus, in most matrilineal societies, the maternal uncle proves to be one of the most important figures in the life of the individual, for he is the person from whom an individual will receive her or his status and wealth. Characteristically, women in matrilineal cultures have more economic and political power, and the men in these kinship systems display less aggressive behavior. Matrilineality should not be confused with matriarchy; in matrilineal societies, men often still control a greater amount of culturally recognized power than do women.

Many of the North American tribes, including the Cherokee, Chickasaw, Choctaw, Creek, Crow, Delaware, Hopi, Iroquois, Laguna, Mandan, Minnitaree, Missouri, Mohican, Natchez, Navajo, Otoe, Tlingit, Wyandote, Yuchi, and most of the sub-Arctic Indian cultures, were matrilineal before contact with Western society. Many of these cultures, however, have lost their characteristic descent patterns as a result of the interference of U.S. inheritance laws, which undercut the matrilineal basis of their society. By mandating that property rights go to a man's children after his death, instead of to his sister's children, U.S. government policy has erected a barrier to conservation of original cultural patterns. *(See also: Matriarchy; Native American Women; Sex-Gender System)*

—Steven Mandeville-Gamble

Further Reading
Eggan, Fred. "Historical Changes in the Choctaw Kinship System." In *Essays in Anthropology*, edited by Fred Eggan, 71-90. Chicago: University of Chicago Press, 1975.
Lévi-Strauss, Claude. *Elementary Structures of Kinship*. Edited by R. Needham; translated by James Harle Bell and John Richard von Sturmer. Boston: Beacon, 1969.
Morgan, Lewis Henry. *Ancient Society*. New York: Holt, 1877. Reprint, Tucson: University of Arizona Press, 1985.
Schneider, David Murray, and Kathleen Gough. *Matrilineal Kinship*. Berkeley: University of California Press, 1961.

∞ McCarthy, Mary (1912–1989)

Novelist, essayist, critic, and journalist, Mary McCarthy was raised in Minneapolis. After graduating from Vassar College, she began publishing fiction. Her first success was *The Company She Keeps* (1942), a collection of satiric stories. McCarthy's widely acclaimed novels include *The Groves of Academe* (1952), *A Charmed Life* (1955), and *Cannibals and Missionaries* (1979). Her novel *The Group* (1963), which probed the lives of well-educated, middle-class women, was made into a successful feature film. She has also written fine travel books such as *Venice Observed* (1956) and *The Stones of Florence* (1959) and astute essays on the Vietnam War and the so-called Watergate affair. *(See also: Hellman, Lillian; Vietnam War; Women Writers)*

—Jonathan W. Zophy

Further Reading
Brightman, Carol, ed. *Between Friends: The Correspondence of Hannah Arendt and Mary McCarthy, 1949–1975*. New York: Harcourt Brace, 1995.

Gelderman, Carol. *Mary McCarthy: A Life.* New York: St. Martin's, 1988.

McCarthy, Mary. *Memories of a Catholic Girlhood.* New York: Harcourt Brace, 1957.

———. *The Seventeenth Degree.* New York: Harcourt Brace, 1974.

McCullers, Carson (1917–1967)

Author Carson McCullers was born Lula Carson Smith in Columbus, Georgia, the oldest of three children. When she was thirteen, McCullers dropped "Lula" from her name. Her mother, Marguerite, encouraged her to study the piano, believing that McCullers was destined to become a musical genius. An attack of rheumatic fever at fifteen, however, forced McCullers to abandon the study of music. At the age of seventeen, she moved to New York City to study writing at Columbia University. In 1936, she again contracted rheumatic fever and was forced to return to Columbus. Two short stories, "Wonderkind" and "Like That," were published that year in *Story.* She married Reeves McCullers in 1937.

In 1940, her first novel, *The Heart Is a Lonely Hunter,* was published, winning the young author literary acclaim. The book introduced the theme around which McCullers based all of her fiction—that of the individual's isolation and loneliness and inability to find redeeming love. She was also concerned with the issues of anti-Semitism, economic exploitation, racism, and sexism, but McCullers did not write overtly political novels. Her fascination with the presence of evil and her use of deformed and abnormal characters earned her a place in the southern Gothic school of literature.

The McCullerses moved to New York City where, in 1941, her novel *Reflections in a Golden Eye* was published. The book brought her fellowships from the Guggenheim Foundation, the Yaddo Colony, and the American Academy of Arts and Letters. The McCullers's already strained marriage ended in 1941 when Carson fell in love with Annmarie Clarac-Schwarzback, a Swiss writer.

In February 1942, McCullers suffered the first of many strokes. Excessive drinking contributed to the steady decline of her health throughout her life. In 1944, "The Ballad of the Sad Cafe" was included in *Best American Short Stories.* She and her former husband remarried in 1945. Her novel *The Member of the Wedding* was published in 1946, and McCullers won another Guggenheim. She had a second stroke in Paris in 1947, partially paralyzing the right side of her body. She had another stroke a few months later and was diagnosed as having a damaged rheumatic heart. In 1948, she and her husband separated again, and she attempted to commit suicide. Her dramatized version of *The Member of the Wedding* opened in 1949, starring Ethel Waters and Julie Harris. It received rave reviews and ran for fourteen and a half months on Broadway. She and her husband reunited that year, but in 1953, he killed himself. In 1961, McCullers published *Clock without Hands,* her last novel. She had a heart attack in 1959, after which her health rapidly declined. In 1962, her right breast was removed, and she died in 1967 from a final stroke.

John Huston directed the film version of *Reflections in a Golden Eye* in 1967. *The Mortgaged Heart* was published posthumously in 1971, and *The Member of the Wedding* was produced as a musical. In addition to novels, McCullers published many short stories, poems, and nonfiction articles. *(See also: Women Writers)*

—Victoria L. Shannon

Further Reading

Budick, Emily Miller. *Engendering Romance.* New Haven, CT: Yale University Press, 1994.

Carr, Virginia Spencer. *Lonely Hunter: A Biography of Carson McCullers.* New York: Doubleday, 1975.

Evans, Oliver. *The Ballad of Carson McCullers.* New York: Coward-McCann, 1966.

Rubin, Louis D., Jr. "Carson McCullers: The Aesthetics of Pain," *Virginia Quarterly Review* 53 (Spring 1977): 265-83.

McDowell, Mary Eliza (1854–1936)

Mary Eliza McDowell began her life of service as a teenager during the Chicago Fire of 1871 when she assisted her Methodist minister to feed and care for the survivors. The relief and aid society they founded at that time would become, 25 years later, the United Charities of Chicago.

McDowell attended kindergarten training school and in 1890 found a position teaching at Jane Addams's Hull House. In 1894, with Addams's recommendation, McDowell became head resident at the new University of Chicago Settlement "back of the yards." The square mile of stockyards and its surrounding neighborhood had the highest infant mortality rate and the worst health record in the city. Besides the stench and smoke of the slaughterhouses, it was within blocks of the city dump and of Bubbly Creek, a dead branch of the Chicago River that had become an open sewer. "Mary the Magnificent" spent the next thirty years working to solve these problems. As a member of the City Waste Commission, she finally saw the garbage dumps closed and covered in 1913; Bubbly Creek was eventually filled in and turned into a manufacturing district.

Believing in the union movement and especially in the rights of working women, she helped to found the National Women's Trade Union League in 1903 and served as the Chicago branch's president from 1904 to 1907. During the 1904 Stockyards strike, McDowell firmly supported the union while working to prevent violence on either side. The Chicago Race Riots of 1919 moved her to found the Interracial Cooperative Committee, encompassing eighty black and white women's clubs that sought racial justice and worked on civic and legislative projects while building racial understanding.

On the assumption that a thorough understanding of any problem was the first step toward its solution, McDowell accepted Mayor Dever's appointment as Commissioner of Public Welfare from 1923 to 1927, where she established a Bureau of Social Surveys that provided valuable information on housing, women's problems, and immigrants.

Before retiring from the settlement in 1929, McDowell had established clubs for women and youth, a kindergarten, a nursery, English and citizenship classes, a municipal bathhouse, a branch library, a playground, and manual training in the local school. After her death in 1936, both the settlement house, which survived until 1973, and Gross Avenue on which it was built were renamed for Mary McDowell. She had been an important part of every movement for progress and social justice for more than thirty years. *(See also: Addams, Jane; Black Women's Clubs; Hull House; National Women's Trade Union League; Settlement House Movement; Social Welfare; Social Work; Unions)*

—**Tamerin Mitchell Hayward**

Further Reading

Mary McDowell and the University of Chicago Settlement, 3 vols. Archives of the Chicago Historical Society.

Taylor, Lea D. "The Social Settlement and Civic Responsibilities— The Life Work of Mary McDowell and Graham Taylor," *Social Science Review* 28 (March 1954): 31-40.

Wilson, Howard E. *Mary McDowell, Neighbor.* Chicago: University of Chicago Press, 1928.

∾ McKinnon, Edna (Rankin)
(1893–1978)

Edna McKinnon was a pioneer birth control advocate. Born the seventh and last child of a prominent Montana family (her sister, Jeannette Rankin, was the first woman elected to the U.S. Congress), Edna Rankin grew up fearing that her parents had not wanted another child and that she was less significant than some of her older siblings. Driven to succeed, she attended Wellesley College and the University of Wisconsin before becoming the first Montana-born woman to graduate from the University of Montana's law school. She had little interest in the law, however, and never practiced it. Rather, after an unsuccessful marriage to Jack McKinnon, she embarked on a lifelong career of educating women and health care providers on the available means of birth control and the economic, psychological, and medical advantages of having only the number of children one wants and can raise without straining the family budget or damaging the mother's health.

Beginning in 1937, McKinnon worked in various parts of the United States as a paid employee of family planning organizations. After she "retired" at the age of sixty-five, however, she spent the next eight years traveling throughout Asia, the Middle East, and Africa—organizing family planning groups, lobbying government officials and medical personnel for support, and setting up family planning clinics. Her greatest achievement, she believed, was in convincing a few of the world's women who had previously known

little or nothing about birth control that they could plan the number and spacing of their children and, in the process, improve their quality of life while reducing suffering—their own and their children's. *(See also: Birth Control; Rankin, Jeannette Pickering)*

—**Roger D. Hardaway**

Further Reading

Dykeman, Wilma. *Too Many People, Too Little Love; Edna Rankin McKinnon: Pioneer for Birth Control.* New York: Holt, Rinehart & Winston, 1974.

∾ McPherson, Aimee Semple
(1890–1944)

Aimee Semple McPherson, evangelist and founder of the International Church of the Foursquare Gospel, was the daughter of a prosperous Canadian father and a devout mother. McPherson's mother, Mildred Kennedy, orphaned and raised in the family of a Salvation Army captain, dedicated her daughter to the service of God when she was only six weeks old. When she was seventeen, McPherson was converted at a Pentecostal revival, and a year later, she married the evangelist who had converted her, Robert James Semple.

She and her husband became traveling evangelists, and in 1909, she was ordained at a Pentecostal ceremony in Chicago. The next year, her husband felt called to preach in China, but he died in Hong Kong, a mere three months after his arrival in Asia. McPherson returned to the United States with her newly born daughter, Roberta, and began a series of missionary lectures while assisting her mother in New York City with Salvation Army work. In 1912, she married Harold Stewart McPherson, a bookkeeper; they had a son, Rolf, who later succeeded his mother as head of the church she founded.

After a long period of illness, McPherson was inspired to resume her career as an evangelist. In August 1915, she began conducting revival meetings in a Pentecostal mission in Mount Forest, Ontario, Canada. She demonstrated great skill in preaching, "speaking in tongues," and faith healing. She spent the next several years in tent revivals up and down the eastern seaboard. Her personal charm, religious zeal, and considerable abilities as a preacher and performer led to the expansion of her revival circuit to include cross-country tours to California and back. Indeed, wearing her preacher's "uniform" of a white dress, white shoes, and a flowing blue cape, McPherson preached her way across the country and back eight times between 1918 and 1923. She also made a preaching tour of Australia, attracting large and enthusiastic crowds wherever she went. During this period, she became the first female to preach a sermon on the radio.

Wanting a base for her operations, McPherson began the construction of the Angelus Temple near Echo Park in Los Angeles in April 1921. The temple became the headquarters of her new "Church of the Foursquare Gospel," which eventually became a separate Pentecostal denomination. From 1923 to 1926, she preached every night and three times on Sunday to large crowds of five thousand or more crowded into the Angelus Temple. McPherson also operated a free food and clothing commissary, a magazine, a radio station, a telephone counseling service, and a Bible college, housed next to the temple. Although she plowed most of the large sums of money she took in back into her ministry, McPherson bragged that she "ruled like a queen in my kingdom."

In May 1926, the evangelist disappeared while swimming at a beach near Los Angeles, only to reappear one month later in Mexico. She claimed to have been kidnapped, but her kidnappers were never found, and little evidence has ever been found to sustain her charges. Evidence that she had staged her kidnapping for publicity purposes or to escape temporarily from her frenetic ministry was insufficient for the courts to prosecute her for fraud. The international news attention helped stimulate the growth of her church, and in the late 1920s, McPherson took to the revival circuit across the United States with stops in Paris and the British Isles.

In 1930, she suffered a nervous breakdown that seriously damaged her health. Her troubles were compounded by a third marriage, which ended in divorce four years later, a break with her mother and daughter, and numerous lawsuits over her badly managed business affairs. Aimee Semple McPherson died of an overdose of sleeping pills in an Oakland hotel room in 1944. At the time of her death, the church had over four hundred branches in the United States and Canada, nearly two hundred missions abroad, and around 22,000 members. It has continued to grow since her death. Never a profound thinker, McPherson was rigidly conservative, sharing many of the ideas of the Ku Klux Klan, although not its racism. However, there has never been any question about the sincerity of her religious convictions. Novelist Sinclair Lewis denied that he used McPherson for the model for his famous evangelist, Sharon Falconer, in *Elmer Gantry. (See also: Christianity; Religion)*

—**Jonathan W. Zophy**

Further Reading

Bahr, Robert. *Least of All Saints: The Story of Aimee Semple McPherson.* Englewood Cliffs, NJ: Prentice Hall, 1979.

Blumhofer, Edith. *Aimee Semple McPherson: Everybody's Sister.* Grand Rapids, MI: Eerdmans, 1994.

McPherson, Aimee Semple. *In the Service of the King: The Story of My Life.* New York: Boni & Liveright, 1927.

———. *This Is That: Personal Experiences, Sermons, and Writings.* Los Angeles: Echo Park Evangelists Association, 1923.

Thomas, Lately. *Storming Heaven: The Lives and Turmoils of Minnie Kennedy and Aimee Semple McPherson.* New York: Morrow, 1970.

———. *The Vanishing Evangelist.* New York: Viking, 1959.

☙ Mead, Margaret (1901–1978)

One of the first American women to earn a Ph.D. in anthropology, Margaret Mead became a world-renowned anthropologist; her most famous works include *Coming of Age in Samoa* (1928) and *Sex and Temperament* (1935). With anthropologist Ruth Benedict, Mead helped establish culture and personality studies as an intellectual force in American anthropology; she was dedicated to showing that culture molded personalities and that many supposedly "innate" qualities in human beings, such as gender roles and the traumas of adolescence, were the result of cultural patterning, not biology.

Both of Mead's parents were academics; at the time of her birth in 1901, her father was a professor of economics at the University of Pennsylvania, Philadelphia, and her mother was working on a master's degree. Mead began college at DePauw University as an English major but decided to transfer to Barnard College in autumn of 1920 after being rejected by the sorority system at DePauw, which she later said was her only experience of rejection in her life.

During her senior year at Barnard, Mead attended a course in anthropology taught by Franz Boas, one of the founders of American anthropology. At that time she met Ruth Benedict, then Boas's teaching assistant, who invited her to continue her studies as a student of Boas. Mead agreed and began her graduate program at Columbia University under the tutelage of Boas.

In 1923, Mead married Luther Cressman, her first husband; they divorced in 1926 after Mead returned from her fieldwork in Samoa. In 1928, she married Reo Fortune, with whom she did fieldwork among the Manus (1928–1929); the Omaha (summer 1930); and three New Guinean cultures—the Arapesh, the Mundugumor, and the Tchambuli (1931–1933). During the last part of their collaborative field research, Mead and Fortune met Gregory Bateson, who was studying the Iatmul at that time in New Guinea. Mead and Bateson fell in love, and after she obtained a divorce from Fortune, she and Bateson married in 1935. Together, they did fieldwork in Bali (1936–1938, 1939) and among the Iatmul of New Guinea (1938). Eventually, Bateson felt that his marriage to Mead was stifling his own intellectual creativity, and he divorced her in 1943.

In 1926, after returning from her first field experience in Samoa, Mead was appointed assistant curator of ethnology for the American Museum of Natural History, a position she maintained between field trips. In 1942, Mead was made an associate curator of the Museum, and by 1969, she had been named curator emeritus.

Perhaps more than any other single anthropologist, Margaret Mead contributed to a popular understanding of anthropology and the concept of "culture," and made both household terms by the 1960s. Although her books were academic in nature, she wrote them with the American public firmly in mind. She applied her professional perspective to her own contemporary culture, and her scientific approach to discerning the origins of women's roles caused her to revise, by the 1960s, the conservative interpretation of those origins that she had voiced in the 1950s. *(See also: Higher Education)*

—**Steven Mandeville-Gamble**

Further Reading

Bateson, Mary Catherine. *With a Daughter's Eye.* New York: Washington Square, 1984.
Mead, Margaret. *Blackberry Winter.* New York: Washington Square, 1972.
———. *Coming of Age in Samoa.* New York: Quill, 1928.
———. *Sex and Temperament in Three Primitive Societies.* New York: Quill, 1935.
Metraux, Rhoda. "Margaret Mead: A Biographical Sketch," *American Anthropologist* 82 (June 1980): 262-69.

∼ Menarche

Menarche (the onset of menstruation) is a milestone in every woman's life that usually occurs about two years after the adolescent growth spurt. It is a tangible indicator of sexual maturity and the capacity to reproduce. Although potentially fertile, a young woman's early cycles are often irregular and anovulatory.

The social significance of female puberty in all world societies is evident by the extreme practices that accompany it. In some native cultures, the young girl is put into seclusion (to protect herself and the society), which could be for a few days or five years. Many societies practice rituals of chastity control for young girls experiencing puberty, including female genital mutilation (FGM) and public virginity tests at the time of marriage. Some cultures in parts of Asia and Africa perform FGM at the time of menarche or earlier; it usually involves the removal of the clitoris and stitching the vulva together, leaving only a tiny hole for urination and menstruation (infibulation). This patriarchal practice results in numerous grave health complications yet is accepted as a way to preserve a woman's purity and to curb her sexual appetite. At least eight countries have legislation that outlaws FGM, yet those who practice this ritual do not see their actions as inhuman or barbarous and resent efforts to stop it.

In the United States, the average age of menarche is about thirteen years, with a range from nine to seventeen years. Studies indicate that the onset of menstruation is influenced by genetic factors, health and nutrition, endocrine function, skeletal and biological maturation, physical activity, and percentage of body fat.

The cycles are started by hypothalamic signals to the pituitary, which secretes follicle-stimulating hormone (FSH) and luteinizing hormone (LH). A group of maturing follicles in the ovary begins to secrete estrogen, which can cause a surge of LH; this results in the first ovulation and, about fourteen days later, the first menstruation.

The following factors are associated with delayed menarche: malnutrition, diabetes mellitus, cystic fibrosis, anorexia nervosa, and intense exercise, such as gymnastics, ballet, running, and dancing. Conversely, some conditions are linked with advanced menarche such as obesity, low levels of physical activity, brain tumors, and hypothyroidism.

It is evident that the age of menarche is highly variable and very sensitive to both internal and external influences. These complex interactions make it very difficult to identify all the relevant associations. *(See also: Menopause; Menstrual Cycle)*

—**Esther K. Wilson**

Further Reading

Delaney, Janice, Mary Jane Lupton, and Emily Toth. *The Curse: A Cultural History of Menstruation.* Urbana: University of Illinois Press, 1988.
Golub, Sharon, ed. *Lifting the Curse of Menstruation: A Feminist Appraisal of the Influence of Menstruation on Women's Lives.* New York: Haworth, 1983.
———. *Menarche, The Transition from Girl to Woman.* Lexington, MA: D. C. Heath, 1983.
Rees, Margaret. "Menarche When and Why?" *The Lancet* 342 (1993): 1375-76.
Reynolds, Barbara. "The Move to Outlaw Female Genital Mutilation," *Ms.* 5 (1994): 92-93.

∼ Mennonite Women

Mennonite women are affiliated with the largest of the three historic Christian peace churches (Mennonite, Quaker, Brethren). Approximately 574,000 Mennonites live in North America as part of a global movement of 1.5 million people. American Mennonites are ethnically and linguistically diverse. They represent a spectrum of denominations, from conservative Old Order groups to others that embrace technology and higher education.

Mennonites trace their spiritual roots to the sixteenth-century Anabaptists of Switzerland who challenged the authority of Catholic and Protestant leaders. Beginning in 1525, Anabaptists rejected infant baptism and insisted on the separation of church and state. Church and civil officials denounced them as heretics. As the Anabaptists fled persecution, they established small congregations across the continent.

Descendants of the early Anabaptists called themselves "Mennonites" after the Dutch leader Menno Simons (1496–1561). Mennonites continued their pattern of migration in search of religious freedom and economic opportunity. A few made the trans-Atlantic crossing as early as 1643, and forty years later, American Mennonites established their first permanent settlement at Germantown, near Philadelphia. In this Germanic subculture, women's roles centered on domestic responsibilities and child rearing. Rich traditions in *fraktur* (calligraphy done in the Pennsylvania Dutch style), quilting, and other decorative arts remain a legacy of generations of Mennonite women in America.

Historically, American Mennonites have derived much of their identity in dissenting from the larger culture. Mennonites generally opposed slavery and refused to bear arms. Yet they divided themselves along several lines. Separatist-minded groups parted from those more receptive to cultural accommodations in dress, language, economic practices, and civic responsibility.

By the late nineteenth century, American Protestantism's thrust toward revival and reform influenced progressive Mennonites to establish mission posts overseas, among Native Americans, and in urban areas. This emphasis on service created openings for Mennonite women as missionaries, teachers, and nurses. Although patriarchal traditions kept most women from exercising religious leadership, a few created alternative institutions, including deaconess orders, to promote health care. During World War II, the threat of women's conscription led pacifist nurses to establish the Mennonite Nurses Association, the first organization of Mennonite professional women.

More recently, the feminist movement has influenced many Mennonite groups to remove restrictions on women in leadership and to explore feminist theology, domestic violence, and related issues. Although conservative Mennonites retain patriarchal practices, seminary-trained women have pastored Mennonite congregations for over a quarter century. *Women's Concerns Report,* a bimonthly newsletter published since 1973 by the Mennonite Central Committee, offers perspectives on issues of interest for Mennonite women internationally. At the August 6 New York Mennonite Conference in 1992, the all-male Ministerial Committee wrote and approved as a study paper "Women in Ministry," which, in exploring female leadership throughout Biblical history, argues that gender should not be a stumbling block against church members becoming church leaders. In 1998, upper leadership of the American Mennonite Church (The Mennonite Church Board) includes a female Associate General Secretary and a female Minister of Peace and Justice. *(See also: Christianity; Religion; Society of Friends)*

—**Rachel Waltner Goossen**

Further Reading

Epp, Marlene. "Women in Canadian Mennonite History: Uncovering the 'Underside,'" *Journal of Mennonite Studies 5* (1987): 90-107.

Goossen, Rachel Waltner. "Mennonite Women and Civilian Public Service," *Mennonite Quarterly Review* 66 (October 1992): 525-38.

———. "Piety and Professionalism: The Bethel Deaconesses of the Great Plains," *Mennonite Life* 49 (March 1994): 4-11.

Juhnke, James C. *Vision, Doctrine, War: Mennonite Identity and Organization in America, 1890–1930.* Scottdale, PA: Herald, 1989.

Klassen, Pamela. "What's Bre(a)d in the Bone: The Bodily Heritage of Mennonite Women," *Mennonite Quarterly Review* 68 (April 1994): 229-47.

Klingelsmith, Sharon. "Women in the Mennonite Church, 1900–1930," *Mennonite Quarterly Review* 54 (July 1980): 163-207.

Schlabach, Theron F. *Peace, Faith, Nation: Mennonites and Amish in Nineteenth-Century America.* Scottdale, PA: Herald, 1988.

Sprunger, Keith L. "God's Powerful Army of the Weak: Anabaptist Women of the Radical Reformation." In *Triumph over Silence: Women in Protestant History,* edited by Richard L. Greaves, 45-74. Westport, CT: Greenwood, 1985.

Women's Concerns Report. Bimonthly newsletter published by the Mennonite Central Committee U.S., Akron, PA, from 1973 to the present.

∞ Menopause

Menopause is the cessation of menstruation that occurs around the age of fifty. This biological milestone marks the end of reproductive capacity. For some, the transition is smooth; for others, it is both physically and emotionally difficult.

Menopause is beset with fear, stereotypes, and misconceptions. Due in large part to aging baby boomers, it has become a topic of mainstream books, articles, talk shows, hotlines, and support groups. Young women are advised to begin early prevention (a diet with calcium, exercise, smoking abstinence) for a better quality of life.

An integral part of a woman's menopausal experience is the cultural influence on her feelings of self-worth. In some primitive societies, women were given special spiritual status, while in others they became nonpersons without worth. A century ago, few women lived beyond their reproductive years; today, a woman can expect to live an additional thirty years. In our youth-oriented society, older women are often stigmatized and undervalued. Unlike pregnancy, women have no choice about menopause. Some mourn their lost fertility, while others welcome new sexual freedom.

The final menstrual phase begins as the ovaries age. The follicles, once numbering 300,000 at puberty, are near depletion, and estrogen levels are declining. Hormone levels are in disequilibrium, which can cause hot flashes, sleeping problems, memory loss, genital and urinary system atrophy, accelerated bone loss and skin aging, loss of libido, and vaginal dryness.

For women taking responsibility for their health, education is essential. Some choose to experience menopause naturally (diet, exercise, herbal remedies); others try hormone replacement therapy (HRT). Natural remedies include herbal combinations, increase in vitamin intake, supplementation of diet with soy and phytoestrogens (naturally occurring estrogen-like compounds found in food), relaxation and mind techniques, and cultural remedies, such as the Japanese healing art of Reiki. HRT involves a regimen of introducing (topically or by ingestion) hormones such as estrogen, progesterone, testosterone, and/or other prescription drugs into the body.

The benefits and risks of HRT are being debated. The popularity of HRT was highest in the 1960s when it was taken by millions to delay aging. HRT has been linked with preventing bone loss (osteoporosis) and reducing the risk of heart disease, the atrophy of sex organs, and the frequency and severity of hot flashes. It can also increase sex drive. The treatment became controversial after 1975 when cancer risks were acknowledged. HRT has also been linked with gallbladder disease and can complicate blood-clotting problems. Medical testing has shown that prescribing low doses or different combinations of hormones can reduce the risks while still providing some benefits. HRT has undergone extensive testing and is closely watched by the American media. Long-term risks and results, however, have yet to be determined. Until results of long-term testing are complete, millions of women are taking advantage of their available options and are always on the lookout for more. Drug companies and health food stores alike are seizing a billion-dollar market for products and information as baby boomers reach the age of menopause.

Menopause is a physical, emotional, and psychological transition. Rather than adhering to predetermined cultural or medical definitions, each woman needs to be in tune with her body and trust her own experience. *(See also: Menarche; Menstrual Cycle)*

—Esther K. Wilson

Further Reading

Buchsbaum, Herbert J., ed. *The Menopause.* New York: Springer-Verlag, 1983.

Callahan, Joan C., ed. *Menopause: A Midlife Passage.* Bloomington: Indiana University Press, 1993.

Cutler, Winnifred B., and Celso-Ramon Garcia. *Menopause, A Guide for Women and Those Who Love Them.* New York: Norton, 1992.

Greer, Germaine. *The Change: Women, Aging, and the Menopause.* New York: Knopf, 1992.

Korenman, Stanley G., ed. *The Menopause.* Norwell, MA: Serono Symposia, USA, 1990.

McCain, Marian Van Eyk. *Transformation through Menopause.* New York: Bergin & Garvey, 1991.

Notelovitz, Morris, and Diana Tonnessen. *Menopause and Midlife Health.* New York: St. Martin's, 1993.

Sand, Gayle. *Is It Hot in Here or Is It Me?* New York: HarperCollins, 1993.

Sheehy, Gail. *The Silent Passage: Menopause.* New York: Random House, 1992.

Utian, Wulf H., and Ruth S. Jacobowitz. *Managing Your Menopause.* New York: Simon & Schuster, 1990.

⤳ Menstrual Cycle

Menstrual cycle refers to monthly changes of the ovaries and uterus orchestrated by fluctuating hormonal levels. Each woman's cycle is variable (frequency, amount of flow, symptoms) and is affected by factors such as stress, oral contraceptives, and loss of body fat (athletes, models, etc.). Very lean women often experience amenorrhea and risk premature bone loss.

Throughout history, menstrual taboos and superstitions have restricted women's behavior. In some primitive societies, menstruating women were considered supernatural, powerful, and dangerous and were sequestered during menses.

Antimenstrual attitudes have persisted in Western culture. The topic of menstruation is usually avoided or addressed using negative euphemisms such as "the curse." In the past, mother-daughter talks were the primary source of menstrual information until schools began to supplement this tradition with educational books and films. In the 1920s, disposable sanitary napkins began to replace reusable cotton diapers; a disposable tampon soon followed. Yet until 1972, advertisements for sanitary protection were banned from radio and television. Despite the slow development and marketing of feminine products, it has become a billion-dollar industry.

This uniquely female cycle is governed by a hypothalamus-pituitary-ovarian feedback system. The pituitary is signaled by the hypothalamus to release follicle-stimulating hormone (FSH), which initiates a group of ovarian follicles to begin maturing and secreting estrogen. About mid-cycle, the pituitary releases a surge of luteinizing hormone (LH), which triggers ovulation. Progesterone and estrogen (from the ovary) induce the uterus to thicken for possible implantation of a fertilized egg. If no fertilization occurs, a sharp decline in ovarian hormones triggers the shedding of the superficial uterine lining (menses) as the subsequent cycle begins.

Most women report menstrual symptoms that range from minor inconveniences to severe effects that disrupt their personal and professional lives. In this country, women's medical problems have gotten short shrift. Physicians often underestimate and downplay the pain and discomfort that women experience, treating their complaints as psychological disorders or imaginary.

Practitioners of "menstrual politics" believe that women are irrevocably limited by their biology and their destiny is to bear children. Despite sexist attacks on their abilities, there are few jobs in the male-oriented workforce that women are excluded from. They do, however, pay a price. Survival has meant developing highly sophisticated coping mechanisms to ignore, suppress, and override the cyclical biological rhythms and changes that occur in their bodies, feelings, moods, energies, and abilities. *(See also: Menarche; Menopause)*

—Esther K. Wilson

Further Reading

Asso, Doreen. *The Real Menstrual Cycle.* New York: John Wiley, 1984.

Delaney, Janice, Mary Jane Lupton, and Emily Toth. *The Curse: A Cultural History of Menstruation.* Urbana: University of Illinois Press, 1988.

Knight, Chris. *Blood Relations: Menstruation and the Origins of Culture.* New Haven, CT: Yale University Press, 1991.

Norris, Ronald V., and Colleen Sullivan. *PMS/Premenstrual Syndrome.* New York: Rawson, 1983.

Snowden, Robert, and Barbara Christian, eds. *Patterns and Perceptions of Menstruation.* New York: St. Martin's, 1983.

⁊ Mentor-Protégée Relationships

Mentor-protégée relationships between women, such as Susan B. Anthony and Abigail S. Duniway, Anne Sullivan and Helen Keller, and Margaret Mead and Gail Sheehy, have been chronicled throughout history. The notion of wise people counseling the young was first introduced when the Greek poet Homer's "faithful and wise" Mentor advised Odysseus. According to Fenelon's *Telemaque,* Mentor (who was actually the goddess Athena in disguise) played a prominent role by giving her protégé good advice, to the extent that before departing for the Trojan War, Odysseus appointed Mentor as the sage guardian of his house and his son Telemachus. On one occasion, Mentor's advice saved Telemachus from death, and after the wars were over, she aided in the search for the lost Odysseus.

The concept of mentor includes being a teacher, sponsor, adviser, counselor, developer of skills and intellect, host, guide, and exemplar who assists a protégée in the transition from the child-parent relationship to that of adult-peer. A number of researchers contend that mentors tend to choose protégées with whom they identify and are socially compatible. Most studies agree that the presence or absence of a mentor has significant impact on adult development.

As is the case with all intense long-term interactions, mentor-protégée relationships proceed through some broadly defined stages. The first contact of the protégée with her mentor/teacher at a young age is followed by a demonstration of independence on the part of the protégée; the protégée then provides guidance to others; and, finally, the protégée, in turn, becomes a mentor to some young person.

Studies indicate that mentors are essential for women's success in organizations; that women, over a lifetime, average three mentors to men's two; and that when women indicate having had mentors in their lives, they often cite their therapists. Recent studies on the impact of mentor-protégée relationships in work environments provide conclusive evidence that productivity and retention rates are higher for female employees when they have access to positive mentor situations. Despite the fact that the first mentor was a woman and that there are numerous historical and contemporary examples of successful female mentor-protégée relationships, management studies indicate that in the workplace, most women prefer male mentors over female mentors. Mentors in the workplace provide women with networking opportunities, occasions to gain insight into the cultural environments of the organizations in which they work, and a safe place to vent frustrations or seek advice about work-related concerns.

The systematic study of mentor-protégée relationships within the workforce and among women's greater societal associations offers a clearer understanding of the importance of female mentoring, its significance in women's lives, and its impact on women's history. *(See also: Friendships; Networking)*

—**Susan H. Koester**

Further Reading

Bolton, E. B. "A Conceptual Analysis of the Mentor Relationship in the Career Development of Women," *Adult Education* 30 (1980): 195-207.

Halcomb, Ruth. *Women Making It: Patterns and Profiles of Success.* New York: Atheneum, 1979.

Kalbfleisch, Pamela J., and Andrea D. Davies. "Minorities and Mentoring: Managing the Multicultural Institution," *Communication Education* 40 (1991): 266-71.

Ragins, B. R. "Barriers to Mentoring: The Female Manager's Dilemma," *Human Relations* 42 (1989): 1-22.

Reisman, J. M. "Intimacy in Same-Sex Friendships," *Sex Roles* 23 (1990): 65-82.

⁊ Mesmerism

Mesmerism surfaced in prerevolutionary France as a healing system for all manner of nervous and physical ailments and emerged as the first great pseudoscientific self-improvement craze. Dubbed "animal magnetism" by its founder, Viennese physician Franz Anton Mesmer (1733–1815), the theory propounded a fluid link between "celestial bodies, the earth, and animated bodies." Mesmer and his followers believed that by harnessing this universal magnetic fluid, first with magnets, then with a bathtub-like contraption called a *baquet,* and finally through trance, not only could the human body be healed, but the human mind would be literally connected to a universe of mysterious powers.

American practitioners readily seized Mesmerism's implicit connection between healing and religious revelation. By the 1840s, Mesmerism had been incorporated into two of the period's most important alternative religious sects. The "mind cure" movement first experimented with the clairvoyant possibilities of mesmeric trance. Its leader, former clockmaker P. P. Quimby, gave popular demonstrations of his ability to both diagnose and prescribe for disorders while mesmerized. He believed that disease could be cured by altering toxic thoughts that he could also discern while in "rapport" with the patient. One of his patients, Mary Patterson (later Mary Baker Eddy) went on to found the most influential of the mind cure religions, Christian Science.

The development of spirit mediumship in 1848 took Mesmerism to its ultimate conclusion. The Spiritualists, following the example of eighteenth-century Swedish mystic Emmanuel Swedenborg, used trance to contact the spirits of the dead, thus completing the interconnecting bond between the celestial and the corporeal. The movement involved a subtle shift of emphasis, for even as Spiritualism made claims to scientific legitimacy, its success and mystique relied on the sensitivity of the medium, usually a woman.

In America, Mesmerism acted largely as a conduit through which several mid-nineteenth-century alternative religions and cures found their fullest expression. Although Mesmerism failed both as a healing system and as a means of revelation, its techniques remain, in modern hypnosis, an important tool in psychotherapy. *(See also: Eddy, Mary Baker; Mind Cure; Spiritualism)*

—**Catherine Mason**

Further Reading

Carpenter, William. *Mesmerism and Spiritualism: Historically and Scientifically Considered.* New York: Appleton, 1889.

Darnton, Robert. *Mesmerism and the End of the Enlightenment in France.* New York: Schocken, 1970.

Fuller, Robert. *Mesmerism and the American Cure of Souls.* Philadelphia: University of Pennsylvania Press, 1982.

Podmore, Frank. *From Mesmerism to Christian Science.* New York: University Books, 1965.

℘ Methodist Women in the Nineteenth Century

In the nineteenth century, Methodist women acted on John Wesley's belief that the rule of female silence based on the teachings of the apostle Paul "admits of some exceptions." They sometimes acquired local fame for exhorting, as did Lydia Hawes, a particularly eloquent speaker in Indiana in the 1830s. Such "female ranting" declined as the Methodist Episcopal Church grew affluent and conventional in the mid-nineteenth century. Bishop Jesse Truesdell Peck's *The True Woman* (1857) prescribed decorous roles for women, especially Sunday school teaching, but also suggested that women who needed exceptional opportunities try foreign missions. That became especially attractive after the Women's Foreign Missionary Society began its highly independent service to the denomination in 1869.

Missionaries and other women challenged the limits that men such as Peck set for them. Phoebe Palmer was the best-known prophet of "holiness" and argued, in *Promise of the Father* (1859), for expanding women's ministries; Margaret Van Cott became the denomination's first licensed woman preacher in 1868; Anna Oliver and Anna Howard Shaw sought full ordination in 1880. The denomination's legislative body, the General Conference, refused ordination and then barred women from licensed preaching. In 1888, Frances Willard and four other women presented themselves as lay delegates to the General Conference. After they were turned away, the conference recognized the new order of deaconesses. Women were given opportunities to serve but no share of authority.

Smaller bodies in the broad Wesleyan tradition, particularly the African Methodist Episcopal Zion Church, some of the Holiness churches, the New York Conference of the Methodist Protestant Church, and the United Brethren ordained women in the nineteenth century. The largest Methodist denomination did not fully ordain women until 1956, but all branches of the Wesleyan tradition had women who challenged the Pauline rule and made exceptions to it throughout the nineteenth century. *(See also: Christianity; Religion; Shaw, Anna Howard; Willard, Frances E.)*

—**Donald B. Marti**

Further Reading

Keller, Rosemary S., Louise L. Queen, and Hilah F. Thomas, eds. *Women in New Worlds: Historical Perspectives on the Wesleyan Tradition,* 2 vols. Nashville, TN: Abingdon, 1981, 1982.

Richey, Russell E., Kenneth E. Rowe, and Jean Miller Schmidt, eds. *Perspectives on American Methodism: Interpretive Essays.* Nashville, TN: Kingswood, 1993.

Rowe, Kenneth. *Methodist Women: A Guide to the Literature.* Lake Junaluska, NC: United Methodist Commission on Archives and History, 1980.

℘ Mexican War (1845–1848)

Despite its short duration and a limited military and diplomatic significance, the Mexican War became a catalyst for major changes in the lives of women in the United States. The terms of the Treaty of Guadalupe-Hidalgo of 1848, which ended the war, directly affected Chicana and Native American women who lived in the more than half-million square miles of territory that Mexico ceded to the United States for 15 million dollars, as well as mainstream and immigrant women who were part of the settlement of the trans-Mississippi west. The subsequent organization of the newly acquired territories into states according to the stipulations of the Compromise of 1850 incited and inflamed the national debate over the institution of slavery, thus affecting the fate of the black women who were slaves as well as free black and white women who were part of the antislavery movement.

Chicanas were a significant proportion of the 73,500 Hispanics who inhabited California and the Utah and New Mexican Territories in 1848. These women remained unassimilated into Victorian American society because of their ethnic, cultural, and religious differences. Their difficulties under internal colonialism in the nineteenth century translated into the triple jeopardy of being female, Hispanic, and poor in twentieth-century American society. Native American women in the acquired territories and on the Great Plains shared the dislocation of their tribes as the federal government facilitated white settlers' claim to those areas for ranching and farming. Mainstream, free black, and immigrant women were a significant proportion of the pioneer population that settled the plains; their presence brought social and economic stability to the area that would become the heartland and breadbasket of the nation.

The conveniently compelling doctrine that rationalized western expansionism as "Manifest Destiny" during the 1840s justified the war with Mexico as a means of diverting internal domestic conflict over the issue of the existence and expansion of slavery; however, the national debate over the "slave" or "free" status of the added southwestern territory exacerbated the rise of a divisive sectionalism. Women were part of the anti-imperialistic peace movement that particularly opposed this war. Black and white women within the antislavery and abolition movements were not deterred by the fierce and often physically violent reaction of the supporters of the extension of slavery into the territories.

Fought on foreign soil and in the sparsely populated southwest, the Mexican War offered women less opportunity to become camp followers. Moreover, in the late 1840s, women lacked the model of Florence Nightingale's organized nursing facilities for the wounded during the Crimean War of 1852 that inspired Clara Barton during the Civil War. Therefore, women's actual participation in the Mexican War was considerably less than that in the Civil War. *(See also: Abolition and the Antislavery Movement; Chicana; Migration and Frontier Women; Native American Women; Pacifism and the Peace Movement; Triple Jeopardy)*

—**Wendell L. Griffith**
—**Angela M. Howard**

Further Reading

Bauer, K. Jack. *The Mexican War.* New York: Macmillan, 1974.

Billings, Eliza Allen. "The Female Volunteer, or The Life and Adventures of Miss Eliza Allen, A Young Lady of Eastport, Maine." Unpublished memoir.

Johannsen, Robert W. *To the Halls of the Montezumas.* New York: Oxford University Press, 1985.

Lyons, James Gilborne. "The Heroine Martyr of Monterey," *American Quarterly Register* (June 1849): 483-84.

Stewart, Miller. "Army Laundresses: Ladies of the 'Soap Suds Row.' " *Nebraska History* 51 (Winter 1980): 421-36.

Tutorow, Norman. *The Mexican-American War: An Annotated Bibliography.* Westport, CT: Greenwood, 1982.

Wecter, Dixon. *The Hero in America: A Chronicle of Hero Worship.* Ann Arbor: University of Michigan Press, 1941.

✍ Meyer, Annie Nathan (1867–1951)

Annie Nathan Meyer was a writer, a founder of Barnard College, a civic and cultural activist, and an antisuffragist. Born into a prominent Sephardic Jewish family in New York City, Meyer nevertheless had a difficult childhood marked by financial troubles and her mother's early death. At eighteen, determined to become a writer, she attended Columbia University's Collegiate Course for Women but found it unsatisfactory because women had access only to examinations, not to classes. After her marriage to Dr. Alfred Meyer in 1887, she left Columbia but subsequently organized a drive to found Barnard College (1889), the women's undergraduate division of the university. She became a Barnard trustee and remained active in the college's affairs throughout her life.

Meyer's literary career began with her editorship of *Woman's Work in America* (1891), a collection of essays, followed by novels (*Helen Brent, M.D.* in 1892 and *Robert Annys, Poor Priest* in 1901); works of nature (*My Park Book,* 1898); twenty-six plays (a few produced on Broadway and elsewhere); a two-volume autobiography, and hundreds of articles, essays, short stories, and letters to the editors of New York City newspapers. Her themes ranged from art, nature, and literature to the position of modern women, Jewish issues, interracial love and lynching, and the proper clothing for working girls. Although her earliest writing supported "New Women," Meyer ultimately took a more conservative position and worked actively for antisuffrage, deriding what she termed "spreadhenism," the idea that women's innate moral superiority would purify politics. Her sister, New York Consumers' League founder Maud Nathan, took an equally strong prosuffrage stance.

A member of the Daughters of the American Revolution, Meyer took pride in her heritage and in the achievements of American Jews. She wrote frequently for Jewish publications and was an early and vociferous opponent of Hitler. Meyer believed in assimilation, spoke against Jewish "particularism," deplored the manners and customs of Eastern European Jewish immigrants, and feared that Zionism would create problems of dual allegiance. She accepted Barnard's policy of limiting Jewish admissions, believing that the college should accept no socially embarrassing students. Her concern for human dignity extended to other minorities. She sponsored Zora Neale Hurston as Barnard's first black student, donated books on black history and culture to Hunter College, and contributed to civil rights organizations.

Strong-willed and eccentric, particularly after the death of her only child, Margaret Meyer Cohen in 1923, she never forgot a slight, real or imagined, and engaged in many feuds. Yet her warmth and generosity brought her the devotion of lifelong friends and a very happy marriage. Embittered over Barnard's reluctance to recognize her as its founder, she never understood the role that anti-Semitism played in denying her that title. *(See also: Barnard College; Jewish Women; Women Writers)*

—**Lynn D. Gordon**

Further Reading

Annie Nathan Meyer Papers. American Jewish Archives. Cincinnati, OH. New York: Barnard College Archives.

Goldenberg, Myrna. "Annie Nathan Meyer: Barnard Godmother, Gotham Gadfly, and American Jewish Woman of Letters." Ph.D. diss., University of Maryland, 1990.

Gordon, Lynn D. "Annie Nathan Meyer and Barnard College: Mission and Identity in Women's Higher Education, 1889–1950," *History of Education Quarterly* 26 (Winter 1986): 503-22.

Meyer, Annie Nathan. *Barnard Beginnings.* Boston: Houghton Mifflin, 1935.

———. *It's Been Fun.* New York: Schumann, 1951.

Taylor, Robert Lewis. "Profiles: The Doctor, the Lady, and Columbia University," *New Yorker* 19 (October 23 and 30, 1943): 27-32; 28-32.

✍ Midwifery

Midwifery is the practice of a midwife, a woman who effects delivery of babies or assists at women's childbirths. Traditionally, such assistance was based on empirically based knowledge. Midwives learned their skills from other midwives, often their mothers or aunts, and passed on to other women information about healing herbs, soothing potions, and ways of handling birth difficulties. Among the usual skills of early midwives were turning a fetus in utero or successfully delivering a fetus in a breech position.

Midwifery had long been a lay or domestic skill, one of the important health care resources possessed by women that were critical to community settlement and survival. By the mid-eighteenth century, however, health care was moving out of the household and into the realm of the apothecary and the physician. Midwifery came under the purview of doctors and the influence of medical and scientific understanding and intervention. Increasingly, doctors claimed that their understanding of anatomy and their special tools—forceps, for example—for speeding up or bringing childbirth to a close made them essential attendants. Midwives, meanwhile, were excluded from the educational institutions in which scientific midwifery, or obstetrics, was being taught.

Midwifery/obstetrics was one of the four major areas of medical instruction, and new doctors were eager for midwifery cases that could profitably serve them as entries into the rest of a family's medical business. The traditional midwife continued to serve, but increasingly she attended only the poor and the inaccessible, women whom doctors could not profitably attend. Immigrant midwives, some of whom had had medical training themselves, were also shunted into secondary roles as birth care providers. The obstetrics that replaced female midwifery was activist and interventive: Doctors positioned women flat on their backs, administering drugs to speed up or slow down labor and to deaden or to eradicate its pain.

During the early decades of the twentieth century, doctors and state and national medical and public health associations joined forces to legislate traditional midwives out of legitimate business. As the traditional midwife was being forced out, the nurse-midwife was emerging as a medically certified, often hospital-trained substitute for a physician. A resurgence of traditional midwifery in the home birth and lay midwife movements in the 1970s arose in reaction to the physician-dominated hospitalized birth process that had been established during the baby boom era. The rise of the women's health movement of the 1960s and 1970s as well as the renewed interest in "natural childbirth," which dated back to the 1950s, converged with the desire of women to reassert control and to participate more actively in the birth process, all of which brought an openness to midwifery as a reasonable alternative to hospital delivery by the 1980s.

Over a twenty-year period, births attended by nurse-midwives have increased significantly in the United States from 19,686 in 1975 to 196,977 in 1994 (Gabay 386). Certified nurse-midwives are licensed registered nurses who have studied in an accredited graduate program and have passed a certification examination. The principal philosophy underlying midwifery service and care is that childbirth is a normal, natural event that in most cases, for women with few health risks, requires no medical intervention. Midwifery practice is oriented toward individualized care and is highly cost-effective, based on an average savings of $3,000 per

midwife-attended birth (Brodsky 47). Midwifery is legal in all fifty states, but significant restrictions occur in much individual state legislation. Midwifery advocates claim that there are numerous advantages to home births with midwives, including fewer medical interventions, increased comfort and personal attention, a greater autonomous feeling of control for the woman, and the enriched experience of giving birth in a familiar environment. Throughout the 1990s, there was a movement within hospitals to establish birthing centers that simulate a home environment, suggesting that midwifery practice and principle are becoming more mainstream. *(See also: Childbirth; "Granny" Midwifery; Immigrant Midwifery; Lying-In)*

—**Janet Carlisle Bogdan**

Further Reading
Bogdan, Janet Carlisle. "The Transformation of American Birth." Ph.D. diss., Syracuse University, 1987.
Brodsky, Archie. "Midwifery's Rebirth," *National Review* 49 (August 1997): 46-47.
Donegan, Jane. *Women and Men Midwives.* Westport, CT: Greenwood 1978.
Gabay, Mary. "Nurse Midwifery: The Beneficial Alternative," *Public Health Report* 112 (September/October 1997): 386-95.
Kobrin, Frances E. "The American Midwife Controversy: A Crisis in Professionalization," *Bulletin of the History of Medicine* 40 (1966): 350-63.
Litoff, Judy Barrett. *American Midwives.* Westport, CT: Greenwood, 1978.
Ulrich, Laurel Thatcher. *A Midwife's Tale.* New York: Knopf, 1990.

Migration and Frontier Women

The presence and contribution of women to the Anglo settlement of the frontier ensured the success of the great western migration in North America. Especially in the southern colonies, fewer women than men migrated to British North America. An initial assumption that a "Golden Age" of sexual equality for colonial women resulted from this unbalanced sex ratio during the early colonial period has not been supported by further research. Frontier women experienced a de facto equality that allowed them to do "men's work" to ensure the survival of the settlement; however, this situational tolerance, which violated the patriarchal gender system, did not produce a de jure equality for women under reformed legal or property statutes. Few frontier women ventured beyond their domestic sphere on a permanent basis, although there were less notorious women than Calamity Jane and Belle Starr, who used the freedom of the frontier to pursue nontraditional occupations.

The majority of women who participated in the western expansion did so as a consequence of their fathers' or husbands' decision to migrate; especially by the mid-nineteenth century, women's move into the frontier usually resulted in a reversion of the quality of their lives to the rugged and hazardous circumstances of their colonial predecessors. As resourceful co-workers and managers, frontier women were crucial to the survival of the family and the farm through their performance of field work, carpentry, and husbandry chores, as well as household and child care duties.

Women shared their families' belief in the opportunities for economic and social advancement in the West, but the journey tested their physical and psychological endurance. As part of a wagon train, women created a female community that provided support and assistance through their mutual obstacles and endless chores. As frontier homesteaders, women experienced isolation from far-distant relations and scattered rural neighbors. Women who settled the Great Plains confronted a vast and often bleak expanse of land unlike the terrain to which they were accustomed. Once arrived at the new location, women first faced the challenge of establishing an adequate shelter until the family could build a more permanent home. The larger homestead tracts placed the nearest neighbor beyond ready call in case of emergency. With determination and resourcefulness, women homesteaders weathered both the physical and economic hardships of the prairie, and as the farm prospered, women attempted gradually to reintroduce the domesticity they had left "back home" or about which they read in women's magazines such as *Godey's Lady's Book*. Homesteads that survived the first two years usually prospered and endured.

At the final stage of western settlement, women turned their attention to the development of towns as social as well as commercial centers. Early on, women used their religious activities not only for spiritual renewal but for crucial social interaction. The insistence of women brought the establishment of churches, public schools, and other institutions of "civilization" to the frontier and prairie towns by the latter quarter of the nineteenth century. The frontier "schoolmarm" served as the particular agent of the concept of true womanhood in her role as teacher in the one-room schoolhouse. As individuals and in organized groups, western women demanded and astutely pursued whatever civic and political reform was necessary to "civilize" their community. As an acknowledgment of their contribution to the development of the new states, western women were the first to be given the vote. In the popular mythology of the American West, the frontier woman stands larger than life beside the cowboy and the Native American as a symbol of courage and endurance. *(See also: Asian Women; Black Women; Common Law; Cult of True Womanhood; Demography; Great Awakening; Morrill Land-Grant Act of 1862; Native American Women; Patrons of Husbandry)*

—**Angela M. Howard**

Further Reading

Armitage, Susan, and Elizabeth Jameson, eds. *The Women's West.* Norman: University of Oklahoma Press, 1987.

Faragher, John Mack. *Women and Men on the Overland Trail.* New Haven, CT: Yale University Press, 1979.

Jeffrey, Julie Roy. *Frontier Women: The Transmississippi West, 1840–1880.* New York: Hill & Wang, 1979.

Limerick, Patricia Nelson. *The Legacy of Conquest: The Unbroken Past of the American West.* New York: Norton, 1987.

Myres, Sandra L. *Westering Women and the Frontier Experience, 1800–1915.* Albuquerque: University of New Mexico Press, 1982.

Pacific Historical Review 49 (1980); 61 (1992).

Schlissel, Lillian. *Women's Diaries of the Westward Journey.* New York: Schocken, 1982.

Schlissel, Lillian, Vicki L. Ruiz, and Janice Monk, eds. *Western Women: Their Land, Their Lives.* Albuquerque: University of New Mexico Press, 1988.

❧ Military Service

Women have served officially or unofficially with the U.S. armed forces since the American Revolution. The first women to gain official status as a corps were the nurses. The Army Nurse Corps was created in 1901, the Navy Nurse Corps in 1908. Approximately 11,275 yeomen (F) served with the Navy and Marine Corps during World War I, but the loophole in legislation that permitted this was closed in 1925. Originally, nurses in the military suffered from poor pay and nebulous status, and even though they received better pay and disability benefits after World War I, they were awarded only relative rank (approximate rank with fewer benefits and pay than men in the same rank) in 1944.

Not until after Pearl Harbor did women begin serving in nonnurse corps. The Army took the lead by creating the Women's Army Auxiliary Corps on May 15, 1942. The Navy, Coast Guard, and Marine Corps followed suit within the year. At peak strength of the military during World War II, 271,600 women served in some service branch; a total of 350,000 women voluntarily entered the services at some point during the hostilities.

With the passage of the Women's Armed Services Integration Act in June 1948, the women's corps were made a permanent part of the armed forces. Women served in the military during the Korean War and the Vietnam War, but their exact numbers are unknown. It was not until 1984 that the Veterans Administration sponsored its first survey to determine how many women veterans there were in this country, but the best estimate is that 6 percent of living veterans are women. After long debate and much soul searching, the "separate but equal" women's corps were abolished in 1978 when women were integrated into the services.

In 1976, the first women were admitted to U.S. military academies, and by 1990, they constituted approximately 10 percent of the cadets/midshipmen and 10 to 12 percent of the active duty U.S. military. Today, there are almost 200,000 women on active duty in the military services and the Coast Guard, making up 13.4 percent of the total armed forces.

The role played by servicewomen during the Persian Gulf war educated the general public about their capabilities. Mobilization in the Gulf War was the largest female deployment in U.S. history, with women serving as 7 percent of the active forces and 17 percent of the Reserve and National

Figure 39. Women in the Military Service Stamp
A postage stamp honoring women in the military was unveiled by the U.S. Postal Service at Arlington National Cemetery on October 18, 1997. Used by permission of Agence France and Corbis/Bettmann.

Guard. Between 1992 and 1994, legislative and policy changes were made to increase opportunities for women in military service. Congress then lifted the barrier to allow women to fly combat planes, and the Navy began to allow women to fly combat aircraft and serve on combat ships. The U.S. military continued the increased the presence of women in combat roles throughout the 1990s; during the U.S.-Iraq conflict of 1998, for the first time, women pilots carried out bombing missions. However, the 1994 prohibition of women in ground combat assignments has prevailed. The Army still excludes women from direct ground combat; they cannot serve in the infantry, armor, cannon field artillery, and short-range defense artillery. Combat service on submarines is also closed to women. Controversy continues over the integration of men and women during basic training and in barracks, despite legislation requiring that they train together in boot camp.

During the 1990s, sexual harassment of women in the military emerged as an important issue. Sexual misconduct by Navy and Marine Corps aviators at the 1991 Tailhook Association convention in Las Vegas and at the Aberdeen Proving Ground training installation in Maryland were two of the most visible incidents.

Another milestone in the 1990s was the admission of women to The Citadel and Virginia Military Institute, the country's last state-funded, all-male military colleges. After the U.S. Supreme Court upheld an order requiring her admission, Shannon Faulkner became the first female in the Corps of Cadets at The Citadel. Although she resigned five days later, her place was taken by Nancy Mellette. Women have also played increasingly visible roles in peacekeeping operations worldwide. In 1995, more than 1,200 women were deployed to Haiti, and more than 5,000 women have served in peacekeeping operations in Bosnia. *(See also: Army Nurse Corps; Marine Corps, Women's Reserve; SPARS; WAVES; Women's Army Auxiliary Corps; Women's Army Corps; U.S. Military Academy)*

—D'Ann Campbell

Further Reading

Bach, Shirley, and Martin Binlin. *Women and the Military.* Washington, DC: Brookings Institution, 1977.

Beeraft, Carolyn. *Women in the U.S. Armed Services: The War in the Persian Gulf.* Washington, DC: Women's Research and Education Institute, March 1991.

Bérubé, Allan. *Coming Out under Fire: The History of Gay Men and Women in World War Two.* New York: Free Press, 1990.

Campbell, D'Ann. *Women at War with America: Private Lives in a Patriotic Era.* Cambridge, MA: Harvard University Press, 1984.

De Panio, Linda Grant. *Seafaring Women.* Boston: Houghton Mifflin, 1982.

Ebbert, Jean, and Marie-Beth Hall. *Crossed Currents: Navy Women from WWI to Tailhook.* Washington, DC: Brasseys/Macmillan, 1993.

Enloe, Cynthia. *Does Khaki Become You? The Militarization of Women's Lives.* Boston: South End Press, 1983.

Goldman, Nancy Loring, ed. *Female Soldiers—Combatants or Noncombatants and Contemporary Perspectives.* Westport, CT: Greenwood, 1982.

Holm, Jeanne. *Women in the Military.* Rev. ed. Novato, CA: Presidio, 1982, 1992.

Litoff, Judith B., and Dave Smith. *We're in This War, Too: World War II Letters from American Women in Uniform.* New York: Oxford University Press, 1994.

McIntosh, Elizabeth P. *Undercover Girl.* Alexandria, VA: Time-Life, 1993.

Morden, Colonel Bette. *The Women's Army Corps, 1945–1978.* Washington, DC: Center of Military History, U.S. Army, 1990.

Presidential Commission on the Assignment of Women in the Armed Forces: Report to the President, November 15, 1992. Washington, DC: Government Printing Office, 1992.

Schneider, Dorothy. *Sound Off: American Military Women Speak Out.* New York: E. P. Dutton, 1988.

Segal, David R., and H. Wallace Senaiko. *Life in the Rank and File: Enlisted Men and Women in the Armed Forces of the United States, Australia, Canada, and the United Kingdom.* McLean, VA: Pergamon-Brassey's International Defense Publishers, 1986.

Stiehm, Judith Hicks. *Arms and the Enlisted Women.* Philadelphia: Temple University Press, 1989.

Treadwell, Mattie E. *The Women's Army Corps.* Washington, DC: Office of the Chief of Military History, Department of the Army, 1954.

U.S. Department of the Army. Medical Department. *Highlights on the History of the Army Nurse Corps.* Washington, DC: U.S. Department of the Army, 1975.

Willenz, June A. *Women Veterans: America's Forgotten Heroines.* New York: Continuum, 1983.

~ Millay, Edna St. Vincent
(1892–1950)

Renowned as a poet and as a personality, Edna St. Vincent Millay captured a mood of a time and place in American history as well as providing a strong female voice in American literature.

Born in 1892 and reared by her mother, Millay achieved literary success early with the publication of her long poem *Renascence* in a collection in 1912. The poem was an immediate critical success, especially as the product of an eighteen-year-old poet. Sent to Vassar College by the generosity of Caroline Dow, executive secretary of the YWCA training school in New York, Millay graduated in 1917 and moved to Greenwich Village in New York City, where she embodied the spirit of the post–World War I days.

Her life and her poetry in these years (see especially poems in *A Few Figs from Thistles,* 1920, and *Second April,* 1921) reflect a witty, sophisticated view of life; her well-known quatrain, "My candle burns at both its ends," is typical. The female speaking voice of the poems, like Millay herself, is independent, even cocky, and as sexually free as her male counterpart. Although she wrote in traditional forms, she clearly spoke for the spirit of the 1920s.

Millay was actively engaged in social issues. She was one of those who protested the unjust conviction and executions in the renowned Sacco-Vanzetti case, and until the approach of World War II, she was a pacifist (see her verse drama *Aria da Capo*). With the rise of fascism, however, her writings focused on her rage at the horrors being committed. Although not her best poems, they are nevertheless witness to her strong connection with history and politics.

Many of her works show feminist themes. Relying on highly personal material, Millay creates voices of strong, attractive, clever, sexually liberated women in her poems. Often, especially in her later poems, nature is called on as a source of power and regeneration. Her works provide examples of personal independence and friendships between women, as did her career. *(See also: Women Writers)*

—**Mabel Benson DuPriest**

Further Reading

Britten, Norman. *Edna St. Vincent Millay.* New York: Twayne, 1967. Rev. ed., 1982.

Cheney, Anne. *Millay in Greenwich Village.* University: University of Alabama Press, 1975.

Freedman, Diane P., ed. *Millay at 100: A Critical Reappraisal.* Urbana: University of Illinois Press, 1995.

Millay, Edna St. Vincent. *Collected Poems.* New York: Harper, 1956.

Nierman, Judith. *Edna St. Vincent Millay: A Reference Guide.* Boston: G. K. Hall, 1977.

Yost, Karl. *A Bibliography of the Works of Edna St. Vincent Millay.* New York: Harper, 1973.

ᴄᴀ Mind Cure

Mind cure, also known as metaphysical healing, psychotherapy, and mental therapeutics, was practiced by followers of a variety of scientific religions, such as Christian Science, Theosophy, and New Thought, that emerged after the Civil War. These "metaphysical movements" sought to rejuvenate religious life by replacing the "old revelation" contained in Scripture with the "new revelation" that the mind has the power to heal the body. Cures were effected, it was claimed, by bringing one's mental attitude and physical state into harmonious balance with the laws of nature.

Philosophically eclectic, mind cure drew from Swedenborgianism, the popular science and health movements, Spiritualism, and above all Transcendentalism. Mind cure technique was developed in the 1850s by Phineas Parkhurst Quimby, an itinerant clockmaker turned healer from New Hampshire. After experimenting with Mesmerism, he rejected the idea that his cures resulted from the manipulation of some invisible "magnetic fluid," arguing instead that both the cause and the cure of disease originated in the patient's state of mind. Mary Baker Eddy, one of his patients, elaborated on Quimby's insights in the 1870s and made metaphysical healing the cornerstone of a new religion, the First Church of Christ, Scientist, or Christian Science.

While Christian Science was the most powerful and long-lived of the mind cure sects, it was not necessarily the most representative. Deeply antiauthoritarian and anti-institutional in spirit, many mind curists regarded the tightly organized infrastructure of the Christian Science Church with hostility. These liberationist impulses may be accounted for by the large number of women who were drawn to mind cure in even larger proportions than in the already "feminized" Protestant denominations. Not incidentally, most of these sects—anticipating late-twentieth-century feminist spirituality—venerated a gender-neutral "Father-Mother" God, endorsed women's rights, valued women's traditional role of healer, and were founded by and gave positions of authority to women, many of whom themselves became objects of devotion.

Mind cure gave rise to pastoral counseling in the 1910s and so may be regarded as a precursor to modern humanist psychotherapy as well as to psychosomatic medicine and popular "success literature" emphasizing the power of positive thinking. In all these ways, mind cure was deeply implicated in the rise of mass consumer culture and the modern cult of personality. *(See also: Eddy, Mary Baker; Spiritualism; Transcendentalism)*

—**Catherine Tumber**

Further Reading

Braden, Charles S. *Spirits in Rebellion: The Rise and Development of New Thought.* Dallas, TX: Southern Methodist University Press, 1963.

Dresser, Horatio W. *A History of the New Thought Movement.* New York: Crowell, 1919.

Hale, Nathan G. "Mind Cures and the Mystical Wave: Popular Preparation for Psychoanalysis, 1904–1910." In *Freud and the Americans: The Beginnings of Psychoanalysis in the United States, 1876–1917.* New York: Oxford University Press, 1971.

Judah, J. Stillson. *The History and Philosophy of the Metaphysical Movements in America.* Philadelphia: Westminster, 1967.

Meyer, Donald. *The Positive Thinkers: Religion as Pop Psychology from Mary Baker Eddy to Oral Roberts.* New York: Pantheon, 1980.

Parker, Gail Thain. *Mind Cure in New England: From the Civil War to World War I.* Hanover, NH: University Press of New England, 1973.

Minimum Wage Laws

Minimum wage laws were an important form of protective legislation for women and children from the first law in Massachusetts in 1912 until the passage of the Fair Labor Standards Act in 1938. Initiated by social feminists during the Progressive Era, these state laws typically established a wages board with the duties of identifying industries with female workforces in which the payment of below-subsistence wages was habitual, then of calculating a living-wage rate, and finally of imposing this rate on designated industries and enforcing its implementation. Minimum wage laws covered shop workers and the so-called sweated trades—the garment industry and those involving the unskilled hand assembly of small items such as boxes, buttons, and trimmings. Enforcement varied because these boards were grossly underfunded, oversight of scattered workshops and homeworkers was difficult, and the penalties were negligible. Nonetheless, the politics of the minimum wage generated landmark debates on the status of women workers and the role of the state in regulating women's employment.

The heyday of minimum wage laws was 1912 through 1919, when laws were passed for fourteen states (mainly in the Midwest and on the West Coast) and the District of Columbia. Coalitions of women's and progressive organizations, with leadership from Florence Kelley as secretary of the National Consumers' League (NCL), supported passage of minimum wage laws, while most employers and much of organized male labor opposed such legislation. The NCL adopted a plan for the minimum wage for women in 1908 that deliberately deviated from the British model of a gender-neutral law. The tactic of proposing gender-specific protective legislation for women undermined the major opposition: The American Federation of Labor (AFL) reluctantly endorsed the policy as strictly for women only in 1913; employers' resistance wavered because they were vulnerable to hostile public reaction to poignant stories of exploited women; and the courts in 1908 permitted economic regulation for women on the grounds of their unique vulnerability.

However, employers continued to oppose the laws through litigation, objecting less to application of the principle of women's weakness than to the precedent set by limiting freedom of contract. In *Stettler v. O'Hara* (1917), the Oregon law survived on a tied vote in the Supreme Court. In *Adkins v. Children's Hospital* (1923), the Court overturned a D.C. law, arguing that woman suffrage victory and social progress removed the necessity of state protection and ignoring the claim of a state interest in the "mothers of the race."

In the meantime, new opposition to any special status for women emerged with the formulation of an equal rights amendment in 1921 by the National Woman's Party. The debate among women over the issue of minimum wage as protective legislation centered on three controversies:

(a) whether the defense of the minimum wage denigrated women, (b) whether the policy had calculable costs in job losses and the development of a gender-segregated labor market or benefits in raised wages, or (c) whether there were viable alternatives for dealing with the appalling poverty that had given rise to these laws.

Demoralized by setbacks in the courts, the minimum wage campaigners retreated into defensive tinkering with the laws until the concept was revived by the New Deal spirit of 1933; five eastern states passed a modified version, still for women, during the 1930s. The Court followed the Adkins precedent and struck down the New York law in *Morehead v. New York ex rel. Tipaldo* (1936). However, in 1937, in *West Coast Hotel Co. v. Parrish,* the justices changed their position on economic regulation and upheld the Washington state law. Their argument was gender neutral, rejecting an absolute right of freedom of contract where a public interest could be shown. This cleared the way for a minimum wage regardless of sex—the principle legislated in the Fair Labor Standards Act of 1938.

When it was enacted in 1938, the act set the minimum wage at 25 cents an hour. This amount has increased over the years to the current level of $5.15 per hour. In 1998, the U.S. Senate rejected a bill to raise the minimum wage to $6.15 an hour by January 1, 2000, but the principle of the original legislation remains an important element in U.S. labor policy. *(See also: Adkins v. Children's Hospital; Equal Rights Amendment; Fair Labor Standards Act; Garment Industries; National Consumers' League; Progressive Era; Protective Legislation; Social Feminism; Wages)*

—**Vivien Hart**

Further Reading

Baer, Judith. *Chains of Protection: The Judicial Response to Women's Labor Legislation.* Westport, CT: Greenwood, 1978.
Beyer, Clara M. *History of Labor Legislation for Women in Three States.* Bulletin of the Women's Bureau, 66. Washington, DC: Government Printing Office, 1929.
Hart, Vivien. *Bound by Our Constitution: Gender and Federalism in New Deal Public Policy.* Ithaca, NY: Cornell University Press, 1998.
Lehrer, Susan. *Origins of Protective Labor Legislation for Women, 1905–1925.* Albany: State University of New York Press, 1987.
Steinberg, Ronnie. *Wages and Hours: Labor and Reform in Twentieth-Century America.* New Brunswick, NJ: Rutgers University Press, 1982.

Minor v. Happersett (1874)

Virginia Minor was an officer in the National Woman Suffrage Association whose attorney husband was equally committed to woman's rights. Together, they developed the constitutional argument that women citizens were protected in their right to vote under the Fourteenth Amendment. As Virginia Minor said, "I believe that the Constitution of the United States gives me every right and privilege to which every other citizen is entitled; for while the Constitution gives the States the rights to regulate suffrage, it nowhere gives them power to prevent." This approach, which began to be used by suffragists in 1869, was called the "new departure."

Their strategy was adopted by the National Woman Suffrage Association and became the foundation of an extraordinary campaign of civil disobedience, in which hundreds of women across the country broke state laws by voting or bringing suit against registrars who refused to let them vote. A number of court cases followed, including Susan B. Anthony's trial for voting, and the suffragists lost them all.

The final test case of woman suffrage under the Fourteenth Amendment began in 1872 when Reese Happersett, the St. Louis registrar of voters, refused to place Virginia Minor's name on the list because "she was not a 'male' citizen, but a woman" and therefore ineligible to vote in the state of Missouri. Because married women under the common law were unable to bring suit independently of their husbands, in association with her husband Francis, Virginia sued for $10,000 damages in the circuit court at St. Louis, lost, and subsequently lost on appeal to the Missouri Supreme Court. They carried the case to the U.S. Supreme Court, with Francis Minor as the chief attorney arguing this landmark woman suffrage case. Chief Justice Morrison R. Waite's opinion declared that suffrage was not coexistent with citizenship, that states had the absolute right to grant or deny suffrage, and that "the Constitution of the United States does not confer the right of suffrage upon any one." The Court's decision was unanimous: "If the courts can consider any question settled, this is one," these nine white men agreed.

Virginia Minor continued her resistance. During the summer of 1879, she refused to pay her taxes, explaining to the board of assessors, "I honestly believe and conscientiously make oath that I have not one dollar's worth of property subject to taxation. The principle upon which this government rests is representation before taxation. My property is denied representation, and therefore can not be taxable."

This Supreme Court decision marked the end of the nineteenth-century quest for woman suffrage through judicial fiat. After *Minor v. Happersett* in 1874, supporters agreed that only a federal amendment to enfranchise women or a state-by-state campaign for individual suffrage statutes would secure the vote for women. Therefore, this decision marked a turning point in the strategy of the nineteenth-century woman suffrage movement as well as the end of the "new departure" strategy. *(See also: National Woman Suffrage Association; Suffrage)*

—Sally Roesch Wagner

Further Reading

DuBois, Ellen Carol. "Taking the Law into Our Own Hands: *Bradwell, Minor,* and Suffrage Militants in the 1870s." In *Visible Women: New Essays on American Activism,* edited by Nancy A. Hewitt and Suzanne Lebsock, 19-40. Urbana: University of Illinois Press, 1993.

MacGregor, Molly Murphy. *Women and the Constitution.* Santa Rosa, CA: National Women's History Project, 1987.

Minor v. Happersett. 53 No., 58, and 21 Wallace, 162 (1874).

Stanton, Elizabeth C., Susan B. Anthony, and Matilda J. Gage, eds. *The History of Woman Suffrage.* Vols. 1-3. New York: Fowler & Wells, 1881–1886.

Wagner, Sally Roesch. *A Time of Protest: Suffragists Challenge the Republic, 1870–1887.* Aberdeen, SD: Sky Carrier Press, 1998.

ə Misogyny

Misogyny is traditionally defined as hatred, dislike, or mistrust of women. Anthropological studies have identified avoidance behavior patterns in many cultures that involve men's shunning of women in particular situations and in particular roles; however, recent scholarship regarding misogyny in American culture extends into a number of disciplines in addition to women's history and gender studies, including psychology, history of religion, theology, literary criticism, and literary history. Studies of misogyny in American literature examining the roles of women as depicted by male authors are numerous, while recent psychological studies stress the role of Western patriarchal culture in limiting and restricting women's self-images and men's images of women. New studies within the fields of history of religion and theology explore the significance of patriarchal religions' characterizations of women. *(See also: Christianity; Feminist Literary Criticism; Psychology; Religion; Theologians; Women's Studies)*

—Mary G. Hodge

Further Reading

Cooey, Paula M. *Religious Imagination and the Body: A Feminist Analysis.* New York: Oxford University Press, 1994.

Cooey, Paula M., Sharon A. Farmer, and Mary Ellen Ross, eds. *Embodied Love: Sensuality and Relationship.* New York: Harper & Row, 1987.

Harding, M. Esther. *The Way of All Women.* 1975. Reprint, New York: Colophon, 1990.

Millett, Kate. *Sexual Politics.* 1970. Reprint, New York: Doubleday, 1990.

Rogers, Katherine M. *The Troublesome Helpmate, A History of Misogyny in Literature.* Seattle: University of Washington Press, 1966.

Smith, Joan. *Misogynies: Reflections on Myths and Malice.* New York: Fawcett, 1992.

Woodman, Marion. *Addiction to Perfection: The Still Unravished Bride, A Psychological Study.* Toronto: Inner City Books, 1982, 1988.

———. *Leaving My Father's House: A Journey to Conscious Femininity.* Boston: Shambhala, 1992, 1993.

———. *The Pregnant Virgin.* Toronto: Inner City Books, 1985.

❧ Mitchell, Maria (1818–1889)

Maria Mitchell was the preeminent woman scientist of her generation and devoted much of her life to assisting other women to enter scientific fields. Trained by her astronomer father William Mitchell, she was a librarian at the Nantucket Athaneum when in 1847 she identified a comet and won a medal from the Danish King. That event catapulted her into prominence, which led to a number of female "firsts" (including membership in the American Association for the Advancement of Science) and a position as professor of astronomy at Vassar College. She continued scientific observations as a field researcher and for nineteen years was a data compiler for the *Nautical Almanac,* which asked her to compute the position of the planet Venus.

Once at Vassar, Mitchell trained the first generation of women astronomers who went on to prominent observatories and to other professorships, and she more generally encouraged her students into scientific careers. In addition, she was an active member and president (in 1875) of the American Association for the Advancement of Women, whose annual peripatetic meetings inspired middle-class women and their daughters to voluntary activism and advanced education. Mitchell herself used the association as a podium to advance the idea that women could achieve prominence in scientific and medical pursuits. A friend of reformers Mary Livermore and Antoinette Brown Blackwell, Maria Mitchell supported suffrage for women but concentrated her public efforts on other immediate and practical concerns for women's education at Vassar and elsewhere. She believed that women required personal encouragement in a supportive environment to gain the confidence as well as the expertise necessary to participate in the competitive and often hostile professions of science. *(See also: Blackwell, Antoinette; Higher Education; Livermore, Mary Ashton; Science; Vassar College)*

—**Sally Gregory Kohlstedt**

Further Reading

Kendall, Phoebe. *Maria Mitchell: Her Life, Letters and Journals.* Boston: Lee & Shepard, 1896.

Kohlstedt, Sally Gregory. "Maria Mitchell and the Advancement of Women in Science." In *Uneasy Careers and Intimate Lives: Women in Science 1789–1979,* edited by Pnina G. Abir-Am and Dorinda Outram, 129-46. New Brunswick, NJ: Rutgers University Press, 1987.

Oles, Carole. *Night Watches: Inventions on the Life of Maria Mitchell.* Cambridge, MA: Alice James Press, 1985.

Rossiter, Margaret. *Women Scientists in America: Struggles and Strategies to 1940.* Baltimore: Johns Hopkins University Press, 1982.

Wright, Helen. *Sweeper in the Sky: The Life of Maria Mitchell. First Woman Astronomer in America.* New York: Macmillan, 1949.

Figure 40. Maria Mitchell
Known as the preeminent woman scientist of her day, Maria Mitchell was the first woman elected to the American Academy of Arts and Sciences. She encouraged legions of women to pursue careers in the sciences. Used by permission of UPI/Corbis-Bettmann.

❧ Mobilization

During periods of war, women have played important roles both within the home and in the workplace. While women have always assisted war efforts by conserving resources and food as well as maintaining homes and farms, many women moved beyond the domestic sphere and into activities that offered direct support to the war effort. During the Revolutionary War, women in towns such as Boston and Philadelphia worked in textile factories to support a boycott of British goods. Women also served as nurses during both the Revolutionary War and the Civil War. Women such as Clara Barton and Dorothea Dix received recognition for their hospital work.

During the Revolutionary War and the Civil War, women offered their services to the cause as opposed to being recruited for work. World War I, however, saw the U.S.

government use several agencies to mobilize women for war work. During 1918, the government created a special division within the Department of Labor to oversee female laborers. The War Advertising Council was set up to encourage war-related advertising, much of it directed at women. Women were recruited by the Department of Labor to work in machine shops, factories, mills, and refineries. Women were also recruited for agricultural jobs, which led to the founding of the American Woman's Land Army.

The greatest push for the mobilization of women in the United States, however, occurred during World War II. With the onset of World War II, women were needed to replace the male workers drafted into military service. The U.S. government set up several agencies to coordinate the mobilization of women for war work. Although the War Manpower Commission was established to mobilize both men and women, much of its work was directed solely at women. The Women's Bureau, which had been created in 1920 to investigate women's special needs in the workforce and had become dormant during the 1930s, reemerged during World War II as the watchdog for female workers. The War Advertising Council was set up to encourage war-related advertising. Its official position was that war advertising was the best way to sell products and win goodwill.

At the start of the war, the primary emphasis was on high wages. Although the government policy of equal pay to women was never rigidly enforced, in general, women's pay increased significantly during the war. This approach was abandoned in 1943 because of the fear of overspending and inflation. The main appeal then became patriotism, which had two directions. Positive appeals encouraged women to "do your part." Negative appeals fed on guilt: "A soldier may die if you don't help out." These appeals were later personalized as women were encouraged to "take a job for your husband/son/brother" and "keep the world safe for your children." Day care centers were established for the children of working mothers; however, most were never used. Of the 4.5 million children under the age of four with working mothers, only 130,000 attended the three thousand day care centers throughout the country.

The aim of the government was to bring as many women into the workforce as possible. The success of these efforts is evidenced by the increase of working females from 27.6 percent to 37 percent by the end of World War II. These agencies were also successful in bringing women into traditionally male jobs. Women in factory work increased 460 percent during World War II.

The mobilization effort was abruptly halted in 1945, as many women were forced out of their jobs to make room for returning male veterans. Many other women voluntarily abandoned the workforce to welcome returning husbands and to start long-delayed families. *(See also: War Manpower Commission; Women's Bureau; World War II)*

—**Judy Sydow Schmidt**
—**Pamela F. Wille**

Further Reading

Campbell, D'Ann. *Women at War with America.* Cambridge, MA: Harvard University Press, 1984.

Culpepper, Marilyn Mayer. *Trials and Triumphs: Women of the American Civil War.* East Lansing: Michigan State University Press, 1991.

Hartmann, Susan M. *The Homefront and Beyond: American Women in the 1940's.* Boston: Twayne, 1982.

Honey, Maureen. *Creating Rosie the Riveter: Class, Gender, and Propaganda during World War II.* Amherst: University of Massachusetts Press, 1984.

Leonard, Elizabeth D. *Yankee Women and Gender: Battles in the Civil War.* New York: Norton, 1994.

Norton, Mary Beth. *Liberty's Daughters: The Revolutionary Experience of American Women, 1750–1800.* Ithaca, NY: Cornell University Press, 1996.

ᔪ *Modern Woman: The Lost Sex*

Modern Woman: The Lost Sex (1947) was an example in both tone and substance of post–World War II antifeminist literature. Coauthored by sociologist Marynia Farnham and historian Ferdinand Lundberg, this best-seller employed Freudian sexology to define women's proper place in postwar American society. Authoritatively citing women's presence in the workforce and absence from the home as the source of problems ranging from the Great Depression to war, Farnham and Lundberg's book defined an "independent woman" as an oxymoronic concept, and thereby, these self-designated experts relegated women to passivity in their social and sexual lives.

The more dominant presence within this influential antifeminist book, Farnham played the role of spokesperson for well-adjusted womanhood. A Ph.D. herself, Farnham warned her readers that education increased the possibility of sex disorders among women, and although Farnham was a practicing psychoanalyst, she categorically stated that women's mental health depended on their performance and acceptance of their domestic role. Emphasizing women's "natural" noncompetitive dependence, Farnham decreed "self-acceptance" of a sexually based inferiority, dependency on men, and passive fulfillment in both sex and motherhood for the well-adjusted woman. However, she argued that passivity in sexuality on the part of women did not relieve them from the responsibility of their own frigidity.

A frontal assault on feminism as a sickness, *Modern Woman* upheld as neurotic any challenge to male dominance. Thus, Farnham dismissed feminism as a psychic disorder, a pathological denial of women's instinct that produced in feminist women hatred of their fathers, rejection of motherhood, and unfeminine behavior—a refrain used by evangelist Pat Robertson in the backlash era of the late 1980s. The authors' proposal for supplemental state support of the woman in the home implied a tacit recognition of the economic factors involved in the contemporary undermining of the traditional women's role in the post-Industrial Era. The impact of *Modern Woman* stemmed not from its original or salient criticism of feminism but, rather, from the timing of its publication. The book's influence was enhanced not only by post-World War II antifeminism but also by the lack of a contemporary, articulate feminism to counter its pseudopsychological propaganda. *(See also: Antifeminism; Freudianism; Psychiatry; Psychology)*

—**Angela M. Howard**

Further Reading

Lundberg, Ferdinand, and Marynia Farnham. *Modern Woman: The Lost Sex.* New York: Harper, 1947.

Mitchell, Juliet. *Psychoanalysis and Feminism.* New York: Vintage, 1975.

~ Mohr, Nicholasa (b. 1935)

Artist, novelist, essayist, juvenile and adult short-fiction writer, Nicholasa Mohr is the first Puerto Rican woman on the mainland to write in English about her own ethnic origins as the child of island migrants to New York City. She wrote and designed the book jackets for *Nilda* (1973), an award-winning children's novel, and *El Bronx Remembered* (1975, reprinted 1993), which were followed by two other semiautobiographical books: *In Nueva York* (1977, reprinted 1997) and *Felita* (1979, reprinted 1996). Recent publications include *The Song of El Coqui and Other Tales of Puerto Rico* (1995) and *All for the Better: A Story of El Barrio* (1996).

Mohr's stories serve as an excellent primary source for interpreting the labyrinth of Puerto Rican family and community life in the ethnic ghetto during the four post-World War II decades. Her skills as both a graphic artist and an author enable her to depict visually and realistically the lifestyles of people who, as citizens, did not face migration quotas but who nonetheless were "strangers in their own country [having brought with them a different language, culture, and racial mixture]." Mohr remembers "how unjust it was for my mother . . . to conform to the role of wife and mother, always sacrificing." Mohr herself, born during the Great Depression as the only daughter in a family with seven children, worked as a waitress while studying art before embarking on a writing career.

Mohr's thematic focus is in detailing her people's plight, the problems of a rural migrant group suddenly thrust into an industrial society, with many large female-headed welfare households living in rat-infested, crumbling tenements, often with no male role model for rebellious street children. Coming to the mainland with few skills, Puerto Ricans are forced into menial jobs where racial and religious discrimination add to adjustment problems. Her anecdotal tales describe failed marriages, illegitimacy, illness, insensitive teachers and social workers, police brutality, and superstitious subculture life within a powerful Anglo community. Realistically sketched vignettes, frequently told from an innocent, questioning, resigned child's vision, unfold like documentaries without artificial solutions or contrived endings,

giving her stories unique credibility. Warm family solidarity and joyous neighborhood participation in the colorful pageantry of religious celebrations help her proud protagonists cope creatively with hardships, finding the strength to survive. Hispanics represent the largest ethnic group in the United States, and Nicholasa Mohr's stories give readers the opportunity to learn about Puerto Rican contributions to American social history. *(See also:* Chicana; *Female-Headed Households; Immigration; Women Writers)*

—**Edith Blicksilver**

Further Reading

Miller, John. "Nicholasa Mohr: Neorican Writings in Progress 'A View of the Other Culture,' " *Revista InterAmerican* 9 (1979-80): 543-49.

Mohr, Nicholasa. "An Awakening . . . Summer 1956, for Hilda Hidalgo." In *Revista Chicano-Riqueña, Women of Her Word, Hispanic Women Write,* edited by Evangelina Vigil, 107-12. Houston, TX: University of Houston Press, 1983.

———. "Christmas Was a Time of Plenty." In *Revista Chicano-Riqueña, New York City Special,* edited by Nicolás Kanellos and Luis Dávilla, 33-34. Houston, TX: University of Houston Press, 1980.

———. *El Bronx Remembered.* New York: Harper & Row, 1975, 1993.

———. *Felita.* 1979. Reprint, New York: Dial, 1996.

———. *Going Home.* 1986. Reprint, New York: Dial, 1997.

———. *In Nueva York.* 1977. Reprint, New York: Dial, 1994.

———. *Nilda.* 1973. Reprint, New York: Harper & Row, 1986.

———. *Rituals of Survival: A Woman's Portfolio.* 1985. Reprint, University Park, TX: University of Houston Press, 1994.

———. "A Special Gift." In *Revista Chicano-Riqueña, New York City Special,* edited by Nicolás Kanellos, 91-100. Houston, TX: University of Houston Press, 1981.

———. "A Very Special Pet." In *The Ethnic American Woman: Problems, Protests, Lifestyle,* edited by Edith Blicksilver, 101-6. Dubuque, IA: Kendall/Hunt, 1978.

Mohr, Nicholasa, and Antonio Martorell (illustrator). *The Song of El Coqui and Other Tales of Puerto Rico.* New York: Viking Children's Books, 1995.

Mohr, Nicholasa, Nicholas Mohr, and Rudy Gutierrez (illustrator). *All for the Better: A Story of El Barrio* (Stories of America). Austin, TX: Raintree/Steck-Vaughn, 1996.

~ Monroe, Marilyn (1926–1962)

An American film star whose career spanned a mere dozen years and eleven major film roles, Marilyn Monroe attained legendary status as a result of her magnetic sexuality, her powerful screen presence, and her mysterious death.

Born Norma Jean[e] Baker/Mortensen in Los Angeles, she grew up fatherless from birth and motherless from the age of seven when her mother, Gladys Mortensen, was institutionalized for mental illness. Cared for by several of her mother's friends, Monroe married James Dougherty, a neighbor boy and aircraft factory worker, when she was sixteen. While he was overseas during the war, she began her career as a model, and after their divorce in 1946, she began appearing in minor film roles, changing her name to Marilyn Monroe.

As a contract player at Twentieth Century Fox, she appeared in John Huston's *Asphalt Jungle* (1950), which produced a flood of fan mail; by 1952, when her nude photograph on a calendar caused a scandal that brought nationwide publicity, she was receiving over five thousand fan letters a week and starring in films such as *Niagara* and *Gentlemen Prefer Blondes*. In 1953, she married Joe DiMaggio, America's baseball hero; the marriage lasted nine months. In 1954, she made *There's No Business like Show Business* and *The Seven Year Itch* and headed for New York to study her craft at Lee Strasberg's Actors Studio and to negotiate a better contract with Fox. That contract, signed in January 1956, gave her more money, the freedom to make films at other studios, and her own production company, Marilyn Monroe Productions at Fox. By the standards of the time, when the studio system was still alive and formidable, it was a triumph.

Between 1956 and 1960, while married to playwright Arthur Miller, she made only four films: *Bus Stop* (1956) and *The Prince and the Showgirl* (1957), both for MM Productions; *Some Like It Hot* (1959); and *Let's Make Love* (1960). As her marriage to Miller entered its final throes, her visits to psychiatrists and doctors and her use of prescription drugs increased, yet she began work on *The Misfits* (1961), with a screenplay by Miller from an *Esquire* short story he had written three years before. It was to be the last film either Monroe or costar Clark Gable would ever make.

In 1961, she resumed her friendship with DiMaggio and, during that same year, had a brief sexual encounter with President John F. Kennedy. Early in 1962, she began work on *Something's Got to Give,* but from the outset, the production was under a cloud caused primarily by Fox's financial woes but blamed on Monroe. That summer, she revitalized her image with photo/interview sessions with *Life, Vogue,* and *Cosmopolitan,* began reading scripts and planning other projects, and set a date for her wedding to DiMaggio. On August 4, 1962, she was found dead from an overdose of sleeping medication, prescribed and perhaps administered by her psychiatrist. Ever since, suicide and conspiracy rumors have flourished.

This brief public life had a disproportionate impact. For men, Monroe seems to be the embodiment of the ideal lover. Norman Mailer is eloquent on the subject:

> She was our angel, the sweet angel of sex, and the sugar of sex came up from her like a resonance of sound in the clearest grain of a violin. Across five continents the men who knew the most about love would covet her, . . . Marilyn was deliverance, a very Stradivarius of sex, so gorgeous, forgiving, humorous, compliant and tender that even the most mediocre musician could relax his lack of art in the dissolving magic of her violin. (15)

Women's reactions have been more complex. In life, Marilyn Monroe was a threat—the ultimate rival for men's affections and a blatant acknowledgment of one's own weaknesses. As Gloria Steinem acknowledges, she

> embodied . . . the fear of a sexual competitor who could take away men on whom women's identities and even livelihoods might depend; the fear of having to meet her impossible standard of always giving—and asking nothing in return; the nagging fear that we might share her feminine fate of being vulnerable, unserious, constantly in danger of being a victim. (14-15)

Decades after her death, books and articles still appear regularly, as the mysteries of Marilyn Monroe continue to engross successive generations. With distance and hindsight, however, those generations are able to appreciate her film work more fully to enjoy and be awed by one who, more than any other, represents the postwar feminine ideal. *(See also: The Fifties; Movie Stars)*

—**Frances M. Kavenik**

Further Reading

Leaming, Barbara. *Marilyn Monroe.* New York: Crown, 1998.
Mailer, Norman. *Marilyn.* New York: Warner, 1973.
Steinem, Gloria. *Marilyn.* Photography by George Barris. New York: Henry Holt, 1986.
Spoto, Donald. *Marilyn Monroe: The Biography.* New York: HarperCollins, 1993.

⮥ Montana State Federation of Negro Women's Clubs

A regional example of the black women's club movement, the Montana State Federation of Negro Women's Clubs resulted from the belief that "effective recognition can only be gained by unity at home." Citing the fact that black women across the country were organizing for "uplift" work, the Pearl Club of Butte, Montana, issued an invitation to its sister black women's clubs to form a state federation. Eight clubs from Kalispell, Butte, Helena, Anaconda, Billings, and Bozeman met in Butte from August 3 to 5, 1921, to form the federation. (Some years later, the federation substituted Colored for Negro in its name.) The federation adopted the motto "Unity and Perseverance" and voted to establish a college scholarship for black students and to send delegates to the National Convention of Negro Women's Clubs. The Dunbar Art and Study Club of Great Falls, an extremely active group, subsequently joined the federation.

For over fifty years, the federation supported the work of women's clubs on a local level as well as the national efforts of the Anti-Lynching League and the National Association for the Advancement of Colored People (NAACP). In Montana, local clubs lobbied for civil rights legislation at the state level, fought discrimination in school athletics and social events, visited black patients in hospitals and rest homes, sponsored Frederick Douglass Day programs to honor the famed black abolitionist, placed books by black authors in public libraries, organized interracial clubs to foster better race relations, and supported the efforts of blacks to join trade unions. The federation met in convention each year, addressing topics such as "Possibilities of the Negro Woman in Business and Industry," "The Achievement of the Negro," and "Fear." The Montana State Federation finally disbanded in the mid-1970s because of a lack of members. *(See also: Black Women's Clubs; National Association for the Advancement of Colored People)*

—**Mary Murphy**

Further Reading

Montana Federation of Colored Women. Records, 1921–78. Montana Historical Society Archives, Helena, MT.

Slauson, Lena Brown. Oral History Interview. Montana Historical Society Archives, Helena, MT.

ᕤ Moore, Anne Carroll (1871–1961)

Anne Carroll Moore, children's librarian and writer, was an innovator in public library services to children. In her position as supervisor of work with children in the New York Public Library (NYPL), 1906 to 1941, she influenced the development of such services worldwide. Furthermore, her extensive contacts with New York publishing houses and authors, her column titled "The Three Owls" that appeared in the *New York Herald Tribune* (1924–1930) and later in the *Horn Book,* and her reviews in the *Bookman* (1918–1941) influenced publishing for children. Her two books for children were *Nicholas: A Manhattan Christmas Story* (1924) and *Nicholas: The Golden Goose* (1932). She fought successfully to obtain professional status for librarians working with children in the NYPL and for the establishment of a section devoted to children's librarianship within the American Library Association. Among the techniques now widely accepted that are associated with her are story hours, cooperation with the schools and teachers, and vibrant exhibits and presentations of music and dance.

Anne Carroll Moore was one of ten children born to a lawyer and his highly cultivated wife in Limerick, Maine. She had intended to read law with her father after completion of her formal education at Bradford (Massachusetts) Academy, but the deaths of her parents and a sister-in-law left her burdened with domestic chores. After her brother's remarriage, she began her library studies at Pratt Institute in Brooklyn.

Although a woman of wide-ranging interests and compassion, she alienated many with her eccentricities and self-centeredness. Moore participated in the campaign to save Leo Frank, who had visited her library as a boy, when he was falsely accused and unjustly convicted of the 1913 murder of Mary Phagan in Atlanta, Georgia. She encouraged the translation and use of foreign materials and supported the work of the American Committee for Devastated France in establishing services for French children after World War I. How-

ever, in her later years, resentful of mandatory retirement, she became quite difficult, distressing many colleagues and friends, especially her successors, as she continued to revisit "her" department. *(See also: Children's Library Movement; Librarianship)*

—**Suzanne Hildenbrand**

Further Reading

Jagusch, Sybille A. "First among Equals: Caroline M. Hewins and Anne C. Moore. Foundations of Library Work with Children." Ph.D. diss., University of Maryland–College Park, 1990.

Lundin, Anne. "Anne Carroll Moore: 'I Have Spun a Long Thread.'" In *Reclaiming the American Library Past: Writing the Women In,* edited by Suzanne Hildebrand, 187-204. Norwood, NJ: Ablex, 1996.

Moore, Anne Carroll. *My Roads to Childhood: Views and Reviews of Children's Books.* Boston: Horn Book, 1961.

ᕤ Moore, Marianne Craig (1887–1972)

A key figure in modern American poetry, Marianne Moore wrote with a disdain for conventional poetry, renouncing elaborate diction and subjectivity and relying on the observation of details to discover "the genuine." To Moore, good poems were "imaginary gardens with real toads in them."

Moore's life was as conventional as her verse was original. Born in Kirkwood, Mississippi, she spent much of her adult life living with her mother in New York City. Although she specialized in biology in college and once considered becoming an artist, she instead became a shorthand and typing teacher and then a librarian. She never lost interest in biology and art, however, and they became two sources of power in her poetry. Her editorship of *Dial* from 1925 until its demise in 1929 also strengthened her natural skills. During this period and throughout her life, she was respected for her literary reviews and her editorial judgment.

Moore's first poems were published in *Poetry* and the *Egoist* in 1915, and her first book of poems, simply titled *Poems,* was published in 1921 in London, without her knowledge, by H. D. (Hilda Doolittle) and Bryher (Winifred Ellerman). Moore wrote on a wide range of topics, but her favorite subjects were animals, ranging from the common to the exotic. While she did publish a translation of La Fontaine's fables in 1954, her animal poems are not fables. Rather, they are observations that make her readers think about themselves and, perhaps, look at life differently.

Moore's greatest contributions to poetry are her poetic language, which is at once poetry and prose, and her prosodic innovations. Eschewing the formal metrical and rhyme schemes of traditional verse, Moore devised her own formal patterns, which were unlike anything else in modern American poetry. She treated the stanza rather than the line as the poetic unit and arranged lines according to the number of syllables rather than by a specific meter, creating an elaborate and thoroughly regular verse pattern. Rhymes occur frequently, although at unexpected places—unaccented syllables and middles of words, for example. All the while, however, Moore's verse remains quiet and unpretentious. *(See also: Doolittle, Hilda; Women Writers)*

—**Kenneth E. Gadomski**

Further Reading

Costello, Bonnie. *Marianne Moore: Imaginary Possessions.* Cambridge, MA: Harvard University Press, 1981.
Parisi, Joseph M. *Marianne Moore: The Art of a Modernist.* Ann Arbor: UMI Research Press, 1990.
Slatin, John M. *The Savage's Romance: The Poetry of Marianne Moore.* University Park: Pennsylvania State University Press, 1986.

ꝏ Moral Reform

Moral reform has been a continuing theme in American history. In Jacksonian America, it featured organizations such as the New York Female Moral Reform Society, founded in May 1834 at the Third Presbyterian Church in New York City. Members of this society wanted to convert New York's large population of prostitutes to evangelical Protestantism and to close the city's many brothels. More fundamentally, these reformers were also interested in confronting the sexual double standard that made it socially acceptable for some men to have mistresses and/or frequent the more attractive houses of pleasure, while women were denied such diversions.

Staff members of the Moral Reform Society began systematically visiting New York bordellos in the fall of 1834 to pray with and exhort both inmates and their patrons to change their "sinful ways." Mild forms of intimidation of customers were also used, as well as street-corner preaching and proselytizing. The society also opened a House of Reception as a refuge for prostitutes who wished to leave "the life." Few took advantage of the opportunity.

The New York Moral Reform Society made perhaps its biggest national impact through publication of its weekly *The Advocate of Moral Reform,* which became one of the nation's most widely read evangelical reform papers, having a circulation of 16,500 by the late 1830s. Other reformers and reform groups were inspired by the efforts of the society, which continues to exist today as the Woodycrest Youth Service.

Moral reform crusades have continued in a variety of locations and time periods down to the present moment even if they have failed repeatedly to eliminate or reform social vices such as prostitution or drug abuse. They have, however, allowed women to play a more public role than was traditionally assigned to them prior to the nineteenth century in the United States. *(See also: Prostitution; Religion)*

—**Jonathan W. Zophy**

Further Reading

Burnham, John. *Bad Habits: Drinking, Smoking, Taking Drugs, Gambling, Sexual Misbehavior, and Swearing in American History.* New York: New York University Press, 1993.

Smith-Rosenberg, Carroll. "Beauty, the Beast and the Militant Woman: A Case Study in Sex Roles and Social Stress in Jacksonian America," *American Quarterly* 23 (1971): 562-84.
———. *Disorderly Conduct: Visions of Gender in Victorian America.* New York: Knight, 1985.
———. *Religion and the Rise of the American City.* Ithaca, NY: Cornell University Press, 1971.

ꝏ Moravian Seminary for Young Females

The Moravian Seminary for Young Females was one of the first boarding schools for girls in the United States. The seminary, also known as Bethlehem Female Seminary, grew out of a school opened on May 4, 1742, in Germantown, Pennsylvania, by the Moravians, or Church of the United Brethren, a religious group from Germany. This school and others were opened as part of the Moravians' commitment to "spread knowledge of Christ." During the first several years, the seminary was moved between three communities before being located in Bethlehem, Pennsylvania, on January 6, 1749. Since then, it has remained in that community.

The reputation of the school grew quickly, and a number of non-Moravians attended. By 1757, for example, eighty-nine pupils were enrolled, as the seminary absorbed the girls' schools of the neighboring congregations. The seminary included an elementary and secondary boarding school and a town day school. It continued to grow because, as a church official later wrote, "In those early days it was a privilege highly prized to have a daughter under such care and training, taken from the remote backwoods homes in many cases and brought in contact with gentle, pious women of refinement." The school, as the guidelines from September 1785 recorded, kept girls "from their fifth to their twelfth or sixteenth year," and taught them "the Admonition of the Lord in every good habit," along with "reading and writing in both the German and English languages, also arithmetic, sewing, knitting, and other feminine crafts." They were also instructed in "history, geography, and music, with great care and faithfulness, and as their health and strength may permit." In 1788, the church prepared "statutes" for the school, which identified the duties of the pupils and their course of study. The daily regimen was strict; pupils were closely monitored and directed by the teachers. Over the next two decades, the growth in enrollment caused the construction of three additional buildings. With the opening of a new facility in 1805, the school became known as the Young Ladies Seminary. Throughout the nineteenth century, the school continued to grow as its reputation spread. By 1853, for example, more than 150 pupils were enrolled at the school. The upper division gained accreditation as the Moravian Seminary and College for Women in 1913, while the lower grades continued to offer college preparatory work. In 1949, the grades seven through twelve were moved to a new facility located outside Bethlehem on an estate donated to the school. *(See also: Education; Female Academies; Linden Hall Seminary; Religion)*

—Robert G. Waite

Further Reading

Haller, Mabel. "Early Moravian Education in Pennsylvania," *Transactions of the Moravian Historical Society* 15 (1953): 1-397.

Mulhern, James. *A History of Secondary Education in Pennsylvania.* Philadelphia: Science Press, 1933.

Norton, Mary Beth. *Liberty's Daughters: The Revolutionary Experience of American Women, 1750–1800.* Ithaca, NY: Cornell University Press, 1996.

Reichel, William C. *A History of the Rise, Progress, and Present Condition of the Moravian Seminary for Young Ladies at Bethlehem, Pa.* Philadelphia: J. B. Lippincott, 1870.

Moreno, Luisa (1907–1992)

Luisa Moreno was a labor leader, union organizer, and a Chicana civil rights activist. Born in Guatemala, she was from an upper-middle-class family. She was educated in the United States at the College of the Holy Name in Oakland, California.

In the 1920s, she was a newspaper reporter in Mexico City. She began her career as a union organizer in New York City in the 1930s, working in Spanish Harlem with garment factory workers. She joined the Congress of Industrial Organizations (CIO) in 1937 and became an organizer and a newspaper editor for the CIO affiliate, the United Cannery, Agricultural, Packing, and Allied Workers of America (UCAPAWA). She traveled extensively throughout the country organizing cigar workers in Florida, pecan shellers in Texas, and cotton, beets, and cannery workers in Michigan, Colorado, and California.

In 1938, she focused primarily on Mexican American civil rights. She participated in founding El Congreso de los Pueblos de Habla Española (Congress of the Spanish Speaking People), also known as El Congresso. This organization fought discrimination and poor working conditions and was committed to the social, economic, and cultural improvement of Mexican Americans. El Congresso was active from 1938 to 1941 and had over 70,000 members at its height. Moreno remained an active union organizer throughout the 1940s and became vice president of the CIO and the international vice president of the UCAPAWA.

Her activism in unions and her radicalism made her a natural target for McCarthyism in the 1950s, and she was forced to leave the United States under the terms of the McCarran-Walter Immigration Act. She originally went to Mexico and then to Cuba, where she participated in the Castro Revolution. She eventually settled in Guadalajara, Mexico. She continued her interest in unions and Mexican American civil rights until her death in 1992. *(See also: American Federation of Labor; Chicana; Congress of Industrial Organizations; Garment Industries)*

—Joyce Ann Kievit

Further Reading

Delgado Campbell, Delores. "Shattering the Stereotype: Chicanas as Labor Union Organizers," *Berkeley Women of Color* 11 (1983): 20-23.

Duran, Livie Isaurom, and Russell Bernard, eds. *Introduction to Chicano Studies.* New York: Macmillan, 1973.

Ruiz, Vicki. "A Promise Fulfilled: Mexican Cannery Workers in Southern California," *Pacific Historian* 30 (Summer 1986): 51-61.

Mormonism

The role of women in the Church of Jesus Christ of Latter-Day Saints, or Mormon Church as it is popularly known, has been a complex and often paradoxical one since the founding of the group in 1830. Mormonism, seeing itself as both a religion and a culture system, has attempted to encompass the whole of life. Under the leadership of the group's prophet-founder, Joseph Smith, Mormons in the 1830s and 1840s reacted against the religious and social disorder of Jacksonian America by developing a patriarchal family system that drew heavily on Old Testament models. Influenced also by the New Testament, Mormonism stressed the "priesthood of all believers" for men, setting up a hierarchical structure in which all worthy adult males had some direct leadership role within the lay governance structure of the church. Women were linked to this structure only indirectly through association with their husbands, but during the first two decades, they did secure the right to participate in public meetings of the church, to vote on important proposals brought before the group, to operate their own women's organization (albeit under ultimate direction of the male priesthood), to receive various "spiritual gifts," and to be "ordained" to administer to the sick.

Religiously, earliest Mormonism fell midway between the most conservative confessional churches such as the Episcopalians, in which women were almost totally excluded from leadership, and the extreme wing of revivalistic and sectarian movements such as the Shakers, which permitted a high degree of equality for women. Until the early 1840s, Mormon women's roles most closely approximated those in mainstream revivalist Protestant groups such as the Methodists and Baptists.

Joseph Smith's effort to introduce a patriarchal polygamous system among his closest associates during the early 1840s was associated with radical changes in Mormon theology and practice. The new temple ceremonies, designed in part to validate plural marriage, emphasized that no person could reach full exaltation in the afterlife without being sealed under the authority of the Mormon Church in a celestial marriage to a worthy spouse. Committed Mormons were privately told that polygamy was the highest form of such celestial marriage because it allowed greatly expanded kinship ties. Such ties were considered the primary source of status and power, both in this life and throughout eternity.

Despite efforts to promulgate beliefs and practices that seemed strikingly at variance with the American norm,

Mormon attitudes toward women nevertheless remained extraordinarily fluid during the turbulent transitional period immediately prior to Joseph Smith's assassination in 1844. Only following the Mormon arrival in the Great Basin region of the West in 1847 was the group, under Brigham Young's leadership, able to set up and develop to the fullest extent its own distinctive way of life. Although Young was a patriarchal leader par excellence and the key individual responsible for institutionalizing and defending polygamy, he also recognized the vital role that women would have to play in developing frontier Utah, and he encouraged women to exercise a remarkable degree of power, influence, and independence in helping to build the Mormon Zion. Utah established one of the first coeducational colleges in the country in 1850; Mormon women voted in Utah earlier than women in any other state or territory of the United States, including Wyoming; women of the Mormon church were active in the professions, including medicine and teaching; and leading Mormon women established a distinguished woman-written, -edited, and -distributed newspaper of their own, the *Woman's Exponent,* which ranged far and wide over issues of concern to women of the period. Through their powerful women's organization, the Relief Society, and numerous other economic and cultural ventures, Mormon women became a key force in frontier Utah at the very time when the outside society viewed them as oppressed and degraded because of the practice of polygamy.

In response to the intense federal antipolygamy crusade of the 1880s that threatened the very survival of Mormonism, the group in the 1890s began to give up polygamy, direct control over Utah politics, and many other controversial practices. As part of this effort to accommodate to American society, Mormons increasingly adopted Victorian notions of gentility and women's role. The gradual end of frontier conditions in the Mormon West around the turn of the century also contributed to the movement away from the older ideals of the versatile pioneer wife and mother toward that of the Victorian homemaker with no legitimate work role outside the home.

Since World War II, and especially since 1960, attempts to limit Mormon women's sphere of influence have become increasingly pronounced. In an effort to deal with the staggering increase of membership from approximately one million in 1945 to over six million in 1985, Mormon church organization has been restructured and further centralized. As part of reducing duplication of magazines, "correlating" the church educational curriculum, and placing all channels of authority under direct male hierarchical control, the Relief Society has lost its independence in funding and programming, as well as its *Relief Society Magazine,* the only officially approved woman's magazine in the church.

Many of the recent converts to Mormonism have been fundamentalist Christians or Catholics dissatisfied with what they perceived as the failure of their parent churches to hold the line against forces contributing to social and family disorder since the 1960s. Mormon church leaders, responding to concerns about disorder in the outer society as well as in their own church, where approximately half of all married women work outside the home, have aggressively promulgated the notion that woman's only significant role is as a wife and mother and that work outside the home is harmful to the family. Through a variety of front organizations, the Mormon Church played a key role in defeating the Equal Rights Amendment to the Constitution, which it viewed as a threat to the family and to its particular family practices. Mormonism's increasingly aggressive political role has been publicly opposed by Mormon or ex-Mormon feminists such as Marilyn Warenski and Sonia Johnson, as well as privately by some Mormon intellectuals, but the overall trend toward further centralization under the patriarchal church structure appears unlikely to be reversed in the near future. *(See also: Complex Marriage; Equal Rights Amendment; Plural Marriage; Religion; Suffrage in the American West)*

—**Lawrence Foster**

Further Reading

Beecher, Maureen Ursenbach, and Lavina Fielding Anderson, eds. *Sisters in Spirit: Mormon Women in Historical and Cultural Perspective.* Urbana: University of Illinois Press, 1987.

Burgess-Olson, Vickie, ed. *Sister Saints.* Provo, UT: Brigham Young University Press, 1978.

Bushman, Claudia, ed. *Mormon Sisters: Women in Early Utah.* Cambridge, MA: Emmeline, 1976.

Foster, Lawrence. "From Activism to Domesticity: The Changing Role of Mormon Women in the Nineteenth and Twentieth Centuries." In *Women, Family, and Utopia: Communal Experiments of the Shakers, the Oneida Perfectionists, and the Mormons,* edited by Lawrence Foster, 202-19. Syracuse, NY: Syracuse University Press, 1991.

Gottlieb, Robert, and Peter Wiley. *America's Saints: The Rise of Mormon Power.* New York: Harcourt Brace Jovanovich, 1986.

Hanks, Maxine, ed. *Women and Authority: Re-emerging Mormon Feminism.* Salt Lake City, UT: Signature, 1992.

Johnson, Sonia. *From Housewife to Heretic.* Garden City, NY: Doubleday, 1981.

Newell, Linda King. "The Historical Relationship of Mormon Women and Priesthood," *Dialogue: A Journal of Mormon Thought* 18 (Autumn 1985): 21-32.

Warenski, Marilyn. *Patriarchs and Politics: The Plight of the Mormon Woman.* New York: McGraw-Hill, 1978.

Whittaker, David J., and Carol C. Madsen. "History's Sequel: A Source Essay on Women in Mormon History," *Journal of Mormon History* 6 (1979): 123-45.

⟡ Morrill Land-Grant Act of 1862

The Morrill Land-Grant Act of 1862 provided a generous federal land grant to establish agricultural and mechanical arts colleges in every state. Each state was allotted thirty thousand acres of public land for each of its congressional representatives on which to create separate A&M (agricultural and mechanical) institutions or adjunct institutions to be added to existing state universities. Considered the most important piece of education legislation enacted at the federal level, the Morrill Land-Grant Act of 1862 was significant for women's education because of the coeducational institutions established in the midwestern and far western states after the Civil War. *(See also: Coeducation; Education; Higher Education; Smith-Lever Act)*

—**Angela M. Howard**

ॐ Morrison, Toni (b. 1931)

Toni Morrison, winner of the 1993 Nobel Prize for literature, a Pulitzer (1988), and the National Book Critics Circle Award (1987), is widely recognized as one of the finest U.S. fiction writers of the late twentieth century. She is the author of seven novels that span 300 years of U.S. history. Her subject is the lives of African Americans, from the torments of the deadly slave ship journeys and the overseers' whips to the African Americans' twentieth-century struggles to earn a living, sustain families, and come to value themselves despite the omnipresence of a nearly all-powerful white culture that defines them as "other" and inferior.

Born Chloe Anthony Wofford, Morrison grew up in Lorain, Ohio, the daughter of former sharecroppers who had migrated north from Alabama. Morrison's father became a ship welder and her mother a homemaker. Morrison took an undergraduate degree in English at Howard University (1953) and an M.A. at Cornell (1955), taught English at Texas Southern University in Houston and at Howard University, and then became an editor for Random House where she worked for eighteen years. She married in 1959 but divorced five years later and raised her two sons as a single mother. Since 1987, she has been a professor in the Council of the Humanities at Princeton University. In addition to her novels, she has written a book of literary criticism (1992) analyzing the portrayal of African Americans in American literature, and a children's book, *The Big Box* (1999).

Morrison is a master both of realism and of lyrical, mythmaking prose steeped in magic and poetry. Her novels concern families and relationships that have been hideously scarred by slavery and deformed by racism, and the people and situations she portrays are so extreme that in the hands of a lesser novelist they would be sensational. The tragic central figure of *The Bluest Eye* (1970), Morrison's first novel, for instance, is a young girl who thinks her life would be livable if only she had blue eyes. Growing up in extreme poverty with a mother and father who beat each other, she has been raped and impregnated by her drunken father who has succumbed to powerlessness and his wife's rejection of him. By the end of the novel, the young girl retreats from reality altogether and believes she has the blue eyes that will transform her into someone lovable. Morrison's best-known novel, *Beloved* (1987), tells the story of Sethe, a runaway slave who tries to kill all four of her children to prevent the slave owner from repossessing them, and succeeds in sawing her baby's throat with a hacksaw. In *Song of Solomon*

Figure 41. Toni Morrison
Recipient of the Pulitzer Prize in 1988 and the Nobel Prize in 1993, Toni Morrison is one of the mostly widely read and influential novelists of today. Used by permission of UPI/Corbis-Bettmann.

(1977), the prosperous, powerful family of the male central figure has turned its back on its blackness with such life-destroying finality that the young man must retrace the steps of his ancestors to find roots to make his own life livable. Morrison's most recent novel, *Paradise* (1998), studies the spiritual impact of ingrownness on an all-black, isolationist town that tries to sustain its crumbling purity by attacking a group of women who live together seeking refuge from their disaster-fraught lives.

Although Morrison creates many memorable and sympathetically portrayed male characters, her mythical and magical figures are most often women. In *Song of Solomon,* for instance, the young man is helped on his quest by his mysteriously powerful aunt who refuses to release her hold on black ways and roots. She has no navel; her father's bones hang in a bag from the rafters of her ceiling; she can teach her nephew to find the secret of his ancestors; and in the last scene of the novel her nephew discovers that she is able to fly. In *Beloved,* the murdered daughter comes back as a ghost, first as a baby and then as a beautiful young black woman who is both the dead child returning to reclaim the love she lost and black suffering under slavery incarnate in a single consciousness. When she lapses into reverie, the reader is immersed in the moment-to-moment experience of the slave crossings from Africa.

Despite Morrison's subject matter, her novels are not polemical. They are an epic of African American life: the loving depiction of the triumphs and failures in everyday living of blacks in the United States. *(See also: Black Women; Slavery; Women Writers)*

—**Gretchen Mieszkowski**

Further Reading

Bloom, Harold, ed. *Toni Morrison*. New York: Chelsea House, 1990.

Butler-Evans, Elliott. *Race, Gender, and Desire: Narrative Strategies in the Fiction of Toni Cade Bambara, Toni Morrison, and Alice Walker.* Philadelphia: Temple University Press, 1989.

Gates, Henry L., Jr., and K. A. Appiah. *Toni Morrison: Critical Perspectives Past and Present.* New York: Amistad, 1993.

Harding, Wendy, and Jacky Martin. *A World of Difference: An Inter-Cultural Study of Toni Morrison's Novels.* Westport, CT: Greenwood, 1994.

Harris, Trudier. *Fiction and Folklore: The Novels of Toni Morrison.* Knoxville: University of Tennessee Press, 1991.

McKay, Nellie Y. *Critical Essays on Toni Morrison.* Boston: G. K. Hall, 1988.

McKay, Nellie Y., and Kathryn Earle, eds. *Approaches to Teaching the Novels of Toni Morrison.* New York: Modern Language Association of America, 1997.

Middleton, David L., ed. *Toni Morrison's Fiction: Contemporary Criticism.* New York: Garland, 1997.

Otten, Terry. *The Crime of Innocence in the Fiction of Toni Morrison.* Columbia: University of Missouri Press, 1989.

Rigney, Barbara. *The Voices of Toni Morrison.* Columbus: Ohio State University Press, 1991.

Weinstein, Philip M. *What Else But Love? The Ordeal of Race in Faulkner and Morrison.* New York: Columbia University Press, 1996.

Wyatt, Jean. "Giving Body to the Word: The Maternal Symbolic in Toni Morrison's *Beloved,*" *PMLA* 108 (1993): 474-88.

Moskowitz, Belle Lindner Israels
(1877–1933)

Belle Moskowitz, social reformer and political strategist, was born in Harlem, New York, and educated at city schools, Horace Mann High School for Girls, and for a year at Teachers' College of Columbia University. She then took a job at the Educational Alliance, a Lower East Side settlement. In 1903, she resigned to marry Charles Henry Israels, an architect, with whom she had three children. When he died suddenly in 1911, she returned to work.

During her marriage, Moskowitz had worked part-time for the social work journal *The Survey* and pursued social reform issues, primarily through the New York Section of the Council of Jewish Women. This work led her into dance hall reform, an experience she parlayed into salaried work when she was widowed. In 1912, she worked in the Progressive Party campaign. In 1913, she became grievance clerk and then Labor Department head for the Dress and Waist Manufacturers' Association. In 1914, she married Henry Moskowitz, a former settlement worker and industrial reformer.

In 1918, the Moskowitzes supported Alfred E. Smith for governor because of his pro-labor legislative record. As New York women were voting for the first time, Moskowitz organized the woman's vote for Smith. After he won, she proposed that he appoint a "Reconstruction Commission" to plan the state's future after the close of World War I. The reports of this commission, which she ran, formed the core of Smith's subsequent legislative program. In 1923, she became director of publicity for the Democratic State Committee. She managed Smith's subsequent reelection campaigns and

his nomination for the presidency in 1928. During the 1928 race, as the only woman on the executive committee of the Democratic National Committee, she directed campaign publicity. After Smith's defeat for the presidency, Moskowitz stayed on as his press agent as he tried, in vain, to remain the Democratic Party's leader. In December 1932, she fell down the steps of her house and, while recovering from broken bones, suffered an embolism. She died on January 2.

Belle Moskowitz's political role was both extraordinary and standard for women of her time. She achieved an unprecedented level of power in a male-dominated political party, yet also maintained close ties to the women's associations and groups that had introduced her to the field of social reform. Moreover, in the belief that remaining behind the scenes was more appropriate to women, she always declined offers of public office. Thus, she serves as a transitional figure in the history of American political women. (*See also: Democratic Party; Politics*)

—**Elisabeth Israels Perry**

Further Reading

Perry, Elisabeth Israels. *Belle Moskowitz: Feminine Politics and the Exercise of Power in the Age of Alfred E. Smith.* New York: Oxford University Press, 1987; Routledge, 1992.

Mothers' Pensions

Mothers' pensions were funds provided by the states to allow widows, deserted wives, or other single mothers to raise their children at home. The first mothers' pension law was passed in 1911 in Kansas City, Missouri; Illinois issued the first statewide measure later that year. Reflecting progressive concern with child welfare, thirty-nine states had enacted mothers' aid laws by 1919. Widowed mothers with children under fourteen were eligible for assistance in all states; some states also aided divorced mothers, deserted wives, and women whose husbands were imprisoned or disabled.

The mothers' pension movement grew out of a 1909 White House Conference on the Care of Dependent Children called by President Theodore Roosevelt. Inspired by a sentimental view of mother love, conference participants proposed paying mothers so that they could keep their children at home rather than having to place the children in institutions. A coalition of women's clubs, settlement workers, trade unions, and politicians lobbied for mothers' pensions, which they claimed was not charity but an entitlement—a salary for raising children to be good citizens.

The early rhetoric of the mothers' pension campaign differed from the actual administration of aid. Despite efforts to define mothers' pensions as a salary for mothers who stayed at home, the allowances were never high enough to support a family, and most states required recipients to work outside the home. Like welfare mothers today, recipients were harassed by investigators trying to determine that they maintained "suitable" homes. Several southern states denied assistance to black mothers. Nevertheless, the mothers' pension program recognized for the first time government's responsibility to aid poor women and children. It was incorporated into the Social Security Act of 1935 as Aid to Dependent Children. *(See also: Progressive Legislation; Social Security Act of 1935)*

—Molly Ladd-Taylor

Further Reading

Abramovitz, Mimi. *Regulating the Lives of Women: Social Welfare Policy from Colonial Times to the Present.* Boston: South End Press, 1988.

Goodwin, Joanne. "An Experiment in Paid Motherhood: The Implementation of Mothers' Pensions in Early Twentieth Century Chicago," *Gender and History* 4 (Autumn 1992): 323-42.

Ladd-Taylor, Molly. *Mother-Work: Women, Child Welfare and the State.* Urbana: University of Illinois Press, 1994.

Skocpol, Theda. *Protecting Soldiers and Mothers: The Politics of Social Provision in the United States, 1870s to 1920s.* Cambridge, MA: Harvard University Press, 1992.

～ Mott, Lucretia Coffin (1793–1880)

Abolitionist and leader of the nineteenth-century woman suffrage movement, Lucretia Mott traced her lifelong interest in woman's rights to her reading of Mary Wollstonecraft's *A Vindication of the Rights of Woman.* She committed whole passages to memory, and as she was fond of telling friends, throughout her life she kept the book "on the center table," frequently urging others to read it. Mott's appearance and demeanor challenged the derisive contemporary stereotype of the suffragists. Radical in her antislavery and feminist views, she nevertheless presented a public image of domestic virtue. Mott often sat quietly knitting on speakers' platforms as she waited her turn at the podium, where her commanding presence as an insightful, incisive, and persuasive critic of the conditions of slaves and women frequently startled her audiences.

Barely into her twenties and newly married to James Mott, she was recognized as a Quaker minister with a gift for preaching. Active in Quaker women's societies, she helped found the Female Anti-Slavery Society of Philadelphia in 1833 and was instrumental in organizing a national meeting of antislavery women in 1837.

Although Mott was elected a delegate to the World's Anti-Slavery Convention held in London in 1840, the assembly there voted to exclude her. Elizabeth Cady Stanton, the wife of another delegate, paid a call on Mott to commiserate. From their shared indignation grew a friendship and a commitment to activism that resulted in the calling of the Seneca Falls (New York) convention of 1848, the first formal woman's rights convention in America. Mott contributed to the writing of the Declaration of Sentiments and the drafting of the resolutions approved at that meeting. By 1848, Mott was widely known and admired as lecturer and preacher, and her presence at the convention helped ensure its success.

In 1850, Mott published her *Discourse on Women,* a treatise that argued for equal political and legal rights for women and for changes in the married women's property laws. Following passage of the Fugitive Slave Act, she opened her home to slaves fleeing via the Underground Railroad and continued her public speaking and writing on abolitionism and woman's rights.

After the Civil War, Mott directed her energies to obtaining the franchise for women and for the black freedmen. She also became increasingly involved in the peace movement. A tireless, widely esteemed spokeswoman and reformer, Mott delivered her last public address at the age of eighty-seven at the Society of Friends' annual meeting in May 1880. She died at home on November 11 that same year, and the nation mourned the loss of this eloquent, beloved leader. *(See also: Abolition and the Antislavery Movement; Cult of True Womanhood; Declaration of Sentiments and Resolutions; European Influences; Public Speakers: Nineteenth Century; Seneca Falls Convention; Society of Friends; Women's Rights Movements: Nineteenth and Twentieth Centuries)*

—Andrea Moore Kerr

Further Reading

Bacon, Margaret Hope. *Valiant Friend.* New York: Walker, 1980.

Cromwell, Otelia. *Lucretia Mott.* New York: Russell & Russell, 1971.

Mott, Lucretia. *Lucretia Mott: Her Complete Speeches and Sermons.* New York: E. Mellen, 1980.

Sterling, Dorothy. *Lucretia Mott: Gentle Warrior.* Garden City, NY: Doubleday, 1964.

～ Mount Holyoke Seminary

Mount Holyoke Seminary was among the best known and most successful female academies (or "seminaries," as women's schools were then called) in the United States during the antebellum period. Founded in South Hadley, Massachusetts, by Mary Lyon in 1837, Mount Holyoke was distinctive because of its large endowment and commitment to educating girls from families of modest means. Mary Lyon was also among the first women educators to recognize the important role that women could play as teachers in the nation's schools, and Mount Holyoke became famous for providing capable and highly dedicated women teachers in this period. Lyon personally supervised the school until her death in 1849. Her successors gradually expanded the curriculum to include Latin, Greek, and other collegiate studies, and in 1893, the school became known as Mount Holyoke College.

Perhaps the most distinctive feature of Mount Holyoke was Mary Lyon's commitment to keeping tuition and other school-related expenses substantially below those charged at other women's schools in this period. The school's substantial endowment, raised through Lyon's personal appeals to prominent men in western Massachusetts and elsewhere, was one factor that helped to reduce costs. More important, however, was Lyon's "domestic plan," which saved money by requiring students to perform the various housekeeping functions associated with maintaining a sizable residential academy. In addition to keeping expenses down, Lyon argued that this policy also helped build character and constituted a vital element of preparing young women for their future roles as wives and mothers. Lyon drew criticism from other women educators in this period both for her domestic plan and her policy of paying low salaries to her teachers. She defended both by maintaining that her school functioned as a family and that the promotion of responsibility and personal loyalty were more important than (and perhaps antithetical to) personal wealth.

Much of the success of Mount Holyoke can be attributed to the close personal attention that Mary Lyon gave the school—and many of its students—through most of its first decade of existence. Historian Thomas Woody has estimated that about sixteen hundred girls attended Mount Holyoke during Mary Lyon's lifetime and that some twelve thousand or more had enrolled by 1887. A survey of alumnae conducted in 1877 found that more than half had worked as teachers (and half of those for five or more years) and about 6 percent had served as foreign missionaries. Twenty-one were doctors. With its policy of lowering the costs of education for women from modest backgrounds, Mount Holyoke offered an opportunity for an advanced education to thousands of American women in the nineteenth century who might otherwise never have received one. In this regard, it represented a significant contribution to the development of women's education in American history. *(See also: Education; Female Academies; Higher Education; Normal Schools; "Seven Sisters"; Teaching)*

—**John L. Rury**

Further Reading

Cole, Arthur C. *A Hundred Years of Mount Holyoke: The Evolution of an Educational Ideal.* New Haven, CT: Yale University Press, 1940.

Green, Elizabeth Alden. *Mary Lyon and Mount Holyoke: Opening the Gates.* Hanover, NH: University Press of New England, 1979.

～ Movie Stars

Women have performed in front of the motion picture camera since the birth of the movies, scandalously showing their legs as dancers and acrobats or posing for *The Kiss* in William K. L. Dickson and Thomas A. Edison's Kinetoscope shorts in the 1890s. But their names were deliberately withheld from the public by the newly formed film companies, whose owners rightly feared that star status would lead to star salaries. The situation changed radically in 1910 when the Independent Producers, led by Carl Laemmle, in their continuing war against the Motion Picture Patents Company (known as the Trust), stole the "Biograph Girl" and began featuring her in films under her real name, Florence Lawrence. This strategy was so successful that they continued the practice with "Little Mary" Pickford and other formerly anonymous players. In 1912, *Photoplay,* America's first fan magazine, was launched, and by 1917, two movie stars—Pickford and Charlie Chaplain—were the highest paid performers in the business, signing contracts for $1 million a year. The movie star was born.

During the heyday of the studio system, stars were "found," manufactured, bought, and sold by the major studios; as contract players, their offscreen activities were choreographed and restricted by publicity departments and their transgressions punished by paternalistic bosses such as Louis B. Mayer and Jack Warner. Stardom was a double-edged sword for those who possessed it, providing financial and emotional security but also requiring absolute obedience. The more independent-minded stars such as Bette Davis and Katharine Hepburn chafed under its confines and made efforts to free themselves.

The star system was a particularly harsh taskmaster and judge of female talent and salability; several stars labeled "box office poison" in the late 1930s (Hepburn among them) were forced off the screen for a while, unable to get jobs in Hollywood. Even those who benefited from and seemingly acquiesced to the system, like Marilyn Monroe, might find themselves rendered obsolete or gradually eased out by newer stars in a culture that revered youth and a narrow concept of female beauty. It was rare that a female star remained a top box-office draw for more than a decade, astonishing if she lasted more than two. A child star like Shirley Temple, the top moneymaker in America in 1938, lost her appeal when she reached adolescence.

The breakup of the studios and the confusion that reigned during the 1950s and 1960s gave new status to movie stars who could guarantee audiences, but all of them were male: Paul Newman, John Wayne, Glenn Ford, Steve McQueen, Sidney Poitier. It was not until the 1970s and 1980s that female stars such as Jane Fonda, Barbra Streisand, and Meryl Streep began to be able to command top billing once again. But by that time, these women were demanding more than big salaries; they also wanted some measure of creative control, if only the power to say "no" or wait for the right vehicle to come to them.

This power has been demonstrated by the top female stars of the 1990s—Michelle Pfeiffer, Meg Ryan, Demi Moore, Whoopi Goldberg, Julia Roberts—all of whom command big salaries and get star vehicles. But stars such as Streisand, Jodie Foster, Goldie Hawn, Emma Thompson, and Oprah Winfrey demand even more. They seek their own opportunities and may be the initiators and controlling agents of the film's production from start to finish, sometimes in the multiple roles of producer, director, and performer. If the old star system produced, almost despite itself, memorable roles and films for women, the new star system will do so because of women's conscious efforts in their own behalf. *(See also: Davis, Bette; Fonda, Jane; Hepburn, Katharine; Monroe, Marilyn; Woman's Film)*

—**Frances M. Kavenik**

Further Reading

Dyer, Richard. *Stars.* London: British Film Institute, 1979, 1986.

Haskell, Molly. *From Reverence to Rape: The Treatment of Women in the Movies,* 2d ed. Chicago: University of Chicago Press, 1987.

"Hollywood, 1998," *Vanity Fair* 452 (April 1998) [Special Issue].

Rosen, Marjorie. *Popcorn Venus.* New York: Coward, McCann, & Geoghegan, 1973.

Todd, Janet, ed. *Women and Film.* New York: Holmes & Meier, 1988.

⮾ Ms. Magazine

Ms. magazine represented a unique application of the women's magazine format to a specific feminist agenda. Although women's magazines as a separate genre dated to the nineteenth century and had, from the outset, employed women editors, *Ms.* was the first national publication created and controlled by women for women. An outgrowth of the raised consciousness of the late 1960s, it was founded early in 1971, in the living room of Gloria Steinem's New York City apartment by a group of dedicated feminist journalists and writers. While many women's liberation groups of the era published newsletters and journals, *Ms.* was to be a nationally distributed magazine that aimed at broadening the audience for feminist interests. Focusing on the mainstreaming of the women's movement, *Ms.* editorial policy dispensed with the usual fare of recipes, advice columns, and handicrafts found in contemporary women's magazines, yet avoided the partisan feminist debates or strong ideological stances of journals established by various women's liberation groups.

The founders of *Ms.* used networking and their previous professional experience to launch their ambitious project. Since Steinem, the publication's first editor, had been instrumental in starting *New York* magazine, *New York* editor and publisher Clay Felker agreed to insert preview copies into the year-end issue of that magazine before the spring premier issue of *Ms.* hit the newsstands in January 1972. The *Ms.* insert—with an appropriate "Wonder Woman" cover—boosted *New York* magazine's sales to an all-time high, and the projected eight-week supply of 300,000 copies sold out in eight days.

Where other women's magazines ridiculed or ignored feminist concerns, *Ms.* addressed forthrightly and without condescension the concerns of women in the home and the workplace and provided articles on women's history. As a feminist forum, *Ms.* offered the works of well-known and struggling contemporary women poets, journalists, and writers in all fields. A major innovative policy excluded advertising that was demeaning to or limiting of women.

Ms. also published collections of its stories and news features and produced television documentaries such as *Woman Alive!* (1973, 1974) and *She's Nobody's Baby: American Women in the Twentieth Century* (1981). As a means for returning profits to the community of women to empower them further, *Ms.* founders established the *Ms.* Foundation for Women, Inc. in 1975 as a public, educational, and charitable organization with tax-exempt status to assist women's projects through direct grants and advisory and referral services. The Free to Be Foundation was established in 1976 to administer the educational "Free to Be . . . You and Me" project, conceived by Marlo Thomas to promote individual human growth and child development in an unbiased way. Named after Thomas's successful children's television special, record album, and book, which provided the initial foundation revenue from royalties, this foundation funds multimedia projects that focus on nonsexist education and child development. In 1997, grants made by the foundation totaled over $2,534,000 according to the *Ms.* Foundation's annual report. These funds and technical assistance aid feminist projects as well as evaluate and support programs to improve the status of women and help to eliminate discrimination based on sex. The *Ms.* Foundation also created "Take Our Daughters to Work Day," complete with materials. This event was created to increase awareness of the needs of young women in their introduction to the workplace.

Ms. magazine celebrated its first decade of publication in 1982 and had succeeded as a national commercial publication that covered the issues of the contemporary women's movement. However, *Ms.* began its second decade during a period of national economic difficulties and conservative backlash against the women's movement. Increased publication costs and added competition for subscribers compounded the problem, as did the fact that the founding members of the staff were ready to pursue other projects and individual careers. After a major reorganization that did not prove sufficient to ensure the publication's future, *Ms.* magazine was sold in 1988. The revised publication further mainstreamed the contents of *Ms.* by including some of the more traditional women's magazine features but did not abandon the editorial policy of covering women's social, political, legal, and economic issues as hard news items or of consciously patronizing women and feminist writers.

At the twentieth anniversary of *Ms.,* Robin Morgan, then editor, reported that the staff was more culturally and ethnically mixed than ever before, including diversity in sexual preference, marital status, age, and race as well as in viewpoint, providing news on international women's issues and movements. In 1993, Marcia Gillespie became the first African American editor-in-chief.

The best of the old *Ms.* remained, while the rebirth of *Ms.* with its no-ad policy as a bimonthly liberated the magazine editorially. Each 100-page issue includes news, coverage of the arts, book reviews, action alerts, and special reports, and is highly recommended. *Ms.* has become a virtual activist clearinghouse tool for women around the world. *(See also: Magazines; Steinem, Gloria; Women's Liberation Movement; Women's Rights Movements: Nineteenth and Twentieth Centuries)*

—**Saundra K. Yelton-Stanley**
—**Angela M. Howard**

Further Reading

Calvacca, Lorraine. "Sisterhood Is Evolving," *Folio: The Magazine for Magazine Management* 23 (May 15, 1994): 6313.

Katz, Bill, and Linda Sternberg-Katz. *Magazines for Libraries,* 7th ed., p. 1129. New Providence, RI: R. R. Bowker, 1992.

Lyons, Harriet. "A History of *Ms.*" Unpublished manuscript, commissioned for *Ms.* magazine's tenth anniversary, 1982.

Morgan, Robin. "Behind the Scenes at *Ms.*," *Ms.* 3 (July/August 1992): 1-2.

Ms. Foundation for Women, Inc. and Free to Be Foundation, Inc. *Ms. Foundation for Women 1983/1985 Annual Report.* New York: *Ms.* and Free to Be Foundations, 1985.

Papachristou, Judith. *Women Together: A History in Documents of the Women's Movement in the United States.* New York: Knopf, 1976.

http://www.msmagazine.com

⚭ *Muller v. Oregon* (1908)

Muller v. Oregon dealt with an Oregon maximum-hours statute that constrained the employment of women in factories, laundries, or other "mechanical establishments" to no longer than ten hours a day. Louis D. Brandeis (later a Supreme Court associate justice) presented the case to the Supreme Court for Oregon; his argument centered on a heavily statistical brief that discussed the relationship between hours of labor and the health and morals of women. Writing for a unanimous court, Justice David J. Brewer upheld the constitutionality of the regulations as a reasonable exercise of the state's police powers. Brewer emphasized the consideration that "woman's physical structure and the performance of maternal functions place her at a disadvantage in the struggle for subsistence" and that her physical well-being "becomes an object of public interest and care in order to preserve the strength and the vigor of the race." The court concluded that the limitations the statute "placed upon her contractual powers, upon her right to agree with her employer as to the time she shall labor" were "not imposed solely for her benefit, but also largely for the benefit of all."

The *Muller* case does not represent a repudiation of substantive due process; the court strictly judged that the economic regulations in question were reasonable use of the state's police powers. *(See also: Kelley, Florence; Progressive Era; Progressive Legislation; Protective Legislation; Wages)*

—**Sue E. Strickler**

Further Reading

Goldstein, Leslie Friedman. *The Constitutional Rights of Women.* New York: Longman, 1987.

Muller v. Oregon, 208 U.S. 412 (1908).

Rossum, Ralph A., and G. Alan Tarr. *American Constitutional Law.* New York: St. Martin's, 1987.

Woloch, Nancy. *Muller v. Oregon: A Brief History with Documents.* Boston: Bedford Books of St. Martin's, 1996.

⚭ Music

Women who have aspired to musical success have encountered many barriers to training, publishing, and performance; yet from colonial days to the present, women have made a rich contribution to American music.

As music spread from church to theater to concert stage in the 1700s, women's names began to appear on the programs. One woman who sang professionally in Charleston and Boston for many years was Catherine Hellyer Graupner (d. 1821). One of the first well-known instrumentalists was Sophia Hewitt (1800–1846), who became the organist for Boston's Handel and Haydn Society in 1820 and remained there for a decade. She also made concert tours with her husband, a violinist.

By the mid-nineteenth century, organ, piano, and harp were generally accepted as instruments appropriate for women as well as men. The same could not be said of many other instruments, including the violin. This was all changed by Camilla Urso (1842–1902), a native of Nantes, France, who spent much of her life in the United States. She established herself as a violin virtuoso comparable to any of the males of her day. Even more successful was American-born violinist Maud Powell (1867–1920). Trained in Leipzig and Berlin, Powell performed not only in major cities but also in the western mining towns of the United States, and she made a 42-concert tour of South Africa. Powell championed works by American composers, black composers, and women composers. Both Powell and Urso had to perform with all-male orchestras. Women were not admitted to the Musician's Union until 1903, and to this day, women occupy only a small percentage of the chairs in major orchestras. Some women found positions in all-female groups; the Boston Fadette Orchestra, organized in 1888 was the most famous of more than a dozen such ensembles.

The latter half of the nineteenth century found a number of female piano virtuosos thrilling American audiences. These gifted performers included Teresa Carreño (1844–1917), Julia Rivé-King (1854–1937), and Fannie Bloomfield-Zeisler (1863–1927). Some brilliant concert artists also excelled as composers and teachers. For example, Rosalyn Tureck (b. 1914) has combined a performance career on piano, harpsichord, organ, and clavichord with conducting, writing, and teaching. Tureck was the first woman invited to conduct the New York Philharmonic Orchestra in a subscription concert in 1958 and has conducted major orchestras on six continents. She performs and lectures annually at the Tureck Bach Institute in New York City and is also exploring electronic music and instruments.

One of the earliest known American women composers was Mary Ann Pound (1751–1796), a singer and actress who wrote songs. Faustina Hasse Hodges (1822–1895) wrote piano pieces and songs; one of her songs, "Rose Bush," sold over 100,000 copies. One of the first American women to compose in large forms was Amy Mary Cheney Beach (1867–1944), a native of Henniker, New Hampshire. Her *Gaelic Symphony* was performed by major orchestras for decades beginning in 1896 when it was premiered by the Boston Symphony. Beach's music has enjoyed a great revival, marked by new recordings of *Gaelic Symphony, Grand Mass in E-flat,* and a multitude of songs, piano, and chamber works.

Ruth Crawford (1901–1953) from East Liverpool, Ohio, studied at the American Conservatory in Chicago and then in 1930 became the first American woman composer to win a Guggenheim Fellowship, which enabled her to study in Berlin and Paris. Crawford won early fame for her innovative works, such as *String Quartet* (1931), and *Three Songs* to texts by Carl Sandburg (1932). After her marriage to Charles Seeger, she devoted most of her energies to transcribing and arranging nearly 300 American folk songs. Crawford-Seeger returned to the writing of dissonant counterpoint shortly before her death, but she completed only one significant work, the prize-winning *Suite for Wind Quintet* (1952).

A contemporary of Crawford-Seeger, Louise Talma (1906–1996) was the first woman to win the coveted Sibelius Award in composition, the first woman to win a Guggenheim on two occasions, the first woman to have a major work staged by a major European opera house, and the first woman to be elected to the Music Department of the National Institute of Arts and Letters.

Vivian Fine (b. 1913) was born in Chicago and studied theory with Ruth Crawford-Seeger. An accomplished pianist, Fine worked in New York as a dance accompanist and collaborated as a composer with Martha Graham and other famous dancer-choreographers. Despite a busy career at several colleges and universities, Fine has proved to be a prolific writer of ballets, chamber works, and choral and orchestral pieces. Her works include two compositions celebrating the women's movement, *Meeting for Equal Rights 1866* (1976) and *The Women in the Garden* (1977).

Pauline Oliveros (b. 1932) is known as one of the most versatile of experimenters among American composers. A native of Houston, Texas, Oliveros has embraced electronic music, sound sculpture, and multimedia presentations. She also writes music for meditation. Performance artists Laurie Anderson (b. 1947) and Meredith Monk (1942–1993) have also expanded traditional concepts of composition and performance. Monk's opera *Atlas* uses nonverbal vocalization for a particularly theatrical effect.

Two of the outstanding black American composers were Florence Smith Price (1888–1953) and Margaret Bonds (1913–1972). A native of Little Rock, Arkansas, Price wrote art songs, spiritual arrangements, keyboard works, four symphonies, three piano concertos, and a violin concerto. Price also taught students, including Margaret Bonds, who went on to her own distinguished career. As musicologist

Christine Ammer has shown, Margaret Bonds "made a conscious effort to develop black idioms in larger musical forms and to promote the music of black Americans." Bonds wrote over two hundred works for chorus, orchestra, and piano, as well as popular songs, some imbued with the jazz style of poet Langston Hughes. Other famous black composers include Undine Smith Moore (1904–1989), best known for choral compositions and spiritual arrangements, and Mary Lou Williams (1910–1981), whose career as a jazz pianist and composer led to a professorship at Duke University.

America has produced dozens of outstanding women composers, including Marion Eugenie Bauer (1887–1955), Mary Carlisle Howe (1882–1964), Dika Newlin (b. 1923), and Emma Lou Diemer (b. 1927). One of today's most celebrated composers is Ellen Taaffe Zwilich (b. 1939). In 1983, she became the first woman to win the Pulitzer Prize in music for *Symphony No. 1.* Her *Symbalon,* commissioned by the New York Philharmonic, was the first work by an American composer to receive its premiere in the Soviet Union. Israeli-born Shulamit Ran (b. 1947) has settled in this country and has won both the Pulitzer Prize and the Friedheim Award. Other highly successful contemporary composers include Joan Tower (b. 1938), Gwyneth Walker (b. 1947), and Libby Larsen (b. 1950).

American women have long found vocal music to be more hospitable to them than instrumental music. Women operatic singers have been onstage since the early eighteenth century. In the twentieth century, singers such as Marian Anderson, Kathleen Battle, Marilyn Horne, Jessye Norman, Roberta Peters, Leontyne Price, Beverly Sills, and Dawn Upshaw have achieved great success and recognition. Women have also enjoyed great commercial success in country and western music, jazz, rock and roll, and other forms of popular music.

In addition to great singers, women have contributed to the operatic world through their compositions since the time of Constance Fount Le Roy Runcie (1836–1911), who wrote a romantic opera, *The Prince of Asturias,* in the late 1860s. She was followed by Eleanor Warner Everest Freer (1865–1942), who wrote nine operas; Mary Carr Moore (1873–1957), who wrote six operas and four operettas; and Emma Roberto Steiner (1852–1929), whose opera *Fleurette* was produced in San Francisco in 1889 and in New York in 1891. Steiner wrote other successful operas and established herself as a conductor despite the incredible prejudices against women at the podium.

On January 13, 1976, Sarah Caldwell (b. 1924) became the first woman to conduct an opera at the Met (Metropolitan Opera Company in New York). The obstacles that women conductors have had to overcome are dramatically illustrated by Judy Collins's award-winning 1974 documentary film, *Antonia: A Portrait of the Woman,* based on the life of Dr. Antonia Brico (1902–1989). As the film documents, despite Brico's enormous talents, music managers would not accept her. Even today, while conductors such as Eve Queler, Catherine Comet, JoAnn Falletta, and Victoria Bond have achieved national reputations, none of the major orchestras in this country has a female music director. Women choral conductors have fared slightly better, as evidenced by the career of Margaret Hillis (1921–1998), director of the Chicago Symphony Chorus beginning in 1957.

Given the persistent pattern of discrimination against women in music, their achievements are remarkable and will continue to enrich the world even more in the future as opportunities are expanded. *(See also: Baez, Joan C.; Beach, Amy Marcy Cheney; Holiday, Billie; Jazz; Popular Vocalists; Price, Leontyne; Smith, Bessie)*

—**Linda Burian Plaut**
—**Jonathan W. Zophy**

Further Reading

Ammer, Christine. *Unsung: A History of Women in American Music.* Westport, CT: Greenwood, 1980.

Block, Adrienne Fried, and Carol Neuls-Bates. *Women in American Music: A Bibliography of Music and Literature.* Westport, CT: Greenwood, 1979.

Cohen, Aaron I. *International Encyclopedia of Women Composers,* 2d ed. New York: Books & Music, 1987.

Dahl, Linda. *Stormy Weather, a Century of Jazz Women.* New York: Limelight, 1984, 1989.

Drinker, Sophie Lewis. *Music and Women: The Story of Women in their Relation to Music.* New York: Coward McCann, 1948.

Jezic, Diane Peacock. *Women Composers: The Lost Tradition Found.* New York: Feminist Press, 1988.

Lepage, Jane Weiner. *Women Composers, Conductors, and Musicians of the Twentieth Century: Selected Biographies.* Vols. 1, 2. Metuchen, NJ: Scarecrow, 1980, 1988.

Pendle, Karin, ed. *Women and Music: A History.* Bloomington: Indiana University Press, 1991.

Tick, Judith. *American Women Composers before 1870.* Ann Arbor: UMI Research Press, 1983.

Zaimont, Judith Lang, and Karen Famera. *Contemporary Concert Music by Women.* Westport, CT: Greenwood, 1981.

Naming Systems

Nothing is so personal as a person's name. The ways in which names are acquired are as varied as the world's cultures, and each culture usually creates a specific naming system. No study has yet found a society that did not have a tradition of assigning personal names. The conferring of a name on a child is typically an outward indication of the child's acceptance into society. An interesting feature of several Native American cultures is the provision for ac quiring permanent names during adolescence or adulthood.

Surnames did not come into common usage until the need arose to distinguish individuals, usually for bureaucratic purposes such as taxation. Use of surnames began in Europe about the twelfth century. Four generally accepted types of surnames are patronymics, local names, occupational names, and nicknames.

A patronymic is a name derived from the father's given name—for example, Robertson, Fitzgerald, Nilsdottir. Less common are matronymics, which derive from the mother's given name—for example, Sean Peig, Ginny ni Carthy. Variations exist even within patronymic systems, and sometimes the name depends on the child's gender. In Scandinavian societies, children of Nils would be named Eric Nilssen (son of Nils) or Ingrid Nilsdottir (daughter of Nils). Arabic speakers use *ibn* in the same way, for example, Faisal ibn Saud (Faisal, son of Saud). In both cases, the father himself uses a different second name referring to *his* father. In contrast, some African cultures call parents after their children: "father of John" and "mother of John." Celtic surnames reflected clan affiliation: MacDonald or O'Leary.

A local name derives from a place-name and is usually either a topographic name (describing a physical feature: Hill, Brook) or a habitation name (describing a known place or house: Oldham, Schwarzschild). An occupational name originates from a specific trade or activity, for example, Smith or Carpenter. Nicknames are descriptive of a person's character or attributes, such as Brown or Rich.

Traditional Hispanic naming patterns give children the paternal surnames of both parents linked with *y* (and)—for example, Elena Garcia y Chavez. They may receive additional names at baptism, first communion, and confirmation. Daughters drop their mothers' names at marriage, linking their fathers' and husbands' paternal names with *de* (of).

If, for example, Elena Garcia y Chavez marries Orlando Vasquez y Morales, her name changes to Elena Vasquez de Garcia. Their child might then be named Ana Vasquez y Garcia.

While some cultures' naming traditions preserve the woman's surname, the tradition of a woman taking her father's surname at birth and her husband's surname at marriage is firmly entrenched in Western culture. Middle-class white women in nineteenth-century America characteristically took their husbands' names completely. Even female friends addressed each other as "Mrs. Ralph Davis"—literally, "wife of Ralph Davis."

Some nineteenth-century feminists, however, refused to change their names after marriage, thus defying the legal submersion of the wife's identity under common law. Lucy Stone and her husband, Henry Blackwell, added a signed protest to their marriage ceremony in 1855. By 1856, Lucy Stone Blackwell had decided to be known again as Lucy Stone. In 1921, Ruth Hale founded the Lucy Stone League to assist twentieth-century women in keeping their original names and to provide a center of research and information on the status of women. Famous "Lucy Stoners" were Margaret Mead, Amelia Earhart, and Edna St. Vincent Millay.

After the progress of the 1920s, the social climate changed again, and women reverted to the more traditional usage of adopting a husband's surname. The issue of social title and name resurfaced during the 1960s with the modern women's movement. Feminists coined "Ms." as a generic title for all women, single and married. Some married women, especially those in a profession, kept their maiden names, since it was custom rather than law for a woman to change her name on all her legal and formal documents after marriage.

In the 1970s, feminist and professional women often used their maiden surnames as their middle names or resorted to the hyphenation of their original surnames with those of their husbands. More radical feminists legally changed their names to reflect their matrilinial heritage rather than use a name that reinforced the patriarchal system. These women adopted descriptive surnames such as "Marthaschild," or tried to create entirely new identities by selecting innovative names that focused on their own lives, as seen in the name change of artist Judy Chicago. The trend for a woman to keep her own name after marriage continued throughout the 1980s and 1990s.

Names and naming patterns reflect a culture or society and ultimately affect an individual's sense of self and the society's view of the person. For American women, the naming system indicates in a direct and fundamental way the status of women, and it provides an individual expression of each woman's perception of her identity. *(See also: Chicago, Judy; Common Law; Earhart, Amelia; Mead, Margaret; Millay, Edna St. Vincent; Native American Women; Stone, Lucy)*

—Gay E. Carter
—Gracia Clark
—Angela M. Howard

Further Reading

Alford, Richard D. *Naming and Identity: A Cross-Cultural Study of Personal Naming Practices.* New Haven, CT: HRAF, 1988.

Hanks, Patrick, and Flavia Hodges. *A Dictionary of First Names.* Oxford, UK: Oxford University Press, 1990.

———. *A Dictionary of Surnames.* Oxford, UK: Oxford University Press, 1988.

Kupper, Susan J. *Surnames for Women: A Decision-Making Guide.* Jefferson, NC: McFarland, 1990.

Lawson, Edwin D., comp. *Personal Names and Naming: An Annotated Bibliography.* Bibliographies and Indexes in Anthropology, No. 3. Westport, CT: Greenwood, 1987.

Schroeder, Lella Obier. "A Rose by Any Other Name: Post-Marital Right to Use Maiden Name, 1934–1982," *Sociology and Social Research* 70 (1986): 290-93.

Smith, Elsdon C. *Personal Names: A Bibliography,* 1952 New York Public Library. Reprint, Detroit, MI: Gale Research, 1965.

Stannard, Una. "Manners Make Laws: Married Women's Names in the United States," *Names* 32 (1984): 114-28.

❧ Nashoba (1825–1830)

Nashoba was a utopian community founded for slaves by Frances Wright in November 1825 in western Tennessee and was the only secular commune founded by a woman in nineteenth-century America. Its purpose was to serve as an example of how blacks in the American South could be gradually emancipated.

During the early 1820s, Wright became interested in the communal movement and abolition. Wright agreed with the proponents of the colonization movement who believed that slaves would eventually be free and, afterward, should be sent to colonies in Africa or Asia, but she believed blacks should first be taught some means of self-sufficiency. In creating Nashoba, she combined this belief with her interest in starting a community patterned after New Harmony, a "village of cooperation" established earlier by socialist Robert Owen. Wright assumed that slaves would be donated to Nashoba by sympathetic planters and settled on a goal of fifty. Each slave would work off his or her price by a credit system that would take five years; meanwhile the slaves were to be educated to prepare them for freedom. Afterward,

they would be sent to a foreign colony to begin their new lives.

From the start, Nashoba was plagued with problems. Only one slave family was donated, and Wright could afford to buy only eight other slaves. The agricultural potential of the two thousand acres of uncleared swampy frontier near Memphis was limited, as was the ability of the slaves to distinguish between the nobly inspired compulsive servitude at Nashoba and the exploitation of their former experiences. Public disdain was exacerbated by the disclosure of an interracial relationship between a teacher and slave within the experimental community. Wright's defense of the arrangement rendered her subject to verbal abuse and threats against her life.

By 1830, Wright decided the experiment at Nashoba was a failure. She now believed society as a whole had to be reformed, not just a part of it. The remaining slaves at Nashoba were given their freedom, and Wright accompanied them to Haiti, then returned to the United States to focus her energies on women's issues. *(See also: Abolition and the Antislavery Movement; Slavery; Utopian Communities)*

—Rose Kolbasnik Callahan

Further Reading

Eckhardt, Celia Morris. *Fanny Wright: Rebel in America.* Cambridge, MA: Harvard University Press, 1984.

Kissel, Susan S. *In Common Cause: The "Conservative" Frances Trollope and the "Radical" Frances Wright.* Bowling Green, OH: Bowling Green State University Press, 1993.

Lane, Margaret. *Frances Wright and the "Great Experiment."* Manchester, UK: Manchester University Press, 1972.

❧ Nathoy, Lalu (Polly Bemis) (1853–1933)

Lalu Nathoy as a girl was kidnapped ("sold" for two bags of seed) by bandits from her family home in a northern Chinese village. She was sold as a prostitute to a procurer for a Chinese saloon owner in the American mining town of Warrens, Idaho, in 1872, just three years before the 1875 passage of the Page Law that excluded Chinese prostitutes and wives from entry into the United States. She became one of eleven women and the only Chinese woman in the town of twelve hundred Chinese and four hundred white men. In the state of highest Chinese immigration, California, women made up only one in every fourteen immigrants in 1870. Sixty percent of these were prostitutes— *lougeui* ("always holding legs up") or *baak haak chai* ("hundred men's wife").

Nathoy, like other Chinese prostitutes who worked in the mining outposts, railroad camps, agricultural villages, and Chinatowns of the West, was in debt peonage, a virtual slave to her master. Desperate to gain her freedom, she stole a shotgun and was prepared to kill her master, when a white saloon owner "won" her in a poker game. Unwilling to be owned by any man, Nathoy became a successful boarding-house owner and eventually married the man who "won" her. She became widely known and admired throughout the region as a model pioneer woman, accomplished in farming, medicine, and homemaking. When she died, her effects were donated to St. Gertrude's Museum in Grangeville, Idaho. Photographs and records of Nathoy have been preserved by the Idaho Historical Society. *(See also: Asian American Women; Migration and Frontier Women; Prostitution)*

—**Marjorie King**

Further Reading

Hirata, Lucie Cheng. "Chinese Immigrant Women in Nineteenth-Century California." In *Women of America: A History,* edited by Carol Berkin and Mary Norton, 223-44. Boston: Houghton Mifflin, 1979.

McCunn, Ruthanne Lum. *Thousand Pieces of Gold.* San Francisco: Design Enterprises, 1981.

Takaki, Ronald. *A Different Mirror: A History of Multicultural America.* Boston: Little, Brown, 1993.

Tsuchida, Nobuya, ed. *Asian and Pacific American Experiences: Women's Perspectives.* Minneapolis: University of Minnesota, Asian-Pacific American Learning Resource Center and General College, 1982.

Wu, Cheng-Tsu. *"Chink!": A Documentary History of Anti-Chinese Prejudice in America.* New York: World, 1972.

Yung, Judy. *Chinese Women of America: A Pictorial History.* Seattle: University of Washington Press for the Chinese Culture Foundation of San Francisco, 1986.

⚬ Nation, Carry (1846–1911)

A well-known figure in the Woman's Christian Temperance Union (WCTU), Carry Nation publicized the temperance cause by smashing saloons with a hatchet. The daughter of George and Mary Campbell Moore, Carry Amelia Moore was born in Garrard County, Kentucky, and moved to near Belton, Missouri, when she was a young child. She inherited the religious fervor of her father, a leader in the Christian church, and the eccentricity of her mother, a victim of serious mental disorders.

In 1867, she married Charles Gloyd, an alcoholic physician and ex-Union captain. He died a short time later. In 1877, she married David Nation, a lawyer, minister, and journalist, nineteen years her senior. When he accepted a pastorate at the Christian church in Medicine Lodge, Kansas, she began her religious and charitable activities in earnest, becoming a founder of the local WCTU. Working as a jail evangelist, she once again encountered the ill effects of alcohol. Although Kansas law prohibited the sale of liquor, the law was not enforced. She and another WCTU member took matters into their own hands when they marched down to the local saloon, singing hymns and attracting a crowd of well-wishers and curious spectators. The bar closed its doors, and Nation realized she had found her calling.

Wielding a hatchet that eventually became her trademark, she began her crusade in Kansas, singing temperance songs, preaching to the saloon patrons, and smashing bottles, bar furniture, and nude wall hangings. In 1901, at a WCTU convention, she was awarded a gold medal inscribed "To the Bravest Woman in Kansas."

Carry Nation later traveled from coast to coast on the lecture circuit, occasionally smashing saloons along the way. She collapsed while lecturing in Eureka Springs, Arkansas, in January 1911, and died six months later. She was buried near Belton, Missouri. Her tombstone reads: "Faithful to the Cause of Prohibition: She Hath Done What She Could." Her life illustrated what one woman could accomplish for a cause in which she believed. Her publicity for prohibition contributed to the eventual passage of the Eighteenth Amendment. *(See also: Prohibition; Temperance Movement; Woman's Christian Temperance Union)*

—**Mary K. Dains**

Further Reading

Beals, Carleton. *Cyclone Carry, The Story of Carry Nation.* Philadelphia: Chilton, 1962.

Caldwell, Dorothy J. "Carry Nation, A Missouri Woman, Won Fame in Kansas," *Missouri Historical Review* 63 (July 1969): 461-88.

Marlow, Lydia. "Carry Nation." In *Show Me Missouri Women: Selected Biographies.* Vol. 1, edited by Mary K. Dains, 236-37. Kirksville, MO: Thomas Jefferson University Press, 1989.

⚬ National American Woman Suffrage Association

Formed in 1890 through the merger of the American and National Woman Suffrage associations, the National American Woman Suffrage Association (NAWSA) was dominated during its first decade of existence by the aging Susan B. Anthony, who took over the presidency from Elizabeth Cady Stanton in 1892. Yet the course of the organization was profoundly influenced by a new generation of suffrage leaders, many of them university-educated professional women. At the suggestion of Alice Stone Blackwell, and over Anthony's protests, the NAWSA resolved in 1893 to hold its annual conventions outside Washington, D.C., in alternate years. The granting of suffrage to Colorado women in 1893 encouraged those who felt that suffrage could be won state by state, and "Aunt Susan," assisted by her younger lieutenants, strenuously joined in massive but unsuccessful statewide campaigns in New York (1894) and California (1896). Anthony went so far as to tone down her personal support for black civil rights in the interest of recruiting more southern women in the NAWSA, and the increasingly upper-middle-class and nativist tone of the organization was reflected in speeches and resolutions condemning unrestricted immigration and favoring educational requirements for suffrage. In 1896, after a bitter internal debate, the NAWSA formally dissociated itself from Stanton's *Woman's Bible,* a radical feminist critique of religion.

At the annual convention of 1900, coinciding with Anthony's eightieth birthday, her chosen successor, Carrie Chapman Catt, took over the leadership from 1900 to 1904, when the ill health of her husband led her to relinquish the presidency. Her husband died the following year. Between 1904 and 1915 Methodist minister Anna Howard Shaw served as president of the NAWSA. Catt resumed direction of the organization from 1915 until the passage of the Nineteenth Amendment in 1920. A shrewd administrator and forceful orator, Catt was somewhat conservative in her views on domestic issues and was at first a strong supporter of the state-by-state approach. She argued that, in the absence of a firm commitment to suffrage from any president or from either major party, it was unrealistic to throw the NAWSA's weight behind the demand for a federal amendment.

A serious challenge to the Catt wing of the NAWSA was posed by Alice Paul, a young Philadelphian who had been jailed several times in England for her participation in Mrs. Emmeline Pankhurst's militant suffragette campaign. Paul, who joined the NAWSA in 1912, created the NAWSA Congressional Committee, which became a rallying point for younger members impatient with the snail's pace of state-based work and eager to revive the fight for a federal measure. The American scene was soon enlivened by suffrage processions, pickets, and other colorful publicity stunts borrowed from the English militants; a few NAWSA members were even imprisoned briefly. Paul eventually left to found her own National Woman's Party in 1916, and while the vast majority of suffragists remained loyal to the NAWSA, Paul's influence was still felt. At its Louisville convention in 1917, the NAWSA once again officially pledged itself to work for a constitutional amendment, and its efforts were crowned with success in the passage (1919) and ratification (1920) of the Nineteenth Amendment. After the gala victory celebrations, the NAWSA transformed itself, and many of its members continued to work for the political education of women and for various feminist social concerns through a new organization, the League of Women Voters. *(See also: Anthony, Susan B.; Catt, Carrie Chapman; League of Women Voters; National Woman's Party; Nineteenth Amendment; Paul, Alice; Suffrage)*

—Gail Malmgreen

Further Reading

Fowler, Robert B. *Carrie Catt: Feminist Politician.* Boston: Northeastern University Press, 1986.

Fuller, Paul E. *Laura Clay and the Woman's Rights Movement.* Rev. ed. Lexington: University Press of Kentucky, 1975, 1992.

Harper, Ida Husted. *The Life and Work of Susan B. Anthony.* Vols. 1-2. Indianapolis, IN: Bowen-Merrill, 1898.

Shaw, Anna Howard. *The Story of a Pioneer.* New York: Harper, 1915.

Stanton, Elizabeth C., Susan B. Anthony, and Matilda J. Gage, eds. *History of Woman Suffrage,* 6 vols. Rochester, NY: Privately Printed, 1881–1922.

⌒ National Association for the Advancement of Colored People (NAACP)

The National Association for the Advancement of Colored People (NAACP) is the oldest civil rights organization in the United States. It grew out of the Niagara movement organized by black educator and author W. E. B. Du Bois to pursue equality in the face of white segregation. On May 30, 1909, an organization known as the Negro National Committee emerged, holding four public meetings during the year. In 1910, at their second annual meeting, the participants chose the name National Association for the Advancement of Colored People. The organization was incorporated in 1911 under the laws of the state of New York. Its basic goal was to gain full equality for blacks as guaranteed by law through litigation, legislation, and education. The NAACP has won many victories in the federal courts, most notably the U.S. Supreme Court decisions protecting the franchise for blacks (1915) and ending school segregation (1954). The organization was also instrumental in securing passage of the Civil Rights Acts of 1957, 1960, and 1964.

Three women who were contributors both in the formative and early years of the NAACP were Ida B. Wells-Barnett, Mary Church Terrell, and Mary White Ovington. All three were well-educated, courageous, articulate speakers, and committed to social change.

Wells-Barnett attended Fisk University and Lemoyne Institute. She was known for her meticulous and detailed documentation of acts of lynching, which provided the NAACP with its greatest thrust during its first decade of operation. She was the most significant crusader, and her twenty-year passionate opposition to lynching was heard through her lectures and eloquent pen. Wells-Barnett was known for her candor and uncompromising stance on the rights of blacks. Because this demeanor was not perceived as appropriate for a woman, she was often excluded and shunned by her contemporaries.

Terrell graduated from Oberlin College and furthered her studies abroad. She and her husband knew Booker T. Washington and usually sided with the "Bookerites" who advocated black acceptance through achievement. They were active members in the Republican Party. The NAACP challenged the ideology and philosophy of both Booker T. Washington and President William Howard Taft, a Republican. Terrell broke ties with the black middle-class establishment and became a founder of the NAACP. She served on the NAACP's Executive Committee for a number of years and organized the first District of Columbia branch.

Ovington is credited with the idea of starting the NAACP. Although she was white, she deplored the state of race relations reflected in William English Walling's account of the Springfield, Illinois, race riots of 1908. She was instrumental in calling a conference to discuss these problems. Among the sixty names of persons of distinction to sign the "call to arms" were those of Wells-Barnett, Ovington, and Terrell.

Ovington was also known for her research that depicted the social and economic conditions of blacks in New York State.

Today, the NAACP consists of more than 2,200 branches that make up seven regions covering all 50 states, the District of Columbia, Japan, and Germany. Its headquarters are in Baltimore, Maryland, and it is governed by a National Board of Directors. The total membership of the NAACP exceeds 500,000. *(See also: Civil Rights; Terrell, Mary Church; U.S. Supreme Court; Wells-Barnett, Ida B.)*

—**Constance H. Timberlake**
—**Merri Scheibe Edwards**

Further Reading

Duster, Alfreda M., ed. *Crusade for Justice: The Autobiography of Ida B. Wells.* Chicago: University of Chicago Press, 1970.
Hughes, Langston. *Fight for Freedom: A Story of the NAACP.* New York: Norton, 1962.
Morris, Milton D. *The Politics of Black America.* New York: Harper & Row, 1975.
Ovington, Mary White. *Half a Man: The Status of the Negro in New York.* New York: Negro Universities Press, 1969.
———. *The Walls Came Tumbling Down.* New York: Arno, 1969.
Sterling, Dorothy. *Black Foremothers: Three Lives.* Old Westbury, NY: Feminist Press, 1979.
Terrell, Mary Church. *A Colored Woman in a White World.* Washington DC: Randell, 1940. Reprint, New York: Arno, 1980.
http://www.naacp.org [NAACP Website]

National Association of Colored Women (NACW)

The National Association of Colored Women (NACW) was organized in July 1896 in Washington, D.C., from a merger of the National Federation of Afro-American Women and the Colored Women's Clubs. The main objective of the NACW was to secure unified action among black club women and to uplift home, morals, and civic life. The motto "Lifting as We Climb" characterized the association's aims.

Mary Church Terrell was elected its first president. For her, the NACW symbolized the unity of black women's efforts toward progress and reform. The vice presidents included Josephine Ruffin, Fanny J. Coppin, and Frances E. W. Harper. Victoria Matthews was elected national organizer, and Margaret Washington was chosen to chair the executive board and to edit the association's news organ, *National Notes.*

The NACW was composed of nearly 200 clubs, with 113 from the Colored Woman's League of Washington. The NACW encouraged the local women's clubs to engage in educational and social service projects and philanthropy. Local clubs emphasized mothers' clubs, the establishment of kindergartens and day nurseries, night classes, and sewing and cooking classes. Self-reliance was promoted through the establishment of penny savings banks. The NACW supported antilynching, temperance, and suffrage movements through departments within the national organization.

The NACW held its first convention in Nashville in 1897. Thereafter, national conventions were held biennially. NACW membership increased steadily from five thousand women in 1896 to fifteen thousand by 1904. By 1906, there were forty thousand members. In 1916, NACW membership was nearly sixty thousand, and in 1924 the goal of 100,000 women was achieved. The NACW continued to expand, but the present enrollment of 45,000 is approximately what it was at the turn of the century. The significance of the NACW lies in the fact that its members challenged individuals and groups who acted unjustly and discriminatorily toward black Americans. *(See also: Black Women; Black Women's Clubs; Colored Woman's League; National Federation of Afro-American Women; Terrell, Mary Church)*

—**Floris Barnett Cash**

Further Reading

Cash, Floris Barnett. "Womanhood and Protest: The Club Movement among Black Women, 1892–1922." Ph.D. diss., State University of New York, Stony Brook, 1986.
Davis, Elizabeth. *Lifting as They Climb.* Washington, DC: National Association of Colored Women, 1933.
Records of the National Association of Colored Women's Clubs: Part 1. 1895–1992. Bethesda, MD: University Publications of America, 1993. Microfilm.
Salem, Dorothy. *To Better Our World: Black Women in Organized Reform, 1890–1920.* New York: Carlson, 1990.
Terrell, Mary Church. *A Colored Woman in a White World.* Washington, DC: National Association of Colored Women, 1968.
Wesley, Charles W. *The History of the National Association of Colored Women's Clubs, Inc.: A Legacy of Service.* Washington, DC: National Association of Colored Women, 1984.
Yates, Josephine. "The National Association of Colored Women," *Voice of the Negro* 1 (July 1904): 283-87.

National Association of University Women (NAUW)

The National Association of University Women (NAUW) was an outgrowth of the College Alumnae Club, which was organized in 1910. Twenty-four university graduates joined Mary Church Terrell in her home in Washington, D.C., for the first meeting. The aim of the College Alumnae Club was to stimulate young women "to attain professional excellence, to exert influence in various movements for the civil good, and to promote a close personal and intellectual fellowship among professional women." The club participated in activities to raise the standards of Negro colleges and to achieve woman suffrage. From 1910 to 1923, the organization expanded, forming branches, and in 1924 became the National Association of College Women, later changed to the National Association of University Women.

Today, the NAUW includes ninety-two local groups and over 4,000 members whose goals are to (a) promote constructive work in education, civic activities, and human relations; (b) study educational conditions with emphasis on problems affecting women; (c) encourage high educational standards; and (c) stimulate intellectual attainment among women in general. The association's theme is "Women of Action: Reaching, Risking, Responding." It is affiliated with the Leadership Conference on Civil Rights and the United Negro College Fund and maintains a program called "After High School—What?" Publications include a *Bulletin* and *Journal of the National Association of University Women*. *(See also: Higher Education; Higher Education for Southern Women; Terrell, Mary Church)*

—**Sandra M. Fox**

Further Reading

"The National Association of University Women: A Membership Pamphlet." Washington, DC: National Association of University Women.

Terrell, Mary Church. *A Colored Woman in a White World*. Washington, DC: Randell, 1940.

✍ National Consumers' League (NCL)

Formed in 1899, the National Consumers' League (NCL) spearheaded a movement of upper- and middle-class white women to improve the working conditions, hours, and wages of working people, particularly wage-earning women. Led until 1932 by the remarkable Florence Kelley, the league was initially concerned with the exploitation of department store clerks but expanded its focus over time to include workers in all occupations. In its early years, the league pressured employers using tactics such as its "White List" and "White Label" to identify compliance with its standards on wages, hours, and health and safety conditions. Urging affluent women to become agents of social reform through enlightened shopping habits, the NCL called itself the "consumers' conscience."

When few employers voluntarily raised labor standards, the NCL shifted to legislative methods. It drafted bills, lobbied state and federal legislatures, and frequently supplied the personnel to administer the new laws. The NCL also defended legislation in court, playing key roles in landmark test cases such as *Muller v. Oregon* (1908). League efforts helped create a body of state laws abolishing child labor and establishing maximum hours and minimum wages for women; it also helped to create the U.S. Children's Bureau (in 1912) and the U.S. Women's Bureau (in 1920). During the New Deal, the NCL backed the federal, sex-neutral Fair Labor Standards Act (1938), and it also campaigned for improved labor laws in the southern states, under the new leadership of Lucy Randolph Mason.

Although ardent suffragists before 1920, NCL activists eschewed the label "feminist" because they associated it with the National Woman's Party (NWP) and the Equal Rights Amendment (ERA), which the NWP introduced in 1923. The NCL believed the ERA would serve the needs of professional and propertied women at the expense of women wage earners, by invalidating women-only labor laws. Although

the NCL underestimated the negative effects on women of sex-based labor laws, it was correct that the ERA did not directly address women's exploitation as wage earners.

Inspired leadership and good connections gave the league an influence larger than its numbers. Close associates over the years included Frances Perkins, Eleanor Roosevelt, and future Supreme Court justices Louis Brandeis and Felix Frankfurter. The NCL's role in creating new laws and agencies exemplifies the crucial contribution of women reformers from the Progressive Era through the New Deal in expanding governmental obligations to protect the public welfare. *(See also: Adkins v. Children's Hospital; Equal Rights Amendment; Kelley, Florence; Muller v. Oregon; National Woman's Party; Perkins, Frances; Protective Legislation; Roosevelt, Eleanor; Social Feminism; Women's Bureau)*

—**Landon R. Y. Storrs**

Further Reading

Boris, Eileen. *Home to Work: Motherhood and the Politics of Industrial Homework in the United States*. New York: Cambridge University Press, 1994.

Chambers, Clarke A. *Seedtime of Reform: American Social Service and Social Action, 1918–1933*. Minneapolis: University of Minnesota Press, 1963.

Kessler-Harris, Alice. *Out to Work: A History of Wage-Earning Women in the United States*. New York: Oxford University Press, 1982.

Sklar, Kathryn Kish. "Two Political Cultures in the Progressive Era: The National Consumers' League and the American Association for Labor Legislation." In *U.S. History as Women's History*, edited by Linda Kerber, Alice Kessler-Harris, and Kathryn Kish Sklar, 36-62. Chapel Hill: University of North Carolina, 1995.

Storrs, Landon. "Civilizing Capitalism: The National Consumers' League and the Politics of 'Fair' Labor Standards in the New Deal Era." Ph.D. diss., University of Wisconsin–Madison, 1994.

✍ National Council of Jewish Women (NCJW)

Founded in 1893 by Hannah Solomon at Chicago's 1893 World Exposition, the National Council of Jewish Women (NCJW) was the first nationwide organization of Jewish women to organize for religious purposes. It provided a conduit through which Jewish women's voices could be heard in their own community, which had traditionally denied women a public role. Simultaneously, it helped Jewish women to Americanize by forging an expression of Jewish identity that fit into the structures of American notions of "proper" womanhood as envisioned by women's clubs and social reformers.

That identity emphasized a domestic feminist approach to women's rights and the centrality of motherhood to all its work, especially the fight against assimilation. The focus on motherhood continues to determine the issues on which NCJW's 100,000-strong membership focuses, including its current emphasis on child welfare and reproductive rights.

(See also: Domestic Feminism; Jewish Women; Solomon, Hannah Greenebaum)

—Faith Rogow

Further Reading

NCJW: Proceedings of the First Convention. Philadelphia: Jewish Publication Society, 1897.

Papers of the Jewish Women's Congress, 1893. Philadelphia: Jewish Publication Society, 1894.

Rogow, Faith. Gone to Another Meeting: The National Council of Jewish Women, 1893–1993. Tuscaloosa: University of Alabama Press, 1993.

∾ National Council of Negro Women (NCNW)

The National Council of Negro Women (NCNW) was founded in 1935 for the purpose of coordinating the activities of black women's organizations and improving black women's status. The organization was established by Mary McLeod Bethune and twenty-nine women representing fourteen black women's organizations. Some of the founding members included Dr. Dorothy Ferebee, Mabel Staupers, Charlotte Hawkins Brown, and Mary Church Terrell. The women met at the YWCA in Harlem in New York City to create an umbrella organization that would unify black women's efforts and affect national public policy.

The leader behind the NCNW was Mary McLeod Bethune, who became its first president. Bethune was the founder of Bethune-Cookman College in Florida. She was also the first black woman to be appointed to a federal government post when President Franklin D. Roosevelt made her head of the Division of Negro Affairs at the National Youth Administration in 1936. Bethune hoped to use her connections in the federal government to advance the rights of black women through the NCNW. The organization lost much of its strength when Bethune retired from the presidency in 1949.

The NCNW has represented over 1 million African American women. During World War II the council pushed for racial equality in federal wartime policies, including the integration of black women into the military. The women also sent a letter to President Roosevelt in support of Jewish rights and in opposition to the Nuremberg Laws in Germany. During the 1960s, the council created rural projects to aid impoverished African Americans in the South. Two important Mississippi programs were Project Home, which addressed poor housing, and Operation Daily Bread, designed to alleviate the food shortage. The NCNW has remained a major force in the advancement of women's rights. (See also: Bethune, Mary McLeod; Terrell, Mary Church)

—Susan Lynn Smith

Further Reading

Collier-Thomas, Bettye. N.C.N.W., 1935–1980. Washington, DC: National Council of Negro Women, 1981.

Giddings, Paula. When and Where I Enter: The Impact of Black Women on Race and Sex in America. New York: William Morrow, 1984.

Hine, Darlene Clark. When the Truth Is Told: A History of Black Women's Culture and Community in Indiana, 1875–1950. Indianapolis, IN: National Council of Negro Women, 1981.

∾ National Education Association (NEA)

The National Education Association (NEA) is the most influential education organization in the United States and is the largest professional organization in the world. It was organized in Philadelphia, Pennsylvania, in 1857 and originally called the National Teachers' Association. Forty-three educators from a dozen states met on August 26, 1857, under the leadership of Daniel B. Hagar and Thomas W. Valentine and adopted a constitution stating that the purpose of the organization is "to elevate the character and advance the interests of the profession of teaching, and to promote the cause of popular education in the United States."

Although women were not admitted to membership until 1866, the constitution was signed by two women, H. D. Conrad and A. W. Beecher. By the time of the 1884 convention in Madison, Wisconsin, women composed 54 percent of the nearly six thousand educators in attendance.

Until 1957, the association's policy was to take official positions only on matters directly affecting education. As a result of the policy, the association's executive committee in 1956 voted to advise its representative assembly to withhold support of a U.S. constitutional amendment on the equal status of women. In contrast to this earlier action, the NEA became a militant advocate of the equal rights of women in the years from 1957 to 1979. In 1975, the representative assembly voted not to hold meetings in states that had not ratified the Equal Rights Amendment, as well as to refuse support to candidates for political office who opposed ratification of the ERA. During that same year, it also amended and strengthened a previous resolution (a) endorsing the use of nonsexist language, (b) supporting the Supreme Court decisions on reproductive freedom and family planning, and (c) advocating the elimination of sexism and sex discrimination from the school curriculum. In 1978, the assembly reaffirmed its position to work for ratification of the ERA as a major legislative priority.

Today, the NEA includes over 2 million educators and is able to create a strong professional, social, and political influence. One of its standing committees is on women's concerns. Publications include the NEA Handbook, Issues, NEA Today, Almanac of Higher Education, NEA Higher Education Advocate, and Thought and Action.

Delegates to the NEA's 1998 national convention rejected the "Principles of Unity," a document outlining the steps that would have united the NEA with the American Federation of Teachers. The NEA delegates, representing the 2.4 million members of the organization, did adopt, however, a measure supporting unity and continued union cooperation on key education issues that allowed state-level mergers to go forward. (See also: Education; Teaching; Unions)

—Sandra M. Fox

Further Reading

Fenner, Mildred Sandison. NEA History. Washington, DC: National Education Association, 1945.

Wesley, Edgar Bruce. NEA: The First Hundred Years. New York: Harper, 1957.

West, Allan M. The National Education Association: The Power Base for Education. New York: Free Press, 1980.

⟨ National Farmers' Alliance

With a southern branch and a northern branch, the National Farmers' Alliance was one of the first mixed-sex organizations to provide opportunities for rural women to hold office. From 1888 through the mid-1890s, alliance women and men gathered to organize cooperatives; to discuss the economic concerns of farm families, including low crop prices, high shipping rates, the lack of land, and increased mortgage foreclosures; and to lay the foundation for the Populist Party.

Women constituted at least one-fourth of the alliance membership. By-laws of the two national alliances, of several state alliances, and of many local suballiances specified that women were eligible for membership although they were exempted from paying dues. Women were often elected to serve as secretaries or treasurers of their suballiances and, more important, as lecturers. Lecturers planned meetings, chose educational materials for study, gave speeches, and solicited members for new suballiances. In eight states, women held state alliance offices. Kansas and Nebraska each boasted six women state officers. In Nebraska, the Zion suballiance elected a woman president, Ella Hall. Fourteen percent of 105 suballiances in Nebraska (the only midwestern state for which membership records exist) had more female members than male members; one-fourth of the Nebraska suballiances had women officers. State officers included Luna Kellie and Elsie Buckman in Nebraska, Eva McDonald Valesh in Minnesota, Fannie Vickery and Bina Otis in Kansas, Sophia Hardin in South Dakota, Fannie Leak in Texas, and Martha Southworth in Colorado. Valesh, Marion Todd, Mary Elizabeth Lease, and Sarah Emery frequently spoke at alliance functions and picnics and were among the many women elected as delegates to state and national conventions.

In addition, women often edited alliance newspapers and wrote popular didactic novels and economic tracts explain-

ing the economic worries of farmers and the ways in which these problems could be solved by the National Farmers' Alliance. The novels included Shylock's Daughter (1894), by Margaret Holmes Bates; A Kansas Farm (1892), by Fannie McCormick; and Richard's Crown (1882), by Anna D. Weaver. Alliance members studied finance, legislation, and economics from the books of Sarah Emery (Seven Financial Conspiracies, 1887), Stella Fisk (The Condition and the Remedy, 1894), Mary Hobart (A Scientific Exposure of the Errors of Our Monetary System, 1891), and Marion Todd (Protective Tariff Delusions, 1886; Honest (?) John Sherman, 1894). (See also: Agriculture: Preindustrial and Nineteenth-Century United States; Emery, Sara Elizabeth Van de Vort; Kellie, Luna Elizabeth Sanford; Lease, Mary Elizabeth Clyens; Populist Party; Valesh, Eva McDonald)

—MaryJo Wagner

Further Reading

Nebraska Farmers' Alliance Papers, 1887–97. Nebraska State Historical Society, Lincoln.

Jeffrey, Julie Roy. "Women in the Southern Farmers' Alliance," Feminist Studies 3 (Fall 1975): 72-91.

McMath, Robert C. Populist Vanguard: A History of the Southern Farmer's Alliance. New York: Norton, 1977.

Wagner, MaryJo. "Farms, Families, and Reform: Women in the Farmers' Alliance and Populist Party." Ph.D. diss., University of Oregon, 1986.

⟨ National Federation of Afro-American Women (NFAAW) (1895–1896)

The National Federation of Afro-American Women (NFAAW) was the first national organization of black women's clubs. It was organized July 29-31, 1895, in Boston during a nationwide conference of black women. The conference convened under the leadership of Josephine St. Pierre Ruffin, founder and president of the Woman's Era Club of Boston and editor of its newsletter, The Woman's Era. She sent a circular letter to women's clubs, leagues, and societies requesting delegates and explaining the purpose of the meeting. The immediate stimulus for organization was a letter to the British Anti-Lynching Society written by a southern editor, John W. Jacks, which slandered the moral character of all black women.

Social activists from communities across the country attended the historic conference, as did 104 black women representing thirty-two clubs from fifteen states and the District of Columbia. Addresses by prominent women such as Anna J. Cooper, Victoria Matthews, and Margaret Washington reflected the concerns of black women. The women's conference attracted a small number of male supporters, including T. Thomas Fortune, the editor of New York Age; Henry B. Blackwell, husband of the feminist Lucy Stone; and William Lloyd Garrison, son of the abolitionist.

The conference culminated with the formation of the National Federation of Afro-American Women and the selection of Margaret Washington, the wife of Booker T. Washington, as president of the new organization. Victoria Earle Matthews was chosen to chair the executive board. According to its constitution, the NFAAW aimed to unify the energies of Afro-American women into one broad sisterhood for the purpose of establishing needed reforms. The following year, both the NFAAW and the Colored Woman's League, a rival organization, held national conventions in Washington, D.C. After a compromise, a united National Association of Colored Women emerged. *(See also: Black Women's Clubs; National Association of Colored Women; Ruffin, Josephine St. Pierre; Washington, Margaret Murray)*

—**Floris Barnett Cash**

Further Reading

Cash, Floris Barnett. "Womanhood and Protest: The Club Movement among Black Women, 1892–1922." Ph.D. diss., State University of New York, Stony Brook, 1986.

Davis, Elizabeth. *Lifting as They Climb.* Washington, DC: National Association of Colored Women, 1933.

Neverdon-Morton, Cynthia. *Afro-American Women of the South and the Advancement of the Race, 1895–1925.* Knoxville: University of Tennessee Press, 1989.

Wesley, Charles W. *The History of the National Association of Colored Women's Clubs, Inc.: A Legacy of Service.* Washington, DC: National Association of Colored Women, 1984.

ᷡ National Federation of Business and Professional Women's Clubs, Inc. of the United States of America (BPW/USA)

The National Federation of Business and Professional Women's Clubs, Inc. (BPW/USA) was founded in St. Louis in 1919 by Lena Madeson Phillips, who challenged her colleagues: "Make no small plans. They have no power to stir the blood." Some independent businesswomen joined those who worked in office white-collar jobs and constituted the majority of the BPW membership. Throughout the 1930s and 1940s, the BPW defended the right of married women in office jobs to continue to work for pay, reflecting both the growth of white-collar jobs and women's presence in that sector of the labor force. In 1940, women constituted half of the 500,000 clerical workers in the United States. The BPW also participated in Red Cross work, the conference to draw up the U.N. Charter, and efforts to create women's military organizations. In the 1950s, the organization focused on job-related issues of concern to its members, most of whom were still salaried clerical workers. The BPW therefore lacked the political clout of comparable men's groups, yet began to assert its place in the community economy. In the 1960s, the BPW led the fight for the Equal Pay Act. By the 1970s, the local BPW chapters exerted political and economic influence in their communities and provided a milieu for networking among its members.

In 1937, the BPW became one of the first women's organizations to endorse the Equal Rights Amendment. The group also participated in the 1977 International Women's Year Conference in Houston and was an influential group in the fight for the successful passage of Title IX, aimed at ending discrimination in education.

By the 1980s, the BPW had become the largest organization of working women in the world, with 150,000 members and 3,500 local organizations and chapters. Male members were admitted to the organization. The Retirement Equity Act and Leadership Training became priorities. In addition to providing personal and professional development opportunities for its members, the organization became committed to developing their political skills and awareness. A national political action committee was created at its 1980 national convention to assist, through contributions and endorsements, candidates for federal office who supported the organization's principles, including ratification of the Equal Rights Amendment. The organization also created the National Council on the Future of Women in the Workplace, composed of one councillor from each BPW state federation and chaired by black Democratic Party leader Eleanor Holmes Norton, to play a vigorous role in exploring the implications for women of new patterns in the workplace regarding pay equity, better child care, and technological change in jobs traditionally held by BPW members. In the 1990s, issues such as child care, elder care, violence against women, and health insurance became of interest to the organization.

The organization annually sponsors National Business Women Week in the third week in October and is affiliated with the Business and Professional Women's Foundation, a nonprofit research and education organization that conducts and supports research on all aspects of women's workforce participation, sponsors scholarship and loan programs for women at critical points in their lives, and supports the Marguerite Rawalt Resource Center on women's employment issues, which provides daily service to the public. *(See also: Business; Equal Rights Amendment)*

—**Anne Statham**

Further Reading

BPW/USA: The Voice of Working America. A pamphlet produced by BPW/USA, Washington, DC., 1987.

BPW/WI History. 1995. Microfiche. Contact BPW Business Office, P.O. Box 2267, Green Bay, WI 54306.

Lemons, J. Stanley. *The Woman Citizen.* Urbana: University of Illinois Press, 1973.

ᷡ National Federation of Settlements

The National Federation of Settlements was officially founded on June 11, 1911, by leaders of the settlement house movement, which encouraged educated young people to "settle" among and associate with the urban poor, serving as catalysts for social reform. At this time, the majority of settlement residents, staff, and heads—and the movement's most prominent leaders—were women. Jane Addams of Hull House in Chicago served as the federation's first president. The new organization improved communication among member houses and helped to coordinate members' social action efforts. These included promoting the creation of the U.S. Children's Bureau, a continual concern for day care, and early endorsement of national health insurance. Lillian Wald of New York's Henry Street Settlement directed a study of prohibition (1927), and Helen Hall published the federation-sponsored *Case Studies of Unemployment* (1931).

While women had ceased to be a majority of settlement heads by the early 1950s, they tended to dominate the administration of the federation from 1934 to 1971. In 1934, the federation appointed Lillie Peck as its first full-time, paid executive. Peck headed the administrative office until 1947, when John McDowell replaced her. As social welfare reform increasingly centered on the federal government, the role of the federation in lobbying became more important. Peck also systematically developed field service to member settlements.

Under McDowell, women filled key positions. Between 1950 and 1968, Fern Colborn authored a federation study of urban renewal, wrote another book on the design of neighborhood centers, and lobbied effectively for housing and welfare programs, including model cities. In 1952, Margaret Berry became assistant director, then executive director from 1959 to 1971. Since Berry, no woman has served as executive director.

During Berry's tenure, the federation enjoyed its strongest years. The national headquarters grew to six and a half paid positions, and the federation ran a training center from 1960 to 1971. The federation office continued to push for social reform, with individual leaders sometimes being ahead of a board that had been dominated by nonprofessionals since the early 1950s. For example, the federation did not speak out on birth control until 1965. While the subject was too controversial for settlements in Catholic neighborhoods, some settlements in Protestant neighborhoods actually housed birth control clinics. Membership in the federation was voluntary for local settlements, which retained complete autonomy. In 1979, it became United Neighborhood Centers of America. *(See also: Addams, Jane; Henry Street Settlement; Hull House; Settlement House Movement; Wald, Lillian)*

—**Judith Ann Trolander**

Further Reading

Archives of the Settlement Movement. 74 microfilm reels. Woodbridge, CT: Research Publications, 1990.

Trolander, Judith Ann. *Professionalism and Social Change: From the Settlement House Movement to Neighborhood Centers, 1886 to the Present.* New York: Columbia University Press, 1986.

———. "The Response of Settlements to the Great Depression," *Social Work* 18 (September 1973): 92-102.

⟨◈⟩ National Labor Union (1866–1873)

The National Labor Union was founded as a national labor federation with representatives from labor unions in thirteen states and Washington, D.C. There were no women present at the first convention in Baltimore, but there were advocates for women among the delegates.

The most important of these was William Sylvis, the union's cofounder and probably the most important labor leader of the time. Sylvis was president of the Iron Molder's International Union, and during his travels on its behalf, he learned firsthand of the struggles of working women and of their difficulties trying to get represented in men's unions or trying to organize their own unions. Like most men of the post-Civil War period, Sylvis did not fully support the presence of women in the labor force. He felt that woman's place was in the home, but he came to believe that if women were going to work, they should be entitled to equal working conditions and equal pay with men. This was part of his belief in social reform for all people. Likewise, Sylvis did not originally support woman suffrage but later came to do so.

The National Labor Union's interest in helping working women had support from the woman suffrage movement. Elizabeth Cady Stanton and Susan B. Anthony, for example, looked to the labor movement for support at a time when most people, including some feminists, felt that the woman suffrage movement should wait until the newly emancipated black man had won the right to vote. In 1868, Stanton attempted to be seated as a delegate at the national convention of the National Labor Union even though she did not represent a labor union. Instead, she represented the Woman Suffrage Association of America, an organization formed just for the convention. With Sylvis's support, she was finally seated.

Several other women were also seated at the convention. Most represented unions that had been formed for the purpose of gaining women's entrance to the convention. The convention did not vote in favor of woman suffrage but did urge equal pay for equal work and women's right to join the labor unions that belonged to the National Labor Union. The only member union that actually carried out this policy was the National Union of Cigar Makers. The convention also praised the efforts of Kate Mullaney, president of the Collar Laundry Union of Troy, for her efforts on behalf of women laborers. In fact, Mullaney was elected second vice president, but this action was later annulled because the first vice president came from the same state. Finally, in 1870, Mrs. E. O. G. Willard of the Sewing Girls' Union of Chicago was elected second vice president of the National Labor Union, the first woman to attain this honor. However, economic hardships brought to National Labor Union members by the Panic of 1873, an economic depression, completed its demise in the face of competition from another labor organization, the Knights of Labor. *(See also: Knights of Labor; Suffrage; Unions; Women's Work: Nineteenth Century)*

—Judith Pryor

Further Reading

Foner, Philip S. *Women and the American Labor Movement: From Colonial Times to the Eve of World War I.* New York: Free Press, 1979.

Grossman, Jonathan Philip. *William Sylvis, Pioneer of American Labor: A Study of the Labor Movement during the Era of the Civil War.* New York: Octagon, 1973.

Kenneally, James J. "Women and the Trade Unions, 1870–1920: The Quandary of the Reformer," *Labor History* 14 (1973): 42-55.

Sylvis, James C. *The Life, Speeches, Labors, and Essays of William H. Sylvis.* Philadelphia: Claxton, Remsen & Happlefinger, 1972.

National Museum of Women in the Arts

The National Museum of Women in the Arts was founded in 1981 to promote awareness of and to educate the public about the achievements of women in the arts through the ages. The museum opened to the public on April 7, 1987, in the former Masonic Temple of Washington, D.C. Designed by architect Waddy Wood in 1907, the Renaissance Revival building is on the National Register of Historic Places. The museum has won several awards for the interior and exterior restoration.

The permanent collection of the museum, whose core of over five hundred pieces was donated by founders Wilhelmina C. and Wallace F. Holladay, ranges from Renaissance to contemporary and includes paintings, sculptures, photographs, Native American pottery, Georgian silver, and works of art on paper. Special exhibitions highlight women and their artistic achievements in a particular area or time period. The museum also houses a Library and Research Center with over eleven thousand books and exhibition catalogues and seventeen thousand files on women artists and institutions, making it one of the most comprehensive research collections on women artists in the world.

The museum has a national and international membership of about sixty-five thousand members. The museum has a unique program of state committees that promotes the museum's mission on a popular level and provides a forum for local artists to show their work in state shows in the nation's capital. *(See also: Art)*

—Mary Louise Wood

Further Reading

Wood, Mary Louise, and Martha McWilliams. *The National Museum of Women in the Arts.* New York: Abrams, 1987.

http://www.nmwa.org

National Negro Health Movement (1915–1950)

The National Negro Health Movement began under the leadership of Booker T. Washington at Tuskegee Institute in Alabama to call national attention to the pressing need for better health among African Americans. In the tradition of black self-help efforts, it was a response to the inadequate provision of health services in the first half of the twentieth century. Among other projects, the movement sponsored an annual health week that focused community involvement in clean-up campaigns and health examinations for black people. By 1922, National Negro Health Week was celebrated nationwide in fifteen states and, by 1945, in forty-five states, with much of the focus of the health movement on the rural South. Black women played an active role in the movement as public health nurses, doctors, teachers, club members, home demonstration agents, midwives, and volunteers in the various health projects. Women and children were the major recipients of services provided by these programs.

Many major black organizations joined the health effort. By the 1930s, the federal government took an increasing interest in black health projects, and the U.S. Public Health Service coordinated black health activities through its new Office of Negro Health Work. *(See also: Black Women)*

—Susan Lynn Smith

Further Reading

Beardsley, Edward H. *A History of Neglect: Health Care for Blacks and Mill Workers in the Twentieth-Century South.* Knoxville: University of Tennessee Press, 1987.

Jones, James. *Bad Blood: The Tuskegee Syphilis Experiment.* New York: Free Press, 1981.

Smith, Susan Lynn. *Sick and Tired of Being Sick and Tired: Black Women's Health Activism in America, 1890–1950.* Philadelphia: University of Pennsylvania Press, 1995.

Torchia, Marion M. "The Tuberculosis Movement and the Race Question, 1890–1950," *Journal of the History of Medicine and Allied Sciences* 32 (1977): 252-79.

National Organization for Public Health Nursing (NOPHN)

The National Organization for Public Health Nursing (NOPHN) was founded in 1912 by nurses who wanted to distinguish themselves from those engaged in private-duty and hospital nursing. It was part of the movement to professionalize nursing but was unique in its close links to the nineteenth-century reform movement. Unlike other professional nurse associations, it welcomed lay members who were dedicated to the goals of preventive medicine. The organization provided a support network and strengthened the sense of professional identity of nurses who practiced in isolation as they visited the homes of the sick among the poor and worked in neighborhood dispensaries, settlement houses, and factories. The organization published a journal, *The Public Health Nurse,* later titled *Public Health Nursing.*

After World War II, employment opportunities for public health nurses declined precipitously as voluntary agencies lost their funding, and due largely to efforts by physicians and insurance companies, medical care was increasingly delivered in hospitals or through physicians' private practice. The NOPHN reacted to the situation by voting to dissolve its organization in 1953. Members were directed to the National League of Nursing Education and the Association of Collegiate Schools of Nursing, two organizations that subscribed to the activist principles of the NOPHN and admitted lay members. *(See also: Nursing)*

—**Jane Crisler**

Further Reading
Fitzpatrick, M. Louise. *The National Organization for Public Health Nursing, 1912–1952: Development of a Practice Field.* New York: National League for Nursing, 1975.
Melosh, Barbara. *"The Physician's Hand": Work, Culture and Conflict in American Nursing.* Philadelphia: Temple University Press, 1982.

⚭ National Organization for Women (NOW)

The National Organization for Women (NOW) is the largest and most influential women's rights organization in the United States, with over 250,000 members and more than 550 chapters, with organizations in each of the fifty states. The main goal of the group is to act to bring women into the mainstream of American society as full and active participants who exercise their responsibilities and their privileges as equal partners to men. NOW is pledged to advance women who work both outside and inside the home, to hasten enforcement of sex discrimination legislation, to improve women's rights and political representation, to establish marriage as a genuine partnership, and to alleviate poverty, largely a women's issue. NOW was organized in October 1966 by a group of twenty-eight women who had attended a conference of state representatives from the various commissions on the status of women in Washington, D.C. These women were frustrated first by the government's approach to women's issues. They realized they needed an "NAACP for women." Betty Friedan, author of *The Feminine Mystique* (1963), became the chief organizer and named the organization.

The general approach of the organization can be described as pragmatic, exerting pressure on the social structure. NOW seeks legal reform in concert with attitudinal and behavioral changes leading to societal change. Methods employed range from consciousness-raising, information giving, marching, picketing, letter writing, petitioning, public opinion influencing, and candidate endorsement to lobbying efforts on all levels of government. The following list

displays the magnitude of these efforts: in 1978, 100,000 marched on Washington, D.C. for ERA; in 1986, 100,000 joined NOW's pro-choice march in Washington, D.C.; in 1989, 300,000 to 500,000 joined NOW's pro-choice march; in 1992, more than 750,000 joined NOW's march for reproductive freedom in Washington, D.C. (the largest single demonstration for reproductive freedom ever).

Local chapters have a great deal of autonomy. Participatory democracy is recognized as crucial in this organization and may explain its longevity. A chapter consists of at least eight members. Before 1973, locals adopted and added to the standard national bylaws, but since 1970, chapters have been encouraged to be experimental as long as goals do not go against existing policy. This enables local chapters to personalize for their particular locales, needs, and interests. This also allows the local chapters to try out more radical ideas and then influence the national organization. At the 25th anniversary celebration of NOW in January 1992, held at the Washington Hilton with the Global Feminist Conference, it was announced that a new feminist political party would be formed to compete with the two major political parties in the United States.

Throughout the 1990s, NOW campaigned for change. The group is currently focused on national governmental elections, abortion rights, lesbian rights, affirmative action, and expanding ideas globally. In 1997, NOW expressed its dedication to young women in their Young Feminists Summit, and in 1998, NOW organized a Women of Color and Allies Summit to support diversity among women. Patricia Ireland is the current president of NOW. *(See also: Friedan, Betty; Women's Liberation Movement)*

—**Saundra K. Yelton-Stanley**

Further Reading
Carden, Maren Lockwood. *The New Feminist Movement,* pp. 103-32. New York: Russell Sage Foundation, 1974.
Leidner, Robin. "Stretching the Boundaries of Liberalism: Democratic Innovation in a Feminist Organization (National Women's Studies Association)," *Signs* 16 (Winter 1991): 263-89.
National NOW Times.
"NOW Herstory in *The Feminist Chronicles 1953–1993,*" *National NOW Times* 26 (January 1994): 9.
"NOW: The Silver Anniversary and the Global Feminist Conference," *Off Our Backs* 22 (February 1992): 1.
Special Insert Time Line: 20 Years of Feminism, *Ms.* 3 (July-August 1992), Commemorative insert between pages 48-49.
http//:www.now.org/index.html [NOW Website]

⚭ National Park Service, National Site Preservation, and Women's History

The preservation of women's history in the United States has been served by the National Park Service, the National Historic Landmarks Program, and the National Register of Historic Places.

The National Park Service was established in 1916 to preserve the nation's significant natural, cultural, and historical resources. At present, there are 369 units in the national park system, five of which are dedicated to women's history.

Women's Rights National Historical Park in Seneca Falls, New York, was created (a) to interpret the first women's rights convention in United States history (1848) and the movement that grew from it and (b) to preserve buildings related to the early struggle for women's rights. Included in the park are the Wesleyan Chapel, site of the convention; the home of Elizabeth Cady Stanton, leader of the nineteenth-century movement; the home of Jane Hunt, where the convention was planned; and the home of Mary Ann McClintock, where the Declaration of Sentiments and Resolutions for the convention was written.

Maggie L. Walker National Historical Site in Richmond, Virginia, was created to preserve the home and neighborhood of an important African American civic and financial leader. Walker was the first woman bank president in America and a central figure in Richmond's African American community for over forty years. Eleanor Roosevelt National Historic Site in Hyde Park, New York, preserves Val-Kill Cottage and associated buildings and grounds. Beginning in 1925, the complex was Eleanor Roosevelt's refuge from the demands of a busy career in public service and the place where she met with numerous world leaders. Clara Barton National Historic Site in Glen Echo, Maryland, preserves and interprets the home where the humanitarian and founder of the American Red Cross resided for the last fifteen years of her life. Mary McLeod Bethune Council House National Historic Site in Washington, D.C., commemorates the life and work of an important educator and leader in the struggle for African American civil rights.

The Sewall-Belmont House in Washington, D.C., is a site associated with the National Park Service but is still privately owned by the National Woman's Party. The house interprets the work of Alice Paul, founder of the National Woman's Party and author of the Equal Rights Amendment. Two other national park sites deal substantively with women's history. Whitman Mission National Historic Site near Walla Walla, Washington, interprets the mission established along the Oregon Trail by Narcissa and Marcus Whitman in 1836. Narcissa Whitman and a colleague, Eliza Spalding, were the first white women to cross the continent overland. Lowell National Historical Park in Lowell, Massachusetts, preserves and interprets the early industrial history of the Northeast, with a focus on the lives and labor activism of early female factory workers.

Interpretation of women's history is being incorporated into existing programs at many national park areas. For example, the role of women in military encampments is interpreted at Morristown National Historical Park in New Jersey, and the contributions of Sacagawea, the Shoshone Indian guide, to the Lewis and Clark expedition are interpreted at Fort Clatsop National Park in Astoria, Oregon. The wives of men whose homes are preserved are often interpreted as well, as at Carl Sandburg National Historic Site at Flat Rock, North Carolina, where Paula Sandburg's

career is extensively discussed. Women's vital domestic roles and activities are interpreted at many sites, including George Washington Birthplace National Monument in Virginia; Martin Van Buren National Historic Site in Kinderhook, New York; and George Washington Carver National Monument in Diamond, Missouri.

Also among the federal government's historic preservation initiatives are two key programs: the National Historic Landmarks Program and the National Register of Historic Places. Both programs are designed to encourage private and state efforts in historic preservation to complement federal activities.

Established in 1935, the National Historic Landmarks Program is designed to identify and encourage the preservation of nationally significant historic sites, buildings, structures, districts, and objects. There are nearly two hundred national historic landmarks, less than 5 percent of which commemorate women's experiences and contributions to the nation. Among national historic landmarks dedicated to women are the homes of reformers Susan B. Anthony, Mary Ann Shadd Cary, Mary Church Terrell, Julia Ward Howe, Harriet Beecher Stowe, Charlotte Forten Grimké, Frances Ellen Watkins Harper, Ida B. Wells-Barnett, and Mary McLeod Bethune. Also included are Harriet Tubman's Home for the Aged and the homes of artists and intellectuals such as Emily Dickinson, Emma Willard, Margaret Fuller, Florence Mills, and Pearl Buck.

Many of these homes were preserved through the efforts of women, as were the homes of Maggie L. Walker, Eleanor Roosevelt, and the sites that make up Women's Rights National Historical Park. More traditionally significant sites such as Mount Vernon, the Old South Meeting House, Mesa Verde, Valley Forge, and the home of Frederick Douglass were also saved by groups of women.

The National Register of Historic Places, established in 1966, officially lists and provides initiatives for the preservation of historic resources of national, state, or local significance. Thirteen percent of all National Register properties are nationally significant; these include all national historic landmarks, which are automatically listed on the National Register. There are over 45,000 properties on the National Register, and women are vastly underrepresented.

Part of the reason for women's underrepresentation is that the criteria for historical significance, particularly in the landmarks program, are based largely on traditional historical categories and periodizations that ignore or exclude women. Sites are evaluated for their economic, political, or military associations, and women's contributions in these areas, as well as more traditionally female fields, are neglected.

In 1987, the National Park Service and other national historical organizations, including the National Coordinating Council for the Promotion of History, embarked on a program to increase women's representation in the landmarks program. The commencement of this project indicated a recognition that a redefinition of "significance" was required if the experiences and accomplishments of women in the United States were to be adequately preserved and interpreted. This reconceptualization of history has begun, in collaboration with the Organization of American Historians, and has resulted in a series of reports revising the thematic frameworks underlying the park system. In 1995, the Park Service also began work on a "Women's History Education Initiative" intended to integrate women's history into the service's preservation and interpretation programs. *(See also: Women's History)*

—**Margaret T. McFadden**

Further Reading

Hosmer, Charles B. *Presence of the Past: A History of the Preservation Movement in the United States before Williamsburg.* New York: Putnam, 1965.

———. *Preservation Comes of Age, from Williamsburg to the National Trust, 1926–1949,* 2 vols. Charlottesville: University of Virginia Press, 1981.

Miller, Page Putnam, ed. *Reclaiming the Past: Landmarks of Women's History.* Bloomington: Indiana University Press, 1992.

National Park Service, U.S. Department of the Interior. *Catalog of National Historic Landmarks.* Washington, DC: Government Printing Office, 1985.

———. *Index of the National Park System, 1993–94.* Washington, DC: Government Printing Office, 1993.

Savage, Beth L., ed. *African-American Historic Places.* Washington, DC: Preservation Press, 1994.

Tinling, Marion. *Women Remembered: A Guide to Landmarks of Women's History in the United States.* Westport, CT: Greenwood, 1986.

∾ National Welfare Rights Organization (NWRO)

The National Welfare Rights Organization (NWRO), a federation of local groups, was formed in April 1967 to represent the needs of welfare recipients and others in need of economic assistance. The membership, made up almost exclusively of mothers receiving Aid to Dependent Children grants through the welfare system, stood at 5,000 in 1967, but by 1969, it reached a peak of 25,000 to 30,000. The majority of members were black welfare mothers. The organization can be said to have represented in excess of 100,000 people at its apex if the children of these women are considered. The requirements for membership were poverty and current or previous welfare recipient status.

The goals of the organization were "adequate income for all Americans" (a guaranteed annual income) welfare and guarantees that the welfare system accord "dignity, justice, and democracy to all recipients." These goals were to be pursued by attempting to eliminate restrictive welfare requirements and generally increasing welfare benefits within their own plan called Guaranteed Adequate Income (GAI) based on the Department of Labor's own statistics of adequate income.

The initial plan of attack called for the local groups to protest particular complaints, usually regarding withheld entitlement payments. Creation and distribution of handbooks, advocacy, sit-ins, and demonstrations are examples of the methods employed.

The NWRO tested welfare policy and law in the courts. It also lobbied for a guaranteed annual income of $6,500 a year for a family of four in 1971, in direct opposition to the punitive Family Assistance Plan being proposed by President Richard M. Nixon. During the Nixon presidency, concessions to welfare recipients began to be withdrawn, cutbacks were increased, and NWRO membership declined. The organization went bankrupt, and the national office closed early in 1975.

It is difficult to assess the real achievements of the organization, but in general, it is fair to say that its efforts did help produce a more humane system and helped expand benefits to welfare recipients. Although the NWRO fell short of its goal of a guaranteed annual income, it at least helped to defeat Nixon's program. According to NWRO activists and social scientists Frances Fox Piven and Richard A. Cloward, members wanted "to build an enduring mass organization through which the poor could exert influence." Perhaps the failures of this organization can be summed up with a question to be pondered still: How can the powerless exert power?

Johnnie Tillmon Blackstone, although no longer on welfare, still holds the title of Director of the NWRO, which continues only locally in a few U.S. cities. *(See also: Female-Headed Households; Mothers' Pensions)*

—**Saundra K. Yelton-Stanley**

Further Reading

Evans, Sara. *Personal Politics: The Roots of Women's Liberation in the Civil Rights Movement and the New Left.* New York: Vintage, 1979, 1980.

Roach, Jack L., and Janet K. Roach. "Mobilizing the Poor: Road to a Dead End," *Social Problems* 26 (December 1978): 160-71.

"Welfare," *Ms.* 6 (July/August 1995): 50-55.

∾ National Woman Suffrage Association (NWSA)

The National Woman Suffrage Association (NWSA) was founded in New York City in May 1869 by Elizabeth Cady Stanton and Susan B. Anthony, who were angered at the refusal of abolitionist leaders to give priority to feminist demands until black rights (including black male suffrage) were secured. The organization took shape at a reception at the New York Woman's Bureau where some one hundred women, representing eighteen states, joined on the spot. Feminist notables such as Lucretia Mott, Martha Wright, Paulina Wright Davis, and Ernestine Rose lent their support to the new venture. It was agreed that men should not hold office in the new association and that its program would emphasize the need for a federal woman suffrage amendment. Stanton was elected president, and Anthony served first on the executive committee and later as vice president at large. The two women tirelessly publicized the wide-ranging feminist aims of the NWSA in the pages of their short-lived newspaper, *Revolution,* through weekly discussion meetings in New York, and in a series of cross-country lecture tours. Their efforts encouraged the proliferation of state and local suffrage associations, and the NWSA soon outstripped its rival, the more moderate American Woman Suffrage Association (AWSA).

The NWSA brought its demand for a proposed Sixteenth Amendment to grant woman suffrage to center stage by holding national conventions each winter in Washington, D.C. NWSA members submitted a flood of petitions and resolutions to Congress and the White House and regularly testified before congressional committees. A delegation from the NWSA boldly disrupted the July 1876 Centennial celebrations in Philadelphia by presenting a "Woman's Declaration of Rights" drafted by Stanton and read aloud by Anthony. Beginning in 1878, at the NWSA's urging, a woman suffrage amendment was introduced every year in Congress.

Stanton remained as president, but from the early 1880s, Anthony increasingly exercised day-to-day leadership of the organization. Early criticism of NWSA's informal, amateurish style and sometimes undemocratic procedures gave way as Anthony promoted an increasingly sophisticated and efficient constitutional structure. In her efforts to build a broad-based, nonpartisan membership, she worked hard to smooth over dissension in the ranks. To Anthony's dismay, Stanton persisted in introducing controversial resolutions, calling, for example, for divorce reform or denouncing sexism in the churches. But NWSA membership continued to grow, as Anthony reached out to other mass women's organizations such as the Woman's Christian Temperance Union and women's clubs. International contacts generated by Stanton's several visits to Europe and Anthony's tour of Britain in 1883 were consolidated by the creation of the International Council of Women, launched at the NWSA convention of 1888.

Over the years, the ideological gap between the AWSA and the NWSA narrowed. In response to pressure from younger NWSA activists such as Rachel Foster Avery and Carrie Chapman Catt, Anthony at last yielded to pleas for unity, and in 1890, the two organizations joined forces to become the National American Woman Suffrage Association. *(See also: Anthony, Susan B.; National American Woman Suffrage Association; Revolution; Stanton, Elizabeth Cady; Suffrage)*

—Gail Malmgreen

Further Reading

Harper, Ida Husted. *The Life and Work of Susan B. Anthony.* Vols. 1-2. Indianapolis, IN: Bowen-Merrill, 1898.

Moynihan, Ruth Barnes. *Rebel for Rights: Abigail Scott Duniway.* New Haven, CT: Yale University Press, 1983.

Stanton, Elizabeth C., Susan B. Anthony, and Matilda J. Gage, eds. *History of Woman Suffrage,* 6 vols. Rochester, NY: Privately printed, 1881-1922.

Wagner, Sally Roesch. *A Time of Protest: Suffragists Challenge the Republic, 1870-1920.* Sacramento: Spectrum, 1987.

Wheeler, Marjorie Spruill, ed. *Votes for Women! The Woman Suffrage Movement in Tennessee, the South, and the Nation.* Knoxville: University of Tennessee Press, 1995.

～ National Woman's Loyal League

In early 1863—when Charles Sumner and other Republican leaders were working toward a federal amendment to abolish slavery—Susan B. Anthony, Elizabeth Cady Stanton, Ernestine Rose, and Lucy Stone proposed the creation of a woman's organization to assist the men of the Union in finding an acceptable political solution to the Civil War. In response to their call, thousands of delegates gathered for an organizational meeting of the National Woman's Loyal League in New York City on May 14, 1863. After Stanton delivered an opening address, a number of the more conservative delegates spoke against injecting questions of women's rights and abolition into the debate, insisting that the sole object of the society should be confined to supporting the war policies of President Abraham Lincoln. The conservative voices, however, were voted down following pleas by Anthony, Stone, Rose, and Angelina Grimké Weld, who adamantly opposed curtailing the jurisdiction of the league. The convention passed a resolution that pledged to support the government but only so long as it continued to wage a war for freedom. The league also established the goal of collecting 1 million signatures on a petition supporting congressional approval of the Thirteenth Amendment, which abolished slavery.

Under the direction of President Stanton and Secretary Anthony, the National Woman's Loyal League grew to a membership of five thousand strong. Operating on a shoestring budget, the league's officers drafted nearly two thousand volunteers to circulate the petitions. While failing to meet its ambitious goal, by the time the league disbanded in August 1864 it had gathered nearly 400,000 signatures supporting the proposed amendment. As a training school for volunteers, the league also provided hundreds of workers with valuable organizational skills that they would use in subsequent crusades for social reform. *(See also: Anthony, Susan B.; Civil War; Stanton, Elizabeth Cady; Stone, Lucy; United States Sanitary Commission)*

—Terry D. Bilhartz

Further Reading

Dorr, Rheta Childe. *Susan B. Anthony.* New York: Stokes, 1928.

Harper, Ida Husted. *The Life and Work of Susan B. Anthony,* 3 vols. Indianapolis, IN: Bowen-Merrill, 1898-1908. Reprint, Salem, NH: Ayer, 1983.

Stanton, Elizabeth Cady, Susan B. Anthony, and Matilda Joslyn Gage, eds. *The History of Woman Suffrage.* Vol. 2. Rochester, NY: Privately printed, 1881.

⮞ National Woman's Party (NWP)

The National Woman's Party (NWP) was established by Alice Paul and Lucy Burns in 1916 as an outgrowth of their efforts within the National American Woman Suffrage Association (NAWSA) and their own Congressional Union (CU) during the previous four years. Infused with the enthusiasm and schooled in the militant tactics of the British Women's Social and Political Union (WSPU), Paul and Burns reorganized the NAWSA Congressional Committee in January 1913 to develop a campaign that would focus the attention of the nation on the drive to secure a federal amendment to give women the vote. Paul and Burns—frustrated by the slow progress of the strategy of the staid and mainstream NAWSA during the war years—applied many of the WSPU tactics to the American suffrage struggle, including civil disobedience, which resulted in arrests, hunger strikes, and forced-feedings of Woman's Party suffragists. Moreover, the committee followed the British WSPU "suffragette" policy of holding the entire party in power responsible for its leaders' failure to adopt a woman suffrage amendment and immediately sponsored a parade of five thousand women, which upstaged the inauguration of President Woodrow Wilson, a Democrat, and evoked a riot among the spectators that brought public sympathy to the women and their cause. The momentum of the committee's pressure on the new Democratic administration continued through the spring in the form of grassroots petition campaigns and suffragist pilgrimages to the Capitol, as well as continual delegations of different groups of women to meet with President Wilson.

In April 1913, while chairpersons of the NAWSA Congressional Committee, Paul and Burns established the CU as an affiliate national organization that was to be committed entirely to securing a federal suffrage amendment and that began publishing its own weekly, *Suffragist,* in November of that year. During the national convention in 1913, however, differences of opinion over policies and practices brought formal separation of the CU from the NAWSA.

An auxiliary of the NAWSA, the CU successfully supported federal legislation that allowed the use of state initiatives to secure state referenda on woman suffrage, but this strategem required many exhausting state campaigns in 1914. Urging western women with partial suffrage to use their vote against all Democratic candidates regardless of their individual stand on suffrage, the CU claimed credit for the defeat of twenty-three of the forty-three who ran for office in 1914 bi-elections, while maintaining a stream of women's delegations to pressure President Wilson to support a federal amendment. Between 1913 and 1916, the CU contributed significantly by resuscitating the languishing suffrage movement while the NAWSA was reorganizing its leadership, priorities, and plan of action for a federal woman suffrage amendment. By 1915, the CU was organizing chapters in all the states in conjunction with its national automobile caravan from San Francisco to Washington and its year-long petition campaign to bring the federal suffrage amendment to a vote in Congress. Although the amendment was voted down in both the House and the Senate in January 1915, the CU efforts drew national publicity to congressional actions regarding federal enfranchisement of women.

In June 1916, the CU organized the National Woman's Party in the twelve states that had already given women the presidential vote. Holding President Wilson personally responsible for the failure of the federal amendment effort, the NWP unsuccessfully opposed the incumbent and the Democratic ticket in the 1916 election. Having failed to revive the amendment in Congress as well, the NWP initiated its famed campaign of militancy in 1917.

The NWP engaged in militant and flamboyant activities, using publicity stunts, marches, open-air meetings, watch fires, strikes, picketing of both the Capitol and the White House, lobbying of legislators as well as the president, and calling on women who were franchised to penalize "the party in power" until a constitutional suffrage amendment was acquired. While the NAWSA used U.S. entry into World War I as a means to enlarge the support base for woman suffrage, the NWP evoked mob violence with its pickets and banners that castigated the Wilson administration for not ensuring democracy's safety at home with woman suffrage. Although guilty at most of creating a nuisance for city and federal officials, the NWP's pickets were the first victims of the early tide of the World War I home front assault on civil liberties that culminated in the Red Scare of 1919.

The illegal arrests of women, which finally totaled 216, began in June 1917 and eventually brought 97 suffragists harsh sentences of as much as six months in the infamous Occoquan, Virginia, workhouse or the deplorable District of Columbia jail. Although perceived as an embarrassment to the NAWSA efforts by that leadership as well as to the Wilson administration, the women who endured forced-feedings and other inflicted hardships were nationally respected settlement house workers and nurses, wives of prominent men, and members of Quaker families. Widespread publicity of their plight and treatment, in addition to their demand to be given "prisoner of war" status, resulted in the unconditional release of the prisoners by exasperated officials in late November. Their innocence was vindicated when the District of Columbia Court of Appeals invalidated all of their arrests and their sentences in March 1918.

The public sympathy for these suffragists coincided with Carrie Chapman Catt's "Winning Plan" of the NAWSA, which brought Woodrow Wilson to support the cause of woman suffrage by September 1918, but the Senate voted it down. In response, both the NWP and the NAWSA openly campaigned against senators who voted against the franchise bill in the bi-elections of 1918.

The NWP membership numbered between 35,000 and 60,000 members at its peak between 1919 and 1920, as its efforts for the federal amendment paralleled those of the NAWSA. However, in 1921, after the ratification of the suffrage amendment, the single-issue politics of the woman suffrage movement took its toll on the NWP, which had only 151 paid members remaining. The leaders of the NWP continued their concern for broader issues that encompassed the whole of the nineteenth-century woman's rights movement. At its 1923 convention to mark the seventy-fifth anniversary of the Seneca Falls (New York) Convention for woman's rights, the NWP presented a draft of a federal Equal Rights Amendment that was introduced in Congress on December 10, 1923. NWP members felt that such a constitutional amendment was the most expedient and far-reaching method of gaining women's equality under the law. This so-called Alice Paul amendment of the NWP initiated an ongoing campaign for the Equal Rights Amendment (ERA).

Thus, the NWP has served as a transition group between the nineteenth-century woman's movement and the twentieth-century women's movement. Its continued support of the ERA placed it at odds with the social feminists who feared the loss of the protective legislation secured during the Progressive Era. Enduring into the 1990s, the NWP still focused its efforts toward the attainment of equal rights for women. Its headquarters, the Sewall-Belmont House in Washington, D.C., is a national landmark and contains a museum of NWP, ERA, and suffrage memorabilia. An anecdote reflecting the constancy of the NWP surfaced during the ERA ratification effort in the early 1970s: Members of the National Organization for Women who were to be hosted at the Sewall-Belmont House arrived late one night and were greeted by venerable women in quaint nightclothes and caps; when the NOW women remarked on their hostesses's state of excitement, the NWP members were said to reply, "You'd be excited, too, if you had been waiting fifty years for reinforcements!" *(See also: Equal Rights Amendment; National American Woman Suffrage Association; Paul, Alice; Suffrage; Women's Rights Movements: Nineteenth and Twentieth Centuries)*

—**Saundra K. Yelton-Stanley**
—**Neil W. Hogan**
—**Angela M. Howard**

Further Reading

Cott, Nancy F. "Feminist Politics in the 1920s: the National Woman's Party," *Journal of American History* 71 (1984): 43-68.

Fair, John D. "The Political Aspects of Women's Suffrage during the First World War," *Albion* 8 (Fall 1976): 274-95.

Ford, Linda G. *Iron-Jawed Angels: The Suffrage Militancy of the National Woman's Party, 1912–1920.* Lanham, MD: University Press of America, 1991.

Irwin, Inez Haynes. *The Story of the Woman's Party.* New York: Harcourt Brace, 1921.

Rupp, Leila J. "The Women's Community in the National Woman's Party, 1945 to the 1960's," *Signs* 10 (1985): 715-40.

◆ National Women's Hall of Fame

Located at 76 Fall Street and housed in a historic building in the heart of Seneca Falls, New York, the National Women's Hall of Fame honors and celebrates the achievements of extraordinary women from Bella Abzug to Mildred "Babe" Didrikson Zaharias. In the summer of 1998, 21 women were inducted as part of the celebration of the 150th anniversary of the first Women's Rights Convention. Elizabeth Cady Stanton (a Seneca Falls resident), Lucretia Mott, and 300 other women and men held the first convention at the Wesleyan Chapel, now the site of the Women's Rights National Historical Park in Seneca Falls.

The Hall of Fame was founded in 1969 to honor women whose contributions "have been the greatest value for the development of their country." In addition to offering historical exhibits, displays on inductees, and a research library, the hall regularly hosts special events, including art shows, author lectures and book signings, speeches, and social presentations. The Museum Shop offers a wide variety of commemorative materials and gift items, including T-shirts, posters, materials for children, and books.

The National Women's Hall of Fame is the only national membership organization devoted exclusively to the accomplishments of American women. Visitors are invited to join the hall and receive quarterly newsletters, a Museum Shop Catalogue, and invitations to special events. Contact: National Women's Hall of Fame, 76 Fall Street, P.O. Box 335, Seneca Falls, New York 13148-0335; (315) 568-8060; e-mail: womenshall@aol.com; Website: http://www.greatwomen.org. *(See also: National Park Service, National Site Preservation, and Women's History; Seneca Falls Convention)*

—**Mary Gratton**

Further Reading

National Women's Hall of Fame Education Committee. *Classroom Ideas for Teaching Women's History from the National Women's Hall of Fame.* Seneca Falls, NY: National Women's Hall of Fame, 1992.

———. *The Faces and Phases of Women.* Seneca Falls, NY: National Women's Hall of Fame, 1983.

———. *National Women's Hall of Fame Resource Catalogue.* Published annually.

———. *The Times and Triumphs of American Women.* Seneca Falls, NY: National Women's Hall of Fame, 1986.

◆ National Women's History Project (NWHP)

The National Women's History Project (NWHP) was established in 1980 by Molly MacGregor, Mary Ruthsdotter, Bette Morgan, and Maria Cuevas to promote gender equity by increasing public awareness of multicultural women's history. The NWHP originated and continues to promote National Women's History Month, a March focal celebration proclaimed since 1987 through a Joint Congressional Resolution. During the month, informative programs focusing on women's contributions and experiences are held at worksites, schools and colleges, public libraries, and other locations throughout the country.

The NWHP serves as a women's history information clearinghouse, providing factual information, referrals, and program-planning assistance on a year-round basis. Their extensive research library and archive of biographical, topical, and photo files are open to the public. Research and writing services are available on a fee-for-service basis.

While working with publishers to increase the representation of women in new publications, the NWHP itself has developed and produced scores of multicultural resources: curriculum units for kindergarten through high school students, comprehensive program-planning guides, posters and display sets, videos, a teacher-training module, and celebration items specifically for National Women's History Month.

To make the best women's history materials available to people everywhere, the NWHP initiated the Women's History Resource Service in 1981. Project staff review all newly published books and educational materials in the field of U.S. women's history, selecting items for inclusion in a mail-order catalog that is distributed widely.

As consultants to county and state offices of education, NWHP staff members provide on-site training services for teachers and equity officers. They also conduct four-day summer conferences in Santa Rosa, California, for educators from across the country.

The NWHP established the Women's History Network in 1984, linking educators, librarians, workplace and community organizers, and other interested people. The network publishes a quarterly eight-page newsletter and provides semiannual, annotated directories to enable members to locate and communicate with others having similar interests. *(See also: International Women's Day; Women's History; Women's Studies)*

—**Mary Ruthsdotter**

⮜ National Women's Political Caucus

The National Women's Political Caucus was established in 1971 to increase the participation of women in public and political life. By the late 1980s, over three hundred affiliates nationwide and over 77,000 people were encouraging women to become politically active at all levels: to run for office, appointments, political convention delegate positions, and judgeships; to become involved as lobbyists and voters; or to be active in any political campaign. This reflects the belief of many women, since the failure of the Equal Rights Amendment to win passage, that equality will come only through equal representation. The Caucus recruits and trains women for the political arena and meets with political candidates to advocate fair representation of women throughout the political process. Through lobbying efforts, it also strives to gain pledges of support for female candidates and concerns.

Founded by a distinguished group of activists—including Fannie Lou Hamer, Gloria Steinem, Shirley Chisholm, Bella Abzug, Dorothy Height, and LaDonna Harris—the Caucus sponsored the first national political convention of women in over one hundred years in 1973. Held in Houston, Texas, it served as a groundbreaker, emphasizing women's political visibility and importance. In 1997, Anita Perez Ferguson was reelected to her second term as the ninth president and first Hispanic head of the National Women's Political Caucus.

The success of the Caucus is reflected in that the number of women in state legislatures more than tripled in 15 years—from 4 percent in 1971 to 14.8 percent in 1986 and grew to 21.8 percent in 1997. Political activity throughout the 1990s proved that comparable gains are being made at other levels of government. The Caucus has also been successful in bringing women's issues to the forefront of American politics.

Known nationally as NWPC or the Caucus, the National Women's Political Caucus maintains the status of being the only national grassroots organization "dedicated to increasing the number of pro-choice women in elected and appointed office at all levels of government, regardless of party affiliation." The Caucus's activities draw the participation of over 50,000 women each year. The membership drive of the mid-1990s yielded modest results in terms of increased membership. The guild's survival into the next century will depend on its ability to focus its mission and programming to attract new and younger members as well as retain its current membership. *(See also: Abzug, Bella Savitsky; Chisholm, Shirley; Politics; Steinem, Gloria)*

—**Saundra K. Yelton-Stanley**

Further Reading

Broder, David S. "Women: Power in Politics," *Washington Post* (July 3, 1985): A17.

Feit, Rona F. "Organizing for Political Power: The National Women's Political Caucus." In *Women Organizing: An Anthology,* edited by Bernice Cummings and Victoria Schuck, 184-208. Metuchen, NJ: Scarecrow, 1979.

Morris, Celia. "Waiting for Ms. President," *Harper's Bazaar* 125 (July 1992): 86-89, 118.

Toner, Robin. "Gains for Women Predicted in Races for Statewide Office," *New York Times* 135 (May 19, 1986): 1.

http://www.nwpc.org [National Women's Political Caucus Website]

⮜ National Women's Trade Union League (NWTUL)

The National Women's Trade Union League (NWTUL) was founded in 1903 by Mary Kenney O'Sullivan. Its purpose was to bring together women from various industries so they could work for higher wages and improved working conditions. The motto of the NWTUL was "The Eight-Hour Day; A Living Wage; to Guard the Home." Not limited to union workers, the league welcomed women who were not in the workforce but who believed in the goals of the trade unions. These women—called "allies" because of their financial and personal contributions—were educated, able to organize and speak before large groups. The league also educated its worker members for leadership and informed the public of union goals.

The first convention of the NWTUL endorsed six primary points: equal pay for equal work, woman suffrage, full unionization, the eight-hour day, a minimum wage, and the economic programs of the American Federation of Labor (AFL).

The Women's Trade Union League (WTUL) was established on the local level, in places such as New York City, Chicago, and Boston. At the workplace, the WTUL established meeting rooms and rest areas for workers to discuss problems, form friendships, or just rest between shifts. The New York league had to cope with its inability to change women's status and the failures of organized labor. When it attempted to affiliate with the AFL, a predominantly male craft union, the New York WTUL was not accepted because it was a trade union, composed of unskilled, poorly paid, irregularly employed female workers. The New York WTUL also confronted the cultural, social, and language differences among the many Jewish and Italian immigrants in the factories. Beginning in 1913, the New York WTUL emphasized woman suffrage and protective legislation, focusing on women's specific needs and difficulties. This represented a shift in league emphasis; previously, women had been regarded simply as workers, not different in their employment needs from men workers. The WTUL continued to work for social reform through the 1950s, by which time working women in New York had achieved a minimum wage and a forty-eight-hour week. *(See also: American Federation of Labor; O'Sullivan, Mary Kenney; Unions; Wages)*
—**Rosemary Herriges**

Further Reading

Dye, Nancy Schrom. *As Equals and as Sisters*. Columbia: University of Missouri Press, 1980.

Foner, Philip S. *Women and the American Labor Movement*. New York: Free Press, 1979.

———. "Women and the American Labor Movement: A Historical Perspective." In *Working Women: Past Present Future*, edited by Karen Shallcross Koziara, Michael H. Moskow, and Lucretia Dewey Tanner, 154-86. Washington, DC: BNA Books, 1987.

Kessler-Harris, Alice. *Out to Work: A History of Wage-Earning Women in the United States*. New York: Oxford University Press, 1982.

∾ Native American Mythology

A culture's mythology reveals its deepest values and most sacred conceptions of ultimates: birth, death, rebirth, and the beginnings of things. The powerful figures in Judeo-Christian sacred stories are virtually exclusively male. The important characters in Native American myths, on the other hand, are both male and female. Both sexes perform the great acts of creation, and the fecundity of the earth is regularly associated with females. Native American sacred stories include a number of impressive female figures who exercise varied and interestingly conceived kinds of power.

The earth itself is female for most tribes—female and a grandmother. In one Cheyenne myth, for instance, Maheo, a male creator god, begins to create earth from a ball of mud but is stymied because he has nowhere to put the mud. The fish and water creatures all try to bear the weight of earth's beginnings, but they are either too small or their fins stick up through the mud. Finally, Grandmother Turtle offers to help, and while she is very old and very slow, she turns out to be the only being who can succeed with this task. The ball of mud flattens out into the earth itself, and she carries it on her back through all time. When trees, grass, and flowers spring up to cover earth's sides, Maheo acknowledges that they are the product of Earth Woman's power as well as his.

Grandmother Turtle assists Maheo; she does not create independently. Estanatlehi, however, another female creator figure, works alone. Although she is the wife of the sun, her story celebrates her capacity to create, not his. Estanatlehi is the source of human life in the Navajos' complex creation story, and she creates human beings in a distinctively womanly way. Using flour from a different color of maize to make each of the different Navajo tribes, she mixes the flour with skin from the center of her breasts and produces human beings.

The most common female figure of power in Native American mythology is a grandmother figure. Many of these, like Grandmother Turtle, appear to be inconsequential, but they perform essential heroic feats. In a Cherokee myth, for instance, a grandmother brings sun to this side of the world. When the earth was new, the animals bumped into each other in primordial darkness. They knew there was sun on the other side of the earth, but they could not figure out how to get any of it. Two confident, assertive males try first: Possum, who hides a little sun in his tail, but loses it when it burns off all his tail-fur; and Buzzard, who swoops out of the sky to steal some sun from the Sun People, but hides it in his head feathers and loses it when they catch fire. Then meek, unassertive Grandmother Spider offers to try. After pointing out that she is so tiny that the Sun People won't notice her, and so unimportant that if she burns up, it won't matter, she makes a little bowl of clay to carry a tiny bit of sun, spins a thread behind her so that she can find her way back, and succeeds in bringing light to this world. Grandmother Spider is wise, humble, and resourceful; these are not the qualities of a great warrior, but, as Grandmother Spider's story acknowledges, they are essential qualities for life on this earth.

A third grandmother story celebrates women's fertility and its fundamental connections with earth's miracle of cyclical resurrection: the essential patterns of life, death, and regeneration, of woman's miracle of enduring through giving birth. In this Mikasuki myth, when two grandsons complain that they are tired of eating meat, their grandmother promises them a new dish. That night, she serves them boiled corn, and they say they have never tasted anything as good. The next day she fixes grits, and the grandsons are amazed again. Finally, on the third day they pretend to go hunting but instead double back to try to find out the source of this mysterious food. They are horrified when they see that the corn is a magical product of their grandmother's body; it appears as she rubs her hands down her sides. When she realizes that they know her secret, she dies, after giving them detailed instructions about burying her body and then cultivating the corn plants that will grow from it.

In Native American mythology, then, female figures supply the foundation for the newly created world and help make it livable. Female force permeates the earth and female fecundity yields corn, the staple of much Native American life. As these few stories illustrate, women as well as men are powerful figures in Native American mythology. *(See also: Mythology; Native American Women)*

—**Gretchen Mieszkowski**

Further Reading

Alexander, Hartley Burr. *The World's Rim: Great Mysteries of the North American Indians.* Lincoln: University of Nebraska Press, 1953.

Burland, Cottie. *North American Indian Mythology.* Feltham, Middlesex, England: Hamlyn, 1965.

Marriott, Alice, and Carol K. Rachlin. *American Indian Mythology.* New York: Crowell, 1968.

Underhill, Ruth M. *Red Men's Religion: Beliefs and Practices of the Indians North of Mexico.* Chicago: University of Chicago Press, 1965.

⮿ Native American Women

Although the lives of Native American women have been ignored by many historians and Indian women have been stereotyped as squaws and princesses, research continues to establish the importance of their roles in both traditional and contemporary cultures. Cultural determinants, as well as the diversity of Indian cultures, established the roles and position of women within their tribes. Generally, in agricultural societies such as the Iroquois or the Navajo, women were accorded more status than they received in the primarily hunting societies of the Great Plains. In every case, however, women had clearly defined and valuable roles within the societies.

Women's status within the Iroquois before contact with whites has been a subject of much interest. The Iroquois organized their kinship groups into matrilineal clans, whose members traced their descent from a common female ancestor. Mothers usually arranged their children's marriages, and newlyweds customarily went to live with the bride's clan. Iroquois women owned the longhouses in which they lived and passed them on to their descendants. They also had a great deal of power because they controlled the agricultural life of their tribes by managing the farming activities of the tribe. Among the Seneca, women elected the tribe's male leaders and participated in many other political decisions.

Before white contact, women also had a great deal of power among the Cherokee in the South. Women had the right to speak in village councils, and some accompanied the men when the tribe went on the warpath. Cherokee women also had a crucial role in agriculture.

All this began to change between 1790 and 1840 as missionaries and government agents urged Native Americans to value individual ownership of land, European gender roles, and the patriarchal family. Native Americans in many cases altered their traditional ways of life, and in the process, the traditional base of women's power among groups such as the Iroquois and the Cherokee was eroded.

Many of the negative images of Indian women developed as a result of contact with Euro-American society. The assault on traditional practices took many forms. Fur trappers and traders changed the material culture of the tribes by introducing and developing a demand for iron, glass beads, cloth, and dyes. The missionaries judged Indian women by traditional Judeo-Christian views that denigrated the power women held in some tribes in favor of European-style patriarchy. Often, Native Americans were judged on the basis of how helpful they could be to whites. Pocahontas, who saved Captain John Smith in 1607 and married John Rolfe, a leader of the English colony in Virginia, is one famous example of an Indian woman valued by whites. Sacagawea of the Shoshone, who guided and interpreted for the Lewis and Clark expedition between 1804 and 1806, was another Native American woman who has gained fame among whites.

Efforts to assimilate Native American women into Euro-American society through education also changed the status of women. Schools run by missionaries and the Bureau of Indian Affairs established curricula along stereotypical lines, training women in homemaking skills while punishing them for speaking their native languages or wearing traditional clothing. In the twentieth century, American Indian women have been victims of medical practices that resulted in mass sterilizations, and social agencies tend to define the family as nuclear and ignore the extended family prevalent in Indian societies. There has been some redress for grievances in recent times, however. Bureau of Indian Affairs schools now give preference to Indian teachers, and the curriculum has become more diversified, resulting in far more Indian women attending colleges and professional schools after high school. The American Indian Religious Freedom Act of 1978 and the Indian Child Welfare Act that same year recognized tribal rights.

The most serious issues affecting Indian women today are those that also affect their children. The rate of infant mortality exceeds that of the national norm of all races, and the rate of fetal alcohol syndrome is three to six times higher than the national average. Native American children with handicapping conditions are less likely to receive services than other American children. Until the passage of the Indian Child Welfare Act, preservation of the Indian family was not considered a priority by government agencies. Many Indian children were placed in non-Indian foster care and adoptive homes or boarding schools without consultation with the families or tribes involved.

Tribal laws are frequently in conflict with federal and state laws, especially regarding women's civil rights issues. One of the most significant court cases affecting Indian women was *Santa Clara Pueblo v. Martinez*, 436 U.S. 49 (1978) in which the Supreme Court ruled that the federal government should not interfere in intratribal issues even where women's rights were at stake.

In 1985, a group of Native Americans in South Dakota formed the Native American Community Board (NACB) to address pertinent issues of health, education, land and water rights, and economic development of Native American people. In 1988, this group opened the Native American Women's Health Education Resource Center, the first resource center located on a reservation in the United States. Today, many organizations provide information and resources for those interested in Native American issues. Many of these organizations also include information on women's health and legal issues. Increasingly, Indian women are becoming active in politics (Ada Deer, Wilma Mankiller), in education (Clara Sue Kidwell, Bea Medicine), in medicine (Annie Wauneka, Connie Uri), and in literature (Paula Gunn Allen, Leslie Marmon Silko, Louise Erdrich). *(See also: Berdache; Bonnin, Gertrude Simmons; Deer, Ada; Erdrich, Louise; Hopkins, Sarah Winnemucca; Indian Child Welfare Act; Mankiller, Wilma; Matriliny; Naming Systems; Native American Women's Literature; Sacagawea; Sandoz, Mari; Silko, Leslie; Triple Jeopardy)*

—Gretchen M. Bataille

Further Reading

Albers, Patricia, and Beatrice Medicine, eds. *The Hidden Half: Studies of Plains Indian Women.* Washington, DC: University Press of America, 1983.

Allen, Paula Gunn. *The Sacred Hoop: Recovering the Feminine in American Indian Traditions.* Boston: Beacon, 1986.

Anderson, Owanah. *Ohoyo One Thousand: A Resource Guide of American Indian/Alaskan Native Women.* Wichita Falls, TX: Ohoyo Resource Center, 1982.

Bataille, Gretchen M., ed. *Native American Women: A Biographical Dictionary.* New York: Garland, 1993.

Bataille, Gretchen M., and Kathleen M. Sands, eds. *American Indian Women: A Guide to Research.* New York: Garland, 1991.

Bruchac, Carol, Linda Hogan, and Judith McDaniel. *The Stories We Hold Secret: Tales of Women's Spiritual Development.* Greenfield Center, NY: Greenfield Review, 1986.

Conference on the Educational and Occupational Needs of American Indian Women. Washington, DC: National Institute of Education, 1980.

Green, Rayna. *Native American Women: A Contextual Bibliography.* Bloomington: Indiana University Press, 1983.

Native Self-Sufficiency 4 (September 1981). [Special issue on women]

Verble, Sedelta, ed. *Words of Today's American Indian Women: Ohoyo Makachi: A First Collection of Oratory by American Indian/Alaskan Native Women.* Washington, DC: U.S. Department of Education, 1981.

⌇ Native American Women's Literature

The literature of Native American women was originally an oral literature—songs and stories that expressed personal emotions and carried on religious and secular traditions of the tribe. This oral tradition continues to exist, but now it coexists with an expanding collection of written poems, stories, novels, autobiographies, and criticism.

In 1883, Sarah Winnemucca Hopkins, a Paiute woman, published her autobiography, *Life among the Paiutes,* and during the first years of the twentieth century, Gertrude Bonnin (Zitkala-Sa) published stories in *Atlantic Monthly.* There were others: Hum-ishu-ma (Chrystal Quintasket), who wrote a novel, *Co-go-wea, the Half-Blood* (1927); Ella Deloria, who did fine work in linguistics and anthropology in addition to publishing Dakota stories; and Pauline Johnson, a Canadian Mohawk who published several collections of poetry and stories. At the end of the nineteenth century and into the twentieth century, Indian women were also relating tribal literature and personal accounts to anthropologists such as Truman Michelson, Ruth M. Underhill, Gilbert Wilson, and A. L. Kroeber.

Increasingly, however, Indian women have chosen to tell their own stories and write poetry and fiction. Indian women writers have gained particular notice since the late 1970s. Leslie Marmon Silko received the prestigious MacArthur Award in recognition of her poetry, stories, and the novel *Ceremony* (1977). Silko's latest works include *Laguna Woman* (second edition, 1994), *Yellow Woman and a Beauty of the Spirit* (1997), and *Gardens in the Dunes* (1999). Louise Erdrich has captured several literary awards since the publication of *Love Medicine* (1984), *The Beet Queen* (1986), and *Tracks* (1988). Her latest novel, titled *The Antelope Wife,* was published in 1998. Paula Gunn Allen has achieved recognition for her poetry, her novel *The Woman Who Owned the Shadows* (1983), and for her criticism, most notably *The Sacred Hoop* (1986). Among her latest works is a young people's collection of biographies titled *As Long as the Rivers Flow: The Stories of Nine Native Americans,* published in 1996. Several collections of contemporary literature and critical studies attest to the growth and development of literature of Indian women. Joy Harjo, Wendy Rose, Linda Hogan, Carol Lee Sanchez, Anna Lee Walters, Beth Brant, Luci Tapahonso, and Mary Tall Mountain are among the names frequently seen in current anthologies. The contemporary literature takes many forms and, like the traditional material, is sometimes personal narrative and sometimes an expression of tribal history or politics. *(See also: Bonnin, Gertrude Simmons; Erdrich, Louise; Hopkins, Sarah Winnemucca; Native American Women; Silko, Leslie Marmon; Women Writers)*

—Gretchen M. Bataille

Further Reading

Allen, Paula Gunn. *Grandmothers of the Light.* Boston: Beacon, 1991.

———. *The Sacred Hoop: Recovering the Feminine in American Indian Traditions.* Boston: Beacon, 1986.

Bataille, Gretchen M., and Kathleen Mullen Sands. *American Indian Women, Telling Their Lives.* Lincoln: University of Nebraska Press, 1984.

Bataille, Gretchen M., and Laurie Lisa, eds. *Native American Women: A Biographical Dictionary.* New York: Garland, 1993.

Brant, Beth, ed. *A Gathering of Spirit: Writing and Art by Native American Women.* Rockland, ME: Sinister Wisdom, 1984.

Fisher, Dexter. *The Third Woman: Minority Women Writers of the United States.* Boston: Houghton Mifflin, 1980.

Green, Rayna. *That's What She Said: Contemporary Poetry and Fiction by Native American Women.* Bloomington: Indiana University Press, 1984.

Katz, Jane B., ed. *I Am the Fire of Time: Voices of Native American Women.* New York: E. P. Dutton, 1977.

Niethammer, Carolyn. *Daughters of the Earth: The Lives and Legends of American Indian Women.* New York: Collier, 1977.

⮜ Nature Study

Nature Study was the name given to a curriculum for science teaching widely discussed and implemented in the elementary (and some secondary) schools in the United States between about 1895 and 1925. Anna Botsford Comstock recalls that nature study began as a way to support agriculture and the development of children's love for gardens and agriculture. The curriculum evolved into a New York syllabus for nature study and agriculture nurtured by Cornell College of Agriculture's extension program. It was a flexible course of study intended to stimulate and expand the teaching of science for children in ways appropriate to their local experiences, whether in the countryside of upstate New York or in urban centers such as Chicago. By combining teaching (in which women were a majority) with science (in which women were scarcely represented), nature study provided an unprecedented opportunity for women to study, teach, and contribute to science.

By the time nature study was implemented, women constituted 90 percent of the teaching staff in most schools and were also prominent on the faculty of normal schools. An analysis of the Nature Study Association in 1908 reveals that approximately 60 percent of its members were women. Men tended to be on college or normal school faculties, while women were more likely to be in the classroom, where some took advantage of opportunities to do fieldwork and gather data. Women also served as superintendents of citywide nature study programs, and a few even held positions on university faculties. Anna Botsford Comstock of Cornell was the single best-known leader in the movement, combining nature study there with extension programs that provided short courses and educational leaflets for teachers. She also wrote the best-selling text (still in print) *Handbook of Nature Study* and was editor of *Nature Study Review* for a decade. She wrote her book from the point of view that nature study leads to both science and aesthetic experience. Other programs were designed for city schoolchildren and sometimes coordinated through a local museum, such as the Brooklyn Children's Museum run by Anna Billings Gallup from 1904 to 1937.

Just as elements of progressivism lost ground in the 1920s, so the nature study curriculum lost out to elementary science, whose goals were to prepare students for advanced work on terms prescribed by academic professors. The specific techniques introduced by nature study teachers—school terrariums and aquariums, nature walks, school museum cabinets, weather data collection—continued in use, but among scientists and social scientists there was a reaction against a science that seemed too "sentimental." For its thirty years of prominence, however, the nature study program provided unprecedented opportunities for individual women teachers and also established methods for teaching about the natural world that persist to the present day in both voluntary clubs and more formal school activities. *(See also: Education; Science; Teaching)*

—**Sally Gregory Kohlstedt**

Further Reading

Burstyn, Joan. "Early Women in Education: The Role of the Anderson School of Natural History," *Journal of Education* 159 (1977): 50-64.

Comstock, Anna Botsford. *The Comstocks of Cornell: John Henry Comstock and Anna Botsford Comstock.* Ithaca, NY: Cornell University Press, 1953.

———. *Handbook of Nature Study.* 1911. Reprint, 1939. Reprint, Ithaca, NY: Cornell University Press, 1986.

Henson, Pamela M. "The Comstocks of Cornell: A Marriage of Interests." In *Creative Couples in the Sciences,* edited by Helena M. Pycior, Nancy G. Slack, and Pnina G. Abir-Am. New Brunswick, NJ: Rutgers University Press, 1994.

Kohlstedt, Sally Gregory. "In from the Periphery: Women in Science, 1830–1880," *Signs* 4 (1978): 81-96.

Minton, Tyree G. "The History of the Nature-Study Movement and Its Role in the Development of Environmental Education." Ph.D. diss., University of Massachusetts, 1980.

⮜ Naylor, Gloria (b. 1950)

Author Gloria Naylor is one of America's most acclaimed Afro-American twentieth-century novelists. Naylor's novels, *The Women of Brewster Place* (1982), *Linden Hills* (1985), *Mama Day* (1988), and *Bailey's Cafe* (1992), focus on Afro-Americans, with an emphasis on women. Naylor writes with power and honesty of the evils of sexism, racism, and greed and their effects on Afro-American culture. Critics often compare her explorations of the Afro-American female experience with the works of Toni Morrison and Alice Walker.

Before beginning a career in writing, Naylor spent five years as a Jehovah's Witness missionary in Florida, New York, and North Carolina. After leaving her missionary work, Naylor studied at Brooklyn College of the City University of New York and received an M.A. in Afro-American studies from Yale University. Naylor's first novel *The Women of Brewster Place* was published while she was still a student at Yale and received the American Book Award for First Fiction in 1983. *The Women of Brewster Place* was made into an Emmy-nominated miniseries and inspired the weekly dramatic series *Brewster Place*.

In 1994, the Hartford Stage Company premiered Naylor's stage adaptation of her novel *Bailey's Cafe*. Naylor is also president of One Way Productions, which produced a film version of *Mama Day*. Naylor's newest novel, *The Men of Brewster Place*, was published in 1998.

Naylor is the recipient of Guggenheim and National Endowment for the Arts fellowships for her novels and a New York Foundation for the Arts fellowship for screenwriting. *(See also: Black Women; Morrison, Toni; Walker, Alice; Women Writers)*

—Preston Lane

Further Reading

Goldstein, William. "A Talk with Gloria Naylor," *Publishers Weekly* 225 (September 9, 1983): 35-36.
Naylor, Gloria. *Bailey's Cafe*. New York: Harcourt Brace Jovanovich, 1992.
———. *Linden Hills*. New York: Ticknor & Fields, 1985.
———. *Mama Day*. New York: Ticknor & Fields, 1988.
———. *The Men of Brewster Place*. New York: Hyperion, 1998.
———. *The Women of Brewster Place*. New York: Viking, 1982.

☙ Neel, Alice (1900–1984)

Alice Neel painted incisive portraits of the decadent, the famous, the poor, and the downtrodden that chronicle the diversity of urban society. Although she also painted brightly colored still lifes, stark interiors, and bucolic landscapes, she is best known for her original and expressive figure paintings.

She enrolled at the Philadelphia School of Design for Women, now the Moore College of Art, in 1921 and completed her studies in 1925. During the summer of 1924, she attended Chester Springs Summer School of the Pennsylvania Academy of Fine Arts, where she met her future husband, Carlos Enriquez, a Cuban art student. Neel's life was not easy. Her first child died of diphtheria in December 1927, and she was abandoned by Enriquez, who took their second child to Cuba in May 1930. Following a nervous breakdown in August of that same year, she was hospitalized for a year.

After her release, Neel went to New York's Greenwich Village to paint. There, she took a series of lovers and developed an interest in leftist politics. She attended meetings of the John Reed Club and briefly joined the Communist Party in about 1935. Her portraits of left-wing activists and intellectuals and her cityscapes of Depression-era New York vividly disclose her political interests. During the Depression, she moved to Spanish Harlem, where she supported herself and two sons on her meager income from the Federal Art Project of the Works Progress Administration (WPA). She remained in Spanish Harlem for twenty-five years, painting her neighbors and her surroundings.

A dark palette and resigned facial expressions are typical of her works of the 1940s. In her later paintings, her palette became increasingly lighter; she used bold, direct, and economical brushstrokes to reveal the inner tensions of her wealthier, more famous subjects. Areas of the canvas were left unpainted, and background elements were less articulated; the viewer is forced to focus on the subject.

Neel, who was neglected and ignored by the art establishment during the reign of abstract expressionism, finally attained recognition when she began to paint the luminaries of art, politics, and business. The poet Frank O'Hara, who posed for her in 1959, was the first of many famous people to do so. Among her other subjects were Andy Warhol, Bella Abzug, Red Grooms, Ed Koch, and Linus Pauling. *(See also: Art)*

—Susan Keyes

Further Reading

Alice Neel, Paintings since 1970. Philadelphia: Pennsylvania Academy of Fine Arts, 1985.
Allara, Pamela. *Alice Neel, Exterior/Interior*. Medford, MA: Tufts University Art Gallery, 1991.
Bauer, Denise. "Alice Neel's Female Nudes," *Woman's Art Journal* 15 (Fall/Winter 1994-95): 20-26.
Castle, Ted. "Alice Neel," *Artforum* 22 (October 1983): 36-41.
Harris, Ann Sutherland. *Alice Neel*. Los Angeles: Loyola Marymount, 1983.
Hills, Patricia. *Alice Neel*. New York: Abrams, 1983.

☙ Networking

Networking is the practice of developing and using contacts with other people for information and support while serving as a resource oneself; the purpose is to help everyone involved get ahead together. Networking is an old idea. In the business world, men have been using this technique for many years, but the "old boys network," as it has sometimes been called, grew naturally out of contacts men made through organizations already in place, such as men's clubs and fraternities. The old boys network has also flourished because men have historically dominated supervisory and managerial positions in the workplace and because men learn early in life to form mutually beneficial contacts—for example, through participation in sports. Women have historically not been socialized in the same way and have tended not to attain high management positions.

Networking for women grew out of the active feminist movement in the 1970s, when women were forming self-help and professional groups of various kinds. While the concept of networking does not require an organization, many formal women's networks have been organized. Some of these have made an effort to bring influential women in a particular city together; others have been organized along professional lines. The number of women's networks has grown in the last few years, and many books, including directories of women's networks in the United States, have been published.

The idea of networking has been perceived by many women to be a good way of moving ahead in one's chosen field, but some factors have kept the idea from being more successful. Some women have trouble becoming involved in networking because they feel more comfortable in a helping relationship with others and less comfortable admitting they joined a group or called a contact because this can be useful to their careers. One expert in the field found that for the women above the middle-manager position in her organization, networking with other women did not work well because there were so few women contacts at that level. Also, surveys have shown that while women at the top felt that they were providing support to women below them, the women lower in the organizational hierarchy did not perceive such support.

In the 1990s, a second meaning of the term *networking,* relating to computer wiring and systems, has overtaken the first, but both senses of the word operate simultaneously when people use the Internet for communication. Surveys of Internet users have found that communicating tops the list of on-line activities for women, followed by information seeking and shopping. Besides Internet "chatting," women interested in discussing women's issues, women's history or related topics have some 450 gender-related discussion forums to choose from. As of 1998, for example, over 4,000 women (and a few men) were participating in WMST-L, a women's studies list.

The number of women using the Internet for networking and other purposes grew throughout the 1990s, with a reported doubling from 1995 to 1997. In 1998, more than 40 percent of Internet users were women, with market research projecting that they would constitute 60 percent of users by the year 2005. *(See also: Business; Consciousness-Raising: Mentor-Protégée Relationships; Women's Liberation Movement)*

—Judith Pryor
**Adapted for the second edition by
Phyllis Holman Weisbard.**

Further Reading

"Internet Drawing More Women for Research, Purchases," *Media Report to Women* (Winter 1998): 4.

Kleinman, Carol. *Women's Networks: The Complete Guide to Getting a Better Job, Advancing Your Career, and Feeling Great as a Woman through Networking.* New York: Lippincott & Crowell, 1980.

Korenman, Joan. "Gender-Related Electronic Forums." Available at http://research.umbc.edu/korenman/wmst/forums.html

Spender, Dale. *Nattering on the Net: Women, Power, and Cyberspace.* North Melbourne, Victoria: Spinifex, 1995.

Stern, Barbara B. *Is Networking for You? A Working Woman's Alternative to the Old Boy System.* Englewood Cliffs, NJ: Prentice Hall, 1981.

Taylor, H. Jeanie, Cheris Kramarae, and Maureen Ebben, eds. *Women, Information Technology and Scholarship.* Urbana: University of Illinois, Women, Information Technology and Scholarship Colloquium Center for Advanced Study, 1993.

Warthay, Philomena D. "The Climb to the Top: Is the Network the Route for Women?" *The Personnel Administrator* 25 (April 1980): 55-60.

Welch, Mary Scott. *Networking: A Great New Way for Women to Get Ahead.* New York: Harcourt Brace Jovanovich, 1980.

↝ New Century Guild for Working Women

The New Century Guild for Working Women in Philadelphia evolved out of low-cost evening classes started in 1882 by the New Century Club. Under the dynamic leadership of club member Eliza Sproat Turner, the guild expanded the scope of its activities, and its classes rapidly grew in popularity. Members of the guild came from a wide range of occupational backgrounds, including dressmaking, sales, mill work, bookbinding, and office work. Women took classes refining their domestic skills in areas such as cooking, home singing, and home elocution, as well as classes in marketable skills such as shorthand, typing, and stenography. The guild's headquarters and its branch facility offered members opportunities to use the well-stocked library, have an inexpensive meal, relax in a gymnasium, and socialize with friends. Lecture series on female hygiene and physiology offered many members a rare opportunity to learn about their bodies.

In 1887, the guild began publishing *Working Woman's Journal,* which contained articles about work from the employees' point of view. This unusual magazine had subscribers in nineteen states. Guild members collected statistics on the hours, wages, regulations, and conditions in those Philadelphia stores that employed women. In 1887, in response to pressure from the guild, the city's major morning papers published a list of proprietors who treated women fairly. The success of the guild's School of Women's Trades, which opened in 1891 offering a professional certificate for a full-time day course of study in dressmaking and millinery, persuaded A. J. Drexel to open Drexel Institute (now Drexel University). At the turn of the century, the guild's early activism on behalf of working women served as a model for other organizations across the United States. In recent decades, the guild has become primarily a social gathering place for a decreasing membership not energized by new recruits. Concern over the steady decline of members and interest in recent decades prompted the guild's 1995 leadership to mount an energetic membership drive aimed at both women and men. The membership drive of the mid-1990s yielded modest results in terms of increased membership. The guild's survival in the twenty-first century will depend on its ability to focus its mission and programming to attract new and younger members as well as retain its current membership. *(See also: Education)*

—Cynthia Jeffress Little

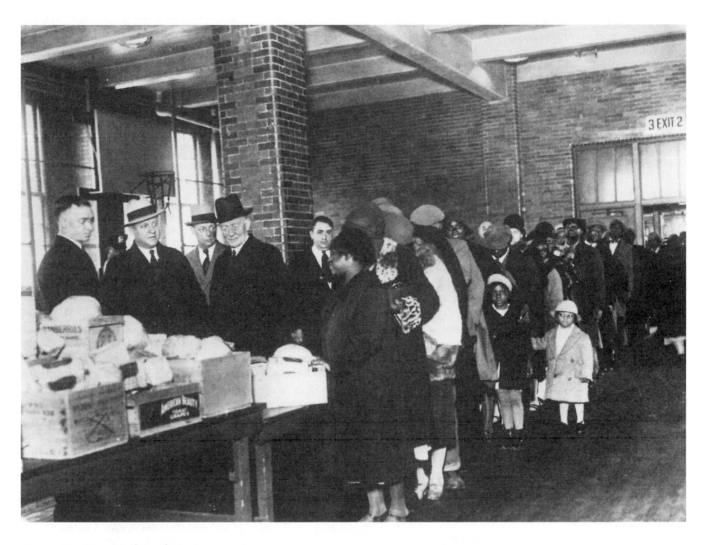

Figure 42. New Deal Food Line
Although the Great Depression left many unemployed and standing in line for food, women gained in political force during the New Deal era. Both legislative gains and an increased role in the workforce helped account for this. Used by permission of UPI/Corbis-Bettmann.

Further Reading

Cooper, Patricia. "Historical Significance Statement: New Century Guild." National Historic Landmark Nomination, 1992.

The New Century Club: Miscellaneous. Historical Society of Pennsylvania, Philadelphia.

Samuels, Gayle Brandow. *Women in the City of Brotherly Love and Beyond: Tours and Detours in Delaware Valley Women's History.* Philadelphia: G. B. Samuels, 1994.

∽ New Deal

In 1929, the United States began its slide into total economic depression. This national crisis reached its peak by the time Franklin D. Roosevelt was elected president in 1932. Roosevelt instituted the New Deal, built on the principles and policies of the Progressive Era, with breathless rapidity. He created relief programs to prevent starvation, as well as plans for recovery of business and agriculture and a series of reforms to make sure that such a depression could never happen again.

In many ways, the Great Depression was worse for women than for men. As the unemployment reached higher into the middle class, more women were faced with the problem of making ends meet. Women had always worked outside the home, usually in low-paid, sex-typed service jobs, and therefore their unemployment rate was lower than that of men. While the inability of unemployed husbands to perform as breadwinners inflicted a psychological toll, wives had the task of keeping the family together, of making the food stretch, of clothing the children. A higher percentage of married women worked outside the home in low-paid, often part-time jobs during the Depression while simultaneously continuing their management of the household on meager incomes.

Women had an important role in Roosevelt's New Deal. When he became president in 1933, his First Lady, Eleanor

Roosevelt, brought to Washington a number of Progressive Era activists and social feminists from within the Democratic Party. Together they influenced the appointment of Frances Perkins, one of this group, to the post of secretary of labor—the first woman appointed to a cabinet-level post. In 1932 and 1936, these women organized a small army of precinct canvassers, demonstrating their potent political power and reaping political appointments such as postmasterships and also ensuring that women would be given equal representation on the Democratic Platform Committee in 1936.

Little New Deal legislation applied specifically to women. Created in 1933 to alleviate suffering during the first winter of the Roosevelt administration, the Civil Works Administration (CWA) employed some 300,000 women, but its emphasis on large-scale construction projects mainly created jobs thought to be unsuitable for women. The Federal Emergency Relief Administration (FERA) provided federal funds to the states to run relief projects until 1935, at which time women constituted about 12 percent of its recipients. The New Deal emphasis shifted in 1935 as the Works Progress Administration (WPA), an agency created by Congress, performed federal oversight and allocated federal funds for building projects that included positions that even women qualified in nontraditional construction trades had difficulty securing. As head of the Women's and Professional Projects Division of the WPA, Ellen Sullivan Woodward sought projects that offered positions for women in research, recreation, health and nutrition, and food processing, as well as in clerical and library services. Women worked in sewing rooms to repair old clothes and to make new ones for distribution to the poor. Married women were often ineligible for relief because husbands were regarded as heads of households, yet women composed 400,000 of the WPA beneficiaries at the peak of the program.

Women benefited from relief programs in the arts. Female artists such as Louise Nevelson, Alice Neel, and Agnes Tait benefited from the Federal Art Project, which provided money for murals and other kinds of painting. The Federal Theatre Project and Federal Music Project promoted the work and talent of women, allowing them to make enough money to avoid starvation. Through publications such as the state guidebooks and other works, the Federal Writers Project enabled writers such as Katherine Dunham and Zora Neale Hurston to survive and expand their talents.

The National Industrial Recovery Act (NIRA) set business codes from 1933 to 1935 for maximum hours and minimum wages that treated men and women equally. The codes did not apply to the traditional jobs of women such as domestic service, secretarial employment, and agricultural labor; nonetheless, the garment industry sweatshops were curbed. After the NIRA was declared unconstitutional in part, the Fair Labor Standards Act of 1938 created permanent hour and wage regulations that applied equally to men and women in a limited portion of the workforce. The Social Security Act (1935) provided for aid to dependent children that included pediatric and maternity care for many mothers, yet exempted dependent spouses, most of whom were women.

Women made gains in the New Deal era: Their political force was recognized. Some benefited through legislation and others through the improvement in the climate for the trade union movement as more women, married and single, entered the paid labor force. *(See also: Democratic Party; Fair Labor Standards Act; Perkins, Frances; Roosevelt, Eleanor)*

—Donald F. Tingley

Further Reading

Ware, Susan. *Beyond Suffrage: Women in the New Deal.* Cambridge, MA: Harvard University Press, 1981.
———. *Holding Their Own: American Women in the 1930's.* Boston: Twayne, 1982.

⮜ New England Non-Resistance Society (1838–1856)

The New England Non-Resistance Society was a radical abolition organization devoted to pacifism, where women participated equally with men. Founded in September 1838 by William Lloyd Garrison (1805–1879) and others, this abolition group, confined to the New England area, attracted some extremely prominent abolitionists. Women activists were drawn to Garrison's principles of equal participation in the movement for women. For example, Maria Weston Chapman (1806–1885) acted as recording secretary and edited the society's bimonthly publication *Non-Resistant* (1839–1842). Abigail Kelley Foster (1810–1887) was a member of the business committee within the society. Woman suffrage movement leader Lucretia Mott (1793–1880) was also a member.

The New England Non-Resistance Society was founded on the principles of pacifism and evangelicalism. Unlike those in other abolition organizations, these members denounced human organized government. They believed the only effective government was God's government, claiming the people's government functioned on violence and force, which society should resist. Members further believed that slavery epitomized the abuse of government, which held its power by force. Because they objected to force of any kind, members were expected to sign a Declaration of Sentiments (1838), promising to renounce all political participation, including voting. This declaration prevented abolition and woman suffrage activist Sarah Grimké (1792–1873) from participating in the society in 1838, because she believed it would endanger the antislavery cause.

The women in the New England Non-Resistance Society, by denouncing the male-dominated government and advocating pacifism, rejected authority and patriarchy. However, by 1842, the New England Non-Resistance Society lost membership and eventually disappeared in 1856 as the country approached sectionalism and war. *(See also: Abolition and the Antislavery Movement; Garrisonians; Grimké,*

Sarah Moore; Mott, Lucretia Coffin; Pacifism and the Peace Movement)

—**Monica L. Everett**

Further Reading

Hanson, Debra Gold. *Strained Sister: Gender and Class in the Boston Female Anti-Slavery Society.* Boston: University of Massachusetts Press, 1993.

Perry, Lewis. *Radical Abolition: Anarchy and the Government of God in Anti-Slavery Thought.* Ithaca, NY: Cornell University Press, 1973.

Nye, Russel B. *William Lloyd Garrison and the Humanitarian Reformers.* Boston: Little, Brown, 1955.

Yacovne, Donald. *Samuel Joseph May and the Dilemmas of the Liberal Persuasion, 1797–1871.* Philadelphia: Temple University Press, 1991.

❧ New Era Club

The New Era Club was formed in 1893 by Josephine Ruffin, who belonged to the prestigious New England Women's Club, which had been founded by Julia Ward Howe. Her association with this club led her to see the need for organizing a club for black women. In many ways, the New Era Club was a result of the interest among educated black and white women in forming clubs during this time. The members tended to be middle-class, educated women who shared cultural interests. But the New Era Club also had a strong educational and social reform focus and issued a newspaper, *Women's Era.*

Ruffin was also instrumental in promoting a national organization for black women's clubs. One of the reasons for the organization came from a letter sent to *Women's Era* by John W. Jacks, editor of a small Mississippi newspaper denouncing the morality of American black women. Although the letter was apparently never published, it received wide circulation among influential black women, and the New Era Club sent out invitations to other black women's clubs to discuss the issue raised in the letter. A meeting was held in Washington, D.C., in 1895 that resulted in the formation of the National Federation of Afro-American Women. The federation was one of two black federated clubs organized during this time, the other being the National League of Colored Women under the leadership of Mary Church Terrell. The two groups united in 1896 and became the National Association of Colored Women.

An incident that occurred during the 1900 convention of the General Federation of Women's Clubs (GFWC) further convinced the black club women of the need to organize their own federations. Ruffin was a delegate representing not only the New England Press Association but the Massachusetts Federation of Women's Clubs, of which the New Era Club was a member. At the convention, Ruffin was permitted to represent the New England Press Association but was not permitted to represent the New Era Club since this would have meant that the club would have to be recognized as a member of the GFWC. The president of the GFWC,

Rebecca Lowe, tried to evade the issue of permitting black clubs to join by calling roll by club names rather than by individuals. Northern delegates who supported Ruffin were surprised by the move and were not able to gather enough votes to have Ruffin accepted as a delegate from the New Era Club. The event caused great controversy and was widely reported in the press. Some newspapers and many readers were strongly in favor of Ruffin's position. One reader blasted women who had been victims of discrimination for not supporting another woman for no other reason than that she was black. The GFWC continued its segregationist policy for several decades after this incident. *(See also: Black Women's Clubs; General Federation of Women's Clubs; National Federation of Afro-American Women; Ruffin, Josephine St. Pierre)*

—**Judith Pryor**

Further Reading

Harley, Sharon, and Rosalyn Terborg-Penn. *The Afro-American Woman: Struggles and Images.* Port Washington, NY: Kennikat, 1978.

Kennedy, Shelagh Rebecca. "New Era Club." In *Black Women in America: An Historical Encyclopedia.* Vol. 2, edited by Darlene Clark Hine, 878-80. New York: Carlson, 1993.

Lerner, Gerda. "Early Community Work of Black Club Women," *Journal of Negro History* 59 (April 1974): 158-68.

Logan, Rayford W. *The Negro in American Life and Thought: The Nadir, 1877–1901.* New York: Dial, 1954.

Woloch, Nancy. *Women and the American Experience.* New York: Knopf, 1984.

❧ New Harmony (1824–1827)

New Harmony was a utopian community established by Robert Owen, a socialist and pioneer of the cooperative movement, in New Harmony, Indiana. This experiment in utopian reform of society required a redefinition of marriage, the family, and gender roles. Although Owen spoke out against monogamous relationships, he believed that the nuclear family was the chief cornerstone of civil society and he therefore attempted to adapt the family unit to a standard consistent with his ideas of communal living. As defined in Owen's "Declaration of Mental Independence," marriage was a dissoluble institution if the mutual affection of the couple ceased. Asserting that conventional society exploited women by making them economically dependent on their husbands, Owen felt that women had to be given equality in all matters pertaining to livelihood and that children should be the wards of society rather than of their individual parents.

Owen's biggest crusade focused on taking away some of the power and influence of the private family without alienating the members of New Harmony. Owen's thoughts on women's rights attracted Frances Wright, who in 1826 founded the Woman's Social Society, the first fully organized woman's club in America, at New Harmony. But Owen was not successful in curtailing the influence of the nuclear family at New Harmony, and in 1827 he left the community and placed Robert Dale Owen, his son, in charge. Robert Dale Owen was an even stronger advocate of women's rights than his father was, and he supported their demands for equality at the 1850 convention to revise the Indiana state constitution. The principle of equality, which had been espoused by Robert Owen at New Harmony twenty-five years before the Indiana Constitutional Convention, was affixed in the state laws of Indiana due to the diligence of Robert Dale Owen and other staunch supporters of women's rights. *(See also: Marriage; Nashoba; Utopian Communities)*

—**Karen Loupe Gillenwaters**

Further Reading
Moment, Gairdner B., and Otto K. Kraushaar, eds. *Utopias: The American Experience.* Metuchen, NJ: Scarecrow, 1980.
Muncy, Raymond Lee. *Sex and Marriage in Utopian Communities—19th Century America.* Bloomington: Indiana University Press, 1973.
Young, Marguerite. *Angel in the Forest.* New York: Scribner, 1945.

~ New Left

New Left is a generic term that refers to a political movement associated with the youth and counterculture movements of 1960s. The New Left represented the merging of several political movements, some of which began in the 1950s and included the antisegregation protests in the South that fostered a national civil rights movement, as well as the free speech movement that attracted undergraduate as well as graduate students who increasingly protested the draft and the Vietnam War.

Initially led by the Student Non-Violent Coordinating Committee (SNCC) and Students for a Democratic Society (SDS), which worked for change within the system, the New Left pursued a socialist, existentialist, humanist reform of contemporary American capitalism and society through a form of participatory democracy. However, after the police riot at the 1968 Democratic convention in Chicago discouraged the prospects for working for reform within the system, the leadership of the ultrademocratic "leaderless" New Left came from the Maoist/Leninist Progressive Labor Party, the Trotskyite Young Socialist Alliance, and the second- and third-generation communists in the DuBois Clubs of America. The turbulence of the late 1960s produced dissension and division within the New Left no less than in American society generally and resulted in radical leftist separatist groups such as the Black Panthers and Yippies. Media coverage of campus antiwar protests made it possible for the SDS to extend the impact of its tactics of teach-ins and demonstrations to confront a nationwide audience with the issues of the New Left.

The women within the New Left came from the same affluent middle-class social and economic backgrounds as the men and were politicized and radicalized by the same issues.

They believed in the political philosophy of the New Left that emphasized an egalitarian, leaderless reform movement to establish a participatory democracy. Involved at the grassroots level of all the New Left projects, they made direct contact with the people in the target communities where they worked. However, the New Left women increasingly noticed and questioned the persistence of sexist discrimination by the male leaders toward women co-workers in the movement. Although civil rights, poverty, and the Vietnam War were designated as the priority issues, the men of the New Left condescended to address philosophically, if not practically, the secondary concerns of New Left women and included articles of feminist criticism in the movement's *New Left Notes.* The women themselves applied both the theory and the strategy that they had practiced as part of the New Left challenge to establishment authority to critique women's position in society as well as in the New Left movement itself.

Thus, the New Left women eventually focused on women's issues as significant instances of injustice that required an autonomous women's movement; they became the radical feminists of the late 1960s and early 1970s who were on the cutting edge of the modern women's movement. They provided this emerging movement with confrontational tactics and theoretical leadership as they articulated and developed a provocative feminist perspective that reflected their socialist background in their efforts to define and address the issues of the modern women's movement. The term New Left thus came to refer to a particular generation of youthful social reformers and critics who flourished in the 1960s and 1970s. *(See also: Civil Rights; Radical Feminism; Vietnam War; Women's Liberation Movement)*

—**Angela M. Howard**

Further Reading
Diggins, John P. *The American Left in the Twentieth Century.* New York: Harcourt Brace Jovanovich, 1973.
Evans, Sara. *Personal Politics: The Roots of Women's Liberation in the Civil Rights Movement and the New Left.* New York: Knopf, 1979.
O'Neill, William. *Coming Apart.* New York: Quadrangle, 1971.

~ New Morality

The term *new morality* may be used generically to designate any deviation from traditional moralities within given cultures. With respect to the American ethical context, new morality commonly refers to the moral revolution evidenced in the antiestablishment movements of the 1960s and 1970s. For example, anti-Victorian sexual freedom found expression in increased premarital, extramarital, and communal/group sex. Fashion trends exhibited the new morality by displaying originality and transformations in style. Such creativity and spontaneity at times scoffed at traditions so forcefully that seminudity and nudity came to the fore.

Opposition to established norms, the status quo, and forms of authoritarianism was another modality for the expression of the antitraditionalism of the new morality. This antiauthoritarianism found a medium for elucidation in the arts. For example, rock music embodied antipathy to authorities through its gyrations and explosive sounds and lyrics. The use of psychedelic drugs provided a biochemical avenue for the avoidance of the status quo and a vehicle to indicate disgust for rigid authoritarianism. Protests against the Vietnam War offered a major collective cause and tragedy for the advocates of the new morality to rally around.

Women's liberation as a cause enlisted the ranks of numerous women who sensed the freedom and the potential for new identity formation present in the late 1960s and into the present. Women found that they could no longer tolerate the idea of gender being tied to particular types of careers so that numerous professional positions as well as blue-collar positions previously restricted to males were slowly but gradually being opened to females. Role reversal in relationships became apparent as the equality of the sexes gained repute. Most important, remarkably gifted women found leadership positions in government, business, and education that provided platforms for numerous key spokespersons to arise, articulate, and solidify the emerging power and place of women in the society.

In theoretical ethics, the new morality found a less volatile, yet significant proponent in the form of morality known as "situation ethics." Joseph Fletcher's groundbreaking *Situation Ethics: The New Morality* sought to elicit a morality from the individual situation within which one is involved rather than any external authoritarian ethic. Only the situation itself could provide ethical answers because all "norms" had been called into question. External authorities could never be trusted in themselves. For Fletcher, J. A. T. Robinson, and others, only love could be the hermeneutical key—not laws, not rules, not principles, not ideals, not norms.

The new morality insistence on freedom and self-expression broke some chains of oppression. Certainly, women benefited to some degree from this new openness. Common terms such as *women's rights, equal pay/equal work, househusband, feminism,* and *liberation* indicated not only new jargon but new opportunities for the women of the 1960s to the present. Along with new freedoms and new experiments in living came new responsibilities, some resilient and not-so-resilient responses, and a metamorphosis that brought much new growth yet concomitant ambiguity and even trauma. Opposition to the new morality, among some segments of the population, gained momentum during the 1990s as a movement toward more traditional values. The Religious Right, particularly through movements such as the Christian Coalition, gained political power in underscoring its opposition to liberal moralities. The influx of Eastern philosophies provided new ideological data for defining morality at the close of the twentieth century. The impact of these movements, although certain, will need elucidation in the twenty-first century. *(See also: Free Love; New Left; Sexual Revolution; Women's Liberation Movement)*

—**Barry Arnold**

Further Reading

Aitken, Robert, and David Steindl-Rast. *The Ground We Share: Everyday Practice, Buddhist and Christian.* Boston: Shambhala, 1996.

Arnold, Barry. *The Pursuit of Virtue.* New York: Peter Lang, 1988.

Fletcher, Joseph. *Situation Ethics: The New Morality.* Philadelphia: Westminster, 1966.

Laney, James, and James Gustafson. *On Being Responsible.* New York: Harper & Row, 1968.

Seller, James. *Essays in American Ethics.* Edited by Barry Arnold. New York: Peter Lang, 1992.

⚭ New Woman

New Woman was a term used at the turn of the twentieth century to refer to the young single woman who was the beneficiary of the nineteenth-century improvement and progress in women's education and employment opportunities. The New Woman defined her womanhood in more secular terms than her mother's generation had defined their true womanhood, allowing the New Woman to experience life as an autonomous individual and self-sufficient worker before she married to become a full-time homemaker and middle-class society matron. Socially active and economically independent, the New Woman was educated, having graduated from high school or even college. She did not reject marriage or the concept of a maternal destiny for women, yet she tacitly asserted her individualism as she adjusted her domesticity in marriage to accommodate her increased social and economic opportunities. These included the use of birth control and the pursuit of civic and intellectual interests apart from those of her husband and children. In her exercise of this choice to maintain a partially separate identity, the New Woman represented a crucial transitional phase of American womanhood before World War I. *(See also: Social Feminism; Socialism; Woman Question)*

—**Angela M. Howard**

Further Reading

May, Henry F. *The End of American Innocence.* Chicago: Quadrangle, 1959, 1962.

Raub, Patricia. "A New Woman or an Old-Fashioned Girl? The Portrayal of the Heroine in Popular Women's Novels of the Twenties," *American Studies* 35 (Spring 1994): 109-30.

Sochen, June. *The New Woman.* New York: Quadrangle, 1972.

⚭ Nichols, Mary Gove (1810–1884)

Mary Gove Nichols was a lecturer, author, and avid proponent of health reform for women. Best known as a water cure enthusiast, at various times she embraced dress reform, Grahamism, temperance, Mesmerism, vegetarianism, Fourierism, Spiritualism, anarchism, pacifism, Swedenborgianism, and free love.

Born Mary Sargent Neal in Goffstown, New Hampshire, she became a Quaker and married Hiram Gove, a family friend and fellow Quaker, at twenty. She later described their unhappy marriage in *Mary Lyndon or, Revelations of a Life* (1865), a fictionalized autobiography. Following four failed pregnancies, she became an adherent of Grahamism and began to lecture to women on sexuality and hygiene. After leaving Gove, she operated a Grahamite boardinghouse with her one surviving child. A second marriage in 1848 to fellow health reformer Thomas Low Nichols resulted in their establishing a series of water cure institutes. They also lectured on socialism and Spiritualism and operated a short-lived health magazine. Nichols ran a girls' school and published articles on women's health and books, including *Experience in Water Cure* (1850) and *Marriage* (1854), which criticized conventional wedlock. The Nicholses studied various communes before establishing their own utopian settlement, Memnomia, in Yellow Springs, Ohio, in 1857. The commune, which broke with Nichols's earlier championing of free love by proclaiming "Freedom, Fraternity, [and] Chastity," broke up following Nichols's religious visions and conversion to Roman Catholicism. At the outbreak of the Civil War, the couple moved to England, where Nichols ran a water cure establishment until her death.

Nichols's feminism was explicit in her concern for women's health. Drawing on varying ideas of women's place, she urged women to both educate themselves about health for the sake of their families and to become physicians and change the existing medical system. Her ideas about female sexuality were similarly contradictory: She both advocated sexual pleasure for women and condemned masturbation and advised chastity, because she believed that the economic and social constraints of marriage did not allow for female orgasm and mutual love. These teachings resulted in her own and her husband's expulsion from leadership of the hydropathic movement in 1856, largely because of their writings against traditional marriage and in favor of sexual self-determination for women. *(See also: Grahamism; Homeopathy; Utopian Communities; Water Cure)*

—**Miriam Reumann**
—**William G. Shade**

Further Reading

Blake, John B. "Mary Gove Nichols, Prophetess of Health." In *Women and Health in America,* edited by Judith Walzer Leavitt, 359-75. Madison: University of Wisconsin Press, 1984.

Cayleff, Susan. *Wash and Be Healed: The Water-Cure Movement and Women's Health.* Philadelphia: Temple University Press, 1987.

Nichols, Mary Gove. *Mary Lyndon or, Revelations of a Life. An Autobiography.* New York: Stringer & Townsend, 1860.

Figure 43. Anaïs Nin
Anaïs Nin's writings were influential in their frank attempts to reconcile femininity with independence. Used by permission of UPI/Corbis-Bettmann.

Nin, Anaïs (1903–1977)

Anaïs Nin was a French-born American author who reached her largest audience through her autobiographical diary, *The Diary of Anaïs Nin* (1966), which detailed her life through character sketches and colorful vignettes. Originally a cult figure because of her symbolic, poetic novels, she attracted a wider readership in later years as a female author attempting to reconcile the nurturing woman and the egotistical artist.

Nin epitomizes the struggling female writer who became established in America without commercial publishers' support. She was the oldest child of Joaquin and Rosa Nin. Her father was a well-known concert pianist and philanderer who deserted the family when Nin was eleven. In 1914, as she traveled to New York with the rest of her family, she began a journal—which became the famous *Diary*—that she believed would entice her father to rejoin them. She dropped out of New York public schools at the age of fifteen following criticism of her writing as "too literary," educated herself through constant reading, and worked as an artist's model to support her family. At the age of twenty, she entered a conflicted marriage to Ian Hugo, a banker and later a film director, who illustrated her books with copperplate engravings. In the early 1930s, Nin returned to Paris and became involved in the Villa Seurat Circle, a group of avantgarde writers that published their own works. There, she met novelist Henry Miller. Nin was Miller's chief literary mentor, and they influenced each other's writings for three decades. In the mid-1930s, she studied psychoanalysis under Otto Rank. Later, she practiced psychoanalysis with Rank in New York. Psychoanalysis proved a lifelong interest that she pursued in dream and fantasy sequences and that endowed her characters with a powerful psychological reality.

Nin returned to New York in 1939 with her husband. She experienced rejection as an author, deemed "uncommercial" by publishers. Nin called on her previous publishing skills with the Seurat Circle and, using a secondhand, foot-controlled printing press, began to publish her own works. The prose poem *House of Incest* (1931) preceded *Winter of Artifice* (1939), which detailed the relationship between a father and daughter and included autobiographical elements. Her third self-published work appeared as a collection of short stories titled *Under a Glass Bell* (1944) and brought her critical acclaim and publishers' attention for its dreamlike atmosphere. In 1946, *Ladders of Fire,* the first of a series of five novels dealing with similar characters, examined the lives of three women. Nin then wrote approximately five more novels before her most famous and first nonfiction work, *The Diary,* was published. Her literary career ended with a literary criticism of her contemporaries, *The Novel of the Future* (1968). In later years, her writings gained much support, particularly among feminists, and until her death in 1977, she remained a frequent lecturer at colleges and universities.

Anaïs Nin's literary vision spoke through female characters, and her purpose was to efface the barriers between the inner and outer self. In life, her exultation in her femininity and her independent will cast her as an influential figure in the 1960s and 1970s. Her six-volume *Diary,* a premier women's autobiographical work, and her rediscovered novels have established Nin's eminence among female writers. *(See also: Women Writers)*

—**Suzette Chapman**
—**Camille Jaski Popliolek**

Further Reading

Dubow, Wendy, ed. *Conversations with Anaïs Nin.* Jackson: University of Mississippi Press, 1994.

Franklin, Benjamin. *Anaïs Nin, an Introduction.* Athens: Ohio University Press, 1979.

Hinz, Evelyn J., ed. *A Woman Speaks: The Lectures, Seminars, and Interviews of Anaïs Nin.* Chicago: Swallow, 1975.

Irgang, Margit, and Gunther Stuhlmann. "Of Veils and Unveiling: Two Biographical Approaches to Anaïs Nin," *Anaïs: An International Journal* 12 (1994): 88-90.

Knapp, Bettina Liebowitz. *Anaïs Nin.* New York: Ungar, 1978.

Nin, Anaïs. *The Diary of Anaïs Nin.* Vol. 1, *1931–1934.* Chicago: Swallow, 1966.

Spencer, Sharon. *Collage of Dreams: The Writings of Anaïs Nin.* Chicago: Swallow, 1977.

⪧ 1950s

During the Cold War, the nuclear family became a symbol of security against the looming threats of atomic war and international communism. American women married younger, had several children close together, and focused on full-time child rearing and homemaking in appliance-equipped suburban homes. In a deviation from long-term demographic trends, after World War II, fertility rates increased dramatically among women of all classes and racial groups, producing the baby boom, which peaked in 1957. One popular advice book warned women, "The family is the center of your living. If it isn't, you've gone far astray."

The ability of women to attain this kind of family life was affected by class, race, and sexuality. Many married women joined the labor force, ignoring pressure to relinquish jobs to returning veterans and despite decreasing opportunities and wages. White women took clerical and service jobs to be able to purchase the new consumer goods their families desired. Most African American women did not have the luxury of becoming full-time homemakers living on their husbands' income. Instead, they combined paid labor, often as domestic workers, with their own household responsibilities.

Fear of unleashed female sexuality permeated postwar culture. Sex was to be contained within an erotic, heterosexual, monogamous marriage. For single women, sexual activity could be dangerous; contraceptives were not available for unmarried women, and safe abortions were increasingly difficult to obtain. Lesbians found postwar America a hostile place, despite Alfred Kinsey's finding that homosexuality was widespread. In the ideological context of a virulent Cold War against communism, lesbians (and gay men) were perceived as national security threats and faced harassment, stigma, job loss, and violent attacks. Despite—or perhaps because of—this persecution, lesbians (and gay men) established strong communities in many urban centers in the 1950s. In 1955, Del Martin and Phyllis Lyon founded the nation's first support and advocacy groups for lesbians in San Francisco.

While white, middle-class women retreated to the suburbs, African American women like Rosa Parks and Ella Baker were active in the birth of the civil rights movement. Women played essential roles as organizers of the Montgomery, Alabama, bus boycott and ensured its success, walking many miles to and from work in the homes of white employers for an entire year. In Little Rock, Arkansas, fifteen-year-old Elizabeth Eckford and five other African American teenage women were among the "Little Rock Nine" who confronted white mobs to attend Central High School in 1957. *(See also: Abortion; Baby Boom; Civil Rights; Consumerism; Female Sexuality; Kinsey Report; Parks, Rosa)*

—**Cynthia Mills Richter**

Further Reading

Coontz, Stephanie. *The Way We Never Were: American Families and the Nostalgia Trap.* New York: Basic Books, 1992.

Faderman, Lillian. *Odd Girls and Twilight Lovers: A History of Lesbian Life in Twentieth-Century America.* New York: Penguin, 1991.

Jones, Jacqueline. *Labor of Love, Labor of Sorrow: Black Women, Work and the Family, from Slavery to the Present.* New York: Vintage, 1995.

May, Elaine Tyler. *Homeward Bound: American Families in the Cold War Era.* New York: Basic Books, 1988.

Solinger, Rickie. *Wake Up Little Susie: Single Pregnancy and Race Before* Roe v. Wade. New York: Routledge, 1992.

Spigel, Lynn. *Make Room for TV: Television and the Family Ideal in Postwar America.* Chicago: University of Chicago Press, 1992.

ఇ. Nineteenth Amendment to the United States Constitution (1920)

The Nineteenth (Woman Suffrage) Amendment provides that "the right of citizens of the United States to vote shall not be denied or abridged by the United States or by any State on account of sex." It also stipulates that "the Congress shall have power, by appropriate legislation, to enforce the Provisions of this article."

The struggle for the "woman vote" had begun at the Seneca Falls (New York) Convention of 1848, the first woman's rights convention in Victorian America, which produced the Declaration of Sentiments and Resolutions that listed the franchise as the primary goal of the nineteenth-century woman's rights movement. By 1890, the suffrage campaign focused on securing a federal amendment to the U.S. Constitution as the proper means to ensure women the franchise.

The ratification of the Nineteenth Amendment ended a schism that had weakened the woman suffrage movement since 1869, when Elizabeth Cady Stanton and Susan B. Anthony founded the National Woman Suffrage Association (NWSA), dedicated to national enfranchisement, while Lucy Stone and Elizabeth Blackwell established the American Woman Suffrage Association (AWSA), which focused on a state-by-state strategy. Although this schism was officially healed by the formation of the National American Woman Suffrage Association (NAWSA) in 1890, the issue still divided suffragists. Southerners, especially, opposed nationwide enfranchisement, out of fear that it would reopen the debate over blacks, who had been successfully disfranchised despite the requirements of the Fifteenth Amendment. The opposition of southern congressmen, of the Democratic Party, and of President Woodrow Wilson postponed proposal of the amendment until 1919, even though the House of Representatives acted formally to pass the amendment on January 10, 1918. The pressures applied by NAWSA, the National Woman's Party (NWP), and other suffrage organizations finally led to the amendment's proposal by the House on May 19, 1919 (by a vote of 304-89) and by the Senate on June 4 (66-30).

Ratification took just over one year, as many legislators and organizations had been converted to the cause by the pressure of suffrage organizations, the active role played by women in World War I, and the requirements of practical politics. The ratification of the Eighteenth Amendment (Prohibition) rendered irrelevant males' fears that female enfranchisement would strengthen Prohibition's chances. Following the "Winning Plan" of its president, Carrie Chapman Catt, the NAWSA and the NWP effectively lobbied in crucial state legislatures. Opposition centered largely in the southern states, but it was a southern state, Tennessee, that became the necessary thirty-sixth state to ratify, despite the frantic efforts of business and liquor interests who, according to Catt and NWSA vice president Nettie Rogers Shuler, "dispensed Old Bourbon and moonshine whiskey with boorish insistence." Legend has it that the deciding vote in the assembly was cast by a young legislator whose mother had urged him to help Mrs. Catt.

The amendment became part of the Constitution on August 26, 1920, allowing women to vote in the November elections. *(See also: American Woman Suffrage Association; Catt, Carrie Chapman; Declaration of Sentiments and Resolutions; National American Woman Suffrage Association; National Woman's Party; Prohibition and the Volstead Act; Seneca Falls Convention; Suffrage)*

—John D. Buenker

Further Reading

Anthony, Susan B., Elizabeth Cady Stanton, Matilda Joslyn Gage, and Ida Husted Harper. *History of Woman Suffrage,* 6 vols. Rochester, NY: Mann, 1881–1922.

Barry, Kathleen. *Susan B. Anthony: A Biography of a Singular Feminist.* New York: New York University Press, 1988.

Catt, Carrie Chapman, and Nettie Rogers Shuler. *Woman Suffrage and Politics.* New York: Scribner, 1923.

Scott, Anne Firor, and Andrew M. Scott. *One Half the People: The Fight for Woman Suffrage.* Philadelphia: J. B. Lippincott, 1975.

Kraditor, Aileen. *Ideas of the Woman Suffrage Movement.* New York: Columbia University Press, 1965.

McBride, Genevieve G. *On Wisconsin Women: Working for Their Rights from Settlement to Suffrage.* Madison: University of Wisconsin Press, 1993.

ఇ. Ninety-Nines, Inc.

The Ninety-Nines, Inc., is an international organization of women pilots. In the fall of 1929 following the Women's Air Derby, the first major cross-country race for women pilots, several women expressed their desire for an organization that would be "dedicated to assist women in aeronautical research, air racing events, the acquisition of aerial experience, and the administration of aid through aerial means in times of emergency." At the instigation of Clara Trenchmann of the Curtiss Flying Service on Long Island, New York, four female Curtiss demonstration pilots wrote to the 126 licensed women pilots in the United States to invite their views on such an organization. Ninety-nine of

Figure 44. The Ninety-Nines
The Ninety-Nines, the oldest aviation organization in the United States, was founded in 1929 to provide encouragement and assistance to women pilots. Shown above are flyers who would compete in the Cleveland Ladybird Air Derby, including Amelia Earhart (fourth from right), the organization's first president, and Florence "Pancho" Barnes (far right). Used by permission of UPI/Corbis-Bettmann.

them responded favorably. On November 2, 1929, twenty-six women met in a Curtiss hangar and formed the Ninety-Nines, named in honor of the charter members. Today the Ninety-Nines, Inc., headquartered in Oklahoma City, has over 6,600 members in thirty-nine countries and continues its dedication to support women pilots worldwide in all their endeavors. *(See also: Aviation)*

—**Claudia M. Oakes**

Further Reading
Brooks-Pazmany, Kathleen. *United States Women in Aviation 1919–1929.* Washington, DC: Smithsonian Institution, 1983.

✑ Noether, Emmy (1882–1935)

Emmy Noether was born in Erlangen in southern Germany. Her father Max Noether was a mathematics professor at the University of Erlangen, and there she completed her doctoral dissertation in mathematics in 1907. In 1916, she moved to the University of Göttingen, Germany, to collaborate with mathematicians David Hilbert and Felix Klein. Hitler's rise forced her move to the United States in 1933. She accepted the position of visiting professor of mathematics at Bryn Mawr College and died there in 1935 from complications following surgery.

Noether was at the forefront of the development of the axiomatic approach in abstract algebra. She developed a general theory of ideals in arbitrary rings and developed the concept of cross products. Through her work on hyper-complex systems and representation theory, she proved results in algebra of great depth and beauty. Albert Einstein wrote of her (*New York Times,* May 4, 1935): "In the judgment of the most competent living mathematicians, Fraulein Noether was the most significant creative mathematical genius thus far produced since the higher education of women began. In the realm of algebra, in which the most gifted mathematicians have been busy for centuries, she discovered methods which have proved of enormous importance in the development of the present-day younger generation of mathematicians." *(See also: Mathematics)*

—**Jonell Duda Comerford**

Further Reading

Brewer, James W., and Martha K. Smith, eds. *Emmy Noether*. New York: Marcel Dekker, 1981.

Campbell, Douglas M., and John C. Higgins, eds. *Mathematics: People, Problems, Results*. Belmont, CA: Wadsworth, 1984.

Dick, Auguste. *Emmy Noether, 1882–1935*. Boston: Birkhauser, 1981.

Grinstein, Louise S., and Paul J. Campbell, eds. *Women of Mathematics: A Biobibliographic Sourcebook*. New York: Greenwood, 1987.

Osen, Lynn M. *Women in Mathematics*. Cambridge: MIT Press, 1974.

⤳ Normal Schools

The term *normal school* was used to describe teacher training institutions in the United States during the nineteenth and early twentieth centuries and was derived from the French term for teacher training institutes—*Normale*. The first normal schools were established in New England prior to the Civil War, but in the latter nineteenth century, they appeared in the Midwest and Pacific states as well. The vast majority of students in the normal schools in virtually all parts of the country were women. Usually, women were represented among normal school students to about the same extent as local teaching forces were feminized. As teaching became more feminized through the latter nineteenth century, so did these schools. By the turn of the century in many parts of the country, normal school education was virtually synonymous with women's education.

A major supporter of the concept of the normal school for teacher training was Horace Mann (1796–1859), one of the most prominent early promoters of educational reform. In 1837, Mann was elected secretary of the Massachusetts Board of Education and began his travels on horseback across the state gathering support for his new idea: the normal school. His goal was a number of teachers' colleges that would prepare teachers in a secular, humanistic environment free from religious and denominational influences. After a number of setbacks, the normal schools flourished in Massachusetts, and the idea spread to neighboring states.

Throughout the nineteenth century, most normal schools were state supported and offered about the same level of education as the high schools of that time. Toward the end of the century, when demand for trained teachers became acute in many parts of the country, it became commonplace for high schools to establish normal departments where young women could receive the requisite training in pedagogy to prepare them for positions as teachers. Still, the number of normal school graduates lagged far behind the demand for teachers well into the twentieth century.

Who were the women students attending normal schools at this time? Historians Richard Bernard and Maris Vinovskis have analyzed enrollment records for Massachusetts normal schools in the 1850s and found that the largest groups were the daughters of farmers and skilled tradesmen, both middling occupational groups in nineteenth-century New England. Other studies of teachers in the nineteenth and early twentieth century have produced similar results. In general, it appears that the women who attended normal schools were from middle- and lower-middle-class backgrounds. To a certain degree, in that case, the normal schools can be said to have served as a sort of popular higher education.

With time, the normal schools shifted their orientation from secondary to higher education. This appears to have been partly due to the efforts of teacher educators to enhance their status, partly due to the efforts of educational leaders to demand higher qualifications of teachers, and in some parts of the country, it may have been due to local political interests wanting to have college-level instruction available for a particular area's youth. By the opening years of the twentieth century, there was a movement to introduce college courses in normal schools across the country. By the 1920s, normal schools in some states had been renamed state teachers colleges, and by the post–World War II period, most normal schools had become state colleges or universities. Today, teacher education is simply one part of the educational mission of most former normal schools, and present-day state universities bear little resemblance to their nineteenth-century predecessors. The early normal schools, however, played a critical role in providing education to tens of thousands of young women at a time when women had relatively few educational alternatives and in training successive generations of women teachers for service in the nation's schools. *(See also: Education; Higher Education; Teaching)*

—**John L. Rury**
—**Lynn E. Lipor**

Further Reading

Bernard, Richard, and Maris Vinovskis. "The Female School Teacher in Antebellum Massachusetts," *Journal of Social History* 10 (Spring 1977): 332-45.

Herbst, Jurgen. *And Sadly Teach: Teacher Education and Professionalization in American Culture*. Madison: University of Wisconsin Press, 1989.

———. "Nineteenth Century Normal Schools in the United States: A Fresh Look," *History of Education* 9 (March 1980): 219-27.

Mann, Horace. *Horace Mann on the Crisis in Education*. Edited, with an introduction by Louis Filler. Yellow Springs, OH: Antioch, 1965.

⤳ Nurse, Rebecca (Towne) (1621–1692)

Rebecca Nurse, a victim of the Salem (Massachusetts) witch trials, was the wife of Francis Nurse and the mother of four sons and four daughters. A respected, intelligent, and pious matron, Nurse was particularly vulnerable because her mother had previously been accused of witchcraft although never brought to trial. Nurse's two younger sisters—Sarah, wife of Peter Cloyse, and Mary, wife of Isaac Easty—were also charged with witchcraft. At seventy-one,

Nurse was accused of being a witch on a complaint by Edward and Jonathan Putnam, the sons of John Putnam.

Nurse was charged with having committed acts of witchcraft on Mrs. Ann Putnam, her daughter Ann Putnam, and Abigail Williams. A hearing on March 24, 1692, resulted in Nurse's internment in the Salem jail until June 2, but a petition filed on her behalf delayed the trial until June 28. Several of the afflicted girls then testified that "Goody" Nurse was the specter who had tormented them. The court appointed a jury of three women to examine Nurse's body for any identifying mark of the devil. Although they found a mark, two of the women stated that the mark was explainable by natural causes. The other woman disagreed.

The jury returned a verdict of not guilty. The accusers demonstrated disapproval with renewed energy and more violent fits. Because of a hearing loss, Nurse failed to respond to a question made to her by the jury. As a result, the jury brought in a second verdict of guilty. After she learned that her silence was misconstrued as a confession of guilt, she wrote a statement explaining her silence; nevertheless, she was sentenced to be hanged. The governor granted her a reprieve; later, the church where she had been a lifelong member excommunicated her. After hearing of the reprieve, the accusers renewed their clamors with the additional support of some Salem gentlemen. The governor recalled the reprieve. On July 19, Nurse was carted to the summit of Gallows Hill and hanged.

The bodies of witches were thrust into shallow graves on Gallows Hill, but Nurse's body did not remain there. Her children bided their time, and under the shroud of darkness took their mother's body home. After her death, she was vindicated, and the sentence of excommunication was erased from the church book in 1712. Later, a granite shaft was raised to Rebecca Nurse, and beside it, another was erected with the names of those courageous friends who spoke in her defense at a time when doing so might have caused them to be accused of witchcraft. (See also: Salem Witch Trials; Tituba)

—Judith Lucas

Further Reading

Boyer, Paul, and Stephen Nissenbaum. *Salem Possessed—The Social Origins of Witchcraft.* Cambridge, MA: Harvard University Press, 1974.

Gragg, Larry. "Under an Evil Hand," *American History Illustrated* 27 (March/April 1992): 54-59.

Nevins, Winfield S. *Witchcraft in Salem Village in 1692.* Salem, MA: Northshore, 1892.

Starkey, Marios L. *The Devil in Massachusetts—A Modern Inquiry into the Salem Witch Trials.* Garden City, NY: Doubleday, 1969.

Upham, Charles W. *Salem Witchcraft.* Vol. 2. New York: Ungar, 1959.

∿ Nursing

Nursing emerged as a paid profession for American women in the mid-nineteenth century. Previously, most nursing was done as part of the traditional female role within the immediate or extended family. Pioneering public hospitals employed charwomen in quasi-nursing roles, while Catholic sisters provided the most exemplary nursing care during the 1850s in denominational institutions. The factors shaping the early direction of professional nursing included the advent of antiseptic and scientific medicine, the gradual increase in the numbers and respectability of hospitals, the example of Florence Nightingale's successes in the Crimea, and the demands of the Civil War.

Recognition of the need for trained nurses came first in Massachusetts in 1850 when the legislature established the New England Medical College and encouraged aspiring nurses to attend lectures. In 1888, the American Medical Association called for improved nurses' training and urged that such training schools be attached to hospitals. The dramatic growth of community hospitals that continued throughout the 1800s kept the demand for a steady source of cheap labor high, and the introduction of scientific medical practices increased the need for educated nurses. The training programs at most hospital-based schools consisted primarily of a long apprenticeship on the wards and inculcating trainees with a strict adherence to the hospital hierarchy. Most students received minimal classroom instruction. This system meant that most hospitals functioned with an essentially untrained corps of nurses. The landmark Goldmark Report (1923) pointed out the fundamental faults in the hospital schools, which emphasized menial tasks while relegating education to a low priority. The Rockefeller Foundation established a prestigious Committee for the Study of Nursing Education. Authored by U.S. Sanitary Commission secretary Josephine Goldmark, the report recommended that the hospital schools be recognized as separate educational departments devoted to providing a thorough nursing education, not merely training. This sparked a trend toward nursing programs leading to baccalaureate degrees in the 1920s. Opposition to the collegiate nursing movement came from private physicians and hospital administrators, who argued that the new nurses would be overtrained and too costly.

The struggle for women to participate formally as nurses in America's war effort began during the Civil War when an estimated ten thousand women, mostly untrained, signed up for nursing duty. Their impressive service record, despite trying conditions and outright opposition from many military physicians, proved their importance to the North's ultimate victory. Nevertheless, it took valiant service during the Spanish-American War and much lobbying before the creation of the Navy Nurse Corps in 1908, which pioneered the creation of a similar service in each branch of the military. These elite corps offered nurses a unique opportunity to demonstrate skilled nursing techniques. World Wars I and II brought thousands of women into nursing, both on the home front and abroad on the front lines. By the end of World War II, women military nurses had become integral to the effective functioning of the American military.

In the post-World War II period, the trend in nursing education was toward professionalization. Diploma schools attached to hospitals moved toward becoming full-fledged educational institutions. More collegiate nursing programs were established, and their enrollments gradually increased as a result of the 1964 Nurses Training Act, created to alleviate a critical shortage of nurses, especially those capable of taking on administrative and teaching roles.

The reforms of the Progressive Era and programs of the Great Depression period created a wide array of nonhospital jobs for nurses in industrial and public health nursing. These positions were especially appealing because they offered nurses the potential for independence and an active role in confronting larger socioeconomic problems. Such quasi-independent practitioners foreshadowed nursing in the late twentieth century, when more health care was done outside the hospital, now a place for emergency care and the treatment of major acute illnesses. In the future, nursing will become increasingly professionalized, with practitioners developing skills as health managers, diagnosticians, and independent health providers working in new relationships with physicians and patients. *(See also: Army Nurse Corps; Barton, Clara; Civil War; Crowell, Frances Elisabeth; Henry Street Settlement; Military Service; National Organization for Public Health Nursing; Philadelphia Training School for Nurses at Philadelphia General Hospital; U.S. Sanitary Commission; Visiting Nurses; Wald, Lillian)*

—Cynthia Jeffress Little

Further Reading

Ashley, J. A. *Hospitals, Paternalism, and the Role of the Nurse.* New York: Teachers College Press, 1976.

Kalisch, Philip A., and Beatrice J. Kalisch. *The Advance of American Nursing,* 2d ed. Boston: Little, Brown, 1986.

Melosh, Barbara. *The Physician's Handbook: Work, Culture, and Conflict in American Nursing.* Philadelphia: Temple University Press, 1982.

Reverby, Susan M. *Ordered to Care: The Dilemma of American Nursing, 1850–1945.* New York: Cambridge University Press, 1988.

Oberlin College

Oberlin College was founded in 1833 as the Oberlin Collegiate Institute, southwest of Cleveland, Ohio, by Yankee missionaries John J. Shipherd and Philo P. Stewart, who named the community in honor of Alsatian pastor John Frederick Oberlin. It was the first coeducational college in the country, the first to accept students regardless of race, and the first to award an undergraduate degree to an African American woman (Mary Jane Patterson, 1862). It was also the first college to grant undergraduate degrees to women. From the outset, women constituted a sizable student minority, and Oberlin became a leader in physical education for women.

Oberlin began as an evangelical experiment in Christian living and education, and women were an integral part of that experiment. The college replicated the family, with women providing moral uplift while serving in a traditional supportive role to men—washing their clothes, cleaning their rooms, waiting on them at meals, and even listening to their public speeches in respectful silence. Not all women, of course, accepted that role. Lucy Stone, Antoinette Brown, Betsey Mix Cowles, and a few other militant women's rights advocates chafed under such restrictions, Stone going so far as to refuse to write a commencement address that she would not be permitted to read publicly.

More typical of Oberlin women was their participation in moral reform movements designed to protect and purify the family. Faculty wives and female students were active in the Oberlin Female Moral Reform Society, early leaders of which included Alice Welch Cowles, Esther Shipherd, and Mary Atkins, founder of Mills College in California. The first three women to receive college degrees—Caroline Rudd, Mary Hosford, and Elizabeth Prall—were also members. Society members were concerned with any action that might promote immorality—immodest dress, dancing, novel reading, and theater attendance. Equally important was the Oberlin Maternal Association, formed to improve family life and child rearing.

Student life was tightly regulated for women, perhaps in an effort to offset public criticism about the experiment in coeducation. Except for attendance at approved activities, such as literary societies or choir, women students were expected to remain in their rooms after the beginning of evening study hours and to retire by ten o'clock. Even their walking was governed by a series of prohibitions. Nevertheless, Oberlin set the example for coeducation followed by a large number of midwestern religious colleges and Big Ten universities.

The original missionary aims of the school provided the foundation for a social conscience that has characterized the history of both the town of Oberlin and the college. Oberlin was a major center of abolitionism, a stop on the Underground Railroad, and a source of volunteers to teach freedmen after the Civil War. In more recent times, Oberlin has become known for its exceptional conservatory and for its support of civil rights, women's liberation, and gay rights. The fortunes of the college have declined somewhat since the Ivy League schools became coeducational. The current presidency of Nancy Dye aims to recognize and preserve the best of Oberlin's past while reshaping the school to compete with the many schools that now offer the diverse, coeducational experience that once made Oberlin unique. *(See also: Blackwell, Antoinette; Coeducation; Education; Higher Education; Moral Reform; Stone, Lucy)*

—**Nicholas C. Burckel**

Further Reading

Fletcher, Robert Samuel. *A History of Oberlin College from Its Foundation through the Civil War*, 2 vols. Oberlin, OH: Oberlin College, 1943.

Ginzberg, Lori D. "Women in an Evangelical Community: Oberlin 1835–1850," *Ohio History* 89 (1980): 78-88.

Hosford, Frances Juliette. *Father Shipherd's Magna Charta: A Century of Coeducation in Oberlin College.* Boston: Marshall Jones, 1937.

Lasser, Carol. *Educating Men and Women Together: Co-education in a Changing World.* Urbana: University of Illinois Press, 1987.

Obscenity

Obscenity provides society with one of its most powerful instruments of social control. Cultures use the notion of obscenity to drive out deviant ideas from public discussion and to dismiss them as vulgar and ridiculous. Furthermore, fighting obscenity provides the legal system with a lever to clamp down on behavior considered unhealthy by the dominant interests of communities. Through this reinforcement of social mores' influence on the legal system, the concept of obscenity has played and continues to play an important role in the history of women in America.

The development of women's roles during the nineteenth century illustrates the power of the label of obscenity. During this time, American society dictated that women should be innocent, dependent on men, self-sacrificing, and devoid of sexual urges and interests. America pushed any opposition to this image of women into the realm of obscenity, making even knowledge of alternatives to this ideal vulgar, ridiculous, and out of reach to most of its citizens. The legal system further limited challenges to this concept by banning activities and the transmission of materials deemed obscene. The Comstock Law of 1873 provided the most striking example of this by specifically banning all devices and information relating to birth control as part of a sweeping prohibition against "obscene, lewd, or lascivious" articles. The government employed this logic to enact similar restrictions on abortion, homosexuality, and other activities deemed harmful to the sexual purity and innocence of the American people.

Despite changing social mores and the shifting status of women, the notion of obscenity continues to play an important role. In a series of decisions, the U.S. Supreme Court left the authority to define obscenity to local communities using local standards. Some feminists, recalling earlier government abuses, view antiobscenity campaigns and obscenity laws with suspicion and pressure local governments to adopt as narrow a definition of obscenity as possible. Others, however, view the notion of obscenity as potentially empowering to women. They believe that violence and degradation against women and children can be banished to the realm of obscenity, and therefore they pressure local governments to adopt stricter obscenity laws. *(See also: Birth Control; Comstock Law; Pornography)*

—Sethuraman Srinivasan, Jr.

Further Reading

Abraham, Henry J. *Freedom and the Court,* 4th ed. New York: Oxford University Press, 1982.

Gordon, Linda. *Woman's Body, Woman's Right: Birth Control in America.* New York: Grossman, 1976.

Kennedy, David. *Birth Control in America: The Career of Margaret Sanger.* New Haven, CT: Yale University Press, 1970.

Lacombe, Dany. *Blue Politics: Pornography and the Law in the Age of Feminism.* Toronto: University of Toronto Press, 1994.

Pritchett, C. Herman. *Constitutional Civil Liberties.* Englewood Cliffs, NJ: Prentice Hall, 1983.

⋙ O'Connor, Flannery (1925–1964)

Fiction writer Flannery O'Connor was a devout Catholic whose religious faith pervaded all of her writing. Realizing that her audience did not always share her belief, O'Connor often used violence and the grotesque to shock her reader into recognition of the need for God's grace. In justification of this style, O'Connor wrote that "for the hard of hearing you shout; for the almost blind, you draw large and startling figures." In her works, those figures included a phony Bible salesman, a crafty one-armed tramp who marries a woman's idiot daughter to get her car, and a little boy who drowns while returning to the river of his baptism, where he "counted." O'Connor's fiction was intended to be unsettling.

Born in Savannah, Georgia, into one of Georgia's oldest Catholic families, Mary Flannery O'Connor attended parochial schools there, moving to Milledgeville, Georgia, in 1938. She attended Peabody Laboratory School and was graduated from Georgia State College for Women in 1945 with a degree in social science. An avid cartoonist and writer in her undergraduate years, O'Connor attended the famous Writers' Workshop at the State University of Iowa, from which she received an M.F.A. in 1947. Her master's thesis was a collection of short stories titled *The Geranium,* and the title story became O'Connor's first published story (*Accent,* summer 1946). From 1948 to 1950, O'Connor lived as the boarder of Sally and Robert Fitzgerald in Ridgefield, Connecticut. The Fitzgeralds, also devout Catholics, provided the fledgling author with the balance of solitude and communion necessary for her art. In 1950, however, O'Connor was stricken with the disease that had killed her father, disseminated lupus erythematosus, and she was forced to return to Milledgeville. There she remained for the rest of her life, living with her mother at Andalusia, the family farm just outside of town. O'Connor's novel *Wise Blood* was published in 1952, followed by an acclaimed collection of short stories, *A Good Man Is Hard to Find* (1955), and a second novel, *The Violent Bear It Away* (1960). At the time of her death in 1964, she had completed the stories for the posthumous collection *Everything That Rises Must Converge* (1965). For her works, O'Connor was many times the recipient of the O. Henry Award, and she received grants from the Ford Foundation and the National Institute of Arts and Letters. The posthumous collection *The Complete Stories* (1971) received the National Book Award in 1972.

A Catholic writer in the Bible Belt South, Flannery O'Connor was largely concerned with southern fundamentalist Protestants and the integrity of their search for salvation. From Hazel Motes, the protagonist of *Wise Blood,* through the tattooed Obadiah Elihue Parker of "Parker's Back," O'Connor presented characters beset by a hunger for God, which manifested itself in bizarre and often wildly humorous behavior. O'Connor described a world in which technology and progress inevitably fail to satisfy the deepest human needs, a world in which, as she put it, "the good is under construction." With a sharp ear for southern dialect and a fine sense of comic timing, Flannery O'Connor is now acknowledged as one of America's foremost writers of the short story. Her letters, published as *The Habit of Being* (1979), afford valuable insight into the qualities that shine through her writing, the depth of her faith, the discipline of her creative life, and her unfailing sense of humor. *(See also: Southern Lady; Women Writers)*

—Sarah Gordon

Further Reading

Asals, Frederick. *Flannery O'Connor: The Imagination of Extremity.* Athens: University of Georgia Press, 1982.

The Flannery O'Connor Bulletin, 1972–. Milledgeville: Georgia College.

Martin, Carter W. *The True Country: Themes in the Fiction of Flannery O'Connor.* Nashville, TN: Vanderbilt University Press, 1969.

May, John R. *The Pruning Word: The Parables of Flannery O'Connor.* Baton Rouge: Louisiana State University Press, 1976.

O'Connor, Flannery. *Collected Works by Flannery O'Connor.* Edited by Mary Jo Salter. New York: Library of America, 1989.

———. *Everything That Rises Must Converge.* New York: Farrar, Straus & Giroux, 1965.

———. *A Good Man Is Hard to Find.* New York: Harcourt Brace, 1955.

———. *The Habit of Being: Letters of Flannery O'Connor.* Edited by Sally Fitzgerald. New York: Farrar, Straus & Giroux, 1979.

———. *Mystery and Manners: Occasional Prose.* Selected and edited by Sally and Robert Fitzgerald. New York: Farrar, Straus & Giroux, 1969.

———. *The Violent Bear It Away.* New York: Farrar, Straus & Cudahy, 1960.

———. *Wise Blood.* New York: Harcourt Brace, 1952.

∽ O'Hair, Madalyn Murray (b. 1919)

Madalyn Murray O'Hair became America's most prominent atheist in 1962 when she filed the lawsuit *Murray v. Curlett,* 374 U.S. 203 (1963), which led to the Supreme Court's ban on prayer in schools. Although her fight for the separation of church and state made her one of the most hated women in America, she has never wavered in her beliefs.

She was born Madalyn Mays, daughter of John Irvin Mays, a prosperous industrial engineer, and Lena Scholle Mays in Pittsburgh, Pennsylvania. As a child, she attended the local Presbyterian church for services and Sunday school. When the stock market crashed in 1929, John Mays was forced to leave Pittsburgh and take his family on the road to find work, resulting in sporadic schooling for Madalyn. After high school graduation, she attended the University of Toledo and the University of Pittsburgh. When World War II began, she joined the U.S. Women's Army Corps, serving as a cryptographer for the staff of General Dwight D. Eisenhower and earning five battle stars in her travels to Africa and Italy. She married William J. Murray in the mid-1940s, and they had two sons, William J. Murray III and Jon Garth Murray. The marriage ended in divorce in the 1950s.

In 1948, Murray graduated from Ashland College, a small liberal arts school affiliated with the Church of the Brethren. Ashland College required two years of Bible study for graduation, and this, she later remarked, informed her later criticism and doubts. After graduation, Murray studied intellectual history for one year at Western Reserve (Case Western) University. She went on to study law at Ohio Northern University, later transferring to South Texas College of Law in Houston and receiving her LL.B. in 1953. She traveled to Washington, D.C., and spent two years at Howard University studying social work on a scholarship from the National Institutes of Health. Murray became a psychiatric social worker and attorney for family and child welfare agencies, probation departments, mental health clinics, and the U.S. Department of Health, Education, and Welfare.

In October 1960, Murray was working for the department of public welfare in Baltimore, Maryland. Her oldest son Bill, who attended Woodbourne Junior High School, voiced his objection to his forced participation in daily prayer to his mother, who wrote a letter to the school board asking for her son to be excused from the daily prayer ritual. When the school board refused her request on the basis of a policy directive that had gone unchallenged for almost fifty years, Murray withdrew both her sons from the Baltimore schools. The school board asked the Maryland Attorney General's office to review the case; it ruled that even though prayer and Bible reading were constitutional, a student who objected had the right to be excused from participation. This seemed to satisfy both parties, but when the Murray children returned to school, they were subjected to taunts and abuse by their fellow classmates as well as to discriminatory treatment by their teachers. Murray received hate letters and telephone calls. Furious at the treatment of her children and herself and outraged at her family's lack of privacy, she hired an attorney. On December 7, 1960, a lawsuit was filed in the Superior Court of Baltimore asking that prayer be removed from the Baltimore public schools. When the case was dismissed some four months later on the grounds that it would subject all students to atheistic beliefs, Murray took it to the Maryland Court of Appeals and then to the Supreme Court of the United States. Twenty-four hours after Murray filed with the Supreme Court, she was dismissed from her job at the welfare department on the grounds that her supervisor had evaluated her as incompetent.

On June 17, 1963, the Supreme Court ruled in favor of Murray on the basis that the Baltimore directive was unconstitutional. Although this was a victory for Murray, her family had suffered. Repeatedly, she and her sons were threatened with violence, and their property was destroyed. She formed the Freethought Society of America, Inc., and then the Other Americans, Inc., to try to find support. Her objective, she later stated, was not to curtail discussion or study of any subject, including religion but, rather, to oppose the imposition of religion.

In 1965, Murray moved to Austin, Texas, and married local artist Richard Franklin O'Hair. There, she founded the

American Atheist Center and the Society of Separationists. She also established the American Atheists Press.

In 2000, federal prosecutors brought to trial Gary Paul Karr as a co-conspirator with David Roland Waters in the 1995 murder of Madalyn Murray, her son John Garth Murray, and her grandaughter Robin Murray O'Hair May, and in the theft of Murray O'Hair's $500,000 in gold coins. *(See also: Christianity; Civil Rights; Religion; United States Supreme Court)*

—Susanne Grooms

Further Reading

O'Hair, Madalyn Murray. *The American Atheist.* Austin, TX: American Atheist Press, 1967.

———. *An Atheist Epic: Bill Murray, the Bible, and the Baltimore Board of Education.* Austin, TX: American Atheist Press, 1970.

———. *Let Us Pray: An Atheist Looks at Church Wealth.* Austin, TX: American Atheist Press, 1970.

———. *Why I Am an Atheist.* Austin, TX: American Atheist Press, 1965.

Stein, Gordon, ed. *The Encyclopedia of Unbelief.* New York: Prometheus, 1985.

Wright, Lawrence. *Saints and Sinners.* New York: Knopf, 1993.

⮞ O'Hare, Kate Richards (1876–1948)

Kate Richards O'Hare, socialist agitator and journalist, was one of the most popular American public speakers in the years 1900 to 1920, especially in the Plains states and the Southwest. She dedicated herself to promoting socialism and sought to solve contemporary problems, focusing especially on worker exploitation, tenant farmers' impoverishment, women's rights, working children, inadequate education, prison conditions, and armed conflict. She believed that all of these problems would ultimately be rectified by the triumph of socialism over capitalism.

As the daughter of Kansas homesteaders, she made her youthful commitments to temperance and missionary activism, but she soon emulated and even went beyond her father's lifelong devotion to political and social reform. She joined the expansive socialist movement in 1901 and, marrying a comrade, Francis P. O'Hare, became widely identified with the Socialist Party of America. While rearing four children, she conducted organizing tours, held party offices, worked on socialist newspapers with Eugene V. Debs, and ran for public office on her party's ticket, becoming the first woman candidate for the U.S. Senate when she was nominated in 1916 in Missouri. During World War I, she opposed U.S. intervention and became an outspoken critic of the war as a capitalist adventure. She was indicted under the Espionage Act for an antiwar speech in 1917, found guilty, and became one of the few women to be sentenced under that act. Receiving a five-year sentence, she served fourteen months in the Missouri State Penitentiary.

During O'Hare's incarceration, she sought with some success to upgrade prison conditions. Thereafter, discouraged by her party's factionalism and antagonistic to the emerging American communist movement, she devoted herself to penal reform. In 1938, she was assistant to the director of the Department of Penology of the State of California. At that time, she no longer considered herself a socialist and was married to Charles C. Cunningham, an engineer. By then, she was viewed as a critic who called public attention to many twentieth-century social problems. *(See also: Pacifism and the Peace Movement; Prison Reform; Socialist Party of America)*

—Sally M. Miller

Further Reading

Foner, Philip S., and Sally M. Miller, eds. *Kate Richards O'Hare: Selected Writings and Speeches.* Baton Rouge: Louisiana State University Press, 1982.

Miller, Sally M. *From Prairie to Prison: The Life of Social Activist Kate Richards O'Hare.* Columbia: University of Missouri Press, 1993.

⮞ O'Keeffe, Georgia (1887–1986)

A key figure in the development of American modernism, Georgia O'Keeffe is known mainly for her paintings of flowers and those of skulls, horns, and pelvises against a stark but colorful New Mexican background. She also painted the New York skyline and a series of abstractions reminiscent of landscapes. Common to all of these subjects is a rejection of conventional notions of perspective. Her flowers, for example, are magnified so that a single flower or part of a flower fills an entire canvas. These unusual subjects and unique perspectives are O'Keeffe's attempts to increase people's awareness of common things, revealing a reality often overlooked.

Another distinguishing characteristic of O'Keeffe's work, one she vehemently denied, is its rich, erotic imagery. The fleshy folds and projections of her flowers, the contours and sensuous colors of her landscapes, the holes and horns of the pelvises and skulls, and the juxtaposition of the circles, curves, and lines of her abstractions are all very sexual. This sensuousness often added to the mystical quality of O'Keeffe's paintings. Doors open into the same landscapes that surround them; lines draw the observer's eye off the canvas; skyscrapers radiate and reflect a mysterious sunlight.

Born in Sun Prairie, Wisconsin, O'Keeffe got her "big break" in 1916 when Alfred Stieglitz, renowned pioneer in photography and sponsor of modern art, showed her work in a three-artist exhibition at his avant-garde "291" gallery in New York City. O'Keeffe and Stieglitz married in 1924 and, while theirs was not a conventional marriage, the more than five hundred photographs he took of her between 1917 and 1937 have been called the greatest love poem in the history of photography. After Stieglitz's death in 1946, O'Keeffe made her home in Abiquiu, New Mexico, where she continued to paint until well into her nineties.

O'Keeffe was out of step with popular taste during much of her life, but the retrospective exhibit of her work at the Whitney Museum of Modern Art in 1970 brought the American public to recognize her unique artistic vision and style and the important impetus she provided for a number of contemporary American artists. Her autobiography is an important verbal and visual record of her life and art.

Among other places, O'Keeffe's work is on permanent display at the Georgia O'Keeffe Museum in Santa Fe, New Mexico, which opened in 1997. The museum's holdings include more than one hundred oil paintings, watercolors, charcoals, pastels, pencil and ink drawings, and sculptures created by the artist from 1916 to 1980. In July 1998, the Museum received the gift of O'Keeffe's personal belongings, including easels, canvas, papers, pastels, watercolors, oils, charcoals, hundreds of paint brushes, a library, and her wardrobe. *(See also: Art)*

—**Kenneth E. Gadomski**

Further Reading

Lisle, Laurie. *Portrait of an Artist: A Biography of Georgia O'Keeffe.* Albuquerque: University of New Mexico Press, 1986.
Merrill, Christopher, and Ellen Bradbury, eds. *From the Faraway Nearby: Georgia O'Keeffe as Icon.* Reading, MA: Addison-Wesley, 1992.
O'Keeffe, Georgia. *Georgia O'Keeffe.* New York: Viking, 1976.
http://www.okeeffemuseum.org [Georgia O'Keeffe Museum Website]

✑ Olmsted, Mildred (Scott) (1890–1990)

Mildred Scott Olmsted, social worker, pacifist, and long-time advocate of equal rights for women and minorities, was a national officer of the U.S. Section of the Women's International League for Peace and Freedom (WILPF) for over fifty years.

Born and raised in eastern Pennsylvania, Olmsted graduated from Smith College in 1912 and married Allen Olmsted, a founder of the American Civil Liberties Union, in 1921. They had one child, Peter, and adopted two more, Enid and Anthony. Following World War I, Olmsted volunteered for overseas work, first with the YMCA in France and later with the American Friends Service Committee in Germany. Converted to pacifism as a result, she returned to the United States in 1920 and joined the WILPF.

Committed to the WILPF's philosophy that there can be no lasting or just peace without freedom and no freedom without peace, Olmsted was the WILPF's national organization secretary in the 1930s and 1940s and its executive director in the 1950s and 1960s. In 1965, she was honored as the only member to serve on the organization's national board of directors for life, and in 1966, she was named executive director emeritus.

Olmsted's firm belief in democracy as both process and goal and her concern with overpopulation, environmental deterioration, and civil rights led her to active involvement in the American Civil Liberties Union, the National Association of Social Workers, the Joint Friends Peace Committee, Planned Parenthood, and the International Wildlife Federation. She was also a member of numerous ad hoc organiza-

tions and conferences: the U.N. Non-Governmental Organizations (1949), the Conference on Church and Peace (1953), the Soviet-American Women's Conference (1961), and the International Woman's Congress (1970). The recipient of many awards, she received honorary Doctor of Law degrees from Smith College in 1974 and Swarthmore College in 1987. *(See also: Pacifism and the Peace Movement; Women's International League for Peace and Freedom)*

—**Carrie Foster**

Further Reading

Bussey, Gertrude, and Margaret Tims. *Pioneers for Peace: Women's International League for Peace and Freedom, 1915–1965.* London: George Allen & Unwin, 1965. Reprint, London: WILPF British Section, 1980.
Foster-Hayes, Carrie. "The Women and the Warriors: Dorothy Detzer and the WILPF." Ph.D. diss., University of Denver, 1984.
Mildred Scott Olmsted Papers. Women's International League for Peace and Freedom Papers. Swarthmore College Peace Collection, Swarthmore, PA.
Women's International League for Peace and Freedom Papers. University of Colorado, Boulder.

✑ Olsen, Tillie (b. 1913)

Fiction writer and commentator on women writers, Tillie Olsen won the 1961 O. Henry Award for her 1961 novella *Tell Me a Riddle.* Olsen's career encapsulates the history of the women's movement and the field of women's literature. A working-class voice bound in traditional maternity and wage earning, Olsen came to attention with powerful stories originally published by small presses. At the beginnings of the Feminist Press in 1970, Olsen encouraged the rediscovery and reprinting of lost women's fiction—identifying Rebecca Harding Davis's *Life in the Iron Mills* and writing an extensive biographical and critical interpretation, a new kind of involved, speculative, empathetic criticism that explained rather than judged the absences and lapses of a writer's career. The recipient of foundation awards, visiting professorships, and lecture invitations, Olsen became the spokesperson for "lost" and silenced women in literature.

Born in Omaha, Nebraska, and graduated from high school, Olsen continued her education by reading at local public libraries. The daily demands of her adult life—motherhood and paid work—occupied the next twenty years. In the work recovered from this period of public "silence" and in the fiction and criticism of later life, Olsen has written of the disappointments of hard-pressed lives. *Yonnondio: From the Thirties* (1974) reprints pieces of a novel manuscript begun during Olsen's own period of silence, added to but still unfinished—re-creating, in a Depression Era story, the struggles of family, the strivings and defeats of parents.

Her nonfiction collection, *Silences* (1978), brought together fifteen years of informal talks and a lifetime of reading, explaining why only "one in twelve" writers were women. With the publication of *Silences,* Olsen was recognized as both spokeswoman and embodiment of the silences limiting the work of women writers. While *Silences* emphasized that most women writers had no children and that most women with children did not/could not write, many of Olsen's own publications focus on the relations of mothers and daughters. The confessional "I Stand Here Ironing" is the first and earliest work in the standard collection of Olsen's short fiction, *Tell Me a Riddle* (1976). "Ironing" painfully conveys a mother's regrets and fearful knowledge that she could have done more for her daughter. For the fifteenth anniversary of the Feminist Press, Olsen selected readings for *Mother to Daughter, Daughter to Mother, Mothers on Mothering: A Daybook and Reader* (1984), a collection that Florence Howe described as "a quilt—in words." Essays by Olsen also accompany a photography collection, *Mothers and Daughters: That Special Quality* (1987).

Still to some degree silenced by daily obstacles, more of her work consists of scattered pieces rather than sustained wholes. Along with the stunningly powerful short fiction, the more recent reprinted talks or lectures, calendar, and photography books are icons to silences. *(See also: Women Writers)*

—**Carol Klimick Cyganowski**

Further Reading

Davis, Rebecca Harding. *Life in the Iron Mills and Other Stories.* Edited and with a biographical interpretation by Tillie Olsen. Old Westbury, NY: Feminist Press, 1972, 1985.

Faulkner, Mara. *Protest and Possibility in the Writing of Tillie Olsen.* Charlottesville: University Press of Virginia, 1993.

Olsen, Tillie. *Silences.* New York: Delacorte, 1978.

———. *Tell Me a Riddle.* New York: Dell, 1976.

———. *Yonnondio: From the Thirties.* New York: Delacorte, 1974.

Pearlman, Mickey, and Abby H. P. Werlock. *Tillie Olsen.* Boston: Twayne, 1991.

Trendsky, Anne. "The Unnatural Silences of Tillie Olsen," *Studies in Short Fiction* 27 (Fall 1990): 509-16.

ᐍ Oneida Community (1848–1881)

The Oneida Community was established by John Humphrey Noyes on Oneida Creek between Syracuse and Utica, New York. This community was notable because it was one of the first "utopias" to grant full equality of position to women. Noyes subscribed to the doctrine of perfectionism, a notion that humans could be freed from sin. This belief led to the unique social structure of Oneida. The perfectionist view of marriage promoted the practice of "complex marriage" as a remedy for marital selfishness. In complex marriage, each person was "married" to every other person, thereby, in theory, eliminating jealousy and possessiveness. Sexual relations were viewed by the Oneida members as strengthening the spiritual bonds of the community.

Since Noyes and his followers abandoned the concept of original sin, women in particular benefited from the resulting belief that sexual shame was irrational. Women were encouraged to take the initiative in sexual couplings; indeed, older women often assumed the role of introducing young men to sexual intercourse. Noyes's ideas concerning marriage and the role of women were manifested in various ways: in the clothes the women wore, loose skirts to the knee with pantalets below; in birth control, the advocation of male continence; and in selective breeding to replace random propagation, eugenic experimentation known as *stirpiculture*. Although the Oneida residents were often criticized by society as immoral in their sexual practices, the social and sexual innovations practiced at Oneida did not result in promiscuous behavior because most of the inhabitants were sincere in their quest for truth and a life without sin.

The hostility and harassment from mainstream religious denominations drove Noyes to resettle in Canada in 1879. In his absence, the Oneidans abandoned his radical community system and reinstituted marriage and property rights among its members. A model of welfare capitalism under its reorganization as a joint-stock company, the Oneida Community became famous for its tableware and was still prospering a century after Noyes's death in 1886, although the community was officially "dissolved" on January 1, 1881. *(See also: Complex Marriage; Utopian Communities)*

—**Karen Loupe Gillenwaters**

Further Reading

Carden, Maren Lockwood. *Oneida: Utopian Community to Modern Corporation.* Baltimore: Johns Hopkins University Press, 1969.

Kern, Louis. *An Ordered Love: Sex Roles and Sexuality in Victorian Utopias—The Shakers, the Mormons and the Oneida Community.* Chapel Hill: University of North Carolina Press, 1981.

Klaw, Spencer. *Without Sin: The Life and Death of the Oneida Community.* New York: Allen Lane, Penguin, 1993.

Parker, Robert Allerton. *A Yankee Saint: John Humphrey Noyes and the Oneida Community.* New York: Putnam's, 1935.

Robertson, Constance Noyes. *Oneida Community: An Autobiography, 1851–1876.* New York: Syracuse University Press, 1970.

ᐍ Orgasm, Female

The pleasurable release of sexual tension through a series of muscular contractions, orgasm is considered the climax of sexual activity. How does one measure orgasm? Like sexuality itself, women's experiences and definitions of orgasm vary. Advice manuals have simultaneously insisted on the naturalness of orgasm and advised women in detail on what they feel like and how to attain them.

Ideas about women's capacity for orgasm have long been tied to ideologies of femininity. Throughout Western history, medical experts debated whether female orgasm was necessary for conception. Nineteenth-century medical writings diverged on whether women could or should experience orgasm. Some writers held that respectable women were incapable of sexual pleasure, while sexual radicals argued that all women were as orgasmic as men if properly stimulated. During the twentieth century, as sex surveys documented a rising awareness and experience of orgasm for women, many marriage manuals preached the importance of specific kinds of orgasms for women, defining some as normal and others as abnormal. In the 1920s and 1930s, experts recommended simultaneous orgasm by husband and wife as the only proper sexual climax. Freud believed that orgasms originated in the vagina, and American psychiatry followed suit, preaching that all orgasms were vaginal, and that they resulted from women's acceptance of their traditional role. Despite the findings of Alfred Kinsey (1953) and William Masters and Virginia Johnson (1966) that all orgasms originated in the clitoris, many experts believed that clitoral orgasms marked a woman as immature and possibly lesbian.

Anne Koedt's "The Myth of the Vaginal Orgasm" (1969) added a feminist twist to the findings of sexologists. Koedt questioned prevailing medical and psychiatric wisdom and argued that since all orgasms originated in the clitoris, the model of the vaginal orgasm was inaccurate and was based on a male definition of sexuality that equated it with penetration. Like other feminists, she encouraged women to experiment with their sexuality and to feel entitled to orgasms. More recently, advice books have counseled practice alone or with a partner for "preorgasmic" or "anorgasmic" women. Most current medical and sexual literature assumes that orgasm is the appropriate ending to sexual activity.

Women's experience, medical findings, and psychological theories about female orgasm have often diverged. The messages directed to women about the type of orgasms they should have, their frequency, and the methods for attaining orgasm, whether vaginal, clitoral, multiple, G-spot, or some combination of these, speak volumes about attitudes toward women's sexuality. (See also: Female Sexuality; Kinsey Report; Lesbianism; Marriage Manuals; Masturbation)

—**Miriam Reumann**

Further Reading

D'Emilio, John, and Estelle B. Freedman. *Intimate Matters: A History of Sexuality in America,* 2d ed. Chicago: University of Chicago Press, 1997.

Irvine, Janice. *Disorders of Desire: Sex and Gender in Modern American Sexology.* Philadelphia: Temple University Press, 1990.

Kinsey, Alfred et al. *Sexual Behavior in the Human Female.* Philadelphia: W. B. Saunders, 1953.

Koedt, Ann. "The Myth of the Vaginal Orgasm." In *Radical Feminism,* edited by Anne Koedt et al., 198-207. New York: Quadrangle, 1973.

Laqueur, Thomas. *Making Sex: The Body and Gender from the Greeks to Freud.* Berkeley: University of California Press, 1990.

Masters, William H., and Virginia E. Johnson. *Human Sexual Response.* New York: Bantam, 1966.

~ O'Sullivan, Mary Kenney
(1864–1943)

Pioneer labor organizer and feminist, Mary Kenney O'Sullivan was one of the principal founders of the National Women's Trade Union League (NWTUL) in November 1903. The original goals of the NWTUL were to organize women wage earners into unions and to win acceptance of women from established male labor organizations. The NWTUL provided the impetus for the successful fusion of the labor movement and the woman's movement.

O'Sullivan began working in a printing and binding factory while she was a child. In Chicago during the 1880s, her experiences and firsthand knowledge of the conditions under which women worked convinced her that women must organize into trade unions to improve hours and working conditions. First a member of Ladies Federal Local Union #2703, she began organizing other women bookbinders into the Woman's Bookbinding Union #1, which affiliated with the American Federation of Labor (AFL). She was subsequently elected a delegate to the Chicago Trades and Labor Assembly and soon after was invited to Hull House, a center of social reform activity. Working with Jane Addams and other social reformers, O'Sullivan coordinated efforts to promote trade unionism among women. Impressed with O'Sullivan's dedication and enthusiasm, Samuel Gompers, president of the AFL, appointed her the AFL's first woman general organizer in 1892; however, she served as an organizer for only five months. Suspicious of feminist involvement in the labor movement, the AFL refused to renew her appointment.

In 1893, she successfully lobbied for the first factory laws in Illinois, which regulated the employment of women and children and set up a state factory inspection department; Florence Kelley was appointed chief inspector with O'Sullivan her assistant. O'Sullivan also tried to persuade the legislature to pass a woman suffrage act, arguing that working women needed to vote to protect themselves with labor legislation, but she was unsuccessful.

She married Jack O'Sullivan, a trade union activist and labor editor of the *Boston Globe,* in 1894. The O'Sullivans lived at the Denison House social settlement in the Boston slums, where they had four children. Jack O'Sullivan encouraged his wife's continued work in the labor movement. She became the executive secretary of the Union for Industrial Progress, which she organized to investigate industrial working conditions. In 1902, her husband was killed when hit by a train. To support herself and her children, she managed a model tenement, the Improved Dwelling Association's Ellis Memorial in Boston; in its basement, she taught English to the tenants' families for many years.

By 1910, new leadership within the NWTUL had shifted its emphasis away from trade union organization and toward education and legislation. This, coupled with the AFL's indifference to women workers, convinced O'Sullivan to search for a more direct and concrete route than trade union activity to improve working conditions for women. While she continued her work with the social reform movement, in 1914 she became a factory inspector for the Massachusetts Department of Labor and Industries, a post she held until she was seventy. Although she remained committed to institutionalizing the place of women within the mainstream of organized labor, in the absence of labor interest in recruiting women, she felt that government action offered the best hope for safeguarding female industrial workers. *(See also: American Federation of Labor; Hull House; Kelley, Florence; National Women's Trade Union League; Settlement House Movement; Unions)*

—**Sandra J. Weidner**

Further Reading

Dye, Nancy Schrom. *As Equals and as Sisters: Feminism, the Labor Movement, and the Women's Trade Union League of New York.* Columbia: University of Missouri Press, 1980.

Foner, Philip S. *Women and the American Labor Movement, From the First Trade Unions to the Present.* New York: Macmillan, 1979.

❧ Our Bodies, Ourselves

Our Bodies, Ourselves, a medical guidebook written by the Boston Women's Health Book Collective, Inc., was one of the first outspoken and informative publications on women's health when it was released three decades ago. Since the first book was published in 1971, women have continued to develop their awareness of the injustices that prevent women from experiencing full and healthy lives. The volume grew out of collaborative efforts by women to share information on health, childbearing, and sexuality. Based on research drawn from medical books, journals, and life experiences, the initial work's basic emphasis was on questioning past medical treatment of women and informing readers of more positive ways to deal with individual health concerns. The Boston Women's Health Book Collective republished the volume in 1984 and 1992 as *The New Our Bodies, Ourselves.* These editions provided updated information and added new topics, including AIDS, new reproductive technologies, environmental and occupational health, and violence against women.

The newest volume, *Our Bodies, Ourselves for the New Century,* was thoroughly revised, and every chapter contains new and updated information along with Website addresses. It is based on and has grown out of women's experiences. It questions the medicalization of women's bodies and lives, while highlighting contrasts between holistic and conventional health practices. Women are challenged to use this information to question the assumptions underlying the care women receive, so that they can effectively deal with the health care system. It reflects the vital health concerns of women of diverse ages, ethnic and racial backgrounds, and

sexual orientations. Topics explored range from living a healthy life to relationships, sexuality, reproduction, growing older, and organizing for life changes.

The original book gave birth to three others by some of the same authors: *Ourselves and Our Children,* published in 1978, focusing on parenting skills; *Changing Bodies, Changing Lives,* published in 1981 and updated in 1987, providing sex information for teenagers; and *Ourselves, Growing Older* in 1987, revised in 1994 as *The New Ourselves, Growing Older,* addressing the neglected health concerns of middle-aged and older women. *Nuestras Cuerpos, Nuestras Vidas,* the Spanish-language adapation of *Our Bodies, Ourselves,* is scheduled to be published in 2000.

The Boston Women's Book Collective sponsors many projects and services including a Women's Health Information Center for distribution of free materials to women and organizations in the United States and elsewhere. *(See also: AIDS; Birth Control; Gynecology; Women's Liberation Movement)*

—**Sandra Riese**

Further Reading

Bell, Ruth. *Changing Bodies, Changing Lives.* New York: Random House, 1981, 1987.

Boston Women's Health Book Collective. *The New Our Bodies, Ourselves.* New York: Simon & Schuster, 1984, 1992.

———. *Our Bodies, Ourselves.* New York: Simon & Schuster, 1976.

———. *Our Bodies, Ourselves for the New Century: A Book by and for Women.* Rev. ed. New York: Touchstone, 1998.

———. *Ourselves and Our Children.* New York: Random House, 1978.

Doress-Worters, Paula B., and Siegal, Daina Laskin. *The New Ourselves, Growing Older.* New York: Simon & Schuster, 1994.

———. *Ourselves, Growing Older.* New York: Simon & Schuster, 1987.

❧ Ouvroirs (Workrooms)
(c. 1914/18)

Ouvroirs were the first attempts by American expatriates, mainly women, to offer civilians relief during World War I, predating American Red Cross work by three years.

Many long-term American expatriates, male and female, reacted to the declaration of the Great War by leaving the Continent and returning to the United States, or at least leaving France. Some returned after a short period, and propelled by love of their adopted country and concern for the already deprived civilians, established *ouvroirs.* Mary King Waddington established an *ouvroir* in early 1914, but credit is still given Edith Wharton for starting the first workroom to relieve unemployed civilian seamstresses, offering not only pay but also medical care, noon meals, and coal in winter; she later broadened her civilian relief work to include the homeless and refugees in France and Belgium.

Wharton was only one of many active American expatriates in Europe before 1917. Others concentrated on employment and day nurseries, hospital supplies, war charities, or war work. Groups included the American Fund for French Wounded (Gertrude Stein and Alice B. Toklas, for instance, drove a delivery truck for them), American Hostels for Refugees, the Franco-American General Committee, the Children of Flanders Rescue Committee, and the American Distributing Service. Among those active in these organizations were Elizabeth Cameron, Mildred Bliss, Elisina Royall Tyler, Anne Morgan, and Elsie de Wolfe; in acknowledgment of their dedicated and frequently dangerous work, European governments awarded honors to many of these expatriates.

After the entry of the United States into World War I, many more Americans became involved in nonmilitary work in Europe, and the American Red Cross played a more active role. *(See also: American Red Cross; Wharton, Edith; World War I)*

—**Maureen R. Liston**

Further Reading

Benstock, Shari. *Women of the Left Bank: Paris, 1900–1940.* Austin: University of Texas Press, 1986.

Earnest, Ernest. *Expatriates and Patriots: American Artists, Scholars and Writers in Europe.* Durham, NC: Duke University Press, 1968.

Schneider, Dorothy, and Carl J. Schneider. *Into the Breach: American Women Overseas in World War I.* New York: Viking, 1991.

✑ Pacifism and the Peace Movement

Women have long considered pacifism and the peace movement important. Pacifism, generally understood as "the refusal on grounds of principle to perpetrate or sanction acts of violence" (Chatfield 13), more specifically has meant the "absolute refusal to participate in, or support in any way, the waging of war" (Mayer 11). A philosophy of noncooperation and nonresistance, pacifism has its roots in the pre-Christian writings of the ancient Chinese and the Jewish prophet Isaiah. With Christianity came the Sermon on the Mount and Jesus' admonishment to "love thine enemy" and "turn the other cheek."

The pacifist envisions a world of equality and cooperative love wherein violence is totally repudiated. The pacifist perceives violence as the grossest immorality and places responsibility for change in the individual rather than in institutional arrangements. Through education and example, each individual must convert to a life of nonviolence; only then will society follow suit.

The pacifist's strategy of passive resistance to initiate political change assumes the natural goodness of all people and that even those who exercise power through both overt and covert violence are at heart persons of morality and ethically based rationality. Thus, the pacifist believes in ultimate triumph through the appeal by example to the adversary's conscience.

Most closely associated with pacifism in women's history were twentieth-century advocates Jane Addams and Dorothy Day. Day was cofounder of the *Catholic Worker.* Her opposition to militarism and her support of conscientious objectors reflected her Roman Catholic religious beliefs.

Addams was part of the less militant secular-humanist position of liberal pacifism active between World Wars I and II. She became chief spokesperson for female pacifists, and her book, *The Newer Ideals of Peace* (1907), was their main contribution to pacifist literature.

Addams led the formation of the nationwide Woman's Peace Party in January 1915. In April, Addams and a delegation of forty-seven women attended the International Congress of Women in The Hague, The Netherlands. The congress resulted in the formation of the Women's International League for Peace and Freedom (WILPF), which remains active. Although not all of its members today adhere to pacifism, the WILPF has been the most active and enduring of the women's peace organizations in modern history.

Over the next few years, other peace groups formed. The Women's Peace Society, created in 1919 under the leadership of Fanny Garrison Villard, believed in more extreme nonresistance than the WILPF. The year 1921 saw the birth of the Women's Peace Union of the Western Hemisphere and the Women's Committee for World Disarmament. That year, members of the Parent-Teacher Association (PTA) lobbied for peace. They believed one of the roles of public schools should be to educate the next generation to prevent war. In 1925, Carrie Chapman Catt organized the National Conference on the Cause and Cure of War. It consisted of the leaders and members of the major women's organizations with peace departments.

A resurgence of peace movements occurred in the 1960s in protest of the Vietnam War. Under the leadership of Bella Abzug and Dagmar Wilson, Women Strike for Peace (WSP) formed in 1962 to work for disarmament and a nuclear test ban treaty. The WSP led the way for other groups in demonstrating at the Pentagon and protesting the use of napalm against the Vietnamese. It was the first peace group to meet formally with representatives from North Vietnam.

Another group that continues to work in the tradition of nonviolence is the Martin Luther King, Jr. Center for Nonviolent Social Change in Atlanta, Georgia, established in 1968 by Mrs. Coretta Scott King. Dedicated to "building a world community of justice, peace, brother and sisterhood," the center is an official nongovernmental organization of the United Nations, with observer status. In recent decades, women have also been active in forming grassroots organizations, such as Grandmothers for Peace International, that employ nonviolent civil disobedience to protest the manufacture, testing, stockpiling, and transport of nuclear weapons. *(See also: Abzug, Bella Savitsky; Addams, Jane; Balch, Emily Greene; Catt, Carrie Chapman; Day, Dorothy; Huerta, Dolores; Vietnam War; Woman's Peace Party; Women's International League for Peace and Freedom; Women's Peace Union)*

—**Carrie Foster**
—**Merri Scheibe Edwards**

417

Further Reading

Addams, Jane. *Newer Ideals of Peace.* New York: Macmillan, 1907.

Brock, Peter. *Twentieth-Century Pacifism.* New York: Van Nostrand Reinhold, 1970.

Chatfield, Charles, ed. *International War Resistance through World War II.* New York: Garland, 1975.

Hartmann, Susan M. *From Margin to Mainstream.* New York: Knopf, 1989.

Mayer, Peter, ed. *The Pacifist Conscience.* Chicago: Regnery, 1967.

O'Neill, William L. *Everyone Was Brave.* New York: Quadrangle, 1971.

⟶ Paley, Grace (b. 1922)

Grace Paley, writer, teacher, and political activist, has authored three collections of highly original short stories illumining "the dark lives of women." Her first volume, *The Little Disturbances of Man* (1956), published in advance of the women's movement, broke new ground by rendering the extraordinary feel of women's daily experience with children and men. *Enormous Changes at the Last Minute* (1974) and *Later the Same Day* (1985) continue to concentrate on the ordinary lives of women as they encounter "life, death, desertion, loss, divorce, failure, love." In her most recent publications, Paley pays particular attention to women's lifelong bonds with one another—their friendships, family ties, and political associations.

Writing to articulate a woman's version of experience, Paley has forged a distinctive, widely acclaimed style. Her narrative structures show a contingency and openness that seem to arise from a feminine tolerance for surprising developments: Lovers come and go in these stories, children grow up, families divide, and women persist in changing. Most of Paley's stories take place in a busy interracial neighborhood in New York City and feature speakers from a variety of backgrounds. Paley has fashioned a verbal style that allows these new ethnic and female voices to be raised. Her female speakers best convey her style; they are good listeners and apt talkers, adept at making fresh remarks and posing unsettling questions. Her men are poor listeners and explainers, verbal self-appreciators. This ironic difference in the way men and women speak their way through life is the point of many of Paley's stories. In her work, women under very modern pressures express comic and candid understandings of sex, power, motherhood, work, community, and intimacy.

Although Paley's stories respect the unavoidable tragedy that touches most lives, her fiction is hopeful and her protagonists engaged. Paley herself has always participated in antiwar and feminist causes, a stance she traces to a family tradition of socialism and activism. At Sarah Lawrence College and City College of New York, where she holds faculty appointments, Paley's goal is to teach not only writing but listening, an activity that in Paley's view has important political dimensions.

Paley has two grown children and one grandchild. She is married to Robert Nichols, a writer, and lives with him in Vermont part of the year. Long admired by other writers, Paley has recently received more widespread recognition for the unmistakable voice that characterizes her fiction. Her latest work, *In the South Bronx of America* (1999), is a pictorial essay produced in conjunction with photographer Mel Rosenthal. *(See also: Women Writers)*

—Carol Snyder

Further Reading

Bach, Gerhard, and Blaine Hall, eds. *Conversations with Grace Paley.* Jackson: University Press of Mississippi, 1997.

Halfman, Ulrich, and Phillip Gerlach. "Grace Paley: A Bibliography," *Tulsa Studies in Women's Literature* 8 (1989): 339-54.

Hulley, Kathleen, ed. *Delta, Revue du Centre d'Etudes et de Recherches sur les Ecrivains du Sud aux Etats-Unis,* 14 (1982). [Special issue devoted to Paley]

Lidoff, Joan. "Clearing Her Throat: An Interview with Grace Paley," *Shenandoah* 32 (1981): 3-26.

Paley, Grace. *The Collected Stories.* New York: Farrar, Straus & Giroux, 1994.

———. *Enormous Changes at the Last Minute.* New York: Farrar, Straus & Giroux, 1974.

———. *Later the Same Day.* New York: Farrar, Straus & Giroux, 1985.

———. *Long Walks and Intimate Talks.* New York: Feminist Press, 1991.

———. *New and Collected Poems.* Gardiner, ME: Tilbury, 1992.

———. Preface. *A Dream Compels Us: Voices of Salvadoran Women,* edited by New Americas Press. Boston: South End Press, 1989.

Paley, Grace et al. *Ergo! The Bumbershoot Literary Magazine* 7 (1992).

Schleifer, Ronald. "Grace Paley: Chaste Compactness." In *Contemporary American Women Writers,* edited by Catherine Kainwater and William J. Scheick, 31-49. Lexington: University Press of Kentucky, 1985.

Taylor, Jacqueline. *Grace Paley: Illuminating the Dark Lives.* Austin: University of Texas Press, 1990.

⟶ Parent-Teacher Association (PTA)

The National Parent-Teacher Association (PTA) was founded in 1897, the end result of the "mothers' congress" held in Washington, D.C., in 1897 to involve mothers in public education. The founders, Phoebe Apperson Hearst and Alice McLellan Birney, devoted their lives to the cause of education. Birney emerged as the first president of the National Congress of Mothers, which became the National Congress of Parents and Teachers in 1924. A similar organization for blacks, the National Congress of Colored Parents and Teachers, was founded in 1927 by Selena Sloan Butler to foster improvements in the segregated school system in the South. Both organizations merged in 1970. In 1997, the National PTA celebrated its 100th anniversary. That same year, Lois Jean White was inaugurated as the first African American president of the National PTA.

For over a century, the vision of the PTA has remained virtually unchanged. It is one of the oldest, largest, and most powerful child advocacy groups in the nation. Its objectives are not only to secure a strong relationship between parents and teachers but to implement higher standards for children in the home, within the legal system, and in health care, as well as in the schools. The PTA continues to expand its goals for parents' involvement in their children's schools to reflect the changes in society and education.

Recommendations to improve the conditions of children are promulgated at the national level. Three commissions—education, health and welfare, and individual development—act as conduits for programs passed from the National PTA through the state level to the local level. Historically, the National PTA has contributed significantly to the passage of child labor and mandatory school attendance laws and to the development of juvenile courts, kindergartens, and school lunch programs. In 1997, the National PTA succeeded in getting content information included in TV ratings. Local PTA chapters foster the basic relationship between the teachers and parents and monitor social problems, such as drug abuse, in addition to working in cooperation with school districts and the community.

PTA membership numbers in the millions. Almost every area involving children's education has benefited from this organization. Dues are nominal, and any adult interested in the education of children is encouraged to join. Traditionally, women as the cultural guardians of children have constituted the working membership, but with the changing family in the last few years, men are taking a greater part.

The laudable objectives of the PTA fit nicely into the woman's sphere concept of the nineteenth and the early twentieth centuries, enabling women to work in a cooperative mode rather than in an adversarial one. *(See also: Education)*

—Jean M. Hayes

Further Reading

Birney, Mrs. T. W. *Childhood.* Introduction by G. Stanley Hall. New York: Frederich A. Stokes, 1905.

Golden Jubilee History, 1897–1947. Chicago: National Congress of Parents and Teachers, 1947.

National PTA Directory. Chicago: National Congress of Parents and Teachers. [published quarterly]

PTA Today. Chicago: National Congress of Parents and Teachers. [published seven times annually]

http://www.pta.org [National Parent-Teacher Association Website]

❦ Parker, Bonnie (1910–1934)

Bonnie Parker became one of the best-known gangsters of the early 1930s after a brief and bloody crime spree with her partner, Clyde Barrow. Born in Rowen, Texas, she completed high school there as an honor student. While working as a waitress in a Dallas cafe in 1930, she met Clyde Barrow and fell in love immediately. A month later, Barrow was sentenced to two years in jail for burglary. Parker smug-

Figure 45. Bonnie Parker
Bonnie Parker claims the dubious distinction of being one of the first notorious women gangsters. As portrayed by Faye Dunaway in the 1960s film *Bonnie and Clyde,* she served as a proto-feminist icon—an anti-heroine. Used by permission of UPI/Corbis-Bettmann.

gled a gun into the prison, and Barrow escaped but was recaptured within a few days. When Barrow gained parole in 1932, they picked up where they had left off.

In March 1932, the pair stole a car, but police spotted them and after a spectacular chase arrested Parker. Her partner escaped. She served three months in jail and then rejoined Barrow. They soon gained national attention as their crime rampage moved across the South and Midwest. A day after their reunion, the pair took a New Mexico sheriff hostage, dropping him off in Texas the next day. In September, their crime spree began in earnest; they raided a National Guard Armory in Fort Worth, Texas, stealing boxes of machine guns, automatic rifles, and shotguns.

The crime spree of Bonnie and Clyde took them across Texas and into bordering states. They robbed grocery stores and small-town banks, their biggest haul netting only $1,500. Bonnie and Clyde killed indiscriminately, murdering fifteen individuals. They were joined by several accomplices, including Barrow's brother, and the gang received national attention throughout 1933 and 1934, largely because of the brutal killing of several police officers and shoot-outs with authorities. Their crime spree was slowed only briefly because of wounds from gunfights with the police. Parker enjoyed the publicity, and she composed a poem titled "The

Story of Suicide Sal," a term given her by a journalist. The pair also took many photographs of each other holding guns from their small arsenal.

As their crime spree mounted, police stepped up their efforts to find Bonnie and Clyde, who narrowly escaped twice in early 1934. Their luck, however, would not hold much longer. On May 23, 1934, a well-armed posse killed Bonnie Parker and Clyde Barrow at a roadside ambush near Gibland, Louisiana. Their dramatic demise ensured them a prominent place in folk legend and popular culture. *(See also: Criminals; Depression Era)*

—**Robert G. Waite**

Further Reading

Frost, H. Gordon, and John H. Jenkins. *"I'm Frank Hammer." The Life of a Texas Peace Officer.* Austin, TX: Pemberton, 1968.

Hinton, Ted. *Ambush: The Real Story of Bonnie and Clyde.* Austin, TX: Shoal Creek, 1979.

Treheerne, J. E. *The Strange History of Bonnie and Clyde.* New York: Stein & Day, 1985.

⚬ Parker, Dorothy (Rothschild)
(1893–1967)

Dorothy Parker was known for her sharp wit, which she loosed on friends and in her writing. This legendary wit earned her a position as one of the first writers for Harold Ross's *New Yorker* magazine (founded in 1925), and it also gave her status with the Algonquin Round Table, a clique of popular New York writers that met informally during the 1920s.

Parker's stories and poems, along with plays and book reviews, appeared in the *New Yorker* throughout her lifetime, and she can be credited with helping to mold the magazine's recognizable style. Her stories, which depict middle- and upper-class Americans engaged in a battle of the sexes, emphasize that love is fickle and that men, especially, are unfaithful. Insecure in their love and in themselves and afraid to show either pain or desire, her women characters agree on the surface to treat love as a game that must be played with calculated wit, not candor. Not surprisingly, Parker's concomitant theme in her stories, and especially in her poems, underscores life's mutability and women's sexual mortality, in the face of which it is best to die young and pretty. Her poems revolve around suicidal themes but usually with an ironic twist that attempts to make light of serious truths. For example, one love poem ends: "My own dear love, he is all my heart-/And I wish somebody'd shoot him."

Parker's personal unhappiness influenced her writing about the tentative and unhappy nature of male-female relationships and of modern life. She was born into a well-to-do family (her father was a garment manufacturer in New York), but her Scottish mother died while Parker was an infant. Her sense of loss was complicated by the strict upbringing imposed by her father and stepmother, and she welcomed the chance to strike out on her own. In 1916, she

Figure 46. Dorothy Parker
Acerbic both in her writing and in her personal style, Dorothy Parker crafted sharply observed plays, short stories, and poems, largely about the problematic male-female relationship. Used by permission of UPI/Corbis-Bettmann.

began writing for Frank Crowninshield (at *Vogue* magazine and then at *Vanity Fair*) before joining the *New Yorker* in 1925. Parker's first marriage, to Edwin Pond Parker II in 1917, was short-lived, and she married actor-writer Alan Campbell (she continued to use Parker's name) in 1933. Although they divorced in 1947, they remarried three years later; and overall, they maintained a personal and professional relationship (Campbell served ably as her manager) that afforded her a degree of personal stability, despite several unsuccessful suicide attempts by Parker.

Although some critics see Parker's work as limited (her verse clever but slight and her stories sharp and telling but scanty in number), she is still read today as one who was unafraid to treat female issues truthfully, if sardonically. Many of her one-liners, such as "Men seldom make passes/At girls who wear glasses," have worked their way into the canon of American popular speech, and Parker herself became identified with the 1920s flapper image that outwardly bespoke a new liberation. Inwardly, this image was fed by the restlessness and the romantic and spiritual yearning that characterized the era for which Dorothy Parker became an ironically clever spokeswoman. *(See also: Flapper; Hellman, Lillian; Women Writers)*

—**Linda Patterson Miller**

Further Reading

Frewin, Leslie. *The Late Mrs. Dorothy Parker.* New York: Macmillan, 1987.

Gill, Brendan, ed. and intro. *The Portable Dorothy Parker.* Rev. ed. New York: Viking, 1973.

Keats, John. *You Might as Well Live: The Life and Times of Dorothy Parker.* New York: Simon & Schuster, 1970.

Kinney, Arthur F. *Dorothy Parker.* Boston: G. K. Hall, 1978.

Meade, Marion. *Dorothy Parker: What Fresh Hell Is This?* New York: Penguin, 1989.

✦ Parks, Rosa (b. 1913)

Civil rights leader and community activist Rosa Parks was born in Tuskegee, Alabama, but spent much of her formative years in or near Montgomery. Her father was a carpenter; her mother, Leona, was a teacher. They instilled in their daughter a sense of the injustice of racial discrimination. She attended Alabama State College until a few weeks before her twentieth birthday, when she married Raymond Parks, a young barber.

The young couple resided in Montgomery, where Parks became an active member and frequent officer of the local chapter of the National Association for the Advancement of Colored People (NAACP). She was also active in church affairs and with the Montgomery Voters League, an organization trying to register more blacks. Her sense of the possibilities for interracial harmony had been strengthened by attending for two weeks the Highlander Folk School, an interracial academic community in Tennessee.

While working as a tailor's assistant at the Montgomery Fair Department Store in 1955, Parks was thrust into the national spotlight. On the evening of December 1, 1955, while riding home on a public bus, she firmly but quietly refused to give up her seat to white passengers, as was the custom in Montgomery. The bus driver summoned the police, and Parks was arrested, jailed, and brought to trial. The arrest of this respectable, churchgoing, forty-two-year-old woman galvanized the black community of Montgomery into action. Led by her friend E. D. Dixon, the president of the Montgomery NAACP, and the local black clergy, a Montgomery Improvement Association was quickly organized under the presidency of Rev. Martin Luther King, Jr.

A successful bus boycott was soon organized, and thirteen months after the boycott began, a federal court order ended the racial segregation of buses in Montgomery. King's Gandhian "passive resistance" policy had won its first major victory. Despite threats, bombings, and other forms of intimidation, the civil rights movement had begun. Parks had been fired from her job as a result of the controversy, and her husband became ill as a result of the pressures put on the family. Nevertheless, she continued to work for the Montgomery Improvement Association until the family relocated to Detroit in 1957.

In Detroit, Parks worked as a dressmaker and continued her civil rights and community activities. She has been particularly active with youth work and job guidance. A fre-

Figure 47. Rosa Parks

Her simple, dignified refusal to sit at the back of the bus in 1955 led to her arrest and was a catalyst for the Montgomery bus boycott, a key struggle in the civil rights movement. Used by permission of UPI/Corbis-Bettmann.

quent public speaker, Parks has also continued to be active in church work, serving as a deaconess at St. Matthews' African Methodist Episcopal Church in Detroit. Still hailed as the "mother of the civil rights movement," Rosa Parks also worked on the staff of Representative John Conyers in Detroit. *(See also: Civil Rights; National Association for the Advancement of Colored People)*

—Jonathan W. Zophy

Further Reading

Friese, Kay. *Rosa Parks.* Englewood Cliffs, NJ: Silver-Burdette, 1990.

Garrow, David. *Bearing the Cross: Martin Luther King, Jr., and the Southern Leadership Conference.* New York: Morrow, 1986.

King, Jr., M. L. *Stride toward Freedom: The Montgomery Story.* New York: Harper, 1958.

Parks, Rosa. *Rosa Parks, Mother to a Movement.* New York: Dial, 1992.

Stevenson, Janet. "Rosa Parks Wouldn't Budge," *American Heritage* 23 (1972): 56-64, 85.

✦ Parsons, Lucy González (1852–1942)

Lucy González Parsons was an orator, writer, and organizer for the American labor movement. A posthumous tribute to her in the *Daily Worker,* the newspaper for the International Labor Defense, described her as a "proud woman of Negro and Mexican ancestry." However, throughout her lifetime she denied any African heritage. Her actual background is unknown. She used three different maiden names, Hull, Carter, and González, and no known records exist of her birth or marriage.

Born in Johnson County, Texas, she married Albert R. Parsons and moved to Chicago in 1874. There, they opened a dress and suit shop and became involved in the Workingmen's Party, the Workingwomen's Party, the Socialist Labor Party, and the Knights of Labor. Her first known writings appeared in the December 7, 1878, *Socialist,* a semiofficial newspaper of the Socialist Labor Party. She later wrote for the *Alarm,* the *Denver Labor Enquirer,* and the *Labor Defender* and edited several books on anarchist leaders. In 1879, they had a son, Albert, Jr., and in 1881, a daughter, Lulu Eda. From 1884 to 1886 she and Lizzy Swank-Holmes worked to organize seamstresses demanding an eight-hour day and improved working conditions.

In 1886, the Parsons received national attention as anarchists when the Chicago police arrested Albert and seven other men for their role in the Haymarket Riot, a bloody confrontation between police and labor radicals in which seven policemen and several workers died. All eight of those arrested were convicted; seven received death sentences. For the next eighteen months, Lucy waged a massive campaign to save the Haymarket martyrs, speaking throughout the nation to gather financial and moral support. The campaign was unsuccessful; Albert and three other Haymarket co-conspirators were executed on November 11, 1887.

After her husband's death, she continued to write articles, led numerous protests and marches, and made stirring speeches. She was militant, initially advocating workers to arm themselves for the purpose of self-defense against attacks by management or police, and later recommended violent revolution against capitalism. She helped found the Industrial Workers of the World in 1905. Russian communism became attractive to Lucy in the 1920s, and in 1925, she proclaimed that the Communist Party was the legitimate successor to prior radical movements. In 1926, she helped found the International Labor Defense, an organization that provided legal defense for workers and political dissidents.

She believed oppression of women resulted from capitalism and women's economic dependence on men. She saw life from a working-class perspective and analyzed society in terms of class struggle. Although she advocated a woman's right to divorce, the availability of birth control and contraceptive devices, freedom from rape, and economic equality, women's issues were secondary to the class struggle. She remained active in the labor movement until her death at eighty-nine in a house fire. *(See also: Chicana; Communist Party; Industrial Workers of the World; Journalism; Knights of Labor; Socialism)*

—**Joyce Ann Kievit**

Further Reading

Ashbaugh, Carolyn. *Lucy Parsons: American Revolutionary.* Chicago: Charles A. Kerr, 1976.

Dubofsky, Melvyn. *We Shall Be All: A History of the Industrial Workers of the World.* Chicago: Quadrangle, 1969.
Foner, Philip S. *History of the Labor Movement in the United States.* New York: International Publishers, 1969.
Knights of Labor Collection. State Historical Society. Madison, WI.
Parsons, Lucy E., ed. *Altgeld's Reasons for Pardoning Fielden, Schwab, and Neebe.* Chicago: Lucy E. Parsons, 1915.
———, ed. *The Famous Speeches.* Chicago: Lucy E. Parsons, 1909.

➴ Patriarchy

As a term describing the origins of the gender system, *patriarchy* was initially employed in the narrow historical context that referred to the development of the legal prerogatives of men within the male-headed households under Greek and Roman law. The male head of household had both legal and economic control over the female and minor dependent males within the family. According to some historians, patriarchy was established in antiquity and expired by the turn of the twentieth century, as married women's property rights and women's civil rights were granted in Western nations. However, women's historians in particular have traced the beginning of patriarchy to the third millennium and challenge the presumption of the demise of patriarchy by citing that its adaptation of the gender system through limited legal reforms during the Victorian and Progressive Eras actually ensured its continued presence into the twentieth century. As the historical debate over patriarchy progressed through the 1980s, women's historian Gerda Lerner asserted that the term patriarchy properly referred to the institutionalized system of male dominance over women and children in the family, which extended male dominance over women into society as well. *(See also: Marriage; Married Women's Property Acts; Sex-Gender System; Sexism)*

—**Angela M. Howard**

Further Reading

Engels, Friedrich. *The Origins of the Family, Private Property, and the State.* Chicago: Kerr, 1902. Reprint, New York: International Publishers, 1970.
Lerner, Gerda. *The Creation of a Feminist Consciousness from the Middle Ages to 1870.* New York: Oxford University Press, 1993.
———. *The Creation of Patriarchy.* New York: Oxford University Press, 1986.

➴ Patrons of Husbandry

The Patrons of Husbandry, better known as the Grange, began in 1867 and almost immediately provided larger roles for women than had any previous agricultural association. Local, or subordinate, granges included women members from their beginning; the first representative National Grange, which met in 1873, had no women members but adopted a constitution that admitted the wives of subordinate grange masters to the state granges and the wives of state grange masters to the National Grange. Women were not at first expected to hold offices in their own right, but four women's offices existed by 1869. These offices—Ceres, Flora, Pomona, and Lady Assistant Steward—were mainly ornamental; they had little responsibility and no authority. A few women held the important working offices starting in the 1870s, and their share of leadership rose steeply after 1895, when Sarah G. Baird started her seventeen years as master of the Minnesota State Grange. In 1901, an informed observer guessed that a majority of local grange lecturers, the officers who planned programs, were women.

The order's Declaration of Purposes, adopted in 1874, called for a "proper appreciation of the abilities and sphere of women." Early leaders denied that they had any sympathy with "women's rights"; they simply wanted to help farm women overcome the stultifying effects of drudgery and rise to the period's ideal of true womanhood. But the order attracted some committed feminists, such as Flora M. Kimball of California, who persuaded it to support equal suffrage. The California State Grange passed an equal suffrage resolution in 1878; other states, and eventually the National Grange, followed. The "home protection" argument that women needed the vote to protect the domestic sphere, which the Woman's Christian Temperance Union (WCTU) employed so effectively, was also persuasive in the Grange. Many women Grange leaders, notably Eliza C. Gifford of New York, were active in the WCTU.

The order never expended much of its energy on equal suffrage; instead, it has consistently stressed purely domestic concerns. The Declaration of Purposes, for example, promises to "enhance the comforts and attractions of our homes," and calls for "domestic science" courses in the agricultural colleges. The order's emphasis on domesticity has been especially strong since 1910, when Elizabeth H. Patterson of Maryland persuaded the National Grange to create a standing committee on home economics.

Charles Gardner, the order's own best historian, claims that it "turned on the radiant light of hope for rural woman." That may be a little fulsome, but it is typical of grangers' pride in their service to women. *(See also: Agriculture: Preindustrial and Nineteenth-Century United States; Cult of True Womanhood)*

—**Donald B. Marti**

Further Reading

Gardner, Charles. *The Grange—Friend of the Farmer, 1867–1947*, pp. 191-207. Washington, DC: National Grange, 1949.

Hebb, Douglas Charles. "The Woman Movement in the California State Grange, 1873–1880." Master's thesis, University of California—Berkeley, 1950.

Marti, Donald B. *Women of the Grange: Mutuality and Sisterhood in Rural America*. Westport, CT: Greenwood, 1991.

Figure 48. Alice Paul
Alice Paul, broadcasting from the National Woman's Party headquarters in Washington, D.C., on April 4, 1922. Used by permission of UPI/Corbis-Bettmann.

⚘ Paul, Alice (1885–1977)

A tough and single-minded reformer on behalf of equal rights for women, Alice Paul militantly challenged political thinking in the twentieth century. She was educated at Swarthmore College (B.A.), the University of Pennsylvania (M.A., Ph.D.), Washington College of Law (L.L.B., L.L.M.), and American University (D.C.L.). While Paul was studying in England from 1907 to 1909, Emmeline Pankhurst introduced her to suffrage philosophy and militant activism. Returning to Washington, D.C., Paul lobbied for enfranchisement. She and Lucy Burns organized the first major suffrage parade in Washington on the eve of the presidential inauguration in 1913.

In the period from 1913 to 1917, Alice Paul organized the final drive to secure woman suffrage. In 1913, she established the Congressional Union, which was singularly and militantly committed to securing a federal woman suffrage amendment by lobbying Congress and pressuring the president. In 1915, she organized an "auto pilgrimage" to carry a petition with a half-million signatures from San Francisco to Washington. Because of her insistence on approaching suffrage for women through a federal amendment only, she broke with the National American Woman Suffrage Association and founded the National Woman's Party (NWP).

Paul ruthlessly applied to the Democrats the British suffragist strategy of "holding the party in power" responsible, and as early as 1917, the National Woman's Party began using militant tactics, which included sending delegations to the president and picketing the White House when denied that access. Picketing suffragists were arrested. To contest their incarceration, these women staged hunger strikes that brought publicized forced-feedings of the prisoners. Public outcry resulted in the release of the suffragists. Some of her contemporaries believed that Alice Paul's militancy and NWP opposition to World War I delayed success in attaining woman suffrage; others credited the value of NWP tactics as adding urgency to the Wilson's conversion to the cause.

With the ratification of the Nineteenth Amendment, the National Woman's Party began to focus on "equal rights for women." In 1923, Paul wrote an earlier version of the Equal Rights Amendment (ERA), which sparked a four-decade division among the supporters of women's rights. Some women supported the concept of an ERA that would grant unconditional legal equality to women, while others were committed to the hard-won "protective legislation" of the Progressive Era, which assumed that gender was a legitimate distinction in formulating the regulation of working hours and conditions for women. Paul's last years were spent lobbying for the ERA that emerged from Congress in 1972 and failed to achieve ratification by the extended 1982 deadline.

In the intervening 1930s and 1940s, Alice Paul turned to international affairs as chairman of the Nationality Committee of the Inter-American Commission of Women, which worked to grant equal national rights to women in the Western Hemisphere. She also lobbied the League of Nations for women's equality and assisted in creating the World Woman's Party. This group sent delegates to the convention that drafted the charter of the United Nations, which included equal rights in its preamble. *(See also: Equal Rights Amendment; National Woman's Party; Suffrage)*

—**Ted C. Harris**

Further Reading

Blatch, Harriott Stanton, and Alma Lutz. *Challenging Years: The Memoirs of Harriott Stanton Blatch*. New York: Putnam, 1940.

Cott, Nancy F. "Feminist Politics in the 1920s," *Journal of American History* 71 (June 1984): 43-68.

Irwin, Inez Hayes. *The Story of the Woman's Party*. New York: Harcourt, Brace, 1921. Reprint, New York: Krans Reprint, 1971. Also republished as *Up Hills with Banners Flying*. Penobscott, ME: Traversity, 1964.

Lunardini, Christine. *From Equal Suffrage to Equal Rights: Alice Paul and the National Woman's Party, 1910–1928*. New York: New York University Press, 1988.

Zimmerman, Loretta Ellen. "Alice Paul and the National Woman's Party, 1912–1920." Ph.D. diss., Tulane University, 1964.

———. "The Jurisprudence of Equality," *Journal of American History* 28 (June 1991): 185-225.

∾ Peabody, Elizabeth Palmer
(1804–1894)

Elizabeth Palmer Peabody, author and educator, successfully promoted the transplanting of German philosopher Friedrich Froebel's concept of the kindergarten to the United States. As one who had struggled to refine her own ideas about education, development, and the woman's sphere over a lifetime of experiences and conversations with the likes of transcendentalists William Ellery Channing, Margaret Fuller, and Bronson Alcott, Peabody

quickly perceived the wisdom of Froebel's thought when she was first introduced to it in 1859. Seeing the validity of his process of infant culture, schoolteacher Peabody established the first American kindergarten in Boston in 1860 as a showcase for Froebelian methodology.

Continually dissatisfied with the results of her infant culture experiment, Peabody went to Europe in 1867 to study the original kindergarten. While in Germany, she began to understand the kindergarten in a new light. It was clear to her that Froebel had intended the kindergarten to be totally distinct in both purpose and methodology from the traditional school. The true Froebelian kindergarten was structured so that the young child was enabled to unfold inherent intellectual, moral, and artistic capabilities. Such development was to be assisted by the careful nurture of a woman who had been intensively trained in both the art and the science of an ideal form of maternal instinct and method. Understanding the relationship that Froebel envisioned between his concept of child nurture and an educated, enabled womanhood, kindergartner Peabody returned to Boston and repudiated all of her earlier efforts of infant culture.

She set to work writing, lecturing, and organizing exhibits that promoted genuine kindergartens. Relying on her wide network of influential friends, she advocated the kindergarten cause before prominent audiences throughout the East and Midwest. Peabody successfully garnered philanthropic support for the young movement and persuaded German kindergartners Maria Kraus-Boelte, Emma Marwedel, and Alma Kriege to emigrate to the United States to train American women in Froebelian principles. She argued for endowed professorships of kindergartening in each of the nation's normal schools. Peabody courted the favor of publishers Milton Bradley and Ernst Steiger and convinced them to manufacture kindergarten materials and to publish books about Froebel. Eventually, the kindergarten concept was incorporated into public education.

Through her successful appeals to society to provide for the appropriate nurture of children through intensive training for maternal duties, Peabody established a reservoir of hope that the kindergarten would gain acceptance as a unique profession for women. *(See also: Blow, Susan Elizabeth; Education; Teaching)*

—**Catherine Cosgrove**

Further Reading

Baylor, Ruth. *Elizabeth Palmer Peabody*. Philadelphia: University of Pennsylvania Press, 1965.

Peabody, Elizabeth. *Lectures in the Training School for Kindergartners*. Boston: Heath, 1893.

———. "Origin and Growth of Kindergartens," *Education* 2 (May/June 1882): 507-27.

∾ Peace Corps

The Peace Corps was established as an independent bureau of the U.S. government in 1961 to send American volunteers to foreign countries that have requested assistance. The stated purposes of the Peace Corps are (a) to help the people of interested countries meet their needs for trained men and women, (b) to promote a better understanding of the people of the United States on the part of the people served, and (c) to promote within American society a better understanding of people in other countries. Peace Corps volunteers are assigned for two-year tours of duty, and they work on projects in education, health, agriculture, environment, and small business development.

Although many give Congressman Henry Reuss credit, the idea for such a program came from several different people over a period of time, gaining most attention when John F. Kennedy proposed it during his presidential campaign. Under the direction of its first director, Sargent Shriver, the corps grew rapidly at first, from an initial 750 by the end of 1961 to over 15,000 volunteers deployed in the late 1960s. President Nixon took a dim view of the Peace Corps, however, in part because many volunteers opposed the Vietnam War and his other policies. He took away its independence by merging it into ACTION, a new federal agency, along with VISTA (Volunteers in Service to America), also referred to as the "domestic Peace Corps," and other volunteer programs. In 1977, President Carter appointed as director Carolyn R. Payton (b. 1925), an African American woman who was then dean of counseling at Howard University and former deputy director of the corps. She resigned after only a year, however, because she did not see eye to eye with the head of ACTION, Sam Brown, who wanted a Peace Corps of highly trained technical specialists. This resulted in a largely white and male applicant pool. Payton's vision included paraprofessionals, including more women and African Americans, who could be trained to be better teachers. In terms of women's issues, 1978 was an important year because "women in development" was added to the Peace Corps' official aid categories.

Although the Peace Corps reemerged on its own in 1981, support during the years of President Reagan and President Bush was quite problematic. That the corps continued at all was due in large measure to the efforts of its second woman director, Loret Miller Ruppe (1936–1996), who served from 1981 to 1989, longer than any other director to date. With no paid work experience to her credit before being appointed by President Reagan, she seemed to have been chosen because she was of the Miller brewing family, had cochaired the Reagan-Bush campaign in Michigan, and was the wife of a six-term former Republican congressman, but she quickly proved herself to skeptics. On her first visit to the White House as director, Ruppe was introduced to her liaison, who informed her that he had recommended that the Peace Corps be abolished. She promptly requested another contact person. She promoted the Peace Corps in terms of self-sufficiency and volunteerism, language understood by conservatives, and effectively used her familiarity with Congress to obtain increases in the corps budget. At her death in 1996, Ruppe bequeathed a generous sum to the Peace Corps to provide women in developing countries with small

grants to support grassroots developmental projects. Besides Payton and Ruppe, the Peace Corps is unusual in having had two more women among the fourteen people who have headed the agency: Elaine L. Chao (b. 1953) from 1991 to 1992 and former Peace Corps volunteer Carol Bellamy (b. 1942) from 1993 to 1995.

Women volunteers have played a major role in the Peace Corps throughout its history. In the early years, they were drawn to the corps because they found less sex discrimination and more rapid advancement than in other government agencies. Hapgood and Bennett attribute this openness to the fact that the Peace Corps was originally headed by people outside the government, who fostered an esprit they described as "creative anarchy," free from tradition and less discriminatory by race, age, or sex. Nevertheless, fewer women than men served in the early days. In 1965, for example, only 40 percent of the volunteers were women. By 1998, the percentage had changed dramatically and almost reversed (59 percent women to 41 percent men).

Peace Corps returnees can opt to continue their volunteer service by speaking to schools participating in the Peace Corps' "World Wise Schools" program or by entering the Crisis Corps, which responds to natural disasters and humanitarian crises. Dr. Mae Carol Jemison (b. 1956), the nation's first African American woman astronaut, is one of many former corps volunteers who have gone on to serve the country in other capacities.

In the 1990s, the number of volunteers hovered around 6,500 to 7,000 per year. President Clinton proposed raising the number of volunteers from 7,000 to 10,000 for the year 2000.

AmeriCorps is a newer "domestic Peace Corps" begun under President Clinton. It is run by the Corporation for National Service, a public-private partnership that also absorbed VISTA. In October 1998, the fifth class of AmeriCorps members was sworn in, bringing the total number of current and former members to more than 100,000. A total of 40,000 members served in 1998-99. Student participants in AmeriCorps earn funds to apply toward college expenses by working on projects such as housing renovations, neighborhood policing, or child immunization. The AmeriCorps National Civilian Community Corps (NCCC) works on environmental issues. In 1998, nearly three-fourths of the NCCC volunteers were women. (See also: Vietnam War; Voluntarism)

—Phyllis Holman Weisbard
—Judith Pryor

Further Reading

Hapgood, David, and Meridan Bennett. *Agents of Change: A Close Look at the Peace Corps.* Boston: Little, Brown, 1968.

Moore, Honor. "The Heiress Who Saved the Peace Corps," *New York Times Sunday Magazine* (December 29, 1996): 34.

Schwartz, Karen. *What You Can Do for Your Country: An Oral History of the Peace Corps.* New York: William Morrow, 1991.

http://www.peacecorps.gov [Peace Corps Website]

ᴂ Peale Family, Women Artists of the

There are several notable women artists in the family of Charles Willson Peale, an important American artist and cultural leader of the Federalist period. Best known are his three nieces, Anna Claypoole Peale (1791–1878), Margaretta Angelica Peale (1798–1882), and Sarah Miriam Peale (1800–1885), and a granddaughter, Mary Jane Peale (1827–1902).

Anna, Margaretta, and Sarah were the daughters and pupils of James Peale, a miniaturist. Anna was primarily an extremely skillful painter of miniature portraits. Her works were in great demand and were exhibited at the Pennsylvania Academy of Fine Arts. In 1824, she and Sarah were the first women elected to membership in the academy. Her painting career ended following her second marriage in 1842.

Sarah Peale is America's first professional woman artist. She went from the family home in Philadelphia to Baltimore to study with her cousin, Rembrandt Peale. Establishing a studio in Baltimore, she became a leading portrait painter. In 1847, she traveled to St. Louis, where she stayed for three decades painting portraits and still-lifes, for which she received many prizes. In 1878, she returned to Philadelphia. Her portrait style is realistic, with firm drawing, rich color, and elegant rendering of texture.

Margaretta Peale was a talented still-life painter who also did some portraiture. Her work was exhibited at the Pennsylvania Academy from 1828 until 1837.

Mary Jane Peale, the only daughter of Rubens Peale, studied painting with her uncle, Rembrandt Peale, and with Thomas Sully. She was building a career as a portrait painter in New York City but returned in 1855 to Pennsylvania to care for her elderly parents. She is best known for her still-lifes, which usually consist of a rich array of fruit on a table in soft, diffused light.

Of the lesser-known Peale women artists, Harriet Cany Peale (c. 1800–1869), the second wife of Rembrandt Peale, was his pupil prior to their marriage in 1840. She was primarily a copiest, often assisting her husband in the production of his many "porthole" portraits of George Washington. Rosalba Carriera Peale (1799–1874), Rembrandt's daughter, became a painter in oils and a lithographer. Mary Jane Simes, granddaughter of James Peale, was a miniaturist in the style of her aunt and teacher, Anna Claypoole. She exhibited miniatures at the Pennsylvania Academy between 1825 and 1830 but retired from painting after her marriage. Anna Peale Sellers (1824–1905), a granddaughter of Charles Willson Peale, studied art in Rome during the 1860s and attended classes at the Pennsylvania Academy, where she exhibited from 1866 until 1878. *(See also: Art)*

—Joan Jacks Silverman

Further Reading

American Painting from the Collection of James H. Ricau. New York: Richard York Gallery, Nov. 4, 1993–Jan. 8, 1994.

Born, Wolfgang. "The Female Peales, Their Art and Its Tradition," *The American Collector* 15 (August 1946): 12–14.

A Century of Philadelphia Artists. Sale catalog, Frank Schwartz & Son, Philadelphia. Philadelphia Collection XXXVII, Summer, 1988.

Elam, Charles H., ed. *The Peale Family: Three Generations of American Artists.* Detroit, MI: Detroit Institute of Arts, 1967.

Hirshorn, Anne Sue. "Legacy of Ivory: Anna Claypoole Peale's Portrait Miniatures," *Bulletin of the Detroit Institute of Arts* 64 (1989): 17–27.

Huber, Christine Jones. *The Pennsylvania Academy and Its Women.* Philadelphia: Pennsylvania Academy of the Fine Arts, 1974.

Huntly, Wilbur H., and John Mahey. *Miss Miriam Peale, 1800–1885: Portraits and Still-Lifes.* Baltimore, MD: Peale Museum, 1967.

In This Academy. The Pennsylvania Academy of the Fine Arts, 1805–1976. Philadelphia: Pennsylvania Academy of the Fine Arts, 1976.

Rubenstein, Charlotte Streifer. *American Women Artists.* New York: Avon Books, 1982.

Schwartz, Robert Devlin. *American Miniatures.* Philadelphia: Robert Schwartz, Philadelphia Collection, XLIV December, 1990.

———. *A Gallery Collects Peales.* Philadelphia: Frank Schwartz & Son, 1987.

Tufts, Eleanor. *American Women Artists, 1830–1930.* Washington, DC: National Museum of Women in the Arts, 1987.

———. *Our Hidden Heritage: Five Centuries of Women Artists.* New York: Paddington, 1974.

ᴂ Peratrovich, Elizabeth (1911–1958)

Born in 1911 to the Raven clan of the Tlingit Indians of Southeast Alaska, Elizabeth Peratrovich played a significant role in Tlingit politics until her untimely death in 1958 from cancer. Described by one newswriter in the mid-1950s as a "chic, well-groomed modern woman possessing great charm and an eye for the practical," Peratrovich was the college-educated mother of three children, an active member of the Presbyterian church, and a grand president of the Alaska Native Sisterhood (ANS).

During her tenure as ANS grand president, Peratrovich took up the Native equal rights issue along with her husband, Roy, and the skillful Tlingit lawyer William L. Paul. She effectively argued that the unfair treatment of Natives in restaurants, movie houses, and other business establishments in Juneau was particularly repugnant, given the country's present emergency (World War II), when unity was being stressed. In a letter to the editor of the Southeast Alaska Empire, she suggested to the readers that such treatment was "very un-American," particularly since "our Native boys" were being called on to defend their country and "lay down their lives," just like the white boys, to protect the freedom that only the whites currently enjoyed. Demonstrating her own commitment to the war effort, Peratrovich raised money for the American Red Cross War Fund.

Her efforts in the equal rights battle moved from newspaper editorials to the halls of the Juneau legislature.

According to the late Governor Ernest Gruening, she actively lobbied politicians, testified at public hearings, and was largely responsible for convincing the legislators to pass the Anti-Discrimination Bill of 1945. In addition, as a member of the executive committee of the Alaska Native Brotherhood/Alaska Native Sisterhood, Peratrovich received support from the Office of Indian Affairs for improvement of the health and sanitary conditions of Native homes and villages, secured funding for nursery schools throughout southeast Alaska from the Federal Works Agency, and at her own expense, traveled throughout Alaska organizing new ANS camps and throughout other states seeking markets for Indian- and Eskimo-made products. Shortly before her death, she served as the Alaskan representative to the National Congress of American Indians. *(See also: Native American Women)*

—**Susan H. Koester**

Further Reading

Koester, Susan H. " 'By the Words of Thy Mouth Let Thee Be Judged': The Alaska Native Sisterhood Speaks," *Journal of the West, Western Speakers: Voices of the American Dream* 27 (April 1988): 35-44.

Oleksa, Michael. *Six Alaska Native Women Leaders: Pre-Statehood.* Edited by Connie Munro and Anne Kessler. Juneau, AK: Department of Education, 1991.

"A Recollection of Civil Rights Leader, Elizabeth Peratrovich, 1911–1958." Compiled by Central Council of Tlingit-Haida Tribes of Alaska, Juneau, 1991.

Perkins, Frances (1880–1965)

When Frances Perkins was appointed the first woman cabinet member (secretary of labor), a Washington reporter asked her if her sex would be a disadvantage in the nation's capital; she replied, "Only when climbing trees." Although she admitted she felt "a little odd," she was President Franklin Roosevelt's most important adviser and held her post as secretary of labor from 1933 until shortly after his death in 1945.

The daughter of an old Maine family, Fanny Caralie Perkins was born April 10, 1880, in Boston, grew up in Worcester, and graduated from Mount Holyoke College. Inspired by reformer Florence Kelley, Perkins left a teaching career for settlement work—in which educated people lived and worked among the urban poor, advocating social reform—first in Chicago and later in Philadelphia. However, she first established her reputation as a researcher in New York on *The Survey* in 1910. She earned a master's degree in political science at Columbia University, then settled into social work as a factory inspector, where she earned a reputation as a tireless advocate for working women.

In 1926, Governor Alfred Smith appointed her chairperson of the state's Industrial Board, and two years later when Franklin Roosevelt became New York's governor, he promoted her to become the first woman state industrial commissioner. Perkins first introduced the idea of unemploy-

ment insurance in 1931 and promoted a series of conferences nationwide on the problems of unemployment. An early proponent of Roosevelt's bid for the presidency, she was rewarded with the cabinet post, which sent AFL president William Green into a rampage of protest. Twelve years later, Green paid tribute to Perkins as one of the most accomplished labor secretaries to hold the office. She contributed to the making of the Wagner Act, the Social Security Act, and the Fair Labor Standards Act. After her retirement from the cabinet, she worked as civil service commissioner under the Truman administration. In 1955, she began lecturing at the School of Industrial and Labor Relations at Cornell University. She published a popular memoir of FDR, *The Roosevelt I Knew,* and was working on a biography of Al Smith at the time of her death in 1965.

Always one to keep her personal life out of the press, Perkins was married in 1913 to Paul C. Wilson, a New Yorker deeply involved in municipal government. They had a daughter in 1915, but shortly thereafter, Wilson began suffering from periodic depressions that after 1929 left him hospitalized. Perkins kept her husband's malady from the press and protected her daughter, Susanna, from public scrutiny. She had very close female friends, notably Mary Dewson, who is said to have engineered Perkins's cabinet appointment. She also roomed in Washington with Mary Rumsey, the daughter of prominent railroad executive E. H. Harriman and a chairperson of the National Recovery Administration Consumers' Advisory Council. Florence Kelley had been her inspiration in earlier years, and Perkins devoted herself to Kelley's favorite cause, the prohibition of child labor. Grace Abbott, Katharine Lenroot, and Clara Beyer were co-workers, part of that unique set of New Deal women whose years of reform work earned them a place in Roosevelt's new experiment in government. Among all of them, Perkins was an inspiration; independent yet caring, she combined family and career obligations in an age when few women dared to hope for both. *(See also: Democratic Party; New Deal; Politics; Settlement House Movement; Social Feminism; Social Work)*

—**Marjorie Murphy**

Further Reading

Martin, George. *Madam Secretary.* Boston: Houghton Mifflin, 1976.

Perkins, Frances. *The Roosevelt I Knew.* New York: Viking, 1946.

Perry, Lilla Cabot (1848–1933)

Painter and poet Lilla Cabot Perry was also among the first to introduce the work of the French impressionists to America. A member of the wealthy Boston Cabot family, she married Thomas Sergeant Perry, grandnephew of the distinguished U.S. naval officer Commodore Matthew C. Perry.

Perry studied at the Cowles School of Art in Boston and also in Paris at the Académie Colarossi and the Académie

Julian. Her work was shown in Paris, Berlin, Florence, Dresden, and Munich. Perhaps the greatest influence on her development as an artist was her friendship with Claude Monet. The two met in 1889, and Perry and her family spent ten summers during the next twenty years in a cottage near Monet's home in Giverny. Although Monet did not officially take in pupils, he encouraged Perry and took a great interest in her work. Perry's painting *Alice on the Path* (1891) hangs in the bedroom of Monet's home, which has been preserved. When in America, Perry lectured and wrote articles on the French impressionists and encouraged other wealthy Americans to buy their work.

Three years spent in Japan, where her husband was professor of English literature, also influenced Perry's artistic development. She had the opportunity to become acquainted with Japanese art and to paint the Japanese landscape and portraits of Japanese people. She also frequently used her three daughters as subjects during this time. After her return to Boston in 1901, Perry became a founder of the Guild of Boston Artists. She painted portraits, landscapes, and genre scenes and exhibited her work throughout the United States. Between 1886 and 1923, she also published four volumes of poetry.

In 1903, Perry purchased a summer home near Hancock, New Hampshire, an area that reminded her of Normandy, and painted many beautiful landscapes. She died there in 1933. *(See also: Art)*

—**Christine Miller Leahy**

Further Reading

King, Alma S. *Lilla Cabot Perry, Days to Remember.* Santa Fe, NM: Santa Fe East Galleries, 1983.

Lilla Cabot Perry: A Retrospective. Exhibition catalog. New York: The Galleries, 1969.

Martindale, Meredith. *Lilla Cabot Perry: An American Impressionist.* Washington, DC: National Museum of Women in the Arts, 1990.

∾ Persian Gulf War

The Persian Gulf War exposed 540,000 U.S. armed personnel to the dangers of battle, including 40,782 servicewomen. Dubbed the "Mommy's War" by the news media as military mothers bade tearful good-byes to their families, this brief conflict showcased the changing roles of American military women, who constituted 11 percent of active duty and 13 percent of reserve forces. As the distinction between combat and noncombat functions blurred, female warriors found themselves closer to the front lines than they could ever have imagined before.

President George Bush implemented Operation Desert Shield immediately following the Iraqi invasion of Kuwait on August 2, 1990, rapidly deploying service personnel to nearby Saudi Arabia. Operation Desert Storm, a combined ground and air attack on Iraqi targets destined to liberate Kuwait, rolled forward on January 17, 1991. The push into

Iraq in February placed servicewomen perilously close to front lines. Brief but intense fighting ensued, culminating in a cease-fire on February 28.

Although congressional legislation and military policy forbade females from flying combat missions, serving aboard fighting ships, and participating in infantry and artillery assaults, servicewomen nonetheless found themselves in harm's way. Thirteen women died in the Gulf theater, including five killed in action. Two fell into enemy hands as prisoners of war.

Women in uniform provided vital support services. Many evacuated and rendered medical aid to wounded warriors, while others ferried food, fuel, and troops by helicopter and truck through combat zones. Serving as military police, some females guarded bases, harbors, and prisoners of war. At military installations throughout the world, servicewomen outfitted combat aircraft and prepared arms and supply shipments.

In the glowing afterlight of the international coalition's swift victory over the Iraqis, Congress and the American public lauded U.S. servicewomen for their outstanding contributions to the war effort and reevaluated their role within the military complex. Most telling is the overwhelming Senate vote on July 31, 1991, to overturn a 1948 law barring women from flying combat missions despite the grave reservations of the chiefs of the Army, Navy, Air Force, and Marine Corps.

Although 56 percent of the American public favored women's participation in combat during the Persian Gulf War, 64 percent opposed fighting roles for women with young children. Despite the apparent gains that female military personnel made during this conflict, servicewomen still face the maternity barrier—one that is unlikely to fall in the near future.

Another dimension of military service in the Persian Gulf War involves the illnesses that have come to be known as Gulf War syndrome. Studies are under way to determine the effect that deployment in the gulf has had on gynecology-related problems among female veterans. *(See also: Military Service)*

—**Amy E. Blackwell**

Further Reading

Addis, Elisabetta, Valerie E. Russo, and Lorenza Sebesta, eds. *Women Soldiers: Images and Realities.* New York: St. Martin's, 1994.

Blacksmith, E. A., ed. *Women in the Military.* New York: H. H. Wilson, 1992.

Cornum, Rhonda. *She Went to War: The Rhonda Cornum Story.* Edited by Peter Copeland. Novato, CA: Presidio, 1992.

Holm, Maj. Gen. Jeanne. *Women in the Military: An Unfinished Revolution.* Rev. ed. Novato, CA: Presidio, 1992.

∾ Pesotta, Rose (1896–1965)

Charismatic labor organizer, union official, garment worker, and writer, Rose Pesotta was born Rachelle Peisoty in the Jewish ghetto of the Ukrainian city of Derazhyna. She attended elementary school in Derazhyna and studied at home with a progressive tutor who introduced her to the works of social critics and the writings of Tolstoy and Dostoevsky. The young Pesotta soon followed her older sister Esther into the ghetto's anarchist underground. She carried with her for the rest of her life the lessons she learned there.

To escape an arranged marriage, in 1913 the self-reliant teenager joined her sister in New York, where she got work in a shirtwaist factory in lower Manhattan and attended night school. Soon afterward, she joined Local 25 of the International Ladies Garment Workers Union (ILGWU). In 1915, she helped start the union's first education department and five years later was elected to the local's executive board. By the start of the 1920s, she was a committed anarchist and anti-Communist and very active in support of Sacco and Vanzetti.

Pesotta attended the Bryn Mawr Summer School for Women in Industry, the Brookwood Labor College, and the Wisconsin School for Workers, afterward becoming a paid general organizer for the ILGWU, working throughout the United States and Canada. In the early years of the Great Depression, she organized Mexican and Chinese garment workers in Los Angeles and San Francisco. Her work caught the attention of John L. Lewis who borrowed her in the late 1930s to work alongside three of the Congress of Industrial Organizations' (CIO's) top organizers—Powers Hapgood, Adolph Germer, and Leo Kryzcki—with striking rubber workers in Akron, Ohio, and autoworkers in Flint, Michigan. During these years, the seemingly inexhaustible Pesotta also worked in behalf of her stateless friend Emma Goldman and, with Carlo Tresca and others, established a colony in Ecuador for Spanish Republican refugees.

As a result of her experiences as an organizer, she became a champion of the rank and file and reproached the ILGWU hierarchy for having so few women at the top levels of leadership. Angered by the union's unconcern, in 1942 she returned to her former work in the garment industry and two years later left the office of vice president. Always a wide-ranging and prolific writer, during her later years she had two autobiographies published, *Bread upon the Waters,* based on her years as an organizer, and *Days of Our Lives,* about her childhood in Russia. *(See also: Congress of Industrial Organizations; Garment Industries; Goldman, Emma; International Ladies Garment Workers Union; Jewish Women; Unions)*

—**Richard Salvato**

Further Reading

Kessler-Harris, Alice. "Organizing the Unorganizable: Three Jewish Women and Their Union," *Labor History* 17 (Winter 1976): 5-23.
Pesotta, Rose. *Bread upon the Waters.* New York: Dodd, Mead, 1944.
———. *Days of Our Lives.* Boston: Excelsior, 1958.
———. *Justice.* Newspaper. ILGWU. [various issues]
———. *Letters, 1920s.* Jewish Labor Fund Archives.

———. *Papers.* Rare Books and Manuscripts Division, New York Public Library.
Seller, Maxine. "Beyond the Stereotype: A New Look at the Immigrant Woman, 1880–1924," *Journal of Ethnic Studies* 3 (Spring 1975): 59-70.
Shepherd, Naomi. *A Prize below Rubies: Jewish Women as Rebels and Radicals.* London: Weidenfeld & Nicolson, 1993.

❧ Peterson, Esther (1906–1997)

Esther Peterson was assistant secretary of labor and director of the Women's Bureau, U.S. Department of Labor, in the Kennedy administration. She remained in the federal government during the Johnson administration, maintaining her position of assistant secretary of labor while also serving as Johnson's special assistant for consumer affairs.

Peterson's position as the highest-ranking woman in the Kennedy administration culminated a career in education and the labor movement. She received a Bachelor of Arts degree from Brigham Young University in 1927 and a Master of Arts degree from Teachers College, Columbia University, three years later. Her teaching career began in 1927 at the Branch Agricultural College in Cedar City, Utah, and continued during the 1930s within the labor movement through teaching positions at the Bryn Mawr Summer School for Women Workers, the Hudson Shore Labor School, and with the International Ladies Garment Workers Union. In 1939, she became assistant director of education and organizer for the Amalgamated Clothing Workers of America (ACWA), a post she held until she became the ACWA's Washington lobbyist in 1945. She became a lobbyist for the AFL-CIO in 1957. In her capacity as a labor union lobbyist, Peterson forged relationships with John F. Kennedy and the Women's Bureau.

The Women's Bureau grew in stature under Peterson's leadership, achieving a long-term legislative goal, passage of the Equal Pay Act (1963) and functioning as the administrative arm of the President's Commission on the Status of Women (PCSW). As historian Cynthia Harrison documents, Esther Peterson herself was instrumental in the passage of the Equal Pay Act, as well as responsible for Kennedy's executive order creating the President's Commission on the Status of Women. As executive vice chair of the PCSW, Peterson was also a key player in the formation of recommendations in its final report, *American Women. (See also: Equal Pay Act of 1963; International Ladies Garment Workers Union; President's Commission on the Status of Women; Unions; Women's Bureau)*

—**Kathleen Laughlin**

Further Reading

Harrison, Cynthia. *On Account of Sex: The Politics of Women's Issues, 1945–1968.* Berkeley: University of California Press, 1988.
Sealander, Judith. *As Minority Becomes Majority: Federal Reaction to the Phenomenon of Women in the Workforce, 1920–1963.* Westport, CT: Greenwood, 1983.

⚬ Phelps, Elizabeth Stuart (Ward)
(1844–1910)

Elizabeth Stuart Phelps, author, was born Mary Gray Phelps to Austin Phelps, a professor of homiletics at Andover Seminary, and Elizabeth Stuart Phelps, an author of religious books for children. In 1852, when Mary was eight, her mother died. During that year, her mother had written her fourth book, given birth to her third child, and experienced the death of her father, Moses Stuart, a biblical scholar at Andover Seminary. The child, a boy, was baptized at her coffin, according to his mother's wishes, an experience that left its imprint on young Mary, who took her mother's name, Elizabeth Stuart Phelps.

Phelps took on the literary task as well as the name of her mother. She became a major author of sentimental fiction, beginning with her most famous novel, *The Gates Ajar,* published in 1868. She published fifty-seven books, none of which equaled the popularity of the first, although many shared its homey description of heaven. Phelps pioneered a language and theology congenial to a mostly female readership searching for religious consolation outside of orthodox Calvinism.

Phelps's task as a writer was to "represent the age." Her heroines were New England girls who took part in various religious crusades and reform movements. The theme of temperance was treated in *A Singular Life* (1895), while the conflict for women between marriage and writing provided the story lines of *The Story of Avis* (1877) and *Dr. Zay* (1882). Phelps took an active personal role in movements she wrote about and maintained a reformer's zeal even to the end of her life, when she was devoted to the cause of antivivisection.

In 1888, Phelps married biblical scholar Herbert Dickenson Ward, a man seventeen years her junior. Although they collaborated on three biblical romances, their marriage was far from compatible. Publicly, Phelps led a successful life, and her private frustrations did not quiet her voice as a major author of sentimental fiction, a moral reformer, and a teacher of religion. *(See also: Religion; Women Writers)*

—**Maria E. Erling**

Further Reading
Douglas, Ann. *The Feminization of American Culture.* New York: Knopf, 1977.
Kelly, Lora Duin. *The Life and Works of Elizabeth Stuart Phelps: Victorian Feminist Writer.* Troy, NY: Whitson, 1983.
Phelps, Elizabeth Stuart. *Chapters from a Life.* Boston: n.p., 1897.
———. *The Gates Ajar.* Boston: Houghton Mifflin, 1868.

⚬ Philadelphia Female Anti-Slavery Society (PFAS)

The Philadelphia Female Anti-Slavery Society (PFAS) was founded in 1833 to raise public consciousness about slavery and to work for its abolition. Considered one of the first political organizations for women, it served as an important training ground for leaders in the movement for women's rights.

The interracial composition of this mainly Quaker group, which held meetings together and visited in each other's homes, shocked even the abolitionist community. The members became involved in the black community by developing an early welfare system in 1839, supporting black schools, and working with the secular, all-black Vigilance Committee, a principal supporter of the Underground Railroad, to warn free blacks of the approach of kidnappers. In later years, the PFAS became involved in petitioning the government and other forms of protest. Throughout its long history, vocal members such as Lucretia Mott and Angelina and Sarah Grimké spoke out against slavery in public forums. The organization supported its programs, including lectures and subscriptions to antislavery publications, by holding annual fairs. At these fund-raising events, members sold pillows and reticules bearing the motto "Am I Not a Woman and a Sister?" over the image of a kneeling slave with shackled wrists. Sister organizations in New Jersey, Great Britain, and Boston contributed articles to this sale, which often earned sums of approximately $2,000.

After thirty-seven years in the forefront of the antislavery movement, the PFAS formally disbanded in March 1870, following the passage of the Fourteenth Amendment. *(See also: Abolition and the Antislavery Movement; Grimké, Angelina Emily; Grimké, Sarah Moore; Mott, Lucretia Coffin; Society of Friends)*

—**Cynthia Jeffress Little**

Further Reading
Bacon, Margaret Hope. *Valiant Friend: The Life of Lucretia Mott.* New York: Walker, 1980.
Lerner, Gerda. *The Grimké Sisters from South Carolina: Pioneers for Women's Rights and Abolition.* New York: Schocken, 1971.
Pennsylvania Abolition Society Collection. The Historical Society of Pennsylvania, Philadelphia.
Soderlund, Jean R. "Priorities and Power: The Philadelphia Anti-Slavery Society." In *The Abolitionist Sisterhood: Women's Political Culture in Antebellum America,* edited by Jean Fagan Yellin and John C. Van Horne, 67-88. Ithaca, NY: Cornell University Press, 1994.

⚬ Philadelphia Training School for Nurses at Philadelphia General Hospital

The Philadelphia Training School for Nurses at Philadelphia General Hospital (called Blockley until 1902) was the first American school of nursing to have a Florence Nightingale-trained nurse at its head. Nightingale had previously revolutionized and professionalized nursing care in Britain in the mid-1850s, during and after the Crimean War.

In 1884, an Englishwoman, Alice Fisher, was hired to reorganize the nursing services and to set up a school of nursing at the hospital. Fisher's original two-year training program, which included classes in both nursing theory and ethics, also emphasized the importance of using aseptic techniques. The program required first-year students to work as private nurses, graduating in their second year to the more demanding work on the wards, where their rigid adherence to aseptic techniques brought about a marked drop in maternal mortality.

Fisher's death in 1888, just two years after the first class graduated, did not break the program's continuity because her colleague and friend Edith Horner Hawley took over as her successor. Hawley continued with the Nightingale approach Fisher had instituted but also expanded the program to train students in nursing practice as well as administration. By 1910, the program had graduated two thousand trained nurses, reflecting the growing popularity of nursing as a career option for women as well as the school's good reputation. In 1909, the program was expanded to three years, and its curriculum was standardized to meet the requirements of the state board of examiners.

The Philadelphia Training School for Nurses graduated its last class in 1977, when Philadelphia General Hospital closed its doors. During its ninety-two-year history, the Philadelphia Training School for Nurses educated a corps of nurses who took leadership roles in nursing education and administration around the world. *(See also: Nursing)*

—Cynthia Jeffress Little

Further Reading

Stachniewicz, Stephanie. *The Double Frill: The History of the Philadelphia General Hospital School of Nursing.* Philadelphia: Stickely, 1978.

~ Photography

Photography was invented in 1839, and from the beginning, women in the United States participated in its development. They worked as semiskilled labor in the industry, producing paper, plates, and film, and they also worked as assistants to their husbands, taking over a studio in the event of the husband's death or a divorce. These women's names are often unrecorded either because they were anonymous workers or they worked under a husband's name even after taking over the studio. Some women took up photography to supplement their incomes. Jane Cook of New York City was both an artist and a daguerreotypist. The San Francisco directory of 1850 listed Mrs. J. Shannon as a midwife and a daguerreotypist. Combining professions such as painting or medicine with daguerrotype was common in the early days of photography for both men and women. Yet even then, examples of named women professional photographers could be found. In 1846, for example, Sarah Holcomb of New Hampshire prevailed over difficult winters and often hostile competition from male photographers.

By the 1880s, technological advances in photography, such as dry plates, roll film, and the hand-held camera created a mass amateur market. Women's entry into photography was also influenced by its status as an art form. In this controversy, which extended from photography's inception into the first quarter of the twentieth century, many perceived the medium as a mechanical recording device. Others, however, notably the photographer and art patron Alfred Steiglitz, promoted photography as a fine art equivalent to painting. Photography was not accepted by art academies as a fine art in the nineteenth and early twentieth centuries. Women were rarely accepted into academies as well. Photography's status in the academy was congruent with women's status in the visual arts and society, thus photography was accessible to women.

In both the nineteenth and twentieth centuries, women practiced photography within their domestic environments as well as in the field. Many professional women photographers opened home studios where they specialized in portraiture as well as other subjects. In the nineteenth and early twentieth centuries, professional and amateur women were predominantly attracted to domestic subjects—women, children, gardens, pets, and genre subjects. Yet photographers such as Gertrude Käsebier produced domestic scenes that commented on the status of women and the disadvantages of marriage. She also had a successful portrait studio. Women were also early photojournalists, such as Frances Benjamin Johnston and Jessie Tarbox Beals. In the early twentieth century, California photographer Anne Brigman expressed a pagan and feminine sensibility in her images of free-spirited female nudes.

By 1900, over 3,500 women are recorded as having worked as professional photographers. Thousands more were dedicated amateurs. These photographers helped establish women in professional photography. By the mid-twentieth century, many women were important photographers. Berenice Abbott worked as a portraitist and as an architectural and scientific photographer. Dorothea Lange and Marion Post Wolcott worked for the Farm Security Administration, documenting the American Depression. During this same period, Margaret Bourke-White was one of the most successful and highest paid photojournalists in the world. Late twentieth century photography has produced internationally important photographers such as Diane Arbus, who received two Guggenheim awards to document American rites and manners. *(See also: Abbott, Berenice; Arbus, Diane Nemerov; Art; Bourke-White, Margaret; Boyd, Louise A.; Eakins, Susan Hannah; Johnston, Frances Benjamin; Käsebier, Gertrude Stanton; Sontag, Susan)*

—C. Jane Gover
Adapted for the second edition by Diana Emery Hulick.

Further Reading

Gover, C. Jane. *The Positive Image: Women Photographers in Turn of the Century America.* Albany: State University of New York Press, 1987.

Newhall, Beaumont. *The History of Photography.* New York: Museum of Modern Art, 1982.

Quitslund, Toby. "Her Feminine Colleagues—Photographs and Letters Collected by Frances Benjamin Johnston in 1900." In

Women Artists in Washington Collections, edited by Josephine Withers, 97-109. College Park: University of Maryland Art Gallery and Women's Careers for the Arts, 1979.

Sullivan, Constance, ed. Essay by Eugenia Parry Janis. *Women Photographers.* New York: Abrams, 1990.

Tucker, Ann. *The Woman's Eye.* New York: Random House, 1973.

⚭ Physicians

Women have had great difficulty becoming physicians. The first formal medical training facilities in the country, which began in 1765, refused to admit female students. Finally, in 1849, Elizabeth Blackwell (1821–1910) became the first woman in the United States to receive a medical degree from a recognized medical school. After the initial publicity surrounding Blackwell's entrance into the profession had died down, medical colleges for women were founded in Philadelphia in 1850 and shortly thereafter in Boston. In 1863, Clemence Sophia Lozier (1813–1988), an M.D. from the Syracuse Eclectic Medical College, succeeded in getting the New York Medical College for women incorporated in 1863.

These institutions trained a number of women doctors, including Rebecca Lee, who in 1864 was the first black woman to receive her degree from a medical school. Her graduation from the New England Female Medical College in Boston set the stage for other black women to follow. Ann Preston (1813–1872) was among the first women to graduate from the Woman's Medical College of Pennsylvania in Philadelphia in 1851. She went on to a successful career as the first female professor at a traditional medical school and later became the first woman dean at a medical college. Mary Edwards Walker (1832–1919) was another of the early pioneers in American medicine. During the Civil War, she served as an assistant surgeon and became the first woman to win the Congressional Medal of Honor.

Despite these successes, the number of women going into medicine remained small. By 1920, women made up only 5 percent of the profession; by 1976, women were still only 8.6 percent of the physicians in the United States; by 1987, women composed 15.2 percent of the profession. By 1900, there were 160 black women physicians of approximately 7,000 women physicians. However, by 1920, the number had dropped to 65.

The drop can be attributed to several factors. Even though coeducation had been introduced in medical schools, black women still faced discriminatory barriers due to the increased competition for medical school slots by minorities. In 1910, the Flexner Report, authorized by the Carnegie Foundation, assessed all medical training institutions in the United States, using the Johns Hopkins Medical School as the model for minimum standards. As a result of this report, many medical schools were closed; at least five were black medical schools, all of which were located in the South. This eliminated access to a formal medical education

for a large population of blacks. Meharry Medical School, Nashville, founded in 1876, and Howard University Medical School, Washington, D.C., founded in 1868, managed to survive the Flexner Report and maintain financial stability. Howard, however, actually graduated more white women than black women during its first twenty-five years.

The Flexner Report was also detrimental to women's medical schools. Indeed, by 1920, of at least seventeen medical schools founded for women, the Woman's Medical College of Pennsylvania was, and still is, the only surviving one begun exclusively to educate women in medicine. During the nineteenth century, the Woman's Medical College of Pennsylvania helped finance the medical education of several black women and graduated at least a dozen black women.

Discrimination also existed for black women physicians in acquiring hospital appointments and membership in medical associations and societies. After graduation, the majority of the nineteenth-century black women physicians set up practice in the South, while white women often interned in a hospital. Since opportunities for hospital appointments were not readily available to black women physicians, they had to begin treating patients immediately with limited experience, while the white women physicians were accepted in some hospitals, affording them the opportunity to gain additional clinical experience under the guidance of an established physician. When internships were made mandatory during the late 1920s, black women were still discriminated against; they were unable to secure internships in the white institutions.

The exclusion of black women physicians from hospitals forced and spurred them to found clinics and hospitals. Blacks were also forced to found their own organizations and associations. The exclusion of blacks from the American Medical Association led to the establishment of the National Medical Association, founded in 1895 in Atlanta, Georgia. Women were involved with the association from the beginning.

Women of all colors have faced numerous obstacles and challenges in all segments of the medical profession. The percentage of women physicians in the United States remained relatively static from 1920 into the 1970s. However, the number of women physicians more than doubled between 1970 and 1980. By 1990, the number of women physicians had increased nearly 92 percent over ten years. In the 1990s, women also played important new leadership roles in medicine. In 1993, Joycelyn Elders became the first African American U.S. Surgeon General. She was succeeded by another African American woman, Audrey Forbes Manley, who served as Acting Surgeon General until assuming the presidency of Spelman College in 1997.

As of 1994, only 19 percent of practicing physicians were women; this fact indicates that not all barriers to women's full participation in the medical community have been overcome. Nevertheless, according to the American Medical Women's Association, women physicians are expected to constitute 30 percent of all physicians and 50 percent or more of all medical students by 2010. *(See also: Blackwell, Elizabeth; Preston, Ann; Woman's Medical College of Pennsylvania; Walker, Mary Edwards)*

—**Margaret Jerrido**

Further Reading

Abram, Ruth J., ed. *Send Us a Lady Physician: Women Doctors in America: 1835–1920.* New York: Norton, 1985.

Chaff, Sandra, Ruth Haimbach, Carol Fenichel, and Nina Woodside. *Women in Medicine: A Bibliography.* Metuchen, NJ: Scarecrow, 1977.

Davis, Marianna, ed. *Contributions of Black Women to America.* Columbia, SC: Kenday, 1982.

Morantz-Sanchez, Regina, ed. *In Her Own Words: Oral Histories of Women.* Westport, CT: Greenwood, 1982.

———. *Science and Sympathy: Women Physicians in American Medicine.* New York: Oxford University Press, 1985.

Walsh, Mary. *"Doctors Wanted: No Women Need Apply": Sexual Barriers in the Medical Profession, 1835–1975.* New Haven, CT: Yale University Press, 1977.

∿ Pinckney, Eliza Lucas (1722–1793)

Eliza Pinckney, agricultural innovator, provided the supreme example of republican motherhood—which emphasized both patriotic and domestic virtues—in early America. Pinckney's two sons, Charles Cotesworth and Thomas, had illustrious political careers in the national arena and were considered exemplary patriots who had surely learned the necessary virtues from their mother. But Pinckney accomplished much more than raising notable children. A successful planter in her own right, she was responsible for the introduction of indigo as a viable cash crop into the South Carolina economy.

Born in the West Indies in 1722, she attended school in England before moving to South Carolina with her family in 1737; two years later, her father, George Lucas, departed to become governor of Antigua. Because his wife was an invalid, Lucas left his South Carolina estates (five thousand acres and eighty-six slaves) under the supervision of his oldest child, sixteen-year-old Eliza. She not only succeeded as business manager of her father's three plantations but undertook a series of agricultural experiments in hopes of improving production. Her most successful effort was the introduction of indigo.

In 1744, she married widower Charles Pinckney and embarked enthusiastically on a new life as the wife of a wealthy planter. But she continued her interest in agricultural improvements, conducting a series of experiments with flax and hemp and reviving silk culture. When Charles died of malaria in 1758, leaving Pinckney a widow of thirty-six with three young children, she again took on the job of managing the family plantations. Once more, she succeeded in her task, her only major setbacks being the losses created by the American Revolution, particularly the British seizure of Charleston in 1780.

Following the Revolution, Pinckney went to live with her daughter, Harriet, at Hampton, South Carolina, devoting most of the rest of her life to her grandchildren. Stricken with cancer, she went to Philadelphia in search of medical help and died there on May 26, 1793, at the age of seventy.

Eliza Lucas Pinckney succeeded in everything she did. She took advantage of every opportunity presented and worked to instill a desire for success in her children. Her triumphs as wife, mother, and planter reserve her a place among the strong, successful women in American history. *(See also: Agriculture: Preindustrial and Nineteenth Century United States; Business; Republican Motherhood)*

—**Carol Sue Humphrey**

Further Reading

Baskett, Sam S. "Eliza Lucas Pinckney: Portrait of an Eighteenth Century American," *South Carolina Historical Magazine* 72 (October 1971): 207-19.

Pinckney, Eliza. *The Letterbook of Eliza Lucas Pinckney, 1739–1762.* Edited by Elise Pinckney and Marvin R. Zahniser. Chapel Hill: University of North Carolina Press, 1972.

Ravenal, Hariott Horry. *Eliza Pinckney.* New York: Scribner, 1896. Reprint, Spartanburg, SC: Reprint Co., 1967.

∿ "Pitcher, Molly" (1754–1832)

"Molly Pitcher" was an American Revolutionary War heroine. On June 28, 1778, at the battle of Monmouth, New Jersey, Pitcher earned her nickname by carrying water from a nearby spring to the American troops and to her husband, John Caspar Hays. After Hays was wounded, Pitcher manned the cannon of Colonel William Irvine's Seventh Company of Pennsylvania Artillery until the American victory.

Born Mary Ludwig, she was the daughter of John George Ludwig, a German dairyman of Mercer County, New Jersey, but had become a domestic in 1769 for Dr. William Irvine of Carlisle, Pennsylvania. After her husband John Hays's death, Pitcher was married in 1792 to George McCauley. On February 21, 1822, the Pennsylvania legislature voted her a pension for life for her services during the Revolutionary War. *(See also: American Revolutionary Era)*

—**Ginger Rae Allee**

Further Reading

Green, Henry Clinton, and Mary Wolcott Green. *The Pioneer Mothers of America.* Vol. 2, pp. 217-23, 342. New York: Putnam, 1912.

Leonard, Eugene Andruss, Sophia Drinker, and Miriam Young Holden. *The American Women in Colonial and Revolutionary Times, 1765–1800,* p. 118. Philadelphia: University of Pennsylvania Press, 1962.

Logan, Mary Simmerson. *The Part Taken by Women in American History.* 1912. Reprint, pp. 162-65. New York: Arno, 1972.

McDowell, Bart. "The Revolutionary War," *National Geographic* 148 (October 1975): 483-84.

Muir, Charles Stothard. *Women, the Makers of History,* pp. 144-46. New York: Vantage, 1956.

☙ Planned Parenthood Federation of America, Inc. (PPFA)

In 1942, Margaret Sanger protested loudly when the American Birth Control League became the Planned Parenthood Federation of America. Sanger claimed to have coined the term *birth control* and justifiably argued her proprietary rights over the organization she had founded and named in 1921. In the early 1940s, however, Sanger no longer had controlling interest in the organization, and its staff of—predominantly male—officers believed that "planned parenthood" made a more positive appeal to the American public than "birth control." Furthermore, the services of the organization, originally aimed exclusively at providing contraceptive information and materials, had been expanded to include aid to infertile couples.

Sanger had worked through the original organization to persuade federal and state governments to include birth control in public health programs. That goal is yet to be entirely realized. Religious and political controversy still dictates birth control policies in many American communities. PPFA continues to be funded largely by donations from corporations, foundations, and individuals. Today, the organization's multimillion-dollar budget supports 900 centers and 137 affiliates nationwide, with a staff and volunteer base that approaches 17,000. The current president of PPFA is Gloria Feldt.

While the range of services varies among individual centers, a typical menu includes question-and-answer educational aids for use by parents in discussing sexual issues with their children, information on contraception, abortion, sterilization, AIDS and other sexually transmitted diseases, infertility, and menopause. Initially appealing primarily to low-income married women, today PPFA services attract a significant number of unmarried teenagers. A typical teenage female client is required to provide her medical history, undergo a pelvic examination, and view films and accept literature on topics relevant to sexual health and fertility. She may then purchase birth control materials at low cost.

In 1966, Alan F. Gutmacher, a highly respected obstetrician and then president of PPFA, urged the medical profession to work closely with the organization. He furthermore called on individual centers to enroll a nucleus of female physicians to oversee clinic activities. The guidelines Gutmacher established are still followed whenever possible.

Currently, PPFA sponsors biomedical, socioeconomic, and demographic research. At its annual convention in the fall, the results of this research are presented. At its official headquarters in New York City, PPFA publishes an annual *Affiliates Directory* and maintains the Katharine Dexter McCormick Library, a renowned collection of 5,000 volumes, over 50,000 articles and clippings, and 125 scholarly journals. In addition, the PPFA presents the Margaret Sanger Award, the Maggie Awards for media excellence in representing the case for fertility control, and the Arthur and Edith Wippman Scientific Research Award. The tribute to Sanger implicit in the titles of these awards indicates that Sanger's reputation as the driving force behind the American birth control movement has been reestablished since the 1940s, when her voice had become too strident for many of the conservative male directors of the federation.

Since 1952, PPFA has been affiliated with the International Planned Parenthood Federation (IPPF). This international coalition, represented in over 180 countries worldwide, is the world's largest voluntary sexual/reproductive health and family planning organization. While a focus on family planning services remains at the core of IPPF's philosophy of sexual and reproductive health care, the organization's many affiliates have agreed to adopt a number of other services. These include education and counseling on sexuality; providing care during pregnancy, delivery, and postpartum; monitoring infant growth and development, with particular attention to the nutrition and health of girl children; promoting environments conducive to the sexual development of girls; prevention of HIV and AIDS; prevention and management of unsafe abortion; and provision of safe abortion services where legal. *(See also: Birth Control; Sanger, Margaret)*

—**Mary Lowe-Evans**

Further Reading

Gray, Madeline. *Margaret Sanger: A Biography of the Champion of Birth Control.* New York: Richard Marek, 1979.

Kennedy, David M. *Birth Control in America: The Career of Margaret Sanger.* New Haven, CT: Yale University Press, 1970.

McCann, Carole R. *Birth Control Politics in the United States, 1916–1945.* Ithaca, NY: Cornell University Press, 1994.

Planned Parenthood Federation of America, Inc. *Seventy Years of Family Planning in America: A Chronology of Major Events.* New York: Planned Parenthood Federation of America, 1986.

Reed, James. *The Birth Control Movement and American Society: From Private Vice to Public Virtue.* Princeton, NJ: Princeton University Press, 1983.

http://www.plannedparenthood.org [Planned Parenthood Federation of American Website]

http://www.ippf.org [International Planned Parenthood Federation Website]

☙ Plath, Sylvia (1932–1963)

Poet and novelist Sylvia Plath is one of the most startling and original voices of the mid-twentieth century and, most critics agree, one of the best. Her reputation rests on a single novel and the poems she wrote in the last two years of her brief life. These were published posthumously in *Ariel* (1965), a collection of forty-three poems, later augmented by her *Collected Poems* (1981). Her one surviving novel, *The Bell Jar* (1963), published pseudonymously a month before her death, is a satirical portrayal of U.S. society in the 1950s and a semiautobiographical account of Plath's breakdown and suicide attempt between her junior and senior years of college.

Plath's Polish-born, German-speaking father, a socio-biologist and expert on bees, died when his daughter was eight, and she was raised in Wellesley, Massachusetts, by her widowed mother, who taught medical secretarial procedures. Plath was an outstanding student and graduated Phi Beta Kappa and summa cum laude from Smith College, despite being hospitalized with manic-depressive illness. In 1956, during a Fulbright year at Cambridge University, she married Ted Hughes, the Yorkshire poet. They had two children, a daughter and a son, and for most of the six years of their marriage, they lived and wrote in London and Devon. Hughes and Plath separated in 1962, and Plath committed suicide in February 1963.

Many of Plath's great *Ariel* poems date from the last months or even weeks preceding her suicide. Characterized by taut, austere manipulations of rhythm and exceedingly precise, arresting, and often violent imagery, the most famous of them are lacerating verbal explosions of emotion: rage, jealousy, despair, fear, hatred, and loathing—of herself as well as of others.

Plath's tumultuous poetry was fueled by her extreme feelings about herself and her family and her equally extreme shifts in mood, from excitement and elation to furious depression. Repeatedly, her subject matter was death and loss. "Death & Co." and the extraordinary poem "Edge" look forward to her final successful suicide, and her previous suicide attempts appear in "Lady Lazarus": "Dying/Is an art,/like everything else./I do it exceptionally well." Her rejection of father and husband, coalesced into a single figure—if something so virulent can be called rejection—stokes the fires of "Daddy," her best known poem, and in "Elm" she turns her imagery against herself: "I am inhabited by a cry./Nightly it flaps out/Looking, with its hooks, for something to love."

Plath lived her married life in the white-picket-fence era and died just as the most recent women's movement was about to begin. As her letters and journals make clear, she was tormented by the conflicting claims of her ambitions for herself as a poet and the idealized domestic life she thought she should be living with a man she could lean on who would be stronger and more successful than she. Although *The Bell Jar* satirizes brilliantly assumptions such as these and the ideas about men and women that lie behind them, and many of Plath's poems concern issues a later generation would call feminist, she apparently could not escape the dictates of her culture in her own life and self-concept. *(See also: Women Writers)*

—**Gretchen Mieszkowski**

Further Reading
Alexander, Paul, ed. *Ariel Ascending: Writings about Sylvia Plath.* New York: Harper, 1985.
Bloom, Harold, ed. *Sylvia Plath.* New York: Chelsea, 1989.
Bundtzen, Lynda. *Plath's Incarnation: Women and the Creative Process.* Ann Arbor: University of Michigan Press, 1983.
Lant, Kathleen Margaret. "The Big Strip Tease: Female Bodies and Male Power in the Poetry of Sylvia Plath," *Contemporary Literature* 34 (1993): 620-69.
MacPherson, Pat. *Reflecting on the Bell Jar.* New York: Routledge, 1991.
Plath, Sylvia. *The Bell Jar.* New York: Harper, 1971.
———. *The Collected Poems.* New York: Harper, 1981.
Ramazani, Jahan. " 'Daddy, I Have Had to Kill You': Plath, Rage, and the Modern Elegy," *PMLA* 108 (1993): 1142-56.
Rose, Jacqueline. *The Haunting of Sylvia Plath.* Cambridge, MA: Harvard University Press, 1993.
Stevenson, Anne. *Bitter Fame: A Life of Sylvia Plath.* Boston: Houghton Mifflin, 1989.
Van Dyne, Susan R. *Revising Life: Sylvia Plath's Ariel Poems.* Chapel Hill: University of North Carolina Press, 1993.
Wagner, Linda W., ed. *Critical Essays on Sylvia Plath.* Boston: G. K. Hall, 1984.

❧ Plural Marriage

Plural marriage, a form of polygyny based on Old Testament patriarchal models, was introduced during the nineteenth century by the Mormons (Church of Jesus Christ of Latter-Day Saints). Joseph Smith, the Mormon prophet-founder, initiated both the theory and practice of polygyny among his leadership cadre in Nauvoo, Illinois, during the early 1840s.

Under Smith's successor, Brigham Young, the main group of Mormons made a great trek west to Utah in the late 1840s and in 1852 publicly announced their commitment to plural marriage as an integral part of their religious and social system. By the 1880s, there were more than 100,000 Mormons in the Intermountain West ideologically committed to polygyny as the highest form of marriage, and between 20 and 30 percent of all Mormon families were polygynous. Intense federal pressure nevertheless forced the Mormon church in 1890 to discontinue sanctioning further plural marriages in the United States, and after 1904, recalcitrant polygynists were excommunicated from the church. Today, Mormons are among the staunchest defenders of monogamy, although Mormon splinter groups with perhaps tens of thousands of adherents continue to advocate and practice plural marriage.

Mormon polygyny in the nineteenth century was the focus of bitter controversy. Non-Mormons denounced it as a system of debauchery perpetrated on Mormon women by an unscrupulous male Mormon leadership, while Mormons defended it as a way of enlarging kinship ties and conforming to God's will. Recent Mormon and non-Mormon scholarship on polygyny has recognized the difficult emotional challenges that plural marriage posed for women but has also stressed the paradoxical ways in which polygyny sometimes could "liberate" women to play a more active role in society. In the absence of their husbands, plural wives sometimes acted as heads of households, taking on a variety of tasks usually open only to men. Plural wives frequently developed close ties of sisterhood with each other, and they could cooperate in tasks such as child care, freeing an able or ambitious plural wife to obtain advanced education or develop an independent career. Mormon women, many of them plural wives, edited, published, and distributed a distinguished independent women's newspaper, *Woman's Exponent,* during the late nineteenth and early twentieth centuries. Only in the mid-twentieth century in a staunchly monogamous church has the Mormon quest for respectability led the group to advocate an essentially neo-Victorian domesticity as the only legitimate role for women. *(See also: Mormonism)*

—Lawrence Foster

Further Reading

Bitton, Davis. "Mormon Polygamy: A Review Article," *Journal of Mormon History* 4 (1977): 101-18.

Casterline, Gail Farr. " 'In the Toils' or 'Onward for Zion': Images of the Mormon Woman, 1852–1890." Master's thesis, Utah State University, 1974.

Embry, Jessie L. *Mormon Polygamous Families: Life in the Principle.* Salt Lake City: University of Utah Press, 1987.

Foster, Lawrence. *Religion and Sexuality: The Shakers, the Mormons, and the Oneida Community,* pp. 123-247. Urbana: University of Illinois Press, 1984.

———. *Women, Family, and Utopia: Communal Experiments of the Shakers, the Oneida Community, and the Mormons.* Syracuse, NY: Syracuse University Press, 1991.

Hardy, B. Carmon. *Solemn Covenant: The Mormon Polygamous Passage.* Urbana: University of Illinois Press, 1992.

Newell, Linda King, and Valeen Tippets Avery. *Mormon Enigma: Emma Hale Smith—Prophet's Wife, "Elect Lady," Polygamy's Foe.* Garden City, NY: Doubleday, 1984.

Warenski, Marilyn. *Patriarchs and Politics: The Plight of the Mormon Woman.* New York: McGraw-Hill, 1978.

Young, Kimball. *Isn't One Wife Enough? The Story of Mormon Polygamy.* New York: Henry Holt, 1954.

Pocahontas (1595–1616?)

Pocahontas, a Native American princess, is best known for her dramatic role in the rescue of John Smith, one of the leaders of Jamestown, England's first permanent settlement in the new world. Smith himself believed she saved his life. Pocahontas also played a less romantic but more crucial part in the success of the precarious English colony. She headed groups of Native Americans who brought the settlers supplies and repeated gifts of food—deer, turkey, and cornbread—without which they probably would have starved, according to Smith's account. Finally, as a young woman of 17, Pocahontas married an Englishman, bore his son, visited England with him, had an audience with Queen Anne, and died at 21 as she was about to sail back to Virginia.

Pocahontas was the favorite daughter of Powhatan, ruler of a confederacy of between eight and nine thousand Native Americans. Late in 1607, when Pocahontas was 12 years old, Powhatan's braves captured John Smith and took him to Powhatan's long house in Werowocomoco (Royal Court). There, Smith first saw this great chieftain sitting on a throne, arrayed in raccoon skins and ropes of pearls, and surrounded by advisers, lesser chieftains, shamans, and a crowd of young women with red-painted heads and shoulders and feathers in their hair. After sharing a feast with Smith, Powhatan and his advisers debated at length, and finally dragged Smith to two large stones, held his head on them, and brandished clubs above him as if about to kill him. At this moment, Pocahontas ran to Smith, took his head in her arms, and laid her head on his—as he believed, saving him from death. Immediately afterward, Powhatan pardoned Smith, and two days later, he formally adopted him, promising to "for ever esteeme him as his son Nantaquoud."

Popular versions of the Pocahontas story, including the 1995 Disney film, picture this preteen acting out of love at first sight of Smith, a 27-year-old hard-bitten soldier of fortune from another culture. Scholars now argue, however, that when Pocahontas rushed forward to save Smith, she was playing an assigned part prescribed for her by her father. Powhatan was showing his absolute power over this white man, forcing Smith to undergo a near-death experience similar to those that new braves endured to test their valor. Then, once Powhatan had brought Smith to the edge of life, he would give a different meaning to the life he had saved; he was claiming Smith ritually as his son. Smith himself, of course, never understood the meaning of the episode.

This interpretation of the Pocahontas story seems particularly likely because from this point on, Powhatan's people treated Smith differently from the other settlers. Pocahontas would come close to Jamestown only if Smith came out to greet her, and the Native Americans supplied the settlers with food until September, 1609, when Smith returned to England. From that point on, Powhatan refused to trade with the colony or have anything to do with its inhabitants.

In 1613, Pocahontas was again involved with the British. This time they took her hostage, proposing to exchange her for several English captives and some stolen weapons. When Powhatan heard that Pocahontas was well treated, however, he refused the trade. She remained the guest of the English, who dressed her in their clothes, converted her to their religion, and renamed her Lady Rebecca. Before long, John Rolfe, a widower in his late twenties, fell in love with Pocahontas; they married with Powhatan's blessing, and in 1616, Rolfe took Pocahontas and their infant son to England where Pocahontas died, probably of tuberculosis.

The story of Pocahontas has captured the imaginations of centuries of Americans, from pageant-performing schoolchildren to major poets such as Carl Sandburg and Hart Crane. She may well have saved the Jamestown settlement, but her contact with white men cost her her life. *(See also: Native American Women)*

—Gretchen Mieszkowski

Further Reading

Barbour, Philip. *Pocahontas and Her World.* Boston: Houghton Mifflin, 1970.

Mossiker, Frances. *Pocahontas: The Life and the Legend.* New York: Knopf, 1976.

Smith, John. *Complete Works of Captain John Smith.* Edited by Philip Barbour, 3 vols. Chapel Hill: University of North Carolina Press, 1986.

———. *Travels and Works of Captain John Smith.* Edited by Edward Arber, 2 vols. Edinburgh: John Grant, 1910.

Tilton, Robert S. *Pocahontas: The Evolution of an American Narrative.* Cambridge, UK: Cambridge University Press, 1995.

⋙ Politics

Politics can be defined narrowly as party politics or broadly as organized methods of negotiating differences in power. Understanding the history of women's political party activity requires both definitions. Women have always been politically active in this broader sense. Although women could not participate directly in party politics until they could vote, they worked outside of party politics in ways that, in turn, influenced agendas within political parties. Furthermore, this female tradition of working outside the mainstream of political processes did not end with woman suffrage. Nonparty politics remains the most important political arena for women because women have used it to create the gender-exclusive space necessary to produce and connect critical analysis and theory with strategy. Moreover, although women continue to be underrepresented in political offices, nonparty activism remains an important crucible of feminist consciousness for women who enter party politics.

Historically, women's nonparty politics can be divided into its two general goals. Some activism sought to gain women access to existing power structures, such as the economy, education, and government. Other efforts sought to eliminate male privilege and the organization of institutions around masculine values. Since the second women's movement, the latter goal has included efforts to eliminate hierarchies among women based on race, class, sexual orientation, age, and ableness. While issues of access have mattered to many women activists, others moved beyond that goal to question the institutionalization of stereotypes about women and to challenge the ground rules by which power structures function. A women's rights focus usually stopped short of these aims, even though the ideas women used to guide their organizing for women's rights posed radical challenges to conventional wisdom.

The first women's movement, especially from the late nineteenth century on, developed much of its political activism around a startling revision of the meaning of women's assignment to the domestic sphere, in effect reviving the Revolutionary War idea of "republican motherhood." Recognizing the social significance of child rearing and using it to argue for mothers' own greater influence in the broader society, the first women's movement established a wide range of gender-exclusive organizations through which many women politicized motherhood: settlement houses, temperance movements, trade unions, peace organizations, and an enormous variety of religious and secular service clubs. Working in service organizations educated women to the need for governmental involvement to solve the problems that concerned them. Jane Addams of Hull House regarded women's activism in this era as "municipal housekeeping"; contemporary historians have argued that the vastness of this activity constituted at least a vision, if not the reality, of a "maternal commonwealth." The difficulties of influencing governmental agencies that fell under the sway of party political machines led some women to organize direct challenges to party politics, including but by no means exclusively the demand for woman suffrage. Political parties entered into the vision of maternal commonwealth by engaging the issues that organized women raised, albeit usually by co-opting and narrowing the parameters of the debate.

Other women's organizations aimed at challenging traditional male bastions from their beginnings, and some drew on politicized motherhood first as an expedient rather than as a guiding principle. As the first industrial labor force, in textile manufacturing, women organized the nation's first labor union for unskilled workers in the 1830s. Post-Civil War women's labor unions organized because men's unions barred them from membership, but women's unions directly challenged male employers (and sometimes female employers, as domestic service workers' unions did), over unsafe work conditions, long hours, production changes, and low salaries. Like men's labor unions, women's unions suffered increasing levels of resistance from industrialists; women laborers in coalition with other workers sought legislation, particularly to limit the length of the workday. By the late nineteenth century, however, increasing levels of hostility against unions, often supported by government, led women's unions to politicize motherhood to gain protective legislation on problems that they could not solve by what had become the traditional union methods of pressuring and negotiating with employers.

Some black women's organizations pursued a different analytical strategy. The antilynching campaign led by Ida B. Wells-Barnett exposed the refusal of white male government officials to enforce the equal protection and due process guarantees of the Fourteenth Amendment but also exposed racists' use of stereotypes about both black male and white female sexuality to justify brutal murders of black men, pointing out these interrelated systems of oppression to white women who, resisting claims on their sexuality for this purpose, lent emotional and financial support to the campaign. The first women's rights movement included multitudes of women, many involved in more than one organization. The issues they raised brought them face to face with governmental bodies, laws, and party politics and brought male politicians face to face with organized women.

The critique of power differences that the first women's movement produced led some women to develop or to reassert feminist critiques late in this era, claiming the term *feminist* from about 1915. Politicized motherhood, as radical as it was for some women of the era, did not effectively challenge women's subordinated status vis-à-vis men; in the opinion of newly emerging feminists, it built on a gilded cage within the gender stereotype, locking women permanently into motherhood as their only significant social role and enforcing a particular kind of mothering as well. Moreover, women's rightists did not explicitly seek to change the shape of institutionalized power structures or the methods of doing business in the institutions into which they gained access. The distinction between women's rightists and feminists is not always obvious in this period: Sometimes women's rights activists simply assumed that processes would change as a natural consequence of mothers' presence in them, but other times, even the same woman did not proceed that far in her vision of the future. The difficulty of claiming feminist positions stemmed in part from the growth of the progressive movement that women had been so instrumental in initiating. By the late 1800s, male-dominated organizations, particularly political parties, co-opted the issues that women had raised, ignored women's analyses, and undermined women's empowerment at the same time that women's disenfranchisement remained largely in place.

A handful of states had opened the possibility for women to run for office by enfranchising them even before the Nineteenth Amendment passed. Montana elected Jeannette Rankin to the federal House of Representatives in 1916, the first woman elected to Congress. Rankin, noted for the women's rights activism that she embedded within the ideology of politicized motherhood, distinguished herself as the only person to vote against U.S. entry into both world wars, serving two brief terms that coincided with these decisions and for her stance on which her political career suffered both times. She worked throughout her life in the women's peace movement.

Activism in nonparty politics during the first women's movement had produced thousands of other women leaders, skilled in administration, public speaking, and organizing. Some of those women, predominantly coming from a women's rights perspective, became the first to hold governmental offices above the municipal level, primarily as political appointees rather than as elected officials. Nonparty organizing produced the Women's Bureau as a permanent agency within the Department of Labor in 1920. Woodrow Wilson appointed a longtime nonparty activist to the top post, trade unionist Mary Anderson, who led the bureau from 1920 to 1944. Anderson staffed the agency with other women nonparty activists who conducted research into the working conditions of women and to recommend legislation based on their analysis of the data they collected. Some Women's Bureau appointees moved into academic posts, while others came to the bureau from academia. The Women's Bureau provided working-class women with their most effective direct access to government. During World War II, the Women's Bureau coordinated the movement of millions of women into new jobs replacing absent men. Frances Perkins, the first woman to hold a cabinet-level post, served as the secretary of labor under Franklin D. Roosevelt, who appointed her because of her expertise gained through nonparty organizing on labor issues for women and children. During the Great Depression, Perkins coauthored important New Deal laws and implemented enormous labor programs.

During the period of public quiet between the first and second women's movements, feminist politics more clearly moved toward challenging sex hierarchy and the values that underlay it. Because the subordination of women had long been justified by women's biological role as childbearers, early twentieth-century feminists looked elsewhere to justify their claims to activity beyond the domestic sphere. Still, middle-class white women who claimed the feminist label tended to seek solutions to women's oppression based on what middle-class white men could do, and the media often subverted their arguments about interconnected goals. Therefore, working-class women viewed the feminist ideal of employment sufficient for economic autonomy from husbands as a singular goal and thus controversial and exclusionary, since an adequate wage for economic independence was impossible and work itself not clearly an empowering experience for most working-class women. Nevertheless, this emerging politics produced, among other things, the Equal Rights Amendment (ERA), written by Alice Paul's National Woman's Party and first introduced to Congress in 1923. The ERA intended to eliminate the sex hierarchy embedded into law. It passed Congress in 1972, but failed ratification in 1982. It represents, however, an important connection between the first and second women's movements. The conversion of the National American Woman Suffrage Association into the League of Women Voters following ratification of the Nineteenth Amendment equally connects the two waves of the women's movement. The league continues to play an important role in informing voters about candidates' positions on important issues of the day, including women's issues.

If any single element can be said to characterize the enormous diversity of the second women's movement, it would surely be the concept of "identity politics" that developed as a result of grassroots analyses of the personal consequences of the ideologies of inequality that shaped women's lives. The second wave of public protest by women emerged from a broad range of experiences, most notably from women's apolitical paid labor in private sector employment and their unpaid political labor in the civil rights and New Left movements. The second women's movement gained its vitality from millions of small consciousness-raising groups across the nation, as well as from more formally structured organizations. The grassroots style of the second women's movement allowed women to cooperate, rather than compete, in producing more sophisticated analyses of their situations and in relating individual experiences to larger systems of oppression. This grassroots style tended to produce heterogeneous groupings, and while feminist theory seemed to advance rapidly, it often assumed that women's experiences were uniform. Eventually, however, small groups encountered one another in larger forums over critical issues, and differences related to race, class, and sexual orientation emerged within the movement. Negotiating differences through nonparty activism has provided the continuing energy for the second women's movement in the face of a conservative backlash, and the struggle to create an inclusive politics has prompted the most dramatic advances in feminist thinking.

Some activists sought to create a feminist presence within the dominant institutions. For example, the National Organization for Women organized to disseminate feminism and focused early on legislative priorities. Rather than working to reform the existing sexist institutions, other activists designed feminist institutions that could serve women's particular needs outside the dominant systems and model nonhierarchical processes at the same time. Among the institutions with the broadest impact were women's health centers, women's presses, women's musical organizations, and battered women's shelters. Carried into academia, feminism also guided the creation of the new discipline of women's studies to document, analyze, critique, refine, and teach the meaning of feminist ideas.

In party politics, women have faced greater barriers to their participation than in grassroots organizing. As elected officials, women face a very thick glass ceiling: The higher the office, the less likely a woman is to hold it. That may in part explain why Walter Mondale's selection of Geraldine Ferraro as his vice presidential running mate in the 1984 election generated such enormous enthusiasm among feminists. The Mondale-Ferraro ticket lost rather resoundingly, and women continue to be underrepresented at all levels. From 1972 to 1991, according to the National Women's Political Caucus, the proportion of women serving in state legislatures or as mayors increased from 1 percent in each category to 18 and 17 percent, respectively. In 1972, two women served in the federal Senate; in 1994, the number increased to six. Women's proportion in the federal House of Representatives remained under 10 percent, a slight improvement from 3 percent in 1971.

Voter prejudice against women in authoritative positions partially explains these results, although surveys indicate that the proportion of eligible voters who claim that bias— that they would not vote for a woman—has declined since the 1970s. The slight increases in women's numbers in elective offices reflects these changing attitudes. But since party politics is a system, something more may explain women's poor representation beyond voter bias. By the 1990s, election results for state legislators, governors, and federal representatives indicated that women were as likely as men to win elections when they sought open seats rather than opposing incumbents. These results suggest that the most important reason for a continuing dearth of women in political offices was that women do not run for office in the same proportion that men do.

One critical reason for that is child rearing, for which women still feel primary responsibility, while men still do not. If women delay their political careers until their children are grown, and most women politicians do, they are less likely to reach high political office because they lack the exposure and the experience of male politicians who started political careers in their twenties. Another vital problem for women in politics is money. Since the 1960s, the cost of running for office has skyrocketed at all levels of the political system, while women's income remains, on average, substantially lower than men's. Unlike numerous men, wealthy women have not claimed a right to run for the highest political office without any prior political experience.

Party support for women candidates, therefore, is critical to fund-raising. Political appointments have often served as a gauge for party attitudes toward and party support for women, and women appointees, from judgeships to White House aides, declined markedly under the Reagan and Bush administrations. In his second term, President Reagan eliminated the agencies that identified eligible women, causing an even more precipitous decline. The Clinton administration not only increased appointments of men and women of color and of white women, improving on representation of these groups over any previous administration, but appointed women to very prominent positions, including Ruth Bader Ginsberg to the Supreme Court, Jocelyn Elders to Surgeon General, and Janet Reno to Attorney General. On the other hand, President Clinton capitulated very publicly to conservative attacks on several of his nominees for offices requiring Senate approval by withdrawing the nominations. He fired Jocelyn Elders in the face of a conservative outcry over her position on teenage sexuality.

Political attacks on women seeking high political offices are not new. When Geraldine Ferraro accepted the Democratic Party nomination to run as Walter Mondale's vice presidential candidate in 1984, she became a target of a probe into her husband's finances. Attacks on political wives have sent a message to women considering political careers as well: Eleanor Roosevelt and Hillary Rodham Clinton, both career women in their own right, stand out as targets of their husbands' political opponents, but historically, most presidents' wives suffered personal attacks as consequences of their husbands' political careers. All of these factors depress the numbers of women entering politics.

A countervailing force for women running for office has been EMILY's List, a nonpartisan political action committee that contributes money to women candidates early in their campaigns. EMILY's List carefully selects the candidates it funds: The race must be winnable, which has usually meant a race for an open seat, and the candidate herself must be viable, which excludes token women nominated by their party for unwinnable seats or to run as last-minute emergency candidates. By infusing money early in the campaign, EMILY's List has mitigated a number of the problems that women politicians face. Women with less political experience can win elective offices with early funds that allow them to circulate their message through campaign ads and appearances, reducing the impact of child rearing on women's ability to run for national offices. Early funds help to raise later funds so that the early infusion of money reduces the consequences of a candidate's lack of personal wealth while it also helps to focus party support. As a result of EMILY's List, more women are now positioned more securely on the political ladder.

Whether women's presence in the halls of government will change the traditional ways of doing business within them remains to be seen. The proportion of feminist women in elective office remains too small to assume that the changes they have already made will be permanent, but many of the women who have held state and federal offices brought with them roots in women's rights and feminist nonparty politics, and their influence has already been felt. Ronald Reagan's election in 1981 sounded a wakeup call to feminists in Congress, who reorganized their Congressional Caucus for Women's Issues into a viable coalition. While important legislation that the caucus supports remains to be enacted, the caucus is an important mechanism for keeping women's issues visible within the federal government.

Women's participation at the polls in the 1998 elections revealed the persistence of the gender gap: More women than men voted; 53 percent of the women voted Democratic, while 45 percent voted Republican. Blanche Lincoln (D-Ark) became the only new woman senator; among the six women newly elected to the House of Representatives, one was African American and another was Latina, and only one was Republican. The number of women in the U.S. Senate remained nine; in the House, there are now 57 women representatives. No woman was elected governor in 1998. Generally, the electorate focused on local issues as well as the economy, Social Security, taxes, and health care. *(See also: Abolition and the Antislavery Movement; Addams, Jane; Barnard, Kate; Baxter, Annie; Benevolence; Bosone, Reva Beck; Chisholm, Shirley; Curtis, Emma Ghent; Democratic Party; Diggs, Annie LePorte; Douglas, Helen Mary; Emery, Sarah Elizabeth Van de Vort; Equal Rights Amendment; Ferraro, Geraldine; Gender Gap; Haley, Margaret A.; Jewish Women; Jordan, Barbara; Kahn, Florence Prag; Kreps, Juanita Morris; League of Women Voters; Lease, Mary Elizabeth Clyens; Lockwood, Belva Ann Bennett McNall; Lusk, Georgia Lee; Lytle, Lutie; Married Women's Property Acts; Moral Reform; National Farmers' Alliance; National Organization for Women; National Woman's Party; National Women's Political Caucus; Patrons of Husbandry; Perkins, Frances; Populist Party; Progressive Party; Rankin, Jeannette Pickering; Republican Motherhood; Republican Party; Right-Wing Political Movements; Socialist Party of America; Suffrage; Temperance Movement; Todd, Marion Marsh; Unions; Valesh, Eva McDonald; Voting Rights; Wells-Barnett, Ida B.; Woman's Peace Party; Women's Bureau; Women's Rights Movements: Nineteenth and Twentieth Centuries; Women's Studies)*

—Deb Hoskins

Further Reading

Collins, Patricia Hill. *Black Feminist Thought: Knowledge, Consciousness, and the Politics of Empowerment.* Boston: Unwin Hyman, 1990.

Cott, Nancy F. *The Grounding of Modern Feminism.* New Haven, CT: Yale University Press, 1987.
Echols, Alice. *Daring to Be Bad: Radical Feminism in America, 1967–1975.* Minneapolis: University of Minnesota Press, 1989.
Evans, Sara M. *Born for Liberty: A History of Women in America.* New York: Free Press, 1989.
———. *Personal Politics: The Origins of Women's Liberation in the Civil Rights Movement.* New York: Vintage, 1979.
Fout, John C., and Maura Shaw Tantillo, eds. *American Sexual Politics: Sex, Gender, and Race since the Civil War.* Chicago: University of Chicago Press, 1993.
Freeman, Jo. *The Politics of Women's Liberation: A Case Study of an Emerging Social Movement and Its Relation to the Policy Process.* New York: McKay, 1975.
Ginzberg, Lori D. *Women and the Work of Benevolence: Morality, Politics, and Class in the Nineteenth-Century United States.* New Haven, CT: Yale University Press, 1995.
Hartmann, Susan M. *From Margin to Mainstream: American Women and Politics since 1960.* New York: Knopf, 1989.
Hewitt, Nancy A., and Suzanne Lebsock, eds. *Visible Women: New Essays on American Activism.* Urbana: University of Illinois Press, 1993.
Kerber, Linda K., and Jane Sherron De Hart, eds. *Women's America: Refocusing the Past,* 4th ed. New York: Oxford University Press, 1995.
Norton, Mary Beth. *Liberty's Daughters: The Revolutionary Experience of American Women, 1750–1800.* Boston: Little, Brown, 1980.
Orleck, Annelise. *Common Sense and a Little Fire: Women and Working-Class Politics in the United States, 1900–1965.* Chapel Hill: University of North Carolina Press, 1995.
Phelan, Shane. *Identity Politics: Lesbian-Feminism and the Limits of Community.* Philadelphia: Temple University Press, 1989.
Ware, Susan. *Beyond Suffrage: Women in the New Deal.* Cambridge, MA: Harvard University Press, 1981.
Yellin, Jean Fagan, and John C. Van Horne, eds. *The Abolitionist Sisterhood: Women's Political Culture in Antebellum America.* Ithaca, NY: Cornell University Press, 1994.

❧ Popular Culture

Women's relationship to popular culture has been an important area for analysis by feminist activists and scholars. Women (in particular, white women) have long been central objects in popular culture artifacts; women have played central roles as consumers of certain popular culture forms (such as novels and soap operas); and in some cases and time periods, women have been significant creators and producers of popular culture.

Feminists have been most concerned about how women are portrayed in popular culture, which is seen as an expression and construction of women's status and position in society. For example, white women have been shown as the sexual object for men to view in advertisements and movies and as symbols of good and evil, while African American women have been either invisible or portrayed as mammy figures. At the same time, many women enjoy some forms of popular culture, particularly those in which women are shown as central subjects rather than objects. Feminists have debated whether or not these forms represent a conservative reinforcement of women's role in patriarchy or a creative expression of women's culture and a desire for alternatives to present gender arrangements.

In those cases where women have been the active creators or consumers, the cultural forms are generally the least valued by mainstream scholars. Alternatively, feminists suggest that it is the association with women and women's experience that leads to the trivialization and devaluation of these cultural forms.

Feminist scholars have struggled to understand the complex and perhaps contradictory relationships between audiences and popular texts. Beginning with the identification of the concept of the "male gaze," which establishes women as the objects of men's look, attention shifted to the possibilities for a "female gaze." Differences of race, class, and sexuality among women have problematized the search for a general explanation of the effect of popular culture on women or the meaning of any particular text. *(See also: Advertising; Domestic Literature in the United States; Movie Stars; Soap Operas; Television)*

—Lana F. Rakow

Further Reading

Edwards, Audrey. "From Aunt Jemima to Anita Hill: Media's Split Image of Black Women," *Media Studies Journal* 7 (Winter-Spring 1993): 214-23.

Ganguly, Keya. "Alien[ated] Readers: Harlequin Romances and the Politics of Popular Culture," *Communication* 12 (1991): 129-50.

Kuenz, Jane. " 'The Bluest Eye': Notes on History, Community, and Black Female Subjectivity," *African American Review* 27 (Fall 1993): 421-32.

Mulvey, Laura. "Visual Pleasure and Narrative Cinema," *Screen* 16 (1975): 6-18.

Press, Andrea L. *Women Watching Television: Gender, Class, and Generation in the American Television Experience.* Philadelphia: University of Pennsylvania Press, 1991.

Radway, Janice. *Reading the Romance: Women, Patriarchy and Popular Literature.* Chapel Hill: University of North Carolina Press, 1984.

Rakow, Lana F. "Feminist Approaches to Popular Culture," *Communication* 9 (1986): 19-41.

Shiach, Morag. "Feminism and Popular Culture," *Critical Quarterly* 33 (Summer 1991): 37-47.

Shoos, Diane. "The Female Subject of Popular Culture," *Hypatia* 7 (Spring 1991): 215-26.

Popular Vocalists

The history of popular singing in America can be divided into pre- and postelectronic eras. At first, vocalists adapted an operatic approach to the projection of sound so that melody and lyrics would carry over the orchestra and be heard in spacious theaters and clubs. Just as the castrati, who combined male lungs with the penetrating sound of the soprano register, were the stars of seventeenth- and eighteenth-century Italian opera, the best known early popular singers were female "belters" like Sophie Tucker and Marion Harris. Even with the introduction of microphones, the devices, except for recording purposes, were largely eschewed by blues singers such as Bessie Smith or by musical theater performers such as Ethel Merman.

It was inevitable, however, that the microphone would dramatically alter the course of popular singing in America. The contained melodic line, colloquial diction, and informal thematic material of the American popular song as developed by composers such as Irving Berlin, George Gershwin, Rogers and Hart, Cole Porter, and Harold Arlen called for an intimate, personal style best realized by singers capable of approaching the microphone not merely as an amplification but as an extension of the human voice. Moreover, the preoccupation in the content of the songs with romantic love and, in particular, with repressed desire ensured that among vocalists of the "golden age" of American popular song, females would remain the dominating, most influential performers. Even the notable exception, Frank Sinatra, was quick to acknowledge his primary debt to two women stylists, Mabel Mercer and Billie Holiday.

With the popularity of big bands along with movie and Broadway musicals in the 1930s and 1940s, American popular song flourished, bringing to the public's attention definitive women interpreters such as Helen Forest, Judy Garland, Lena Horne, and Dinah Shore. Even with the waning of the golden age of popular song in the 1950s, a number of female vocal artists kept the tradition alive. Rosemary Clooney, Peggy Lee, and Sarah Vaughan were among the first to take advantage of the new long-playing record format, but none exploited this technical innovation more productively than the "first lady of song," Ella Fitzgerald. Her set of LPs recorded for the Verve label may be said to constitute a great American songbook, representing the best work of the major American songwriters of the first half of this century.

The rock revolution of the 1960s changed the role of female as well as male vocalists, shifting the emphasis from the song itself to the performer and performance. Although drawing to a limited extent on Bessie Smith and the blues tradition, Janis Joplin, the prototypal rock performer of the period, was best known for her flamboyant, self-destructive lifestyle and raw, frenetic concert performances. Besides the "hard rock" style of Joplin, a white performer, another direction in rock music derived from the rhythm and blues as well as gospel roots of black music. Featuring a mellower sound and more modulated passion, the "soul" rock of women vocalists first reached mass audiences through the recordings of Aretha Franklin and Diana Ross. A third and final direction of female popular singing in the 1960s was introduced by Barbra Streisand. A performer who bridges many styles, Streisand primarily reflects the tradition of Broadway and musical theater, updating it with dramatic effects and a sense of exhibitionism that, however controversial among music critics, have won her the steadfast devotion of a legion of fans.

Although Streisand continues to set box office records, the two most important pop divas for the MTV generation of the past fifteen years have been Whitney Houston and Madonna. The former combines considerable range and power with questionable musical taste, while the latter masks minimal vocal equipment with an undeniable sense of theater and the deft employment of various personae and gender roles.

Finally, as country-western music increasingly absorbs mainstream pop and rock influences, it continues to broaden its audience while remaining the popular music of choice for perhaps most Americans over the age of 40. To the ranks of long-established C&W queens such as Loretta Lynn, Tammy Wynette, and Dolly Parton can be added new stars such as k. d. lang (now considered mainstream), a self-professed lesbian in a musical arena once considered inalterably conservative and reactionary. *(See also: Holiday, Billie; Jazz; Smith, Bessie; Waters, Ethel)*

—Samuel L. Chell

Further Reading

American Popular Song: Six Decades of Songwriters and Singers. Smithsonian Collection of Recordings. New York: CBS, 1984.

Balliett, Whitney. *American Singers.* New York: Oxford University Press, 1988.

Gaar, Gillian G. *She's a Rebel: The History of Women in Rock & Roll.* Seattle, WA: Seal, 1992.

Pleasants, Henry. *The Great American Popular Singers.* New York: Simon & Schuster, 1985.

∂ Populist Party

The Populist Party, a radical third party of the 1890s that had evolved from the National Farmers' Alliance in the 1890s, was one of the few political parties to accept women delegates to its state and national conventions and to employ women in its speakers' bureau. Women who had previously been active in the Farmers' Alliance now endorsed and worked for the People's Party.

When farm, labor, and reform organizations gathered in 1891 in Cincinnati to begin forming the Populist Party, women delegates were in force, delivering speeches on economic issues facing farmers and laborers, lobbying among male delegates for woman suffrage and temperance, drawing up the party's platform, and negotiating political compromises. Frances Willard of the Woman's Christian Temperance Union (WCTU) and Helen Gougar, a delegate from the Prohibition Party, joined the Populist women at the convention. The women delegates and many male delegates believed that the convention would pass, with a large majority, resolutions endorsing suffrage and temperance. Both resolutions, however, were defeated. Undaunted by this defeat, the women attended the National Conference of Industrial Associations in February 1892 in St. Louis to help plan the Populist Party nominating convention to be held in Omaha in July. In addition to representing county and state alliances, women also represented the National Women's Alliance and the WCTU. Annie Diggs and Mary Elizabeth Lease were delegates for the National Citizen's Alliance. Other women served on the executive committee. Again the convention failed to pass resolutions on woman suffrage and temperance.

Nevertheless, most of the women continued supporting the party, attending state Populist conventions, and campaigning for Populist candidates. Although a significant number of the delegates at the July nominating convention in Omaha were women, few women were elected to party committees. The activities of the women at this convention were now symbolic gestures and politically less significant than had been the case at previous alliance, Populist, and other third-party conventions. Susan B. Anthony attended the convention to lobby for woman suffrage and was annoyed that Populist women continued to support the party despite the omission of a suffrage plank. After the July convention, Marion Todd, Sarah Emery, Annie Diggs, Mary Elizabeth Lease, and Eva McDonald Valesh toured the country campaigning for James Weaver, the Populist presidential candidate, and other Populists. Other women ran for office on the Populist ticket in state and local elections. Florence Olmstead and Clara Hazelrigg were elected as county school superintendents in Kansas. Mary Elizabeth Lease, Lutie Lytle, Emma Ghent Curtis, and other women received spoils jobs in return for campaigning for Populist governors in Kansas and Colorado. In both states, legislatures with Populist majorities passed women suffrage referenda that then went to the electorate.

In 1893, Colorado women attained suffrage. The suffrage referendum was defeated in Kansas. After the 1892 presidential election and the state elections of 1892 and 1893, women's involvement with Populist politics dwindled in most states. The party joined with the Democrats in 1896 to support the presidential candidacy of William Jennings Bryan, and the radical economic demands of the Populists that women had endorsed were ignored. Women, nevertheless, had gained important organizing, campaigning, and lobbying experience, which many would use in future political work. *(See also: Curtis, Emma Ghent; Diggs, Annie LePorte; Emery, Sarah Elizabeth Van de Vort; Lease, Mary Elizabeth Clyens; Lytle, Lutie; National Farmers' Alliance; Politics; Todd, Marion Marsh; Valesh, Eva McDonald)*

—MaryJo Wagner

Further Reading

Buhle, Mari Jo. *Woman and American Socialism, 1870–1920.* Urbana: University of Illinois Press, 1981.

Jensen, Joan M. *With These Hands.* Old Westbury, NY: Feminist Press, 1981.

Wagner, MaryJo. "Farms, Families, and Reform: Women in the Farmers' Alliance and Populist Party." Ph.D. diss., University of Oregon, 1986.

∂ Pornography

"Obscenity" and "pornography" are often used interchangeably, but there are important distinctions. The category of obscenity (from the Latin meaning "filth") has been used by the courts to proscribe some sexual material based on offensiveness and violation of accepted moral standards. Contemporary feminists use the term *pornography* (from the Greek meaning "whore" and "to write") to describe materials that eroticize domination and subordination.

Writing about sexuality and depicting it are not modern inventions, but the large-scale production of commercial pornography is a modern phenomenon. By the mid-nineteenth century, pornography was widely available in the United States, and laws were passed outlawing obscenity. Not until the 1950s did challenges to such laws begin to successfully frame obscenity as a First Amendment issue. At the same time, magazines such as *Playboy* (first published in 1953) began to market pornography that would become more socially acceptable. Throughout the 1960s and into the 1970s, the issue was typically framed as a battle between liberal free-speech advocates and the forces of repression.

That framework changed in the 1970s and 1980s with the emergence of a feminist critique that focused on the harm to women caused by mass-marketed, misogynist pornography. While the evidence from laboratory studies on pornography and violence is generally thought to be inconclusive, the testimony of women who have been injured by pornography has made clear the links between pornography and the sexual aggression of some men and has highlighted the way in which domination and subordination are made sexy.

In 1983, the Minneapolis City Council considered an ordinance that would have given plaintiffs injured by pornography the right to seek damages and injunctions by suing pornography producers, traffickers, and some consumers in civil court. The ordinance's authors, legal scholar Catharine MacKinnon and writer Andrea Dworkin, rejected criminal obscenity law as useless in stopping pornography's harms and argued that pornography—defined as the "graphic sexually explicit subordination of women through pictures and/or words"—was a practice of sex discrimination and violated the civil rights of women. The ordinance would have created causes of action for anyone (a) coerced into the making of pornography, (b) forced to view pornography, (c) victimized by an assault directly caused by specific pornography, (d) defamed through his or her unauthorized use in pornography, or (e) subordinated through trafficking in pornography. The Minneapolis City Council approved the ordinance twice, but it was vetoed by the mayor. Indianapolis passed a similar ordinance in 1984, but it was rejected by the federal courts on First Amendment grounds. Efforts to write it into law at the local, state, and federal levels continued into the 1990s.

The radical feminist critique of pornography sparked a pro-pornography/anticensorship response from some women, such as the Feminist Anti-Censorship Taskforce (FACT) formed to oppose the Minneapolis ordinance. While the ordinance is a civil remedy available to the people injured by pornography and would not empower police or prosecutors, opponents branded it as censorship and argued that women's interests would not be served by restricting pornography.

In the 1990s, the debate concerning censorship took on a new dimension as pornography became increasingly available on the Internet. In 1996, Congress enacted the Telecommunications Act, one portion of which—the Communications Decency Act—made it illegal to make indecent material accessible to minors on the Internet. Civil liberties groups challenged the bill, which was struck down by a three-judge federal district court. The decision was upheld by the U.S. Supreme Court in *ACLU v. Reno* (929 F. Supp. 824, E.D. Penn, 1996). Congress subsequently enacted the Child Online Protection Act 9 (H.R. 3783, 1998), which lawmakers described as more narrowly tailored to minors. However, this legislation has also been challenged as a violation of free speech. *(See also: Comstock Law; Female Sexuality; Moral Reform; Obscenity; Sexual Revolution)*

—**Robert W. Jensen**

Further Reading

Burstyn, Varda, ed. *Women against Censorship*. Vancouver: Douglas & McIntyre, 1985.

Dworkin, Andrea. *Letters from a War Zone*. London: Secker & Warburg, 1988.

———. *Pornography: Men Possessing Women*. New York: E. P. Dutton, 1989.

Itzin, Catherine, ed. *Pornography: Women, Violence and Civil Liberties*. Oxford, UK: Oxford University Press, 1992.

Lederer, Laura, ed. *Take Back the Night: Women on Pornography*. New York: William Morrow, 1980.

MacKinnon, Catharine A. *Feminism Unmodified: Discourses on Life and Law*. Cambridge, MA: Harvard University Press, 1987.

———. *Only Words*. Cambridge, MA: Harvard University Press, 1993.

Russell, Diana E. H., ed. *Making Violence Sexy: Feminist Views on Pornography*. New York: Teachers College Press, 1993.

Segal, Lynne, and Mary McIntosh, eds. *Sex Exposed: Sexuality and the Pornography Debate*. London: Virago, 1992.

Stoltenberg, John. *Refusing to Be a Man: Essays on Sex and Justice*. New York: Meridian, 1990.

Strossen, Nadine. *Defending Pornography: Free Speech, Sex, and the Fight for Women's Rights*. New York: Scribner, 1995.

Post-World War II (1945–1960)

The explosion of the atomic bombs at Hiroshima and Nagasaki ended World War II and ushered in a new age of prosperity and paranoia. As the United States entered the Cold War, Americans turned to a policy of containment and conservatism both abroad and at home in response to the perceived monolithic communist conspiracy. Overseas, the United States appointed itself the guardian of democracy and free trade, while on the domestic front, the Red-baiting of the McCarthy era of the 1950s attempted to root out suspected communist infiltration into American culture. After a decade and a half of economic uncertainty and war, the Great Depression and World War II, young Americans faced corporate anonymity and fears of nuclear holocaust. Many of them turned inward, to the safety of their homes and families, moved to the suburbs, and produced the baby boom generation. The secure image of the 1950s, however, camouflaged an undercurrent of social unrest that produced the emerging civil rights movement.

Women were forced to define themselves in terms of class and race. The Cold War revitalized the patriotic concept of "republican motherhood" and the cult of domesticity, glamorizing the role of wife and mother as caretaker of the future of American civilization. Not only did the new domesticity require traditional gender roles, but options for women outside the home were limited, and the activities of "respectable" women were circumscribed.

Higher education for women no longer implied their commitment to a career. Few women finished college because they married and began to have children much earlier than had previous generations. Although women had entered the workforce in unprecedented numbers during World War II, they were demobilized to make way for returning veterans. After the war, labor unions did little to advance the rights of women in the workplace. Employers offered women lower wages and restricted advancement opportunities, regardless of their skill or education. Women's employment outside of the home was considered temporary, to supplement the family income. As a result, women turned their creative energies toward their families and children, elevating motherhood and housewifery to professional status. Women also found an outlet for their talents and energies in the PTA, the YMCA, and other voluntary organizations within their communities.

Mainstream women's magazines flourished, offering a steady stream of implicitly antifeminist fiction and features. But social, political, and economic conditions after the war also set the stage for the resurgence of the women's movement in the 1960s. The overwhelming conservatism of the 1950s horrified women activists. Betty Friedan's accurate description of the frustration of postwar housewives in *The Feminine Mystique* (1963) helped a new generation of feminists to find their voices.

While white, middle-class women strained against the limits of domesticity, women of other races and classes struggled to overcome other kinds of oppression. African American women worked in rural fields or, more often, as domestic laborers. In the South, they developed leadership and grassroots organizations to confront Jim Crow laws, building the backbone of the civil rights movement. Women like Rosa Parks attained national celebrity. Black women also suffered harsh, often brutal attacks by local racist police and citizens. The Chicano and Latino civil rights movement that began in the 1950s among the migrant workers in the American southwest was also led by women, such as Dolores Huerta. Other working-class women joined labor unions, despite the intense suspicion of any liberal reform activity during the McCarthy era. Issues of class and race were more important than gender issues for most women of color. Only in the 1960s did minority women begin to develop a distinct feminist voice that could speak for them.

A dearth of legislation on women's issues and a cultural backlash against the expansion of women's roles character-ized the postwar era. In general, women of all races and classes were legally and economically unprotected. Jobs for women were temporary or menial, and the wages of "women's work" were never meant to support a family. The economy made it impossible for most women, especially women of color, to fulfill the ideal of full-time homemaker and mother. *(See also: Baby Boom; Black Women; Chicana; Civil Rights; Friedan, Betty; Higher Education; Huerta, Dolores; Parks, Rosa; Republican Motherhood; Women's Rights Movements: Nineteenth and Twentieth Centuries)*

—**Leigh Fought**

Further Reading
Harrison, Cynthia Ellen. *On Account of Sex: The Politics of Women's Issues, 1945–1968.* Berkeley: University of California Press, 1988.

Lynn, Susan. *Progressive Women in Conservative Times: Racial Justice, Peace, and Feminism, 1945 to the 1960s.* New Brunswick, NJ: Rutgers University Press, 1992.

May, Elaine Tyler. *Homeward Bound: American Families in the Cold War Era.* New York: Basic Books, 1988.

Rupp, Leila J. *Survival in the Doldrums: The American Women's Rights Movement, 1945 to the 1960s.* New York: Oxford University Press, 1987.

⊷ Premarital Sex

Premarital sex usually refers to heterosexual intercourse before marriage, although the term can also refer to a range of behaviors, including gay or lesbian sex and degrees of petting. Pregnancy rates have long been the easiest way for historians to measure premarital sex levels; however, they leave out a great range of nonprocreative sexual behaviors and offer little information on how premarital sex is judged and treated.

Attitudes toward premarital sex have varied across cultures, shaped by the gender, age, and class of participants; their access to marriage partners; the likelihood of pregnancy and its prevention; the economic and social value of children; legal strictures against fornication; and religious and moral teachings. Among African American slaves, who were denied legal marriage, community standards allowed unwed sex and pregnancy. Among middle-class whites during the same period, community strictures against women who were premaritally sexually active were harsh. In many cultures that officially forbade premarital sex, eventual marriage legitimized both sex between engaged partners and any children born from it. As urbanization and industrialization weakened the force of community and moral regulation, rates of premarital pregnancy among whites rose from 10 percent in the 1850s to 23 percent in 1910.

During the twentieth century, a sexual philosophy of "permissiveness with affection" dominated American patterns of premarital sex. The increased availability of birth control, a general rise in the age of marriage, and a changing cultural climate for women's sexuality played major roles in this trend. The Kinsey reports documented that at mid-century, 90 percent of men and half of women surveyed had engaged in premarital sex, although many of the women did so only with future marriage partners. The rate of premarital sex continued to rise, escalating dramatically among women from the mid-1960s on. In the 1990s, premarital sexuality was both more widely accepted than ever before and subject to a backlash; it was blamed for social problems, including AIDS, economic demands on the welfare system, and the decline of the nuclear family. *(See also: AIDS; Dating; Female Sexuality; Marriage)*

—**Miriam Reumann**

Further Reading

Bailey, Beth. *From Front Porch to Back Seat: Courtship in Twentieth Century America.* Baltimore: Johns Hopkins University Press, 1988.

Brumberg, Joan Jacobs. " 'Ruined' Girls: Family and Community Responses to Illegitimacy in Upstate New York, 1890–1920," *Journal of Social History* 18 (1984): 247-72.

D'Emilio, John, and Estelle Freedman. *Intimate Matters: A History of Sexuality in America,* 2d ed. Chicago: University of Chicago Press, 1997.

Kunzel, Regina. *Fallen Women, Problems Girls: Unwed Mothers and the Professionalization of Social Work, 1890–1945.* New Haven, CT: Yale University Press, 1993.

Reiss, Ira. *The Social Context of Premarital Sexual Permissiveness.* New York: Holt, Rinehart & Winston, 1967.

Wells, Robert V. "Illegitimacy and Bridal Pregnancy in Colonial America." In *Bastardy and Its Comparative History,* edited by Peter Laslett et al., 349-61. Cambridge, MA: Harvard University Press, 1980.

⧁ Presbyterian Women's Groups

Women's participation in the Presbyterian church was affected by a schism between the Presbyterian Church in the USA (PCUSA; later, United Presbyterian Church in the USA, or UPCUSA) and the Presbyterian Church in the United States (PCUS, or Southern Presbyterian Church) in 1862. In the early nineteenth century, women organized independent benevolent societies to support foreign and domestic missionaries, teachers, doctors, orphans, and widows, breaking with male organizations.

The General Assembly of the PCUSA in 1811 first publicly supported the work of "pious females," but warned the societies to engage only in services for women and children. After the Civil War, the missionary societies concentrated their efforts exclusively on foreign or home missions or on work with freedmen. The societies organized regional boards to which auxiliaries in local churches belonged. The first denominational woman's board, the Women's Executive Committee of Home Missions (WEC), was formed in 1878, with F. E. H. Haines as president, to benefit and cooperate with the Board of Home Missions. Katherine Bennett led the board to incorporate in 1915, making it the first women's organization to report directly to the General Assembly. The regional foreign missionary societies operated independently until 1885, when they united to form the Committee of Presbyterian Women for Foreign Missions; it joined with the Board of Foreign Missions in 1920.

In the 1920s, the General Assembly Council of the PCUSA eliminated the separate women's boards and later created the Women's Joint Committee. The Presbyterian Women's Organization (later, United Presbyterian Women) oversaw women's activities and advocated representation for and ordination of women. The Cumberland Presbyterian Church (CPC; merged with the PCUSA in 1906) and the United Presbyterian Church of North America (UPNA) created similar structures for their women members.

The campaign to ordain women as deacons, elders, and ministers arose in response to discussions about women being allowed to address mixed-sex audiences. The office of deacon opened to women first, and only later were women ordained to elder status.

There were isolated attempts to ordain women to the ministry. Louisa Woosley (CPC), ordained in 1889, and Elizabeth Brinton Clark (UPNA), ordained in 1944, both had their ordinations invalidated soon after. The PCUSA rejected ordination amendments to its constitution twice before such an amendment finally passed in 1955-56.

After the southern presbyteries of the PCUSA split off in 1861 over a theological difference, southern women continued their fund-raising work for home and foreign missions and auxiliary societies; however, conservative ministers feared the creation of a "women's church." Nonetheless, Jennie Hanna and Mrs. Josiah Sibley formed the first "presbyterial" in 1888; "synodicals" were started in 1904. Despite opposition from some men, the General Assembly in 1912 approved a superintendent of women's work at the denomination level to coordinate women's efforts and promote the educational, spiritual, and mission programs of the entire church. Hallie Paxson Winsborough, as first superintendent (1912–29; later, secretary), renamed the organization the Women's Auxiliary, drawing together the various local church societies into one group.

The auxiliary and Women of the Church (WOC) sponsored conferences, leadership workshops, and literature for Bible and mission studies along with the Board of Women's Work (BWW, later the Office of Women's Work and other successors). The program grew to include special committees on race and community relations, and ecumenical and interdenominational efforts.

In the 1950s, WOC and the BWW lobbied for equal representation of women on all boards, agencies, and committees in the PCUS. Although women had been appointed to executive and special committees since 1923, the BWW wanted to have at least one-third representation. The ordination of women became a priority after the defeat of an ordination amendment in 1955. It had been opposed by conservatives who thought it unscriptural for women to preach, lead prayer, or speak before mixed-sex audiences. In 1963, the committee rewriting the church's constitution deleted gender references in the section on qualifications for ordination; the change passed in 1964. Rachel Henderlite was ordained to the ministry in May 1965.

In 1983, the UPCUSA and the PCUS reunited after a 121-year split. In July 1988, United Presbyterian Women and WOC became Presbyterian Women. *(See also: Christianity; Religion)*

—**Diana Ruby Sanderson**
Adapted for the second edition by Paula Williams Webber.

Further Reading

Annual Reports of the Women's Auxiliary, Committee on Women's Work, the Board of Women's Work, the Office of Women's Work and Office of Women (1913–83). PC (USA) Department of History (Montreat), Montreat, NC.

Annual Reports of Women's Executive Committee of Home Missions, Woman's Board of Home Missions, Woman's Board of Foreign Missions, United Presbyterian Women. PC (USA) Department of History, Philadelphia, PA.

Boyd, Lois A., and R. Douglas Brackenridge. *Presbyterian Women in America: Two Centuries of a Quest for Status.* Westport, CT: Greenwood, 1983.

Farrior, Louise H. *Journey toward the Future.* Atlanta, GA: Williams, 1987.

Miller, Page Putnam. *A Claim to New Roles.* Metuchen, NJ: Scarecrow, 1985.

Minutes of the General Assemblies of the Presbyterian Church in the United States (1912-83), Presbyterian Church in the United States of America (1811–1957), the United Presbyterian Church of North America (1858–1957), United Presbyterian Church in the United States of America (1957–83).

Vanwijk-Bos, Johanna W. H. *Reformed and Feminist: A Challenge to the Church.* Louisville, KY: Westminster/John Knox, 1991.

Verdesi, Elizabeth Howell. *In But Still Out: Women in the Church.* Philadelphia: Westminster, 1976.

Winsborough, Hallie Paxson. *Yesteryears.* Atlanta, GA: Assembly's Committee on Women's Work, 1937.

᭡ Prescriptive Literature

Prescriptive literature was a peculiarly American literary form written during the first half of the nineteenth century. As the industrial age began, America struggled tentatively to evolve new democratic forms. Gender roles were seen as the most effective means of channeling and controlling potentially explosive social change; consequently, men's and women's roles were undergoing deliberate redefinition in a variety of prescriptive texts. The mass production of literary texts, made possible and economical by the newly developed printing press, facilitated this process. Although the American male was undergoing a similar redefinition, these prescriptive texts primarily advocated a specific role for the American female. Jacksonian Democracy, while expanding opportunity for men, actually resulted in a contraction of opportunity for women. The need for coherence and stability during this period of change was believed to be found in the home, a belief that further entrenched the stereotypical view of a woman's place. Ministers such as William Alcott initiated the movements by preaching the virtues of the submissive woman and codifying, along the lines of scientific rationalism, the rules of domesticity and

housekeeping. In addition, in their sermons and published tracts, they taught that a woman's role was to be a moral touchstone in family and society.

Men were not the only advocates of this new prescription for gender identity. Many women, most notably Lydia Maria Child, Susan Warner, and Elizabeth Oakes Smith, wrote similarly focused tracts or incorporated the domestic role of a woman into their fiction; however, their writings differed from those of the ministers. Even as they tacitly accepted their prescribed role, these writers strove to expand women's cultural and national influence. Sarah Josepha Hale was particularly influential; she edited *Godey's Lady's Book,* which, while embracing the domestic sphere as women's particular domain, sought to increase their influence by using the power of the role. This literary response to the ideology of domesticity is a conservative one (when compared with the radical efforts of Elizabeth Cady Stanton), yet even as these writers reaffirmed their prescribed place in the family, their resistance and impatience with the ideological contradictions underlying the disparity of opportunity are clearly present. *(See also: Child, Lydia Maria Francis; Cult of True Womanhood; Domestic Literature; Hale, Sarah Josepha; Stanton, Elizabeth Cady; Women Writers)*

—**Max Gavin Schulz**

Further Reading

Berkin, Carol Ruth, and Mary Beth Norton. *Women of America: A History.* Boston: Houghton Mifflin, 1979.

Cott, Nancy. *The Bonds of Womanhood: "Woman's Sphere" in New England, 1780–1835.* New Haven, CT: Yale University Press, 1977.

Douglas, Ann. *The Feminization of American Culture.* New York: Knopf, 1977.

Tompkins, Jane P. *Sensational Designs: The Cultural Work of American Fiction, 1790–1860.* New York: Oxford University Press, 1985.

᭡ President's Commission on the Status of Women

The President's Commission on the Status of Women was established by President John F. Kennedy in 1961 as a result of the persuasion of Esther Peterson of the U.S. Women's Bureau and other influential women within the Democratic Party who voiced their concern regarding the lack of women appointees to significant federal positions within the Kennedy administration.

The ailing but venerable Eleanor Roosevelt chaired this advisory commission of thirteen women and eleven men, which used seven investigatory committees, assisted by scores of consultants as well as the Women's Bureau staff, as it conscientiously conducted a formal federal inquiry into women's legal and social status. To honor its late chairperson, who died in 1962, the commission presented its report, titled *American Women,* to President Kennedy on October 11, 1963, Eleanor Roosevelt's birthday.

The sixty-page report reflected the social and political agenda of its appointees and the political preference of the Kennedy administration in its rejection of the Equal Rights Amendment (ERA) as the appropriate means for securing women's legal equality, which, the report suggested, could be achieved under the existing Fourth and Fourteenth amendments. Both the social feminists and organized labor opposed the ERA as a threat to their hard-won protective legislation for women workers.

In this, the first comprehensive federal review of the social, legal, and political status of women, the commission endeavored simultaneously to support both women's special role in the family and their increased access to paid employment. After citing as unacceptable existing discriminations against women and offering suggested reforms, the report endorsed equal and increased opportunity for women in education as well as in full- and part-time employment, paid maternity leave, day care, and other crucial community services for working mothers. The report challenged the federal government to demonstrate through its federal programs a working model of equal employment opportunity for women. As a result of this report, the Equal Pay Act of 1963 amended the Fair Labor Standards Act and became the first federal ban on wage discrimination based solely on sex.

This report initiated and delineated a national discussion of women's issues that coincided with the resurgence of the women's movement in the mid-1960s. Moreover, each state subsequently followed this federal precedent for statute and policy review by establishing similar commissions that provided state governmental access and support for the efforts of feminists to remedy inequities for women at the state level. Finally, as a result of exasperation at the snail's pace of actual achievement of reform by the Third National Conference of the Commissions on the Status of Women in 1966, the National Organization for Women was founded as a result of an informal caucus of twenty-eight conference women in the hotel room of feminist leader and author Betty Friedan. *(See also: Equal Pay Act of 1963; Equal Rights Amendment; Friedan, Betty; National Organization for Women; Protective Legislation; Roosevelt, Eleanor; Social Feminism)*

—**Angela M. Howard**

Further Reading

Harrison, Cynthia. *On Account of Sex: The Politics of Women's Issues, 1945–1968.* Berkeley: University of California Press, 1988.

Hartmann, Susan. *From Margin to Mainstream: American Woman and Politics since 1960.* New York: Knopf, 1989.

President's Commission on the Status of Women. *American Women.* Washington, DC: Government Printing Office, 1963.

∞ Preston, Ann (1813–1872)

Quaker reformer, physician, and educator, Ann Preston became the first woman professor at a "regular" medical college in the United States and the first woman dean of a medical school. As dean of the Female Medical College of Pennsylvania from 1865 to 1872, Preston was responsible for a significant increase in the opportunities available for women to train and practice as physicians. A member of the first graduating class of the Female Medical College of Pennsylvania in 1851, Preston returned as a faculty member and repeatedly and unsuccessfully sought admission for her students to clinics at the many hospitals in Philadelphia in the 1850s. Her requests were denied by male physicians and administrators who sought to keep women out of organized medicine. In response to the need for clinical training for women medical students, Preston founded the Woman's Hospital of Philadelphia in 1861. There, also, she began the first nurses' training school in America.

Like so many of the women reformers of the latter half of the nineteenth century, Preston was a persuasive speaker and writer, talents she placed in the service of the social issues of abolition, temperance, and woman's rights. On this last issue, Ann Preston made her most lasting contributions. As a Quaker, she believed in the traditional role of women in the household; she herself lived at home until well into her thirties, taking care of her mother and siblings. As a Hicksite Quaker, one who followed the liberal preacher Elias Hicks, she also believed in a woman's right to speak and travel in public and to engage in the same professions as males, be it the ministry or medicine. Following the direction of her own inner light, at the age of thirty-seven she enrolled in the first class of students at the newly incorporated Female Medical College of Pennsylvania, the first woman's medical college in the modern world. After graduation and for the twenty-one remaining years of her life, she devoted herself to the survival and continued improvement of the college (renamed the Woman's Medical College of Pennsylvania in 1867) and to the advancement of sound medical education for women.

Although ideologically radical, Preston used traditional methods to attain her goals. Believing in the concept of woman's sphere, she urged the expansion of that sphere to whatever extent necessary to provide women with the opportunity to live independent, productive lives. By the time of her death in 1872, many of the goals she had worked toward, including increased clinical opportunities for women medical students, higher scholastic standards at the college, and recognition of women physicians by the male medical profession, had been successfully realized in Philadelphia, the center of medical education in the United States at that time. *(See also: Nursing; Physicians; Society of Friends; Woman's Hospital of Philadelphia)*

—**Sandra L. Chaff**

Further Reading

Archives and Special Collections on Women in Medicine. Medical College of Pennsylvania, Philadelphia. Records of the Medical College of Pennsylvania. (Formerly the Female Medical College of Pennsylvania and the Woman's Medical College of Pennsylvania)

Chaff, Sandra L., Ruth Haimbach, Carol Fenichel, and Nina Woodside. *Women in Medicine: A Bibliography of the Literature on Women Physicians.* Metuchen, NJ: Scarecrow, 1977.

Foster, Pauline. "Ann Preston, M.D. (1813–1872): A Biography. The Struggle to Obtain Training and Acceptance for Women Physicians in Mid-Nineteenth Century America." Ph.D. diss., University of Pennsylvania, 1984.

⮌ Price, Leontyne (b. 1927)

Leontyne Price is an operatic soprano whose life exemplifies the possibilities of women, particularly of American black women. She was born into a musical family, and Price's southern upbringing in Laurel, Mississippi, was full of her mother's solos in the church choir and her father's tuba playing. Having begun piano lessons at the age of four, Price soon joined her mother in the church choir. When she was nine, she heard a concert by Marian Anderson that inspired her plan for a career in music.

The young singer obtained her musical training at Central State College in Wilberforce, Ohio (1949), and the Juilliard School of Music in New York (1949–1952), where she studied voice with renowned concert vocalist and mentor Florence Kimball. In 1952, after she appeared in a Juilliard production, composer Virgil Thompson invited her to appear in his opera *Four Saints in Three Acts* on Broadway and in Paris at the International Arts Festival. Her career developing quickly. Price was invited to sing the role of Bess in a revival of Gershwin's *Porgy and Bess,* and she toured with the company in Europe. In 1953, she sang the premieres of works by major composers such as Samuel Barber and Igor Stravinsky, and in November 1954, she made her concert debut at Town Hall in New York.

From then on, honors came swiftly. In 1955, she made her television debut in Puccini's *Tosca* with the NBC Opera, thereby becoming the first black singer to appear in a televised opera. In 1957, she made her operatic debut in Poulenc's *Dialogues of the Carmelites* with the San Francisco Opera, and her debut at the Metropolitan Opera in New York in 1961 as Leonora in Verdi's *Il Trovatore* was the occasion of a historic forty-two-minute ovation. During the 1960s, she sang no fewer than 118 operas at the Metropolitan.

Price's uniqueness seems an extension of her personal independence. She has said that the secret to her whole being is that what she is as a woman is what she hears in the sound of her voice. In the years after her divorce from bass-baritone William Warfield in 1973, Price developed a liking for her independence. National committees and organizations across the country have recognized her with numerous honors, including fifteen Grammy awards, four honorary doctorates, the Presidential Medal of Freedom (1964), the NAACP Springarn Medal (1965), and the Order of Merit from Italy. She also received the Kennedy Center Honor in 1980 and the National Medal of Art in 1985. In 1989, the National Academy of Recording Arts and Sciences presented her with their Lifetime Achievement Award, and she continues to be honored by many national and international groups.

Figure 49. Leontyne Price
Shown here rehearsing for a Metropolitan Opera production of Verdi's *Il Trovatore* in 1969, Leontyne Price is an influential artist and exemplar. Used by permission of UPI/Corbis-Bettmann.

Well into her fifties, Leontyne Price revived her unsurpassed *Aida* in 1981 in San Francisco. She continues to give benefit recitals when possible and encourages and supports young artists in her field. *(See also: Black Women; Music)*

—**Mary Frances Concepción**
Adapted for the second edition by Robynne Rogers Healey.

Further Reading

Cliburn, Van, and Richard Mohr. "In Praise of Leontyne," *Opera News* 46 (January 23, 1982): 8-11.

Lyone, Hugh L. *Leontyne Price: Highlights of a Prima Donna.* New York: Vantage, 1973.

Rubin, Stephen E. "Price on Price," *Opera News* 40 (March 6, 1976): 16-20.

Southern, Eileen. "Leontyne Price." In *Biographical Dictionary of Afro-American and African Musicians,* pp. 313-14. Westport, CT: Greenwood, 1982.

⮌ Prison Reform

The 1840s marked the beginning of a broad movement to reform the prisons in which women were incarcerated. In New York City, for example, Protestant missionaries Phoebe Palmer and Sarah Platt, concerned with the spiritual needs of women inmates, began to visit them in the Tombs, one of the city's jails. At the same time, members of the New York Female Moral Reform Society used their religious message to convert and reform young jailed prostitutes. Reform-minded women also joined the Female Department, the auxiliary of the Prison Association of New York, and worked to strengthen religious beliefs among women prisoners. This group was led by Abby Hopper Gibbons, and it opened a halfway house in 1845. The Women's Prison Association and Home was established in that same year. Also in the 1840s, Abby Gibbons joined with Josephine Shaw Lowell to campaign in New York for separate women's prisons operated by women. In Massachusetts, Hannah Chickering founded the Dedham Asylum for Discharged Female Prisoners. Chickering and Mary Pierce Door served on the Massachusetts Prison Commission and, with Ellen Cheney Johnson and Clara Temple Leonard, led a campaign for a separate prison for women. Connecticut, New York, and Massachusetts appointed women to the state prison boards. Women participated increasingly in professional prison associations, such as the National Prison Congress and National Conference on Charities and Corrections.

The efforts of individuals grew into a broader reform movement after the Civil War. By the late 1800s, this work led to an increased professionalism among these reformers, who also began formulating a new view of female criminals, one emphasizing the social causes of crime rather than the idea of "the fallen woman." A more sympathetic view of women offenders was developed, which identified economic conditions and sexual exploitation as principal causes of crime.

By World War I, a second generation of women prison reformers had emerged. Among the most prominent was Frances Kellor, a criminologist who argued against biological determinism. Other reformers expanded this research, and they also challenged the methods of operating women's prisons. Many favored preventive services rather than incarceration as the best means of curbing crime. In addition, organizations such as the YWCA, Immigrant Protective League, and Big Sisters worked hard to keep young women away from crime. Some reformers from the Women's Prison Association advocated probation rather than incarceration for females, and the number of women placed on probation doubled from 1907 to 1913. Women's courts were established, and new versions of prisons were developed by Katharine Bement Davis and Jessie Donaldson Hodder. These institutions were organized on the cottage system, and they offered academic and vocational classes.

During the 1920s and 1930s, attitudes and emphasis shifted. For example, the crackdown on prostitution that followed World War I sent a large number of women to jail. New women's prisons were constructed. During Prohibition, women were sentenced to terms in reformatories for alcohol and narcotic offenses. Popular views of female offenders hardened. The 1930s marked an end to a century of women's prison reform, as the nation's penal institutions moved away from reform and became custodial in nature.

Only after the emergence of the women's movement of the 1960s and 1970s did a renewed professional and scholarly interest in female incarceration emerge. Critics challenged the legitimacy of separate prisons for women, exposing their inequities, and triggering the reintroduction of prisons housing both males and females.

In the 1990s, as more women than ever before entered the prison system, studies of women in prison began to expose overcrowding, physical and sexual abuse, health care inadequacies, and various social and economic impacts on greater American society. Statistics in 1998 revealed a tripling of women in state and federal prisons since 1980, resulting in overcrowding and stimulating economies as the number of women's prisons continued to increase. In addition, prison systems that evolved for the incarceration of men have not been adapted to meet the general and prenatal health care needs of women. Approximately 8 percent of women entering prison are pregnant. Those who carry their babies to term are subjected to uncomfortable, unhealthy, and dangerous conditions and are usually separated from their newborns within hours of giving birth. Greater public attention is being paid to the conditions of women prisoners as the female inmate population continues to rise. *(See also: Barnard, Kate; Criminals; Farnham, Eliza Wood Burham; Leonard, Clara Temple; O'Hare, Kate Richards; Washington, Margaret Murray; Women's Prisons)*

—**Robert G. Waite**

Further Reading
Burkhart, Kathryn Watterson. *Women in Prison.* Garden City, NY: Doubleday, 1973.

Freedman, Estelle B. *Their Sisters Keepers: Women's Prison Reform in America, 1830–1930.* Ann Arbor: University of Michigan Press, 1981.

McKelvey, Blake. *American Prisons: A History of Good Intentions.* Montclair, NJ: Patterson Smith, 1977.

Siegal, Nina. "Women in Prison: What's Behind the Rising Numbers?" *Ms.* 9 (September/October 1998): 64-72.

Sullivan, Larry E. *The Prison Reform Movement: Forlorn Hope.* Boston: Twayne, 1990.

❧ Progressive Era

The Progressive Era is the designation that historians have bestowed on that period of U.S. development between the "gilded age" of the late nineteenth century and the 1920s, years characterized by an extraordinary commitment to "reform" and "progress." Although marked by such incredible complexity and diversity that scholars still debate furiously over its origins, nature, persistence, and legacy, the Progressive Era is best understood as a period of broad-gauged, multifaceted reforms set against the backdrop of the emergence of the United States as a modern, urban, industrial, multicultural world power. Many of these efforts involved voluntary action by private groups or organizations acting out of perceived self-interest, altruism, or ideological conviction, ranging from labor unions and trade associations to settlement houses and social gospel churches. At the same time, the era was characterized by an unprecedented flurry of political activism and legislative enactments at the municipal, state, and, to a lesser extent, federal levels of government. Historians have traditionally divided the era's reforms into those aimed at efficiency and the regulation of industry and those focused on social justice, an area where women reformers were particularly active.

Whatever their disagreements regarding the contours of this critical reformist era, historians generally concur that women played an unprecedented major role in reform. This was especially true of the emerging class of well-educated professional women, of those upper- and middle-class females with greatly increased leisure time due to technological innovation, and of those in the industrial working class struggling to improve the conditions of their labor. Although the majority of women, especially in rural and small-town areas, remained uninvolved in these wider currents, millions became either "feminists," committed to improving their own status, or "social feminists," who were convinced that women should play a critical role in the betterment of all society.

Women were especially active in the contest over woman suffrage, constituting not only the National American Woman Suffrage Association, successfully led by Carrie Chapman Catt, the National Woman's Party of Alice Paul and Lucy Burns, and the Political Equality League, but also the National Association Opposed to Woman Suffrage. Through the settlement house movement, which encouraged educated youth to "settle" and work among the urban poor, Jane Addams, Sophonisba Breckenridge, and other women activists created the profession of social work; their practical experience and involvement in aiding the poor and ethnic minorities brought them into political and organized-labor activities. Working-class females, often with the cooperation and encouragement of professionals and socialites, fought to improve their wages, hours, and working conditions through organizations such as Florence Kelley and Mary Dreier's Women's Trade Union League, which worked with Clara Lemlich and the International Ladies Garment Workers Union, the American Association for Labor Legislation, and various teachers' federations and central labor unions. Women led the lobby against child labor abuses in the National Child Labor Committee and against shoddy products and exorbitant prices in the National Consumers' League, led by Josephine Shaw Lowell and Alice Woodbridge.

Women helped found and operate a variety of organizations designed to aid ethnic minorities, including the North American Civic League for Immigrants; the Immigrants' Protective League of Chicago, directed by Grace Abbott; the National Association for the Advancement of Colored People, which benefited from the participation and leadership of Ida Wells-Barnett and Mary Church Terrell; and the National Urban League. The General Federation of Women's Clubs, most notably during the presidency of Mrs. Sarah Platt Decker, involved hundreds of thousands in a wide variety of reform movements, including conservation, public health, education, and library extension work. Especially under the leadership of Frances Willard, the Woman's Christian Temperance Union crusaded for a myriad of social reforms in addition to prohibition. Women were also prominent in the movements for mental health, social hygiene,

and birth control, and many, such as Elizabeth Gurley Flynn and Kate Richards O'Hare, joined radical organizations such as the Industrial Workers of the World and the Socialist Party. During World War I, women escalated their social involvement in a variety of causes, including nursing, morale building, selling war bonds, or peace advocacy, accomplishments that convinced many previously skeptical men of the legitimacy of woman suffrage and feminism. *(See also: Antisuffragism; Black Women's Clubs; General Federation of Women's Clubs; Immigrant Protective League; Minimum Wage Laws; National American Woman Suffrage Association; National Consumers' League; National Woman's Party; National Women's Trade Union League; Politics; Progressive Legislation; Protective Legislation; Settlement House Movement; Social Feminism; Social Housekeeping; Socialism; Suffrage; Teaching; Unions; Woman's Christian Temperance Union; World War I)*

—**John D. Buenker**

Further Reading

Buenker, John D., and Nicholas C. Burckel. *Progressive Reform: A Guide to Information Sources.* Detroit, MI: Gale, 1980.

Chambers, John Whiteclay II. *The Tyranny of Change.* New York: St. Martin's, 1980.

Link, Arthur S., and Richard L. McCormick. *Progressivism.* Arlington Heights, IL: Harlan Davidson, 1983.

Muncy, Robyn. *Creating a Female Dominion in American Reform, 1890–1935.* New York: Oxford University Press, 1991.

Painter, Nell. *Standing at Armageddon: The United States, 1877–1919.* New York: Norton, 1987.

Scott, Anne Firor. *The Southern Lady: From Pedestal to Politics, 1830–1930.* Chicago: University of Chicago Press, 1972.

❧ Progressive Legislation

The Progressive Era was characterized by a veritable flood of legislation, especially at the state level, that dealt directly with the interests and concerns of women. Between 1911 and 1919, thirty-nine states enacted some type of "mothers' pension" laws providing financial aid to widows with dependent children. The majority of states also passed legislation regulating the wages, hours, and conditions of employment for women who labored in factories, in response to pressure from organizations such as the National Consumers' League, the National Women's Trade Union League, and the American Association for Labor Legislation.

Organized labor, dominated by men, was ambivalent about such legislation, fearing that the minimal standards enacted by law would become the norm, undermining collective bargaining, but union leaders generally supported such efforts for female workers. Some staunch feminists were similarly ambivalent, fearing that such "preferential" treatment might undermine their arguments in favor of sexual equality, but these were far outnumbered by the "social feminists," who believed that such concerns were trivial compared with the immediate plight of laboring women.

The beginnings of these reforms predate the Progressive Era. In 1893, the Illinois legislature mandated a maximum eight-hour day for women, but the state supreme court found it to be unconstitutional. In *Lochner v. New York* (1905), the U.S. Supreme Court struck down a New York "ten-hour law" for women, on the grounds that it violated their freedom of contract. The same fate befell other such attempts until 1908, when the Supreme Court, at the urging of the National Consumers' League and its attorney, Louis D. Brandeis, upheld an Oregon law providing for a ten-hour day for women (*Muller v. Oregon*, 1908). Thirty-nine states adopted maximum-hours laws by World War I. Minimum wage laws were slower to materialize, but several studies by government agencies and private foundations between 1910 and 1913 clearly documented the effect of low wages on women, especially the recourse of many to prostitution. Beginning with Massachusetts in 1912, several states enacted minimum wage laws. Most industrial states also passed laws regulating the conditions of labor for women in industry, with the New York Factory Investigating Commission providing the model legislation between 1911 and 1914. Working women also benefited from the workman's compensation systems and industrial commissions that most industrial states established. Nearly every state, and the federal government, enacted laws to suppress prostitution, culminating in the passage of the Mann Act, also known as the White Slave Traffic Act, in 1910.

Beginning with Wyoming in 1890, several western states passed woman suffrage laws, while others, such as Wisconsin, allowed women to vote in school board elections only, since that was perceived as an extension of women's nurturing role. In 1913, Illinois became the first major urban industrial state to enact woman suffrage, albeit for offices not created by the state constitution. All told, twenty states adopted some form of woman suffrage prior to the adoption of the Nineteenth Amendment in 1920. The Progressive Era was a pioneering period in terms of legislation designed to meet the needs of women, one that established important precedents but that left much to be done. *(See also: Minimum Wage Laws; Mothers' Pensions;* Muller v. Oregon; *Progressive Era; Social Feminism)*

—**John D. Buenker**

Further Reading

Baer, Judith A. *The Chains of Protection: The Judicial Response to Women's Labor Legislation.* Westport, CT: Greenwood, 1978.

Buenker, John D., and Nicholas C. Burckel. *Progressive Reform: A Guide to Information Sources.* Detroit, MI: Gale, 1980.

Lochner v. New York, 198 U.S. 45, 25 S.Ct. 539, 49, L.E.D. 937 (1905).

Muller v. Oregon, 208 U.S. 412 (1908)

Skocpol, Theda. *Protecting Soldiers and Mothers: The Political Origins of Social Policy in America.* Cambridge, MA: Harvard University Press, 1992.

⁊ Prohibition and the Volstead Act

Although prohibition, like temperance, had become identified as a woman's issue by 1900, it was enacted before the passage of the Nineteenth Amendment, which gave women the vote. The movement to prohibit the sale, manufacture, and/or transportation of alcoholic beverages by law dates from 1846, when Maine passed the first statute, with twelve other states following suit by 1855. By the end of the Civil War, however, nine of these states either repealed their "Maine Laws" or had had them declared unconstitutional. The movement entered its second phase with the formation of the Prohibition Party in 1869 and with the founding of the Woman's Christian Temperance Union (WCTU) in 1874. Kansas became the first state to incorporate prohibition into its constitution in 1880, a move emulated by Oklahoma in 1907. The Anti-Saloon League (ASL) completed the triad of prohibition organizations in 1893, and several states responded with local option or statewide laws. By 1907, however, only Kansas, Maine, Nebraska, North Dakota, and Oklahoma remained prohibition states.

Spearheaded by the ASL and the WCTU, the prohibition movement became an integral part of the reformist surge of the Progressive Era, benefiting from its association with other movements, such as those to eliminate industrial accidents, curb prostitution, restrict immigration, and uplift African Americans, American Indians, and immigrants. In part a response to the serious drinking problems that plagued the United States, prohibition was also an effort to scapegoat ethnic minorities and to protect putative rural and small-town virtue against modern, urban, industrial life. Its association with woman suffrage was a mixed bag for both movements but probably harmed the suffrage cause more than it did prohibition. The enactment of the Eighteenth Amendment eventually allowed many opponents of prohibition to endorse woman suffrage since the ultimate horror had already been wrought. The WCTU also contributed to the movement's success among women by addressing its concern to many other socioeconomic and cultural reforms.

By 1917, there were thirteen totally dry states and thirteen more with local option or other limited prohibition laws. The entry of the United States into World War I added the arguments of patriotism and economy to the prohibitionist arsenal. By December 1917, both houses of Congress had approved the proposal of the Eighteenth Amendment, which provided that "after one year from the ratification of the article, the manufacture, sale, or transportation of intoxicating liquors within, the importation thereof into, or the exportation thereof from the United States and all territory subject to the jurisdiction thereof for beverage purpose is hereby prohibited." The ratification process consumed thirteen months, with the only significant opposition occurring in populous urban industrial states with polyglot populations, such as Rhode Island and Connecticut. Because the Eighteenth Amendment also provided that "Congress and the States shall have concurrent power to enforce the article by appropriate legislation," Congress followed with the Volstead Act, introduced by a Minnesota Republican in 1919, which defined intoxicating liquor as any that contained .5 percent of alcohol, fixed penalties for liquor sales, provided for injunctions against all the violating establishments, and contained a search-and-seizure provision. Curiously, it also continued the federal tax on alcoholic beverages, making the Treasury Department partly responsible for its enforcement.

In practice, enforcement proved to be a national scandal that gave rise to bootleggers and gang wars, police corruption, "speakeasies," and general disrespect for law and order. Public drinking by women became acceptable behavior, as speakeasies replaced saloons. By the outbreak of the Great Depression, however, disillusionment with prohibition had proceeded so far that several states repealed their enforcement statues, while many political leaders called for repeal. In 1932, the victorious Democrats, led by President Franklin D. Roosevelt, made repeal a top priority, and the new Congress responded by proposing the Twenty-First Amendment on February 20, 1933. It was ratified within less than a year, and the states regained total control over the liquor traffic. *(See also: Progressive Era; Temperance Movement; Woman's Christian Temperance Union)*

—**John D. Buenker**

Further Reading

Blocker, Jack S. *Retreat from Reform: The Prohibition Movement in the United States, 1890–1913.* Westport, CT: Greenwood, 1976.

Bordin, Ruth B. A. *Women and Temperance: The Quest for Power and Liberty, 1873–1900.* Philadelphia: J. B. Lippincott, 1981.

Clark, Norman H. *Deliver Us from Evil: An Interpretation of American Prohibition.* New York: Norton, 1976.

Paulson, Ross Evans. *Woman Suffrage and Prohibition: A Comparative Study of Equality and Social Control.* Glenview, IL: Scott, Foresman, 1973.

Timberlake, James H. *Prohibition and the Progressive Movement.* Cambridge, MA: Harvard University Press, 1963.

⨪ Project Head Start

As a federal program designed to assist and educate impoverished children, Project Head Start has had an impact on the lives of mothers in poverty. It began in 1965 as a summer program in President Lyndon B. Johnson's "War on Poverty." The emphasis of the project was on diagnosis, remediation, and developmental guideposts. The efforts focused on health, social, nutritional, and psychological services for the child and his or her family. The project was to be an enriching preschool learning experience at which at least one full meal was to be provided. Parents were encouraged to participate in every phase.

At the conclusion of the summer program, it was announced that the project would continue throughout the year with support for the children as they attended public school. The project was intended to ensure that the young impoverished child who might lack environmental stimulation would develop to the fullest of his or her potential.

In 1967, there were 3,000 programs throughout the United States, with 1,500,000 children involved. In 1968, there were full-year programs in 756 communities and summer programs in 1,100 communities. The emphases and approaches varied depending on the needs of the communities. The common goals were serving disadvantaged children and families and being responsible for the development of basic programs that met these goals. Additional training opportunities for parents were made available. Parents were to be offered appropriate counseling, legal services, and job and open-housing opportunities.

By 1985, more than 8,500,000 children had been served by Project Head Start, which had proved that it could have a positive immediate effect on the cognitive development of young children. Studies indicate that children who have attended Head Start programs develop the ability to adapt more readily to the school environment and experience more academic success. The project has also been successful in improving the general health of the child by providing needed health care and improving the existing health care services. As reported in the *Project Head Start Statistical Fact Sheet,* the project has been less successful in the areas of parent health education and parent involvement. The most effective programs have proven to be the ones in which the parents take an active role. Such participation has also produced beneficial changes in the community.

Although funding for Project Head Start was severely cut by the Reagan budget in 1989, it was restored under the Bush administration after the passage of the Head Start Expansion and Quality Improvement Act of 1990. The Silver Ribbon Panel of the National Head Start Association document titled *The Nation's Pride, A Nation's Challenge: Recommendations for Head Start in the 1990s* stated that by the year 2000, Head Start should build the capacity to serve children under the age of three, raise income eligibility guidelines, increase efforts to provide parent support services, and conduct needed research on the components of quality within the program. Although Head Start is now at a crossroad in terms of future responsibilities, it remains the nation's most successful educational and social experiment.

President Clinton's 1998 proposal, *Child Care That Strengthens American Families,* increased the investment in Head Start and doubled the number of children served by Early Head Start to 80,000. Since 1993, Head Start funding has increased by more than 57 percent. Over 830,000 children and their families are served by Project Head Start.

Head Start has played a major role in directing attention to the importance of early childhood development and has had a dramatic impact on child care. Studies have indicated that children who have participated in Head Start programs score higher than comparable non-Head Start children in preschool achievement tests and perform better in the early grades. Head Start provides outreach and training programs for low-income parents and increases their awareness of policy-making procedures that can serve to benefit their children. *(See also: Child Rearing; Education)*

—Bonnie Lou Rayner
—Sandra M. Fox

Further Reading

Child Care That Strengthens American Families. The White House at Work, January 7, 1998.

Head Start: A Child Development Program. Washington, DC: U.S. Department of Health and Human Services, Administration for Children and Families, Head Start Bureau.

Hymes, Jr., James. *Living History Interviews.* Carmel, CA: Hacienda, 1979.

McKey, Ruth Hubbell, and Larry Condelli. *The Impact of Head Start on Children, Families, and Communities.* Washington, DC: CSR, Inc., 1985.

Project Head Start 1969–1970: A Descriptive Report of Programs and Participants. Washington, DC: O.C.D. HEW Research Division, 1972.

Zigler, Edward, and Susan Muenchow. *Head Start: The Inside Story of America's Most Successful Educational Experiment.* New York: HarperCollins, 1992.

～ Prostitution

Prostitution, the practice of engaging in sexual relations for payment, has existed in the United States since the colonial period. Among the first victims of prostitution in America were female indentured servants and black female slaves. Although condemned by some of the clergy and outlawed by statute as early as 1672, prostitution grew as the country grew and accelerated significantly in the second half of the nineteenth century.

As historian Ruth Rosen has observed, rapid industrialization brought drastic changes in economic and family life and contributed to increased prostitution, which reached a peak of activity between 1850 and 1900. Furthermore, westward expansion, the transportation revolution, and growing militarization created all-male populations with a keen appetite for the services of female prostitutes in many areas of the United States. For some women, especially those from the working classes, prostitution seemed a lesser evil than poorly paid legitimate jobs or deprivation. While prostitution offered a dangerous, degrading, and short-lived occupation, it promised some material comfort and the myth of upward mobility. The existence of forced prostitution, or white slavery, while exaggerated by reformers, has been documented.

Efforts to curtail or eliminate prostitution—from the efforts of the New York Magdalen Society in the 1830s to the wave of Progressive reforms in the early twentieth century—have been almost continuous, and unsuccessful. Efforts at regulation, as have occurred with some success in Europe, have been limited in scope and duration. On the national level, the major accomplishment of the Progressive reformers in the area of prostitution was the passage of the White-Slave Traffic Act of 1910 (the Mann Act), which outlawed transporting a woman across a state line for immoral pur-poses. While the Mann Act may have reduced the instances of white slavery, it certainly did not eliminate forced prostitution.

On the local level, reformers in the 1900 to 1918 period succeeded in closing most public brothels and "red light" districts, some of which were quite extensive, such as the Storyville district of New Orleans, which had over 230 brothels prior to its closing in 1917. One of the most famous brothels closed in this period was the one in Chicago operated by Aida and Minna Everleigh. Tragically, the closing of most public brothels resulted in prostitution assuming even worse forms, such as an increase in streetwalking, and new forms, such as massage parlors and call-girl operations. Control of illicit, commercial sex has tended to shift from female madams and the prostitutes themselves to mostly male pimps or procurers and organized crime syndicates. These vice "employers" have tended to be less humane than many of the old-style madams, who had usually been former prostitutes themselves and knew firsthand the difficulties of the trade. Problems of disease and of safety for the prostitutes also increased with the closing of the bordellos and the scattering of prostitution. This has also increased the traditional problems of police harassment, selective law enforcement, and the corruption of public officials.

Not all brothels disappeared from the American scene, despite the efforts of reformers and the discouragement of their use by federal military policy during both world wars. Sally Stanford, for example, ran a popular house of prostitution in San Francisco between 1938 and 1945 before going on to achieve additional fame as a restaurateur, a member of the Sausilito City Council, and a best-selling memoirist. Among other madams who have written popular accounts of their careers in vice are Polly Adler, Nell Kimball, Pauline Tabor, and, more recently, Xaviera Hollander, who has written a large number of sex books, including the best-selling *Happy Hooker,* and socialite Sidney Biddle Barrows, who wrote *The Mayflower Madam.* In the 1990s, new forms of prostitution emerged that do not involve genital contact or penetration, such as computer sex, phone sex, erotic massage, and lap dancing, with phone sex becoming a multimillion-dollar industry.

Despite efforts to glamorize prostitution in some books and films, it remains an often grim reality, frequently compounded by problems such as drug and alcohol addiction and abuse, AIDS, teenage runaways, broken homes, child abuse, social ostracism, disease, police harassment, thievery, and sometimes serious violence. While prostitution as an industry generates vast sums of money, most of the profits have gone to pimps, taxi drivers, members of organized crime, lawyers, physicians, liquor and drug dealers, law enforcement officials, landlords, and real estate speculators. Even a highly successful call girl is not immune to some of the danger and degradation involved in prostitution, including psychiatric disorders and a limited earning span with no health or retirement benefits. Efforts to unionize prostitutes have not succeeded, nor have the efforts of

Margo St. James and her organization, COYOTE (Call Off Your Old Tired Ethics), to decriminalize prostitution. Prostitution is legal in the United States only in Nevada. *(See also: AIDS; Criminals; Moral Reform)*

—Jonathan W. Zophy

Further Reading
Bullough, Vern. *The History of Prostitution.* Hyde Park, NY: University Books, 1964.

Bullough, Vern, and Barret Elcano. *Bibliography of Prostitution.* New York: Garland, 1977.

Butler, Anne. *Daughters of Joy, Sisters of Misery: Prostitution in the American West.* Urbana: University of Illinois Press, 1985.

Connelly, Mark. *The Response to Prostitution in the Progressive Era.* Chapel Hill: University of North Carolina Press, 1980.

Elias, James, Vern Bullough, Veronica Elias, and Gwen Brewer. *Prostitution: On Whores, Hustlers, and Johns.* Amherst, NY: Prometheus, 1997.

Hobson, Barbara. *Uneasy Virtue: The Politics of Prostitution and the American Reform Tradition.* New York: Basic Books, 1987.

Rosen, Ruth. *The Lost Sisterhood: Prostitution in America, 1900–1918.* Baltimore: Johns Hopkins University Press, 1982.

Shrage, Laurie. *Moral Dilemmas of Feminism: Prostitution, Adultery, and Abortion.* New York: Routledge, 1994.

Winick, Charles, and Paul Kinsie. *The Lively Commerce: Prostitution in the United States.* Chicago: Quadrangle, 1971.

～ Protective Legislation

Protective legislation included a variety of state laws regulating the conditions under which women worked. In the nineteenth century, workers and reformers sought laws to improve conditions for both men and women, but the courts ruled such legislation an unconstitutional interference with the right of adult males to make contracts. Judges, however, were sympathetic to arguments that women's physical inferiority and roles as childbearers and child rearers warranted state protection. Ohio passed the first maximum-hours law for women in 1852, and by 1900, a number of states had enacted protective legislation for women workers. In 1908, in *Muller v. Oregon,* the U.S. Supreme Court affirmed that women's special roles and physical vulnerability justified protective measures.

By 1920, most states imposed some regulations on employers who hired women, although the majority of the occupations of women workers were never covered. Almost every state limited the hours of work, and most prohibited women from night work. Other kinds of laws banned women from various jobs such as selling liquor, carrying mail, working in foundries and mines, and operating elevators. A fourth type of protective measure was aimed at promoting a safe and clean work environment by requiring, for example, seats, rest periods, and adequate ventilation and lighting. While a number of states passed minimum wage laws for women, the Supreme Court ruled such legislation unconstitutional in 1923.

The U.S. Women's Bureau and most women's organizations strongly supported protective legislation. Labor unions, too, promoted such laws for women, but not for men. Reluctant to launch organizing drives among women, labor leaders saw such laws as a substitute for collective bargaining and a way of reducing competition for jobs. Opposing protective legislation on grounds that it limited women's employment opportunities were a relatively small group of feminists in the National Woman's Party and some professional women's organizations, which sought equal treatment of men and women through an equal rights amendment to the Constitution.

The Supreme Court's acceptance of the gender-neutral Fair Labor Standards Act of 1938 paved the way for applying regulatory laws to both male and female workers. But protective legislation for women endured until the 1970s, when federal courts ruled such laws in violation of the ban on sex discrimination in employment enacted in Title VII of the Civil Rights Act of 1964. *(See also: Civil Rights Act of 1964; Equal Rights Amendment; Fair Labor Standards Act; Minimum Wage Laws;* Muller v. Oregon; *Progressive Era; Progressive Legislation; Social Feminism)*

—Susan M. Hartmann

Further Reading
Babcock, Barbara A. et al. *Sex Discrimination and the Law.* Boston: Little, Brown, 1975.

Baer, Judith A. *The Chains of Protection.* Westport, CT: Greenwood, 1978.

Hill, Ann C. "Protection of Women Workers and the Courts," *Feminist Studies* 5 (Summer 1979): 247-73.

Kirkby, Diane. " 'The Wage-Earning Woman and the State': The National Women's Trade Union League and Protective Legislation, 1903–1923," *Labor History* 28 (1987): 54-66.

Lehrer, Susan. *Origins of Protective Legislation for Women, 1905–1925.* Albany: State University of New York Press, 1987.

Muller v. Oregon, 208 U.S. 412 (1908).

～ Pruitt, Ida (1888–1985)

Ida Pruitt was a missionary educator in China (1912–1918), the founder and head of the Department of Social Services at the Peking Union Medical College (1921–1939), the coauthor of *A Daughter of Han: The Autobiography of a Chinese Working Woman,* the American executive secretary of the American Committee for the Chinese Industrial Cooperatives (1939–1952), and a vocal supporter of the People's Republic of China.

The daughter of American missionaries living in an interior Chinese village during the heyday of the American foreign missionary movement, Pruitt spent much less time at boarding school than most missionary children. Perhaps because of her long and intimate association with her Chinese "amah" (nurse/nanny), neighbors, and friends, she identified to an unusual degree with the traditional Chinese, especially women. Her oral histories, essays, fiction, and professional social work articles were unusual for American authors of any period in portraying the Chinese as having strength, dignity, and the capacity for self-rule. In particular, her treatment of women challenged long-standing Western stereotypes of Asian women. Her translations of Chinese authors have been called exceptional.

Pruitt's unique position at the intersection of traditional Chinese and modern American cultures inspired her unusually strong opposition to foreign political and cultural intervention in China. During the Japanese occupation of the 1930s, she was one of a handful of Westerners who participated in the anti-Japanese underground. The American Committee of the Chinese Industrial Cooperatives, under her leadership, was unique among China relief agencies in maintaining a genuinely nonpartisan stance between Chinese political factions during World War II.

Ida Pruitt's commitment to China's independence and her role in interpreting China to Americans extended into the postwar anti-Communist period dominated by the sensational investigations of Republican Senator Joseph R. McCarthy of alleged Communist subversion of American life. In defiance of a State Department ban on American travel to Communist countries, she visited China in 1959 and spoke publicly about the country when it was off limits to Americans. For thirty years, from 1949 to 1979, she was one of few Americans openly advocating U.S. diplomatic recognition of the People's Republic of China. *(See also: American Missionary Association)*

—Marjorie King

Further Reading

Anna and Ida Pruitt Papers. The Arthur and Elizabeth Schlesinger Library. Radcliffe College, Cambridge, MA.

Crouch, Archie R., comp. *Christianity in China: A Scholars' Guide to Resources in the Libraries and Archives of the United States.* Armonk, NY: M. E. Sharpe, 1988.

King, Marjorie. "Missionary Mother and Radical Daughter: Anna and Ida Pruitt in China, 1887–1939." Ph.D., diss., Temple University, 1984.

Pruitt, Ida. *A China Childhood.* San Francisco: Chinese Materials Center, 1978.

———. *A Daughter of Han: The Autobiography of a Chinese Working Woman.* New Haven, CT: Yale University Press, 1945. Reprint, Stanford, CA: Stanford University Press, 1967.

———. "Day by Day in Peking," *Atlantic Monthly* 147 (January-June 1931): 611-19.

———. "Faith," *Atlantic Monthly* 150 (July-December 1932): 782-83.

———, trans. *The Flight of an Empress by Wu Yung.* New Haven, CT: Yale University Press, 1936.

———. "New Year's Eve in Peking," *Atlantic Monthly* 149 (January-June 1932): 47-53.

———. *Old Madam Yin: A Memoir of Peking Life, 1926–1938.* Stanford, CA: Stanford University Press, 1979.

———, trans. *Yellow Storm by Lao She (Lau Shaw).* New York: Harcourt Brace, 1951.

~ Psychiatry

Psychiatry is a specialized branch of medicine that deals with the treatment of mental and personality disorder. Because of its close links with medicine, psychiatry relies heavily on the concept of organismic (physiological) causes of disorders. Consequently, most psychiatrists seek to treat their patients with a combination of drug therapy and psychotherapy.

The psychotherapeutic method currently used by most psychiatrists has its roots in the psychoanalytic work of Sigmund Freud and his disciples. By means of intensive interview and analysis of symbolic behaviors, such as dreams, the analyst seeks to guide the patient to an understanding of the underlying causes of the dysfunctional symptoms she exhibits.

Traditional psychoanalytic theory describes women as weak beings whose lives are dominated by the psychological shock of not being male (castration complex). Women's experience of the Oedipal conflict and their envy of male power (penis envy) dooms them to a life dominated by a desire to emulate men. Hence, women's neuroses are seen as being caused by an ill-formed ego unable to withstand these id-based impulses. Women thus are perceived as narcissistic, masochistic, and passively aggressive. This imagery has formed the basis for psychoanalytic treatment of women since the turn of the century.

However, for the past twenty years, psychiatry has been struggling to revise its approach to the treatment of women. Work by male psychiatrists on the existence of "womb envy" in males began to challenge the belief that normalcy was related to masculinity. Moreover, work by feminist psychotherapists began to present an alternative framework for explaining women's psychology and their experience of psychological depression and other disorders. Jean Baker Miller, a psychiatrist, was the first person to provide a feminist interpretation of the social forces that impel women to develop symptoms of psychological disorder. She describes the way in which traditional female socialization forces a young woman to deny her own self-fulfillment. And she explains that being seen as "psychologically healthy" requires that a woman be willing to devote herself to the nurturance and care of others, while at the same time neglecting herself. Miller's perceptions were strongly supported by research by Broverman et al. (1970) demonstrating that women and men therapists alike evaluated traditionally male characteristics (e.g., independence, objectivity) as more positive and more psychologically healthy than traditionally female characteristics (e.g., emotionality, subjectivity). Current research demonstrates that women are susceptible to being channeled into dependency on prescribed drugs, and these gender differences in psychotropic drug use are manifestations of the gendered construction of society (Ettorre and Riska).

Miller and her associates at the Stone Center at Wellesley College continue to develop the self-in-relation theory to offer healthy descriptions of women's development. Theories such as this, and the plethora of feminist research that has followed from these works, have defined the ways in which psychiatry needs to change to serve its women patients better. Sex and gender differences exist in response to psychotropic medications, such as those used for psychotic, anxiety-related, and depressive disorders (Hamilton and Jensvold). We now know more clearly the relationships between female hormonal systems and neocortically induced mood states. We also understand more clearly the psychological and societal factors related to women's eating disorders and drug and alcohol dependence patterns. However, this research has had little effect on the traditional discipline of psychiatry. Despite the emergence of feminist models of successful therapeutic methods, the medical model that underlies psychiatry has been little changed. Moreover, millions of women still suffer from major clinical psychological depression and seek the help of psychiatrists who do not subscribe to a socially induced model of psychological disorder. It is hoped that the newly emerging field of feminist psychiatry will have a strong influence on this branch of medicine in the future. *(See also: Deutsch, Helene; Eating Disorders; Freudianism; Horney, Karen; Modern Woman: The Lost Sex; Physicians; Psychology; Satir, Virginia)*

—Teresa Peck
—Susan C. Turell

Further Reading

Broverman, Inge et al. "Sex Role Stereotypes in Clinical Judgements of Mental Health," *Journal of Consulting and Clinical Psychology* 34 (1970): 1-7.

Ettorre, Elizabeth, and Elianne Riska. *Psychotropics and Society.* London: Routledge, 1996.

Hamilton, Jean A., and Margaret F. Jensvold. "Sex and Gender as Critical Variables in Feminist Psychopharmacology Research and Pharmacotherapy," *Women and Therapy* 16 (1995): 9-30. [Special issue on psychopharmacology from a feminist perspective]

Miller, Jean Baker, ed. *Psychoanalysis and Women.* New York: Brunner/Mazel, 1973.

———. "Women's Psychological Development." In *Women beyond Freud: New Concepts of Feminine Psychology,* edited by Milton Berger, 79-97. New York: Brunner/Mazel, 1993.

Russell, Denise. *Women, Madness, and Medicine.* Oxford: Polity, 1995.

◈ Psychology

Psychology is the study of the individual's mental and observable behavior. In the United States in the mid-nineteenth century, psychology was considered to be a subfield of philosophy, but the emerging work of the psychophysicists in Europe and a growing awareness of the physiological bases of some behaviors led to the reconceptualization of psychology as a science. The development of departments of psychology at major U.S. universities, most notably Cornell, Chicago, Columbia, and Harvard, established the discipline as a legitimate field of academic study by the last decade of the nineteenth century. Since that time, psychology has grown in stature as a discipline that combines the rigor of science with the empathy and sensitivity of clinical insight.

Psychology has always been a discipline that has attracted women scholars. Some of the distinguished foremothers of

American psychology had to endure academic insult and enormous hurdles in the pursuit of their careers. For example, Christine Ladd-Franklin and Mary Calkins were both denied their doctoral degrees—by Johns Hopkins and Harvard, respectively—in the late nineteenth century despite their having completed all necessary coursework and the dissertation. Many early women psychologists were denied teaching posts at coeducational or Ivy League universities because they were considered to be unable to meet the demands of academic life. Consequently, most of them took positions at women's colleges and started a tradition of excellence in undergraduate training of women psychologists that ensured their students places in the best graduate schools a generation later. This in turn ensured that women's role in psychology would become one of vigorous participation and valuable contribution. For example, in 1891, Mary Calkins founded one of the first psychological research laboratories in the United States at Wellesley College; Margaret Washburn, after becoming disillusioned with the way women were treated at Cornell, left her teaching position there to found the psychology department at Vassar, her alma mater, in 1903. Since that time, women have continued to find psychology an attractive field of study, such that by the mid-1980s women composed about 30 percent of the recipients of Ph.D. degrees awarded in that field. Leading lights in the field have included Helen Durkin, Henriette Glatzer, Karen Horney, Edith Jacobson, and Margaret Mahler.

However, although psychology has been a moderately receptive discipline for women scholars, it has, until recently, been insensitive to the role of gender bias in its scholarship. The push for scientific exactness that dominated U.S. psychology from the 1930s to the late 1960s created a situation wherein much of what was considered to be psychological "fact" was based on data from studies of male subjects only. Frequently, this situation occurred because the paradigms under which the investigators were functioning made interpretation of data from women subjects difficult. In many cases, the female data directly contradicted the thesis under investigation and was therefore ignored by the investigator. Thus, established theories such as Lawrence Kohlberg's theory of moral development and Stanley Coopersmith's theory of self-esteem were developed from male data. When women subjects were evaluated by these theories, they were found to be "morally immature" or lacking in self-esteem.

The reemergence of feminist consciousness in the 1960s allowed women psychologists to begin to question the established findings in the field. A major turning point for psychology came with the publication, in 1974, of *The Psychology of Sex Differences* by Eleanor Maccoby and Carol Jacklin. In this book, hundreds of studies that investigated gender-based differences were reanalyzed. The resulting conclusions strongly challenged accepted lore in psychology concerning the extent and pervasiveness of gender as a causative factor in human behavior. The scholarship in this book captured the spirit of change within psychology that had started in the late 1960s with the formation of a splinter group of the American Psychological Association, the major professional association for academic and practicing psychologists in the United States. The Association for Women in Psychology was formed to provide a professional forum for women psychologists to present their work and to identify areas of psychology in need of redefinition and reconstruction. Membership in this organization grew quickly, and by 1973, the field of psychology of women was recognized by the parent organization, and a division of the American Psychological Association devoted to scholarship in feminist psychology (Division 35, Psychology of Women) was formed. This division developed its own scholarly journal *Psychology of Women Quarterly,* dedicated to the promulgation of research about women's psychology.

Concurrent with the political emergence of women psychologists in the late 1960s came a vigorous burst of scholarly activity dedicated to the identification of women's psychological characteristics. The need to "set the record straight" led to the publication of research about women and to the development of psychology courses on college campuses based on this new research. Since that time, courses in the psychology of women have become standard offerings in undergraduate and graduate psychology departments in most colleges and universities in the United States. *(See also: Family Violence; Freudianism; Higher Education; Horney, Karen; Modern Woman: The Lost Sex; Psychiatry; Satir, Virginia; Women's Studies)*

—**Teresa Peck**

Further Reading

American Psychological Association, Membership Office. Personal communication, Washington, D.C., 1988.

Maccoby, Eleanor, and Carol Jacklin. *The Psychology of Sex Differences.* Palo Alto, CA: Stanford University Press, 1974.

Russo, Nancy F., and Agnes N. O'Connell. "Models from Our Past: Psychology's Foremothers," *Psychology of Women Quarterly* 5 (1980): 11-54.

Scarborough, Elizabeth, and Laurel Furumoto. *Untold Lives: The First Generation of American Women Psychologists.* New York: Columbia University Press, 1989.

Williams, J. *Psychology of Women: Behavior in a Biosocial Context.* New York: Norton, 1977.

∿ Public Speakers: Nineteenth Century

"But I suffer not a woman to teach, nor to usurp authority over the man, but to be in silence" (1 Tim., 2:12). From colonial times, Puritan/Protestant clergy, in the name of St. Paul, curtailed almost all public roles for women. Although certain evangelical sects and Quakers had long encouraged women to proselytize (and many of the best of the women orators were Quakers), the Protestant ban on women's public speaking continued far into the nineteenth century, when the era's Victorian notions about woman's nature further encouraged the belief that a female wanting to

speak in public must be unwomanly as well as irreligious. Nevertheless, important exceptions emerged out of the reform impulse or religious fervor over a specific cause—usually abolition, temperance, or woman suffrage. Advocate of sexual freedom and atheism Frances Wright spoke in public in the 1820s, while abolitionists Frances Maria W. Stewart and the Grimké sisters (Sarah and Angelina) did so in the 1830s. After the 1848 Seneca Falls Convention and the several women's rights conferences and conventions it spawned, an increasing number of women took to the platform: Sojourner Truth, Lucy Stone, Ernestine Rose, Lucretia Mott, and Abby Kelley. In 1853, Susan B. Anthony, Amelia Bloomer, and the Reverend Antoinette Brown were the first women to lecture in public in Manhattan—to an audience of over three thousand.

Both the Civil War and postwar conditions forced women into more public roles. Although few were trained in classical rhetoric or oratory, some turned their occasional speeches for special causes into careers—as agents for temperance or suffrage groups and, later in the century, as speakers in the increasingly popular lyceum and Chautauqua movements, series of lectures and public forums presented by local and traveling speakers. Anna Dickinson and Mary Livermore moved from war effort work to Redpath's Lyceum circuit. Olympia Brown, Elizabeth Cady Stanton, Stone, and Anthony campaigned for a woman suffrage referendum in Kansas in 1867. Phebe Hanaford, contemporary historian of women speakers, claims that more than thirty women had achieved national prominence through public speaking by 1876, while many more had gained local recognition. *(See also: Abolition and the Antislavery Movement; Christianity; Politics; Populist Party; Religion; Society of Friends; Suffrage; Temperance Movement)*

—**Nan Nowik**

Further Reading

Campbell, Karlyn Kohrs, ed. *Women Public Speakers in the United States, 1800–1925: A Bio-Critical Sourcebook.* Westport, CT: Greenwood, 1993.

Hanaford, Phebe. *Women of the Century.* Boston: Russell, 1877.

Kennedy, Patricia S., and Gloria H. O'Shields, eds. *We Shall Be Heard: Women Speakers in America 1828–Present.* Dubuque, IA: Kendall/Hunt, 1983.

O'Connor, Lillian. *Pioneer Women Orators: Rhetoric in the Ante-Bellum Reform Movement.* New York: Columbia University Press, 1954.

Stanton, Elizabeth Cady, Susan B. Anthony, and Matilda Joslyn Gage, eds. *History of Woman Suffrage,* 2d ed. Rochester, NY: Mann, 1889.

∿ Pure Food Act (1906)

The first line of the Pure Food Act of 1906 states its purpose as "an act for preventing the manufacture, sale, or transportation of adulterated or misbranded or poisonous or deleterious foods, drugs, medicines, and liquors, and for regulating traffic therein, and for other purposes." The passage of this act was a testimonial to one of the earliest realizations of women's political power to enact change in American society.

Annie Whittenmyer, a helper in Civil War hospitals, sparked the first public interest in pure foods. Upset by the monotonous diet and nonnutritious fillers given to patients, she argued for a healthier, more varied diet specialized for patients' needs. Her arguments persuaded Harvey Wiley to make the study of food additives and processing his life's work. When he became chief chemist in the U.S. Department of Agriculture, the fight against impure food and unsafe food processing began in earnest. Wiley asked the women of the United States to help him force the enactment of legislation to make processed foods and medicines safe for their families' consumption.

In the 1890s, a group of women formed the Food Consumers' League. Alice Lakey began a publicity campaign against the use of aniline, a poisonous, oily liquid made from coal, used in food-coloring dyes. Florence Kelley, the secretary of the National Consumers' League in 1899, became the first woman in the United States to lead a state factory inspection service. She encouraged increased food and drug legislation at city, state, and federal levels.

In 1902, the Woman's Christian Temperance Union (WCTU) joined the fight. Members were enraged by a Professor Atwater of Wesleyan University, who claimed that alcohol was a food, and by the charge of the editors of *American Medicine* that the WCTU was inconsistent in campaigning against beer but not against medicines that contained ten times as much alcohol. Martha Allen, the woman in charge of WCTU's national Department of Nonalcoholic Medication, led an information dissemination campaign against the medical use of alcoholic drinks and the misbranding of patent medicines. The popular press quickly picked up the WCTU's cry, and a flood of articles lambasting the unethical use of patent medicines appeared in the *Ladies' Home Journal* and *Collier's* between 1903 and 1906.

In early 1905, the public's concern was echoed by North Dakota Senator Porter McCumber, who introduced a pure food and drug bill. This bill died when the Senate session ended without taking action on it. However, the public demands for food and drug regulation legislation turned to an uproar with the publication in February 1906 of Upton Sinclair's *The Jungle,* which exposed the horrors of the Chicago meat-packing industry. Congress heard these demands. Senator Albert Beveridge of Indiana wrote a meat inspection bill that was signed into law on June 30, 1906. Senator Weldon B. Heyburn of Idaho wrote a forceful pure food and drug bill for Senate consideration. Representative William Peters Hepburn of Iowa introduced similar measures in the House. A combination of the Heyburn and Hepburn bills passed both houses on June 29, 1906, and became the Pure Food Act (Public Law No. 384). *(See also: Kelley, Florence; Woman's Christian Temperance Union)*

—**Mari Lynn Dew**

Further Reading

Jackson, Charles O. *Food and Drug Legislation in the New Deal.* Princeton, NJ: Princeton University Press, 1970.

May, Charles Paul. *Warning! Your Health Is at Stake.* New York: Hawthorn, 1975.

"Report of the Pure Food Committee of the General Federation of Women's Clubs," *Annals of the American Academy of Political and Social Sciences* 28 (September 1906): 296-301.

Wood, Donna J. *Strategic Uses of Public Policy: Business and Government in the Progressive Era.* Marshfield, MA: Pitman, 1986.

Qoyawayma, Polingaysi (1892–1990)

Polingaysi Qoyawayma, a pioneer in American Indian education, was born in the Hopi village of Oraibi in Arizona in 1892. Her autobiography, *No Turning Back* (1964), describes her early education, her teaching career, and the difficulty she faced as a Hopi woman living in two worlds.

After the final military defeat of the Indians in the 1800s, Indian children had been sent away to white-run boarding schools, often hundreds or even thousands of miles from their homes. These government schools were usually operated by Christian churches and attempted to assimilate the Indians into white society by separating them from their Indian communities, by insisting on instruction in English, and by forcing the children to adopt white dress and manners. The result was that when the children returned to the reservations after years of such instruction, they were alienated from their tribes.

As a child, Qoyawayma was sent to California where she worked and studied for four years. She recalls the harsh treatment on the reservation and at the government-run schools. She recounts how Hopi women were forced to march naked through a dipping vat because of a suspected epidemic. She remembers how Hopi men wept because they were forced to cut their hair and how a classmate at school was forced to sit in front of the class with an eraser stuffed into her mouth because she had been talking.

In 1924, Qoyawayma began teaching Hopi and Navaho children. Fifty years before it would become fashionable to do so, she insisted on teaching in Hopi and Navaho as well as English. She knew how difficult her education had been, and she taught her students by using lessons from their own heritage. Moreover, she did this at a time when there were few defenders of American Indian cultures. Eventually, however, Qoyawayma won the support of John Collier, commissioner of the Bureau of Indian Affairs. She retired from teaching in 1954.

Throughout her life, Qoyawayma promoted education for Indian people. She was not opposed to assimilation into the white world, but she knew that the various Indian cultures offered valuable lessons as well. Her autobiography, like those of Black Elk, Lame Deer, and Mountain Wolf Woman, ranks as one of the important accounts of American Indian life in the twentieth century. *(See also: Native American Women; Native American Women's Literature; Women Writers)*

—John Snider

Further Reading

Linder, Jo., ed. *When I Met Polingaysi Underneath the Cottonwood Tree*. Mesa, AZ: Discount Printer, 1983.

Qoyawayma, Polingaysi (Elizabeth Q. White), as told to Vada F. Carlson. *No Turning Back*. Albuquerque: University of New Mexico Press, 1964.

Quilts

Quilts, or quilting, appeared in Europe as a result of the Crusades, when men discovered the practicality and warmth of wearing padded clothing during their travels. Women saw the usefulness of this procedure and applied this craft to their own clothing and cloth used in the bedchamber.

When the colonists began settling in America, they brought with them quiltmaking techniques. In the seventeenth and early eighteenth centuries, quilts were extremely rare and usually imported. By the 1750s, American women were making quilts. In the next century, they developed the block style as well as distinct designs and pattern names.

There are three types of quilts: whole cloth, pieced, and appliquéd. Whole-cloth quilts are made from two pieces of the same colored fabric to form the front and back of the quilt. Pieced quilts are formed by sewing geometric pieces of fabric together in a repeated design. Appliquéd quilts use a plain front onto which are stitched pieces of fabric to form a picture or stylized design. In each, the common link is the quilting stitches.

Women made quilts both for necessity and for pleasure. While they sewed everyday quilts quickly and inexpensively, quiltmakers spent months designing, making, and quilting special quilts that they kept for display or gave to friends to mark important occasions. Quilts were shown with great pride. Quilting bees were a major social event for women. Their hands would be busy creating a work of art that also provided an opportunity for interaction. Quilts were made by hand even after the invention of the sewing machine. A high social value was placed on handwork. With the onset of the Victorian era, a different emphasis and value was placed on quilts. Quilt tops began to be made out of silk and other types of fabrics that were more elegant than practical.

After World War II, quiltmaking gradually lost importance as the society turned to mass-produced merchandise. In the 1970s, museums first hung American quilts as art. Today, quiltmaking is a million-dollar business as people make both art quilts and traditional quilts for sale and for personal satisfaction.

—Suellen Meyer
—Bonnie Lou Rayner

Further Reading

Cooper, Patricia, and Norma Buferd. *The Quilters: Women and Domestic Art*. New York: Doubleday, 1977.

Horton, Laurel, ed. *Quiltmaking in America*. Nashville, TN: Rutledge Hill, 1994.

Orlofsky, Patsy, and Myron Orlofsky. *Quilts in America*. New York: McGraw-Hill, 1974. Reprint, New York: Abbeville, 1991.

ᔌ Quimby, Harriet (1875–1912)

Harriet Quimby was the first licensed female pilot in the United States. A stunning beauty of her day, Quimby was also an early feminist who chose careers in male-dominated fields over a husband and family.

She began as a writer for the *San Francisco Dramatic Review* in 1902 and also did features for local newspapers, the *Call-Bulletin* and the *San Francisco Chronicle*. She later moved to New York City to take the job of drama critic for *Leslie's Illustrated Weekly*. Her circle of friends included members of New York's growing aviation community, and as a result of their influence, she began flying lessons at the Moisant School on Long Island in early 1911. She received her pilot's license, the first for an American woman, on August 1, 1911.

Quimby joined the Moisant International Aviators, putting on demonstration flights and competing with her fellow female aviators for records and prize money. On April 16, 1912, she became the first woman to pilot an aircraft across the English Channel. Unfortunately, at the peak of her resulting fame, she was killed on July 1, 1912, while taking part in an air meet in Boston. A leading aviation periodical asked several prominent pilots of the day to comment on the causes of the accident. None, not even those opposed to women pilots, ever mentioned the possibility of pilot error, a posthumous tribute to Quimby's flying skills. *(See also: Aviation; Journalism)*

—Claudia M. Oakes

Further Reading

Gwynn-Jones, Terry. "For a Brief Moment the World Seemed Wild About Harriet," *Smithsonian* 14 (January 1984): 112-26.

Moolman, Valerie. *Women Aloft*. Alexandria, VA: Time-Life Books, 1981.

Race Suicide

Race suicide was an antifeminist theory developed between 1905 and 1910 in reaction to lower birthrates and changes in family structure and sexual practices believed to be caused by birth control use and the feminist adoption of the concept of "voluntary motherhood." Race suicide proponents believed upper-class, educated women were shirking their duty by not having large families—or any families at all—and allowing the upper class to be overtaken by immigrants and the poor. The hysteria was escalated by the leadership position taken by President Theodore Roosevelt, who condemned birth control and smaller families, declaring that women who chose not to have children were "criminal against the race . . . the object of contemptuous abhorrence by healthy people." In actuality, the birthrate had begun to decline as early as the 1880s, but by 1905, large families, particularly within the upper classes, were considered necessary to maintain the stability of the country.

Feminists were accused of selfishness and indulgence for supporting the issue of birth control and for practicing voluntary motherhood. In response to the race suicide issue, many feminists rejected the cult of motherhood and more aggressively defended birth control and the smaller-family issue by arguing that some women made better contributions to society through their work. But there was also an inherent economic problem that transcended the attack against feminism: Many lower-class women used birth control because they could not afford to raise large families. Children were considered an "expensive luxury" in many working-class families, whether immigrant or native-born. Few women gave up birth control as a result of the race suicide issue. *(See also: Antifeminism; Birth Control; Education; Progressive Era; "Voluntary Motherhood")*

—**Karen C. Knowles**

Further Reading

Gordon, Linda. *Woman's Body, Woman's Right.* New York: Grossman, 1976.

Kennedy, David. *Birth Control in America.* New Haven, CT: Yale University Press, 1970.

King, Miriam, and Steven Ruggles. "American Immigration, Fertility, and Race Suicide at the Turn of the Century," *Journal of Interdisciplinary History* 20 (1990): 347-69.

Roosevelt, Theodore. *Presidential Addresses and State Papers.* Vol. 3, pp. 282-91. New York: Review of Reviews, 1910.

Radcliffe College

Radcliffe College is an elite women's college associated with Harvard University. Although it was officially founded in 1894, Radcliffe actually began much earlier, with the efforts of influential women and men to open Harvard to study for women in the 1870s.

There was considerable opposition to coeducation in Harvard's administration and in its governing body, the Harvard Corporation. Consequently, the first arrangements for educating women at Harvard were informal. Private lessons were offered by Harvard faculty members to individuals or to small groups of women who were interested in studying at Harvard. Eventually, this arrangement evolved into a full course of study offered under the auspices of the "Harvard Annex," the name given to the faculty group giving instruction to interested women.

In 1882, a number of influential Boston and Cambridge women incorporated the Society for the Collegiate Instruction of Women, an organization dedicated to opening Harvard to women for study leading directly to a Harvard degree. Despite raising more than a quarter of a million dollars to help establish a course of study for women at Harvard in 1892, however, the Harvard Corporation refused to allow women admission to the university in a degree-seeking capacity. This led the society to charter Radcliffe two years later, with the Harvard Corporation serving as "visitors," responsible for appointing instructors and examiners, and Harvard's president countersigning Radcliffe diplomas. Nonetheless, many champions of women's higher education were outraged by the refusal of Harvard's administration and trustees to admit women directly to the university for study.

Radcliffe was the epitome of a "coordinate college," one that drew its resources from a larger, all-male university. There were some women who taught at Radcliffe and who did not hold appointments at Harvard. By and large, however, Radcliffe did not offer young women the opportunity to study under the guidance of a largely female faculty, as did Wellesley, Smith, and other independent women's colleges.

Radcliffe continued its life as Harvard's small "sister college" until the early 1960s, when Radcliffe graduates were finally given Harvard degrees. Throughout nearly the first fifty years of the college's existence, its students were restricted to Radcliffe courses, but during World War II, the entire Harvard curriculum was opened to Radcliffe students. In 1970, a coresidency between Harvard and Radcliffe students began, and in 1975 a joint admissions process with no gender quotas was initiated. In 1977, Radcliffe and Harvard signed an agreement that reaffirmed Radcliffe's status as an independent college but delegated to Harvard responsibility for undergraduate education. Students were admitted to Radcliffe but then enrolled in Harvard College.

In 1999, Harvard and Radcliffe officially merged, and women undergraduates are now admitted directly to Harvard College. At the same time as the merger, the Radcliffe Institute for Advanced Study was established as a faculty alongside Harvard's nine other schools and faculties. As an interdisciplinary center for scholars in a variety of fields, the Institute builds on Radcliffe College's historic commitment to the study of women, gender, and society, offering nondegree educational programs and executive education programs as well as symposia, colloquia, workshops, and conferences for the university community as a whole. The Institute includes the Bunting Fellowship Program, the Murray Research Center, the Public Policy Center, and the Schlesinger Library, which is one of the premier libraries for women's history in the country. As part of the merger, Harvard and Radcliffe each dedicated approximately $150 million to support the programs on the Institute. The remainder of Radcliffe's current endowment, about $50 million, continues to be dedicated to undergraduate education. *(See also: Archives and Sources; Education; Higher Education; "Seven Sisters")*

—**John L. Rury**
Adapted for the second edition by Diana E. Axelsen.

Further Reading
Solomon, Barbara Miller. *In the Company of Educated Women: A History of Women and Higher Education in America.* New Haven, CT: Yale University Press, 1985

❧ Radicalesbians

Radicalesbians was a New York City-based, 1970s lesbian-feminist political group. Like the Furies Collective of Washington, D.C., and Gay Women's Liberation in San Francisco, Radicalesbians was formed out of anger and frustration with the sexism of male-dominated gay-liberation groups and the homophobia of many women's rights organizations.

Radicalesbians stated their philosophy in "The Woman-Identified Woman" (1970), an essay that continues to be an important statement of lesbian-feminist politics. The essay begins by asking, "What is a lesbian? A lesbian is the rage of all women condensed to the point of explosion." The es-

sence of women's liberation, according to the women of Radicalesbians, lay in the creation of new consciousness and the challenge to patriarchy that arises when women identify with and relate to other women. In naming the connection between the oppression of women and the structure and practice of heterosexuality, Radicalesbians brought a new theoretical perspective to feminism and enabled women to view lesbian sexuality as a positive personal and political choice. *(See also: Lesbianism; Radical Feminism; Women's Liberation Movement)*

—**Mary Battenfeld**

Further Reading
D'Emilio, John. *Sexual Politics, Sexual Communities: The Making of a Homosexual Minority in the United States, 1940–1970.* Chicago: University of Chicago Press, 1983.

Echols, Alice. "The Radical Feminist Movement in the United States, 1967–1975." Ph.D. diss., University of Michigan, 1986.

Radicalesbians. "The Woman-Identified Woman." In *Out of the Closets: Voices of Gay Liberation,* edited by Karla Jay and Allen Young, 172-77. New York: Quick Fox, 1972.

❧ Radical Feminism

Radical feminism reflected the agenda of radical women leaders of the women's movement in the 1960s, many of whom came from a socialist background or who had served in the civil rights, student, and antiwar movements of that decade. Both politicized and radicalized through their participation in the Student Non-Violent Coordinating Committee (SNCC), Students for a Democratic Society (SDS), and other New Left organizations, radical feminists reshaped and expanded socialist doctrine to develop a radical feminist ideology as well as their own style of organization and strategy. They sought to eliminate male dominance from society.

Adamantly committed to a leaderless participatory democratic approach, these feminists eschewed the mainstream political approach for direct confrontation in the form of street theater. The first major demonstration in protest of the sexism of the Miss America Pageant in September 1968 earned them national media coverage. Their bonfire of the symbolic "traditional" trappings of femininity produced the image of the "bra-burning" feminist, which critics used to impugn all activist and outspoken feminists of the era. Employing such outrageous spectacles, the demonstrations of the radical feminists alienated mainstream women and provided fodder for a hostile establishment press to censure and ridicule the cause of feminism as well as its supporters. However, the proponents of radical feminism compelled public attention to focus on the fundamental inequality of women.

The development of radical feminism began with the 1964 position paper of the women in SNCC that anonymously questioned the sexist relegation of women workers to subordinate and auxiliary status within the organization.

By 1968, radical feminism had spread nationwide, although it was centered in the larger cities; radical feminists engaged in dynamic discussions in their intellectual quest for a nonsexist definition of women's position in society generally. Increasingly a minority philosophy within the national feminist movement, radical feminism provided scope for the leftist tacticians and theoreticians within the feminist movement. Radical feminists within the Redstockings, a famous New York group, first advanced the effective use of consciousness-raising as a process of educating women to the origins of their limited status and sex stereotyping and were the first feminists to confront publicly the issue of abortion rights and to seek a comprehensive analysis of women's oppression within the sex gender system.

Paralleling the evolution of the women's liberation movement, internal dissension over the issues of elitism and leadership among the radical feminist groups lessened the effectiveness of their organizations. Nonetheless, radical feminism provided the "shock troops" of activists and theoreticians within the modern women's movement to stimulate provocative and profound scholarly and intellectual inquiry into feminism itself, as well as into the purpose and goals of the feminist movement. In the 1980s, the popular press seldom mentioned the concerns and issues of radical feminism except to charge the complicity of its intense social and political criticism in the demise of feminism generally or to blame the "extremism" of radical feminism for the much-discussed and celebrated backlash against the gains and goals of the women's movement since the 1960s. However, the influence of economic and social changes in the last decade of the twentieth century spurred radical feminist theorists to consider achieving the fundamental feminist goal of eliminating the effects of persistent misogyny and residual sexism within mainstream culture. *(See also: Consciousness-Raising; New Left; Women's Liberation Movement)*

—Angela M. Howard

Further Reading

Bachwald, Emily, Pamela R. Fletcher, and Martha Roth, eds. *Transforming a Rape Culture.* Minneapolis, MN: Milkweed Editions, 1993.

Bryson, Valerie. *Feminist Political Theory: An Introduction.* Houndmills, Basingstoke, Hampshire: Macmillan, 1992.

Crow, Barbara, ed. *Radical Feminism.* New York: New York University Press, 1997.

Daly, Mary. *Gyn/Ecology: The Metaethics of Radical Feminism.* Boston: Beacon, 1990.

Echols, Alice. *Daring to Be Bad: Radical Feminism in America, 1967–1975.* Minneapolis: University of Minnesota Press, 1981.

Evans, Sara. *Personal Politics: The Roots of Women's Liberation in the Civil Rights Movement and the New Left.* New York: Knopf, 1970.

Firestone, Shulamith. *The Dialectic of Sex.* New York: Bantam, 1972.

Greer, Germaine. *The Female Eunuch.* New York: Bantam, 1972.

Koedt, Anne, Ellen Levine, and Anita Rapone, eds. *Radical Feminism.* New York: Quadrangle, 1973.

Rowbotham, Sheila. *Women in Movement: Feminism and Social Action.* New York: Routledge, 1992.

Russo, Ann, and Cheris Kramarae, eds. *The Radical Women's Press of the 1850's.* New York: Routledge, 1991.

Whittier, Nancy. *Feminist Generations: The Persistence of the Radical Women's Movement.* Philadelphia: Temple University Press, 1995.

～ Rainey, Gertrude Pridgett "Ma" (1886–1939)

Gertrude "Ma" Rainey, pioneer American classic blues performer, composer, and the "Mother of the Blues," brought blues to a broader audience through performance and the recording industry. For her role in shaping the blues, Ma Rainey earned the right to her stage billing, Mother of the Blues. Born April 26, 1886, to minstrel troopers, Thomas Pridgett, Sr. and Ella Allen, she became part of a family that included five children. Columbus, Georgia, was her home of birth, baptism (First African Baptist Church), and death. In this family and setting, young Pridgett received exposure to the emerging blues tradition that began as one-verse songs repeating a single line several times that had evolved from field hollers and work songs.

She appeared for the first time on stage at the age of 12 as both a singer and a dancer in a talent show at the Springer Opera House in Columbus. While still a teenager, she married an older man, dancer-comedian "Pa" Rainey, and became "Ma" Rainey in 1904. The couple became featured performers with the Rabbit Foot Minstrels, a team that provided entertainment for black audiences by black performers. The Raineys had one adopted son, Danny, who worked in the family touring troupe during the 1920s. While traveling through a small town in Missouri, she heard a local girl singing about a man who had left her. She learned the song and incorporated it into her act. The response from the audience that night led to regular use of this new form of music that Rainey called "the blues," although the term was not so named at the time. She heard similar songs throughout her performances in the South.

Descriptions of this great performer varied. She performed in extravagant gowns, wore feather boas and plumes to decorate her short, squat body. Jewelry and tiaras of gold and diamonds surrounded her sweet, round face, unruly hair, and gold-lined teeth. This image created a picturesque figure on stage, according to John Wesley Work, a musicologist from Fisk University. Her deep contralto voice provided an authentic manner of singing the blues. Ma Rainey was a person of the folk. Champion Jack Dupree, a blues pianist, described her as "an ugly woman" who made the audience forget everything once she opened her mouth and "got into your heart."

Rainey took the folksy country blues and incorporated them into her sophisticated professional performances, creating an expressive and bold professional style of expression often referred to as "classic blues." Working with her young protégée, Bessie Smith, in the same show with the Rabbit

Street Minstrels, Ma Rainey helped to created the Empress of the Blues, as Bessie Smith came to be called.

Blues mushroomed in the 1920s, affecting both southern-born and those recently uprooted and living in northern ghettos hungry for down-home music. The themes of blues included life's highs and lows: infidelity, alienation, death, poverty, injustice, love, sex, loneliness, and the range of male-female emotions, regularly in Rainey's songs. She recorded prolifically between 1923 and 1928, mostly for Paramount, and mostly her own compositions. Her entire output consisted of some ninety-four blues compositions, only twenty-six of them attributed to other songwriters. She especially reflected the problems met by black women coming to the cities, where alliances with men were usually as temporary as the jobs the men held. Cabarets, whiskey joints, and brothels arose for relief from social and emotional problems. Absence of family and community ties often erupted in domestic violence, a theme reflected in her songs.

Although she recorded with some of the best, such as Louis Armstrong, her down-home material had gone out of fashion by the late 1920s. She continued to perform in the Theatre Owners Booking Association, the TOBA Circuit. The performers changed the meaning of the acronym to Tough on Black Asses because of the constant movement and many performances. She created her own road show, *Arkansas Swift Foot*, and continued to draw audiences until the Great Depression hurt the ability of her audiences to pay for entertainment. In 1933, the family-minded performer returned home to Columbus, Georgia, to care for her brother after the sudden deaths of her mother and sister. She died of coronary heart disease on December 22, 1939, leaving the billing to her protégé Bessie Smith. *(See also: Jazz; Popular Vocalists; Smith, Bessie; Thornton, Willie Mae)*

—**Dorothy C. Salem**

Further Reading

Barlow, William. *Looking Up at Down: The Emergence of Blues Culture*. Philadelphia: Temple University Press, 1989.

Dall, Christine, prod. and dir. *Wild Women Don't Have the Blues*. Videotape. San Francisco: California Newsreel, 1989. [California Newsreel, 149 Ninth Street, San Francisco, CA 94103; http://www.newsreel.org]

Ellison, Mary. *Extensions of the Blues*. New York: Riverrun, 1989.

Evans, David. *Big Road Blues: Traditional Creativity in the Folk Blues*. Berkeley: University of California Press, 1982.

Harrison, Daphne D. *Black Pearls: Blues Queens of the 1920s*. New Brunswick, NJ: Rutgers University Press, 1988.

Lieb, Sandra R. *Mother of the Blues: A Study of Ma Rainey*. Amherst: University of Massachusetts Press, 1983.

Walton, Ortiz M. *Music: Black, White & Blue*. New York: William Morrow, 1972.

✒ Ramírez, Sara Estella (1881–1910)

Sara Estella Ramírez was a Chicana political activist, teacher, labor organizer, author, and feminist. She was born at Villa de Progresso, in the state of Coahuila, Mexico,

and educated at Ateneo Fuentes, a teachers college in Saltillo, Mexico. In 1898, she began teaching at Seminario de Laredo in Laredo, Texas, where she taught Spanish and started to study English.

Shortly after arriving in Laredo, Ramírez began to publish her poems, essays, and literary articles in *La Cronica*, a local Spanish language newspaper. In 1901, she became associated with Ricardo Flores Magon, a Mexican anarchist leader and head of the Partido Liberal Mexicano (PLM). She organized an association for supporters of the PLM and began to publish a liberal newspaper, *La Corregidora*, and a literary periodical, *Aurora*. In 1904, when Magon fled the repressive regime of Mexican dictator Porfirio Diaz, he went to Ramírez's home. She was part of a network of organizers that maintained a link between Mexican revolutionaries north and south of the Rio Grande.

Ramírez was a popular literary figure in the Laredo area from 1901–1910. She encouraged workers to organize and staunchly defended human rights in her writings. In a 1908 speech given to Sociedad de Obreros (Society of Workers), a mutualistic society, she urged solidarity, goodwill, and cooperation among workers. In her poem "Surge," she articulated decidedly feminist ideas, challenging women to become involved in the struggle for democratic rights and take control of their lives.

Ramírez suffered from multiple illnesses throughout her life and died at the age of twenty-nine. At her funeral, she was eulogized as "la mujer mexicana mas ilustrada de Texas" (the most illustrious Mexican woman of Texas) and "La Musa Texana." *(See also:* Chicana; *Journalism)*

—**Joyce Ann Kievit**

Further Reading

Hernández Tovar, Inez. "Sara Estella Ramírez: The Early Twentieth Century Texan-Mexican Poet." Ph.D. diss., University of Houston, 1984.

Zamora, Emilio. "Sara Estella Ramírez: Una Rosa Roja en El Movimiento/A Red Rose in the Movement." In *Mexican Women in the United States: Struggles Past and Present*, edited by Magdalena Mora and Adelaida R. Del Castillo, 163-69. Los Angeles: UCLA Chicano Studies Research Center, 1980.

✒ Randall, Margaret (b. 1936)

Poet, oral historian, essayist, translator, editor, teacher, photographer, feminist, activist, and public lecturer, Margaret Randall was born in New York City and raised in New Mexico. Randall lived in Mexico, Cuba, and Nicaragua for twenty-three years. She has written, edited, and translated sixty books of prose and poetry. She has exhibited her photography, read her poetry, and lectured widely in the United States and abroad.

In Mexico, she founded and coedited, first with Sergio Mondragon and then Robert Cohen, the bilingual quarterly *El Corno Emplumado/The Plumed Horn*, 1962 to 1969, which became an important literary bridge between the cultures of the United States and Latin America throughout the decade of the 1960s.

Randall left Mexico after government repression of the 1968 student protests. She lived in Cuba with her children, worked for the Cuban Book Institute, joined the militia, and wrote the first of her oral histories of Latin American women. In 1980, she accepted an invitation to work for the Nicaraguan Ministry of Culture and then at the Foreign Press Center.

Randall returned to the United States in 1984 and applied to regain her American citizenship, which she had exchanged for Mexican citizenship to find work. The Immigration and Naturalization Service (INS) denied her citizenship, having found opinions in some of her books critical of U.S. policy in Southeast Asia and Central America. The INS ordered her deported under the "ideological exclusion" clause of the 1952 McCarran-Walter Immigration and Nationality Act. Randall, backed by many well-known writers and others, challenged the INS ruling. After a five-year fight, an immigration appeals court ruled that Randall did not need to give up her citizenship and therefore she had never lost it. *(See also: Women Writers)*

—**Marjorie King**

Further Reading

Crawford, Joan, and Patricia Smith. *This Is about Vision—Interviews with Writers of the Southwest,* pp. 71-81. Albuquerque: University of New Mexico Press, 1990.

Randall, Margaret. *Gathering Rage: The Failure of Twentieth Century Revolutions to Develop a Feminist Agenda.* New York: Monthly Review, 1992.

Still, Gloria. "Writers of Conscience: Meridel LeSueur and Margaret Randall." Ph.D. diss., Indiana University, 1993.

Warmbold, Carolyn Nizzi. "Women of the Mosquito Press: Louise Bryant, Agnes Smedley, and Margaret Randall as Narrative Guerrillas." Ph.D diss., University of Texas at Austin, 1990.

⋧ Rankin, Jeannette Pickering
(1880–1973)

Politician and pacifist Jeannette Rankin was the first woman to serve in Congress. Rankin was born on a ranch in Montana Territory, graduated from the University of Montana, and taught school briefly before earning a graduate degree in social work from the New York School of Philanthropy (now part of Columbia University). Beginning in 1910, she worked in several state suffrage campaigns and eventually became chairperson of the movement in Montana, where women won the right to vote in 1914, six years before the Nineteenth Amendment was enacted.

Rankin, who never married, was wealthy enough to survive without working steadily. A progressive Republican, she launched a campaign for the U.S. House of Representatives in 1916. With strong support from women of both parties, Rankin won election handily to one of Montana's two at-large seats in the House.

Within days of her historic swearing-in in 1917, Rankin opposed President Woodrow Wilson's call for a declaration of war against the Central Powers of Europe. Meanwhile, the Montana legislature divided the state into two single-member districts for the 1918 congressional election. This reapportionment put Rankin and her congressional colleague in the same district, a move designed to defeat her in a bid for a second term. This prompted Rankin to run for the U.S. Senate in 1918 so that she could campaign throughout the state, but she lost the election.

Rankin spent the next several years engaged in working for various social causes, especially peace. In 1940, when another world war was being fought in Europe, Rankin capitalized on the isolationist leanings of her fellow citizens and ran for Congress from Montana again. She won and began her second term in the House of Representatives in 1941, twenty-two years after her first had ended in 1919. On December 8, 1941, she cast the sole vote in either house of Congress against U.S. entry into World War II. This action was extremely unpopular in Montana and ruined her political career. Rankin never ran for public office again.

For the remainder of her life, Rankin was a crusading pacifist. In 1968, she was thrust into the national limelight one last time when, at the age of eighty-eight, she led a march on Washington to protest the Vietnam War. *(See also: Pacifism and the Peace Movement; Politics; Republican Party; Suffrage in the American West)*

—**Roger D. Hardaway**

Further Reading

Harris, Ted Carlton. "Jeannette Rankin: Suffragist, First Woman Elected to Congress, and Pacifist." Ph.D. diss., University of Georgia, 1972.

Josephson, Hannah. *Jeannette Rankin: First Lady in Congress.* Indianapolis, IN: Bobbs-Merrill, 1974.

Schaffer, Ronald. "Jeannette Rankin, Progressive-Isolationist." Ph.D. diss., Princeton University, 1959.

⋧ Rape/Sexual Assault

Rape or sexual assault became a major feminist issue in the 1970s. It was considered a "crime of passion" to which men were driven by seductive and wanton women. Although it is the case that men can be rape victims, the vast majority of victims are female; according to U.S. Department of Justice statistics for 1997, only 6 percent of rape victims are male.

Both sexist stereotypes and common law conspired to make rape a criminal proceeding in which the victim and her behavior were tried rather than the defendant. Under common law, women had been regarded as chattel of men, and therefore sexual assault of a woman was considered a crime against the patriarchal state or the man who owned her, either her father or husband. Rendered a mere witness in the judicial proceedings, the victim was at the mercy of the defense attorney, whose client's rights were protected and took precedence. For their part, the victims were reluctant to file charges or take cases to court given that only one case in ten ever reached trial and only one in ten of those cases resulted in convictions. To the feminists of the 1970s, the crime of rape became a key example of sexist society's debasement of women. Feminists secured reformed statutes that redefined rape as sexual assault in several states by the 1980s.

Rape is defined as the use of force or the threat of force to have some form of sexual intercourse (vaginal, oral, or anal) with another person. The key to prosecuting a rape/sexual assault case remains the issue of consent, particularly if the perpetrator is known to the victim/survivor. The rape victim must be an individual who has not consented to the sexual activity in that she or he (a) was forcibly compelled to engage in the act, (b) experienced the threat of forcible compulsion to an extent that could not be resisted, (c) was unconscious, or (d) was below the "age of consent" specified by the state in which the activity occurred (statutory rape).

Although sexual assault is not a gender-specific crime for its victims or its perpetrators, women continue to be the most frequent victims and men the most frequent perpetrators. Estimates in the 1990s indicated that one-third of all American women will become victims of rape sometime during their lives.

The victims of a sexual assault commonly experience "rape trauma syndrome" in the aftermath of the attack. This is a three-stage process in which initially (the acute stage) the victim/survivor experiences feelings of shock, fear, embarrassment, humiliation, and often guilt. She may also experience other psychological and physical reactions such as insomnia, headaches, nausea, and loss of appetite. A second stage is often experienced in which the victim/survivor will try to forget about the assault or deny its impact on her life, as a defense to the psychological trauma. During the third stage (the integration stage), the victim/survivor will realize that she must psychologically work through the trauma related to the assault, and come to some specific meaning of the rape to her life and self-identity.

Posttraumatic Stress Disorder (PTSD) is a recent construct used to describe the constellation of behaviors observed in many rape victims/survivors. PTSD includes intrusive reexperiencing of the trauma with a cyclicity of symptoms, creating intense psychological distress. Rape victims may be the largest group of PTSD sufferers. This construct is limited, however, as it may not adequately describe the complexity of the psychological reactions to sexual assault.

Despite these severe reactions, rape/sexual assault is one of the least reported violent crimes. The reasons for this include the victim/survivor's feelings of shame and embarrassment as well as her fear of reprisals from her attacker. Reluctance to report is also due to the traditional responses of the police, courts, and hospital personnel to the rape victim/survivor. It has been found that the rape victim often experiences a second victimization at the hands of these institutions. She must convince the authorities that her complaint is both legitimate and prosecutable in that she is visibly traumatized and that she in no way contributed to her victimization. The rise of the incidence and labeling of "date rape" in the late 1970s fueled confusion regarding the issue of consent, especially in cases in which the women knew or had previous relationships with their alleged rapists.

The insensitivity and skepticism that frequently characterize official responses to rape/sexual assault victims are indicative of the institutionalization of popular myths about this crime. These include the ideas that (a) all women unconsciously want to be raped; (b) women enjoy being taken by force; (c) many women "ask for it" by the way they dress, walk, or otherwise behave; and (d) women sometimes falsely accuse men of rape either out of revenge or because of guilt feelings over agreeing to have sex with them. The expanding commercial pornography market uses the male fantasy that women want and deserve to be raped as a common theme in literature, movies, and videos. Even rock videos perpetuate this message.

Since the 1970s, the treatment of sexual assault victims has improved considerably, to a large extent because of the grassroots efforts of feminists. Rape crisis counselors and hotlines are available to provide support; many police agencies now have specially trained officers to respond to sexual assault complaints; state laws have been amended to eliminate unreasonable and sexist definitions and evidentiary rules, and witness support services have been added to district attorney offices. Despite these changes, unfortunately, there has been no noticeable decrease in the number of sexual assaults in the United States. *(See also: Acquaintance/Date Rape; Common Law; Marital Rape)*

—Claire M. Renzetti
—Susan C. Turell

Further Reading

Estrich, Susan. *Real Rape*. Boston: Harvard University Press, 1987.

Madriz, Esther I. "Images of Criminals and Victims: A Study of Women's Fear and Social Control." *Gender and Society* 11 (1997): 342-356.

McCann, I., and L. Perlman. *Psychological Trauma and the Adult Survivor: Theory, Therapy, and Transformation*. New York: Brunner/Mazel, 1990.

Schwartz, Martin D., and Walter S. DeKeseredy. *Sexual Assault on the College Campus*. Thousand Oaks, CA: Sage, 1997.

⸱ Rationalism

Many of the leading thinkers of seventeenth- and eighteenth-century Europe were rationalistic. They believed that reason was the faculty that separated humans from beasts and that the triumphs of seventeenth-century science proved that reason could be trusted. Many concluded that men and, later, women of reason could know and understand the world.

The emphasis on reason was popularized by thinkers such as René Descartes (1596-1650) in France and John Locke (1632-1704) in England. The ideas of Descartes and

Locke had a widespread influence among intellectuals throughout Europe and, later, the Americas, helping to make the Enlightenment the Age of Reason. Although most male Enlightenment philosophers did not think women should share identical rights with men, the French philosopher Condorcet (1743–1794) argued on the basis of reason that women should have citizenship, the right to vote, and the right to hold office.

Although such enlightened views on women were in the minority, the glorification of reason in the early modern period still contributed greatly to the improvement of women's lives on both sides of the Atlantic. Late medieval writer Christine de Pisan (c. 1363–1431) had foreseen the utility of reason as a tool for the liberation of females in her *City of Ladies,* where Lady Reason is an important character in shaping a world where women have all the jobs so long denied them. As Juana Inez de la Cruz, a Mexican intellectual of the colonial era, wrote in 1691, "Since I first gained the use of reason my inclination toward learning has been so violent and strong that neither the scoldings of other people . . . nor my own reflections . . . have been able to stop me from this natural impulse that God gave me."

In short, reason became a valuable tool by which men and women could free themselves from the limitations and superstitions of the past and attempt to construct a more rational and humane society. While women's capacity for rational thought was still denied by most men and women until well into the twentieth century in the West, advanced thinkers were well aware of its potentialities. Writings such as Mary Wollstonecraft's *A Vindication of the Rights of Woman* (1792) and John Stuart Mill's *The Subjection of Women* (1861) must be understood against the background of the rise of rationalism. The light of reason has exposed many of the arguments used to hold women in bondage as totally illogical and unreasonable. Women have proved to be as capable of rational thought as men. We now should know that reason has no gender. *(See also: European Influences)*

—**Jonathan W. Zophy**

Further Reading

Commager, Henry Steele. *The Empire of Reason: How Europe Imagined and American Realized the Enlightenment.* Garden City, NY: Doubleday, 1977.

Gay, Peter. *The Bridge of Criticism.* New York: Harper, 1970.

Koch, Adrienne, ed. *The American Enlightenment.* New York: Braziller, 1970.

May, Henry. *The Enlightenment in America.* New York: Oxford University Press, 1976.

🔊 Reconstruction and the Gilded Age (1865–1880s)

This period traditionally has been defined in terms of the postwar federal policies of the Radical Republicans and the political consequences of the triumph of laissez-faire economics. The emphasis on the class divisions among men ignored the gender-specific aspects of accelerated industrialization, commercialization, and urbanization. For example, Native American women and Chicanas were displaced and degraded by the impact of the transportation revolution, which coincided with the completion of the trans-Mississippi settlement of the West and Southwest. Economic changes encouraged the increased participation of women in the paid labor force despite the vaunting of the ideals of the Victorian cult of domesticity.

The assertion that the franchise was crucial to ensure the social, political, and economic independence of men belied the patriarchal arguments for denying the vote to women. The common purpose of congressional reconstruction legislation from 1865 to 1871 was to force white men in the South to accept the enfranchisement of the freedmen. The exclusion of black and white women from the specific federal protection of their citizenship and voting rights had split suffragists into two separate national organizations by 1870, the National Woman Suffrage Association (NWSA) and the American Woman Suffrage Association (AWSA). Supporters of the NWSA pursued a strategy deemed the "new departure," which sought to use the Constitution and the Fourteenth and Fifteenth Amendments to assert that women required only that the federal government recognize and protect their preexisting right to the franchise. This strategy produced Victoria Woodhull's unsuccessful bid for the presidency in 1872, as well as many women's attempts to vote in that and other federal elections. The ensuing federal trial of Susan B. Anthony was intended to discourage such political actions by women. Nevertheless, the NWSA presented its protest on behalf of women at the Philadelphia Centennial Celebration in 1875. The new departure was abandoned after the Supreme Court decision *Minor v. Happersett* (1874), which ruled that citizenship and the franchise were not coexistent.

African American women were particularly affected by the failure of reconstruction legislation and the hostile opinions of the postwar Supreme Court, which denied them the franchise because of their sex and the federal guarantee of their civil rights because of their race. Freed black women in the South had benefited from the education efforts of the Freedmen's Bureau, which Congress terminated in 1869, and had steadily built up their communities, their churches, and their black women's clubs. Developing an alliance between middle-class and poor women within the black community, black women created and supported segregated educational institutions for women and men and thereby established parallel advances in black women's education and employment opportunities beyond domestic service and agriculture. Women such as Ida B. Wells-Barnett fought Jim Crow practices and campaigned against lynching by exposing its economic motivation. The rise of segregation in the South presented the national suffrage movement with the dilemma of how to use black women's support without triggering southern white racism against woman suffrage.

White women, too, used voluntary associations and religious activities to breach the prewar limitations established for woman's sphere. Women who attended women's colleges and coeducational institutions founded throughout the 1870s strengthened women's presence and preeminence in the professions of teaching and nursing as well as medicine, ministry, and law. Church women funded the education and activities of "female foreign missionaries." These women's missionary societies flourished in the 1870s and first articulated the agenda of "home protection" which became a focal program of the Woman's Christian Temperance Union (WCTU). During the 1870s, the WCTU mobilized women to support not only the temperance movement but many woman's rights issues, such as suffrage, especially under the leadership of Frances Willard, who became WCTU president in 1870.

In the years following the Civil War, women's entry into industrial, commercial, and sales occupations included all ethnic groups. White women lost many wartime government office jobs but managed to increase their hold on clerical and sales positions. Some immigrant women became domestics; others joined working-class women in the industrial workforce. Tied to their homes by childbearing and child-rearing responsibilities, married immigrant women supplemented family incomes by taking in boarders or doing piecework for a pittance. Those women who could, worked in factories and sweatshops for wages even less than immigrant men but in equally unsavory and dangerous conditions. The loss of a husband or father meant certain destitution, and many immigrant women turned to prostitution for survival. Women's groups such as the Working Women's Protective Union and the Immigrant Protective League addressed the condition of these women workers during the 1870s. Other women's groups, such as local Young Women's Christian Associations (YWCAs) and Hull House, offered courses to develop white-collar job skills among immigrant and working-class girls. These reform efforts stemmed from a concern to keep young women out of prostitution, as well as to offer the means for job mobility.

Immigrant women who participated in the settlement of the West shared the rural hardships of the frontier. Women's presence in the limited populations of the western territories prompted the relative success of woman suffrage, especially in school board or partial suffrage rights for women. However, the racism of Anglo settlers along the West Coast contributed to the appalling condition of Chinese women brought to the United States as prostitutes to service the barely tolerated Chinese men whose labor was required, especially on the Transcontinental Railway and in the mining camps. Some of these women survived and escaped their servitude through marriage or by establishing independent businesses. Fear of the development of a permanent Chinese-American community if women emigrated from China to become wives contributed to the success of the lobby for the Chinese Exclusion Act of 1882.

Native American women and Chicanas experienced the consequences of internal colonialism as the settlement of the West resumed after the Civil War. Their cultures were undermined by the various homestead acts, confrontation with the U.S. Army, and forced relocation that produced the Indian wars that raged on the Great Plains during the 1870s and the 1880s. Indian Bureau policymakers developed the concept of *severalty* to break up reservation lands into individually owned homesteads. Thus, severalty further diminished the status of Native American women as tribal leaders and transferred their economic power based on control of agricultural activities to the men to impose further the patriarchal gender system on Native American society.

Therefore, the seemingly lackluster postwar decades teemed with events and developments that proved fundamental to the significant trends that flourished during the Progressive Era. Many of the best-known nineteenth-century women authors were inspired by their experiences and observations of this period to produce some of their major publications. Among these authors were Louisa May Alcott, Kate Chopin, Edith Wharton, Frances Ellen Watkins Harper, and Sarah Winnemucca Hopkins. *(See also: Asian American Women; Black Women; Black Women's Clubs; Education; Higher Education; Immigrant Protective League; Immigration; Institute for Colored Youth; Native American Women; Nursing; Politics; Progressive Era; Suffrage; Suffrage in the American West; Suffrage in the South; Woman's Christian Temperance Union; Women's Missionary Societies; Women's Rights Movements: Nineteenth and Twentieth Centuries; Women's Work: Nineteenth Century; Working Women's Protective Unions; Young Women's Christian Association)*

—**Leigh Fought**
—**Angela M. Howard**

Further Reading

Bodnar, John. *The Transplanted: A History of Immigrants in Urban America.* Bloomington: Indiana University Press, 1986.

DuBois, Ellen Carol. "Taking the Law into Our Own Hands: *Bradwell, Minor,* and Suffrage Militance in the 1870s." In *Visible Women: New Essays on American Activism,* edited by Nancy A. Hewitt and Suzanne Lebsock, 19-40. Urbana: University of Illinois Press, 1993.

Goodwyn, Lawrence. *The Populist Movement: A Short History of the Agrarian Revolt in America.* New York: Oxford University Press, 1978.

Minor v. Happersett. 53 No., 58, and 21 Wallace, 162 (1874).

Solomon, Martha, ed. *A Voice of Their Own: The Woman Suffrage Press, 1840–1910.* Tuscaloosa: University of Alabama Press, 1991.

⤚ Red Scares (1917–1922)

Red scares were caused by fears of political subversion in the United States and concerns over the impact of the Bolshevik revolution. Soon after the United States entered World War I, Congress passed laws that strengthened the federal government's control of speech and opinion. Congress also strengthened immigration laws, leading to the deportation of aliens who were members of political organizations that the Justice Department claimed advocated the overthrow of the government. These laws helped create an atmosphere in which individuals were subject to arrest and harassment for simply criticizing the government or belonging to socialist or workers' organizations.

There are no reliable statistics for the number of women arrested in this period, but cases from World War I suggest that women accounted for 10 percent of the total number of cases. In almost all cases, women convicted under these laws were political leaders, teachers, or doctors. Over half were unmarried; only two had children.

Those arrested included the most prominent leaders of the left, such as Emma Goldman, Kate Richards O'Hare, and Rose Pastor Stokes, as well as previously unknown women arrested for their associations or speech. Women were involved in the most important First Amendment cases to emerge from this period. Dr. Elizabeth Baer was a defendant in the *Schenck* case (1919), which established the "clear and present danger" test for subversive speech. Mollie Steimer was a primary defendant in the *Abrams* (1919) case, in which Justice Oliver Wendell Holmes set the groundwork for future challenges of the government's regulation of political speech.

While countersubversive laws were not used to prosecute the leaders of women's organizations, the sum result of the Red scares was to push women's politics further right. Local chapters of the National Woman Suffrage Association cut ties with socialist members and declared themselves to be at war with domestic subversion. Conservative organizations such as the Daughters of the American Revolution played important roles in recruiting women into antisubversive activities.

Those women or women's organizations that failed to join loyalty campaigns were harassed and defined as subversive. The Lusk Report, which detailed subversive organizations operating in New York State, listed feminist organizations such as the Woman's Peace Party and its leaders Lillian Wald and Jane Addams as potentially dangerous. Such charges, combined with continued assaults on civil liberties throughout the period, caused women such as Crystal Eastman and Elizabeth Gurley Flynn to found the modern civil liberties movement. *(See also: Addams, Jane; Civil Liberties Movement during World War I; Eastman, Crystal; Flynn, Elizabeth Gurley; Goldman, Emma; O'Hare, Kate Richards)*

—Kathleen Kennedy

Further Reading

Abrams et al. v. United States, 250 U.S. 616 (1919).

Jensen, Joan. "All Pink Sisters: The War Department and the Feminist Movement in the 1920's." In *Decades of Discontent: The Women's Movement, 1920–1940,* edited by Lois Scharf and Joan Jensen, 199-222. Boston: Northeastern University Press, 1983.

Kennedy, Kathleen. "Loyalty and Citizenship in the Wisconsin Woman's Suffrage Association, 1917–1919," *Mid-America* 76 (Spring/Summer 1994): 109-31.

———. " 'We Mourn for Liberty in America': Socialist Women, Anti-militarism, and State Repression, 1914–1922." Ph.D. diss., University of California, Irvine, 1992.

Polenberg, Richard. *Fighting Faiths: The Abrams Case, the Supreme Court, and Free Speech.* New York: Penguin, 1987.

Schenck v. United States, 249 U.S. 47 (1919).

Religion

Religion includes ideological, ritual, and institutional dimensions, hence a consideration of women in religion touches on their participation—or lack thereof—in religious leadership, administrative decision making, theology, and liturgy. Women's access to these dimensions of the religious life has frequently been restricted. But the predominating religion has also proven to be empowering to women in the course of American history, and this is the story accented here.

During the colonial period, the established churches prescribed a Puritan social order that was patriarchal in nature, defining women's proper place in the home under the authority of their husbands. Male clergy guarded their authority over church affairs with equal firmness. Pushing these limits made a woman suspect and potentially subject to clerical as well as civil punishment, as illustrated by Anne Hutchinson, who challenged Puritan theology and ignored the church's disapproval of her theological teaching at women's meetings conducted in her home. She was tried for heresy, excommunicated, and banished from the Massachusetts Bay Colony in 1638.

A change of attitude toward women's nature began during this period, however. A move away from the identification of women with Eve, the personification of evil and temptation, led first to seeing women as men's equals in moral and spiritual matters and, eventually, as their superiors. Consequently, women became spiritual guides to their husbands and providers of religious instruction to their children, servants, and in the case of property-owning white women in the southern colonies, to their slaves as well.

Women's subordinate status in the churches came to be contested by utopian and radical sects in the colonies and by utopian and millennialist sects of the nineteenth century. These groups' theological views effected more egalitarian relations between women and men, frequently providing women with leadership and teaching roles. The Quakers' emphasis on the inner light and the Shakers' expectation of both a male and a female Messiah are two examples of such sectarian perspectives. It should come as no surprise that a number of nineteenth-century abolitionists and early feminists, including Susan B. Anthony and Lucretia Mott, were Quaker ministers.

Evangelical revivalism of the eighteenth and nineteenth centuries also expanded both black and white women's religious participation. Since evangelicalism stressed the experience of conversion that led to personal transformation, all converted people, women and men alike, were expected to tell others about it. As a result, women became group leaders in certain forms of evangelicalism, such as Methodism, where they engaged in public speaking through prayer, personal testimony, discussions of religious literature, and preaching. As a result of women preaching in some evangelical churches, a major debate about the propriety of women's preaching emerged among Protestant denominations during the course of the nineteenth century. Biblical, theological, and sociological arguments were used on both sides, but most American Christians opposed it. In parallel fashion, the question of the ordination of women to the ministry arose at that time as well. A few women were ordained in a few denominations, but most denominations did not consider this move until the twentieth century.

The evolving colonial view that women were the spiritual and moral superiors of men came to full fruition in the nineteenth century with the development of the cult of true womanhood, whereby women's purported natural moral virtue and spiritual sensitivity justified their involvement in social reform work intended to transform society itself. Despite some of the restrictive features of this ideology, under its auspices women came to be involved in the significant social movements of the nineteenth century, including abolition, temperance, prison reform, and woman suffrage. Within the churches, women came to form their own mission boards, before under the administration of men. In this new capacity, women collected money for the missions, developed and administered national organizations, improved the status of missionary wives, and made overseas mission work a possibility for many single women. Catholic women in religious orders founded and oversaw social services, taught in parochial schools, and served as nurses. In these ways, Catholic sisters did much to change American anti-Catholic sentiments.

The most dramatic transformation for American women in religion was triggered by the second wave of feminism. Mary Daly's book *The Church and the Second Sex,* published in 1968, catapulted Christian women into a thoroughgoing evaluation of women's status in the churches, past and present. The last thirty years have seen a virtual explosion of feminist religious challenge, thought, and praxis across religious traditions. Some of these developments are in continuity with the concerns expressed by nineteenth-century feminists. The struggle for women's ordination has been won in most Protestant denominations and in all branches of Judaism, except Orthodoxy. It remains to be seen, however, whether established religions will give free reign to the creativity of their female religious leadership. Catholic women continue to campaign for the ordination of female priests, while many pursue alternative, grassroots, feminist liturgical communities known as women-church.

Feminists have not been satisfied with the mere inclusion of women in leadership positions of existing religious institutions. All facets of religious thought and practice have been submitted to reexamination, followed, in many cases, by suggested revisions. Feminist scholarship has been ambitious in its scope. It includes historical and archeological studies of women's status and experience in religion from ancient Israel to the present; a revisiting and reinterpreting of scriptural texts, designed to reconstruct women's roles and contributions in ancient communities; feminist critiques of traditional theologies and liturgies and the development of alternatives (especially noteworthy has been the challenge to male God-language and imagery); and contributions to the new field of feminist religious ethics. Some feminists have rejected Judaism and Christianity as hopelessly patriarchal, calling, instead, for a revival of ancient Goddess religions.

Feminist work in religion has been transformed in recent years by the challenge of womanists (African American feminists), *mujeristas* (Hispanic feminists), and others, who have charged that white women's work has excluded the concerns of women of color. Consequently, feminist work in religion today, as in other fields, is increasingly moving to the recognition that all forms of oppression are interstructured. The most recent development in this direction is the emphasis on global education in seminaries and, elsewhere, dialogue among religious women of the First, Second, and Third Worlds for purposes of mutual understanding and collaboration in activist and scholarly pursuits. Within the United States, contributions by Jewish, Muslim, Buddhist, Hindu, and Native American women are also significantly expanding the nature and content of feminist religious discourse. *(See also: Christianity; Cult of True Womanhood; Daly, Mary; Episcopal Women; Fiorenza, Elizabeth Schussler; Hutchinson, Anne Marbury; Jewish Women; Lutheran Women; Mennonite Women; Methodist Women in the Nineteenth Century; Mormonism; Native American Mythology; Presbyterian Women's Groups; Ruether, Rosemary Radford; Shakers; Society of Friends; Theologians; Unitarian-Universalism)*

—**Frida Kerner Furman**

Further Reading

Adler, Rachel. *Engendering Judaism: An Inclusive Theology and Ethics.* Philadelphia: Jewish Publication Society, 1998.

Christ, Carol P. *Rebirth of the Goddess: Finding Meaning in Feminist Spirituality.* New York: Routledge, 1997.

Christ, Carol P., and Judith Plaskow, eds. *Womanspirit Rising: A Feminist Reader in Religion.* San Francisco: Harper San Francisco, 1979, 1992.

Daly, Mary. *The Church and the Second Sex.* Boston: Beacon, 1968, 1985.

Fiorenza, Elisabeth Schussler. *In Memory of Her: A Feminist Theological Reconstruction of Christian Origins.* New York: Crossroads, 1986.

Isasi-Díaz, Ada María. *En la Lucha/In the Struggle: A Hispanic Women's Liberation Theology.* Minneapolis, MN: Fortress, 1993.

Plaskow, Judith. *Standing Again at Sinai: Judaism from a Feminist Perspective.* San Francisco: Harper & Row, 1990.

Plaskow, Judith, and Carol P. Christ, eds. *Weaving the Visions: New Patterns in Feminist Spirituality.* San Francisco: Harper & Row, 1989.

Proctor-Smith, Marjorie, and Janet R. Walton, eds. *Women at Worship: Interpretations of North American Diversity.* Louisville, KY: Westminster/John Knox, 1993.

Ruether, Rosemary Radford. *Sexism and God-Talk: Toward a Feminist Theology.* Boston: Beacon, 1983.

———. *Women and Redemption: A Theological History.* Minneapolis, MN: Fortress, 1998.

Ruether, Rosemary Radford, and Rosemary Skinner Keller, eds. *Women & Religion in America,* 3 vols. San Francisco: Harper & Row, 1981–1986.

Williams, Delores. *Sisters in the Wilderness: The Challenge of Womanist God-Talk.* Maryknoll, NY: Orbis, 1993.

⨳ Republican Motherhood

Republican motherhood is a concept referring to women's role in society after the American Revolution that valued women's role as mothers and formulated the foundation for women's education.

Women contributed substantially to the patriotic efforts of the Revolutionary period from the nonimportation of British goods to running family farms and even collecting money and producing supplies for the war effort. Nonetheless, women's political and legal status did not change despite the promise of the republican ideals of the Declaration of Independence.

However, while women's sphere remained domestic after the Revolution, the concept of republican motherhood represented a change in attitude toward the image of women and emphasized their roles as mothers. Seventeenth- and eighteenth-century American women were not idealized for motherhood; they were seen simply as helpmates.

Women's piety, on the other hand, was considered valuable. American women were expected to protect the morality and virtue of American society. Women's piety, as well as their patriotic efforts during the war, changed their role in American society; motherhood became more valued.

It was the republican mother's duty to impart morals and values to her children. Furthermore, motherhood was valuable to American society because the republican mother was expected to engender loyalty and patriotism in her children, to raise her sons to be good citizens and her daughters to be domestic. This version of motherhood was, therefore, important to the development of the new American nation.

While republican motherhood was eventually restrictive for American women in that it defined them domestically, the concept of republican motherhood encouraged support for the education of women. For a woman to teach morals to her children, she must be able to read the Bible. A republican mother also needed an education to educate her children about republican ideals. Thus, intellectuals such as Benjamin Rush (1745–1813) argued for women's education on the basis of women's important role as mothers.

Another proponent of women's education based on the concept of republican motherhood was Abigail Adams (1744–1818). She was the most renowned example of a republican mother in that she managed the farm in Braintree, Massachusetts, while her famous husband John Adams (1735–1826) was involved in the American Revolution. In addition, she educated her children to be patriotic; one son, John Quincy, became the sixth president of the United States. Adams wrote frequently to her son while he was in Europe, instructing him on the virtues of morality, loyalty, and duty. This was the responsibility of a republican mother. *(See also: Adams, Abigail; American Revolutionary Era; Education; Rush, Benjamin and "Thoughts on Female Education")*

—Monica L. Everett

Further Reading

Adams, Abigail. "To John Quincy Adams." In *Early American Women: A Documentary History, 1600–1900,* edited by Nancy Woloch, 175-80. Belmont, CA: Wadsworth, 1992.

Kerber, Linda K. "The Republican Mother." In *Women's America: Refocusing the Past,* edited by Linda K. Kerber and Jane Sherron DeHart, 87-95. New York: Oxford University Press, 1982, 1991.

Rush, Benjamin. "Thoughts upon Female Education." In *Early American Women: A Documentary History, 1600–1900,* edited by Nancy Woloch, 180-85. Belmont, CA: Wadsworth, 1992.

⨳ Republican Party (GOP)

The Republican Party has had a checkered record with regard to its support for women's issues and its recruitment of women to public office. Most of the original nineteenth-century feminists were Republicans because of the party's antislavery stand. When the Radical Republicans failed to endorse woman suffrage after the Civil War, the feminists were disillusioned, but for the most part, they were unwilling to join the Democrats with their close ties to southern racial supremacists and northern big-city bosses.

With the advent of a renewed woman suffrage movement after 1910, both political parties faced increasing pressure to endorse a constitutional amendment, but in fact, it was Theodore Roosevelt's Progressive Party that first endorsed woman suffrage in 1912. As late as 1916, neither major party was willing to back a constitutional amendment in its platform, instead leaving the decision to the states. At the end of World War I, both parties had supporters and opponents of woman suffrage, but the Republican side had fewer diehards than the Democrats, whose southern congressional delegation provided the bulk of the opposition to the Women's Suffrage Amendment in votes taken in both 1918 and 1919.

Following ratification of the Nineteenth Amendment in August 1920, the majority of the new women voters opted for the Republicans in every presidential election until 1964. Most of the more educated women were Republicans and tended to vote regularly, while many immigrant women who might have supported the Democrats never voted at all. Despite this strong vote of confidence by women voters, the Republican Party did little to recruit women candidates or officeholders before the 1970s. Although the first woman in Congress, Jeannette Rankin of Montana, elected in 1916, was a Republican, she was followed by few others. No Republican president appointed a woman to his cabinet until Eisenhower made Oveta Culp Hobby his Secretary of Health, Education and Welfare in 1953. In Congress, a few Republican widows managed to develop a reputation for independence and political expertise. Chief among these was Margaret Chase Smith of Maine, who served in the House from 1940 until 1949 and in the Senate from 1949 to 1973.

With the coming of the second wave of feminism in the 1970s, Republicans began to recruit more women candidates, especially at the state and local levels. Few of these women moved up to Congress since, by and large, most were considered too liberal by either the voters in the primaries or the party organizations. Nevertheless, the GOP achieved a major coup in 1978 when Nancy Landon Kassebaum of Kansas became the first woman elected to the Senate who was not a widow of a former member of Congress.

The capture of the party by the Radical Right in 1980 and the rejection of its forty-year record of support for the Equal Rights Amendment caused defections of moderate and liberal women who had fought only a few years earlier for an increased female role. Despite the Reagan landslides in 1980 and 1984, polls showed the development of a significant gap between the votes of men and women. Most college-educated women as well as the overwhelming majority of black women have voted Democratic since 1980. Both Presidents Reagan and Bush tried to counter their poor image among women by making a few female appointments to cabinet-level or similar positions. The most important of these was Sandra Day O'Connor, named by President Reagan in 1981 as the first woman to serve on the Supreme Court. None of the cabinet-level positions were among the most influential departments, and at lower judicial and administrative levels, there were few female appointments.

The influence of the Religious Right, particularly over the abortion issue, and Anita Hill's treatment by the Senate Judiciary Committee during the Clarence Thomas hearings in 1991 widened female alienation from the GOP. The Republican landslide in the 1994 election only confirmed earlier patterns. National exit polls showed women supporting Democrats by a margin of about 5 percent, but when comparative age groups of men and women are considered, the gender gap became a canyon. For example, among voters aged eighteen to twenty-four, 18 percent more women than men favored Democrats.

For the first time, the 1994 election saw the election of a number of conservative Republican women who were antiabortion and strongly supported the right-wing agenda. Still, the Republicans failed to attract significant numbers of women as either successful candidates or voters except in the most conservative states. By the summer of 1998, there were three GOP females compared with six Democrats in the Senate and sixteen in the House compared with thirty-seven Democrats, even though the Republicans held majorities in both houses of Congress. The Republicans also held one of the nation's two female governorships, Christine Todd Whitman of New Jersey.

Probably the most significant example of the continuing gender gap occurred in the 1996 presidential election when women favored President Clinton by more than fifteen percentage points, while men narrowly supported Senator Dole. For the first time, women had clearly elected a president. Much of Clinton's support came from moderate Republican women in the suburbs who found the GOP's platform unappealing, and Dole was unable to change the party's image before the election. *(See also: Gender Gap; Longworth, Alice Roosevelt; Politics; Rankin, Jeannette Pickering; Schlafly, Phyllis MacAlpin; Smith, Margaret Chase; Suffrage)*

—**Neil W. Hogan**

Further Reading

Carroll, Susan J. *Women as Candidates in American Politics.* Bloomington: Indiana University Press, 1985.

Carroll, Susan J., Debra L. Dodson, and Ruth B. Mandell. *The Impact of Women in Public Office: An Overview.* New Brunswick, NJ: Center for the American Woman and Politics, 1991.

Chafe, William H. *The Paradox of Change.* New York: Oxford University Press, 1992.

Chamberlain, Hope. *A Minority of Members.* New York: Praeger, 1973.

Dodson, Debra L., and Susan J. Carroll. *Reshaping the Agenda: Women in State Legislatures.* New Brunswick, NJ: Center for the American Woman and Politics, 1991.

Griffith, Elizabeth. *In Her Own Right: The Life of Elizabeth Cady Stanton.* New York: Oxford University Press, 1984.

Hartman, Susan M. *From Margin to Mainstream: American Women and Politics since 1960.* New York: Knopf, 1989.

Rule, Wilma. "Why Women Don't Run: The Critical Controversial Factors in Women's Legislative Recruitment," *Western Political Quarterly* 34 (March 1981): 60-77.

Scott, Anne F., and Andrew M. *One Half of the People.* Philadelphia: J. B. Lippincott, 1975.

ᴠ Revolution

Revolution was a women's rights periodical published and edited by Susan B. Anthony and Elizabeth Cady Stanton from 1868 to 1870. The journal appeared during a time of national upheaval over Reconstruction, deep political schisms, and the push for suffrage for black men. While some suffragists were willing to postpone the struggle for woman suffrage, *Revolution* served as a visible and vocal proponent for woman suffrage, black as well as white. Although the journal had a circulation of only three thousand in 1870, its impact on the women's rights movement and on coverage of the movement by the rest of the country's press was disproportionate to its circulation. It was an important forum for the discussion of issues and the focus of heated criticism and support from abolitionists, newspaper editors, suffragists, and readers all over the country. In addition to suffrage news and arguments, the journal advocated marriage reform and changes in divorce laws, championed the plight of working women, and argued in favor of practical dress for women. The journal was considered to represent the radical arm of the women's rights movement and figured in the split of the movement into the National Woman Suffrage Association and the American Woman Suffrage Association.

In 1870, the financial burden Anthony had shouldered with *Revolution* became too great for the journal to continue. In addition, the more conservative and financially stable *Woman's Journal,* started by the American Woman Suffrage Association in 1870, proved to be too much competition. *Revolution* was therefore transferred to Edwin Studwell (publisher) and Laura Curtis Bullard (editor) for the sum of $1, leaving Anthony with a personal debt of $10,000. *Revolution* continued under Bullard as a literary and social journal until it was sold to the *New York Christian Enquirer* in 1872. *(See also: Anthony, Susan B.; Journalism; Stanton, Elizabeth Cady; Suffrage)*

—**Lana F. Rakow**

Further Reading

Masel-Walters, Lynne. "Their Rights and Nothing More: A History of the *Revolution,* 1868–70," *Journalism Quarterly* 53 (Summer 1976): 242-51.

Mitchell, Catherine. "Historiography: A New Direction for Research on the Woman's Rights Press," *Journalism History* 19 (Summer 1993): 59-63.

Rakow, Lana F., and Cheris Kramarae. *The Revolution in Words: Righting Women, 1868–1871.* London: Routledge, 1990.

Solomon, Martha M., ed. *A Voice of Their Own: The Woman Suffrage Press, 1840–1910.* Tuscaloosa: University of Alabama Press, 1991.

⟶ Ribbonwork or Silk Appliqué

Ribbonwork or silk appliqué is a term applied to the use of silk ribbons on clothing for decorative purposes. As an art form, it was begun by American Indian women of the Great Lakes and Mississippi Valley tribes after the French brought bright silk taffeta ribbons to them as gifts and trade goods. Although historians are not sure of the exact dates of ribbonwork's start, trading posts began in the late 1600s, ribbons were popular worldwide in the 1700s, and crude silk ribbonwork appears in paintings of Indians made in 1788.

The earliest examples of ribbonwork in museums date from the early 1800s, and the best are from the Woodland tribes, including the Prairie Potawatomie, Miami, Kickapoo, Sac and Fox, Menomini, and Winnebago. The art form spread to other tribes and areas and today is done by Indian women coast to coast.

The earliest ribbonwork was silk stitched to wool, linen, or cotton fabric and birch bark; then, early seamstresses used flower sacks as patterns or templates. Today, newspaper or other household items are used to create the design patterns. Designs used by the Woodland tribes are mostly of the floral family—to reflect their heritage—and some make the patterns such as flowers and leaves join together to represent the continuation of life.

In the early days, women sewed the design down with silk thread in a color that contrasted with the pattern. This was effective in the cross-stitch because it resulted in an X-shaped pattern. In later years, they began sewing the ribbonwork strips on the sewing machine. Colors are often selected to reflect religious symbolism, and much Woodland ribbonwork is created with a positive and negative side to each flower or design. Many of the designs being used today have been preserved, kept, and used by families and clans for many generations, and it is often necessary to ask an elder's permission to use them.

The skills of women appliqué artists are being preserved within families and clans, with older seamstresses teaching the younger ones. Classes in ribbonwork and silk appliqué are being taught in American Indian communities. Galleries and shops are selling ribbonwork clothing and panels to buyers of all kinds. *(See also: Native American Women)*

—**Jan Vassar**

Further Reading

Hartman, Sheryl. *Indian Clothing of the Great Lakes: 1740–1890.* Ogden, UT: Eagle's View, 1978.

Kelly, Helen. *Scarlet Ribbons, American Indian Technique for Today's Quilters.* Paducah, KY: American Quilter's Society, 1987.

Marriott, Alice M. "Ribbon Appliqué Work of North American Indians, Part I," *Bulletin of the Oklahoma Anthropological Association* 6 (March 1958): 49-59.

Ritzenthaler, Robert E., and Pat Ritzenthaler. *The Woodland Indians of the Western Great Lakes,* 1970. Reprint, Milwaukee, WI: Milwaukee Public Museum, 1983.

⟶ Rich, Adrienne (b. 1929)

Adrienne Rich, author of nineteen volumes of poetry, is a major voice of twentieth-century poetry and the most famous twentieth-century feminist poet. She is also a prolific and prominent feminist cultural critic. In her poems, essays, and speeches, as well as in a volume of meditations on poetry, politics, and life in America, she has denounced racism, sexism, anti-Semitism, homophobia, and the military-industrial complex. Her feminist analysis of motherhood, *Of Woman Born: Motherhood as Experience and Institution* (1976), remains one of the outstanding theoretical works of the women's movement, and two outstanding essays, "It Is the Lesbian in Us" (1976) and "Compulsory Heterosexuality and Lesbian Existence" (1980), have established her as one of lesbianism's most distinguished conceptualizers.

Born in 1929 in Baltimore, Maryland, Rich is the daughter of a Jewish father and a Protestant mother; she describes herself as "split at the root" (*Blood, Bread, and Poetry,* 1987). Her first publication was *A Change of World* (1951), a collection of poetry written while she was a Radcliffe undergraduate which won the Yale Younger Poets Prize, judged by W. H. Auden. In 1953, Rich married Alfred Conrad, an academic economist. They had three sons in five years, and her experience of trying to survive as a poet and intellectual while living the life of a suburban housewife forms the basis

Figure 50. Adrienne Rich
One of the major American poets of the twentieth century, Adrienne Rich has also made her mark as a radical lesbian feminist theorist. Used by permission of UPI/Corbis-Bettmann.

of both *Of Women Born* and many of the poems in *Necessities of Life* (1966), *The Will to Change* (1971), and *Diving into the Wreck* (1973).

In one often quoted passage from *Of Woman Born,* Rich says, "I could only go on working as a writer if I could fuse the woman and the poet, the woman and the thinker." This is the poetic stance that has placed her at the forefront of feminist poetry. Especially in volumes such as *The Dream of a Common Language: Poems 1974–1977* (1978) and *A Wild Patience Has Taken Me This Far* (1981), her work is rich with women's experience and imagery: slicing beets, looking after children, brewing coffee, shopping, talking with a mother-in-law. Her poems repeatedly evoke great women of the past: Willa Cather, Susan B. Anthony, Jane Addams, Elizabeth Barrett Browning, Emily Dickinson, Elizabeth Cady Stanton, and the suffragettes.

Although Rich is a lesbian and writes strongly and openly about her personal life, she is not at all a confessional poet. Her most personal poems are more nearly mediations than *cris de coeur.* Very often she achieves distance from their emotion by addressing them to an implied audience. For instance, the woman Rich loved appears repeatedly as the audience of Rich's extraordinary *Twenty-One Love Poems* (1976). In "From a Survivor" (1976), Rich speaks to her dead husband about their marriage two years after her husband's suicide.

Rich's more recent volumes focus less on women and women's issues and more on Rich's dark verdict on late-twentieth-century Western civilization. Her principal subjects in *An Atlas of the Difficult World* (1991) are victims, survivors, "the light of history," and our shared responsibil-

ity to create a livable world. The holocaust, war, deportations, torture, and the undertow that drags the swimmer out to sea figure prominently in these poems. In *What Is Found There: Notebooks on Poetry and Politics* (1993), Rich resumes in prose the immediate, personal voice of *Of Woman Born* to denounce U.S. culture and its "waste, greed, brutality, frozen indifference." Finally, violence and physical and societal decay haunt Rich's poems in *Midnight Salvage: Poems 1995–1998,* her most recent collection, which includes "Shattered Head" and "Rusted Legacy." A second theme emerges in this volume besides Rich's condemnation of the dark truths of our civilization: her responsibility as a poet to expose them. Her poems are our midnight salvage.

Rich's work has been honored repeatedly with awards, including two Guggenheims, a MacArthur Fellowship, and the Academy of American Poets Tanning Prize. More memorable, however, are the prizes she has refused and her reasons for refusing them. In 1997, she refused the National Medal for the Arts from President William Clinton because of "the increasingly brutal impact of racial and economic injustice in our country" (letter to Jane Alexander, National Endowment for the Arts, July 3, 1997). In 1974, Rich refused the National Book Award as an individual, accepting it instead, along with Alice Walker and Audre Lorde, in the name of all women unheard of in this patriarchal world. *(See also: Androgyny; Lesbianism; Lorde, Audre; Women Writers)*
—**Gretchen Mieszkowski**

Further Reading

Grahn, Judy. *The Highest Apple: Sappho and the Lesbian Poetic Tradition.* San Francisco: Spinster's Ink, 1985.

Heilbrun, Carolyn G. "Woman's Autobiographical Writings: New Forms," *Prose Studies: History, Theory, Criticism* 8 (1985): 14-28.

Keyes, Claire. *The Aesthetics of Power: The Poetry of Adrienne Rich.* Athens: University of Georgia Press, 1986.

Martin, Wendy. "Adrienne Rich: The Evolution of a Poet." In *American Writing Today,* edited by Richard Kostelanetz, 334-42. Troy, NY: Whitston, 1991.

———. *An American Triptych: Anne Bradstreet, Emily Dickinson, Adrienne Rich.* Chapel Hill: University of North Carolina Press, 1984.

Ostriker, Alicia. *Stealing the Language: The Emergence of Women's Poetry in America.* Boston: Beacon, 1986.

Ratcliffe, Krista. *Anglo-American Feminist Challenges to the Rhetorical Traditions: Virginia Woolf, Mary Daly, Adrienne Rich.* Carbondale: Southern Illinois University Press, 1996.

Rich, Adrienne. *Blood, Bread, and Poetry: Selected Prose 1979–1985.* New York: Norton, 1987.

———. *Diving into the Wreck: Poems, 1971–1972.* New York: Norton, 1973.

———. *Of Woman Born.* New York: Norton, 1976.

———. *Snapshots of a Daughter-in-Law: Poems, 1954–1962.* New York: Harper & Row, 1963.

Stimpson, Catharine. "Adrienne Rich and Lesbian/Feminist Poetry," *Parnassus: Poetry-in-Review* 12-13 (1985): 249-68.

Templeton, Alice. *The Dream and the Dialogue: Adrienne Rich's Feminist Poetics.* Knoxville: University of Tennessee Press, 1994.

❧ Richmond, Mary Ellen
(1861–1928)

Mary Ellen Richmond was a social work practitioner and educator and a key figure in the transition from the nineteenth-century charity organization society "friendly visitors" to professional social work. Richmond was born in Belleville, Illinois, and graduated from high school in Baltimore. Unlike many early social workers, Richmond came from lower-middle-class origins and did not attend college. Her mother died of tuberculosis when Richmond was three, and she was raised by her widowed maternal grandmother and two unmarried aunts.

She began her long and varied career in social work as assistant treasurer of the Baltimore Charity Organization Society (COS) in 1891. For the next 14 years, she served as COS general secretary in Baltimore and Philadelphia. In the latter position, she is credited with leadership in securing state legislation on behalf of deserted wives and was a founder of the Pennsylvania Child Labor Committee, the Public Charities Association, the Philadelphia juvenile court, and the Housing Association. She was also active in establishing institutional care for feeble-minded women and children.

In 1909, she was appointed Director of the Department of Charity Organization of the Russell Sage Foundation, a position that established her among the national leadership of the emerging social work profession. Her two classic books are *Social Diagnosis* (1917) and *What Is Social Casework?* (1922). In the latter, she defined social casework as "those processes which develop personality through adjustments consciously effected, individual by individual, between men and their social environment."

Richmond has long been associated with casework as "retail reform." (She is credited with coining this phrase for individual casework to distinguish it from "wholesale reform," or community organization and social action efforts at more wide-scale social change.) As such, she has often been held up as the symbol of casework as Emersonian individual change over against Jane Addams as symbol of the settlement house movement devoted to social change.

Recent scholarship has begun to see Richmond as more than a symbol of social casework. Her own career was largely one devoted to administration, advocacy, theory, and education, and her published work includes various indications of a broad perspective on the field. For example, her published works include *The Good Neighbor in the Modern City* (1907), which includes a paean to the contributions of the citizen-volunteer. *(See also: Higher Education; Social Work)*

—**Roger A. Lohmann**

Further Reading

Deutch, J. A. "Mary E. Richmond: A Compassionate Scholar Was in Our Midst," *Journal of Independent Social Work* 2 (1987): 45-55.

Drew, Patricia. *"A Longer View": The Mary E. Richmond Legacy.* Baltimore: University of Maryland, School of Social Work and Community Planning, 1983.

Lieberman, F. "The Immigrants and Mary Richmond," *Child and Adolescent Social Work Journal* 7 (April 1990): 61-64.

Pittman-Munke, Peggy. "Mary E. Richmond: The Philadelphia Years," *Social Casework* 66 (1985): 160-66.

———. "Mary Richmond: Wider Social Movement, 1900–1909." Ph.D diss., University of Texas at Austin, 1985.

Pumphrey, Muriel W. "Mary Richmond and the Rise of Professional Social Work in Baltimore." Ph.D diss., Columbia University School of Social Work, 1956.

Rich, Margaret. "Mary E. Richmond, Social Worker," *Social Casework* 9 (November 1952): 363-70.

Richmond, Mary. *The Long View*, edited by Joanna C. Colcord and Ruth Z. S. Mann. New York: Russell Sage Foundation, 1930.

❧ Ride, Sally Kristen (b. 1951)

Sally Ride was the first American woman in space. She graduated from Stanford University in 1973 with degrees in both English and physics. After graduation, she remained at Stanford as a teaching assistant and did research in laser physics. While completing work on her dissertation, she read an article in the campus newspaper announcing that NASA was looking for scientists to train as mission specialists. For the first time, the space administration would accept women into the program. Ride put in her application, and in 1978, she was accepted into the astronaut training program. In 1981, she became the first woman to act as capsule communicator for a shuttle mission. Later, she was selected by Commander Robert Crippen to serve on the crew of the space shuttle *Challenger*.

In the media blitz that occurred before the flight, Ride fielded questions about her emotional stability and her fitness for the mission. The media was far more concerned with the fact that she was a woman than with her performance as an astronaut. On June 18, 1983, Sally Ride lifted off aboard the space shuttle for a six-day mission. In her capacity as mission specialist, she executed the first deployment and retrieval of satellites with the Remote Manipulator System, a huge robotic arm that she had helped design. In 1984, Ride made her second shuttle flight on the first mission to include two women. Ride was in training for her third mission when the shuttle *Challenger* exploded in 1985. She ended her astronaut training in 1986 to become a member of the commission that investigated the *Challenger* disaster. In 1987, Ride resigned from the space program to become a science fellow at Stanford University. She is currently the head of the California Space Institute at the University of California in San Diego.

The advances made by the woman's movement in the 1960s and 1970s made it possible for Sally Ride to succeed in a field that had been previously closed to women. She immediately became a heroine to thousands of young women. Although she accepted her position as a role model, breaking the gender barrier was not her primary goal. Becoming an

Figure 51. Sally Ride
Ride became the first American woman in space on June 18, 1983, when she joined the crew of the space shuttle *Challenger* on a six-day mission. Used by permission of UPI/Corbis-Bettmann.

astronaut had been a childhood dream for Sally Ride. She did not set out to become the "first woman astronaut"; she simply did not let the fact that she was a woman stand in the way of that dream. *(See also: Aviation; Science)*

—**Rae Fuller Wilson**

Further Reading

Adler, Jerry, with Pamela Abramson. "Sally Ride: Ready for Lift-off," *Newsweek* (June 13, 1983): 36-43.

Golden, Frederic. "Sally's Joy Ride into the Sky," *Time* (June 13, 1983): 56-58.

Ride, Sally, with Susan Okie. *To Space and Back.* New York: Beech Tree Books, 1991.

Sanborn, Sarah. "Sally Ride, Astronaut: The World Is Watching," *Ms.* 11 (January 1983): 45-48.

Stott, Carole. *Into the Unknown.* New York: Hampstead, 1989.

❧ Right-Wing Political Movements

Women have been active in many right-wing causes in the twentieth century. Some of these political movements have sought to preserve traditional gender and family relationships, while others have stressed values of competition and individualism. Many right-wing organizations with large numbers of women have been formed to counter gender, racial, or social class equality.

In the early twentieth century, a small number of middle-class and elite women were active in the struggle against female suffrage. They claimed that women's special place in the family and home would be threatened by granting women access to the public sphere of politics. Antisuffragists argued that women and men should not have separate, individual public identities but that the family, as represented by husband and father, should be the primary unit of society.

In the 1920s, women joined a different kind of right-wing movement, the Ku Klux Klan. Hundreds of thousands of white, native-born Protestant women participated in a movement against Catholics, African Americans, socialists, and Jews. Yet they also favored limited gender equality, arguing that white Protestant women should be active participants in both politics and the home. Klanswomen worked against parochial schools, racial integration, and immigration but favored increased rights for white, Protestant women in the economy and in politics.

In World War II, women participated in two opposing right-wing movements: patriotic societies that stressed nationalistic allegiance to the United States and pro-Nazi groups that favored European fascism. These movements had little interest in issues of gender or family, except in support of the war effort or partisan politics.

From the 1950s to the present, right-wing women primarily have been involved in self-proclaimed "pro-family" movements. These movements oppose social changes such as legalized abortion or recognition of lesbian and gay relationships, which are seen as threatening to the traditional nuclear heterosexual family. They argue either that women should be subservient to men in the family and in the public sphere or that women's primary base of power and influence should remain that of home and family life. In the 1990s, a number of men's organizations developed large constituencies in opposition to women's gains in the workplace and in support of men's claims to authority in the family. *(See also: Abortion; Antifeminism; Antisuffragism; Equal Rights Amendment; Schlafly, Phyllis MacAlpin)*

—**Kathleen M. Blee**

Further Reading

Blee, Kathleen M. *Women of the Klan: Racism and Gender in the 1920s.* Berkeley: University of California Press, 1991.

Klatch, Rebecca E. *Women of the New Right.* Philadelphia: Temple University Press, 1987.

Luker, Kristin. *Abortion and the Politics of Motherhood.* Berkeley: University of California Press, 1984.

Marshall, Susan. *Splintered Sisterhood: Gender and Class in the Campaign against Woman Suffrage.* Madison: University of Wisconsin Press, 1997.

∾ Ritter, Frances (Fanny) Raymond (1840–1890)

Frances Ritter was a music educator, writer, translator, and singer. She was most noted for the publication in the *Woman's Journal* of 1876 of "Woman as a Musician: An Art-Historical Study," an expanded version of a text presented before the Centennial Congress of the Association for the Advancement of Woman in Philadelphia earlier that year. In this work, she traced women's otherwise neglected share in the history of music.

Although excluded from the music of the medieval church, the creativity of women could be found in folk songs and troubadour ballads. With the invention of opera in the seventeenth century, women began to have great public careers in music, although not yet excelling in musical composition. Ritter advocated the inclusion of a composition course in women's college education, more attention by women to the study of instruments other than the piano, and the study of singing as physically and morally healthful. She pointed out that good music teachers and performers commanded excellent salaries. Finally, she reserved special praise for the vast army of nonprofessional women who supported music and musicians through admiration and friendship, financial generosity, collecting musical literature and instruments, and generally influencing the musical taste of society. Thus, she became the first champion of American women's cultural support of art.

Ritter was an associate professor of music at Ohio Female College in Cincinnati and later moved to Vassar College with her husband, Frédéric Louis Ritter, a composer, historian of music, and Vassar professor. She translated Ludwig Ehlert's *Letters on Music, to a Lady* (1870) and Robert Schumann's *Music and Musicians* (1877). Her own works included *Some Famous Songs: An Art-Historical Sketch* (1878), *Songs and Ballads* (1887), and a volume of poetry. (*See also: Music*)

—Anne O. Dzamba (Sessa)

Further Reading

Block, Adrienne Fried, and Carol Neuls-Bates, eds. and comps. *Women in American Music.* Westport, CT: Greenwood, 1979.

Petrides, Frederique Joanne. "Some Reflections on Women Musicians," *American Music Lover* 1 (February 1936): 291-94, 314-15.

Ritter, Frances Raymond. *Woman as a Musician: An Art-Historical Study,* pp. 15-17. New York: Edward Schuberth, 1876.

Stratton, Stephen S. "Women in Relation to Musical Art," *American Art Journal* 44 (13-27 March 1886): 355-56, 373-74, 391-92.

∾ Rivlin, Alice Mitchell (b. 1931)

Economist Alice Rivlin was the first director of the Congressional Budget Office. The CBO was created in 1975 to provide Congress with assistance in evaluating and developing policy on federal income and spending. When this department was created to provide analytical support similar to that enjoyed by the executive branch, it was advisable to appoint a political economist who would not only be knowledgeable but experienced.

Rivlin was chosen after she made an eloquent presentation in Senate Budget Committee hearings. She displayed a greater understanding of the CBO's function than any other candidate. There was some doubt that she would be appointed, both because of her gender and her liberal political bent. However, Rivlin has been able to work in both Republican and Democratic administrations and more recently has been characterized as a "fanatical, card-carrying middle-of-the-roader."

In Rivlin's age group, there are not great numbers of female economists. In fact, when Rivlin earned her Ph.D. in 1958 from Radcliffe, there were few academic posts open to women, and this prompted her to take her first position at the Brookings Institution as a research fellow. More recently, she has been a member of the faculty at George Mason University. Because of the example individuals such as Rivlin have set, the ranks of women economists have expanded over time.

At Brookings, her research expertise expanded to include budget analysis. She was assistant secretary for planning and evaluation in the Department of Health, Education, and Welfare during the Johnson administration. She then returned to Brookings, where she continued to examine public decision making in relation to the federal budget. This broad background and experience provided the necessary tools for the position at CBO. She directed this department, with its staff of approximately two hundred, for eight years and consistently viewed the office as a neutral organization designed to provide information. At the completion of her second term, she returned to Brookings as director of economic policy studies, where she has been a senior research fellow in the Economic Studies program.

She has expanded her public service commitment by serving on and chairing numerous committees in Washington, D.C., that have investigated unpopular issues such as bloated city government. During her career, Rivlin has been a prolific author. In 1992, she authored *Reviving the American Dream*, which examined the responsibility of all levels of government and espoused "dividing the jobs" through cooperative federalism as the twenty-first century approaches.

Through dedication to providing information to guide public policy, Rivlin has been able to advance her career, serving as deputy director of the Office of Management and Budget (OMB) under Leon Panetta at the outset of the Clinton administration. In June 1994, President Clinton named Rivlin to the number-one post in the OMB, a position she had aspired to for some time. In June 1996, Rivlin was selected as vice chairperson of the Federal Reserve Board. In 1998, President Clinton appointed her chairwoman of the District's Financial Control Board. Although she has described herself as an "official purveyor of bad news to Congress," she has gained the respect of liberals and conservatives alike through her straightforward delivery of information and analyses. *(See also: Higher Education; Politics)*

—**Patricia M. Duetsch**

Further Reading

"Alice's Adventures in Budgetland," *Time* 105 (June 23, 1975): 57.

"The Fed's Iron Lady," *The International Economy* 10 (September 1996): 10.

"Grounding of Alice Rivlin," *Economist* 334 (February 4, 1995): 28.

"Her Hand Is on the Future," *Time* 113 (June 18, 1979): 58.

Rivlin, Alice M. *Reviving the American Dream.* Washington, DC: Brookings Institution, 1992.

"The Rivlin Diet: A Cure for Bloat in D.C.?" *Washington Post* (December 9, 1990): A1.

ᔕ Robinson, Harriet Hanson
(1825–1911)

Woman's rights activist, woman's club organizer, and writer, Harriet Hanson Robinson spent her early years in Boston. The death of her father sent the family to Lowell, Massachusetts, in 1832, where Mrs. Hanson managed a boardinghouse and Harriet and her brother went to school and worked in the mills. Like other mill girls, Harriet was eager to take advantage of the educational opportunities Lowell offered, and she became an occasional contributor to *Lowell Offering.*

In 1848, she married William S. Robinson, newspaper editor and dedicated activist in the "free soil" movement, which opposed the extension of slavery into territories newly acquired from Mexico. William's commitment to the abolitionist cause cost him jobs, but although there was often little money, the marriage was a happy one as Harriet's lively and detailed journal shows. William became well-known as the author of the "Warrington" papers in the *Springfield* (Massachusetts) *Republican;* after a variety of editorial jobs, he was elected clerk of the Massachusetts House of Representatives. They lived for a few years in Concord, William's hometown, and settled in Malden, then a country suburb of Boston. William was active in politics and retained his clerkship until 1873, when a coup by his political opponents ousted him. He never recovered from the shock and died in March 1876.

During the years of her marriage, Harriet wrote occasionally (and at length in her journals), but her energies were directed toward her home, her four children, and her husband. Theirs was a marriage of deep affection; Harriet's first act after his death was to collect his "Warrington" essays, write a biographical introduction, arrange publication (paying the costs herself), and actively sell the book.

There is a ten-year gap in her journal after William's death; by the time she resumed writing, she had become active in the woman suffrage movement. As early as the 1860s, both she and William had been interested in women's causes; now she devoted herself to suffrage work. She wrote articles, and she and her daughter Harriette (Shattuck) joined the National Woman Suffrage Association (NWSA), working with Susan B. Anthony; Harriet's book, *Massachusetts in the Woman Suffrage Movement* (1881), became part of a larger suffrage history sponsored by the national group. She formed the National Women's Suffrage Association of Massachusetts and was the first woman to speak before the U.S. Senate Committee on Women's Suffrage. When the two major and sometimes rival groups, the NWSA and the American Woman Suffrage Association (AWSA), merged in 1891, Harriet and her daughter resigned, chiefly because of their dislike of Lucy Stone, an AWSA founder.

Her writing during this time concerned women's issues. A paper, "The Life of the Early Mill Girls," was presented to the American Social Science Association (1882) and was followed by *Early Factory Labor in New England* (1883). She wrote a play, *Captain Mary Miller* (1886), about the wife of a riverboat captain who takes over his job when he is ill; it was performed and favorably reviewed in Boston.

When they left the NWSA, Harriet and her daughter founded a woman's club in Malden, introducing a rule for rotation in office and actively supporting women's right to sit on school committees and to vote for school committee members. She wrote another suffrage play, *The New Pandora* (1889), a revision of the Pandora myth that claimed Pandora (woman) brought civilization into the world. In 1896, she published *Loom and Spindle, or Life among the Early Mill Girls, with a Sketch of "The Lowell Offering" and Some of Its Contributors,* a book of personal reminiscences that has since become a major source of information about the Lowell mill girls. She held national office in the General Federation of Women's Clubs, remaining active until her death. *(See also: Lowell Mill Girls; Lowell Offering; Suffrage; Women Writers)*

—**Shirley Marchalonis**

Further Reading

Bushman, Claudia L. *"A Good Poor Man's Wife."* Hanover, NH: University Press of New England, 1981.

Robinson, Harriet Hanson. *Loom and Spindle.* Boston: Crowell, 1896.

ᔕ Robinson, Julia Bowman
(1919–1985)

Julia Bowman Robinson was one of the most outstanding American women mathematicians of the twentieth century. She received her Ph.D. in mathematics from the University of California, Berkeley, in 1948 and remained on the research faculty there throughout her life. She was the first woman mathematician elected to the National Academy of Sciences (1975) and the first woman president of the American Mathematical Society (1982). She received in 1983 the prestigious MacArthur fellowship of $60,000 per year for five years in recognition of her contributions to mathematics. In her research, she used methods of number theory to attack problems in mathematical logic. She is best known for her contribution to the solution of Hilbert's tenth problem, that there exists no generalized method to decide which equations have integer solutions. *(See also: Higher Education; Mathematics)*

—**Jonell Duda Comerford**

Further Reading

Grinstein, Louise S., and Paul J. Campbell, eds. *Women of Mathematics: A Biobibliographic Sourcebook.* Westport, CT: Greenwood, 1987.

Notices of the American Mathematical Society (Providence, RI) 32 (October 1985): 590.

Osen, Lynn M. *Women in Mathematics.* Cambridge: MIT Press, 1974.

Press, Jaques Cattell, ed. *American Men and Women of Science.* New York: Bowker, 1986.

Reid, Constance. "The Autobiography of Julia Robinson," *College Mathematics Journal* 17 (1986): 2-21.

～ Rochester Women's Anti-Slavery Societies (1835–1868)

The women of Rochester, New York, established five antislavery societies in the mid-nineteenth century. Differentiated by race, religion, wealth, and ideology, these associations were united in "the one great object of converting the entire public to abolitionism." A black and a white women's society, founded in 1834 and 1835, respectively, joined local men's societies in upholding William Lloyd Garrison's demand for immediate emancipation. The black women's efforts, however, gained little public notice. White middle-class women, stirred by the religious revivals of the early 1830s, soon collected hundreds of signatures on antislavery petitions. Yet by 1840, their society disbanded amidst ministerial and editorial controversy about unwomanly behavior.

Five years later, a small circle of Quakers formed the Western New York Anti-Slavery Society (WNYASS) with the aid of Abby Kelley Foster. Sexually and racially integrated, the WNYASS was headquartered in Rochester but forged bonds with agrarian co-worshipers across the state. Fundraising fairs organized by women sustained the society's activities and supported publication of Frederick Douglass's abolitionist newspaper *North Star.* Organizers as well of the Rochester Woman's Rights Convention of 1848, WNYASS women shocked their more conservative neighbors. Still, in 1851 a massive WNYASS-organized fund-raising festival attracted support from several groups of women: the newly formed Union Anti-Slavery Sewing Society, composed of

black women; white evangelical women active in the 1830s; and white Presbyterian and Unitarian women new to the cause.

Despite the success of the event, white female abolitionists soon broke into opposing camps as their black co-workers once again faded from public record. Feminist-abolitionists continued to labor in the WNYASS, to push for racial equality in addition to emancipation and to favor the abolition of sexual inequality, capital punishment, and the land monopoly. Their more moderate evangelical and Unitarian sisters formed the all-female Rochester Ladies' Anti-Slavery Sewing Society, which focused on the two goals of emancipation and uplift for blacks. The first goal was promoted through funding men's political and legislative campaigns; the latter, by sending female agents to work with newly freed slaves in the contraband camps of Alexandria, Virginia.

By 1868, all of Rochester's female antislavery societies had disbanded, although many members remained active in other causes for several decades. Despite their diversity, these women's societies collectively provided the kinds of political pressure, publicity, funds, and moral and material assistance to blacks that gave the antislavery movement its visibility and power in New York State. *(See also: Abolition and the Antislavery Movement; American Antislavery Societies)*

—**Nancy A. Hewitt**

Further Reading

Hewitt, Nancy A. *Women's Activism and Social Change: Rochester, New York, 1822–1872.* Ithaca, NY: Cornell University Press, 1984.

Rochester Ladies' Antislavery Papers. University of Michigan, Ann Arbor.

Samuel D. Porter Family Papers and Isaac and Amy Post Family Papers. University of Rochester, Rochester, NY.

Yellin, Jean Fagan, and John VanHorne, eds. *The Abolitionist Sisterhood: Women's Political Culture in Antebellum America.* Ithaca, NY: Cornell University Press, 1993.

～ Rockford Female Seminary/ Rockford College

Located in Rockford, Illinois, the Rockford Female Seminary was founded by a consortium of Congregational and Presbyterian churches, receiving its charter in 1847. The first principal, Anna Sill, modeled Rockford on the women's colleges of the East. Rockford was referred to as the "Mount Holyoke of the West," in that the founders wished to provide for their daughters the same education that they would have had if their families had remained in the East. Rockford initially shared with Beloit College in Wisconsin an all-male board of trustees, composed equally of clergy and lay members. The religious dimension remained a significant force at Rockford; many of the early teachers left to marry missionaries, and Miss Sill encouraged social activities with the young men of Beloit College, favoring those who were embarking on careers as missionaries and were seeking wives to accompany them.

Rockford students took the initiative in advancing the cause and character of women's education. In 1874, "assuming the prerogative of our college brethren," alumnae gathered for a public dinner in the first event of its kind for a women's college in the United States. This was the origin of the Chicago-Rockford Alumnae Association. The class of 1878 began the tradition of Class Day, "in the manner of celebrating [commencement] in male colleges."

Rockford's role in women's education cannot be told apart from its most distinguished alumna, Jane Addams. When Addams entered Rockford in 1877, the curriculum consisted of classical and modern languages, the sciences, music, American literature, medieval history, and religion, a course of study Addams later criticized: "[It] is at fault in that it failed to recognize certain needs . . . [that is] to cultivate and guide the great desires of which all generous young hearts are full" (*Democracy and Social Ethics*). Nevertheless, Addams and a classmate undertook additional preparation to be eligible to receive the B.A. degree. In 1882, Rockford received the necessary charter, giving it the right to confer degrees, and the seminary thus attained college status.

Addams remained "unresponsive to the evangelical appeal" of Rockford, but she and her classmates were captivated by the "social faith," taking as their motto the word *Breadgivers*. The college woman, she told a class assembly, "wishes not to be a man, nor like a man. . . . We still retain the old ideal of womanhood—the Saxon lady whose mission it is to give bread unto her household. So we have planned to be breadgivers throughout our lives, believing that in labor alone is happiness." The settlement at Hull House, founded by Addams and classmate Ellen Gates Starr, drew on these "boarding school ideals," not the least in that it re-created the world of the women's college that Jane Addams had so cherished at Rockford.

Rockford College admitted male students during World War II and became officially coeducational in 1958. In 1964, the college moved to its present modern campus, and the original seminary buildings were demolished. In honor of its most distinguished alumna, Rockford College regularly confers the Jane Addams Medal on "women who . . . have achieved pre-eminence . . . and made significant contributions to culture and society." *(See also: Addams, Jane; Education; Female Academies; Higher Education)*

—**Laura Gellott**

Further Reading

Addams, Jane. "The College Woman and the Family Claim," *Commons* (Chicago) 3 (September 1898): 3-7.
———. *Democracy and Social Ethics*. New York: Macmillan, 1902.
———. *Twenty Years at Hull House*. New York: Macmillan, 1910.
Cederborg, Hazel. "A History of Rockford College." M.A. thesis, Wellesley College, 1915.
Lagemann, Ellen Condliffe, ed. *Jane Addams on Education*. New York: Teachers' College Press, 1985.
Lasch, Christopher. "Jane Addams: The College Woman and the Family Claim." In *The New Radicalism in America, 1889–1963*, pp. 3-37. New York: Knopf, 1966.

~ *Roe v. Wade* (1973)

On January 23, 1973, the U.S. Supreme Court announced its decision in *Roe v. Wade;* the impact was generally to legalize abortion throughout the United States.

Prior to *Roe*, in most states abortion was an illegal medical procedure. A few states, such as New York and California, allowed abortions in a variety of situations; some states, such as Georgia, allowed abortions in very limited circumstances (such as rape, incest, and to save the life or health of the woman) after various procedural hurdles were cleared. However, many states had very restrictive laws that made abortion illegal except to save the life of the woman.

Texas had that restrictive law when a pregnant woman given the name Jane Roe sued in a class action, on behalf of all Texas women who were or might become pregnant and would want all options, asking that the Texas law be declared unconstitutional and that Defendant Henry Wade, the District Attorney of Dallas, be told to stop prosecuting doctors for performing abortions.

The Court's opinion outlined a right of privacy protecting the ability of women to make their own decisions about whether to continue or terminate a pregnancy. That right was based primarily on the Fourteenth Amendment, which protects against having one's liberty taken without due process of law, but the Ninth Amendment, which says that rights not given to the government are reserved to the people, was also mentioned.

In addition, the Court said that Texas had not proven a compelling reason to regulate abortion and pointed out that experts in various fields could not agree on the answer to the question of "when life begins" and thus said that decision should be left to the individual.

The seven-to-two decision in dictum, or advisory language, talked about a trimester approach to pregnancy. In the first trimester, a state could not regulate abortion except in regard to the medical qualifications of the person performing it; in the second trimester, a state could regulate regarding the safety of the procedure; and in the third trimester, a state could regulate to prohibit abortion in all but very exceptional cases, such as to save the life of the woman.

Instead of ending the public, political, and legal conflict over abortion, the *Roe* decision increased the intensity of the debate. Those opposed to abortion began to organize with more determination and more success. States began to pass laws to test how broad the Supreme Court would allow restrictions to be. Clinics and abortion providers became targets for harassment, arson, acid attacks, and other violence.

As Presidents Ronald Reagan and George Bush, each elected on an antiabortion platform, began to appoint Supreme Court Justices, the balance of the Court began to shift. By 1992, when Governor Bill Clinton was running against President Bush, four of the justices were saying "get rid of the *Roe* decision," but five were saying "leave it alone"; however, Justice Henry Blackmun, who wrote the *Roe* decision, had written "I cannot last forever" and was believed to be close to retirement. Justice Blackmun did in fact retire in 1994.

Due to Clinton's election and appointments, the current Court vote count is probably three willing to overturn *Roe,* three unwilling to overturn but willing to allow the states to regulate more broadly; and three preferring to leave *Roe* as it has been. In the most recent major case related to abortion restrictions, *Planned Parenthood of Southeastern Pennsylvania v. Casey* (1992), the Court approved state regulations, including the requirement that minors involve at least one parent or obtain court permission before an abortion, the requirement for a 24-hour waiting period between contacting an abortion provider and having the procedure, and the requirement that a patient be told state-mandated information.

While *Roe* has not been overturned, access to abortion since the 1980s has been more limited for American women. Eighty-six percent of all counties and ninety-five percent of nonmetropolitan counties in the United States have no abortion provider. In forty-four states, the number of physicians who performed abortions declined between 1992 and 1996.

Although the 1994 Freedom of Access to Clinic Entrances Act (FACE) provides federal protection against unlawful tactics used by abortion opponents and has led to a decrease in some types of clinic violence, attacks at clinics remain a major concern. Since 1993, seven persons working or volunteering at abortion clinics have been killed; sixteen attempted murders have occurred since 1991. Between 1977 and 1999, at least 40 bombings, 161 arsons, 77 attempted bombings and arsons, and 513 bomb threats have been directed at abortion providers nationwide (www. naral.org/ issues/issues_violence.html).

In 2000, abortion remains a high-profile issue with those seeking election and with many voters. The extent to which abortion will be legal and available in the United States may well rest on the decisions of the voters. *(See also: Abortion; United States Supreme Court)*

—**Sarah Weddington**
Updated for the second edition by Diana E. Axelsen.

Further Reading

Roe v. Wade, 410 U.S. 113, 35 L. Ed. 2d, 147. 93 S. Ct. 705 (1973).
Garrow, David J. *Liberty, Sexuality, the Right to Privacy, and the Making of* Roe v. Wade. New York: Macmillan, 1994.
Planned Parenthood of Southeastern Pennsylvania v. Casey, 112 S. Ct. 2791 (1992).
Pojman, Louis P., and Francis J. Beckwith, eds. *The Abortion Controversy: 25 Years after* Roe v. Wade, *A Reader,* 2d ed. Belmont, CA: Wadsworth, 1998.
Rubin, Eva R. *Abortion, Politics, and the Courts.* Westport, CT: Greenwood, 1982.
Weddington, Sarah. *A Question of Choice.* New York: Putnam, 1992.
http://www.naral.org/issues/issues_violence.html

ᴀ Rollins, Charlemae (1897–1979)

Black librarian, educator, author, and editor, Charlemae Rollins was born in Yazoo, Mississippi, and studied at Columbia University and the University of Chicago. Rollins was a tireless worker in the struggle to end the stereotypes of blacks that were so widespread in children's books. Her most notable effort in this endeavor was *We Build Together* (1947, 1951, 1967), published by the National Council of Teachers in English, a guide to children's literature in which blacks were depicted accurately and honestly.

Rollins worked for thirty-six years in the Chicago Public Library, most of those years in the children's department at the George C. Hall Branch. She also taught children's literature at Roosevelt University and for several summers at Fisk University and Morgan State College.

Many of Rollins's books for children dealt with notable blacks. Probably the most famous of these was *Black Troubadour: Langston Hughes* (1971), which received the Coretta Scott King award the year it was published. Other similar titles by Rollins include *Famous American Negro Poets for Children* (1965) and *Famous American Negro Entertainers of Stage, Screen, and TV* (1967). Rollins also edited a collection of Christmas songs and stories by or about blacks and wrote numerous journal articles.

Rollins received numerous awards and honors. Among these were the prestigious Grolier Award (1956)—Rollins being the first black so honored—and an honorary doctorate from Columbia University (1974). She was the first black elected president of the Children's Services Division of the American Library Association. *(See also: Black Women; Librarianship; Women Writers)*

—**Suzanne Hildenbrand**

Further Reading

"Rollins, Charlemae." In *Something about the Author.* Detroit, MI: Gale Research, 3 (1972), 175-76; 26 (1982), 171.
Saunders, Doris. "Charlemae Rollins," *ALA Bulletin* 49 (February 1955): 68-69.

ᴀ Roosevelt, Eleanor (1884–1962)

Eleanor Roosevelt was the niece of Theodore Roosevelt and the politically active wife of Franklin Delano Roosevelt. She was also an author and social activist. Orphaned at the age of ten and deeply affected by other personal tragedies, she was compassionate toward the underprivileged, the impoverished, and the downtrodden. Roosevelt espoused many liberal causes, chief among them peace and human rights, especially the rights of minorities, youth, and women. She worked actively for groups such as the National Association for the Advancement of Colored People (NAACP), the League of Women Voters, the National Women's Trade Union League, Americans for Democratic Action, and the International Student Service.

Educated at Allenswood, a girls' school outside of London, England, Anna Eleanor Roosevelt returned to the United States at the age of seventeen determined to be of service to the less fortunate. She plunged into settlement house work—in which educated young people, worked among the poor, and espoused social reform—and at eighteen she joined Florence Kelley's National Consumers' League. After marrying Franklin Roosevelt in 1905, she devoted herself to furthering her husband's career and the welfare of her children.

When her husband was paralyzed by polio in 1921, she became politically active. During the 1932 campaign that led to her husband's election to the presidency, she coordinated many of the activities of the Women's Division of the Democratic National Committee, working with social feminist Molly Dewson to mobilize thousands of women precinct workers. Together, they brought a diverse group of women activists to Washington, many of whom served in the Roosevelt administration.

During the more than twelve years she spent as First Lady, she was able to further her causes through her influence with her husband and his subordinates and through her loyal work with the Democratic Party. Acting as the eyes, ears, and legs of the president, she visited Great Britain, Chile, the Caribbean, and the Pacific theater of war. She earned the nickname "Eleanor Everywhere" while touring diverse places such as Appalachian coal mines, Nisei detention camps, and the 1933 encampment of the Veteran's Bonus Army. By keeping the pressing need for social reform constantly before the president, she also served as his conscience.

After her husband's death, Roosevelt was appointed to the U.N. delegation by President Harry S. Truman in 1946, served until 1953, and was reappointed by President John F. Kennedy in 1961. Her major accomplishment while serving as chairperson of the Commission on Human Rights was the creation in 1948 of the Universal Declaration of Human Rights, and she became the first recipient of the U.N. Human Rights prize, which was awarded posthumously. She traveled the world in support of peace and international understanding.

A prolific writer, she published a dozen books, including a three-volume autobiography. For over twenty years, she wrote a daily syndicated newspaper column titled "My Day" and published extensively in the leading periodicals of her day. The bibliography of those articles fills thirty-three pages. Roosevelt also hosted several regular radio and television programs, appeared frequently on NBC's *Meet the Press,* and filmed educational television programs at Brandeis University.

Although originally opposed to both woman suffrage and an equal rights amendment that she feared might jeopardize the protective legislation previously enacted for women, Roosevelt's dedication to social justice and her friendship with feminists such as Molly Dewson, Elizabeth Read, Esther Lape, and Helen Gahagan Douglas broadened her perspective. Her acceptance of such feminist political goals was strengthened by her personal and possibly intimate relationship with Associated Press reporter Lorena Hickok. Through a lifetime of service working from within to improve the democratic system and by her immense courage in fighting for what she believed, Eleanor Roosevelt enhanced the power, stature, and the self-perception of women throughout the world. By 1948, according to a Gallup Poll, she was America's most admired woman. *(See also: Democratic Party; Dewson, Mary Williams; Douglas, Helen Mary; New Deal; Social Feminism)*

—**Tamerin Mitchell Hayward**

Further Reading

Cook, Blanche Wiesen. *Eleanor Roosevelt.* Vol. 1, *1884–1933.* New York: Viking, 1992.

Goodwin, Doris Kearns. *No Ordinary Time: Franklin and Eleanor Roosevelt: The Home Front in World War II.* New York: Simon & Schuster, 1994.

Hoff-Wilson, Joan, and Marjorie Lightman. *Without Precedent: The Life and Career of Eleanor Roosevelt.* Bloomington: Indiana University Press, 1984.

Kearny, James R. *Anna Eleanor Roosevelt: The Evolution of a Reformer.* Boston: Houghton Mifflin, 1968.

Lash, Joseph P. *Eleanor and Franklin.* New York: Norton, 1971.

———. *Eleanor: The Years Alone.* New York: Norton, 1972.

Roosevelt, Eleanor. *The Autobiography of Eleanor Roosevelt.* 1961. Reprint, New York: Da Capo, 1992.

———. *It's Up to the Women.* New York: Stokes, 1933.

Scharf, Lois. *Eleanor Roosevelt: First Lady of American Liberalism.* Boston: Twayne, 1987.

❧ Rose, Ernestine Louise Potowsky (1810–1892)

Ernestine Rose was a leading nineteenth-century feminist, abolitionist, and social activist and a colleague of Ralph Waldo Emerson, William Lloyd Garrison, Elizabeth Cady Stanton, Susan B. Anthony, and other noted reformers.

Born in Piotrkow, Poland, in 1810, Rose was the only child of an Orthodox rabbi who taught her Torah and Talmud (Bible and Jewish religious law), an education traditionally reserved for males. A rebel against the religious world of her childhood, she rejected an arranged marriage, sued her father in the Polish courts for control of her inheritance, and left home at the age of sixteen. After traveling through Europe on the proceeds of an air freshener she invented, she arrived in England in 1830. Here, she met social reformer Robert Owen, whose radical ideas influenced her own. Here, too, she met and married William Rose, also a follower of Owen. A talented silversmith and jeweler, William Rose provided financial and moral support for his wife's political activities.

Ernestine and William Rose immigrated to New York City in 1836, where she plunged almost immediately into the social and political reform movements of the antebellum United States. She traveled throughout the East, lecturing on government and religion (she was a free thinker) and championing the causes of free public education, woman's rights, and the abolition of slavery. At a time when it took courage for a woman to speak in public anywhere on any topic, she spoke out against slavery on lecture tours in the South as well as the North. Although English was not her native language, she became an accomplished and sought after public lecturer, earning renown as "queen of the platform."

From 1843 to 1846, Rose and her husband lived in an Owenite commune near Syracuse, New York, while she continued her political activities. Her first successful political project was her leadership of the campaign for women's property rights in New York State, a campaign that culminated in legislative victory in 1848. Two years later, she helped organize the first National Women's Rights Convention. In the decades that followed, she campaigned throughout the United States for women's rights, focusing her energies on property rights, divorce law, and suffrage. An eighteenth-century-style rationalist, she did not argue for women's rights on the basis of romantic views of women's special virtues or moral mission, the popular "cult of domesticity" or "separate spheres" ideologies of the day. Instead, she demanded gender equality on the grounds that women were human beings and therefore had the same "inalienable" human rights as men. She did not participate in organized Jewish life and paid little, if any, attention to her Jewish heritage. However, in 1863 she responded repeatedly and vigorously in writing to anti-Semitic remarks published by Horace Seaver, editor of the *Boston Investigator.*

After the Civil War, Rose joined Susan B. Anthony as a leader in the more radical wing of the suffrage movement. She attacked the Fourteenth and Fifteenth Amendments because they gave citizenship and suffrage to African American men but not to women, white or black, and in 1869, she was a founder of the radical Women's Suffrage Society. In 1869, she and her husband returned to England where poor health forced her into a life of semiretirement. She continued to speak out on issues of women's rights, however, until her death in 1892. *(See also: Abolition and the Antislavery Movement; Anthony, Susan B.; Jewish Women; Public Speakers: Nineteenth Century; Suffrage; Women's Rights Movements: Nineteenth and Twentieth Centuries)*

—**Maxine Schwartz Seller**

Further Reading

Stanton, Elizabeth Cady, Susan B. Anthony, and Matilda Joslyn Gage, eds. *History of Woman Suffrage.* New York: Fowler & Wells, 1881.

Suhl, Yuri. *Eloquent Crusader: Ernestine L. Rose.* New York: J. Messner, 1970.

———. *Ernestine L. Rose and the Battle for Human Rights.* New York: Reynal, 1959.

~ Rosenberg, Anna M. (1902–1983)

Anna M. Rosenberg was one of the leading public women in the period between the New Deal and the Korean War, serving in a wide variety of local, state, and national posts,

including the highest office ever held by a woman in the Defense Department. Born Anna Marie Lederer in Budapest, Hungary, where her father was a furniture manufacturer and her mother a writer of children's stories, she immigrated to New York in 1912 following family financial reverses. While still in high school, she came to public attention when she mediated a strike of students protesting a longer school day because of wartime military training. Even though she was just a teenager, she also became an advocate for women suffrage, facing down the opposition of a hostile New York ward boss. She later entered New York Tammany Hall politics by running a campaign for this very same ward leader. In 1918, she married Julius Rosenberg, who later became a successful businessman. They had a son, Thomas, who served as a partner in her public relations and marketing firm after World War II.

Meanwhile, Anna Rosenberg was developing a career as a private labor mediator and public relations consultant. With the advent of the New Deal, she was appointed assistant director and then director of the New York regional office of the National Recovery Administration. Following its demise, she served as a regional director of the Social Security Administration between 1937 and 1942, while continuing her private work as mediator and labor consultant for a number of large firms. Charming, with a strong sense of humor, she could also be a tough negotiator when bargaining with union and business leaders. New York's Mayor Fiorello La Guardia once said of her that she knew "more about unions and labor relations than any man in the country."

During World War II, she was appointed as a regional director of the War Manpower Commission, where she successfully organized the recruitment of women and African Americans for defense work over the objections of union leaders. As a result of two missions in Europe in 1944-45 to study the problems of demobilization, she met Generals Dwight D. Eisenhower, George Patton, and George Marshall, all of whom were impressed with her expertise in personnel matters. Her experience on these visits led her to encourage President Franklin D. Roosevelt to support the GI Bill of Rights for returning veterans.

Facing a severe shortage of available men during the Korean War, General Marshall, then Secretary of Defense, handpicked Rosenberg as the most capable individual to deal with the crisis, asking President Harry S. Truman to appoint her assistant secretary of defense. Facing a smear campaign from anti-Semites and Red-baiters, who maintained she was once a member of the Communist-controlled John Reed Club, she skillfully defended herself and was overwhelmingly confirmed by the Senate. Her most important work at the Pentagon centered on the draft and universal military training legislation and its implementation.

Although she returned to the private sector in 1953, Rosenberg continued to accept a large number of public posts, particularly in New York City, and also served on the boards of a number of private foundations and philanthropic organizations. Divorced from her first husband in 1962, she married Paul G. Hoffman, industrialist and the first administrator of the Marshall Plan, that same year. She was awarded the Medal of Merit by President Harry S. Truman and the Medal of Freedom by President Dwight D. Eisenhower. She worked at her firm until a month before her death in May 1983. *(See also: Mobilization; New Deal; War Manpower Commission; World War II)*

—Neil W. Hogan

Further Reading

"Anna Rosenberg Hoffman Dead: Consultant and 50's Defense Aide," *New York Times* 122 (May 10, 1983): 25D.

George C. Marshall Research Library, Lexington, Virginia. Interview and papers in the National Archives Collections.

Pouge, Forrest C. *George C. Marshall: Statesman.* New York: Viking Penguin, 1987.

"The Woman—What a Woman!—Who Bosses the Men," *Newsweek* 37 (February 26, 1951): 20-24.

~ Rosenberg, Ethel Greenglass
(1915–1953)

Ethel Rosenberg, housewife and mother, was executed, along with her husband, Julius, in the electric chair at Sing Sing prison at the age of thirty-seven for conspiracy to commit espionage in what the FBI termed "the crime of the century."

The daughter of Jewish immigrants, Rosenberg grew up on New York City's Lower East Side and attended its public schools. Her early ambitions to become a singer were thwarted by her mother's disapproval and by the Great Depression. After graduating from high school in 1931, she performed office work for a series of business firms. However, she continued voice lessons, appeared with an amateur theatrical group, and was the youngest member of the Schola Cantorum, a professional choir. At the same time, Rosenberg was an active participant in left-wing political activities and union organizing. In 1939, she married Julius Rosenberg, a graduate engineer of the City College of New York, and continued her activism until the birth of her first child, Michael, in 1943. A second son, Robert, was born in 1947, and Rosenberg devoted her time and energy to her family.

Accused by Ethel's younger brother of passing atomic secrets to the Soviet Union, Julius Rosenberg was arrested and imprisoned in 1950. The following month, she, too, was arrested. Six months later, charges were made, based on the testimony of her sister-in-law, who claimed that Ethel Rosenberg typed the information allegedly given her husband by her brother, although no such typed material was ever found. Despite the flimsy case against her, the government persisted in charging her, hoping this would force her husband into confessing. Convicted of conspiracy, the two were sentenced to death. Held in virtual solitary confinement at Sing Sing prison for two years, Ethel Rosenberg was allowed weekly visits with her husband and only sporadic contact with her children. Vilified as a domineering, unnatural wife and mother and subjected to enormous pressure from her family, the government, and the press to admit her

guilt, Rosenberg steadfastly insisted on her innocence. Her letters to her husband and sons, published as *Death House Letters* in an effort to raise money for her sons' future, provide a poignant account of her anguish over the loss of her family, as well as her awareness that she was a symbol of anti-Communist hysteria. In her final letter to her sons, she wrote: "Always remember that we were innocent and could not wrong our conscience."

—Ruth Jacknow Markowitz

Further Reading

Meeropol, Robert, and Michael Meeropol. *We Are Your Sons: The Legacy of Ethel and Julius Rosenberg.* Boston: Houghton Mifflin, 1975.

Philipson, Ilene. *Ethel Rosenberg: Beyond the Myths.* New York: Franklin Watts, 1988.

Rosenberg, Ethel, and Julius Rosenberg. *Death House Letters.* New York: Jero, 1953.

Schneir, Walter, and Miriam Schneir. *Invitation to an Inquest: Reopening the Rosenberg "Atom Spy" Case,* 2d ed. New York: Praeger, 1983.

~ "Rosie the Riveter"

"Rosie the Riveter" symbolized the woman worker in American defense industries during World War II. Facing a simultaneous manpower drain and increased production demands, the federal War Manpower Commission and the Office of War Information undertook a recruitment campaign to bring more women into the labor force. Lured by higher wages, women took men's places in factories that produced aircraft, ordnance, and ships. Although only 8 percent of the workers employed in the production of durable goods had been women in 1940, this figure jumped to 25 percent in 1945.

Between 1940 and 1945, the number of female workers rose from 12 to 18 million. Clerical positions for women almost doubled, although critical shortages developed in the nursing and teaching professions. The entry of large numbers of married women and women thirty-five and older also helped to transform the labor force.

Still, female workers faced hurdles. They encountered wage discrimination and were denied access to hazardous occupations, such as sandblasting. In factories, women tended to stay in lower-level jobs that required less training. Black women worked as janitors and sweepers and in other bottom-rung jobs. Unions often welcomed females reluctantly. Working mothers of young children faced disapproval based on a fear that they were contributing to juvenile delinquency.

Working women faced a double standard. Government and industry appealed to their patriotism to enter the labor force, yet both expected them to leave once the war ended. Nevertheless, female employment in the United States stood at 17 million in 1947, higher than it had been before the war began. *(See also: Mobilization; War Manpower Commission; World War II)*

—Casey Edward Greene

Further Reading
Campbell, D'Ann. *Women at War with America: Private Lives in the Patriotic Era.* Cambridge, MA: Harvard University Press, 1984.
Field, Connie, prod. and dir. *The Life and Times of Rosie the Riveter.* Film, 1980. [DIRECT; 60 min; color; 16mm]
Gluck, Sherna B. *Rosie the Riveter Revisited: Women, the War, and Social Change.* Boston: Twayne, 1987.
Hartmann, Susan M. *The Home Front and Beyond: American Women in the 1940s.* Boston: Twayne, 1982.
Honey, Maureen. *Creating Rosie the Riveter: Class, Gender, and Propaganda during World War II.* Amherst: University of Massachusetts Press, 1984.
Wise, Nancy Baker, and Christy Wise. *A Mouthful of Rivets: Women at Work in World War II.* San Francisco: Jossey-Bass, 1994.

∽ Ross, Elizabeth Griscom (Betsy) (1752–1836)

Elizabeth (Betsy) Ross was the legendary seamstress and alleged designer of the first official American flag. The daughter of Quaker parents, Elizabeth Griscom was born January 1, 1752, in Philadelphia, Pennsylvania. She married John Ross November 4, 1773; he died during militia duty in 1776. Afterward, she supported herself by making flags for the state of Pennsylvania. On June 15, 1777, she married Joseph Ashburn and later had two children. Ashburn, a seaman, was captured by the British and died in a British prison in 1782. Ross married John Claypoole in 1783, with whom she had five children. Claypoole, her last husband, died in 1817 in Philadelphia, where Ross lived until her death in 1836 at the age of eighty-four.

The legend of Betsy Ross was first told by her grandson, William Canby, in 1870, thirty-four years after her death and almost a century after her alleged creation of the first flag. Canby claimed his grandmother told him she was visited by George Washington, Robert Morris, and George Ross of the Continental Congress in June 1776, when she suggested a five-pointed star for the flag rather than a six-pointed one and was commissioned to sew and produce the first flag for the new nation.

By the mid-1880s, the story reached school textbooks where it has remained. The veracity of Canby's claim that Ross actually made the first American flag is a highly controversial subject. Some scholars contend that the U.S. Navy was flying the "Stars and Stripes" before Ross could have been commissioned to sew the first American flag. But this too is refutable. Today, most historians believe the Ross family's story is doubtful. *(See also: American Revolutionary Era)*

—**Monica L. Everett**

Further Reading
McCandless, Byron. "The Story of the American Flag," *National Geographic Magazine* 32 (October 1917): 286-302.
Miller, William C. "The Betsy Ross Legend," *Social Studies* 37 (November 1946): 317-23.

∽ Ross, Nellie Tayloe (1876–1977)

Nellie Tayloe Ross became the first woman governor and the first woman director of the U.S. Mint. A native of Andrew County, Missouri, she was the daughter of James Wynne Tayloe and Elizabeth Green Tayloe. The family later moved to Omaha, Nebraska. Little is known of her education. Some sources say she taught school a few years before her marriage to William Bradford Ross, a young Tennessee lawyer, in 1902.

Her husband established a law office in Cheyenne, Wyoming, where they lived for many years, rearing three sons. Ross was active in the Women's Club, the Episcopal church, and the Boy Scouts.

William Bradford Ross was elected governor of Wyoming in 1922. When he died two years later, Ross decided to run for governor to fill his unexpired term. She won by a landslide, although she never made a speech or left her home because she was in mourning. The election made her the first woman governor in the United States along with "Ma" Ferguson of Texas, elected on the same day. Ross served as governor from 1925 to 1927. In 1926, she ran for reelection but did not campaign and suffered defeat in a close race.

Ross became more active in political affairs. In 1934, she directed the women's division of Franklin D. Roosevelt's presidential campaign. He appointed her to head the U.S. Mint, the first woman to hold that post. She served in that position from 1933 to 1953. After her retirement in 1953, Ross remained in Washington, D.C., where she died in 1977, shortly after her 101st birthday. Her contributions as a pioneer woman in public life paved the way for other women in American politics and government office. *(See also: Politics)*

—**Mary K. Dains**

Further Reading
The Good Housekeeping Woman's Almanac, p. 480. New York: Newspaper Enterprise Association, 1977.
Wachtel, Ina. "Nellie Tayloe Ross." In *Show Me Missouri Women: Selected Biographies.* Vol. 2, edited by Mary K. Dains and Sue Sadler, 196-97. Kirksville, MO: Thomas Jefferson University Press, 1993.

∽ Rudolph, Wilma Glodean (1940–1994)

Wilma Rudolph was the first American woman to win three gold medals in running in the Olympic games. Rudolph's achievements were a consequence of incredible personal determination, as well as tenacious and loving support from her parents and Tennessee State track coach Ed Temple.

Rudolph overcame being black, female, and poor in a small Tennessee town. She experienced a sickly childhood that included several years in a leg brace and, later, a high school pregnancy. Rudolph became a superior high school

Figure 52. Wilma Rudolph
Wilma Rudolph overcame great poverty and childhood sickness to capture three gold medals in the 1960 Olympics. Used by permission of UPI/Corbis-Bettmann.

basketball player and a world-class runner. She won a bronze medal the summer before her junior year in high school at the 1956 Olympics and went on to win three gold medals, in the 100-meter and 200-meter dashes and 400-meter relay, at the 1960 Olympics in Rome. In both 1960 and 1961, she was voted Female Athlete of the Year by the Associated Press. In 1961, she was named outstanding amateur athlete and received the Sullivan Award from the Amateur Athletic Union. Rudolph was elected to the National Track and Field Hall of Fame in 1974.

In her autobiography, she reports that in 1963 she graduated from Tennessee State and married her childhood sweetheart, Robert Eldridge. In the ensuing years, she shared her time parenting her four children, teaching, and working with young people to encourage both athletic participation and success in life. Rudolph died of brain cancer in 1994. *(See also: Athletics/Sports; Black Women)*

—**Margaret Konz Snooks**

Further Reading

Biracree, Tom. *Wilma Rudolph.* New York: Chelsea House, 1988.

Rudolph, Wilma, with Martin Ralbovsky. *Wilma.* New York: New American Library, 1977.

Salem, Dorothy C., ed. *African American Women, A Biographical Dictionary,* pp. 431-35. New York: Garland, 1993.

⚕ Ruether, Rosemary Radford
(b. 1936)

Rosemary Radford Ruether is a twentieth-century feminist scholar of religious history who has played a major role in the reconstruction of Jewish and Christian thought in the wake of the second wave of feminism in America.

Her early works were largely focused on Christian, specifically Catholic, representations of women and deity and their ramifications for religious praxis and on the development of religious dogma from the patristic period onward and serving patriarchal ends at the expense of more inclusive strands of tradition. Her *Sexism and God-Talk* (1983) and *Women-Church* (1985) discuss the ways in which the traditionally male deity of Western monotheism, and his manifestation in Jesus of Nazareth, can be reinvisioned more inclusively and how feminist revisionist sensibilities can be integrated into Christian liturgical worship and praxis. Her *Gaia and God* (1992) is an attempt at opening a discursive space for ecofeminism within a particularly religious sensibility, Christian or otherwise.

Ruether's work since then has gradually broadened to include more intense reflection on the interface between religion and politics, specifically regarding the Catholic Church in democratic America and the manifestation of religious nationalism in the Israeli/Palestinian conflict. Overall, Ruether's work is important for its often quite interdisciplinary discussion of religion and culture in a way that highlights the destructive power of religious ideas and, simultaneously, indicates options for a retheorizing of religion so as to minimize its negative effects and retain its possible value for human society at large. *(See also: Christianity; Religion; Theologians)*

—**B. Jill Carroll**

Further Reading

Bianchi, Eugene C., and Rosemary Ruether, eds. *A Democratic Catholic Church: The Reconstruction of Roman Catholicism.* New York: Crossroad, 1992.

Ellis, Marc H., and Rosemary Ruether, eds. *Beyond Occupation: American Jewish, Christian and Palestinian Voices for Peace.* Boston: Beacon, 1990.

Hall, Douglas John, and Rosemary Ruether. *God and the Nations.* Minneapolis, MN: Fortress, 1995.

Holler, Barry Penn. *On Being the Church in the United States: Contemporary Theological Critiques of Liberalism.* New York: Peter Lang, 1994.

Hurcombe, Linda, ed. *Sex and God: Some Varieties of Women's Religious Experience.* New York: Routledge & Kegan Paul, 1987.

Ramsay, William M. *Four Modern Prophets: Walter Rauschenbusch, Martin Luther King, Jr., Gustavo Gutierrez and Rosemary Radford Ruether.* Atlanta, GA: John Knox, 1986.

Ruether, Rosemary Radford. *Disputed Questions: On Being a Christian.* Nashville, TN: Abingdon, 1982.

———. "Feminist Interpretation: A Method of Correlation." In *Feminist Interpretation of the Bible,* edited by Letty M. Russell, 111-24. Philadelphia: Westminster, 1985.

———. "Feminist Theology and Spirituality." In *Christian Feminism,* edited by Judith L. Weidman. San Francisco: Harper & Row, 1984.

———. *Gaia and God: An Ecofeminist Theology of Earth Healing.* San Francisco: Harper's, 1992.

———. *New Woman, New Earth.* New York: Seabury, 1975.

———, ed. *Religion and Sexism: Images of Women in the Jewish and Christian Traditions.* New York: Simon & Schuster, 1974.

———. *Sexism and God-Talk: Toward a Feminist Theology.* Boston: Beacon, 1983.

———. "Theologizing from the Side of the Other: Women, Blacks, Indians and Jews." In *Faith That Transforms: Essays in Honor of Gregory Baum,* edited by Mary Jo Leddy and Mary Ann Hinsdale. New York: Paulist Press, 1987.

———. *Women and Redemption: A Theological History.* New York: Fortress, 1998.

———. *Women-Church: Theology and Practice of Feminist Liturgical Communities.* San Francisco: Harper & Row, 1985.

———. *The Wrath of Jonah: The Crisis of Religious Nationalism in the Israeli-Palestinian Conflict.* New York: Harper & Row, 1989.

Sands, Kathleen. *Escape from Paradise: Evil and Tragedy in Feminist Theology.* Minneapolis, MN: Fortress, 1994.

Tardiff, Mary. *At Home in the World: The Letters of Thomas Merton and Rosemary Ruether.* Maryknoll, NY: Orbis, 1995.

∾ Ruffin, Josephine St. Pierre (1842–1924)

Josephine Ruffin was a lecturer, suffragist, and social activist. She was the founder of the Woman's Era Club of Boston and the editor of the club newsletter *The Woman's Era.* Ruffin organized the first national conference of black women in 1895.

Born in Boston, Josephine was the sixth child of John and Eliza St. Pierre. She attended public school in Charleston and Salem, Massachusetts, and a private school in New York City because her mother refused to allow her to attend segregated schools in Boston. In 1858, she married George Ruffin, a graduate of Harvard Law School and Boston's first black municipal court judge. Active in the crucial causes of her day, Ruffin recruited soldiers for the Civil War, worked with the U.S. Sanitary Commission, and helped organize the Boston Kansas Relief to help persons who chose to move to Kansas in 1879. After her husband's death in 1886, Ruffin devoted her life to charities and philanthropic work. She served on the executive board of the Massachusetts Moral Education Association and the Massachusetts School Suffrage Association, and was a visitor for the Associated Charities of Boston. While editor of the *Boston Courant,* a weekly black newspaper, she joined the New England Press Association.

Ruffin envisioned a women's movement directed toward the good of all, regardless of gender or race. Yet she herself was a victim of discrimination in 1900 when she attended a convention of the General Federation of Women's Clubs (GFWC) as a representative of the New England Woman's Club, the Massachusetts State Federation of Women's Clubs, and the Woman's Era Club. The GFWC rejected the credentials of the Woman's Era Club, and Ruffin refused to enter the convention solely as a delegate from white clubs. Afterward, Ruffin initiated the movement for the first national organization of black women, the National Federation of Afro-American Women. She was a vice president of the National Association of Colored Women and president of the Woman's Era Club from 1894 to 1903. *(See also: Black Women; Black Women's Clubs; National Association of Colored Women; National Federation of Afro-American Women)*

—Floris Barnett Cash

Further Reading

Brown, Hallie Q. *Homespun Heroines and Other Women of Distinction.* Freeport, NY: Books for Libraries Press, 1971.

Cash, Floris Barnett. "Josephine St. Pierre Ruffin." In *Notable Black American Women,* edited by Jessie Carney Smith, 961-66. Detroit, MI: Gale Research, 1992.

Giddings, Paula. *When and Where I Enter: The Impact of Black Women on Race and Sex in America.* New York: Bantam, 1984.

Scruggs, L. A. *Women of Distinction.* Raleigh, NC: Scruggs, 1893.

∾ Rukeyser, Muriel (1913–1980)

Known primarily as a protest poet, Muriel Rukeyser was equally a poet of the human soul, writing as earnestly about the need for communication among people and the exhilaration of life and love as about social injustice. She believed intensely in life, encouraging others through her poetry to look within themselves to discover the strength and self-knowledge necessary to live full, productive lives rather than to hide from progress and change. Using images of technology and energy extensively in her early volumes of poetry, she searched for a place for the self in a modern technological society.

Born in New York City, Rukeyser led a quiet, sheltered childhood, which became a source of her insistence on experience and communication in poetry. Her political involvement bore witness to her verse. She was arrested while attending the Scottsboro Trials in Alabama in 1933; personally investigated the mining tragedy in Gauley Bridge, West Virginia; reported for *Life and Times Today* on the Fascist Olympics in Barcelona as the Spanish Civil War broke out around her; demonstrated for peace in Hanoi and Washington, D.C., in 1972; and later that year flew to Korea to plead for the life of imprisoned poet Kim Chi-Ha.

While critics have linked her poetry with that of W. H. Auden, Stephen Spender, and other political poets, she considered Emerson, Melville, and Whitman her mentors. Her visionary quality and organic poetic theory are clearly Transcendentalist, her outrage with injustice Melvillean, and her long, rhythmic lines, her optimism, her poetic altruism, and her expression of the power and beauty of sensuality Whitmanesque. Yet a feminine consciousness is also evident throughout Rukeyser's poetry, linking her work with that of Denise Levertov and Adrienne Rich. She sees with a feminist point of view, which adds vitality to her revisualizations of history and myth.

In addition to poetry, Muriel Rukeyser also published several volumes of translations, three biographies, two volumes of literary criticism, a number of book reviews, a novel, five juvenile books, several documentary film scripts, and a play. In each, she urges her readers to look within themselves for the common ground on which all human beings stand. *(See also: Women Writers)*

—**Kenneth E. Gadomski**

Further Reading

"Craft Interview with Muriel Rukeyser." In *The Craft of Poetry,* edited by William Packard, 53-76. Garden City, NY: Doubleday, 1974.

Kertesz, Louise. *The Poetic Vision of Muriel Rukeyser.* Baton Rouge: Louisiana State University Press, 1979.

Terris, Virginia R. "Muriel Rukeyser: A Retrospective," *American Poetry Review* 3 (May/June 1974): 10-15.

⚭ Rush, Benjamin and "Thoughts on Female Education"

Benjamin Rush (1745–1813), an eighteenth-century advocate of improving American women's education, influenced the advancements in and set the standards for the curriculum of female academies and seminaries during the Federalist Era. Proudly nationalistic and intensely critical of servile imitation of the British "ornamental" education for women, Rush promoted a comprehensive curriculum that surpassed that of the "finishing school," feeling that the duties of Republican Motherhood required that American women have both the formal education and the practical training to rear patriotic sons and dutiful daughters. Rush was a founder of the trend-setting Young Ladies' Academy of Philadelphia, which offered a curriculum for girls that acknowledged their equal capacity to learn without challenging the gender system of colonial and revolutionary American society.

"Thoughts on Female Education" (1787) was given by Rush as a commencement address at the Young Ladies' Academy of Philadelphia on July 28, 1787, and later published at the request of members of that audience in his *Essays, Literary, Moral, and Philosophical* (1798). In it, Rush, a co-founder of the academy, outlined the "first principles" of female education that he felt must accommodate the peculiar position of American women in the new nation.

In "Thoughts on Female Education," Rush listed certain aspects of American life that required women's education to prepare them for the particular circumstances of late-eighteenth-century America: early marriages that allowed only limited time for education, the cultural materialism of the middle class that presumed a wife capable of prudent management of the family assets, the teaching requirements of the maternal role, and the domestic arts needed to manage the household successfully without competent domestic

servants. Rush deemed the British approach of ornamental education for women inadequate for the role American women must play in the development of the new nation. Therefore, he urged that American women's education include English language arts, basic mathematics and bookkeeping skills, geography and travel, history and biography (to provide both amusement and instruction), and rudimentary natural and physical sciences (as useful in the domestic arts). Rush did not eschew all the ornamental arts: Vocal but not instrumental music could be pursued in a disciplined setting, and dancing would provide wholesome exercise.

Rush and his colleagues such as Horace Bushnell established that women had the capacity to learn and thereby laid a foundation on which Victorian promoters could seek increasing advances in women's education throughout the nineteenth century. Rush acknowledged to the graduates of the Young Ladies' Academy that the success of this expanded curriculum for women's education depended on their womanly conduct, lest their use of that education fuel the fears that education would "unsex" women. Thus, Rush's opinions and his pamphlet influenced the supporters of advances in women's education at the end of the eighteenth century and throughout the nineteenth century. *(See also: Education; Female Academies; Republican Motherhood; Young Ladies' Academy of Philadelphia)*

—**Angela M. Howard**

Further Reading

Good, Harry G. *Benjamin Rush and His Service to American Education.* Berne, IN: Witness, 1918.

Rush, Benjamin. *Essays, Literary, Moral, and Philosophical.* Philadelphia: Thomas & Samuel Bradford, 1798.

Woody, Thomas. *A History of Women's Education in the United States,* 2 vols. New York: Science Press, 1929.

⚭ Russell, Maud Muriel (1893–1989)

Maud Russell, an advocate of the policies of the People's Republic of China and the editor of the *Far East Reporter,* was born in Hayward, California, and graduated from the University of California at Berkeley in 1915. Interested since childhood in missionary work, she accepted a position with the Young Women's Christian Association in China in 1917 and served there until 1943. During those years, Russell became increasingly skeptical of the roles played by foreigners, including missionaries, in China, while at the same time the political upheavals she witnessed brought her to the conclusion that China's needs for social and economic reform would best be met by the Chinese Communist Party.

From 1946 to 1952, Russell was the executive director of the Committee for a Democratic Far Eastern Policy (CDFEP), an organization that opposed American aid to China's Nationalist government and, after the founding of the People's Republic of China in 1949, advocated diplomatic recognition of and trade with that nation. When

McCarthyism forced the CDFEP's disbandment in 1952, Russell continued to work independently to publicize the positive achievements of "new" China, feeling the need to present Americans with a perspective not provided by the mainstream press. With her own money and the help of some of her former CDFEP colleagues, she began the publication of a newsletter, the *Far East Reporter*, and from 1953 to 1978, made annual cross-country lecture tours, speaking on China, showing slides, and distributing literature.

Russell's audiences during the 1950s and 1960s were small and occasionally hostile, but the establishment of friendly relations with China in the early 1970s and the con-comitant renewal of widespread American interest in that country made her an increasingly popular speaker. Although failing eyesight forced her to give up her cross-country trips in 1978, she continued to publish the *Far East Reporter* until a few months before her death. *(See also: Young Women's Christian Association)*

—Laura K. O'Keefe

Further Reading

Maud Russell Papers. Rare Books and Manuscripts Division. New York Public Library.

❧ Sacagawea (1784/9–?)

Despite uncertainty about the place and date of her death and even disagreement about the spelling and meaning of her name, the Shoshoni Indian woman Sacagawea is one of America's best-known Native heroines. As Bernard DeVoto noted in *The Course of Empire,* more monuments have been erected in her honor than for any other American woman, and "she has received what in the United States counts as canonization if not deification: she has become an object of state pride and interstate rivalry." The spelling of her name as "Sacajawea" derives from an 1814 narrative of the Lewis and Clark journey published by Nicholas Biddle. However, most Lewis and Clark scholars, together with the U.S. Geographic Names Board, the U.S. National Park Service, the National Geographic Society, and *World Book Encyclopedia,* have adopted the "Sacagawea" spelling. According to these accounts, her name is derived from the Hidatsa words for "bird" and "woman," and in the Lewis and Clark journals, she is referred to as "Bird Woman."

Sacagawea was born circa 1786 in east-central Idaho near present-day Salmon in Lemhi County as a woman of the Shoshoni (also Shoshone) or Snake nation. When she was about twelve, she was captured and enslaved by a raiding band of the Hidatsu (Minnetaree) Indians of Knife River, North Dakota. The Hidatsu in turn sold her to a French-Canadian fur trader, Toussaint Charbonneau, who claimed her as his wife. Captain Meriwether Lewis and Captain William Clark spent the winter of 1804-1805 with the friendly Mandan Indians near what is today Bismarck, North Dakota. There, they met Charbonneau and Sacagawea, who was pregnant and who gave birth to a son, Jean Baptiste Charbonneau, in February 1805 at Fort Mandan. Lewis and Clark hired Toussaint, who was conversant in French and Hidatsa, as an interpreter. They recognized that the presence of a woman and child would establish the peaceful nature of the party; in addition, Sacagawea spoke both Shoshoni and Hidatsa and could serve as a Native translator. So, they instructed Charbonneau to bring Sacagawea and her son with him, and, in the spring of 1805, the Corps of Discovery set out for the Pacific.

Although Lewis did not often mention Sacagawea in his journals, Clark recorded many instances in which Sacagawea contributed to the success of the journey. In August 1805, the Lewis and Clark party met a band of Shoshoni led by Sacagawea's brother. She was able to negotiate for fresh horses and guides that were essential for the crossing of the Idaho and Oregon mountains. Sacagawea's knowledge of mountain terrain saved much travel time. In addition, she gathered and prepared roots, nuts, berries, and other plants that provided nourishment when food was scarce.

The details of Sacagawea's life after the expedition are a matter of much controversy. She did take her son to St. Louis, where he was raised by Clark, and she did leave the abusive Charbonneau and spend time in St. Louis. According to Clark's records, her death occurred sometime between 1825 and 1828. Other accounts, including that of trader John C. Luttig, record her death on December 20, 1812, at Fort Manuel, South Dakoka. However, Native accounts, especially Shoshoni oral history, report that she remarried, rejoined the Shoshoni people, and moved to the Wind River reservation in Wyoming, where she was reunited with her son and where she died in April 1884. According to this history, she was buried in the white cemetery at Fort Washakie, Wyoming, as a final show of respect for her role in the Lewis and Clark expedition. In the notes for her novel *Sacajawea,* published in 1979, Anna Lee Waldo presents evidence to support this account.

In 1998, the U.S. Congress passed a bill authorizing the U.S. Mint to place into circulation a new dollar coin bearing "a design of Liberty represented by a Native American woman, inspired by Sacagawea." The design for the coin was based on the recommendation of the Dollar Coin Design Advisory Committee, appointed by Secretary of the Treasury Robert E. Rubin to present a design for a coin to replace the Susan B. Anthony dollar. The coin, gold in color with a distinctive edge, was introduced in 2000. In providing extensive input to the Design Advisory Committee, the public played a unique role in selecting the new coin, ensuring an important place for Sacagawea in the nation's history. Whatever the questions about her later life, Sacagawea's role in the Lewis and Clark expedition rightly earned great respect and admiration for this Native American woman. *(See also: Native American Women)*

—Diana E. Axelsen

Further Reading

Anderson, Irving. "Probing the Riddle of the Bird Woman," *Montana: The Magazine of Western History* 23 (1973): 2-17.

Anderson, Irving W. "Sacajawea?—Sakakawea?—Sacagawea?" *We Proceeded On,* 1975, Summer. Retrieved August 10, 1999, http://www.lewisandclark.org/pages/sactext.htm

Chuinard, E. G. "The Actual Role of the Bird Woman: Purposeful Member of the Corps or Casual 'Tag Along,'" *Montana: The Magazine of Western History* 26 (Summer 1976): 18-29.

DeVoto, Bernard. *The Course of Empire.* Boston: Houghton Mifflin, 1952.

Diehl, Philip N. *Editorial, "The New Dollar Coin," by the Director of the U.S. Mint, June 24, 1998.* Available at http://www.usmint.treas.gov/dollarcoin/editorial_saca.cfm

Dye, Eva Emery. *The Conquest.* Portland, OR: Metropolitan Press, 1963. (Original edition published in 1902)

Eastman, Charles A. *A Report of the Commission of Indian Affairs.* Washington, D.C.: Department of the Interior, 1925.

Hebard, Grace Raymond. *Sacajawea, A Guide and Interpreter of the Lewis and Clark Expedition.* Glendale, CA: Arthur H. Clark, 1957.

Howard, Helen Addison. "The Mystery of Sacajawea's Death," *Pacific Northwest Quarterly* 58 (1967): 1-6.

Luttig, John C. *Journal of a Fur-Trading Expedition of the Upper Missouri, 1812-1813.* Saint Louis, MO: Missouri Historical Society, 1920.

Matthews, Washington. *Ethnography and Philology of the Hidatsa Indians.* Washington, D.C.: Government Printing Office, 1877.

Remley, David. "Sacajawea of Myth and History." In *Women and Western American Literature,* edited by Helen Winter Stauffer and Susan J. Rosowski, 70-89. Troy, NY: Whitston, 1982.

Waldo, Anna Lee. *Sacajawea.* New York: Avon, 1979.

White, Julia. "Sacajawea (Boat Launcher) or Sacagawea (Bird Woman)—Shoshoni. Retrieved August 10, 1999, http://www.powersource.com/powersource/gallery/womansp/shoshoni.html

❧ Salem Witch Trials

In the fall of 1692, a group of adolescent girls in Salem, Massachusetts, were "afflicted" by a strange hysteria that resulted in seizures and accusations of witchcraft. The precise causes of the girls' sickness, and whether feigned or real, continue to be debated; one theory is that they were teenagers rebelling against hidebound Puritan strictures, another that they were ingesting hallucinogenic chemicals from the ergot fungus in rye flour. As the frenzy began, the Salem minister's daughter, Betty Parris, and niece Abigail accused the family's black slave woman Tituba of witchcraft. Tituba, a native of Barbados, finally gave way under intense pressure and, in fear of her life, confessed to bewitching the young girls. With her confession, the accusations spread to include many women and three men of Salem who were already suspected of being less than pious Puritans.

The witchcraft court, convened by the government of the colony of Massachusetts, met at Salem in 1692 and 1693 to hear the cases. Led by Puritans such as Cotton Mather and Samuel Sewall, the court handed down a guilty verdict and death sentence in nineteen cases. Eighteen people were hanged, and one man, Giles Corey, was pressed to death with stones. As the hysteria spread beyond Salem, the pattern repeated itself; there was no presumption of innocence and virtually no effective defense against the charge of witchcraft. Within another year, there were hundreds of accused witches in jails throughout eastern Massachusetts, awaiting sentencing or execution.

At that time, a new royal governor, William Phips, arrived in Massachusetts to find the colony seized with hysteria that had gone beyond the control of the Puritan theocracy itself. Phips dismissed the Puritan witchcraft court, freed the remaining jailed witches, and ended the accusations. That his own wife had also been named may have added to his general displeasure. Following his action, the power of the Puritan church over the colony government rapidly declined, leading modern historians to argue that the witchcraft hysteria was the last demonstration of theocracy in Massachusetts and that its ending began the movement toward separation of church and state. *(See also: Nurse, Rebecca; Tituba)*

—Ellen D. Langill

Further Reading

Boyer, Paul, and Stephen Nissenbaum. *Salem Possessed.* Cambridge, MA: Harvard University Press, 1974.

Burr, George L., ed. *Narratives of the Witchcraft Cases, 1658–1706.* New York: Scribner, 1914.

Starkey, Marion L. *The Devil in Massachusetts.* New York: Knopf, 1949.

Upham, Charles W. *Salem Witchcraft.* 1867. Reprint, New York: Ungar, 1959.

❧ Sampson, Deborah (Gannett) (1760–1827)

Deborah Sampson, American Revolutionary War soldier and heroine, was the oldest of three daughters and three sons of Jonathan Sampson and Deborah Bradford, both of whom were descended from the early Pilgrims.

On September 3, 1782, Sampson was excommunicated from the First Baptist Church of Middleborough, Massachusetts, for enlisting as a soldier in the Army. The previous May 20, she had enlisted in the Fourth Massachusetts Regiment under the name Robert Shutleff/Shirtliff. Sampson fought in several engagements and was wounded at Tarrytown, New York. While hospitalized with a fever in Philadelphia, her sex was discovered, and General Henry Knox discharged her at West Point on October 25, 1783. In 1792, the state of Massachusetts awarded her a pension, and in 1805, the United States placed her on the pension list. After she died, her heirs received compensation from an act of Congress in 1838.

She married Benjamin Gannett in April 1785 and bore three children. In 1797, Herman Mann published her biography, titled *The Female Review.* Later, she toured on a theater circuit telling of her adventures in the war. *(See also: American Revolutionary Era; Military Service)*

—**Ginger Rae Allee**

Further Reading

Bruce, H. Addington. *Women in the Making of America*. Rev. ed., pp. 91-96. Boston: Little, Brown, 1928.

Green, Henry Clinton, and Mary Wolcott Green. *The Pioneer Mothers of America*. Vol. 2, pp. 265-79. New York: Putnam, 1912.

Leonard, Eugene Audress, Sophia Drinker, and Miriam Young Holden. *The American Women in Colonial and Revolutionary Times, 1765–1800*, pp. 120-21. Philadelphia: University of Pennsylvania Press, 1962.

Logan, Mary Simmerson. *The Part Taken by Women in American History*. 1912. Reprint, pp. 105-06. New York: Arno, 1972.

Revolutionary War. "Military Pension File X32722, Deborah Gannett (Alias Robert Shurtleff)." National Archives, Washington, D.C.

Whitton, Mary Ormsbee. *These Were the Women, U.S.A. 1776–1880*, pp. 14-16. New York: Hastings House, 1954.

Wright, Richardson. *Forgotten Ladies*, pp. 94-120. Philadelphia: J. B. Lippincott, 1928.

Sandoz, Mari (1896–1966)

Mari Sandoz, historian and novelist, did perhaps more than any other white writer to destroy the destructive stereotype of American Indians. Her Great Plains series is not only a classic in the history of the American West but portrayed the American Indians on their own terms long before it had become fashionable to do so. The six works in their historical chronology are *The Beaver Men* (1964), *Crazy Horse* (1942), *Cheyenne Autumn* (1953), *The Buffalo Hunters* (1954), *The Cattlemen* (1958), and *Old Jules* (1935), which is autobiographical.

Sandoz possessed several qualities that made her uniquely qualified to write about the Plains Indians. She attempted to enter into the cultures she was writing about. In 1930 and 1931, she traveled three thousand miles in Sioux territory, interviewing and living with Sioux and Cheyenne who knew Crazy Horse. Moreover, before she wrote *Cheyenne Autumn,* she retraced the fifteen-hundred-mile flight north and talked with the old Cheyenne who had survived the ordeal. In addition, she adopted an Oglala and Cheyenne perspective in her writing, using idioms and metaphors to capture, in her words, "the underlying rhythm pattern to say something of the things of the Indian for which there are no white-man words, suggest something of his innate nature, something of his relationship to the earth and the sky and all that is between."

Sandoz was accused by critics of endorsing the Noble Savage stereotype and being too partisan in favor of the Indians. However, Sandoz wrote from the assumption that Oglala and Cheyenne cultures were as varied and complex as white/Anglo culture, and she illuminated the good as well as the bad, the heroic as well as the mundane. We see Little Wolf as the culture hero of his people, and finally we see him

Figure 53. Mari Sandoz

Author of the six-volume Great Plains series, published from 1935 to 1964, Mari Sandoz wrote in a balanced and sympathetic way about American Indians. Used by permission of UPI/Corbis-Bettmann.

disgraced when he kills a tribesman in a drunken rage. We see Crazy Horse as the self-sacrificing leader as well as the jealous lover. We see the Oglala warriors as courageous fighters against the whites and obsequious toward the whites once they are captured. *(See also: Migration and Frontier Women; Women Writers)*

—**John Snider**

Further Reading

Clark, Laverne Harrell. "The Indian Writings of Mari Sandoz: 'A Lone One Left from the Old Times.'" *American Indian Quarterly* 1 (1974): 183-92, 269-80.

Sandoz, Mari. *Sandhill Sundays and Other Recollections*. Lincoln: University of Nebraska Press, 1970.

Snider, John. "Mari Sandoz' *Crazy Horse* and *Cheyenne Autumn:* Destroying the Stereotype." In "The Treatment of American Indians in Selected American Literature: A Radical Critique," pp. 160-92. Ph.D. diss., University of Illinois—Urbana, 1983.

Stauffer, Helen Winter, ed. *Letters of Mari Sandoz.* Lincoln: University of Nebraska Press, 1992.

———. *Mari Sandoz.* Boise, ID: Boise State University Press, 1984.

———. *Mari Sandoz: Story Catcher of the Plains.* Lincoln: University of Nebraska Press, 1982.

⚭ Sanger, Margaret Louise (Higgins)
(1879–1966)

Margaret Sanger was the most notable leader in the twentieth-century birth control movement. After marrying artist William Sanger in 1902 and bearing three children, Sanger went to work as a home nurse in the slums of New York City. Appalled by the plight of the women she encountered, Sanger recognized that only birth control could free these women from the physical hardships, fear, and dependency inherent in being unable to separate sexual experience from reproduction.

Convinced that birth control was the key to gaining female autonomy, Sanger sought to challenge the laws prohibiting it. In March 1914, she began publishing *The Woman Rebel,* a monthly journal devoted to socialist and anarchist issues. Emblazoned with the slogan, "No Gods, No Masters," *The Woman Rebel* was intended as a call to arms for working-class women. Each issue included not only discussions of radical issues such as the uses of violence as a tool of striking workers but dramatic statements on the rights of women, particularly their right to sexual freedom. For Sanger, every woman had a right to be "absolute mistress of her own body." This included the right to practice *birth control,* a term first coined for *The Woman Rebel.*

An appearance in the first issue of an unsigned article by Sanger announcing her intention to publish contraceptive information in *The Woman Rebel* quickly drew the attention of the postal authorities who told her that she had violated the nation's Comstock laws and could not continue to distribute the journal. Although Sanger soon decided to publish the birth control information in a separate pamphlet titled *Family Limitation,* the postal authorities, unaware of this, continued to focus on *The Woman Rebel.* In August, Sanger was formally indicted, not for publishing birth control material, but, rather, for printing an article by William Thorpe titled, "A Defense of Assassination." Unwilling to stand trial on this indictment, she fled to England in November 1914.

Once safely off U.S. soil, Sanger authorized the release of *Family Limitation,* a sixteen-page pamphlet that offered clear, frank descriptions of various contraceptive methods. Although Sanger addressed *Family Limitation* to working women, she asserted the right of *all* women to own and control their bodies. With its simple straightforward prose and graphic illustrations, *Family Limitation* was the most useful guide to birth control and reproduction then available to American women.

Sanger was aware that distributing this pamphlet would violate the Comstock law's prohibition on the dissemination of birth control material and had been prepared to break the law in order to challenge it. However, because she was on her way to England when the first copies of *Family Limitation* were circulated, it was not Margaret Sanger but her husband, William Sanger, who was arrested for possessing a copy of the offending pamphlet. In a nationally publicized trial, William Sanger was found guilty and sentenced to thirty days in jail. However, further efforts to suppress *Family Limitation* failed. Some 10 million copies of the pamphlet were distributed in the next two decades, and it was translated into thirteen languages.

Anxious to keep the public focused on her cause, Margaret Sanger returned to the United States in 1915 to face her own trial for *The Woman Rebel.* Within a few weeks of her return, Sanger's daughter Peggy died of pneumonia, and letters of sympathy and support began pouring in. Close friends such as H. G. Wells and other notables sent a letter to President Woodrow Wilson affirming their support for Sanger, while others raised funds for her defense. With intensified press coverage of Sanger, the *Woman Rebel* trial, and the birth control movement, the government decided to avoid further publicity and dropped the charges.

In 1916, Sanger embarked on a nationwide lecture tour to promote birth control and continued to draw the attention of both local authorities and the press. In the wake of the controversy generated by her speeches and the continued distribution of the now-infamous *Family Limitation* pamphlet, Margaret Sanger soon emerged as the leader of the new birth control movement. When she returned to New York in 1916, she was arrested for opening the nation's first birth control clinic in Brownsville, Brooklyn. This time, she was convicted and jailed for thirty days.

While these law-defying tactics brought national prominence to the birth control movement, Sanger recognized that the birth control movement was still too marginalized and too radical to succeed. She began seeking more broadly based support among wealthy professional, business, and philanthropic communities. During these years, she also secured a divorce from first husband William Sanger and in 1921 married wealthy oil producer J. Noah Slee, who provided much of the birth control movement's financing.

Sanger's growing financial base enabled her to found the American Birth Control League in 1921 and launch a campaign to legalize birth control. Insisting that birth control be treated as a medical as well as a social and economic issue, she pressed for passage of a bill exempting doctors from the legal prohibitions on contraceptives. Her efforts were rewarded in the Supreme Court's *United States v. One Package* (1936) decision, which permitted the importation and dissemination of contraceptive materials intended for physicians. In 1923, Sanger opened the Birth Control Clinical Research Bureau, the first doctor-staffed birth control clinic in the nation. These efforts resulted in the transformation of the birth control movement into a respectable social reform movement, a shift reflected in the 1942 reorganization of the American Birth Control League and its successors into the Planned Parenthood Federation of America.

Beginning in the 1920s, Sanger also brought her birth control message to China, Japan, India, and the Soviet Union. She sought to build international networks of birth control advocates through the London-based Birth Control International Information Centre, which she cofounded with Edith How-Martyn in 1929. In the years following World War II, Sanger emerged from semiretirement in Tucson, Arizona, to reclaim leadership of global birth control efforts. She was instrumental in the founding of the International Planned Parenthood Federation in Bombay in 1952, serving as its president until her retirement in 1959. Margaret Sanger's ongoing efforts to support and encourage contraceptive research also led to the eventual development of the first birth control pill.

Margaret Sanger persevered in the face of numerous legal, religious, and social obstacles. By remaining consistently dedicated to ensuring that safe and reliable birth control was available to all women, she helped effect a social revolution that transformed women's lives. *(See also: American Birth Control League; Birth Control; Birth Control Clinical Research Bureau; Obscenity; Planned Parenthood Federation of America)*

—**Esther Katz**

Further Reading

Chesler, Ellen. *Woman of Valor: Margaret Sanger and the Birth Control Movement in America.* New York: Simon & Schuster, 1992.

Gordon, Linda. *Woman's Body, Woman's Right: A Social History of Birth Control in America.* New York: Grossman, 1976.

Kennedy, David. *Birth Control in America: The Career of Margaret Sanger.* New Haven, CT: Yale University Press, 1970.

McCann, Carole, R. *Birth Control Politics in the United States, 1916–1945.* Ithaca, NY: Cornell University Press, 1994.

Reed, James. *From Public Vice to Private Virtue: The Birth Control Movement and American Society Since 1830.* Princeton, NJ: Princeton University Press, 1978.

Sanger, Margaret. *An Autobiography.* New York: Norton, 1938.

———. *Margaret Sanger: My Fight for Birth Control.* New York: Farrar & Rinehart, 1931.

———. *The Woman Rebel,* compiled and with an introduction by Alex Baskin. Stony Brook: State University of New York, 1976.

United States v. One Package, 13 F.Supp. 334 (1936).

Sargent, Jesse Irene (1852–1932)

Jesse Sargent was professor of the history of fine arts at Syracuse University, 1895 to 1932, and a leading advocate of the American arts and crafts movement. Sargent taught Romance languages, aesthetics, and art history at Syracuse University and received honorary degrees from that institution in 1911 and 1922. In 1926, she became the second woman to be awarded an honorary membership by the American Institute of Architects. For twenty-five years, Sargent contributed articles on jewelry, metalwork, glass, and ceramics to *The Keystone* (Philadelphia). Her most significant work, however, appeared in *The Craftsman* (Syracuse), a magazine published by furniture manufacturer Gustav Stickley.

Sargent's main themes were typical of much arts and crafts writing. She condemned the effects of the "moral earthquake" wrought by industrialism. For example, she believed that the increasing reliance on machines and on an elaborate division of labor had transformed factory workers into slaves. Degraded labor, in turn, cheated consumers by producing poorly designed and cheaply constructed objects. Most alarming, industrialism threatened to destroy urban civilization because it fostered an excessive individualism that was blind to mutual obligations and the corporate life of the municipality.

Influenced by the writings of British reformers such as John Ruskin and William Morris and by her own extensive reading in thirteenth-century history and literature, Sargent believed that certain principles gleaned from Europe's Middle Ages could guide modern Americans toward a better society. The life of the medieval craftsman, she argued, consisted of an ideal mixture of art, labor, and recreation. The guilds of that era were models of brotherhood, civic spirit, and quality workmanship. And the balanced, interdependent structure of the cathedral mirrored both the religious faith and secular aspirations of an organically unified society. Sargent's thoughts on social reform were also powerfully affected by Russian anarchist Peter Kropotkin, who proposed an "integral education" that would combine manual training with the usual academic studies. Finally, she was very impressed by the simple dignity of Gustav Stickley's house and furniture designs. Such dwellings could serve the middle class as soothing havens from the "storm and stress" of modern life.

Sargent wrote more than eighty articles for *The Craftsman* during its first years, 1901 to 1905, and played a crucial role in molding a magazine ostensibly devoted to the "household arts," into the principal journal of arts and crafts social thought. *(See also: Art; Higher Education)*

—**Bruce R. Kahler**

Further Reading

Gabriel, Cleota Reed. "Irene Sargent: Rediscovering a Lost Legend," *The Courier* 16 (Summer 1979): 3-13.

Reed, Cleota. "Irene Sargent: A Comprehensive Bibliography of Her Published Writings," *The Courier* 18 (Spring 1981): 9-25.

Satir, Virginia (1914–1989)

An acknowledged pioneer in the area of family therapy and best known for her books *Cojoint Family Therapy* and *Peoplemaking,* Virginia Satir contributed much to the understanding of family dynamics and communication patterns. She was in great demand as the premier trainer of family therapists at AVANTA in Menlo Park, California, and a pivotal force in the field of family therapy because of her exceptional skills and innovative thinking.

Born in Neilsville, Wisconsin, to Reinhold and Minnie Pagenkopf, Satir began a brief teaching career after receiving a B.E. from Wisconsin State University in 1936. She worked as a social worker and received her M.A. in psychiatric social work from the University of Chicago in 1948. She married Norman Satir in 1951, raised two children, and was divorced in 1961.

In 1955, Satir became an instructor in family dynamics at the Illinois State Psychiatric Institute. At the institute, she introduced the revolutionary idea of working with the patient's family instead of doing individual therapy with the hospitalized person. Satir moved to California in 1959 and cofounded the Mental Research Institute in Palo Alto, an interdisciplinary group of therapists, communication experts, and social scientists committed to the study of family interaction in relation to illness and health. In the mid-1960s, after establishing the first training program in family therapy, Satir went on to develop a human growth center at the Esalen Institute. She founded the AVANTA network in 1976 in Menlo Park as a training center for teachers of family systems.

When *Cojoint Family Therapy* was published in 1964, Satir described to therapists her unorthodox techniques, which emphasized the reestablishment of communication patterns between family members. Seeing mental illness as "distorted communication," Satir emphasized social rather than intrapsychic factors. When she first developed her theories, Satir was criticized as being too confrontational, but over the years, her ideas have won wide acceptance. In 1974, Satir published *Peoplemaking* so that families could recognize and analyze their own rules and make behavioral changes. She did not emphasize mental illness but discussed concrete interventions to improve the self-esteem of family members.

Virginia Satir helped revolutionize the field of psychotherapy by treating clients within the context of their families rather than as individuals. As author and productive social worker, she has contributed more to the professional development of family therapy than any other woman. *(See also: Psychiatry; Psychology; Social Work)*

—**Linda Noer**

Further Reading

Goldenberg, Irene, and Herbert Goldenberg. *Family Therapy.* Monterey, CA: Brooks/Cole, 1980.

ᷲ Schlafly, Phyllis MacAlpin (Stewart)
(b. 1924)

Author, speaker, and crusader for conservative causes, Phyllis Schlafly was instrumental in defeating ratification of the Equal Rights Amendment. As editor of the *Phyllis Schlafly Report* and the *Eagle Forum Newsletter,* she rallied nonworking women to antifeminist causes. Without a paid staff or large contributions, she wrote hundreds of articles and delivered speeches in every state condemning femi-

nism as destructive of the family. Schlafly has published nine books, including *A Choice, Not an Echo,* which promoted the presidential candidacy of Senator Barry Goldwater in 1964.

Schlafly was born in St. Louis in 1924 and educated at the Convent of the Sacred Heart. She graduated Phi Beta Kappa from Washington University in 1944, while working at a war plant forty-eight hours a week, and won a scholarship to Radcliffe College, where she earned an M.A. in government in 1945. At the age of fifty-four, she received a law degree from Washington University.

She did research in Washington, D.C., managed a successful campaign for a Republican congressional candidate in St. Louis, and edited a bank newsletter before marrying John Fred Schlafly, Jr., an Alton, Illinois, attorney, in 1949. Having borne four boys and two girls, Schlafly has stated that raising a family is the most important career for a woman and that she enjoyed nothing more than caring for a baby.

A conservative Republican, Schlafly ran for Congress in 1952 and 1970 but lost both races. She served as a delegate or alternate to Republican national conventions in 1956, 1960, and 1964 and ran for president of the National Federation of Republican Women in 1967 but was defeated. She collaborated with Rear Admiral Chester Ward on five books between 1964 and Ward's death in 1978, including *Kissinger on the Couch* and *Ambush at Vladivostok.* She opposed the Nuclear Test Ban Treaty of 1963 and arms control agreements with the Soviet Union.

As founder and chairperson of STOP ERA, Schlafly was the most prominent woman opponent of the Equal Rights Amendment, which fell short of ratification in 1982. As president of the Eagle Forum, a conservative political activist organization, she crusaded against abortion, pornography, and violence and sex on television. Even though her son is an open homosexual, she still is adamantly opposed to gay rights legislation. In addition, she also supported movements that oppose affirmative action and preferential status under the Civil Rights Act. Furthermore, Schlafly was influential in the defeat of the Family and Medical Leave Act in 1988.

Considered one of the founding mothers of the New Moral Majority, Schlafly was a major speaker at the GOP convention in 1992. Consequently, she was instrumental in the adoption of the anti-abortion, antigay Republican platform for the 1992 presidential election.

Schlafly is a devout Catholic and a member of the Daughters of the American Revolution. She was also a member of the Commission on the Bicentennial of the United States Constitution. Currently, Schlafly is working to prevent the implementation of programs on AIDS education and sex education, claiming that they promote promiscuity and "safe sodomy." *(See also: Antifeminism; Equal Rights Amendment; Republican Party; Right-Wing Political Movements)*

—**Glen Jeansonne**
—**Michelle Novak**

Further Reading

Felsenthal, Carol. *The Sweetheart of the Silent Majority: The Biography of Phyllis Schlafly.* Garden City, NY: Doubleday, 1981.

Klemesrud, Judy. "Opponent of the E.R.A. Confident of Its Defeat," *New York Times* (December 15, 1975): 44: 1.

Schlafly, Phyllis. *A Choice, Not an Echo.* Alton, IL: Pere Marquette Press, 1964.

———. "Family and Medical Leave Act." Speech to Congress. *Congressional Digest* 67 (May 1988): 145-49.

———. Interview. *Meet the Press* 92 (September 27, 1992): 11-17.

～ Schneiderman, Rose (1882–1972)

Rose Schneiderman, a Jewish immigrant, became a union organizer and leader after working in a cap factory from 1898 to 1903. Schneiderman's involvement with the trade union began with her job in the cap factory. Her experience in chartering the first female local of the United Cloth Hat and Cap Maker's Union and her participation in the thirteen-week capmaker's strike inspired her dedication to the spirit of trade unionism. To Schneiderman, this spirit meant friendship among workers through serving others; she felt that because the struggle of one member was the responsibility of all the members, the group benefited from the work of each individual.

Schneiderman joined the New York Women's Trade Union League (WTUL) in 1905, and three years later, she became a salaried full-time union organizer through the generosity of a benefactor of the New York league. As a union organizer, she stressed sisterhood in speaking to the factory women, emphasizing that they were not alone in their struggle but joined by many others. By 1913, woman suffrage was a major issue. Schneiderman saw suffrage as a tool to pass legislation to improve working conditions and chaired the industrial section of the Women's Suffrage Party of New York City. She was now addressing the male union membership and urging them to vote for the Nineteenth Amendment. While president of the New York WTUL, 1918 to 1949, Schneiderman worked for an eight-hour day and a minimum wage, developed a summer school for working women, and opened a new clubhouse for evening classes, meetings, and social gatherings.

Schneiderman was president of the National Women's Trade Union League, 1926 to 1950. As president, she met prominent people such as Eleanor Roosevelt and was a frequent guest in the Roosevelt home. She seemed to have enlightened Franklin Delano Roosevelt with regard to trade unions, and he appeared to understand and favor unions. Roosevelt appointed Schneiderman the only woman member on the advisory board of the National Recovery Administration (NRA) in 1933.

When Schneiderman retired in 1955, she had played a significant role in the development of trade unionism in the United States for fifty years. She was a worker, an organizer, and a leader, but above all, she was a believer in unionization. Her belief in unions and the zeal with which she spoke inspired many women to join unions. As more women joined the unions, the unions became stronger, and the strength of those unions resulted in improved working conditions for women. *(See also: Jewish Women; National Women's Trade Union League; New Deal; Unions)*

—**Rosemary Herriges**

Further Reading

Lagemann, Ellen Condliffe. *A Generation of Women: Education in the Lives of Progressive Reformers.* Cambridge, MA: Harvard University Press, 1979.

Schneiderman, Rose. "A Cap Maker's Story." In *The Female Experience: An American Documentary,* edited by Gerda Lerner, 300-02. Indianapolis, IN: Bobbs-Merrill, 1980.

Schneiderman, Rose, and L. Goldthwaite. *All for One.* New York: Eriksson, 1967.

～ School Board Suffrage

School board suffrage was a minimalist strategy used both by suffragists and male legislators who wanted to appear progressive by giving women a vote in school elections. By the mid-nineteenth century, the doctrine of separate spheres had already expanded to consider school teaching, at least at the elementary level, as suitable work for single women. By extension, the regulation of schools, particularly in rural districts, could be seen as another aspect of women's role as mothers. Many males, especially in western and midwestern states, found that the enfranchisement of women in school elections provided an acceptable level of female participation without threatening the traditional male control of politics. Some twenty-three states gave women the vote in school elections, but some of them for only brief periods. Many states hedged even this limited form of woman suffrage by creating barriers involving marital status, property ownership, or geography. Most southern states barred women of any race from any form of suffrage, but one surprising exception was Kentucky. As early as 1838, it passed a law allowing widows with children in school to vote on school issues. The law was later expanded to include spinsters who were guardians of children, but this insignificant change did not apply to Louisville and some other large towns. Mississippi also gave widows voting rights in school elections, but most state restrictions were geographic, confining women's vote to rural districts. Towns and cities often had the power in their charters to exclude women from voting even though state law might allow it in the countryside. For example, New York women could vote only in country districts and in eleven third-class cities whose charters permitted female voting on several matters. In Illinois, women won a hard-fought battle for school suffrage in 1891 only to find it an empty victory since many cities, including Chicago, had appointed school boards.

Women also discovered that what was granted by a state legislature could be taken away by the courts and male voters. The classic case occurred in New Jersey where in 1887 the legislature after a long struggle by woman suffrage forces gave women the right to vote in rural school meetings. Seven years later in 1894, the state Supreme Court ruled that the legislation violated New Jersey's constitution. For the next three years, an alliance of suffrage groups, including the Woman's Christian Temperance Union and the General Federation of Women's Clubs, waged a massive campaign to restore this modest advance for woman suffrage. After they pressured the legislature into passing a constitutional amendment in two successive sessions, a special state referendum was held in September 1897, but it lost by almost 10,000 votes.

The defeat in New Jersey illustrated just how difficult it was to secure even a minimal level of woman suffrage through state constitutional referendums. As the suffrage movement renewed itself after 1900, the strategy turned toward the presidential vote and, after 1916, a federal constitutional amendment. Furthermore, social feminists such as Jane Addams saw that the interests of poor and immigrant women transcended the narrow limits of the school and involved social problems requiring help from city, state, or national governments where women had no vote.

School board suffrage not only gave many women their first opportunity to vote but also provided thousands of them with an opportunity to serve in an elective office. Again, many states limited this right by excluding county superintendents from the list of school offices for which women were eligible. In the era of the one-room rural schoolhouse, the county superintendents were often the most important local school officials. North Dakota was the most progressive state in giving women the vote for county superintendents as well as the state superintendent of public instruction, the highest school office in the state. In the first decade of its statehood in the 1890s, two women were elected to serve in this post.

Only six states—Kansas, Illinois, Nebraska, North Dakota, Tennessee, and Vermont—went to the next intermediate step and gave women a vote in municipal elections. Except for Kansas (1887) and Illinois (1913), these laws were passed during the final push for a federal amendment during World War I. *(See also: Addams, Jane; Education; Politics; Suffrage; Suffrage in the American West; Suffrage in the South; Teaching; Voting Rights)*

—**Neil W. Hogan**

Further Reading

Anthony, Susan B., Matilda Joslyn Gage, Ida Husted Harper, and Elizabeth Cady Stanton, eds. *The History of Woman Suffrage,* 6 vols. New York: Fowler & Walker/National Woman Suffrage Association, 1881-1922. Reprint, Salem, NH: Ayer, 1985.

Brown, Victoria Bissell. "Jane Addams, Progressive and Woman Suffrage." In *One Woman, One Vote,* edited by Marjorie Spruill Wheeler, 179-202. Troutdale, OR: New Sage Press, 1995.

Buechler, Steven M. *The Transformation of the Woman Suffrage Movement: The Case of Illinois, 1850-1920.* New Brunswick, NJ: Rutgers University Press, 1986.

Gordon, Felice D. *After Winning: The Legacy of the New Jersey Suffragists, 1920-1947.* New Brunswick, NJ: Rutgers University Press, 1986.

～ Science

Women's contributions to American science are remarkable in light of a history of limited access to higher education, restricted job opportunities, and constraining societal conceptions of women's work.

Science in colonial America was characterized by the work of interested amateurs, both men and women, because there were few chances for focused science education or professional development. Scientific exploration began at home, with the immediate natural environment serving as textbook. Eliza Pinckney (1722?–1793) worked from her plantation in South Carolina to develop new methods in the cultivation of indigo, and Martha Logan (1704–1779) turned her interest in her garden into popular writings on horticulture.

As would be true in later times, colonial women who became active in science often had fathers or husbands who introduced them to the subject. One of the best-known women scientists of the time was Jane Colden (1724–1766), who, like her brothers, received botanical instruction from her father, the famous Cadwallader Colden. Cadwallader believed that women were unable to learn Latin and refused to teach it to his daughter, with the result that he reported all of her classifications and discoveries for her.

Following American independence and the stabilization of the new democracy, the early nineteenth century was a time of a popular enthusiasm for science. Traveling lyceum lectures provided affordable introductory science instruction for men and women, and universities replaced the "classical" education of Latin and Greek with a new curriculum that included natural and physical sciences. The rise of interest in science in America was influential for women's education as well as men's. Botany was considered especially suitable to the temperament of women, but women were also educated in astronomy, chemistry, and physics.

The 1820s saw a sudden growth in the number of institutions devoted to women's education. Teaching posts at these women's seminaries and colleges became the only form of employment in the sciences for almost all women. Most women's schools included collections of scientific instruments and materials for demonstrations, and American women received better education in the sciences than their counterparts in Northern Europe. Yet it was not intended that women should go on to careers in the fields they were studying. On the contrary, science education had purely domestic aims, because it was believed that an introduction to science would improve women as mothers, wives, and teachers in the common schools springing up across the republic.

Some women did manage to support themselves through research and upper-level teaching in the sciences, however.

Lydia Shattuck (1822–1889), one of fifteen women chosen by naturalist Louis Agassiz to participate in his 1873 Anderson School of Natural History, made outstanding contributions toward botanical classification and collections while working at Mount Holyoke Seminary. She was also notable as an early advocate of the theory of evolution. Her pupil Cornelia Clapp (1849–1934) also attended the Anderson School and became a prominent zoologist, participating in the research projects at the Marine Biological Laboratory in Woods Hole, Massachusetts. Another example of a successful female scientist of the time was Almira Phelps (1793–1884), who wrote extremely popular texts on botany, chemistry, and other topics.

Most famous was Maria Mitchell (1818–1889), whose work in her father's observatory led to her 1847 discovery of a comet, an event honored by the awarding of a gold medal from the King of Denmark. She was inducted into the American Academy of Arts and Sciences and chosen to direct the observatory at Vassar College, where she encouraged other women to become involved in science.

In the second half of the nineteenth century, however, increasing specialization and professionalization of the sciences threatened the position of women in science by making access to graduate school and laboratories more important. For example, botanical classification, once based on morphology, or the appearance of a plant, now moved toward a basis in physiology, or plant function. As a result, botanists who formerly required only magnifying glasses and plant presses now needed fully equipped laboratories.

The first doctorates of philosophy were given at Yale in 1861, and the degree soon became a prerequisite to teaching and doing research in the sciences. Between 1861 and 1893, however, women were only sporadically granted Ph.D.s, often from less prestigious institutions. Ellen Swallow Richards (1842–1911), the first woman admitted to the Massachusetts Institute of Technology, was given her B.S. in chemistry in 1873. However, she was told during her years of graduate work that the department would not grant a doctorate to a woman. Richards, who coined the term *ecology*, had hoped that she might gain advances for women by demonstrating that science could support traditional feminine spheres of work. From her studies on water quality and concern for creating a healthy home, Richards founded the field of home economics.

Other women who were denied degrees were more outspoken. Christine Ladd-Franklin (1847–1930), mathematician and color theorist, studied at Johns Hopkins from 1879 to 1882 without receiving a doctorate. As a consequence, she became an agitator for the cause of women in science and set up a fellowship with the Association of Collegiate Alumnae to send women graduate students abroad to study at respected universities in Britain and Germany.

In 1893, the year that geologist Florence Bascom (1862–1945) was given a doctorate by "special dispensation" at Johns Hopkins, six of the most renowned graduate schools in the country announced that they would give graduate degrees to women, opening the gates for women across the country. Once women began to receive doctoral degrees, however, they found that there was still little chance for them to make a career in science. Teaching positions in women's colleges were limited in number, and the only research positions available to women were as low-status assistants performing repetitive work. Some scientists even argued that women were particularly suited to these kinds of tasks.

Only occasionally did women placed in these positions gain recognition for their achievements. At the Harvard College Observatory, a group of women became notable for the astronomical discoveries they made as computing assistants. Edward Pickering, head of the observatory, hired women because he had noticed the patience and attention to detail of his housekeeper, Williamina Fleming (1857–1911). "Pickering's harem" began with Fleming in 1881, who eventually became the first female officer of Harvard and hired many other women to work in the observatory. Besides her tireless efforts to discover and classify stars, Fleming also refined Pickering's system of classification and demonstrated that spectral lines proved certain stars to be variable. Her employees included Annie Jump Cannon (1863–1941), who created the spectral classification system adopted by the International Solar Union in 1910, and Antonia C. Maury (1866–1952), who did pioneering work on the component stars of spectroscopic binaries.

World War I offered new opportunities for women, who took jobs during the war effort that had previously been unavailable to them. Women's work in chemistry, physics, psychology, and other fields during the war led to general excitement about women in science. The enthusiasm was further increased by Marie Curie's tour of America in 1921. Although there were still many who preferred to keep women out of science, more women were able to find employment in the sciences than ever before.

Unfortunately, the Great Depression was a difficult time for scientific study in general and for women scientists in particular. When jobs were scarce, employers were more likely to hire men, because men were considered to be responsible for the finances of an entire family. The steady rise of antinepotism regulations also meant that married women often lost their positions with universities, even if they had been employed by the university prior to marriage.

Women in World War II gained few of the benefits that women had during World War I. Although women were involved in every aspect of scientific research during the war, including at least eleven women who worked on crucial elements of the Manhattan project, most women scientists were given only routine, administrative assignments.

Following the Second World War, women scientists faced some of their biggest setbacks. Although science was booming as a field of study and employment, women were excluded at every turn. Women who had been given teaching and research positions during the war quickly lost them, regardless of their achievements. The GI Bill and quotas placed on female enrollment kept the numbers of women receiving higher education low. Professors were often reluctant to take women as graduate students, not only because they were doubtful of the women's abilities but also because they feared that female students were more likely to drop their pursuit of science after marriage or childbirth. Within research projects, women were generally invisible to the public, given only entry-level positions and almost never advanced. At universities, not only did departments rarely hire single women, but antinepotism rules continued to keep women out of teaching and research positions.

Indeed, although the Cold War sometimes resulted in governmental propaganda encouraging women to learn about science for reasons of national defense, the prevailing sentiment was that women's roles should be supporting husband and son. Women scientists were portrayed as unfeminine and potentially un-American. Given this environment, it is unsurprising that whereas women received approximately 11 percent of all science doctorates during the 1920s, the number had dropped to 5 percent during the 1950s.

Happily, the women's movement of the late 1960s brought about legal reform in women's education and employment rights. Title VII of the Civil Rights Act of 1964 prohibits sex discrimination in employment, and in 1970, psychologist Bernice Sandler brought a class-action lawsuit against 250 colleges and universities for discriminatory hiring practices. By the 1970s, women had the legal protection they needed to guarantee equal treatment in education and employment, and certain affirmative action policies even encouraged the hiring of women.

Despite the obstacles, six American women have been honored with Nobel prizes for their achievements in the sciences. Gerty Cori (1896–1957) received a prize in medicine or physiology in 1947 with her husband and Bernardo Houssay for their work in studying carbohydrate metabolism. In 1963, Maria Goeppert Mayer (1906–1972) shared the prize in physics for describing atomic structure with the concept of shell layers housing protons and neutrons. Rosalyn Sussman Yalow (b. 1921) won for medicine or physiology in 1977 with Andrew Schally and Roger Guillemin. She worked on radioimmunoassay, a technique that allowed doctors to measure with great accuracy the concentration of substances in fluid samples.

Barbara McClintock (1902–1992) was given a Nobel prize for medicine or physiology in 1983 for her discovery that some genetic material was mobile. In 1986, Rita Levi-Montalcini (b. 1909) won the Nobel in medicine or physiology with Stanley Cohen for their discovery of nerve growth factor (NGF). Last, in 1988, the prize in medicine or physiology was awarded to Gertrude B. Elion along with George Hitchings and James Black for their work in developing drugs that would leave healthy cells alone while attacking the abnormal ones. This work has had impact on treatments for everything from leukemia to herpes and AIDS.

As in other academic fields, access to work and study in the sciences has been especially restricted for minority women. The first African American woman to receive a science Ph.D. was Ruth E. Moore, who studied bacteriology at Ohio State University and was awarded a degree in 1933. In 1973, Shirley Ann Jackson became the first African American woman to receive a doctorate in physics. She completed her graduate work at MIT.

Today, the situation has greatly improved for women in the sciences. It is true that women continue to be better represented in the biological sciences than the physical, and statistics show that women have trouble gaining tenure at some of the most elite universities. On the whole, however, women have far greater opportunities for study and work in all fields of science now than at any previous time. Yet old conceptions of science as a masculine activity have not disappeared entirely, and today's struggle may well be to prevent girls and young women from being discouraged early on in their schooling. The American Association of University Women has shown that elementary and high school teachers still tend to favor boys and young men in the science classroom. Although the most dramatic victories for women in science may have already occurred, the more subtle process of reconceptualizing the meaning of gender and the nature of science is ongoing. *(See also: Benedict, Ruth Fulton; Blackwell, Elizabeth; Carson, Rachel; Education; Geology; Higher Education; Home Economics; Mathematics; Mead, Margaret; Mitchell, Maria; Nature Study; Physicians; Pinckney, Eliza Lucas; Preston, Ann; Walker, Mary Edwards; Woman's Medical College of Pennsylvania)*

—Caroline Reynolds Sherman

Further Reading

Abir-Am, Prina G., and Outram, Dorinda, eds. *Uneasy Careers and Intimate Lives: Women in Science, 1789–1979*. New Brunswick, NJ: Rutgers University Press, 1987.

Arnold, Lois Barber. *Four Lives in Science*. New York: Schocken, 1984.

Bertsch McGravne, Sharon. *Nobel Prize Women in Science: Their Lives, Struggles, and Momentous Discoveries*. New York: Birch Lane, 1993.

Bleier, Ruth, ed. *Feminist Approaches to Science*. Elmsford, NY: Pergamon, 1986.

Cole, Jonathan R. *Fair Science: Women in the Scientific Community*. New York: Free Press, 1979.

Gornick, Vivian. *Women in Science: 100 Journeys into the Territory*. New York: Simon & Schuster, 1990.

Hanson, Sandra L. *Lost Talent: Women in the Sciences*. Philadelphia: Temple University Press, 1996.

Keller, Evelyn Fox. *Reflections on Gender and Science*. New Haven, CT: Yale University Press, 1985.

Oglivie, Marilyn. *Women in Science: Antiquity through the 19th Century: A Biographical Dictionary with Annotated Bibliography*. Cambridge: MIT Press, 1986.

Rossiter, Margaret W. *Women Scientists in America: Before Affirmative Action, 1940–1972*. Baltimore: Johns Hopkins University Press, 1995.

———. *Women Scientists in America: Struggles and Strategies to 1940*. Baltimore: Johns Hopkins University Press, 1982.

✑ Scientific Motherhood

Scientific motherhood, an ideology developed in the late nineteenth century, defined motherhood as woman's most significant role. It declared that mothers were both responsible for the health and well-being of their children and incapable of carrying out their duties alone. Initially, advocates of scientific motherhood maintained that mothers needed scientific information; by the twentieth century, they increasingly insisted that women had to be directed, some would say controlled, by scientific and medical experts. While the tradition of women as the moral guardians of the home (and by extension of society) continued, scientific motherhood stressed the physical and psychological nurturance of children rather than moral training.

Several factors fostered the spread of scientific motherhood. With industrialization and urbanization, the home lost many productive functions; mothers became consumers, not producers. Child care did remain in the home, even though family size was shrinking. (In 1800, white families averaged slightly more than eight children; by 1850, about five and a half; and by 1900, little more than three and a half.) At the same time, scientific knowledge held a privileged position in American culture.

Many mothers embraced the central tenets of scientific motherhood. After all, science provided the latest, the best information about child care. Furthermore, the prestige of science added status to maternal activity. The ideology presented a positive image of motherhood: acclaiming mothers for using science to raise their children. At the same time, however, scientific motherhood disparaged mothers, representing them as incapable of successfully rearing their children without scientific experts.

Scientific motherhood was disseminated through many channels. Women's magazines were especially influential. Some, such as *Babyhood*, were devoted exclusively to child care, while others, such as *Good Housekeeping*, featured child care articles and columns. Magazine advertisements used the aura of science to promote their products, reminding readers of the importance of scientific advice. In addition, physicians, nurses, and others concerned with child welfare wrote baby books and pamphlets. Working-class women learned the principles of scientific motherhood at "well baby" clinics; more affluent women attended college courses. In the twentieth century, home economics courses flourished in primary and secondary schools and in colleges. Child welfare organizations distributed pamphlets, such as the U.S. Children's Bureau's *Infant Care*, first published in 1914 and still in print today. Such sources emphasized women's huge responsibility for the health of their families and the necessity of mothers' following the direction of scientific authorities.

Scientific motherhood continues to influence us. Books on child care sell very well. Prenatal classes and home economics courses enroll many people, males as well as females. Journals such as *Baby Talk* enjoy wide circulation. And not surprisingly, we are still evaluating the appropriate role of science in child care. *(See also: Child Rearing; Magazines)*

—**Rima D. Apple**

Further Reading

Apple, Rima D. "Constructing Mothers: Scientific Motherhood in the Nineteenth and Twentieth Centuries," *Social History of Medicine* (Summer 1995): 161–78.

———. *Mothers and Medicine: A Social History of Infant Feeding, 1890–1950.* Madison: University of Wisconsin Press, 1987.

Ladd-Taylor, Molly. *Raising a Baby the Government Way: Mothers' Letters to the Children's Bureau, 1915–1932.* New Brunswick, NJ: Rutgers University Press, 1986.

✑ Scudder, Vida Dutton (1861–1954)

Vida Scudder was a Christian socialist, scholar, and activist. She attended Girls Latin School (Boston), Smith College, and Oxford University, where she was moved by the lectures of John Ruskin on social privilege and the need for reform. Between 1887 and 1928, she taught English at Wellesley College. She demonstrated her literary and social concerns in a popular course on social ideals in English literature and occasionally came into conflict with college authorities over her political activities. She joined with others to initiate the College Settlements Association and was a primary organizer of Denison House in Boston's South End. She founded the Church League for Industrial Democracy, took an active role in organizing the National Women's Trade Union League, and joined the Socialist Party.

According to her biographer, although Scudder was often labeled a communist, she actually prefigured recent Christian and Marxist dialogue. By the mid-1930s, she had also declared herself a pacifist. From 1889 to her death, she belonged to the Society of the Companions of the Holy Cross, a spiritually minded, socially concerned, autonomous group of Episcopalian laywomen from whom she drew much personal support. Her major scholarly work was *The Franciscan Adventure* (1931), and she was the author of sixteen other books on religion, literature, history, and politics. Her splendid autobiography *On Journey* (1937) is a powerful spiritual and intellectual history as well as a story of American social politics in the first half of the twentieth century. *(See also: Christianity; National Women's Trade Union League; Religion; Settlement House Movement; Society of the Companions of the Holy Cross)*

—**Anne O. Dzamba (Sessa)**

Further Reading

Corcoran, Theresa S. *Vida Dutton Scudder.* Boston: G. K. Hall, 1982.

Darling, Pam. *New Wine: The Story of Women Transforming Leadership and Power in the Episcopal Church.* Boston: Cowley, 1994.

Donovan, Mary S. *A Different Call: Women's Ministries in the Episcopal Church.* Ridgefield, CT: Morehouse, 1986.

Scudder, Vida Dutton. *On Journey.* Boston: E. P. Dutton, 1937.

──. *Social Ideals in English Letters.* Boston: Houghton Mifflin, 1898.

∾ Seamen's Aid Society

Founded in 1833, the Seamen's Aid Society was an example of women's benevolence efforts in antebellum America. The image of seamen has been shaped by tales of seagoing, vessels, foreign ports, brothels, boarding houses, "bethels" or shelters for homeless seamen, churches, institutions, homes, missions, and societies. Early seamen were followed by a plethora of human problems related to isolation from family members and hardship of life at sea. Perhaps worse off than the men at sea, wives and children were followed by destitution and often had no regular sources of financial support or health care and sometimes no food or shelter. Historically, sea trade was second only to agriculture in economic importance, yet seamen were transients in ports other than their own and usually were in need of a variety of social welfare services. Seamen's mission societies emerged in response to the plight of seamen but without attention to the tragic conditions of their wives and children.

Recognizing the suffering of seamen's families, Sarah Josepha Hale, a widow herself and mother of five children, founded the Seamen's Aid Society in Boston in 1833. This society was a major women's movement identifying employment as a main solution to poverty for destitute women and children. The society employed seamen's wives to sew garments for the poor and sold complete outfits for seamen. The ladies of the society produced and sold garments at lower cost than the slop-shop operators, the manufacturers of seamen's wear, and at lower prices than merchants.

The Seamen's Aid Society, under the direction of Mrs. Hale from 1833 to 1840, became a powerful organization of women on behalf of women and opened a trade school for girls, day nurseries for working mothers to leave their children in safe care, and free libraries. The Seamen's Aid Society and its followers addressed housing, food, and clothing needs of poor women and children and advocated for health care, particularly for women who had little access to health care and little willingness to risk indignities of the medical examination.

In 1847, the Seamen's Aid Society opened the Mariner's House, a boarding house in Boston. The Mariner's House began the boarding house movement by independent societies that fostered boarding houses and missions in coastal cities around the nation. The Seamen's Aid Society boarded more seamen than any other independent society in the 1850s, about 1,800 boarders annually. Merging with the Boston Port Society in 1867 to form the Boston Port and Seamen's Aid Society, the society has continued to serve seamen and their families. *(See also: Benevolence; Boarding/Housekeeping System; Hale, Sarah Josepha)*

—Karen V. Harper-Dorton

Further Reading

Finley, Ruth E. *The Lady of* Godey's. Philadelphia: J. B. Lippincott, 1931.

Kverndal, Roald. *Seamen's Missions: Their Origin and Early Growth.* Pasadena, CA: William Carey Library, 1986.

Zophy, Angela Howard. "A True Woman's Duty 'To Do Good...': Sarah Josepha Hale and Benevolence in Antebellum America." In *Moment of Decision: Biographical Essays on American Character and Regional Identity,* edited by Tandall M. Miller and John R. McKivigan, 155-69. Westport, CT: Greenwood, 1991.

∾ Sellins, Fannie (Mooney) (1870–1919)

Labor union organizer and socialist Fannie Sellins was shot and killed on August 26, 1919, by Allegheny Coal and Coke Company deputy sheriffs in West Natrona, Pennsylvania. Born Fannie Mooney in New Orleans, she later moved to St. Louis, where she was president of Local 67 of the United Garment Workers. In 1909, she traveled across the country gathering support for the locked-out garment workers of the Marx and Hass Clothing Company of St. Louis. Her efforts to encourage a boycott of the company's products brought about a settlement in 1911.

This boycott campaign brought Sellins to the attention of Van Bittner, president of United Mine Workers Subdistrict 5 of Western Pennsylvania and West Virginia. In 1913, on Bittner's recommendation, she went to work in Colliers, near Wierton, West Virginia, aiding families who had been driven out of their homes by the Pennsylvania and West Virginia Coal Company and were living in the woods outside the town. Her support defied an injunction against the United Mine Workers to supply aid to the miners, and she was arrested and jailed. Although the Colliers' strike was settled in 1914, Sellins's case was not cleared until 1916, when she was pardoned by President Woodrow Wilson.

Sellins's work with the miners' wives and families proved to be an effective organizing method. She was also able to recruit black workers who were originally brought up from the South as strikebreakers with the promise of higher wages. Sellins was able to show them that they had been hired under false pretenses. This effort brought her into conflict with the coal companies and made her a target for the violence that eventually ended her life in 1919.

A monument to Fannie Sellins was erected and dedicated by the United Mine Workers of America at her gravesite in Arnold, Pennsylvania. An annual tradition of commemorating her death by workers of the area has recently been renewed. *(See also: Garment Industries; Socialism; Socialist Party of America; United Mine Workers)*

—Abby Schmelling

Further Reading

Huntington Socialist and Labor Star. Huntington, WV, 1913–1915.

Korson, George. *Coal Dust on the Fiddle.* Philadelphia: University of Pennsylvania Press, 1943.

Meyerhuber, Carl. "Fannie Sellins and the Events of 1919." Paper given at meeting of the Pennsylvania Labor History Society, September 17, 1986.
St. Louis Labor. St. Louis, MO, 1909–1911.

⟂ Seneca Falls Convention

Held July 19-20, 1848, in Seneca Falls, New York, the Seneca Falls Convention was the first formal U.S. woman's rights convention. Lucretia Mott, Elizabeth Cady Stanton, and Quaker abolitionist women organized the convention and advertised it in the July 14 issue of the *Seneca County Courier* as one that would "discuss the social, civil, and religious conditions and rights of woman." Between one hundred and three hundred women and men attended. The first day's meeting was chaired by Mott's husband, James. The women made speeches and presented a Declaration of Sentiments and Resolutions, modeled after the Declaration of Independence, that listed eighteen resolutions regarding woman's rights. All except the elective-franchise resolution for woman suffrage passed unanimously; Stanton and Frederick Douglass, however, persuaded a minimally adequate majority to carry that resolution as well. The second day concluded the meeting with the signing of the Declaration of Sentiments by sixty-eight women and thirty-two men, many of whom later withdrew their names in response to public ridicule and criticism of the convention proceedings. *(See also: Declaration of Sentiments and Resolutions; Mott, Lucretia; Stanton, Elizabeth Cady)*

—**Angela M. Howard**

Further Reading

Boylan, Anne M. "Women and Politics in the Era Before Seneca Falls," *Journal of the Early Republic* 10 (Fall 1990): 363-82.
Sherr, Lynn. *Failure Is Impossible: Susan B. Anthony in Her Own Words.* New York: Times Books, 1995.
Stanton, Elizabeth Cady, Susan B. Anthony, and M. J. Gage, eds. *The History of Woman Suffrage,* 6 vols. New York: National American Woman Suffrage Association, 1888–1922.

⟂ Seton, Elizabeth Ann (Bayley)
(1774–1821)

Elizabeth Ann Seton, wife, mother, young widow, and convert to Catholicism, founded the first "native" American Catholic sisterhood, the first American Catholic parochial school, and the first American Catholic orphanage and was the first native-born American saint.

She was born on August 28, 1774, in New York to a well-established New York Episcopalian family. Elizabeth and her sister Mary were enrolled in a private school called "Mama Pompelion's." In 1794, she married William Magee Seton, a wealthy New York importer and merchant. The marriage was a happy one, and they had five children. A series of unfortunate events forced her husband into bankruptcy. In 1803, William, Elizabeth, and their daughter Anna went to visit friends, the Filicchis, in Leghorn, Italy, where William died of tuberculosis in December 1803. During her stay with the Filicchis, Elizabeth was exposed to and began her conversion to Catholicism.

Back in New York in 1804, she announced to her shocked family and friends that she was thinking of becoming a Catholic. Despite efforts to dissuade her, she officially converted in 1805. In 1808, she went to Baltimore, where she opened a school. Thinking of establishing a community of "sisters," she pronounced vows of poverty, chastity, and obedience in March 1809. In June, the community was founded when five women, including Seton, put on the formal religious habit. Later that month, the small community moved to Emmitsburg, Maryland, where in early 1810 the first Catholic parochial school in the United States was established. On January 17, 1812, Archbishop John Carroll confirmed the rules and constitution of Mother Seton's Sisters of Charity, the first American community of sisters.

As the community grew, it accepted new responsibilities. The sisters took charge of orphanages in Philadelphia in 1814 and in New York in 1817. These were the first of many educational and charitable institutions that Seton's sisters would establish and staff over the years. Elizabeth Seton died on January 4, 1821. In 1975, she became the first native-born U.S. citizen to be canonized. *(See also: Christianity; Religion)*

—**Edward C. Stibili**

Further Reading

Bailly de Barberey, Helen. *Elizabeth Seton.* Translated by Joseph B. Code. New York: Macmillan, 1927.
Dirvin, Joseph I. *Mrs. Seton: Foundress of the American Sisters of Charity.* New York: Farrar, Straus & Cudahy, 1962.
Feeney, Leonard. *Elizabeth Seton: An American Woman.* New York: America Press, 1938.
Melville, Annabelle M. *Elizabeth Bayley Seton, 1774–1821.* New York: Scribner, 1951.

⟂ Settlement House Movement

The settlement house movement was launched in London in 1884 when a group of Oxford University students opened Toynbee Hall to alleviate the suffering produced by rapid industrialization and urbanization. It served as a model for like institutions in America. Among the more famous were Jane Addams's Hull House, located in the midst of one of Chicago's densest immigrant ghettos, and New York's Henry Street Settlement, founded by public health nurse Lillian Wald. According to Addams, the settlements had two objectives: (a) to improve the quality of life in their neighborhoods and (b) to offer their residents, most of whom were women, a socially acceptable and useful outlet for their newly acquired education and ambition.

Like the hundreds of settlements that proliferated across the country at the turn of the century, Hull House and Henry Street were centers for civic, educational, social, and philanthropic reform. By 1893, for instance, Hull House was home to over forty different groups, which drew over two thousand participants to the settlement on a weekly basis. There was a day nursery, gymnasium, dispensary, and playground; cooking, sewing, and language classes; and a cooperative boardinghouse for working women. In addition, there was an art gallery, a Plato Club, a theatrical company, and a variety of bands and choruses. As one historian noted, the settlement house was a veritable department store of reform. Moreover, the settlements were magnets for scholars embarking on studies of the nation's growing cities. In other words, the settlements were urban outposts, offering students a vantage point from which to conduct their inquiries while also meeting the needs of their neighbors and residents. *(See also: Addams, Jane; College Settlement; Henry Street Settlement; Hull House; Social Work; Wald, Lillian)*

—**Rebecca L. Sherrick**

Further Reading

Chambers, Clarke A. *Seedtime of Reform.* Minneapolis: University of Minnesota Press, 1963.

❧ "Seven Sisters"

The "Seven Sisters" refers to a group of elite, private eastern liberal arts colleges originally for women only, most of which were established in the late nineteenth century: Mount Holyoke (1836), Vassar (1861), Wellesley (1870), Smith (1871), Radcliffe (1879), Bryn Mawr (1880), and Barnard (1893). In 1926, these schools became formally affiliated within the Seven College Conference, from which the name Seven Sisters was derived.

The Seven Sisters colleges were all established at a time when women's higher education was still rather controversial. Mount Holyoke was an especially important school for young women in the nineteenth century, although it did not gain collegiate status until the 1890s. The men and women who founded the Seven Sisters colleges were committed to the proposition that women were generally as capable of scholarship as men. They were also committed to the idea that women could use higher education to fulfill a growing range of roles in society. The most important of these were associated with the cult of domesticity, a battery of responsibilities assigned to wives and mothers in the nineteenth century, particularly caring for and educating their own children. The Seven Sisters colleges generally aimed to educate women so that they could perform such domestic functions well. The most important exception to this pattern was at Bryn Mawr during the presidency of M. Carey Thomas (1894–1922), who believed that women should be educated to perform the same professional roles as men. At other Seven Sisters colleges, however, there was often considerable tension between the academic, intellectual side of college life and the domestic sex role socialization purposes of these institutions.

Because these colleges were private and derived most of their revenue from tuition, they generally drew students from middle- and upper-class families. The women who attended these schools, moreover, were typically white, Protestant, native-born Americans. With time, the Seven Sisters became known as a female counterpart to the largely all-male Ivy League, partly because two of the Seven Sister schools—Radcliffe and Barnard—were in fact associated with Ivy League universities and partly because the others were also seen as socially and academically exclusive. The generally homogeneous quality of the student body invariably affected the character of life and education at these schools.

Although they enjoyed great success and prestige throughout most of the twentieth century, the Seven Sisters colleges came under sharp attack in the 1960s with the development of the modern feminist movement. Betty Friedan, a graduate of Smith, attacked such schools in her best-selling book *The Feminine Mystique* for allegedly discouraging intellectual accomplishment in young women. In the past few decades, several of the Seven Sisters colleges have considered making their programs—to one extent or another—coeducational, and some have joined forces with their formerly all-male counterparts. Today, there is little emphasis on domestic socialization among the Seven Sisters, many of which are routinely ranked among the top colleges in the country. Although the education provided by these institutions is still elite, the schools have opened their doors to women of diverse backgrounds. *(See also: Barnard College; Bryn Mawr College; Higher Education; Mount Holyoke Seminary; Radcliffe College; Smith College; Vassar College; Wellesley College)*

—**John L. Rury**

Further Reading

Horowitz, Helen Lefkowitz. *Alma Mater: Design and Experience in the Women's Colleges from Their Nineteenth Century Beginnings to the 1930s.* New York: Knopf, 1984.

Solomon, Barbara Miller. *In the Company of Educated Women: A History of Women and Higher Education in America.* New Haven, CT: Yale University Press, 1985.

❧ Sewing Machines

Louis Godey, founder of *Godey's Lady's Book,* said, "Next to the plow the sewing machine is perhaps humanity's most blessed instrument." Before the invention of the sewing machine, women spent half their waking time handsewing and mending clothes. Sewing was one of the few occupations open to women who had to support themselves in the early 1800s. At that time, most sewing was done at home, but some factories existed where women handsewed garments. The working conditions were poor, because employers knew that the women had no other options.

American Elias Howe, Jr. is credited with the invention of the sewing machine in 1846. His machine and others made by his contemporaries did not catch on immediately. The early machines were expensive, clumsy, and seemed too troublesome to use. In 1850, when the yearly average family income was $500, a machine cost $125. Mass production innovations brought the price down to $64 by 1870. In 1856, poor women who earned their living by sewing could lease a sewing machine with the option to own. Middle-class women had barriers other than financial to overcome in order to acquire a sewing machine. Some saw no need to buy a machine to do what women could do by hand, especially if it gave women more leisure time; others thought that women should not or could not operate machinery.

Women in the 1850s were already showing a tendency to want to take more control of their lives. As early as 1852, *Scientific American* predicted a social revolution caused by the lessening of women's sewing labors. At the 1892 Patent Centennial, Robert Taylor credited the sewing machine with women's advance in careers in law, medicine, business, and other professions that were once closed to them.

While the sewing machine freed middle-class women to pursue new careers and causes, lower-class women were enslaved by it. Often, sewing factories were firetrap sweatshops, with poor working conditions. The immigrant movement to America in the 1880s provided the factories with plenty of cheap labor. The poor conditions led to the formation of unions. In 1909, the first women's strike in the shirtwaist industry occurred when 20,000 women walked out, demanding better conditions. The horrible Triangle Shirtwaist Factory fire of 1911, which caused the deaths of 146 women, led to new protective labor laws. Unions succeeded in eliminating sweatshop conditions from union shops by 1929.

Today, the sewing machine continues to provide the world with an abundance of homemade and ready-made goods. *(See also: Garment Industries; International Ladies Garment Workers Union; Shirtwaist Makers Strike, 1909; Triangle Fire)*

—Ellen Wolcott

Further Reading

Brandon, Ruth. *A Capitalist Romance: Singer and the Sewing Machine.* Philadelphia: J. B. Lippincott, 1977.

Daves, Jessica. *Ready-made Miracle: The American Story of Fashion for the Millions.* New York: Putnam, 1967.

Ley, Sandra. *Fashion for Everyone: The Story of Ready-to-Wear, 1870s–1970s.* New York: Scribner, 1975.

Siegel, Beatrice. *The Sewing Machine.* New York: Walker, 1984.

～ Sex Discrimination

Sex discrimination is the institutionally rooted practice of favoring one sex over the other. For many feminists, recognizing that we live in an institutionally patriarchal society clearly limits the definition of sex discrimination to favoring men over women. Historically, discrimination against women has been encoded directly into numerous laws, although silence on women in other laws has also produced sex discrimination. The first women's rights convention, held at Seneca Falls, New York, in 1848, recognized sex discrimination as a primary barrier to women's full participation in society. The Declaration of Sentiments and Resolutions produced by that convention listed a wide range of "unjust laws," including the unequal status of married women and women's disenfranchisement, just as the Declaration of Independence had listed the King of England's injustices toward the American colonists.

While most of the laws cataloged in the Declaration of Sentiments have been struck down and women successfully waged a seventy-year struggle for the right to vote, sex discrimination did not and has not ended. The National Woman's Party and subsequent feminist organizations expected the Equal Rights Amendment, first introduced into Congress in 1923, to eliminate legal sex discrimination in one bold stroke and at the federal level in the same way that Congress had intended the Fourteenth and Fifteenth Amendments to eliminate racial discrimination, by establishing a national definition for citizenship that lower-level laws would not be permitted to diminish on the basis of race. The Fourteenth Amendment was much abused by the Supreme Court until the 1960s, but the ERA is still not part of the Constitution. That has meant that sex discrimination largely continues to be fought case-by-case and law-by-law.

In the contemporary women's movement, feminists sought to draw together the combined power of all three branches of government so that legislation, enforcement, and interpretation might all work to the benefit of women. In the courts, they successfully argued three important judicial concepts to dismantle sex discrimination in general, even before the ERA's demise in 1982. Thus, since the 1970s the Supreme Court has extended its interpretation of both the "equal protection" and the "due process" clauses of the Fourteenth Amendment to include groups in addition to the former slaves for whom the amendment was written. In the 1970s as well, feminist lawyers and legal theorists successfully argued to extend the judicial concept of a right to privacy to women.

The three-branched strategy produced important achievements in employment. Title VII of the 1964 Civil Rights Act prohibited sex discrimination in hiring, firing, and promotion, and numerous Supreme Court cases clarified that provision by defining what constituted discrimination and determining whether a variety of business practices were justified or illegal. The Equal Employment Opportunity Commission (EEOC) under Eleanor Holmes Norton's leadership filed numerous class action suits and supporting briefs. Activists pursued one troublesome issue, the practice of demoting, firing, or furloughing pregnancy women, to additional legislation: The Pregnancy Discrimination Act of 1978 specifically prohibited discrimination against pregnant women. In 1980, the EEOC issued a clear definition of sexual harassment and asserted its illegality under Title VII. This executive branch policy not only prohibited unwanted sexual advances by superiors, colleagues, or clients but also provided women with remedies against a work environment rendered intimidating or uncomfortable, allowing individual women to determine what inhibits their ability to work effectively. In *Meritor Savings Bank v. Vinson* (1986), the Supreme Court upheld this "chilly climate" section of the EEOC guidelines. While the Court had broadened its interpretation of Title VII through the 1970s, it had retrenched on some issues under a more conservative Court beginning in the 1980s. The *Meritor* victory demonstrated that, despite conservative backlash, basing the legal argument in terms of rights would remain the most effective means of contesting sex discrimination in employment.

While innovative legal approaches such as the definition of sexual harassment provided women with necessary tools to combat sex discrimination, the rights approach also served the growing backlash. Affirmative action proved vulnerable to a Court attack. As originally envisioned by John F. Kennedy, the policy responded to anger and resentment among employers produced by punitive restrictions on hiring practices, the "you may not" attitudes of previous policy. First clearly mandated by Lyndon Johnson and extended by Richard Nixon through executive orders, affirmative action intended to provide a legal means for employers to do something positive, hence the term *affirmative,* to end racial and sex discrimination in the workforce. The order outlined procedures and required employers to make "every good-faith effort" to eliminate discrimination. Yet a series of court cases in the 1980s that successfully argued "reverse discrimination" against white males threatened this policy. Conservatives continued to label affirmative action a "quota system" that they defined as requiring an employer to hire a particular proportion of women or racial minorities whether they were qualified or not, even though the federal policy did not mandate quotas and even though the Supreme Court had consistently struck down quota-based business policies. While many feminists questioned the very idea of "reverse discrimination," many also questioned the ease with which employers could manipulate affirmative action in ways that pit white women against men and women of color.

Since the early 1980s, both governmental policies and internal business policies combined to constrict educational and employment opportunities and to concentrate wealth to the highest levels since the Great Depression. As a result and in combination with the decline of the EEOC as an effective advocate, the willingness of women and racial minorities to file discrimination suits and their ability to win them diminished. Even the battles that feminists believed were already won had to be rejoined. Nevertheless, feminist development of the concept of interlocking or interrelated oppressions, advanced by feminists of color, provided new keys to a multicultural struggle against sex discrimination in all its many forms. *(See also: Affirmative Action; Civil Rights; Civil Rights Act of 1964; Equal Employment Opportunity Commission; Equal Rights Amendment; Fourteenth Amendment to the U.S. Constitution; Politics; Seneca Falls Convention;* *Suffrage; United States Supreme Court; Voting Rights; Women's Rights Movements: Nineteenth and Twentieth Centuries)*

—Deb Hoskins

Further Reading

Crenshaw, Kimberle et al., eds. *Critical Race Theory.* New York: New Press, 1995.

Hoff, Joan. *Law, Gender, and Injustice: A Legal History of U.S. Women.* New York: New York University Press, 1991.

Lefcourt, Carol, ed. *Women and the Law.* New York: Clark Boardman, 1990.

MacKinnon, Catherine A. *Feminism Unmodified: Discourses on Life and Law.* Cambridge, MA: Harvard University Press, 1987.

———. *Sexual Harassment of Working Women: A Case of Sex Discrimination.* New Haven, CT: Yale University Press, 1978.

Meritor Savings Bank v. Vinson, 477 U.S. 57 (1986).

Rubenstein, William B., ed. *Lesbians, Gay Men, and the Law.* New York: New Press, 1993.

Sex Equity/Comparable Worth

Sex equity or comparable worth represents a major effort by women's groups and unions from the late 1970s to the middle 1980s to bridge the wage gap between men and women. Even with the vast influx of women into nontraditional jobs and despite affirmative action programs, the gap had not changed significantly in the previous fifty years.

Over twenty years after their enactment, neither the Equal Pay Act of 1963 nor Title VII of the Civil Rights Act of 1964 had achieved pay equity for most women. The Equal Pay Act has been interpreted by the courts as granting equal pay for the same or largely similar work. Most women, however, do not have jobs similar to men's. About 80 percent of working women are concentrated in only 20 of the some 427 existing job categories that the U.S. Labor Department has established. These jobs include clerical and secretarial workers, teachers, nurses, and retail workers. Thus, most women are employed in sex-segregated jobs where their experience, skills, and education are consistently undervalued.

Under these circumstances, equal pay legislation has had little impact on the mass of working women. Comparable worth goes beyond equal pay and requires employers to grant equal pay to employees doing different work of comparable value. This determination requires a complex program of job evaluations, a procedure that has been used by management for over fifty years to structure pay differentials among workers. For purposes of comparable worth, this procedure considers factors such as skill, responsibility, training, and working conditions. Each factor is given a numerical value, and jobs that have the same or similar scores are considered comparable.

In the United States, comparable worth advocates have focused on state and local governments as initial targets for implementation of the concept. Most notable successes have been in states and localities where unions have been long accepted and where women play important roles in the state legislatures or on local councils. Over twenty states have either implemented or studied some kind of comparable worth procedures for their employees, but only Minnesota mandated it for all of its local government units.

Initial success at the state level was not replicated in Washington, where opposition from business and the Reagan and Bush administrations blocked legislation. Furthermore, fearing competition from other states without comparable worth laws, there was little impetus at the state level to move beyond public employees into the private sector. Business interests, in particular, opposed the idea, not only because of its potential cost but also because they believed that comparable worth was incompatible with a free market economy. With a backlash from male members who sometimes found their pay frozen or reduced as a result of comparative studies and facing state budget cuts or even layoffs, even the public employee unions lost interest in expanding the concept in the 1990s.

In the 1980s, the gender gap between the pay of men and women narrowed considerably, so by 1991, the average weekly wages of women were 74 percent of men's compared with 64.6 percent in 1981. By 1997, women's wages had risen to only 74.1 percent of men's ("About the National Committee on Pay Equity"). At the same time, wages of women in managerial and professional occupations have remained at the level of 65 percent or less of men's earnings. In some occupations, including physicians, the gap actually widened considerably. Consequently, most feminists have, at least temporarily, lost interest in comparable worth legislation and focused on other factors of discrimination, including the penalty women pay for motherhood when they take time off from their careers to care for their children.

By the late 1990s, opposition from conservative forces and business interests had slowed the earlier impetus of the comparable worth movement even among public employees. Only the unions had continued to demonstrate much interest in the issue. An AFL-CIO financial survey in 1994 showed that 94 percent of working women considered equal pay to be very important to them, ranking above child care, paid leaves, and health insurance. At the same time, 64 percent of these women provided over half their family's income, providing a rationale for men to support equal pay. Even with the prosperity of the 1990s, women were still making only 75 percent of men's pay in 1996. Comparable worth and equal pay seem to be issues that will not go away despite the myth that women have achieved pay equity. *(See also: Affirmative Action; Equal Pay Act; Wages)*

—**Neil W. Hogan**

Further Reading

"About the National Committee on Pay Equity (NCPE)." Available at http://www.feminist.com/fairpay.htm

Acker, Joan J. *Doing Comparable Worth: Gender, Class, and Pay Equity.* Philadelphia: Temple University Press, 1989.

Figat, Deborah N., and June Lopidus. *How Women Can Earn a Living: The Effects of Pay Equity Remedies and a Higher Minimum Wage.* Washington, DC: Institute for Women's Policy Research, 1997.

Hartmann, Heidi, I., ed. *Comparable Worth: New Directions for Research.* Washington, DC: National Academy Press, 1985.

Hutner, Frances C. *Equal Pay for Comparable Worth: The Working Women's Issue of the Eighties.* New York: Praeger, 1986.

Kelly, Rita Mae, and Jane Bayes, eds. *Comparable Worth, Pay Equity, and Public Policy.* New York: Greenwood, 1988.

Remick, Helen. *Comparable Worth and Wage Discrimination: Technical Possibilities and Political Realities.* Philadelphia: Temple University Press, 1984.

Schmid, Gunter, and Renate Wertzel. *Sex Discrimination and Equal Opportunity.* Aldershot, England: Gower, 1986.

Thompson, Roger. "Women's Economic Equity," *Editorial Research Reports* 1 (May 10, 1985): 335-58.

U.S. Department of Labor, Bureau of Labor Statistics. *Employment Characteristics of Families in 1997.* Washington, DC: U.S. Department of Labor, 1998.

⪼ Sex-Gender System

The sex-gender system, a concept developed by anthropologist Gayle Rubin in the 1970s, has been influential in feminist theory and women's history. Drawing on literature on kinship and social organization, especially the work of Claude Lévi-Strauss, Rubin argued that biological differences such as menstruation, pregnancy, and lactation are translated into gender roles—codes of conduct for men and women—that differ across cultures. She defined this "sex-gender system" as a "set of arrangements by which a society transforms biological sexuality into products of human activity" and further asserted that in many cultures, relationships between men are mediated by the exchange of women.

The concept of the sex-gender system was influential in feminist theoretical writings of the 1970s and 1980s. Some historians of women and gender adopted Rubin's theory to ground their discussions of sexuality and gender. Rubin later criticized her idea that sexual difference formed a basis for gender ideology. Reasoning that feminism was a theory of gender, not of sexuality, she wrote that "although sex and gender are related, they are not the same, and they form the basis of two distinct arenas of social practice." Her argument that sexuality and gender must be understood as separate analytical categories has been echoed by most historians of women, gender, and sexuality. *(See also: Gender Role Socialization; Gender Roles; Patriarchy; Sexism)*

—**Miriam Reumann**

Further Reading

Rubin, Gayle. "The Traffic in Women: Notes on the Public Economy of Sex." In *Towards an Anthropology of Women,* edited by Rayna R. Reiter, 157-210. New York: Monthly Review Press, 1975.

———. "Thinking Sex: Notes for a Radical Theory of the Politics of Sexuality." In *Pleasure and Danger: Exploring Female Sexu-*

ality, edited by Carole Vance, 267-319. New York: Routledge, 1984.

ᔡ Sex in Education; or, A Fair Chance for the Girls

Sex in Education; or, a Fair Chance for the Girls was a pseudoscientific treatise published in 1873 by Edward H. Clarke, M.D., former professor of medicine at Harvard University. It warned that young women who studied rigorously ("in a boy's way") risked atrophy of the uterus and ovaries, sterility, insanity, and death. Widely read and reviewed, Clarke's book affected higher education for women well into the twentieth century.

In the decades following the Civil War, increasing numbers of women limited their families, campaigned for suffrage, and worked outside the home. Women also enrolled in high schools, land grant colleges, and universities and tried to enter prestigious male institutions such as Harvard, where Clarke served on the board of overseers. *Sex in Education* expressed Clarke's opposition to women's demands for admission to Harvard Medical School and his discomfort, shared by many, at women's generally expanding roles.

To an age that revered science and professional expertise, Clarke announced that women's sphere must be determined by physiology. Using quotations from unnamed "experts" and seven case studies from his medical practice, he maintained that American women were sickly and unable to bear and nurse children because the "vital force" needed to develop the reproductive system had been diverted to the brain. He recommended no more than four hours of study a day for women and complete rest during menstruation, making coeducation impossible. Critics noted that this regime precluded not only coeducation but all higher education and all employment outside the home as well.

Within a year, articles, reviews, and at least four books refuted Clarke's views. Mothers, teachers, college professors and administrators, feminists such as Caroline Dall and Lucy Stone, public figures such as Julia Ward Howe, and physicians such as Mary Putnam Jacobi argued that Clarke's physiology was antiquated, his evidence flawed, and his motives suspect. Noting that "scientific" writers such as Clarke could have a hidden social agenda, these authors assembled their own data on the health, careers, marriage, and fertility of educated women. Anticipating socialization theory, they argued that if women were sickly, it was because society limited their lifestyles and expectations.

Coeducation expanded because women demanded it and it was cheaper than single-sex education. Clarke's view that women's physiology limited their ability to study and work survived, however, to influence twentieth-century educational psychologists, to help justify protective legislation for working women and special living arrangements and courses for college women, and to support conservative attitudes about women's roles. Meanwhile, Clarke's critics

were the forerunners of an oppositional female research tradition—including Dr. Celia Mosher, Leta Hollingworth, and Margaret Mead—that refuted charges of female incapacity and supported equal education and equal rights. *(See also: Coeducation; Education; Higher Education)*

—**Maxine Schwartz Seller**

Further Reading

Clarke, Edward H., M.D. *Sex in Education; or, A Fair Chance for the Girls.* Boston: James R. Osgood, 1873.

Duffy, E. B. *No Sex in Education, or An Equal Chance for Both Girls and Boys.* Philadelphia: J. M. Stoddard, 1874.

Howe, Julia Ward. *Sex and Education: A Reply to E. H. Clarke's "Sex in Education."* Boston: Roberts Brothers, 1874.

Rosenberg, Rosalind. *Beyond Separate Spheres: The Intellectual Roots of Modern Feminism.* New Haven, CT: Yale University Press, 1982.

Smith-Rosenberg, Carroll, and Charles Rosenberg. "The Female Animal: Medical and Biological Views of Woman and Her Role in Nineteenth-Century America," *Journal of American History* 60 (September 1973): 334-56.

ᔡ Sexism

Sexism refers to a belief in the superiority of men and the discriminatory behavior resulting from that belief. Although theoretically women might be "sexist" in their treatment of men, in fact, the term arose in the 1960s to express discrimination against women. In this regard, the concept of sexism developed as an analogue to racism, then a powerful charge of the civil rights movement against American whites. Feminists saw sexism operating on a broad range of fronts. In particular, they pointed to overwhelming manifestations of sexism in language—for instance, in the use of *man* to refer to human beings in general. Sexism also operated, social scientists found, in the preferential treatment of boy children, in all aspects of institutional education, and in preadult literature used in the schools. Such an early introduction to sexism, feminists believed, only mirrored the society at large—its culture, political system, and employment patterns. All of these rested on sexist premises, belittling the abilities of women and therefore allocating positions of power, prestige, and wealth to men. The modern feminist movement has spent its efforts in an ongoing battle with the detrimental effects of sexism on individual human lives and on the society at large. *(See also: Gender Role Socialization; Patriarchy; Sex-Gender System; Sexual Division of Labor)*

—**Bonnie G. Smith**

Further Reading

Bem, Sandra L. *The Lenses of Gender: Transforming the Debate on Sexual Inequality.* New Haven, CT: Yale University Press, 1993.

Bowles, Gloria, and Renate Duelli Klein, eds. *Theories of Women's Studies.* Boston: Routledge & Kegan Paul, 1983.

Fausto-Sterling, Anne. *Myths of Gender: Biological Theories about Women and Men,* 2d ed. New York: Basic Books, 1992.

Hunter College Women's Studies Collective. *Women's Realities, Women's Choices: An Introduction to Women's Studies.* New York: Oxford University Press, 1983.

Nilsen, Alleen Pace et al. *Sexism and Language.* Urbana, IL: National Council of Teachers of English, n.d.

Segal, Lynne, ed. *Sex Exposed: Sexuality and the Pornography Debate.* New Brunswick, NJ: Rutgers University Press, 1993.

❧ Sexton, Anne (1928–1974)

Anne Sexton, doyenne of the confessional mode in poetry, has been celebrated and condemned with equal vehemence for the frank, intimate, sometimes lacerating self-revelations in her works. She was born Anne Bray Harvey on November 9, 1928, in Newton, Massachusetts, to parents who might have inspired an F. Scott Fitzgerald novel: attractive, wealthy party-goers. On the surface a glamorous socialite, Sexton was a profoundly troubled woman beneath the veneer.

She began writing poetry as a teenager. But it wasn't until 1956 on the advice of her psychiatrist that she began to take her writing seriously, finding in it a catharsis for feelings of guilt, inadequacy, and despair. Following the birth of her second daughter and failing (in her own view) to live up to the 1950s image of good wife and mother, Sexton experienced "terrible spells of depression" and outbursts of violence that placed her two babies in jeopardy. On the day before her twenty-eighth birthday, Sexton made her first suicide attempt.

For eighteen years Sexton fended off attacks of depression by exploring in writing her own psychic disorders and manic behavior. The result is a body of poems hauntingly beautiful although paradoxically scarred by wounds of self-doubt. In the poems, Sexton encounters her parents, doctors, children, and lovers. Most touchingly, she confronts versions of herself that have been betrayed. Her subjects are quintessentially female as evidenced in titles such as "Her Kind," "The Farmer's Wife," "Unknown Girl in the Maternity Ward," "The Abortion," "Woman with Girdle," "Housewife," "Cinderella," and "Divorce Thy Name Is Woman." In her poems as in her single play Mercy Street, Sexton employs startlingly fresh, apt metaphors for the frightened, trapped, middle-class, modern American woman that she was. Incidents in her life, such as a drugged fall down stairs, inspired her:

> For the soft, soft bones that were laid apart
> and were screwed together. They will knit.
> And the other corpse, the fractured heart,
> I feed it piecemeal, little chalice, I'm good to it.

Among her poet friends and influences (many of whom were also her lovers) were Robert Lowell, George Starbuck, James Wright, W. O. Snodgrass, Anthony Hecht, Tillie Olsen, Maxine Kumin, and the other Massachusetts-born confessional suicidal woman poet, Sylvia Plath. Toward the end of her life, Sexton was also inspired and

perplexed by the life of Jesus as her collection *The Jesus Papers* suggests. Even more than his life, however, the crucifixion intrigued her.

On Friday, October 4, 1974, a fresh glass of vodka in hand, Sexton entered her garage, climbed into her 1967 red Cougar, turned on the ignition, and took her place among the far too many suicidal woman poets of the century. *(See also: Women Writers)*

—Mary Lowe-Evans

Further Reading
Middlebrook, Diane Wood. *Anne Sexton: A Biography.* Boston: Houghton Mifflin, 1991.

Sexton, Anne. *Anne Sexton: The Complete Poems.* Boston: Houghton Mifflin, 1981.

❧ Sexual Division of Labor

The sexual division of labor is universal in human society, although the particular forms it takes vary widely. This variation is most evident in North America through comparisons of the sexual division of labor in Native American and European societies, free labor and slave communities, and agrarian and industrial areas and eras.

Initially rooted in, or at least justified by, women's childbearing capacity, the sexual division labor has affected nonchildbearing women and has survived technological advances in birth control. In general, this division has limited the types of work performed by women, their access to education, and the conditions and remuneration of their employment. The most fundamental division has been between work performed in the household by women (including piecework, care of boarders, and gardening as well as domestic labor and child care) and that performed outside the household by men (including labor in fields, factories, mines, and offices). As North American women entered the wage labor force in ever larger numbers after 1820, the links between the sexual division of labor within the household and that in society at large became increasingly visible.

The sexual division of labor has often proved to be less rigid for women than for men, who rarely serve as domestic laborers. In times of economic necessity—harvesting and planting seasons, war, or the development or rapid expansion of new fields of labor—women have been encouraged to ignore preexisting, gender-based definitions of work. Then, farm wives and housewives, female slaves and immigrants, young single women and widows are thrust into corn and cotton fields, munitions factories, textile mills, insurance offices, and schoolrooms. Yet even when women perform "men's" work, the sexual division of labor ensures that they will receive lower wages, less status, and have more limited occupational mobility. Only in times of severe economic crisis, such as the Great Depression and then only to a limited extent, has this division of labor served to maintain rather than restrict women's labor force participation.

In addition, this division of labor has shaped men's and women's voluntary labors, from the organization of charitable societies to the mobilization of grassroots movements. Finally, as the United States extends its economic domain into the Third World, the American form of the sexual division of labor is being exported to those countries along with American capital. *(See also: Housework; Wages)*

—**Nancy A. Hewitt**

Further Reading

Baron, Ava, ed. *Work Engendered: Toward a New History of American Labor*. Ithaca, NY: Cornell University Press, 1991.

Hartmann, Heidi. "The Family as a Locus of Gender, Class and Political Struggle: The Example of Housework," *Signs* 6 (Spring 1981): 366-94.

Milkman, Ruth. *Gender at Work: The Dynamics of Job Segregation by Sex during World War II*. Urbana: University of Illinois Press, 1987.

Signs: Journal of Women in Culture and Society. Special Issue on "Development and the Sexual Division of Labor," 7 (Winter 1981).

❧ Sexual Politics

Sexual Politics, by Kate Millett (1970), studies the "political" relationship between men and women in a sexist society and maintains that most gender differences are culturally conditioned. Begun as a Ph.D. thesis, *Sexual Politics* developed into a book that studies the inadequate and dehumanized presentation of women in what passed for standard (patriarchal) literature. Millett's seminal work in feminist literary criticism both popularized the questioning of male authority that characterized the modern women's movement and contributed to the rise of women's studies in academe. Millett used the writings of Sigmund Freud and other major psychologists and of modern literary giants to trace many of society's outdated sexual habits and customs as well as their subsequent effects on various generations of women. In a scholarly manner, Millett established that the predefined sexual roles of women deserved revision.

Written within a socialist context, *Sexual Politics* examines the patriarchy as an institutionalized and ideological system that subjugates women; it also offers one of the most comprehensive analyses of the concept of sexism. The book begins with a discussion of patriarchy. Through examples from the works of D. H. Lawrence, Henry Miller, Norman Mailer, and Jean Genet, Millett demonstrates how "sex" determines both the personalities and the dependent social and legal status of woman characters. The second section traces the history of the sexual revolution. Here, the author studies the effects of Freudian theory on feminism and draws on Nazi Germany and Soviet Russia to illustrate the link between authoritarianism and patriarchy. In the final section, Millett returns to Lawrence, Miller, Mailer, and Genet to analyze the role of women as reflected in female characters and to emphasize the need for change. Millet proposes

Genet as the reformer; only he personifies female characters as humans, as opposed to sex objects.

Sexual Politics stands among the first works of the period to examine the exploitation of women, to record the history of sexual reform, and to state the need for revolution. Millett's examination of the socially pervasive power relationship between the sexes provokes reevaluation of engrained assumptions. *(See also: Feminist Literary Criticism; Freudianism; Gender Role Socialization; Sex-Gender System; Women's Rights Movements: Nineteenth and Twentieth Centuries; Women's Studies)*

—**Suzette Chapman**
—**Camille Jaski Popliolek**

Further Reading

Millett, Kate. *Flying*. New York: Knopf, 1974.
———. *Sexual Politics*. New York: Doubleday, 1970.
———. *Sita*. New York: Ballantine, 1978.
Mitchell, Juliet. *Woman's Estate*. New York: Pantheon, 1971.

❧ Sexual Revolution

Sexual revolution has swept America twice in the twentieth century, in the 1920s and the 1960s. During the first "revolution in manners and morals," the key words were *Fords, flappers,* and *jazz;* during the later one, they were *drugs, Vietnam,* and *generation gap.*

Although outspoken writers exaggerated the depth of change, in this century the evolution of sexual behavior has generally followed a slow and steady pace punctuated by dramatic incidents. Yet the 1920s and the 1960s deserve some of the notoriety they have received. Both were periods of sexual openness facilitated by mobility and social freedom for youth. They were times in which adolescents and young adults had "a sense of a separate destiny, of experiencing what no one had ever experienced before." Music—whether jazz or rock and roll—acted as a symbolic protest in both eras and was part of the secret language of emergent sexuality.

More women than ever before seemed to be having more sex and enjoying it more. In the 1920s, this involved an increase in "petting," premarital intercourse, and extramarital sex. In the 1960s, the age of first intercourse dropped dramatically, oral-genital stimulation became commonplace, and middle-class parents had to accept the idea that their daughters were "living with" someone. Most women enjoyed their new sexual freedom, but many saw major elements of the "sexual revolution" of the 1960s as essentially hostile to women. Poor women were left to care for the children, while middle-class women found themselves dealing with psychic scars, a by-product of their misperception of males' casual attitudes toward "relationships." Women were not sure that they had been a part of the revolution, and in the 1960s, feminists coined the slogan "The Sexual Revolution Is Not OUR War" to emphasize that women had to be free to say "yes" or "no" to sexual advances. Throughout the

1970s, the women's movement supported women's right of choice when and whether to be sexually active. The AIDS crisis of the 1980s hammered the last nail into the coffin of the carefree and careless sexual abandon of the 1960s sexual revolution for the sexually active, regardless of particular sexual preference. The concept of a sexual revolution has been rendered unnecessary in an increasingly tolerant, if not actually permissive society. *(See also: Female Sexuality; Flapper; New Morality; Premarital Sex)*

—**William G. Shade**
—**Angela M. Howard**

Further Reading

D'Emilio, John, and Estelle B. Freedman. *Intimate Matters: A History of Sexuality in America.* New York: Harper & Row, 1988.

Dench, Geoff, ed. *Rewriting the Sexual Contract.* New Brunswick, NJ: Transaction Publishers, 1998.

Fass, Paula. *The Damned and the Beautiful: American Youth in the 1920s.* New York: Oxford University Press, 1977.

Kinsey, Alfred et al. *Sexual Behavior in the Human Female.* Philadelphia: W. B. Saunders, 1953.

Smith, Daniel Scott. "The Dating of the American Sexual Revolution: Evidence and Interpretation." In *The American Family in Social-Historical Perspective,* edited by Michael Gordon, 321-35. New York: St. Martin's, 1973.

∿ Sexual Suicide

In 1973, George Gilder, a Republican speech writer and protégé of the Rockefellers, published *Sexual Suicide.* The book is an attack on feminist thought and a defense of traditional gender roles based on the proposition that women as wives and mothers are all that stands between civilization and a descent into total chaos. (To be fair to Gilder, many nineteenth-century American women reformers seemed to make much the same point.) Gilder argues that only the socializing force of the family can turn children into civilized human beings and only the institution of traditional marriage can keep men from turning into destructive, antisocial, ravaging beasts. The small price women pay for this civilizing role, which, of course, comes out of their female sexual superiority rooted both in their ability to conceive and nurture and their "enormous power over man," is that they must allow men to assume the roles of "provider and achiever." If women fail to concede to men the control of the marketplace, which Gilder assures us is a minor benefit compared with the daily joys of childbearing, child raising, and suburban homemaking, set-adrift males will disrupt the community.

When he is not making quasi-anthropological defenses of the nuclear family and male dominance of the public sphere, Gilder makes ad feminem attacks on prominent feminists and their followers. He characterizes feminists as negative thinkers, women intent on revenging themselves against men. He also says they are spoiled and remote from the experience of ordinary women. He describes American housewives as among the happiest people in the world and dis-

misses malcontents as intellectuals. Gilder defends discrimination against women in the workplace because they have another role to play that is much more valuable to society, while men must work to support their families and remain connected to the community. Gilder advocates unequal pay on grounds that men need more money to counterbalance female sexual superiority (i.e., her ability to seduce men and give birth), men need to be encouraged to create families and support them, and men have a greater propensity to spend money on the opposite sex. Gilder, unlike practically any of his feminist or nonfeminist contemporaries, claims to be seriously worried about the failure of Americans to reproduce themselves and thus views employment discrimination and unequal pay as efficient ways to solve the "population problem."

In 1974, Gilder published *Naked Nomads,* in which he continued his argument that single men have myriad social and psychological problems that can be solved only through marriage to traditional women. Gilder contends that men must be allowed to be providers or their marriages—and eventually civilization—will fall apart, and he cites as proof the fact that career women and ghetto women have the highest divorce rates. He also claims that liberated women's rejection of marriage has increased the rate of male homosexuality. *(See also: Antifeminism; Race Suicide)*

—**Barbara McGowan**

Further Reading

Gilder, George. *Naked Nomads.* New York: Quadrangle, 1974.
———. *Sexual Suicide.* New York: Quadrangle, 1973.

∿ Shakers

The Shakers, a religious group known officially as the United Society of Believers in Christ's Second Appearing, originated during the mid-eighteenth century near Manchester, England, among a small schismatic group of "shaking Quakers" led by Ann Lee. Lee's driving sense of mission resulted primarily from four traumatic experiences in childbirth and the deaths of her children in infancy or early childhood. She became convinced that only through celibacy and total devotion to God could humanity achieve salvation. Emigrating to America, Lee attracted several thousand followers in New York State and New England after the Revolutionary War.

Under Lee's American successors Joseph Meacham and Lucy Wright, the Shakers instituted full-scale celibate communal living, brought their pentecostal "shaking" and other revivalistic excesses under control, and established a dual system of government in which both sexes had parallel and equal leadership roles at every level of the religious hierarchy. Shaker theology stressed a dual godhead in which female and male elements were equally represented. Ann Lee was viewed by many of her followers as embodying God's spirit in female form in the same way that Jesus earlier had embodied God's spirit in male form. Despite equal Shaker leadership roles for men and women, traditional economic divisions between the sexes remained unchanged within the group.

Shaker theological and social unorthodoxy—including their requirements of celibacy, communal living, and equality for women in religious leadership—provoked much controversy. By the 1830s, however, when the group achieved the peak of its temporal success with as many as four thousand members living in more than sixty semiautonomous communities at eighteen different sites in New York, New England, and the Midwest, the Shakers were widely praised for their industry, quality of workmanship, and fine products. This religion proved especially attractive to capable women who failed to find outlets for their talents in the larger society, and they in turn served as an inspiration for a host of other communal experimenters during the nineteenth century.

Although totally dependent for their survival on a diminishing supply of converts from the outside world, the Shakers nevertheless have persisted to the present. Feminists increasingly have looked to the Shakers as exemplars of a more active role for women in religious liturgy and leadership. *(See also: Christianity; Lee, Mother Ann; Religion; Society of Friends)*

—**Lawrence Foster**

Further Reading

Andrews, Edward Deming. *The People Called Shakers.* New York: Dover, 1963.

Brewer, Priscilla. *Shaker Communities, Shaker Lives.* Hanover, NH: University Press of New England, 1986.

Campbell, D'Ann. "Women's Life in Utopia: The Shaker Experiment in Equality Reappraised," *New England Quarterly* 51 (March 1978): 23-38.

Foster, Lawrence. *Religion and Sexuality: The Shakers, the Mormons, and the Oneida Community,* pp. 21-71, 226-47. Urbana: University of Illinois Press, 1984.

Humez, Jean M., ed. *Mother's First-Born Daughters: Early Shaker Writings on Women and Religion.* Bloomington: Indiana University Press, 1993.

Mercadente, Linda A. *Gender, Doctrine, and God: The Shakers and Contemporary Theology.* Nashville, TN: Abingdon, 1990.

Proctor-Smith, Marjorie. *Women in Shaker Community and Worship: A Feminist Analysis of the Uses of Religious Symbolism.* Lewiston, MA: Mellen, 1985.

Rourke, Constance. "The Shakers." In *The Roots of American Culture and Other Essays,* edited by Van Wyck Brooks, 195-237. New York: Harcourt Brace, 1942.

Stein, Stephen J. *The Shaker Experience in America.* New Haven, CT: Yale University Press, 1992.

White, Anna, and Leila S. Taylor. *Shakerism: Its Meaning and Message.* Columbus, OH: F. J. Heer, 1904.

⌇ Shange, Ntozake (b. 1948)

Poet, playwright, novelist, and dancer, Ntozake Shange is best known for performance pieces expressing the thoughts and voices of young African American women

Figure 54. Ntozake Shange

A poet, playright, novelist, and dancer, Ntozake Shange (right) appears here in her landmark 1975 chorepoem *for colored girls who have considered suicide/ when the rainbow is enuf.* Used by permission of UPI/Corbis-Bettmann.

characters. Her choreopoem, *for colored girls who have considered suicide/when the rainbow is enuf, Spell #7* (1975), brought national attention both to Shange's innovative subject of young women's lives and to her innovative dramatic form, uniting drama and dance.

Frequently produced, *for colored girls* presents seven women and their realities of heartache, frustration, and inequality. None of the women are given names; they are addressed by the colors they wear. Movement or dancing by the women accompanies and counterpoints their stories. Shange comments that physical performance, "the freedom to move in space, to demand of my own sweat a perfection that could continually be approached, though never known, was poem to me, my body and mind."

Born Paulette Williams, daughter of Paul Williams, a surgeon, and Eloise Williams, a psychiatric social worker and educator, she graduated from Barnard College in 1970 with honors in American Studies. In 1971, she decided to take an African name. "Ntozake" means "she who comes with her own things," and "Shange" means "who walks like a lion." In 1973, Shange received her master's degree in American Studies from the University of Southern California, but her interest in the stories of black women's lives grew in the Women's Studies Program at Sonoma State College, where she taught from 1972 to 1975. Shange's attention to women's untold stories brought a productive career of performance pieces, fiction, poetry and essay collections—all stretching expectations as they articulate women's experiences. Of her novels, *Betsey Brown* (1985, also in a musical adaptation) shows racism and human nature through the eyes of a thirteen-year-old, while *Sassafrass, Cypress and Indigo* (1982) has been described as a "blues narrative." Her latest novel, also adapted for the stage, *The Resurrection of* the Daughter: Liliane (1994) continues Shange's interest in adolescent girls and coming of age, developing a new form through a series of dialogues between Liliane and her psychoanalyst. Other volume publications, including performance pieces and poetry, are *Three Pieces; From Okra to Greens; Beneath the Necessity of Talking; A Photograph: Lovers in Motion; Nappy Edges; A Daughter's Geography; Ridin' the Moon in Texas; Some Men; Melissa and Smith; The Love Space Demands: A Continuing Saga,* and the essay collection *See No Evil.*

Most recently, she has turned her attention to children's literature. *Whitewash* (1998), loosely based on incidents in the Bronx, tells the story of Helene-Angel, a grade school girl, and her big brother Mauricio and tackles the issues of racism and hate crimes. Shange has also presented a one-woman show, *Ellington Is Not a Street,* dealing with Duke Ellington. *(See also: Black Women; Dance; Theater; Women Writers)*

—**Carol Klimick Cyganowski**

Further Reading

Cronacher, Karen. "Unmasking the Minstrel Mask's Black Magic in Ntozake Shange's Spell #7," *Theatre Journal* 44 (May 1992): 177-93.

Elder, Arlene. "*Sassafrass, Cypress and Indigo:* Ntozake Shange's Neo-Slave/Blues Narrative," *African American Review* 26 (Spring 1992): 99-107.

Lester, Neal A. "At the Heart of Shange's Feminism: An Interview," *Black American Literature Forum* 24 (Winter 1990): 717-30.

Shange, Ntozake. *Betsey Brown.* New York: St. Martin's, 1985.

———. *for colored girls who have considered suicide/when the rainbow is enuf.* New York: Macmillan, 1977.

~ Sharp, Katharine Lucinda
(1865–1914)

Katharine Lucinda Sharp was a librarian and library educator whose career reflected the ambiguous reality confronting women completing the new professional training programs in female-intensive fields during the late nineteenth and early twentieth centuries. Although, accompanied by elaborate rhetoric, educational and health institutions were expanding, they lacked fiscal support for such expansion. Women professionals often had to choose between self-sacrifice and self-fulfillment. A revolutionary new kind of library service was required by the emerging research universities; yet inadequate financial support and only limited autonomy were available to the women charged with achieving the revolution. After years of trying to reconcile her ideas of modern academic library service with the reality of her budgets and an unresponsive educational bureaucracy, Sharp, a victim of overwork that compromised her health, resigned and left librarianship.

An only child, born in Elgin, Illinois, Sharp was an excellent student, graduating from Northwestern University at the age of twenty. After a brief career in secondary school teaching, she studied at the New York State Library School under Melvil Dewey, originator of the Dewey Decimal System of library classification. Her first position (1893) was at the newly opened Armour Institute in Chicago, where she was both head librarian and professor of library economy. In 1897, Sharp and the library school moved to the University of Illinois, where she was professor of library economy, head librarian, and director of the Illinois State Library School. As head librarian, she replaced an untrained man uncommitted to service who had alienated the faculty. Although lauded for the improvements she made, she was exhausted by continual staff shortages due to low salaries, overwork, and battles with the administration, and in 1907, she resigned from the University of Illinois. She joined the Deweys at Lake Placid, New York, becoming vice president of the Lake Placid Corporation, and died after an auto accident at the resort.

Despite heavy responsibilities during her professional life, Sharp wrote much, including *Illinois Libraries* (1906–1908), and lectured widely on professional issues, frequently calling for higher standards of librarianship. *(See also: Librarianship)*

—**Suzanne Hildenbrand**

Further Reading

Grotzinger, Laurel Ann. *The Power and the Dignity: Librarianship and Katharine Sharp.* New York: Scarecrow, 1966.

———. "The Proto-feminist Librarian at the Turn of the Century: Two Studies," *Journal of Library History* 10 (July 1975): 195-213.

Howe, Harriet E. "Katharine Lucinda Sharp." In *Pioneering Leaders in Librarianship,* edited by Emily Danton, 165-72. Chicago: American Library Association, 1953.

~ Shaw, Anna Howard (1847–1919)

Anna Howard Shaw, a central figure in the late-nineteenth- and early-twentieth-century struggles for woman's rights, was born in Newcastle, England. At the age of four, she moved with her family to America, settling in Massachusetts; then, shortly before the Civil War, the Shaw family moved to the Michigan frontier. Shaw spent her teenage years caring for her sickly mother while her father and brothers were away at war. At the age of twenty-four, Shaw left home to attend high school in Big Rapids. At this time, she came under the influence of Reverend Marianna Thompson and decided to prepare for the Methodist ministry. She spent two years at Albion College before moving to Boston to attend divinity school at Boston University. Following graduation in 1878, Shaw served as a pastor for several years and in 1880 was ordained as an elder in the Methodist Protestant church.

Having successfully entered a clerical profession traditionally dominated by men, in 1883 Shaw began part-time work toward a medical degree. After completing her studies in 1886, Shaw became the first American woman to hold divinity and medical degrees simultaneously.

At the age of thirty-nine, Shaw left the preaching and healing ministry for another career. Joining first the Massachusetts Suffrage Association and later Lucy Stone's American Woman Suffrage Association, Shaw became a full-time organizer and lecturer for the causes of suffrage and temperance. At the urging of Frances Willard, Shaw accepted the position as chairperson of the Franchise Department of the Woman's Christian Temperance Union (WCTU). In 1888, as a delegate of the WCTU to the first meeting of the International Council of Women, Shaw met Susan B. Anthony, who persuaded her not to waste her talents on temperance but to commit herself totally to the grand cause of suffrage.

Shaw remained Anthony's friend and disciple for the remainder of her life. Their friendship had a profound impact on the future direction of the suffrage movement. In 1892, Anthony became president and Shaw vice president of the National American Woman Suffrage Association (NAWSA). An odd-looking couple, good-naturedly ridiculed by friends as "the ruler and the rubber-ball," Anthony and Shaw were strikingly different in appearance, style, and talent. Unlike the tall and slender, highly organized, and agnostic Anthony, Shaw was a roly-poly Methodist preacher with a quick wit and a golden tongue. Anthony groomed Shaw to play a particular role in the suffrage campaign—that of a moderate reformer whose life and reputation would help counteract the popular image of suffragists as unreligious and un-American militants. Shaw accepted her role graciously. Together, Anthony and Shaw were able to extend each other's outreach and effectiveness.

In 1904, at Anthony's request, Shaw became president of the NAWSA. She held this office until stepping down to become president emeritus in 1915. She remained a moderate throughout her presidency, opposing those who advocated campaigning against the political party in power rather than individual candidates unfriendly to suffrage, picketing the White House, calling hunger strikes, and pressing for immediate suffrage elections, even if there were no prospect for victory.

In May 1917, President Woodrow Wilson called on Shaw to chair the Woman's Committee of the Council of National Defense. Two years later, in appreciation for her war services, Wilson awarded her the Distinguished Service Medal. Shaw spent the remaining months of her life campaigning for the creation of the League of Nations. She died on July 2, 1919, at her home in Moylan, Pennsylvania. *(See also: Anthony, Susan B.; National American Woman Suffrage Association; Suffrage)*

—**Terry D. Bilhartz**

Further Reading

McGovern, James R. "Anna Howard Shaw: New Approaches to Feminism," *Journal of Social History* 3 (1969/70): 135-53.

Shaw, Anna Howard. *The Story of a Pioneer.* New York: Harper, 1915.

Spencer, Ralph W. "Anna Howard Shaw: The Evangelical Feminist." Ph.D. diss., University of Boston, 1972.

～ Shaw, Anna Moore (1898–1978)

Anna Moore Shaw (also known as Chehia) was born on the Gila River Pima Reservation, the youngest child of Josiah (Red Arrow) and Rose (Haus Molly) Moore. Her parents were among the first Pima to be converted to Christianity, and she belonged to the first generation of Pima children sent to boarding school. She attended one year at the Tucson Indian Mission before being sent in 1908 to the Phoenix Indian School. In 1920, Shaw was the first Pima female to graduate from Phoenix Union High School. While still in high school, she married Ross Shaw, from the Salt River Pima Reservation. They settled in Phoenix, where her husband went to work for the Santa Fe Railroad.

Shaw was determined to bring the white version of a higher standard of living to her family while remaining sensitive to her cultural heritage. At first, the family lived in a racially mixed neighborhood, but during World War II, the Shaws broke the restricted neighborhood code in Phoenix by buying a house in a white neighborhood. Shaw was the first Pima to join the Parent-Teacher Association and was the first Pima to join the United Church Women (later the Church Women United), in which she was very active. She was the first woman to be ordained an elder in her Phoenix church. A devoted follower of Carlos Montezuma's teachings about the need for multiethnic understanding among all peoples, she devoted her life to the fulfillment of that goal through her community and church activities.

When Shaw finally agreed to her husband's wish to retire on his land on the Salt River Reservation, she was shocked by the squalor and poverty she saw on the reservation and, as a result, helped found many social service programs. Once back on the reservation, her interest in Pima traditions was revived. She began teaching these traditions and assisted in the founding of a cultural museum. She edited the monthly newsletter "Awathm Awahan [Pima Letters]" for three years. As part of her renewed cultural interest, she had been collecting traditional Pima tales and in 1968 published a collection of them as *Pima Legends*. In 1974, she published her autobiography, *A Pima Past*, a collection of reminiscences of her life, with special emphasis on the effects of Christianity.

Shaw spent the last years of her life living on the reservation. Her advocacy of interracial harmony was recognized in 1981 when she was posthumously inducted into the Arizona Hall of Fame. *(See also: Christianity; Native American Women; Native American Women's Literature)*

—**Susan L. Rockwell**

Further Reading

Bataille, Gretchen, ed. *Native American Women: A Biographical Dictionary,* p. 232. New York: Garland, 1993.

Bataille, Gretchen, and Kathleen M. Sands. *American Indian Women: A Guide to Research,* pp. 101, 152, 264, 351-52. New York: Garland, 1991.

———. "Two Women in Transition." In *Native American Women Telling Their Lives,* edited by Gretchen M. Bataille and Kathleen M. Sands, 83-112. Lincoln: University of Nebraska Press, 1985.

Greene, Rayna. *Native American Women: A Contextual Bibliography,* p. 94. Bloomington: Indiana University Press, 1983.

Shaw, Anna Moore. *Pima Legends.* Tucson: University of Arizona Press, 1968.

———. *A Pima Past.* Tucson: University of Arizona Press, 1974.

Tsosie, Rebecca. "Changing Women: The Cross-Currents of American Indiana Feminine Identity," *American Indian Culture and Research Journal* 12 (1988): 1-37.

⨳ Sheppard-Towner Act of 1921

The Sheppard-Towner Act of 1921 established federal matching funds for state health clinics, midwife education, and visiting nurse programs. The nation's first social welfare program, it aimed at reducing the national infant mortality rate. Activists such as Mary Anderson and Julia Lathrop of the Children's Bureau argued that infant mortality and ill health were directly related to low wages, crowded housing, and parental ignorance. Conservative groups, including the American Medical Association, opposed the measure on the basis that federal funding violated states' rights.

Sponsored in 1918-19 by Congresswoman Jeanette Rankin, the bill originally met with failure. Finally, Harriet Upton, vice chairperson of the Republican Party, threatened members of Congress with retaliation at the polls if they did not approve it. An editorial in *Good Housekeeping* magazine on infant mortality in America provided timely support. That the bill passed Congress by a wide margin reveals the growing political clout of the nation's recently enfranchised women.

Mortality rates did decline for white infants between 1921 and 1928. They declined nominally, if at all, for minority infants. Despite this promising outlook, Congress repealed the act in 1929, bowing to pressure applied by the act's conservative opposition. *(See also: National Organization for Public Health Nursing; Protective Legislation; Visiting Nurses)*

—Karen Raines-Pate
—Jonathan W. Zophy

Further Reading

Chambers, Clark. *Seedtime of Reform.* Ann Arbor: University of Michigan Press, 1967.

Cooper, Donald G. "Save the Babies: The Passage of a Federally-Supported Maternal and Infant Health Act," *UCLA Historical Journal* 8 (1987): 25-39.

"Herod Is Not Dead," *Good Housekeeping* 71 (December 1920): 4.

Ladd-Taylor, Molly. " 'Grannies' and 'Spinsters': Midwife Education under the Sheppard-Towner Act," *Journal of Social History* 22 (Winter 1988): 255-75.

Lindenmeyer, Kriste. "Saving Mothers and Babies: The Sheppard-Towner Act in Ohio, 1921–1929," *Ohio History* 99 (Sum/Aut 1990): 105-27.

⨳ Shirtwaist Makers Strike of 1909

On November 23, 1909, twenty thousand shirtwaist makers launched the largest women's strike in American history. The first mass job action of its kind, the strike focused national attention on "sweatshop" workers and launched the unionization of the garment trade, the nation's third largest industry and largest employer of women. It was an immigrant woman's strike at a time when immigrants were despised as strikebreakers and women were considered unorganizable. Most of the strikers were Eastern European Jews, a sizable minority were Italian, and almost all were young, in their teens or early twenties.

Anger at the treatment of women already on strike against the Triangle and Leiserson companies contributed to the general strike. The underlying causes, however, were oppressive conditions throughout the industry—a fifty-six-hour week with unpaid overtime; fees for use of thread, machinery, and lockers; piecework; and low wages paid in tiny, redeemable "tickets." The goals were better hours and pay and, most important, the union shop.

Although male officials negotiated with the employers, the strike was led and carried out by the women. Hungry, inadequately dressed, harassed by the police, and attacked by thugs and prostitutes hired by the companies, the women marched, rallied, picketed, and raised money for their cause. Financial and moral support came from progressive reformers; from the Jewish immigrant community with its strong, radical working-class subculture and tradition of women's activism; and from women, including college students, Socialist Party women, suffragists; and most important, from the National Women's Trade Union League.

The strike ended February 15, 1910, with mixed results. Most companies signed with the union, although often not meeting all the union demands, but nineteen, including the largest, remained unorganized. Labor benefited, as subsequent strikes, inspired by the shirtwaist makers, organized the garment trades; but benefits for women were less clear. Publicity surrounding the strike encouraged protective legislation for women workers, but the strikers had fought for self-governing unions, not paternalistic laws. The strike contributed to the personal growth of many participants, and leaders such as Clara Lemlich, Pauline Newman, Theresa Malkiel, and Rose Schneiderman continued suffragist and labor activism. But although the strike demonstrated that women could be assets to the labor movement, the American Federation of Labor failed to devote adequate attention to

Figure 55. Shirtwaist Makers Strike
In the largest women's strike in American history, twenty thousand workers staged a job action that focused national attention on the inhumane treatment of garment employees. Here, four women picket in front of a New York factory. Used by permission of UPI/Corbis-Bettmann.

them. *(See also: Garment Industries; National Women's Trade Union League; Unions)*

—Maxine Schwartz Seller

Further Reading

Henry, Alice. *The Trade Union Woman.* New York: Appleton, 1915.

Levine, Louis. *The Women's Garment Workers: A History of the International Ladies Garment Workers.* New York: B. W. Huebach, 1924.

Malkiel, Theresa. *Diary of a Shirtwaist Striker.* New York: Cooperative Press, 1910.

Seller, Maxine S. "The Uprising of the Twenty Thousand: Sex, Class, and Ethnicity in the Shirtwaist Makers Strike of 1909." In *Struggle a Hard Battle: Essays on Working-Class Immigrants,* edited by Dirk Hoerder, 254-70. Dekalb: Northern Illinois University Press, 1986.

Tax, Meredith. *The Rising of the Women: Feminist Solidarity and Class Conflict, 1880–1917.* New York: Monthly Review, 1980.

⮿ Silko, Leslie Marmon (b. 1948)

Native American novelist, poet, essayist, and short-story writer Leslie Marmon Silko was born in Albuquerque to Lee H. Marmon of the Laguna and Virginia of the Plains tribes. Of Native American, Anglo, and Mexican ancestry, Silko grew up on the Laguna Pueblo Reservation where she learned the cultural traditions of the Lagunas through the oral tales told by her grandmother. She uses her heritage as the inspiration for her stories. She writes that "the core of my writing is the attempt to identify what it is to be a half-breed . . . to grow up neither white nor fully traditional Indian." She asserts, however, that "what I know is Laguna. This place I am from is everything I am as a writer and human being."

Silko draws from the oral traditions and folklore of her heritage to interpret Native American moral codes and experiences. She recounts in her works what happens when a way of life that has flourished for generations rapidly undergoes cataclysmic and brutal changes with the coming of the Caucasians. Community and tribal life broke down, pressured by the advent of reservation life and the removal of children to missionary boarding schools where speaking their tribal language was forbidden.

Insightfully interpreting her people's plight, Silko writes about broken treaties, relocation, disease, alcoholism, and promiscuity, but her characters are seldom embittered or defeated. Instead, they cope with adversity, using survival tactics learned from their past to strengthen their resolution to triumph. Although a sense of loss and nostalgia haunts her stories and poems, they end on an optimistic note with diverse ethnic groups learning to respect each other's cultures.

A strong moral connection exists between Silko's artistic delight in crafting a story and the therapeutic functional purpose she hopes it will serve in the Native American community. In *Ceremony* (1977), the first full-length novel published by an Indian woman, and in *Storyteller* (1981), a collection of poems, short stories, and photographs, Silko sensitively sketches realistic people living in harmony with nature, respecting the animals in their environment.

"Lullaby" (1974), included in *The Best American Short Stories* (1975) and *Two Hundred Years of Great American Short Stories* (1975), describes the tough, devoted perseverance of an old woman, Ayah, sitting with her sickly husband, both wrapped in a blanket, their backs against a rock as a storm beats down. She sings a lullaby from her childhood as the story ends: "The earth is your mother, she holds you. The sky is your father, he protects you. Sleep, sleep. Rainbow is your sister, she loves you. The winds are your brothers, they sing to you. Sleep, sleep. We are together always." Thus, Silko uses religious and philosophic themes from her Native American oral and cultural storytelling tradition to craft poignant artistic creations.

She has received numerous grants and awards, including a National Endowment for the Arts Fellowship and a MacArthur Foundation Award in 1981 to complete her second novel, *Almanac of the Dead*. After receiving a B.A. from the University of New Mexico in 1969, Silko has taught in Arizona, New Mexico, and was a visiting scholar at Vassar, the University of Washington, and Emory University. *(See also: Native American Women; Native American Women's Literature; Women Writers)*

—**Edith Blicksilver**

Further Reading

Allen, Paula Gunn. "The Feminine Landscape of Leslie Marmon Silko's *Ceremony*." In *Studies in American Indian Literature*, edited by Paula Gunn Allen, 127-33. New York: MLA, 1983.

Blicksilver, Edith. "Traditionalism vs. Modernity: Leslie Silko on American Indian Women," *Southwest Review* 64 (1979): 149-60.

Herzog, Kristin. "Thinking Woman and Feeling Man: Gender in Leslie Marmon Silko's *Ceremony*," *MELUS* 12 (Summer 1985): 25-36.

Hirsch, Bernard A. "The Telling Which Continues: Oral Tradition and the Written Word in Leslie Marmon Silko's *Storyteller*," *American Indian Quarterly* 4 (Winter 1988): 1-26.

Sands, Kathleen M., ed. "A Special Symposium Issue on Leslie Marmon Silko's *Ceremony*," *American Indian Quarterly* 5 (February 1979): 1-75.

Seyersted, Per. *Leslie Marmon Silko*. Boise, ID: Boise State University Press, 1980.

Silko, Leslie Marmon. *Almanac of the Dead*. New York: Simon & Schuster, 1991.

———. *Ceremony*. New York: Viking, 1977.

———. *The Delicacy and the Strength of Lace: Letters between Leslie Marmon Silko and James Wright*. St. Paul, MN: Greywolf, 1986.

———. *Laguna Woman*. Greenfield Center, NY: Greenfield Review, 1974.

———. "Lullaby." In *The Ethnic American Woman: Problems, Protests, Lifestyle*, edited by Edith Blicksilver, 54-60. Dubuque, IA: Kendall/Hunt, 1978.

———. *Storyteller*. New York: Seaver, 1981.

～ Singing Bird (1761–1846)

Singing Bird, which translates to *As she we qua* in the Sauk language, was married to the famous Sac war chief Black Hawk and stayed by his side for half a century. She was born in 1761 in the area of Green Bay, Wisconsin. Her mother was half French and half Sauk, and nothing is known of her father. At an early age, she moved with her husband to Saukenuk village near Rock Island, Illinois.

According to custom, Singing Bird helped process and store the kill from annual hunts, looked after the children, made clothes for the family, and helped the other village women tend the productive 800 cultivated acres of fruits and vegetables in Saukenuk. She also made woven mats for ceremonial and household use. During their long marriage, Singing Bird bore Black Hawk five children. When two of them died young, Singing Bird went alone, as was the custom, to weep over and tend their graves at the edge of the large Saukenuk village. These graves and cornfields meant that she and the other women were probably the greatest motivators for her husband's decision to protect and defend the tribe's land by waging the Black Hawk War against the United States in 1832.

Monogamy was not often practiced among the headmen and chiefs of Black Hawk's time. Keokuk, a war and government chief of the Sac and Fox during the same era, was said to have five wives at one time. "This is the only wife I ever had or will have. She is a good woman, and teaches my boys to be brave," wrote Black Hawk of Singing Bird in his autobiography in 1833.

When Singing Bird and Black Hawk grew old, they moved with two sons and one daughter to a cabin on the Des Moines River near Iowaville, Iowa. As was her practice, she accompanied her husband on what would be his last public outing on July 4, 1838, when he spoke to an Independence Day celebration in Fort Madison. Later, she confided to neighbors that "the end is near. He is getting old. Monito calls him home." Black Hawk died on October 3, 1838, and his devoted wife saw that his burial was in the tradition of his Thunder Clan. The family continued to live in the lodge until the fall of 1845 when they were removed to a reservation in Kansas.

Singing Bird died in Kansas on August 29, 1846. *(See also: Native American Women)*

—**Jan Vassar**

Further Reading

Black Hawk. *Autobiography of Ma-ka-tai-me-she-kia-kiak or Black Hawk,* through the interpretation of Antonine LeClaire. Edited by J. B. Patterson, with Introduction and Notes, Critical and Historical by James D. Rishell. Rock Island, IL: American Publishing Company, 1912.

Eckert, Allan W. *Twilight of Empire.* New York: Bantam, 1988.

Flowers, Sheila. "The Man, the Husband, the Father." From a Sheila Flowers manuscript, Houston, TX, 1985.

Hagan, William T. *The Sac and Fox Indians.* 1958. Reprint, Norman: University of Oklahoma Press, 1980.

Iowa Writers' Program. "Chief Black Hawk Finds Peace at Iowaville." Van Buren County, IA: Works Progress Administration, 1940.

McKenney, Thomas L., and James Hall. *A History of the Indian Tribes of North America,* with *Biographical Sketches and Anecdotes of the Principal Chiefs,* 3 vols. Philadelphia, 1838.

⚘ Single Women

Old maid and *spinster,* pejorative terms used for unmarried women, have been boldly accepted, vociferously rejected, and quietly suffered by such women. Both terms reinforce the norm of marriage when attached to the woman who remains single past the conventional age for marrying or who seems, in appearance or by temperament, unlikely ever to marry. Spinster is still the legal term for an unmarried woman in Britain.

Spinster originally described anyone whose occupation was spinning. More women than men, and especially unmarried women and adolescent girls, were associated with spinning as a home occupation. As the demand for and popularity of homespun declined with the manufacture of cloth in industries, the spinster's status dropped; thereafter, she was connected with a "useless" or "mindless" task. Victorian notions of respectability prohibited the middle- and upper-class spinster from seeking education and other employment. Thus, the spinster's economic "uselessness" paralleled her social uselessness as a woman who did not fulfill her "normal" and "natural" function in life by marrying and mothering children.

Her apparent rejection of the married state threatened or challenged a society that, in turn, scorned the spinster. The "old maid" is ridiculed in legend, joke, and song as the lonely woman left behind in the race to marry. In the child's card game *Old Maid,* the loser is the player left with the Old Maid card (a spare queen in a regular deck) when all the other cards have been paired up. The stereotype of the old maid or spinster is a prim, petty, nervous, gossipy woman, devoted to pets, jealous of married women, who fears men but nonetheless pines for one.

As educational and economic opportunities for women increased, and particularly when wars created a surplus of unmarried women, more freedom, approval, and recognition for the old maid or spinster followed. In the antebellum United States, the cult of single blessedness balanced the cult of domesticity somewhat by glorifying the spinster while also suggesting new constraints through the ideals of service, selflessness, and celibacy. Many spinsters were active in the women's rights movement, a movement that invited a reassessment of marriage. For those who saw marriage as an economic association devoid of nobility, a submission to male dominance, a sacrifice of individual goals, or an otherwise imperfect institution, spinsterhood emerged as a positive and viable choice. *(See also: Marriage)*

—**Kathleen Kirk**

Further Reading

Adams, Margaret. *Single Blessedness.* New York: Basic Books, 1976.

Chambers-Schiller, Lee Virginia. *Liberty, A Better Husband: Single Women in America, the Generations of 1780–1840.* New Haven, CT: Yale University Press, 1984.

Hutton, Laura. *The Single Woman.* 1935. Reprint, New York: Roy, 1960.

Jeffreys, Sheila. *The Spinster and Her Enemies: Feminism and Sexuality, 1880–1930.* Boston: Pandora, 1985.

O'Brien, Michael, ed. *An Evening When Alone: Four Journals of Single Women in the South, 1827–67.* Charlottesville: University Press of Virginia, 1993.

Peterson, Nancy L. *Our Lives for Ourselves: Women Who Never Married.* New York: Putnam, 1981.

⚘ Slavery

Slave women were perhaps the most vulnerable women in America during the eighteenth and nineteenth centuries, before emancipation. Enslaved, black, and female, they lived in a society ruled by free white men, and their experience of slavery was different from black men's. The differences began with the "middle passage," the transportation of African blacks to the New World, when the enslaved African women were sometimes isolated from the men and forced to serve the crew on deck. These differences continued through the imbalanced sex ratio of the early colonial period and extended through the end of slavery, as slave women came to develop a mother-child-centered social universe within the slave community.

More than anything else, slave women's reproductive capacities determined their place in bondage. Women were especially vulnerable to sexual exploitation. While rape was not uncommon (although probably declining in frequency through the nineteenth century), the principal abuse was more subtle and universal. After the close of the legal African slave trade in 1807, slaveholders relied on slave women's childbearing capacity to replenish the farm/plantation workforce. Slave men served principally as laborers, but slave women were expected both to work in the fields or the "big house" and to bear and raise children for the master's profit. Their role as mother confined them to their farms/plantations, for with children they were less mobile than were slave men, and this caused slave women to practice different strategies of resistance than did men. Slave women, for example, played on the slaveholders' "property" interest (e.g., slave women's reproductive capacity) by feigning sickness to gain relief from overwork. As nurses and cooks, slave women had opportunities to poison their masters.

The work cycle of slave women also differed from that of men. Slave girls did odd chores in the big house and in the yards, which introduced them to the domestic service that would be part of their obligations thereafter. On plantations, where the majority of slaves lived by the late antebellum period, slave girls worked in "trash" gangs with boys, performing the lighter chores such as weeding and clearing stubble, but not until they reached their teens did they join a work gang that was usually composed entirely of women. Some adult slave women performed heavy agricultural labor along with the men throughout the South (plowing, hoeing, picking cotton, or cutting rice or sugar cane), but most slave women usually worked in female work groups apart from the men (spinning, weaving, sewing, quilting, and hoeing). Thus, slave women spent most of their time with other women, and given the high percentage of slave marriages in which the husband and wife lived on separate farms/plantations, the slave women relied on female and kin networks and themselves rather than husbands/fathers to raise and define the world of the slave children.

On large plantations especially, female slaves were socialized into clearly defined sex roles, drawn from African culture and American experience. Afro-American cultural imperatives, for example, dictated that women delay childbearing for at least two years after they experienced menarche (generally about the age of fifteen). Motherhood marked the woman's rite of passage, and as in many African societies, the Afro-American slave woman married the father of her first child only after the child was born, thus demonstrating her ability to have children.

Slave marriages were of necessity egalitarian, for women assumed much of the responsibility for care and even the provisions grown in the slave gardens. In the slave community, the mother-child relationship superseded that of the husband-wife, in part due to the master's vested interest in the former (which sometimes protected the slave mothers by discouraging the sale of small children away from their mothers) and in part due to the circumstances of slave life. Without property, slave men could not claim traditional male authority over their wives. Still, many slave women revealed a special strength by deferring to their menfolk when they were present, thus bolstering the husband/father's esteem and maintaining the semblance of the two-parent, monogamous household that would form the basic social unit among blacks after emancipation. That many ex-slaves sought to formalize their marriages after emancipation suggests that the unions established during slavery were based

on mutual affection. The emergence of patriarchal households among ex-slaves in the post-Civil War rural South coincided with new economic and social arrangements, especially the blacks' movement into sharecropping and tenancy, which isolated women from previous female networks and stressed individual family cohesion.

As slaves, black women could not share a sympathetic relationship with white women. Black slave women might attend the same church as their mistresses (and submit to the same discipline), they might suffer the same female complaints and the same dangers attending childbearing, and in some instances, they might earn the confidences of their white mistresses, but they could not escape the authority of white women. Whippings, beatings, scourges, and other punishments inflicted on slave women by white women bore grim witness to the discrepancies in power separating black from white. The myth of the "faithful mammy" notwithstanding, slave women cast their lot with their own families and the slave community. During the Civil War, slave women fled the farms/plantations at the first opportunity to lay claim to as much freedom from whites as was possible, leaving their white mistresses to fend for themselves. *(See also: Abolition and the Antislavery Movement; Black Women)*

—**Randall M. Miller**

Further Reading

Blassingame, John W. *The Slave Community: Plantation Life in the Antebellum South*. Rev. ed. New York: Oxford University Press, 1979.

Campbell, Edward D. C., Jr., and Kym S. Rice, eds. *Before Freedom Came: African-American Life in the Antebellum South*. Charlottesville: University Press of Virginia, 1991.

Fox-Genovese, Elizabeth. *Within the Plantation Household: Black and White Women of the Old South*. Chapel Hill: University of North Carolina Press, 1988.

Genovese, Eugene G. *Roll, Jordan, Roll: The World the Slaves Made*. New York: Pantheon, 1974.

Gutman, Herbert G. *The Black Family in Slavery & Freedom, 1750–1925*. Oxford, UK: Basil Blackwell, 1976.

Jones, Jacqueline. *Labor of Love, Labor of Sorrow: Black Women, Work, and the Family from Slavery to the Present*. New York: Basic Books, 1985.

Kolchin, Peter. *American Slavery, 1619–1877*. New York: Hill & Wang, 1993.

White, Deborah Gray. *Ar'n't I a Woman? Female Slaves in the Plantation South*. New York: Norton, 1985.

～ Smedley, Agnes (1892–1950)

Agnes Smedley, journalist and social activist, was born near Campground, Missouri, and grew up in a series of western mining camps in an atmosphere of poverty that she later credited with her lifelong identification with the powerless. She went to work at the age of fourteen but persevered at acquiring an education, eventually graduating from San Diego Normal School (now California State University at San Diego) in 1914.

Involved in the American Socialist Party since the early 1910s, Smedley moved to New York in 1919 and found work on the Socialist Party paper, *The Call*. She was also active in the birth control movement headed by Margaret Sanger and in the crusade for Indian independence from Great Britain, traveling to Berlin in 1920 to work with the Indian Revolutionary Committee. She remained in Europe for another seven years, writing extensively on Indian nationalism and other social issues for German and American periodicals and completing her first book, the autobiographical novel *Daughter of Earth* (1927).

In early 1928, Smedley arrived in China as a correspondent for the *Frankfurter Zeitung*. Almost immediately, she was drawn to the cause of the Chinese Communist Party as the means to end the intense poverty of China's citizenry. She remained in China for the most part until 1941, reporting on conditions among peasants and factory workers, the Chinese Red Army, and the Sino-Japanese War for a variety of publications.

After her return to the United States, Smedley continued to write on the contemporary situation in China. *Battle Hymn of China,* an account of her years there, was published in 1943. With the beginnings of the Cold War, however, Smedley's popularity with American readers began to dwindle. In late 1948, community complaints over Smedley's alleged Communist activities forced her to leave Yaddo, the writers' colony in upstate New York where she had lived for the previous five years.

The Communist victory in China in 1949 and increasing antileftist sentiment in the U.S. caused Smedley to resolve to return to China, which she had begun to regard as her spiritual home. She was in England, trying to arrange a visa when she became seriously ill; she died in London in May 1950. *The Great Road,* her biography of Zhu De (Chu Teh), commander-in-chief of the Red Army, was posthumously published in 1956. *(See also: Journalism; Socialist Party of America; Women Writers)*

—Laura K. O'Keefe

Further Reading

MacKinnon, Janice R., and Stephen R. MacKinnon. *Agnes Smedley: The Life and Times of an American Radical.* Berkeley: University of California Press, 1988.

Smedley, Agnes. *Battle Hymn of China.* New York: Knopf, 1943.

———. *Daughter of Earth.* 1927. Reprint, Old Westbury, NY: Feminist Press, 1973.

⚬ Smith, Bessie (1898?–1937)

American blues singer who was also known as "The World's Greatest Blues Singer" and "The Empress of the Blues," Bessie Smith is considered second in importance only to the "Mother of the Blues," Gertrude "Ma" Rainey. Born in Chattanooga, Tennessee, into a poor family, Smith lost both parents by the time she was nine. Smith sang as a child and entered show business at an early age. She was

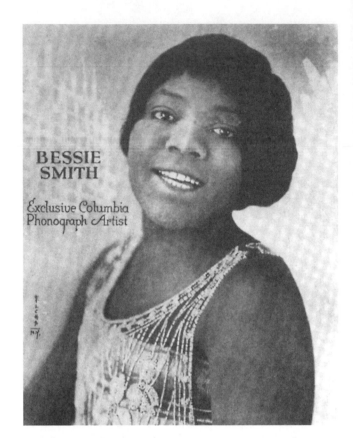

Figure 56. Bessie Smith
Known as "The World's Greatest Blues Singer" during her heyday in the 1920s, Bessie Smith was hugely influential as a blues musician, and her popularity helped spur on the mass marketing of popular music recordings. Used by permission of Frank Driggs/Corbis-Bettmann.

first "discovered" at a local amateur contest by the manager of Chattanooga's Ivory Theater and later by pianist-composer Clarence Williams, a representative of Columbia Records. She toured with one of F. C. Woolcott's Rabbit Foot Minstrel groups managed by Will Rainey, husband of Gertrude Rainey. It is widely assumed that Ma Rainey took care of Smith and helped her career, although Smith rarely acknowledged the debt in later years. Smith began her recording career in 1920, recording for the "Race Records" series of Okah and Paramount record labels; she made her first recording for Columbia in 1923.

Smith combined recording trips to New York with radio shows and live performances for the rest of her career. Her fame spread rapidly among both black and white audiences, from the black vaudeville circuits throughout the South into major northern cities such as New York and Chicago. Langston Hughes wrote of Smith; Louis Armstrong, Fletcher Henderson, Benny Goodman, and others recorded with her.

Smith sang of the love, poverty, pain, and perseverance that made up the classic blues repertoire, and her interpretation of works such as "Nobody's Blues but Mine," "Chicago Bound," and "St. Louis Blues" embodied what has been called the "classic blues style." Her emotional, technically skillful voice (so powerful she often refused a microphone) and arresting physical presence were captured at least in part in the short motion picture *St. Louis Blues* in 1929.

Toward the end of the 1920s and into the 1930s, however, Smith's recording career declined. Her music grew artistically and she continued to tour, but changes in popular music taste, together with her problems with alcohol, ended her "glory days." John Hammond produced what became Smith's last recordings in 1933. In 1936, she announced plans for a comeback, but on September 26, 1937, she was killed in an automobile accident. The circumstances are a mystery, but many blamed local segregation policies for her untimely death. Edward Albee based his play *The Death of Bessie Smith* on that theory. Smith remains, however, an artist whose influence continues to the present. Columbia Records released a five-volume, two-record set of Smith's recordings, under the title *Bessie Smith*, which was produced by John Hammond in 1972. (*See also: Holiday, Billie; Jazz; Music; Popular Vocalists; Rainey, Gertrude "Ma"*)

—**Elizabeth H. Coughlin**

Further Reading

Albertson, Chris. *Bessie.* Briarcliff Manor, NY: Stein & Day, 1972.
Bessie Smith: Any Woman's Blues. Columbia, GP 30126, 1972.
Bessie Smith: The Empress. Columbia, GP 30818, 1972.
Bessie Smith: Empty Bed Blues. Columbia, GP 30450, 1972.
Bessie Smith: Nobody's Blues but Mine. Columbia, GP 31093, 1972.
Bessie Smith: The World's Greatest Blues Singer. Columbia, GP 33, 1972.
Harris, S. *Blues Who's Who.* New Rochelle, NY: Arlington House, 1979.
Hughes, Langston. "The Negro Artist and the Racial Mountain," *Nation* 122 (June 23, 1926): 692-94.
Rampersad, Arnold. *The Life of Langston Hughes,* 2 vols. New York: Oxford University Press, 1986, 1988.
Stearns, Marshall W. *The Story of Jazz.* London: Oxford University Press, 1970.

∽ Smith, Margaret Chase (1897–1995)

Businesswoman and politician Margaret Chase Smith was born in Skowhegan, Maine, and worked as a dimestore clerk, telephone operator, newspaperwoman, and teacher, eventually managing the town woolen mill. Her stature as a businesswoman led to the 1930 presidency of the State Federation of Business and Professional Women's Clubs. That same year, she also married politician Clyde Smith (1876–1940). Following his death in 1940, she successfully ran for his congressional seat. After four House terms, Smith won a Senate seat in 1948, the first woman senator elected on her own merit.

While most women politicians generally avoided hard issues and followed party lines, Smith, an Air Force Reserve Officer, demonstrated her independence by vocally encouraging a strong defense, often voting against the GOP major-

ity. In 1947, she cast the lone Republican House vote approving Truman's budget. Refusing to label herself a feminist, she supported the incorporation of women in the military and publicly admonished her own Republican Party for its condescending attitude toward women.

In 1950, Wisconsin Republican Senator Joseph McCarthy received national notoriety by hurling unwarranted charges of communist affiliations against individuals. Outraged, Smith hoped to enlist Senate colleagues to thwart the Wisconsin senator. Fearing political retaliation, no Democrats and only a few Republicans voiced support. Undaunted, on June 1, 1950, the first-term senator and lone female stood before her peers and attacked the immorality of a fellow Republican's so-called investigations in a "Declaration of Conscience." Bernard Baruch claimed "if a man made the speech, he would be the next President." The address marked the pinnacle of her career, with the possible exception of her pioneering attempt to become the 1964 Republican presidential nominee.

Current women's historians often ignore Smith because she entered the political office of a deceased husband and because she avoided labeling herself a feminist. These historians fail to take into account that Smith won her Senate seat eight years after her husband's death or that she refused to be intimidated by other party members. Furthermore, Smith considered herself a senator who happened to be female; she focused on issues of justice, whether those issues involved the status of women or the rights of any individual in a fight against tyranny. (*See also: The 1950s; Politics; Republican Party*)

—**Dennis L. Morrison**

Further Reading

"Margaret Chase Smith Interview." Videocassette produced by Dennis L. Morrison, January 10, 1990. Special Collections, Margaret Chase Smith Library. Skowhegan, Maine.
Morrison, Dennis L. *Woman of Conscience: Senator Margaret Chase Smith of Maine.* St. James, NY: Brandywine, 1994.
Rovere, Richard. *Senator Joe McCarthy.* New York: Harcourt Brace, 1959.

∽ Smith, Mary Rozet (1871–1934)

Best friend of Jane Addams and a benefactress of Chicago's Hull House settlement founded by Addams, Mary Rozet Smith was one of several society women who gave money to Hull House and volunteered to help operate its many clubs, classes, lectures, receptions, and other activities. Although never a resident at the settlement, she was, after 1895, one of its trustees and also Addams's personal adviser on financial matters. Smith frequently paid off Hull House's debts and provided funds for new ventures, most notably the Children's Building (1895).

Smith's far greater claim to historical significance, however, was her long and intimate friendship with Addams. She was a shy and gentle woman who, for more than forty years, made a career of tending to Addams's personal needs. For example, Walton Place, Smith's family residence in Chicago, was a constant refuge for Addams. Each summer the two lived together in a house they purchased near Bar Harbor, Maine. Smith also gave clothing and countless other gifts to Addams and accompanied her on her many extensive travels around the globe. Allen F. Davis, Addams's biographer, argues that Smith's unquestioning devotion gave Addams an emotional support that was crucial to her growth as a reformer and a celebrity.

The intense and durable relationship shared by Smith and Addams exemplified a type of passionate bonding commonly found among the "New Women" of the Progressive Era. As these young, single, well-educated women from middle-class families developed public careers in education and social reform, they often came to prefer their female colleagues as private companions as well. Although there is no evidence of a sexual relationship between Smith and Addams, for all other intents and purposes they were married. Beyond that, Hull House residents and the settlement house movement at large served them as a support group, a surrogate family. *(See also: Addams, Jane; Hull House; New Woman; Progressive Era; Settlement House Movement)*

—**Bruce R. Kahler**

Further Reading

Davis, Allen F. *American Heroine: The Life and Legend of Jane Addams.* New York: Oxford University Press, 1973.

D'Emilio, John, and Estelle B. Freedman. *Intimate Matters: A History of Sexuality in America.* New York: Harper & Row, 1988.

Linn, James Weber. *Jane Addams: A Biography.* New York: D. Appleton-Century, 1943.

❧ Smith College

Smith College, an institution of higher education for women in Northampton, Massachusetts, opened in September 1875 with fourteen students. Founded according to the testament of Sophia Smith (1796–1870), who inherited a fortune from her brother Austin in 1861, the college aimed at providing an educational program for women comparable to that of men, without, according to the wishes of the founder herself, upsetting conventional notions of femininity. To this end, the college worked in two directions. First, it organized a curriculum based on standard university offerings and eliminated elements of secondary school preparation offered by other women's institutions. To maintain femininity, the trustees and administrators proposed a system of living in familylike cottages that would duplicate patterns of sociability and order prevalent in the society at large. Both the house system and the high standards of education continued into the late twentieth century, when Smith was selected as one of the fifteen best liberal arts colleges in the country.

Under the presidency of L. Clark Seelye, the college expanded from the original small student body to close to two thousand by his retirement in 1910. The largest independent women's college in the world, Smith had an enrollment of close to 2,500 women by the mid-1970s. Seelye was concerned with a comprehensive program and thus offered not only science but also a strong program in the arts. In 1921, the college added a School of Social Work, which awarded a master's degree. Other than that, Smith College maintained its commitment to the liberal arts, despite pressures to expand or to reorient its offerings. In addition, it maintained its commitment to women's education when the administration decided in the mid-1970s to resist the trend toward coeducation. The selection of the first woman president, Jill Ker Conway, in 1975, seemed to confirm that commitment.

The Smith College endowment grew from the original bequest of $400,000 to close to $80 million in the mid-1970s. By 1997, the endowment had reached $683 million. Like other women's colleges, Smith has experienced the financial pressures of competing with men's institutions for endowment money. Not only were alumnae less able or willing to give than graduates of male colleges, but parents were sometimes less interested in paying hefty fees for daughters. Today, however, Smith is consistently among the top private liberal arts institutions in gift income, and 56 percent of Smith students receive need-based financial aid, with average grants of about $16,078.

Smith continues to attract a stable but increasingly diverse student body. More students in the 1970s and 1980s had backgrounds in science, math, and technical subjects, and their interests shifted away from traditional areas such as art history and history. Smith has more than 43,000 alumnae in all 50 states and more than 100 other countries. Betty Friedan, Julia Child, Margaret Mitchell, Sylvia Plath, Nancy Reagan, and Gloria Steinem are among its graduates.

With more than 1.3 million items, Smith's Neilson Library is the largest of any liberal arts college in the United States. It is also home to outstanding collections of books and manuscripts by Sylvia Plath and Virginia Woolf. *(See also: Higher Education; "Seven Sisters")*

—**Bonnie G. Smith**

Further Reading

Hanscom, Elizabeth Deering. *Sophia Smith and the Beginnings of Smith College.* Northampton, MA: Smith College, 1926.

Horowitz, Helen L. *Alma Mater. Design and Experience in the Women's Colleges from their Beginnings to the 1930s,* 2d ed. Amherst: University of Massachusetts Press, 1993.

Lincoln, Eleanor Terry. *This, the House We Live In: The Smith College Campus from 1871–1982.* Northampton, MA: Smith College, 1983.

Mendenhall, Thomas C. *Chance and Change in Smith College's First Century.* Northampton, MA: Smith College, 1976.

Rothman, David J. *The Dangers of Education: Sexism and the Origins of Women's Colleges.* New York: Garland, 1987.

Toth, Susan Allen. *Ivy Days: Making My Way Out East.* Boston: Little, Brown, 1984.

Smith-Hughes Act of 1917

The Smith-Hughes Act of 1917 established the Federal Board for Vocational Education to promote training in home economics as well as in agriculture, vocational subjects, commerce, trades, and industry in secondary schools. Rural high schools could now offer agricultural and home economics courses that serviced student organizations such as the Future Farmers of America and the Future Home-makers of America, while urban schools established vocational training for boys and commercial "business" courses for girls. Thus, high school curricula that previously emphasized college preparation for middle-class students adapted education for girls to suit the sex-segregated job market that awaited them. The social mobility of non-minority working-class girls was increased through their access to white-collar positions. As postsecondary education under the Smith-Lever Act of 1914 focused curricula for women students on their future role in marriage and the family, the modifications of high school curricula under the Smith-Hughes Act reinforced the concentration of young women in those jobs within the pink-collar ghetto. *(See also: Coeducation; Home Economics; Smith-Lever Act)*

—Angela M. Howard

Smith-Lever Act of 1914

The Smith-Lever Act of 1914 provided federal financing of home economics curricula in the coeducational state colleges and universities that had been established as land grant institutions under the Morrill Land-Grant Act of 1862. This act reflected a twentieth-century trend in women's education in both public and private institutions to accommodate the curriculum to women's domestic role. The specialized field of home economics was intended to prepare the young middle-class woman for her "professionalized" role of wife and mother, which implied that women were not in colleges or universities to pursue nontraditional careers as they had been encouraged to do during the last decades of the nineteenth century and into the Progressive Era. *(See also: Coeducation; Education; Home Economics; Morrill Land-Grant Act)*

—Angela M. Howard

Further Reading

U.S. Congress. *Joint Resolution to Recognize the Seventy-Fifth Anniversary of the Smith-Lever Act of May 8, 1914 and Its Role in Establishing Our Nation's System of State Cooperative Extension Services.* 101st Cong., 1st sess., 1989.

Snow, Helen Foster (1907–1997)

Helen Foster Snow was an author, a journalist, and a certified genealogist. She was also an instrumental figure within the Chinese industrial cooperatives. Often writing under the name of Nym Wales, many of her works, such as *Inside Red China* (1939), *Red Dust* (1952), and *The Chinese Labor Movement* (1945), are firsthand accounts of the people and political climate that she met and experienced while living in China from 1931 to 1940.

After passing the foreign service exam, she went to China in August of 1931, intending to stay for only one year. Her plans included working, traveling, and writing; however, shortly after arriving, she met and married Edgar Snow, an American foreign correspondent and journalist. They remained in China to write about its current political situation, which included the developing Communist Party.

In 1937, Snow spent four months in the then Communist capital of Yenan as one of the few non-Chinese to enter this city. Her interviews of the Communist members and leaders helped both China and the outside world better understand the backgrounds and goals of these people. Although she was not a Communist, she believed that a socialist form of government was the best way to bring China into the modern world. Snow helped modernize and strengthen China by working with the Chinese industrial cooperatives. In 1937, she conceptualized setting up industrial cooperatives to bring both democracy and industrialization to China. She worked with Edgar Snow, Rewi Alley, Ida Pruitt, and many others to organize and implement this nonpartisan venture. The cooperatives were shut down in 1951.

After leaving China, Snow moved to Connecticut to continue writing. Shortly after her divorce in 1949, she started a career as a certified genealogist. In 1981, Snow, Rewi Alley, and Liu Guangmien were key people in restoring the American Committee for Industrial Cooperatives.

Snow's writings brought a better understanding of the complexity and passion of China during the 1930s, and her work with Chinese industrial cooperatives has been a testimony to her dedication. *(See also: Journalism)*

—Michelle Maack Friederichs

Further Reading

Indusco Inc. Files. Box 31. Snow, Helen Foster (Nym Wales), 1938–1947. Rare Book and Manuscript Library. Columbia University, New York.
Nym Wales Collection. Hoover Institution. Stanford University, Stanford, California.
Snow, Helen Foster [Nym Wales, pseud.]. *The Chinese Labor Movement.* 1945. Reprint, Freeport, NY: Books for Libraries Press, 1970.
——— [Nym Wales, pseud.]. *Inside Red China.* 1939. Reprint, New York: Da Capo, 1979.
———. *My China Years.* New York: William Morrow, 1984.
———. *New York Times Oral History Program.* Columbia University Oral History Collection Part IV, no. 187, 1977. Reprint, Sanford, NC: Microfilming Corporation of America, 1979.

———— [Nym Wales, pseud.]. *Red Dust*. Stanford, CA: Stanford University Press, 1952.

ᵔ Soap Operas

Soap operas are a form of popular entertainment, traditionally associated with women audiences (85-90 percent) and domestic themes of love and family, with roots in serialized radio drama but now primarily a daytime television phenomenon. They were called "soap operas" because the programs were frequently sponsored or owned by detergent manufacturers. Their origins are found in serialized stories of literary journals, in romances of the nineteenth century, in novels of the eighteenth century, and even in popular drama of the late Middle Ages and the Renaissance.

Soap opera story lines are never ending, thus differentiating daytime "soaps" such as *All My Children, Guiding Light, The Young and the Restless, General Hospital, As the World Turns,* and *Days of Our Lives* from nightime or prime-time dramatic series of the 1980s and 1990s such as *Dallas, Knots Landing, L.A. Law,* and *ER,* all of which presented self-contained narrative episodes each week while "continuing" portions of the plot and character interrelationships. The themes of daytime soap operas have, in recent years, included more violence, exotic travel, and politics, but the stories still center on the domestic and the intimate: romantic love, marriage (yearned for, planned, begun, failed, regretted, and missed), the family (immediate and extended), friendship, companionship, business associations, and the related social issues with attendant values, choices, commitments, and concerns of the day.

Aside from developing strong personalities, creating almost allegorical heroines and villains, and providing viewers with fantasy, escapism, and surrogate love, soaps also educate by giving practical knowledge of the day on diseases such as breast cancer, AIDS, alcohol/drug addictions and mental illness, and social concerns such as homophobia, divorce, domestic violence, rape, fertility technology, adoption, and abortion. This didacticism links them with the older tradition of popular culture. The genre has been criticized for easy solutions to difficult problems; some criticism is warranted, yet soaps treat many social issues in greater depth than other forms of pop culture, and several achieve poignant and sophisticated dramatic scenes. Also criticized for prolonging plots, soaps, on the contrary, reveal the density and complexity of domestic and moral issues and relationships by showing numerous points of view and by involving the viewer in the "psychological time" as well as "chronological time" of the crisis or character. A once largely female audience now includes men; a growing audience in recent years is that of college students and teenagers, which has caused substantial alterations of story lines and characters. *(See also: Popular Culture; Television)*

—**Travis DuPriest**

Further Reading

Allen, Robert C. *Speaking of Soap Operas.* Chapel Hill: University of North Carolina Press, 1985.

Buckman, Peter. *All for Love.* Salem, NH: Salem House, 1985.

Cassata, Mary, and Thomas Skill. *Life on Daytime Television: Tuning-in American Serial Drama.* Norwood, NJ: Ablex, 1983.

Edmondson, Madeleine, and David Rounds. *The Soaps: Daytime Serials of Radio and T.V.* New York: Stein & Day, 1973.

Modleski, Tania. *Loving with a Vengeance.* Hamden, CT: Archon, 1982.

Mumford, Laura Stempel. *Love and Ideology in the Afternoon: Soap Opera, Women, and Television Genre.* Bloomington: University of Indiana Press, 1995.

Schemering, Christopher. *Guiding Light: A 50th Anniversary Celebration.* New York: Ballantine, 1986.

————. *The Soap Opera Encyclopedia.* New York: Ballantine, 1985.

ᵔ Social Feminism

Social feminism refers to the activities and goals of the New Woman of the Progressive Era. Distinctive because of its emphasis on social justice and social reform, social feminism dates from the late-nineteenth-century settlement house movement—in which educated young people worked for social reform among the urban poor—and the rise during the early twentieth century of women's groups such as the Association of Collegiate Alumnae, the General Federation of Women's Clubs, the Woman's Christian Temperance Union, the National American Woman Suffrage Association, the National Consumers' League, and the National Women's Trade Union League.

The women who led and worked within these groups were predominately educated and middle to upper class and were capable of deploying considerable influence, even in those areas where women had no legitimate access to actual economic or political power. Using a cooperative ethic and motivated by a sense of mission, social feminists were dedicated to social action and supported the vote for women as a means of advancing their social reform efforts. As was true of the previous generations' domestic feminism, the approach of social feminism created a framework for women's participation in the public sphere that neither assumed nor allowed for women's full emancipation. The benevolent enterprises of social feminism offered a sense of usefulness and fulfillment that accommodated the needs of social feminists without requiring a radical analysis of the "woman question."

Social feminism waned during the New Deal and World War II eras; during the civil rights and New Left period, a resurgence of that urge so characteristic of educated middle-class women to be active and useful in achieving social justice spawned the leadership of both the radical women's liberation movement and the more mainstream modern women's movement of the 1960s and 1970s. *(See also: Domestic Feminism; Feminism; Progressive Era; Socialist Feminism)*

—**Angela M. Howard**

Further Reading

Cott, Nancy F. "What's in a Name? The Limits of Social Feminism; or Expanding the Vocabulary of Women's History," *Journal of American History* 76 (December 1989): 809-29.

O'Neill, William L. *Everyone Was Brave: A History of Feminism in America.* New York: Quadrangle, 1969, 1971.

✿ Social Housekeeping

Social housekeeping referred to the immigrant working-class and "native" educated middle-class reformers who took the traditional domestic values of woman's sphere into their community as necessary to fulfill their social and economic responsibility to minister to the needs of families within urban industrial areas at the end of the nineteenth century. As part of the Progressive Era, the social housekeepers made significant contributions as individuals and in women's groups to the definition and realization of progressive goals as well as to the establishment of social work as a profession. The settlement house movement, the woman's club movement, the political and economic reforms associated with the Progressive Era, and the early-twentieth-century peace movement were all aspects of social housekeeping that legitimized women's participation within the public sphere.

Although these reform movements occurred beyond the domestic sphere, social housekeepers applied the tactic and goals of both domestic feminism (to justify these dutiful women's entrance into these movements) and of social feminism (to alter political and economic policies and practices to achieve social justice). The influence of the generation of social housekeepers and their social feminism survived the political fundamentalism and unfettered business economics that characterized the conservative reactionism of the 1920s to resurface in the 1930s and again after the 1950s. Social housekeeping embodied the reform-minded New Woman of the twentieth century and established women's place beyond the home without redefining the concept of womanhood as centered within women's maternal and nurturing role in the family. *(See also: Domestic Feminism; Pacifism and the Peace Movement; Progressive Era; Settlement House Movement; Social Feminism; Social Welfare; Social Work)*

—**Angela M. Howard**

Further Reading

O'Neill, William L. *Everyone Was Brave: A History of Feminism in America.* New York: Quadrangle, 1969, 1971.

✿ Socialism

Socialism is a doctrine that particularly focuses on the condition of the working class and the arrangement of production in the modern world. Initially, in the early nineteenth century, socialists came from all parts of the political spectrum and took the name "socialist" because of a concern for society and social questions in an age of economic transformation. By the twentieth century, however, Marxian ideas definitively shaped socialist beliefs.

Outraged at the injustice of early industrialization, German-born Karl Marx (1818–1883) developed theories about the conflictual nature of historical processes and the class-based nature of society that depended on one's relationship to productive organization or "mode of production." Conflicts arising between master and slave, lord and serf, bourgeoisie and proletariat drove economic arrangements to newer forms such as feudalism, capitalism, and finally socialism, respectively. Under socialism, the theory ran, economic distinctions would disappear as society came to rest on the common ownership of the means of production—that is, on all the tools, factories, land, and machines on which society depended for sustenance.

In addition, gender inequality would disappear along with such private ownership. Marx's collaborator, Friedrich Engels (1820–1895), presented a detailed socialist analysis of the subjection of women in *Origin of the Family, Private Property, and the State* (1884). In it, he postulated that women's oppression stemmed from the need to ensure the legitimacy of heirs to property and thus to power. The minute private property disappeared, so would the "woman question." The secondary nature of gender posited by socialist theory and defended strongly by socialist leaders made specific attention to women's issues a vexing question. Sexual emancipation, suffrage, separate women's organizations, the struggle for equal wages, the division of labor in the household—all of these were hotly debated, routinely dismissed as trivial, or deliberately ignored. Moreover, socialist leaders sometimes saw little use in recruiting women to the cause in the first place.

Nonetheless, women joined the socialist movement late in the nineteenth century because of the promised end to social as well as gender injustice. While many socialist leaders hardly welcomed women to the cause, others propounded ideas of equality in work and an end to domestic drudgery. At the same time, women found socialist activities a way of maintaining ethnic traditions and developing networks in the urban environment. There developed from these interests and the interest in economic justice an elite group of activist women around the turn of the century and later, among them Kate Richards O'Hare, Ida Crouch Hazlett, Caroline Lowe, and Rose Pastor Stokes, to name a few. Many of them, however, found themselves conflicted after the Russian Revolution posed other questions. In general, some chose to follow the Russian lead into a Communist Party heavily influenced by Moscow. Others remained socialists—attached, that is, to a Socialist Party vastly diminished in strength by the split. A series of purges of left-wing thinkers and activists after World War I and continuing through the anti-Communist hysteria of the McCarthy period in the 1950s also reduced socialist organizations to virtual impotence in political life. Soon after, however, socialist questions again appeared on the agenda, as feminists in the new women's movement of the late 1960s tried to pose again the question of gender in a socialized and socialist world.

In 1989, socialism collapsed as a political system in Eastern Europe and the Soviet Union. At this point, many U.S. women developed a completely different relationship to socialism. Academic feminists hastened to chart the rapidly declining status of women in the formerly socialist countries, while U.S. foundations sent activists to teach women how to defend their rights politically and how to thrive in the new market economy. However, many women in the former Soviet Empire rejected U.S.-style feminism as imperialistic and completely out of touch with their needs. At the end of the 1990s, the legacy of socialism was uncertain. *(See also: Socialist Feminism; Socialist Party of America)*

—**Bonnie G. Smith**

Further Reading

Barrett, Michele. *Women's Oppression Today: The Marxist-Feminist Encounter.* Rev. ed. London: Verso, 1988.

Buhle, Mari Jo. *Encyclopedia of the American Left.* Urbana: University of Illinois Press, 1992.

———. *Women and American Socialism, 1870–1920.* Urbana: University of Illinois Press, 1981.

Engels, Friedrich. *Origin of the Family, Private Property, and the State in the Light of New Researches by Lewis H. Morgan* (1884). Edited by Eleanor B. Leacock. New York: International Publishers, 1972.

Funk, Nanette, and Magda Mueller, eds. *Gender Politics and Post-Communism.* New York: Routledge, 1993.

Laclau, Ernesto, and Chantal Mouffe. *Hegemony and Socialist Strategy: Towards a Radical Democratic Politics.* Translated by Winston Moore and Paul Cammack. London: Verso, 1985.

Sayers, Janet, Mary Evans, and Nanneke Redclift. *Engels Revisited: New Feminist Essays.* London: Tavistock, 1987.

⌐ Socialist Feminism

Socialist feminism can be viewed as the nexus of Marxist, radical, and psychoanalytic threads of feminist thought. It is largely the result of Marxist feminists' dissatisfaction with the essentially gender-blind character of Marxist thought. Socialist feminists challenge Marxist feminism in its inability to explain adequately why capitalism results in the public-private sphere split along gender lines. In addition, socialist feminists are reluctant to embrace the universality of patriarchy espoused by radical feminists and believe that psychoanalytic feminism fails to include a material base for women's oppression, instead pointing only to psychic factors.

Socialist feminists have developed two hypotheses regarding women's oppression. A dual-system approach, in which patriarchy and capitalism are distinct forms of social relations that intersect to oppress women, suggests that woman's status and function are jointly determined by her role in production and in reproduction. The economic aspects of patriarchy can be altered by material means, but its biosocial and ideological aspects can be altered only by non-

material means. A Marxist analysis of capitalism needs to be complemented with a feminist analysis of patriarchy, since men's desire to control women is at least as strong as capital's desire to control workers.

A unified-system approach attempts to analyze capitalism and patriarchy together through use of a singular concept. One such concept, the sexual division of labor, implies a gender-based capitalism; one can observe a decline in women's relative status as they moved from a precapitalist economy into a capitalist one. Marriage as an economic partnership was dissolved, creating a separation of public and private spheres and the marginalization of women.

Another concept used as a unifying concept in socialist feminism is that of alienation, expanded from the original Marxist meaning. Women, in special gender-specific ways, are alienated from those processes and people they need to achieve wholeness as persons. A woman is alienated from the product on which she works: her body. Women's bodies become objects for men. A woman is alienated from the product of her reproductive labor when someone decides how many children she ought to bear. Women are also alienated from the process of their reproductive labor when it is controlled through medical expertise and technology. And women are alienated from their intellectual capacities.

In attempting to find a conceptual umbrella, socialist feminists try to resolve the existing differences among the many threads of feminism. Any unifying theory, however, runs the risk of making the differences that exist among women invisible. *(See also: Radical Feminism; Sexual Division of Labor; Socialism; Women's Work: Nineteenth Century)*

—**Susan C. Turell**

Further Reading

Eisenstein, Zillah, ed. *Capitalist Patriarchy and the Case for Socialist Feminism.* New York: Monthly Review, 1979.

Hartmann, Heidi. "The Unhappy Marriage of Marxism and Feminism: Towards a More Progressive Union." In *Women and Revolution: A Discussion of the Unhappy Marriage of Marxism and Feminism,* edited by L. Sargent, 1-41. Boston: South End Press, 1981.

Jaggar, Alison M. *Feminist Politics and Human Nature.* Totowa, NJ: Rowman & Allenheld, 1983.

Mitchell, Juliet. *Women's Estate.* New York: Pantheon, 1971.

Tong, R. *Feminist Thought,* 2d ed. Boulder, CO: Westview, 1998.

⌐ Socialist Party of America

Locus of a growing national movement between 1901 and World War I, the Socialist Party of America stood for equal civil and political rights for men and women, including universal suffrage. The earlier recognition by international socialism of the exploitation of women led to the party's position, which became a factor in its ability to attract women to its banner. About 10 percent of the membership was female. Women were convention delegates, party journalists, speakers, and organizers and were more visible than in any other political party of the era. However, women lacked any real power. Furthermore, the party always subsumed the "woman question" within the so-called labor question and, in practice, assigned the former no serious priority. Consequently, women organized to build their own sector within the party.

Native-born American women who joined the Socialist Party often had prior organizational experience through the Bellamyite (nationalist clubs), Populist, or women's club movements and other activities, such as temperance or missionary work. Immigrant women, numbering as much as one-third of the membership of a few foreign-language branches of the party, were working class or intellectuals. Some women came to the party from a background in autonomous female socialist study groups. In 1908, the Woman's National Committee was established, and it prodded all locals to organize woman's committees, promoted the election of more women to party offices, issued propaganda leaflets, and sought to convert women from all areas of society to socialism. A profile of the most well-known activists suggests that they tended to be middle-class, native-born, college graduates, usually of middle age, often rural in upbringing, and from the Midwest or the West. The leading women socialists—not all of whom were involved in the woman's sector—were Kate Richards O'Hare, Mary Wood Simons, Lena Morrow Lewis, and Rose Pastor Stokes.

The woman's sector was a vibrant party mechanism, attracting new members, energizing locals, and improvising innovative organizational techniques. But some socialist women as well as men opposed its existence as irrelevant and counterproductive. In 1915, it was abolished, and within a few years, leftist factionalism virtually destroyed this national movement, while women once again played only a minor role in it. *(See also: O'Hare, Kate Richards; Socialism; Woman Question)*

—**Sally M. Miller**

Further Reading

Buhle, Mari Jo. *Women and American Socialism, 1870–1920.* Urbana: University of Illinois Press, 1981.

Miller, Sally M., ed. *Flawed Liberation: Socialism and Feminism.* Westport, CT: Greenwood, 1981.

———. "Other Socialists: Native-Born and Immigrant Women in the Socialist Party of America," *Labor History* 24 (Winter 1983): 84-102.

⟪ Social Purity Movement

The social purity movement describes a loose coalition of reformers, primarily middle-class women, who campaigned for a series of civic and moral reforms affecting family and public life after the Civil War. In their quest to rid America of vice, social purity reformers pressed for a single sexual standard, lobbied against alcohol and prostitution, and proclaimed woman's role as guardian of the home.

Reformers—a coalition of clergy, women's clubs, temperance workers, and former abolitionists—were often motivated by a blend of moral, nationalist, and feminist motives. Although all shared an opposition to prostitution and alcohol, the aims of different segments of the movement varied. Many pressed for the reformation of marriage, as reflected in critiques of male sexual excess and in the popular theme of "The White Life for Two," a slogan of the Social Purity Division of the Woman's Christian Temperance Union. Other reformers aided unwed mothers and prostitutes or advocated voluntary motherhood. Some promoted sex education and public discussions of sex and sexual politics, while others advocated censorship.

The movement's stance on women's rights was similarly complex and often contradictory, as social purity reformers drew simultaneously on Victorian notions of women's separate sphere and on suffrage rhetoric. By proclaiming their moral authority in the public realm, reformers both elaborated traditional ideas about women's place and extended that sphere by advocating political power for women. Reformers split over the issue of women's political rights, with some advocating suffrage and others opposing it or promoting a limited suffrage for women. Their concern for women unlike themselves varied: Some reformers fought against domestic violence and helped minority women to leave prostitution, but others scapegoated African Americans, Jews, and recent immigrants in their crusades against vice.

The social purity movement met with some national success, including Prohibition (1920–1933) and the Mann Act (1910). Many cities and states rejected regulated prostitution and passed legislation raising the age of consent for girls. Although the movement suffered from internal contradictions and uneasy coalitions, many of its themes shaped twentieth-century middle-class ideologies of marriage and sexuality, and its concerns remained at the forefront of women's reform through the Progressive Era. *(See also: Age of Consent; Comstock Law; Moral Reform; Obscenity; Prostitution)*

—**Miriam Reumann**

Further Reading

D'Emilio, John, and Estelle Freedman. *Intimate Matters: A History of Sexuality in America,* 2d ed. Chicago: University of Chicago Press, 1997.

Gilfoyle, Timothy. *City of Eros: New York City, Prostitution, and the Commercialization of Sex.* New York: Norton, 1992.

Pivar, David J. *Purity Crusade: Sexual Morality and Social Control, 1860–1900.* Westport, CT: Greenwood, 1973.

Rosen, Ruth. *The Lost Sisterhood: Prostitution in America, 1900–1918.* Baltimore: Johns Hopkins University Press, 1982.

Smith-Rosenberg, Carroll. *Disorderly Conduct: Visions of Gender in Victorian America.* New York: Oxford University Press, 1985.

Social Security Act of 1935

The New Deal's legislative response to the economic devastation wrought on the middle and working classes by the Great Depression, the Social Security Act provided federal unemployment and old-age insurance, as well as "relief," or social welfare, for dependent women and children that was unprecedented in its scope. This was not the first form of social insurance to be introduced to the American public. An earlier attempt that occurred in 1908 provided workmen's compensation for federal employees; also, a few states' statutes and workmen's compensation laws dated from the Progressive Era.

Among the many factors involved in the creation of the Social Security Act, there were two overriding forces. First, this act represented a belated and begrudging acknowledgment that the national economy had changed from one characterized by the Jeffersonian agricultural self-sufficiency of the nineteenth century to one of urban interdependence on the wage and market system in the twentieth. Second, the social welfare aspects of this legislation reflected the presence of influential women in high political positions during Franklin Roosevelt's New Deal. Among these women, many of whom were social feminists, an agenda for reform emerged. They developed a network that served as a major policy-influencing group determined to achieve social reform programs of vital concern to women as homemakers and as paid workers. Maternal and child welfare, health insurance, mothers' pensions, minimum wage and maximum-hour reforms were priorities for women in the network throughout their political lives because these reforms eliminated the necessity for special protective legislation for women.

The Social Security Act of 1935 established retirement pensions for workers aged sixty-five or older, including women, and provided benefits to wives, mothers, and children. The inclusion of maternal and child welfare with mothers' pensions in this bill marked the final outcome of the social feminists' struggle to protect women in the home, which dated back to the 1920s, and of the thirty-year fight for governmental protection of the basic welfare rights of both the individual and the family.

In general, this act worked to preserve the patriarchal gender system of the "traditional family." In the 1970s, issues of sex equity within the Social Security system were raised by feminists with varying degrees of success. Ultimately, homemakers' rights were incorporated into modifications to the Social Security Act that protected the homemaker-wife's share of the pension of the employed spouse in case of divorce.

Initially, the greatest impact of the Social Security Act appeared to be in the decreasing number of women workers over the age of sixty-five. Of secondary impact was the support of dependent widows and children, especially in education benefits for the latter. However, the number of single and married working women in predominantly "women's jobs" as well as in nontraditional occupations has increased throughout the second half of the twentieth century, thus rendering crucial the retirement benefits for women workers. Cutbacks in Social Security benefits, the major source of support for elderly women, during the 1980s further accelerated the feminization of poverty, since women's longevity continued to exceed that of men's.

Because of the rising life expectancy of American workers (from 61 in 1935 to 76 today), benefits paid out by Social Security are expected to exceed payroll taxes collected by the system by 2012. A wide variety of approaches to the problem are being considered, ranging from tax reform to privatization to raising the age for receiving Social Security benefits. Yet two-thirds of Social Security recipients count on the system for at least half their income, so it seems likely that some form of Social Security will continue as an important program during the 21st century. (See also: New Deal; Protective Legislation; Social Feminism)

—Arlie Roy Bice III

Further Reading

Burkhauser, Richard, and Karen Holden. *A Challenge to Social Security: The Changing Roles of Women and Men in American Society.* San Diego, CA: Academic Press, 1982.

Burns, Eveline M. *The American Social Security System.* Dallas, TX: Houghton Mifflin, 1949.

Cohen, Wilbur, and William Haber. *Readings in Social Security.* New York: Prentice Hall, 1948.

Ware, Susan. *American Women in the Thirties: Holding Their Own.* Boston: Twayne, 1982.

Witte, Edwin E. *Development of the Social Security Act.* Madison: University of Wisconsin Press, 1962.

Social Work

Social work is a twentieth-century service profession found in most countries of the world today. Social workers are concerned with the interactions between people and social institutions that affect their abilities to accomplish life tasks, realize their personal aspirations, and alleviate distress. Social work has three principal purposes: (a) to enhance personal problem-solving, coping, and developmental capacities; (b) to promote effective and humane operation of service delivery systems; and (c) to link people with resources, services, and opportunities.

Traditionally, social work activities have been broadly divided into casework, group work, and community organization. In recent decades, however, social workers have branched out into a broad range of intervention strategies targeted at individuals, groups, organizations, communities, and societies.

Social work had its origins in nineteenth-century voluntary activities and offered important career opportunities for early cohorts of women graduating from college. Contemporary social service continues to be done by a mixture of those with specialized training, certification, and licensure who call themselves social workers and those without such education or credentials. An estimated 2,727,000 workers were employed in social services jobs in the United States in 1992, the majority of them lacking formal training and occupying paraprofessional positions (U.S. Bureau of the Census 409). Approximately one in six social service positions was held by a professional social worker. Of the 427,697 social workers in the United States in 1990, 61 percent (252,930) were employed in service industries, 38 percent (164,732) were employed in government, and less than 2 percent (10,000) were engaged in private practice (Ginsberg 188).

In the 1970s, social work education expanded to embrace the baccalaureate degree (B.S.W.), along with the more traditional graduate (M.S.W.) and doctoral (Ph.D. and D.S.W) degrees. By 1990, there were nearly 500 B.S.W. programs and 100 M.S.W. programs in the United States, graduating approximately 17,000 B.S.W.s and 10,000 M.S.W.s (and fewer than 300 doctorates) each year. Social work education continues to attract primarily women students, with the percentage declining at each level. In 1995, for example, 89.7 percent of B.S.W. graduates were women, together with 78.5 percent of M.S.W. graduates, and 58.5 percent of Ph.D. graduates (Ginsberg 189, 194).

Social service workers became increasingly self-conscious, reflective, and critical in the period after the Civil War, under the influence of "scientific charity." Mary Richmond, Jane Addams, and other early professional leaders in social work are pivotal figures in the transition from the "moral certainties" of nineteenth-century friendly visiting to the deliberate and reasoned investigations advocated by professional social workers.

Beginning in the 1870s, the National Conference of Charities and Corrections met annually and published volumes of papers on issues of current interest. Initially a predominantly male gathering, this conference and its changing attendance at annual meetings offer testimony to the growing importance and expanding opportunities for women in the emerging social service field.

Efforts to gain understanding of the causes of poverty was a major dynamic of early social work efforts and gave rise to emphasis on the individual in his or her social environment. The emphasis on individual growth and development, in turn, led to the pervasive influence of Freudian psychology roughly during the half century after 1920. The social work profession recovered earlier interests in poverty, community, research, and policy in the 1960s and experienced substantial growth during the 1970s.

The "social work profession" as a single entity really came together only in 1955 with the creation of the National Association of Social Workers (NASW) from seven separate constituency groups for hospital, group, psychiatric, and other social workers. In 1995, the NASW had 155,000 members, the majority of whom were women.

One of the continuing characteristics of social work as a "women's profession" is that although eight of ten social work professionals today are women, the majority of leadership positions in education and organizations where social work is practiced continue to go to men. *(See also: Addams, Jane; Benevolence; Kelley, Florence; Perkins, Frances; Satir, Virginia; Settlement House Movement; Wald, Lillian)*

—**Roger A. Lohmann**

Further Reading

Ginsberg, L. *The Social Work Almanac.* Silver Spring, MD: National Association of Social Workers, 1992.

U.S. Bureau of the Census. *Statistical Abstract of the United States: 1992.* Washington, DC: Government Printing Office, 1992.

✌ Society of Friends

The Society of Friends, or Quakers, is a religious group founded in England by George Fox in 1652 that persisted into the twentieth century. From the beginning, women were considered equal in the eyes of the church, and Fox's wife, Margaret Fell, championed female ministries. Quakers believed in the Divine Light, or God in everyone, and men and women were therefore spiritually equal since there was nothing to prevent women from experiencing this spiritual rebirth. The Quakers believed in a lay ministry, and both men and women served as lay ministers.

When William Penn brought Quaker beliefs to Pennsylvania in 1681-82, a system of government was set up very much like the governments of other colonies and of England, and equality for women was not reflected in this government. However, the religious organization was different from other Protestant sects. Women's meetings were a very important part of church governance. These meetings were about business, and through them, Quaker women addressed their responsibilities for marriage, family matters, and helping the poor. Women who wanted to marry first went to a women's meeting, and the couple were interviewed to make sure they were both Quakers and would raise their family in the society. As in other families of the seventeenth century, the man was seen as the head of the household, but men and women both had to submit to the discipline of the church. If there was trouble in a marriage, a women's meeting might try to resolve the problem.

In the eighteenth and nineteenth centuries, Quaker women remained active. They continued to serve as lay ministers and traveled more to visit Friends' groups in the United States and England. However, there is not much evidence that there were many changes in women's status in secular areas of their lives. Even though many Quaker women maintained both religious and secular responsibilities, the nineteenth century had a high proportion of Quaker women reformers active in the abolitionist and feminist movements. There may have been several reasons for this. Leadership roles in the religious group prepared such women to speak in public and made it more comfortable for them to assume the same roles in other areas of their lives. Lucretia Mott, a well-known Quaker, formed an abolitionist group for women and was one of four Quaker women to convene the women's rights conference at Seneca Falls, New York, in 1848. Mott found different reasons for equality of women than some of her contemporaries. She was not so much interested in the need for suffrage but worked for a new image of women as moral, responsible people. Mott was probably more of an activist than the typical Quaker woman, but she was not unique in carrying her religious beliefs into the other parts of her life. *(See also: Christianity; Mott, Lucretia Coffin; Public Speakers: Nineteenth Century; Religion)*

—**Judith Pryor**

Further Reading

Bacon, Margaret. *Mothers of Feminism: The Story of Quaker Women in America.* New York: Harper, 1986.

Cadbury, Henry J. "George Fox and Women's Liberation," *The Friends' Quarterly* 19 (October 1974): 370-76.

Calvo, Janis. "Quaker Women Ministers in Nineteenth-Century America," *Quaker History* 63 (1974): 75-93.

Dunn, Mary Maples. "Women of Light." In *Women of America: A History,* edited by Carol Ruth Berkin and Mary Beth Norton, 114-33. Boston: Houghton Mifflin, 1979.

Ford, Linda. "William Penn's Views on Women: Subjects of Friendships," *Quaker History* 72 (1983): 75-102.

Greene, Dana. "Quaker Feminism: The Case of Lucretia Mott," *Pennsylvania History* 48 (1981): 143-54.

Mack, Phyllis. *Visionary Women: Ecstatic Prophecy in Seventeenth-Century England.* Berkeley: University of California Press, 1992.

～ Society of the Companions of the Holy Cross

The Society of the Companions of the Holy Cross is an international "companionship" of over seven hundred women united in the search for inner spiritual life and communal worship. These women share a deep interest in literature and the arts as forms of spiritual experience and a dedication to social service and social justice. Not a monastic order, the society consists of Episcopalian laywomen living in the world "under a Rule of intercessory prayer, simplicity of life, thanksgiving, and special concern for Christian unity, mission, and social justice."

The society was founded in 1884 by Emily Malbone Morgan, a pioneer in social work among women factory workers, as a means of providing Adelyn Howard, her childhood friend and an invalid of uncommon grace and fortitude, with the support of community and the activity of praying for others. The membership has included women of varying backgrounds, occupations, and races. Although many have been active in the settlement house and labor movements, in civil rights, suffrage campaigns, and similar activities, the degree to which the society should take public stands on social issues has often been a matter of debate. Membership is determined not by slant of opinion but by keenness of concern. The group is autonomous and self-governing and maintains Adelynrood, a conference center and retreat house, in Byfield, Massachusetts. *(See also: Christianity; Religion; Scudder, Vida Dutton)*

—**Anne O. Dzamba (Sessa)**

Further Reading

Chrisman, Miriam U. *"To Bind Together," A Brief History of the Society of the Companions of the Holy Cross.* Privately printed, 1984.

Morgan, Emily Malbone. *Letters to Her Companions.* Edited by Vida Scudder. Privately published, 1944.

～ Solomon, Hannah Greenebaum (1858–1942)

Progressive reformer and club woman Hannah Solomon was best known for founding the National Council of Jewish Women (NCJW, 1893). Her parents were affluent German Jewish immigrants and founders of Chicago's influential Reform Jewish community. Solomon herself was a follower of prominent Reform rabbi Emil Hirsch. Claiming that she "consecrated" every day, Solomon supported his attempt to change Jewish Sabbath observance from Saturday to Sunday, thereby causing a destructive split within the NCJW that nearly cost her the presidency of that organization. She held the presidency from 1893 until 1905, when she was elected honorary president for life.

In the council's early years, Jewish publications recognized Solomon as spokesperson for American Jewish women and frequently published her work. Most often, she wrote of the need for a renewed Jewish womanhood, arguing that only committed Jewish mothers could raise committed Jewish children. She believed it was woman's responsibility to save Judaism from the destructive effects of increasing assimilation. The NCJW used that view to justify demands for religious education for women (training previously reserved for males) and for a voice in synagogue policy, particularly in areas concerning synagogue schools. Solomon was also known for promoting preventive social work practiced by professional social workers. She frequently cooperated with Jane Addams and in 1897 founded the council's Bureau of Personal Service, an immigrant aid organization.

Solomon (with her sister Henriette) also gained fame as the first Jew to join the prestigious Chicago Women's Club (in 1877). Through that club, Solomon was instrumental in establishing Cook County's juvenile court (1899) and the Illinois Industrial School for Girls (1905). She was also a founding member of the Illinois Federation of Women's Clubs (1905) and treasurer of the Council of Women of the United States (1899), an organization she later represented

Figure 57. Hannah Solomon

Hannah Solomon (left) is shown congratulating Mrs. Maurice Goldman of San Francisco after the latter was elected in 1940 to a second term as president of the National Council of Jewish Women. The Council, which Solomon founded in 1893, promotes the goals of American Jewish women. Used by permission of UPI/Corbis-Bettmann.

at the 1904 International Council of Women in Berlin, where she acted as translator for the other U.S. representatives, Susan B. Anthony and May Wright Sewall. Solomon dubbed herself "a confirmed woman's rights-er" and supported nonmilitant efforts to win suffrage.

Despite her commitment to social reform work, Solomon's main allegiance was to her family. She frequently cautioned other club women not to let club activities lead to neglect of home duties. A domestic feminist, she glorified mothers as the shapers of future generations and motherhood as the most effective tool for societal change. She argued that social work was an extension of motherhood and based her demands for women's rights on this view. *(See also: Domestic Feminism; Jewish Women)*

—**Faith Rogow**

Further Reading

NCJW: *Proceedings of the First Convention.* Philadelphia: Jewish Publication Society, 1897. (Also see proceedings for each subsequent Triennial Convention)

Papers of the Jewish Women's Congress—1893. Philadelphia: Jewish Publication Society, 1894.

Solomon, Hannah Greenebaum. *Fabric of My Life: The Story of a Social Pioneer.* 1946. Reprint, New York: Bloch, 1974.

———. *A Sheaf of Leaves.* Chicago: Privately printed, 1911.

～ Sonneschein, Rosa Fassel
(1847–1932)

Rosa Sonneschein, writer, editor, publisher, feminist, and Zionist, was best known for the paper she wrote for, edited, and published from 1895–1899, *The American Jewess*. Born in Moravia, she was the youngest and most adored child of a prominent rabbi who was a Talmudic master and moderate reformer. She immigrated to the United States with her husband, Solomon Sonneschein, a radical Reform rabbi, and in 1869 moved to St. Louis.

For twenty years, Sonneschein participated in the Jewish community, Jewish-Christian relations, and club circles. She was active in the Germania Club and Temple Israel's Ladies' Aid Society and was a founder of The Pioneers, a Jewish women's literary club, and Temple Israel's Choral Society. She also wrote for publications such as the *Jews' Annual* (1884) and the *Jewish Messenger* and covered various world fairs for the German- and English-language press in St. Louis.

After an acrimonious marriage, the Sonnescheins divorced in 1893. Partially to support herself, she founded *American Jewess* in Chicago in 1895 after declaring the need for a magazine for Jewish women at the 1893 World's Fair. Through the magazine, Sonneschein advocated women's participation in Jewish public life, woman suffrage, and women's right to education and work. Progressive in the Jewish community, she was not a radical in terms of the wider woman's rights movement. *American Jewess* reflects the position of those who struggled to reconcile their version of woman's accepted place in Judaism and American society with the need for change.

Sonneschein was one of the first prominent Reform Jews to advocate Theodor Herzl's brand of political Zionism. In an 1896 article, she suggested that the National Council of Jewish Women take up Zionism as its central focus (members rejected her suggestion). She attended the First and Second Zionist Congresses in 1897 and 1898. She covered the first congress for *American Jewess*, publishing a speech by Herzl's colleague, Max Nordau.

The cause of *American Jewess*'s demise in 1899 has not been adequately explained. Financial difficulties, backlash against her criticisms, and Sonneschein's growing deafness probably all played some part. Little is known about her life after 1899. Although she occasionally wrote a piece for a local paper, her public involvement virtually ceased. Until 1916, she lived in Chicago and St. Louis, often with her daughter's family. From that time until her death in 1932, she lived alone in St. Louis. *(See also: American Jewess; Jewish Women; National Council of Jewish Women)*

—**Jane H. Rothstein**

Further Reading

American Jewess 1-9 (April 1895–August 1899).

Kraut, Benny. "A Unitarian Rabbi? The Case of Solomon H. Sonneschein." In *Jewish Apostasy in the Modern World*, edited by Todd M. Endelman, 272-303. New York: Holmes & Meier, 1987.

Loth, David. "The American Jewess," *Midstream* 31 (1985): 43-46.

———. "Notes on the Marital Discord of Solomon and Rosa Sonneschein." Small Collections, American Jewish Archives. Cincinnati, OH.

———. "Supplementary Memoir of the Sonnescheins." Small Collections, American Jewish Archives. Cincinnati, OH.

Porter, Jack Nusan. "Rosa Sonnenschein [sic] and *The American Jewess:* The First Independent English Language Jewish Women's Journal in the United States," *American Jewish History* 67 (September 1978): 57-63.

———. "Rosa Sonneschein and *The American Jewess* Revisited: New Historical Information on an Early American Zionist and Jewish Feminist," *American Jewish Archives* 32 (1980): 125-31.

Sonneschein, Solomon H. Letterbooks 1882–1893. Solomon H. Sonneschein Papers. Collection #360, American Jewish Archives. Cincinnati, OH.

⮂ Sontag, Susan (b. 1933)

Susan Sontag is a writer who has explored a dazzling range of genres and interests since emerging in the 1960s as one of the United States's most prominent public intellectuals. Following childhood in Arizona and California, Sontag graduated from the University of Chicago at the age of 18 and earned master's degrees in both English and philosophy at Harvard before continuing graduate studies at Oxford and at the Sorbonne. In the 1960s, Sontag's articles and reviews began to appear in elite journals such as *Partisan Review* and *The New York Review of Books.* Her early positions on aesthetics are staked out in *Against Interpretation* (1966): The famous "Notes on Camp" espouses "a good taste of bad taste," and "On Style" rejects overly intellectualized meaning in favor of a direct appreciation of sensory beauty. In *Styles of Radical Will* (1969), Sontag continues to explore relations between aesthetics and ethics and to argue that sensibilities determine moral choices.

Sontag expresses and develops these stances in a variety of fields and genres. A film director in Sweden and Israel, she has written criticism of cinema and photography (*On Photography,* 1977) that again explores the power of art to influence morality and public life. Following her recovery from breast cancer, Sontag in *Illness as Metaphor* (1978) exposed Western culture's equations of morality and health, a critique she controversially updated in 1989 with *AIDS and Its Metaphors.* Sontag has remained in the forefront of intellectual discourse also by promoting European artists and writers such as Walter Benjamin in *Under the Sign of Saturn* (1980) and by editing *The [Roland] Barthes Reader* (1982). In yet another dimension to her polymath career, Sontag has authored a considerable body of fiction, from experimental novels (*The Benefactor,* 1963, and *Death Kit,* 1967) and short stories (*I, etcetera,* 1978) to *The Volcano Lover: A Romance* (1992), a historical novel of ideas that revisits the eighteenth-century affair between Lady Hamilton and Lord

Nelson. Her most recent novel, *In America: A Novel* (2000), is the story of a Polish diva who abandons the stage and attempts to start a utopian community in California.

Sontag's status as an American woman intellectual is unchallenged, yet she stands somewhat apart from mainstream feminism. Her fiction is narrated by male characters; most of her criticism concerns male artists and writers; indeed, she entered the public stage in advance of the feminist revolution. In "The Third World of Women" (*Partisan Review,* 1973), however, Sontag, like Charlotte Perkins Gilman earlier in the century, attacks "the mystique of 'nature'" and the sexist division of "home" and "the world"; advocating a socialistic women's movement that institutionalizes child care, she also endorses subversive acts like whistling at men and "collecting pledges to renounce alimony and giggling."

As an important essayist, critic, filmmaker, director, playwright, and political activist, Sontag has contributed much to social, political, and cultural changes since the 1960s. During the past few decades, she has received numerous foundation grants and fellowships to support her work. *(See also: Photography; Women Writers)*

—Craig White

Further Reading
Hardwick, Elizabeth, ed. *A Susan Sontag Reader.* New York: Farrar, Straus & Giroux, 1982.

Kimball, Roger. "The New Sensibility," *New Criterion* 16 (February 1998): 5-7.

Nelson, Cary. "Soliciting Self-Knowledge: The Rhetoric of Susan Sontag's Criticism," *Critical Inquiry* 6 (Summer 1980): 707-26.

Poague, Leland. *Conversations with Susan Sontag.* Jackson: University of Mississippi Press, 1995.

Schor, Esther H. "Susan Sontag." In *Modern American Women Writers,* edited by Elaine Showalter, 471-84. New York: Scribner, 1991.

⮂ Southern Baptist Woman's Missionary Society

In 1845, the Southern Baptist Convention organized in the First Baptist Church, Augusta, Georgia. The convention established two mission boards—the Foreign Mission Board with headquarters in Richmond, Virginia, and the Domestic Mission Board with headquarters in Marion, Alabama. The commissioning and sending of early missionaries to China by the Foreign Mission Board led to female prayer support groups in the local churches. When Ann Baker Graves's son became a missionary to China in 1855, Ann began a prayer group, Female Missionary Prayer Meeting, to pray for his ministry.

In 1868, the first general meeting of women, led by Ann Graves, gathered at the Southern Baptist Convention in Baltimore, Maryland, to pledge support to missions. In 1871, the women formed the Woman's Mission to Woman, the first federation of missionary organizations among Southern Baptist women.

By 1874, H. A. Tupper, corresponding secretary of the Foreign Mission Board, recommended the appointment of a central committee of Baptist Women in each state. Within three years, similar central committees were appointed by I. T. Tichenor, secretary of the Home Mission Board (formerly the Domestic Mission Board).

Baptist women met once again in 1884 prior to the Southern Baptist Convention in Waco, Texas. There, the secretaries of the Central Committees of Baptist Women resolved that the societies represented would make the meeting an annual event at each Southern Baptist Convention. By 1888, three women from each state had been appointed as delegates to the convention. The next step involved organizing as an entity. Many women had been advised by their respective state conventions not to vote in favor of organization; therefore, only ten states voted to organize the "Executive Committee of Woman's Missionary Societies (auxiliary to the Southern Baptist Convention)," later known as Woman's Missionary Union. Miss M. E. McIntosh of South Carolina was elected the first president, and Baltimore, Maryland, was named headquarters for the Executive Committee.

In 1889, at the first annual meeting of the Executive Committee, the organizational structure for graded missionary organizations was adopted. The organizations that were to make up the Woman's Missionary Union included Woman's Missionary Society, Young Woman's Auxiliary, Girls' Auxiliary, Sunbeam Band, and the Order of Royal Ambassadors. In 1957, the Order of Royal Ambassadors, the organization for boys, was transferred to the Brotherhood, the Baptist men's organization. In 1970, the age-level organizations were reorganized. The new age-level organizations were Baptist Women for women thirty-five years and up, Baptist Young Women for women eighteen to thirty-five; Acteens for girls seventh grade through twelfth grade, Girls in Action for girls first grade through sixth grade, and Mission Friends for preschool-age children. In October 1995, another reorganization took place in the age-level groups. The new organizations are Women on Mission, Acteens, Girls in Action, and Mission Friends.

Woman's Missionary Union supports mission efforts through offerings and prayer emphases. The union sponsors two seasons of prayer during the year. The Foreign Mission season of prayer is held annually in December, concluding with the Lottie Moon Christmas offering for Foreign Missions. The Home Mission season of prayer is held annually in March, culminating with the Annie Armstrong Home Missions offering. The Woman's Missionary Union offers prayer support and financial support for over 4,913 home missionaries and 4,078 foreign missionaries. The headquarters are now in Birmingham, Alabama. *(See also: Benevolence; Christianity; Religion)*

—**Paula Williams Webber**

Further Reading

Allen, Catherine B. *A Century to Celebrate: History of Woman's Missionary Union.* Birmingham, AL: Woman's Missionary Union, 1987.
Durham, Jacqualine. *And Some Had Dreams: A History of WMU.* Birmingham, AL: Woman's Missionary Union, 1987.
Hunt, Alma. *Woman's Missionary Union.* Birmingham, AL: Woman's Missionary Union, 1964.

∿ Southern Christian Leadership Conference (SCLC)

The Southern Christian Leadership Conference (SCLC) was organized in January 1957 in Atlanta in the wake of the Montgomery, Alabama, bus boycott, which began when Rosa Parks, a black woman, was arrested for refusing to go to the back of the bus, where blacks in the South were expected to sit. The SCLC grew in influence under the leadership of Martin Luther King, Jr., who served as its head until his assassination in 1968. Under King, the SCLC played an important role in major civil rights events such as the March on Washington (1963) and the antisegregation campaigns in Birmingham and Selma, Alabama, and Albany, Georgia. The southern black Baptist ministers in the SCLC dominated the leadership, but Ella Baker, Dorothy Cotton, Diane Nash, Septima Clark, and Jane Stembridge were members of the executive staff. Baker is credited with a major role in organizing the 1960 conference of student activists in Raleigh, North Carolina, that became known as the Student Non-Violent Coordinating Committee (SNCC). *(See also: Civil Rights; King, Coretta Scott; New Left; Parks, Rosa)*

—**Linda Ray Pratt**

Further Reading

Branch, Taylor. *Parting the Waters: America in the King Years, 1954–65.* New York: Simon & Schuster, 1988.
———. *Pillar of Fire: American in the King Years, 1963–65.* New York: Simon & Schuster, 1997.
"Dorothy Cotton." In *My Soul Is Rested: Movement Days in the Deep South Remembered,* edited by Howell Raines, 432-34. New York: Putnam, 1977.
Evans, Sara. *Personal Politics: The Roots of Women's Liberation in the Civil Rights Movement and the New Left.* New York: Random House, 1979.
Fairclough, Adam. *To Redeem the Soul of America: The Southern Christian Leadership Conference and Martin Luther King, Jr.* Athens: University of Georgia Press, 1987.
Lyon, Danny. *Memories of the Southern Civil Rights Movement.* Chapel Hill: University of North Carolina Press, 1992.
Sellers, Cleveland, with Robert Terrell. *The River of No Return.* New York: William Morrow, 1973.

∿ Southern Lady

The Southern Lady was an ideological concept in which southern women embodied standards of moral and social conduct supportive of white racist society. Like the nineteenth-century "lady" elsewhere, the Southern Lady was the moral vessel whose piety, modesty, and wisdom were the bulwark of the family. She was the tamer of men's brute instincts, the guardian of the young, and the source of religious values in the home and community. Ideally, she was also beautiful, charming, accomplished in music and with the needle, and submissive to her male masters. In the context of slave society, the Southern Lady was placed on a pedestal as proof of the purity and piety of a society under attack for the immorality and exploitation inherent in its economic structure. The Southern Lady's image was intended to personify all that was moral and civilized in white culture, and she became the chief symbol of what southerners defended as "our way of life."

The dynamics of miscegenation in slave culture added to the cult of the lady a rigid sexual repression because the image of the "virtuous wife" was used to counter the image of the profligate husband. Thus, the ideology of the Southern Lady became an instrument whereby harsh and violent punishments were meted out to black men who were considered to have violated rules of conduct designed to protect the interests of white supremacy.

Although only a small fraction of the southern population was ever part of the elite white planter class with which the image of the Southern Lady is most associated, the ideal of conduct that she embodied was commonly shared by other classes of whites. Fiction of southern plantation life first gave the image wide popular appeal in the 1830s in both the North and South, and it continued to be popular into the twentieth century through best-sellers such as *Gone with the Wind*. Mary Boykin Chesnut's *A Diary from Dixie* (1905), covering the years from 1861 to 1865, is perhaps the most noted account of the life of a Southern Lady. Fanny Kemble's *A Residence on a Georgian Plantation*, published in 1863, was a sharply critical and iconoclastic picture of slave society that influenced antisouthern opinion during the Civil War. *(See also: Ames, Jessie Daniel; Association of Southern Women for the Prevention of Lynching; Chesnut, Mary Boykin; Cult of True Womanhood; Kemble, Fanny; Slavery; Southern Women's History)*

—**Linda Ray Pratt**

Further Reading

Bernhard, Virginia, Betty Brandon, Elizabeth Fox-Genovese, and Theda Perdue, eds. *Southern Women: Histories and Identities*. Columbia: University of Missouri Press, 1992.

Clinton, Catherine. *Plantation Mistress: Woman's World in the Old South*. New York: Pantheon, 1983.

Fox-Genovese, Elizabeth. *Within the Plantation Household: Black and White Women of the Old South*. Chapel Hill: University of North Carolina Press, 1988.

Jordan, Winthrop D. *White over Black*. Chapel Hill: University of North Carolina Press, 1968.

Scott, Anne Firor. *The Southern Lady: From Pedestal to Politics, 1830–1930*. Chicago: University of Chicago Press, 1970.

Welter, Barbara. "The Cult of True Womanhood 1820–1860," *American Quarterly* 18 (1966): 151-74.

Woodward, C. Vann, ed. *Mary Chesnut's Civil War*. New Haven, CT: Yale University Press, 1981.

Southern Women's History

Southern women's history has evolved in the past 150 years from printed paeans to the ideal of white southern womanhood to serious scholarly studies with multicultural dimensions. Southern women's history begins with the region—eleven Confederate states as well as Missouri, Kentucky, and Maryland—and includes the fact that the South before World War II was overwhelmingly rural. The institution of slavery and its aftermath, issues of race and class, strongly entrenched notions of patriarchy, defeat in the Civil War, the rise of populism, progressivism, the Great Depression, and the civil rights movement also affected the lives of southern women and constitute important subjects of study in the field of southern women's history. Scholars pursuing the history of women in the South ask several questions: What part did women take in critical events that affected the region? What role did women play in the economic and social changes that occurred? What values, behaviors, life experiences, and expectations did southern women hold? How did the existence of a multiracial and class-stratified society affect women's thoughts and actions? Southern women's history explores these and all questions related to gender within the context of the South's distinctive history.

The twentieth-century study of southern women by historians began with a group of women scholars in the late 1920s and 1930s, who examined the lives of southern women as they moved from private realms to public spaces. Among these scholars, Julia Cherry Spruill, in her study, *Women's Life and Work in the Southern Colonies* (1938, 1972), advanced the understanding of the role of southern women by using colonial newspapers as well as legal documents and travel accounts. Her work was followed in the 1970s with renewed vigor by a school of seventeenth-century Chesapeake scholars who questioned the status of Chesapeake women in relation to their counterparts both in England and New England. Higher death rates and an unequal sex ratio in southern colonies enhanced the status of women survivors but ultimately led to more family instability for both white and slave women. Native American women in the South lived with more privileges it seems than their European or African counterparts, despite contemporary accounts that distorted this reality.

Antebellum southern women's history was given new life by Anne Firor Scott's *The Southern Lady* (1970), which depicts southern plantation mistresses as hard workers who handled the great domestic responsibilities of the plantation but not without complaint. Discovering these women's discontentment with isolation, miscegenation, slavery, and patriarchal authority, she encouraged scholars to continue exploring the lives of southern mistresses. Studies of white and black antebellum women were pursued by Catherine Clinton, Elizabeth Fox-Genovese, Jean Friedman, Carol Bleser, and Sally McMillen. Cross-class and race studies conducted by Suzanne Lebsock, and Victoria Bynum discussed notions of status, culture, and disorder in a slave society. The history of slave women has been enhanced by Deborah G. White's *Ar'n't I a Woman?* (1985), wherein she discovered a matrifocal family system where sex roles among slaves did not mirror those of the white community.

Women in the Civil War first received modern consideration in Mary Elizabeth Massey's *Bonnet Brigades* (1966); her work was followed by a host of reprints of women's diaries and family papers, showing the significant changes and responsibilities that devolved on women during the war. George Rable's *Civil Wars* (1989) offers the most comprehensive history of southern women during the war years and elucidates the role of Confederate women in the creation of nationalism and civic religion. Emancipated slave families are surveyed by Leon Litwack, Jacquelyn Jones, and Herbert Gutman, who shed light on the integrity of family unity in the face of economic transition.

Women in the rural and industrial postwar South constitute important but understudied areas: Margaret J. Hagood's *Mothers of the South* (1939, 1977) remains the classic work on tenant farm women. Mary Frederickson, Dolores Janiewski, Jacquelyn D. Hall et al., and Julia K. Blackwelder have studied the roles of black, white, and Hispanic working women; they point to strict racial segregation in the workplace while exploring women's resistance to or compliance with patriarchal authority in the mills and factories.

Anne Scott's *The Southern Lady* and *Natural Allies* (1991) serve as standard texts for the study of postwar middle-class women's history; she argues for a connecting link between women's church societies, education, and women's reform organizations. The rise of women's missionary societies, benevolent associations, literary and civic clubs, patriotic societies, the Woman's Christian Temperance Union, the Young Women's Christian Association, suffrage societies, and antilynching and race relations efforts are explored against a New South backdrop by Jacquelyn Dowd Hall, Cynthia Neverdon-Morton, Jacquelyn Rouse, Rosalyn Terborg-Penn, A. Elizabeth Taylor, Mary Martha Thomas, and Marjorie S. Wheeler, among others.

Race relations and women's history intersect at various points in the late nineteenth and twentieth centuries, but more needs to be written about this subject, especially in the formative years between 1920 and 1954. Vicki Crawford's *Women in the Civil Rights Movement* (1990), several volumes in Darlene Clark Hine's *Black Women in American History* (1990), and Anne C. Loveland's *Lillian Smith* (1986) provide excellent overviews of the period after the *Brown v. Board of Education* decision, while Sara Evans's *Personal Politics* (1980) makes clear the connection between liberal ideology, the civil rights movement, and the emergence of women's liberation. Finally, members of the religious right and opponents of the Equal Rights Amendment have been analyzed by Jane de Hart and Donald Mathews.

Southern women's history is a relatively new but exciting field of study in which there is yet much to discover about the women who carved out lives for themselves and their families in the nation's southland. *(See also: Black Women; Civil Rights Movement; Civil War; Equal Rights Amendment; Native American Women; Progressive Era; Slavery; Southern Women's Organizations/Leaders; Suffrage in the South; Woman's Christian Temperance Union; Women's History; Young Women's Christian Association)*

—**Elizabeth Hayes Turner**

Further Reading

Bernhard, Virginia et al. *Hidden Histories of Women in the New South.* Columbia: University of Missouri Press, 1994.

———. *Southern Women: Histories and Identities.* Columbia: University of Missouri Press, 1992.

Blackwelder, Julia Kirk. *Women of the Depression: Caste and Culture in San Antonio, 1929–1939.* College Station: Texas A&M University Press, 1984.

Bleser, Carol, ed. *In Joy and in Sorrow: Women, Family, and Marriage in the Victorian South.* New York: Oxford University Press, 1991.

Bynum, Victoria E. *Unruly Women: The Politics of Social and Sexual Control in the Old South.* Chapel Hill: University of North Carolina Press, 1992.

Clinton, Catherine. *The Plantation Mistress: Women's World in the Old South.* New York: Pantheon, 1982.

Clinton, Catherine, and Nina Silber, eds. *Divided Houses: Gender and the Civil War.* New York: Oxford University Press, 1992.

Crawford, Vicki et al., eds. *Women in the Civil Rights Movement: Trailblazers and Torchbearers, 1941–1964.* Brooklyn: Carlson, 1990.

Evans, Sara. *Personal Politics: The Roots of Women's Liberation in the Civil Rights Movement and the New Left.* New York: Random House, 1980.

Fox-Genovese, Elizabeth. *Within the Plantation Household: Black and White Women of the Old South.* Chapel Hill: University of North Carolina Press, 1988.

Frederickson, Mary. *A Place to Speak Our Minds: The Southern School for Women Workers, 1927–1950.* Bloomington: University of Indiana Press, 1990.

Friedman, Jean E. *The Enclosed Garden: Women and Community in the Evangelical South, 1830–1900.* Chapel Hill: University of North Carolina Press, 1985.

Green, Rayna. *Native American Women: A Contextual Bibliography.* Bloomington: Indiana University Press, 1983.

Hagood, Margaret J. *Mothers of the South: Portraiture of the White Southern Farm Woman.* 1939. Reprint, New York: Norton, 1977.

Hall, Jacquelyn Dowd. *Revolt against Chivalry: The Women's Campaign against Lynching.* 1979. Reprint, New York: Columbia University Press, 1993.

Hall, Jacquelyn Dowd et al. *Like a Family: The Making of a Southern Cotton World.* New York: Norton, 1987.

Harley, Sharon, and Rosalyn Terborg-Penn, eds. *The Afro-American Woman: Struggles and Images.* Port Washington, NY: Kennikat, 1978.

Hine, Darlene Clark et al., eds. *Black Women in American History,* 8 vols. Brooklyn, NY: Carlson, 1990.

Janiewski, Dolores E. *Sisterhood Denied: Race, Gender, and Class in a New South Community.* Philadelphia: Temple University Press, 1985.

Jones, Jacquelyn. *Labor of Love, Labor of Sorrow: Black Women, Work, and the Family from Slavery to the Present.* New York: Basic Books, 1985.

Land, Aubrey C., Lois Carr, and Edward C. Papenfuse, eds. *Law, Society, and Politics in Early Maryland.* Baltimore: Johns Hopkins University Press, 1977.

Lebsock, Suzanne. *The Free Women of Petersburg: Status and Culture in a Southern Town, 1784–1860.* New York: Norton, 1984.

Loveland, Anne C. *Lillian Smith: A Southerner Confronting the South.* Baton Rouge: Louisiana State University Press, 1986.

Massey, Mary Elizabeth. *Bonnet Brigades: American Women and the Civil War.* New York: Knopf, 1966.

McMillen, Sally G. *Motherhood in the Old South: Pregnancy, Childbirth, and Infant Rearing.* Baton Rouge: Louisiana State University Press, 1990.

Neverdon-Morton, Cynthia. *Afro-American Women of the South and the Advancement of the Race, 1895–1925.* Knoxville: University of Tennessee Press, 1989.

Rable, George. *Civil Wars: Women and the Crisis of Southern Nationalism.* Urbana: University of Illinois Press, 1989.

Rouse, Jacquelyn Anne. *Lugenia Burns Hope: Black Southern Reformer.* Athens: University of Georgia Press, 1989.

Scott, Anne Firor. *Natural Allies: Women's Associations in American History.* Urbana: University of Illinois Press, 1991.

———. *The Southern Lady: From Pedestal to Politics, 1830–1930.* Chicago: University of Chicago Press, 1970.

———. *Unheard Voices: The First Historians of Southern Women.* Charlottesville: University of Virginia Press, 1993.

Spruill, Julia Cherry. *Women's Life and Work in the Southern Colonies.* 1938. Reprint, Chapel Hill: University of North Carolina Press, 1972.

Tate, Thad W., and David L. Ammerman, eds. *The Chesapeake in the Seventeenth Century: Essays on Anglo-American Society.* Chapel Hill: University of North Carolina Press, 1979.

Taylor, A. Elizabeth. *The Woman Suffrage Movement in Tennessee.* New York: Bookman, 1957.

Thomas, Mary Martha. *The New Woman in Alabama: Social Reforms and Suffrage, 1890–1920.* Tuscaloosa: University of Alabama Press, 1992.

Wheeler, Marjorie Spruill. *New Women of the New South: The Leaders of the Woman Suffrage Movement in the Southern States.* New York: Oxford University Press, 1993.

White, Deborah Gray. *Ar'n't I a Woman? Female Slaves in the Plantation South.* New York: Norton, 1985.

↻ Southern Women's Organizations/ Leaders

Because the South remained predominantly rural well into the twentieth century, southern women had fewer opportunities than women in other regions to participate in voluntary associations. Nevertheless, southern women, like women elsewhere, joined together for self-improvement, service, and reform.

Before the Civil War, white women in the South's towns and cities participated in benevolent, religious, and temperance associations. In 1853, Ann Pamela Cunningham of South Carolina founded the first national women's patriotic society, the Mount Vernon Ladies' Association of the Union. During the Civil War, Southern women banded together in hospital and sewing circles; after the war, many of these same associations cared for the graves of Confederate dead.

Southern women's organizations multiplied in the decades following the Civil War, with church missionary societies leading the way. Methodists, Baptists, and Episcopalians formed state or regional women's auxiliaries in the 1870s and 1880s. The Woman's Christian Temperance Union (WCTU) and the King's Daughters, a philanthropic organization, established southern branches. In the 1890s, white southern women joined patriotic societies such as the Colonial Dames, the Daughters of the American Revolution, and the United Daughters of the Confederacy. They also organized local literary and civic clubs and state federations of women's clubs. As women's voluntary associations grew in the first decade of the twentieth century, they gained respectability and power and played an important role in southern progressive reform.

At the same time that white women were organizing, a parallel network of associations appeared among black women. The WCTU and Young Women's Christian Association (YWCA) sponsored separate branches for blacks. Black women had their own local civic clubs and in 1896 organized the National Association of Colored Women. After World War I, white and black women—frequently acting through the Methodist church, the YWCA, and federations of women's clubs—began working together to ease racial tensions. At a historic meeting in Memphis in 1920, black and white women created the Woman's Committee of the Commission on Interracial Cooperation. At the Memphis meeting, black women attempted to enlist white women in their antilynching campaign. In the 1930s, under the leadership of Jessie Daniel Ames, white southern women organized the Association of Southern Women for the Prevention of Lynching.

Voluntary associations in the South, as elsewhere, enabled women to move outside their homes without openly challenging the domestic ideal. They gave southern women the public voice denied them as individuals. Acting together, southern women established a place for themselves in politics long before they got the vote. *(See also: Ames, Jesse Daniel; Association of Southern Women for the Prevention of Lynching; Commission on Interracial Cooperation; National Association of Colored Women; Southern Lady; Southern Women's History; United Daughters of the Confederacy; Woman's Christian Temperance Union)*

—Anastatia Sims

Further Reading

Friedman, Jean E. *The Enclosed Garden: Women and Community in the Evangelical South, 1830–1900.* Chapel Hill: University of North Carolina Press, 1985.

Giddings, Paula. *When and Where I Enter: The Impact of Black Women on Race and Sex in America.* New York: Bantam, 1985.

Hall, Jacquelyn Dowd. *Revolt against Chivalry: Jessie Daniel Ames and the Women's Campaign against Lynching.* New York: Columbia University Press, 1979.

Lebsock, Suzanne. *The Free Women of Petersburg: Status and Culture in a Southern Town, 1784–1860.* New York: Norton, 1984.

Neverdon-Morton, Cynthia. *Afro-American Women of the South and the Advancement of the Race, 1895–1925.* Knoxville: University of Tennessee Press, 1989.

Roth, Darlene Rebecca. *Matronage: Patterns in Women's Organizations, Atlanta, Georgia, 1890–1940.* Brooklyn, NY: Carlson, 1994.

Scott, Anne Firor. *Natural Allies: Women's Associations in American History.* Urbana: University of Illinois Press, 1991.

———. *The Southern Lady: From Pedestal to Politics, 1830–1930.* Chicago: University of Chicago Press, 1970.

~ Spalding, Eliza Hart (1807–1851)

In 1836, Eliza Spalding and Narcissa Whitman became the first white women to reach the Continental Divide and to cross the Rocky Mountains. Spalding and her husband, Henry Harmon Spalding, had joined the Whitmans to establish a Presbyterian mission among the Indians of the Oregon Territory. While the Whitmans settled among the Cayuse near Fort Walla Walla, Washington, the Spaldings chose to live with the Nez Perce at Lapwai, in what is now Idaho.

Born in Berlin, Connecticut, and raised on a farm in upstate New York, Spalding was skilled in the usual farm and home crafts. She attended a local female academy, then taught school for a few years before marrying in 1833. Spalding was converted and joined the Presbyterian church when she was nineteen; she remained an intensely religious woman until her death. Her husband, an equally religious man, attended Lane Theological Seminary.

The Spaldings opened a school in Lapwai a few months after their arrival. While her husband preached and taught the Nez Perce Indians farming skills, she took charge of the school. Daily lessons included English, spinning, weaving, sewing, and knitting, as well as Bible lessons. Her school became very popular, averaging a daily attendance of one hundred Nez Perce women and children. Spalding gave birth to four children who lived to maturity and suffered one miscarriage while living at Lapwai.

On November 29, 1847, the Cayuse rose up against and massacred the Whitmans and twelve other members of their mission. When this occurred, the Nez Perce protected the Spalding family and led them safely to the Willamette Valley. The mission was closed, and the family settled on a farm at Brownsville, Oregon. Spalding, always a victim of poor health, was at that time suffering from tuberculosis. Never fully recovering from the disease, she died on January 7, 1851, at the age of forty-four. *(See also: Christianity; Migration and Frontier Women; Religion)*

—Deborah Dawson Bonde

Further Reading
Dawson, Deborah Lynn. "Laboring in My Savior's Vineyard: The Mission of Eliza Hart Spalding." Ph.D. diss., Bowling Green State University, 1988.

Drury, Clifford, ed. *The First White Women over the Rockies.* Vol. 1, *The Diaries of Narcissa Whitman, Eliza Spalding, and Mary Gray.* Glendale, CA: Arthur H. Clark, 1963.

Jeffrey, Julie Roy. *Converting the West: A Biography of Narcissa Whitman.* Norman: University of Oklahoma Press, 1991.

~ Spanish Civil War (1936–1939)

The largely untold story of U.S. women volunteers in the Spanish Civil War began in 1936 when the Spanish people elected a Popular Front government. This government sought to establish a liberal democracy in Spain. Within three months, the young republic came under attack by Spanish General Francisco Franco, who had turned to Hitler and Mussolini for aid. Antifascists from all over the world went to Spain to defend the republic and formed the International Brigades; among them were some 3,200 volunteers from the United States, who became known as the Abraham Lincoln Battalion.

Over sixty women, primarily medical personnel, volunteered to serve in Spain, thus becoming the first group of women in U.S. history to go overseas to aid in a civil war. They played a major role in providing health care and support services for the republican (Loyalist) forces, despite opposition to their going by the overwhelmingly male organizers of the Lincoln Battalion. That they could go was a result of women's greater economic independence since the wave of feminism in the 1920s. Many were under thirty; some were recent graduates of nursing schools. At considerable risk to their careers, their health, and even their lives, they left families and jobs for an uncertain future in a bloody civil war.

Brutality reached new heights during the Spanish Civil War as Franco's Falangist troops introduced tactics such as the bombing of civilian targets and hospitals. Medical supplies were extremely limited, antibiotics such as penicillin were unknown, and working hours were endless. The young U.S. volunteers worked relentlessly, carrying out nursing tasks as well as training Spanish civilians and even running hospitals. Cecilia Seborer, a lab technician, aided in the surgical pioneering of the technique of whole-blood transfusions. Other women drove ambulances, served as war correspondents—Mary Hemingway and Josephine Herbst—worked as translators, and aided refugee children. Many women were sent home suffering from fatigue and other illnesses before the official withdrawal of the International Brigades in October 1938.

As "premature antifascists," these women faced the same harassment after their return as did the men, including visits by the FBI and loss of jobs and friends. Their experiences in Spain, despite the defeat of the Spanish Republic, proved to be a catalyst for future involvement in the women's movement and other progressive issues. *(See also: Journalism; Nursing)*

—Karel Kilimnik

Further Reading

de Vries, Lini. *Up from the Cellar*. Minneapolis, MN: Vanilla, 1979.

Gerassi, John. "During the Civil War." In *The Premature Anti-Fascists: An Oral History—North American Volunteers in the Spanish Civil War, 1936–1939*. New York: Praeger, 1986.

Hutchins, Evelyn. "A Woman Truck Driver." In *Our Fight: Writings by Veterans of the Abraham Lincoln Brigade, Spain, 1936–1939*, edited by Alvah Bessie and Albert Prago, 175-78. New York: Monthly Review, 1987.

Martin, Fredericka. "The American Hospital Unit." In *Our Fight: Writings by Veterans of the Abraham Lincoln Brigade, Spain, 1936–1939*, edited by Alvah Bessie and Albert Prago, 142-47. New York: Monthly Review, 1987.

(O'Reilly) Kea, Salaria. " 'While Passing Through': Health and Medicine," *Journal of the Health and Medicine Policy Research Group* 4 (Spring 1987): 113–15.

Wyden, Peter. "The Bloody Jarama." In *The Passionate War: A Narrative History of the Spanish Civil War, 1936–1939*. New York: Simon & Schuster, 1983.

⟋⟍ SPARS

SPARS, the women's corps of the U.S. Coast Guard, was created in November 1942, four months after the U.S. Navy created its women's corps, known as WAVES. The women were called SPARS, from Semper Paratus (Always Prepared), the Coast Guard's motto, and were accepted on the same basis as male reservists.

SPARS served in a variety of jobs to release men for the front lines. A major source of pride for the SPARS was their participation during World War II in Unit 21, which oversaw the top-secret project, LORAN, or Long Range Aid to Navigation. Unit 21 was at first manned by men. Within a month, SPARS completely staffed the unit except for one veteran radio technician who acted as their instructor. Six months later, he had also shipped out. At peak strength of the armed forces during World War II, ten thousand women served as SPARS; in all, thirteen thousand served during the war.

The first director, Dorothy Stratton, formerly dean of women at Purdue University, was serving as a senior officer in the WAVES training program in Wisconsin when the Coast Guard created its women's corps. WAVES director Mildred McAfee, who had been a dean of women before becoming president of Wellesley, recommended Stratton for the position. The second director, Helen Schleman, had also served as dean of women at Purdue. The third director, Katherine A. Towle, went from the SPARS to become dean of students at the University of California at Berkeley in the 1960s.

After the passage of the Women's Armed Services Integration Act in June 1948, the SPARS remained distinct within the service until 1978, after which women could enter the Coast Guard Academy and command cutters with male and female crews. Since the Coast Guard reports to the Department of Transportation instead of the Navy during peacetime, it is not restricted by law as is the Navy in training women in combat roles. The Coast Guard has consequently given its women more opportunity than the other services to gain a wide range of technical and leadership experiences. *(See also: Military Service; WAVES; Women's Army Auxiliary Corps; Women's Army Corps)*

—**D'Ann Campbell**

Further Reading

Campbell, D'Ann. *Women at War with America: Private Lives in a Patriotic Era*. Cambridge, MA: Harvard University Press, 1984.

The Coast Guard and the Women's Reserve in World War II. Washington, DC: Coast Guard Historian's Office, 1992.

Lyne, Mary C., and Kay Arthur. *Three Years behind the Mast: The Story of the United States Coast Guard SPARS*. Washington, DC: U.S. Coast Guard, 1946.

Stratton, Dorothy. "Recollection with Dorothy Stratton." Oral History Collection, United States Naval Institute, Annapolis, MD, 1971.

U.S. Coast Guard. *The Coast Guard at War: Women's Reserve XXII A*. Washington, DC: U.S. Coast Guard Headquarters, Historical Section, Public Information Division, 1946.

⟋⟍ Spelman College

Spelman College, now part of the historically black Atlanta University Center, was founded in 1881 by two New England women, Sophia B. Packard and Harriet E. Giles. The original aim of the institution, which began as the Atlanta Baptist Female Seminary, was to educate women and girls who had gained their freedom from slavery. Reverend Frank Quarles, pastor of Friendship Baptist Church in Atlanta, gave Miss Packard and Miss Giles his full support, arranging for the school to meet for the first two years in the basement of his church. On April 11, 1881, eleven black girls attended the first classes. On the second day, there were 25 students, and the number had grown to 80 by the time the school closed for the year on July 15. By year's end, enrollment had grown to 200 students between the ages of 15 and 52. From the beginning, the founders' aim was not only to provide an elementary education to those who had been deprived of schooling during slavery but also to prepare Spelman students to serve as teachers, missionaries, and church workers. However, practical skills were also stressed as part of preparing students to be good homemakers and mothers.

Packard and Giles gave a presentation on their school to the Cleveland, Ohio, Wilson Avenue Church in the summer of 1882. One of the church members, John D. Rockefeller, heard their speech and became a lifelong contributor not only to the school but to African American education in general. With additional support from the American Baptist Home Mission Society and its women's auxiliary, nine acres of land and five buildings were purchased at the site of Fort McPherson, former Union Army barracks. The financial support of Mr. and Mrs. John D. Rockefeller, Sr., together with other gifts ranging from $1.00 to $1,000, made it possible to complete payment of the mortgage.

The school moved to its new location in February 1883, and Packard and Giles fought a proposal to merge the female seminary with the Atlanta Baptist Seminary, a school for males. Packard and Giles knew from experience that courses in coeducational schools focused on males, and they believed that their female students would be better served by keeping the schools separate. To do so, they had to raise enough money to support separate schools. Baptists in the North and African American Baptists in Georgia contributed, and the Rockefellers donated the remaining amount needed. In 1884, the school's name was changed to Spelman Seminary, in honor of Mrs. Harvey Buel Spelman, mother of Laura Spelman Rockefeller and of Miss Lucy Spelman.

The curriculum expanded to include college preparatory classes equivalent to high school. In these early years, the main purpose of the school was to provide students with practical and vocational training straining. A high priority was the establishment of a printing office in 1884, with a printing press provided by the Slater Fund. The first issue of *The Spelman Messenger* appeared in March 1885. Students were trained in typesetting and composition, with an emphasis on accuracy. This experience opened up new employment opportunities for Spelman students. A Nurse Training Department opened in 1886, the first nurses' school for African American students in the United States, followed in 1891 by the Missionary Training Department. A new building was dedicated in 1918 to house the expanded home economics program. Spelman Seminary started a College Department in 1897, although most of the college work was at nearby Morehouse College. Rockefeller gave $200,000 in 1900, which was spent on buildings, including MacVicar Hospital, used both as a nurses' training hospital and as a hospital for black women.

One of the most significant occurrences in Spelman's history occurred in 1924, when it changed from a seminary to a full-fledged college aimed at providing a first-rate liberal arts education to its students. Under the leadership of Florence Matilda Read, who served as president from 1927 to 1953, the curriculum was expanded, with college courses established in the humanities, fine arts, social sciences, and natural sciences. In 1927, the elementary and nursing schools closed; in 1930 the high school closed.

Prior to 1920, most of the teachers were unmarried, white, New England women, with a few African American teachers who were former Spelman students. Albert E. Manley succeeded Read as president in 1953, ending nearly a half century of New England leadership. During his tenure, Spelman continued its commitment to a liberal arts education, but it was strengthened by the addition of non-western and ethnic studies courses. Within the broader context of the civil rights movement, students and faculty during the 1960s demanded that the colleges in the Atlanta University Center take account of black experience. In 1970, the first stage of a comprehensive Afro-American Studies Program was implemented. At Spelman, courses were added to address economic, social, political, and cultural developments in Africa and the Caribbean as well as in the African American community within the United States.

In the 1974-75 school year, the Spelman academic program was reorganized on a divisional basis, and the Education, Fine Arts, Humanities, Natural Sciences, and Social Sciences divisions were formed. The divisional structure also provided a framework for the development of interdisciplinary courses. During Dr. Manley's administration, several other new programs were implemented in the 1970s, including Freshman Orientation and Freshman Studies, the Health Careers Program, the Family Planning Program, and cooperative programs with non-black institutions. Cooperation among the institutions within the Atlanta University Center dramatically increased during Dr. Manley's presidency. One milestone was the creation in 1964 of the Atlanta University Center Corporation. Between 1972 and 1978, financial support from the Ford Foundation totaling $20 million enabled the AUC institutions to implement a number of collaborative programs.

In *A Legacy Continues: The Manley Years at Spelman College, 1953–1976,* Dr. Manley describes the participation of students at Spelman College and the other AUC institutions in the civil rights movement. He notes that "although much has been written about the direct action techniques of students who were enrolled at Berkeley, Antioch, the University of Chicago, and other colleges and universities, . . . it has not been emphasized sufficiently that black students were the first to apply the direct action techniques of the civil rights movement [to the academic environment]" (p. 175). When Dr. Manley announced his retirement, many faculty and students assumed that in this time of new opportunities for women, the next Spelman president would be a woman. When the Board of Trustees announced the appointment of an African American man, Donald Mitchell Stewart, students tied the doors of the board room to block all exits. Despite the lockup, Stewart assumed the presidency in 1976.

In 1987, Johnnetta Betsch Cole stepped into the role of seventh president of Spelman College, the first African American woman to do so in its 106-year history. Under the leadership of Dr. Cole, or "Sister President," as she was known, Spelman achieved national status as one of the leading liberal arts colleges in the United States, becoming the first African American college to receive a number one ranking in *U.S. News and World Report*'s annual college issue. She presided over a fund-raising campaign that brought in $114 million, the largest amount ever raised by a black college or university. The endowment was tripled, rising from $42 million to $143 million. With a grant from Camille and Bill Cosby, the Camille Cosby Center was built. It now houses the Women's Research and Resource Center, as well as an art gallery, a media center, and additional classrooms and faculty offices. In 1999, Dr. Cole, currently the Presidential Distinguished Scholar at Emory University, received the Radcliffe medal, presented each spring by the Radcliffe

College Alumnae Association to an individual whose life and work have had a significant impact on society.

In 1998, Audrey Forbes Manley, a Spelman graduate, became the first alumna to serve as president of Spelman. She had made significant contributions to the college in her role as First Lady during Albert Manley's presidency. After his retirement, the Manleys moved to Washington, D.C., where Audrey Manley became the first African American female to serve as Acting Assistant Secretary for Health. She subsequently served as Acting Surgeon General of the United States until her appointment as president of Spelman.

Today, Spelman is ranked fifth among the one hundred colleges ranked by *Money Magazine* as best buys, and first among both historically black and women's colleges. It continues to develop innovative programs ranging from the Center for Scientific Applications in Mathematics to the Summer Art Colony in Portobello, Panama. Spelman plays a leadership role in training African American women in the sciences; nearly forty percent of the school's students concentrate in the natural sciences. A $30 million Science Center is near completion. A two-semester course, The African Diaspora and the World, is both interdisciplinary and gender informed. This course is an example of Spelman's continued commitment to providing students with an introduction to their own background and culture, an understanding of their relationship to other communities of African descent, and the ability to reflect critically on methods of addressing the need for social change. *(See also Black Women; Education; Higher Education for Southern Women; Nursing)*

—Diana E. Axelsen

Further Reading

American Baptist Historical Society. Valley Forge, Pennsylvania.
Rockefeller Archives Center. Tarrytown, New York.
Spelman College Archives. Spelman College. Atlanta, Georgia.
Cole, Johnnetta B. *Conversations: Straight Talk With America's Sister President.* New York: Doubleday, 1994.
———. *Dream the Boldest Dreams: And Other Lessons of Life.* Marietta, GA: Longstreet, 1997.
Guy-Sheftall, Beverly. "Spelman College." In *Black Women in America: An Historical Encyclopedia,* edited by Darlene Clark Hine. Vol. pp. 1091-95. Brooklyn, NY: Carlson, 1993.
Guy-Sheftall, Beverly, and Jo Moore Stewart. *Spelman: A Centennial Celebration.* 1981.
Manley, Albert E. *A Legacy Continues: The Manley Years at Spelman College, 1953-1976.* Lanham, MD: University Press of American, 1995.
Read, Florence. *The Story of Spelman College.* Princeton: Princeton University Press, 1961.
The Spelman Messenger. Division of Special Collections and Archives. Woodruff Library, Clark Atlanta University. Atlanta, Georgia.

Spencer, Anna Garlin (1851–1931)

Anna Garlin Spencer was a minister, feminist, educator, pacifist, and writer on ethics and social problems. Born in Rhode Island, Spencer dedicated her life to social reform. She was the first woman minister in her home state and served in the Bell Street Chapel, a liberal church, from 1891 to 1902. From 1902 until her death, Spencer held a series of teaching posts at the University of Wisconsin, the University of Chicago, and Columbia University. She taught and wrote extensively on the issues of religion, aspects of marriage and the family, the role of women, sexuality, and philanthropy. Her work on these issues appeared in the scholarly and popular press.

Spencer was active in the woman's rights movement for more than forty years. In the 1890s, she served as the president of the Rhode Island Equal Suffrage Association. An early participant in the National Council of Women, Spencer was president of that organization in 1920.

Spencer's interest in pacifism also led her to prominent positions in the cause of peace. She was on the executive committee of the National Peace and Arbitration Congress in 1907 and was a founding member of the Woman's Peace Party in 1915. She also became the first chairman of the national board of the U.S. section of the Women's International League for Peace and Freedom in 1919. In this position, she steered the group through the difficult period of reorganization after the first World War. Spencer was able to combine women's peace activity with women's new voting rights.

Spencer died in 1931 of a heart attack while attending a dinner at the League of Nations Association in New York City. She had been active in many causes up to the time of her death. *(See also: Pacifism and the Peace Movement; Religion; Women's International League for Peace and Freedom; Women's Rights Movements: Nineteenth and Twentieth Centuries)*

—Wendy E. Chmielewski

Further Reading

Pivar, David J. *Purity Crusade: Sexual Morality and Social Control, 1868–1900.* Westport, CT: Greenwood, 1973.
Smith, Christine Brittle. *Anna Garlin Spencer.* Including Local Council of Women of Rhode Island, 1983.

Spencer, Lilly Martin (1822–1902)

Lilly Martin Spencer was not only one of the most popular American artists of the nineteenth century but also one of the most important and best-known American woman painters. Spencer's reputation and popularity were established with her warm and humorous portrayals of everyday family life as well as her still-life works. She had a special eye and ability to create paintings using common objects. Many of Spencer's works were sold to popular art unions of the mid-nineteenth century, which operated as consumer co-ops and widely disseminated the works of many women artists. Spencer's reputation increased as her works were reproduced as engravings and lithographs and widely distributed to subscribers, making her name a household word. Her genre paintings are an example of the type popular before the Civil War, at which time they earned as much as works by George Caleb Bingham, a famous genre painter of the time.

Spencer was born in England; her parents were French intellectuals who later emigrated to Ohio. They were active in the main causes of the period and encouraged her art, even allowing her to make charcoal murals on the plaster walls of their farmhouse. She is considered to be self-taught, although she had some lessons from itinerant painters and artists in Cincinnati and New York City.

Although not traditional, her marriage to Benjamin Rush Spencer, an English tailor, lasted forty-six years beginning in 1844. Early in the marriage, her husband recognized Spencer's ability to support the family better than he could and therefore took over domestic responsibilities and assisted her with the business side of her work. They had thirteen children, seven of whom survived. Her husband and children were often the subjects of Spencer's paintings.

Spencer held her first public exhibition in 1841. The attention given to her and her work by critics led to an offer from a wealthy patron to finance her training in Boston and Europe, but she refused. She was quite successful in the Midwest but decided to move to New York in 1848 to seek fame in the center of the art world. The stiff competition led her to take night classes and to improve her drawing and knowledge of perspective.

With the demise of art unions, the decreasing popularity of her special type of genre, and the increasing use of photography for portraits, the Spencers' income dropped. In her later years, Spencer worked hard but was forced to barter her paintings for bread to stay alive. Nonetheless, she produced an incredible number of works and painted up to her death at the age of eighty. *(See also: Art)*

—**Holly Hyncik Sukenik**

Further Reading

Bolton-Smith, Robin. "The Sentimental Paintings of Lilly Martin Spencer," *Antiques* 104 (July 1973): 108-15.
Bolton-Smith, Robin, and William H. Truettner. *Lilly Martin Spencer 1822–1902: The Joys of Sentiment.* Washington, DC: Smithsonian Institution, 1973.
Chadwick, Whitney. *Women, Art, and Society.* New York: Thames & Hudson, 1990.
Rubinstein, Charlotte Streifer. *American Women Artists: From Early Indian Times to the Present,* pp. 50-53. Boston: Avon, 1982.

～ Spiritualism

The belief that the dead can communicate with the living is a very old one in Eastern and Western cultures. The modern phenomenon of Spiritualism is a product of the religious enthusiasm and social reformism that swept an area of western New York known as the "burned-over district" in the 1840s. Although it spread quickly to Europe, in many respects, Spiritualism remained a quintessentially American cultural trend, combining as it did wide-ranging European ideals such as those of French social philosopher Charles Fourier and Swedish mystic Emmanuel Swedenborg with an American individualist sensibility.

In 1847, itinerant Mesmerist Andrew Jackson Davis presented a prophetic vision of world history in *The Principles of Nature, Her Divine Revelation; and a Voice to Mankind,* in which he predicted that the imminent communion of dead and living souls would result in the betterment of humankind. The next year, his prophecy was revealed when two young sisters apparently received messages from a murdered peddler buried beneath their rural upstate New York home. Encouraged by an elder sister, Catherine and Margaretta Fox became the first Spiritualist mediums when they created a sensation in nearby Rochester with their "spirit rappings." A medium, by virtue of her extraordinary sensitivity, would hold forth in a small circle of believers, enter into a trance, and receive messages from the "invisibles," often reproducing the voice or handwriting of the deceased. Despite the Fox sisters' unhappy personal lives and their eventual admission of fraudulence, Spiritualism remained one of the most significant and widespread of alternative religions, with up to one million followers in the United States by the 1850s. In the Progressive Era, when inventions such as the telegraph facilitated instant communication between great distances, the "spirit telegraph" alleviated age-old fears with comforting messages emanating from beyond the grave.

Women were largely in control of the seance as the mediums through which the spirits of loved ones and historical actors spoke to the living. The center of Spiritualist life was not the church or the market but the home, and messages conveyed from the other world were personal ones. From its inception, Spiritualist communication provided a forum for politically radical ideas, giving a critical voice to advocates of abolition, women's rights, and temperance.

Spiritualism professed to offer tangible proof of the immortality of the soul, creating controversy within both scientific and religious orthodoxy. It culled many of its followers from the ranks of the disaffected or from alternative religious sects such as the Quakers. In 1882, believers in the scientific community, eager to explain material phenomena such as automatic writing and spirit photography, established the Society for Psychical Research in London (followed quickly by an American society) to gather evidence and eliminate fraud. In the late nineteenth century, Russian-born adept Helena Blavatsky incorporated Spiritualist tenets into the broadly syncretic practice of Theosophy, and in South America, the teachings of French reincarnationist Alan Kardec survive in the practice of "spiritism." *(See also: Mesmerism; Religion)*

—**Catherine Mason**

Further Reading

Brandon, Ruth. *The Spiritualists.* New York: Knopf, 1986.
Braude, Ann. *Radical Spirits: Spiritualism and Women's Rights in Nineteenth-Century America.* Boston: Beacon, 1989.

Doyle, Arthur Conan. *The History of Spiritualism,* 2 vols. New York: George H. Doran, 1926.

Hardinge, Emma. *Modern American Spiritualism.* 1870. Reprint, Hyde Park, NY: University Books, 1970.

Isaacs, Ernest. "The Fox Sisters and American Spiritualism." In *The Occult in America: An Historical Perspective,* edited by Howard Kerr and Charles Crow, 79-110. Urbana: University of Illinois Press, 1983.

Jackson, Herbert G. *The Spirit Rappers.* Garden City, NJ: Doubleday, 1972.

Moore, Robert L. *In Search of White Crows: Spiritualism, Parapsychology, and American Culture.* New York: Oxford University Press, 1977.

Podmore, Frank. *Mediums of the Nineteenth-Century,* 2 vols. Hyde Park, NY: University Books, 1963.

～ Stanton, Elizabeth Cady (1815–1902)

Suffragist, lecturer, and writer, Elizabeth Cady Stanton was the foremost critic of legal and cultural forms of women's subordination in the nineteenth century. As initiator of the Seneca Falls (New York) Convention in 1848—the first such gathering for women's rights in America—and author of its demand for woman suffrage, Stanton became the most prominent advocate of women's legal equality and political activism. Her arguments began where the American Revolution left off, with a social contract to which women, like men, should be parties because they were imbued with the same natural rights and rational minds. Not limiting herself to the right of women to have a voice in government, Stanton explored the implications of true equality for the most intimate human relations and most pervasive cultural norms. At every opportunity, she criticized male political culture on the one hand and woman's culture on the other for perpetuating female dependency in a society premised on individualism and self-sovereignty.

Born in Johnstown, New York, the daughter of a lawyer and judge, Stanton attended Emma Willard's Seminary, but her legal and political education at home left the clearer mark. Marriage to abolitionist orator Henry B. Stanton in 1840 introduced her to the most advanced circles of reform, and from that date, she also confronted a burdensome domestic life. Seven children limited her early activism, but Stanton polished her gifts as a writer to exert great influence over the new woman's rights movement, whose meetings she could rarely attend. A close collaboration with Susan B. Anthony, beginning in 1851, allied Stanton with a person more interested in and skillful than herself at organizing people to carry out their shared ideas.

After the Civil War, Stanton achieved a national reputation as a popular lecturer on the lyceum circuit, an outspoken social and political commentator, and the venerable president of the National Woman Suffrage Association (NWSA). Her topics included maternity, the woman's crusade against temperance, child rearing, and divorce law, as well as constitutional questions, presidential campaigns, and woman suffrage. Thriving on controversy, she championed

Figure 58. Elizabeth Cady Stanton
Stanton (right, pictured here with Susan B. Anthony), was a prominent advocate of legal equality for women. A lecturer, writer, but perhaps first and foremost an activist, Stanton initiated the Seneca Falls Convention in 1848—the spark that ignited the movement for women's suffrage. Used by permission of UPI/Corbis-Bettmann.

notorious victims of the double standard. Witty and personable on the platform, she entertained her audiences while exposing them to advanced discussion of full equality.

In the 1880s, tired of travel and organizational leadership, Stanton intensified her writing, producing one of her greatest legacies, three volumes of the *History of Woman Suffrage* (1881–1886), prepared with Anthony and Matilda Joslyn Gage. Still the single most important source on the ideas and people of the early movement for equality, the *History* project showed a remarkable grasp of how important history would be to the survival of this political movement.

Stanton also returned to her lifelong examination of how religion structured women's subordination. Scores of articles as well as the better-known *Woman's Bible* (1895, 1898) set forth her convictions that religious faith blocked progress toward women's self-sovereignty, that churches threatened the fabric of republican government, and that ecclesiastical domination subordinated women more effectively than the state itself. Commentaries on biblical passages about women written by Stanton and a small committee, the *Woman's Bible* exposed the book's patriarchal values and drew attention to its exceptional women. As she had done in 1848, Stanton expanded a men's debate—this time about the historical Bible—to analyze anew what held women back and what directions their rebellion should take. Although celebrated by freethinkers for her work, Stanton found herself sharply criticized by a majority of suffragists who wanted no conflict over religion. Nearing the end of her life, but still the quintessential reformer, Stanton reexperienced the isolation and criticism of 1848 but died without the chance to lead in the new direction. *(See also: Anthony, Susan B.; National Woman Suffrage Association; Public Speakers: Nineteenth Century; Religion; Seneca Falls Convention)*

—**Ann D. Gordon**

Further Reading

Banner, Lois. *Elizabeth Cady Stanton: A Radical for Women's Rights.* Boston: Little, Brown, 1980.

DuBois, Ellen C., ed. *Elizabeth Cady Stanton and Susan B. Anthony: Correspondence, Writings, Speeches,* 2d ed. Boston: Northeastern University Press, 1993.

Gifford, Carolyn DeSwarte. "Politicizing the Sacred Texts: Elizabeth Cady Stanton and *The Woman's Bible.*" In *Searching the Scriptures.* Vol. I, *A Feminist Introduction,* edited by Elisabeth Schussler Fiorenza, 52-63. New York: Crossroad, 1993.

Gordon, Ann D., ed. *The Papers of Elizabeth Cady Stanton and Susan B. Anthony.* Vol. 1, *In the School of Anti-Slavery, 1840-1866.* New Brunswick, NJ: Rutgers University Press, 1997.

———. "The Political Is the Personal: Two Autobiographies of Woman Suffragists." In *American Women's Autobiography: Fea(s)ts of Memory,* edited by Margo Culley, 111-27. Madison: University of Wisconsin Press, 1992.

Griffith, Elisabeth. *In Her Own Right: The Life of Elizabeth Cady Stanton.* New York: Oxford University Press, 1984.

Holland, Patricia G., and Ann D. Gordon, eds. *The Papers of Elizabeth Cady Stanton and Susan B. Anthony.* Microfilm edition. Wilmington, DE: Scholarly Resources, 1991, 1992.

Kern, Kathi L. "Rereading Eve: Elizabeth Cady Stanton and *The Woman's Bible,* 1885-1896," *Women's Studies* 19 (Winter 1991): 371-83.

Lutz, Alma. *Created Equal: A Biography of Elizabeth Cady Stanton, 1815-1902.* New York: Day, 1940.

Stanton, Elizabeth Cady. *Eighty Years and More: Reminiscences, 1815-1897.* Introduction by Ellen C. DuBois, afterward by Ann D. Gordon. 1898. Reprint, New York: Schocken, 1971.

Stanton, Elizabeth Cady et al. *The Woman's Bible.* Foreword by Maureen Fitzgerald. 1898. Reprint, Boston: Northeastern University Press, 1993.

Stanton, Elizabeth Cady, Susan B. Anthony, and Matilda Joslyn Gage, eds. *History of Woman Suffrage,* 3 vols. 1881-1886. Reprint, New York: Arno, 1969.

Starr, Ellen Gates (1859–1940)

Ellen Gates Starr, settlement worker, bookbinder, and labor activist, is best known as the cofounder, with Jane Addams, of Chicago's Hull House settlement in 1889. Although Addams proved to be the main force behind the nation's most famous settlement house—the third established in a movement that encouraged educated young people to live and work among the urban poor—Starr's enthusiastic support and professional contacts during the early years were perhaps decisive in establishing the institution. As a resident of Hull House for nearly thirty years, Starr made the fate of art and labor in the modern city her prime concern.

During the mid-1890s, Starr had become dissatisfied with her earliest attempts at Hull House to preserve dignified labor and an artistic impulse among Chicago's immigrants. She recognized that in joining the trade unions in their demands for higher wages, shorter hours, and better working conditions, workers had failed to address the fact that the very nature of factory work had been degraded. Likewise, cultivating in her neighbors an appreciation for European painting through exhibitions at the settlement or the circulation of reproductions in local schools now seemed ineffectual in preventing the fine arts from becoming irrelevant to urban industrial life. Although Starr continued to participate in these activities, she was increasingly drawn to the current revival of the handicrafts as the best way of making art and labor once again meaningful to the working class. For fifteen months (1897–1898), she served as an apprentice at the Doves Bindery in London under the supervision of T. J. Cobden-Sanderson, a leading figure in the British arts and crafts movement. She then returned to Hull House, established her own bookbindery, and developed during the next two decades a national reputation as a superior craftsman.

Starr succeeded in making beautiful books and probably thought of herself as that "happier and more rational human being" that she had said all workers could become once they took up a handicraft. Unfortunately, she never fulfilled her dreams of influencing the commercial production of books or of extending the pleasures of handcraftmanship to the masses. Thus, by the 1920s, Starr concluded sadly that she had been naive to hope that by practicing a handicraft one could help drive out the "hideousness and joylessness" of modern industrialism. *(See also: Addams, Jane; Bookbinding; Hull House; Progressive Era; Settlement House Movement)*

—**Bruce R. Kahler**

Further Reading

Kahler, Bruce R. "Art and Life: The Arts and Crafts Movement in Chicago, 1897–1910." Ph.D. diss., Purdue University, 1986.

Starr, Ellen Gates. "Art and Labor," *Hull-House Maps and Papers,* pp. 165-79. New York: Crowell, 1895.

———. "The Renaissance of Handicraft," *International Socialist Review* 2 (February 1902): 570-74.

Stearns, Lutie Eugenia (1866–1943)

Lutie Stearns, whom Edna Ferber once called "a terrific and dimensional human being," was an outspoken advocate for a variety of social issues, especially the establishment of public libraries.

Born in Staughton, Massachusetts, she emigrated to Wisconsin in 1871 and was hired at the Milwaukee Public Library as head of the circulation department in 1888. During her free time, she worked to get the Wisconsin Free Library Commission established in 1895. She became its secretary for two years, then library organizer when the commission restructured in 1897. From 1903 to 1914, she was head of the commission's Traveling Library Department. Estimates indicate she helped establish 150 public libraries, 1,400 traveling libraries, and 14 county library systems in Wisconsin in a ten-year period.

By 1914, her drive for libraries waned, and she resigned from the commission to pursue other causes. Despite a noticeable stutter, she developed into a skilled lecturer on topics of keen interest to her. Between 1914 and 1932, she traveled to thirty-eight states to speak on prohibition, women's rights, the League of Nations, industrial reform, peace, and education, all of which she favored. She was an active member of the Federation of Women's Clubs and the Women's International League for Peace and Freedom. From 1932 to 1935, she wrote a column for the *Milwaukee Journal* titled "As a Woman Sees It." She died on Christmas Day in 1943. (*See also: General Federation of Women's Clubs; Librarianship; Women's International League for Peace and Freedom*)

—**Wayne A. Wiegand**

Further Reading

Stearns, Lutie Eugenia. "My Seventy-Five Years," *Wisconsin Magazine of History* 42 (1958/59): 211-18, 282-87; 43 (1959/60): 97-105.
Tannenbaum, Earl. "The Library Career of Lutie E. Stearns," *Wisconsin Magazine of History* 39 (1955/56): 159-65.

Stein, Gertrude (1874–1946)

Author Gertrude Stein was born in Allegheny, Pennsylvania, but she did not remain a small-town American girl. She lived as a child with her family in Europe and then in California, and she spent most of her adult years in France, where she gained recognition as a writer of experimental literature and as a collector of art—and artists. At 27 Rue de Fleurus, her apartment in Paris, which she shared with her brother Leo and then, after 1909, with her lifelong companion and lover, Alice B. Toklas, she held court with many of the promising artists and writers of the day. She and Leo were among the first Americans to recognize modernist painting, and visitors to their salon apartment could see, in profusion, works by Pablo Picasso, Juan Gris, and others, as they heard Stein and the other artists gathered there discuss matters of art and life. The gatherings at her salon during the early decades have assumed almost legendary status because of who was there and because of Stein herself, a Buddha-like woman with talent and a formidable personality. Ernest Hemingway, in his posthumously published Paris memoirs (*A Moveable Feast,* 1964), gave credit to Stein's artistic genius, which was innovative and trend setting, as he also recognized the judgmental role she sometimes assumed regarding the art and artists of the day.

Stein's personality and legendary status in modern art have tended to overshadow her own writing, which writers such as Hemingway, Sherwood Anderson, and others first helped her to publish. Although Stein had studied to become a medical doctor at Johns Hopkins University, she tired of her studies and applied her scientific mind to her art. Throughout most of her career, Stein wrote for a limited audience, largely due to her unconventional style as well as the length of her works. Her *Making of Americans,* which was almost a decade in the writing, began as the history of an American family and then became the history of mankind (at 550,000 words). Influenced by psychologist William James's theory of consciousness as well as her own awareness that modernist art should show what reality is, not what one would like it to be, Stein violated conventional narrative structures so as to re-create on the printed page what she called the "continuous present." She believed that traditional word and sentence patterns inhibited meaning, and she experimented with variations on word groups (which she called word portraits), which might move beyond their prescribed meanings to take on a fresh resonance. Her style was marked by its repetitive qualities, and many today identify her work with Stein's own phrase: "A rose is a rose is a rose." Because of the highly experimental and sometimes undisciplined nature of her writing, some critics have faulted Stein's work for verbosity and obscurity, and her writing is less often regarded on its own merits than for the impact it had on other writers. Save for the successful *Autobiography of Alice B. Toklas* (published in 1933 and written in the persona of Alice, who engagingly comments on life at 27 Rue de Fleurus), Stein was, and continues to be, primarily a writer's writer.

Following the publication of *Alice B. Toklas,* Stein was greeted in America as a celebrity, as she undertook a national lecture tour wherein she talked to enthusiastic audiences about life and art in postwar Paris. During World War II, Stein and Toklas opened their French country home to American GIs, and Stein died quietly there at the end of the war. Stein is often remembered for her classification of Hemingway and his compatriots as the "Lost Generation." (*See also: Toklas, Alice B.; Women Writers*)

—**Linda Patterson Miller**

Further Reading

Brinnin, John Malcolm. *The Third Rose: Gertrude Stein and Her World.* Boston: Little, Brown, 1959.
Hoffman, Frederick J. *Gertrude Stein.* Boston: G. K. Hall, 1961.
Mellow, James R. *Charmed Circle: Gertrude Stein and Company.* New York: Praeger, 1974.
Stein, Gertrude. *The Autobiography of Alice B. Toklas.* New York: Harcourt Brace, 1933.
———. *Fernhurst, Q.E.D. and Other Early Writings.* Edited by Leon Katz. New York: Liveright, 1971.
———. *Lectures in America.* New York: Random House, 1934.
———. *The Making of Americans.* Paris: Contact Editions, 1925.
———. *Paris, France.* New York: Scribner, 1940.
———. *Picasso.* New York: Scribner, 1939.
———. *Selected Writings of Gertrude Stein.* Edited, with an introduction by Carl Van Vechten. New York: Random House, 1946, 1962.
———. *Three Lives.* New York: Grafton, 1910.
———. *Wars I Have Seen.* New York: Random House, 1944.

———. *Writings and Lectures, 1911–1945.* Edited by Patricia Meyerowitz. Baltimore: Penguin, 1967.

Weinstein, Norman. *Gertrude Stein and the Literature of the Modern Consciousness.* New York: Ungar, 1970.

~ Steinem, Gloria (b. 1934)

Since the 1960s, Gloria Steinem has been a central figure in the women's movement both nationally and internationally. She was born in Toledo, Ohio, the daughter of Ruth Nuneviller Steinem, a journalist, and Leo Steinem, who had a variety of real estate investments, including a summer resort in Michigan. Her parents met as students at the University of Toledo and married in 1921. Steinem's mother had her first breakdown in 1930 and suffered throughout her life from mental illness. After her parents separated in 1944, Steinem assumed responsibility for the care of her mother until Ruth's death in 1981. Steinem described their relationship in an essay, "Ruth's Song," published in *Outrageous Acts and Everyday Rebellions,* a collection of her essays that appeared in 1983.

Steinem entered Smith College in 1952, spending her junior year abroad and graduating magna cum laude in 1956. She was awarded a Chester Bowles fellowship to travel in India. By obtaining assignments to write pamphlets and newspaper supplements on India, she was able to remain until 1958. She became a member of the teams organized by Mahatma Gandhi to travel from village to village to try to stop riots based on caste distinctions. Her experience in India influenced her entire life and fostered her lifelong commitment to nonviolence and her opposition to class distinctions. Her career as a journalist took a great leap forward in 1963 when she did an undercover exposé of the Playboy nightclub empire of Hugh Hefner, editor and publisher of *Playboy* magazine. The essay, which appeared in *Show* magazine, helped to raise people's consciousness about the sexism inherent in the Playboy nightclubs' treatment of their uncomfortably clad waitresses, whose real working lives contrasted sharply with the glamorous image that the Playboy corporation attempted to give them. In 1968, she helped found *New York* magazine, for which she wrote many articles and the column "City Politic."

In the late 1960s, Steinem was active in the antiwar movement. She took part in the Vietnam War tax protest in February 1968 and went to the 1968 Democratic convention in Chicago to promote George McGovern as a peace candidate. She also became active in the campaigns of the United Farm Workers, which were rooted in the nonviolence she had experienced with Gandhi's teams in India. However, she was increasingly aware of the limitations of working inside male-dominated institutions and movements. Her feminist consciousness was further galvanized by her attendance at an abortion hearing in 1969 organized by the radical women's group Redstockings. Steinem, who had an abortion in London in 1956, wrote later in *Outrageous Acts* that "it wasn't until I went to cover a local abortion hearing for New York that the politics of my own life began to explain my interests. . . . Suddenly, I was no longer learning intellectually what was wrong. I knew."

Her concerns for women soon translated into actions, as Steinem became one of the founders of the Women's Action Alliance in 1970 and joined the National Women's Political Caucus in 1971.

She also became increasingly involved in the civil rights movement and went on the road with a black woman, Dorothy Pitman Hughes, speaking out against both racism and sexism. She was a cofounder of *Ms.* magazine, for which she served as a contributing editor for fifteen years, and she helped establish the *Ms.* Foundation for Women. Her essay "Sex, Lies, and Advertising" describes the evolution of *Ms.* into an ad-free publication for which she still serves as a consulting editor. Although critical of its early reluctance to support lesbian and gay rights, Steinem also became active in the National Organization for Women. In 1974, she joined the Coalition of Labor Union Women, and she became a member of the International Women's Year Committee in 1977. Since then, she has campaigned for numerous women candidates, including Shirley Chisholm, Bella Abzug, and Carole Moseley-Braun.

Her political effectiveness has been enhanced by the success of her journalistic and literary career. *Outrageous Acts and Everyday Rebellions* became a best-seller in 1983. Her book *Marilyn,* an imaginative study of the legendary movie star, also became a best-seller, as did her autobiographical *Revolution from Within* (1992), which discussed her problems with self-esteem. Another collection of her essays, *Moving beyond Words,* appeared in 1994. She also is a coeditor of *The Reader's Companion to U.S. Women's History* (1998).

Gloria Steinem has become one of the most influential and celebrated of modern North American feminists. Germaine Greer assessed Steinem's influence as a feminist activist, journalist, and role model: "There are hundreds and thousands of women out there who still look to her." For women of all ages, she continues to explore what it means to be a woman. In her essay "Doing Sixty," Steinem celebrates the last third of life as a time for the "full, glorious, alive-in-the-moment, don't-give-a-damn yet caring-for-everything sense of the right now." She continues to speak and write on women's issues, including economic empowerment for women and minorities. She also serves as president of Voters for Choice. *(See also: Journalism; Ms. Magazine; National Organization for Women; Women's Liberation Movement)*

—Jonathan W. Zophy

—Diana E. Axelsen

Further Reading

Carter, Betsey. "Liberation's Next Wave According to Gloria Steinem," *Esquire* 101 (June 1984): 202-6.

Cohen, Marcia. *The Sisterhood.* New York: Simon & Schuster, 1988.

Harrison, Cynthia. *On Account of Sex: The Politics of Women's Issues, 1945–1968.* Berkeley: University of California Press, 1988.

Heilbrun, Carolyn. *The Education of a Woman: The Life and Times of Gloria Steinem.* New York: Dial, 1995.

Langway, Lynn. "Steinem at 50: Gloria in Excelsis," *Newsweek* 103 (June 1984): 27.

Mankiller, Wilma, Gwendolyn Mink, Marysa Navarro, and Gloria Steinem, eds. *The Reader's Companion to U.S. Women's History.* New York: Houghton Mifflin, 1998.

Steinem, Gloria. *Marilyn.* New York: Henry Holt, 1986.

———. *Moving beyond Words.* New York: Simon & Schuster, 1994.

———. *Outrageous Acts and Everyday Rebellions.* New York: Henry Holt, 1983.

———. *Revolution from Within: A Book of Self-Esteem.* New York: Little, Brown, 1992.

———. "The Birth of *Ms.*" *New York* 26 (April 19, 1993): 134-136.

ॐ Stewart, Elinore (Pruitt) Rupert
(1876–1933)

Elinore Pruitt Stewart, author of *Letters of a Woman Homesteader* and *Letters on an Elk Hunt by a Woman Homesteader,* chronicled her early-twentieth-century experience on a southwest Wyoming ranch. Stewart intended her life as a woman homesteader to serve as a central theme of her work and offered homesteading as a panacea to the problems of wage-working urban women, suggesting her own example as encouragement. For this reason, her work appeals to modern readers because it offers a feminist perspective (although Stewart might have resisted that label) on the prospects of homesteading, and it offers an alternative to the stereotypes of western women as reluctant, depressed pioneers. The movie *Heartland* (1979), based on Stewart's story, underscores its contemporary appeal.

Stewart was born in 1876 in Indian Territory. At the age of fourteen, she was orphaned and working as a cook and laundress for railroad crews. By 1909, she was a widow and a mother, living in Denver and looking for an alternative to wage earning. She answered Clyde Stewart's newspaper ad for a housekeeper, moved to his ranch in Wyoming, and filed on an adjoining homestead. Soon thereafter, Elinore and Clyde married, but she maintained her determination to "prove up" on the homestead without any help from her spouse. In the end, she relinquished her homestead in 1912, and her widowed mother-in-law took it up, finally receiving the title to the property in 1915. In 1920, Ruth C. Stewart sold the land to her son Clyde.

Elinore Stewart, then, failed to achieve her goal of independent land ownership. But her importance lies less in the details of her land transactions than in her ability to express through writing the hopes and aspirations of men and women of her generation. She was a writer who also ranched in partnership with her husband. She chose homesteading and its supposed opportunities for working-class women as a literary device or vehicle for her optimism. She was a spirited woman who saw the West and its rugged landscape as a challenge. In her literature and her imagination, if not always in her day-to-day life, she met and overcame many of these challenges. *(See also: Migration and Frontier Women)*

—**Sherry L. Smith**

Further Reading
Garceau, Dee. *The Important Things of Life: Women, Work and Family in Sweetwater County, Wyoming, 1880–1929.* Lincoln: University of Nebraska Press, 1997.

George, Susanne. *The Adventures of the Woman Homesteader: The Life & Letters of Elinore Pruitt Stewart.* Lincoln: University of Nebraska Press, 1992.

Smith, Sherry L. "Single Women Homesteaders: The Perplexing Case of Elinore Pruitt Stewart," *Western Historical Quarterly* 22 (May 1991): 163-83.

Stewart, Elinore Pruitt. *Letters of a Woman Homesteader.* 1913-14. Reprint, Boston: Houghton Mifflin, 1976.

———. *Letters on an Elk Hunt by a Woman Homesteader.* Boston: Houghton Mifflin. 1915. Reprint, Lincoln: University of Nebraska Press, 1979.

ॐ Stewart, Maria (1803–1879)

Abolitionist, journalist, and educator, Maria Stewart was the foremother to a generation of black women political activists. Considered America's first black woman political writer, Stewart spoke militantly and eloquently in the struggle against racial and gender oppression. Little is known about her family life except that she was born free in Hartford, Connecticut in 1803. Orphaned at the age of five, by her own testimony, she was "bound out in a clergyman's family" for whom she worked until the age of fifteen. Stewart's formal education consisted of Sabbath school, which she attended until the age of twenty. By the age of twenty-three, she had moved to Boston where she married James W. Stewart, an independent businessman and veteran of the War of 1812. The Stewarts settled in Boston's small, but politically active, free black community. Within a few years following their marriage, James Stewart died, and through unscrupulous legal means, some local white businessmen swindled Stewart out of her inheritance. Following the death of her friend David Walker, a militant speaker for African American freedom, Stewart "experienced a religious conversion" which led her to devote her life to the struggle for the liberation of the African people. In 1831, Stewart contacted William Lloyd Garrison and Isaac Knapp, founders and editors of the *Liberator,* a Boston abolitionist newspaper. She brought them a completed manuscript, which Garrison and Knapp published as *Religion and the Pure Principles of Morality, the Sure Foundation on Which We Must Build.* In 1832, Stewart's address to the Afric-American Female Intelligence Society of America, the first recorded public speech made by an American-born woman, launched her speaking career. In her speeches, Stewart spoke directly to the black community, invoking images of Africa's historic legacy. She filled her speeches with militant appeals to African women to join the struggle against racial oppression and for woman's rights, calling on them to become educated and to build schools and other institutions to serve the race. Thus, she provided the ideological basis for the African American women's club movement in the century that followed. However, criticism from members of the black community, who disapproved of Stewart's "religious exhortations and her audacity as a woman," led her to leave Boston and abandon the podium.

Although Stewart gave up her public speaking career, she continued to work for her community through teaching and institution building in New York City, Baltimore, and Washington, D.C. In the late 1870s, Stewart secured a widow's pension for her late husband's service in the War of 1812. She used the modest funds to publish her collected works, which remain a valuable resource for understanding the development of black feminist thought. *(See also: Abolition and the Antislavery Movement; African Benevolent Societies; Black Women; Black Women's Clubs; Public Speakers: Nineteenth Century; Women Writers)*

—**Barbara Shircliffe**

Further Reading

Giddings, Paula. *When and Where I Enter*. New York: William Morrow, 1984.

Richardson, Marilyn. *Maria Stewart: America's First Black Woman Political Writer*. Bloomington: Indiana University Press, 1987. [Contains *Meditations from the Pen of Mrs. Maria Stewart*]

Yee, Shirley J. *Black Women Abolitionists, A Study in Activism, 1828–1860*. Knoxville: University of Tennessee Press, 1992.

ᵔᵕ Stinson, Katherine (1891–1977)

Katherine Stinson was the oldest member of a family that was very prominent in aviation in the early twentieth century. After receiving her pilot's license in 1912, she began making public flights in San Antonio, where she also lectured on aviation to school groups and recommended that it be made part of their curriculum. Her list of records and firsts includes being the first woman to loop an aircraft, the first woman to fly in the Orient, and the first pilot to make a nonstop flight from San Diego to San Francisco. In 1915, she helped her family found the Stinson Flying School in San Antonio, where she and her sister Marjorie were the principal flight instructors.

Stinson was an outspoken advocate of U.S. women pilots being allowed to fly for their country during World War I, but she was unsuccessful and was allowed to fly only on behalf of Red Cross and Liberty Loan Bond drives. She eventually went to France to serve as an ambulance driver. Although Katherine Stinson's pleas for active participation by women pilots in World War I fell on deaf ears, an idea was planted that may have assisted her successors in convincing the government to allow women to fly as part of the war effort at the outbreak of World War II. *(See also: Aviation)*

—**Claudia M. Oakes**

Further Reading

Oakes, Claudia M. *United States Women in Aviation through World War I*. Washington, DC: Smithsonian Institution, 1978.

ᵔᵕ Stone, Lucy (M. Blackwell) (1818–1893)

Lucy Stone was in her time the most admired and politically effective of the pioneer feminists. As a student at Oberlin College in the mid-1840s, Stone declared her intention to become a lecturer for woman's rights following her graduation. Employed at first by the New England Anti-Slavery Society, she divided her time between speaking for women and against slavery, and her lectures often drew crowds of two and three thousand. In 1850, she helped organize the first national woman's rights convention, held in Worcester, Massachusetts.

In 1855, despite her objections to married women's legal disabilities, Stone married Henry Blackwell, brother of the medical doctors Elizabeth and Emily. At their wedding ceremony, the couple presented their marriage protest, which drew widespread public attention to the gender-based inequities of the marriage laws. Motherhood and the Civil War temporarily slowed Stone's career, but in 1867, she resumed active campaigning for a woman suffrage amendment. A schism within the woman suffrage movement in 1869 divided her from Elizabeth Cady Stanton and Susan B. Anthony and their National Woman Suffrage Association (NWSA); continuing animosity resulted in her near-exclusion from the *History of Woman Suffrage,* prepared by Anthony, Stanton, and Matilda Joslyn Gage. Following the split, Stone and others founded the American Woman Suffrage Association (AWSA), an organization that developed strategic and tactical sophistication, eventually providing the political prototype for the lobbying effort led by Carrie Chapman Catt, which culminated in the passage of a woman suffrage amendment in 1920.

Stone was active in the national movement for woman suffrage; she also lobbied various state legislatures on behalf of a number of feminist and reform causes—the enactment of married women's property laws, equal rights statutes, divorce law reform, and school and municipal suffrage bills. However, Stone's most lasting contribution to the woman's movement is the *Woman's Journal,* which she founded in 1870 and edited until her death in 1893. This extraordinary archive of women's history provided a weekly chronicle of woman's progress—political, vocational, economic, cultural, and legal—both in the United States and abroad; the *Woman's Journal* enjoyed continuous publication for sixty-one years.

Stone's death on October 18, 1893, attracted worldwide attention. For generations afterward, grateful women continued to make pilgrimages to the birthplace of the woman known as the "morning star" of the woman's rights movement. *(See also: American Woman Suffrage Association; Anthony, Susan B.; National American Woman Suffrage Association; National Woman Suffrage Association; Social*

Purity Movement; Stanton, Elizabeth Cady; Woman's Journal)

—**Andrea Moore Kerr**

Further Reading

Blackwell Family Papers. Manuscript Division, Library of Congress, Washington, D.C.

Blackwell, Alice Stone. *Lucy Stone: Pioneer of Woman's Rights.* Boston: Little, Brown, 1930.

Hays, Elinor Rice. *Morning Star: A Biography of Lucy Stone.* New York: Harcourt Brace & World, 1961.

Kerr, Andrea Moore. *Lucy Stone: Speaking Out for Equality.* New Brunswick, NJ: Rutgers University Press, 1992.

Lasser, Carol, and Marlene Deahl Merrill, eds. *Friends and Sisters: Letters between Lucy Stone and Antoinette Brown Blackwell, 1846–93.* Urbana: University of Illinois Press, 1987.

Merk, Lois Bannister. "Massachusetts in the Woman Suffrage Movement." Ph.D. diss., Radcliffe College, 1961.

Wheeler, Leslie, ed. *Loving Warriors: Selected Letters of Lucy Stone and Henry B. Blackwell, 1853–1893.* New York: Dial, 1981.

ᴥ Stowe, Harriet Beecher (1811–1896)

Author Harriet Beecher Stowe was born in Litchfield, Connecticut, the seventh of nine children, to Roxana Foote and the famous Congregational minister Lyman Beecher. In 1836, she married Calvin Ellis Stowe, a professor of biblical literature at Lane Theological Seminary in Cincinnati.

Stowe was a prolific writer. She began publishing in 1833 and quickly became known as a regional, local-color author because of her New England novels such as *The Minister's Wooing* (1859), *The Pearl of Orr's Island* (1892), *Oldtown Folks* (1870), and *Poganuc People* (1878). In addition to novels, Stowe wrote poetry, children's books, religious treatises, and a travel book. She is best known, however, for *Uncle Tom's Cabin,* written in 1852, subtitled *Or Life among the Lowly.* This novel is the most widely read and influential antislavery novel ever written, but the book is equally significant as a domestic critique of slavery's threat to mainstream American family values. Inspired by Stowe's outrage over the Fugitive Slave Law of 1850, the book is a sentimental, melodramatic tale of a slave, Uncle Tom, who has converted to Christianity. He is sold and forced to part from his family. Stowe exposes the separation of families that the slave laws permitted and portrays the resulting horrors in such a manner as to appeal to the Christian ethics of her readers. The political effects of *Uncle Tom's Cabin* were immediate and remarkable. Antislavery sentiment in the North increased dramatically because of Stowe's portrayal, and hostile responses from southerners were vicious in their defense of "the peculiar institution."

Uncle Tom's Cabin appeared in serial form in the *National Era* from June 1851 through April 1852. In the first year after publication, the book existed in forty different editions and had sold over 350,000 copies in the United States. It was issued in England by over forty publishers, and English reviewers called it "the Iliad of the blacks." It has

Figure 59. Harriet Beecher Stowe
Seen here with her brother, prominent clergyman Henry Ward Beecher, Stowe's landmark novel, *Uncle Tom's Cabin,* played a major role in building support for the abolitionist movement, and it has remained in print since its publication in 1852. Used by permission of Corbis-Bettmann.

been translated into over twenty languages. Since taking over publication in 1862, Houghton Mifflin Company has never allowed the book to go out of print.

In 1853, Stowe published *A Key to Uncle Tom's Cabin* in an attempt to defend herself against over thirty anti-*Uncle Tom* novels that had appeared. In 1903, Edwin S. Porter produced the first film version of *Uncle Tom's Cabin;* Paramount produced another in 1918, and in 1927, Universal produced a third. Today, the novel is still part of the canon of literature taught in American public schools.

In 1896, Stowe died in Hartford, Connecticut. In 1903, her works were collected in the library of the Women's Building at the World's Columbian Exposition in Chicago. The collection included a twenty-volume set of her complete works and forty-two translations of *Uncle Tom's Cabin.* (See also: *Beecher, Catharine; Women Writers*)

—**Victoria L. Shannon**

Further Reading

Fetterly, Judith. *Provisions: A Reader from 19th-Century American Women.* Bloomington: Indiana University Press, 1985.

Hedrick, Joan D. *Harriet Beecher Stowe: A Life*. New York: Oxford University Press, 1994.

Wagenknecht, Edward. *Harriet Beecher Stowe: The Known and the Unknown*. New York: Oxford University Press, 1965.

✑ Striptease

Striptease is a form of entertainment in which a woman or man gradually undresses to music before an audience. In the United States, it derived from a tradition that included music halls and vaudeville. As early as 1847, the American Theater in New York City presented reviews that featured "dancing girls" in various states of undress. In the spring of 1904, the exotic dancer "Little Egypt" became the sensation of the St. Louis Exposition. In 1908, Anna Held, the first wife of show business impresario Florence Ziegfeld, disrobed behind a screen at the Mason Opera House in Los Angeles as an orchestra played "I'd Like to See a Little More of You." By the following year, New York's Columbia Theater was staging shows with titles such as "Tease for Two" and "Strip, Strip, Hooray."

Other entertainers in the 1920s were consciously developing more elaborate striptease routines. Mae Dix, for example, while clad in folded newspapers, read headlines to music and permitted box-seat patrons to tear sheets off her costume. In 1928, Hinda Wassau in Chicago and Carrie Finnell in Cleveland set the style that almost all strippers have followed since. Their acts featured staples of stripping such as formal evening gowns with long gloves at the onset of the routine, the bump and grind, the slow removal of garments down to a G-string (originally a nineteenth-century term for the *cache-sexe* of Native Americans) and pasties (nipple covers), and the musical accompaniment of a small band featuring a torpid but pronounced drumbeat. Finnell later embellished her striptease further with the invention of breast tassel twirling.

The 1930s were the halcyon days of stripteasing with stars such as Gypsy Rose Lee, Ann Corio, Margie Hart, Yvette Dare, Lois De Fee, Georgia Southern, and Zoritz, who used a boa constrictor in her act. Not only did strippers display themselves in a variety of imaginative ways, but they also appeared in comedy sketches with burlesque comedians such as Bud Abbott, Lou Costello, Jimmy Durante, Phil Silvers, and Looney Lewis. The most famous exotic dancer of the period was Gypsy Rose Lee, the author of three best-selling books, whose life was the subject of a popular Broadway musical and later a Hollywood film starring Natalie Wood.

Even in gradual decline as a theatrical entertainment, striptease produced a number of stars in the 1950s and 1960s such as Lily St. Cyr; Tempest Storm, who never once removed her G-string in four decades of stripping; Sally Rand, the legendary fan dancer; Blaze Starr, whose romance with Louisiana governor Earl Long became the subject of the 1991 film *Blaze;* and Jennie Lee, who started an Exotic Dancers Hall of Fame in 1961. In the 1970s and 1980s, strippers achieved more fame for their offstage antics than their onstage performances. Examples include Fannie Foxe, whose involvement with powerful Congressman Wilbur Mills in 1974 helped end his political career (the "Tidal Basin Affair"), and Morganna Roberts, known as baseball's "kissing bandit."

Stripping has also been kept in the public eye by the frequent appearances of exotic dancers on television talk shows and several popular novels, including Carl Hiassen's *Striptease* (1993), made into a Demi Moore film in 1996. Today's striptease headliners such as Venus De Light, Porsche Lynn, Hypatia Lee, and Teri Weigel also appear in X-rated movies and magazines. The 1990s also witnessed a dramatic increase in the number of so-called gentlemen's clubs, which employ large numbers of dancers in upscale, plush surroundings. In 1967, an estimated 7,000 women worked as strippers in the United States; today, more than 200,000 women work as exotic dancers and lingerie "models." Houston, Texas, alone has more than 40 striptease clubs and 20 lingerie studios.

Striptease is associated increasingly with prostitution, drink hustling, drugs, and the objectification and dehumanization of women. It is also linked to serious medical problems caused by silicone breast implants. Many exotic dancers have followed the lead of Carol Doda, one of the first women in the United States to have breast implants in 1966. Women often enter stripping because of the lure of "easy money," but they often leave it after a few years because of the many dangers inherent in the activity. *(See also: Popular Culture; Pornography; Prostitution)*

—Jonathan W. Zophy

Further Reading

Futterman, Marilyn. *Dancing Naked in the Material World*. Buffalo, NY: Prometheus, 1992.

Lewin, Lauri. *Naked Is the Best Disguise: My Life as a Stripper*. New York: William Morrow, 1984.

Skipper, J. K., and C. H. McCaghy. "Stripteases: The Anatomy and Career Contingencies of a Deviant Occupation," *Social Problems* 17 (1970): 391-405.

Wortley, Richard. *A Pictorial History of Striptease*. Secaucus, NJ: Chartwell, 1976.

✑ Strong, Anna Louise (1885–1970)

Considered "one of the most significant journalists of the twentieth century" by *Le Monde*, Anna Strong wrote more than thirty books on the development of socialist revolution and political upheaval in the Soviet Union, Poland, Lithuania, Spain, Tibet, Vietnam, and most notably, China. Her 1946 interview with Chairman Mao Tse-tung in Yenan, the Communist wartime headquarters, made known to the Western world Mao's famous reference to American imperialism as a "paper tiger," as well as his contempt for the atomic bomb.

Strong was born in Friend, Nebraska, the daughter of Rev. Sydney Strong, a Congregational minister, activist, and liberal thinker, and Ruth Tracy Strong, a college graduate who encouraged her independence. Strong attended Bryn Mawr and Oberlin Colleges, graduating summa cum laude and Phi Beta Kappa. She received an M.A. and Ph.D. in philosophy from the University of Chicago and worked in a canning plant to "come up hard against life." She also held positions at the Russell Sage Foundation, the National Child Labor Committee, and the U.S. Children's Bureau.

Joining her widowed father in Seattle, she took up mountain climbing and became involved with middle-class women's organizations as well as labor and antiwar activism. Her public support for activists arrested under the 1917 Espionage Act resulted in her recall from the Seattle School Board and her transformation from liberal reformer to radical activist. As a reporter for the Socialist *Union Record,* she covered the 1919 Seattle General Strike and became a member of the Strike Committee, for which she was arrested. Her articles about the events in the Soviet Union provided the only positive coverage of the Russian Revolution in the United States between 1917 and 1919.

In 1921, disillusioned by the failure of the "Seattle revolution," Strong became one of the first Americans to travel to the Soviet Union. She lived in the U.S.S.R. until 1949 as correspondent for *Hearst's International Magazine* and, later, as the Russian correspondent for the North American Newspaper Alliance. She also taught English to Trotsky and interviewed Stalin. By the 1930s, Strong was considered a Soviet expert. During her yearly visits to the United States, she gave public lectures and consulted with American businessmen as well as First Lady Eleanor Roosevelt.

Strong visited China several times to report major labor strikes, particularly noting women's participation. Strong helped smuggle Sun Yat-sen's widow, Soong Ching-ling, to the Soviet Union. In 1949, after Strong reported how little aid the Soviet Union had given the Chinese Communists, she was denounced as an American spy and deported from the U.S.S.R. Although American Communists and other leftists ostracized her, and the American press hounded her for anti-Soviet statements, Strong resisted the temptation to use her personal experience for political or monetary gain. In 1956, at the age of seventy-one, Strong returned to China, where she lived until her death. She published seventy issues of her newsletter, *Letters from China,* which offered first-hand accounts of the Cultural Revolution and the Red Guards. *(See also: Communist Party; Journalism; Unions)*

—**Marjorie King**

Further Reading

Duke, David T. "Anna Louise Strong and the Search for a Good Cause," *Pacific Northwest Quarterly* 66 (1975): 123-37.
History Committee of the General Strike Committee; Anna Louise Strong, historian. *The Seattle General Strike.* 1918. Reprint, Seattle, WA: Shorey Bookstore, 1972.
Jaffe, Philip. "The Strange Case of Anna Louise Strong," *Survey* 53 (1964): 129-39.
Niew, Judith. *Seven Women: Portraits from the American Radical Tradition.* 1977. Reprint, New York: Penguin, 1978.
Pringle, Robert. "The Making of a Communist: Anna Louise Strong, 1885-1925." Master's thesis. University of Virginia, 1967.
Reece, Bob. "An Octogenarian Red Guard," *Far Eastern Economic Review* 69 (1968): 456-58.
Strong, Anna Louise. *China's Millions: The Revolutionary Struggles from 1927-1935.* Rev. ed. 1935. Reprint, Beijing: Knight, 1965.
———. *The Chinese Conquer China.* Garden City, NY: Doubleday, 1949.
———. *I Change Worlds: The Remaking of an American.* 1935. Reprint, Seattle, WA: Seal, 1979.
———. *Letters from China,* 4 vols. Beijing: New World, 1961-1970.
———. *Peoples of the U.S.S.R.* New York: Macmillan, 1944.
———. *The Rise of the Chinese People's Communes—and Six Years After.* Beijing: New World, 1959, 1964.
———. *When Serfs Stood Up in Tibet.* Beijing: New World, 1960.
Strong, Tracy B., and Helene Keyssar. *Right in Her Soul: The Life of Anna Louise Strong.* New York: Random House, 1983.
Trotsky, Leon. Preface to *The First Time in History: Two Years of Russia's New Life,* by Anna Louise Strong, pp. 5-7. New York: Boni & Liveright, c. 1924.
Willen, Paul. "Anna Louise Strong Goes Home Again," *The Reporter* 12 (April 7, 1955): 28-31.

✒ Suffrage

In the United States, the right or opportunity to express a political opinion or participate in a ballot decision was considered a states' rights issue limiting woman's involvement until the ratification of the Nineteenth Amendment in August 1920. Woman's franchise developed slowly throughout the United States, beginning on local and state levels following the American Revolution. The first opportunities for women to cast ballots often occurred in the form of limited or partial suffrage that involved school board elections and taxation issues.

Some of the first women to experience limited suffrage were from Kentucky. In 1838, Kentucky gave school suffrage to widows who had school-age children. Michigan and Minnesota voted the same limited school suffrage to widows in 1875. Kansas expanded school suffrage, which was granted in 1861, to allow municipal suffrage in 1887, thereby allowing women to vote in city elections. By 1890, nineteen states added limited school suffrage, while three states granted women tax and bond suffrage if the women were taxpayers.

In 1848, women's rights became a national issue. The movement, headed by Elizabeth Cady Stanton and Susan B. Anthony, publicly aired grievances against the condition of women in society. One such grievance was the franchise. Although the original U.S. Constitution did not withhold voting privileges from women, it empowered individual states with jurisdiction over voting qualifications. Most states endorsed men as the only privileged voting class. In 1864, the Fourteenth Amendment used the word *male* in its definition of those persons enfranchised by identifying voters as male inhabitants of a state, twenty-one years of age, and citizens the passage of state amendments that would allow women the right to vote as a result of an approved state referendum. Many state referendum campaigns failed.

After World War I, a major push for national enfranchisement gained momentum. President Woodrow Wilson endorsed suffrage along with many noted women's clubs, such as the General Federation of Women's Clubs and the Young Women's Christian Association (YWCA). A proposed amendment referred to as the Susan B. Anthony Amendment passed the U.S. House of Representatives in 1918 and finally was approved by the U.S. Senate in 1919. The Nineteenth Amendment achieved ratification on August 26, 1920, when Tennessee became the thirty-sixth state to ratify, thus making all citizens, including women, enfranchised. *(See also: American Woman Suffrage Association; Equal Rights Association; Fourteenth Amendment; General Federation of Women's Clubs; National American Woman Suffrage Association; National Woman Suffrage Association; National Woman's Party; Nineteenth Amendment to the U.S. Constitution; Suffrage in the American West; Suffrage in the South)*

—**Paula Williams Webber**

Further Reading

Haley, Caroline, and Melanie Nolan, eds. *Suffrage and Beyond: International Feminist Perspectives.* New York: New York University Press, 1994.

Darcy, R., Susan Welch, and Janet Clark. *Women, Elections and Representation.* New York: Longman, 1987.

Ostrogorski, Moisei. "Women Suffrage in Local Self-Government," *Political Science Quarterly* 6 (December 1981): 677-710.

Stanton, Elizabeth Cady, Susan B. Anthony, and Matilda Joslyn Gage, eds. *History of Woman Suffrage.* Vol. 1. Rochester, NY: Charles Mann, 1887.

Webber, Paula Williams. "The Early Houston Woman Suffrage Movement." Master's thesis. University of Houston—Clear Lake, 1995.

Figure 60. Suffragist Fola LaFollette

Fola LaFollette, daughter of Wisconsin Senator Robert LaFollette and suffragist Belle Case LaFollette, worked for women's suffrage and also was sympathetic to labor concerns. She is shown here taking part in a march during the New York City garment strike near the culmination of the woman suffrage movement. Used by permission of Corbis-Bettmann.

of the United States. This statement suggested that women were neither inhabitants of the state nor citizens. The Fifteenth Amendment, introduced six months later, proposed that "the right of citizens of the United States to vote shall not be denied or abridged by the United States or any State, on account of race, color, or previous condition of servitude," thereby giving freedmen the right to vote.

In 1869, two woman's organizations evolved, the National Woman Suffrage Association (NWSA) and the American Woman Suffrage Association (AWSA). Although these two organizations differed in strategy and leadership, they both worked to further woman's rights. In 1890, the two organizations merged as the National American Woman Suffrage Association (NAWSA). Also in 1890, Wyoming became a member of the United States and was the first state admitted to the union as a full-suffrage state. In 1893, Colorado followed and was admitted as the second state granting women full-suffrage opportunities.

By 1900, several individual city and state suffrage associations had been established. Most suffrage organizations were affiliated with the work of the NAWSA and worked for

⚓ Suffrage in the American West
(1869–1896)

The political franchise was extended to women in the United States in 1920 with the ratification of the Nineteenth Amendment, but in some areas of the American West, women had been voting for half a century. While late-nineteenth-century organized efforts to achieve woman suffrage were concentrated in New England and New York and centered around personalities known for their activism in the abolition movement and the post-Civil War effort to obtain full citizenship for women and freedmen, women were first allowed to vote in the Rocky Mountain West.

The Democratic-led territorial legislature of Wyoming, seeing female suffrage as a means to advertise the region and to embarrass the puritanical Republican governor, extended the franchise to Wyoming women in December 1869. Two months later the Mormon-dominated Utah

Territorial Legislature voted in the affirmative on a woman suffrage measure. Here the principal motives were to counter accusations that Mormon women were the downtrodden, ignorant slaves of the male hierarchy; to recruit the national suffrage organization to lobby against antipolygamy legislation pending in Congress; and to promote Utah's bid for statehood. But in both Utah and Wyoming, the franchise was restricted by the territorial status of these two areas, since citizens of territories were not allowed to vote in gubernatorial or presidential elections. Moreover, in 1887, with the passage of the Edmunds-Tucker Act, which was designed to eliminate plural marriage as practiced by the Mormons, the U.S. Congress took the vote from the women of Utah territory.

Later, when Wyoming joined the union in 1890, it reaffirmed its two decades of experience with woman suffrage by adopting a constitution that carried a clause including women in the elective process; thus, it became the first state to allow its adult female citizens to participate in all political elections.

Despite suffragists' petitions and territorial governors' requests for a woman suffrage bill, from 1869 to 1876, the Colorado Territorial Legislature was unwilling to extend political privileges to women. Even in 1876, when Colorado joined the union as the Centennial State, its constitution limited women's political participation to school district elections; moreover, repeated attempts over the next seventeen years to extend women full electoral privileges met with failure. It was not until 1893 that a Populist-supported woman suffrage referendum was approved. Thus, Colorado became the second state to allow its women to vote.

Utah joined the Union in 1896 with a constitution reinstating woman suffrage. The same year, Idaho amended its constitution to allow women access to the ballot. In 1896, women were allowed full voting rights in these four Rocky Mountain states, but it would be fourteen years before any other state would extend such privileges to its female citizens and twenty-four years before women's right to the ballot would be recognized by an amendment to the federal Constitution.

Why did women first realize the goal of the elective franchise in the nineteenth-century American West? First, female suffrage was seen as a means to advertise a region and improve the image of a particular society or to attract investors and settlers. Second, it was often proposed as a political hoax to embarrass the opposition or was undertaken as an effort by a political faction to recruit women to its cause and thus gain or hold political supremacy. Third, the move for woman suffrage drew support from the reaction to the enfranchisement of black men in the Reconstruction era. Fourth, territorial residents saw that it could be used to recruit eastern support in their campaigns for statehood. Finally, it seemed to be a safe place to experiment with woman suffrage, and there was little organized opposition to women voting in these areas at that time.

In the West, the vote was generally viewed as a privilege bestowed by the governing body, not an inherent right. More often than not, western women and the eastern suffrage movement were used by those in power to achieve other goals, and women were granted the ballot at a specific time, not for the liberal principles lauded by the eastern movement, but for more pragmatic purposes, usually political. In short, women were enfranchised in the nineteenth-century American West as a matter of expediency, not ideology. *(See also: Migration and Frontier Women; Suffrage; Suffrage in the South)*

—Beverly Beeton

Further Reading

Beeton, Beverly. *Women Vote in the American West: The Woman Suffrage Movement, 1869–1896.* New York: Garland, 1986.

Jensen, Billie Barnes. "Colorado Woman Suffrage Campaigns of the 1870s," *Journal of the West* 12 (April 1973): 254-71.

Larson, T. A. "Emancipating the West's Dolls, Vassals, and Hopeless Drudges: The Origins of Woman Suffrage in the West." In *Essays in Western History in Honor of T. A. Larson,* edited by Roger Daniels, 1-16. Laramie: University of Wyoming Press, 1971.

ᐧᐧ Suffrage in the South

There was little suffrage activity in the South until the latter part of the nineteenth century, when state-level associations were organized as auxiliaries of the National American Woman Suffrage Association (NAWSA). The first large assemblage of suffragists in the region was the annual convention of the NAWSA in Atlanta in 1895. Other southern cities in which the NAWSA held conventions were New Orleans (1903), Louisville (1911), and Nashville (1914).

During 1916 and 1917, the National Woman's Party (NWP) organized branches in the southern states. Unlike the NAWSA, the NWP employed militant tactics in its crusading. Opinion in the South was hostile toward militancy, however, and the southern branches of the NWP did not engage in it. Some southern women were arrested and jailed for picketing the White House in Washington, but apparently there were no imprisonments for suffrage activities in the southern states.

The movement in the South was complicated by the area's large number of black women. The southern prejudice against black voting made the prospect of black women at the polls abhorrent to many. The focus of the suffrage movement was sex, not race. Nevertheless, the two issues were intertwined in southern thinking, and woman suffrage was rarely discussed without the injection of its real and imagined racial implications.

Southern women often stated that they wished to be enfranchised by their states rather than by the federal government. They asked that state constitutions be amended to eliminate sex as a qualification for voting, but in no state did they succeed in gaining the adoption of such an amendment. They did win a few concessions, however. As a result of their efforts, the legislatures of Arkansas (1917) and Texas (1918) opened primary elections to women voters, and the Tennessee legislature (1919) authorized their voting for presidential electors and in municipal elections.

Despite their preference for enfranchisement through state action, most of the southern suffragists supported the Nineteenth, or "Susan B. Anthony," Amendment. The South as a whole opposed it, however. Many southerners considered the proposed amendment an infringement on state's rights. Others feared that it would mean federal control of elections. When it was submitted for ratification, only four southern states approved: Texas (June 1919), Arkansas (July 1919), Kentucky (January 1920), and Tennessee (August 1920). Since Tennessee's ratification was the thirty-sixth and since thirty-six was the number required at that time, its action made the Nineteenth Amendment part of the U.S. Constitution. With woman suffrage a reality, the other southern states belatedly ratified, the last being Mississippi in 1984. *(See also: National American Woman Suffrage Association; National Woman's Party; Southern Women's History; Suffrage; Suffrage in the American West)*

—A. Elizabeth Taylor

Further Reading
Fuller, Paul E. *Laura Clay and the Woman's Rights Movement.* Lexington: University of Kentucky Press, 1975.
Johnson, Kenneth R. "Kate Gordon and the Woman Suffrage Movement in the South," *Journal of Southern History* 38 (August 1972): 365-92.
Scott, Anne Firor. *The Southern Lady: From Pedestal to Politics, 1830–1930.* Chicago: University of Chicago Press, 1970.
Stanton, Elizabeth Cady, Susan B. Anthony, M. J. Gage, and I. H. Harper, eds. *The History of Woman Suffrage,* 6 vols. New York: National American Woman Suffrage Association, 1881–1922.
Taylor, A. Elizabeth. "The Woman Suffrage Movement in Mississippi, 1890–1920," *Journal of Mississippi History* 30 (February 1968): 1-34.
———. *The Woman Suffrage Movement in Tennessee.* New York: Twayne, 1957.
Wheeler, Marjorie Spruill. *New Women of the New South: The Leaders of the Woman Suffrage Movement in the Southern States.* New York: Oxford University Press, 1993.

～ Suffrage Memorial Tablets

To mark the tenth anniversary of the founding of the National League of Women Voters in 1920, which followed the passage of the federal woman suffrage amendment, the league proposed a tenth anniversary memorial fund plan to perpetuate the memory of former suffrage leaders. The league had been created by the National American Woman Suffrage Association as its only descendant. The plan called for establishment of national and state rolls of honor, recording the names of those whose work and influence brought women "a new day of partnership in public life."

Gifts of $1,000 for national listing and $100 for state would provide a capital fund to help carry on league work,

perpetuating the influence of suffrage leaders. The honorees were nominated according to local league interest, based on association with suffrage leaders and inspiration from them in their local communities as well as in the state.

At the 1930 convention, nineteen members of the National Honor Roll attended the convention banquet, including James Lees Laidlaw of New York State, the only male honoree. His name, honoring all men allied to the suffrage cause, was placed on a separate plaque adjacent to the National Honor Roll. The national memorial, a five-foot-high bronze tablet, was installed in league headquarters in 1931 during a National League Council meeting. Seventy-one women's names were listed under twenty-five states and the District of Columbia. The states were California, Colorado, Connecticut, Illinois, Indiana, Iowa, Kansas, Kentucky, Massachusetts, Michigan, Minnesota, Missouri, Nebraska, New Hampshire, New Jersey, New Mexico, New York, Ohio, Oregon, Pennsylvania, Rhode Island, Tennessee, Texas, West Virginia, and Wisconsin.

Carrie Chapman Catt, one of three presidents of the suffrage organization, spoke at the tablet's dedication, recalling that all but a few of the names had been familiar friends. Her name was listed as a president, as well as under Iowa, where she grew up, and New York, where she later lived.

Designed by Gaetano Cecere, this work depicted pioneers stopping in their steady forward march to pass a torch to fresher, more youthful hands. The rays of a sun surmounting the design symbolized the spread of their achievements. Ten stars marked the first ten years of the league. The names of the three suffrage associations' presidents were immediately below the classic scene: Susan B. Anthony, Anna Howard Shaw, and Carrie Chapman Catt. Later disposition of the memorial, as the league moved its headquarters, is unknown.

Twenty-one states also established state memorial tablets. At least two—New York and Ohio—still occupy walls in their state capitols. *(See also: League of Women Voters; Suffrage)*

—Hilda R. Watrous

Further Reading
League of Women Voters Collection. Library of Congress, Washington, D.C.
National League of Women Voters. Proceedings of the Tenth Anniversary Convention of the National League of Women Voters. Washington, DC, 1930.
New York (State and City) Woman Suffrage Collection. Butler Library, Columbia University.
"Unveiled at Headquarters," *New York Times* (April 16, 1931): 5.
Woman's Journal 14 (December 1929): 28-9; 15 (March-May 1930): 26-27; 16 (May 1931): 25.

～ Swenson, May (1913–1989)

Poet, naturalist, and implicit feminist, May Swenson was an incessant experimenter with poetic structure and language, often pushing her poems to their limits to strengthen the bond between reader and poem. Poetry is neither ideas nor philosophy, she contended but is, instead, "a happening" that the poet "makes," one that leads the reader beyond appearance and flux to the essence of the thing perceived.

Swenson's experiments are an extension of Ralph Waldo Emerson's organic theory of poetic structure. Many experiments focus directly on line placement and division, but she also used space and shape liberally for the same purposes. Because she believed that something can be felt about a poem even before one begins to read it, shape becomes a kind of objective correlative that reinforces the experience the poet presents through language and imagery. Yet she seldom sacrificed content to shape as concrete poets often do, since she finished the poem linguistically before imposing any shape on it.

While experimentation was more important to Swenson than any consistent technique, her most beautiful poems are semantic still lifes describing common objects, events, and scenes. They are deceptively unassuming; however, there is always an undercurrent of movement hidden within, structurally or linguistically, a tension waiting for contact with the reader to come alive.

Animals, especially birds and horses, are Swenson's most common poetic subjects and serve as oblique comments on the physical, social, sexual, and intellectual natures of human beings. By carefully studying animals and using them as epistemological tools, she believed, we can discover what it means to be human.

Swenson's few poems about women, however, are probably her most important ones, for they are attempts to come to terms with what it really means to be a woman. She examines women's place in society; she discusses their relationships with parents, with children, with men, and with other women; and she considers what it means to have a woman's body. This exploration was a painful one, for it took a good part of her career as a poet for her to come to her most powerful statements about life as a woman. *(See also: Women Writers)*

—**Kenneth E. Gadomski**

Further Reading

Gadomski, Kenneth E. "May Swenson's Poetry: A Discussion with Checklist." Ph.D. diss., University of Delaware, 1984.
Ostriker, Alicia. "May Swenson and the Shapes of Speculation," *American Poetry Review* 7 (March/April 1978): 35-38.
Russell, Sue. "A Mysterious and Lavish Power: How Things Continue to Take Place in the Work of May Swenson," *Kenyon Review* 16 (Summer 1994): 128-39.

❧ Synagogue Sisterhoods

Synagogue sisterhoods grew out of the domestic feminism of middle- and upper-class women's clubs at the turn of the century. Prior to the establishment of sisterhoods, Jewish women had developed their own local literary and social clubs and had founded the National Council of Jewish Women (NCJW) to promote Judaism. However, religious divisions within the NCJW rendered it ineffective as a religious organization, and it changed its emphasis to social reform work. Religious women developed sisterhoods as their alternative, because synagogues were the center of Jewish religious life in America and because working through one's synagogue posed no conflicts over religious practice or interpretation. Since most women active in Jewish women's groups were also synagogue members and since many of those groups already held their meetings in the synagogue building, the transition was easy.

As the number of local sisterhoods grew, each movement developed its own national organization to coordinate efforts. The Women of Reform Judaism (until 1994 called the National Federation of Temple Sisterhoods), an affiliate of the Union of American Hebrew Congregations (the umbrella organization for Reform synagogues), was founded January 22, 1913. The conservative movement followed with the founding of the Women's League of the United Synagogue of America on January 21, 1918. The Union of Orthodox Jewish Women's Organizations of America was organized on April 19, 1920. All three groups were largely founded by the wives of prominent clergy and lay leaders of the organizations with which each sisterhood federation was affiliated.

Initially, women were not permitted to serve on synagogue boards or in the clergy. Sisterhoods provided women with their only participation in synagogue policy, usually by their basing demands for power on the argument that one could not be a good Jewish mother without a voice in the religious training of one's children. In addition to supporting synagogue religious schools, sisterhoods educated their own members, ran cultural and social service programs, and raised vital funds for synagogue buildings and projects and for their movements' seminaries. Today, women serve on synagogue boards and in the clergy, so sisterhoods are no longer women's sole voice in the arena of synagogue decision making. Many sisterhoods have changed meeting times from afternoons to evenings to accommodate working women. Its continued role as a vital fund-raiser has preserved the strength of the sisterhood movement. *(See also: Jewish Women; Religion)*

—**Faith Rogow**

Further Reading

American Jewish Yearbook. Philadelphia: Jewish Publication Society, 1913–1985.

Talbert, Mary Burnett (1866–1923)

Mary Burnett Talbert, educator, activist in prison reform, human rights leader, and community organizer for the National Association for the Advancement of Colored People (NAACP), National Association for Colored Women (NACW), and the YWCA, used organizations to improve conditions for the race. Mary Morris Burnett was born on September 17, 1866, the last of eight surviving children to Cornelius J. Burnett and Caroline Nichols Burnett of Oberlin, Ohio. Natives of North Carolina, her parents moved to the college town in 1860 to enable their children to have the educational opportunities offered there. They established several businesses that catered to the Oberlin College clientele.

The home and town nurtured social activism in Mary Burnett. She attended the public schools of Oberlin through high school, graduated in 1883 at the age of sixteen, and then enrolled in Oberlin College. She completed her training in three years to begin her professional career by accepting a position as liberal arts instructor in the segregated school system of Little Rock, Arkansas. In 1887, she became the first female assistant principal in the state, the highest position a black person or a woman had been given. One year later, she became principal of the Union High School of Little Rock, remaining in the city until her marriage in 1891 to William Herbert Talbert. They moved to Buffalo and raised their daughter, Sarah May (b. 1892).

She became a charter member of the Buffalo Phillis Wheatley Club in 1899 and soon became active in the NACW. By 1911, the Empire State Federation of Women's Clubs was formed. She served as its second president, 1912 to 1916, during which time she served as NACW vice president (1914) and president (1916 and 1918).

While leading the NACW, Talbert addressed issues of national and international priorities. Her career showed the multiplicity of reforms engaged in simultaneously by black women in this era. While she was a national organizer for the NACW in 1913, Talbert also helped to organize branches and increase circulation for the newsletter of the NAACP. While raising over 5 million dollars in the Liberty Bond Drive among African American women, Talbert spread the message of the NAACP in the South. Following her presidency of the NACW, she became a field-worker for the NAACP and raised funds for a church-affiliated home for black working girls.

Talbert was an ambassador of goodwill during the World War I era when she served as YMCA secretary and Red Cross nurse in Romagne, France in 1919, teaching classes for African American soldiers. Following the war, Talbert attended the Pan-African Congress in Paris and the International Congress of Women in Zurich. After her return to the United States, she traveled under the auspices of the U.S. government and lectured to black women's groups on food preservation and conservation. She served as the club's first elected delegate to the quinquennial conference of the International Council of Women that met in Christiana, Norway in 1920, informing European audiences about the discrimination against African Americans. Talbert was one of the American women appointed to the League of Nation's Committee on International Relations. She joined the 1921 delegation of prominent blacks who petitioned President Warren Harding to grant clemency to the members of the African American 24th Regiment falsely accused of inciting the Houston, Texas, riots of 1917. In 1922, she joined other NACW members in organizing the International Council of Women of the Darker Races of the World to address the needs of people of color around the globe and served on the organization's Committee on Education. As NAACP vice president and board member from 1918 until her death in 1923, she served as the national director of the Anti-Lynching Crusaders, a national network of black women working to raise money and consciousness about lynching and for passage of a federal antilynching bill. She was the first woman to receive the NAACP's Spingarn Medal for her dedicated service in preserving the Frederick Douglass home and for her other human rights activities.

She died at the age of fifty-seven on October 8, 1923, of coronary thrombosis in Buffalo, New York, where she is buried in Forest Lawn Cemetery. *(See also: National Association for the Advancement of Colored People; National Association of Colored Women)*

—Dorothy C. Salem

Further Reading

Brown, Hallie Q. *Homespun Heroines and Other Women of Distinction*, pp. 216-19. Xenia, OH: Aldine, 1926.

Logan, Rayford. "Talbert, Mary." In *The Dictionary of American Negro Biography,* edited by Rayford Logan and Michael Winston, 576-77. New York: Norton, 1985.

Wesley, Charles. *The History of the National Association of Colored Women's Clubs, Inc.* Washington, DC: National Association of Colored Women's Clubs, 1984.

Williams, Lillian S. "Talbert, Mary Morris Burnett." In *Encyclopedia of World Biography.* Vol. 16, edited by David Eggenberger, 396-98. Palatine, IL: McGraw-Hill/Heraty, 1973.

❧ Talbot, Marion (1858–1948)

Marion Talbot was a leading advocate of educational equality for women. As a college administrator and professor, Talbot sought advancement for graduate women within academia and encouraged women to accept the challenge of higher learning.

Early in her career, Talbot tried to dispel the myth that women could not handle the pressures of college work. Graduating in 1880 from Boston University with a bachelor of arts degree, Talbot organized a survey that questioned the medical view of Dr. Edward Clarke in his controversial *Sex in Education, or A Fair Chance for the Girls* (1873) that the mental and physical strain of college work would damage the reproductive system of young women. Talbot's survey of college graduates and nongraduate women found no evidence to support Clarke's view. The survey revealed that college graduate women were just as fertile as nongraduate women. In 1881, with the support of friends, Talbot founded the Association of Collegiate Alumnae, which later became known as the American Association of University Women. This organization had a twofold purpose: to provide fellowship to women attending college and to assist women wanting to attend college.

In 1884, Talbot graduated with a bachelor of science degree from Massachusetts Institute of Technology, where she became interested in the new field of domestic science. Talbot believed that science could be a foundation to deal with the problems of sanitation and consumer protection. In 1887, she collaborated with Ellen Richards in editing *Home Sanitation: A Manual for Housekeepers,* the first of several publications on this topic. In 1890, Talbot was appointed as instructor in domestic science at Wellesley College. However, New England's conservative attitude toward educating women and Wellesley's disinterest in supporting development of sanitary science left Talbot dissatisfied, and she accepted an offer to teach and act as dean of undergraduate women and assistant professor of sanitary science at the University of Chicago.

From 1892 until 1899, when she was appointed dean of university women, Talbot was in charge of the day-to-day activities of the women students and development of the sanitary science program. Her support of coeducation led to an unsuccessful campaign against an internal proposal to establish a separate junior college for women at the University of Chicago. Her persistent support for coeducation continued despite administrative resistance.

Marion Talbot's fight for women's educational equality inspired others to continue the struggle for coeducation. Through her support of women's education, she offered young women an alternative to the domestic sphere. *(See also: Association of Collegiate Alumnae; Coeducation; Higher Education;* Sex in Education, or A Fair Chance for the Girls; *University of Chicago)*

—**Michael A. deLeón**

Further Reading
Berkin, Carol Ruth, and Mary Beth Norton. *Women of America: A History.* Boston: Houghton Mifflin, 1979.

Rosenberg, Rosalind. *Beyond Separate Spheres: Intellectual Roots of Modern Feminism.* New Haven, CT: Yale University Press, 1982.

Storr, Richard J. *Harper's University: The Beginning.* Chicago: University of Chicago Press, 1966.

❧ Tallchief, Maria (b. 1925)

Maria Tallchief was the first native-born American prima ballerina. Born in Fairfax, Oklahoma, to Ruth Porter and Alex Tall Chief, an Osage Indian, she moved to Beverly Hills, California, with her family in 1933. There, she and her sister studied music and dance with Ernest Belcher. Tallchief went on to study with Bronislava Nijinska and, in 1942, she went to the Ballet Russe de Monte Carlo. She was married to George Balanchine from 1946 to 1952, and trained with him at his School of American Ballet. After one brief season with the Paris Opera Ballet in 1947, she danced with the New York City Ballet from 1947 to 1960. She was the prima ballerina with the New York company and again for one season with the American Ballet Theater in 1960. She was the artistic director for the Chicago City Ballet until 1987. She was married to Henry Paschen, Jr., in 1957. *(See also: Dance; Native American Women)*

—**Susan Kinnell**

Further Reading
Kufrin, Joan. *Uncommon Women: Gwendolyn Brooks, Sarah Caldwell, Julie Harris, Mary McCarthy, Alice Neel, Roberta Peters, Maria Tallchief, Mary Lou Williams, Eugenia Zukerman.* Piscataway, NJ: New Century, 1981.

Livingston, Lili C. *American Indian Ballerinas.* Oklahoma City: University of Oklahoma Press, 1997.

Maynard, Olga. *Bird of Fire: The Story of Maria Tallchief.* New York: Dodd, Mead, 1961.

Tallchief, Maria, and Larry Kaplan. *Maria Tallchief: America's Prima Ballerina.* New York: Henry Holt, 1997.

Tobias, Tobi. *Maria Tallchief.* New York: Crowell, 1970.

❧ Tarbell, Ida (1857–1944)

Ida Tarbell belonged to the generation of American women who attended college after the Civil War, did not marry, and devoted themselves to a career in public life. Tarbell's decision to work as a writer and pioneering investigative reporter was influenced by her participation in the late-nineteenth-century Chautauqua movement that promoted self-improvement and by her father's experience in the oil business.

Franklin Tarbell, like many small businessmen at the turn of the century, was forced out of business by a monopolistic conglomerate that undercut his prices. Ida never forgave the man who ruined her father's fortunes; as a young journalist employed by *McClure's Magazine,* she wrote a series of articles exposing the ruthless practices of John D. Rockefeller and his Standard Oil Company. The sensational series earned Tarbell the reputation of "muckraker" and fueled the demand for "trust-busting" reform in the Progressive Era. Her diligence as an editor of and contributor to *McClure's Magazine* and *American Magazine* affirmed the role of the press as a public watchdog.

Tarbell's articles and books describing American business at the turn of the century—such as *The History of the Standard Oil Company* (1904) and *The Tariff in Our Times* (1911)—offer a vivid portrait of society during the Gilded Age. Although she did not identify herself as a militant feminist, concern for the welfare of women was a recurrent theme in her writings. Her investigations into business and trade practices took the point of view of the consumer and showed the ways in which women and children were victimized. Tarbell herself was a hard-working but always controversial personage, whose pen offered hope to the downtrodden and inspired terror in the hearts of the privileged. *(See also: Journalism; Magazines; Progressive Era)*

—**Jane Crisler**

Further Reading

Brady, Kathleen. *Ida Tarbell: Portrait of a Muckraker.* New York: Putnam, 1984.

Tarbell, Ida. *All in a Day's Work.* New York: Macmillan, 1939.

———. *The Business of Being a Woman.* New York: Macmillan, 1912.

———. *The History of the Standard Oil Company.* New York: McClure, Phillips, 1904.

———. *The Life of Abraham Lincoln.* New York: Doubleday & McClure, 1900.

———. *The Tariff in Our Time.* New York: Macmillan, 1911.

⚞ Taylor, Rebecca (fl. 1930–1980)

Rebecca Taylor led efforts to improve the conditions of working women in Texas during the first half of the twentieth century. Taylor began her career in the early 1930s as a teacher of night classes. Knowing of Taylor's mastery of Spanish, Meyer Perlstein recruited her in 1934 to represent the International Ladies Garment Workers Union (ILGWU) in San Antonio, where most of the garment workers were either Mexican or Mexican American. Over the next two years, Taylor worked to bring the union to local factories, but employers' resistance and plant closures frustrated her efforts. From 1937 through 1940, the ILGWU thrived in San Antonio under Taylor's guidance.

Successful strikes in 1937 and 1938 helped the union win a contract without a strike in 1939. The fortunes of the ILGWU in San Antonio declined during the 1940s, and membership in San Antonio locals had fallen to about six hundred when Taylor left her post in the early 1950s. From the 1950s until the late 1970s, Taylor represented employers rather than employees as a personnel manager for garment manufacturers.

Taylor's principal strengths as a union organizer were her bilingual abilities and the confidence that she inspired among the business leaders with whom she negotiated. Because of her middle-class Anglo heritage, Hispanic workers did not immediately trust Taylor, and the leadership of Taylor's Hispanic co-workers, who were themselves garment workers, was an essential element in the ILGWU's success in San Antonio. At the national level, Taylor stressed the importance of drawing union organizers from among the Mexican and Mexican American women in the Southwest, but union officials failed to appreciate the importance of cultural ties among rank-and-file industrial workers. This weakness and the passage of the Texas right-to-work law of 1947 were understood by Taylor to spell disaster for the ILGWU in San Antonio. *(See also: Garment Industries; International Ladies Garment Workers Union)*

—**Julia Kirk Blackwelder**

Further Reading

Blackwelder, Julia Kirk. *Women of the Depression: Caste and Culture in San Antonio, 1929–1939.* College Station: Texas A&M University Press, 1984.

⚞ Taylor, Valerie (b. 1913)

Valerie Taylor is a pioneer lesbian writer and public speaker. Born Velma Nacella Young in Aurora, Illinois, Taylor was inspired by her own pacifist parents, her distant Potawatomie Indian ancestry, and her two great-grandmothers. One marched in a woman suffrage parade in 1889, carrying Valerie's father on her back; the other started a community library and women's club.

Taylor lived in a construction camp in Indiana before attending Blackburn College at Carlinville, Illinois, from 1935 to 1937. She taught country school for three years, married in 1938, and bore three sons. After fifteen "disastrous" years, she divorced and supported her three sons by office work, editing, and ad writing. By night, she produced confession stories. (The single mothers in her office called themselves the "mother tigers.")

Taylor also began to write poetry and fiction. Much of her work draws from her experiences on a midwestern farm during the Great Depression. Over three hundred poems, a variety of short pieces, and a Gothic romance have been published. She is best known, however, as an early lesbian novelist during a time, the 1950s, when most lesbian literature was written by men—badly. Taylor wanted to read about real lesbians' lives. Of her thirteen published novels, her best known are the Erica Frohmann trilogy, *Prism,* and *Rice and Beans.*

Taylor became an outspoken lesbian activist, appearing on many radio and television programs in the Chicago area, where she had moved in 1956 to become an assistant editor at Henry Regnery Co. She was interviewed by Studs Terkel and Phil Donahue. As a member of the Socialist Party and the Women's International League for Peace and Freedom, she was active in antiracist and antiwar movements. Since moving to Tucson, Arizona, in 1979, Taylor has continued to write and to support progressive causes and gay rights, including a coffee house for lesbians and sanctuary for refugees. *(See also: Lesbianism; Pacifism and the Peace Movement; Women Writers)*

—**Marjorie King**

Further Reading

Foster, Jeannette H., and Valerie Taylor. *Two Women Revisited: The Poetry of Jeannette Foster and Valerie Taylor.* Rev. ed. Austin, TX: Banned Books, 1991.

Grier, Barbara. *The Lesbian in Literature,* 3d ed. Tallahassee, FL: Naiad, 1981.

Taylor, Valerie. *Girls in Three-B.* New York: Fawcett-Cress, 1959, 1965.

———. *Journey to Fulfillment.* Vol. 1, Erica Frohmann Trilogy. 1964. Reprint, Tallahassee, FL: Naiad, 1982.

———. *Love Image.* Bates City, MO: Naiad, 1977.

———. *Prism.* Tallahassee, FL: Naiad, 1981.

———. *Return to Lesbos.* Vol. 3, Erica Frohmann Trilogy. 1963. Reprint, Tallahassee, FL: Naiad, 1982.

———. *Rice and Beans.* Tallahassee, FL: Naiad, 1989.

———. *Ripening.* Austin, TX: Banned Books, 1988.

———. *Stranger on Lesbos.* London: Spearman, 1960. (Precursor to Erica Frohmann trilogy.)

———. *Unlike Others.* 1963. Reprint, Tallahassee, FL: Naiad, 1976.

———. *Whisper Their Love.* London: Spearman, 1959.

———. *World without Men.* Vol. 2, Erica Frohmann Trilogy. 1963. Reprint, Tallahassee, FL: Naiad, 1982.

Teaching

Ever since the latter nineteenth century—and even earlier in some parts of the country—the majority of teachers in the United States have been women. The development of teaching as female occupation began in the late eighteenth and early nineteenth centuries, when new conceptions of female roles began to change women's lives. The emerging ideology of true womanhood held that women played an especially critical role in the moral and intellectual development of children. As larger numbers of women began to attend school in the period following the American Revolution, it became commonplace in certain areas—New England in particular—to hire women to teach a short summer session in schools for younger children and girls who were not needed for work on farms. This was associated with the notion that women carried a special responsibility and talent for rearing children. Influential early women

educators, most notably Emma Willard and Catharine Beecher, argued that teaching was an especially appropriate occupation for women because of this. Other educators agreed. By 1850, the majority of teachers in New England, the nation's most educationally developed region, were young women.

The feminization of teaching proceeded quickly to other parts of the country in the latter nineteenth century. Many historians have argued that feminization occurred because women commanded smaller salaries than men teachers and thus offered schools an inexpensive way of expanding. Others have emphasized factors that caused men to move out of teaching, such as the lengthening of school terms—which made it impossible for men to combine teaching with other jobs—and new educational requirements, making it easier for relatively well-educated women to get teaching positions. Feminization appears to have occurred first and fastest in urban areas, where school terms were longest and enrollments grew fastest; and it proceeded most slowly in the largely agricultural South, where school terms were short and teacher turnover was high. Like other working women in this period, most women teachers were quite young. The spinster schoolmarm was a rarity through most of American history. For most women, teaching was a job taken during the interlude between school and marriage. This pattern seems to have persisted until the post-World War II period, when rapidly expanding enrollments and a set of new attitudes about women's work resulted in larger numbers of women remaining in teaching after marriage.

Women continue to dominate teaching today in roughly the same proportions as at the turn of the century. Although about three of four teachers are women, school administration continues to be dominated by men. Like other "female" professions in that regard, teaching has afforded educated women an opportunity to develop and employ their skills and knowledge, but it has not offered them a high level of autonomy for professional development. With the improvement of salaries and benefits in teaching brought on by unionization over the past several decades, there has been a slight defeminization of teaching since 1970. But in the public mind, teaching continues to be "women's work," and teachers receive less remuneration and are assigned lower status than other professional groups, despite the critical social and cultural roles they play in modern society. *(See also: Beecher, Catharine; Cult of True Womanhood; Education; Female Academies; Mount Holyoke; Normal Schools; Willard, Emma Hart)*

—**John L. Rury**

Further Reading

Herbst, Jurgen. *And Sadly Teach: Teacher Education and Professionalization in American Culture.* Madison: University of Wisconsin Press, 1989.

Rousmaniere, Kate. *City Teachers: Teaching and Social Reform in Historical Perspective.* New York: Teachers College Press, 1997.

Rury, John L. "Who Became Teachers: The Social Background of American Teachers." In *American Teachers, Histories of a*

Profession at Work, edited by Donald Warren. New York: Macmillan, 1989.

Strober, Myra H., and Audry Gordon Lanford. "The Feminization of Public School Teaching: Cross-Sectional Analysis, 1850–1880," *Signs: Journal of Women in Culture and Society* 11 (Winter 1986): 212-35.

♆ Technology

Technology and science are the new religions of the twentieth century, and women have not been allowed behind the altar rail. Brought up on dolls and makeup kits rather than trucks and chemistry sets, plagued by math anxiety, and underrepresented in engineering and physics departments, they are ill prepared for positions of power and influence in the technological marketplace. Crucial issues concerning the future of reproductive technologies, hazardous waste, depletion of the ozone layer, and nuclear weapons will be decided by those who understand the intricacies of their development, and women are rarely members of this high priesthood.

Some women have broken through the barriers and made significant technological contributions. Such women usually receive no credit for this blasphemous behavior, or if given credit at the time, they are written out of history, lost forever as role models for coming generations. The cotton gin, the circular saw, the clothes wringer, and the astrolabe—all owe their existence to creative women.

While it is often assumed that technology has been and continues to be a liberating force for women, the evidence is decidedly mixed. Current theorists also argue that the technical competence of men, which women traditionally lack, is a more subtle form of domination than overt physical control, but one with the same results. Although more women than men work with machines, men as a gender control the design and implementation of new technologies. In short, men create technological change, and women react to it.

New technologies in the workplace have lessened the need for heavy lifting, so that, potentially, many new fields have opened up for women. However, the workforce is still highly sex segregated: Women constitute over 90 percent of all nurses, child care workers, and secretaries. Computers that allow huge increases in productivity are replacing many women clerical workers. Thus, many women lose their jobs, while the remaining workers find that the new jobs require less skill than the previous secretarial positions. The jobs become more routinized: A word processor operator simply enters keystrokes and does not have the variety of duties of the former secretary.

Women are concentrated in occupations that often lend themselves to computerization. Bank teller, telephone operator, and airline reservation clerk are other female-dominated jobs that have been replaced or decimated by computers. The new hi-tech industries that design, build, and repair computers do employ large numbers of women, yet the vast majority of them work at the lowest skill and pay levels. Another unfortunate trend is that as women gain access to some hi-tech, all-male jobs, the jobs become obsolete. Women became computer programmers, and now sophisticated computers program other computers; women learned to climb telephone poles, and now plug-in phones are the norm. In general, technology in the workplace does not seem to have upgraded women's disadvantaged position.

The unpaid workplace of the housewife has been the site of many technological innovations that have replaced or eased many of her functions, yet the middle-class homemaker finds that the amount of work in the home has actually increased. Thus, household technology is labor-saving but not time-saving. New standards of cleanliness, fewer servants, extended family members in the home, and her new duties as consumer, chauffeur, and family psychologist contribute to her hectic day. Ironically, one final reason for the increased workload of the "everyday housewife," employed outside the home or not, is that other family members feel less compelled to offer help to one surrounded by technology. They mistakenly feel that it has considerably lightened her load.

Reproductive technologies and birth control have undoubtedly given women more control over this crucial aspect of their lives. Yet feminists worry about their implications. They see a link between genetic and reproductive technologies and wonder to what ends genetic technologies will be used. They see surrogate motherhood more subject to legal control and emotional argument than sperm donorship. Some argue that these reproductive technologies—largely under the control of male scientists, doctors, ethicists, and legal experts—are another instance of the shifting of male control over women. They fear that these technologies may entrench current class and race divisions between women and that the well-documented preference for male children could reach new heights as couples may soon be able to implement these preferences.

The United States is facing a shortage of mathematicians and scientists, and women and minorities form an untapped source of recruits. Thus, both feminists searching for equality for women and government researchers searching for potential scientists would like to see more women involved in the design, implementation, and assessment of technology. Both groups are currently addressing problems such as the higher incidence of math anxiety among women, the small number of women in technical fields, and the lack of retraining opportunities for women workers displaced by technological change. The secular religions of science and technology will have much to gain from these new high priestesses: The values, insights, and goals of both sexes and all races will surely give us a more balanced view of the world we are trying to understand. *(See also: Mathematics; Physicians; Science)*

—**Susan Lee Weeks**

Further Reading

Bindocci, Cynthia Gay. *Women and Technology: An Annotated Bibliography.* New York: Garland, 1993.

Figure 61. Telephone Operators
The invention of the telephone created the need for operators and was a major factor in women's increased participation in the workforce during the early 20th century. Telephone operators are shown here in a photograph circa 1915. Used by permission of UPI/Corbis-Bettmann.

Cockburn, Cynthia. *Machinery of Dominance: Women, Men and Technical Know-how.* London: Pluto, 1985.

Cockburn, Cynthia, and Susan Ormrod. *Gender and Technology in the Making.* Thousand Oaks, CA: Sage, 1993.

Hacker, Sally. *Pleasure, Power and Technology: Some Tales of Gender, Engineering, and the Cooperative Workplace.* Boston: Unwin Hyman, 1989.

Macklin, Ruth. *Surrogates and Other Mothers: The Debates over Assisted Reproduction.* Philadelphia: Temple University Press, 1994.

Stanley, Autumn. *Mothers and Daughters of Invention: Notes for a Revised History of Technology.* Metuchen, NJ: Scarecrow, 1993.

ᨑ Telephone Operators

The telephone, along with the typewriter, was a major contributor to women's rapid increase in labor-force participation at the beginning of the 20th century. In the earliest days of the telephone industry in the 1870s, boys were hired to service switchboards, but they were rapidly replaced by women, until women accounted for almost 99 percent of the country's switchboard operators by World War I. Women ostensibly were more polite and reliable than boy operators, but in addition, women were eager to find work, were believed less likely to unionize, and were hired to work at half to a quarter of men's wages.

The telephone industry generally hired young, attractive, single, native-born white women as operators. The work was considered to be safe, clean, and respectable, particularly in comparison with other types of women's work under industrialization. The pace of the work, long and irregular hours, and rigid supervision over the operators' vocabulary, diction, and physical movements, however, made operating work physically and mentally monotonous and exhausting. The ideal operator was as machinelike as possible. Despite the realities of the job, public fancy was caught by the romantic and heroic image of the operator as portrayed by the telephone industry and in songs and visual images until the passing of the old operator era in the middle of the twentieth century.

While women initially found operator work attractive, they became increasingly active after the turn of the century in labor union organizing for better working conditions and wages and for protection against the consequences of automation. Operating remained a sex-segregated job until AT&T signed a consent decree in 1973 with the Equal Employment Opportunity Commission, after which men were slowly added to the operator force. Telephone operators continued to lose their jobs to automation, especially with the introduction of computers that understand human speech. *(See also: Technology)*

—Lana F. Rakow

Further Reading

Lipartito, Kenneth. "When Women Were Switches: Technology, Work, and Gender in the Telephone Industry, 1890–1920," *American Historical Review* 99 (October 1994): 1074-1111.

Maddox, Brenda. "Women and the Switchboard." In *The Social Impact of the Telephone,* edited by Ithiel de Sola Pool, 262-80. Cambridge: MIT Press, 1977.

Norwood, Stephen H. *Labor's Flaming Youth: Telephone Operators and Worker Militancy, 1878–1923.* Urbana: University of Illinois Press, 1990.

Schmitt, Katherine M. "I Was Your Old 'Hello' Girl," *Saturday Evening Post* 203 (July 12, 1930): 18-19.

Television

From the earliest days of television, women have played important roles as program creators, performers, and viewers. While the medium is an influential purveyor of stereotypes about gender, the family, romance, race, and sexuality and has been reluctant to take feminism seriously, it has also created major women stars and remains a powerful tool for changing perceptions of women's lives. The industry's dependence on ratings has also made women crucial to the success of individual programs, broadcast networks, cable services, and the advertisers that support commercial television.

Women have been featured in every TV genre but have been especially visible in domestic situation comedies. Series such as *Father Knows Best* (1954–1963), *Leave It to Beaver* (1957–1963), and *The Donna Reed Show* (1958–1966) presented an idealized version of traditional family life, while comedians such as Gracie Allen and Lucille Ball offered somewhat more complicated visions of femininity. *The Mary Tyler Moore Show* (1970–1977) challenged convention with an unmarried woman protagonist whose life centered on the workplace, and stars such as Roseanne Barr wielded substantial control as creators and producers of their own series, yet the sexual politics of the sitcom remained essentially unchanged into the 1990s.

The milestones in prime-time drama have been even more paradoxical. For example, the emphasis on glamour in *Charlie's Angels* (1976–1981) tended to undermine its innovative focus on a trio of women crime fighters. Women have only slowly been integrated into network news broadcasts, with some fifteen years elapsing between the first and second women—Barbara Walters and Connie Chung—to coanchor the evening news. Other nonfiction formats have been more welcoming, particularly the daytime talk show, where host-producer Oprah Winfrey swiftly became one of television's wealthiest and most powerful figures.

Because they often control household purchasing decisions, women have been crucial target audiences since the 1950s, when radio soap operas moved to television, becoming one of daytime's dominant genres. In prime time, an increasing emphasis on demographics has led to strategies such as CBS's famous 1980s Monday night lineup, which countered ABC's *Monday Night Football* with women-oriented sitcoms and the female-buddy police drama *Cagney and Lacey,* a series saved from network cancellation in part by its women fans' letter-writing campaign. With the rise of cable television in the 1980s, services such as Lifetime began to air original and syndicated shows aimed at women. *(See also: Mass Communication Media; Popular Culture; Soap Operas)*

—Laura Stempel

Further Reading

Allen, Robert C., ed. *Channels of Discourse, Reassembled: Television and Contemporary Criticism,* 2d ed. Chapel Hill: University of North Carolina Press, 1992.

———. *Speaking of Soaps.* Chapel Hill: University of North Carolina Press, 1992.

D'Acci, Julie. *Defining Women: Television and the Case of Cagney and Lacey.* Chapel Hill: University of North Carolina Press, 1994.

Faludi, Susan. *Backlash: The Undeclared War against American Women.* New York: Anchor Books, 1991.

Feuer, Jane, Paul Kerr, and Tise Vahimagi, eds. *MTM: "Quality Television."* London: BFI, 1984.

Mellencamp, Patricia. "Situation Comedy, Feminism, and Freud: Discourses of Gracie and Lucy." In *Studies in Entertainment: Critical Approaches to Mass Culture,* edited by Tania Modleski, 80-95. Bloomington: Indiana University Press, 1986.

Spigel, Lynn. *Make Room for TV: Television and the Family Ideal in Postwar America.* Chicago: University of Chicago Press, 1992.

Temperance Movement (1790s–1900)

The temperance movement was one of the many reforms to interest women in the nineteenth century. It was born in the late eighteenth century along with the American Republic, out of the need for a sober citizenry to provide moral governance. Women, responsible for moral training, were the natural persons to train a temperate citizenry. Moral suasion—convincing drinkers of the error of their ways—was the movement's primary tactic.

From the inception of temperance organizations, women were major participants in them, but the pervasiveness of the cult of domesticity denied women a leadership role. Organized religion, which reinforced this notion of spheres while allowing active participation and limited opportunities for leadership by women, performed a role that cannot be downplayed. Virtually all temperance supporters were churchgoers, but the movement itself was nondenominational. The Woman's Crusade of 1873 and 1874 is but one example of the Christian nature of the temperance cause. Women were not violent, nor did they lecture. Instead, they publicly prayed for the redemption of saloon keepers and their patrons.

Temperance developed and transformed woman's role in Victorian America. Taking as their model the active role women played in the abolition movement, temperance women began to speak publicly on the evils of drink. Temperance was advocated to protect home and family, the two foundations of women's sphere. By taking this approach, women created and legitimized a greater role for themselves.

Born of the Woman's Crusade, the Woman's Christian Temperance Union (WCTU), under the leadership of Frances E. Willard, became the preeminent temperance organization of the last quarter of the nineteenth century. The predominantly Protestant and middle-class WCTU championed temperance under the banner of "Heart and Home and Native Land." Yet even as the WCTU grew in size and influence, conflict developed over the issue of temperance and its effectiveness. Because moral suasion had not produced the desired results, legal suasion (or prohibition) became a popular alternative among many reformers. By the 1880s, the WCTU supported the Prohibition Party while still advocating temperance.

As the Progressive Era developed, prohibition became the favored solution to the woes caused by drink, and the Anti-Saloon League became its leading proponent. The WCTU worked for the Eighteenth Amendment along with the league and celebrated its passage, but it was a pyrrhic victory. Temperance became a national laughingstock, ridiculed in nearly all aspects of society. The movement would not again gain widespread support until the 1980s. *(See also: Christianity; Cult of True Womanhood; Moral Reform; Prohibition and the Volstead Act; Willard, Frances E.; Woman's Christian Temperance Union)*

—Anita M. Weber

Further Reading

Alexander, Ruth M. " 'We Are Engaged as a Band of Sisters': Class and Domesticity in the Washingtonian Temperance Movement, 1840–1850," *Journal of American History* 75 (1988): 763-88.

Bordin, Ruth. *Women and Temperance: The Quest for Power and Liberty, 1873–1900.* Philadelphia: Temple University Press, 1981.

Epstein, Barbara Leslie. *The Politics of Domesticity: Women, Evangelism, and Temperance in Nineteenth-Century America.* Middletown, CT: Wesleyan University Press, 1981.

Tyrell, Ian. *Sobering Up: From Temperance to Prohibition in Antebellum America.* Westport, CT: Greenwood, 1979.

⨀ Tenayuca, Emma (b. 1917)

Emma Tenayuca played a short but dramatic role as a leader of Mexican and Mexican American workers in San Antonio during the 1930s. Heavily influenced by her socialist grandfather, she proved herself a charismatic speaker during her years as a schoolgirl. After graduating from high school in 1934, she went to work as an elevator operator and became active in the labor movement. Through her participation in worker movements, she met Homer Brooks, one-time Communist Party candidate for the Texas governorship, whom she later married.

In 1936, Tenayuca and others held a rally to organize all of San Antonio's Hispanic workers into a single and independent union. At this rally, Tenayuca was selected as head of the women's division, but the organizational efforts soon failed. Thereafter, Tenayuca organized the Workers' Alliance, a group that disseminated civil rights literature and staged demonstrations. During a 1937 Workers' Alliance sit-in at San Antonio City Hall, Tenayuca was arrested for refusing to leave the building. She also played a controversial role in the 1938 San Antonio pecan shellers' strike. In 1939, she retired from labor activism after a Workers' Alliance rally ended in a riotous attack by the movement's Anglo opponents. *(See also: Chicana; Unions)*

—Julia Kirk Blackwelder

Further Reading

Blackwelder, Julia Kirk. *Women of the Depression: Caste and Culture in San Antonio, 1912–1939.* College Station: Texas A&M University Press, 1984.

Calderon, Roberto R., and Emilio Zamora. "Manuela Solis Sager and Emma Tenayuca: A Tribute." In *Chicana Voices: Intersections of Class, Race, and Gender,* pp. 30-41. Austin: University of Texas Press, 1990.

Wertenbacker, Green Peyton. *San Antonio: City of the Sun.* New York: Crowell, 1946.

⨀ Terrell, Mary ("Mollie") Church (1863–1954)

Club leader, speaker, and social activist in peace, suffrage, and racial advancement organizations, Mary Church Terrell spent her adult life in efforts to clarify and correct racial and gender discrimination. She was born on September 23, 1863, in Memphis, Tennessee, to Robert R. Church, the first black millionaire in the South, and Louisa Ayers Church, owner of a fashionable hair salon. She received her early education at the "Model School" associated with Antioch College and in the public schools of Yellow Springs, before moving to Oberlin, Ohio, to attend the high school and Oberlin College. After earning her A.B. degree from Oberlin in 1884, she taught at Wilberforce University and the Preparatory School for Colored Youth (later the M Street High School) in Washington, D.C. With a leave of absence from the high school (1888–1890), she traveled and studied abroad in England, Belgium, Switzerland, France, and Germany. After her return, she rejoined the teaching faculty of the M Street High School and shortly thereafter married the principal, Robert H. Terrell, who was later appointed a municipal judge in the District of Columbia. As Mary Church Terrell, she began an active public career as a lecturer in this country and abroad, often appearing on the Chautauqua circuit.

Terrell served in many leadership roles: an appointee to the first Washington, D.C., board of education (1895–1901/ 1906–1911), the first female president of the Bethel Literary and Historical Society of D.C. (1892–1893), a member of John Milholland's Constitution League, a founder and member of the NAACP executive committee, a founder of the Washington Colored Women's League, the first president of the National Association of Colored Women (NACW), a founder of Delta Sigma Theta, and the second vice president of the Council of Women of the Darker Races. During this active career, Terrell raised two daughters, Mary Terrell (Tancil Beaupreu) and Phyllis Terrell (Langston), and remained active in Republican politics.

Mary Church Terrell was in one writer's words a "genteel militant" who was active in social reform efforts to overcome racism and sexism in this country. She was a member of many women's groups seeking suffrage, rights, and peace: the National American Woman Suffrage Association, the Women's International League for Peace and Freedom, the National Woman's Party, and the Association of Collegiate Alumnae (later the American Association of University Women or AAUW). She helped prepare for demobilization during World War I through the War Camp Community Service and served as a delegate to the International Peace Congress held in Zurich in May 1919 and at the World Fellowship of Faith in London in 1937.

Honorary degrees from Oberlin College, Wilberforce University, and Howard University reflected her lifetime of community commitment. At the age of eighty-six, she launched a three-year battle for membership in the Washington chapter of the AAUW to challenge its racial exclusionary policies. As she won that battle, she assumed leadership of a coordinating committee for the Enforcement of the District of Columbia Anti-Discrimination Laws. On February 28, 1950, she participated in an early "sit-in" at Thompson Restaurant in Washington, D.C., later bringing suit to end segregation. She participated in picketing and protest marches until the June 1953 ruling ending segregated eating establishments in the nation's capital. She lived to see the Supreme Court decision, *Brown v. Board of Education, Topeka, Kansas,* which ended legal segregation in schools in May 1954. She died on July 24, 1954, and rests at Lincoln Memorial Cemetery, Suitland, Maryland. *(See also: Colored Woman's League; National Association for the Advancement of Colored People; National Association of Colored Women; National Woman's Party; Women's International League for Peace and Freedom)*

—Dorothy C. Salem

Further Reading
Davis, Elizabeth L. *Lifting as They Climb.* Washington, DC: National Association of Colored Women, 1933.

Giddings, Paula. *When and Where I Enter: The Impact of Black Women on Race and Sex in America.* New York: Bantam, 1984.

Harley, Sharon. "Beyond the Classroom: Organized Lives of Black Female Educators, 1890–1930," *Journal of Negro Education* 51 (Summer 1982): 254-65.

———. "Mary Church Terrell: Genteel Militant." In *Black Leaders of the Nineteenth Century,* edited by Leon Litwack and August Meier, 307-21. Chicago: University of Illinois Press, 1988.

Holland, Endesha Ida Mae. "The Autobiography of a Parader without a Permit." Ph.D. diss., University of Minnesota, 1986.

Jones, Beverly Washington. "Quest for Equality: The Life of Mary Eliza Church Terrell, 1863–1954." Ph.D. diss., University of North Carolina—Chapel Hill, 1980.

Salem, Dorothy. *To Better Our World: Black Women in Organized Reform, 1890–1920.* Brooklyn, NY: Carlson, 1990.

Sterling, Dorothy. *Black Foremothers, Three Lives,* 2d ed. New York: Feminist Press, 1979, 1994.

Terrell, Mary. *A Colored Woman in a White World.* Washington, DC: Ransdell, 1940.

Wesley, Charles Harris. *The History of the National Association of Colored Women's Clubs: A Legacy of Service.* Washington, DC: Mercury, 1984.

✑ Textiles: North and South

The American textile industry provides a kind of summary of the American working experience. Some of the earliest factories developed in textiles; their labor forces first attempted organization; immigration fostered change in the source of those laborers; and the industry itself changed regional emphases as it moved from its New England origins to the South in the 1880s and after.

Women have made up the core of the textile labor force from the beginning of the industry. Early textile mills were located to take advantage of both sources of water power and readily available supplies of labor. Those laborers were drawn from rural New England families and were largely female. Representing predominantly single women between the ages of fifteen and thirty, the female "operatives" were attracted by higher wages and the relative mobility that came with textile work. They worked for a variety of reasons, including contributions to a family wage, savings for a dowry, subsistence in an otherwise declining agricultural economy, and independence. Most worked for relatively short periods and an average of five years of often discontinuous labor before leaving the paid workforce for marriage. Although it delayed the age of marriage, the work experience provided opportunity for young women.

Factories using female labor developed boardinghouses that provided a paternalistic watch over the workers. Modeled after the early mills established by Francis Lowell at Waltham, Massachusetts, the system of boardinghouses was known as the Waltham system. The controls provided a hoped-for docile and controlled labor force and an environment that countered criticism of the early factories. Autonomy for the women was so circumscribed, however, that rebellions against the system were frequent by the 1830s. In the 1840s and 1850s, immigrant labor gradually replaced native-born female workers, and while women continued to occupy a prominent place, they ceased to dominate the textile labor force.

Southern textile mills began to develop with William Gregg's famous South Carolina Graniteville mills and those at Roswell in Georgia in the two decades before the Civil War. The decided expansion of southern textiles came as part of the New South enunciated by journalist and orator Henry Grady and others in the 1880s and 1890s. As the mills were brought to the cotton, textile mill owners engaged in some of the same hiring practices used in northern mills a half-century earlier, and their textile mills drew on the labor of women as a source of docile, relatively cheap labor that would not compete with men's. In the biracial South, however, textile workers were largely white, and the southern mill owner quickly supplemented the Waltham-style boardinghouse with the mill village so that entire families would come to work in the mills. In contrast to the earlier northern experience, then, the female southern mill workers did not gain extrafamily experience or relative autonomy before marriage; rather, the mill work became a factory version of the family economy and the family wage in the tightly controlled paternalistic yet exploitative setting of the company towns in which 75 percent of the workers labored.

Conditions in the mill towns became infamous for poverty, deprivation, and disease. Southern progressive Edgar Gardner Murphy summarized the workers' condition in 1904:

> [I know] . . . mills in which children and all were called to work before sunrise, laboring from dark to dark. I have repeatedly seen them at labor twelve, thirteen and even fourteen hours a day. . . . I have seen children eight and nine years of age leaving the factory as late as 9:30 at night, and finding their way . . . through the unlighted streets of the mill villages, to their squalid homes.

Southern textile mills would deteriorate and become the object of intense labor struggles in the 1920s and 1930s as well as the focus of considerable investigative energy that ultimately resulted in protective legislation for the women and children workers of the mills. Ironically, the difficult conditions of textile work produced protective legislation

that circumscribed the legal and social autonomy that women might have gained from the wages they earned in the mills.

Although evidence of women's long association with the workplace, the textile industry also illustrates the ironies of women's paid labor. Hired for docility, expected to be either short-term workers or participants in a family wage, women found the work brought with it the adjustments typical of shifts from a preindustrial to an industrial economy but seldom brought the advantages of wage-based independence, workplace autonomy, or alleviation of domestic expectations. (See also: *Industrial Revolution; Lowell Mill Girls; Protective Legislation*)

—**Thomas F. Armstrong**

Further Reading

Cohn, David L. *Life and Times of King Cotton.* New York: Oxford University Press, 1956.

Dublin, Thomas. *Women at Work.* New York: Columbia University Press, 1979.

Janiewski, Dolores E. *Sisterhood Denied: Race, Gender and Class in a New South Community.* Philadelphia: Temple University Press, 1985.

Kessler-Harris, Alice. *Out to Work.* New York: Oxford University Press, 1982.

~ Thanksgiving

As a national commemoration, Thanksgiving represented the convergence of nineteenth-century woman's influence and mainstream patriotism with the precolonial Amerindian autumnal custom that emerged as the regional New England tradition that honored the Pilgrim's first celebration of the survival of the Plymouth settlement in the autumn of 1621. President George Washington proclaimed a national day of thanksgiving for the new nation in 1789, but it was not observed on the same day nor in all of the states. President Abraham Lincoln's wartime proclamation in the fall of 1863 designated the last Thursday in November as Thanksgiving Day for the nation. Subsequently, Thanksgiving Day was observed annually on that day as a celebration of enduring Victorian domestic, religious, and patriotic values until the mid-twentieth century, when the fourth Thursday of November was designated the national holiday.

As the unrivaled spokeswoman of the cult of true Womanhood as well as an adroit practitioner of woman's influence, editor Sarah Josepha Hale (1788–1879) pursued a dual strategy from 1827 until 1863: She wrote personal letters to presidents and governors of states and territories, urging that they proclaim the last Thursday of November as Thanksgiving Day. Both the cuisine and the customs established as traditional for this regional holiday would become the standard for the patriotic and pious nondenominational (although distinctly Protestant) national day of thanksgiving. As editor of the influential *Godey's Lady's Book,* Hale annually offered recipes for traditional Yankee dishes to extol the patriotic domesticity of Thanksgiving and demurely lobbied her readers to support the establishment of a national day of thanksgiving in her editorial columns of *Godey's* November issues. Hale modified her yearly request for Thanksgiving in 1861 with an apolitical suggestion that such a holiday might also be observed as a day of peace. In 1863, Hale succeeded in securing a presidential proclamation following her personal audience with Abraham Lincoln in Washington, D.C.

Thus, the establishment of a national Thanksgiving Day represented several trends within Victorian domestic culture. As a symbol of nineteenth-century patriotic fervor, the post-Civil War celebration of Thanksgiving Day fostered, or at least gave lip service to, national unity. As an elevation and equation of the regional customs and values of New England as the national standard for mainstream America, the celebration of Thanksgiving Day reinforced the status of New England as the "cradle of the nation." Finally, with her powerful example of domestic feminism, Hale's successful campaign proved the efficacy of woman's influence to apply moral suasion to male authorities at the national political level. In the face of the social, political, and economic impact of late-nineteenth-century industrialism and urbanism on the middle-class family and the women within it, Thanksgiving Day represented annual national homage paid to the importance of the family, consecrated the Victorian ideals of nostalgic agrarianism and righteous patriotism, and thereby fortified the cult of domesticity by emphasizing the centrality of the domestic domain to which women were relegated. *(See also: Cult of True Womanhood; Hale, Sarah Josepha)*

—**Angela M. Howard**

Further Reading

Douglas, Ann. *The Feminization of American Culture.* New York: Knopf, 1977.

Finley, Ruth E. *The Lady of* Godey's. Philadelphia: Lancaster, 1931.

Travers, Carolyn. "The American Thanksgiving: The Evolution of a Tradition," *New England Journal of History* 48 (1991): 30-35.

Zophy, Angela Howard. "A True Woman's Duty 'To Do Good': Sarah Josepha Hale and Benevolence in Antebellum America." In *The Moment of Decision: Biographical Essays on American Character and Regional Identity,* edited by Randall M. Miller and John R. McKivigan, 154-69. Westport, CT: Greenwood Press, 1994.

∿ Theater or Drama

For over a century, U.S. literary critics have lamented the state of American drama, neglecting or ignoring the dramatic writing that could answer their complaints: the work of U.S. women playwrights. At every stage of U.S. history, women's plays have marked important phases in theater evolution.

Mercy Otis Warren, the earliest American playwright, supported revolutionary politics and pilloried royalists in *The Adulateur* (1772) and *The Group* (1775). Anna Cora Mowatt, in *Fashion* (1845), produced what a 1908 essay on "Our Infant Industry" acknowledged as "perhaps the first native drama of any considerable merit." Mowatt followed her success as a playwright with an acting career, bringing middle-class respectability to stage performance. Through the nineteenth century, stage adaptations of women's fiction (most notably, versions of Harriet Beecher Stowe's *Uncle Tom's Cabin*) supplied national stages, along with original drama. By the turn of the century, Martha Morton (probably the first U.S. woman career playwright) had founded the Society of Dramatic Authors, an alternative to the all-male American Dramatists Club.

For all of U.S. women's benchmark contributions to the national theater, relatively few have made a consistent success of the commercial stage. Notable exceptions include Clare Kummer, author of *Good Gracious, Annabelle* (1916) and other farces, who was commercially successful throughout her career; Anne Nichols, whose *Abie's Irish Rose* (1922) entered American folklore; Rachel Crothers—director, actor, and set designer, as well as playwright—who was the earliest steadily flourishing woman playwright of serious problem plays on modern women's issues, from *A Man's World* 1909) through *Susan and God* (1937); Clare Boothe, whose *The Women* (1936) attracted audiences for decades; Mary Chase, whose *Harvey* (1945) played for almost 2,000 performances; Lillian Hellman, who captured notice with *The Children's Hour* (1934) and sustained an exceptional dramatic career; and contemporary feminist playwrights such as Beth Henley.

But for many other playwrights and women in other theater professions, support and production has come in regional and little theaters and through specialized prize competitions and publication in magazines. Contests have been important in introducing and establishing innovative women playwrights. For example, early in the century, Josephine Preston Peabody, author of *The Piper* (1909), won the Stratford competition. Alice Brown (biographer of Mercy Otis Warren), author of *Joint Owners in Spain* and *Children of Earth* (1913), won the $10,000 Ames Prize. Because their commercial opportunities were especially restricted, African American women playwrights were encouraged by prize competitions, magazine publication, and production in noncommercial theaters. For example, Georgia Doublas Johnson's *Plumes* (1927) won an *Opportunity* prize; Marita Bonner's *The Purple Flower* was published in *Crisis.* Women playwrights have also won the Pulitzer Prize for drama, although not as regularly as their numbers and productivity would predict: Zona Gale for her adaptation of her own story, *Miss Lulu Bett,* in 1921; Susan Glaspell for *Alison's House* in 1931; Zoe Akins, for her adaptation of Edith Wharton's *The Old Maid* in 1935; Mary Chase for *Harvey* in 1945; and Beth Henley for *Crimes of the Heart* in 1980. New York drama critics, disturbed that Akins won the

Pulitzer over Maxwell Anderson's *Winterset*, rebelled and formed their own, competing prize: the New York Drama Critics Circle Award. The New York critics infrequently honored women's work—for example, Lillian Hellman's *Watch on the Rhine* (1941) and *Toys in the Attic* (1960); Carson McCullers's dramatization of her own novel, *The Member of the Wedding* (1950); Lorraine Hansberry's pathbreaking *A Raisin in the Sun* (1959); and Henley's *Crimes of the Heart*.

As much as regional and small theaters have supported women, women directors, actors, playwrights, designers, and producers built the regional and small theater movement in the U.S. As Joseph Zeigler comments, "Modern American regional theatre began with Margo Jones in Dallas in 1947 . . . her book *Theatre-in-the-Round* . . . is the nearest thing to a bible in the regional theatre" (17). In the last thirty years, feminist drama and feminist theater companies have provided the cutting edge of performance and form. And earlier in the century, women in the Provincetown Players, the Theatre Guild, and a national range of ethnic and community theaters established U.S. dramatic practice that was inventive, directed to contemporary issues, and inclusive.

Susan Glaspell was a founder of the Provincetown Players—as well as a director, actress, reporter, novelist, and playwright of innovative dramas (*Trifles*, 1916; *Women's Honor*, 1918; *Bernice*, 1919) that directly challenged stereotypical conceptions of women. Provincetown drama and dramatists reshaped U.S. theater in the early twentieth century, with women writers, including Djuna Barnes, Neith Boyce, Louise Bryant, Edna Ferber, Edna St. Vincent Millay, and Rita Wellman. Women's dramatic achievements through Provincetown have tended to be erased in traditional drama histories, as critics focus on male playwrights, particularly Eugene O'Neill, and ignore women's accomplishments. For example, O'Neill's recognition as the creator of American expressionist drama in *The Hairy Ape* overlooks Provincetown colleague Glaspell's earlier expressionist play, *The Verge*.

From the 1960s onward, feminist and other alternative theater groups reshaped American drama and vastly increased the numbers of women in theater. Megan Terry, for example, developed innovative forms, using theatrical transformations in *Calm Down Mother* and other plays that emphasized the transmutations of actors and characters from role to role and thus the roles we play in society. Other feminist playwrights and theorists developed women-centered plays and focused on the presumptive male gaze, the normalizing effect of realistic reifications of social conditions antagonistic to women, and the theater's often assumed "compulsory heterosexuality." Women playwrights, directors, and producers have become so numerous that names such as Beth Henley, Maureen Duffy, Tina Howe, and Marsha Norman only begin to suggest the new rosters and the variety and productivity of women's theater. Productions of women's plays still remain a small part of the commercial season and the high-income productions.

Growth in women's drama has brought, if not a string of commercial successes, increased lesbian representation to focused and mainstream theater, including a whole series of gay transformations of traditional, heterosexual-assuming plays and a variety of subgenres, including the coming-out play, the lesbian romance, and the activist play. Anthologies of gay and lesbian plays outnumber the lesbian-only or single-playwright volumes, but the existence of anthologies has spread recognition of this significant work beyond the cities and theaters where it is produced. Mainstream theaters in the 1990s have begun to produce lesbian plays as part of their standard repertoire and subscription seasons. Experimental lesbian theater more than gay theater seems to focus on representations of the body, how lesbianism is embodied, and how the audience gaze affects the drama. A major critical debate continuously revolves around the question of whether realism is an effective (or even appropriate) mode for lesbian and feminist drama.

Women of color, often missing or underrepresented on stages and in drama anthologies before the 1980s and 1990s, have come to be recognized for the significant role they play in transforming the subjects, characterizations, and forms of the American stage. Increasing numbers of readily available anthologies have brought their work into more theaters and classrooms and have begun to focus critical attention on distinctive woman of color playwriting, for example, Kathy A. Perkins and Roberta Uno's *Contemporary Plays by Women of Color* (1996).

African American women, who had been writing and producing drama since the Harlem Renaissance of the 1920s, are the largest critical presence and influence. Alice Childress brought a wide range of black women's experiences to the stage, challenging stereotypes of interracial relationships, poor black women, and the black intelligentsia, among others. Ntozake Shange introduced new forms, including the choreopoem. Adrienne Kennedy, Pearl Cleage, Anna Deavere Smith, and scores of other African American playwrights have joined in developing a rich and various tradition. Mainstream regional theaters now can find it obligatory to include an African American woman's play in their seasons.

Anthologies of Hispanic women playwrights (e.g., Migdalia Cruz, Cherríe Moraga) and Asian American women playwrights (e.g., Brenda Wong Aoki, Elizabeth Wong) are now filling in the shelves of theater bookstores, along with the multiethnic, multiracial collections. The categories of race and sexual orientation, ethnicity, and experimental technique or subject matter continually overlap, so descriptive references often become multiply hyphenated, and many critics refuse to see a play as primarily Latina or primarily lesbian. This focus on individual playwrights and their messages and presentations exists alongside the anthology or theater by ethnicity. We have yet to see, however, any move in the academy to give this drama the standing now accorded to the fiction and poetry of women of color.

Appraising women's role in the American theater—both reconsidering the milestones of dramatic history in terms of women's plays and acknowledging the tremendous variety and innovation of "breathing" playwrights of today—portrays a different story of our drama: different periods, different credit for dramatic innovation, different names and subjects for our attention. As new, inclusive histories of drama begin to be written, women's historical development of dramatic forms seems clearly the mother of theater innovations of feminist drama (reversing gender roles, splitting private and public personae) and the abundant richness of today's women playwrights.

—Carol Klimick Cyganowski

Further Reading

Berney, K. A., and N. G. Templeton, eds. *Contemporary Women Dramatists.* Detroit, MI: St. James, 1994.

Chinoy, Helen Kirch, and Linda Walsh Jenkins, eds. *Women in American Theatre.* New York: Crown, 1981.

Mahone, Sydne, ed. *Moon Marked & Touched by Sun: Plays by African American Women.* New York: Theatre Communications Group, 1994.

Perkins, Kathy A., and Robert Uno, eds. *Contemporary Plays by Women of Color.* New York: Routledge, 1996.

Peterson, Jane T., and Suzanne Bennett. *Women Playwrights of Diversity: A Bio-Bibliographical Sourcebook.* Westport, CT: Greenwood, 1997.

Robinson, Alice M., Vera Mowry Roberts, and Milly S. Barranger, *Notable Women in the American Theatre: A Biographical Dictionary.* New York: Greenwood, 1989.

Zeigler, Joseph Wesley. *Regional Theatre: The Revolutionary Stage.* Minneapolis: University of Minnesota Press, 1973.

⤙ Theologians

Although it is true that men have been the voice of authority throughout American religious history, women have consistently distinguished themselves in matters of faith. In early American history, women had limited access to both the academic world and institutional structures. In the nineteenth century, the abolition and suffrage movements began to have an impact on religion and theology. From the early voices of women such as the Grimké sisters, Sojourner Truth, Harriet Livermore, Phoebe Palmer, and Elizabeth Cady Stanton (*The Woman's Bible*), new religious perspectives were developed, bringing with them challenging interpretations of Scripture and broadened theological perspectives.

It is ironic that the first people who settled American lands, many in pursuit of religious freedom, quickly and forcefully subdued women who expressed religious beliefs and values that deviated from perceived norms, charging such women with heresy and witchcraft. The oppression of women that characterized the early church still exists today in tension with the liberating powers of religious thought.

The twentieth century has brought with it a theological revival for women, again spurred by secular feminist voices.

Emerging in increasing numbers from religious and professional schools, women have challenged the male-centered theological tradition by illuminating the denigrating powers of patriarchal structures, exclusive language, limited imagery of the Sacred, and misogynist interpretations of religious texts. Such women theologians include Mary Daly, who now calls her work "post-Christian." As a prolific historian of Christian thought, Rosemary Radford Ruether has recovered many significant texts by and about women, which both provide us with insight into the liberating traditions within Christianity and expose those that have degraded and suppressed women. Biblical exegete Elisabeth Schussler Fiorenza has attempted to use the biblical text, not as an authority in itself, but as a source for reconstructing the history of women in early Christianity. Building on the work of these pathbreakers, many other American women theologians such as Sallie McFague, Phyllis Tribble, Jaqueline Grant, Elizabeth Clarke, and Anne Carr, among others, are adding depth, texture, and diversity to the American feminist theological corpus.

These challenges have brought with them new and creative interpretations of our religious past, even as they serve to reveal contemporary theological perspectives that recognize the liberating promises of religious texts and systematics. Religious words are being redefined or replaced; religious imagery is becoming multifaceted; religious values are being clarified from feminist perspectives; religious structures are being formed that include women in leadership positions while simultaneously fostering a positive regard for all women of religion. (*See also: Christianity; Daly, Mary; Fiorenza, Elisabeth Schussler; Religion; Ruether, Rosemary Radford; Salem Witch Trials*)

—Joanne S. Richmond
—Cynthia Jurisson

Further Reading

Carr, Anne. *Transforming Grace.* New York: Harper, 1990.

Daly, Mary. *Beyond God the Father.* Boston: Beacon, 1973.

———. *The Church and the Second Sex.* New York: Harper & Row, 1968.

———. *Gyn/Ecology.* Boston: Beacon, 1978.

Fiorenza, Elisabeth Schussler. *Bread Not Stone.* Boston: Beacon, 1984.

———. *In Memory of Her.* New York: Crossroads, 1983.

Ruether, Rosemary Radford. *Religion and Sexism.* New York: Simon & Schuster, 1974.

———. *Sexism and God-Talk: Toward a Feminist Theology.* Boston: Beacon, 1983.

———. *Womanguides.* Boston: Beacon, 1985.

———. *Women of Spirit.* New York: Simon & Schuster, 1979.

Stanton, Elizabeth Cady. *The Woman's Bible,* 2 vols. New York: European Publishing, 1895–1898. Reprint, vol. 1, 1898.

⤙ Thomas, Alma (1891–1978)

Alma Thomas was an artist and art educator whose late-life emergence as an abstract artist of the Washington Color School brought her national recognition. Born in

Columbus, Georgia, she moved with her family to Washington, D.C., as a child and attended Armstrong High School, a trade school. She continued her education at Howard University and was its first art school graduate in 1924. In 1934, she obtained an M.A. from Teachers College of Columbia University, with a thesis on marionettes.

Her thirty-five-year career teaching art at Shaw Junior High School in Washington was complemented by her career as an exhibiting artist and art gallery director. She studied painting at American University in the 1950s and began to develop an interest in abstract art. For a retrospective at Howard University in 1966, she broke free from the realism of her earlier work and produced several new works in an abstract style inspired by leafy trees in the sunlight outside the window of her inner-city town house. This breakthrough led to solo exhibitions at the Whitney Museum in New York (the first at that museum for a black woman) and the Corcoran Gallery in Washington. She also exhibited her work at the Boston Museum of Fine Arts and the National Collection of American Art. One painting was purchased by the Metropolitan Museum of Art in New York City. Under the auspices of the Tyler School of Fine Arts at Temple University, she toured the art capitals of Europe. In 1976, she received the International Women's Year Award for Outstanding Contributions and Dedication to Women and Art. *(See also: Art; Black Women)*

—**Susan Kellogg Portney**

Further Reading

Fine, Elsa Honig. *The Afro-American Artist.* New York: Holt, Rinehart & Winston, 1973.

Munro, Eleanor. *Originals: American Women Artists.* New York: Simon & Schuster, 1979.

Thomas, M. Carey (1857–1935)

M. Carey Thomas is best known for building Bryn Mawr College into a premier institution for women's higher education, but by the beginning of the twentieth century, she had also become the nation's leading advocate for excellence in women's education generally. The eldest of ten children in a prominent Baltimore Quaker family, she was never called by her first name, Martha; her family called her Minnie until she adopted Carey while at college. After she went through a long childhood convalescence resulting from a serious burn, her mother, Mary Witall Thomas, was more willing to give in to her daughter's increasing demands for an independence and education well beyond what was considered acceptable for a young Quaker woman in the middle of the nineteenth century.

She graduated from Cornell with a B.A. in 1877, but her desire to do graduate work at Johns Hopkins was frustrated by male opposition. She was allowed to study privately with a faculty member, but was not allowed to participate in seminars with the male students. Undaunted, Thomas then traveled to Germany with a close friend, Mamie Gwinn, to study at the University of Leipzig despite hostility from the male students. After two years, she was told that the faculty at Leipzig would not grant degrees to women. Continuing in her pursuit of a doctorate, she tried again at Gottingen. Finally, she succeeded at Zurich, where she earned a Ph.D. in philosophy, summa cum laude, in 1882, the first woman to receive this honor that had previously been awarded only to a handful of men. It was all the more amazing since she had begun German and other languages needed for her research only four years earlier.

Thomas then applied for and was rejected for the presidency of the new Quaker women's college in Bryn Mawr, Pennsylvania, but settled at first for the position as dean of the college in 1884. Even in her role as dean with her forceful personality and a carefully conceived plan, she was able to shape Bryn Mawr in her own image. Carey Thomas wanted more than a woman's college that would equal the elite Ivy League men's colleges. Instead, she saw Bryn Mawr as a research institution similar to the European universities where she had recently studied. Limited financial resources prevented the fulfillment of her dream; nevertheless, graduate programs, fellowships, and the development of a scholarly tradition set Bryn Mawr apart from other women's colleges. Despite opposition from some of the Trustees, M. Carey Thomas was named president in 1894 and ran the college almost single-handedly until her autocratic style provoked a faculty rebellion in 1916.

Thomas's influence as an educator spread far beyond the campus of Bryn Mawr College. With the help of a number of friends, she organized the Bryn Mawr School in Baltimore in 1885, providing girls with an academically demanding secondary education that included the classics. In 1893, with the assistance of Mary Garrett, a lifelong friend who was a wealthy railroad heiress, Thomas arranged for the new Johns Hopkins Medical School to admit women. After fundraising efforts by a woman's committee and a large gift from Garrett, the Trustees agreed to open their doors to female students, but if they reneged on their promise, the money with interest was to go to Bryn Mawr College.

By the turn of the century, Carey Thomas had become the spokeswoman for equality and excellence in women's higher education. She was highly critical when Harvard President Charles Eliot called for a different and, "by implication," inferior education for women. Thomas maintained that women's education not only had to be held to the same standards as men's but that women should study the same subjects as men. At the same time Thomas realized that family responsibilities and motherhood had blocked women from the full attainment of their intellectual abilities. Consequently, she saw the need to dismantle the collection of man-made laws that worked against the interests of women. Abandoning her earlier reluctance, Carey Thomas became a prominent suffragist. She helped to organize and then headed the National College Equal Suffrage League between 1908 and 1917. Acting as a strong supporter of

Anna Howard Shaw, she also became a powerful force in the National American Woman Suffrage Association.

Her last important work prior to her retirement in 1922 was the establishment of the Bryn Mawr Summer School for Women Workers in 1921. Carey Thomas was one of the most influential women of her time, but like many others of her economic and social background she was an elitist who held racist and anti-Semitic views. Her prejudices cannot be condoned. On the other hand, she also foreshadowed the future of feminism in seeing that barriers beyond suffrage had to be removed before women could fulfill their intellectual and creative potential. During her retirement, she worked for peace and promoted the work of the League of Nations. M. Carey Thomas died in December 1935. *(See also: Bryn Mawr College; Bryn Mawr Summer School for Women Workers; Higher Education; National American Woman Suffrage Association; "Seven Sisters")*

—Neil W. Hogan

Further Reading

Bryn Mawr College Archives, Bryn Mawr, PA.

Dobkin, Marjorie, Houseplan, ed. *The Making of a Feminist: Early Journals and Letters of M. Carey Thomas.* Kent, OH: Kent State University Press, 1979.

Finch, Edith. *Carey Thomas of Bryn Mawr.* New York: Harper & Brothers, 1947.

Horowitz, Helen Lefkowitz. *Alma Mater.* New York: Knopf, 1984.

———. *The Power and Passion of M. Carey Thomas.* New York: Knopf, 1994.

West, Lucy Fisher, ed. *The Papers of M. Carey Thomas in the Bryn Mawr College Archives.* Woodbridge, CT: Research Publications International, 1982.

∿ Thompson, Dorothy (1893–1961)

Dorothy Thompson, journalist, columnist, radio broadcaster, and lecturer, grew up in a western New York home of very modest means, the oldest of three children born to a Methodist minister and his wife. She studied at the Lewis Institute in Chicago, graduated from Syracuse University, cum laude, in 1914, and worked as a suffrage activist and for social service organizations and advertising agencies. In 1920, she sailed for Europe, planning to support herself through freelance journalism. Thompson became an expert on Central European politics, was named Vienna correspondent for the *Philadelphia Public Ledger,* and in 1924 moved to Berlin as head of the Central European bureaus of the *Ledger* and the *New York Evening Post.*

An attractive and dynamic woman, with many male and female admirers, Thompson married Josef Bard, a Hungarian Jewish writer and journalist, in 1923. Bard showed little inclination to limit himself to one woman, and they were divorced in 1927. In 1928, Thompson married American novelist Sinclair ("Red") Lewis and resigned her position to return to America, determined that this marriage would succeed. They had one child, Michael, born in 1930.

Thompson's column of political and foreign affairs, "On the Record," first appeared in 1936 in the *New York Herald Tribune.* Initially an anti-New Dealer, she supported Franklin D. Roosevelt in his bid for a third term (1940) because she approved of his foreign policy. Before the pro-Republican *Tribune* could drop her, she switched to the *New York Post* and the Bell Syndicate; her columns appeared across the country and in Canada. Best known for denunciations of fascism abroad and at home and for her work on behalf of European refugees, she also contributed monthly essays to *Ladies' Home Journal,* writing about education, materialist activism, and American culture.

Although acclaimed as America's most prominent woman (next to Eleanor Roosevelt) during the late 1930s and 1940s, Thompson's personal life fell apart during the years of her greatest fame. Sinclair Lewis's alcoholism, his rages, and his inability to tolerate either the presence of his son or his wife's success made their life together intolerable. The couple separated in 1937 and divorced in 1942. In 1943, Thompson married Maxim Kopf, a Czech refugee sculptor. She described the fifteen years of their marriage as the happiest in her life.

After the war, Thompson's influence waned. The *New York Post* dropped her column in 1947 because she advocated the renaissance of a strong Germany as a buffer against the Soviet Union; gradually, she lost other influential outlets for her column. She noted that Americans became less interested in the complexities of world affairs, wanting only to enjoy the peace. Her unwavering, and some argued, unreasoning, support of the Arab cause in the Middle East also diminished her popularity.

In 1958, following her husband's death, Thompson retired from writing her column; she died two and a half years later of a heart attack. *(See also: Journalism; Women Writers)*

—Lynn D. Gordon

Further Reading

Dorothy Thompson Papers. George Arents Research Library. Syracuse University, Syracuse, NY.

Gordon, Lynn D. "Why Dorothy Thompson Lost Her Job: Political Columnists and the Press Wars of the 1930s and 1940s," *History of Education Quarterly* 34 (Fall 1994): 281-303.

Kurth, Peter. *American Cassandra: The Life of Dorothy Thompson.* Boston: Little, Brown, 1990.

Sanders, Marion K. *Dorothy Thompson: A Legend in Her Time.* Boston: Little, Brown, 1973.

Sheean, Vincent. *Dorothy and Red.* Boston: Houghton Mifflin, 1963.

Thompson, Dorothy. *Courage to Be Happy.* Boston: Houghton Mifflin, 1957.

———. *Dorothy Thompson's Political Guide: A Study of American Liberalism and Its Relation to Totalitarian States.* New York: Stackpole, 1938.

———. *I Saw Hitler.* New York: Farrar & Rinehart, 1932.

———. *Listen, Hans!* Boston: Houghton Mifflin, 1942.

Thornton, Willie Mae (1926–1984)

American singer, musician, and songwriter, also known as "Big Mama" Thornton, Willie Mae Thornton is considered one of the premier singers of the blues. The daughter of a preacher, she was born in Montgomery, Alabama. Thornton began touring at the age of fourteen with Sammy Green's Hot Harlem Review. She toured extensively and began her recording career in 1950. Although Thornton performed works by others, she composed many of the songs she performed. Her first major success, in 1952, was her own composition, "Hound Dog." Despite her formidable reputation as a performer of the blues, Thornton is perhaps most popularly known as the composer of two works that came to be identified with two white performers whose commercial successes and status in popular culture far overshadowed the African American artists from whose repertoire they drew. "Hound Dog" became an enormous hit for Elvis Presley. Fifteen years later, another one of her compositions, "Ball and Chain," became one of Janis Joplin's biggest hits. Joplin was known to speak of her indebtedness to the contributions of female African American blues artists, especially Thornton and Bessie Smith, and to describe her own work in terms of that tradition.

Thornton was a direct descendant of classic blues singers such as Ma Rainey, Bessie Smith, and especially Memphis Minnie, the 1930s blues singer whose style Thornton's most closely resembled. Like Bessie Smith, Thornton combined her recording career with extensive touring, appearing with bluesmen Johnny Otis, Muddy Waters, and others. She made her first tour of Europe in 1965 with the American Folk Blues Festival and appeared in major festivals throughout Europe and the United States, performing, among other works, what is perhaps her third most popular and most widely recorded composition, "Little Red Rooster."

Thornton was among the "big voiced" female singers whose careers were revived during the blues revival in the United States of the 1960s and early 1970s. Willie Mae Thornton remains significant as one of many African American and female writers who contributed to the "cross-over" successes of rhythm and blues even though some of their more widely known work came to be associated with others. She continued to record for Vanguard, Mercury, and other small labels until her death in 1984, the same year she was inducted into the Blues Hall of Fame. Willie Mae Thornton and her body of work stand among the most respected and influential interpreters of the blues. *(See also: Holiday, Billie; Jazz; Music; Popular Vocalists; Smith, Bessie)*

—**Elizabeth H. Coughlin**

Further Reading

Cohn, Lawrence. *Nothing but the Blues.* New York: Abbeville, 1993.

Friedman, Myra. *Buried Alive: The Biography of Janis Joplin.* New York: William Morrow, 1973.

Harris, S. *Blues Who's Who.* New Rochelle, NY: Arlington House, 1979.

Stearns, Marshall W. *The Story of Jazz.* London: Oxford University Press, 1970.

Thurman, Sue Bailey (1903–1996)

Sue Bailey Thurman, author, lecturer, historian, and organizational leader, was born the youngest and only surviving child of ten to educators the Reverend Isaac and Susie (Ford) Bailey in Pine Bluffs, Arkansas, on August 26, 1903. She received bachelor's degrees in music and liberal arts from Oberlin College in 1926.

Renowned for her advocacy of interracial, intercultural, and international understanding, she worked for the YWCA from 1926 to 1932. As national traveling secretary for the college division, she lectured throughout Europe in 1928 and established the first World Fellowship Committees of the YWCA. In 1932, she married religious leader and social critic Dr. Howard Thurman, with whose ministry her own work was deeply entwined until his death in 1981. She was the founder and editor (1941–1944) of the *Aframerican Women's Journal,* the first published organ of the National Council of Negro Women, as well as the founder and first chairperson of the Council's National Library, Archives, and Museum. In the 1950s, she founded the Museum of Afro-American History in Boston. She also established women's organizations at Howard University in the 1930s and at Boston University in the 1950s. Thurman wrote several books, including *Pioneers of Negro Origin in California* (1949) and *The Historical Cookbook of the American Negro* (1958).

She also traveled around the world in pursuit of her vision of international peace and fellowship. In 1935-36, she traveled to India, Burma, and Ceylon as part of the first Negro Delegation of Friendship to the East, which her husband chaired. The Thurmans were the first African Americans to meet Mahatma Gandhi and to discuss with him the use of nonviolent resistance to effect social change. In 1940, she led the first Delegation of Negro Women to Cuba, and in 1947 she was a representative to the first Inter-American Congress of Women held in Guatemala. In 1949, she led a delegation of members of the Church for the Fellowship of All Peoples, the first interracial, interreligious church in the United States, of which her husband was cofounder and copastor, to the Fourth Plenary Session of the United Nations Educational, Scientific and Cultural Organization (UNESCO) in Paris.

She received honorary doctorates from Livingston College and Boston University. In 1991, she received a formal citation from the Indian government at the centennial celebration of Gandhi's birth. From 1981 until her death, she served as honorary chair of the Howard Thurman Educational Trust. *(See also: Black Women; National Council of Negro Women; Religion; YWCA)*

—**Catherine Tumber**

Further Reading

Bailey-Thurman Papers, 1882-1995, Special Collections. Robert W. Woodruff Library, Emory University, Atlanta, GA.

"Sue Bailey Thurman: In Her Own Right," *Bostonia* (Spring 1992): 49.

Sue Bailey Thurman Papers. Boston University and personal collection.

Thurman, Howard. *With Head and Heart: The Autobiography of Howard Thurman.* New York: Harcourt Brace Jovanovich, 1979.

Thurman, Sue Bailey. Interview by Beth Rhude. Black Women Oral History Project. Schlesinger Library. Radcliffe College, Cambridge, MA.

❦ Title IX of the Education Amendments of 1972

Title IX of the Education Amendments of 1972 prohibits gender discrimination for federally funded education programs. By passing Title IX, Congress extended the protection of Title VII of the Civil Rights Act to educational institutions. (An additional protection is the Fourteenth Amendment, which prohibits schools from discriminating against students on the basis of sex.) Title IX provides that "no person in the United States shall, on the basis of sex, be excluded from participation in, be denied the benefits of, or be subjected to discrimination under any education program or activity receiving Federal financial assistance." In 1982, the Supreme Court ruled that the prohibition for sex discrimination was extended to employment and admission practices of schools. In 1984, in a narrowing interpretation of the statute, *Grove City College v. Bell* (1984), the Supreme Court held that Title IX did not apply to programs (such as athletics) that did not receive direct financial assistance. Hundreds of Title IX complaints were dropped as a result of that court decision. Then Congress passed the Civil Rights Restoration Act of 1987 (P.L. 100-259, 102 Stat. 28, 1988) that provided that all aspects of education are covered by Title IX.

The Office for Civil Rights (OCR) investigates complaints, initiates compliance reviews, and provides guidance on how to effect adherence to the law. To understand the labyrinth through which various issues have traveled requires sorting through the statutes, letters of finding, rules and regulations, memorandums, and the OCR investigator's manual, as well as court decisions and out-of-court settlements.

A major effect of Title IX implementation has revolved around institutional compliance in sports programs. According to OCR records, two particularly significant issues are athletic scholarships and athletic benefits. Historically, the OCR requires that athletic scholarships be awarded to members of each sex in proportion to the number of students of each sex participating in interscholastic sports (not in proportion to enrollment). The second issue, athletic benefits, must conform to "equal opportunity and effective accommodation of interests and abilities" of members of both sexes in equipment, supplies, game and practice schedules, travel and per diem, coaching and tutoring, assignment and compensation of coaches and tutors, locker rooms, practice and competitive facilities, medical and training facilities and services, housing and dining facilities and services, and publicity. OCR analysis finds compliance if the institution (a) ensures that participation opportunities are provided substantially proportionate to enrollment or (b) can show a history of program expansion responsive to interests and abilities or (c) if one sex is underrepresented, can demonstrate that the interests and abilities of that sex have been fully and effectively accommodated by the present program. The OCR has tolerated continuing spending discrepancies between the sexes in athletic programs.

In 1993, an important gender-equity lawsuit was settled out of court. The Office for Civil Rights found Auburn University in violation of Title IX, and Auburn paid damages and legal fees and added a women's soccer team as a consequence. Over 50 lawsuits or complaints were filed in 1993. However, in *Cohen v. Brown* (1993), the court required that all three aspects of the test (substantial proportionality, program expansion, and accommodation of interest and abilities) must be met. This is a direct contradiction of the current OCR approach. Pending and future court decisions may make Title IX an affirmative action mandate rather than an antidiscrimination statute by requiring that the athletic participation rate by gender reflect the enrollment rate of educational institutions.

While statistical comparisons vary, there is little doubt that interscholastic and intercollegiate athletic participation by females has increased significantly since the passage of Title IX. There is also little doubt that parity has yet to occur. With regard to females holding athletic administrative and coaching positions, there have actually been losses. As coaching salaries for female sports rose in response to Title IX, male coaches moved into the limited number of coaching slots. As athletic departments merged their female and male components, males tended to be hired as athletic directors and to other administrative positions.

Initially, the National Collegiate Athletic Association (NCAA) opposed Title IX but, later, initiated studies that appear to encourage gender equity (percentage of female athletes reflecting percentage of female undergraduate enrollment), and a preliminary report was issued in 1993. The major opposition to Title IX implementation, as affirmative action legislation, seems to lie in the fear that gender equity in athletics will diminish athletics for males, particularly for the revenue-generating sports of men's football and basketball that may support both male and female athletics.

Although athletics has certainly been the most noted arena in which the drama of Title IX implementation has played, many other arenas brought Title IX into the limelight in the 1990s. In 1997, the National Coalition for Women and Girls in Education (NCWGE) published "The Report Card," a progress report on Title IX's first 25 years.

The report "grades" the effects of Title IX in nine general areas. The NCWGE ratings range from slightly above average in the areas of higher education, math and science, and treatment of pregnant and parenting students; to average in the areas of athletics, career education, and standardized testing; and below average in the areas of employment, improved learning environments, and sexual harassment. While it recognizes how far the United States has to go before achieving gender equity in education, "The Report Card" also praises the progress of Title IX thus far. Also in 1997, the U.S. Department of Education released a Title IX progress report. This report commends Title IX for making the United States a world leader in granting educational opportunities to women. The government report also recognizes that huge strides must still be made in the areas of sexual harassment, wages, and athletics. History assures us that Title IX implementation will continue to break barriers as it evolves, affecting issues in a variety of settings. *(See also: Affirmative Action; Athletics/Sports; Education)*

—**Margaret Konz Snooks**

Further Reading
Carlino, Salvatore. "Title IX: A Legislative History, Selected Court Cases and the Future of Women's Athletic Programs." Ph.D. diss., Pennsylvania State University, 1985.
Cohen v. Brown, 991 F.2nd 888 1st Cir. (1993).
Grove City College v. Bell, 465 U.S. 555 (1984).
National Coalition for Women and Girls in Education. "The Report Card." 1997. Available at http://www.aauw.org/1000/summary.html#anchor584966
National Collegiate Athletic Association. "Preliminary Report of the Task Force on Gender Equity." 1993.
Riley, Richard W., U.S. Secretary of Education. "Title IX: 25 Years of Progress." June 1997. Available at http://www.ed.gov/pubs/TitleIX
Thro, William E., and Brian A. Snow. "Cohen v. Brown University and the Future of Intercollegiate and Interscholastic Athletics," *Education Law Reporter* 84 (1993): 611-29.
20 U.S.C. §§ 1681-85 (1992).

ᴥ Tituba (c. 1648–1692)

Tituba was a Carib Indian woman slave who was brought to Salem Village, Massachusetts, by the Reverend Samuel Parris. She came from the Spanish settlements in the West Indies, as did her husband, John Indian. A group of local girls and women frequently came to visit Parris's young daughter and listen to Tituba tell stories. When the stories she told of voodoo rituals, prophecy, and spirit life seemed to "possess" those young girls, Tituba was accused of witchcraft. Tried and presumed guilty, Tituba was finally acquitted because of her genuine penitence and because the governor's wife intervened by calling the trials a disgrace.

A curious debate has arisen over the ethnic origin of Tituba, described in Ann Petry's children's book *Tituba of Salem Village* as a black but elsewhere described as half-black and half-Indian. *(See also: Nurse, Rebecca; Salem Witch Trials)*

—**Susan Kinnell**

Further Reading
Conde, Maryse. *Tituba, Black Witch of Salem.* Foreword by Angela Davis. Charlottesville: University Press of Virginia, 1992.
Hansen, Chadwick. "The Metamorphosis of Tituba, or Why American Intellectuals Can't Tell an Indian Witch from a Negro," *New England Quarterly* 47 (1974): 3-12.
Robbins, Peggy. "The Devil in Salem," *American History Illustrated* 6 (1971): 44-48.

ᴥ Todd, Marion Marsh (1841–?)

Born in Plymouth, New York, Marion Marsh Todd was a lawyer and writer who supported woman suffrage, temperance, the Greenback Labor Party, the Union Labor Party, and the Populist Party. Todd moved to Michigan in 1851 with her family. A few years later, she entered Ypsilanti State Normal School and at seventeen began teaching school. In 1868, she married Benjamin Todd of Boston, a lawyer who advocated women's rights and political and economic reform. The couple had one daughter, Lulu.

After a move to California, Todd entered Hastings Law College in San Francisco but was unable to finish law school because her husband's death in 1880 left her in financial difficulty. She was, nevertheless, admitted to the California Bar and opened a law office in San Francisco, specializing in finance law. In 1883, Todd stopped practicing law and devoted herself to writing, lecturing, and political campaigning. Todd attended the state convention of the Greenback Labor Party and was nominated for the office of state attorney general. She also attended conventions of the Anti-Monopoly Party and the Knights of Labor. In 1886, she returned to the Midwest and became one of the editors of *Chicago Express,* a reform newspaper with a national circulation, and helped to organize the Union Labor Party. With the demise of these early reform parties, Todd then took an active part in the newly formed Populist Party, attending conventions, speaking from the platform, and lecturing on the national campaign trail.

Her nonfiction included *Protective Tariff Delusions* (1886), *Professor Goldwin Smith and His Satellites in Congress* (1890), *Pizarro and John Sherman* (1891), *Railways of Europe and America* (1893), and *Honest (?) John Sherman, or a Foul Record* (1894). Her books about Senator John Sherman were used extensively in Populist Party campaigns, and many Populists believed that Todd's work had caused the defeat of the hated Sherman, who was considered responsible for financial legislation that had been hard on farm and working-class families. Todd also wrote several romantic novels: *Rachel's Pitiful History* (1895), *Phillip: A Romance* (1900), and *Claudia* (1902). The last known record of Todd indicates that she was living in Springport, Michigan, in 1914. *(See also: Legal Profession; Populist Party; Women Writers)*

—MaryJo Wagner

Further Reading

Diggs, Annie. "Women in the Alliance," *Arena* 6 (July 1892): 161-79.
Willard, Frances E., and Mary A. Livermore, eds. *A Woman of the Century*, p. 718. New York: Charles Wells Moulton, 1893.

∞ Todhunter School

The Todhunter School, 66 East 80th Street, New York City, was begun by British-born and Oxford-educated Winifred Todhunter as an exclusive girls' finishing school. The education offered at Todhunter School was intended to prepare students for college, but it also had a broad cultural aim and was meant to instill feminist principles. The educational techniques combined progressive project-oriented assignments and traditional testing.

When she returned to England in 1926, Todhunter offered to sell the school to her vice principal, Marion Dickerman, a graduate of the University of Syracuse and formerly dean of New Jersey State College. A woman of high principles, Dickerman was a leader in the suffrage movement and a pacifist. Lacking the funds to purchase the school by herself, Dickerman turned to her friends and colleagues from the Women's Division of the New York State Democratic Committee, Eleanor Roosevelt and Nancy Cook.

The purchase was completed, and although Cook was never an active participant, from 1927 to 1939 Roosevelt was active in various capacities at Todhunter School: as a teacher of government, literature, American History, and drama; as associate principal with Dickerman; and as fundraiser and publicist. Teaching was a fulfillment of Eleanor Roosevelt's lifelong dream. During her own education at Allenswood School, Headmistress Marie Souvestre had been a formative influence on her life, and she hoped to assist other students in a similar fashion. Troubled by the narrowness of private school education, Roosevelt initiated a course titled Modern Trends in Government. Her teaching methods were personal and informal, using current events and newspapers to teach lessons in citizenship and taking her students on field trips to varied places—from plays and museums to tenements and settlement houses—to increase their firsthand knowledge of the world. Roosevelt wished to provide her students with both the tools and the inspiration to make their lifelong learning an ongoing adventure. Her motto was summed up in her own words, "Be Somebody, Be Yourself, Be All You Can Be!"

Even when her husband became the governor of New York, Roosevelt continued teaching two and a half days per week, commuting once a week from Albany to New York City. Later, during the Roosevelt presidency, she felt it necessary to limit her teaching activities but remained involved until 1939.

On July 28, 1939, the Todhunter and Dalton Schools consolidated, receiving an absolute charter on October 18, 1939. Dalton School continues to provide private school education to elementary and secondary school students at its current location 108 E. 89th Street, New York City. *(See also: Education; Roosevelt, Eleanor; Teaching)*

—Tamerin Mitchell Hayward

Further Reading

Cook, Blanche Wiesen. *Eleanor Roosevelt*. Vol. I, *1884–1933*. New York: Viking, 1992.
Lash, Joseph P. *Eleanor and Franklin*. New York: Norton, 1971.
Office of Non-Public School Services. State Education Department. Albany, NY.

∞ Toklas, Alice B(abette) (1877–1967)

Known principally as Gertrude Stein's companion, Alice B. Toklas was a translator, publisher, journalist, letter writer, and biographer/autobiographer, as well as a cook, secretary, and housekeeper.

The first thirty years of Toklas's life have only become of interest because of her final sixty years. The only daughter of a Polish and a German Jew, Toklas was born, raised, and educated in San Francisco and Seattle. Her only sibling was ten years her junior. The Toklas family was relatively prosperous; Alice received her education in private schools and a conservatory, which she had to leave because of her mother's illness in 1893. She spent the next fourteen years keeping house and, after her mother's death in 1897, took over full responsibility for the male household while trying to retain her own interests.

In 1907, Toklas journeyed to Europe, where she met Gertrude Stein, who became her lifelong companion. It remains unclear when Toklas finally established herself in the Rue de Fleurus dwelling of Gertrude and her brother Leo, but Leo had moved out by 1912. Stein and Toklas traveled, fostered Stein's career, continued the salon tradition, delivered hospital supplies after the American entry into World War I, and patronized modern art. Toklas's only return to the United States was with Stein in 1934-35, to promote Stein's *An Autobiography of Alice B. Toklas* and to be at the opening of Stein's *Four Saints in Three Acts*. During World War II, Toklas and Stein remained in German-occupied France. Stein died in 1946.

After having established Plain Editions to publish Stein's writings privately in the late 1920s, Toklas translated a few works in the late 1930s. Supporting Stein's posthumous career, Toklas attempted to have her friend's unpublished writings published. She continued letter writing and fostering artistic talents and began writing cookbooks and articles. With or without Stein, Toklas was an important Parisian expatriate.

Her activities did not relieve her loneliness after Stein's death, and illness and legal battles with Stein's heirs increased it. *(See also: Stein, Gertrude; Friendships)*

—**Maureen R. Liston**

Further Reading

Liston, Maureen R. *An Essay to Introduce Gertrude Stein's A Novel of Thank You.* Essen: Die Blaue Eule, 1986.

———. *Gertrude Stein: An Annotated Critical Bibliography.* Kent, OH: Kent State University Press, 1979.

Simon, Linda. *The Biography of Alice B. Toklas.* Garden City, NY: Doubleday, 1977.

Toklas, Alice B. *The Alice B. Toklas Cookbook.* New York: Harper & Row, 1954.

———. *Staying on Alone: Letters of Alice B. Toklas.* Edited by Edward Burns. New York: Liveright, 1973.

———. *What Is Remembered.* New York: Holt, Rinehart & Winston, 1963.

⮜ Transcendentalism

Transcendentalism was the philosophy of a small, loose association of middle-class intellectuals and reformers active in Boston and Concord from 1836 to 1860. Predominantly Unitarians or ex-Unitarians, leaders such as William E. Channing, Ralph Waldo Emerson, and Theodore Parker rejected the strictly rationalist emphasis of the Enlightenment and instead sought to cultivate the intuitive moral and intellectual powers in humans. Combining Immanuel Kant's romanticism with elements of East Asian mysticism, the transcendentalists were critical of the materialism and alienation from nature that the new industrial order seemed to foster. While Emerson and Henry David Thoreau advocated radical individualism and withdrawal from society, other transcendentalist thinkers, such as Theodore Parker, felt that society must be reformed so as to nurture all individuals in their search for development and transcendence. Rejecting Emerson's radical individualism, some members of the group experimented in communal living on George Ripley's Brook Farm (1841–1847) and Bronson Alcott's Fruitlands (1843), but neither of the experiments proved long-lasting. Of more consequence was the participation of many of the transcendentalists in the reform movements of the era, most notably abolition and the nascent woman's movement.

Transcendentalism offered women both leadership opportunities and an ideological base from which they would critique the basis of gender inequality and celebrate the potential for woman's full and "authentic" development. Elizabeth Peabody ran a book collective in Boston, and Margaret Fuller was dubbed the "priestess of transcendentalism" for her leadership in a five-year series of "conversations" on social and literary topics and for her editorship of the transcendentalists' quarterly journal *The Dial* from 1840 to 1843. In *Woman in the Nineteenth Century* (1845), Fuller argued that the universal material/spiritual dualism was replicated in the sexes; she attributed "energy, power, and intel-

lect" to men, and "harmony, beauty, and love" to women. Women's oppression, she argued, tended to throw the world off balance, thereby reifying the materialistic, intellectual side of human nature. Women's emancipation from such oppression would thus restore the natural equilibrium and combat the materialism and loss of spirituality that the transcendentalists perceived in the emerging industrial order.

Elizabeth Cady Stanton, although not active as a transcendentalist per se, was also deeply influenced by its leaders, especially Theodore Parker. Unlike Fuller, however, Stanton argued that because woman's development had been suppressed historically, it was impossible to speculate about her true nature. Only after active reform to eradicate the economic, political, and cultural barriers to women's collective self-development would women's real potential become manifest. Louisa May Alcott, Bronson's daughter, grew up in the ideological mood of transcendentalism and offers both respectful and ironic reactions in her fiction. *(See also: Alcott, Louisa May; Fuller, Margaret; Rationalism; Stanton, Elizabeth Cady; Utopian Communities)*

—**Maureen Fitzgerald**
Adapted for the second edition by John Gorman.

Further Reading

Cooper, James L., and Sheila M. Cooper. *The Roots of American Feminist Thought.* Boston: Allyn & Bacon, 1974.

Douglas, Ann. *The Feminization of American Culture.* New York: Avon, 1977.

Fitzgerald, Maureen. "In Search of Self: The Religious Basis of Elizabeth Cady Stanton's Feminism." Paper presented at the Seventh Berkshire Conference on the History of Women, Wellesley, MA, June 1987.

Rose, Anne C. *Transcendentalism as a Social Movement, 1830–1850.* New Haven, CT: Yale University Press, 1981.

⮜ Triangle Fire of 1911

On Saturday afternoon, March 25, 1911, a fire broke out in the Triangle Shirtwaist Company, which occupied the top three floors of a tenement in New York City's Washington Place district. It began on the eighth floor of the Asch Building, when a cigarette or sparks from defective wiring ignited a pile of material scraps. Before the fire had run its course, 147 employees, most of them women of Italian or Jewish immigrant antecedents, had died, either from smoke inhalation or by jumping to their deaths to avoid suffocation, smashing into the pavement with sickening thuds. It was the worst industrial tragedy in the history of New York, and one of the worst ever, anywhere. Some escaped by reaching the roof and climbing to an adjacent building, but most tried to reach safety via two elevators, an enclosed staircase, and a single-ladder "fire escape" that led only to an enclosed courtyard that quickly filled with smoke. Because the doorway to the staircase was locked, dozens of bodies piled up behind it. Those who reached the courtyard survived only because firemen smashed in other locked doors.

Despite those circumstances, neither the proprietors of the factory nor the owners of the building were found liable or negligent, since these practices satisfied existing fire regulations for loft factories. The National Women's Trade Union League (NWTUL), however, organized a public funeral demonstration in which 100,000 people marched through the city and joined other labor, business, civic, and religious leaders in a mass protest meeting at the Metropolitan Opera House. The meeting delegated a Committee of Fifty to deliver a petition to the legislature demanding investigation of working conditions. The petition led Senate Majority Leader Robert F. Wagner and Assembly Majority Leader Alfred E. Smith to propose a joint resolution establishing the New York State Factory Investigating Commission, popularly known as the Triangle Fire Commission.

With Wagner as chairman and Smith as vice chairman, the commission membership also included NWTUL President Mary E. Drier, American Federation of Labor President Samuel Gompers, and several legislators and prominent businessmen. During its four-year tenure, the commission held scores of public hearings, heard the testimony of several hundred witnesses, and produced thirteen volumes of carefully prepared reports. It drafted sixty bills, fifty-six of which were enacted into law, giving New York the best system of factory legislation of any state in the union. None of these was ever overturned by the courts. *(See also: Garment Industries; National Women's Trade Union League; Shirtwaist Makers Strike of 1909)*

—**John D. Buenker**

Further Reading

Goldmark, Josephine. *Impatient Crusader: Florence Kelley's Life Story.* 1953. Reprint, Westport, CT: Greenwood, 1976.

Kerr, Thomas J., IV. "The New York Factory Investigating Commission and the Minimum Wage Movement," *Labor History* 12 (1971): 373-91.

Lagemann, Ellen C. *A Generation of Women: Education in the Lives of Progressive Reformers.* Cambridge, MA: Harvard University Press, 1979.

Stein, Leon. *The Triangle Fire.* New York: Caroll & Graf, 1962.

～ Triple Jeopardy

A term widely used in the 1970s and 1980s but since fallen out of use, *triple jeopardy* refers to the social and economic disfranchisement of poor minority women. The position of being in "triple jeopardy" arises out of membership in three low-status communities—women, minorities, and the underclass. The three terms of disfranchisement are interrelated and difficult to separate in describing the low structural status of poor minority women. Black, Native American, and Mexican American women occupy a disproportionate number of low-paying unskilled and semiskilled jobs in service positions. Social disfranchisement is evidenced by a lack of power in both public and private spheres. The relationships between minority women and majority men, minority women and majority women, and

minority women and minority men have been historically based on the exploitation of minority women, who have been sexual objects for both minority and majority men (the most blatant example is the sexual exploitation of female slaves by slaveowners), have functioned as servants and nannies for majority women (relieving the latter of household drudgery), and have suffered inequality at home.

The way in which ethnicity, class, and sex combine to block opportunity for minority women has been the subject of theoretical debate. A Marxist-derived approach situates all domination within the capitalist system. Racism and sexism are based in the jockeying for economic ascendancy. Racism serves as justification for economic exploitation, while sexism arises out of women's position as unpaid domestic labor. Much of black and Mexican American women's literature identifies racism (as opposed to class or sex) as the guiding force behind lack of economic power. Black women especially focus on economic dislocation, based on racist hiring practices, to explain the unequal relationship between black men and women.

The "mainstream" women's movement explores the dialectic of powerlessness in the public and private realms. The lack of access women have traditionally had to political and economic structures is partially based in inequality in the domestic realm, and the symbols surrounding women as primarily domestic contribute to lack of access to the public arena—one aspect of which is economic. *(See also: Asian American Women; Black Women; Chicana; Native American Women; Socialist Feminism)*

—**Priscilla Weeks**

Further Reading

Britain, Arthur, and Mary Maynard. *Sexism, Racism, and Oppression.* New York: Basil Blackwell, 1984.

Etienne, Mona, and Eleanor Leacock, eds. *Women and Colonization: Anthropological Perspectives.* New York: Praeger, 1980.

Lerner, Gerda, ed. *Black Women in White America.* New York: Pantheon, 1972.

Melville, Margarita, ed. *Twice a Minority.* London: C. V. Mosby, 1980.

Stromberg, Ann H., and Shirley Harkness, eds. *Women Working: Theories and Facts in Perspective.* Mountain View, CA: Mayfield, 1978.

～ Troy Female Seminary

Troy Female Seminary began offering a rigorous educational program in 1821, and it rapidly became one of the foremost schools in the United States. The founder, Emma Hart Willard, came to Troy, New York, at the invitation of that community's Common Council. Willard had moved to nearby Waterford in 1819 with the expectation that New York State would provide financial support for the school. Although the legislature was receptive to her plans, aid was not forthcoming. Then, on March 26, 1821, the Troy Common Council passed a resolution to raise $4,000 by special tax for the purchase or construction of a building for a female seminary. Additional funds were raised by subscription, and a building was purchased. The community was firmly behind Willard's efforts. When the school opened in September 1821, it enrolled ninety girls from across the nation. Willard continued to appeal to the legislature for support but in vain. Citizens of Troy came to the seminary's assistance, and no outside aid was needed.

Willard was highly successful in her teaching. She was assisted by a professor and by a number of teachers trained by her. The curriculum was repeatedly improved at her initiative, and the school offered advanced courses in history and natural philosophy. No other girls' school in the nation offered such a complete program of study. By the mid-1820s, the success of the seminary prompted the city of Troy to expand the size of its building. In 1838, Willard retired as director of the seminary, handing over its direction to her son and daughter-in-law. Under their guidance, which lasted until 1872, the Troy Female Seminary continued to flourish and grow. The courses of study included modern languages, the Bible, composition, elocution, mathematics, astronomy, literature, history, and other subjects. The students' success challenged and firmly refuted the widely accepted point of view that such courses would, as Willard put it, "unsex us." The ability of females to master these disciplines was clearly demonstrated twice each year in the public examinations. Held in February and July, they drew crowds of spectators, as prominent scholars were invited to conduct the testing.

After the school's fifty-year lease on the buildings ended in 1872, the trustees purchased the site from the city and added new buildings. The school continued to gain widespread interest. In 1872, Emily T. Wilcox took over as principal, a post she held until 1895. In that year, the school changed its name to the Emma Willard School, and under that name it continues to be a leading educational institution. (See also: Education; Female Academies; Willard, Emma)

—Robert G. Waite

Further Reading

Emma Willard and Her Pupils or Fifty Years of Troy Female Seminary, 1822–1872. New York: Mrs. Russell Sage, 1898.

Lutz, Alma. Emma Willard: Pioneer Educator of American Women. Boston: Beacon, 1964.

Woody, Thomas. A History of Women's Education in the United States. Vol. 1-2. New York: Science Press, 1929.

ᕯ Truth, Sojourner (c. 1797–1883)

Sojourner Truth was a public speaker representing a commitment to both the nonviolent abolition of slavery and the emancipation of women, her commitments being rooted in Christian faith. Her mother, Elizabeth, a slave, named her Isabella. Years later, Isabella obtained her freedom, and believed that God called her to be a witness of God's truth to others; it was then, in 1843, that she changed her name. She began traveling and preaching, and the gentle power of her words (as well as her delivery and six-foot height) impressed people throughout the country. With the power of the truth that she spoke, she was able to confront boldly, as well as support, men as authoritative and respected as Frederick Douglass.

Even as she is an anomaly, Sojourner Truth has become an archetype for the thousands of black women who lived in slavery. In her lifetime, she journeyed from her birthplace in a root cellar to the prominent stages of the abolition and emancipation movements. She delivered her most famous speech in response to hecklers at the 1851 Women's Rights Convention in Akron, Ohio, where she declared the strength of all women when she asked, "Ain't I a woman?" Truth incorporated the experiences of her mother into her speeches to make her point, as in her claim to have borne thirteen children only to see most of them sold off to slavery.

A victim of the laws of her time, she still maintained a steady belief in the law and used the courts to fight injustice. In 1828 in Kingston, New York, Truth successfully sued Solomon Gedney for the freedom of her son, Peter, the youngest of her five children. In the mid-1830s, after she was accused and acquitted of poisoning her employer, she sued the press and became the first black person to win a slander suit against a white person. The court decided in her favor and awarded her $125 in damages. In 1865, Truth filed suit in Washington, D.C., against the City Railway to affirm the legal right of blacks to ride the public transport.

Truth worked with the Freedmen's Bureau and lobbied Congress to establish a program to resettle freed blacks in the West after the Civil War. She deemed her meeting with President Abraham Lincoln a highlight of her life. She died in Battle Creek, Michigan, in 1883. (See also: Abolition and the Antislavery Movement; Black Women; Public Speakers: Nineteenth Century; Slavery)

—Joanne S. Richmond
—Merri Scheibe Edwards

Further Reading

Litwack, Leon, and August Meier, eds. Black Leaders of the Nineteenth Century. Urbana: University of Illinois Press, 1988.

Ortiz, Victoria. Sojourner Truth, A Self-Made Woman. Philadelphia: J. B. Lippincott, 1974.

Pauli, Hertha. Her Name Was Sojourner Truth. New York: Avon, 1962.

Robinson, Wilhelmena S. Historical Negro Biographies. In Library of Negro Life and History, pp. 130-31. New York: Publisher's Company, 1967.

Staples, Robert. The Black Women in America. Chicago: Nelson Hall, 1973.

Truth, Sojourner. Narrative of Sojourner Truth. 1878. Reprint, New York: Arno, 1968.

ᕯ Tubman, Harriet (1821?–1913)

Born a slave, Harriet Tubman became one of the best-known leaders of the Underground Railroad, an organized network of abolitionists who helped slaves escape

Figure 62. Harriet Tubman
Shown here at far left, holding a pan, Harriet Tubman was a leader of the Underground Railroad, a network of abolitionists who aided slaves in their flight to freedom. "Mother Harriet" became heavily involved in women's suffrage organizations in her later years. Used by permission of Corbis-Bettman.

to freedom. She served as a spy, scout, and nurse for the Union Army during the Civil War. Abolitionist, suffragist, and militant black leader, Tubman was known as "Moses" because of her untiring efforts on behalf of black emancipation.

Tubman was born in the early 1820s on a plantation on the Eastern Shore of Maryland. In about 1844, Tubman married a free black man, while still enslaved herself. When her master died in 1849, it was rumored that she would be sold, so she decided to escape. Her husband and her brothers refused to go with her, so she journeyed alone to freedom in the North. By hiding during the daytime and walking at night, she arrived safely in Pennsylvania.

Tubman was not content with her own freedom, and over a ten-year period she made nineteen trips into the South to free others. At least three hundred men, women, and children escaped slavery through her efforts on the Underground Railroad. None of the people she assisted were ever caught, leading anxious slaveowners to offer $40,000 in reward for her capture. Tubman risked reenslavement to free others, but she cautiously carried a hidden revolver to protect herself and spur on reluctant fugitives.

Tubman was well known to abolitionist leaders and even aided John Brown in his plans to raid Harper's Ferry in Virginia. She aided the Union Army in the South during the Civil War as a cook, nurse, spy, guerrilla fighter, and commander of scouts. Like many women, she worked in makeshift hospitals attending to wounded soldiers. Yet unlike most women, Tubman, only five feet tall, commanded soldiers on raiding expeditions, most notably on one up the Combahee River in South Carolina in 1863, when three hundred black soldiers rescued more than seven hundred slaves. She also organized networks of spies among slaves in Confederate territory.

Following the war, Tubman helped establish schools to educate ex-slaves and even founded the Home for Indigent and Aged Negroes in her own house in New York. She used her government pension to help defray the cost, and she had her friend Sarah Bradford write her biography in 1869 to raise money for the home.

Known as "Mother Harriet" in her later years, she actively participated in women's organizations and attended woman suffrage conventions. She was at the founding conference of the National Association of Colored Women in 1896, the first national black women's organization. Honored by many, she died in Auburn, New York, in 1913. *(See also: Abolition and the Antislavery Movement; Black Women; Civil War; National Association of Colored Women; Slavery)*

—Susan Lynn Smith

Further Reading

Bradford, Sarah. *Harriet Tubman: The Moses of Her People.* 1886. Reprint, New York: Corinth, 1961.

Conrad, Earl. *Harriet Tubman: Negro Soldier and Abolitionist.* New York: International Publishers, 1942.

❦ Turner, Mrs. E. P. (1856–1938)

Mrs. E. P. Turner was a club woman and community builder in Dallas, Texas, during the Progressive Era. Born and reared near Jefferson, Texas, Adella Kelsey met Edward P. Turner, who was employed by the Texas and Pacific Railroad. Shortly after their marriage in 1879, the Turners moved to Dallas; they had four sons, only two of whom survived.

While president of the City Federation of Women's Clubs (1903–1904), the Texas Federation of Women's Clubs (1904–1906), and the Dallas Woman's Forum (1906–1908), Turner launched her campaign for correcting wrongs and abuses wherever woman's influence was needed. Because of her expanding interest in the welfare and education of children, in 1908 she became one of the first women to serve on the Dallas County School Board.

In 1910, when her term of office on the school board expired, Turner once again became president of the Dallas Woman's Forum. From 1910 to 1919 she organized and built the Woman's Forum into an institution that had a major impact on the reform of sanitary conditions and the welfare of delinquent and underprivileged children in Dallas. In 1921, her interest in the legal rights of women led to the formation of the Women's Good Citizenship Association, which later became the Dallas League of Women Voters. After over fifty years of involvement in the women's club movement, Mrs. E. P. (Adella P. Kelsey) Turner died on June 6, 1938, in Dallas. *(See also: General Federation of Women's Clubs; Progressive Era)*

—Diana Church

Further Reading

Church, Diana. "Mrs. E. P. Turner: Clubwoman, Reformer, Community Builder," *Heritage News* (Summer 1985): 9-14.

Hazel, Michael V. "Dallas Women's Clubs: Vehicles for Change," *Heritage News* (Spring 1986): 18-21.

———. "A Mother's Touch: The First Two Women Elected to the Dallas School Board," *Heritage News* (Spring 1987): 9-12.

❦ Turnout

Turnout was a nineteenth-century term used interchangeably with strike by the early female operatives in the Massachusetts mills. It was actually a work stoppage or walkout en masse from their stations into the streets. The turnouts followed announcements of wage cuts. Harriet Hanson Robinson, a bobbin doffer in the mills at the age of eleven and later a suffragist, led one of the early turnouts (1836) and proudly recollected this event many years later in addressing a group of mill girls. *(See also: Lowell Mill Girls; Robinson, Harriet Hanson; Textiles: North and South)*

—Virginia Beattie Mattes

Further Reading

Dublin, Thomas. *Women at Work, The Transformation of Work and Community in Lowell, Massachusetts, 1826–1860.* New York: Columbia University Press, 1979.

Josephson, Hannah. *The Golden Threads, New England's Mill Girls and Magnates.* New York: Duell, Sloan & Pearce, 1949.

Robinson, Harriet H. *Loom and Spindle.* Kailua, HI: Press Pacifica, 1976.

❦ Tuskegee Normal and Industrial Institute

As the result of a political deal, blacks in Macon County, Alabama, obtained a small state appropriation for a school at Tuskegee, Alabama, and in 1881, Booker T. Washington arrived there to become its first principal. By the time of his death in 1915, he had built Tuskegee Institute into the second-best-endowed black school in the nation and had become widely recognized by whites as a national spokesman for Afro-Americans. The school's combination of teacher and vocational training became a model for numerous other schools.

In his rise to prominence, Washington was aided by two strong women who became his second and third wives. Olivia Davidson was the first teacher he hired, and Margaret Murray served as lady principal and director of Industries for Girls. They directed the training programs for women, which were geared to producing teachers with knowledge of domestic arts such as dressmaking and cooking.

Tuskegee graduates were expected to share the benefits of their education, and most women graduates became teachers in rural areas—usually continuing to work after marriage. Quite a few made significant contributions. Petra Pinn, a nurse training graduate in 1906, held several responsible positions before opening and supervising a private hospital in West Palm Beach, Florida. Elizabeth Evelyn Wright founded Vorhees Normal and Industrial Institute in Denmark, South Carolina, in 1897—three years after her graduation. Many others have had similar success as the nature and program of Tuskegee have evolved. *(See also: Higher*

Education; Higher Education for Southern Women; Teaching; Washington, Margaret Murray)

—**Linda O. McMurry**

Further Reading

Booker T. Washington Papers. Library of Congress. Washington, DC.

Butler, Addie Louise Joyner. *The Distinctive Black College: Talladega, Tuskegee, and Morehouse.* Metuchen, NJ: Scarecrow, 1977.

Harlan, Louis R. *Booker T. Washington: The Making of a Black Leader, 1856–1901.* New York: Oxford University Press, 1972.

———. *Booker T. Washington: The Wizard of Tuskegee, 1901–1915.* New York: Oxford University Press, 1983.

Thrasher, Max Bennet. *Tuskegee: Its Story and Its Work.* New York: Negro University Press, 1969.

Una (1853–1855)

Una, a Boston-based monthly magazine "Devoted to the Elevation of Woman," provided an alternative viewpoint to the popular woman's magazines of the mid-nineteenth century. Editor Paulina Wright Davis commented in the first issue of February 1853, "Women have been too well, and too long, satisfied with Ladies' Books, Ladies' Magazines and Miscellanies; it is time they should have stronger nourishment." From the start, the intent of the Una was to address the questions of woman's rights and duties in a straightforward, honest manner. The Una, translated as "truth," was considered the first woman's suffrage paper and preceded the longer-lived Woman's Journal by almost two decades.

During the two years of Una's publication, its contributors included well-known suffragist Elizabeth Cady Stanton, popular poet Sarah Helen Whitman, writer Miss Leslie, and a host of other writers and editorialists, including Davis and assistant editor Caroline Dall. Even Sarah Josepha Hale, editor of a less nourishing "ladies' magazine," Godey's Lady's Book, contributed her thoughts. Una played an important role in providing information on issues of concern to suffragists by reporting on questions of legal rights for women, providing notes and commentaries on woman's rights conventions, and discussing issues pertaining to health, literature, education, and religion. Political rights for women, particularly Massachusetts women, were consistently addressed in Una, with published excerpts from the constitutional convention meetings of Massachusetts. In 1855, after two years of publication, Davis was no longer able to finance Una, and it ceased publication. (See also: Dall, Caroline Wells; Davis, Paulina Kellogg Wright; Magazines; Suffrage)

—Karen C. Knowles

Further Reading

Riegel, R. E. American Feminists. Lawrence: University of Kansas Press, 1968.
Stanton, Elizabeth C., Susan B. Anthony, and Matilda J. Gage, eds. The History of Woman Suffrage, 6 vols. New York: National American Woman Suffrage Association, 1888–1922.
Stearns, Bertha M. "New England Magazines for Ladies, 1830–1860," New England Quarterly 3 (October 1930): 653-54.

Stein, Karen F. "Paulina Kellogg Wright Davis." In American Women Writers: A Critical Reference Guide from Colonial Times to the Present. Vol. 1, edited by Lina Mainiero, 475-76. New York: Frederick Ungar, 1979.
Una. Vols. 1-3. Boston: Sayles, Miller & Simons, 1853–1855.

Unions

The earliest recorded union was the New York United Tailoresses Society, formed in 1824, which struck in 1825 and again in 1831, but left no records of the results. Mill women in Lowell, Massachusetts, organized the Factory Girls' Association in 1834, followed by the Female Labor Reform Association in 1845. Sarah Bagley, a mill worker from New Hampshire, appears to have been the multi-talented force behind both of these organizations. She was extremely active between 1836 and 1846, when she became the first woman telegrapher and then disappeared from recorded history. Sewing machine operators in New York established the Working Women's Union in 1863, electing Ellen Patterson president and M. Trimble recording secretary. After the Civil War, Kate Mullaney led the Troy Collar Laundry Union (1866) in a strike supported by Troy union men. A series of labor disasters for the men, coupled with the introduction of paper collars, effectively ended the strike, and the union was dissolved.

Throughout the 1860s, mill workers continued to organize under the guidance of Jennie Collins. She was active with the New England Labor Reform League and organized the Working Women's Club of Boston. In 1869, the Typographical Union admitted women for the first time. Augusta Lewis, corresponding secretary (1870), was the first woman to hold national office. The Daughters of St. Crispin (1869) was the first national union for women. These unions, for the most part, failed because the women lacked the education, expertise, and financial resources needed for long-term growth. Their male counterparts in the labor movement did not take the women seriously until the Knights of Labor and the American Federation of Labor agreed to allow them to organize ladies' assemblies. For ten years (1881–1890), Leonora Kearney Barry worked as a general investigator, educator, and organizer of women for the Knights of

Labor. When she retired, no one took up the work, and it was abandoned.

However, the women had opened the door, and their unions began to proliferate: the Ladies Federal Labor Union (1888), led by Elizabeth Morgan; the Retail Clerks International (1890), led by Mary Burke; and the International Boot and Shoemakers, led by Mary Anderson, later first director of the Women's Bureau, U.S. Department of Labor (1895). By 1892, Mary E. Kenney was the national organizer of women for the American Federation of Labor. Helen Campbell was appointed to Massachusetts' Bureau of Labor. The National Women's Trade Union League (1903), guided by its president, Margaret Dreier Robins, trained women whose names became legend in early union history: Rose Schneiderman, Women's Trade Union League; Pauline Newman, International Ladies Garment Workers Union; Marie Van Vorst and her sister Bessie, labor reformers; Mary Harris "Mother" Jones, labor activist and investigator; Helen Gurley Flynn, Industrial Workers of the World; and Mary Anderson and Leonora O'Reilly.

Black women and minorities were not represented in the unions until the last thirty-five or forty years. When white women and immigrants replaced them in the trades, black women were forced to take menial work that was impossible to organize. National Labor Union/Cincinnati Colored Teachers Cooperative Association (1870) was an exception. Today, almost all teachers belong to the National Education Association, established in 1870. By 1918, as a result of employment during World War I, 35,000 women were members of the railroad unions, with many occupying administrative positions.

By the 1920s, women had finally become accepted as members in male labor unions. But unions were decimated by the worldwide depression of the 1930s: Unemployed workers could not pay their dues, and impoverished unions could not help their members. World War II saw a union renewal, and by 1945, there were 3 to 3.5 million women union members in organizations such as the National Teachers Association, International Brotherhood of Electrical Workers (telephone employees), and nurses' unions.

The percentage of union members who are women doubled since 1960, from 20 percent to 39.5 percent in 1998. Powerful labor legislative lobbying groups, the civil rights movement, and sophisticated technology aided in bringing workers out of the dark ages of industrialization. But the modern woman union member also owes her equal work status to the determination, tenacity, and dedication of early women activists. *(See also: American Federation of Labor; Bagley, Sarah G.; Congress of Industrial Organizations; Flynn, Elizabeth Gurley; Industrial Workers of the World; International Ladies Garment Workers Union; Huerta, Dolores; Jones, "Mother"; Knights of Labor; Lowell Mill Girls; Moreno, Luisa; National Education Association; National Women's Trade Union League; O'Sullivan, Mary Kenney; Schneiderman, Rose; United Farm Workers; Women's Protective Union)*

—**Jean M. Hayes**

Further Reading

Greenwald, Maurine Weiner. *Women, War and Work*. Westport, CT: Greenwood, 1980.

Ware, Norman. *The Industrial Worker: 1840–1860*. 1924. Reprint, Chicago: Quadrangle, 1964.

⟨ Unitarian–Universalism

Unitarianism and Universalism both evolved from the Congregational churches of New England around the time of the American Revolution. Both religions believed in the "natural freedom of human beings," and traced their earliest ideas to the Renaissance, the Reformation, and the spirit of individualism found in the New World. They also accepted the total equality of women and men. Some of the early women encouraged by this view to achieve their full potential were Louisa May Alcott, Susan B. Anthony, Clara Barton, Elizabeth Blackwell, Dorothea Dix, and Julia Ward Howe. Olympia Brown became, in 1863, the first woman to be ordained in any organized church in the United States.

The first Universalist church in the colonies was founded by John Murray in Gloucester, Massachusetts, in 1774. He was a devoted believer in universal salvation as described by James Relly in his *Union* (1843). Man, it was believed, was a product of natural forces and therefore God was revealed in the natural universe and in man, not just in the Bible. Universalism appealed to many in the lower classes and the less educated.

Unitarianism appealed to members of the educated upper classes such as the Transcendentalists. It emphasized an intellectual and critical study of the Bible and other sources of enlightenment. Unitarians preached toleration and Arminianism (individualism in each person's relationship to God). They revered Jesus as a teacher but not as God; hence, they were not Trinitarians.

In 1961, the Unitarian and Universalist churches consolidated, believing that they were united by their purposes, their values, and their ethical principles. They maintained no religious creed and accepted no dogma but gave ultimate authority to the reason, the insight, and the experience of each individual. Their avowed aim is to encourage humans to use their full potential to secure peace and justice and to be mindful of the needs and worth of others, irrespective of their gender, race, or other distinctions. *(See also: Brown, Olympia; Christianity; Religion)*

—**Tamerin Mitchell Hayward**

Further Reading

Cassara, Ernest, ed. *Universalism in America: A Documentary History*. Boston: Beacon, 1971.

Cooke, George Willis. *Unitarianism in America: A History of Its Origin and Development*. Boston: Unitarian Association, 1902.

Gittlin-Emmer, Susan. "Roots of Our Strength: A Heritage of Unitarian and Universalist Women." Unpublished manuscript. 1980.

Scholenfield, Harry Barron, ed. *The Unitarian Universalist Pocket Guide.* Boston: Beacon, 1963.

⚘ United Auto Workers (UAW)

As was the case with several industrial unions, the United Auto Workers grew out of the struggles to organize workers in heavy industry during the 1930s. In 1936, the UAW united with the Congress of Industrial Organizations (CIO) and faced the formidable task of organizing autoworkers in the Big Three: Ford, General Motors, and Chrysler. Walter Reuther, one of the most committed and impressive leaders of the union during the early days, first worked to organize workers in the Detroit area. He remained an important leader in the union throughout his life, serving thirty-five years as a union officer, twenty-four of those as president. Perhaps the most memorable legacy of the United Auto Workers' early organizing efforts was the sit-down strike. Workers refused to leave the auto plants, set up barriers to prevent siege from outside, and presented the threat of wrecking expensive machinery within the factories. Scabs could not be used effectively in this situation, and workers bonded with the sense of solidarity, since they lived together in the plant. The most famous sit-down strike occurred at the GM plant in Flint, Michigan, and lasted from December 1936 until February 1937.

During the Flint GM sit-down strike, the women whose husbands, sons, and brothers were in the plant formed an auxiliary. This group got food to the workers, mended wounds, ran picket lines, and coordinated publicity. After a confrontation between workers and police on January 11, 1937, some of the women's auxiliary members established the Women's Emergency Brigade, whose purpose, according to leader Genora Johnson, was to be on hand when emergencies arose during the strike. Organized to mimic a military organization and wearing colored armbands and berets, these women could be called on a moment's notice to ring a plant with a picket line to protect the workers inside, break windows in a plant that was being tear gassed, or create a diversion to allow workers to take over a plant to sit-down. Because of the major contribution of the auxiliaries and emergency brigade in keeping up the morale and determination of the strikers, women's auxiliaries received the full support of the UAW leadership during this era of organizational efforts.

In more recent times, the UAW was the first major union to condemn protective legislation for women, declaring such laws discriminatory. As early as 1970, the union took a strong stand on women's issues in a resolution passed at the national convention that year that supported a woman's right to abortion, the establishment of a network of day care centers, and the passage of an equal rights amendment to the U.S. Constitution. In 1979, the UAW also took the issue of sexual harassment to the bargaining table and got language written into contracts addressing it. In 1991, the UAW won a U.S. Supreme Court case against the Johnson Controls battery plant in Louisville, Kentucky, in a ruling that made "fetal protection policies" illegal. The UAW also lobbied for the Pregnancy Disability Amendment (an amendment to Title VII of the Civil Rights Act of 1964) and for the Family and Medical Leave Act (FMLA).

In 1966, Olga Madar became the first woman to be elected to the UAW Executive Board, first as a member-at-large and then as a UAW vice president in 1970. More recently, Carolyn Forrest became a UAW vice president in 1992 and has since headed a number of UAW departments, including bargaining and grievance handling in the "competitive shops" sector that includes auto suppliers. Women now make up the majority of 22,000 members of the UAW's biggest local union, UAW Local 6000, public employees of the State of Michigan. *(See also: Congress of Industrial Organizations; Flint Auto Workers' Strike; Unions)*

—**Mariann L. Nogrady**

Further Reading

Foner, Philip S. *Women and the American Labor Movement, From World War I to the Present.* New York: Free Press, 1980.

Gabin, Nancy Felice. *Feminism in the Labor Movement: Women and the United Auto Workers, 1935–1975.* Ithaca, NY: Cornell University Press, 1990.

Vorse, Mary Heaton. *Labor's New Millions.* New York: Modern Age, 1938.

⚘ United Daughters of the Confederacy

Organized in 1894 by Caroline Meriweather Goodlett of Nashville and Anna Davenport Raines of Savannah, the United Daughters of the Confederacy (UDC) was one of the most popular voluntary associations for white southern women in the early twentieth century. UDC claimed seventeen thousand members by 1900 and continued to grow. There were 44,000 Daughters in 1910 and 68,000 in 1920. Membership peaked in the early 1920s and declined thereafter.

UDC grew out of local memorial associations and auxiliaries to veterans' groups. The Daughters undertook a variety of projects to commemorate the "Lost Cause." They offered relief to needy Confederate veterans, widows, and orphans; lobbied for higher pensions for veterans; constructed monuments; held pageants and ceremonies on Confederate holidays; cared for graves of Confederate soldiers; and collected documents and artifacts pertaining to the Civil War. Much of their work was educational. They sponsored essay contests for schoolchildren and college students, monitored textbooks to ensure that "true" history was being taught in the public schools, and funded scholarships for descendants of veterans.

The Daughters honored the heroines of the Confederacy along with its heroes. They stressed women's contributions to the war effort and praised southern women for their strength, resourcefulness, and courage. When Confederate veterans wanted to build a monument to southern women, UDC insisted that practical assistance to women of the present would be the most fitting memorial to the women of the past. They suggested scholarships, homes for Confederate widows, or industrial schools as alternatives, indicating that perhaps the Civil War experience offered different lessons to women than to men. Women learned during the war that men would not always be there when needed, and the Daughters' practical proposals suggest that they wanted to be prepared to take care of themselves. In this instance, however, the men prevailed, and several southern states erected statues to the women of the Confederacy.

UDC played an important, if ambiguous, role in determining the place of white women in the New South. In the name of preserving tradition, UDC members moved beyond the traditional domestic role into public life. While glorifying the Old South, they modified the southern feminine ideal to emphasize strength and competence. The Daughters perpetuated the myth of the Southern Lady, but they portrayed her as steel magnolia rather than clinging vine. *(See also: Civil War; Southern Lady; Southern Women's History; Southern Women's Organizations/Leaders)*

—**Anastatia Sims**

Further Reading

Davies, Wallace Evan. *Patriotism on Parade: The Story of Veterans and Hereditary Organizations in America, 1783–1900.* Cambridge, MA: Harvard University Press, 1955.

Foster, Gaines M. *Ghosts of the Confederacy: Defeat, the Lost Cause, and the Emergence of the New South.* New York: Oxford University Press, 1987.

Poppenheim, Mary B. et al. *The History of the United Daughters of the Confederacy.* Raleigh, NC: Edwards & Broughton, n.d.

Roth, Darlene Rebecca. *Matronage: Patterns in Women's Organizations, Atlanta, Georgia, 1890–1940.* New York: Carlson, 1994.

⤫ United Farm Workers (UFW)

Farmworkers in the United States, largely seasonal Hispanic workers, were the last large group of workers to be organized. Early attempts at organization had failed, but in 1962, César Chávez, assisted by Dolores Huerta, formed the National Farm Workers Association (NFWA). Plagued by low wages, long hours, and poor working conditions, the workers, through the NFWA, came to strength as a result of the Delano grape strike, which started in California in September 1965 and lasted until May 1970. Symbolized by a black Aztec eagle on a red flag, emblazoned with the Spanish word for strike—*Huelga*—the Delano strikers of the NFWA received support from Robert F. Kennedy, other powerful U.S. unions, and civil rights organizations. However, La Causa, as the movement came to be known, made slow progress until Chávez and Huerta organized a nationwide consumer boycott of California grapes that dramatized and publicized the conditions of the farmworkers.

During this strike, the NFWA merged with the Agricultural Workers Organizing Committee of the AFL-CIO, to form the United Farm Workers Organizing Committee, AFL-CIO. After more struggles and boycotts, the UFW in 1977 had over seventy contracts and represented about thirty thousand workers.

By the 1970s, the United Farm Workers depended on women in the fields and in positions of leadership. Once women learned to do pruning, a previously male-dominated job, the union sent men and women out to jobs based on their availability, ending any sex-determined work in the fields. Dolores Huerta, an early union organizer, became the union's first elected vice president in 1974. Although women did not win the acceptance of the male leadership easily, Chávez wanted women like Huerta on the picket line. Women, for example, led the picketing against the union-busting efforts of the growers and Teamsters and refused to retaliate when provoked by the Teamsters' violent beatings and attacks. As a result, the women established themselves as a mainstay of the union's nonviolent philosophy. Huerta also acted as chief negotiator for the first contract and did negotiations herself for five years. Other important self-taught women in this union include Jessie Lopez de la Cruz, the first woman to organize workers in the field; Marie Sabadado, the director of the Robert F. Kennedy Farm Workers Medical Plan; and Helen Chávez, the head of the Credit Union.

Since 1994, the UFW has signed seventeen contracts with growers of grapes, lettuce, roses, strawberries, mushrooms, and other vegetables. The total membership of the organization is estimated at 26,000 members. In 1998, the UFW targeted the strawberry industry, especially in California, raising awareness of the plight of seasonal strawberry field workers. UFW members have organized to establish security for workers by informing consumers, vendors, and growers about injustices in working conditions and wages. The founder of the United Farm Workers Organization, César Chávez, died in 1994. Dolores Huerta is currently acting as secretary/treasurer of the UFW. *(See also: Chicana; Huerta, Dolores)*

—**Mariann L. Nogrady**

Further Reading

Altman, Linda Jacobs. *Migrant Farm Workers: The Temporary People.* New York: Franklin Watts, 1994.

Baer, Barbara L., and Glenna Mathews. "You Find a Way: The Women of the Boycott," *The Nation* 218 (February 23, 1974): 233-34.

de la Cruz, Jessie Lopez. "My Life: Jessie Lopez de la Cruz as told to Ellen Cantarow," *Radical America* 12 (November/December 1978): 34-35.

De Ruiz, Dana Catharine. *La Causa: The Migrant Farmworkers' Story.* Austin, TX: Raintree Steck-Vaughn, 1993.

Foner, Philip S. *Women and the American Labor Movement: From World War I to the Present.* New York: Free Press, 1980.

Wirpsa, Leslie. "UFW Targets Strawberry Fields," *National Catholic Reporter* 34 (May 1998): 3-5.

❧ United Mine Workers of America (UMWA)

Founded in 1890, the United Mine Workers of America (UMWA) is an industrial labor union. Unlike today, when women work side by side with men in the ore mines of the United States, superstition once made it "unlucky" for a woman even to be near a mine. Nevertheless, women suffered just as much as their fathers, husbands, brothers, and sons from the difficult physical conditions of the company town, where there were inadequate sanitary conditions, everything was covered with coal dust, and water had to be carried from nearby streams. Women were always fearful of injury or death to their male relatives and husbands, which would make their lives even more difficult. In this atmosphere, two strong women labor union organizers were recruited by the United Mine Workers to improve the conditions of the miners and their families.

By the time Mary Harris "Mother" Jones attended the founding convention of the IWW (Industrial Workers of the World) in Chicago in 1905, she had already been a union activist for many years. To the mine workers, she was known as the "Miners' Angel" because of her participation in labor conflicts in West Virginia, Colorado, and Pennsylvania. In one especially successful campaign, she helped the Paint Creek miners gain union recognition and a contract during the southern West Virginia conflict of 1912-13. Although she was held in custody by the military authorities of West Virginia for quite a bit of this time, she was able to gain a great deal of publicity, which resulted in getting a congressional subcommittee to investigate the conditions surrounding the strike. This made it difficult for Governor Henry Hatfield to retaliate with martial law. As a result, the coal operators granted the strikers' original demands, and the strike was settled.

Fannie Sellins was recruited by Van Bittner, subdistrict director of District 5 of the United Mine Workers, after successfully campaigning for a boycott of a St. Louis clothing company whose workers had been locked out from 1909 to 1911. Otto Kaemmerer, a former president of a United Garment Workers local in St. Louis, said that she visited nearly every national, state, and district convention of the United Mine Workers and the Western Federation of Miners throughout the country. By 1913, Sellins was in West Virginia helping the families of miners on strike in Colliers. Later, she helped prevent violence between union and nonunion coal miners working in the Penn Salt pits near Pittsburgh. In the tradition of Mother Jones, she was an outspoken advocate of the miner and the United Mine Workers.

In the early part of the century, the socialist-influenced United Mine Workers organized extensive women's auxiliaries with a distinctive cultural flavor, like the Dante Alligheri Clubs of the Kansas "Little Balkans" coal mining district, and *Lavoratore Italiano* (UMW's newspaper), which helped Italian Americans emerge as an important force. *(See also: Industrial Workers of the World; Jones, "Mother"; Sellins, Fannie; Socialism)*

—Abby Schmelling

Further Reading
Buhle, Mari Jo. *Women and American Socialism, 1870–1920.* Urbana: University of Illinois Press, 1983.
"Fannie Sellins Dies on the Battlefield of Labor," *St. Louis Labor* (August 30, 1919): 1.
Fetherling, Dale. *Mother Jones, the Miners' Angel: A Portrait.* Carbondale: Southern Illinois University Press, 1979.
Meyerhuber, Carl. "Fannie Sellins and the Events of 1919." Paper given at meeting of the Pennsylvania Labor History Society, September 27, 1986.
Williams, John A. *West Virginia: A History.* New York: Norton, 1984.

❧ United States Children's Bureau

The United States Children's Bureau was created as an agency of the federal government in 1912 to "investigate the questions of infant mortality, the birth rate, orphanages, juvenile courts, desertion, dangerous occupations, accidents and diseases of children, employment, [and] legislation affecting children" in the United States and its territories. The legislation signed by President William Howard Taft reflected the concerns of the Progressive Movement, which advocated protective measures for women, children, and other members of society who suffered under adverse social and economic conditions.

Early child welfare advocates maintained that the nation should care as much about its children as it did about its food. Accordingly, the first specific project undertaken by the bureau was one to reduce infant mortality. It was modeled on the Department of Agriculture's public education program that provided information to farmers on how to improve their crops. After studying the incidence of infant mortality in various geographic locations and among different social groups, the bureau sponsored maternal education programs that improved prenatal care, infant care and feeding, and medical consultation among women who previously had no access to such resources.

The bureau maintained its dual mission of research and program development by adapting its programs through the years to accommodate changing social conditions, the dislocations caused by two world wars and the Great Depression, and medical advances. The bureau's many studies and the precedents set by its administration laid the groundwork for the Social Security Act and other health and welfare programs enacted during the Roosevelt administration. During World War II, the bureau worked to keep children in school and protect them from unfair labor practices while it expanded its maternal care program into the single most extensive medical care program ever undertaken by the government. The Emergency Maternity and Infant Care Program ensured that the pregnant wives and newborn children of absent servicemen received the best medical treatment available. After the war, the bureau's programs focused on qualitative issues of child welfare: mental health, delinquency, and rehabilitation from crippling or debilitating diseases, especially polio. The bureau also made its expertise available to the world as it participated in international child welfare congresses and provided training and information to other countries. In the 1980s, most of the Children's Bureau programs were curtailed by reductions in social programs.

The success of the bureau's programs was due in large part to its leaders. Julia Lathrop, a close associate of Jane Addams and Lillian Wald, was the first chief of the bureau. She was succeeded in 1921 by Grace Abbott, a leader in child labor protection. Katharine F. Lenrott was named chief in 1934 and carried out the New Deal reforms and emergency wartime programs. She was succeeded by Martha Eliot, a physician, who served from 1952 to 1956. The final director of the bureau was Katherine Oettinger, who headed the bureau from 1957 until its absorption into the Office of Child Development of the Department of Health, Education and Welfare in the 1970s.

Originally conceived as a holistic advocacy agency for children, the Children's Bureau literally disappeared over the decades of its existence as the federal government reorganized, redefined departments and programs, and specialized their mission. The sense of mission and personal professional commitment exhibited by the bureau's directors was replaced by anodyne agency administrators. Child advocacy moved into the realm of nongovernmental organizations, which can focus on the needs of children, regardless of the governmental jurisdiction involved. *(See also: Abbott, Grace; Lathrop, Julia Clifford; Progressive Era)*

—**Jane Crisler**

Further Reading

Abel, Emily K. "Benevolence and Social Control: Advice from the Children's Bureau in the Early Twentieth Century," *Social Service Review* 68 (March 1994): 1-19.

Parker, Jacqueline K. "Women at the Helm: Succession Politics at the Children's Bureau," *Social Work* 39 (September 1994): 551-59.

The United States Children's Bureau, 1912–1972. New York: Arno, 1974. [Reprinted collection of articles]

United States Military Academy

Located in West Point, New York, the United States Military Academy was established as part of the U.S. Army Corps of Engineers in 1802. An act in 1912 reorganized the academy from an apprentice school to a four-year program with an expanded faculty and student body. The most famous of the early West Point superintendents was Colonel Sylvanus Thayer (1817–1833), who designed an academic structure that is still generally in place today.

The most radical change in the academy in the twentieth century was the admission of women beginning in 1976. Military leaders and cadets were most resistant to this change, which was mandated by Congress in a 1975 law that applied to the Naval and Air Force academies as well. The three academies reacted to this integration in different ways. West Point focused on maintaining "standards" and tried to ignore anatomical or physiological differences between the sexes. Annapolis tried for "low" visibility of the women cadets to make them less conspicuous; the Air Force strove for "high" visibility to instill an esprit de corps among the women. Only the Air Force had concrete plans for this transition. In part, this resulted in a lower attrition rate for the Air Force.

The first class of women graduates has been carefully followed by psychologists and sociologists. They graduated in 1980 and have now put in their required time, but there is no discernible trend regarding career service as yet. Leaders of the U.S. Military Academy as well as of the other academies worried about pregnancy among women officers. This concern was as unfounded in the 1980s as it was in the 1940s when, as Mattie Treadwell's book on the Women's Army Corps showed, pregnancy rates were low even though getting pregnant at the end of the war was the easiest way to "devolunteer." Sexual harassment has been a much larger problem, but the branches of the service have given this issue much attention in an attempt to address and eliminate the problem.

Women cadets and graduates have had to face the fact that the Army has closed many highly prestigious careers to them because of restrictions on women in combat. Since the war in the Persian Gulf, women are now allowed to be trained as combat airplane and helicopter pilots. The Army has recently opened up other military occupational specialties to women but has continued to close all positions for women in the infantry and armory branches. *(See also: Military Service)*

—**D'Ann Campbell**

Further Reading

Barkalow, Carol, with Andrea Raab. *In the Men's House: An Inside Account of Life in the Army by One of West Point's First Female Graduates.* New York: Poseidon, 1990.

A Comparison of Faculty and Cadet Attitudes towards Women. No. 76-017. Washington, DC: Office of Institutional Research, 1976.

Durning, Kathleen P. *Women at the Naval Academy: The First Year of Integration.* San Diego: Navy Personnel Research and Development, 1978.

Lovell, John. *Neither Athens Nor Sparta?* Bloomington: Indiana University Press, 1979.

Priest, Robert F., and John W. Houston. *Analysis of Spontaneous Cadet Comments on the Admission of Women.* No. 76-104. Washington, DC: Office of Institutional Research, 1976.

Stauffer, Robert. *Comparison of USMA Men and Women on Selected Physical Performance Measures . . . "Project Summertime."* Washington, DC: U.S. Military Academy, 1976.

Stiehm, Judith Hicks. *Bring Me Men and Women: Mandated Change at the U.S. Air Force Academy.* Berkeley: University of California Press, 1981.

United States. Office of the Chief of Naval Operations. Navy Women's Study Group. *An Update Report on the Progress of*

Women in the Navy. Washington, DC: Chief of Naval Operations, 1990.

Vitters, Alan G., and Nora Scott Kinzer. *Report of the Admission of Women to the U.S. Military Academy (Project Athena).* Washington, DC: Department of Behavioral Sciences and Leadership, 1977.

✨ United States Sanitary Commission

The United States Sanitary Commission was the outstanding public service contribution and accomplishment of Union women during the Civil War, despite the fact that antebellum women's inequality required that the commission itself be run by men. Established in 1861 to coordinate the war relief efforts of seven thousand local northern and western women's aid societies, the U.S. Sanitary Commission provided crucial services, which included providing trained nursing staff to Union hospitals as well as sending medical supplies and arranging transportation for the wounded. Appointed as superintendent of its nurses, Dorothea Dix successfully neutralized the opposition of the Army's male medical corps to the presence of women nurses in the Army hospitals as she oversaw the creation of a modern nursing service under the commission's aegis.

To fund the activities of this most effective women-created institution, its supporters successfully sponsored fairs and bazaars. The proceeds were used to buy food, clothing, and medical supplies that the local aid societies' members could not make themselves; local and state women's relief groups astutely sent designated agents to the front line hospitals to ensure proper distribution of the supplies. The outrage of an Iowa agent at the appalling food served in the military hospitals resulted in a commission-supported campaign for "diet kitchens" to provide the patients with decent nutrition. Commission-sponsored "refreshment saloons," forerunners of the USO canteens of the twentieth century, served soldiers traveling to and from the front. The wartime activities of Mrs. March and her daughters in Louisa May Alcott's *Little Women* exemplified the commission's work at the local level. At the end of the war, commission workers turned their attention to pressuring the government to address the plight of war orphans.

The U.S. Sanitary Commission contributed in excess of $1 million in hospital supplies and countless able and resourceful volunteers for the understaffed and ill-managed military hospitals. The Union benefited from the unstinting dedication of competent middle-class women who contributed their time and talent from the home front to the battlefront. Among the more well-known women who served the medical mission of the U.S. Sanitary Commission were Harriet Tubman, Sojourner Truth, Susie King Taylor, Jane Swisshelm, Mary Livermore, Mary Ann "Mother" Bickerdyke, and Louisa May Alcott. Women's experience with the commission indirectly spurred the professionalization of nursing, further development of institutions to train women physicians, and the creation of the American Red Cross. *(See also: Alcott, Louisa May; American Red Cross; Barton, Clara; Civil War; Dix, Dorothea Lynde; Nursing; Truth, Sojourner; Tubman, Harriet)*

—**Angela M. Howard**

Further Reading

Clinton, Catherine. *The Other Civil War: American Women in the Nineteenth Century.* New York: Hill & Wang, 1984.

Scott, Anne Firor. *Natural Allies: Women's Associations in American History.* Women in America Series. Chicago: University of Illinois Press, 1992.

✨ United States Supreme Court

The U.S. Constitution defines the U.S. Supreme Court as the apex of "judicial power," and all other courts as "lower level." Many of the Constitution's authors, unlike their British predecessors, regarded the Constitution they were writing as fundamental law and acts of Congress as ordinary law. But it took the Court itself, under Chief Justice John Marshall (1801–1835), to establish the principle that the Constitution takes priority over all laws passed by any body, federal, state, or municipal, and to position itself as the final arbiter in sorting out conflicts between ordinary and fundamental law. Civil rights and discrimination issues as a result fall within the Supreme Court's jurisdiction. Although the Court perceives itself as independent of party politics, and often acts that way, politicians do assign membership on the Court: Presidents appoint all federal judges with the consent of the Senate. Appointments are lifetime terms, so that Court decisions can change the shape of women's rights very quickly and can stand for a very long time. Thus, deaths and retirements from the Supreme Court periodically raise or revisit critical issues for women.

The Supreme Court's record on women's rights can be divided into four phases. The first wave of the women's movement looked to the Court to extend to women the rights to "equal protection" and "due process" granted to freed slaves by the Fourteenth Amendment. Not only did the Court fail to do that (*Minor v. Happersett,* 1874, upheld women's disenfranchisement, for example), it also failed to enforce the clear intent of the Fourteenth Amendment on issues of race (*Plessy v. Ferguson,* 1896, upheld segregation in the doctrine of "separate but equal"). Despite years of activism by women of all races, the Court did not distinguish itself as a supporter of women of any race.

By the early 1900s, the Court began to position itself as a guardian of women by upholding a wide range of "protective legislation." Often advocated by women themselves, particularly by women trade unionists and their more privileged supporters and eventually by women in governmental positions, protective legislation most often undermined women's socioeconomic situations by defining them solely as childbearers and child nurturers and protecting them as such. This paternalistic attitude can be viewed, as it was by its supporters, as an attempt to eliminate the worst abuses of working women in industry. Unfortunately, the results of that were mixed, with race and class making an enormous difference in the safety of workplaces where employers hired women. Furthermore, protective legislation led employers to hire fewer women, restricting employment opportunities overall; at the same time, these new laws depressed wages for all Americans as they justified underpaying women.

Not until the third phase, beginning roughly in the 1920s, did the Supreme Court's attitude toward women's issues begin to render it truly an ally for challenging women's position as second-class citizens. Until the 1980s, the arena in which it most reliably distinguished itself lay in its gradual rejection of government's right to interfere with procreation. Over several decades, the Court overturned federal laws prohibiting use of the mail to distribute information about contraceptives and revised its thinking on free speech issues dealing with the publication of contraceptive and sex education information. This part of a women's rights agenda, the right to control one's own body, culminated in the 1960s and 1970s with the Court striking down legal restrictions on the sale and use of contraceptive devices (*Griswold v. Connecticut*), laws banning abortion (*Roe v. Wade* and *Doe v. Bolton*), and laws mandating leaves of absence for pregnant employees (*Cleveland v. LaFleur*).

Also during this third phase, the Court finally revisited the Fourteenth Amendment to decide challenges to Jim Crow segregation mounted by the National Association for the Advancement of Colored People (NAACP) throughout the 1930s and 1940s, eventually establishing itself as a reliable ally of women of color, although this process often assumed that discrimination against women of color resulted solely from racism. The critical shift came under Chief Justice Earl Warren (1953–1969), emerging first in the *Brown v. Board of Education of Topeka* case (1954). The Court established three levels of "scrutiny" that it would use to evaluate the constitutionality of ordinary law on issues of race. The highest level, called "strict scrutiny," required the Court to examine the results of laws under the "equal protection" and "due process" clauses of the Fourteenth Amendment. Strict scrutiny institutionalized a growing role for social science evidence in legal arguments. Thus, if a law had a demonstrable effect of discriminating against persons of color, the intent of the law or the lawmakers became irrelevant; the discriminatory impact was sufficient for the Court the declare the law unconstitutional. The Equal Rights Amendment (ERA) would have established sex as a strict scrutiny category, but the ERA failed ratification in 1982 and is not yet a part of the Constitution.

The fourth phase, characterized by backlash, revisited long-standing controversies over the balance of power among the three branches of the federal government. Since the Constitution does not specify on what the Supreme Court should base its decisions, the Court has always created its own internal mechanisms for deciding constitutional issues. Those mechanisms may or may not become established

judicial principle, but judicial principles are not, at least in theory, subject to democratic or political party influence. This autonomous power of the Court, produced by the Constitution's silence, has therefore generated ongoing arguments with other branches of government over how fundamental law should be interpreted. By the 1970s, conservatives protested an "activist" Court that created law via judicial decision rather than remanding an unconstitutional provision back to Congress or the states. *Roe v. Wade,* the Court case that established a woman's right to choose abortion, is a critical example. Historically, however, even conservative Courts can be viewed as activist, creating law without legislative action by ignoring the intent of Congress in its deliberations, overturning established judicial principles or precedents, or establishing conservative judicial principles. Each and all of these strategies offered hope to right-wing conservatives for overturning a number of judicial results that affect women's rights, in particular, a woman's right to choose. In the 1980s and 1990s, the Court upheld the right of states to impose limitations on women seeking abortions, including mandatory waiting periods and parental consent requirements for minors.

In the fourth phase as well, the appointment of conservative judges throughout the federal court system also produced a backlash against affirmative action. Despite the Court's movement since the 1970s to expand the groups to whom it applies "due process" and "equal protection," the Court's own methods do not require it to scrutinize laws that indirectly or unintentionally result in sex discrimination, and it has held a line on gender relative to a class-, sex-, and race-segmented labor market. The ERA would have established sex as a suspect category, meaning that the nation had acknowledged persistent, historical sexism as it had acknowledged persistent, historical racism with the Fourteenth Amendment. Without the ERA, and with increasingly conservative lawmakers and courts, women's challenges to employment policies since the 1970s usually had to demonstrate an employer's intent to discriminate, a tougher level of proof that less clearly included equity-based evidence. Because the principle of levels of scrutiny is a judicial one rather than a legislative one, an increasingly conservative Supreme Court created under the Reagan and Bush administrations threatened the concept itself. While the Court ruled in *Bakke v. University of California* (1978) that educational institutions could not establish quotas to meet federal affirmative action rules, it nevertheless upheld the basic concept behind affirmative action, that institutions could regard race or ethnicity "as a 'plus' in a particular applicant's file." In 1989, however, the Court seriously undermined affirmative action by reaffirming its stand against "rigid racial quotas" and allowing previously settled affirmative action cases to be reopened.

The Supreme Court was entirely white until President Lyndon Johnson in 1967 appointed Justice Thurgood Marshall, a principal architect of the NAACP's judicial strategy to dismantle de jure segregation. In 1991, to replace retiring Justice Marshall, President George Bush appointed a young, inexperienced federal court judge, an African American conservative, Clarence Thomas. Thomas opposed women's right to abortion as well as affirmative action; he was most noted for eviscerating the Equal Employment Opportunity Commission (EEOC) when President Ronald Reagan appointed him to head it. Anita Hill, a lawyer, law professor, and former employee of Thomas's at the EEOC, challenged his nomination to the highest court in televised confirmation hearings. Hill accused Thomas of sexual harassment, and the treatment she received from an all-male Senate Judiciary Committee angered many women. The Senate approved Thomas's Court appointment.

The Supreme Court was also entirely male until the appointment of Justice Sandra Day O'Connor by President Ronald Reagan in 1981; O'Connor's appointment was opposed by many feminists. In 1993, however, President Bill Clinton appointed a second woman to the Court, Justice Ruth Bader Ginsburg, noted for her lifelong work on behalf of equity for women in the workplace and her role in arguing for the right to privacy as one means of ensuring women's reproductive choices. *(See also: Affirmative Action; Civil Rights; Equal Rights Amendment; Fourteenth Amendment; Griswold v. Connecticut; Minor v. Happersett; National Association for the Advancement of Colored People; Politics; Protective Legislation; Roe v. Wade; Voting Rights)*

—Deb Hoskins

Further Reading

Baer, Judith. *Equality under the Constitution: Reclaiming the Fourteenth Amendment.* Ithaca, NY: Cornell University Press, 1983.

Bakke v. University of California, 438 U.S. (1978).

Brown v. Board of Education of Topeka, 347 U.S. 483 (1954).

Cleveland Board of Education v. LaFleur, 414 U.S. 632 (1974).

Doe v. Bolton, 410 U.S. 179 (1973).

Griswold v. Connecticut, 381 U.S. 479 (1965).

Mezey, Susan Gluck. *In Pursuit of Equality: Women, Public Policy, and the Federal Courts.* New York: St. Martin's, 1992.

Minor v. Happersett, 53 No., 58, and 21 Wallace, 162 (1874).

Plessy v. Ferguson, 163 U.S. 537 (1896).

Roe v. Wade, 410 U.S. 113 (1973).

University of Chicago

The University of Chicago was incorporated in 1890 with substantial funding from John D. Rockefeller and opened for classes in 1892 under the presidency of William Rainey Harper. From the outset, the university was coeducational, and early enrollments indicate that more than a quarter of the students were female. During Chicago's first ten years, women accounted for nearly 50 percent of bachelor's degrees awarded and more than half the Phi Beta Kappa memberships.

Former Wellesley president Alice Freeman Palmer served as professor of history and as the first dean of women, assisted by her eventual successor, assistant professor of sanitary science Marion Talbot. Both were founders of the Association of Collegiate Alumnae (later the American Association of University Women). Talbot became dean in 1898, serving in that position until her retirement in 1925, and was probably the most influential woman at the university during her tenure. Although Talbot did accede to establishment of local "clubs" with no national affiliation, she opposed the formation of sororities and pushed for separate dormitories for women as the focus of their social life. Gifts from Mrs. Nancy Foster, Mrs. Mary Beecher, and Mrs. Elizabeth Kelly provided funding for the first women's residences, each of which, except for Green Hall, bore the name of its donor. Nevertheless, only a minority of the women students lived in dormitories, and many commuted from their parents' homes. Thus, Talbot led the campaign to found the Woman's Union in 1901 to provide day students with a place to rest, read, eat, and become involved with campus life.

Wellesley College provided the largest block of students in the early graduate programs. Chicago's arts and sciences graduate school included a large number of women, including reformers Grace and Edith Abbott, Sophonisba Breckinridge, Katharine Bement Davis, and scholars Myra Reynolds, Helen Bradford Thompson, Elizabeth Wallace, and Madeleine Wallin.

Perhaps because of the proportion of women students and their success, and the related fear that men would not attend a school in which women constituted a majority, in 1902 President Harper, over the objection of Talbot, other women, and some male faculty, imposed sex-segregated classes in the first two years of college. The practice was abandoned as too expensive within a few years.

Chicago has also played an important role in women's athletics. The appointment in 1898 of Gertrude Dudley as director of women's athletics and director of the women's gymnasium marked an early advance in collegiate athletics for women in the United States. It also represented a departure from the traditional view that competitive sports were not proper for women. The oldest women's athletic advocacy organization, the Women's Athletic Association, was formed at the University of Chicago in 1904. Mary Jean Mulvaney became the first female athletic director of a coeducational program and the first woman to serve on a National Collegiate Athletic Association general committee. In 1972, Chicago became the first university to offer athletic scholarships to women.

The appointment in 1978 of Hanna Holborn Gray as president of the university was the first of a woman to a major university presidency in the United States. *(See also: Association of Collegiate Alumnae; Athletics/Sports; Coeducation; Higher Education; Talbot, Marion)*

—Nicholas C. Burckel

Further Reading

Goodspeed, Thomas Wakefield. *A History of the University of Chicago: The First Quarter-Century.* Chicago: University of Chicago Press, 1916.

Gordon, Lynn D. *Gender and Higher Education in the Progressive Era.* New Haven, CT: Yale University Press, 1990.

Talbot, Marion. *More than Lore.* Chicago: University of Chicago Press, 1936.

Rausch, Eileen R. " 'Let Ohio Woman Vote': The Years to Victory, 1900–1920." Ph.D. diss., University of Notre Dame, 1984.

Upton, Harriet Taylor. "Random Recollections." n.p.: Commission for the Preservation of Ohio Suffrage Records, n.d. [1927].

~ Upton, Harriet Taylor (1854–1945)

Harriet Taylor Upton served as a longtime national and Ohio state suffrage leader and organizer. Affectionately called "the Boss" or "the General" by her cadre of workers, Upton was skilled at public speaking and legislative lobbying and was able to direct and organize masses of women, all of which proved invaluable to the suffrage movement. Under her leadership as Ohio Woman Suffrage Association (OWSA) president, the state movement adopted new practices such as open-air meetings and parades, streamlined and strengthened its organizational structure, and faced several serious crises as its membership numbers grew.

Born in Ravenna, Ohio, in 1854, Upton spent most of her life in the small town of Warren. As a young woman, she served as hostess and companion in Washington, D.C., for her widowed father, an Ohio congressman, from 1880 to 1893. In Washington, she met and eventually married attorney George Upton, who joined his father-in-law's Warren law practice. Their thirty-nine-year marriage was an especially close and supportive one; the two did not have children.

Harriet Taylor Upton first became interested in suffrage after attending a lecture given by suffrage leader Susan B. Anthony. Despite their age difference, the two became close friends, and Anthony helped to draw Upton into local and later national suffrage work. For many years, Upton served on the congressional and press committees of the National American Woman Suffrage Association and as national treasurer from 1893 to 1910.

As OWSA president (1890–1908, 1911–1920), Upton directed two unsuccessful referendum campaigns (1912, 1914) to add woman suffrage to the state constitution. A third unsuccessful referendum (1917) lost Ohio women the right to presidential suffrage, which had previously been enacted into law by the state legislature. Despite these defeats, statewide organizational efforts and accompanying congressional lobbying were ultimately successful. Ohio became the fifth state to ratify the Nineteenth Amendment, a testament to the hard work of Ohio's women and their tireless leader.

Following suffrage's victory, Upton served for several years as the first female member of the Republican Party's Executive Committee. *(See also: Anthony, Susan B.; National American Woman Suffrage Association; Suffrage)*

—**Eileen R. Rausch**

Further Reading

Allen, Florence E., and Mary Welles. *The Ohio Woman Suffrage Movement, "A Certain Unalienable Right": What Ohio Women Did to Secure It.* n.p.: Commission for the Preservation of Ohio Woman Suffrage Records, 1952.

~ Urbanization

Urbanization is the historical process whereby cities (densely populated with nonagricultural residents and contained within definite geolegal boundaries) evolve, developing large-scale, complex commercial, financial, industrial, residential, cultural, ecological, political, educational, communication, and transportation systems that transcend municipal boundaries. These systems structure and order internal behavior within the city and link it to its hinterlands. Over time, they unite individual cities in regional, national, and international networks that are extensions of their own internal systems. Urbanization is also the process that ultimately transforms an entire society, even those living in nonurban locales, because everyone and every place is increasingly enmeshed in the economic, financial, cultural, and political networks of the nation's cities.

Since colonial times, this process of urbanization has profoundly affected the lives of women in the United States. The first census, in 1790, showed that only slightly above 5 percent of Americans lived in the nation's twenty-four cities, even though the latter were defined as places of over 2,500 people. By 1840, nearly 11 percent of the population was classified as urban, with New York City exceeding 250,000 people. By 1880, 28.2 percent of the American people lived in cities of over 8,000 people; by 1910, that figure had risen to 45.7 percent. The 1920 census was the first in which urban dwellers outnumbered their rural and small-town cousins; by 1980, the proportion had reached nearly three-quarters. The growth rate of individual cities and their suburbs has been phenomenal, with Chicago going from a village of just over 3,000 in 1840 to a city of over 2 million by 1920, and Los Angeles exploding from about 33,000 in 1880 to over 6 million in 1960.

The influx of so many people into such a relatively small space within such a brief time span engendered a pressing need for expanding urban services, such as transportation, communication, education, recreation, utilities, and sewage and garbage disposal, which cities were often unable to meet adequately. Restrictive state charters that limited bonded indebtedness and tax rates, legislative malapportionment, privatism, and competition among the city's diverse ethnocultural and socioeconomic groups made it extremely difficult to provide an adequate level of urban services, leading to the growing prevalence of slums, poverty, crime, vice, and other urban problems. Yet the continued influx of people into urban areas eloquently testified to the continuing perception of the city as a place of greater economic opportunity and personal fulfillment.

Women, especially, found the city a far more fertile ground for their drive for equality than rural areas or small towns, and leadership in the various women's movements was exercised primarily by urban dwellers. The city also provided many women with new professions and new creative outlets unavailable elsewhere.

As has been the case with most historical processes, urbanization has proved to be a mixed bag so far as the status of women is concerned. On the one hand, the city was a place that promised far greater freedom from the restraints traditionally imposed by the paternalistic society and culture of rural and small-town America. It also generated millions of jobs in the burgeoning industrial and service sectors of the economy that released women from the confines of the narrow occupational niches that existed in villages and on farms. Urban women who achieved a middle-class status through education, occupation, or marriage were much better able to explore new definitions of women's role in society. The proliferation of women's organizations in cities provided their members with unprecedented opportunities for education, propaganda, pressure tactics, and political lobbying on women's issues. The progress enjoyed by the women's movement and feminism in twentieth-century America has clearly had predominantly urban roots, in terms of both leadership and critical mass.

On the other hand, urbanization has been far less kind to millions of women with working-class and ethnic minority backgrounds. Native-born white and African American women from America's farms and villages mingled with female immigrants from Europe, Canada, Mexico, and Asia to form a gender-based urban proletariat and underclass. Whether young and single and living in boarding or lodging houses or older and widowed, divorced, or separated, millions of women were forced to subsist on a wage scale about half that of males of comparable circumstances. Segregated into low-paying occupations in manufacturing, clerical, sales, or other service jobs and generally living apart from family or other support groups, these "women adrift" composed roughly one-fifth of the urban, non-servant, female labor force by 1900. While many were forced to resort to prostitution or other avenues of illegal activity, even those who eschewed such pursuits were frequently branded "immoral" simply because of their independent circumstances.

Remarkably, many of these "women adrift" managed to create elaborate peer subcultures, aided by the efforts of their better-established sisters. Unions, such as the International Ladies Garment Workers, reform organizations, such as the Women's Trade Union League, and social settlements, such as Chicago's Hull House brought together women from a variety of socioeconomic and ethnocultural backgrounds. Their efforts not only produced the beginnings of improved socioeconomic conditions for less fortunate women but also planted the seeds for the evolution of future sisterhood. *(See also: Demography; Friendships; Industrial Revolution; Migration and Frontier Women; Politics; Pro-*gressive Era; Prostitution; "Women Adrift;" Women's Work: Nineteenth Century)*

—**John D. Buenker**

Further Reading

Buenker, John D., Gerald Michael Greenfield, and William J. Murin. *Urban History: A Guide to Information Sources.* Detroit, MI: Gale, 1981.

Chudacoff, Howard, and Judith E. Smith. *The Evolution of American Urban Society,* 3d ed. Englewood Cliffs, NJ: Prentice Hall, 1988.

Furer, Howard B. "The American City: A Catalyst for the Women's Rights Movement," *Wisconsin Magazine of History* 52 (1969): 285-395.

Meyerowitz, Joanne J. *"Women Adrift": Independent Wage Earners in Chicago, 1880–1930.* Chicago: University of Chicago Press, 1988.

Miller, Zane L., and Patrician Mooney Melvin. *The Urbanization of Modern America: A Brief History,* 2d ed. New York: Harcourt Brace Jovanovich, 1987.

~ Utopian Communities

Utopian communities were intentional living and working arrangements organized to change various aspects of society. Most visible in the United States during the nineteenth century, these communities addressed the issues of women's economic function, political rights, marital role, sexuality, and reproduction. Yet no community was entirely successful in creating an equal place for its female members, and not all architects of utopian societies believed in expanding the rights of women. Both religious and secular communities were created in reaction to the upheaval caused by America's transformation from a rural society to an industrial and urban one.

In religious communities, new social arrangements promoted spiritual redemption. Such communities questioned sexuality, marriage, and reproduction. The Shakers, founded by Ann Lee, practiced celibacy and thus freed women from oppressive sexual and reproductive roles. There was equal participation in religious leadership for women in Shaker communities. Work in Shaker communities mirrored the gender divisions of the outside world. At the Oneida Community (1848–1881), a form of complex marriage and community-wide birth control was practiced. Although the men controlled contraception, some attention was paid to female sexual pleasure. However, women were considered spiritually inferior to men. Some women at Oneida had the opportunity to pursue nontraditional work. The Mormons reorganized the family by instituting polygamy. For some women, this meant sharing a husband and forming a household with other women and their children. Some Mormon women entered the professions or performed nontraditional jobs. Only men could become priests and religious leaders.

Architects of many secular communities were influenced by the Enlightenment and theories of natural rights.

At Robert Owen's New Harmony and subsequent communities, and Charles Fourier's "phalanxes"—economic units of people sharing a communal dwelling and dividing work according to their natural inclinations—intellectual equality and the economic and political roles of women were major gender issues. Owenite communities began by guaranteeing equal rights to female members, but in actual practice, women's rights were ambiguous. In the Fourierist phalanxes, women sometimes owned stock in the community on the same basis as men. In these communities, women worked for wages, because lack of economic independence was believed to be a cause of female oppression. But women were still responsible for unpaid domestic work and child care.

Known for its famous adherents, Brook Farm (1841–1847) was based on transcendental philosophy, emphasizing the innate worth of the individual, male or female. The community attracted Margaret Fuller, Nathaniel Hawthorne, and Ralph Waldo Emerson. While sexual and reproductive roles at Brook Farm remained similar to those outside, women participated equally in most aspects of the community. Brook Farm women such as Abby Diaz and Marianne Orvis reported they had expanded intellectual and creative opportunities in the community.

For women, utopian communities held promise of new roles, new responsibilities, and the chance to explore the meaning of gender in a new society. Frequently, however, that promise was not kept or disappeared under the guise of community expediency. (See also: Complex Marriage; Fuller, Margaret; Mormonism; Nashoba; New Harmony; Oneida Community; Shakers; Transcendentalism)

—Wendy E. Chmielewski
—Karen Loupe Gillenwaters

Further Reading

Chmielewski, Louis J. Kern, and Marlyn Klee-Hartzell, eds. Women in Spiritual and Communitarian Societies in the United States. Syracuse, NY: Syracuse University Press, 1993.

Foster, Lawrence. Women, Family and Utopia: Communal Experiments of the Shakers, the Oneida Community, and the Mormons. Syracuse, NY: Syracuse University Press, 1991.

Guarneri, Carl J. The Utopian Alternative: Fourierism in Nineteenth-Century America. Ithaca, NY: Cornell University Press, 1991.

Hayden, Dolores. Seven American Utopias: The Architecture of Communitarian Socialism, 1790–1975. Cambridge: MIT Press, 1976.

Kephart, William M. Extraordinary Groups: An Examination of Unconventional Life-Styles, 4th ed. New York: St. Martin's, 1991.

Kolmerten, Carol A. Women in Utopia: The Ideology of Gender in the American Owenite Communities. Bloomington: Indiana University Press, 1990.

Melville, Keith. Communes in the Counter Culture: Origins, Theories, Styles of Life. New York: Morrow, 1972.

Popenoe, Cris, and Oliver Popenoe. Seeds of Tomorrow: New Age Communities That Work. San Francisco: Harper, 1984.

Wagner, Jon, ed. Sex Roles in Contemporary American Communes. Bloomington: Indiana University Press, 1982.

Valesh, Eva McDonald (1866–1956)

Eva Valesh was born in Orono, Maine, attended high school, worked as a journalist, participated in labor politics, and later became active in the Farmers' Alliance and Populist Party in Minneapolis. As a fledgling journalist using the pen name Eva Gay, Valesh wrote a series of articles on working women in St. Paul/Minneapolis for the *St. Paul Globe* in 1888 and then began attending meetings of the Knights of Labor, where she met John P. McGaughey, master workman of the Minnesota Knights of Labor. McGaughey was so impressed with her talent and her concern for laboring women and men that he trained her in public speaking and introduced her to reform politics.

During the same year, Valesh ran for a seat on the Minneapolis school board. After losing the election, she returned to her job with the *Globe*, where she edited a labor news column, supporting the single-tax movement and the Greenback Labor Party, and continued lecturing at labor meetings. In 1890, she attended the state Farmers' Alliance convention, where she was elected as a state alliance lecturer. She soon became an assistant national lecturer and accepted the clerkship of the Minnesota House Appropriations Committee. As the representative of the Knights of Labor, Valesh attended a national alliance and labor convention in Cincinnati in 1891 where delegates founded the Populist Party. She returned from the convention, married the president of the Minnesota Federation of Labor, Frank Valesh, and began lecturing across the country for the new party. A difficult pregnancy kept her off the lecture circuit, but after the birth of her son, Frank Morgan Valesh, in 1892, she resumed lecturing in Minnesota for the Farmers' Alliance and Populist Party.

In 1896, Valesh divorced her husband, moved to New York with her son, and was hired by William Randolph Hearst as a reporter for the *New York Journal*. She later supported herself as a freelance journalist in Washington, D.C., worked for the Democratic National Committee, assisted Samuel Gompers in editing and publishing the *American Federationist*, and in 1910 returned to New York to work for the National Women's Trade Union League. In 1911, Valesh married Benjamin F. Cross, a wealthy New Yorker, and for seven years they published the *American Club Woman*. When that marriage ended, Valesh, who had suffered a heart attack, was no longer physically able to engage in publishing or labor organizing, and she supported herself for the remainder of her life as a proofreader for *Pictorial Review* and the *New York Times*. She retired from the *Times* in 1951 at the age of eighty-five and died in 1956. *(See also: Journalism; National Farmers' Alliance; Populist Party)*

—MaryJo Wagner

Further Reading

Faue, Elizabeth. "Women, Work, and Union: Eva McDonald Valesh and the Roots of Personal Ideology." Unpublished paper, University of Minnesota, 1982.

Gilman, Rhoda R. "Eva McDonald Valesh: Minnesota Populist." In *Women of Minnesota: Selected Biographical Essays,* edited by Barbara Stuhler and Gretchen Kreuter, 55-76. St. Paul: Minnesota Historical Society, 1977.

Valesh, Eva McDonald. "The Reminiscences of Eva McDonald Valesh." Oral History Transcript. Columbia University, New York, 1972.

Vanderlip, Narcissa Cox (1880–1966)

Categorized as a philanthropist by the Smithsonian's National Portrait Gallery after acceptance of her portrait in 1981, Narcissa Cox Vanderlip was freed by affluence from economic and household worries and directed her energies and skills toward philanthropic and reform activities. She was the wife of world-famed economist Frank Arthur Vanderlip and the mother of six children.

Born in Quincy, Illinois, she entered the University of Chicago in 1899, but after a whirlwind courtship, she left school for marriage in her senior year. In recognition of her many endeavors on behalf of society and the university, she was granted her degree in 1933.

The family resided at their seventy-two-acre estate in Scarborough, New York, where various national and international figures were entertained through the years. They also owned a sizable ranch in California that evolved into the planned community of Palos Verdes. Wayfarer's Chapel, California, designed by Frank Lloyd Wright and dedicated in 1951, was built on land she donated.

In 1916, Vanderlip became an active supporter of woman suffrage. In 1917, she also engaged in war support efforts, including serving as an official of the national War Savings Stamps Committee and speaking across the country in support of war savings certificates. From 1919 to 1923, she served as first president of the League of Women Voters of New York State. Her advocacy activities in this role, as in other later responsibilities, were frequently reported in the *New York Times.*

She visited Japan in 1920 with her husband and a distinguished party invited by Japanese business leaders. Following the Tokyo earthquake in 1923, she raised thousands of dollars to rebuild Tsuda College for women. She also served as a trustee of, and fund-raiser for, Constantinople Women's College in Turkey. She was elected president of the board of trustees of New York Infirmary for Women and Children in 1929 and laid the cornerstone of a new infirmary building in 1953. She received the Peter Stuyvesant Award for outstanding charitable work in greater New York in 1949. Her testimony before Congress in 1954 was influential in allowing women doctors in the armed services. She was awarded a Doctor of Humane Letters degree by the Women's Medical College of Pennsylvania in 1956.

Listed in *Who's Who in America* for several years, she regularly commuted to New York to administer the affairs of the infirmary until shortly before her death at the age of eighty-six. *(See also: League of Women Voters; Suffrage)*

—Hilda R. Watrous

Further Reading

Frank A. Vanderlip Collection. Narcissa Cox Vanderlip Papers. Butler Library. Columbia University, New York.

League of Women Voters of New York State Collection. Butler Library. Columbia University, New York.

New York (City and State) Woman Suffrage Papers. Butler Library. Columbia University, New York.

New York Times, scattered articles, 1917–1966.

Vanderlip Family Papers. Frank A. Vanderlip, Jr. New York.

✍ Vapors

Vapors was the term used by Victorians to describe a form of hysteria. A woman suffering from "the vapors" was incapacitated, unable to function as those around her might expect. A fainting spell followed by bed rest was generally accepted as a recognizable illness, and the patient was excused from the rigors of daily life.

Hysteria, meaning "uterus," had been defined by Hippocrates in ancient Greece to describe a variety of symptoms in women, all caused by the supposed wanderings of the uterus. This notion was refined by Galen, a second-century Greek physician who developed the humoral theory of medicine to refer to the vaporous emissions produced by the "wandering" uterus. As modern medicine revealed precise anatomical and physiological information about the location and functions of internal organs, these ancient theories were gradually discredited.

Discoveries about the nervous system led to new theories of women's behavior, such as mesmerism, which used trances and hypnosis to control the transmission of magnetism in the body. Ironically, neurologists' obsession with what they saw as deviant behavior and their failure to find a physiological cause promoted other theories, both psychological and cultural. Freud's analysis of hysterical women formed the basis of his psychological theories.

All of these theories about hysterical women were gender specific: They were created for women. They proliferated during the Victorian era when middle-class women's behavior was strictly governed by codes of etiquette and social expectations. When women experienced an attack of the vapors, they both conformed to prevailing stereotypes of women as fragile, excitable creatures and escaped, however temporarily, from oppressive social situations. The vapors disappeared as women's roles changed and medical science developed in the twentieth century, but the cultural role played by the malady remains; the vapors were replaced by contemporary syndromes, such as neurosis, depression, and anorexia, that are cultural as well as physiological in origin. *(See also: Eating Disorders; Freudianism; Hysteria; Mesmerism)*

—Jane Crisler

Further Reading

Drinka, George Frederick, M.D. *Myth, Malady and the Victorians.* New York: Simon & Schuster, 1984.

Rousseau, G. S. " 'A Strange Pathology': Hysteria in the Early Modern World, 1500–1800." In *Hysteria beyond Freud,* edited by Sander Gilman et al., 91-221. Berkeley: University of California Press, 1993.

Smith-Rosenberg, Carroll. *Disorderly Conduct: Visions of Gender in Victorian America.* New York: Knopf, 1985.

Veith, Ilsa. *Hysteria: The History of a Disease.* Chicago: University of Chicago Press, 1965.

✍ Vassar College

Vassar College was founded in 1861 with an initial gift of $400,000 by English-born brewer and businessman Matthew Vassar, who, persuaded by Baptist preacher Milo Jewett, used his fortune to build an impressive college for women in Poughkeepsie, New York. The college opened in 1865 with thirty-five students, dedicated to its founder's wish that it not be merely a female "seminary," as women's schools were then called but, rather, a full college competing with the best men's colleges. Initially, however, it had to establish a preparatory department to raise its students to college-level work; eventually, as admissions standards increased, the preparatory school was abolished. Vassar had the largest enrollment of the early women's colleges.

Although early faculty and presidents were men, Vassar included among its faculty astronomer Maria Mitchell, the first woman to be elected to the American Academy of Arts and Science, and Dr. Alida Avery, who also served as the college's physician. In 1898, Vassar established the first chapter of Phi Beta Kappa at a women's college. Sarah Josepha Hale used her *Godey's Lady's Book* to persuade Vassar of the propriety of having female instructors at a women's college.

Figure 63. Vassar College Students
Founded in 1861, this college in Poughkeepsie, New York, is regarded as one of the most important women's institutions of learning. Pictured above are students in 1920; by 1969, the school was coeduational. Used by permission of Corbis-Bettmann.

Hannah Lyman, who as first "lady principal" was second in importance only to the president, imposed a strict regimen on students, stressing etiquette, study, and religious practices, but Vassar, unlike Mount Holyoke, did not require domestic work.

Under president James Monroe Taylor, a leading Baptist educator, Vassar grew in size and quality, the former through the largess of fellow Baptist donors, especially Charles M. Pratt of Standard Oil, and the latter through the introduction of the elective system and through faculty such as Herbert Mills and Lucy Maynard Salmon. Mills introduced a course on the family in 1916, the first such course taught at a women's college; Salmon adopted the German seminar model in the 1880s, using primary sources as the basis for her history courses. In particular, Vassar gained a reputation in astronomy and physics and, later, in chemistry and psychology.

Although its founders vigorously defended Vassar's right to provide an education comparable to men's, they did not question the doctrine of separate spheres for the sexes.

Women then, as later in the 1920s when specific courses were designed to educate women to their "societally defined duties," were expected to uphold moral virtue in the family and attend to the domestic side of life, especially bearing and raising children. The freshman curriculum included physiology and hygiene, courses designed to ensure that education did not impair women's presumed delicate health. The early curriculum also emphasized science, especially the biological sciences. Although the sciences and the classics dominated the curriculum, the advent of the elective system brought a shift toward the social sciences and arts. In 1969, Vassar admitted its first male students.

Although never a bastion of feminism, Vassar numbers among its alumnae many distinguished graduates, among them poet Edna St. Vincent Millay, novelist Mary McCarthy, anthropologist Ruth Benedict, publisher Katharine Graham, actress Meryl Streep, and artist Nancy Graves. *(See also: Hale, Sarah Josepha; Higher Education; Mitchell, Maria; Science; "Seven Sisters")*

—**Nicholas C. Burckel**

Further Reading

Gordon, Lynn D. *Gender and Higher Education in the Progressive Era*. New Haven, CT: Yale University Press, 1990.

Herman, Debra. "College and After: The Vassar Experiment in Women's Education, 1861–1924." Ph.D. diss., Stanford University, 1979.

Horowitz, Helen Lefkowitz. *Alma Mater: Design and Experience in the Women's Colleges from Their Nineteenth-Century Beginning to the 1930's*. New York: Knopf, 1984.

Newcomer, Mabel. *A Century of Higher Education for American Women*. New York: Harper, 1959.

⬧ Venereal Disease/Sexually Transmitted Diseases

Venereal disease, also called sexually transmitted diseases (STDs), comprises several different diseases almost always transmitted through intimate sexual contact. The principal exceptions are infants and young children, who may acquire the disease from contaminated hands of adults, and newborn infants, who may be infected while passing through the birth canal of an infected mother. In recent years the newly discovered STD acquired immune deficiency syndrome (AIDS) has also been spread through contaminated blood given by infected donors and through contaminated needles used by intravenous drug addicts.

Although STDs are the most common communicable diseases, the true causes of venereal infections were not completely understood until the twentieth century. Although venereal diseases (VDs) are caused by bacteria, spirochetes, or viruses, VD has often been used to denote a person or society epitomized by a corrupt sexuality.

One common bacterial-caused venereal disease is gonorrhea. Although complications of gonorrhea can cause sterility in both men and women, gonorrhea can be cured successfully with early detection and treatment. The response to late detection and medication is less successful. Females infected with gonorrhea may experience no symptoms since they apparently build up antibodies in the genital tract.

The most common bacterial STD in America, however, is chlamydia. Most infected women have no symptoms at all. Like gonorrhea, chlamydia can be treated if caught early. If untreated, chlamydia can cause infertility; it can also be passed to babies during birth.

Syphilis is caused by a spirochete, a spiral microorganism similar to bacteria. Like gonorrhea, syphilis can be successfully treated if detected in its earliest stages. Syphilis, known as "the great mimic," can be mistaken on a superficial examination for other diseases such as measles and various skin disorders. Some patients do not develop any of the symptoms during the early stage of the disease. During the late stages of syphilis, however, virtually every organ or body system may be attacked; indications of the disease include heart problems, blindness, and brain damage. Prior to the era of antibiotics, mercury was used to treat syphilis. Its side effects often made the treatment worse than the disease.

Viral STDs are difficult to treat and, as yet, impossible to cure. Human papillomavirus (HPV), herpes simplex virus 2 (HSV 2), and AIDS are caused by viruses. HPV, or genital warts, is thought to be the most common STD in America today. Although most strains of HPV simply cause warts or lesions in the genital area, some are associated with a greater risk of cervical cancer.

Herpes resembles a cold sore or fever blister located in the genital area. It is highly contagious and virtually incurable. Studies indicate that about one of every five Americans has herpes; most are unaware of their infection. AIDS, caused by the human immunodeficiency virus (HIV), attacks the body's natural defense system. Although transmitted sexually, the virus must enter the bloodstream to do its damage. To date, there is no cure for AIDS, and as devastating as the earlier venereal diseases have been, AIDS has proved fatal in all cases.

The arrival of herpes and AIDS ended the social silence that historically followed STDs. Various methods have been employed to heighten awareness of STDs. Historically, STDs have been a matter of both medical and social concern for many: gays, lesbians, feminists, the social hygiene and social purity movements, those seeking to reform prostitution, and the New Right, to name a few. *(See also: AIDS; Prostitution)*

—**Robynne Rogers Healey**
—**David C. Wolf**

Further Reading

Brandt, Allan M. *No Magic Bullet: A Social History of Venereal Disease in the United States since 1880*. New York: Oxford University Press, 1987.

Cartwright, Frederick. *Disease and History*. New York: Crowell, 1972.

Fee, Elizabeth. "Sin vs. Science: Venereal Disease in Baltimore in the Twentieth Century," *Journal of the History of Medicine* 43 (April 1988): 141-64.

Schofield, C. B. S. *Sexually Transmitted Diseases*. Edinburgh, Scotland: Churchill Livingstone, 1979.

Shilts, Randy. *And the Band Played On: Politics, People, and the AIDS Epidemic*. New York: St. Martin's, 1987.

⬧ Victor, Frances Auretta Fuller
(1826–1902)

Author and historian Frances Victor is best known for her collaboration with Hubert Howe Bancroft on his multi-volume series, *History of the Pacific States*. Victor wrote both volumes on Oregon and the volumes on Washington, Idaho, Montana, Nevada, Colorado, and Wyoming; she contributed to the volumes on California, the Northwest coast, and British Columbia. Her histories are notable for their blend of fact and romance. She interviewed many pioneers and also examined written documents.

Victor was born in Rome, New York, and in 1839 moved with her family to Ohio, where she attended a female "seminary," as women's schools were then known. With her younger sister Metta, Victor began to publish poems and tales locally, and in 1848, her first book, *Anizetta, the Guajira: or the Creole of Cuba,* appeared. Her literary career was postponed by her first marriage, which ended in divorce in 1862. Her second marriage, to Henry Clay Victor, whose brother edited Beadle's "dime novels," renewed her interest in writing, and she wrote several books about Nebraska farm life for that series.

In 1863, her husband's job as a Navy engineer took the Victors to California, and the following year they moved to Oregon. Because her husband's work often took him away to sea, Victor turned to history, folklore, and writing. In 1870, she published *The River of the West,* an account of mountain man and Oregon pioneer Joe Meek. This work, along with subsequent publications that included a travel book, a temperance tract, poems, and short stories, brought her to the attention of Bancroft. He offered her a position on his staff, and Victor, who was widowed in 1875, accepted the job and moved to San Francisco. She remained with Bancroft until 1890, when she returned to Portland. There she revised her earlier travel book, wrote *The Early Indian Wars of Oregon,* which was commissioned by the state legislature, and published a final book of poems. Victor died in 1902, leaving a sizable body of work about the American West as her legacy to future historians. *(See also: Women Writers)*

—Sherry L. Smith

Further Reading

Kern, Donna Casella. "Frances Fuller Victor." In *American Women Writers.* Vol. 4, edited by Lina Muiniero, 299-301. Vol. 4. New York: Ungar, 1982

Mills, Hazel E. "Travels of a Lady Correspondent," *Pacific Northwest Quarterly* 45 (October 1954): 105-15.

Victor, Frances Fuller. *All over Oregon and Washington.* San Francisco: J. H. Carmany, 1872.

———. *Atlantis Arisen; or, Talks of a Tourist about Oregon and Washington.* Philadelphia: J. B. Lippincott, 1891.

———. *The Early Indian Wars of Oregon.* Salem, OR: F. C. Baker, 1894.

———. *East and West: or, The Beauty of Willard's Mill.* San Francisco: J. H. Carmony, 1862.

———. *The River of the West: The Adventures of Joe Meek.* Hartford, CT: R. W. Bliss, 1870.

Victor, Frances Fuller, with Hubert Howe Bancroft. *History of Nevada, Colorado and Wyoming, 1540–1888.* San Francisco: History Co., 1890.

———. *History of the Pacific States of North America.* San Francisco: A. L. Bancroft, 1884–1890.

~ Vietnam War (1957–1975)

The Vietnam War demonstrated an increasing role for women in the American military. About 261,000 women served in the U.S. armed forces during the Vietnam era, and over 7,500 women actually participated in Vietnam. Those included 5,000 women in the Army, 2,000 in the Air Force,

500 in the Navy, and 27 in the Marines Corps. Although still denied combat roles, the majority of women in Vietnam served in nurse corps and other medical capacities. One Army nurse, Sharon Lanz, was killed in a rocket attack in 1969. Other women served in administrative positions; some served as advisers to the South Vietnamese Women's Army Corps; and others helped with military intelligence, often serving as photo interpreters.

Women were also serving in Vietnam as part of the staff of the U.S. embassy and the civilian workforce supporting the U.S. military, including foreign service officers, administrative personnel, librarians, and Red Cross and USO volunteers. Among the last U.S. deaths in the war were thirty-seven women civilian employees, killed in the crash of an Air Force evacuation transport on April 4, 1975.

American women were also active in the movement to stop the Vietnam War. Singer Joan Baez, actress Jane Fonda, civil rights activist Coretta Scott King, and many other women actively protested the war. Women were active in all the major groups trying to halt the war, including Mothers for Peace, Students for a Democratic Society, Vietnam Moratorium Committee, New Mobilization Committee to End the War in Vietnam, Vietnam Veterans Against the War, the War Resisters League, and other groups. The war protesters organized mass demonstrations such as the Moratorium Day demonstrations of October 15, 1969, organized by Marge Sklencar among others. They also attempted boycotts, sit-ins, letter-writing campaigns, theatrical and artistic displays, and traditional political lobbying and support for antiwar candidates. Their efforts were successful in shortening the war and achieving the withdrawal of American troops. Rosalynn Carter, wife of former President Jimmy Carter, served on the National Sponsoring Committee for the Vietnam War Memorial. Maya Lin, a Yale architectural student, won the national competition and designed the emotionally moving Vietnam Memorial in Washington, D.C. A Vietnam Women's Memorial was erected in 1992, also in the nation's capital. *(See also: Baez, Joan C.; Fonda, Jane; King, Coretta Scott; McCarthy, Mary; Military Service)*

—Jonathan W. Zophy

Further Reading

Beattie, Keith. *The Scar That Binds: American Culture and the Vietnam War.* New York: New York University Press, 1998.

Burns, Richard Dean, and Milton Leitenberg. *The War in Vietnam, Cambodia, and Laos, 1945–1982: A Bibliographical Guide.* Santa Barbara, CA: ABC-Clio, 1984.

Holm, Jeanne. *Women in the Military: An Unfinished Revolution.* Novato, CA: Presidio, 1992.

Olson, James. *Dictionary of the Vietnam War.* Westport, CT: Greenwood, 1988.

Willenz, June. *Women Veterans: America's Forgotten Heroines.* New York: Continuum, 1983.

Zaroulis, Nancy, and Gerald Sullivan. *Who Spoke Up? America's Protest against the War in Vietnam, 1963–1975.* New York: Doubleday, 1984.

～ Visiting Nurses

For more than a century, visiting nurses have been caring for the sick at home. Hired by an amazing assortment of church groups, charity organizations, and women's clubs, their mission has been to bring health care, social order, and hygiene to the homes of the sick poor.

Most early visiting nurse organizations were located in northeastern cities. In general, they were small undertakings in which a few wealthy women hired one or two nurses who visited eight to twelve patients each day. They provided, among other things, baths, dressing changes, and treatments, and they taught family members how to give care in their absence. The problems encountered by these nurses were usually acute, often infectious, and almost always complicated by family circumstances.

Support for the work of visiting nurses grew rapidly. By 1909, approximately 565 organizations across the country employed a total of 1,416 visiting nurses. Lillian Wald, founder of the Henry Street Settlement in New York City, had even convinced the Metropolitan Life Insurance Company to provide the services of trained nurses as an additional benefit to its industrial policyholders. The mutual advantages of this arrangement were apparent. "Mother Met," as the company was affectionately called, quickly extended its nursing services across the company. Where possible, Metropolitan Life arranged for existing visiting nurse associations to provide care; where that was not possible, the company hired its own nurses. Three years after the service was initiated, Metropolitan was paying for 1 million nursing visits annually at a cost of roughly $500,000 per year. The result was the establishment of the first national system of insurance coverage for home-based care.

By 1910, the work of the visiting nurse had expanded to include numerous preventive programs. While most such programs originated with voluntary organizations, such as visiting nurse societies, activities directed toward prevention were eventually assumed by boards of health and education. Although nursing leaders had campaigned for the creation of an institutional framework that would allow visiting nurses to care for the healthy and the sick, this "division of labor" meant, ultimately, that sick nursing became the domain of voluntary organizations and preventive care became the responsibility of public agencies. The legacy of this dilemma still haunts contemporary visiting nurses. *(See also: Nursing; Wald, Lillian)*

—**Karen Buhler-Wilkerson**

Further Reading

Brainard, Annie. *The Evolution of Public Health*. Philadelphia: W. B. Saunders, 1922.

Buhler-Wilkerson, Karen. "Bringing Care to the People: Lillian Wald's Legacy to Public Health Nursing," *American Journal of Public Health* 83 (December 1993): 1778-86.

———. *False Dawn: The Rise and Decline of Public Health Nursing, 1900–1930*. New York: Garland, 1990.

———. "Public Health Nursing: In Sickness or in Health?" *American Journal of Public Health* 75 (October 1985): 1155-61.

Fitzpatrick, Louise. *The National Organization for Public Health Nursing, 1912–1952: Development of a Practice Field*. New York: National League for Nursing, 1975.

Gardner, Mary Sewall. *Public Health Nursing*. New York: Macmillan, 1916.

Waters, Yassabella. *Visiting Nursing in the United States*. New York: Charities, 1909.

～ Voice of Industry

Voice of Industry, published as a weekly newspaper, was the official organ of the New England Workingman's Association. Sarah Bagley, early feminist labor leader in the Lowell, Massachusetts, textile mills and president of the Lowell Female Labor Reform Association (LFLRA), was associated with *Voice of Industry* in 1845 and 1846. She was one of a three-member publishing committee and for a brief period was its chief editor. *Voice of Industry* became an important tool of the LFLRA with the latter's establishment of a Female Department in *Voice* and the employment of editors who traveled to other mill towns.

At a time when woman's sphere was relegated to home and hearth and it was considered a faux pas for women to speak in public or have their names in print, Bagley's ringing speeches published in *Voice of Industry* brought attention to the plight of women, helped spearhead the ten-hour-workday movement, and paved the way for its success in 1874. *(See also: Bagley, Sarah G.; Lowell Mill Girls)*

—**Virginia Beattie Mattes**

Further Reading

Cantor, Milton, ed. *American Workingclass Culture: Explorations in American Labor and Social History*. Westport, CT: Greenwood, 1979.

Early, Frances H. "A Reappraisal of the New England Labour-Reform Movement of the 1840's: The Lowell Female Labor Reform Association and the New England Workingmen's Association," *Histoire Socials* (Canada) 13 (1980): 25.

～ Voluntarism

The primary vehicle for women's social and political activism throughout American history has been the voluntary association. Inspired by westward expansion, urban growth, moral decay, industrial exploitation, racial inequities, and religious faith, women of the eighteenth and nineteenth centuries donated their labor in local and national societies to promote missionary and charitable efforts, social and political reform, and personal development and transformation. By the turn of the twentieth century, the battle for the ballot engaged much of women's voluntary labor, but the attainment of suffrage in 1920 expanded rather than diminished the extent of female voluntarism.

The most well-known and widely studied voluntary labors have been those performed by middle- and upper-class white women within national societies such as the General Federation of Women's Clubs, the Woman's Christian Temperance Union, the Young Women's Christian Association, the National American Woman Suffrage Association, and, more recently, the National Organization for Women. Yet the success of these societies has always rested on the labors of thousands of women in local communities. Within local communities, moreover, the true diversity and complexity of female voluntarism appeared, as black, ethnic, working-class, and/or working women established their own associations and as sibling rivalry emerged alongside sisterhood in the public domain. Less affluent or minority women were more likely to labor in associations dominated by or including men or to undertake voluntary activities, in the forms of boycotts or strikes, that did not involve permanent organization. Still, these women also established single-sex, permanent associations, such as the National Association of Colored Women.

Characterized by ideological as well as racial, ethnic, and economic diversity, female voluntarists have employed a wide range of techniques to achieve a multiplicity of goals. Petitioning, lobbying, fund-raising, demonstrating, boycotting, striking, and voting have been some of the most often used strategies for voicing and visualizing women's views. Voluntarists have also attacked problems directly—for example, through the collection and distribution of clothing, bedding, and medicine and the provision of child care, health care, and cash. Finally, through the establishment of self-help associations and public institutions such as clinics, shelters, and schools, women have voluntarily constructed much of the infrastructure of social welfare systems. Whether as an extension of women's privatized and unpaid domestic work or as a distinct form of unwaged social labor, female voluntarists placed themselves squarely in the public domain prior to obtaining the vote and expanded their efforts thereafter. *(See also: Benevolence; General Federation of Women's Clubs; National Association of Colored Women; National American Woman Suffrage Association; National Organization for Women; Social Housekeeping; Woman's Christian Temperance Union; Young Women's Christian Association)*

—**Nancy A. Hewitt**

Further Reading

Baker, Paula. "The Domestication of Politics: Women and American Political Society, 1780–1920," *American Historical Review* 89 (June 1984): 620-47.

Blair, Karen J. *A History of American Women's Voluntary Organizations, 1810–1960: A Guide to Sources.* Boston: G. K. Hall, 1989.

Hewitt, Nancy A., and Suzanne Lebsock, eds. *Visible Women: New Essays on American Activism.* Urbana: University of Illinois Press, 1993.

Neverdon-Morton, Cynthia. *Afro-American Women of the South and the Advancement of the Race, 1895–1925.* Knoxville: University of Tennessee Press, 1989.

Scott, Anne Firor. *Natural Allies: Women's Associations in American History.* Urbana: University of Illinois Press, 1991.

❧ "Voluntary Motherhood"

"Voluntary Motherhood" was a slogan used by feminist supporters of reproduction control and women's sexual self-determination in the last third of the nineteenth century. Women's rights advocates at that time did not favor contraception, although traditional contraceptive methods (such as douches, pessaries, and coitus interruptus) were probably still in use. Nor did these feminists publicly approve of abortion, although it was widely practiced and many people, including some feminists, quietly accepted its necessity if women were to have any control over their reproduction. Instead, the means that voluntary-motherhood advocates proposed was abstinence. They recommended two forms of abstinence: a rhythm method (which was not likely to have been very reliable, since at this time women's ovulation cycle had not been accurately plotted), and long-term abstinence when no pregnancy was desired.

The feminist revulsion against contraception was in part a reflection of their dislike for sexual permissiveness and the exploitation of women, which they believed would result from separating sex and reproduction. Most important, however, their insistence on abstinence was their way of asserting women's right to sexual self-determination, even in marriage. The traditional view of marriage required women's sexual submission to their husbands on demand. Even "free love" feminists, who took a more positive view of heterosexual activity than conservative "social purity" feminists, agreed that women could not begin to define their own sexual needs until they had acquired the right to reject men's sexual sovereignty over them.

After about 1910, most feminists began to endorse contraception as a means of birth control. Participants in a "sexual revolution" that praised frequent heterosexual activity as conducive to health and female fulfillment, they derided as prudish the nineteenth-century feminist view that frequent intercourse was a male "need" that had been imposed on women. Thus, until the new women's history of the 1970s and 1980s, the voluntary-motherhood proponents were not taken seriously as birth control advocates. *(See also: Birth Control; Free Love; Social Purity Movement)*

—**Linda Gordon**

Further Reading

Gordon, Linda. "Why Nineteenth-Century Feminists Didn't Support 'Birth Control' and Twentieth-Century Feminists Do: Feminism, Reproduction, and the Family." In *Rethinking the Family,* edited by Barrie Thorne. New York: Longman, 1981.

———. *Woman's Body, Woman's Right: A Social History of Birth Control in America.* New York: Viking/Penguin, 1976. Revised ed., 1990.

⮾ Voluntary Parenthood League (VPL)

The Voluntary Parenthood League (VPL) was a short-lived lobbying organization dedicated to removing contraception from the lists of material classified as obscene in the federal penal codes known as the Comstock laws (1873). The VPL was founded in 1918 after Mary Ware Dennett (1872–1947) resigned from the National Birth Control League (NBCL). In founding the VPL, Dennett effectively dismantled the NBCL, taking many members and officers with her. Dennett thought that once legal obstacles to discussion on birth control were lifted, moral, social, and medical objections would quickly fall away. She sought to distance her movement from that of Margaret Sanger by using the name "voluntary parenthood" rather than "birth control" because it was less objectionable to many legislators and conservatives.

Among its activities, the VPL published *The Birth Control Herald,* lobbied for federal legislation from 1919 to 1924, and amassed a National Council of prominent men and women in support of its legislative campaigns. Based on a free speech justification, the VPL's bills would have enabled any adult to receive and transmit contraceptive information. This broad access contrasted with the legislative repeals argued for by Sanger, who defined contraception as a medical issue and lobbied for legislation that limited transmission of contraceptive information to doctors. Sanger's proposed bill was more attractive to many in the medical profession, although both bills faced stiff opposition from a powerful Catholic lobby. In 1923, the VPL succeeded in having the Cummins-Vaile bill introduced, but it died in committee. Although she pursued them until the mid-1930s, Sanger's "doctors only" bills fared no better.

After the 1924 defeat, the VPL was unable to mount another successful lobbying campaign, and many of its supporters and officers defected in support of Sanger's "doctors only" bills as more likely to be passed. In 1925, Mary Ware Dennett resigned as director, and the VPL slowly faded out of existence, eclipsed by the more wide-ranging American Birth Control League. With the dissolution of the VPL, Sanger stood alone as leader of the American birth control movement. *(See also: American Birth Control League; Birth Control; Comstock Law; Dennett, Mary Coffin; National Birth Control League; Sanger, Margaret)*

—**Cathy Moran Hajo**

Further Reading

Gordon, Linda. *Woman's Body, Woman's Right: A Social History of Birth Control in America.* New York: Grossman, 1976.

Women's Studies Manuscript Collections from the Schlesinger Library, Radcliffe College, Series 3: The Papers of Mary Ware Dennett and the Voluntary Parenthood League. Microform. University Publications of America, Bethesda, 1993.

Voluntary Parenthood League. "The Laws Against Contraceptive Knowledge." New York: Voluntary Parenthood League, 1921.

Vreeland, Francis McClellan. "The Process of Reform with Especial Reference to Reform Groups in the Field of Population." Ph.D. diss., University of Michigan, 1929.

⮾ Voting Rights

Voting rights are an important measure of citizenship. The authors of the Constitution omitted many people from this citizen responsibility in part because they viewed the male-headed family as an economic unit and therefore male heads-of-household as the only political participants. Moreover, since the nation's "founding fathers" actually feared democracy as well as permanent political parties, they restricted political participation to landowning men. In other words, the authors of the Constitution assumed that only a landowning male head-of-household could resist pressure from an employer, a political party, or a representative of government to vote in any particular way, and that he and only he, therefore, could represent the interests of all family "members," including servants and slaves.

Historically, then, politicians have viewed voting rights for men as connected to economic activity. Gradually extending the right to vote to additional groups of men reflected acknowledgment of their need to participate in the polity in order to protect their economic rights and opportunities. The same logic did not apply to women, however, From the colonial era, all married women, and originally single and widowed adult women, were the property of some adult male, a status inherited from English common law. In practice in the North American colonies, free white women by necessity had greater opportunities to act as free citizens in economic arenas than common law implied, but only the adult male whose charge they were had legal status. The American Revolution unleashed ideas of liberty across many levels of society, and in that spirit, some women took quick advantage of the loose wording of the New Jersey state constitution of 1787 that enfranchised "all free inhabitants" who met property requirements. Twenty years later, the state legislature eliminated this oversight, arguing, against all evidence, that the single and widowed women as well as free blacks who had claimed the right to vote were too easily manipulated. The incident reinforced the idea that disenfranchisement for women and nonwhites bore no relationship to their economic autonomy, let alone to their economic contributions. Women, like children, continued to be regarded as dependent, attitudes justified by assumptions about the "nature" of women.

Disenfranchisement compromised women's ability to protect their economic interests and helps explain the early location of voting rights issues in the thinking of the first women's movement. The property restriction in the New Jersey constitution had disenfranchised married women because they could not own property in their own names. Since most women married in the nineteenth century, some early women's rights theorists recognized that full citizenship required breaking down the English common law position of "civil death" that ended a woman's legal existence on marriage. Early activists like Elizabeth Cady Stanton and Susan B. Anthony viewed the right to vote as one, but only one, logical element of women's legal emancipation.

They viewed the vote as necessary but insufficient to women's equality, legal and otherwise.

Married women's property laws, first enacted by New York in 1836 and followed by other state statutes, might seem to represent the breakdown of civil death by allowing married women to hold property in their own names. But these acts provided a means of protecting the property of married men from creditors, and that was the reason why men demanded their enactment. They did not spur male politicians to entertain enfranchising women, in part because they did not challenge either the legal tenet or the underlying assumptions of women's "natural" dependence. So extensively did women themselves believe that men should lead that the first women's rights convention, held in Seneca Falls, New York, in 1848, and called by women abolitionists who were angered by their inferior positions in that movement, was not only chaired by a man but very nearly failed to include the demand for the right to vote in its culminating document, the Declaration of Sentiments and Resolutions.

The argument that women should be dependent since they were already defined as such by common law continued, producing new justifications embedded in old assumptions throughout the nineteenth century. The notion that women were dependent and lacked intelligence by nature, often backed by religious or pseudoscientific arguments, required that women who demanded the vote first demonstrate their intellectual capacity and emotional stability. The women's rights movement at least until the late nineteenth century included the demand for equal access to education and the construction of all-female institutions of higher learning as well as the creation of women-only voluntary associations for self-improvement and civic activism, all of which went hand-in-hand with the demand for the right to vote. Work in voluntary associations radicalized thousands of women who came to understand their own status by working on behalf of others; at the same time it empowered women who found themselves doing what they had been told they could not.

The circular logic of arguments against women's autonomy, in which women's dependence in reality proved that women were dependent by nature, explains why women's increasingly organized struggle to gain the right to vote dragged on for so long. Some women activists, notably white and middle class, increasingly chose to circumvent altogether the broader issues raised by viewing women as property who suffered civil death after marriage, along with the underlying justifications for this status and the limited opportunities to avoid it. That decision resulted in an increasingly singular focus within a large segment of the women's rights movement on gaining the suffrage and contributing to splits on goals, gentility, and tactics that divided woman suffrage organizations twice in the long road to victory. As acrimonious as they were, these divisions actually aided the cause by multiplying the strategies, participants, and public awareness.

The American Woman Suffrage Association (AWSA) initially succeeded in gaining limited voting rights in some municipalities, particularly in school board elections, as well as enfranchisement through state constitutional amendments, most effective early on in the West. When the state-by-state strategy that emphasized behind-the-scenes lobbying ground to a halt, the AWSA joined the National Woman Suffrage Association (NWSA) that had sought a federal amendment with public demonstrations. The National American Woman Suffrage Association (NAWSA) sought a federal amendment. Marches for woman suffrage grew, enhanced by organized women of color and women trade unionists. Membership in the NAWSA grew and would have grown more had it allowed women of color to join. Viewing the NAWSA as too conservative, the National Woman's Party (NWP) soon broke off from it to pursue broader goals and to employ more confrontational tactics on suffrage that included blaming the party in power. When a number of NWP members chained themselves to the gates of the White House, President Woodrow Wilson ordered them arrested. They initiated a hunger strike that jail officials countered with forced-feeding, and media attention to the suffering of NWP prisoners increased public sympathy for woman suffrage.

Women of color and unionized women tended to view voting rights as critical to their lives and largely supported a national amendment as necessary but not sufficient. Their views remained similar to early women's rightists like Cady Stanton, but since the civil death restrictions had little affected them even after slavery, their understanding of their needs focused critically around issues of poverty as intertwined with racism and sexism, as Sojourner Truth had argued. Abandoned by the suffrage organizations whose founders had been radicalized on women's issues through their work in abolitionist movements, women of color organized their own voluntary associations in which they worked for suffrage along with a range of other goals. Excluded from membership in national suffrage organizations, women of color seemed invisible in a movement that increasingly narrowed among white, middle-class women to the vote, but activist women of color along with early women's rightists and the later NWP produced some of the core ideas of contemporary feminism and connect the first wave of women's movement to the second. By studying these activist women, women's historians no longer argue that success, defined as gaining the right to vote, killed the first women's movement. Suffragists did finally prevail with the passage and ratification of the Nineteenth Amendment to the Constitution in 1920.

As basic as it was, the right to vote did not prove to be the panacea that some suffragists believed it would be. Voting rights did not eliminate the concept of women as the property of men; that persistent reality is visible in the many objectifying images of women in popular culture that render women the property, no longer of one man, but presumably of any man who covets them. Suffrage did not destroy the concept of civil death, either; its persistence remains the most evident in the problem of domestic violence. Nor did the Nineteenth Amendment enfranchise all adult women, as states, especially in the South, continued to defy the Fifteenth Amendment intended to enfranchise African Americans, and the woman suffrage organizations that had excluded women of color continued to deny that issues of race were women's issues.

Women needed the additional legislation permitted by both the Nineteenth and the Fifteenth Amendments to enforce their voting rights. During the civil rights movement, women like Rosa Parks, Septima Clark, Fannie Lou Hamer, and Ella Baker, among thousands of others, organized voter registration drives and made other public claims on their right to act as political beings. The Twenty-Fourth Amendment (1964) prohibited poll taxes, under whatever name, from disenfranchising voters in primary elections, a strategy that had been useful in hindering African American voting in the one-party South by defining a political party as a private club and a poll tax as members' dues. The Voting Rights Acts of 1965, 1970, 1975, and 1986 prohibited literacy and other kinds of tests as voter registration requirements, allowed federally authorized registrars to register voters in areas where discrimination seemed evident, established thirty days as a maximum national residency requirement, and standardized absentee procedures for presidential elections. The 1992 Language Assistance Act provided for bilingual ballots. The most recent extension of the right to vote came in the Twenty-Sixth Amendment (1972) that rendered permanent a 1970 act of Congress that had lowered the voting age from twenty-one to eighteen, prompted by anti-Vietnam War protests in which women played crucial roles and that radicalized a significant portion of a new generation of feminists.

Despite all these acts, disenfranchisement remained a reality for some women. By the late 1980s, with the exception of female prisoners disenfranchised for murdering a male abuser, even some feminists believed that women were disenfranchised because of their poverty, their race or ethnicity, or because they were handicapped, rather than because they were female. The interrelatedness of racism, classism, and sexism, however, suggests that these problems of disenfranchisement connect to gender; disenfranchisement remains a feminist issue. Federal court cases since the 1960s endeavored to settle the question of voting outcomes (equity) for racial minorities unable to elect candidates of color despite concentrated voting strength. To counter this unintended result of residential segregation, officials gerrymandered the shape of voting districts in ways that undermined that power. By 1992, court-ordered redrawn voting districts, motor-voter registration laws, and more accessible polling places resulted in the highest proportion of nonwhite elected officials since Reconstruction. Some of these remedies to racism increased the proportion of women in elective offices as well, although that was not the intended outcome. Still, by 1995 the proportion of women in elective office re-

mained well below their proportion in the population, and more women achieved both elective and appointed positions at lower levels of government than at higher ones. In the final argument about how much change in women's status women's right to vote has produced, women remain dependent on men in government because they are still overwhelmingly represented by men. *(See also: American Woman Suffrage Association; Anthony, Susan B.; Catt, Carrie Chapman; Civil Rights; Fourteenth Amendment to the U.S. Constitution; Hamer, Fannie Lou; League of Women Voters; National Association for the Advancement of Colored People; National Woman Suffrage Association; National American Woman Suffrage Association; National Woman's Party; Nineteenth Amendment to the U.S. Constitution; Parks, Rosa; Paul, Alice; Politics; Seneca Falls Convention; Sex Discrimination; Stanton, Elizabeth Cady; Suffrage; United States Supreme Court)*

—Deb Hoskins

Further Reading

Arrington, Karen McGill, and William L. Taylor, eds. *Voting Rights in America: Continuing the Quest for Full Participation.* Washington, DC: Leadership Conference Education Fund, Joint Center for Political and Economic Studies, 1992.

Rogers, Donald W., ed. *Voting and the Spirit of Democracy.* Urbana: University of Illinois Press, 1992.

Rule, Wilma, and Joseph F. Zimmerman, eds. *United States Electoral Systems: Their Impact on Women and Minorities.* Westport, CT: Praeger, 1992.

Thernstrom, Abigail M. *Whose Votes Count? Affirmative Action and Minority Voting Rights.* Cambridge, MA: Harvard University Press, 1987.

Vroman, Mary Elizabeth
(c. 1924/29–1967)

Mary Elizabeth Vroman was a short-fiction writer, novelist, movie script writer, and the first African American woman member of the Screen Writers Guild. Born in Buffalo, New York, Vroman grew up in the West Indies and graduated from Alabama State Teachers College determined to make a difference in her students' lives. She taught for twenty years in Alabama, Chicago, and New York.

In 1951, the editors of *Ladies' Home Journal* found a letter written by a twenty-six-year-old Alabama schoolteacher included with a short story submission, "See How They Run," explaining why she wrote the tale.

> Segregation in the South poses many unique problems in the Negro schools. The Negro teacher bears a responsibility to her students unparalleled by that of any other, for though Negro children are typical of children elsewhere, they develop under greater handicaps and with less outer aid. It is with these problems that the story I am submitting for publication deals. "See How They Run" does not seek to solve these

problems, merely paint an honest picture of possible solutions.

When "See How They Run" appeared in the June 1951 issue of *Ladies' Home Journal*, Vroman was able to share her rural teaching experiences with sympathetic readers.

Vroman's first published tale, regarding experiences by an idealistic African American first-year teacher in a third-grade rural Alabama school, elicited 500 enthusiastic letters from readers. Praised as the "finest story to come out of the South since *Green Pastures*," "See How They Run" was chosen to win the Christopher Award for inspirational magazine writing because of its "humanitarian quality." The story also appeared in the July 1952 issue of *Ebony*.

The protagonist, Jane Richards, describes her interactions with children in a leaky-roofed school with a potbellied stove. Many youngsters come to class without breakfast and share tattered, outdated textbooks. They help their overworked, underpaid teacher haul water from a well down the road, not far from a foul-smelling outhouse. The story serves as an excellent primary source showing the difficulties of educating African American children in the segregated South where the young people walk two miles from home daily to attend school, many too impoverished to purchase a nutritious lunch.

Due to the success of "See How They Run," Vroman was asked, in 1953, to prepare a movie script of her story for a motion picture titled *Bright Road*, featuring Harry Belafonte and Dorothy Dandridge.

Vroman's first book-length story, *Esther* (1963), describes life in a small, rural southern town. It is about a dignified grandmother, Lydia Jones, who saves her money as a midwife to purchase some land and uses her savings to encourage her granddaughter, Esther Kennedy, to pursue a nursing career. For her second book, *Shaped to Its Purpose* (1965), Vroman researched the history of the first fifty years of Delta Sigma Theta, a sorority of 40,000 college-trained professional African American women, to which she belonged. In 1967, her third book, *Harlem Summer*, was published. Intended for young adult readers, it tells the story of John, sixteen, from Montgomery, Alabama, spending the summer living with relatives and working in Harlem.

Vroman honestly depicted African American lifestyles during the decades of the 1950s and 1960s without becoming cynical. In spite of adversities, her characters are proud and resilient. They retain their sense of humanity, finding joy in happy experiences with loving family members and understanding friends.

Married to Oliver M. Harper, a dentist, Vroman died at the age of forty-two in 1967 due to complications following surgery. *(See also: Black Women; Education; Magazines; Teaching; Women Writers)*

—**Edith Blicksilver**

Further Reading

Bachner, Saul. "Black Literature: The Junior Novel in the Classroom—*Harlem Summer*," *Negro American Literature Forum* 7 (Spring 1973): 26-27.

———. "Writing School Marm: Alabama Teacher Finds Literary Movie Success with First Short Story," *Ebony* (July 1952): 23-28.

Blicksilver, Edith. "See How They Run." In *The Ethnic American Woman: Problems, Protests, Lifestyle*, edited by Edith Blicksilver, 125-43. Dubuque, IA: Kendall/Hunt, 1978.

Wages

Pay for women workers in America has always been less than that of their male counterparts. Most sources assume that women were paid approximately one-third to one-half the wages of men doing the same or similar work in the late nineteenth and early twentieth centuries. Consequently, unskilled women workers did not even receive subsistence wages, making them the cheapest pool of American labor. Even in exact work, where women did work identical to that of men, women were paid less. Employers often insisted that this discrepancy was legitimate, based as it was on their assumption that women were merely working for extra income, not to support themselves or a family. But this was not the case in many instances, particularly with young, single women and immigrants whose families desperately needed their wages. Other employer justifications of the wage discrepancy included women's supposed higher absenteeism, shorter working careers with a high turnover rate, lower productivity due to less physical strength, and other similar sexist biases of little validity. The economic reality was simply that women were concentrated in a few key industries as unskilled laborers and were unable to bargain effectively to improve their lot, especially since they could be easily replaced.

Over 80 percent of the working women (c. 265,000), according to the 1860 census (the first to analyze women workers), were employed in the textile industry. By 1900, women constituted one-fifth (5 million) of the American labor force; by 1910, after heavy immigration, the percentage of women in the workforce rose to 25 percent, with all but 9 of the 369 industries listed in federal records employing women. Despite such figures, job categories and wages were still segregated by gender, and women remained the lower paid, largely unskilled pool of American labor. Women's wages rose slowly during the early 1980s but still lagged behind those of men in all job categories. In 1983, women's median earnings were 64 percent of men's, and in 1985 they were 65 percent. By 1997, they had risen to 74.1 percent ("About the National Committee on Pay Equity").

The solution of this wage problem—equal pay for men and women for equal work—was largely discredited because of the inherent assumption that women were less productive. Hence, with equal wages, employers would hire male workers, resulting in the higher unemployment of women and a worse economic situation for them than with unequal wage scales. *(See also: Equal Pay Act of 1963; Minimum Wage Laws; Sex Equity/Comparable Worth; Women's Work: Nineteenth Century)*

—Maureen Anna Harp

Further Reading

Abbott, Edith. *Women in Industry: A Study in American History.* New York: Appleton, 1919.

"About the National Committee on Pay Equity (NCPE)." Available at http://www.feminist.com/fairpay.htm

Hutchins, Grace. *Women Who Work.* New York: International, 1934.

Kessler-Harris, Alice. *Out to Work: A History of Wage-Earning Women in the United States.* New York: Oxford University Press, 1982.

Smuts, Robert W. *Women and Work in America.* New York: Columbia University Press, 1959, 1971.

Wald, Lillian (1867–1940)

Lillian Wald was a social activist of the Progressive and New Deal Eras. Trained as a nurse, Wald established the nation's first nonsectarian visiting nurse service in New York City in 1893. Her program to take health services to the homes of the poor anticipated by two years the antituberculosis programs instituted by the New York health commissioner Dr. Hermann Biggs. Wald based her service in the "Nurses Settlement," first housed on Jefferson Street and subsequently moved to larger quarters at its famous Henry Street address. The Henry Street Settlement was one of the best-known centers of the settlement house movement, which encouraged social reforms to benefit the urban poor.

Wald was a friend of Jane Addams and Alice Hamilton of the Hull House settlement in Chicago and was active in labor movements, especially those devoted to the protection of women and children. In keeping with these priorities, she was a pacifist during World War I and a supporter of woman suffrage. As she learned about social issues on a practical level at Henry Street, she lobbied for political change. Her first national cause was the federal Children's Bureau. She began promoting such an agency under President Theodore

Roosevelt in 1905 and saw its creation in 1912 by President William Howard Taft.

After World War I, Wald followed the same path as many other social activists who had been opposed to the war: She worked for international harmony and well-being within the framework of the Red Cross movement. In 1924, she traveled to Russia at the invitation of the government to advise the Soviets on the care of children who had been orphaned by the revolution. In the late 1920s, she undertook housing reform as a major social cause, one as important as her advocacy for child welfare. Her efforts were obstructed by business and political interest groups and effectively thwarted by the Crash of 1929 and Great Depression of the 1930s.

As the daughter of a wealthy family from Rochester, New York, Wald was a personal friend of Franklin and Eleanor Roosevelt. She shared many of her concerns about social conditions with the Roosevelts and, although physically unable to work in the Roosevelt administration, she communicated frequently with New Deal policymakers on specific issues. Her stories of life at the Nurses Settlement were collected in a book titled *Windows on Henry Street,* which became a classic text for social workers. *(See also: Henry Street Settlement; New Deal; Roosevelt, Eleanor; Social Work; United States Children's Bureau; Visiting Nurses)*

—**Jane Crisler**

Further Reading

Duffus, Robert Luther. *Lillian Wald: Neighbor and Crusader.* New York: Macmillan, 1938.
Wald, Lillian. *Windows on Henry Street.* New York: Holt, 1915. Reprint, Boston: Little, Brown, 1984.

☙ Walker, Alice (b. 1944)

Author of fiction, poetry, and essays, Alice Walker received the Pulitzer Prize in 1983 for *The Color Purple,* an epistolary novel centered on the plight of the black woman in the rural South. The themes of this important novel have concerned Walker throughout her writing career—the effects of racism on blacks and especially on the black woman, who is often a double victim: In addition to the white man's oppression, she must bear the brunt of the black man's desperate need for any sense of power and control. Thus, she suffers pain and violence at the hands of the black male, as well as the white. However, *The Color Purple* presents the possibility for the black woman to extricate herself from this physical and spiritual devastation, gaining independence and a sense of self through productive, self-supporting work.

Born in Eatonton, Georgia, the daughter of sharecroppers, Alice Walker was educated in segregated public schools. She attended Spelman College (1961–1963), where she became involved in the civil rights movement, and graduated from Sarah Lawrence (B.A., 1965). She was married for nine years (1967–1976) to Melvyn R. Leventhal, a civil

rights lawyer; their union produced one daughter, Rebecca Grant. Early in her career, Walker worked with voter registration in Georgia, the Head Start program in Mississippi, and the New York City welfare department, activities that signaled her continuing concern with social issues. She has lectured widely and has received numerous awards, including first prize in *The American Scholar* essay contest (1967), a Radcliffe Institute Fellowship (1971–1973), the Lillian Smith Award for *Revolutionary Petunias* (1973), the Rosenthal Foundation Award from the American Academy and Institute of Arts and Letters (1974), the Guggenheim Award (1977–1978), and the American Book Award (1983) for *The Color Purple,* as well as the Pulitzer Prize.

Because of the commercial and critical success of *The Color Purple,* which was translated into a controversial film by Steven Spielberg in 1985, Walker's earlier work has received increased attention. Most critics agree, however, that *The Color Purple* is a highly original synthesis of material found in earlier works such as *The Third Life of Grange Copeland* (1970), *In Love and Trouble: Stories of Black Women* (1973), and *Meridian* (1976), a novel about the civil rights movement. Most of Walker's fiction centers around black women, and for this she has been acclaimed by feminists such as Gloria Steinem, who asserts that Walker presents "the female experience more powerfully for being able to pursue it across boundaries of race and class." Walker was also a consulting editor of *Ms.* Magazine in the 1970s and has been a frequent contributor since then.

Walker's collection of essays, *In Search of Our Mothers' Gardens* (1983), is a compelling record of the diversity of her concerns and the strength of her passion, especially as she relates in very candid fashion her own experiences as a black woman. Courageous and controversial, Alice Walker continues to provoke all readers to reexamine their assumptions.

Walker has authored twenty-two books and has been labeled "one of the most censored writers in the U.S." Some recent topics of attention and activism for her include the Million Man March on Washington, Native American rights, the U.S. embargo against Cuba, and female genital mutilation.

In 1993, Walker and Pratibha Parmar coauthored the book *Warrior Marks,* an investigation into the practices of female genital mutilation and circumcision based on interviews with women of different cultures deeply involved in the subject matter. This groundbreaking work informed readers worldwide of the cultural traditions and rituals surrounding female genital mutilation. Walker also wrote a powerful novel, *Possessing the Secret of Joy,* about a woman's lifelong experience with female genital mutilation. In 1998, she published another novel, *By the Light of My Father's Smile,* an exploration of female sexuality, and, according to Walker, "a call to fathers to stand with their daughters and help protect them in a world where they are vulnerable" (White 48). Her literary career and her activism continue to inspire and transform women worldwide. *(See* also: *Black Women; Female Genital Mutilation; Ms. Magazine; Women Writers*)

—Sarah Gordon

—Lisa Sirmons Edwards

Further Reading

Davis, Thadious M. "Alice Walker's Celebration of Self in Southern Generations," *Southern Quarterly* 21 (Summer 1983): 39-53.

Tate, Claudia, ed. *Black Women Writers at Work*. New York: Continuum, 1983.

Walker, Alice. *By the Light of My Father's Smile*. New York: Harcourt Brace Jovanovich, 1998.

———. *The Color Purple*. New York: Harcourt Brace Jovanovich, 1982.

———. *Good Night, Willie Lee, I'll See You in the Morning*. New York: Dial, 1979.

———. *Horses Make a Landscape Look More Beautiful*. New York: Harcourt Brace Jovanovich, 1984.

———. *In Love and Trouble: Stories of Black Women*. New York: Harcourt Brace Jovanovich, 1973.

———. *In Search of Our Mothers' Gardens: A Collection of Womanist Prose*. New York: Harcourt Brace Jovanovich, 1983.

———. *Meridian*. New York: Harcourt Brace Jovanovich, 1976.

———. *Once*. New York: Harcourt Brace & World, 1968.

———. *Possessing the Secret of Joy*. New York: Harcourt Brace Jovanovich, 1992.

———. *Revolutionary Petunias and Other Poems*. New York: Harcourt Brace Jovanovich, 1973.

———. *Temple of My Familiar*. New York: Harcourt Brace Jovanovich, 1989.

———. *The Third Life of Grange Copeland*. New York: Harcourt Brace Jovanovich, 1970.

———. *Warrior Marks*. New York: Harcourt Brace Jovanovich, 1993.

———. *You Can't Keep a Good Woman Down*. New York: Harcourt Brace Jovanovich, 1981.

White, Evelyn C. "Alice Walker on Finding Your Bliss," *Ms.* 9 (Sept/Oct 1998): 44-50.

❧ Walker, Madame C. J. (Sarah Breedlove) (1867–1919)

Businesswoman and entrepreneur Madame C. J. Walker was born to black sharecropper parents in Delta, Louisiana, but became the richest self-made woman in America in the early twentieth century. Orphaned at six, married at fourteen, and widowed at twenty, Walker took her daughter, A'Lelia, and went north to seek her fortune. By 1905, she was traveling from St. Louis to Denver and from Pittsburgh to Indianapolis to set up markets for her product, a secret-formula hair straightener for African Americans. In 1910, she founded the Madame C. J. Walker laboratories to manufacture her products in Indianapolis. At the peak of her business, she had more than two thousand agents in the field selling her "Preparations," and the sale of Madame C. J. Walker's Hair Grower (a pomade) alone was bringing in more than $50,000 annually.

Walker moved to New York City in 1913, after her initial success. She built a Harlem town house and an adjacent school of beauty culture. In 1917, she built a $250,000 Italianate mansion designed by Vertner Tandy, a famed Harlem architect, at the exclusive Irving-on-the-Hudson. The estate became known as Villa Lewaro.

During her life, Walker gave generously to charities, and during World War I, she protested the War Department's segregation policy by leading a female delegation to see President Woodrow Wilson. When she died in 1919, she left sums of money to civil rights and missionary groups, as well as two-thirds of net corporate profits to charity. Her daughter, A'Lelia Walker Robinson, became famous for her flamboyant lifestyle, and after the death of her mother, Villa Lewaro became a gathering place for Harlem's intellectual and artistic elite. (*See also: Beauty Industry; Black Women; Business*)

—Rose Kolbasnik Callahan

Further Reading

Levering, David. *When Harlem Was in Vogue*. New York: Knopf, 1984.

Ottley, Roi, and William J. Weatherby, eds. *The Negro in New York: An Informal Social History, 1626–1940*. New York: Praeger, 1969.

❧ Walker, Maggie Lena Mitchell (c. 1867–1934)

Maggie Walker, the nation's first female bank president, club woman, business leader, and civic reformer, reflected the achievements of her generation. Born c. 1867 to former slave Elizabeth Draper and an Irish-born newspaperman who worked for the *New York Herald*, she received her last name in 1868 when her mother married William Mitchell, the butler to the Van Lew family, who served as spies for the Union Army, hid slaves for the Underground Railroad, and harbored Union soldiers during the Civil War.

After the war, the Mitchells moved to the city for more contact with the black community in Richmond's College Alley, which was close to William Mitchell's new job as head waiter at the St. Charles Hotel. In February 1876, a few years after her brother Johnnie was born, her stepfather's body was found in the James River, a victim of a robbery or a suicide. A laundry business supported the family after his death, and Walker helped on deliveries and as a babysitter for her brother.

Educated in the segregated public schools of Richmond, Walker started her business education as a teenager through Richmond's oldest and largest black church, Old First Baptist Church (First African Baptist Church), working with the insurance business connected with the fraternal organization the Independent Order of St. Luke (IOSL). In 1883, she finished at the head of her class at Armstrong Normal and High School after leading her senior class in a request to end Jim Crow segregation for the graduation ceremonies.

She was a teacher at the Lancaster School, while taking classes in accounting and business management to better serve the IOSL. Her marriage September 14, 1886, to Armstead Walker, a young contractor active in her church, ended her teaching career. They started their family in 1890, but she combined family life with her work for the IOSL. She quickly moved from executive secretary to grand secretary-treasurer, a position she held for thirty-five years. She found an organization in need of leadership with inadequate staff, no property, no reserve funds, and only 3,400 members, of whom only 1,080 were paying members. Her efforts to rebuild the organization led to her creation of a fraternal newspaper, the *Saint Luke Herald,* to establish communication, market the services, and heighten the race's awareness of lynching, politics in Haiti, racial discrimination, Jim Crow segregation, and subordination of black women. The newspaper stimulated the formation of a profitable printing business. In 1903, she organized a building project to erect a three-story brick hall, which was then rented to the Right Worthy Grand Council, the central organization of the IOSL. Under her twenty-five-year leadership, the IOSL's financial status improved, membership climbed, and organizational influence spread.

She shifted the organization's initial goals, to provide funeral/burial services and assistance for ill and aged, to savings and investments. Her innovations produced a penny savings bank in 1902, which became the St. Luke Bank and Trust Company in 1903, thereby making her the first female bank president in the United States. She also started the short-lived department store on Broad Street, the St. Luke Emporium, to provide substantial employment for black women.

Walker worked through women's organizations to improve the community. As a leader of the National Association of Colored Women (NACW), she founded the Richmond Council of Colored Women in 1912, which she mobilized for a fund-raising effort to buy land for a girls' reformatory, the Virginia School for Girls and the Virginia Manual Labor School in Hanover County. Her fund-raising also helped establish a tuberculosis sanitorium in Burkeville and both a community center and a nursing home in Richmond. Her financial expertise helped reclaim the Frederick Douglass Home.

Beyond the community, she helped racial advancement organizations. She helped organize the local NAACP in 1917, serving on the national board from 1923 until her death. She served on the Virginia Interracial Commission and became a founder of the International Council of Women of the Darker Races, a global network of women of color. She served as a trustee of the National Training School for Girls in Washington, D.C.; as a board member of the National Urban League; and as a trustee of Hartshorn College.

When her son Russell killed his father, thinking him a burglar, the scandal almost led to her removal from the IOSL post. She rebounded on the eve of the Great Depression when her bank absorbed other black banks, becoming the Consolidated Bank and Trust Company with her as chairman of the board. The 1930s found Walker confined to a wheelchair and dubbed the "Lame Lioness." She died on December 15, 1934, of diabetic gangrene and was buried in the family section of Evergreen Cemetery.

Her legacy continued. As one of the wealthiest African American women of her day, she contributed to the St. Luke Education Fund, which continued to fund black education. Her community center, an affiliate of the National Urban League, eventually became the city's first black library, and in 1991, the Black History Museum. Her bank continues to this time. The City of Richmond has recognized these contributions by naming a street, a high school, and a theater in her honor. Her home on Leigh Street is a national historic site serving as the repository of her papers, diaries, and photographs. *(See also: Black Women; Business; National Association for the Advancement of Colored People; National Association of Colored Women)*

—**Dorothy C. Salem**

Further Reading

Bird, Caroline. "The Innovators: Maggie Walker, Kate Gleason." In *Enterprising Women,* edited by Caroline Bird. 166-75. New York: Norton, 1976.

Branch, Muriel, and Dorothy Rice. *Miss Maggie: A Biography of Maggie Lena Walker.* Richmond: Marlough, 1984.

Brown, Elsa Barkley. "Maggie Lena Walker." In *Encyclopedia of Southern Culture,* edited by Charles Wilson and William Ferris, 1588-89. Chapel Hill: University of North Carolina Press, 1989.

Dabney, Wendell. *Maggie L. Walker and I.O. of St. Luke.* Cincinnati, OH: Dabney, 1927.

Daniel, Sadie. *Women Builders.* Washington, DC: Associated Publishers, 1931.

Davis, Elizabeth L. *Lifting as They Climb.* Washington, DC: National Association of Colored Women, 1933.

⌇ Walker, Mary Edwards (1832–1919)

Dress reformer, woman's rights advocate, suffragist, and Civil War physician, Mary Edwards Walker lectured and wrote on reform movements of the nineteenth century. Walker's life represented the currents of change women were creating and in which they were involved. She argued that no constitutional amendment was necessary to give women the right to vote because such right was implied in the Constitution already and all that was needed was a declaratory statement from Congress to that effect. She wrote of this belief in a tract: "Crowning Constitutional Argument." When the suffragists gave up this approach and began working instead for a constitutional amendment, Walker refused to join them and held fast to her theory.

Walker's commitment to dress reform manifested itself when she began wearing more comfortable, modified dress at the age of sixteen. She continued to experiment throughout her life with healthful dress and lectured extensively on that subject in London, Manchester, Glasgow, and Paris as well as throughout America. Her dress-reform garb, and theories on it, were less successful in America, however, and her income and popularity started to wane. To continue earning a living and expounding her beliefs, she began appearing with the circus as a sideshow attraction, lecturing on medicine and dress reform and ultimately wearing the so-called full male attire for which she is remembered.

Among the first of her sex to receive a medical degree, she graduated from Syracuse Medical College in 1855, after which she maintained a medical practice briefly with Albert Miller, whom she married in 1855. By 1860, she had given up her medical practice and her marriage, seeking a divorce in Iowa because New York State did not permit it. She moved to Washington, D.C., establishing a refuge for women who came to the city destitute. By 1864, she had joined the Union Army as assistant surgeon, the first woman to be so commissioned in the American armed services. Walker was rewarded for her service with the Congressional Medal of Honor, the only woman in the history of the United States to receive that award.

In the fabric of Walker's life can be found the threads that also delineated the woman movement of the nineteenth century: dress reform, equal educational opportunities, women's rights, votes for women, and health and hygiene concerns. Mary Edwards Walker, while appreciated by her closest friends and patients, was increasingly ridiculed and finally discounted by leaders, both female and male, in the worlds of politics and medicine. *(See also: Civil War; Dress Reform: Nineteenth Century; Physicians; Suffrage)*

—**Sandra L. Chaff**
Adapted for the second edition by Sandra Riese.

Further Reading

Chaff, Sandra L. "In Recognition of . . . Mary Edwards Walker (1832–1919)," *Women and Health* 6 (Spring/Summer 1981): 83-90.

Chaff, Sandra L., Ruth Haimbach, Carol Fenichel, and Nina Woodside. *Women in Medicine: A Bibliography of the Literature on Women Physicians.* Metuchen, NJ: Scarecrow, 1977.

Lida Poynter manuscript and notes on Mary Edwards Walker, M.D. Archives and Special Collections on Women in Medicine. Medical College of Pennsylvania, Philadelphia.

Snyder, Charles McCool. *Dr. Mary Walker: The Little Lady in Pants.* New York: Vantage, 1962.

Werlich, Robert. "Mary Walker: From Union Army Surgeon to Sideshow Freak," *Civil War Times Illustrated* 6 (June 3, 1967): 46-49.

☙ War Brides, World War II

While historians have engaged in several invaluable and noteworthy studies of "Rosie the Riveter" and the public role of wartime women, the private and family lives of young war brides remain a relative terra incognita. There were approximately 1 million more marriages from 1940 to 1943 than would have been expected at prewar rates. In

Figure 64. War Bride, World War II
Between four and five million women were married to servicemen during World War II. Some, like the woman pictured here loading live ammunition into turret guns on an unknown tank or aircraft, were able to find work. Many others traveled across the country to be near their husbands. The creation of this sisterhood was an early spark of the feminist movement of the 1950s and 60s. Used by permission of UPI/Corbis-Bettmann.

total, 4 to 5 million women, or 8 percent of all wives, were married to servicemen during the war years. For wives under twenty, this figure rises to 40 percent.

One of the most striking characteristics of these war brides was their mobility. Newly married women traveled thousands of miles across America to be near the military bases where their husbands were stationed. War brides on the move banded together, giving each other the inevitable baby showers, sharing information, anything to fill "the daytime void." They joined the Red Cross, drove in motor pools, worked as volunteers in hospitals and at United Service Organizations (USOs), gave blood and helped at blood centers, and took nurses' aide courses. Many war wives found temporary employment, and approximately one-half of all service wives worked for wages at some time during the war. However, it was often difficult for war brides to find jobs because employers were hesitant to hire transients. Eventually, of course, there was the inevitable move to another posting and, finally, saying good-bye to one's husband as he left for overseas.

During the long and difficult months of separation from their husbands, war brides often sought comfort and solace from each other. They enjoyed informal gatherings where they made ice cream and "swapped stories." They went to the movies together, played cards, met at the local drug store, and participated in a variety of civic and church activities. A 1944 feature story on war brides by Elizabeth Valentine, published in the *New York Times,* described these young women as "wandering members of a huge unorganized club." They recognized each other on sight, exchanged views on living quarters, allotments, and travel, and demonstrated pride in their husbands. The women in their "unorganized clubs" sustained each other and helped make the waiting "for the end of the duration" tolerable.

At present, it is only possible to speculate about the long-term and ultimate meaning of World War II on the lives of young war brides. Historians must scrutinize letters, diaries, journals, advice manuals, the popular literature, and a wide range of other materials from the 1940s and later before a significant assessment of this tantalizing question can be reached. (See also: Mobilization; "Rosie the Riveter"; World War II)

—Judy Barrett Litoff

Further Reading

Campbell, D'Ann. Women at War with America: Private Lives in a Patriotic Era. Cambridge, MA: Harvard University Press, 1984.

Hartmann, Susan M. The Home Front and Beyond. Boston: Twayne, 1982.

Klaw, Barbara. Camp Follower: The Story of a Soldier's Wife. New York: Random House, 1943.

Litoff, Judy Barrett, and David C. Smith. Since You Went Away: World War II Letters from American Women on the Home Front. New York: Oxford University Press, 1991.

Litoff, Judy Barrett, David C. Smith, Barbara Taylor, and Charles Taylor. Miss You: The World War II Letters of Barbara and Charles Taylor. Athens: University of Georgia Press, 1989.

ᖆ War Manpower Commission (WMC)

The War Manpower Commission (WMC) was established by presidential order in April 1942 to mobilize American manpower during the Second World War. The vast majority of adult Americans fell under its jurisdiction, as it possessed the responsibilities of inducting men into the armed forces, reallocating workers from low-priority to high-priority industries for the war effort, and finding, training, and placing new workers for defense industries. This mandate required it to tap previously underused sources of labor, most notably women and racial minorities. Although these groups advanced social and economically as a result, the WMC's reluctance to challenge traditional gender and racial roles limited their opportunities.

The WMC chose not to present the war effort as an opportunity for women to alter their status politically, economically, or socially. Rather, it generally presented employment in the defense industries to women as a patriotic sacrifice to be endured temporarily. It envisioned this burden carried primarily by single women, with those responsible for young children recruited only as a last resort. To that end, the WMC conducted three national campaigns in 1942 and 1943 to recruit women into the workforce. These campaigns concentrated their efforts in areas of the country with chronic labor shortages and used short films, announcements by radio personalities, posters, billboards, and a national effort through popular magazines. Significantly, the WMC did not coordinate its efforts at recruiting or aiding women workers with the Women's Bureau of the Labor Department or traditional feminist organizations.

Due to the high demand for labor and the WMC's efforts, many women obtained relatively high-paying government and manufacturing jobs during the war. These women primarily either were not of childbearing age or held lower-paying clerical or service work prior to the war. The many weaknesses of the WMC, however, limited the opportunities available to women. The WMC's reluctance to accept mothers of young children in the workforce led to the development of a haphazard system of child care. Gender discrimination also exposed a blind spot in the WMC. Although it went to great lengths to encourage local employers to hire women, its reliance on voluntary employer compliance and its willingness to accept discriminatory job orders greatly curtailed opportunities available to women and minorities. This unwillingness to challenge discrimination also undercut the WMC's primary function, as it allowed some defense plants to be chronically understaffed, sacrificing to prejudice the production necessary for the war effort. (See also: Lanham Act; Mobilization; "Rosie the Riveter"; Women's Bureau; World War II)

—Sethuraman Srinivasan, Jr.

Further Reading

Anderson, Karen. Wartime Women: Sex Roles, Family Relations, and the Status of Women during World War II. Westport, CT: Greenwood, 1981.

Rupp, Leila J. Mobilizing Women for War: German and American Propaganda, 1939–1945. Princeton, NJ: Princeton University Press, 1978.

U.S. War Manpower Commission. "Adequacy of Labor Supply in Important Labor Market Areas." 1944–1945.

———. "America at War Needs Women at Work." 1943.

ᖆ Ward, Nancy (1738–1824)

Nancy Ward (also known as Nanke'hi) was the last "Beloved Woman" of the Cherokees and the head of the influential Women's Council made up of representatives from each clan and a voting member of the council of chiefs. She was born into the Wolf Clan in Chota, Monroe County, Tennessee.

In the 1750s, Ward married Kingfisher and they had two children. In 1755, Ward went with her husband to the Battle of Taliwa, a skirmish between the Cherokees and Creek Indians. Ward chewed lead bullets in an effort to make Kingfisher's rifle fire more effective. When Kingfisher was shot and killed, she took his rifle and fought on, rallying the Cherokees to victory. Her battle companions rewarded her efforts by giving her a black slave left by the retreating Creeks. According to legend, this made her the first Cherokee to own a slave. When she returned to Chota, her valor in battle made her the obvious choice to fill the vacant position of Agi-ga-u-e, or "Beloved Woman."

In the late 1750s, she married Bryant Ward, a white English trader. Her husband did not stay long among the Cherokees and returned to the Pendleton district of South Carolina by 1760. They had one daughter.

During the 1760s, the Cherokee Nation was hostile to the encroaching white men who were settling on Cherokee lands in direct violation of a royal decree from England. When the American Revolution broke out, the Cherokee sided with the British. As Beloved Woman, Ward knew the details of an impending attack on the settlement of Watauga. She sent a message to the settlement advising them to flee the area.

Despite the warning, not all the settlers managed to escape. Lydia Bean, the wife of Tennessee's first permanent white settler, was captured and condemned to death by fire. Ward heard about the captured woman and rushed to her aid. As Beloved Woman, she had the right to revoke a death sentence. Ward took Bean home with her and nursed her back to health. During her stay, Bean introduced Ward to dairy farming and the art of making cheese and butter. Shortly thereafter, Ward was the first Cherokee to keep cattle, and she introduced dairy farming to her people.

Throughout the war, Ward befriended many white traders and settlers. She was a negotiator at the 1781 treaty parlays at Little Pigeon River, Tennessee. She was troubled that the Americans had no women negotiators at the meeting and demanded that their leaders return to their people and explain the terms to the women. After the negotiations, Ward purchased and operated a small inn on the Ocowee River at Womankiller Ford.

In 1817, the Cherokee tribal government met for the last time and decided to reorganize its government somewhat like that of the United States. Ward was aged and too ill to attend the meeting, but she sent her walking cane and a letter to the meeting. She told the council that she approved of the new government the Cherokees were adopting and urged the new officials to hold on to the remaining Cherokee lands. This was the last official act of Nancy Ward. She died seven years later. Those present at her death claimed that a white light ascended from her body and flew into the sacred mound of Chota, the place of her birth. *(See also: Native American Women)*

—**Joyce Ann Kievit**

Further Reading

Dockstader, Frederick J., ed. *Great North American Indians: Profiles in Life and Leadership,* pp. 320-21. New York: Van Nostrand Reinhold, 1977.

Felton, Harold W. *Nancy Ward: Cherokee.* New York: Dodd Mead, 1975.

Foreman, Carolyn Thomas. *Indian Woman Chiefs,* pp. 72-84. Norman: University of Oklahoma Press, 1954.

McClary, Ben Harris. "The Last Beloved Woman of the Cherokees," *Tennessee Historical Society Quarterly* 21 (1962): 352-64.

Tucker, Norma. "Nancy Ward, Ghighau of the Cherokees," *Georgia Historical Quarterly* 53 (June 1969): 192-200.

Woodward, Grace Steele. *The Cherokees.* Norman: University of Oklahoma Press, 1963.

☙ Warren, Mercy (Otis) (1728–1814)

Mercy Otis Warren was a historian, poet, and patriot. Warren was the third of thirteen children of James and Mary (Allyne) Otis of Barnstable, Massachusetts. Her father was a justice of the peace, her brother James an advocate of the king, and her husband, James Warren, a member of the Massachusetts legislature. Being surrounded by influential men of the revolutionary cause, Warren wrote political satire.

In addition to writing plays—*The Adulateur, The Motley Assembly,* and *The Group*—Warren also published poems and dramatic poems—*The Sack of Rome* and *The Ladies of Castile.* Encouraged by President John Adams to write her views of the war, Warren penned the three-volume *History of the Rise, Progress, and Termination of the American Revolution.*

Warren was a feminist who objected to the lack of female education; she had to sit in on her brothers' formal education to learn. Until the age of eighty-six, Warren corresponded with the political leaders of her era in the fight for freedom. She left a legacy of manuscript material for future generations about the struggle of the United States for independence. *(See also: American Revolutionary Era; Theater; Women Writers)*

—**Ginger Rae Allee**

Further Reading

The Mercy Otis Warren Papers and Mercy Otis Warren Letter-Box. Massachusetts Historical Society, Boston.

Fritz, Jean. *Cost for a Revolution 1728–1814, Some American Friends and Enemies.* Boston: Houghton Mifflin, 1972.

Norton, Mary Beth. *Liberty's Daughters.* Boston: Little, Brown, 1980

☙ Washerwoman's Strike: Atlanta

In the summer of 1881, laundresses, cooks, and other domestic servants in Atlanta struck for higher wages. The strike was the second attempt both to organize and to insist on these wage demands, and like the first, it originated in the Summer Hill Church, located in Atlanta's black community. Inspired by ministerial preaching and supported by both men and women, the strike lasted for several weeks in a summer during which Atlanta was preparing for the Cotton States Exposition of 1881 and simultaneously struggling with a local water shortage. Atlanta police arrested several of the strike leaders and charged them with disorderly conduct for their practice of visiting working washerwomen and urging them to join the strike effort. Initial fines did not deter the leaders or force strikers back to work, but a combination of a city-council license fee and

the practice of raising rents of washerwomen tenants helped break the strike. By mid-August, most washerwomen seemed to have returned to work.

Although it did not result in a successful organization for domestic workers, this strike action on the part of Atlanta washerwomen was nevertheless significant. The strike represented a transitional labor protest in the years after emancipation. Under slavery, work protests had frequently included spontaneous but often short-lived sabotage inspired by preachers within the slave community. During emancipation, black community cohesiveness centered on the church. The washerwoman's strike was at once a spontaneous reaction to poor working conditions and at the same time inspired by those at the center of the black community. Moreover, the strike symbolically targeted the servant occupations that seemed so much an extension of slavery. Black women, joined by black men, were protesting not just the wages for their work but their perception that emancipation and migration to the cities had not led to a "new South" but to a transfer of the "old slavery." Strikes such as this were not uncommon among black men, and those among black turpentine laborers, stevedores, longshoremen, and others deserve parallel and comparative consideration. *(See also: African American Domestic Workers)*

—**Thomas F. Armstrong**

Further Reading

Atlanta Constitution. July-August, 1881.

Hunter, Tera W. "Domination and Resistance: The Politics of Wage Household Labor in New South Atlanta," *Labor History* 34 (1993), 205-20.

Jones, Jacqueline. *Labor of Love, Labor of Sorrow.* New York: Basic Books, 1985.

Rabinowitz, Howard. *Race Relations in the Urban South, 1865–1900.* New York: Oxford University Press, 1978.

✎ Washington, Margaret Murray
(1865–1925)

Born March 9, 1865, in Macon, Mississippi, Margaret Murray attended the newly created public schools there before going to college at Fisk University in Nashville. After graduation in 1889, she became "lady principal" at Tuskegee Institute in Alabama. Three years later, she became the third wife of Booker T. Washington and Director of Industries for girls at the institute. Better educated than her husband, she became both his partner at the institute and an independent force for black advancement.

A believer in the power of women to bring needed change, she founded the Tuskegee Women's Club and became president of the newly organized National Federation of Afro-American Women in 1895. The next year, the federation merged with another group to form the National Association of Colored Women, of which she became president in 1912. As president, she began the publication of *National Notes* and urged women to go into business: "There are the

professional and business women whose interests are being pushed so that the woman who is inclined to be independent of her father and brothers in her struggle for a living may not be swallowed up."

She was particularly distressed about the plight of young people in adult penitentiaries and was a major force in organizing a reform school for boys at Mount Meigs, Alabama, in 1902 and the Reform Institution for Delinquent Colored Girls of Alabama in 1904. Until her death on June 4, 1925, she remained active in the cause of better conditions for blacks, serving as a member of the Commission on Interracial Cooperation, headquartered in Atlanta, Georgia, and established to improve communication between the races. She also authored three publications on parenting and improving home conditions. *(See also: Black Women's Clubs; Commission on Interracial Cooperation; National Association of Colored Women; Prison Reform; Tuskegee Institute)*

—**Linda O. McMurry**

Further Reading

Margaret Murray Washington Papers. Tuskegee Institute Archives. Tuskegee, AL.

Harlan, Louis R. *Booker T. Washington: The Making of a Black Leader, 1856–1901.* New York: Oxford University Press, 1972.

———. *Booker T. Washington: The Wizard of Tuskegee, 1901–1915.* New York: Oxford University Press, 1983.

✎ Water Cure

Water cure or "hydropathy" flourished as one of many healing sects in America from 1843 to 1900. It reached its peak in the 1850s, with up to 213 water cure establishments catering to the physiological and psychological needs of its patrons. Its proponents believed that water was the source of life and, consequently, prescribed the frequent use of cold water for bathing and drinking in conjunction with a spartan regime of vegetarian diet, exercise, and physical stimulation as remedy for all manners of disease.

Exclusive European spas had long exploited the alleged restorative qualities of minerals in water, but it was only in the 1820s that Vincent Pressnitz of Silesia began to advocate the therapeutic properties of cold water. In the 1840s, New York physicians Joel Shew and R. T. Trall and reformer Mary Gove Nichols introduced the cold water cure to America as part of an overall health regime.

Women especially appreciated water cure's approach to "natural," noninterventionist health care, which in the age of bleeding and purging, instead stressed control over one's own health and body. Water cure establishments, usually located in rural settings far from the bustle and strain of rising urban centers, regularly employed women physicians and therapists in the belief that they best understood the health concerns of other women. The long-lived *Water-Cure Journal* espoused issues of special concern to women, such as the admission of women to medical schools, the wearing of loose-fitting, "rational" dress, temperance, and the reform of child-birthing practices.

Deliberately affordable to the middle class, water cure facilities themselves provided a communal atmosphere, a vigorous routine, and even sensual pleasure in the form of baths, massages, and body wraps. In general, water cure philosophy belied the conventional medical notion that female physiology impaired women's intellect and, by extension, the societal notion of women's inferiority.

The Civil War broke down any philosophical link between the healthy body and a healthy society, effectively ending the utopian dream of water cure as a panacea. Furthermore, the rise of consumer culture in the late nineteenth century required richer accommodations as the new water cure resort featured dancing, dining, and game playing among its genteel leisure activities. The heyday of water cure serves as an important early example of alternative health care, and its fundamental precepts of sensible diet, hygiene, and exercise remain sound today. *(See also: Dress Reform: Nineteenth Century; Grahamism; Mind Cure; Nichols, Mary Gove)*

—**Catherine Mason**

Further Reading

Cayleff, Susan E. *Wash and Be Healed: The Water Cure Movement and Women's Health*. Philadelphia: Temple University Press, 1987.

Donegan, Jane. *Hydropathic Highway to Health: Women and Water-Cure in Antebellum America*. Westport, CT: Greenwood, 1986.

Shew, Joel. *Hydropathy; or the Water-Cure: Its Principles, Modes of Treatment*. New York: Wiley & Putnam, 1845.

Sklar, Kathryn Kish. "All Hail to Pure Cold Water!" In *Women and Health in America,* edited by Judith Walzer Leavitt, 246-54. Madison: University of Wisconsin Press, 1984.

Weiss, Harry B., and Howard R. Kemble. *The Great American Water-Cure Craze: A History of Hydrotherapy in the U.S.* Trenton, NJ: Past Times Press, 1967.

Waters, Ethel (1900–1977)

Singer, comedienne, and actress Ethel Waters was born illegitimate, her twelve-year-old mother a victim of rape, in a slum in Chester, Pennsylvania. She grew up emotionally and economically deprived, often stealing and hanging around street gangs. At an early age, she embraced the stage as a means of escape and began performing a vaudeville act as early as 1909. Later, she toured on the Theatre Owner's Booking Association circuit, which provided entertainment for all-black audiences.

She began working in Harlem nightclubs in the 1920s and became popular with white audiences, who dubbed her "the Ebony Comedienne." She also became the first female to record the blues, eventually recording twenty-six titles for the Black Swan label and, later, forty-seven titles for Columbia. In the 1930s, she developed into the first consequential female jazz singer. Among her famous songs were "Dinah," "Heat Wave," "Suppertime," and her signature song, "His Eye Is on the Sparrow."

Waters also appeared on Broadway, beginning with all-black revues like *Africana* (1927), Lew Leslie's *Blackbirds* (1930), and *Rhapsody in Black* (1931). In 1939, she became the first black woman to appear on Broadway in a dramatic role, in *Mamba's Daughter*. She played the loving and faithful wife, Petunia, in the musical *Cabin in the Sky* (1940), a role she repeated in the film. In 1949, she played the grandmother in the film *Pinky*. Perhaps her greatest role was that of Berenice in *Member of the Wedding* (1950), for which she received the New York Drama Critics Award. She was nominated for an Academy Award as best supporting actress for the same role in the film version. She starred in the short-lived television series *Beulah* and made her last film, *The Sound and the Fury,* in 1958. Waters continued to perform into her seventies, appearing in television roles, stock, and revivals. After a religious experience in the late 1950s, she frequently appeared with the Billy Graham Crusade. *(See also: Black Women; Jazz; Popular Vocalists; Theater)*

—**Rose Kolbasnik Callahan**

Further Reading

McCorkle, Susannah. "The Mother of Us All (Ethel Waters)," *American Heritage* 54 (Feb/March 1994): 60-72.

Mellers, Wilfred. *Angels of the Night: Popular Female Singers of our Time*. Oxford, UK: Basil Blackwell, 1986.

Waters, Ethel. *His Eye Is on the Sparrow*. Westport, CT: Greenwood, 1978.

WAVES

Although U.S. law prohibited women from serving in the armed forces, during World War I, the Navy found a loophole and recruited women to serve as telephone operators and clericals. By the war's end, 11,275 yeomen (F)s had served with the Navy and the Marines Corps, earning high marks for their contributions. Despite their success, Congress, in the 1925 Naval Reserve Act, plugged the loophole, and when World War II broke out, the Navy had to seek new legislation to recruit women.

The first women's corps was authorized for the Army by Congress in May 1942, but the legislation initially granted only partial military status, and women became members of the Women's Army Auxiliary Corps (WAAC). The Navy was most reluctant to allow women in, but realizing that Congress was going to draft such legislation, its leaders designed their own program, which made women recruits comparable with male reservists, not members of a nebulous auxiliary. The WAVES (Women Accepted for Volunteer Emergency Service) were created on July 30, 1942 (Public Law 689). At times, WAVES also seemed to stand for Women Are Very Essential Sometimes. In all, 100,000 women served as WAVES during World War II, but none were allowed overseas. A handful were stationed in Alaska and Hawaii by the end of the war. The largest group of enlisted women performed clerical and administrative assignments. In all, thirty-eight ratings were opened to WAVES. Approximately one-third were assigned to naval aviation; many became trainers of beginning pilots, weather watchers, and parachute packers.

The first WAVES director was Mildred McAfee, who was the president of Wellesley College before and after the war. "Captain Mac," as she was affectionately called by the women, quickly became a legend and until her recent death remained active in college circles and civic organizations.

With the passage of the Women's Armed Services Integration Act in June 1948, WAVES were made a permanent part of the Navy. In the 1970s, the Navy and Army debated whether to maintain a separate corps for women (the Navy Nurse Corps had both men and women in it since the 1950s) or to abolish the WAVES. After long debate, all "separate but equal" women's corps were abolished in 1978. Beginning in 1976, women were allowed to attend the U.S. Naval Academy at Annapolis, Maryland.

Legal barriers prohibiting women from combat roles in planes and on ships are collapsing. Women began serving aboard ships over a decade ago and now are serving aboard combat support logistic ships and being trained as combat pilots. The Navy now has women admirals who command both men and women and has come a long way from believing that any woman aboard a ship was bad luck. *(See also: Marine Corps, Women's Reserve; Military Service; SPARS; Women's Army Auxiliary Corps; Women's Army Corps)*

—**D'Ann Campbell**

Further Reading
Alsmeyer, Marie Bennett. *The Way of the WAVES.* Conway, AR: Hamba, 1981.

Bureau of Naval Personnel, Historical Section. "Women's Reserve." Washington, DC, 1946.

Godson, Susan. "The WAVES in World War II," *Naval Institute Proceedings* 107 (December 1981): 46-51. [Godson has the contract to produce the first full-length book on women in the Navy.]

Hancock, Joy Bright. *Lady in the Navy: A Personal Reminiscence.* Annapolis, MD: Naval Institute, 1972.

ᕦ Way, Amanda M. (1828–1914)

Amanda M. Way, advocate of woman suffrage and temperance, worked for reform and religion in several states. After starting her public life as an abolitionist, she became a leader during the 1850s in both Indiana's women's movement and the predominantly male Good Templar temperance society. After the Civil War, she revived the Indiana women's society as a branch of the American Woman Suffrage Association. In 1867, she became the first woman to head a Good Templar grand lodge. At one time or another, she was elected the chief officer of the Good Templars in Indiana, Kansas, and Idaho. She was also active in other antidrink organizations such as the National Prohibition Party and the Woman's Christian Temperance Union. In 1900, she was the Prohibition candidate for Idaho's seat in the federal House of Representatives.

Way made her living as a teacher, milliner, tailor, and Civil War nurse (for which she received a federal pension). Although born in a Quaker family, she became a Methodist, and in 1871, shortly before she moved to Kansas, the Richmond district of the North Indiana conference of the Methodist Episcopal Church licensed her as a local preacher. In the 1880s, when the general conference expelled women from the pulpit, Way returned to the Society of Friends and served for the rest of her life as a Quaker minister in Kansas, Idaho, and California.

Her unpublished autobiography, last known reported in Oregon, is lost. *(See also: Good Templars; Society of Friends; Suffrage; Temperance Movement; Woman's Christian Temperance Union)*

—**David M. Fahey**

Further Reading
Bader, Robert Smith. *Prohibition in Kansas.* Lawrence: University Press of Kansas, 1986.

Hill, George W. E. *Some Good Templars I Have Known: Brief Biographies of Our Most Eminent Workers.* Grand Valley, MI: Valley City, 1893.

Pacific Friend 21 (March, 1914): 14. [obituary]

ᕦ Weber, Lois (1882–1939)

One of the highest-paid directors in the American film industry during her heyday, Lois Weber directed dozens of films between 1912 and 1927. Her films were immensely popular, and her facility with screen technique "was as characteristic to her audiences as that of Griffith or DeMille," according to one film historian.

After touring as a concert pianist and then serving with the Salvation Army, Weber decided to try the stage on the advice of an uncle. She married the actor-manager of a road company, Phillips Smalley. The couple found work in the then somewhat disreputable motion picture business, playing leads, writing scripts, and directing segments of films at Rex Pictures, the New York-based organization of Edwin S. Porter. In 1912, after Porter's departure, the two took over Rex, which was by then releasing its films nationally through Universal.

Weber was clearly the dominant member of the partnership, which produced between two hundred and four hundred films, according to her. Fewer than fifty titles survive today, but these show Weber experimenting with a full range of techniques in the service of her favorite genre, the modern morality tale. After Universal built Weber her own studio in Hollywood during World War I, she was able to supervise every detail of her own productions. She was known for working closely with her stock company of actors, and this, along with her emphasis on melodrama, showed the continuing influence of her theatrical background.

Weber's work through 1921 showed a flair for spectacular visual treatments of contemporary social themes; her *Where Are My Children?* (1916) treated the then-taboo subject of birth control, and several other titles suggest that Weber regularly grappled with issues of the day. Her flair for the sensational along with the serious—including the use of frontal nudity in the well-publicized *Hypocrites* (1914)—made her films extraordinarily popular. At Universal, Weber was eventually paid $2,500 a week, and her talents were coveted by other studios. In 1920, Famous Players-Lasky (now Paramount) hired her at $50,000 per picture plus one-third of the profits, making her briefly one of the most economically powerful women in the American film industry. However, Weber released only three films under the Lasky banner; two more were released by a smaller independent distribution company. Weber's morality plays, in the post-World War I era, seem to have gone quickly out of favor with the public. She directed only a few more films before her death, although one of her later projects was a grandiose plan for the use of films in education.

Like other female directors, Weber constantly fought her studio's publicity machinery, which focused attention on her so-called woman's touch. But no amount of patronizing could obscure the fact noted by a contemporary interviewer: "She is doing a lion's share toward broadening the horizon of women's endeavors, and her brilliant accomplishments should act as a spur for the ambitious but halting ones who long for the freedom of self-expression found in a vocation of their own." *(See also: Arzner, Dorothy; Blaché, Alice Guy; Woman's Film)*

—Kevin Jack Hagopian

Further Reading

Heck-Rabi, Louise. "Lois Weber: Moralist Moviemaker." In *Woman Filmmakers: A Critical Reception,* edited by Louise Heck-Rabi, 53-71. Metuchen, NJ: Scarecrow, 1984.

Koszarski, Richard. "The Years Have Not Been Kind to Lois Weber." In *Women and the Cinema,* edited by Karyn Kay and Gerald Peary, 146-52. New York: E. P. Dutton, 1977.

"Lois Weber: Whose Role Is It Anyway?" *British Film Institute Monthly Film Bulletin* 49 (May 1982): 100.

Welfare Reform

The way in which a society treats its least fortunate members is an index of its cultural and political values. In the United States, private organizations tended to the needs of the poor and vulnerable until the economic devastation of the Great Depression of the 1930s overwhelmed the capacities of these groups.

Among the New Deal programs initiated by President Franklin D. Roosevelt was the original Social Security legislation, enacted in 1935. It included a program for mothers with dependent children that provided payments for women to stay out of the workforce and raise their children. This solution to the problem of family destitution reflected the prevailing gender division of labor that gave preference to mothers in the home and the need to reduce massive unemployment.

Although it was originally envisioned as a transitional measure made necessary by the Great Depression, the Aid to Dependent Children (later Aid to Families with Dependent Children, AFDC) program endured for more than half a century as the cornerstone of a federal-state government partnership to care for the poor and, in the minds of most citizens, defines the term *welfare.* Welfare reform movements of the 1960s and 1970s focused attention on access limitations, rights issues, and inefficient program administration, but the program endured relatively unchanged throughout the post-World War II period.

During the Republican presidential administrations of the 1980s, assumptions governing the AFDC program came under intense and wide scrutiny. The ethos of the "Reagan Revolution" emphasized individualism and economic self-reliance. At the same time, the massive entrance of mothers, including those with small children, into the paid workforce changed prevailing gender role expectations.

Numerous governmental and academic studies conducted in the 1970s and 1980s identified the inefficiencies of the AFDC program. The government's policy of paying women to stay home with children came under attack as encouraging sloth, dependency, and illegitimacy. At a time of ballooning federal deficits, the entitlement provisions of AFDC were portrayed as a threat to economic order rather than as the solution envisioned under the New Deal.

A major revision in the AFDC program occurred in 1990 when the Family Support Act of 1988 was implemented. The act created the Job Opportunities and Basic Skills Training (JOBS) program, which required women with small children (less than six years of age) to prepare actively for the workforce. The JOBS program also provided child care and transportation needed for mothers to participate in training. The Budget Reconciliation Act of 1990 provided child care tax credits and Medicaid benefits, complementary measures that could assist graduates of the JOBS programs as they moved toward economic self-sufficiency in the labor market.

The presidential and congressional elections of 1992 and 1994 increased debate about the efficacy and fairness of welfare programs in the United States. Shifts from Democratic to Republican Party majorities in the Congress and many state legislatures and governors' offices energized the debate. The issues of "welfare reform" expanded to include the division of labor between the state and federal governments, the role of government in its citizens' lives, the rights of legal and illegal immigrants, and access to abortion and/or contraception.

While *family values* is a popular political term, discussion of welfare reform tends to focus on individual family members: unwed mothers, anonymous or unsupportive fathers, and innocent children. Political promises to "end welfare as we know it" have generally led to proposals to refine or revise the existing AFDC program, such as limiting the term of eligibility for benefits to two years.

The contentious national debate about welfare reform reflects societal conflicts about changing gender roles, sexuality, race and immigration, economic decline, and loss of community. In debating "welfare reform" measures that would alter the reproductive behavior of women and their participation in the workforce, citizens are expressing anxiety about the present and what they perceive to be threats to their future. The desired "reform" expresses a social ideal. It is unlikely that comprehensive legislation can be enacted to satisfy such disparate concerns. "Welfare reform" is likely to continue as incremental revision to existing measures. *(See also: New Deal; Social Security Act of 1935; Welfare Rights Movement)*

—Jane Crisler

Further Reading

Chilman, Catherine. "Welfare Reform or Revision? The Family Support Act of 1988," *Social Service Review* (September 1992): 350-77.

Gordon, Linda, ed. *Women, the State, and Welfare.* Madison: University of Wisconsin Press, 1990.

Lynn, Laurence E., Jr. "The Rhetoric of Welfare Reform: An Essay Review," *Social Service Review* (June 1990): 175-88.

———. "Welfare Reform and the Revival of Ideology: An Essay Review," *Social Service Review* (December 1992): 642-54.

Norris, Donald, and Lyke Thompson, eds. *The Politics of Welfare Reform.* Thousand Oaks, CA: Sage, 1995.

Ozawa, M. N. "Women, Children, and Welfare Reform," *AFFILIA: Journal of Women and Social Work* 9 (Winter 1994): 338-59.

◁ Welfare Rights Movement

The welfare rights movement in the United States grew out of the civil rights movement of the 1960s. The pioneer organization, National Welfare Rights Organization (NWRO, 1967-1973), combined traditional concepts of social welfare with the philosophy of the civil rights movement that citizens are entitled to a minimum level of material comfort. In the 1960s, studies of social inequality focused on populations that had traditionally been disadvantaged in American society due to past history and prejudice: recent urban immigrants who lived in isolated ghettos and the rural poor who did not have access to medical, educational, and social services. In many instances, poverty was exacerbated by racial prejudice.

President John F. Kennedy addressed the problem of poverty with the food stamp program. His effort was succeeded by the more ambitious War on Poverty, initiated by President Lyndon B. Johnson in 1964. Although flawed in its conception and deprived of funding by the escalating Vietnam War, the War on Poverty reflected the embarrassment of an affluent, technologically advanced society that could not eradicate hunger and suffering. As the civil rights movement

developed in the latter half of the decade, welfare concerns meshed with demands for justice in an inequitable society.

After the NWRO disbanded in 1973, welfare rights movements organized on a local basis and to serve different constituencies. The desires of welfare recipients to receive prompt payment of benefits without humiliating treatment by social service personnel, for example, led to intense lobbying of individual offices by local coalitions of recipients, social workers, and community activists. Issues that developed in the late 1980s were the concern with a seemingly permanent underclass of welfare recipients and the "feminization of poverty," a result of wage discrimination, welfare policies that many charge encourage dependency, and divorce law reforms that have a disproportionate effect on women and children.

The public debate about "welfare reform" in the 1990s is changing the perspective from welfare as a "right" or entitlement to a means toward economic self-sufficiency. The Family Support Act of 1988 (implemented in 1990) created the JOBS (Job Opportunities and Basic Skills Training) program requiring employment training for parents (primarily women with small children). Increased emphasis on programs that limit benefits, mandate job training and employment search, and offer incentives to reduce childbearing among welfare recipients raised new rights issues in the 1990s. No one organization or coalition can provide solutions to these issues; the diversity of their stances reflects the redefinition of the very concept of *rights* that is under way in the United States. *(See also: Civil Rights; Female-Headed Households; Mothers' Pensions; National Welfare Rights Organization; Welfare Reform)*

—Jane Crisler

Further Reading

Chilman, Catherine. "Welfare Reform or Revision? The Family Support Act of 1988," *Social Service Review* 66 (September 1992): 350-77.

Gordon, Linda, ed. *Women, the State, and Welfare.* Madison: University of Wisconsin Press, 1990.

Leiby, James. *A History of Social Welfare and Social Work in the United States.* New York: Columbia University Press, 1978.

Morrissey, M. H. "The Downtown Welfare Advocate Center: A Case Study of a Welfare Rights Organization," *Social Service Review* 64 (June 1990): 190-207.

West, Guida. *The National Welfare Rights Movement: The Social Protest of Poor Women.* New York: Praeger, 1981.

◁ Wellesley College

Wellesley College, a leading women's college located in Wellesley, Massachusetts, was founded in 1875 by Henry F. Durant, a Harvard-educated trustee of Mount Holyoke College and champion of women's higher education. Durant was dedicated to the principle of giving young women a collegiate education substantially the same as that given young men, an idea that was sharply criticized at that time. Durant also believed that a woman's college should have a largely female faculty, both to provide women students with positive role models and to give academic women opportunities for employment. Wellesley quickly became recognized as one of the most important women's colleges in the country.

From the very start, tuition and board at Wellesley were high compared with other colleges and universities across the country, and as a consequence, the college attracted a rather elite clientele. Because of its explicit commitment to equality in women's education, Wellesley also attracted a number of older women students interested in receiving first-rate collegiate instruction. For the most part, the Wellesley curriculum was similar to that offered at men's colleges in this period, with heavy emphasis on classical languages, science, and literature. Later, courses on home economics and related issues (such as "consumerism"), hygiene, and physical education were added as Wellesley and other women's colleges responded to charges that college education was harmful to the health of young women and that it was responsible for lower marriage rates among educated women. Wellesley also offered professional instruction in education and helped students interested in medical careers to prepare for medical school.

Perhaps the most important contribution of Wellesley—and other leading women's colleges in this period—was to provide an opportunity for bright young women to learn from the nation's first generation of professionally trained female scholars. Offering a haven for talented women academics who often found it impossible to find appointments elsewhere, Wellesley soon developed distinction in a number of fields, the most prominent being botany and psychology. Historian Patricia Palmieri has described Wellesley as an "Adamless Eden" in the first five decades of its development, a place where women could pursue their intellectual interests in a context of genuine feminine fellowship. More recently, Wellesley has eschewed the example of other women's colleges that have turned coed, choosing instead to develop further its distinctive identity as a woman's college. In recent years, Wellesley has become an important center for scholarship in the newly developing field of women's studies. *(See also: Higher Education; "Seven Sisters"; Women's Studies)*

—John L. Rury

Further Reading

Horowitz, Helen Lefkowitz. *Alma Mater: Design and Experience in the Women's Colleges from Their Nineteenth-Century Beginnings to the 1930s.* New York: Knopf, 1984.

Palmieri, Patricia. "Here Was Fellowship: A Social Portrait of Academic Women at Wellesley College, 1880–1920," *History of Education Quarterly* 23 (Summer 1983): 195-214.

↶ Wells-Barnett, Ida B. (1862–1931)

Journalist, antilynching crusader, community organizer, club woman, and woman suffrage advocate, Ida B. Wells-Barnett worked tirelessly to meet the needs of her race and correct social injustices. She was born on July 16, 1862, in Holly Springs, Mississippi, to Lizzie Bell, a slave cook, and Jim Wells, a slave carpenter. As the eldest of eight children, Wells at the age of sixteen took over the family responsibilities of raising her siblings after the death of her parents and her infant brother in the 1878 yellow fever epidemic. With the help of the black community, Wells attended Rust College to become a teacher, a profession that she pursued first in Holly Springs and then in Memphis, Tennessee.

In May 1884, Wells sued and won a case against the Chesapeake and Ohio Railroad Company for forcefully removing her from a segregated ladies coach. Victory was bittersweet, however, because the state supreme court reversed the lower court's decision. The incident reflected her spirit as a crusader against racial injustices. While earning her living as a teacher, she became part owner and editor of the Memphis *Free Speech and Headlight.* Her column written under the pen name Iola informed about the poor conditions of local schools for black children, a criticism that led to her dismissal in 1891 by the Memphis School Board. After the 1892 lynching of three of her friends, she was diligent in her antilynching crusade. Her research on lynching in the South attempted to destroy the rationale for such barbarism, which was the protection of white women from rape by black men. Her articles led to travels as an antilynching lecturer. In May 1892, following speaking engagements in Philadelphia and New York, her offices and press at *Free Speech* were destroyed and her life threatened. She continued her exposés on lynchings from a safer distance as a writer for T. Thomas Fortune's *New York Age.* By October 1892, her investigative research culminated in publication of *Southern Horrors: Lynch Law in All Its Phases.* She toured England and Scotland lecturing on racial violence, often linking the oppression and exploitation of African Americans to white economic opportunity. International support for the issues swelled and produced conservative reaction in the United States of America. Her work led to her being honored by black club women, the New York Woman's Loyal Union.

She used the international platform of the 1893 World's Fair, the Columbian Exposition, to further educate foreign travelers about racial violence and discrimination. With help from the aged Frederick Douglass, she solicited funds to publish 20,000 copies of a protest pamphlet, *The Reason Why the Colored American Is Not in the Columbian Exposition.* Ensuing attacks against her journalism and public speaking, when coupled with racial exclusion from the World's Fair, led black club women to organize in major cities.

In 1895, she married Chicago lawyer and newspaper owner Ferdinand Barnett. Barnett, a widower, brought two children into this union, which produced four others: Charles Aked, Herman Kahlstaat, Ida B. Wells, Jr., and Alfreda M. Family life did not stifle her reform impulses. She used the family paper, *Chicago Conservator,* as her vehicle to expose racial injustices. Her leadership helped the growth of numerous black and women's reform organizations: the Ida B. Wells Club, the Frederick Douglass Settlement, the Negro Fellowship League, the National Association of Colored Women, and the Alpha Suffrage Club. She was one of two African American women to sign "the Call" for the formation of the National Association for the Advancement of Colored People.

Her anti-Booker T. Washington stance and alliance with T. Thomas Fortune, W. E. B. Du Bois, and Marcus Garvey often placed her at odds with the conservative leadership in Chicago. She remained active in Republican politics. She served as a probation officer in Chicago. In 1913, she marched in a woman suffrage parade in Washington, D.C., with the all-white Illinois contingent and mobilized the black community to support the election of the first black alderman, Oscar DePriest. Her protests during World War I led to the Secret Service labeling her a dangerous radical. She reported on several riots, including the riot in East St. Louis in July 1917 and the Elaine, Arkansas, race riot, which led to the indictment for murder of several black farmers in 1922.

In declining health and somewhat isolated from the mainstream of black leadership during her later years, Wells-Barnett became embittered when some of her organizations became displaced by services from the National Urban League, YMCA, NAACP, and others. She died of uremia on March 25, 1931, and is buried at Oakwood Cemetery in Chicago. Her life symbolized a "crusade for justice," the title of her autobiography published under the editorship of her daughter, Alfreda Duster. *(See also: Black Women's Clubs; National Association for the Advancement of Colored People; National Association of Colored Women)*

—**Dorothy C. Salem**

Further Reading

Davis, Elizabeth Lindsay. *The Story of the Illinois Federation of Colored Women's Clubs.* Chicago: n.p., 1922.

Duster, Alfreda, ed. *Crusade for Justice: The Autobiography of Ida B. Wells.* Chicago: University of Chicago Press, 1970.

Giddings, Paula. *When and Where I Enter: The Impact of Black Women on Race and Sex in America.* New York: Bantam, 1984.

Holt, Thomas C. "The Lonely Warrior: Ida B. Wells-Barnett and the Struggle for Black Leadership." In *Black Leaders of the Twentieth Century,* edited by John Hope Franklin and August Meier, 39-61. Urbana: University of Illinois Press, 1982.

Ida B. Wells Papers. J. Regenstein Library. University of Chicago.

Sterling, Dorothy. *Black Foremothers: Three Lives,* 2d ed. New York: Feminist Press, 1979, 1994.

Thompson, Mildred. "Ida B. Wells-Barnett: An Exploratory Study of an American Woman, 1893–1930." Ph.D. diss., George Washington University, 1979.

⊷ Welty, Eudora Alice (b. 1909)

Eudora Welty is a short-story writer, novelist, and the recipient of numerous honors, including, among others, a Guggenheim Fellowship (1952) and a Pulitzer Prize for *The Optimist's Daughter* (1973). Welty is ranked with the preeminent writers of the Southern Renaissance. As Faulkner incorporated Oxford, Mississippi, into his oeuvre, Welty infuses her work with the linguistical rhythms and social customs of Jackson, Mississippi. Welty's emphasis on locale serves to illuminate the experiences she envisions as central to the world of ordinary life. Her characters' social and personal identities, as well as their search for stability and order in the pastoral tradition, relying on perpetuating their insular agrarian-based values to counteract the looming cultural chaos of an urban industrialized society, brilliantly evoke her uniquely southern vision of twentieth-century America. Merging this regional emphasis with broader cultural and aesthetic concerns, Welty incorporates surrealistic and impressionistic passages to convey how memory and storytelling nurture the collective identity so vital to the survival of the community in a rapidly growing America.

Recent scholarship has finally begun to explore fully Welty's feminism; her fiction represents the physical, psychological, and spatial dimensions that serve to confine the individual. She incorporates marginalized cultural artifacts (folktales, songs, advertisements, and fairy tales) in an effort to challenge the dominant literary conventions and confront the process through which the patriarchy establishes its own myth of authorization. In addition, Welty uses the traditional Gothic motifs of seduction, betrayal, and captivity to construct her narratives around a pattern of enclosure and escape. Her female protagonists either defy the oppressive nature of organized society or attempt to infuse that society with new understanding; in their efforts to break free of the cultural constraints that limit their opportunity and influence, her characters strive to generate wider avenues in self-determination. Welty further dramatizes her characters' struggles to free themselves from the oppressive forces of culture by subverting the conventions of the romance. Within the romance, female characters are generally presented with two possible means of resolution (death or subservience in marriage). Welty resists these limitations by rejecting closure itself. Her narratives frequently end on a definitive note of "openness" that presents her female protagonists with an expanded view of possibility rather than finalizing their individuality within the similarly confining dimensions of subservience or death. Thus, Welty has truly created tales of liberation. *(See also: Women Writers)*

—**Max Gavin Schulz**

Further Reading

Mark, Rebecca. *The Dragon's Blood: Feminist Intertextuality in Eudora Welty's* The Golden Apples. Jackson: University Press of Mississippi, 1994.

Mortimer, Gail L. *Daughter of the Swan: Love and Knowledge in Eudora Welty's Fiction.* Athens: University of Georgia Press, 1994.

Vande Kieft, Ruth M. *Eudora Welty.* Rev. ed. Boston: G. K. Hall, 1987.

Welty, Eudora. *The Collected Stories of Eudora Welty.* New York: Harcourt Brace Jovanovich, 1980.

———. *Delta Wedding.* New York: Harcourt Brace, 1946.

———. *The Eye of the Story: Selected Essays and Reviews.* New York: Random House, 1971.

———. *The Optimist's Daughter.* New York: Random House, 1970.

Weston, Ruth D. *Gothic Traditions and Narrative Techniques in the Fiction of Eudora Welty.* Baton Rouge: Louisiana State University Press, 1994.

✿ Wharton, Edith (1862–1937)

Author Edith Wharton was born Edith Newbold Jones, the youngest of three children, to wealthy New York parents. In 1885, she married Edward Robbins Wharton, but the marriage soon soured. The couple lived together to preserve appearances until 1913, when Wharton divorced her husband because of his mental instability. The Whartons had moved to Paris in 1907, and she remained in Europe for the rest of her life.

Wharton's first book was a collection of short stories called *The Greater Inclination* (1899). Although she wrote novels, novellas, poetry, and travel books, Wharton was most at home with the short story. She wrote eighty-six in her life, and her book *The Writing of Fiction* (1925) is dedicated to a study of the form. Wharton was a realist, concerned with American social life and social change. Many of her novels and stories are set against the background of affluent American society and deal with the uncertainties in private relations between men and women. To Wharton, moral commitment was absolute; to behave immorally endangered society.

Wharton is probably best remembered for *The House of Mirth* (1905) and *Ethan Frome* (1911). In 1920, *The Age of Innocence* won the Pulitzer Prize, making Wharton the first woman to win it. In 1923, she became the first woman to receive an honorary doctorate from Yale. Wharton died of a stroke on August 11, 1937. *(See also: Women Writers)*

—Victoria L. Shannon

Further Reading

Gilbert, S. M., and S. Gubar. *No Man's Land: The Place of the Woman in the Twentieth Century.* Vol. 2, *Sexchanges.* New Haven, CT: Yale University Press, 1989.

Lewis, R. W. B. *Edith Wharton.* New York: Harper & Row, 1975.

Nevius, Blake. *Edith Wharton: A Study of New Fiction.* Berkeley: University of California Press, 1953.

Wharton, Edith. *Age of Innocence.* New York: Appleton, 1920.

———. *Ethan Frome.* New York: Scribner, 1911.

———. *House of Mirth.* New York: Scribner, 1905.

✿ Wheatley, Phillis (Peters)
(c. 1753–1784)

Phillis Wheatley, pioneer of the African American literary tradition, was a poet known for occasional verse written in the English neoclassical manner. Her talents were recognized while she was a slave. Relying on the heroic couplet, she composed more than one hundred poems, half of which were published during her lifetime.

The small African girl was judged to be about eight years old when she was sold in Boston in 1761 as a personal servant to Susannah, wife of prominent Boston merchant-tailor John Wheatley. The Wheatley's teenage daughter, Mary, taught her English. Phillis (named for the slave ship that brought her to America) then studied the Bible, classical history, mythology, and Latin. Her poetry bore the stamp of this education with biblical as well as classical allusions. Although a slave, she was treated like a family member, with a room in the main house and only light household chores. Her first poem was published in 1767, and in 1770, an elegy on English evangelist George Whitefield brought her international recognition. She joined the Old South Congregational Church in 1771 as a communicant, a privilege not generally extended to slaves. Her reputation as an occasional poet grew as Boston's elite requested her services. Yet her proposal in 1772 to publish a book of poetry failed.

The frail poet sailed to England for her health in May 1773, bringing a statement attesting to the authenticity of her writing signed by prominent Bostonians, including John Hancock, who later signed the Declaration of Independence. Preceded by her reputation, she became a London favorite. There, her proposal for a volume of poetry met with success. But by the time *Poems on Various Subjects, Religious, and Moral* was published in September, making her the first American black to publish a volume of poetry, she had returned to her dying mistress. In America, at the request of English acquaintances, she was manumitted.

In 1776, her poem praising George Washington was published. Shortly after John Wheatley's death in 1778, Phillis married John Peters, a free black. She continued to write, but her proposal in 1779 for a volume of poetry and letters was rejected; most of these writings are lost. She had individual poems published until three months before her death. Impoverished, she died December 5, 1784. Although her obituary was published in several newspapers, she was buried in an unmarked grave with her third child. In 1786, *Poems* was printed in America. *(See also: Black Women; Slavery; Women Writers)*

—Therese L. Lueck

Further Reading

Reising, Russell. "The Whiteness of the Wheatleys: Phillis Wheatley's Revolutionary Poetics." In *Loose Ends: Closure and Crisis in the American Social Text,* pp. 73-115. Durham, NC: Duke University Press, 1996.

Renfro, G. Herbert. *Life and Works of Phillis Wheatley: Containing Her Complete Poetical Works, Numerous Letters, and a Complete Biography of This Famous Poet of a Century and a Half Ago.* 1916. Reprint, Freeport, NY: Books for Libraries, 1970.

Robinson, William H. *Phillis Wheatley and Her Writings.* New York: Garland, 1984.

Wheatley, Phillis. *The Collected Works of Phillis Wheatley,* edited by John C. Shields. New York: Oxford University Press, 1988.

White Rose Mission

White Rose Mission was established in 1897 in New York City and incorporated in 1898. The mission, a nondenominational institution, provided lodging and a variety of self-help activities for black women. It aided in their adjustment to the city and their development of the skills necessary to survive in an urban environment. It offered practical courses in sewing, cooking, and dressmaking and maintained a job placement service. A settlement house—one of many urban centers of social reform where educated young people worked among the poor—it provided community services such as mothers' meetings, a kindergarten, and a library of books on black history.

Victoria Earle Matthews, president of the Woman's Loyal Union, was the founder of White Rose Mission and its superintendent for the first decade of its existence. The mission offered lodging to women from the ages of fifteen to forty-five and provided accommodations for one night to six weeks to all women seeking shelter, regardless of their ability to pay the weekly fee of $1.25. It maintained travelers' aid representatives in New York and Norfolk to guide girls and women coming from the South in search of employment, to protect them from fraudulent employment agencies that exploited them and even forced some into prostitution.

The work of the mission was conducted by black women who volunteered their services and taxed themselves when increasing funds were needed for expanded community services, travelers' aid, and larger quarters. Contributions and support came from black and white donors, including Booker T. Washington, Grace Hoadley Dodge, Mrs. William H. Baldwin, and Mrs. C. P. Huntington. After occupying a series of temporary locations in the city, the White Rose Home relocated to permanent quarters on West 136th Street in 1918. *(See also: Black Women; Settlement House Movement)*

—**Floris Barnett Cash**

Further Reading

Best, Lasalle. "History of the White Rose Mission and Industrial Association." WPA Research Paper, n.d. Schomburg Collection. New York Public Library.

Cash, Floris Barnett. "Radicals or Realists: African American Women and the Settlement House Spirit in New York City," *Afro-Americans in New York Life and History* 15, no. 1 (January 1991): 7-17.

Lewis, Mary. "The White Rose Home and Industrial Association," *The Messenger* 7 (January 1925): 158.

Lerner, Gerda. "Early Community Work of Black Club Women," *Journal of Negro History* 59 (April 1974): 158-67.

Meier, August. *Negro Thought in America, 1880–1915.* Ann Arbor: University of Michigan Press, 1978.

Whitney, Adeline Dutton Train
(1824–1906)

Adeline Dutton Train Whitney, who published as Mrs. A. D. T. Whitney, was a well-known novelist from the early 1860s until her death. Although she wrote poems, short stories, and nonfiction, she was primarily a writer of stories about girls for adult as well as juvenile audiences.

Whitney was the daughter of a wealthy Boston merchant and shipowner. She attended George B. Emerson's school, and she credited him with developing her skill in Latin and English composition. Like his famous cousin Ralph Waldo Emerson, George Emerson encouraged individuals to use their talents and fulfill their potentialities. In 1843, when she was nineteen, she married Seth Whitney, an Army officer, and lived for the rest of her life in Milton, Massachusetts. She had four children and began to write when the youngest was eight.

Mother Goose for Grown Folks (1859), a collection of parodies of well-known poems (Mother Goose, for example, spoke as Brahma), attracted attention; her *The Boys at Chequasset* (1862) was written primarily to amuse her children. Her real career began in 1863 with the publication of *Faith Gartney's Girlhood,* which sold over 300,000 copies in its first year and made her famous. She followed it with *The Gayworthys* (1865). In these two novels, she established the subject and treatment she would repeat with modifications in all her stories: the initiation of a young girl into the world of adult responsibility. Whitney was a deeply religious woman, and her concept of woman's role was fairly traditional, if glorified. While recognizing that women to whom God had given unusual talents should be allowed to depart from the norm, she felt that the highest attainment possible for a woman was controller of the home—and therefore the future. Her position typified a popular view of woman that put her role as "light of the home" first but permitted her to use other talents. This belief, together with her conviction that religion is to be lived, not isolated or merely talked, shaped her novels. Her skill at characterization and her ability to tell a good story save her novels from piousness and, even in a culture that no longer shares her values, make them readable. She writes with humor, and her satire, especially of the social class distinctions that work to separate people, has a needlelike quality.

The popular "Real Folks" stories were four books, *A Summer in Leslie Goldthwaite's Life* (1866), *We Girls* (1870), *Real Folks* (1871), and *The Other Girls* (1873). The first two were serialized in *Our Young Folks* before publication; the last of the four is perhaps her most complex novel, for she goes beyond her normal well-bred families to look at the lives of farm girls and city working girls, including the results of the Boston fire that destroyed nearly half the city and the employment places of many working girls. Although they are not sequels, the "Real Folks" books have shared characters, and they are set in the kind of small world that Anthony Trollope created. Most of the early novels were re-issued steadily over a period of forty years.

Other works were *Hitherto* (1867), *Odd or Even* (1880), *Bonnyborough* (1886), *Ascutney Street* (1890), and *Square Pegs* (1899); one way or another, all these stories stressed the need for women to define themselves in terms of active Christianity. Whitney also wrote articles on cooking, the Bible, and women's role, and published several collections of short stories. *(See also: Women Writers)*

—Shirley Marchalonis

Further Reading

Dobson, Joanne. "The Hidden Hand: Subversion of Cultural Ideology in Three Mid-Century American Women's Novels" *American Quarterly* 38 (Summer 1986): 223-42.

Marchalonis, Shirley. "Leaving the Jargons: Adeline D. T. Whitney and the Sphere of God and Women" *Women's Studies* 19 (1991): 309-25.

Stowe, Harriet Beecher. "Mrs. A. D. T. Whitney." In *Our Famous Women*, pp. 652-90. Hartford, CT: A. D. Worthington, 1884.

✎ Willard, Emma Hart (1787–1870)

Emma Hart Willard was the nineteenth century's leading advocate of female education, the author of widely read textbooks, and the founder of one of the earliest schools of higher education for girls in the United States. As a young educator, Willard worked tirelessly to gain educational opportunities for women. Many of her students went on to become teachers throughout the country, and her program of study was widely copied.

Born in Berlin, Connecticut, she learned the lessons of farm life, and her father encouraged the pursuit of intellectual interests. In 1800, she taught herself geometry, a subject then believed to be beyond the capacity of women, and went on to study at the local academy. At the age of seventeen, she began her career in teaching and continued her education. In 1807, she accepted the position of director of a female academy in Middlebury, where she met and married Dr. John Willard. When financial problems hit her husband in 1814, Willard opened a boarding school for girls, Middlebury Female Seminary. Although she established the school as a business venture, she soon "formed the design of effecting an important change in education by the introduction of a grade of schools for women higher than any heretofore known."

Recognizing that women could master the subjects long reserved for men's colleges, Willard advocated state aid for girls' schools, an idea elaborated in her *Plan for Improving Female Education*. Several students from New York State encouraged her to try to gain support there, and in 1819, Willard moved her school to Waterford, New York. She sent the governor a plan titled *An Address to the Public: Particu-*

Figure 65. Emma Hart Willard
Founder of Troy Female Seminary in New York, Emma Hart Willard was a renowned textbook author and tireless advocate of female education in the early nineteenth century. Used by permission of Corbis-Bettmann.

larly to the Members of the Legislature of New York, Proposing a Plan for Improving Female Education. Willard and her husband lobbied the legislature, which was receptive to the plan but failed to provide funds. She published the plan, and it gained widespread acceptance, including the support of Thomas Jefferson.

In 1821, the Common Council of Troy, New York, voted to raise $4,000 for Willard to establish a school in that community. In September, Troy Female Seminary opened. The curriculum was rigorous, as Willard established a serious course of study. The success of the school enabled her to add classes in mathematics and science, courses offered at no other female school. By 1831, the school enrolled more than one hundred boarding students and two hundred day students. Willard managed the school and taught many of the classes while training hundreds of teachers who spread her ideals of education across the nation. Along with her highly effective teaching, Willard wrote successful textbooks.

Having made the seminary an educational and financial success, Willard turned over its direction to her son and daughter-in-law in 1838. She traveled abroad and retired to Connecticut, where she continued to promote female education. In 1844, she returned to Troy and devoted the remainder of her life to that cause. *(See also: Education; Female Academies; Teaching; Troy Female Seminary)*

—Robert G. Waite

Further Reading

Goodsell, Willystine, ed. *Pioneers of Women's Education in the United States.* New York: AMS, 1970.

Lord, John. *The Life of Emma Willard.* New York: Appleton, 1873.

Lutz, Alma. *Emma Willard: Daughter of Democracy.* Boston: Houghton Mifflin, 1929.

ॐ Willard, Frances E. (1839–1898)

Frances E. Willard was president of the Woman's Christian Temperance Union (WCTU) and a leading advocate of social reform in Victorian America. Raised in Wisconsin by two former Oberlin College students in a staunch Methodist environment, Willard absorbed the moral fervor and egalitarianism present in the household. This led her to see women as valid participants in public life with a responsibility to improve American society. Through the WCTU and its "do everything" policy, Willard advocated a wide range of reforms: spousal equality in marriage, woman suffrage, dress reform, social purity, age-of-consent laws, kindergartens, and kitchen gardens. With her demands always couched in the rhetoric of the nineteenth-century concept of true womanhood, she reached a broad spectrum of American and (later) British women. "Home protection" was her rallying cry as she spoke of homes broken by alcohol and tobacco use.

A powerful speaker, Willard was a favorite on the lecture circuit—her reform pulpit. On many issues, Willard was more progressive than her fellow WCTU members. Her acceptance of Fabian socialism and her resulting repudiation of prohibition exceeded WCTU temperance policy. By 1896, Willard had reversed the accepted notion that drink caused poverty. Her solution for drunkenness became not prohibition but economic improvement.

Prior to her reform career, Willard taught in one-room Illinois schoolhouses and at female academies in Pittsburgh; Evanston, Illinois; and Lima, New York. She presided over the Evanston College for Ladies from its inception as a Methodist woman's college in 1870 until Northwestern University absorbed it in 1873. After one year as a dean of women, Willard resigned and devoted her energy to reform.

Although she did not join the WCTU until after the Woman's Crusade of 1873-74, Willard became a leader from the start, first holding the presidency of the Chicago WCTU from 1874 to 1877, then serving concurrently as the first corresponding secretary of the national WCTU, president of the Illinois Union, and head of the national publication committee. Willard's efforts were rewarded with her election as president of the national WCTU in 1879, a position she held until her death in 1898.

As one of the foremost women of the late nineteenth century, Willard united the divergent strains of Victorian reform, setting the stage for women's involvement in the progressive reforms of the twentieth century that culminated in woman suffrage and prohibition. *(See also: Cult of True Womanhood; Public Speakers: Nineteenth Century; Woman's Christian Temperance Union)*

—**Anita M. Weber**

Further Reading

Bordin, Ruth. *Frances Willard: A Biography.* Chapel Hill: University of North Carolina Press, 1986.

Earhart, Mary. *Frances Willard: From Prayers to Politics.* Chicago: University of Chicago Press, 1944.

Slagell, Amy Rose. "A Good Woman Speaking Well: The Oratory of Frances E. Willard." Ph.D. diss., University of Wisconsin—Madison, 1992.

Willard, Frances E. *Glimpses of Fifty Years: The Autobiography of an American Woman.* Chicago: WCTU Publishing, 1889.

ॐ Witherspoon, Frances M. (1887–1973)

Mississippian, Bryn Mawr graduate, feminist, peace and civil liberties proponent, Frances M. Witherspoon was also a talented writer. In 1909, as a new college graduate, she engaged in social work and was a field-worker for the Pennsylvania Woman Suffrage Party. Witherspoon moved to New York City in 1910 with her classmate and lifelong companion Tracy Mygatt; together, they established a child care center for working mothers and launched a series of "church raids" to open church facilities to unemployed and homeless workers.

In 1914 and 1915, Witherspoon and Mygatt campaigned vigorously for the vote under the aegis of the Socialist Party's Women's Suffrage Committee. Absolute pacifists by conviction, they fought preparedness, providing executive leadership in several peace groups. They joined the New York City branch of the Woman's Peace Party in 1915, serving as editors in 1917 for its antiwar journal *Four Lights.* As founder of the New York Bureau of Legal Advice (1917–1920), the first organization to offer free legal aid to conscientious objectors and free-speech victims during World War I, Witherspoon was a key person in the early civil liberties movement in the United States.

After the war, Witherspoon helped to establish the War Resisters League and remained active in this group until the 1960s. She held membership in the Fellowship of Reconciliation, the American Civil Liberties Union, the Women's International League for Peace and Freedom, and the National Committee for a Sane Nuclear Policy (SANE). At eighty-two, Witherspoon organized a protest against the Vietnam War among Bryn Mawr alumnae: In 1968, a full-page antiwar statement appeared in the *New York Times* and the *Philadelphia Evening Bulletin* signed by more than one thousand Bryn Mawr alumnae.

Witherspoon's life and career reflect characteristics common to many women of her race, class, educational attainment, and era. She believed that women and men of "good will" could help to create an equitable, socially just, warless world, and dedicated herself to this ideal. Broad-visioned and optimistic, Witherspoon nevertheless appreciated the immensity of the task she had set herself. An understanding of the interconnections between militarism, sexism, racism, and economic inequalities under capitalism informed all her efforts, as was the case for other feminist peace activists with whom Witherspoon associated, such as Crystal Eastman, Jessie Wallace Hughan, and Emily Greene Balch. Identifying the values and commitments of women such as Witherspoon helps bring into clearer focus an important chapter in the history of feminism that has, to date, been little studied. *(See also: Civil Liberties Movement During World War I; Pacifism and the Peace Movement; Suffrage)*

—Frances H. Early

Further Reading

Early, Frances H. *A World without War: How U.S. Feminists and Pacifists Resisted World War I.* Syracuse, NY: Syracuse University Press, 1997.

Manahan, Nancy. "Future Old Maids and Pacifist Agitators: The Story of Tracy Mygatt and Frances Witherspoon," *Women's Studies Quarterly* 10 (Spring 1982): 10-13.

The Papers of Tracy D. Mygatt and Frances Witherspoon. Swarthmore College Peace Collection. Swarthmore, PA.

"The Reminiscences of Frances Witherspoon and Tracy D. Mygatt." Oral History Research Office. New York: Columbia University, 1966.

❧ Wolff, Sister Mary Madeleva
(1887–1964)

Sister Mary Madeleva Wolff, Sister of the Holy Cross, poet, and president of St. Mary's College, Notre Dame, Indiana, was born Mary Evaline Wolff, the daughter of August Frederick and Lucy (Arntz) Wolff, in Cumberland, Wisconsin. She attended public elementary and high schools and spent one year at the University of Wisconsin. In 1906, she transferred to St. Mary's College, Notre Dame, where she devoted herself to the study of English literature.

She entered the Sisters of the Holy Cross in 1908 and was given the name Mary Madeleva. After graduation in 1909, she taught English and philosophy at St. Mary's. In 1918, she received her master's degree from the University of Notre Dame, and from 1919 to 1922, she was principal of Sacred Heart Academy in Ogden, Utah. In 1922, she was sent for doctoral studies to the University of California, Berkeley. She was the first nun to earn a Ph.D. from Berkeley, and her dissertation, "Pearl: A Study in Spiritual Dryness," was published in 1925. From 1925 to 1933, she was dean and president of Mount Mary-of-the-Wasatch College in Salt Lake City, Utah. In 1933, she was granted a year's sabbatical to study women's colleges in Europe, with some time set aside for English studies at Oxford. There, she became acquainted with literary figures such as Edith Wharton, William Butler Yeats, Wilfred Meynell, Seamus MacManus, and Hilaire Belloc. She also had the opportunity to visit the Holy Land. After her return, she was appointed president of St. Mary's College, Notre Dame, a position she held until 1961.

Sister Madeleva was one of America's best-known religious poets of the twentieth century. Her verse and literary articles appeared in *The Saturday Review, The American Mercury,* and the *New York Times.* Her first book of poems, *Knights Errant, and Other Poems,* was published in 1923 and reflected her own and American Catholicism's general preoccupation with the Middle Ages. Other works of poetry reveal her Franciscan love of nature and her desire to penetrate the mysteries of God through his creation. Her prose works were numerous, covering topics such as nineteenth-century poetry, Catholic literary figures, and poetic composition.

As president of St. Mary's College, Sister Madeleva significantly advanced the cause of education for Catholic women. In addition to a vigorous program of institutional expansion, Sister Madeleva established the first graduate school of sacred doctrine for women in 1943. She also welcomed well-known contemporary artists to share their talents on campus. Sister Madeleva's paper titled "The Education of Sister Lucy," delivered at the annual meeting of the National Catholic Education Association in 1949, stimulated the creation of the "sister formation" movement, a program to upgrade the standards of education for nuns. She received seven honorary degrees and a number of awards for her poetry. She resigned the presidency of St. Mary's in 1961 and died in Boston in 1964. *(See also: Christianity; Higher Education; Religion; Women Writers)*

—Steven M. Avella

Further Reading

Klein, Mary E. "Sister M. Madeleva Wolff, C.S.C., St. Mary's College, Notre Dame, Indiana: A Study of Presidential Leadership, 1934–1961." Ph.D. diss., Kent State University, 1983.

Madeleva, Sister M., C.S.C. *American Twelfth Night and Other Poems.* New York: Macmillan, 1955.

———. *The Four Last Things.* New York: Macmillan, 1959.

———. *My First Seventy Years.* New York: Macmillan, 1959.

Mandell, Gail. *Madeleva: One Woman's Life.* Ramsey, NJ: Paulist Press, 1994.

Werner, Sister Maria Assunta. *Madeleva.* Notre Dame: Sisters of the Holy Cross, 1994.

❧ Woman Question

Woman question was the term that referred to the debate over the position of women in the late nineteenth and early twentieth centuries among the socialist and Marxist theorists as well as the suffragists and antisuffragists. The woman question encompassed all the issues within the woman movement that challenged the gender system—woman suffrage, legal reform of the laws relating to married women's property rights, increased educational and employment possibilities, women's sexuality and control over their reproductive capacity, and women's social and political freedoms. It was a useful term to focus the political and theoretical discussions of the New Woman, regarding woman's role and true nature among both socialists and avowed feminists. *(See also: New Woman; Socialism)*

—**Angela M. Howard**

Further Reading

Bebel, August. *Woman under Socialism.* Translated by Daniel DeLeon. New York: Schocken, 1971. [Original title, *Woman and Socialism,* translated by Meta L. Stern, 1910]

Shulman, Alix Kates, ed. *Red Emma Speaks: Selected Writings and Speeches by Emma Goldman.* New York: Vintage, 1972.

"The Woman Question," *North American Review* 272 (September 1987): 25-92.

The Woman Question: Selections from the Writings of Karl Marx, Frederick Engels, V. I. Lenin, and J. V. Stalin. New York: International Publishers, 1951.

ᔍ Woman's Christian Temperance Union (WCTU) (1874–)

The Woman's Christian Temperance Union (WCTU) began in Cleveland, Ohio, in November 1874. Over one hundred women, many of whom had participated in the women's temperance crusade of 1873-74, gathered to create a permanent national temperance organization whose leadership and membership would be exclusively women. Although the WCTU focused primarily on the issue of temperance through moral suasion and education during its first five years under the presidency of Annie Wittenmyer (1874–1879), its activities broadened to include many women's rights reforms during the presidency of its best-known leader, Frances E. Willard (1879–1898).

With the motto "Do Everything," Willard encouraged her membership, composed mainly of evangelical Protestants, to engage in a variety of reforms ranging from temperance education in public and Sunday schools to agitation for police matrons in city prisons. Her slogan "Home Protection" was the rallying cry for the WCTU's espousal of woman suffrage so that women could help vote in prohibition. In its first two decades, the WCTU developed sophisticated political organizing and lobbying techniques at local, state, and national levels, which it has continued to employ in its century-long struggle for abstinence. During the 1880s, it became an international organization working for prohibition and women's rights in many areas of the world. It was also the first large national organization to bring together southern and northern women after the Civil War.

With Willard's death in 1898, Lillian M. N. Stevens, a trusted Willard lieutenant, became president (1898–1914). Stevens knit together factions within the organization split over financial problems and disagreements about the extent to which the organization should operate in the political sphere. During Stevens's tenure, the WCTU increasingly focused on the struggle for national prohibition, cooperating with other temperance organizations such as the Anti-Saloon League.

Following the passage of the Eighteenth (Prohibition) Amendment in 1919, the WCTU, guided by its fourth president, Anna Gordon (president 1914–1925), turned its attention to child welfare, Americanization of immigrants, and "social purity." As support for repeal of the Prohibition Amendment grew during the late 1920s and early 1930s, the WCTU fought to retain national prohibition. With the repeal of the Eighteenth Amendment (1933), the WCTU lost some of its prestige and power. Yet it has continued to work for "education for total abstinence" through a variety of means, including work with children and youth, production of both printed and filmed materials, and efforts to influence U.S. political processes. *(See also: Prohibition and the Volstead Act; Temperance Movement; Willard, Frances E.)*

—**Carolyn DeSwarte Gifford**

Further Reading

Bordin, Ruth. *Woman and Temperance: The Quest for Power and Liberty, 1873–1900.* Philadelphia: Temple University Press, 1981.

Gifford, Carolyn DeSwarte. "For God and Home and Native Land: The W.C.T.U.'s Image of Woman in the Late Nineteenth Century." In *Women in New Worlds.* Vol. 1, edited by H. Thomas and R. S. Keller, 310-27. Nashville: Abingdon, 1981.

———. "Home Protection: The W.C.T.U.'s Conversion to Woman Suffrage." In *Gender, Ideology, and Action: Historical Perspectives on Women's Public Lives,* edited by Janet Sharistanian, 95-120. Westport, CT: Greenwood, 1986.

Jimerson, Randall et al., eds. "Description of the Microfilm Series: Series III, The W.C.T.U., 1853–1939." In *Guide to the Microfilm Edition of Temperance and Prohibition Papers,* pp. 55-100. Ann Arbor: University of Michigan Press, 1977.

Tyler, Helen E. *Where Prayer and Purpose Meet: The WCTU Story.* Evanston, IL: Signal, 1949.

Tyrrell, Ian. *Woman's World/Woman's Empire: The Woman's Christian Temperance Union in International Perspective, 1880–1930.* Chapel Hill: University of North Carolina Press, 1991.

ᔍ Woman's Commonwealth (The Sanctified Sisters, The True Church Colony) (1867?–1983)

The Woman's Commonwealth (The Sanctified Sisters, The True Church Colony) of Belton, Texas, was a Christian socialist, celibate, and feminist community led by Martha White McWhirter. The commonwealth was a separatist community through which members voiced feminist concern about their religious, economic, social, and sexual roles. The original women first sought only religious independence, but they found that signs of feminine autonomy threatened male relatives and neighbors, who reacted with criticism and violence. The Sisters refused to be intimidated and became more insistent about their rights, discovering the connection between religious freedom and their feminist demands.

In 1867, women from prominent families of Belton had a religious experience of "sanctification," which led them to question the religious leadership of their ministers. These women were also led to question their roles as wives. They claimed they were willing to remain in their homes, but that as perfected and sanctified believers, they could no longer engage in sexual relations with their husbands. By 1879, all the women refused financial support from male relatives as a sign of independence and commitment to their shared principles. A combination of hard work, financial acumen, inherited property, and communal practices soon made them very successful.

Pressure from estranged husbands and outraged townspeople forced the women to make a firmer show of their beliefs. Although religious concerns were still an important focus, a shift toward more communal and socialist concerns occurred. In 1885, the women lived in one household and opened an adjoining house as the Central Hotel. The hotel became the center of the community. It was run communally; each woman worked four hours a day, and all jobs were rotated every month. The women also kept up with feminist, socialist, and other progressive causes of the day.

In 1898, the community moved to Washington, D.C. Four years later, the members drew up a constitution, incorporated themselves, and became known as the Woman's Commonwealth. Soon after the death in 1904 of charismatic leader Martha McWhirter, there were changes in the community. Some women remained in Washington; others moved to semiretirement on the community farm in the Maryland suburbs.

The group had attracted many applications during the Washington years, and the women were careful to select only compatible new members. There were few new applications after 1910. The last surviving member of the community, Martha McWhirter Scheble, died in 1983. With her death, the Woman's Commonwealth Association was dissolved, and community property was deeded to the Washington City Orphan Asylum. *(See also: Christianity; Religion; Utopian Communities)*

—**Wendy E. Chmielewski**

Further Reading

Chmielewski, Wendy E. "Heaven on Earth: The Woman's Commonwealth, 1867–1983." In *Women in Spiritual and Communitarian Societies in the United States,* edited by Wendy E. Chmielewski, Louis J. Kern, and Marlyn Klee-Hartzell, 52-67. Syracuse, NY: Syracuse University Press, 1993.

Constitution and By-Laws of the Woman's Commonwealth of Washington, D.C. Washington, DC: Crane, n.d.

Garrison, George Pierce. "A Woman's Community in Texas," *Charities Review* 3 (November 1893): 26-46.

Kitch, Sally. *This Strange Society of Women: Reading the Letters and Lives of the Woman's Commonwealth.* Columbus: Ohio State University Press, 1993.

❧ Woman's Film

The *woman's film,* also known as the *women's film* or the *women's picture,* was a Hollywood phenomenon particularly during the "classical" period, the 1930s and 1940s. Although the term may be used in connection with any film, serious or comic, that focuses on women protagonists, it is more often applied to tragic or melodramatic films that end unhappily. Thus, critics, often male, have derided these films as "the weepies" and dismissed them as inconsequential, ignoring that most of Hollywood's finest directors, writers, and actors have at one time or another been associated with them. At its worst, the woman's film is self-conscious bathos, but at its best, it is vivid and enthralling, a true artistic collaboration between writer, director, and female star(s).

Although some commentators, such as Charles Higham and Joel Greenberg, associate the woman's film primarily with the 1940s, Molly Haskell and others also include the 1930s and part of the 1950s, as a time when the studios produced woman's films as regularly as westerns, musicals, or other genres. Like comparable male genres—the war film or the western—the woman's film presents a focused worldview that both aggrandizes and sentimentalizes its protagonists and their actions. In so doing, it reaches out, inviting its audiences to respond emotionally to its protagonist(s). If film is primarily an emotional experience, then these kinds of films may well be the apotheosis of its artfulness.

There are many ways to define the woman's film. Jeanine Basinger calls it "a movie that places at the center of its universe a female who is trying to deal with the emotional, social, and psychological problems that are specifically connected to the fact that she is a woman" (20). Molly Haskell identifies four themes—sacrifice, affliction, choice, and competition—that often appear in the woman's film, while Andrea Walsh categorizes by narrative type and affective focus: maternal dramas, "working girl" films, films of suspicion and distrust, and "woman in suffering" films. Woman's films can also be identified by their directors: George Cukor, Max Ophuls, Douglas Sirk, Ernst Lubitsch, John Stahl, Edmund Goulding, and (the early) William Wyler and George Stevens. But it was the stars who made the woman's films extraordinary: Bette Davis, Joan Crawford, Katharine Hepburn, Ingrid Bergman, Rosalind Russell, Olivia de Havilland, Ginger Rogers, Greta Garbo, Barbara Stanwyck, Greer Garson, and others. Without them, the woman's film would never have achieved the level of popularity and distinction that it did. Indelibly imprinted on generations of audiences are the performances of Garbo in *Camille* (1936), Stanwyck in *Stella Dallas* (1937), Davis in *Dark Victory* (1939), Hepburn in *Christopher Strong* (1933), Bergman in *Gaslight* (1944), Crawford in *A Woman's Face* (1941), Garson in *Mrs. Miniver* (1942), Rogers in *Kitty Foyle* (1940), or Russell in *His Girl Friday* (1941).

By the 1950s the woman's film was beginning to fade from the Hollywood scene. Several factors are probably responsible: the tendency of *film noir* to take a male perspective and to feature women as evil temptresses (*femme noir*) or ineffectual background figures, the rise of the television soap opera as an even more accessible emotional medium, the influence of neorealism with its avoidance of romance as a suitable narrative subject, the tendency of 1950s films to become more sexually explicit, which in practice meant the surfacing of what Haskell calls "breast fetishism." Most of the stars of the woman's film who had been active in the 1940s—Davis, Crawford, Garson, Russell—were on the shelf by the mid-1950s; and their replacements—Marilyn Monroe, Doris Day, Debbie Reynolds, the young Audrey Hepburn—could not demand the same kinds of concessions from studio bosses, producers, and directors who were themselves coping with the dying of the studio system. In effect, the majority of 1950s and 1960s films—whether epic or art—were male oriented and dominated. Not until the 1970s would a new crop of strong female actors and sympathetic directors surface to make a new woman's film possible. *(See also: Arzner, Dorothy; Blaché, Alice Guy; Davis, Bette; Hepburn, Katharine; Lupino, Ida; Monroe, Marilyn; Movie Stars; Popular Culture; Weber, Lois)*

—**Frances M. Kavenik**

Further Reading

Basinger, Jeanine. *A Woman's View: How Hollywood Spoke to Women, 1930–1960.* New York: Knopf, 1993.

Gledhill, Christine, ed. *Home Is Where the Heart Is: Studies in Melodrama and the Woman's Film.* London: British Film Institute, 1987.

Haskell, Molly. "The Woman's Film." In *From Reverence to Rape: The Treatment of Women in the Movies,* 2d ed. 1974. Reprint, pp. 153-88. Chicago: University of Chicago Press, 1987.

Higham, Charles, and Joel Greenberg. "Women's Pictures." In *Hollywood in the Forties,* pp. 139-54. New York: A. S. Barnes, 1968.

Todd, Janet, ed. *Women and Film.* New York: Holmes & Meier, 1988.

Walsh, Andrea S. *Women's Film and Female Experience: 1940–1950.* New York: Praeger, 1984.

⋙ Woman's Hospital of Philadelphia

The Woman's Hospital of Philadelphia (today, Hospital of the Medical College of Philadelphia), established in 1861, was one of the many hospitals for women and children that came out of the nineteenth-century women's medical movement. The specific impetus for founding this institution was the ostracizing of Woman's Medical College by the board of censors of the Philadelphia Medical Society; this action barred Woman's Medical College students from attending public teaching clinics and its graduates from joining local medical societies. Dr. Ann Preston, a graduate of the college and a professor there, became the organizing force behind the Woman's Hospital, which was to provide a retreat for women "without violence to their sensibilities" and offer important bedside training to students at Woman's Medical College.

Despite internal dissension over this ambitious venture, Dr. Preston moved forward quickly by establishing a board of lady managers with the help of prominent Quaker leader Lucretia Mott. Much of the initial fund-raising for the hospi-

tal was done by Dr. Preston, who went door to door among her network in the Quaker community. In 1860, the organizing committee sponsored postgraduate training for Dr. Emeline Horton Cleveland at the School of Obstetrics connected with the Maternité of Paris to hone her professional skills and increase her knowledge of hospital management.

After her return to Philadelphia in 1862, Dr. Cleveland took over as chief resident at the Woman's Hospital. During the seven years she held this important position, she inaugurated courses in nurses' training and initiated one of the first programs in bedside techniques for laywomen—forerunners of nurses' aides. Her success in performing some of the first ovarian tumor removals done by a woman surgeon enhanced her reputation and that of the entire staff among the male medical establishment. This helped to lower the barriers against the acceptance of women physicians throughout Pennsylvania. *(See also: Mott, Lucretia Coffin; Nursing; Physicians; Preston, Ann; Society of Friends; Woman's Medical College of Pennsylvania)*

—**Cynthia Jeffress Little**

Further Reading

Abram, Ruth J. *"Send Us a Lady Physician": Women Doctors in America, 1835–1920.* New York: Norton, 1985.

⋙ Woman's Journal (1870–1917)

Woman's Journal, a weekly suffragist newspaper, was founded and edited by Lucy Stone and Henry Blackwell and served as an official publication of the American Woman Suffrage Association until 1890, when it served the National American Woman Suffrage Association. Soon after its inception, *Woman's Journal* merged with the *Agitator,* published in Chicago. *Woman's Journal* was "devoted to the interests of Woman—to her educational, industrial, legal and political Equality, and especially to her right of Suffrage." As a political arm of suffrage associations, *Woman's Journal* reprinted meeting and convention addresses and notes, reported on national and international political and social news, and published columns and editorials concerning suffrage issues, as well as poems, stories, and book reviews. Letters to the editor often provoked prolonged, serious debates on education, voting rights, and social equality.

Although contributors included both inexperienced and experienced writers, the first assistant editors were Julia Ward Howe, W. L. Garrison, and T. W. Higginson, prominent members of the New England Suffrage Association. By 1872, there was little money to pay editors, and so the bulk of the editorial work was done by Lucy Stone and Henry Blackwell; after Stone's death in 1893, her daughter Alice continued the journal. In 1917, *Woman's Journal* merged with *Woman Citizen;* from 1927 to 1931, until it ceased publication, it was again titled *Woman's Journal. (See also: American Woman Suffrage Association; Blackwell, Alice*

Stone; National American Woman Suffrage Association; Stone, Lucy)

—Karen C. Knowles
Adapted for the second edition by Andrea Moore Kerr.

Further Reading
Kerr, Andrea Moore. *Lucy Stone: Speaking Out for Equality.* New Brunswick, NJ: Rutgers University Press, 1992.
Steiner, Linda Claire. "The Women's Suffrage Press, 1850–1900." Ph.D. diss., University of Illinois, 1979.
Woman's Journal. Vols. 1–48. January 8, 1870–May 26, 1917.

Woman's Medical College of Pennsylvania

The Woman's Medical College of Pennsylvania (now Medical College of Pennsylvania) in Philadelphia opened its doors in 1850 to forty women students taught by six male faculty members. Among the members of the first graduating class in 1851 was Ann Preston, who as a teacher, administrator, and physician became a driving force behind the college's many successes during its formative years. Support for this novel experiment in women's education came from Philadelphia's Quaker community, specifically from two of its members, Dr. Joseph Longshore, who obtained the school's charter, and William Mullen, who paid the rent on the classrooms.

This institution blazed many trails in the nineteenth century as a professionally staffed facility for women's medical training. It was the first of the five "regular" medical schools for women, the only one to endure into the twentieth century as a separate entity, and the last of the original five to become coeducational. Early on, it was one of the few schools to offer women of every race, creed, and national origin an opportunity to receive a quality medical education. Even though the college started with an all-male faculty, by 1876, there were enough trained women to compose a faculty of nine professors teaching in all fields of the medical curriculum. Standards were rigorous and comparable to those of the best male medical schools. Long before practical training for medical students had become popular, Woman's Medical College lengthened its program from three to four years so that students would receive ample clinical experience. Toward this goal, and because the male medical establishment had barred its students from attending the regular teaching clinics, the college opened its own dispensary in 1858 and a hospital in 1861, which offered students needed training and patients a rare opportunity to be attended by women physicians. In 1876, the Woman's Medical College dramatically demonstrated its institutional strength by inaugurating the first building ever dedicated to women's medical education.

For over one hundred years, Woman's Medical College has educated generations of women physicians who have used their skills in private practices, as missionary doctors here and abroad, as researchers and teachers, and as physicians in public and private institutions such as orphanages and hospitals. *(See also: Physicians; Preston, Ann; Society of Friends; Woman's Hospital of Philadelphia)*

—Cynthia Jeffress Little

Further Reading
Abram, Ruth J. *"Send Us a Lady Physician": Women Doctors in America, 1835–1920.* New York: Norton, 1985.

Woman's Peace Party (WPP)

The Woman's Peace Party (WPP), the roots of which lay within the International Woman Suffrage Alliance (IWSA), was the first major all-female U.S. peace organization before 1919. Its founding was inspired by two European suffragists, Emmeline Pethick-Lawrence of Great Britain and Rosika Schwimmer of Hungary, who appealed to their U.S. counterparts for aid in peace efforts after World War I began in Europe in August 1914. Pethick-Lawrence's visit to a suffrage meeting in New York City in November 1914 resulted in the creation of the first WPP organization, led by militant suffragists Madeline Doty and Crystal Eastman. Pethick-Lawrence's later visit to Chicago convinced the older and more moderate suffragist and settlement house pioneer Jane Addams to form a nationwide WPP in January 1915. Branches were then organized in many areas of the nation.

From its earliest inception, the WPP stressed the importance of woman suffrage and equal participation in government as a means for curtailing war. Seeing World War I as a failure on the part of male leadership, the WPP stressed the intellectual and moral sentiments developed by "the mother half of humanity" and expressed disillusionment with "the man-run world." Besides working to organize U.S. women against war in general, the WPP also urged President Woodrow Wilson to mediate an end to the European conflict. The women met with IWSA members at The Hague in April 1915, followed by visits throughout Europe with leaders of both neutral and belligerent nations. They also carried on relief work and protested U.S. troops and imperialism in Central America, the Caribbean, and the Philippines.

Once the United States declared war in 1917, however, the WPP ceased its criticism of the government's policy. Although retaining its pacifist rhetoric, the WPP took the position that World War I was "the war to end all wars" and turned its concentration toward postwar plans. In 1919, at an international women's conference held in Zurich, the WPP joined its European sister organizations in founding the Women's International League for Peace and Freedom (WILPF), the name it has retained to this day. *(See also: Addams, Jane; Pacifism and the Peace Movement; Women's International League for Peace and Freedom, Women's Peace Union)*

—Harriet Hyman Alonso

Further Reading

Addams, Jane, Emily G. Balch, and Alice Hamilton. *Women at The Hague: The International Congress of Women and Its Results.* New York: Macmillan, 1915. Reprint, New York: Garland, 1972.

Alonso, Harriet Hyman. *Peace as a Women's Issue: A History of the U.S. Movement for World Peace and Women's Rights.* Syracuse: Syracuse University Press, 1993.

Degen, Marie Louise. *The History of the Woman's Peace Party.* Baltimore: Johns Hopkins University Press, 1939. Reprint, New York: Garland, 1972.

Wiltsher, Ann. *Most Dangerous Women: Feminist Peace Campaigners of the Great War.* Boston: Pandora, 1985.

Woman's Peace Party and Women's International League for Peace and Freedom Papers. Swarthmore College Peace Collection. Swarthmore, PA.

Women's International League for Peace and Freedom Papers. Norlin Library. University of Colorado, Boulder.

∾ Woman's Rights Conventions

The first formal woman's rights convention in the United States occurred in Seneca Falls, New York, in 1848, and established the agenda of woman's rights issues, including suffrage. Throughout the antebellum period, state suffrage associations held subsequent conventions to rally support for state constitutional amendments for woman suffrage and other woman's rights issues. These local conventions produced the nationally known leaders of the nineteenth-century woman's rights movement, such as Lucy Stone, Elizabeth Cady Stanton, Susan B. Anthony, and Sojourner Truth. These gatherings also generated the grassroots organizations that provided the members and the means for educating public opinion regarding women's issues.

The last of these conventions, held in 1866, established the ill-fated American Equal Rights Association to pursue suffrage for both women and blacks through amendments to state constitutions. The failure of the association's all-out effort to win passage of two separate suffrage bills in the Kansas campaign of 1867 impelled the formation of an organization focused solely on woman suffrage. An inability to agree on the best strategy to achieve woman suffrage resulted in the establishment of the National Woman Suffrage Association and the American Woman Suffrage Association in 1869. *(See also: American Woman Suffrage Association; Equal Rights Association; National Woman Suffrage Association; Seneca Falls Convention; Suffrage; Women's Rights Movements: Nineteenth and Twentieth Centuries)*

—**Angela M. Howard**

Further Reading

Chafe, William H. *The Paradox of Change: American Women in the 20th Century.* New York: Oxford University Press, 1992.

Clinton, Catherine. *The Other Civil War: American Women in the Nineteenth Century.* New York: Hill & Wang, 1984.

Cook, Rebecca J., ed. *Human Rights of Women: National and International Perspectives.* Philadelphia: University of Pennsylvania Press, 1994.

Langley, Winston E., and Vivian C. Fox, eds. *Women's Rights in America: A Documentary History.* Westport, CT: Greenwood, 1994.

Schneider, Dorothy, and Carl J. Schneider. *American Women in the Progressive Era, 1900–1920.* New York: Doubleday, 1994.

Sigerman, Harriet. *Laborers for Liberty: American Women 1865–1890.* New York: Oxford University Press, 1994.

Simon, Rita J., and Gloria Danziger. *Women's Movements in America: Their Successes, Disappointments and Aspirations.* Westport, CT: Greenwood, 1991.

West, Guida, and Rhonda L. Blumberg, eds. *Women and Social Protest.* New York: Oxford University Press, 1990.

∾ "Women Adrift"

"Women adrift" was the label middle-class social investigators of the early twentieth century gave to urban wage-earning women who lived apart from family, relatives, and employers. Most of these women were boarders and lodgers in the cities. They included native-born white and black women who migrated from America's farms, towns, and cities and foreign-born women who came primarily from Europe and Canada. While most of these women were young and single, the group included older women and separated, divorced, and widowed women. By all accounts, the vast majority worked in predominantly female service, manufacturing, clerical, and sales jobs. In 1900, the women adrift comprised roughly one-fifth of the urban, non-servant female labor force.

The women adrift attracted public notice in the late nineteenth and early twentieth centuries because reformers feared that low-income women without the moral and economic protection of family would drift into starvation or prostitution. In fact, the women adrift did face obstacles. Most important, employers often paid them the low wages of dependent daughters and wives. In addition, these women found that neighbors and acquaintances suspected them of immoral behavior, associating their independence from family with prostitution.

Many women adrift found substitutes for family support. Some lived as though they were daughters in the homes where they boarded or lodged. Others came to depend on their peers, pooling resources for room and board and depending on higher-paid men for entertainment. Especially in the urban furnished-room districts, areas where lodgers concentrated, early twentieth-century observers noticed elaborate peer subcultures among women adrift. *(See also: Demography; Friendships; Industrial Revolution; Migration and Frontier Women; Progressive Era; Prostitution; Urbanization; Women's Work: Nineteenth Century)*

—**Joanne J. Meyerowitz**

Further Reading

Meyerowitz, Joanne J. *Women Adrift: Independent Wage Earners in Chicago, 1880–1930.* Chicago: University of Chicago Press, 1988.

Neill, Charles P. *Wage-Earning Women in Stores and Factories.* Vol. 5, *Report on Condition of Woman and Child Wage-Earners in the United States.* Washington, DC: Government Printing Office, 1910.

～ Women in the Modern World, Their Education and Their Dilemmas

Published in 1953 by Columbia-Barnard sociologist Mirra Komarovsky, *Women in the Modern World, Their Education and Their Dilemmas* was both a sociological study of contemporary college-educated females and an attack on the new antifeminism of the post-World War II era. Questioning the premises of the neo-Freudians who supported subservient roles for women, Komarovsky pointed out that evidence did not support the idea of inborn mental differences between the sexes, that "penis envy" had social not biological roots, and that the "active" woman was not a neurotic rebelling against her deepest feminine self. Komarovsky also asserted that women who wanted careers shared the same mixture of motives as modern men and did not suffer from personality disorders. The reasons that society viewed such women so harshly and seemed unable to accept their lives were rooted, according to Komarovsky, in unabsorbed social, technological, and moral changes. In short, while social realities and to some extent even sex roles had changed, attitudes toward sex roles remained traditional, trapping women and men in anachronistic, unfulfilling situations.

Komarovsky's survey-interview data provide a good picture of those women Betty Friedan would later describe as victims of the "feminine mystique." Komarovsky found that the majority of college women interviewed believed it was natural for women to have no personal ambitions and to live through their husbands' successes, that motherhood could be totally satisfying and became stultifying only if one lacked imagination or efficiency, that women who worked could not be good mothers, that the ideal number of children was three or more, and that husbands were naturally superior in qualities demanded by the outside world but needed the constant encouragement of wives to achieve their full potential. Those college-age women who wanted to work saw themselves as combining family, marriage, and career usually by pursuing interrupted, discontinuous life patterns.

In her interviews with college-educated housewives, Komarovsky discovered women shocked by the demands of child rearing, discontented with the kinds of volunteer work available, and upset by the contrast between their home-bound lives and the lives of their professional husbands. To solve these dilemmas, Komarovsky recommended more education on family life for both men and women, greater recognition and encouragement of female talents, and marriages based on real equality. Written in the 1950s, the book did not consider the possibility—and problems—of a society where most women with children worked outside the home, nor did the book, by virtue of its subject, take into account the experiences of working-class women. But Komarovsky later explored this subject in *Blue Collar Marriage* (1964). *(See also: Freudianism; Friedan, Betty; Higher Education)*

—Barbara McGowan

Further Reading

Komarovsky, Mirra. *Blue Collar Marriage.* New York: Random House, 1964.
———. *Women in the Modern World, Their Education and Their Dilemmas.* Boston: Little, Brown, 1953.
May, Elaine Tyler. *Homeward Bound.* New York: Basic Books, 1988.
Rupp, Leila, and Verta Taylor. *Survival in the Doldrums.* New York: Oxford University Press, 1987.

～ Women of All Red Nations (WARN)

Women of All Red Nations (WARN), a coalition of American Indian women, grew out of the takeover at Wounded Knee, South Dakota, by members of the American Indian Movement (AIM) in 1973. The association was founded in Rapid City, South Dakota, and over thirty Native nations are represented in its membership. The founding conference in September 1978 delineated the key issues of the women: sterilization abuse, political prisoners, education for survival, the destruction of the family, the theft of Indian children through forced adoptions to nontribal families, and the loss of the Indian land base. Ted Means, a leader of the AIM, called the women of WARN the "backbone of the International Indian Treaty Council . . . and the Federation of National Controlled Survival Schools." WARN, however, is not an auxiliary to any male organization; its purpose is to organize for the liberation of all Native peoples. Among the leaders are Lorelei Means and Madonna Gilbert. The Indigenous Women's Network, which met in the fall of 1985 in Yelm, Washington, affirmed many of the positions taken by WARN, attesting to the continuing strength of the networks among American Indian women. *(See also: Native American Women)*

—Gretchen M. Bataille

Further Reading

Emery, Marg. "Indian Women's Groups Span a Broad Spectrum," *Indian Truth: Special Issue on Indian Women* 239 (May-June 1981): 8.
LaDuke, Winona. "Words from the Indigenous Women's Network Meeting," *Akwesasne Notes* 17 (Early Winter 1985): 8-9.
Tomkin, Merle, Carol Stern, and Margie Bowker. "Listening to Native American Women," *Heresies 13: Feminism and Ecology* 4, no. 1 (1981): 17-21.
Women of All Red Nations. Porcupine, SD: We Will Remember Group, 1978.
"Women of All Red Nations (W.A.R.N.)," *Akwesasne Notes* 10 (Winter 1978): 15.

Figure 66. Women Strike for Peace
Reacting to the impending threat of nuclear war, the group Women Strike for Peace staged a one-day walkout involving some 50,000 women across the country. These and other demonstrations influenced President John F. Kennedy to sign the Limited Test Ban Treaty in 1963. Used by permission of UPI/Corbis-Bettmann.

❧ Women Strike for Peace (WSP)

Women Strike for Peace (WSP) was founded in 1961 by Dagmar Wilson, who called together a group of women concerned about radiation fallout from above ground nuclear testing and dissatisfied with other peace organizations. WSP was nonhierarchical in structure, had no designated leaders or official membership lists, and welcomed supporters regardless of ideology. On November 1, 1961, some 50,000 women in sixty cities, alerted through a wide array of informal contacts, walked off their jobs and out of their homes in a one-day women's peace strike, the largest female peace demonstration in the century. Further activities prompted subpoenas of fourteen of the women by the House Un-American Activities Committee; WSP was charged with harboring Communists. Relying on their roles as mothers, on humor, and on a refusal to be intimidated, WSP succeeded in making the committee look both tyrannical and foolish. WSP has since been given major credit for moving President Kennedy toward signing the Limited Test Ban Treaty of 1963.

WSP continued to lobby for nuclear disarmament, built an international network of similarly oriented women, including Russians, and was active in the movement to end military involvement in the Vietnam War. The first women of WSP were largely well-educated, middle-class homemakers. They have had some success in attracting the younger and more diverse generation of women that followed them. Today, WSP maintains a national office in Washington, D.C. *(See also: Pacifism and the Peace Movement; Vietnam War)*

—**Anne O. Dzamba (Sessa)**

Further Reading

Alonso, Harriet. *Peace as a Women's Issue: A History of the U.S. Movement for World Peace and Women's Rights.* Syracuse, NY: Syracuse University Press, 1993.

Swerdlow, Amy. *Women Strike for Peace: Traditional Motherhood and Radical Politics in the 1960's.* Chicago: University of Chicago Press, 1993.

❧ Women Writers

Women writers have given their voices to English-language literature in America from its earliest beginnings. Supplementing and subverting masculine authority, they write from the privacy of home or step into the public sphere to call for reform. Their voices rise or fall at different periods of American history, but at the beginning of the twenty-first century, women are successfully mediating new and traditional identities for a rapidly changing nation.

Native American women created and memorialized many works of literature before and after the European conquest of America, but the American "canon" of accepted literary "classics" has, like its public leadership, traditionally been dominated by men of European descent. Women wrote Anglo-America's first creative literature, however, and their texts generate paradigms that continue to the present. The poetry of Anne Bradstreet (1612?–1672) of Massachusetts, first published without her knowledge in 1650, shows great historical learning but is now admired chiefly for its depictions of domestic life and family love in a threatening environment. Aphra Behn (1640–1689) of England, who visited Surinam with her family in 1663, wrote the early novel *Oroonoko* (1688) to protest the slave trade and Christian hypocrisy. Thus, women speak from the privacy of home yet also emerge to advocate fair treatment for Americans whose voices, like their own, may be repressed—as, for instance, the Puritan councils of New England silenced Anne Hutchinson (1591–1643) for preaching a personal or intuitional relationship with God.

For European Americans in the seventeenth and eighteenth centuries, the labors of settlement often eclipsed the cultivation of literature. However, settlement precipitated conflicts with Native Americans, which led to the writing of "captivity narratives." In the first and most popular of these, the remarkable *Narrative . . . of Mrs. Mary Rowlandson* (1682), a Puritan woman describes her three-month ordeal in the wilderness with an anthropologist's eye for detail but also with a heart-searching account of her abiding insecurity. Other such narratives, including that told by "the White Woman of the Genesee" Mary Jemison (1743–1833), concern women who are successfully adopted into Indian tribes and families. These private women's voices model an enormously popular genre in American literature, as women's captivity by Indians evolves into a standard plot in classic novels such as James Fennimore Cooper's *The Last of the Mohicans* and films such as John Ford's *The Searchers* (1956).

The "Founding Fathers" of the early United States set boundaries between public manhood and private womanhood, so that women's writing appears less prominently in the eighteenth century. Yet a variety of personal and popular texts survive, some of them published decades after their inscription. Among the most famous is the correspondence between Abigail Adams (1744–1818) and her husband John Adams (later second president of the United States) as he helped lead the American Revolution. Her letters preserve the flavor of the epoch's private life, yet they also intimate rebellion when she urges the Continental Congress to "Remember the Ladies," for [we] will not hold ourselves bound by any Laws in which we have no voice." Also from this period, the journal of Sarah Kemble Knight (1666–1727) and the autobiography of Elizabeth Ashbridge (1713–1755) record changing aspects of women's material and spiritual experience. Perhaps the most extraordinary woman writer of this period—as well as the first "woman of color" to enter the canon of Anglo-American literature—is Phillis Wheatley (1753–1784); bought and educated by a pious Boston family, this slave, kidnapped in Africa, wrote accomplished poems for American newspapers and had a volume of poems published in London.

After the American Revolution, the developing genre of the novel provides the primary vehicle for women's voices, with Susanna Rowson's *Charlotte Temple* (1791) and Hannah Webster Foster's *The Coquette* (1797) exploring social boundaries in a rapidly changing society. During the "American Renaissance" before the Civil War, the first great generation of urban American women wrote bestselling novels—including Susan B. Warner's *The Wide, Wide World* (1850), Maria Susannah Cummins's *The Lamplighter* (1854), and Fanny Fern's *Ruth Hall* (1855)—that trace women's transition from an identity based exclusively on family to one that embraces individual or professional fulfillment.

Antebellum women also contributed their voices to more explicitly political issues. Lydia Maria Child (1802–1880) and other New England women were among the earliest crusaders for the abolition of slavery. African American women's voices also continued to emerge with Harriet Jacobs's *Incidents in the Life of a Slave Girl* (1861) and Harriet E. Wilson's *Our Nig* (1859), the latter being American literature's first full-length novel by a woman of color. Sojourner Truth (1797–1883), an illiterate but charismatic freewoman, spoke of emancipation for slaves *and* for women. Women's abolition writing reached a climax with Harriet Beecher Stowe's phenomenal bestseller, *Uncle Tom's Cabin* (1852).

Perhaps the most versatile and brilliant of all American Renaissance women was Margaret Fuller (1810–1850), who stimulated a wider participation by women in literary and political activities through "conversation circles," journalism, and her study *Woman in the Nineteenth Century* (1844). Also in the mid-1800s, another phenomenal American woman, Emily Dickinson (1830–1886), wrote dazzling verse that, since its posthumous publication, has never lost popular or critical esteem.

In the aftermath of the antebellum union between abolition and feminism, women's writing following the Civil War appears somewhat more fragmented, perhaps reflecting a more diverse national population. Sarah Orne Jewett (1849–1909), Mary E. Wilkins Freeman (1852–1930), and Kate Chopin (1851–1904) were leading practitioners of

"Local Color" or "Regional Writing," which depicted rapidly vanishing rural places and folkways as well as women's roles in these communities. Frances E. W. Harper (1825–1911), who campaigned for abolition before the Civil War, published her novel *Iola Leroy* (1892) to warn of the nation's continuing racial trials and to model their resolution. The first Native American woman writer to enter the Anglo-American tradition, Zitkala-Sa (1876–1938), published stories and recollections in *Atlantic Monthly* that were later collected as *American Indian Stories* (1921). Mary Antin (1881–1949), a Jewish immigrant from Russia, extolled the virtues of assimilation and education in *The Promised Land* (1912). Of all American women writers of the late nineteenth and early twentieth centuries, the most distinguished is Edith Wharton (1862–1937), whose masterful novels of old New York and of international society explore the ironical situations of women who represent wealth but are restricted from earning their own money.

The triumph of woman suffrage in the early twentieth century coincided with another flowering of women's literature. Fiction continued as a major genre, through the varied regional writings of Willa Cather (1873–1947) and Katherine Anne Porter (1890–1980), through the Modernism of Gertrude Stein (1874–1946), and through the exuberant voice of Zora Neale Hurston (1891–1960) during and after the Harlem Renaissance. This period also witnessed a rebirth of poetry, with Edna St. Vincent Millay (1892–1950), Amy Lowell (1874–1925), H. D. (1886–1961), and Marianne Moore (1887–1972) experimenting with traditional and Modernist forms. Lillian Hellman (1905–1984) contributed to the twentieth-century emergence of American drama.

At mid-century, the "feminine mystique," which enshrined women behind white picket fences, momentarily stifled larger movements in women's writing. However, the "southern Gothic" of Flannery O'Connor (1925–1964) and Eudora Welty (b. 1909) expressed the violent tensions repressed by society, and the "confessional style" of poets Anne Sexton (1928–1974) and Sylvia Plath (1932–1963) portended a personal revolution waiting to be born. Also in this period, the supremely intelligent poetry of Elizabeth Bishop (1911–1979) achieved a lasting critical status.

The feminist and civil rights movements of the 1960s and 1970s freed so rich and plentiful a variety of voices and styles that any categories are automatically complicated. The dedicated research of Betty Friedan (b. 1921), the radically psychosexual poetry of Adrienne Rich (b. 1929), the perverse profusion of Joyce Carol Oates (b. 1938), the West Coast journalism and fiction of Joan Didion (b. 1934), and the cosmic gender theory of Mary Daly (b. 1928) opened numerous paths for women's literature, and young European American poets such as Carolyn Forché (b. 1950) have in their turn declared personal and political commitments that attract committed readers.

Probably the most spectacular development in American women's writing at the end of the twentieth century was the literary movement of women of color. African American writers such as Maya Angelou (b. 1928), June Jordan (b. 1936), Alice Walker (b. 1944), and Gloria Naylor (b. 1950) have figured prominently in public consciousness, culminating in the award to Toni Morrison (b. 1931) of the Nobel Prize for Literature in 1993 and the appointment of Rita Dove (b. 1952) as the nation's poet laureate. The achievements of African American women have been joined by popular and critical successes by American Indian novelists Leslie Marmon Silko (b. 1948) and Louise Erdrich (b. 1954), by Latina writers Aurora Levins Morales (b. 1954) and Sandra Cisneros (b. 1954), and by Chinese Americans Maxine Hong Kingston (b. 1940) and Amy Tan (b. 1952). Speaking of herself and sharing with others, the American woman writer combines our nation's most personally affirming and politically subversive identities. *(See also: Adams, Abigail; Angelou, Maya; Ashbridge, Elizabeth Sampson; Bonnin, Gertrude Simmons; Bradstreet, Anne; Cather, Willa; Charlotte Temple, A Tale of Truth; Child, Lydia Maria Francis; Chopin, Kate; Daly, Mary; Dickinson, Emily; Doolittle, Hilda; Erdrich, Louise; Freeman, Mary Eleanor Wilkins; Friedan, Betty; Fuller, Margaret; Harlem Renaissance; Harper, Frances Ellen Watkins; Hellman, Lillian; Hurston, Zora Neale; Hutchinson, Anne Marbury; Incidents in the Life of a Slave Girl; Jewett, Sarah Orne; Kingston, Maxine Hong; Millay, Edna St. Vincent; Moore, Marianne Craig; Morrison, Toni; Naylor, Gloria; O'Connor, Flannery; Plath, Sylvia; Rich, Adrienne; Sexton, Anne; Silko, Leslie; Stein, Gertrude; Stowe, Harriet Beecher; Walker, Alice; Welty, Eudora Alice; Wharton, Edith; Wheatley, Phillis)*

—**Craig White**

Further Reading

Davidson, Cathy N., and Linda Wagner-Martin, eds. *The Oxford Companion to Women's Writing in the United States.* New York: Oxford University Press, 1995.

Gilbert, Sandra M., and Susan Gubar, eds. *The Norton Anthology of Literature by Women: The Tradition in English.* New York: Norton, 1985.

Mainero, Lina, ed. *American Women Writers,* 4 vols. New York: Frederick Ungar, 1979.

Showalter, Elaine et al., eds. *Modern American Women Writers.* New York: Scribner's, 1991.

༝ Women's Airforce Service Pilots (WASPs)

The Women's Airforce Service Pilots (WASPs) were a quasi-military, civilian group of women who towed targets and ferried planes across the United States from September 1942 to December 1944. Most women in the military served in traditionally female occupations. WASPs were different; they were flying planes just as the glamorous "fly boys" were. To become a WASP, a woman had to have a pilot's license (rare among women in this period) and volunteer for a six-month training program. Some women came from elite families who could afford flight lessons; others had been trained under the Civilian Pilot Training Program. Far more applications were received than could be accommodated. The commanding general of the Army Air Force, H. H. "Hap" Arnold, was a strong supporter of the women fliers. WASPs flew seventy-seven different types of aircraft, including the B-17, P-38, F-5, C-4, and B-24, to both coasts so that these planes could be shipped to the combat areas. Thirty-eight WASPs were killed in crashes.

Their colorful commander was Jacqueline Cochran, an experienced pilot who had won two Harmon Trophies by 1939, the highest award for U.S. aviators. She did not want her elite women to be part of the Women's Army Corps nor part of Nancy Love's very experienced Women's Auxiliary Ferrying Squadron (WAFS), whose pilots ferried planes for the Air Corps Ferrying Command, later the Air Transport Command (ATC). On August 5, 1943, the WAFS and women pilot trainees, Cochran's group, were merged in one organization, the WASP. Cochran was director of women pilots, and Love was WASP executive with the Ferrying Division of the ATC. When General Arnold failed to achieve military status for the WASPs late in 1944, he disbanded the organization. It was not until November 23, 1977, that the 1,074 WASPs achieved veteran's status. *(See also: Aviation; Cochran, Jacqueline; World War II)*

—D'Ann Campbell

Further Reading

Chun, Victor K. "The Origins of the WASPs," *American Aviation Historical Society Journal* 14 (Winter 1969): 259-62.

Cochran, Jacqueline. *The Stars at Noon.* Boston: Little, Brown, 1954.

Cochran, Jacqueline, and Mary Ann Bucknum Brinley. *Jackie Cochran.* New York: Bantam, 1987.

Cole, Jean Haseall. *Women Pilots of World War II.* Salt Lake City: University of Utah Press, 1992.

Douglas, Deborah G. *United States Women in Aviation, 1940–1985,* 3 vols. Washington, DC: Smithsonian Institution Press, 1990.

Granger, Byrd Howell. *On Final Approach: The Women Airforce Service Pilots of WWII.* Scottsdale, AZ: Falconer, 1991.

Jaros, Dean. *Heroes without Legacy: American Airwomen, 1912–1944.* Niwot, CO: University of Colorado Press, 1993.

Keil, Sally Van Wegener. *Those Wonderful Women in Their Flying Machines: The Unknown Heroines of World War II.* New York: Rawson, Wade, 1979.

Verges, Marianne. *On Silver Wings: The Women Airforce Service Pilots of World War II, 1942–1944.* New York: Ballantine, 1991.

⟶ Women's Army Auxiliary Corps (WAAC)

With the Japanese bombing of the U.S. Pacific Fleet at Pearl Harbor on December 7, 1941, the American military began to mobilize for war. A handful of admirals and generals argued, based on the successful World War I service of 11,250 yeomen (F)s, that a "few good women" should volunteer to serve in the military for the duration. These women should be in the military and not just working for the military because the Army wanted to be able to "order" them to work long hours in emergencies and to move from site to site as needed; to give them classified information to file, type, and decode; and to know that they would not quit. Representative Edith Nourse Rogers of Massachusetts introduced the bill to establish a women's corps in the Army. The opposition feared that women would lose their femininity. On May 15, 1942, the president signed legislation (Public Law 554) creating the Women's Army Auxiliary Corps, which gave women partial military status.

The WAAC had different names for ranks and different pay scales from the rest of the Army, and its members were an auxiliary, not part of the Army. If WAACs were stationed overseas, they did not have the same legal protection as the men, and a WAAC was not eligible for veterans' benefits—unless she joined the Women's Army Corps (WAC) when it was formed. Plans called for twelve thousand volunteers the first year and double that the second. When generals discovered how well the women performed and how the WAAC freed men for fighting, they demanded thousands more. General Dwight D. Eisenhower sent in a requisition for more WACs than there were in the entire corps.

On July 1, 1943, Congress abolished the WAAC and created the WAC, which gave women the same rank titles and pay as male reservists. Luckily, most WAACs reenlisted as members of the WAC so there was continuity and experience. Oveta Culp Hobby, a prominent Texas civic leader, newspaperwoman, and wife of a former governor, became the WAC's first director. *(See also: Hobby, Oveta Culp; Military Service; Women's Army Corps; World War II)*

—D'Ann Campbell

Further Reading

Pollard, Clarice F. *Laugh, Cry and Remember: The Journal of a G.I. Lady.* Phoenix, AZ: Journeys Press, 1991.

Pollock, Elizabeth R. *Yes, Ma'am!: The Personal Papers of a WAAC Private.* Philadelphia: J. B. Lippincott, 1943.

Stanbury, Jean. *Bars on Her Shoulders: A Story of a WAAC.* New York: Dodd, Mead, 1943.

Treadwell, Mattie E. *The Women's Army Corps.* Washington, DC: Office of the Chief of Military History, Department of the Army, 1954.

⟶ Women's Army Corps (WAC)

The Army was the first of the services during World War II to allow women to serve in the military, albeit with only partial military status, as members of the Women's Army Auxiliary Corps. Women finally achieved the same rank, titles, and pay as male reservists when Congress abolished the WAAC and instead created the Women's Army Corps, on July 1, 1943.

While the generals were delighted with their work, the rank and file—in the states, in Europe, the Mideast, and the

South Pacific—found women in the military a threat to their status. Once they served with the women, they were often willing to say that "their girls" performed well, but they still did not like the idea of women infiltrating such a traditional male bastion. Many warned their friends and relatives away, alleging falsely that women who served in the military had "questionable" moral standards. The sexual innuendos ruined WAC recruitment and demoralized those already in the WAC. The enlisted WACs had more schooling than their male counterparts. Over 70 percent performed jobs in the military that were traditionally labeled "women's work," such as typing and filing. About one-third served with the Army Air Force. The college-educated WAC officers were paid more in the military than they had earned as civilians and learned skills that helped many gain leadership positions after the war in their communities and in the work force. At the peak of World War II, 100,000 women served as WACs; about 140,000 served during the war.

With the passage of the Women's Armed Services Integration Act in June 1948, the WAC was made a permanent part of the Army. In the 1970s, the Army began debating whether to maintain a separate corps for women (the Army Nurse Corps had both men and women in it since the 1950s) or to abolish the WAC. The "separate but equal" women's corps was abolished in 1978, and the members were fully integrated into functional units. In 1976, the first women were admitted to the U.S. Military Academy at West Point, New York. While combat service for women continues to be debated, more military occupational specialties (MOS) are open to women each year. For example, women can now be trained as combat pilots in some planes and helicopters. *(See also: Marine Corps, Women's Reserve; Military Service; SPARs; WAVES; Women's Army Auxiliary Corps; World War II)*

—D'Ann Campbell

Further Reading

Allen, E. Ann. "The WAC Mission: The Testing Time from Korea to Vietnam." Ph.D. diss., University of South Carolina, 1986. [University Microfilms International, 1989]

Campbell, D'Ann. *Women at War with America: Private Lives in a Patriotic Era.* Cambridge, MA: Harvard University Press, 1984.

Dammann, Nancy. *A WAC's Story: From Brisbane to Manila.* Sun City, AZ: Social Change Press, 1992.

Earley, Charity Adams. *One Woman's Army: A Black Officer Remembers the WAC.* College Station: Texas A&M University Press, 1989.

Green, Anne Bosanko. *One Woman's War: Letters Home from the Women's Army Corps, 1944–46.* St. Paul: Minnesota Historical Society Press, 1989.

Holm, Jeanne. *Women in the Military: An Unfinished Revolution.* Rev. ed. Novato, CA: Presidio, 1982, 1992.

Litoff, Judith B., and Dave Smith. *We're in This War, Too.* New York: Oxford University Press, 1994.

Meyer, Leisa. "Creating G. I. Jane: The Women's Army Corps During WWII." Ph.D. diss., University of Wisconsin, 1993.

Mordon, Colonel Bettie. *The Women's Army Corps 1945–1978.* Washington, DC: Center of Military History, U.S. Army, 1990.

Pollard, Clarice F. *Laugh, Cry and Remember: The Journal of a G.I. Lady.* Phoenix, AZ: Journeys Press, 1991.

Prior, Billy. *Flight to Glory.* Belmont, CA: Ponce, 1985.

Putney, Martha S. *When the Nation Was in Need: Blacks in the Women's Army Corps during World War II.* Metuchen, NJ: Scarecrow, 1992.

Spratley, Dorothy R. *Women Go to War: Answering the First Call in World War II.* Columbus, OH: Hazelnut, 1992.

Treadwell, Mattie E. *The Women's Army Corps.* Washington, DC: Office of the Chief of Military History, Department of the Army, 1954.

⤵ Women's Bureau, U.S. Department of Labor

The Women's Bureau of the U.S. Department of Labor was established by Congress in 1920 as a federal agency to represent the interests of wage-earning women. On the heels of the passage of the Nineteenth Amendment, women's organizations interested in state and federal social welfare legislation lobbied Congress to create a permanent women's division in the Department of Labor. The Women's Bureau, with a limited budget and no enforcement authority, functioned as a clearinghouse of information and publicity for women's organizations central to its establishment. From the 1920s to the 1940s, the bureau promoted the social welfare agenda of its founding organizations: passage of protective labor legislation for women and active opposition of the Equal Rights Amendment.

By the 1950s and 1960s, the Women's Bureau had shifted its emphasis from investigating labor conditions to advocating women's employment rights. Under Director Esther Peterson's leadership, bureau advocacy for working women resulted in the formation of the President's Commission on the Status of Women (PCSW) by President Kennedy's Executive Order 10980 issued on December 14, 1961, and passage of the Equal Pay Act (1963). By 1964, the Women's Bureau had become the administrative arm of institutions contributing to the development of grassroots feminism: federal bodies created by the PCSW, the Citizens' Advisory Council on the Status of Women and the Interdepartmental Committee on the Status of Women, and state status of women commissions. In 1970, the Women's Bureau publicly reversed its long-standing opposition to the Equal Rights Amendment when court rulings determined that protective labor legislation violated Title VII of the 1964 Civil Rights Act. *(See also: Civil Rights Act of 1964; Equal Pay Act of 1963; Equal Rights Amendment; President's Commission on the Status of Women; Protective Legislation)*

—Kathleen Laughlin

Further Reading

Harrison, Cynthia. *On Account of Sex: The Politics of Women's Issues, 1945–1968.* Berkeley: University of California Press, 1988.

Sealander, Judith. *As Minority Becomes Majority: Federal Reaction to the Phenomenon of Women in the Workforce, 1920–1963.* Westport, CT: Greenwood, 1983.

http://www.dol.gov/dol/wb/ [Women's Bureau Website]

∾ Women's Educational and Industrial Union (WEIU)

This organization, identified often by its acronym WEIU, was an important social reform influence in Boston during the latter nineteenth century and the beginning of the twentieth. Established in the decade following the Civil War, the WEIU was dedicated to helping working women avoid poverty and all its attendant evils by offering them training and access to reasonably good jobs. Although it provided a number of other services, the WEIU focused its efforts on providing education that could provide young working-class women with stable employment. Among its most successful programs were classes to prepare women for work in the "needle trades" and special classes to help women find employment in retail department stores. The latter program eventually became a course in the Boston public schools.

The WEIU was a somewhat unique variety of what William O'Neill has described as "social feminist" organizations during this period. Like other social feminist groups (such as the National Women's Trade Union League), it concerned itself with practical measures to improve the lot of poor and working women; but, unlike other such groups, the WEIU focused its efforts on education and employment as important avenues for self-improvement among working-class women.

Curiously, the WEIU has yet to receive much attention from historians. No major study has examined the organization's development or its role in the period during which it was active. *(See also: National Women's Trade Union League; Social Feminism)*

—**John L. Rury**

Further Reading

Rury, John L. *Education and Women's Work: Female Schooling and the Division of Labor in American Life, 1870–1930.* Albany: SUNY Press, 1991.

∾ Women's Equity Action League (WEAL)

The Women's Equity Action League (WEAL) was a national, nonprofit membership organization that specialized in women's economic issues. It conducted research and education projects, supported litigation, and lobbied. Publications included the bimonthly *WEAL Washington Report, WEAL Informed,* and various fact sheets and information kits. The organization was founded in Ohio in 1968 and initially cultivated women who viewed NOW as too radical or unconventional. One of its first efforts was a class-action complaint of sex discrimination with the Department of Labor's Office of Contract Compliance against all colleges and universities holding federal contracts. In 1972, it opened a national office in Washington, D.C., and became a primary lobbying group on a broader range of feminist issues than originally envisioned. WEAL disbanded in 1989. *(See also: Affirmative Action)*

—**Anne O. Dzamba (Sessa)**

Further Reading

Freeman, Jo. *The Politics of Women's Liberation.* New York: David McKay, 1975.

Gelb, Joyce, and Marian Lief Palley. *Women and Public Policies.* Princeton, NJ: Princeton University Press, 1982.

Spalter-Ross, Roberta, and Ronee Schreiber. "Outsider Issues and Insider Tactics: Strategic Tensions in the Women's Policy Network during the 1980s." In *Feminist Organizations: Harvest of the New Women's Movement,* edited by Myra Ferree and Patricia Yancey Martin. Philadelphia: Temple University Press, 1995.

∾ Women's Health Protective Association (WHPA)

The Women's Health Protective Association (WHPA) of Galveston, Texas, was founded in March 1901 to promote public health and beautification in a city that had been devastated by the hurricane of 1900. Led by the social elite of the city, the organization invited women of all social and economic classes to join in its efforts.

Flourishing between 1901 and 1920, the WHPA focused early efforts on city beautification. Renowned as a tropical paradise before 1900, Galveston lost nearly all its trees and shrubs in the tidal flooding that accompanied the hurricane. Following the storm, the city embarked on a grade-raising project to fill the low areas and elevate the land. While the project protected the citizens from future flooding, virtually all remaining vegetation in the fill area died under several feet of dredge material.

When the grade-raising project ended in 1911, the WHPA was ready. The women had studied and selected trees and shrubs that could withstand heat, humidity, and salt air. Through dues and fund-raisers such as horse shows and seed sales, the women imported oaks, palms, cottonwoods, and elms to plant along city streets and to sell at cost to private citizens. By 1906, the organization operated its own nursery on land donated by John Charles League, and by 1912, the women had planted nearly 10,000 trees and 2,500 oleanders throughout the city of Galveston.

In 1913, the women shifted their emphasis to public health and sanitation. Joining with the Galveston Commercial Association, they asked Dr. J. P. Simonds, head of Preventive Medicine at the University of Texas Medical Branch, to conduct a sanitation survey. He reported that Galveston lacked strong civic pride and recommended that the city enforce sanitary laws, pass a building ordinance, regularly inspect sources of the city's milk supply, provide regular medical examinations of schoolchildren, establish more playgrounds, and eliminate breeding places for mosquitoes.

Supported by four hundred members, the WHPA successfully lobbied the city to appoint a dairy inspector and a building inspector and to pass ordinances regulating grocery stores and bakeries and requiring property owners and lessors to be responsible for maintaining clean sidewalks and alleys abutting their property. Watchdog committees of the WHPA helped enforce the new ordinances.

Other projects that the WHPA supported during the first two decades of the twentieth century included the establishment of the children's hospital at the University of Texas Medical Branch, the passage of the city's first zoning ordinance, and the annual antituberculosis Christmas stamp campaign. Although the organization did not maintain the extraordinary level of activity established during the first twenty years of the century, it continued for the next fifty years to work for city beautification. In 1924, the association changed its name to the Women's Civic League, and in the 1940s, it became the Galveston Civic League. *(See also: Progressive Era)*

—**Jane A. Kenamore**

Further Reading

Frost, Meigs O. "The Women of Galveston," *Southern Women's Magazine* 2 (June 1914): 9-10.

Kenamore, Jane A., and Michael E. Wilson. *Manuscript Sources in the Rosenberg Library: A Selective Guide.* College Station: Texas A&M University Press, 1983.

Morgan Family Papers. The Rosenberg Library. Galveston, TX. *Report of a Sanitary Survey of the City of Galveston,* c. 1913; in Morgan Family papers (83-0057, Box 10, ff8). Galveston, TX.

Women's Civic League Records. The Rosenberg Library. Galveston, TX.

ᕪ Women's History

While not all writers of women's history have been women's rights activists or feminists, the history of women's history is still largely inseparable from the history of women's rights movements and feminism.

For the most part, the urge to research the history of women has resulted from women's rights activists wanting to record their own accomplishments within a historical context. Even those who were not activists saw value in recording for posterity the accomplishments of notable women, and for generations, women's clubs of various kinds have collected and published books containing biographical sketches of their members or of their ancestors. As early as the 1840s, Elizabeth Cady Stanton wanted to write a history of women's desires for emancipation. The first woman recognized as a historian of women was Elizabeth Fries Ellet, whose *The Women of the American Revolution* appeared in 1848 and consisted of biographical sketches of more than 120 exemplary women. Shortly thereafter, Sara Josepha Hale's *Woman's Record: Sketches of All Distinguished Women from the Beginning till A.D. 1850* admonished readers to recognize women, whom Hale believed were destined to Christianize the world, as the core of world history. By the end of the nineteenth century, the female group biography, or prosopography, was a popular genre. Boston's Roberts Brothers published a series, *Famous Women,* in the 1880s; Scribner's published a six-volume *Women of Colonial and Revolutionary Times* in the 1890s.

The writing of history became increasingly professionalized and divorced from writing that simply praised ancestors, but academically trained historians—female and male—generally did not recognize the existence of a history of women. Activists in white women's rights movements did, and they produced a series of works about the suffrage movement that formed a foundation for mid-twentieth-century historians. Paulina Wright Davis's *A History of the National Woman's Rights Movement* (1871) and Harriet Robinson's *Massachusetts in the Woman Suffrage Movement* (1881) were followed by the six-volume *History of Woman Suffrage,* published between 1881 and 1922 by Elizabeth Cady Stanton, Susan B. Anthony, Matilda Joslyn Gage, and Ida Husted Harper. While documenting both the birth and growth of a reform movement and the efforts of organizations that supported it, these works, written as they were by participants, engaged in a celebratory rather than critical depiction of the movement, its leaders, and their activities. Nevertheless, the link these women established between women's political reform and women's history continued into the twentieth century. As the "woman movement" evolved into feminism, prosopographies and histories of movements gave way to sociological studies (Lucy Maynard Salmon's *Domestic Service,* 1897, and Edith Abbott's *Women in Industry,* 1913) and biographies by iconoclastic authors intent on revealing rather than canonizing their subjects (Katharine Anthony's *Margaret Fuller,* 1920; Paxton Hibben's *Henry Ward Beecher,* 1927; Emanie Sachs's *The Terrible Siren,* about Victoria Woodhull, 1928; and Rheta Childe Dorr's *The Woman Who Changed the Mind of a Nation,* about Susan B. Anthony, 1928).

The transition from activist-amateur to academically trained professional historian is embodied in Mary Ritter Beard, who began but left unfinished a graduate program in sociology at Columbia University in 1904. Active in suffrage and women's trade union reform, Beard wrote *Woman's Work in Municipalities* (1915) and *A Short History of the American Labor Movement* (1920) before collaborating with her husband Charles on *The Rise of American Civilization* (1927), a series that acknowledged women's roles in history more than any previous synthesis. In *On Understanding Women* (1931) and *America through Women's Eyes* (1933), Beard criticized professional historians for fragmenting history by ignoring or distorting women's part in it and attempted to show an alternative, woman-centered view. Throughout the 1930s, Beard worked toward creating the World Center for Women's Archives to preserve and catalog materials related to women's past. Although this dream never materialized, the Sophia Smith Collection at Smith College and the Schlesinger Library at Radcliffe resulted from the project. Beard's best known book, *Woman as Force in History* (1946), asserted that, contrary to many nineteenth-century writers' focus on women's subjection, women had been "a force in making all the history that has been made."

Despite Beard's efforts, the academy largely ignored women's history during Beard's thirty-year career. Arthur Schlesinger chided his colleagues in 1922 for ignoring the history of the women's rights movement. The Berkshire Conference of Women Historians was founded in 1929, and the American Historical Association held the first full session on women's history in 1940, but none of these events sparked significant interest in women's history among scholars. Activist Alma Lutz published biographies of suffragists, but these were criticized as unscholarly.

The near silence in women's history that followed Beard broke with the eruption of the women's liberation movement in the 1960s. As with the nineteenth-century woman's rights movement, an intense interest in women's history accompanied the women's liberation movement. By 1960, thirteen contemporary books related to women's history existed. Perhaps the most notable was Eleanor Flexner's *Century of Struggle: The Woman's Rights Movement in the United States* (1959). During the 1960s, eleven more appeared. Most of these were about white women's fight for equality, such as Aileen S. Kraditor's *The Ideas of the Woman Suffrage Movement: 1890–1920* (1965); Andrew Sinclair's *The Emancipation of the American Woman* (1965); Alan Pendleton Grimes's *The Puritan Ethic and Woman Suffrage* (1967); Kraditor's edited sourcebook *Up from the Pedestal: Selected Writings in the History of American Feminism* (1968); and William O'Neill's *Everyone Was Brave: The Rise and Fall of Feminism in America* (1969). The 1960s were also marked by efforts among academic historians to organize politically. Gerda Lerner noted that in 1969 women "were so marginally represented in professional activities and conventions as to be virtually excluded. . . . [W]omen's history as a field and a content was unrecognized and even the handful of its practitioners were unaware of its history and of its existence in other parts of the world." The Coordinating Committee on Women in the Historical Profession formed in 1969 to provide a vehicle within the American Historical Association to recruit women into the profession, oppose discrimination against women historians, and to help women's history to grow as a field.

Calling Mary Beard her mentor and drawing on Beard's work, Lerner published an essay in 1969, "New Approaches for the Study of Women in American History," to assert that there were more important questions historians should ask about women's history than those related to women's subordination, such as "What were women doing?" and "How were they doing it?" This essay is one of the earliest works

both to caution against regarding women as a monolithic group and to remind historians of the significance of race and class as well as sex.

In 1970, only four academically trained historians defined themselves as women's historians, but the field exploded nonetheless. The biographical dictionary *Notable American Women* appeared in 1971, Sarah Lawrence College offered the first M.A. program in women's history in 1972, and the first revived Berkshire Conference on the History of Women occurred in 1973. By the end of the decade, forty-six books had been published. The works fed from and contributed to a sense of discovery and assertion. Titles such as Anne Firor Scott's "Making the Invisible Woman Visible" (1972); Lerner's *Black Women in White America: A Documentary History* (1972); Sheila Rowbotham's *Hidden from History: Rediscovering Women in History from the 17th Century to the Present* (1973); Mary S. Hartman and Lois Banner's *Clio's Consciousness Raised* (1974); and Lerner's *The Female Experience* (1977) and *Women's History Resources: A Guide to Archives and Manuscript Collections in the United States* (1979) revealed the groundbreaking nature of the work under way. Many publications were documentary histories and collections of primary sources that constituted not only the first step for historians but also the proof that women's history existed. In addition to this broad-and-basic approach, historians such as Linda Gordon and Carroll Smith-Rosenberg studied the particularity of female experience in historic context: the female life cycle, birth control, sex roles, puberty, menopause, and "the female world of love and ritual." In the 1970s, historians began to distinguish between the words *sex* and *gender.* The culturally grounded concept of gender became the key for countering the essentialism of biologically—"sex"—based arguments about women. By the end of the decade, books declared, as did Nancy F. Cott and Elizabeth H. Pleck's *A Heritage of Her Own* and Lerner's *The Majority Finds Its Past* (1979), that women had, without question, discovered and claimed an identifiable past.

The 1970s sense of a common purpose—discovery and documentation—gave way by the end of the decade to interpretation. Much early 1970s women's liberation literature had focused on patriarchy, women's oppression and rights, and on diversity among women (Robin Morgan's *Sisterhood Is Powerful,* 1970; Toni Cade's *The Black Woman: An Anthology,* 1970; Deborah Babcox and Madeline Belkin's *Liberation Now,* 1971; Miriam Schneir's *Feminism: The Essential Historical Writings,* 1972). Increasingly, studies of "separate spheres," woman's culture, or what Cott called *The Bonds of Womanhood* (1977) emerged, bringing with them assumptions about similarities among (white) women and women's differences from men. Eventually, historians' disagreements about these differences were emblemized by the *Sears* case (1978), when Rosalind Rosenberg and Alice Kessler-Harris each invoked women's history in support of opposing positions about sex discrimination in employment.

By 1980, the field had grown enough that Women's History Month was nationally recognized. Its existence spurred regional interest that resulted in popular projects such as Texas's 1981 statewide touring exhibit *Texas Women: A Celebration of History*. Between 1981 and 1987, forty books in the field were published. The first book in women's history to win the Bancroft Prize, Mary Ryan's *Cradle of the Middle Class,* appeared in 1981. In 1987, the International Federation for Research in Women's History formed. In 1988, the National Endowment for the Humanities (NEH) funded the Conference on Graduate Training in U.S. Women's History, and in 1989, the first issue of the *Journal of Women's History* appeared. The 1980s opened with two journals, *Feminist Studies* and the *Pacific Historical Review,* publishing watershed spring issues. *FS* published a symposium on the relationship of politics (particularly feminism) and culture ("many female worlds") in women's history. *PHR* focused on women in the West, included essays about black, Chicana, Japanese, and Native American women, and led with Joan Jensen and Darlis Miller's "Gentle Tamers Revisited: New Approaches to the History of Women in the American West," which not only advocated and limned western history studies that countered stereotypes of women but also called for a multicultural approach to women's history.

Debate characterized the 1980s as historians searched for precise definitions and a theoretical framework. Women of color, from various fields, and a few white historians challenged the essentialism of the notion of a "women's sphere" and countered with studies of class, race, sexuality, and region as well as gender (Cherrie Moraga and Gloria Anzaldúa's *This Bridge Called My Back: Writings by Radical Women of Color,* 1983; bell hooks's *Feminist Theory from Margin to Center,* 1984; Paula Giddings's *When and Where I Enter: The Impact of Black Women on Race and Sex in America,* 1984; Jacqueline Jones's *Labor of Love, Labor of Sorrow: Black Women, Work and the Family from Slavery to the Present,* 1985; Evelyn Nakano Glenn's *Issei, Nisei, War Bride: Three Generations of Japanese American Women in Domestic Service,* 1986; Elizabeth Fox-Genovese's *Within the Plantation Household: Black and White Women of the Old South,* 1988; Elizabeth V. Spelman's *Inessential Woman: Problems of Exclusion in Feminist Thought,* 1988; and Darlene Clark Hine's *Black Women in White: Racial Conflict and Cooperation in the Nursing Profession,* 1989).

"Separate spheres" increasingly became a trope for power relations between women and men. In 1986, Joan Wallach Scott's influential essay "Gender: A Useful Category of Historical Analysis" suggested that poststructuralist theories, particularly Jacques Derrida's use of deconstruction to critique hierarchies, offered more promise for historians of women than did traditional social history. "If we treat the opposition between male and female as problematic rather than known," Scott said, "as something contextually defined, repeatedly constructed, then we must constantly ask not only what is at stake in proclamations or debates that invoke gender to explain or justify their positions but also how *implicit understandings of gender* are being invoked and reinscribed." In 1988, Linda K. Kerber concurred, stating that the use of the language of separate spheres imposed "a static model on dynamic relationships" and that the historian's task was to deconstruct and demystify power. The journal *Gender and History* first appeared in 1989. Poststructuralist analyses of "understandings" or "meaning" encouraged inquiry not so much of women's experiences but of processes underlying them and of language used to describe them and eventually called into question history itself by differentiating between "fact" and "representation." By decade's end, historians seemed divided into methodological and theoretical camps, with historians of women in one and historians of gender in the other.

The 1990s opened with historians openly arguing the merits of each and with some declaring the field had lost its identity. A session on critical theory and the history of women at the Eighth Berkshire Conference on the History of Women in 1990 defined the conflict as a disagreement over categories of analysis and how power should be conceptualized. Joan Hoff declared poststructuralism trendy, dangerous, and a threat to the field because it eschewed chronological narrative and depoliticized gender, effectively divorcing history from its roots in feminist activism. Those who found merit in each camp searched for middle ground. Hoff and other critics, such as Evelyn Brooks Higginbotham, criticized gender theorists for their silence about race. Research in the history of women of color and discussions about multicultural approaches to women's history that had emerged in the 1980s, especially as increasing numbers of women of color entered the profession, continued to bear fruit in the 1990s. In 1990 alone, Vicki L. Ruiz and Ellen Carol DuBois published *Unequal Sisters: A Multicultural Reader in U.S. Women's History,* Darlene Clark Hine's multivolume *Black Women in American History* appeared, and the Western History Association revisited "The Gentle Tamers Revisited" with a panel that assessed progress in multicultural women's history since 1980. In 1991, *Frontiers* published a special issue on "the challenge of writing multicultural women's history." The Berkshire Conference held its first session on Chicana history in 1993.

At mid-decade, women's history was in transition as it moved increasingly from margin to center. Although the history of women is not mainstreamed (some debate whether this is advisable), and discrimination against its practitioners remains, the field has grown and matured to the point that it has produced multiple generations of trained historians, many of whom have tenured positions. One result of the increasing status of the field is that the once clear link between women's history and activism has become blurred. The field experiences the tension of debate over fundamental questions: Who are we? What is our purpose? Can women's history survive separated from feminism? The energy of a field in formation that characterized the 1970s has been largely replaced with questions about the shape of its survival in the twenty-first century. *(See also: Archives and Sources; Beard, Mary; Deconstruction; Feminism; Higher Education; Internet Resources; Suffrage; Women's Liberation Movement; Women's Studies)*

—**Nancy Baker Jones**

Further Reading

Beard, Mary R. *Woman as Force in History.* New York: Collier, 1946.

DuBois, Ellen. "Making Women's History: Activist Historians of Women's Rights, 1880–1940," *Radical History Review* 49 (1991): 61-84.

DuBois, Ellen et al. "Politics and Culture in Women's History: A Symposium," *Feminist Studies* 6 (1980): 26-64.

Gordon, Linda. "What's New in Women's History." In *Feminist Studies/Critical Studies,* edited by Teresa de Laurentis, 29-30. Bloomington: Indiana University Press, 1986.

Hewitt, Nancy A. "Beyond the Search for Sisterhood: American Women's History in the 1980s," *Social History* 10 (1985): 299-322.

Lerner, Gerda. *The Majority Finds Its Past: Placing Women in History.* Oxford, UK: Oxford University Press, 1979.

Pacific Historical Review 49 (1980), 61 (1992).

Rose, Sonya O. et al. "Dialogue," *Journal of Women's History* 5 (1993): 89-128.

Scott, Joan Wallach. *Gender and the Politics of History.* New York: Columbia University Press, 1988.

Vogel, Lise. "Telling Tales: Historians of Our Own Lives," *Journal of Women's History* 2 (1991): 89-101.

⌒ Women's International League for Peace and Freedom (WILPF)

The Women's International League for Peace and Freedom (WILPF) had its origins in the Woman's Peace Party. On January 9, 1915, eighty-six delegates representing major women's organizations in the United States met in New York to establish the Woman's Peace Party. Pacifist sentiment had long been a feature of women's organizations, and when war broke out in 1914, many "expressed astonishment that such an archaic institution should be revived in modern Europe." Under the leadership of Jane Addams, a delegation of forty-seven American women attended the International Congress of Women at The Hague in Holland in April 1915. The conference marked the birth of the International Women's League for Peace and Freedom, the name proposed by Catherine Marshall of England. This name, however, did not replace the older Woman's Peace Party in the United States until 1919.

The peace movement splintered during the war years, with their noisy patriotism and short-term economic gains for women. Those who persisted did so under duress. Emily Greene Balch was fired from her post as economics professor at Wellesley for her antiwar activities, and Jane Addams was cited as "the most dangerous woman in America."

The league, which celebrated its 80th anniversary in 1995, is today the oldest continually active peace organization in the United States. It has 110 branches in the U.S., and sections in 42 countries of the world. Five of its members have won Nobel Peace Prizes, including Jane Addams in 1931 and Emily Greene Balch in 1946.

The league is avowedly feminist in its platforms and activities. It has remained true to the conviction of its founders that peace is not rooted merely in treaties or disarmament but is inextricably linked to issues of justice, freedom, nonviolence, opportunity, and equality for all. To that end, the decade of the 1980s witnessed the league's acting in coalition with movements such as the Nuclear Weapons Freeze Campaign, the Conference on Racism, and the Women's Speaking Tour on Central America. For the 1990s, the U.S. section has identified four main priorities: racial justice, women's rights, ending U.S. global intervention, and disarmament. Specific programs include a campaign to end the economic blockade of Cuba, participation in the Women Versus Violence-Clothesline Project, and work with the Jobs in the Peace Economy-Conversion of Weapons Production Facilities Campaign. In September 1995, the WILPF participated as a nongovernmental organization (NGO) at the U.N. Conference on Women in Beijing, China. The meeting was preceded by a "peace train" in which 232 women from 42 countries traveled to China by way of Helsinki, Finland, across Eastern Europe and the states of the former Soviet Union.

The U.S. section of the WILPF is based in Philadelphia; the international office is in Geneva, Switzerland. *(See also: Addams, Jane; Balch, Emily Greene; Pacifism and the Peace Movement; Woman's Peace Party)*

—**Laura Gellott**

Further Reading

Addams, Jane. *Peace and Bread in Time of War.* New York: Macmillan, 1922.

Spivek, Roberta. *Generations of Courage: The Women's International League for Peace and Freedom, and the 20th Century.* Philadelphia: WILPF U.S. Section, 1995.

Steinson, Barbara J. *American Women's Activism in World War I.* New York: Garland, 1982.

http://www.wilpf.org [Women's International League for Peace and Freedom Website]

⌒ Women's Joint Congressional Committee (WJCC)

The Women's Joint Congressional Committee (WJCC) was formed in 1920 under the auspices of the League of Women Voters to meet the legislative goals of women's organizations in the postsuffrage era. The founding organizations included the National Women's Trade Union League, the General Federation of Women's Clubs, the Woman's Christian Temperance Union, and the National Consumers' League. Established as a clearinghouse to coordinate lobbying efforts toward passage of congressional legislation of interest to women, the WJCC was open to any national women's organization whose mission did not conflict with the goals of member organizations. WJCC work coalesced around social welfare legislation supported by its founding organizations relating to issues such as education, child welfare, public health, labor conditions, and consumer interests. This social reform coalition actively opposed passage of the Equal Rights Amendment, viewing it as a threat to protective labor legislation.

Growing to twenty-four member organizations by the mid-1920s, the WJCC remained active during the 1930s and 1940s. The lobbying group broke apart in the 1950s. The League of Women Voters, following a policy that de-emphasized alliances with women's organizations, left the WJCC in 1954. Another important founding organization, the National Women's Trade Union League, disbanded in 1950. *(See also: General Federation of Women's Clubs; League of Women Voters; National Consumers' League; National Women's Trade Union League; Woman's Christian Temperance Union)*

—**Kathleen Laughlin**

Further Reading

Cott, Nancy. *The Grounding of Modern Feminism.* New Haven, CT: Yale University Press, 1987.

Scott, Anne Firor. *Natural Allies: Women's Associations in American History.* Urbana: University of Illinois Press, 1993.

Young, Louise M. *In the Public Interest: The League of Women Voters, 1920–1970.* New York: Greenwood, 1989.

☙ Women's Liberation Movement

The women's liberation movement flourished in the late 1960s and early 1970s as a variety of independent groups dispersed over the United States with an estimated fifteen thousand members. Demonstrating a New Left flair for publicity through guerrilla theater tactics such as hexing Wall Street on Halloween while dressed as witches, groups such as WITCH (Women's International Terrorist Conspiracy from Hell) and the more intellectual and radical Redstockings drew public and media attention to the issues of the modern women's movement.

Women's liberation groups were generated among the young women (under thirty years of age) within the various radical movements of the 1960s, especially those connected to the civil rights movement and the New Left. As women began to realize their own oppression, they began formulating an ideology of women's liberation that used a radical and often Marxist theoretical framework. However, when they presented it within the movements in which they were working, they found the men unsympathetic at best and hostile at worst. When asked what was the position of women within the Student Non-Violent Coordinating Committee in 1964, the famous reply of Stokely Carmichael was, "The only position for women in SNCC is prone."

An awareness of sexism and women's issues grew among civil rights and New Left women until they felt obliged either to align themselves with the emerging feminist movement or remain as support workers for male leaders rather than as acknowledged capable peers within the earlier movements. As women began to exit the New Left movements, the radical males began to incorporate the women's movement philosophy into their own leftist liberation theory. These New Left women defined their movement as women's liberation and thus ignited the modern women's movement of the 1960s and 1970s. Theirs was a direct feminist challenge to the gender system and the traditional definitions of woman and womanhood, as well as to racism and capitalism.

However, no sooner had the men in the radical movements started to take women and their issues more seriously than the male-dominated media began to ridicule and trivialize the image of women's liberation as "Women's Lib" and to publicize distorted accounts of the women's activities. The classic case of such distortion was the coverage of the "bra burning" protesters at the Miss America Pageant in August 1968. Although the press photograph of the purported incident was staged after the feminists had protested the sexist trappings of women's apparel by symbolically dropping items of clothing into a trash can, the visual stereotype of the bra-burning, man-hating feminist registered and persisted.

The special contribution of women's liberation to the modern women's movement was the development of consciousness-raising (C-R) as a process by adapting tactics once used by the New Left. Women's liberation groups sought to raise women's consciousness regarding sexism and feminism as both related to the lives of C-R group members through this process, which bonded women to their individual C-R groups and produced dedicated feminist activists who gave the relatively small women's liberation groups a national visibility and impact that far exceeded their numbers. The C-R process was adopted successfully by the more mainstream women's movement groups such as the National Organization for Women. Eventually, this process itself filtered into the general culture through various self-help groups that ranged far beyond a strictly feminist perspective, for it was employed not only by groups of rape victims, battered spouses, and displaced homemakers but by groups as diverse as single parents and Mothers Against Drunk Driving.

By 1970, women's liberation groups were converting new members through C-R groups, writing and publishing feminist literature, and developing feminist theory. Shifting their emphasis from direct confrontational actions to education, the women's liberation groups promoted women's independence and self-respect through supporting the development of women's studies as well as the revival and inclusion of women's literature and women's history in the curriculum of both public schools and institutions of higher education. Women's liberation publications focused as well on exploring survival skills crucial to divorced, widowed, or dependent women who faced specific sexist discrimination. In the early 1970s, a wide variety of such publications were produced by these radical women to disseminate important information that was generally unavailable to women.

Mimeographed amateur newsletters of small specialized groups and newly established scholarly journals dedicated to feminist theory or specific issues such as lesbianism flourished. For example, the Boston Women's Health Collective published *Our Bodies, Ourselves,* a classic women's liberation publication, to provide information about women's bodies and particular medical procedures.

Many of the women's liberation approaches and processes were adopted by more mainstream women's movement organizations to attack particular issues pragmatically and piecemeal, while the women's liberationists themselves were working for revolutionary results. However, as feminists of all degrees worked with women who lacked either a theoretical framework or an agenda for radical change to provide specific remedies such as medical care or abortion referral, the radical young women began to fear that these efforts actually thwarted the possibility for permanent change by using temporary solutions to fundamental feminist concerns. By 1971, they recognized the danger of such temporary, immediate solutions and began cooperating and coordinating efforts with other reform groups to work within the system for lasting substantive change on issues such as abortion, prostitution, child care, discrimination, and welfare. This cooperation and efforts to "mainstream" their issues and their energies, as well as attrition and theoretical schisms among the charter members of the original groups, created tensions that diminished the sense of identity and solidarity among the founders of the women's liberation movement, and the movement ceased to exist after 1972.

The impact of this movement, as well as of the process of consciousness-raising, persisted: The National Feminist Organization issued its Statement of Purpose in 1973; the Chicana feminist movement grew out of the Chicano national movement during the late 1970s, as Native American women began to assume their traditional leadership roles in intertribal groups such as the American Indian Movement. The assertion of the women's liberation movement of the importance and significance of women as historical participants in all human activity inspired women students and professors to respond to the questions raised by the radical feminists of the late 1960s; interdisciplinary women's studies programs developed and increased throughout the 1980s although the social and political climate was no longer hospitable to radical social reform. Although the women's liberation movement itself was short-lived, its methodology for questioning patriarchal authority and sexist practices provided a model for protest and reform that vitalized many aspects of the mainstream women's movement, which in turn has survived the vicissitudes of the last quarter of the twentieth century. *(See also: Consciousness-Raising; Feminism; National Organization for Women; New Left; Our Bodies, Ourselves; Women's Rights Movements: Nineteenth and Twentieth Centuries)*

—**Saundra K. Yelton-Stanley**
—**Angela M. Howard**

Further Reading

Carden, Maren Lockwood. *The New Feminist Movement,* pp. 103-32. New York: Russell Sage, 1974.

Dixon, Marlene. "The Rise of Women's Liberation," *Ramparts* 8 (December 1969): 57-63.

Evans, Sara. *Personal Politics: The Roots of Women's Liberation in the Civil Rights and the New Left.* New York: Vintage, 1979.

Freeman, Jo. "The Women's Liberation Movement: Its Origins and Structures, Impact and Ideas." In *Women: A Perspective,* edited by Jo Freeman, 448-60. Palo Alto, CA: Mayfield, 1975.

Garcia, Alma M. "The Development of Chicana Feminist Discourse, 1970–1980." In *Unequal Sisters: A Multicultural Reader in U.S. Women's History,* edited by Vicki L. Ruiz and Ellen Carol DuBois, 2d ed., 531-44. New York: Routledge, 1994.

Hole, Judith, and Ellen Levine. *Rebirth of Feminism.* New York: Quadrangle, 1971.

hooks, bell. *Ain't I a Woman?: Black Women and Feminism.* Boston: South End Press, 1984.

Jones, Beverly, and Judith Brown. "Toward a Female Liberation Movement." In *Voices from Women's Liberation,* edited by Leslie B. Tanner, 362-415. New York: Mentor, 1970.

Pharr, Suzanne. *In the Time of the Right: Reflections on Liberation.* Inverness, CA: Chardon, 1996.

Salper, Roberta. "The Development of the American Women's Liberation Movement, 1967–1971." In *Female Liberation,* edited by Roberta Salper, 169-84. New York: Knopf, 1972.

Snitow, Ann, and Rachel Blau DuPlessis, eds. *The Feminist Memoir Project: Voices from Women's Liberation.* New York: Crown, 1998.

Witt, Shirley Hill. "Native Women Today: Sexism and the Native American Women," *Civil Rights Digest* 6 (1974): 29-35.

http://scriptorium.lib.duke.edu/wlm/ [Documents from the Women's Liberation Movement]

～ Women's Memorial

The Women's Memorial was established in 1997 to honor all women who served and will serve in the United States Military. The memorial is the repository of the collective histories and personal experiences of the 1.8 million women—nurses, trainers, communications specialists, and pilots—who served in the U.S. Armed Forces. Ohio Congresswoman Mary Rose Oakar and Alaska Senator Frank H. Murkowski proposed the enabling legislation in 1985; on November 6, 1986, President Ronald Reagan signed Public Law 99-610, which authorized the Women in Military Service for America Memorial Foundation, Inc. (WIMSA) to establish a memorial on federal land in Washington, D.C.

The president of WIMSA, Brigadier General Wilma L. Vaught, USAF (Ret.), and the National Park Services selected the gateway to Arlington Cemetery, the Grand Entrance and Hemicycle, as the site for the memorial, with full support of the National Capital Memorial Commission, the National Capital Planning Commission, and the Fine Arts Commission. In November 1989, Marion Gail Weiss and Michael Manfredi won a national competition for a design concept for the memorial to adopt. In April 1995, the National Capital Planning Commission and the Fine Arts Commission approved the Weiss/Manfredi memorial design to restore and renovate the Hemicycle, which *Washington Post* architecture critic Ben Forgey described as "a perfect gesture in a proper place at a fitting moment." An estimated six thousand people attended the ground-breaking ceremonies in June 1995; on October 18, 1997, hailed as "an elegant solution to integrating a new purpose with an existing historical structure," the Women's Memorial was formally dedicated.

The Women's Memorial includes the Women's Memorial Education Center, within which is located a computerized register for the names, photographs, service records, and experiences of the women who served in the military. "We Also Served" provides a separate register to honor those women who did not serve in a branch of the armed forces but were assigned overseas during wartime. The Education Center includes a 196-seat theater, a Hall of Honor, and a Memorial Gallery. *(See also: Military Service)*

—**Richard A. Wilson**

Further Reading

Holm, Major Jeanne M., USAF (Ret.), ed. *In Defense of a Nation: Women in World War II.* Washington, DC: Military Women's Press, 1998.

http://www.wimsa.org [Women in Military Service for America Foundation, Inc. Website]

ᔓ Women's Missionary Societies

The first female benevolent societies appeared by the 1790s. Early in the nineteenth century, during the Second Great Awakening, social consciousness flourished, and many women engaged in societies that supported missionary work. Mite societies, cent societies, missionary societies, mutual aid, charitable, and sewing societies were variations on the same central idea. Missionary societies raised funds to aid young male missionaries abroad and in the Western United States. In 1800, the Boston Female Society for Missionary Purposes raised funds to send ministers to "uncivilized areas." By 1817, 187 missionary societies existed, of which 110 were women's organizations.

Often, the societies focused within their own communities, meeting needs among those deemed worthy. Domestic missionary societies also were popular. The Female Charitable Society of 1813, a society of seventeen Presbyterian women, recorded giving to "Irish, Colored, and our own people."

Missionary societies usually affiliated with a church or denomination. In 1871, Maryland was headquarters for the Woman's Baptist Home Mission Society and the Woman's Mission to Woman, a federation of missionary organizations among Southern Baptist women. By 1888, all Southern Baptist missionary societies were unified under one executive union called Woman's Missionary Society auxiliary to the Southern Baptist Convention. The Presbyterian church formed regional boards such as the Women's Foreign Missionary Society of the Presbyterian Church. Auxiliary groups were established in local churches.

Societies gave women opportunities to acquire leadership and organizational skills. This was also true of missionary societies, which allowed women to collect and disburse funds as well as administrate. *(See also: Benevolence; Christianity; Religion; Women's Rights Movements: Nineteenth and Twentieth Centuries)*

—**Paula Williams Webber**

Further Reading

Boyd, Lois A., and R. Douglas Brackenridge. *Presbyterian Women in America: Two Centuries of a Quest for Status.* Westport, CT: Greenwood, 1983.

Clinton, Catherine. *The Other Civil War: American Women in the Nineteenth Century.* New York: Hill & Wang, 1992.

Hunt, Alma. *Woman's Missionary Union.* Birmingham, AL: Woman's Missionary Union, 1964.

Scott, Anne Firor. *Natural Allies: Women's Associations in American History.* Chicago: University of Illinois Press, 1991.

ᔓ Women's Peace Union (WPU)

The Women's Peace Union was an uncompromisingly pacifist interwar organization that evolved out of both the New York Woman's Peace Party and the New York State suffrage campaign. Membership was open to any woman over the age of twenty-one who would sign a pledge not to support war in any way. Although the leadership never exceeded fourteen women, the membership reached over two thousand. The leaders included Elinor Byrns, Caroline Lexow Babcock, Tracy Mygatt, Gertrude Franchot Tone, Mary Winsor, Frieda Langer Lazarus, and for six months, Jeannette Rankin.

Founded in August 1921, the WPU reflected four characteristics present in the 1920s peace movement. First, its leaders believed in a nonresistant philosophy, much like Mahatma Gandhi's, which preached that human life is sacred and all violence and killing are wrong. Second, the WPU was legalistic. Its program consisted of campaigning for a constitutional amendment to outlaw war and the manufacturing and trading of war materiel. This goal was also fostered by the union's senatorial sponsor, Lynn Joseph Frazier of North Dakota, who introduced the amendment into every congressional session from 1926 to 1939. Third, the WPU was feminist in that its roots, contributors, and strategy all lay in the suffrage movement. The WPU leaders chose to emphasize peace through the amendment as their one issue after the suffragists had the vote. Their belief was that winning the vote had been a nonviolent revolution and that peace could be won the same way. They felt that unless there was an end to war and war expenditures, basic social reforms could never be ensured. Finally, the WPU was nationalistic. Its members saw the United States as a progressive, democratic leader that other nations would follow to world disarmament.

The WPU program consisted of extensive lobbying in Washington, D.C., holding three Senate hearings (1927, 1930, 1934), and sending a representative to the League of Nations Disarmament Conference in Geneva in 1932. Although strong and active in the 1920s, the WPU weakened in the 1930s, largely because of the Great Depression and the growth of both fascism in Europe and worldwide militarism. Although never officially disbanded, the WPU ceased operations in 1941 just before Pearl Harbor was attacked. *(See also: Babcock, Caroline Lexow; Pacifism and the Peace Movement; Woman's Peace Party)*

—Harriet Hyman Alonso

Further Reading

Women's Peace Union Papers. Swarthmore College Peace Collection. Swarthmore, PA, and New York Public Library, New York City.

Alonso, Harriet Hyman. *The Women's Peace Union and the Outlawry of War, 1921–1942.* Knoxville: University of Tennessee Press, 1989.

Women's Prisons

With the establishment of the first prisons following the Revolutionary War, few provisions were made for the incarceration of women. Their small number made it possible for prison authorities to place them together in rooms away from the men's cell blocks, where they were frequently neglected.

Throughout the mid-1800s, the conditions remained poor, and little concern was given to the women inmates. The daily routine was characterized by idleness, and they were seldom supervised. Descriptions from the 1820s emphasized the crowded conditions and the intolerable noise. The establishment of New York's Mount Pleasant Female Prison in 1835, the nation's first women's prison, was an improvement, but not widely imitated. Throughout the 1860s, those prisons built to hold females outwardly resembled the male penitentiaries, but the care of the women inmates was decidedly inferior. Little concern was given to their needs.

The first effective effort toward specialized handling of women prisoners came from Zebulon Brockway, a major penal reformer who in 1868 established the House of Shelter for females as part of the Detroit, Michigan, House of Corrections. It offered treatment directed toward the needs of the women inmates. Beginning in the 1860s, reformers turned their attentions to incarcerated females and developed the idea of a women's reformatory. This concept rested on the belief that female inmates could best be reformed through a program of domestic training, a program emphasizing their "feminine" nature. In addition, the state legislation establishing the reformatories made it easier for officials to imprison women for minor offenses. Men convicted for the same crimes were typically not sent to prison. Support for reformatories came slowly, and by 1900, only two additional states, Indiana and Massachusetts, had established

institutions for women. By 1935, as the movement gained strength, the number had risen by seventeen. There are currently over seventy women's prisons in the United States.

Although there are far fewer women in prison than men, the population of incarcerated women is increasing much more rapidly than that of men. The rise in percentage of incarcerated women is a result of legislation adopted in 1987 requiring mandatory minimum prison sentences for drug offenses. Today, federal laws mandate prison sentences for people involved in drug trafficking and conspiracy. Bureau of Justice statistics from 1998 show that 66 percent of women in federal prisons are serving time for drug offenses.

Prison conditions and programs remain inferior to those at male institutions. Few vocational programs are available, and health care is inadequate. Children whose parents are incarcerated are at least three times as likely as other children to become incarcerated themselves. Long-term social and psychological impacts are yet to be realized as the number of women in prison continues to rise. *(See also: Criminals; Prison Reform)*

—Robert G. Waite

Further Reading

Freedman, Estelle B. *Their Sister's Keepers: Women's Prison Reform in America, 1830–1930.* Ann Arbor: University of Michigan Press, 1981.

McKelvey, Blake. *American Prisons: A History of Good Intentions.* Montclair, NJ: Patterson Smith, 1977.

Rafter, Nicole Hahn. *Partial Justice: Women in State Prisons, 1800–1935.* Boston: Northeastern University Press, 1985.

———. *Partial Justice: Women, Prisons, and Social Control,* 2d ed. New Brunswick, NJ: Transaction Publishers, 1990.

Siegal, Nina. "Women in Prison: What's Behind the Rising Numbers?" *Ms.* 9 (September/October 1998): 64-72.

Women's Protective Union (WPU)

The Women's Protective Union of Butte, Montana, was founded in the early 1890s. The origins of the union are obscure. According to some sources, the Western Federation of Miners organized the union in 1893, shortly after its own founding; others claim the Knights of Labor established the women's union. Its original members were the girls and women who worked in Butte's many boardinghouses, catering to the needs of the unmarried copper miners who dominated the city's population. The union eventually encompassed all female restaurant workers and a variety of hotel and motel maids, public building janitresses, hospital maids, girls who sold candy and popcorn in movie theaters, car hops at drive-ins, cocktail waitresses, and women employed at the local tamale factory. Best known of the union's members were the "bucket girls" who worked in boardinghouses and cafes, each day packing thousands of lunch buckets for hard-rock miners.

The Women's Protective Union has a rich history of association with labor movements of the western United States. In 1903, it affiliated with the American Labor Union (ALU), an organization chiefly representing western miners. The WPU submitted to the ALU the proposal that female organizations be taxed at one-half the rate of male unions owing to the lesser wages paid to women. In 1905, after entertaining a variety of speakers from the nascent Industrial Workers of the World, the WPU voted to join that radical labor group. On July 9, 1909, the WPU received a charter from the Hotel and Restaurant Employees International Union but still retained its distinctive local name. For the following sixty-four years, the union remained an exclusively female organization, but in 1973 it was instructed by the international union to merge with the Cooks and Waiters Union, Local 22. After some resistance, the WPU complied, and the two unions formed the Culinary and Miscellaneous Workers Union, Local 457.

Over the years, the WPU not only combated abusive bosses and sought to protect its members' rights as employees, it also served as a social and educational institution for Butte's working women. The union sponsored lectures, theatrical performances, dances, and benefits. Members often went out together for ice cream after union meetings, and as one woman, a member for sixty years, put it, "It was friendship. We loved to go to the union." *(See also: Industrial Workers of the World; Unions)*

—**Mary Murphy**

Further Reading

Cobble, Dorothy Sue. *Dishing It Out: Waitresses and Their Unions in the Twentieth Century.* Urbana: University of Illinois Press, 1991.

Weatherly, Laura Ryan, and Margaret Harrington. "Bucket Girl: Yard Girl, The Women Who Worked in Butte," *Catering Industry Employee* (October 1975): 22-23.

Webster, Valentine C. Oral History Interview. University of Montana Oral History Collection, Missoula, MT.

✑ Women's Rights Movements: Nineteenth and Twentieth Centuries

The struggle for women's rights as an organized reform movement in the United States began in the mid-nineteenth century. Historians of women's history have divided this continuous effort to support the rights of women into two distinct movements: The nineteenth-century woman's movement extended from the first Woman's Rights Convention in Seneca Falls, New York, in 1848, to the ratification of the Nineteenth Amendment, which enfranchised women in 1920; the twentieth-century women's movement began with the initial National Woman's Party attempt to launch the Equal Rights Amendment in 1923. The resurgence of feminist reform in the 1960s has been termed the modern women's movement. Prior to World War I, the members and critics of the movement to advocate or advance the status of women applied the term *feminist* to such activities and groups, and historians thereafter applied the term to advocates and developments in both centuries.

After 1848, the issues and goals of the woman's movement remained remarkably constant and inclusive until the Civil War. This reform movement challenged the limitations of woman's sphere under patriarchy and the gender system. Woman's rights advocates pursued various and significant reforms and improvements in women's education and employment opportunities as well as equal legal and political rights for women, the most-often acknowledged of which was women's enfranchisement through a federal amendment.

Historian Nancy Cott has suggested patterns of participation among those whose efforts improved women's status in Victorian America: Feminists directly challenged the patriarchal gender system and worked to restructure society; "womanist" supporters sought to reform the gender system to ensure a wider sphere and greater esteem for women as the superior gender but did not target an end to patriarchy as a goal; "collectivists" generally were ethnic women and women of color who addressed the needs of their community, confronting racism rather than identifying with the mainstream middle-class woman's movement, although they joined feminist efforts on issues that involved the welfare of their community or pursued parallel reforms. Feminists, nonfeminists, and occasionally antifeminists as individuals and as members of various associations established the goals of the woman's movement as a collective effort that addressed the conditions of every aspect of women's lives, to improve the status of women in antebellum America.

The woman's role of "helpmeet" during the colonial era gave way to the model of Republican Motherhood after the American Revolution, which seemingly promised equality of rights and opportunity for all people. The heritage of English common law allowed only *feme sole* and *feme covert* status to women, who were defined as the chattel property of their fathers and husbands. The citizenship of women was not acknowledged until after the Civil War.

The emphasis of the new nation on middle-class values and the economic and social mobility of the antebellum era produced a commitment to education that included establishing special academies for girls and women. By the 1820s, the social changes that accompanied the rise of industrialization and urbanization in the United States brought large numbers of women into the paid labor force as well as requiring a refinement of the cultural definition of the role of woman. Although marriage remained the only career choice for most middle-class women, educational and employment opportunities increased to compensate for this change in woman's role. Women's displacement from their crucial preindustrial tasks of food processing and clothing production within single-family farming made single young women available for the initial workforce of the textile industries. The presence and treatment of women in the paid labor force emerged early on as an issue of the woman's rights movement; the Lowell Mill Girls were the vanguard of the nineteenth-century industrial labor force and conducted the first strike of women workers.

Meanwhile, a definition of a separate woman's sphere in Victorian America emerged that confined women to a restrictive domestic identification with household chores, child rearing, and managing family consumption of mass-produced goods, especially in the towns and cities. Many women came to an understanding of the basic issues of woman's rights as a result of their unchallenged religious and civic activities in voluntary and benevolent associations. However, women also participated in antebellum abolition, temperance, and other reform movements; their experience in the antislavery and abolition movements particularly politicized their awareness of woman's second-class status and provided seasoned leadership for the emerging woman's rights movement by the 1840s.

While middle-class mainstream supporters of woman's rights in the Northeast and Midwest addressed feminist and urban reform issues, ethnic and minority women faced racist and class discrimination as well as the restrictions of gender. Native American women lost their role and status within their tribes with increased contact with white settlers who encroached on traditional lands and lifestyle. Interactions with federal authority forced the tribes' removal and their adoption of patriarchal power structures. Chicana and Latina reform efforts in the Southwest responded to ruthless displacement and loss of their family colonial land grants, both resulting from the trans-Mississippi migration, spurred by territorial expansion and homestead laws of the U.S. government. The few Asian American women brought to the West continued to live under the patriarchal gender system of their homelands. Women immigrants who arrived on the East Coast, first from Ireland, then from western and southern Europe, joined the industrial workforce or followed their men to establish farms in the Great Plains. Some immigrant women in the eastern urban areas joined the woman's movement, the labor movement, or both, as they sought to improve the living and working conditions among the working poor; but many minority women worked for improvements within their communities rather than formally joining the reform efforts of the woman's movement.

The Seneca Falls (New York) Convention in 1848, the first national woman's rights convention in the United States, formally inaugurated the organized movement to address the discrimination that women experienced under the law and in religion, education, and employment. The *Declaration of Sentiments and Resolutions* of the Seneca Falls Convention provided a summary list of grievances among women who were aware that they were the largest disfranchised group in their society. The issues raised with this protest document included the lack of woman suffrage and women's subordination to men in the family, under the law, and in all social institutions. The founders of the mainstream woman's rights movement were women for whom the purity, piety, domesticity, and submission of the cult of true womanhood proved inadequate as a source of identity and

self-esteem. The woman's rights movement extended beyond the generally acknowledged organized activities of avowed feminists for a women's franchise and dress reform. In the 1840s and 1850s, issues concerning women's admission to the professions of teaching and medicine were supported by conservative women as part of the emerging domestic feminism. Individuals such as Dorothea Dix pursued one-woman, single-issue campaigns to improve the conditions of the less fortunate in society; working-class and middle-class married women worked together for reform of married women's property rights.

By 1860, public as well as private institutions had been created to train women as public school teachers and therefore facilitated women's domination of that field by the 1880s. Women's medical hospitals had been established to train women physicians to care for women and children and medical missionaries to carry the cult of true womanhood throughout the world. More native-born and immigrant women joined the paid labor force, following traditional women's work from the domestic sphere to the industrial marketplace. Married women's property reform, which protected women's wages as well as custody and property rights, had been accomplished in New York State. All these and more issues were part of the woman's rights movement in the mid-nineteenth century, although those feminists who focused on the vote and dress reform continued to draw the attention of both a generally derisive press and of frankly antifeminist conservative critics.

During the Civil War, supporters of woman's rights in the North contributed to the war effort and thus used opportunities to expand women's opportunities especially in previously male-only occupations. Women's groups such as the U.S. Sanitary Commission and local and state organizations gathered and sent medical and other supplies to the wounded as well as volunteers to serve as nurses and aides in military hospitals; this wartime opportunity to serve established nursing as a profession for women. With the Union victory, supporters of woman's rights formed the Equal Rights Association in 1866; they hoped that the enfranchisement of the freedmen would include not only former slave women but all women. Disappointed by the gender limitation to universal manhood suffrage in the Fourteenth Amendment, the proponents of woman suffrage split into the American Woman Suffrage Association (AWSA) and the National Woman Suffrage Association (NWSA) in 1869. The NWSA and the AWSA represented the distinction between feminists and suffragists regarding political theory and practice; the NWSA continued to pursue and address diverse and often controversial feminist issues as well as woman suffrage; the AWSA focused its mainstream efforts on attaining the franchise for women.

After the Civil War, the expansion of public education provided young women with the occupations produced by technological advances in commercial and industrial sectors of the economy. The founding of separate women's colleges in the East and coeducational institutions in the West offered educational opportunities for women that produced a generation of college-educated domestic feminists who furthered the expansion of woman's sphere into public work and activities. As civic-minded middle-class matrons and members of the women's club movement or as career "spinster" teachers, nurses, physicians, or workers in the settlement house movement, these women worked among the urban poor. Women began to enter the professions of law and the ministry.

Working-class and immigrant women continued to join the workforce in factories, offices, and commercial establishments, not in pursuit of careers but to assist in their families' survival in urban industrial America. From their ranks came women leaders in the union and labor movement, who during the Progressive Era would articulate the issues of the woman's movement that addressed the needs of their co-workers. Social feminism emerged as a coalition of the working- and middle-class women who confronted the conditions of women workers in sweatshops and retail stores, through the efforts of the National Women's Trade Union League and the National Consumers' League. The Woman's Christian Temperance Union, following the motto of its president Frances Willard, "Do Everything," supported many women's movement issues. Birth control proved another issue of the woman's rights movement that crossed class and economic lines.

Free black women had participated in the abolition and antislavery movements as well as the antebellum woman's rights movement. Sojourner Truth argued with eloquence and deadly accuracy against the non sequiturs of the critics of women's rights and made universally comprehensible the particular situation of black women both before and after the Civil War. Emancipated black women continued their efforts to forge stable families and to improve the legal status and economic conditions of their communities. In racially segregated voluntary associations, middle-class club women worked for the vote, civil rights, and other issues crucial to their less prosperous sisters in rural areas of the South and in urban northern cities. Black club women provided the community and church leadership to address the need for educational institutions for black women as well as for black men, as part of the woman's rights movement. Excluded from equal participation because of racism within white mainstream woman's rights groups at the turn of the century, black women nonetheless worked for woman suffrage through their own national and community groups. Native American women endured the impact of federal policies of removal, internment, and severalty that impoverished their people and further undermined their traditional tribal roles. Other minority women—Asian American, Chicana and Latina—participated in Progressive Era reform efforts that grew out of their community concerns.

By the last decade of the nineteenth century, the woman's rights movement began to focus on the single issue of woman suffrage. The two national suffrage associations merged in 1890, becoming the National American Woman Suffrage Association (NAWSA), which set its sights on a federal amendment to enfranchise women as it worked piecemeal through individual states to achieve full and partial suffrage for women. The General Federation of Women's Clubs as well as the social feminist organizations joined the campaign for woman suffrage, which was accomplished with the ratification of the Nineteenth Amendment in 1920.

The women progressives such as Jane Addams provided leadership for the Women's International League for Peace and Freedom and endured public and government censure during and after World War I. Chinese American women focused their efforts on support of women who were active in the nationalist movement in China; Puerto Rican women formed their Liga Feminea de Puerto Rico in 1917. Local and neighborhood issues compelled women to join together and thus fostered diversity within the woman's movement, although the general movement was eclipsed by the suffrage movement.

The achievement of that limited goal brought closure to the purpose of the single-issue suffrage movement but left issues of the broader nineteenth-century movement for women's rights unresolved; thus, the presence of an organized woman's rights movement was diffused at the close of World War I. The NAWSA evolved into the nonpartisan League of Women Voters, and a striking difference of opinion emerged and dissolved the coalition of various women's groups that had supported the final drive for the woman vote.

Those Progressive Era women who supported the goals of social feminism defended the gains in protective legislation. They supported the agenda of the Women's Bureau, which built on prewar accomplishments such as *Muller v. Oregon* (1908) that defined women as a special class of workers and produced the Sheppard-Towner Act of 1921; their stance put them at odds with the radical feminism of the members of the National Woman's Party (NWP), who initiated the twentieth-century campaign for the Equal Rights Amendment because the vote alone would not ensure women's equality under the law or in society. The proponents of the politics of domesticity represented the majority opinion regarding the gains of the movement: Women's employment was appropriate in certain occupations and professions on a contingency basis; women's place and future in higher education was defined as limited to woman's duty and service to family, community, and the nation. Women's destiny remained determined by their biology.

Although Alice Paul first initiated the introduction of the Equal Rights Amendment in 1923 to secure complete legal equality for women, the 1920s were not characterized by additional significant gains for the women's movement for several reasons: (a) the rise of political fundamentalism in American society generally, (b) the assumption of the younger generation of women that the franchise signified that the struggle for women's rights had been won and that the vote would automatically bring all the improvements promised by the suffragists, and (c) the disintegration of the coalition of women's groups that had worked for suffrage.

Despite the efforts of the nonpartisan League of Women Voters and contrary to both the fears of the antisuffragists and the hopes of suffragists, women voted according to their class, race, and economic status rather than as a gender bloc. Many of the women who had worked for woman suffrage were either too exhausted to continue the struggle for women's rights, or they devoted their efforts to one-issue causes. Young women in the 1920s took advantage of the advances in educational and employment opportunities, but despite the increase in the numbers of women who received postsecondary educations and worked outside the home, these improvements were limited to jobs deemed appropriate for women who worked conditionally, because of the continued primary identification of women's proper role with marriage, home, and child care. However, the political activists within the National Woman's Party, holdover social feminists from the Progressive Era, and a token number of stalwart women in academe and the professions served as keepers of the flame of feminism throughout the "Roaring Twenties" and into the New Deal era. Minority women who suffered from sexist, racist, and class discrimination worked foremost to improve conditions for the members of their ethnic groups.

The historical context of the 1920s proved as hostile to avowed feminism as to other social reform movements. However, the feminism of the movement persisted and resurfaced sporadically throughout the 1930s and 1940s, finally reasserting its presence during the social ferment of the 1950s and 1960s that sparked the modern or twentieth-century women's movement.

Led by Eleanor Roosevelt, professional women influenced the New Deal administration's social reform programs of the 1930s to improve women's conditions in the family and to a lesser degree in the labor force. Due to these social feminists, women were included as participants and beneficiaries of the relief, reform, and recovery programs of New Deal agencies. After 1941, the ambivalence of the government's wartime recruitment of single and married women to work in the defense plants notwithstanding, women's mass involvement in home front and military mobilizations of World War II offered them unprecedented opportunities and pay scales. The war prompted governmental employment policies and changes in the postwar economy that compounded the wartime experiences of women drawn into the paid labor force. Despite the brutal demobilization dismissal policies regarding women, many single and married women remained in the workforce after 1945, and those who returned to the home did so with the knowledge that once they had been economically self-sufficient as well as part of a great patriotic force of competent and independent women.

As the economic realities of the 1950s strained the ability of the male breadwinner to support the prescribed suburban lifestyle of his middle-class family, the mainstream matron found homemaking less rewarding than the women's magazines had promised. Thus, married women continued to increase both their part-time and full-time participation in the labor force into the 1960s. The convergence of the restlessness of suburban married women from "the problem that had no name" (as it was designated by Betty Friedan in *The Feminine Mystique*), the participation of young and older black and white women in the civil rights movement, and the radical politicization of campus women in the New Left produced a spectrum of activities and groups that focused specifically on women's issues by the mid-1960s. An early indication of the latent political power of women was demonstrated by the Woman's Strike for Peace in 1962; its participants defied the congressional House Un-American Activities Committee and challenged Cold War nuclear policies of the United States.

Myriad militant groups within the women's liberation movement drew the younger women from the New Left, while the National Organization for Women pursued a more mainstream political and legal reform agenda that reflected a membership of middle-class and professional women. The women's liberation movement contributed the process of consciousness-raising (C-R) that promoted the empowerment of grassroots groups that addressed sexism in general, sexual assault in particular, and various other efforts. C-R groups provided a practical application of the feminist slogan "The Personal Is Political," as women from diverse sectors of American society shared their personal experience and developed a sense of solidarity that prompted their political and reform action.

The agenda of the modern women's movement revealed those issues that most concerned women generally: equality of treatment under the law, equal opportunity in education and in the workplace, adequate child care as well as child and maternal welfare policies, abortion rights, and reforms in family and divorce statutes. Many items on this agenda echoed the original concerns in the 1848 *Declaration of Sentiments* and were repeated in the *NOW Statement of Purpose* in 1966. Both avowed feminists and mainstream reformers used political action to secure women's presence in all occupations and endeavors as well as professional networking to ensure the existence and an awareness of women as role models in traditional and nontraditional activities and employment. The issues raised by the women's movement provided support for scholarly inquiry that challenged the general absence of women in traditional curricula and resulted in the establishment of women's studies courses and programs in institutions of higher education. In 1982, for example, after a decade of efforts to improve the opportunities for women of color, Chicana feminists formed the Mujeres Activas en Litras y Cambio Social (MALCS) to further interdisciplinary curriculum and programs as well as to oppose their race, class, and gender oppression in colleges and universities.

The immediate target of the modern women's movement was increased women's access to and equal participation in politics and in all aspects of the economy. Long-established women's groups such as the American Association of University Women and the YWCA joined the newer organizations to support the Equal Rights Amendment, which was sent to the states for ratification in 1972. The Supreme Court's decision *Roe v. Wade* decriminalized abortion in 1973. During the early 1970s, women filed sex discrimination cases at both the state and federal levels under the provisions of the Civil Rights Act of 1963 and used the Equal Employment Opportunity Commission, established by the Civil Rights Act of 1964, to ensure women's equal opportunity in the labor force. Supporters of equal education for women brought class-action suits against academic institutions using Title IX of the Education Act of 1972. Using the leverage of these federal laws and Executive Orders 11246 and 11375, the women's movement had achieved significant success in raising social consciousness regarding the presence and impact of sexism by the mid-1970s.

The nationwide participation of diverse women's groups in the 1977 International Women's Year (IWY) Conference in Houston marked the crest of the twentieth-century women's movement during the 1970s. The result of IWY state conferences that had provided a forum for defining the positions of proponents and opponents of the women's movement, the IWY Conference produced its National Plan of Action that not only supported the ERA but also articulated and addressed the crucial issues of the movement, which included the feminization of poverty and child care; homemakers', minority women's, and lesbian rights; equity in education, employment, and credit; and abortion rights. Support of the ratification of the Equal Rights Amendment drew a variety of women's organizations to work together in a manner similar to the final push for woman suffrage, but the single focus obscured the persistent multiplicity of issues that concerned women in the 1980s.

Minority women reflected the growing sense of ethnic pride and supported cultural diversity that honored their community history, culture, and values. Native American women assumed leadership roles within the tribes as they challenged the federal policies that had denied the cultural values and practices on the reservations. Asian American women as well as Chicanas and Latinas formed groups among their ethnic associations to assert the importance of women's issues within their community. Urban black women assumed leadership of reform issues that were important to improving conditions and opportunities for their communities, as well as developed feminist groups that examined the impact of race, class, and gender on African American women.

However, the 1980s brought economic crisis and a conservative and antifeminist backlash to the social reforms of the 1960s and 1970s. According to critics, the women's movement threatened the patriarchal core of the family, common law, and capitalism and thus was the cause of the breakdown of the family and the rising divorce rate, the disintegration of law and order, and male unemployment. The administrations of Ronald Reagan oversaw the deliberate evisceration of the established and successful federal agencies, programs, and statutes that had facilitated women's struggle for equity under the law, in education, employment, and the family. Phyllis Schlafly's Stop ERA organization led the charge to defeat the Equal Rights Amendment in the last three of the thirty-eight states needed for ratification of the amendment, despite the successful effort of feminists to gain a three-year extension for its ratification. Following their success in thwarting ERA ratification, the New Right coalition of political conservatives and religious fundamentalists consummately orchestrated opposition to women's reproductive rights and thus recruited numerous previously apolitical women into the movement they designated "Right to Life." Reagan-appointed judges in the federal judiciary handed down decisions that threatened women's civil and reproductive rights; the *Webster* decision in 1989, which eroded the protection of *Roe v. Wade,* reinvigorated the pro-choice movement as did the assaults on women's clinics and their staffs.

Thus, by the late 1980s, the course of the women's movement seemed uncertain. Women were fighting setbacks at the state and national level. Attempts to introduce the ERA in 1983 and 1987 failed to achieve the two-thirds congressional vote required; endeavors to halt the erosion of Title IX and the cutback on federal entitlement programs that were desperately needed to reverse the feminization of poverty produced at best a "holding action." Adverse economic conditions limited support for programs for women in employment and in education. As in the 1920s, the young women of the 1980s seemed to feel that the revolution had been won and that the struggle was over, and they took for granted the opportunities secured for them by the feminist activities of the 1960s and 1970s. The 1990s promised more of the same, until the election of Democrat Bill Clinton as president in 1992 revived hopes of feminists that the gains in educational and employment opportunities, in reproductive and legal rights of the modern women's movement of the 1970s and 1980s might be preserved. The development of a global economy nurtured the growth of the international women's movement as a response to significant changes in women's roles around the world. *(See also: Abolition and the Antislavery Movement; American Revolutionary Era; American Woman Suffrage Association; Birth Control; Black Women's Clubs; Civil Rights; Civil Rights Act of 1964; Civil War; Common Law; Cult of True Womanhood; Declaration of Sentiments and Resolutions; Domestic Feminism; Dress Reform: Nineteenth Century; Education; Equal Rights Amendment; Feminism; General Federation of Women's Clubs; Industrial Revolution; International Women's Year Conference of 1977; Legal Profession; Marriage; Married Women's Property Acts; National American Woman Suffrage Association; National Organization for Women; National Woman Suffrage Association; New Deal; New Left; Nursing; Patriarchy; Physicians; Radical Feminism; Roe v. Wade; Seneca Falls Convention; Settlement House Movement; Sex-*

Gender System; Social Feminism; Suffrage; Teaching; Temperance Movement; Title IX of the Education Amendments of 1972; Unions; Wages; Women's Liberation Movement; Women's Studies; Women's Work: Nineteenth Century)

—Angela M. Howard

Further Reading

Clinton, Catherine. *The Other Civil War: American Women in the Nineteenth Century.* New York: Hill & Wang, 1984.

Cott, Nancy F. *The Grounding of Modern Feminism.* New Haven, CT: Yale University Press, 1987.

DuBois, Ellen. *Feminism and Suffrage: The Emergence of an Independent Women's Movement in America.* Ithaca, NY: Cornell University Press, 1978.

Hersh, Blanch. *The Slavery of Sex: Feminist-Abolitionists in America.* Urbana: University of Illinois Press, 1978.

Muller v. Oregon, 208 U.S. 412 (1908).

Roe v. Wade, 410 U.S. 113, 35 L. Ed. 2d, 147. 93 S. Ct. 705 (1973).

Rupp, Leila J. *Worlds of Women: The Makings of an International Women's Movement.* Princeton, NJ: Princeton University Press, 1998.

Scharf, Lois, and Joan M. Jensen, eds. *Decades of Discontent: The Women's Movement, 1920–1940.* Boston: Northeastern University Press, 1987.

Scott, Anne Firor. *Natural Allies: Women's Associations in American History.* Urbana: University of Illinois Press, 1992.

Webster v. Reproductive Health Services, 851 F. 2d 1074 (8th. Cir. 1988), probable jurisdiction noted, 109 S. Ct. 780 (1989).

http://scriptorium.lib.duke.edu/#collections [Rare Book, Manuscript, and Special Collections Library, Duke University]

⭐ The Women's Room

Written by Marilyn French in 1977, *The Women's Room* has as its title an alternative expression for the euphemism "ladies' room." French centers her novel on the nearly autobiographical character of Mira, who leads the life of a typical suburban housewife until her doctor-husband decides he wants a divorce. As a result, Mira must support herself, and she completes college, sends her two children to a boarding school, and enrolls in a graduate program at Harvard. It is in a rest room there that Mira notices a sign on the door that has the term LADIES ROOM scratched out and WOMEN'S ROOM written in its place, as if to signify women's coming of age from a subordinate relationship with men to one of greater relevance and importance.

After becoming involved in several of the late 1960s demonstrations and a certain amount of activism, Mira realizes that she had led a life of social inactivity that included daily kaffeeklatsches and monthly cocktail parties. Basically, she has lost her own identity, but through her fulfilling schoolwork, she gains it back. Prior to Harvard, her friendships with the other suburban housewives were based primarily on common concerns such as household chores and the proper discipline of children, but after her arrival in graduate school, she learns of things that take place outside the limited world she has known. Throughout the story, Mira encounters several groups of women whom she quickly

befriends to gain release through their empathy and understanding discourse. The last group of female friends at Harvard is the one that aids Mira in reaching an acute awareness of life beyond the bounds of a male-dominated marriage and world.

The book is historically significant as a novel that captured many women's experiences, but it has also become a cultural icon of middle-class white feminism; it is read and studied widely in the academic world and became a made-for-television movie that received critical acclaim and several Emmy nominations. *The Women's Room* remains at the forefront of women's literature in America, and shortly after it was published, according to *Virginia Quarterly Review,* several daily and weekly press reviewers claimed that the novel from which the new euphemism was derived was the "major novel in the women's liberation movement." *(See also: Women Writers; Women's Liberation Movement)*

—James A. Howley

Further Reading

French, Marilyn. *The War against Women.* New York: Summit, 1992.

———. *The Women's Room.* New York: Summit, 1977.

Robinson, Paul. "History and Her Story," *Washington Post* (June 2, 1985): 1-14.

Summers, Anne. "Dissidents and Discontents," *Times Literary Supplement* 4412 (October 23, 1987): 1158.

⭐ Women's Studies

Women's studies is an interdisciplinary academic field that examines the experience and achievements of women from a feminist perspective. It had its origin in the movement for women's equality that was revived in the 1960s. In higher education, feminist critiques of the traditional disciplines mirrored agitation for the end of discriminatory treatment of women as students and faculty and, in general, for the transformation of society at large. Flaws in the existing disciplines included both the treatment of the male as the norm and the female as an anomaly and the absence altogether of women's accomplishments and experiences. The primary impetus for development of the field of women's studies came from scholars in the social sciences and humanities; however, scholars from the professions and biological sciences have also made major contributions to the conception and growth of women's studies. These scholars recognized that lasting social change would not occur unless there was a radical transformation in what is known, how it is known, and how value is assigned to areas of knowledge. Women's studies pioneers had to overcome the prejudice in academia that research with a primary or exclusive focus on women was marginal. The field of women's studies began as an interdisciplinary critique that has evolved into an independent method of inquiry and body of knowledge concerned centrally with gender. It is noteworthy that the field of women's studies has matured concurrently with the growth in numbers of women students and faculty in American higher education.

San Diego State University established the first women's studies baccalaureate degree program in 1969. Within two decades, numbers of academic programs surged from 39 in 1974 to 671 by 1993. Since the intention of faculty in women's studies was not only to discover new knowledge about women but also to transform the narrow male bias of the traditional curriculum, women's studies programs most often eschewed departmental status for an interdisciplinary structure that invited faculty with appointments in disciplinary departments to participate. Formal curricula typically have included general introductory courses, women-related courses offered in the traditional departments, and integrative capstone courses to round out the program. Increasingly, feminist theory courses have become part of such formal curricula. Early programs offered submajor options only—special certificates or minors. However, as the field has developed, numbers of formal bachelor's, master's, and doctoral degree programs have been growing steadily.

The new knowledge has changed not only higher education, where feminist theory is firmly established as a methodological approach and has transformed many fields such as literary studies and history, it has also changed the face of publishing. The first scholarly journal devoted to the field, *Women's Studies—An Interdisciplinary Journal*, began publishing in 1972. In 1975, *SIGNS: Journal of Women in Culture and Society* began publication and has become the leading journal of women's studies scholarship. Another publication is the *National Women's Studies Association Journal*. By 1993, the *Women's Studies Index* offered bibliographic guidance on articles in eighty-two women-centered periodicals. Esther Stineman's 1979 annotated *Women's Studies— A Recommended Core Bibliography* could comfortably contain principal monographs pertinent to the field in its 1,763 entries. The 1987 Loeb-Searing-Stineman supplement, covering the period from 1980 to 1985, had to select its 1,211 entries from more than five thousand pertinent publications that had appeared since the original bibliography was published. Not included was the vast volume of periodical literature, from entire issues of nonwomen's studies journals featuring women-related scholarship to individual women-related articles now commonplace in such journals.

In 1979, the National Women's Studies Association (NWSA) was founded and held its first annual conference. By 1993, the NWSA had grown to four thousand members with twelve regional groups. Unlike other professional associations in higher education, the NWSA has had a policy of sponsoring community and feminist-activist aims as well as purely academic functions, a purpose that has been carried out with some difficulty. Within many disciplinary associations, women's caucuses have been formed and often promote disciplinary research on women as well as focus on the status of women in the profession.

Within the field, there has been a degree of tension between the goal of integrating women's studies across the curriculum and that of establishing separate programs. Academic "mainstreaming" projects across the country have attracted federal and private extramural funding, and a range of "how-to" publications and materials have sprung up from these projects to assist interested faculty in integrating the findings of women's studies scholarship into their disciplinary courses. Women's studies practitioners have generally agreed that both integration projects and separate programs are necessary: (a) the programs to serve as an interdisciplinary crossroads at which an independent body of knowledge continues to grow and (b) the mainstreaming projects to fulfill the goal of transformation, of creating bias-free and fully integrated disciplinary curricula. Women's studies has been a major contributor to the burgeoning field of cultural studies. *(See also: Archives and Sources; Higher Education; Internet Resources; Women's Liberation Movement)*

—**Karen Merritt**

Further Reading

Bowles, Gloria, and Renate Buelli Klein, eds. *Theories of Women's Studies.* Boston: Routledge & Kegan Paul, 1983.

Boxer, Marilyn Jacoby. *When Women Ask the Questions: Creating Women's Studies in America.* Baltimore: Johns Hopkins University Press, 1998.

Female Studies I-VI. Old Westbury, NY: Feminist Press, 1970–1972.

Hull, Gloria T., Patricia Bell Scott, and Barbara Smith, eds. *But Some of Us Were Brave: Black Women's Studies.* Old Westbury, NY: Feminist Press, 1986.

Kennedy, Mary, Cathy Lubelska, and Val Walsh, eds. *Making Connections: Women's Studies, Women's Movements, Women's Lives.* London and Washington, DC: Taylor & Francis, 1993.

Minnich, Elizabeth, Jean O'Barr, and Rachel Rosenfeld, eds. *Reconstructing the Academy: Women's Education and Women's Studies.* Chicago: University of Chicago Press, 1988.

O'Barr, Jean, and Kristin Luker. *Feminism in Action: Building Institutions and Community through Women's Studies.* Chapel Hill: University of North Carolina Press, 1994.

∾ WOMENS WAY

WOMENS WAY was established in 1977 as a fund-raising coalition of organizations providing innovative, nontraditional services for Philadelphia-area women. The idea originated with Louise Page, who wanted to start an agency that would bring together a cross section of women inspired by the idea of women helping women and to create a vehicle for funding women's services.

The original members of the coalition were Women in Transition, Women Organized Against Rape, the Elizabeth Blackwell Health Center for Women, CHOICE (health counseling and referral), the Pennsylvania Program for Women and Girl Offenders, the Women's Law Project, and Options for Women (employment counseling). By 1985, the coalition also included Women Against Abuse, the Community Women's Education Project, Women's Alliance for Job Equity, the Domestic Abuse Project of Delaware County, and the WOMENS WAY Discretionary Fund. Two of the founding member agencies, Women in Transition and the Pennsylvania Program for Women and Girl Offenders, had dropped out of the coalition by 1981.

These agencies emerged in the early 1970s as part of the rebirth of the women's movement, which created a demand for services not provided by traditional organizations. Their pioneering activities in areas such as abortion rights and fair treatment for rape victims, coupled with their identification as feminist organizations, had curtailed their ability to raise adequate funds to expand their services. Financial desperation persuaded these agencies to forfeit their fund-raising autonomy to this untried coalition.

The early years of WOMENS WAY were difficult ones, with annual totals under $87,000. Not until WOMENS WAY negotiated a donor option plan with United Way in 1980-81 did the annual total show a substantial increase to $206,000. Access to other payroll deduction plans has further broadened the base of support, along with growing help from the corporate community. WOMENS WAY allocations continued to represent a small percentage of the combined agency budgets of $2.4 million for 1985-86, but the evenly distributed funds are essential to meet expenses not covered in restricted grant allocations. To mark its tenth anniversary in 1987, WOMENS WAY launched a campaign to raise $2 million for the Reserve Fund for the Future to ensure the continuation of the member agencies. By the mid-1980s, WOMENS WAY was considered the most successful women's fund-raising coalition in the country. In 1998, WOMENS WAY had nine full-member agencies and eight associate member agencies that received allocations and technical assistance grants totaling almost $800,000 (*WOMENS WAY 1997-98 Annual Report,* Philadelphia, 1998). In addition, WOMENS WAY awarded a total of $40,000 to twenty-nine smaller, local organizations whose programs and services complement those of the WOMENS WAY agencies. By 1998, WOMENS WAY was close to raising $1 million to endow the Ernesta D. Ballard Fund for WOMENS WAY at the Philadelphia Foundation. The 1998 WOMENS WAY dinner, the organization's largest fund-raising event, netted a record $430,000. As an organization that has just passed its twentieth anniversary, it is increasingly conscious of the need to look to the future in terms of growing its endowment fund and recruiting younger women both as donors and as leaders.

—**Cynthia Jeffress Little**

Further Reading

Little, Cynthia J. "Feminism and Volunteerism in Action: WOMENS WAY." In *Celebrate Women,* edited by Patricia O'Donnell. Philadelphia: Pennsylvania Federation of Women's Clubs, 1986. Exhibition catalog.

~ Women's Work: Nineteenth Century

During the nineteenth century, the Industrial Revolution transformed the labor of women in America. In 1800, few women worked for wages, and the vast majority of female wage earners were domestic workers. By 1900, one-third of the employed women were servants, and one-fifth of all women were wage earners. Single women dominated the world of female employment, but the employment of married women rose significantly in the last two decades of the century. At the time of the 1900 census, 6 percent of American wives were wage earners. Significant numbers of women first entered employments outside the domestic sphere with the emergence of factory spinning and textile production in the 1820s and 1830s. By the end of the century, nearly a million women, or about one-fifth of all female wage earners, were employed in factories. In addition to spinning and textile manufacturing, women worked widely in tobacco factories, boot and shoe factories, glass making, garment manufacturing, and commercial laundries by 1900.

In addition to creating a market for female labor in manufacturing, the Industrial Revolution opened other employment sectors to women as higher-paid male workers were lured elsewhere. Technological changes, including the telephone and the typewriter, dramatically altered means of communication and record keeping and simultaneously created a demand for literate but not highly trained workers, jobs that were offered to women. A sharp rise in the demand for schooling in an industrializing society and the desertion of teaching jobs by men opened the way for women teachers. By the 1860s, women constituted the majority of public school teachers. Although teachers accounted for three-fourths of all the female professional workers in 1900, women also advanced in professions such as nursing, the arts, and religious and welfare work in the late nineteenth century. After the Civil War, retail stores and urban service industries also became employers of women.

The circumstances under which women entered new occupations during the nineteenth century illustrate how strictly employment in America has been segregated by sex and how women have been economically disadvantaged through occupational segregation. The jobs that women came to dominate in the nineteenth century were characterized by a similarity to women's work within the home, a simplification of tasks through mechanization or the reorganization of work, a reduction in wages, or a combination of these factors. Industrial homework, poorly paid manufacturing done at home, persisted longer among women than among men.

Throughout the nineteenth century, the vast majority of women labored at domestic chores, raised food for their families and produced the family clothing, or participated in commercial production on family farms without receiving wages. Both paid and unpaid labor in agriculture was a major field of work for women in the nineteenth century. Until Emancipation, much of this labor was provided by black women, and after the Civil War, black women were the majority of paid female laborers in agriculture. *(See also: African American Domestic Workers; Agriculture: Preindustrial and Nineteenth-Century United States; Cigar Makers/*

Tobacco Workers; Domestic Service; Garment Industries; Industrial Revolution; Nursing; Teaching; Telephone Operators; Textiles: North and South; Wages)

—**Julia Kirk Blackwelder**

Further Reading

Blewett, Mary H. *Men, Women, and Work: Class, Gender, and Protest in the New England Shoe Industry, 1780–1910.* Urbana: University of Illinois Press, 1988.

Kessler-Harris, Alice. *Out to Work: A History of Wage Earning Women in the United States.* New York: Oxford University Press, 1982.

Matthaei, Julie A. *An Economic History of Women in America: Women's Work, the Sexual Division of Labor, and the Development of Capitalism.* New York: Schocken, 1982.

Stansell, Christine. *City of Women: Sex and Class in New York, 1789–1860.* New York: Knopf, 1986.

U.S. Bureau of the Census. *Historical Statistics of the United States, Colonial Times to 1970.* Part 1, Bicentennial ed. Washington, DC: Government Printing Office, 1975.

Weiner, Lynn Y. *From Working Girl to Working Wife: The Female Labor Force in the United States, 1820–1980.* Chapel Hill: University of North Carolina Press, 1985.

ᕕ Woodhull, Victoria Claflin
(1838–1927)

Figure 67. Victoria Woodhull
Spiritualist, financier, reformer, advocate of free love, and candidate for president, Victoria Woodhull was a highly visible figure in the cause of woman suffrage in the nineteenth century. Used by permission of Corbis-Bettmann.

Victoria Claflin Woodhull was a successful businesswoman and reformer. The seventh daughter of Reuben Claflin and Roxanna Hummel, she grew up in central Ohio. As a girl, she worked with her family's "medicine show," which featured her younger sister Tennessee (1846–1923), an accomplished medium.

In 1853, at the age of fifteen, she married Canning Woodhull, a physician, who was no match for her restless spirits. He later divorced Woodhull because of her liaison with Colonel James Harvey Blood, a dashing Civil War veteran. Colonel Blood helped interest Woodhull in a number of reform causes that surrounded nineteenth-century spiritualism. Later, Woodhull and her sister moved to New York and became the first female stockbrokers on Wall Street. The good-looking but somewhat notorious sisters had secured the financial backing of aging railroad magnate Cornelius Vanderbilt. The "Bewitching Brokers" mastered the art of stock wheeling and dealing and soon moved into a splendid mansion on fashionable Murray Hill.

Having conquered the financial world, Woodhull turned her attention to the politics of reform. Influenced by the thought of radical philosopher Stephen Pearl Andrews and her own life experiences, Woodhull wrote in support of Pantarchy—the perfect state, where free love reigned among consenting adults and children and property were managed in common. She regarded marriage as a degrading form of bondage. These conclusions, so shocking to Victorian sensibilities, were published in a series of *New York Herald* articles in 1870 and in book form a year later under the title *Origin, Tendencies and Principles of Government.*

She followed up on her political and social theories by declaring herself a candidate for the presidency of the United States on April 2, 1870. Her platform was articulated in her journal, *Woodhull & Claflin's Weekly,* which gained her further notoriety. Woodhull both shocked and titillated her readers with tales of Wall Street corruption and fraud and her advocacy of sexual rights for women and legalized prostitution, along with tax, housing, and dietary reform. She also published news about working women's efforts to organize and better their conditions. The *Weekly* published the first American version of Marx and Engels's *Communist Manifesto* and openly espoused the cause of socialism.

In 1871, she supported the woman suffrage movement despite the disapproval of Lucy Stone and others. She was the first woman invited to address the House Judiciary Committee, brilliantly arguing that the use of the word *person* in the Fourteenth and Fifteenth Constitutional Amendments already implied female suffrage. Woodhull became the most talked-about figure in the suffrage movement. She kept the presses humming with public calls for "secession" if Congress did not grant women the vote, as well as with her continued defense of sexual freedom. Woodhull's personality, however, began to obscure the issues, and Susan B. Anthony had to oust her in 1872 as the leader of the National Woman Suffrage Association.

Woodhull then went into a period of decline, as she abandoned her spiritualist associations and divorced Colonel

Blood for adultery in 1876. Suffering from ill health and financial setbacks, Woodhull moved to England and resumed her lecture career. Despite her philosophical renunciation, she married John Biddulph Martin, an aristocrat from a leading British banking family, on October 31, 1883. Between 1892 and 1901, Woodhull and her daughter Zula Maud published the *Humanitarian,* a journal devoted to eugenics. She continued her interest in the woman's movement in the United States and returned to her native land on a number of occasions. *(See also: Free Love; Journalism; National Woman Suffrage Association; Socialism)*

—**Jonathan W. Zophy**

Further Reading

Gabriel, Mary. *Notorious Victoria: The Life of Victoria Woodhull, Uncensored.* Chapel Hill, NC: Algonquin, 1998.

Goldsmith, Barbara. *Other Powers: The Age of Suffrage, Spiritualism, and the Scandalous Victoria Woodhull.* New York: Harperperrenial, 1999.

Johnson, Johanna. *Mrs. Satan: The Incredible Saga of Victoria C. Woodhull.* New York: Putnam, 1967.

Marberry, M. M. *Vicky: A Biography of Victoria C. Woodhull.* New York: Funk & Wagnalls, 1967.

Meade, Marian. *Free Woman: The Life and Times of Victoria Woodhull.* New York: Knopf, 1976.

Ocko, Stephanie. "Victoria Woodhull's Siege of New York," *American History Illustrated* 16 (1981): 32-37.

Sachs, Emanie. *"The Terrible Siren": Victoria Woodhull.* New York: Harper, 1928.

Schneir, Miriam. *Feminism: The Essential Historical Writings.* New York: Vintage, 1972.

✑ Workers' Education for Women

Between 1910 and the 1930s, programs to educate women workers were established by labor unions, by government agencies and women's voluntary organizations, and by colleges and universities. For the most part, these efforts were not intended to help working women obtain college degrees but, rather, were designed to provide them with an opportunity to study to understand their world better. An additional motive was to provide women with resources to help them organize unions and other sorts of self-help organizations on the job. Although most of the programs for workers' education for women were established in the opening decades of the century, these activities have continued up to the present.

Among the first workers' education programs to be established for women were those of the National Women's Trade Union League (NWTUL), a largely middle- and upper-class organization of women dedicated to improving the lives of women workers, particularly those working in industry. At about the same time (1914), the International Ladies Garment Workers Union (ILGWU) began its own program of education for women working in the garment trades, teaching them principles of trade unionism and other subjects. Slightly later, other programs were established by the YWCA, by other unions, and by state and local governments

to allow working women to study during summer sessions at colleges and universities. Perhaps the most famous of these was the summer school for women workers held at Bryn Mawr College between 1921 and 1938. Other well-known summer programs were conducted at Barnard College and at the University of Wisconsin. In 1928, a national organization, the Affiliated Schools for Women Workers, was established to coordinate these activities and to provide information about various programs to women and to sponsoring agencies. Less than a decade later, this organization broadened its purview to include education for both men and women workers. It continued to perform this function until 1962 under the title American Labor Education Service.

What did women workers study in these programs? Although many of the worker education courses focused on problems of labor organization, most seem to have been general programs of study in the liberal arts. At Bryn Mawr and other colleges, women (most of them young) studied literature and history, economics (often with a focus on their own problems), politics, and the natural sciences. While these courses were often rather low key and introductory in orientation, both students and teachers remember them as having been especially poignant learning experiences. Only a small fraction of working women ever participated in workers' education programs, but a fairly high percentage of the alumnae of these programs became activists in the labor movement or in other organizations concerned with the welfare of working women. *(See also: Bryn Mawr Summer School; International Ladies Garment Workers Union; National Women's Trade Union League)*

—**John L. Rury**

Further Reading

Kornbluh, Joyce L., and Mary Frederickson, eds. *Sisterhood and Solidarity: Workers' Education for Women, 1914–1984.* Philadelphia: Temple University Press, 1984.

✑ Working Women's Protective Unions (WWPUs)

Several distinct associations in a number of cities organized under this name between the 1840s and the 1870s. In each, benevolent leaders or middle-class reformers joined forces with working women for the latter's protection and improvement. One of the earliest such associations was the Working Women's Protective Unions (WWPUs) formed in Rochester, New York, in 1848. In the aftermath of the Rochester Woman's Rights Convention, feminists and seamstresses jointly declared that women were entitled "equally with men to the products of their labor or its equivalent," although the women's larger purpose was to associate together for their "individual and collective benefit and protection."

During the Civil War, the largest and most successful WWPUs emerged. The prototype was established in New York City in 1863, under the auspices of *New York Sun* editor Moses Beach. There were disagreements between the working women, mainly seamstresses, and the benevolent "gentlemen" over the relative power of each on the WWPU board. Ultimately, the benevolent leaders reserved decision making to themselves while the working women formed an "advisory council." The WWPU advocated shorter hours and higher wages but focused most of its practical energies on providing legal services for women victimized by unscrupulous employers. Similar organizations were soon founded in Chicago, Detroit, St. Louis, San Francisco, and Baltimore and remained active until the mid-1890s.

Most WWPUs organized employment agencies, and some established sickness and death benefit associations, cooperative workshops, and standard price scales. Others, probably under the influence of affluent benefactors, gave more attention to protecting working women's "purity and honor." The WWPUs competed with other mixed-class associations seeking to improve the working women's lot, such as the Working Girls' Clubs, the Working Women's Improvement Societies, the social settlements, and the Working Woman's Associations. The last of these, founded in 1868 under the influence of Susan B. Anthony, sought recognition by the National Labor Union; but most such organizations were substitutes for, not precursors of, unionization. Thus, the legacy of the WWPUs is to be found not in the efforts of working women to organize themselves but in organizations such as the National Women's Trade Union League and in campaigns for protective legislation. *(See also: National Labor Union; National Women's Trade Union League; Women's Work: Nineteenth Century)*

—**Nancy A. Hewitt**

Further Reading

Kessler-Harris, Alice. *Out to Work: A History of Wage-Earning Women in the United States.* New York: Oxford University Press, 1982.

⮾ Works Progress Administration (WPA)

In an effort to combat the widespread poverty and unemployment resulting from the Great Depression, the early programs in President Franklin D. Roosevelt's New Deal concentrated on direct relief (e.g., the Federal Emergency Relief Association). Between 1935 and 1941, the federal Works Progress Administration (WPA) instituted a program of emergency relief based on public works projects for the millions of unemployed Americans who had not received adequate relief through previous or existing governmental relief programs. The WPA exceeded earlier governmental efforts in size, scope, and budgetary allocation. The original allocation for the WPA was $5 billion, and over three and a half million workers were eventually employed by the WPA, completing projects of public works that included over 110,000 public buildings, 100,000

bridges, 500,000 miles of roads, and 600 airports. The salaries paid to the WPA workers were less than those paid in the private sector but more than welfare assistance payments—roughly, fifty dollars a week.

Projects for the WPA were chosen on the basis of material costs and for their noninterference with the activities of the federal government or private industry. For this reason, the WPA is known for its innovative work in the arts and humanities and in providing employment to many difficult-to-employ Americans, including a large number of women.

Among the projects included in the WPA were the Federal Writer's Project, the Federal Arts Project, and the Federal Theater Project. Substantial numbers of women were employed by both the Federal Art and Federal Theater projects. The former provided art instruction and decorative murals in public buildings; the latter was an effort to bring the theater to Americans of all classes in all regions of the country. Hannie Flanagan (the first woman to be awarded a Guggenheim Fellowship) was chosen to head the Federal Theater Project, which produced plays, vaudeville shows, and experimental theater productions for some 30 million Americans. Louise Nevelson was involved with the Federal Arts Project, and Tillie Olsen in the Federal Writer's Project, which turned out state, territory, and regional guides to the United States and a 150-volume "Life in America" series, among other things. Ellen Woodward was head of the Women's and Professional Projects Division of the WPA.

As with other work-relief agencies, the WPA barred women from working in construction-related employment—the major component of public relief work. By 1935, the WPA employed about 35,000 women, which represented about 15 percent of total WPA employment. In 1939, the Federal Theater Project was abolished by the U.S. Congress, and other projects were allowed to continue only if sponsors were located to bear 25 percent of the operating costs. As a tribute to its success, the Federal Writer's Project was able to obtain this support in all of the (then) forty-eight states. *(See also: Depression Era; New Deal; Olsen, Tillie; Theater; Women Writers)*

—**Maureen Anna Harp**

Further Reading

Mangione, Jerre Gerlando. *The Dream and the Deal.* Boston: Little, Brown, 1972.

Mathews, Jane De Hart. *The Federal Theatre.* Princeton, NJ: Princeton University Press, 1967.

McDonald, William J. *Federal Relief Administration and the Arts.* Columbus: Ohio State University Press, 1967.

⮾ World War I

World War I was paradoxical because it brought hardship and loss while at the same time presenting opportunities and benefits to previously disadvantaged groups, with women making up the largest group taking advantage of those new opportunities. The war brought many women out of their homes and into new spheres of action, as well as making it possible for working women to move to more lucrative positions. White women, and to a lesser degree women of color, found jobs open to them in factories and war industries as never before. Four hundred thousand women joined the labor force for the first time, and 8 million women who already held jobs switched from low-paying fields to higher-paying industrial work. Women were employed for the first time in a variety of new areas, including law enforcement, railway operation, and as farm laborers attached to the "women's land army," a reserve of twenty thousand urban and rural women organized by the federal government to replace mobilized men in the Midwest and the Great Plains. One-third of American women physicians sought Army commissions during the war and, when denied, pressed for full civic and professional participation at home through organizations such as the Medical Women's National Association and the American Women's Hospitals Organization.

For middle-class women and professional women, the war provided opportunities outside of the workforce, as women appeared for the first time on government bodies connected with the general war effort. These agencies included the Women's Committee of the Council for National Defense and the Department of Labor. In addition, housewives were crucial to the success of rationing during Herbert Hoover's Food Administration from 1917 to 1919.

While many women served the war effort on the home front, another 25,000 women received the unprecedented opportunity to serve overseas on the front lines in Europe. These women, who had to support themselves and thus were mostly young and wealthy, served with over one hundred different organizations of the United States and its allies. They worked as nurses and communications and supply personnel for the military and held a variety of positions in welfare organizations, such as the American Red Cross and the Young Women's Christian Association. Journalists such as Peggy Hull distinguished themselves despite discrimination from their male peers and the military.

The emergency created by World War I, in addition to providing women with opportunities for service, also provided them with a temporary escape from restrictive societal definitions of woman's sphere and potential. Although their jobs were defined as temporary and "for the duration," women were still able to break through notions of their physical, mental, and emotional capabilities and thus began to open the door of equal opportunity. *(See also: American Red Cross; Journalism; Military Service; Physicians; Young Women's Christian Association)*

—**Leisa Diane Meyer**
—**Robert S. Shelton**

Further Reading

Clarke, Ida Clyde. *American Women and the World War.* New York: Appleton, 1918.

Fraser, Helen. *Women and War Work.* New York: Shaw, 1918.

Greenwald, Maurine. *Women, War and Work.* Westport, CT: Greenwood, 1980.

Jensen, Kimberly. "Uncle Sam's Loyal Nieces: American Medical Women, Citizenship, and War Service in World War I," *Bulletin of the History of Medicine* 67 (1993): 670-90.

Kalisch, Phillip A., and Margaret Scobey. "Female Nurses in American Wars: Helplessness Suspended for the Duration," *Armed Forces and Society* 9 (1983): 215-44.

Meyer, Leisa Diane. "'Miss Olgivy Finds Herself': American Women's Service Overseas During WWI." Master's thesis. University of Wisconsin–Madison, 1986.

More, Ellen S. "'A Certain Restless Ambition': Women Physicians and World War I," *American Quarterly* 41 (1989): 636-60.

Schneider, Dorothy, and Carl Schneider. *Into the Breach: American Women Overseas in World War I.* New York: Viking, 1991.

Steinson, Barbara Jean. *American Women's Activism in World War I.* New York: Garland, 1982.

❧ World War II

World War II saw American women serving their country in a variety of capacities on the home front and overseas. The barriers against married women teachers and "older" women workers (over thirty-five) were removed and never replaced. Women worked as farmhands and farm wives, in factories, and in clerical and sales positions. They began entry into banking positions, found more opportunities in middle-management positions, and entered professional schools. About 5 percent of the women worked as "Rosie the Riveters" and "Winnie the Welders" in positions that had traditionally been held by men and were reserved for men after the war. Half the black women domestics quit their positions and worked in more lucrative, higher-status jobs. The remaining domestics could demand higher wages and better hours. Because of the shortages, both minority women and handicapped women were hired for factory work.

The percentage of married women working jumped from 18 percent to 25 percent for the duration, a trend that continued after the war. During the war, as unemployment dropped to 2 percent and rationing was instituted, the tasks of the housewife were more demanding and time-consuming than ever before. Many housewives also tried to juggle part-time jobs or volunteer work along with raising a family and keeping it clothed and fed.

Women also served as volunteers with the Red Cross and the USO and as members of the Army or Navy Nurse Corps or Women's Army Corps overseas. (Women in other women's corps served only in the United States until late in the war; some were stationed in Alaska and Hawaii.) In total, 350,000 women served in the armed forces at some point during the hostilities. With the passage of the Women's Armed Services Integration Act in June 1948, the women's corps were made a permanent part of the armed forces.

After the war, many of the skilled women workers lost their positions as the wartime factories closed. Unions did not help the women who had held "men's" positions to find new ones. Many who had worked during the war wanted to return to "one job" as housewives in the postwar era. A new generation of women took their place in the workforce, as clerical and secretarial positions increased dramatically after the war.

While some historians view World War II as a watershed, most now agree that there was more continuity than change as a result of the war years. Employers were never again so fearful of hiring women workers. However, the dual, or sex-segregated, labor force continues today, and so does inequity in pay between men and women workers. *(See also: Army Nurse Corps; Marine Corps, Women's Reserve; Military Service; Mobilization; "Rosie the Riveter"; SPARS; War Brides, World War II; WASPs; WAVES; Women's Army Auxiliary Corps; Women's Army Corps)*

—D'Ann Campbell

Further Reading

Anderson, Karen Sue. *Wartime Women*. Westport, CT: Greenwood, 1981.

Campbell, D'Ann. *Women at War with America: Private Lives in a Patriotic Era*. Cambridge, MA: Harvard University Press, 1984.

Elshtain, Jean Bethke, and Sheila Tobias. *Women, Militarism, and War: Essays in History, Politics, and Social Theory*. Savage, MD: Rowman & Littlefield, 1990.

Garbin, Nancy F. *Feminism in the Labor Movement: Women and the United Auto Workers, 1935–1975*. Ithaca, NY: Cornell University Press, 1990.

Gluck, Sherna Berger, ed. *Rosie the Riveter Revisited: Women, the War, and Social Change*. Boston: G. K. Hall, 1987.

Hartmann, Susan. *The Home Front and Beyond: American Women in the 1940's*. Boston: G. K. Hall, 1982.

Higonnet, Margaret et al., eds. *Behind the Lines: Gender and the Two World Wars*. New Haven, CT: Yale University Press, 1987.

Honey, Maureen. *Creating Rosie the Riveter: Class, Gender and Propaganda during World War II*. Amherst: University of Massachusetts Press, 1984.

Kesselman, Amy. *Fleeting Opportunities: Women Shipyard Workers in Portland and Vancouver during World War II and Reconversion*. Albany: State University of New York, 1990.

Litoff, Judy Barrett, and David Smith, eds. *Since You Went Away: World War II Letters from American Women on the Home Front*. New York: Oxford University Press, 1991.

Lutz, Alma, ed. *With Love, Jane: Letters from American Women on the War Fronts*. New York: John Day, 1945.

Milkman, Ruth. *Gender at Work: The Dynamics of Job Segregation of Sex During World War II*. Urbana: University of Illinois Press, 1987.

Rupp, Leila. *Mobilizing Women for War: German and American Propaganda, 1939–1945*. Princeton, NJ: Princeton University Press, 1978.

Seeley, Charlotte Palmer. *American Women and the Armed Forces: A Guide to the Records of Military Agencies in the National Archives Relating to American Women*. Washington, DC: National Archives and Records Administration, 1992.

Shukert, Elfrieda Berthiaume, and Barbara Smith Scibetta. *War Brides of World War II*. Novato, CA: Presidio, 1988.

Thomas, Mary Martha. *Riveting and Rationing in Dixie: Alabama Women in the Second World War*. Tuscaloosa: University of Alabama Press, 1987.

৯ World's Columbian Exposition (1893)

Held in Chicago, Illinois, in 1893, the World's Columbian Exposition was the world's fair that celebrated the four hundredth anniversary of Christopher Columbus's arrival in North America. The largest fair of its time, it ran six months, from May 1 to October 30, and drew more than 27 million people. The fairgrounds were built on former swampland just south of Chicago's major business district. Dubbed the "White City" for their white stucco walls, the great exhibit halls stood as a testament to American ingenuity and energy, exemplified by Chicago's rise from the ashes of the great fire that ravaged a third of it less than twenty years before. In addition to its significance as a showplace for American culture, technology, and industry, the fair was an especially important event for women, for women contributed to its buildings and exhibits on a far larger scale than had ever been seen before.

Inspired by the Women's Pavilion of the Philadelphia Centennial of 1876, the first exposition building planned, funded, and managed entirely by women, the women involved in the Chicago fair seized the opportunity to build on their predecessors' accomplishments. As a result, among the Columbian Exposition's structures stood three buildings designed by and for women and their families: the Woman's Building, the Children's Building, and the Woman's Dormitory.

The Board of Lady Managers, who oversaw the projects, together with many other planners, raised funds, solicited exhibits, arbitrated internal political disputes, negotiated thorny issues of racial and social inclusiveness, and attended to matters of architectural design and decoration.

In the end, the Woman's Building housed an enormous, international collection, including artwork, scientific inventions, a model kitchen, and a library. Speakers addressed issues such as suffrage, technology, poverty, dress reform, international law, and copyright.

The Children's Building was a pioneer day care facility, as well as a kind of museum that exhibited works related to education, child care, pediatrics, and efforts such as lip-reading instruction for deaf children. Significantly, the "color line" was not drawn in the children's nursery. Next door, the Woman's Dormitory offered clean, safe, and affordable lodging for women fair-goers of modest means.

Those responsible for the Woman's Pavilion of 1876 showcased the largest collection of women's accomplishments ever displayed up to that time. Just seventeen years later, the women of the World's Columbian Exposition tripled those accomplishments. The women's buildings proved that a network of women representing virtually every background and ideology could plan, fund, and administer a massive project. *(See also: Art; Woman's Rights Conventions)*

—Elizabeth H. Coughlin

Further Reading

Adams, Henry. *The Education of Henry Adams.* Boston: Houghton Mifflin, 1918. Reprint, New York: Modern Library, 1931.

Bertuca, David J. *The World's Columbian Exposition: A Centennial Bibliographic Guide.* Westport, CT: Greenwood, 1996.

Board of Lady Managers Papers. Chicago Historical Society, Chicago, IL.

Clinton, Catherine. *The Other Civil War: American Women in the Nineteenth Century.* New York: Hill & Wang, 1984.

Ginger, Ray. *Altgeld's America: The Lincoln Ideal versus Changing Realities.* New York: Funk & Wagnalls, 1958.

Harper's Bazaar. c. 1892–1894.

Illinois Woman's Exposition Board. *Report of the Illinois Woman's Exposition Board, from 1891 to 1984.* Chicago: The Board, 1985.

Midwest Women's Collection. University of Illinois Library, Chicago Campus, Chicago, IL.

O'Neill, W. *Everyone Was Brave: The Rise and Fall of Feminism in America.* Chicago: Quadrangle, 1969.

Weimann, Jeanne Madeline. *The Fair Women: The Story of Woman's Building, World's Columbian Exposition: Chicago, 1893.* Chicago: Academy Chicago, 1981.

White, Trumbull, and William Igleheart. *The World's Columbian Exposition, Chicago, 1983.* Philadelphia: P. W. Ziegler, c. 1893.

⚞ Yezierska, Anzia (1880?–1970)

Anzia Yezierska, a Russian-Jewish emigrant to America around the turn of the century, wrote about what she knew best. Most of her novels and short stories involve Russian-Jewish women immigrants struggling to make a new life in America.

In the short story "America and I," from her collection *Children of Loneliness,* a young girl tells her story about becoming Americanized. Like most immigrants, after her arrival she gets a job as a maid for an already Americanized and successful immigrant family. These people treat her unfairly and tell her that she is greedy when she wants to be paid for her work. They argue that she should consider herself lucky because she has a nice place to sleep, food to eat, and a good job. The woman is crushed by the people's behavior and chooses to work in a sweatshop rather than work for them. It was a subject Yezierska wrote about often—the "immigrant characters' struggle with the disillusioning America of poverty and exploitation while they search for the 'real' America of their ideals."

The young girl in "America and I" finds that, contrary to the stories she heard in Russia, the streets of her adopted country are not paved with gold. She finds the work at the sweatshop unsatisfying. She wants a job so that she can "do something with [her] head, [her] feelings." The character is not able to describe specifically what she wants to do, but it is obvious she wants a job that stimulates her both intellectually and emotionally. She wants a job that she can be proud of and that makes her more independent.

The young girl starts to read American history books and begins to see how alike she is to the Pilgrims, who also came to a new world that was unwelcoming. She begins "to build a bridge of understanding between the American-born and [herself]." This is what she had to do to begin to feel a part of America—and what Yezierska herself had done.

Through her stories, Yezierska brought the experiences of many immigrants and the treatment they received to the attention of the American public. *(See also: Immigration; Jewish Women; Women Writers)*

—**Susan Kogen-Mehlman**

Further Reading

Henriksen, Louise Levitas. *Anzia Yezierska: A Writer's Life.* New Brunswick, NJ: Rutgers University Press, 1991.

Schoen, Carol B. *Anzia Yezierska.* Boston: Twayne, 1992.

Wilentz, Gay. "Cultural Mediation and Immigrant's Daughter: Anzia Yezierska's *Bread Givers,*" MELUS: *The Journal of the Society for the Study of the Multi-Ethnic Literature of the United States* 17 (Fall 1991–1992): 33-41.

Yezierska, Anzia. "America and I." In *Women Working, An Anthology of Stories and Poems,* edited by Nancy Hoffman and Florence Howe, 19-32. Old Westbury, NY: Feminist Press, 1979.

⚞ Young, Dora Steel Schexnider (b. 1939)

Dora Steel Schexnider Young, first woman chief of an Oklahoma Indian tribe, was born on January 22, 1939, and was elected Principal Chief of the Sac and Fox Tribe on August 25, 1973. Several Oklahoma newspapers declared her to be the first woman chief ever elected to such a position by any tribe in Oklahoma. She was only thirty-four at the time of her election to the high office, but she had served on the Sac and Fox Business Committee since 1969 and had been active in tribal politics for several years.

Her election as Principal Chief meant she represented the high number of Sac and Fox women who were active at all levels of tribal life. At the time of her first involvement in tribal politics and her election as Principal Chief, the women's liberation movement was not in full swing in the United States and especially in conservative Oklahoma.

Several interviews with Sac and Fox men who lived through Young's tenure as Principal Chief note their displeasure and humiliation at her election. But Young was not daunted by her opposition, and after she was sworn in, she established the first permanent Sac and Fox tribal office in Shawnee, Oklahoma. She kept the office open without a full-time salary and began to work on developing the Sac and Fox reservation located six miles south of Stroud, Oklahoma.

She was responsible for the creation of a long-range plan for reservation property that included economic development projects, housing, recreation, health, and an organized effort to solve water supply problems. Some of these plans became a reality during her two-year term (pow wow and rodeo arenas), and others were completed after she left office (main office complex, museum, water tower). Young was also responsible for the printing of a book that lists tribal enrollment and was instrumental in supporting efforts to preserve the Sac and Fox language through publication of a primer in 1977.

Although she served only one two-year term as Principal Chief (1973–1975), Young has remained active in Sac and Fox politics and was secretary-treasurer from 1978 to 1980. She holds membership on several committees and is chairman of the Sac and Fox Historical Committee. *(See also: Native American Women; Politics)*

—Jan Vassar

Further Reading

"First Lady Chief in Long History of Tribe," *Stroud American* 49 (August 30, 1973): 1.

Mueller, Kerstin. "The Changing Role of Algonkian Women—A Study on the Contemporary Sac and Fox of Oklahoma." Master's thesis. University of Tulsa, 1991.

Reinschmidt, Michael. "Ethnology of the Sauk, 1885–1985, a Socio-political Study on Continuity and Change." Ph.D. diss., Gottingen University, Gottingen, Germany, 1993.

Sac and Fox Business Committee. *Long Range Plans for the Sac and Fox Tribe of Indians of Oklahoma.* Stroud, OK: Sac and Fox Tribe, 1975.

Sac and Fox Tribe of Indians of Oklahoma. *Primer Book: Sac and Fox Language.* Edited by Mary F. McCormick. Shawnee, OK: Sac and Fox Tribe, 1977.

———. *Tribal Enrollment as of April 1, 1975.* Shawnee, OK: Tribal Operations Program of the Shawnee Agency, Bureau of Indian Affairs, 1975.

ᐇ Young, Ella Flagg (1845–1918)

Ella Flagg Young was the first woman to head a major urban school district and the first woman president of the National Education Association. She was born in Buffalo, New York, and her father was a skilled mechanic who moved his family to Chicago during the 1856-57 recession. Trained at Chicago High School in the "normal department"—which specialized in teacher training—she graduated in 1862 and at seventeen began her teaching career in the Chicago city school system. Three years later, she was appointed head teacher of the practice classroom at the Scammon School, the practice school of the Chicago Normal School, where she began a lifetime of interest in the pursuit of teaching excellence. She married William Young in December 1868 and continued her teaching duties.

Chicago was a turbulent city in the late 1800s, and Young stayed in the thick of school politics to achieve a reputation as a staunch defender of rank-and-file teachers and an advocate of teacher training. She advanced rapidly, first as a teacher in the normal department, then as a high school teacher, and eventually as district superintendent. Although

Figure 68. Ella Flagg Young
The first woman president of the National Education Association, Ella Flagg Young was a pragmatic visionary who provided leadership in the Chicago school system, especially in training teachers to handle the influx of immigrant children to the city. Used by permission of UPI/Corbis-Bettmann.

her early career was an astounding success, Young's personal life was filled with tragedy. Her husband died in 1873, and her father and sister died shortly thereafter. In 1899, after being passed over by a field of political appointees for the superintendency of Chicago's overburdened school system, Young announced that she wanted to pursue a higher degree at the University of Chicago.

Educational philosopher John Dewey once attributed his knowledge of school teaching to the work of Ella Flagg Young as she completed her dissertation, "Isolation in the Schools," under his direction. Young helped Dewey set up his experimental laboratory school at the University of Chicago, but she was clearly waiting to get back into the politics and excitement of Chicago education. Her opportunity arose in 1900 when she was chosen to head the brand new Chicago Normal School. Under her guidance, the school grew in enrollment while she worked to achieve college credits for her graduates. She was especially concerned with enabling her teachers to handle the pressures of new immigrant children in Chicago's crowded classrooms, and she pioneered in creating alliances between settlement house workers and schoolteachers.

In 1909, after nine turbulent years of union dissatisfaction under a harsh administrator, the board of education sought to end its school wars by appointing Young as the new superintendent. A year later, she was elected the first woman president of the National Education Association. She again aggressively took the reins of office, immediately setting management and labor relations at ease while she struggled with an unwieldy and corrupt board of education. Facing a budget deficit in 1915, she was harangued by board members who instigated a state legislative investigation of what they charged was "frenzied feminine finance." Young stepped down from office in December 1915. She died on October 26, 1918, in the height of the great flu epidemic, while she was campaigning for war bonds. She left her estate to her constant companion and friend, Laura Brayton. *(See also: Education; National Education Association; Teaching; University of Chicago)*

—Marjorie Murphy

Further Reading

McManus, John T. *Ella Flagg Young and a Half Century of the Chicago Public Schools.* Chicago: A. C. McClurg, 1916.
Munro, Petra. "Educators as Activists: Five Women from Chicago," *Social Education* 59 (September 1995): 274-78.
Smith, Joan K. *Ella Flagg Young: Portrait of a Leader.* Ames: Iowa State University Research Foundation, 1979.

⟶ Young Ladies Academy of Philadelphia

The Young Ladies Academy of Philadelphia was established in 1787 to give girls an education similar to that of boys in academies. Under the direction of head teacher John Poor, students learned grammar, arithmetic, geography, and oratory, which were recognized as the basic skills for functioning in a commercial society. Prominent men in the community took an active interest in the academy, first as school visitors and later as trustees once the school was incorporated in 1792. Their commitment to this experiment reflected the belief that educated wives and mothers were essential to transmit the social and political values of the new republic to future generations.

By 1788, more than one hundred young women had attended this interdenominational, secular school. Although most came from the Philadelphia area, the institution's reputation became such that parents up and down the eastern seaboard and as far away as the West Indies sent their daughters to the Young Ladies Academy. For most students, the experience of living away from the influence of family and the demands of domesticity was unique and important. At the academy, they lived with girls from many religious affiliations, different socioeconomic backgrounds, and educa-

tional levels. The students formed intense friendships with their peers and grew in self-confidence from testing their minds in intellectual pursuits. The Young Ladies Academy played an important symbolic role by asserting that women were capable of learning academic subjects and by affirming society's need to educate women. In the 1800s, similar academies for young women appeared throughout the settled areas of the new nation. *(See also: Education; Female Academies; Rush, Benjamin and "Thoughts on Female Education")*

—Cynthia Jeffress Little

Further Reading

Gordon, Ann. "The Young Ladies Academy of Philadelphia." In *Women of America: A History,* pp. 69-91. Boston: Houghton Mifflin, 1979.

⟶ Young Women's Christian Association of the United States (YWCA)

The Young Women's Christian Association of the United States (YWCA) originated in Boston, Massachusetts, in 1866. Although a forerunner of the YWCA, the Ladies Christian Association of New York, was founded in 1858, the Boston organization was the first to use the name "Young Women's Christian Association." The YWCA sought to assist young working women who were traveling to the larger cities in search of employment. One of the first services provided by the Boston association was a boarding home for women, which was opened in 1868. The board members chose to focus their attention on the younger women who were newly arrived in the city and received the lowest wages. Boarding homes continued to be a very large part of the YWCA program for many years.

As a Christian organization, the early YWCA required its members to belong to an evangelical Protestant church. The association gradually eased the church membership restrictions by the early twentieth century, therefore opening the door for non-Protestant women to become members of the organization. Yet religion continued to play a key role in the vitality of the organization, with Bible study classes and vesper services remaining very popular among members.

Other services and programs offered by the YWCA included employment bureaus for women, health and fitness programs, and cafeterias. The Young Women's Christian Association also organized Travelers' Aid departments within the local associations that assisted women travelers. Grace Dodge, the first president of the National Board of the Young Women's Christian Association, was instrumental in the founding of the Travelers' Aid Society, and Dodge's affiliation with the YWCA led to the organization's association with Travelers' Aid Societies during the early twentieth century.

During World War I, the YWCA was one of seven organizations operating under the direction of the U.S. government, staffing canteens and hostess houses at many military bases and in nearby communities for soldiers and their families. The Patriotic League was also formed by the association, which brought girls and women together to make their contributions to the war effort by means such as sewing and the selling of war bonds. The Patriotic League stressed the importance of strong moral values among women in the military camp communities. Because of their efforts during World War I, the YWCA became one of the founding members of the United Services Organization (USO) during World War II.

Even though the YWCA was an advocate of women's rights in the workplace, it did not actively speak out in favor of woman suffrage or early attempts at the passage of an equal rights amendment. The YWCA was, however, a supporter of protective legislation and advocated changes in the workplace such as minimum wage laws, an eight-hour day, and collective bargaining agreements. The association assisted women employees by offering classes in typing, bookkeeping, stenography, and other business skills that would enhance their chances of employment.

Although the YWCA stressed that its programs were for all women, black women were not a part of the association in the United States until 1893 when the first black YWCA was opened in Dayton, Ohio. By the mid-1900s, the association became one of the leading organizations promoting the end of racism and has continued with the focus up to the present day.

Priding itself on the flexibility of its program, the YWCA expanded its services over the years to include providing day care for children, operating battered women's shelters, and offering programs specifically targeted at teenage girls. The YWCA remains one of the largest women's organizations in the world, focusing on issues that are significantly important to women's lives. *(See also: Christianity; World War I; World War II)*

—Pamela F. Wille

Further Reading

Robinson, Marion O. *Eight Women of the YWCA.* New York: National Board of the Young Women's Christian Association of the U.S.A., 1966.

Scott, Anne Firor. *Natural Allies: Women's Associations in American History.* Urbana: University of Illinois Press, 1991.

Sims, Mary. *First Sixty Years of the Young Women's Christian Association, 1855–1915.* New York: Woman's Press, 1916.

———. *History of a Social Institution: The Young Women's Christian Association.* New York: Woman's Press, 1936.

Wilson, Elizabeth. *Fifty Years of Association Work among Young Women, 1866–1916.* New York: National Board of the Young Women's Christian Association of the U.S.A., 1916.

Wilson, Grace H. *The Religious and Educational Philosophy of the Young Women's Christian Association.* New York: Columbia University Teachers College, 1933.

Zaharias, "Babe" Didrikson
(1911–1956)

"Babe" Didrikson Zaharias was an outstanding athlete and medical humanitarian. The sixth of seven children born to Norwegian immigrants in Port Arthur, Texas, Mildred Ella first distinguished herself in high school basketball. A one-woman "team" at the 1932 Amateur Athletic Union Championships, she placed in seven track and field events, including five firsts. This dubbed her the "Texas Tomboy." She excelled in a variety of sports: baseball throw, javelin, eighty-meter hurdles, shot put, high jump, and discus. At the 1932 Los Angeles Olympics, she won two gold medals (eighty-meter hurdles—setting an Olympic record—and javelin) and a first-place tie in the high jump.

She appealed to the nation. The press reveled in her quick quips and brassiness as much as in her athletic prowess. Meanwhile, her critics (some teammates, press, and public) condemned her as arrogant, boastful, and disturbingly unfeminine.

After the Olympics, she made money as a harmonica-playing stage entertainer, in mock demonstrations of her prowess, and touring with gender-mixed baseball teams. At times these activities had a circuslike atmosphere.

She chose golf as her next domain. Her first tournament (1934) led to others, including the 1938 competition that paired her with George Zaharias, a professional wrestler whom she wed that same year. In one stretch, she won thirteen consecutive amateur golf tournaments. In 1948, she cofounded the Ladies Professional Golf Association. She was voted "the greatest female athlete of the first half of the twentieth century" by the Associated Press in 1950. She was diagnosed with cancer in 1953.

She "went public" with her ailment as a self-help role model, founded the Cancer Research Fund, attended charity golf tournaments, and promoted cancer education. She returned to golf—victoriously—shortly after a colostomy. Repeated hospitalizations from 1954 to 1956 signaled the disease's supremacy. She died at the age of forty-five in Galveston, Texas.

Named Woman Athlete of the Year six times by the Associated Press, her world, national, Olympic, and golf records are booklet length. She was honored by numerous health and political agencies. Her sports and humanitarian artifacts

Figure 69. "Babe" Didrikson Zaharias
Shown here winning the hurdles in the 1932 Olympic Games in Los Angeles, Babe Didrikson Zaharias excelled in virtually every athletic venture available to her. She became the most admired woman athlete in America, an admiration that only grew during her fight against the cancer that claimed her life at age forty-five. Used by permission of UPI/Corbis-Bettmann.

are housed in a memorial museum in Beaumont, Texas. Her life is portrayed in her autobiography *This Life I've Led*, numerous children's books, two biographies, and a major motion picture. Yet little of the private woman is explored. She provided a strong and fiercely competitive role model for other women, and she was the model of unparalleled athletic excellence. *(See also: Athletics/Sports)*

—**Susan E. Cayleff**

Further Reading

Babe Didrikson Zaharias papers. John Gray Library. Lamar University, Beaumont, TX.

Cayleff, Susan E. " 'Babe' Didrikson Zaharias: Her Personal and Public Battle with Cancer," *Texas Medicine* 82 (September 1986): 41-45.

Johnson, William Oscar, and Nancy P. Williamson. *"Whatta-Gal": The Babe Didrikson Story.* Boston: Little, Brown, 1975.

Zaharias, Babe Didrikson (as told to Harry Paxton). *This Life I've Led: My Autobiography.* New York: A. S. Barnes, 1955.

✍ Zorach, Marguerite Thompson
(1887–1968)

Marguerite Thompson Zorach was one of the few artists to introduce fauvism and cubism to America. She was particularly successful at influencing the acceptance of modern art in the United States.

While enrolled at Stanford in 1908, Zorach accepted an invitation from her aunt to join her in Paris. After her arrival, she visited the now-famous Salon D'Automne of 1908. The world was shocked by the distorted images and bold colors in the paintings, and critics referred to the artists as *"fauves"*—wild beasts. Zorach was enthusiastic about the new art and quickly became very successful working in that style, exhibiting several times at the Paris Salon and the Salon D'Automne. Her aunt disapproved of her niece's bizarre paintings and her romance with an unsuitable young man, William Zorach, and decided it was time to take her home. Zorach's later work was influenced by their tour of the Orient and the Middle East.

In California, a show of her avant-garde paintings shocked conservative Fresno. Before joining William in New York, Zorach saved several of her fauve-style pieces and destroyed the rest. In New York, the Zorachs exhibited in many important shows, including the seminal Armory Show of 1913.

After the birth of her children in 1915 and 1917, Zorach began creating rich, complicated needlework pieces, which she sold to support the family. Although highly regarded, these tapestries were considered craft, not art. In 1925, Zorach founded the New York Society of Women Artists for avant-garde painters. The society's exhibits surprised and impressed the critics, but Zorach's art was too revolutionary for most people. Two large murals done in the 1930s for the Federal Arts Project were rejected by her hometown. The Zorachs collaborated on their art all though their lives, and William, who recognized his wife as a great artist, regretted that his own reputation overshadowed hers. In 1968, Zorach gave her son Tessim the early paintings she had saved. These few paintings, exhibited for the first time in 1973, are considered among her most innovative and finest works. *(See also: Art)*

—**Holly Hyncik Sukenik**

—**Marian J. Hollinger**

Further Reading

Chadwick, Whitney. *Women, Art, and Society.* New York: Thames & Hudson, 1990.

Hoffman, Marilyn F. *Marguerite and William Zorach: The Cubist Years, 1915–1918.* Hanover, NH: University Press of New England, 1987.

National Collection of Fine Arts, Smithsonian Institution. *Marguerite Zorach: The Early Years, 1908–1920.* Exhibition catalog. Washington, DC: Smithsonian Institute, December 7, 1973–February 4, 1984.

Rubinstein, Charlotte Streifer. *American Women Artists,* pp. 172-76. Boston: Avon, 1982.

Zorach, Tessim. *Marguerite Zorach—At Home and Abroad.* Exhibition catalog. New York: Kraushaar Galleries, 1984.

✍ Zueblin, Aurora Thompson (Fisk)
(1868–1958)

Aurora Thompson Zueblin was an advocate of the American arts and crafts movement. She was educated at Northwestern University Academy in Evanston, Illinois, where her father Herbert Franklin Fisk was principal and professor of pedagogy. After teaching in public schools for two years, she married Charles Zueblin, a University of Chicago sociologist, founder of Northwestern Settlement, and a prominent figure in movements for civic improvements. She left teaching but remained active in the Chicago branches of the Society for Ethical Culture, the Public School Art Society, and the University Settlement League. She made her greatest mark on the times, however, as a member of the Chicago Arts and Crafts Society and as chronicler and theorist of that organization's ideals.

In 1895, Zueblin visited the Merton Abbey workshop of William Morris, whose revival of numerous handicrafts had inspired the British arts and crafts movement. There, she witnessed workers joyfully making things that were both useful and beautiful. She now understood why many social reformers applauded Morris for having realized the ideal of uniting art and labor. In a series of eleven articles for *The Chautauquan,* 1902 to 1904, Zueblin focused on this practical idealism as the distinctive feature of the arts and crafts movement. She reviewed the leading individuals and organizations in England and on the Continent; praised several American manufacturers of "industrial art," such as Rookwood Pottery in Cincinnati and Gustav Stickley's United Crafts in Syracuse, New York; and examined the potential impact of the movement on art education in public schools. These essays constituted the single most comprehensive survey of the arts and crafts movement to reach a national audience.

Zueblin's "Duties of the Consumer," appearing in *The Craftsman* in 1904, was her most original work. She was alarmed that so many modern consumers complacently accepted the "tyranny of things," living amid a clutter of cheap objects that possessed little meaning for their lives. She called on them, therefore, to develop a more intelligent, caring, and responsible relationship with their physical surroundings. They should purge their homes of unnecessary accumulation and instead create simple and harmonious interiors. Through earnest choice and thoughtful use of household objects, consumers could "humanize" the domestic environment and transform it into an expression of their own personalities. Zueblin had succeeded in outlining an arts and crafts theory of consumption to complement the movement's emphasis on handicraft production. *(See also: Art; Consumerism)*

—**Bruce R. Kahler**

Further Reading

Kahler, Bruce R. "Art and Life: The Arts and Crafts Movement in Chicago, 1897–1910." Ph.D. diss., Purdue University, 1986.

Zueblin, Aurora Fisk. "The Arts and Crafts Movement," *The Chautauquan* 36-37 (October 1902-June 1903). [Special issues]

———. "Duties of the Consumer," *The Craftsman* 7 (October 1904): 88-95.

Index

About the Contributors

CECELIA A. ALBERT, formerly an associate editor at ABC-CLIO, earned a B.A. in philosophy from the University of California at Santa Barbara.

GINGER RAE ALLEE is an operations analyst at Rockwell Space Operations. She is a genealogist and editor of *Allee's All Around Family Newsletter.* She holds an M.A. in history from the University of Houston–Clear Lake.

VICTORIA C. ALLISON is a Ph.D. candidate at the State University of New York at Stony Brook and is completing her dissertation titled "The Bad Neighbor: Media, Narrative, and Foreign Policy in U.S. Relations with Peronist Argentina, 1943–1955." She is an instructor at Tulane University.

HARRIET HYMAN ALONSO is Professor of History at Fitchburg State College in Massachusetts. She is the author of several articles and two books: *The Women's Peace Union and the Outlawry of War, 1921–1942* and *Peace as a Women's Issue: A History of the U.S. Movement for World Peace and Women's Rights.*

RIMA D. APPLE is Professor in the Department of Consumer Science and in the Women's Studies Program at the University of Wisconsin–Madison. She is the author of *Mothers and Medicine: A Social History of Infant Feeding, 1890–1950* and coeditor of *Mothers and Motherhood: Readings in American History.*

THOMAS F. ARMSTRONG is Professor of History, Provost, and Senior Vice President at Texas Wesleyan University. He has published more than thirty articles in journals such as the *Georgia Historical Quarterly* and *Labor History* and has contributed to essay collections and several encyclopedias.

BARRY ARNOLD is Associate Professor of Religious Studies and Philosophy at the University of West Florida. He is the author of *The Pursuit of Virtue,* coauthor and editor of *Essays in American Ethics,* and

editor of a ten-volume series titled *The Reshaping of Psychoanalysis: From Sigmund Freud to Ernest Becker.*

VIVIAN ATWATER is Associate Professor of Art History at the University of Houston–Clear Lake. She has published articles in *Nouvelles de l'estampe* (1995) and the *Dictionary of Art* (1996) and is preparing a book on printmaking of the Enlightenment.

STEVEN M. AVELLA is Associate Professor of History at Marquette University in Milwaukee. His publications include *This Confident Church: Catholic Leadership and Life in Chicago, 1940–1965* and *The Monument of Grace: The History of the North American Province of the Society of the Divine Savior, 1947–1987,* Vol. 2. He has published in the *Catholic Historical Review, Kansas Quarterly,* and *U.S. Catholic Historian.*

DIANA E. AXELSEN is a senior books production editor at Sage Publications. Previously, she taught philosophy and women's studies at Spelman College in Atlanta, Georgia, and at California Lutheran University in Thousand Oaks.

BETH L. BAILEY is Associate Professor of American Studies at the University of New Mexico. She is the author of *From Front Porch to Back Seat: Courtship in 20th Century America* and *Sex in the Heartland* and coauthor of *The First Strange Place: Race and Sex in WWII Hawaii.*

BARBARA BAIR is Associate Editor of the Jane Addams Papers, Department of History, Duke University. She is Associate Editor of *Marcus Garvey: Life and Lessons* and of volumes six and seven of *The Marcus Garvey and Universal Negro Improvement Association Papers.* She earned her Ph.D. in American civilization at Brown University.

JANET G. BALDINGER is a docent at the National Museum of Women in the Arts. She received her training in art education at the University of Maryland.

709

GRETCHEN M. BATAILLE is Professor of English at Washington State University, where she serves as Provost and Academic Vice President. She is the author of *Native American Women: A Biographical Dictionary* and coauthor of *American Indian Women: A Guide to Research; Images of American Indians in Film; American Indian Women Telling Their Lives; The Pretend Indians: Images of Native Americans in the Movies*, and *The Worlds between Two Rivers: Perspectives on American Indians in Iowa.*

MARY BATTENFELD is Assistant Professor of Humanities at Wheelock College. Her most recent publication is a teacher's guide for Zitkala-Sa's *American Indian Stories*. She earned her Ph.D. from the University of Maryland in 1990.

BEVERLY BEETON is retired Professor of History, Provost, and Vice Chancellor for Academic Affairs at the University of Alaska, Anchorage. Her publications include *Women Vote in the West: The Woman Suffrage Movement, 1869–1986* and *The Letters of Elizabeth Wells Randall Cummings.*

ALLISON BERTRAND is an independent art historian. She has taught at Arizona State University, Tempe, Arizona, and is a contributor to *North American Women Artists of the Twentieth Century: A Biographical Dictionary*. Her article "Beaumont Newhall's 'Photography 1839–1937': Making History" appeared in *History of Photography.*

ARLIE ROY BICE III holds a B.A. from the University of Houston–Clear Lake in history and is a graduate student at the University of Texas–Tyler.

TERRY D. BILHARTZ is Professor of History at Sam Houston State University and is the author of *Urban Religion and the Second Great Awakening, Francis Asbury's America*, and *Constructing the American Past.*

JULIA KIRK BLACKWELDER is Head of the Department of History at Texas A&M University. She received her Ph.D. from Emory University and is the author of *Now Hiring: The Feminization of Work in the United States, 1900–1995; Women of the Depression: Caste and Culture in San Antonio, 1929–1939;* and "Race, Ethnicity, and Women's Lives in the Urban South," in *Shades of the Sunbelt: Essays on Ethnicity and Women's Lives in the Urban South.*

AMY E. BLACKWELL received an M.A. in history from the University of Houston in 1997. She has published "Wigwam Metropolis: Camp Ford, Texas" in the *East Texas Historical Journal* under her previous name, Amy L. Klemm.

ELEANOR H. BLAKELY is Associate Professor and Director of the MSW program in the School of Social Work and Public Administration at West Virginia University in Morgantown. She has published articles on sexual harassment and domestic violence. Her current research focuses on impact of welfare reform on families in West Virginia.

KATHLEEN M. BLEE is Professor of Sociology and Director of the Women's Studies Program at the University of Pittsburgh. The author of *Women of the Klan: Racism and Gender in the 1920s*, she is currently completing a book with Dwight Billings on the origins of persistent poverty and violence in rural Appalachia.

EDITH BLICKSILVER is Associate Professor Emeritus of Literature at the Georgia Institute of Technology. She is the editor of *The Ethnic American Woman: Problems, Protests, Lifestyles*, awarded the Best Non-Fiction Book of the Year Award by the Dixie Council of Authors

and Journalists, and the author of *Going Pro*. She completed her graduate work at Smith College as a Sophia Smith Scholar.

JANET CARLISLE BOGDAN is Associate Professor and Chair of the Sociology and Anthropology Department at Le Moyne College in Syracuse, New York. Her essays have appeared in *Feminist Studies; Changing Education: Women as Radicals and Conservators; The American Way of Birth; Women, Health, and Medicine in America;* and *Social Problems.*

ANNE HUDSON BOLIN is Electronic Development Coordinator at Aspen Systems, Rockville, Maryland. She received a master's in library science at the University of Maryland.

DEBORAH DAWSON BONDE, formerly on the faculty at Boise State University, is currently a homemaker. She earned her B.A. at Albertson College of Idaho, her M.A. in American studies at Washington State University, and her Ph.D. in American culture at Bowling Green State University.

KATHLEEN MARY BROWN is Associate Professor of History at the University of Pennsylvania. She holds a Ph.D. in history from the University of Pennsylvania–Madison.

REGINA A. BROWN is Assistant Professor and Head of the Orton Memorial Library of Geology at Ohio State University. She has published a chapter in volume 13 of the *Encyclopedia of Earth Sciences: The Encyclopedia of Applied Geology* and an article on "The Role of Women in the Development of the Earth Sciences, an Historical Survey" in *Advances in Geosciences.*

JOHN D. BUENKER is Professor of History at the University of Wisconsin–Parkside. He is the author of *Urban Liberalism and Progressive Reform; The Income Tax and the Progressive Era;* and *Wisconsin: The Progressive Era* and coauthor of *Progressivism; Immigration and Ethnicity; Multiculturalism in the United States*, and *Progressive Reform*, and *Those United States: International Views American History*, among numerous other writings.

KAREN BUHLER-WILKERSON is Professor of Community Health at the University of Pennsylvania School of Nursing, where she earned her Ph.D. She is the author of *False Dawn: The Rise and Decline of Public Health Nursing* and has published essays in *Nursing Research, American Journal of Public Health*, and *Nursing History Review.*

NICHOLAS C. BURCKEL is Dean of Libraries and Associate Professor of History at Marquette University. He is a Fellow and Past President of the Society of American Archivists. His books include *Immigration and Ethnicity; Racine: Growth and Change in a Wisconsin County; Progressive Reform*, and *Kenosha Retrospective.*

DAVID H. BURTON is Professor of History at St. Joseph's University and author of biographies of *Theodore Roosevelt, Oliver Wendell Holmes, Jr.*, and *William Howard Taft*. He received his Ph.D. in history from Georgetown University.

MARILYN DEMAREST BUTTON is Associate Professor of English at Lincoln University, Pennsylvania. Her published articles have focused on the lives and works of various women writers, including Frances Milton Trollope and Muriel Spark. Following her sabbatical studies at Westminster Seminary, in Pennsylvania, she coedited a collection of articles titled *Foreign Women in British Literature: Exotics, Aliens, and Outsiders.*

ROSE KOLBASNIK CALLAHAN earned her B.A. in history from the University of Wisconsin–Parkside and an M.A. in literature from the University of South Florida. She is currently employed by the Oakland California School District.

D'ANN CAMPBELL is Vice President for Academic Affairs at New Hampshire College, Manchester.. She is the author of *Women at War with America: Private Lives in a Patriotic Era.*

B. JILL CARROLL is Lecturer in Humanities at the University of Houston–Clear Lake. She received a Ph.D. from Rice University and is the author of articles on *Blood Meridian* and Sallie McFague.

GAY E. CARTER is Reference/Documents Librarian at the Alfred R. Neumann Library, University of Houston–Clear Lake. She is the author of two essays in *Twentieth Century Science Fiction Writers,* third edition, and contributes a column on medical genealogy to the *Houston Genealogical Record.*

FLORIS BARNETT CASH is Assistant Professor of Africana Studies and History at the State University of New York at Stony Brook. She was the guest curator at the Brooklyn Historical Society for the exhibit *Black Women of Brooklyn,* author of the exhibition brochure, *Black Women of Brooklyn: Seventeenth Century to the Present,* and author of "Radicals and Realists: African American Women and the Settlement House Spirit in New York City" in *Afro-Americans in New York Life and History.*

SUSAN E. CAYLEFF is Professor and Chair of Women's Studies at San Diego State University. She is the author of *Golden Cyclone: Life and Legend of Babe Didrikson Zaharias* and coeditor of *Wings of Gauze: Women of Color and the Experience of Health and Illness,* and *Wash and Be Healed: The Water-Cure Movement and Women's Health.*

SANDRA L. CHAFF is a consultant for establishing women's collections and libraries. She is the former director of the archives and special collections on women in medicine and research instructor in the history of medicine at the Medical College of Pennsylvania in Philadelphia and one of the editors of *Women in Medicine: A Bibliography of the Literature on Women in Medicine.*

SUZETTE CHAPMAN holds a master's degree in literature from the University of Houston–Clear Lake. In addition to owning an environmentally friendly grounds maintenance business, she is a freelance grant writer, assisting nonprofit organizations on the Texas Gulf Coast.

SAMUEL L. CHELL is Professor of English at Carthage College. His Ph.D. is from the University of Wisconsin–Madison, and he is the author of *The Dynamic Self: Browning's Poetry of Duration* and articles on women and film.

WENDY E. CHMIELEWSKI is the Curator of the Swarthmore College Peace Collection. She is a coeditor of *Women in Spiritual and Communitarian Societies in the United States,* a collection of essays on the experience and role of women in intentional communities.

DIANA CHURCH is Instructor in Art at Richland College in Texas. She earned her M.A. at the University of Texas at Dallas and is the author of a *Guide to Dallas Artists, 1890–1917.*

ANNE L. CLARE was a docent at the National Museum of Women in the Arts in Washington, D.C. for twelve years. She is a graduate of Otterbein College in Westerville, Ohio.

GRACIA CLARK is Assistant Professor of Anthropology at Indiana University, Bloomington. She holds a Ph.D. in social anthropology from Cambridge University. She is the author of a book on Asante market women, *Onions Are My Husband,* and she has edited a volume titled *Traders versus the State.*

ELIZABETH CLARK-LEWIS is Associate Professor of History and Director of the Public History Program at Howard University. Her book, *Living In, Living Out,* was published by the Smithsonian Press in 1994. She produced "Freedom Bags," a documentary broadcast by PBS, which has received the Oscar Micheaux award for the best documentary from the Black Filmmakers Hall of Fame and educational excellence awards from the National Education Association and the American Association of University Women.

CATHERINE CLINTON is the author of several books, including *The Plantation Mistress: Woman's World in the Old South, The Other Civil War: American Women in the Nineteenth Century,* and Fanny Kemble's Cival Wars. She is coauthor of *The Columbia Guide to American Women in the Nineteenth Century.*

JONELL DUDA COMERFORD is Professor of Mathematics at Eastern Illinois University. She earned her Ph.D. in mathematics from the University of Illinois and has published in *Communications in Algebra, Canadian Mathematical Bulletin, UMAP Journal,* and *Information and Control.*

MARY FRANCES CONCEPCIÓN has a B.A. in music from DePaul University. She is a devotee of the operatic arts and hopes to make music her life's work.

ANNE ELIZABETH COOPERMAN holds a bachelor of arts degree in psychology from DePaul University and a bachelor of arts degree in art with a concentration in advertising from Columbia College.

CAROLINE CORTINA is a Ph.D. candidate in the Department of History at Brown University, where she also received her master's degree. Her research area includes the Commission on Interracial Cooperation.

CATHERINE COSGROVE has a doctorate from Northern Illinois University. She teaches in the Hinsdale, Illinois, public schools and is currently working on a history of the American Kindergarten Movement.

GINGER COSTELLO received her M.A. and M.F.A. from the University of Montana and is presently a full-time lecturer in English at Chicago State University where she teaches courses in composition, literature, and creative writing.

ELIZABETH H. COUGHLIN is Assistant Director of the DePaul University Writing Centers and faculty member in the Department of English, from which she received her M.A. She has written a series of Writing Center Handbooks and has written on writing instruction, placement, and assessment.

SUZANNE JONES CRAWFORD is Professor of History at Cameron University and coauthor of essays on Kate Barnard published in *The Historian, Mid-America,* and *An Oklahoma I Had Never Seen Before.* She is currently completing a full-length biography of Barnard.

JANE CRISLER is Dean of the University of Wisconsin–Rock County. She earned the Ph.D. in modern European history at the University of Wisconsin–Madison. Her publications include essays in *College*

Teaching, Rhetoric and Civilization, George Moore in Perspective, and the *Women's Studies Encyclopedia.*

CAROL KLIMICK CYGANOWSKI is Director of the American Studies Program and Associate Professor of English, American Studies, and Women's Studies at DePaul University. She earned her Ph.D. in English language and literature at the University of Chicago and is the author of *Magazine Editors and Professional Authors in Nineteenth Century America: The Genteel Tradition and the American Dream.*

MARY K. DAINS, now retired, was formerly Associate Director of the State Historical Society of Missouri and Associate Editor of the *Missouri Historical Review.* She is the editor of *Show Me Missouri Women: Selected Biographies* (1989) and coeditor of Volume 2 of the same title (1993).

FLORENCE DAVIS was a docent at the National Museum of Women in the Arts in Washington, D.C.

PAMELA DEAN is Director of the Williams Center for Oral History at Louisiana State University. She received her Ph.D. in history from the University of North Carolina–Chapel Hill and is the author of *Women on the Hill: A History of Women at the University of North Carolina.* Her dissertation is titled "Covert Curriculum: Class and Gender at a New South Women's College, 1892–1910."

JAYNE CRUMPLER DEFIORE is the author of *Miracle in the Valley: A History of the University of Tennessee Medical Center at Knoxville, 1944–1995.* Formerly an associate editor of the *Correspondence of James K. Polk,* she earned her Ph.D. from the University of Tennessee in the Department of Independent Study at the University of Tennessee, Knoxville. She has published articles in the *Tennessee Historical Quarterly* in her two fields of interest, women's history and the history of medicine.

MICHAEL A. DE LEÓN was a graduate student in historical studies at the University of Houston–Clear Lake, where he earned a B.A. in history.

MARY E. DEMENY is a graduate of the University of Houston–Clear Lake. She returned to scholarly pursuits as an adult, after thirty years of marriage and having raised five children. When she received her B.A. in U.S. Women's History in 1995, she had thirteen grandchildren.

MARI LYNN DEW graduated with highest honors from Carthage College in 1988. She received an M.A. from Lutheran School of Theology at Chicago in 1992 and is currently an S.T.M. student at the Lutheran Theological Seminary at Philadelphia.

HASIA R. DINER is the Paul S. and Sylvia Steinberg Professor of American Jewish History at New York University, with a joint appointment in the departments of History and Hebrew and Judaic Studies. A specialist in immigration and ethnic history and the history of American women, she is the author of three books: *In the Almost Promised Land: American Jews and Blacks, 1915–1935; Erin's Daughters in America: Irish Women in the Nineteenth Century;* and *A Time for Gathering: The Second Migration, 1820–1880,* the second volume in the series, "The Jewish People in America."

PATRICIA M. DUETSCH is Assistant Vice President of Business Development at Johnson Bank in Racine, Wisconsin. She earned her M.S. in urban affairs at the University of Wisconsin–Milwaukee and her M.B.A. from the University of Wisconsin–Parkside.

MELINDA DUNKER has a B.S. in commerce accountancy from De Paul University and works for a public accounting firm. She is a fiction writer and poet.

MABEL BENSON DUPRIEST is Professor of English and Department Chair at Carthage College in Kenosha, Wisconsin. She earned her Ph.D. in English at the University of Kentucky.

TRAVIS DUPRIEST, Ph.D., is Director of the DeKoven Retreat and Conference Center in Racine, Wisconsin, and Professor of English at Carthage College in Kenosha, Wisconsin. He is the author of five books of creative writing, several scholarly books, and numerous articles.

ANNE O. DZAMBA (SESSA) is Professor of History and Women's Studies at West Chester University in Pennsylvania. She is the author of *Richard Wagner and the English* and essays in *Wagnerism in European Culture and Politics, Women Art Educators,* and *Essays in European History.*

FRANCES H. EARLY teaches North American social history, peace studies, and women's studies at Mount Saint Vincent University, Halifax, Nova Scotia. Her most recent major publication is *A World without War: How U.S. Feminists and Pacifists Resisted World War I* (1997).

JOLYNN EDWARDS studied ballet in Seattle at The Cornish School and in New York at the American Ballet Theatre School with Leon Danieleon and William Griffith, dancing professionally with opera companies in New York City and Philadelphia and the Bar Harbor Festival Ballet. An associate professor at the University of Washington, Bothell, she teaches dance history, art history, and comparative arts in the Interdisciplinary Arts and Sciences Program. Her publications on eighteenth-century cultural history include an article, "Watteau and the Dance," and a monograph on the Parisian art dealer, Alexandre-Joseph Paillet.

LISA SIRMONS EDWARDS holds an M.A. in history from the University of Houston–Clear Lake. She currently teaches world history at Deer Park High School in Deer Park, Texas.

PENELOPE J. ENGELBRECHT is a writer and former academic living in Chicago. Her works have appeared in *Feminist Studies, Sinister Wisdom, Trivia,* and several anthologies. She holds an M.A. in English from DePaul and did doctoral work at Loyola University.

MARIA E. ERLING is a Lutheran pastor who teaches at the Lutheran Theological Seminary in Gettysburg, Pennsylvania. She earned her master's of divinity degree from Yale University and a doctorate in theology from Harvard Divinity School. Her dissertation discusses Swedish immigrant religious culture in New England, 1880–1920.

CELIA ESPLUGAS is Assistant Professor of Spanish at West Chester University. Her areas of research are twentieth-century Latin American, English, and American literature; women's studies; and methodology in foreign language teaching. She has published extensively in the United States and abroad.

MERRI SCHEIBE EDWARDS is a freelance researcher and writer in Galveston, Texas. She received her M.A. in history from the University of Houston–Clear Lake.

MONICA L. EVERETT is an instructor at the International Baccalaureate History at Awty International School in Houston, Texas. She received her M.A. in history at the University from Houston–Clear Lake.

DAVID M. FAHEY is Professor of History at Miami University in Oxford, Ohio. He earned his Ph.D. in history at Notre Dame University. He is the author of *Temperance and Racism: John Bull, Johnny Reb, and the Good Templars* (1996).

ELIZABETH FIELDS is Instructor in the North Harris Montgomery Community College District, Houston, Texas. Her M.A. is from the University of Houston–Clear Lake.

DIANE DEVUSSER FIERO works in Development at the California Institute of Technology. She earned her B.S. in psychology at the University of Houston–Clear Lake and her M.S. in human resource design at Claremont Graduate University.

MAUREEN FITZGERALD is Visiting Assistant Professor of American Studies at the College of William and Mary. She holds M.A. and Ph.D. degrees in history from the University of Wisconsin–Madison.

NANCY FOGELSON taught history at Cincinnati Country Day School, Cincinnati, Ohio. She is the author of *Arctic Exploration and International Relations* and articles in *Fram: The Journal of Polar Studies, Diplomatic History,* and *Journal of Military History.*

JOYCE FOLLET is the U.S. Historian in the Division of Continuing Studies at the University of Wisconsin–Madison. She recently produced the video documentary *Step by Step: Building a Women's Movement.* She earned a Ph.D. in women's history at the University of Wisconsin–Madison.

CARRIE FOSTER is Associate Professor of History at Miami University in Hamilton, Ohio. She earned a Ph.D. in history from the University of Denver. Her history of the Women's International League for Peace and Freedom, *The Women and the Warriors: the U.S. Section of the Women's International League for Peace and Freedom, 1915–1946,* was published in 1995 by Syracuse University as part of its Studies on Peace and Conflict Resolution.

LAWRENCE FOSTER is Professor of American History at Georgia Institute of Technology in Atlanta. He is the author of *Religion and Sexuality: Three American Communal Experiments of the Nineteenth Century* and *Women, Family and Utopia: Communal Experiments of Shakers, the Oneida Community, and the Mormons.* His doctorate in history is from the University of Chicago.

LEIGH FOUGHT is completing her dissertation in U.S. women's history at the University of Houston, where she also served as an intern in the Women's Archive and Research Center in the M.D. Anderson Librtary. She has worked with at-risk students at the University of Houston and has taught at Houston Community College for six years. She volunteers for several women's organizations.

SANDRA M. FOX is Associate Professor and Chair of the Department of Education at Lake Forest College, Illinois.

MARY LOU FRANCE was a student status examiner at the University of Wisconsin–Parkside in Kenosha, Wisconsin, before her retirement.

MICHELLE MAACK FRIEDERICHS is Adjunct Instructor at St. Mary's University in Minnesota, Concordia University in St. Paul, and Minnesota State University in Mankato. She received an M.A. in English from Mankato State University and is working on a doctorate in educational leadership at St. Mary's University in Minneapolis.

FRIDA KERNER FURMAN is Associate Professor of Religious Studies at DePaul University. She is the author of *Beyond Yiddishkeit: The Struggle of Jewish Identity in a Reform Synagogue* and *Facing the Mirror: Older Women and Beauty Shop Culture,* which received the 1997 Eli Longas-Moranda Prize from the American Folklore Society, Women's Section.

KENNETH E. GADOMSKI is a senior technical editor/writer for QMS, Inc., as well as a part-time instructor in the English Department at the University of South Alabama. He has published in *Critical Surveys of Poetry: Supplement, Bulletin of Bibliography, Notes on Modern American Literature, Explicator,* and *Journal of Narrative Technique.* In 1984, he earned his Ph.D. in English from the University of Delaware.

LAURA GELLOTT is Associate Professor of History at the University of Wisconsin–Parkside. She is the author of *The Catholic Church and the Authoritarian Regime in Austria,* a contributor to *Liberalism and Catholicism: Contributions to American Public Philosophy,* and has published in the *Austrian History Yearbook,* the *Catholic Historical Review, Commonweal, Mid-America,* and the *Journal of Contemporary History.*

CAROLYN DESWARTE GIFFORD is the general editor of a reprint series on "Women in American Protestant Religion" and has written essays in *Gender, Ideology and Action: Historical Perspectives on Women's Public Lives; Feminist Perspectives on Biblical Scholarship; Women and Religion in America,* and *Women in New Worlds.* She is the editor of *"Writing Out My Heart": Selections from the Journal of Frances E. Willard, 1855–1896.* She is currently writing a biography of Willard. She earned her Ph.D. in history of religions at Northwestern University.

KAREN LOUPE GILLENWATERS is Professor of English at Brazosport College in Lake Jackson, Texas. She has published in the *Handbook of Texas.* She earned her M.A. in English at Lamar State University.

JOANNA BOWEN GILLESPIE is an affiliated scholar in the Women's Studies Department at the University of Arizona, Tucson. She is the author of *Women Speak of God, Congregations, and Change* (1995) and articles on Martha Laurens Ramsay (1759–1811) and, most recently, Sarah Patton Boyle (1906–1996). Her Ph.D. is from New York University.

RACHEL WALTNER GOOSSEN is Assistant Professor and Chair of the Department of History at Goshen College. She earned her Ph.D. from the University of Kansas. Her publications include an essay on "Feminist Historiography and Teaching Peace" and a book, *Women against the "Good War": Conscientious Objection and Gender on the American Home Front.*

ANN D. GORDON is Associate Research Professor in the history department at Rutgers University and editor of the multivolume *Selected Papers of Elizabeth Cady Stanton and Susan B. Anthony.* She coedited the microfilm edition of the *Stanton and Anthony Papers* with Patricia G. Holland and has written numerous articles in women's history.

LINDA GORDON is Florence Kelley Professor of History at the University of Wisconsin. She has specialized in examining the historical roots of contemporary social policy debates, particularly as they concern gender and family issues. Her books include *Woman's Body, Woman's Right: The History of Birth Control in America; Heroes of Their Own Lives: The Politics and History of Family Violence; Cossack Rebellions: Social Turmoil in the 16th Century Ukraine; Pitied But Not Entitled: Single Mothers and the History of Welfare;* and *The Great Arizona Orphan Abduction.*

LYNN D. GORDON is Associate Professor of Education and History and chair of the Gender and Society Group at the University of Rochester. Her publications include *Gender and Higher Education in the Progressive Era*. Her articles on women in higher education and the professions have appeared in the *History of Education Quarterly*, *American Quarterly*, and the *History of Higher Education Annual*. She is currently working on a biography of Dorothy Thompson.

SARAH GORDON is Professor of English at Georgia College and the editor of *The Flannery O'Connor Bulletin*. She earned her Ph.D. in English at Texas Christian University.

JOHN GORMAN is Professor of English at the University of Houston–Clear Lake. He has published two collections of poetry, *Perry Como Sings* and *Public Places*. His doctorate is from the University of Virginia.

CYNTHIA LYNN GOULD is an M.F.A. candidate at Southern Methodist University. She earned a B.A. in women's studies from the University of Washington in Seattle.

C. JANE GOVER teaches in the Museum Studies Program, New York University. She is the author of *The Positive Image: Women Photographers in Turn of the Century America*.

MARY GRATTON is Operations Manager at the National Women's Hall of Fame.

THERESE M. GRAZIANO is a graduate of the University of Wisconsin–Parkside.

CASEY EDWARD GREENE is an archivist at the Rosenberg Library in Galveston, Texas. He earned his master's degree in library science at North Texas State University and an M.A. in history at the University of Houston–Clear Lake.

WENDELL L. GRIFFITH is a faculty member in history at Okaloosa/Walton Community College in Florida and a Ph.D. candidate at the University of West Florida. He is a graduate of Louisiana Tech University and the University of West Florida.

SUSANNE GROOMS is completing her master's degree in history at the University of Houston–Clear Lake.

DARYL M. HAFTER is Professor of History at Eastern Michigan University. She has published an edited volume, *European Women and Preindustrial Craft* (1995) and essays in *French Historical Studies* and *Cultures of Control*, edited by Miriam Levin. She has been elected vice president of the Society for the History of Technology and holds a Ph.D. in history from Yale University.

KEVIN JACK HAGOPIAN is a lecturer in the School of Communication at Pennsylvania State University. He has published in several journals, including the *Journal of Communication* and *Wide Angle*, and is a former editor of the *Film Literature Index*.

PATRICIA HAIRE was a student at DePaul University with a major in English and with communications as a supporting field of study.

CATHY MORAN HAJO is Assistant Editor of the Margaret Sanger Papers at New York University. She is currently working toward a Ph.D. in comparative U.S.-European history at New York University.

JACQUELYN DOWD HALL is Julia Cherry Spruill Professor of History and director of the Southern Oral History Program at the University of North Carolina–Chapel Hill. Her publications include *Revolt against Chivalry: Jesse Daniel Ames and the Women's Campaign against Lynching* and *Like a Family: The Making of a Southern Cotton Mill World*. She holds a Ph.D. in history from Columbia University.

DEBRA NEWMAN HAM is Professor of History at Morgan State University in Baltimore. Formerly, she was with the Manuscripts Division of the Library of Congress. She is the author of *Black History: A Guide to Archival Records in the National Archives* (1984) and the editor of *The African American Mosaic, a Library of Congress Resource Guide for the Study of Black History and Culture* (1993) and of *The African Odyssey* (1998). She completed her Ph.D. in history at Howard University.

MICHELE A. HANSFORD is Director and Curator of the Powers Museum. She earned her M.A. in historical administration at Eastern Illinois University.

ROGER D. HARDAWAY is Associate Professor of History at Northwestern Oklahoma State University and Chair of the History Department. He earned a law degree at University of Memphis and a doctorate in history at the University of North Dakota. He is the coeditor of *African Americans on the Western Frontier* (1998).

MAUREEN ANNA HARP is on the staff of the Center for American Culture Studies at Columbia University and also teaches at Regis High School in New York City. She is one of the contributors to *American Studies: An Annotated Bibliography*. She did her graduate work in history at Columbia University.

KAREN V. HARPER-DORTON is Professor of Social Work and Public Administration at West Virginia University. She holds the M.S.W. degree and has an M.A. and Ph.D. in social welfare from Ohio State University. She publishes widely in social work and is coauthor of *Cross-Cultural Practice: Social Work with Diverse Populations* (1996) and of *Working with Children and Their Families* (1999).

ROBIN O. HARRIS is Assistant Professor at Georgia College and State University and completing revisions on her dissertation, a full biography of Julia Anna Flisch, which will be published by the University of Georgia Press. She received her B.A. and M.A. in history from Georgia College and State University and her Ph.D. from Georgia Institute of Technology.

TED C. HARRIS is Vice President and Dean of Academic and Student Services at Waycross College, Georgia, where he also serves as Professor of History. He is the author of *Jeannette Rankin: Suffragist, First Woman Elected to Congress, and Pacifist*. He earned his Ph.D. in history at the University of Georgia.

VIVIEN HART is Professor of American Studies at the University of Sussex, England. She is the author of *Bound by Our Constitution: Women, Workers, and the Minimum Wage*. She received her Ph.D. in government from Harvard University.

SUSAN M. HARTMANN is Professor of History and Women's Studies at Ohio State University. She is the author of *From Margin to Mainstream: American Women and Politics since 1960* and *The Other Feminists: Activists in the Liberal Establishment* (1998).

JEAN M. HAYES taught at Galveston College, Galveston, Texas, and is now retired in Arlington, Texas. She served in the U.S. Navy from 1943 until 1946 and earned both a bachelor's and a master's degree in history from the University of Houston–Clear Lake.

MEGAN HAYES graduated from Appalachian State University in 1997 with a B.A. in interdisciplinary studies and a concentration in women's studies. Since 1996, she has worked with a team of women to establish and develop a women's center on the ASU campus and currently serves on the ASU Women's Center Advisory Board.

TAMERIN MITCHELL HAYWARD is Chair of the Social Studies Department and teaches in the International Baccalaureate program at J. I. Case High School in Racine, Wisconsin. Her most recent publication is a curriculum project for *Moving Forward: A Transportation Legacy,* produced by the Kenosha County Historical Society for Wisconsin's sesquicentennial. She earned her M.A. in history at the University of Wisconsin–Milwaukee.

ROBYNNE ROGERS HEALEY is a doctoral candidate at the University of Alberta. She completed her master's degree at the University of Alberta in American women's history.

RITA RUBINSTEIN HELLER is Associate Professor of History and Coordinator of the Local History Program at County College of Morris, New Jersey. Her dissertation on the Bryn Mawr Summer School for Women Workers, 1921–1938 inspired her National Endowment for the Humanities documentary film *The Women of Summer,* which she coproduced. She is the author of essays in *History of Higher Education Annual* and *Sisterhood and Solidarity: Workers Education for Women, 1921–1938.* Her documentary, *Chanceman's Brothers and Sisters: The Origins of the Twentieth Century Morris County Black Community,* won a CINE Golden Eagle and was a Black Maria Film Festival Director's Choice.

PATRICIA R. HENSCHEN earned her M.A. in literature and women's studies at the University of Houston–Clear Lake. She is a published poet and did her thesis on Adrienne Rich. In addition, she is a technical writer at NASA/Johnson Space Center.

ROSEMARY HERRIGES, OSF, is an elementary school principal in Lomira, Wisconsin. She holds a master's degree in education from Carthage College and Edgewood College.

NANCY A. HEWITT is Professor of History at Rutgers University. She is the author of *Women's Activism and Social Change* and *Visible Women: New Essays on American Activism.* Her Ph.D. in history is from the University of Pennsylvania.

SUZANNE HILDENBRAND is Professor in the School of Information and Library Studies at the State University of New York at Buffalo. Her publications include *Reclaiming the American Library Past: Writing the Women In* and articles in *Library Trends* and *Library Quarterly.* Her Ph.D. was earned at the University of California, Berkeley.

ROBERTA A. HOBSON teaches U.S. History and American Literature (from a feminist perspective) at Herbert Hoover High School in San Diego, California. She has an M.A. in history from San Diego State University and is the author of several publications, including "Judith McDaniel, Writer and Activist: Seeking Herself," a biography and literary critique in *Contemporary Lesbian Writers of the United States.*

MARY G. HODGE was Associate Professor of Anthropology at the University of Houston–Clear Lake. She earned her Ph.D. in anthropology with an emphasis on Mesoamerican archaeology at the University of Michigan at Ann Arbor.

NEIL W. HOGAN is Professor of History at East Stroudsburg University in Pennsylvania. His recent publications include *Pride and Promise: A Centennial History of East Stroudsburg University* and numerous articles on women's history and modern British history. He earned his Ph.D. at Ohio State University.

MARIAN J. HOLLINGER, now retired, was the Coordinator of Art History at West Virginia University and a Ph.D. candidate at the University of Toronto.

DEB HOSKINS is Assistant Professor of Women's Studies at the University of Wisconsin–La Crosse. She received her Ph.D. from Indiana University.

ANGELA M. HOWARD, coeditor of this *Handbook,* is Professor of U.S. and Women's History at the University of Houston–Clear Lake. She has written book chapters in *The Moment of Decision, For the General Welfare,* and *Kenosha Retrospective,* plus a number of shorter articles. She is editor for the Garland Press series "Biographical Dictionaries of Minority Women" and coedited *Antifeminism in America, 1963 to the Present* (1977, with Sasha Ranaé Adams Tarrant).

CHARLES G. HOWARD is an independent genealogist who is researching his family history.

JAMES A. HOWLEY received his Ph.D. in sociology from the University of Illinois, Urbana-Champaign and is a Graduate Career Counselor at the University of Chicago.

DIANA EMERY HULICK is a writer, photography consultant, and proprietor of the Hulick Agency, Mesa, Arizona. She has authored some fifty articles on photographic history and is the main author of *Photography: 1900 to the Present.* She has an M.F.A. in photography from Ohio University and a doctorate in the history of photography from Princeton University.

CAROL SUE HUMPHREY is Professor of History at Oklahoma Baptist University. She has published *"This Popular Engine": New England Newspapers during the American Revolution, 1775–1789* (1992) and *The Press of the Young Republic, 1783–1833* (1996) as well as articles in journals such as *American Journalism, Journalism History,* and *Social Science Perspectives Journal.*

DEBRA PRESTON HUTCHINS teaches eighth-grade U.S. history at Thompson Intermediate School in the Pasadena Independent School District in Houston, Texas. She received her B.A. and M.A. in history from the University of Houston–Clear Lake, where she also worked as publication and research assistant to Dr. Angela Howard.

MARY JANE CAPOZZOLI INGUI teaches at Hofstra University. She holds a Ph.D. in history from Lehigh University and has written many articles, including "Mothers and Daughters: Nassau County Italian American Women" in *Immigrant America.* Her book publications include *American History 1877–Present* and *Three Generations of Italian American Women in Nassau County, 1925–1981.*

R. JANIE ISACKSON is Director of the Bridge Program and is a freshman writing instructor at DePaul University. She earned her B.A. at Indiana University, and she holds an M.A. from Goddard College, Plainfield, Vermont.

GLEN JEANSONNE is Professor of History at the University of Wisconsin–Milwaukee. His books include *Gerald L. K. Smith: Minister of Hate; Messiah of the Masses: Huey P. Long and the Great Depression;* and *Women of the Far Right: The Mothers' Movement and World War II.* He has also published more than forty articles, including essays on Jeannette Rankin and the Mothers' Movement. He received his Ph.D. in history from Florida State University in 1973.

ROBERT W. JENSEN is Associate Professor in the Department of Journalism at the University of Texas at Austin. He is coeditor of *Freeing the First Amendment: Critical Perspectives on Freedom of Expression* and coauthor of *Pornography: The Production and Consumption of Inequality.* His research has focused on pornography and the feminist critique of sexuality.

MARGARET JERRIDO is Archivist and Head of the Urban Archives at Temple University, Philadelphia. She has published in *Women and Health* and *Black Women in America* after earning her M.L.S. from Drexel University.

NANCY JOHNS is retired from academia. She earned her Ph.D. from Clayton University.

NANCY BAKER JONES is an independent scholar in women's studies and American civilization in Austin, Texas. She is a coeditor of *Women and Texas History: Selected Essays,* has written scripts for two women's history videos, and is coauthor of *Capitol Women: A Biographical History of Women in the Texas Legislature, 1923–1999.* She earned her doctorate at the University of Texas at Austin.

CYNTHIA JURISSON is Associate Professor of American Church History at the Lutheran School of Theology in Chicago. She received her Ph.D., magna cum laude, from Princeton Theological Seminary in 1994.

BRUCE R. KAHLER is Associate Professor of History at Bethany College, Lindsborg, Kansas. His articles have appeared in *Selected Papers in Illinois History* and *Tiller.* He earned his Ph.D. in history at Purdue University.

HILARY JO KARP is Associate Professor of Psychology at the University of Houston–Clear Lake. Her current research focuses on the biopsychology of nicotine addiction. She completed her Ph.D. in psychology at the University of Chicago.

TERRI EVERT KARSTEN is a freelance writer who teaches English at Cochrane-Fountain City High School in Wisconsin. She has published articles and short stories for children and adults in *Educational Researcher, Highlights, The Friend, Wee Wisdom,* and *Cobblestone.* She earned an M.A. in linguistics from the University of Wisconsin–Madison.

ESTHER KATZ is Editor and Director of the Margaret Sanger Papers, a project sponsored by New York University. She is also Research Scholar and Associate Professor (adjunct) of History at New York University. She edited *The Margaret Sanger Papers Microfilm Edition* (Smith College Collections and Collected Documents Series). She earned her Ph.D. in history at New York University.

EVELYN G. KATZ is a docent at the National Museum of Women in the Arts. She earned an M.S. in biology and education at the City University of New York.

FRANCES M. KAVENIK, coeditor of this *Handbook,* is Professor of English and Director of the ACCESS Program at the University of Wisconsin–Parkside. She is coauthor, with Eric Rothstein, of *The Designs of Carolean Comedy* and author of *British Drama, 1660–1779: A Critical History.* Her Ph.D. in English is from the University of Wisconsin–Madison.

LOUISE M. KAWADA is Associate Professor of Critical Studies at Massachusetts College of Art in Boston, where she teaches courses in American literature, Japanese literature in translation, and women

writers. She has written articles on American women poets and the issue of nuclearism, on comedic form in Lisa Alther and Rita Mae Brown, and on Whitman and his resonance in American women poets. He has also edited *The Apocalypse Anthology.*

CATHERINE E. KELLY is Assistant Professor of History at the University of Oklahoma and is the author of *Between Town and Country.* She earned her Ph.D. at the University of Rochester.

JANE KENAMORE is an archivist at the American Medical Association. Her M.A. in education is from the University of California at Santa Monica.

KATHLEEN KENNEDY is Associate Professor of History at Western Washington University in Bellingham. She has published an article in *Mid-America* titled "Loyalty and Citizenship in the Wisconsin Women's Suffrage Association, 1917–1919" and is the author of a forthcoming book, *Scurrilous Citizens and Disloyal Mothers: Women and Subversion during World War II* (1999).

ANDREA MOORE KERR, Ph.D., is a women's historian and writer whose biography of Lucy Stone was published in 1992.

AMY KESSELMAN is Professor of Women's Studies at the State University of New York at New Paltz. She is the author of *Fleeting Opportunities: Women Shipyard Workers in Portland and Vancouver during World War II and Reconversion* and coeditor, with Lily McNair and Nancy Schniedewind, of *Women: Images and Realities, a Multicultural Anthology.*

SUSAN KEYES is a frequent art exhibition reviewer for the *New Art Examiner,* and her interviews with people in the arts appear in the *Washington Review.* She earned her M.A. and M.F.A. at the University of Iowa.

JOYCE ANN KIEVIT is a Ph.D. candidate at the University of Houston, a graduate of Hope College, Holland, Michigan, and earned her M.A. at the University of Houston–Clear Lake. She is a contributor to *Native American Women.*

KAREL KILIMNIK is a schoolteacher in the Philadelphia Public School System. She did her graduate work at Beaver College.

BOBBY ELLEN KIMBEL is Associate Professor of English at Pennsylvania State University–Abington. She is the editor of four volumes in the *Dictionary of Literary Biography* series on the American short story.

MARJORIE KING is an independent scholar, a member of the faculty at the China Youth College for Political Sciences in Beijing, China, and an instructor of modern Chinese history at the Institute for International Education Studies (IES), based at the Beijing Foreign Studies University. She is a member of the executive committee of the International Committee for the Promotion of the Chinese Industrial Cooperatives, also based in Beijing. She is the author of "Gung Ho! The Chinese Industrial Cooperatives in China's Socialist Market Economy," in *Weaving a New Tapestry* (1999) and is working on a biography of Ida Pruitt, an American born in China who served as a medical social worker.

SUSAN KINNELL is custom publishing manager for the bookstore at the University of California, Santa Barbara, and coauthor of three books: *Hypertext/Hypermedia in Schools: A Handbook for Librarians and Teachers, CD-ROM for Schools: A Directory and Practical Handbook for Media Specialists,* and *Searching America: History and Life and Historical Abstracts on Dialog.* A graduate of Mt. Holyoke College, she has also published a number of journal articles and reviews.

KATHLEEN KIRK teaches literature and writing at DePaul University in Chicago. Her poems, stories, and essays have appeared in *Puerto del Sol, Primavera, Belles Lettres, Mangrove, Spoon River Poetry Review,* and elsewhere. She is an editor for *Rhino, a Literary Annual.*

BARBARA HOPE KLEIN is a graduate of DePaul University.

KAREN C. KNOWLES is the author of *Celebrating the Land: Women's Nature Writings, 1850–1991* (1992). She earned an M.A. in English and American literature at Boston College.

SUSAN H. KOESTER is Professor of Speech Communication at the University of Alaska, Southeast. She is the editor of *Western Speakers: Voices of the American Dream;* has written articles for *Journal of the Northwest Communication Association, Journal of the West,* and *The Speech Teacher;* and has contributed to the anthology *American Portraits: History through Biography.*

SUSAN KOGEN-MEHLMAN is a graduate of DePaul University in Chicago.

SALLY GREGORY KOHLSTEDT is Professor of History of Science at the University of Minnesota and Director of the Center for Advanced Feminist Studies. She is the author of *The Formation of the American Scientific Community: The American Association for the Advancement of Science,* plus many book chapters and scholarly articles. She received her Ph.D. in history from the University of Illinois.

DAVID KUNZLE is Professor of Art History at the University of California at Los Angeles. He is the author of *Posters of Protest, The Early Comic Strip, Nineteenth-Century Comic Strip, Fashion and Fetishism, The Murals of Revolutionary Nicaragua, 1970–92,* and *Che Guevara: Icon, Myth and Message.* He earned his Ph.D at the University of London.

PETER LABELLA has been in educational publishing as an editor for twelve years, the last four with Sage Publications.

BARBARA E. LACEY is Professor of History at Saint Joseph's College in West Hartford, Connecticut. She has written scholarly articles for the *William and Mary Quarterly, Rhode Island History, Connecticut History, Journal of Social History,* and the *New England Quarterly.*

MOLLY LADD-TAYLOR is Associate Professor of History at York University in Toronto, Canada. Her publications include *Mother-Work: Women, Child Welfare and the State, 1890–1930* and *Raising a Baby the Government Way: Mothers' Letters to the Children's Bureau, 1915–1932.*

PRESTON LANE is Artistic Associate and Literary Manager of the Dallas Theater Center. He holds a BFA from the North Carolina School of the Arts and an advanced degree from the Yale School of Drama.

ELLEN D. LANGILL teaches history at the University of Wisconsin–Milwaukee. She is the author of *Carroll College: The First Century* and "Women at the University of Wisconsin 1909–1939." She is the editor of *From Farmlands to Freeways: A History of Waukesha County, Wisconsin* and of the prize-winning book, *Foley and Lardner, Attorneys at Law, 1842–1992,* a legal history of Wisconsin. She also wrote the sesquicentennial history titled *Milwaukee 150: The Greater Milwaukee Story Powered by the Past,* a 150-year history of banking in Wisconsin,

and is coauthor of a forthcoming history of women's studies in the University of Wisconsin system.

KATHLEEN LAUGHLIN is Assistant Professor of History and Women's Studies at Metropolitan State University in Minneapolis. She is the author of an article in *Ohio History* and a forthcoming book, *"Linking Government and the Grassroots": The Public Politicies of the Women's Bureau, U.S. Department of Labor, 1945 to the 1960s.*

CHRISTINE MILLER LEAHY is Coordinator of Elementary School Programs at the National Museum of Women in the Arts. She received an M.A.T. degree from George Washington University.

CRISTINE M. LEVENDUSKI is Associate Professor in the Graduate Institute of Liberal Arts at Emory University in Atlanta, Georgia. Her publications include *Peculiar Power: A Quaker Woman Preacher in Eighteenth-Century America.* She earned her Ph.D. in American Studies at the University of Minnesota–Minneapolis.

DAVID LEVIN is Director of Distance Learning at DePaul University where he is also Associate Professor in the School for New Learning.

LYNN E. LIPOR is a graduate of the University of Wisconsin–Parkside.

LAURIE LISA is coeditor (with Gretchen M. Bataille) of *Native American Women: A Biographical Dictionary.*

MAUREEN R. LISTON is Lecturer in English for Academic Purposes at the Hochschule fuer Technik und Wirtschaft Dresden, Germany. She completed her M.A. in English and American Studies at Case Western Reserve and her Ph.D. at Ruhr-University Bochum.

JUDY BARRETT LITOFF is Professor of History at Bryant College. She is the author of *American Midwives, 1860 to the Present; The American Midwife Debate; Miss You: The World War II Letters of Barbara Wooddall Taylor and Charles E. Taylor; Since You Went Away: World War II Letters from American Women on the Home Front; Dear Boys: World War II Letters from a Woman Back Home; We're in This War, Too; World War II Letters from American Women in Uniform; American Women in a World at War: Contemporary Accounts from World War II; Dear Poppa: The World War II Berman Family Letters;* and many scholarly articles.

CYNTHIA JEFFRESS LITTLE is Vice President for Research Services for the Historical Society of Philadelphia. She is the author of *Women's Historical Philadelphia: A Self-Guided Walking Tour.* She received her Ph.D. in history from Temple University.

ROGER A. LOHMANN is Professor in the School of Social Work at West Virginia University. He is the author of *Breaking Even: Financial Management in Human Services; The Commons: New Perspectives on Nonprofit Organization and Voluntary Action;* and a forthcoming volume on social administration as well as numerous journal articles.

MARY LOWE-EVANS is Professor of English at the University of West Florida. In addition to *Crimes against Fecundity: Joyce and Population Control,* she has authored *Frankenstein: Mary Shelley's Wedding Guest* and articles for *Studies in the Novel, James Joyce Quarterly, Journal of Modern Literature,* and *The Explicator.* She also edited *Critical Essays on Mary Wollestonecraft Shelley.*

JUDITH LUCAS is Chair of Social Studies at Clear Brook High School in Houston, Texas. She is also Teacher Consultant for the National Geographic Society and the Texas Alliance for Geographic Education. In addition, she teaches at the College of the Mainland in La Marque, Texas, and at the University of Houston–Clear Lake. She earned an M.A. in history at the University of Houston–Clear Lake.

THERESE L. LUECK is Associate Professor in the School of Communication at the University of Akron. She earned her Ph.D. in American culture at Bowling Green State University and has published book chapters as well as articles in journals such as *Journalism Educator*. She is coeditor of two volumes, *Women's Periodicals in the United States*.

PIPER MADLAND is an at-home mother in The Woodlands, Texas. She has worked for women's and contemporary arts organizations in Texas. She earned a B.A. in art and history and in sociology from Rice University and has a master's degree in history with a concentration in women's studies from the University of Houston–Clear Lake.

GAIL MALMGREEN is Processing Archivist at the Robert F. Wagner Labor Archives, New York University, and was formerly Associate Editor of the papers of Elizabeth Cady Stanton and Susan B. Anthony at the University of Massachusetts. She is the author of *Neither Bread Nor Roses: Early Feminist Socialists and the Working Class* and *Silk Town: Industry and Culture in Macclesfield, 1750–1835*. She is the editor of *Religion in the Lives of Englishwomen*.

STEVEN MANDEVILLE-GAMBLE is Associate Librarian in the Green Library at Stanford University. He has a B.A. from Stanford and an M.A. from the University of Michigan, both in anthropology, as well as an M.L.S. from the University of California at Berkeley.

AMY YEARY MANGAN is Dean of the Workforce Department at Central Florida Community College. She has an M.A. in American and European history from the University of West Florida.

SHIRLEY MARCHALONIS is Professor Emerita of English and Women's Studies at Pennsylvania State University, Berks campus. She is the author of *The Worlds of Lucy Larcom, 1824–1893*.

RUTH JACKNOW MARKOWITZ is the author of *My Daughter, the Teacher: Jewish Teachers in the New York City Schools* and articles in *Women Educators in the United States, European Immigrant Women in the United States*, and *History of Higher Education Annual*. She received her Ph.D. in history from the State University of New York at Stony Brook.

DONALD B. MARTI is Associate Professor of History at Indiana University at South Bend. He has published articles on women's history in *Agricultural History*. He obtained his Ph.D. at the University of Wisconsin–Madison.

DONALD R. MARTIN is Associate Professor of Communication at DePaul University in Chicago. He published an article on Congresswoman Barbara Jordan in the *Southern Speech Communication Journal*.

CATHERINE MASON is a freelance writer. She earned her doctorate in history at the University of Rochester.

LOU ANN MATOSSIAN is a Ph.D. candidate in linguistics at the University of Pennsylvania. She has published in *Language in Society* and *Women and Language* and earned an M.S. from the University of Pennsylvania.

VIRGINIA BEATTIE MATTES is a journal writer and poet. She has held positions as an auditor, treasury agent, and instructor. She earned both an M.A. and an M.A.T. in history from the University of Chicago.

KAREN P. MATTOX is a graduate of Oberlin College in Ohio, where she studied art history. She was the first education intern at the National Museum of Women in the Arts, Washington, D.C.

MARGARET T. MCFADDEN is Assistant Professor of American Studies at Colby College. She is the author of *Women's Rights Trail: Seneca Falls and Waterloo, New York*. She earned her Ph.D. from Yale University.

THERESA A. MCGEARY is a recent graduate of DePaul University.

BARBARA MCGOWAN is Professor of History and Director of the Women's Studies Program at Ripon College in Wisconsin. She received her Ph.D. in American culture at the University of Michigan.

JOHN R. MCKIVIGAN is the Mary O'Brien Gibson Professor of History at Indiana University–Purdue University at Indianapolis and and Associate Editor of the Frederick Douglass papers at Yale University. He is the author of *The War against Proslavery Religion: Abolitionism and the Northern Churches, 1830–1865*.

LINDA O. MCMURRY is Professor of History at North Carolina State University. She is the author of *George Washington Carver: Scientist and Symbol; Recorder of the Black Experience: A Biography of Monroe Nathan Work; To Keep the Waters Troubled: The Life of Ida B. Wells* and coauthor of *America and Its People*.

KAREN MERRITT is Director of Academic Planning and Program Review for the University of California. She has published essays in *Beyond Intellectual Sexism: A New Woman, a New Reality* and *Frontiers*. She earned her Ph.D. at Harvard University.

LEISA DIANE MEYER is Director of Women's Studies and Associate Professor of History at the College of William & Mary. She is the author of *Creating G.I. Jane: Sexuality and Power in the Women's Army Corps during World War II* (1996).

SUELLEN MEYER is Professor of English at St. Louis Community College–Meramec. She has written a number of scholarly and popular articles about quilts. She earned her master's degree at St. Louis University.

JOANNE J. MEYEROWITZ is Associate Professor of History at the University of Cincinnati. She is the author of *Women Adrift: Independent Wage Earners in Chicago, 1880–1930* and the editor of *Not June Cleaver: Women and Gender in Postwar America, 1945–1960*.

GRETCHEN MIESZKOWSKI is Professor of Literature and Women's Studies and Director of Humanities at the University of Houston–Clear Lake. She is the author of *The Reputation of Criseyde: 1155–1500* and frequent essays in *The Chaucer Review*.

LINDA PATTERSON MILLER is Professor of English at Pennsylvania State University–Abington. She is the editor of *Letters from the Lost Generation: Gerald and Sara Murphy and Friends* and coeditor of *The Book of American Diaries*. She has also contributed articles to numerous literary journals.

RANDALL M. MILLER is Professor of History at Saint Joseph's University and former editor of the *Pennsylvania Magazine of History and Biography*. Among his numerous books are *"Dear Master": Letters of a Slave Family* and *Catholics in the Old South*. He is coeditor of the *Dictionary of Afro-American Slavery*.

SALLY M. MILLER is Professor of History at the University of the Pacific. She is the author of *The Radical Immigrant; From Prairie to Prison: The Life of Social Activist Kate Richards O'Hare,* and the editor of *Flawed Liberation: Socialism and Feminism* and other works.

KAY MILLS is a journalist. Her publications include *This Little Light of Mine: The Life of Fannie Lou Hamer; A Place in the News; From the Women's Pages to the Front Page; and Something Better for My Children: The History and People of Head Start.* She earned an M.A. at Northwestern University.

LESLYE KING MIZE is Associate Professor and Director of Training of the Family Therapy Program at the University of Houston–Clear Lake. She has published many articles in the field of family therapy and feminism and is currently working on a research project on biological adult sisters in families. Her most recent article is "Mother/Daughter Dilemma: Research on Issues of Context for Daughters" in the *Journal of Feminist Family Therapy.* Her Ph.D. in marriage and family therapy is from Texas Woman's University.

COLONEL BETTIE J. MORDEN is a retired army historian who lives in Arlington, Virginia. Her publications include *The Women's Army Corps, 1945–1978.* She earned her M.A. at Columbia University.

DENNIS L. MORRISON is Professor of History and Geography at San Jacinto College South in Houston, Texas. He is also Adjunct Professor of History and Education at the University of Houston. He has just completed his ninth book, *World Geography, A Study Guide.* His prior works include a biography of Henry A. Wallace and *Woman of Conscience,* on Senator Margaret Chase Smith.

MARJORIE MURPHY is Professor of History at Swarthmore College. She is the author of *Blackboard Unions* and holds a Ph.D. in history from the University of California–Davis.

MARY MURPHY is Associate Professor of History at Montana State University–Bozeman, author of *Mining Cultures: Men, Women and Leisure in Butte, 1914–41,* and coauthor of *Like a Family: The Making of a Southern Cotton Mill World.*

LYNN R. MUSSLEWHITE is Professor of History at Cameron University and coauthor of essays on Kate Barnard published in the *Historian, Mid-America,* and *An Oklahoma I Had Never Seen Before.* He is currently completing a full-length biography of Barnard.

ANNE DEHAYDEN NEAL is Vice President and General Counsel of the American Council of Trustees and Alumni, a nonprofit organization based in Washington, D.C., dedicated to academic freedom and excellence. She is a member of the board of All Hallows Guild, Washington National Cathedral; Friends of the U.S. National Arboretum; Paine Art Center and Arboretum; and the Sabre Foundation. She is also a founding member of the National Museum of Women in the Arts. She was formerly coeditor of the American Bar Association publication *Communications Lawyer* and currently edits the quarterly newsletter *Inside Academe.*

JEAN NETTLES holds an M.A. in history from the University of Houston–Clear Lake, where she is a certification analyst.

LINDA NOER is Professor of Social Work at Carthage College in Kenosha, Wisconsin. She earned her Ph.D. at Loyola University, Chicago.

MARIANN L. NOGRADY teaches in the Newton Public Schools in Newton, Massachusetts. She is a graduate of Knox College.

MICHELLE NOVAK is Interim Dean of Academic Development at Houston Community College. She holds an M.A. in history from the University of Houston–Clear Lake and is seeking a Ph.D. in history there.

NAN NOWIK was Associate Professor of English at Denison University and held a Ph.D. in English from Ohio State University. While writing her articles for this book, she was diagnosed as having rapidly growing brain tumors. She heroically completed her *Handbook* (first edition) essays after undergoing two brain surgeries and during radiation treatment.

CLAUDIA M. OAKES is Assistant Director for Operations at the Utah Museum of Natural History. Formerly, she was curator of aeronautics at the Smithsonian Institution. She is the author of *United States Women in Aviation through World War I* and *United States Women in Aviation, 1930–1939.* She earned a master's degree in public administration from George Washington University.

BARBARA OBERLANDER is Professor of History and Honors Program Coordinator at Santa Fe Community College in Gainesville, Florida. She earned her doctorate at Brandeis University and has given many lectures and workshops on women's history. She is coauthor of an article on "Teaching Gender" for the National Collegiate Honors Council Report.

LAURA K. O'KEEFE is a librarian and archivist at the New York Public Library. She is currently a doctoral candidate at the Graduate Center of the City University of New York.

LAURA OREN is Professor of Law at the University of Houston Law Center. Her most recent publication is "Section 1983 and Sex Abuse in Schools: Making a Federal Case Out of It," which appeared in the *Chicago-Kent Law Review.* She has also published essays in *Feminist Studies* and the *Biographical Dictionary of Modern British Radicals.* She holds both a J.D. from the University of Houston Law Center and a Ph.D. in history from Yale University.

MARY PATTERSON is an instructor at Houston Community College. She received her B.A. from the University of Houston–Clear Lake, where she is completing her M.A.

PAMELA PATTERSON was a student at DePaul University.

TERESA PECK was Coordinator of the Women's Studies Program at the University of Wisconsin–Parkside. The author of a number of scholarly articles, she is currently a psychologist in private practice in London.

ELISABETH ISRAELS PERRY is John Francis Bannon Professor of History and American Studies at Saint Louis University and the author of *Belle Moskowitz: Feminine Politics and the Exercise of Power in the Age of Alfred E. Smith.* Her Ph.D. is from the University of California, Los Angeles.

LINDA BURIAN PLAUT teaches humanities and women's studies at Virginia Polytechnic Institute. She gives frequent recitals of violin music by women, and Hildegard Publishing Company has just released her new edition of *Sonate, Op. 18* by Emile Mayer.

CAMILLE JASKI POPLIOLEK is an assistant vice president with Chicago Title Insurance Company in Hillside, Illinois. She earned her bachelor of arts degree at DePaul University and obtained a law degree from Illinois Institute of Technology, Chicago-Kent College of Law in 1990.

SUSAN KELLOGG PORTNEY is a docent at the National Museum of Women in the Arts. She is a graduate of the University of Miami.

PATRICIA L. PRADO-OLMOS is Assistant Professor at California State University–San Marcos. She has published in the *Bilingual Research Journal*. Her doctorate is from the University of California at Santa Barbara.

LINDA RAY PRATT is Professor and Chair of English at the University of Nebraska at Lincoln. She edited *I Hear Men Talking: Stories of the Early Decades by Meridel LeSueur* and has published numerous articles in journals such as *Victorian Poetry* and *Women's Studies*. She is past national president (1992–1994) of the American Association of University Professors. She has also published widely on issues in higher education.

RICHARD PROUTY is an independent scholar in the Chicago area. His dissertation examined issues of gender and class in modernist narratives.

JUDITH PRYOR is the Coordinator of Reference at the Library/Learning Center of the University of Wisconsin–Parkside. She is the coeditor of *Delivering Government Services* and earned her M.L.S. at Indiana University.

KAREN RAINES-PATE earned her B.A. in history at the University of Houston–Clear Lake, where she is currently completing her M.A. in history.

LANA F. RAKOW is Professor in the School of Communication at the University of North Dakota. In addition to numerous articles and book chapters on gender and communication, she is the author of *Gender on the Line: Women, the Telephone, and Community Life,* the editor of *Women Making Meaning: New Feminist Directions in Communication Research,* and the coeditor with Cheris Kramarae of *The Revolution in Words: Righting Women, 1868–1871.*

EILEEN R. RAUSCH is Personnel Manager for the State of Connecticut's Judicial Branch. She earned her Ph.D. at the University of Notre Dame.

BONNIE LOU RAYNER is a volunteer at a sheltered workshop where she directs the computer lab. She retired after teaching for thirty-five years in the Hinsdale (Illinois) Public School system and has written a book about gross motor development in children from birth to six years old. She earned her master's degree in education with a concentration in early childhood leadership and advocacy from the National College of Education in Illinois.

CLAIRE M. RENZETTI is Professor and Chair of Sociology at St. Joseph's University, Philadelphia. She is editor of the international, interdisciplinary journal *Violence Against Women,* coeditor of the Sage *Violence Against Women* book series, and editor of the Northeastern University Press book series *Gender, Crime, and Law.* She is the author or coauthor of ten books and numerous book chapters and articles in scholarly journals.

DIANA DINGESS RETZLAFF is a graduate in history of the University of Houston–Clear Lake.

MIRIAM REUMANN is a graduate student in the Department of American Civilization at Brown University, where she is completing a dissertation on responses to the Kinsey Reports and the construction of American sexual character in the postwar era.

JOANNE S. RICHMOND serves the Evangelical Lutheran Church in America as campus pastor of Dana College in Blair, Nebraska. A graduate of Carthage College, she earned her M.Div. with honors from Pacific Lutheran Theological Seminary. She has also served congregations in Wisconsin and Michigan.

CYNTHIA MILLS RICHTER is a Ph.D. candidate in American studies and feminist studies at the University of Minnesota where she is completing her dissertation on gender, race, and postwar housing. She also holds an M.Arch. from Princeton University and a B.A. from Swarthmore College.

SANDRA RIESE is Director of the Women's Health Center at St. Catherine's Hospital in Kenosha, Wisconsin. She has a B.S. in nursing from Mount Senario College and an M.A. in public administration from the University of Wisconsin.

LOUISE S. ROBBINS is Associate Professor and Director of the School of Library and Information Studies at the University of Wisconsin–Madison. She is the author of a number of articles and *Censorship and the American Library: The American Library Association's Response to Threats to Intellectual Freedom, 1939–1969.* Her new book, *The Dismissal of Miss Ruth Brown: Civil Rights, Censorship, and the American Public Library:* is forthcoming. Her Ph.D. is from Texas Woman's University.

SANDRA E. ROBERTS is Chaplain at the Kenosha County Jail. She earned her M.Div. at Garrett Theological Seminary in Evanston, Illinois.

GWENDALYN KEITA ROBINSON is the author of *Crowning Glory: An Historical Analysis of the Afro-American Beauty Industry and Tradition.* She received a Ph.D. in history from the University of Illinois at Chicago.

SUSAN L. ROCKWELL is a Ph.D. candidate in Native American Literature at Arizona State University. She is a language arts instructor at Cook College and Theological School (a two-year institution for Native American and other indigenous students) and a Faculty Associate in English at Arizona State University. Her articles have appeared in the *American Indian Culture and Research Journal* and *Ethnic Studies Review.*

FAITH ROGOW, Ph.D., is author of *Gone to Another Meeting: A History of the National Council of Jewish Women, 1893–1993.* She is currently the owner of Insighters Educational Consulting and an independent scholar specializing in media education.

JANE H. ROTHSTEIN is a doctoral candidate at New York University. Her dissertation is on the *mikveh* (ritual bath) and Jewish family purity laws in the United States, 1880–1940. She has published articles in *Jewish Women in America: An Historical Encyclopedia* (1997), and is a 2000–2001 dissertation fellow in the Social Science Research Council's Sexuality Research Fellowship Program. She earned an M.A. in history at Case Western Reserve University.

JOHN L. RURY is Professor in the School for New Learning at DePaul University. He is the author of *Education and Women's Work* and has contributed articles to the *History of Education Quarterly, Urban Education,* and the *Journal of Negro Education.* He has served as editor of the *American Educational Research Journal* section on social and institutional analysis.

MARY RUTHSDOTTER is Projects Director and a cofounder of the National Women's History Project. She is a graduate of the University of California at Los Angeles.

CAROL ANN SADTLER is a writer living in Chicago. She earned her M.A. in comparative literature at the University of Maine, Orono.

CAROL LEE SAFFIOTI-HUGHES is Associate Professor of English at the University of Wisconsin–Parkside. She is the author of *Space: The Final Frontier* (TV series), *Basic College Research,* and *Wolf Song Sequence.* She holds a Ph.D. in English from Princeton University.

DOROTHY C. SALEM is Professor of History at Cuyahoga Community College and Cleveland State University in Cleveland, Ohio. Her books include *To Better Our World: Black Women in Organized Reform, 1890–1920; African American Women: A Biographical Dictionary,* and *The Journey: A History of the African American Experience.*

RICHARD SALVATO is Archivist in the Rare Books and Manuscripts Division of the New York Public Library.

DIANA RUBY SANDERSON is Assistant Research Historian for local church history at the Presbyterian Church (U.S.A.) Department of History in Montreal, North Carolina. She is a graduate of Louisiana State University.

J. A. SANDOZ is a freelance writer. She holds master's degrees in recreational administration from Brigham Young University and in general studies from the Episcopal Divinity School.

ROBERTA G. SANDS is on the faculty of the School of Social Work at the University of Pennsylvania. She is the author of over forty publications that address mental health, family, and feminist issues and describe interprofessional discourse.

ABBY SCHMELLING is the Executive Director of the Volunteer Center of Oak Park, Illinois. She has an M.A. in African languages and literature from the University of Wisconsin.

JUDITH SYDOW SCHMIDT earned a B.S. in accounting from the University of Houston–Clear Lake and is a C.P.A. working in industry in San Antonio, Texas.

MAX GAVIN SCHULZ is a full-time lecturer in literature and writing at Houston Community College. He holds a Ph.D. from the University of Southern California and has recently published articles in *Review* and *Gulf Coast.* His book, *The Mask of John Berryman,* is being reviewed for publication.

SUSAN E. SEARING is Visiting Professor of Library Administration at the University of Illinois, Urbana-Champaign. The author of *Introduction to Library Research in Women's Studies,* she completed her M.L.S. at the University of Michigan.

MAXINE SCHWARTZ SELLER is Professor of Educational Organization, Administration, and Policy and Adjunct Professor of History at the State University of New York at Buffalo. Among her publications are *To Seek America: A History of Ethnic Life in the United States; Immigrant Women; Ethnic Theatre in the United States; Women Educators in the United States, 1820–1993; Identity, Community, and Plu-* *ralism in American Life;* and *Beyond Black and White: New Faces in American Schools.*

WILLIAM G. SHADE is Professor Emeritus of History and Director of the American Studies Program at Lehigh University. He is the author of several books, including *Our American Sisters: Women in American Life and Thought* and *Revisioning the British Empire in the Eighteenth Century.* He did his doctoral work in history at Wayne State University.

VICTORIA L. SHANNON is an instructor in English at DePaul University and Columbia College, Chicago. She is also an academic counselor in Columbia's Student Support Services and has contributed to the *Encyclopedia of Women's Studies.* She received her M.A. from DePaul University and is currently doing work toward an Ed.D. there.

ROBERT S. SHELTON is Assistant Professor of History at the University of North Carolina, Greensboro. He earned his M.A. at Rice University. He has published "A Modified Crime: The Apprenticeship in St. Kitts" in *Slavery and Abolition.*

CAROLINE REYNOLDS SHERMAN studied intellectual history at Harvard and graduated summa cum laude in 1999. She is currently working at the Korea Institute of Finance in Seoul.

REBECCA L. SHERRICK is Provost and Associate Professor of History at Carroll College in Waukesha, Wisconsin. Holder of a Ph.D. in history from Northwestern University, she has written articles for *American Studies Quarterly, Women's Studies International Forum,* and a number of other education publications.

BARBARA SHIRCLIFFE is Assistant Professor of Social Foundations at the University of South Florida–Tampa. Her Ph.D. in social foundations was earned at the State University of New York at Buffalo, where her dissertation was on student-run women's studies programs.

JOAN JACKS SILVERMAN, a docent at the National Gallery of Art and former docent at the National Museum of Women in the Arts, earned an M.A. from New York University's Institute of Fine Arts.

JAN STOCKMAN SIMONDS is Professor of Dance and Chair of Humanities and Fine Arts at the University of Houston–Clear Lake. She has choreographed over sixty dance works, has taught dance for forty-one years, and was a member of the José Limón Dance Company.

ANASTATIA SIMS is Professor of History at Georgia Southern University. She is the author of *The Power of Femininity in the New South: Women's Organizations and Politics in North Carolina, 1830-1930.* She has published articles in *North Carolina Historical Review, Women in New Worlds: Historical Perspectives on the Wesleyan Tradition,* and *Tennessee Historical Quarterly.*

BONNIE G. SMITH is Professor of History at Rutgers University. She is the author of many books and articles, including *The Gender of History.*

SHERRY L. SMITH is Associate Professor of History at the University of Texas at El Paso. She is the author of *The View from Officer's Row: Army Perceptions of Western Indians.* She holds a Ph.D. in history from the University of Washington,

SUSAN LYNN SMITH is Associate Professor of History and Women's Studies at the University of Alberta in Canada. She is the author of *Sick and Tired of Being Sick and Tired: Black Women's Health Activism in America, 1890-1950.*

JOHN SNIDER is Professor of English at Montana State University–Northern, in Havre, Montana. He completed his doctoral dissertation at the University of Illinois on "The Treatment of American Indians in Selected American Literature" in 1983.

MARGARET KONZ SNOOKS teaches in the program of Fitness and Human Performance at the University of Houston–Clear Lake. She is coauthor of *American Social Problems: An Institutional View*. She earned her doctorate in sociology at the University of Texas at Austin.

CAROL SNYDER is Associate Professor of English and associate provost of the University of Houston–Clear Lake. She was the editor of the Garland Press series *Gender and Genre in Literature*, and her essays have appeared in *College Composition, Twentieth Century Science Fiction Writers* and *Woman's Art Journal*.

SETHURAMAN SRINIVASAN, JR., earned his M.A. at Stephen F. Austin University. He is a doctoral student in history at the University of Houston.

ANNE STATHAM is Professor of Sociology and Women's Studies at the University of Wisconsin–Parkside and Outreach Administrator for the UW System Women's Studies Consortium. She is the coauthor of *The Worth of Women's Work, Gender and University Teaching: A Negotiated Difference*, and numerous articles in such journals as *Sex Roles, Sociological Quarterly, Social Problems, Social Forces, Journal of Social Issues*, and *Work and Occupations*. She completed her Ph.D. in sociology at Indiana University.

LAURA STEMPEL is a writer living in Chicago. She is the author of *Love and Ideology in the Afternoon: Soap Opera, Women, and Television Genre* (1995).

EDWARD C. STIBILI is Vice President of Academic and Student Affairs at Calumet College of St. Joseph, Whiting, Indiana. He is the coauthor of *Italian-Americans and Religion: An Annotated Bibliography* and essays in *Religious Experience of Italian Americans* and *U.S. Catholic Historian*. He did his Ph.D. in history at Notre Dame University.

LANDON R. Y. STORRS is Assistant Professor of History at the University of Houston. She is the author of a forthcoming book on the National Consumers' League and New Deal Labor Standards Policy. Her doctorate is from the University of Wisconsin–Madison.

SUE E. STRICKLER is Associate Professor of Political Science at Eastern New Mexico University. Holder of a Ph.D. in political science from the University of Iowa, she is the author of a chapter on congressional oversight in *Administrative Discretion: Implementation of Public Policy*.

HOLLY HYNCIK SUKENIK is a graduate of the University of Delaware. As a docent at the National Museum of Women in the Arts, she did research on women artists.

MARIE SCHIRTZINGER TARIS is Associate Director of Admissions at Ohio State University, from which she received her M.A. in guidance and counseling.

SASHA RANAÉ ADAMS TARRANT is an Instructor at Brazosport College in Brazosport, Texas, and is working on her Ph.D. in U.S. social history at Texas A&M University. She coedited *Antifeminism in America* (1997) and holds a B.A. and M.A. in women's history from the University of Houston–Clear Lake.

A. ELIZABETH TAYLOR was Professor of History Emerita at Texas Woman's University. She authored *The Woman Suffrage Movement in Tennessee*, as well as articles in journals such as *Journal of Southern History, Georgia Historical Quarterly, North Carolina Historical Review, Journal of Mississippi History*, and *South Carolina Historical Magazine*.

JACQUELINE TAYLOR is Professor of Communication at DePaul University and Director of the DePaul Humanities Center. She is the author of *Grace Paley: Illuminating the Dark Lives* as well as essays in *Literature in Performance, Southern Speech Communication Journal*, and *Text and Performance Quarterly*. She earned her Ph.D. in communication at the University of Texas at Austin.

ROBIN S. TAYLOR is a graduate student at DePaul University.

KATHERINE TESCHNER is an English major at DePaul University.

CONSTANCE H. TIMBERLAKE is Professor Emeritus in the College for Human Development at Syracuse University and Associate Director of Rowan State College, Camden Campus, Camden, New Jersey. Her scholarship and research in child, family, and community studies has recently focused on adolescent pregnancy prevention as well as her work on "Sexuality Attitudes of Black Adults," which appeared in *The Journal of Family Relations*.

DONALD F. TINGLEY is Professor of History Emeritus at Eastern Illinois University. He is the author of *Social History of the United States, The Structuring of a State: Illinois, 1899–1928*, and, with Elizabeth Tingley, *Women and Feminism in American History*.

BEVERLY G. TOOMEY is Professor of Social Work at Ohio State University. She is the coauthor of *Practice Focused Research, Social Work in the '80s* and *Mentally Ill Offenders and the Criminal Justice System*.

MICHAEL MILLER TOPP is Assistant Professor of History at the University of Texas–El Paso. He has published several articles on the Italian American Left and is the author of a forthcoming book, *I Senza Patri [Those without a Country]: The Transnationalism of the Italian American Left*. He received his Ph.D. in American civilization from Brown University.

JUDITH ANN TROLANDER is Professor of History at the University of Minnesota at Duluth. She holds a Ph.D. from Case Western Reserve University. She is the author of *Professionalism and Social Change: From the Settlement House Movement to Neighborhood Centers, 1886 to the Present* and *Settlement Houses and the Great Depression*.

CATHERINE TUMBER is Associate Editor of the Howard Thurman Papers Project of Morehouse College. She holds a Ph.D. in American history from the University of Rochester and teaches U.S. social, cultural, and intellectual history.

MISTI TURBEVILLE teaches American history at Crawford High School and McLennan Community College in Waco, Texas. She has an M.A. in history.

SUSAN C. TURELL is Assistant Professor of Psychology and Convener of Women's Studies at the University of Houston–Clear Lake. She has published several articles in psychological journals regarding women's issues in general and violence against women specifically.

ELIZABETH HAYES TURNER is Associate Professor of History at the University of Houston–Downtown. She earned her doctorate from Rice University and is the author of *Women, Culture, and Community: Religion and Reform in Galveston, 1880–1920*.

JAN VASSAR is Consultant at the Sac and Fox National Public Library. Her publications include *In Their Name* and articles in *The Daily Oklahoman*. Her B.A. is from Tulsa University, where she is currently a graduate student.

WENDY HAMAND VENET is Associate Professor of History at Georgia State University. She is the author of *Neither Ballots nor Bullets: Women Abolitionists and the Civil War* and the coeditor of *Midwestern Women: Work, Community, and Leadership at the Crossroads*.

MARYJO WAGNER is a professional speaker and trainer and an independent scholar. Her Ph.D. in history is from the University of Oregon. She is the author of articles on frontier women and women's history resources.

SALLY ROESCH WAGNER is Executive Director of the Matilda Joslyn Gage Foundation. Recent publications include a Modern Reader's Edition of Gage's 1893 classic, *Woman, Church and State* and a biographical monograph of Gage, *She Who Holds the Sky*. She earned a Ph.D. from the University of California at Santa Cruz.

ROBERT G. WAITE is a research historian in Washington, D.C. He is the author of numerous articles on the history of law enforcement and crime in the United States and Germany. At present he is writing a book on women and crime in Germany, 1941–1945.

BEVERLY FALCONER WATKINS is Associate Professor and Chair of the Department of Social Work at Savannah State University. She received a Ph.D. from Ohio State University and has published in *Social Work*.

HILDA R. WATROUS is a historiographer and consultant who graduated from the State University of New York at Cortland. She is Historian of the League of Women Voters of New York State.

PAULA WILLIAMS WEBBER is a public school teacher and Department Chair for Special Education at Galena Park High School. She codirects the Woman's Missionary Union for the First Baptist Church in Galena Park, Texas. She earned her B.A. in history from the University of Tulsa in 1980 and her M.A. in history at the University of Houston–Clear Lake in 1995.

ANITA M. WEBER is currently Senior Archivist with History Associates Incorporated. She has an M.A. in history from Northern Illinois University and an M.L.S. from Kent State University.

SARAH WEDDINGTON argued the winning side of *Roe v. Wade* before the U.S. Supreme Court and is the author of *A Question of Choice*, a book describing the case and reviewing the history of choice since then. She practices law in Austin, Texas, and is Adjunct Associate Professor at the University of Texas–Austin. In 1972, she was the first woman elected from Austin to be a member of the Texas House of Representatives, where she served three terms. From 1978 to 1981, she was an assistant to President Jimmy Carter. Her responsibilities included assisting in the selection of women for federal judiciary appointments and helping to implement programs to promote equal treatment of women in the military, in securing business loans, and in social programs. She received her J.D. degree from the University of Texas School of Law.

PRISCILLA WEEKS is a research associate with the Environmental Institute of Houston at the University of Houston–Clear Lake. She received her Ph.D. in anthropology from Rice University. She has done field work on conservation and development issues in the Philippines and India and on the Texas Gulf Coast.

SUSAN LEE WEEKS has more than fifteen years of experience teaching about women's issues in various colleges and universities. She is currently working to recruit more women into technical occupations and is involved with SMARTGirls, a nonprofit organization that encourages girls to explore math, science, and technical fields. She received her master's degree in studies of the future from the University of Houston–Clear Lake, and her Ph.D. in sociology from Washington State University.

SANDRA J. WEIDNER received her B.S. in industrial and labor relations from the University of Wisconsin–Parkside. A former union organizer, she was elected Alderman for the Sixth Ward of the City of Racine, Wisconsin, in April 2000.

PHYLLIS HOLMAN WEISBARD is Women's Studies Librarian of the University of Wisconsin System. She and her staff maintain a comprehensive women's studies Website (http://www.library.wisc.edu/libraries/WomensStudies/) and publish *Feminist Collections: A Quarterly of Women's Studies Resources* and other resource publications. She is the author of a bibliography on American Jewish women's history and coauthor of bibliographies on Jewish Law and on the history of women and science, health, and technology.

LESLIE KANES WEISMAN is Professor and former Associate Dean of Architecture at the New Jersey Institute of Technology. She has also taught at the University of Illinois, Massachusetts Institute of Technology, Brooklyn College, and the University of Detroit, where she held appointments in architecture, planning, and women's studies. Among her numerous publications are the award winning books *Discrimination by Design: A Feminist Critique of the Man-Made Environment* and *The Sex of Architecture*.

CRAIG WHITE is Associate Professor of Literature and Humanities at the University of Houston–Clear Lake. He has published articles in American literature, the history of science, and culture and gender studies. He earned his Ph.D. in English at the University of Wisconsin–Madison.

WAYNE A. WIEGAND is Professor in the School of Library and Information Studies at the University of Wisconsin–Madison. He is the author of *Politics of an Emerging Profession: The American Library Association, 1876–1917*; *"An Active Instrument for Propaganda": The American Public Library during World War I*; and *Irrepressible Reformer: A Biography of Melvil Dewey*.

PAMELA F. WILLE is currently a doctoral candidate in history at Texas Tech University. She received her M.A. in history from the University of Houston–Clear Lake.

ESTHER K. WILSON is Assistant Dean of the College of Liberal Arts and Sciences at the University of Wisconsin–Parkside. She earned her M.S. in biology at Emporia State University in Emporia, Kansas.

RAE FULLER WILSON is a graduate assistant at the University of Houston–Clear Lake. She received her B.A. from Stephen F. Austin State University.

RICHARD A. WILSON is a graduate student in history at the University of Houston–Clear Lake.

ELLEN WOLCOTT is a homemaker. She received her B.S. in mathematics at Ohio University.

DAVID C. WOLF is a doctoral student in history at the University of Florida. He received his B.A. and M.A. in history in the University of West Florida.

MARGARET RIPLEY WOLFE is Professor of History and Senior Research Fellow at East Tennessee State University. She is the author of numerous books, articles, and essays, among them *Kingsport, Tennessee: A Planned American City* and *Daughters of Canaan: A Saga of Southern Women.* She is the general editor of a new series, "Women in Southern Culture," published by the University Press of Kentucky. She completed her Ph.D. in American history at the University of Kentucky.

MARY LOUISE WOOD teaches history of art at Sidwell Friends School in Washington, D.C. She was curator of education at the National Museum of Women in the Arts for four years. The holder of a Ph.D. from the Johns Hopkins University, she is the coauthor of *The National Museum of Women in the Arts.*

SAUNDRA K. YELTON-STANLEY is a counselor for the Kenosha Unified Public Schools in Wisconsin. She has written materials and coordinated curriculum packets for the celebration of Women's History Month (K-12) in conjunction with the Wisconsin Consortium for Sex Equity in Education, with the support of the Wisconsin Department of Public Instruction. She did her graduate work in history at Indiana University–Bloomington.

JUDY YUNG is Associate Professor of American Studies at the University of California, Santa Cruz, and author of *Unbound Feet: A Social History of Chinese Women in San Francisco; Chinese Women of America: A Pictorial History;* and *Island: Poetry and History of Chinese Immigrants on Angel Island, 1910–1940.*

MICHELE WENDER ZAK is Associate Professor of Communication and Organizational Behavior at Saint Mary's College in California. She earned a Ph.D. from Ohio State and is the coauthor of *Women and the Politics of Culture* and the forthcoming book *Leadership and the Art of Communication.*

JONATHAN W. ZOPHY is Professor of History at the University of Houston–Clear Lake. His books include *Patriarchal Politics; The Holy Roman Empire: A Dictionary Handbook; The Social History of the Reformation;* and *A Short History of Renaissance and Reformation Europe.*

DATE DUE